401(k) Answer Book

2016 Edition

by Empower Retirement

401(k) Answer Book is the most comprehensive one-volume desk reference for pension administrators, human resources managers, fund managers, trustees, accountants, attorneys, consultants, financial advisors, and anyone who deals professionally with 401(k) plans. The authors, all experts in the 401(k) field, draw on their years of experience to present the information you need to know in an easy-to-use format.

Highlights of the 2016 Edition

The 2016 Edition of *401(k) Answer Book* brings the practitioner up to date on legal and regulatory measures and other developments that have had significant impact on retirement plans and their administration, including:

- DOL proposed rule redefining the definition of a fiduciary (see chapter 5) and the definition of nonfiduciary investment education (see Qs 8:21–8:37)
- DOL rule extending to 14 months the period for annual participant investment and fee disclosures (Q 19:67)
- DOL Field Assistance Bulletin 2014-01 with updated guidance on making distributions to missing participants in terminated defined contribution plans (Q 21:10)
- IRS guidance regarding documentation that plan sponsors must retain in connection with allowing plan loans and hardship withdrawals (Qs 15:17, 15:52)
- IRS Revenue Procedure 2015-27, modifying EPCRS and clarifying that employers can pursue corrective measures, other than recoupment from participants, in the event of benefit overpayments (Q 20:10)
- IRS Revenue Procedure 2015-28, providing a new set of safe harbor corrections if the employer fails to implement a participant's deferral elections, whether affirmative or pursuant to an automatic contribution arrangement, or it fails to make the 401(k) plan available to an employee who is eligible to participate (Q 20:10, Appendix M)
- IRS Revenue Procedures 2015-6 and 2015-8, updating the IRS determination letter process (Qs 3:32–3:35)

Wolters Kluwer

- DOL Field Assistance Bulletin 2015-02, providing additional guidance on satisfying ERISA fiduciary responsibilities when selecting an annuity provider for benefit distributions (Q 16:42)
- Qualified charitable distributions (QCD) transfers (Q 22:20)
- Expansion of age 50 exception to the 10 percent premature distribution penalty tax for certain governmental plan distributions (Q 18:86)
- Maximum extension lengthened to 3½ months for Form 5500 filings for taxable years after December 31, 2015 (Q 19:13)
- Information regarding the availability of IRS determination letters beginning in 2017 (Q 3:28)
- IRS Notice 2014-54 regarding treatment of distributions sent to multiple destinations (Q 16:106)
- IRS Notice 2014-66 addressing whether a series of target date funds that include deferred annuities could satisfy nondiscrimination requirements as they apply to plan right and features (Q 6:28)
- DOL Information Letter regarding whether a series of target date funds that invest in unallocated deferred annuity contracts could satisfy the requirements of a QDIA (Q 7:53)
- Information on qualifying longevity annuity contracts (QLACs) (Q 6:35)
- Fee leveling and why it is used (Q 4:58)
- IRS guidance on in-plan Roth rollovers and transfers under Notice 2013-74 (Qs 2:84, 18:65, 18:67–18:70, 18:73, 18:78)
- IRS final regulations regarding the reduction or elimination of safe harbor contributions mid-year (Qs 2:253, 2:254)
- IRS Notice 2014-19 with guidance on when 401(k) plans must adopt interim good-faith amendments to comply with IRS guidance issued in connection with the Supreme Court's decision in *United States v. Windsor* (Q 3:25)
- Issuance of IRS Notice 2014-19, IRS Revenue Ruling 2013-17, and DOL Technical Release No. 2013-04 with guidance on how the *Windsor* decision should be implemented in the context of employee benefit provisions (Qs 17:34–17:43)
- Department of Labor (DOL) proposed regulations that would require some service providers to provide a guide or index with their initial 408(b)(2) disclosure (Qs 4:106–4:113)

- IRS guidance limiting 60-day rollovers between multiple IRAs in one calendar year (Q 22:22)
- IRS Revenue Ruling 2014-9 on when a plan administrator is considered to have reasonably concluded that a proposed rollover contribution is valid (Q 2:137)
- Applicable guidance regarding when mid-year amendments to safe harbor plans are permitted (Q 2:269)
- Status of the Internal Revenue Service and Social Security Administration letter-forwarding services (Q 21:11)
- Update on PBGC's program for missing participants in defined contribution plans (Q 21:13)
- SEC final rules applicable to money market funds designed to manage and mitigate potential redemption runs and increase transparency of risk (Q 6:17)
- Discussion of Retirement Readiness reports (Q 8:20)
- IRS Revenue Procedure 2013-12 with updates to the Employee Plans Compliance Resolution System (Q 20:2)
- IRS Revenue Procedure 2013-22 establishing a program for the pre-approval of prototype or volume submitter 403(b) plan documents (Q 22:126)
- The difference between 3(21), 3(38), and 3(16) fiduciaries under ERISA (Qs 5:2–5:4)
- Recent regulatory guidance on target date funds (Qs 6:27–6:29)
- DOL Advisory Opinion on when revenue-sharing payments become plan assets (Q 4:126)
- DOL technical updates to the Delinquent Filer Voluntary Compliance (DFVC) program (Q 19:15)
- DOL proposal to require that retirement income projections be included on participant benefit statements (Q 19:41)
- DOL final regulations requiring investment- and fee-related disclosures to participants in participant-directed plans (Qs 19:56–19:73)
- DOL final regulations on required service provider disclosures regarding fees and services under ERISA Section 408(b)(2) (Qs 4:66–4:113)

- DOL Field Assistance Bulletin 2012-02R providing additional guidance on the participant investment and fee disclosure requirements (Qs 19:74–19:108)
- IRS guidance on application of survivor annuity rules to plans with lifetime income products under IRS Revenue Ruling 2012-3 (Qs 17:5–17:8)
- Updates to disclosure requirements applicable to ERISA Section 404(c) plans (Q 7:22)
- Information on Eligible Investment Advice Arrangements (EIAAs) under DOL Final Regulations Section 2550.408g-1 (Qs 5:95–5:116)
- DOL proposed rule to enhance target-date fund disclosures (Q 7:54)
- DOL developments concerning electronic disclosure of employee benefit plan information (Q 19:125)
- Updates relating to Form 5500 filing requirements (Qs 19:8–19:11)
- IRS guidance regarding contributions of paid time off (PTO) to a 401(k) plan under Revenue Rulings 2009-31 and 2009-32 (Q 2:33)
- Information on lifetime income products in the 401(k) context (Qs 6:35–6:37)
- SEC proposed measures involving 12b-1 fees (Q 6:100)
- Safe harbor time frame for depositing salary deferral contributions under DOL Regulation Section 2510.3-102(a)(2) (Q 5:81)
- Calculation of earnings adjustments in determining corrective allocations or distributions under the IRS's correction programs (Q 20:7)
- Fees for correcting a plan failure to timely amend for changes in the law under IRS correction procedures (Q 20:27)
- Eligible Combined Plans, a design feature for maintaining a defined contribution and defined benefit plan on a combined basis (Qs 2:270–2:274)
- Fiduciary considerations surrounding the selection of target date funds and lifetime income products for a plan (Qs 5:163–5:165)
- Links to IRS information on retirement plans for small businesses (Q 22:86)
- Updates (throughout) to reflect 2015 cost-of-living adjustments
- Guidance on safe harbor exemption from ERISA for 403(b) plans under DOL Field Assistance Bulletin 2010-01 (Qs 22:146–22:153)

- Form 5500 transitional guidance for 403(b) plans under DOL Field Assistance Bulletins 2009-02 and 2010-01 (Qs 22:157–22:158)
- Up-to-date charts comparing 401(k) plans with SEPs, SIMPLEs, 403(b) plans, and nonqualified deferred compensation plans (Tables 22-3, 22-4, 22-5, 22-7, 22-8)
- Automatic enrollment design opportunities: Automatic contribution arrangement (ACA), eligible automatic contribution arrangement (EACA), and qualified automatic contribution arrangement (QACA) (Qs 2:36–2:68)
- Up-to-date automatic enrollment sample notice templates and comparison chart (appendix B)
- Qualified reservist distributions (QRDs) under the HEART Act (Qs 16:27–16:29)
- DOL guidance on ERISA bonding requirements (Qs 5:47–5:56)
- Final DOL regulations and subsequent clarifying guidance on qualified default investment arrangements (QDIAs) under ERISA Section 404(c) (Qs 7:40–7:70)

The *401(k) Answer Book* also offers practitioners a wealth of materials and guidance, including:

- A 401(k) Compliance Calendar (appendix J)
- An IRS Rollover Chart (appendix I)
- A chart on Correcting Missed Deferrals (appendix M)
- A chart of key participant disclosures and notices with cross-references to chapters for detailed information (Table 19-2)
- Up-to-date sample notice templates for safe harbor 401(k) plan notices, automatic enrollment notices, and QDIA notices (appendices A, B, and C)
- Sample Section 404(c) checklist (appendix C)
- Model notice for an EIAA (appendix H)
- Practical information on partial plan terminations, plan mergers, and spinoffs (Qs 21:14–21:27)
- Fiduciary guidelines for selecting an annuity payment option (Q 16:42)
- Fiduciary liability after the Supreme Court's decision in *LaRue v. DeWolff, Boberg & Associates, Inc.* (Q 5:69)

- Qualified optional survivor annuity (QOSA) requirements under Code Section 417 and IRS Notice 2008-30 (Qs 17:12, 17:13)
- DOL guidance on participant statement requirements (Qs 19:40–19:51)
- ERISA Spending Accounts and other ways to manage plan expenses (Qs 4:124–4:127)
- Current rules on the use of electronic technologies for satisfying notice and consent requirements (Qs 19:125, 19:127)
- Final regulations on the Roth 401(k) feature and information on analyzing the Roth 401(k) option (Qs 2:78–2:85)
- Information on selecting service providers, including guidance from the SEC and the DOL (Qs 4:8–4:27)

Additional practice aids include the glossary, tables of cases, statutes, and authorities, and a comprehensive Index.

10/15

For questions concerning this shipment, billing, or other customer service matters, call our Customer Service Department at 1-800-234-1660.

For toll-free ordering, please call 1-800-638-8437.

401(k) Answer Book

2016 Edition

EMPOWER
RETIREMENT™

Wolters Kluwer

Published by Wolters Kluwer in New York.

Wolters Kluwer Legal & Regulatory Solutions U.S. serves customers worldwide with CCH, Aspen Publishers and Kluwer Law International products.

Printed in the United States of America

ISBN 978-1-4548-5600-9

1 2 3 4 5 6 7 8 9 0

FSC
www.fsc.org
MIX
Paper from responsible sources
FSC® C014174

About Wolters Kluwer Legal & Regulatory Solutions U.S.

Wolters Kluwer Legal & Regulatory Solutions U.S. delivers expert content and solutions in the areas of law, corporate compliance, health compliance, reimbursement, and legal education. Its practical solutions help customers successfully navigate the demands of a changing environment to drive their daily activities, enhance decision quality and inspire confident outcomes.

Serving customers worldwide, its legal and regulatory solutions portfolio includes products under the Aspen Publishers, CCH Incorporated, Kluwer Law International, Loislaw, ftwilliam.com and MediRegs names. They are regarded as exceptional and trusted resources for general legal and practice-specific knowledge, compliance and risk management, dynamic workflow solutions, and expert commentary.

WOLTERS KLUWER SUPPLEMENT NOTICE

This product is updated on a periodic basis with supplements and/or new editions to reflect important changes in the subject matter.

If you would like information about enrolling this product in the update service, or wish to receive updates billed separately with a 30-day examination review, please contact our Customer Service Department at 1-800-234-1660 or email us at: *customer.service@wolterskluwer.com*. You can also contact us at:

Wolters Kluwer
Distribution Center
7201 McKinney Circle
Frederick, MD 21704

Important Contact Information

- To order any title, go to *www.wklawbusiness.com* or call 1-800-638-8437.
- To reinstate your manual update service, call 1-800-638-8437.
- To contact Customer Service, e-mail *customer.service@wolterskluwer.com*, call 1-800-234-1660, fax 1-800-901-9075, or mail correspondence to: Order Department—Wolters Kluwer, PO Box 990, Frederick, MD 21705.
- To review your account history or pay an invoice online, visit *www.WKLawBusiness.com/payinvoices*.

Wolters Kluwer

About the Authors

Steven J. Franz is Director of Regulatory Services for Empower Retirement and oversees plan document production and plan compliance-related matters. Steve has more than 30 years of experience in the employee benefits arena. He is a graduate of the University of Wisconsin School of Law. He earned a Master of Law in Estate Planning from the University of Miami (Florida) School of Law and is a member of the Wisconsin Bar Association.

Lisa R. Richardson is Assistant Vice President of Empower. She received a law degree from the University of Minnesota Law School and was granted a Certified Employee Benefit Specialist (CEBS) designation from the International Foundation of Employee Benefit Plans and the Wharton School of the University of Pennsylvania.

Lisa is a member of the Wisconsin Bar Association, the International Society of Certified Employee Benefit Specialists, and the Greater Milwaukee Employee Benefits Council. She has written numerous articles on a variety of employee benefit topics.

Joan C. McDonagh is Senior Director of National Regulatory Policy for Empower. She received her law degree from American University, Washington College of Law and subsequently practiced law in the employee benefits area. Joan's areas of expertise include ERISA compliance, with an emphasis on fiduciary requirements.

Joan is a member of the Wisconsin Bar Association. She is on the Government Relations Committee of the Society of Professional Asset-Managers and Record Keepers (SPARK) and chairs the Public Policy Committee of the Defined Contribution Institutional Investment Association (DCIIA). She is a member and past vice president of Wisconsin Retirement Plan Professionals, Ltd. She has written numerous articles and presented a variety of seminars on retirement plan issues.

Marilyn R. Collister is Senior Director of Legislative and Regulatory Affairs for Empower. Marilyn received her law degree and Master of Law in Taxation degree from the University of Denver College of Law. She is an employee benefits attorney specializing in employer-sponsored defined contribution plans. Her areas of expertise include the unique rules applicable to governmental plans, church plans, tax-sheltered annuities, and fiduciary responsibility. She is a frequent speaker and presents seminars on various issues impacting retirement plans.

Marilyn serves on the Legislative and DC Best Practices Committees for the National Association of Government Defined Contribution Administrators (NAGDCA), the Retirement Income Task Force for the American Benefits Council, the Government Relations and 403(b) Committees for the Society of Professional Asset-Managers and Record Keepers (SPARK), and is a contributing member to a number of other industry associations.

The material in the *401(k) Answer Book* is prepared by the individual authors, contains each author's own views, and does not necessarily reflect, nor should it be construed as, the views of Empower or any of its employees or affiliates. The information contained herein is for general use only and does not constitute legal, tax, or investment advice upon which any party can rely.

Empower Retirement offers market leadership and scale as the second-largest retirement services provider in the United States according to *Pensions & Investments*, March 2015. We partner with 30,000 plans and more than 7 million participants with $435 billion in assets under administration.

We are fully committed to the retirement services industry, with expertise and diversification across all plan types, of every size, in every market segment. Empower imagines a better retirement system because we believe that those who save for their future deserve more. Through a singular focus on income replacement, the Empower experience is one that can take people on a successful journey to and through retirement.

Preface

401(k) Answer Book is designed for professionals who need quick and authoritative answers to help them decide whether to install or continue a 401(k) plan, how to coordinate 401(k) plans with other plans, and how to comply with a vast number of legal and regulatory requirements. It is the most comprehensive one-volume desk reference for pension administrators, benefit managers, fund managers, trustees, accountants, attorneys, human resources professionals, consultants, advisors, and anyone who must deal professionally with 401(k) plans. Each of the 22 chapters provides a tightly organized treatment of a design feature, plan activity, or plan-related topic. Especially convenient to the user is the grouping of all material relating to nondiscrimination testing in chapters 10 through 13. The book strives to provide a balance of formal qualification material with practical considerations for effective 401(k) plan design, administration, and communication.

Question-and-Answer Format. Each chapter begins with a brief introduction, which provides an overview of the issues that are then explored in detail in question-and-answer format.

List of Questions. The List of Questions located at the front of the publication serves as a detailed table of contents, enabling the reader to locate areas of immediate interest.

Practice Aids. The text is interspersed with examples, practice pointers, and sample calculations that help to illustrate the concepts discussed and assist in understanding.

Glossary. A glossary containing definitions of technical terms that have specific legal meaning and commonly used acronyms is provided.

Tables. Compilations of Internal Revenue Code sections, Treasury Regulations sections, ERISA sections, Department of Labor regulations, and other relevant statutes and regulations, agency rulings, opinions, and memoranda discussed in the chapters are provided to assist users in locating regulatory source material referenced in the text. A table of cases is also provided.

Topical Index. A comprehensive index is provided as a further aid to locating specific information.

Acronyms and Abbreviations. Because the subject area covered is replete with technical and legal terms, *401(k) Answer Book* employs acronyms and abbreviations when such terms are mentioned frequently in a chapter. Upon first mention in the chapter, the term or the name of the statute is spelled out in full, and its corresponding abbreviation or acronym is given in parentheses. Subsequent mention of the term or statute will use only the abbreviation or acronym. The most common of these shorthand references are the following:

- Code—Internal Revenue Code of 1986, as amended (Section references unless otherwise qualified refer to the I.R.C.)
- DOL—U.S. Department of Labor
- EBSA—Employee Benefits Security Administration (formerly the Pension Welfare Benefits Administration)
- EGTRRA—Economic Growth and Tax Relief Reconciliation Act of 2001
- ERISA—Employee Retirement Income Security Act of 1974, as amended
- GUST—An acronym applied to GATT, USERRA, SBJPA, and TRA '97
- IRS—Internal Revenue Service
- PBGC—Pension Benefit Guaranty Corporation
- PPA—Pension Protection Act of 2006
- SBJPA—Small Business Job Protection Act of 1996
- TRA '97—Taxpayer Relief Act of 1997
- USERRA—Uniformed Services Employment and Reemployment Rights Act of 1994

As with previous editions, the objective of this edition is to provide accessible, concise discussions of all aspects of 401(k) plan design and administration, as well as the relationship of 401(k) plans with other types of retirement plans.

While the authors have made every attempt to ensure that the material in this book is current, given the regulatory and legislative environment, some rules may change by the time this book is in print.

Steven J. Franz
Lisa R. Richardson
Joan C. McDonagh
Marilyn R. Collister

Contents

List of Questions xxiii

CHAPTER 1

Introduction 1-1

History of 401(k) Plans 1-2

Advantages and Disadvantages of 401(k) Plans 1-4

Taxes and 401(k) Plans 1-8

Analyzing the Roth 401(k) Option 1-12

Types of Entities That May Use 401(k) Plans 1-17

When a 401(k) Plan Is Appropriate 1-18

Multiemployer and Multiple-Employer 401(k) Plans ... 1-20

Multiple-Employer Plans 1-22

Market for and Utilization of 401(k) Plans 1-24

Future of 401(k) Plans 1-25

Legislative and Regulatory Developments Affecting 401(k) Plans 1-27

Proposed Legislation and Regulatory Developments 1-41

CHAPTER 2

401(k) Plan Design 2-1

Design Options and Objectives 2-2

Types of 401(k) Plan Contributions and Automatic Contribution Arrangements 2-11

Qualified Automatic Contribution Arrangements 2-19

Basic Qualification Requirements 2-44

SIMPLE 401(k) Plans 2-66

Safe Harbor 401(k) Plans 2-71

Eligible Combined Plans 2-83

CHAPTER 3

The 401(k) Plan Document 3-1

Plan Document Alternatives 3-1

Advance IRS Approval 3-9

CHAPTER 4

Plan Services and Service Providers 4-1

401(k) Plan Services 4-2

Selecting Plan Administration Services 4-5

Selecting Investment Services 4-11

Allocation of Earnings and Expenses 4-16

Payment of Fees and Expenses 4-20

Legal and Regulatory Initiatives Concerning 401(k) Plan Fees 4-32

DOL Final Rule on Service Provider Fee Disclosure 4-34

Other Activity on Fee Disclosure 4-49

CHAPTER 5

Fiduciary and Prohibited Transaction Rules 5-1

Fiduciary Issues 5-2

Prohibited Transactions 5-28

Managing Fiduciary Liability in a 401(k) Plan 5-48

Managing Personal Liability 5-53

The Voluntary Fiduciary Correction Program 5-58

Fiduciary Concerns Related to Specific Investment Products 5-64

CHAPTER 6

Investing Plan Assets 6-1

Primary Asset Classes 6-2

Investment Vehicles 6-5

Asset Allocation Strategy 6-20

Managed Account Service 6-21

Employer Securities 6-21

Directed Trustee Considerations 6-35

401(k) Stock Ownership Plans 6-37

Self-Directed Options 6-38

Investment Policies 6-42

Selecting and Monitoring Plan Investments 6-43

Mutual Fund Investigations 6-44

Investment Fees and Revenue Sharing 6-45

CHAPTER 7

Participant Direction of Investments—ERISA Section 404(c) 7-1

Participant-Directed Plans 7-1

Broad Range of Investment Alternatives 7-4

Independent Exercise of Control 7-6

Disclosure Requirements 7-7

Investment Change Frequency 7-9

Investment Elections 7-11

Fiduciary Liability Relief 7-12

Qualified Default Investment Arrangements 7-14

Blackouts and Changes in Investment Options 7-29

Litigation Involving Participant-Directed Plans 7-30

CHAPTER 8

Participant Communication and Education 8-1

An Effective 401(k) Communication Program 8-2

Department of Labor Guidance on Participant Investment Education 8-10

Individual Retirement Planning 8-20

CHAPTER 9

Contribution Limits 9-1

Limits on Elective Deferrals 9-2

Code Section 415—Annual Addition Limits 9-14

Code Section 404—Deduction Limits 9-21

CHAPTER 10

Data for Nondiscrimination Testing 10-1

Who Is the Employer? 10-2

What Is a Plan? 10-23

Who Is an Employee? 10-26

Who Is a Highly Compensated Employee? 10-30

What Is Compensation? 10-37

CHAPTER 11

Minimum Coverage Testing 11-1

Minimum Participation 11-1

Minimum Coverage 11-2

Correcting Minimum Coverage Failure 11-15

CHAPTER 12

General Nondiscrimination Testing 12-1

Testing of Employer Nonelective Contributions 12-1

Permitted Disparity 12-7

Nondiscriminatory Availability of Benefits, Rights, and Features 12-11

CHAPTER 13

ADP and ACP Testing 13-1

Avoiding ADP and ACP Testing 13-2

The Actual Deferral Percentage Test 13-2

The Actual Contribution Percentage Test 13-21

CHAPTER 14

Top-Heavy Rules 14-1

Top-Heavy Testing 14-2

Minimum Vesting 14-11

Minimum Contributions 14-12

Top-Heavy Strategy 14-16

CHAPTER 15

Participant Loans, Hardship Withdrawals, and In-Service Distributions 15-1

Participant Loans 15-2

Hardship Withdrawals of Elective Contributions 15-23

In-Service Distributions 15-29

Hurricane Sandy Relief 15-31

CHAPTER 16

Distributions Subsequent to Termination of Employment 16-1

Optional Forms of Benefit 16-2

Minimum Distribution Requirements 16-13

Participants Called to Active Military Duty 16-21

Rollover Rules 16-22

Withholding on Distributions 16-38

Claims for Benefits 16-46

CHAPTER 17

Spousal Rights 17-1

Survivor Annuity Requirements 17-1

Annuity and Other Lifetime Income Products 17-2

Qualified Domestic Relations Orders 17-16

CHAPTER 18

Taxation of 401(k) Plans 18-1

Payroll Taxes 18-2

Taxation and Reporting of Distributions and Pre-Tax Contributions 18-6

Life Insurance 18-16

Loans 18-17

Distribution of Excess Deferrals 18-18

Distributions of Excess Contributions and Excess Aggregate Contributions 18-19

Taxation of Roth Distributions and In-Plan Roth Rollovers 18-20

Other Taxes 18-29

Filing Requirements for Distributions 18-33

Distribution Planning 18-35

CHAPTER 19

Reporting and Disclosure 19-1

IRS and DOL Form 5500 Reporting 19-2

EFAST2 19-9

Special Filing Issues 19-14

Participant Disclosures 19-15

Use of Electronic Technology 19-70

Record Retention Under ERISA 19-82

CHAPTER 20

Correcting 401(k) Plan Qualification Errors 20-1

Employee Plans Compliance Resolution System 20-2

Self-Correction Program 20-7

Voluntary Correction Program 20-11

Audit Closing Agreement Program 20-13

CHAPTER 21

Plan Terminations, Mergers, Spinoffs, and
Abandoned Plans 21-1

Plan Terminations 21-1

Missing Participants 21-4

Partial Termination 21-8

Mergers and Spinoffs 21-10

Plan Considerations During Major Business Transactions 21-14

Abandoned Plans 21-17

CHAPTER 22

401(k) Plan Alternatives 22-1

Individual Retirement Arrangements (IRAs) 22-2

Simplified Employee Pensions (SEPs) and Salary Reduction SEPs (SARSEPs) 22-14

SIMPLE IRAs and SIMPLE 401(k) Plans 22-21

Cash Balance Plans 22-29

Floor-Offset Plans 22-29

Nonqualified Deferred Compensation (NQDC) Plans 22-29

Section 403(b) Plans—Tax-Sheltered Annuities 22-38

Section 457(b) Eligible Deferred Compensation Plans 22-52

APPENDIX **A**

Sample Safe Harbor 401(k) Plan Notice **A-1**

APPENDIX **B**

Automatic Contribution Arrangement Comparison Chart and Sample Notices **B-1**

Automatic Contribution Arrangement Comparison Chart **B-2**

Sample Notice for Plans with an Automatic Contribution Arrangement (ACA) **B-3**

Sample Notice for Plans with an Eligible Automatic Contribution Arrangement (EACA) **B-4**

Sample Notice for Plans with a Qualified Automatic Contribution Arrangement (QACA) **B-9**

Sample Notice for Safe Harbor QACA Plans with an Eligible Automatic Contribution Arrangement (EACA) **B-13**

APPENDIX **C**

Sample Plan Sponsor Fiduciary Manual, Fiduciary Checklist, ERISA Section 404(c) Compliance Checklist, and QDIA Notice **C-1**

Sample Plan Sponsor Fiduciary Manual **C-1**

Sample Plan Sponsor Fiduciary Checklist **C-8**

Sample ERISA Section 404(c) Compliance Checklist **C-10**

Sample Qualified Default Investment Alternative (QDIA) Notice **C-12**

Sample ERISA Section 404(a) Participant Disclosure Checklist C-14

APPENDIX D

Key Indexed Limits (2013–2014) D-1

APPENDIX E

Key Indexed Limits Affected by the Economic Growth and Tax Relief Reconciliation Act of 2001 (EGTRRA) E-1

APPENDIX F

DOL Model Blackout Notice F-1

APPENDIX G

IRS Model Diversification Notice for Plans Holding Publicly Traded Employer Securities G-1

APPENDIX H

Model Participant Disclosure Regarding Eligible Investment Advice Arrangements (EIAAs) H-1

APPENDIX I

IRS Rollover Chart I-1

APPENDIX J

401(k) Plan Compliance Calendar J-1

APPENDIX K

DOL Model Comparative Chart K-1

APPENDIX L

Sample DOL Guide to 408(b)(2) Initial Disclosures L-1

APPENDIX M

Fixing Common Plan Mistakes—Correcting Missed Deferrals M-1

GLOSSARY GL-1

TABLES

Internal Revenue Code Sections T-1

United States Code T-9

ERISA T-11

Pension Protection Act of 2006 .... T-13

Cases T-15

Code of Federal Regulations T-17

Treasury Regulations T-19

Department of Labor Regulations, Opinions, and Field Bulletins T-27

Miscellaneous IRS Announcements, Notices, Memoranda, Rulings, and Procedures T-31

INDEX IN-1

List of Questions

Chapter 1 Introduction

History of 401(k) Plans

Q 1:1	What was the Internal Revenue Service's position on cash or deferred arrangements prior to the addition of Section 401(k) to the Internal Revenue Code?	1-2
Q 1:2	How did the passage of Code Section 401(k) influence the growth of cash or deferred arrangements?	1-3

Advantages and Disadvantages of 401(k) Plans

Q 1:3	How does offering a 401(k) plan benefit the employer?	1-4
Q 1:4	How do competitive pressures motivate an employer to establish a 401(k) plan?	1-5
Q 1:5	What tax-related objectives may an employer have in establishing a 401(k) plan?	1-5
Q 1:6	How can a 401(k) plan replace or supplement a defined benefit plan?	1-5
Q 1:7	What type of employer is most likely to offer both a 401(k) and a defined benefit plan?	1-6
Q 1:8	Are there disadvantages to an employer in sponsoring a 401(k) plan?	1-6
Q 1:9	How does a 401(k) plan benefit employees?	1-6
Q 1:10	How may a 401(k) plan supplement an employee's personal savings program?	1-7
Q 1:11	How is a 401(k) plan viewed by employees in a competitive environment?	1-7
Q 1:12	Are there disadvantages to an employee for participating in a 401(k) plan?	1-7

Taxes and 401(k) Plans

Q 1:13	In a stable tax environment, what are the advantages of accumulating money in a tax-deferred vehicle?	1-8

Q 1:14	Does it make sense to defer compensation in a rising tax environment?	1-8
Q 1:15	If an employee chooses to defer salary for a period of ten years, what impact will tax rate changes have?	1-10
Q 1:16	How does a 401(k) plan compare with an after-tax investment in a tax-deferred investment vehicle?	1-10
Q 1:17	When might a company choose after-tax savings over a 401(k) plan?	1-11

Analyzing the Roth 401(k) Option

Q 1:18	What factors should be considered when deciding whether to contribute on a Roth basis or a before-tax basis?	1-12
Q 1:19	How does ability to maximize deferrals and pay current income tax affect the decision regarding participation in a Roth 401(k) plan?	1-12
Q 1:20	How do anticipated post-retirement tax rates affect the decision whether to participate in a Roth 401(k)?	1-14
Q 1:21	How does a participant's anticipated earnings rate affect the decision regarding the Roth 401(k) option?	1-15
Q 1:22	How does the number of years until benefits are needed affect the decision regarding a Roth 401(k)?	1-15
Q 1:23	How does the level of concern for tax diversification affect the decision regarding the Roth 401(k)?	1-17
Q 1:24	How does the extension of EGTRRA affect a participant's decision regarding the Roth 401(k)?	1-17
Q 1:25	How does a participant's confidence that he or she can avoid taking distributions from the Roth account until the account is "qualified" affect the decision regarding a Roth 401(k)?	1-17

Types of Entities That May Use 401(k) Plans

Q 1:26	What entities may adopt a 401(k) plan?	1-17
Q 1:27	Can other types of cash or deferred arrangements be offered by governmental or tax-exempt employers?	1-18
Q 1:28	What kinds of plans may offer a 401(k) feature?	1-18

When a 401(k) Plan Is Appropriate

Q 1:29	Does it make economic sense for a small business owner to establish or continue a qualified plan?	1-18
Q 1:30	Are 401(k) plans appropriate for unincorporated businesses?	1-19
Q 1:31	When is a 401(k) plan appropriate for a sole proprietorship?	1-19
Q 1:32	What are the considerations in designing a 401(k) plan for a partnership?	1-19
Q 1:33	Can a limited liability company sponsor a 401(k) plan?	1-20

Q 1:34 What are the 401(k) design considerations for a small or professional business? 1-20

Multiemployer and Multiple-Employer 401(k) Plans

Q 1:35 Why do multiemployer units consider 401(k) plans? 1-21
Q 1:36 In replacing a defined benefit plan, how is the 401(k) plan structured? 1-21
Q 1:37 How is a supplemental 401(k) plan structured? 1-21
Q 1:38 What design and administration features are unique to a multiemployer 401(k) plan? 1-21

Multiple-Employer Plans

Q 1:39 How do multiple-employer plans work? 1-22
Q 1:40 What are the benefits to participating employers of joining a MEP? 1-23
Q 1:41 What is an "Open MEP"? 1-23
Q 1:42 What legal concerns arise with Open MEPs? 1-23
Q 1:43 What is the practical significance of the DOL's ruling that Open MEPS are not single-employer sponsored plans? 1-23

Market for and Utilization of 401(k) Plans

Q 1:44 How many 401(k) plans and participants are there in the United States? 1-24
Q 1:45 What are average participation rates in 401(k) plans? 1-24
Q 1:46 Does the fact that a 401(k) plan offers a matching employer contribution noticeably affect 401(k) participation? 1-24

Future of 401(k) Plans

Q 1:47 How are demographic trends affecting 401(k) plans? 1-25
Q 1:48 What economic trends are affecting 401(k) plans? 1-25
Q 1:49 What are the prospects for 401(k) plans?. 1-26

Legislative and Regulatory Developments Affecting 401(k) Plans

The Economic Growth and Tax Relief Reconciliation Act of 2001

Q 1:50 What are the key areas of change to 401(k) plans resulting from EGTRRA?. 1-28
Q 1:51 How has EGTRRA changed plan contribution and benefit limits?. 1-28
Q 1:52 How were employers' deduction limits for plan contributions changed by EGTRRA? 1-29

Q 1:53 How were the rollover rules changed by EGTRRA? 1-30

Q 1:54 How did EGTRRA change the rules for IRAs? 1-30

Q 1:55 How did EGTRRA encourage the use of qualified plans by small employers? 1-31

Q 1:56 How did EGTRRA simplify the rules for plan administration? . . . 1-31

Q 1:57 What was unique about the effective dates for EGTRRA? 1-32

The Pension Protection Act of 2006

Q 1:58 What changes did the PPA make to automatic enrollment plans? 1-32

Q 1:59 What changes did the PPA make with respect to ERISA's fiduciary and prohibited transaction rules? 1-32

Q 1:60 What changes did the PPA make to the rules concerning plan distributions or other withdrawals? 1-33

Q 1:61 What changes did the PPA make to ERISA's notice, reporting, and disclosure requirements? 1-33

Q 1:62 What changes did the PPA make to plans offering employer securities as an investment option? 1-34

Q 1:63 What other changes did the PPA make that significantly impact 401(k) plans? 1-34

Q 1:64 What are some changes made by the PPA that impact plans other than 401(k) plans? 1-35

The Uniformed Services Employment and Reemployment Rights Act of 1994

Q 1:65 What action must an employee take in order to secure reemployment rights under USERRA? 1-35

Q 1:66 Does the rehired employee have the opportunity to make elective deferral contributions with respect to the period of military service? 1-36

Q 1:67 What compensation is taken into account in determining the rehired employee's additional elective deferrals? 1-36

Q 1:68 What contributions must the employer make? 1-36

Q 1:69 Must employee and employer contributions be adjusted for earnings? 1-36

Q 1:70 How are employee and employer contributions treated for testing purposes? 1-37

The Heroes Earnings and Assistance Relief Tax (HEART) Act of 2008

Q 1:71 How did the HEART Act change the rules regarding differential wage payments? 1-37

Q 1:72 How does the HEART Act impact the qualified reservist distribution rules? 1-37

Q 1:73 How does the HEART Act change the rules regarding death and disability benefits available to military personnel and their beneficiaries? 1-38

The Worker, Retiree, and Employer Recovery Act of 2008

Q 1:74 What are the technical corrections to the Pension Protection Act of 2006 included in the WRERA? 1-39

Q 1:75 What new rules in the WRERA are designed to provide economic relief to 401(k) plan sponsors and participants? . . . 1-40

The Dodd-Frank Wall Street Reform and Consumer Protection Act of 2010

Q 1:76 What impact will the Dodd-Frank Act have on 401(k) plans? . . . 1-40

The American Taxpayer Relief Act of 2012

Q 1:77 How did ACT expand in-plan Roth conversion opportunities? 1-41

Establishment of MyRA Accounts

Proposed Legislation and Regulatory Developments

Q 1:78 What proposals are the Obama administration considering? . . . 1-41

Q 1:79 What significant new guidance has the Treasury Department issued? 1-42

Q 1:80 What significant new guidance has the Department of Labor issued? 1-44

Q 1:81 What other significant guidance has been issued affecting 401(k) plans? 1-45

Q 1:82 What did the SEC report recommend regarding a uniform standard of care for brokers and advisers? 1-46

Chapter 2 401(k) Plan Design

Design Options and Objectives

Q 2:1 What elements of employee demographics should be considered in designing a 401(k) plan? 2-2

Q 2:2 How does the size of the workforce affect 401(k) plan design? 2-2

Q 2:3 How do the pay levels of employees affect 401(k) plan design? 2-3

Q 2:4 What is the impact of employee turnover on 401(k) plan design? 2-3

Options That Impact Plan Expenses

Q 2:5 What financial considerations should an employer take into account before adopting a 401(k) plan? 2-3
Q 2:6 How much will matching contributions cost? 2-4
Q 2:7 How is the expected cost of the match computed? 2-4
Q 2:8 What other costs may be incurred in conjunction with a 401(k) plan? 2-4
Q 2:9 Should plan expenses be paid from plan assets? 2-5
Q 2:10 Can plan expenses be used by the employer as a credit against taxes owed by the employer? 2-5

Options That Impact Plan Participation

Q 2:11 What is the impact of matching contributions on plan participation? 2-6
Q 2:12 Should matching contributions be fixed or discretionary? 2-6
Q 2:13 Should matching contributions be ongoing or made at year's end? 2-6
Q 2:14 Should an employer that makes ongoing match contributions do true-up match contributions after the end of the plan year? 2-7
Q 2:15 Why might an employer choose to make discretionary nonelective contributions to its 401(k) plan? 2-7
Q 2:16 How does the employer make a choice between allocating funds to matching contributions and allocating them to discretionary contributions? 2-7
Q 2:17 How may qualified nonelective contributions be used in a 401(k) plan? 2-8
Q 2:18 Is access to plan funds important to encourage participation in 401(k) plans? 2-8
Q 2:19 Are there tax incentives available to lower-paid participants to encourage their participation in 401(k) plans? 2-9
Q 2:20 What is the amount of the saver's credit? 2-9
Q 2:21 Is the saver's credit permanent? 2-9
Q 2:22 Who is an *eligible individual*? 2-9
Q 2:23 What is a *qualified retirement savings contribution*? 2-9
Q 2:24 Can an employer establish a 401(k) plan that will cover just one participant? 2-10
Q 2:25 What special consideration applies to employers that, under the law, can maintain either a 403(b) plan or a 401(k) plan? 2-10

Types of 401(k) Plan Contributions and Automatic Contribution Arrangements

Q 2:26 What types of contributions are generally found in a 401(k) plan? 2-11

Elective Contributions

Q 2:27 What is an *elective contribution*? 2-11

Q 2:28 What is a *cash or deferred election*? 2-11

Q 2:29 Does a cash or deferred election include an arrangement under an employee stock ownership plan, pursuant to which dividends are either distributed or invested pursuant to the election made by the participant in accordance with Code Section 404(k)(2)(A)(iii)? 2-11

Q 2:30 May a contribution pursuant to a cash or deferred election be made before the performance of services with respect to which the contribution is made? 2-12

Q 2:31 Is there an exception to the general rule that contributions made pursuant to a cash or deferred election will be treated as elective contributions only if made after the performance of services with respect to which the elective contributions are made? 2-12

Q 2:32 Is a one-time election to defer a specified amount or percentage of an employee's compensation considered a cash or deferred election? 2-12

Q 2:33 Will the dollar equivalent of a participant's unused paid time off that is contributed by an employer to a 401(k) plan be considered an elective deferral contribution? 2-13

Automatic Enrollment Feature

Q 2:34 Must an employee's cash or deferred election be affirmative? 2-14

Q 2:35 What requirements must an automatic enrollment feature satisfy? 2-14

Automatic Contribution Arrangements Under the Pension Protection Act of 2006

Q 2:36 How does the Pension Protection Act of 2006 affect the use of automatic enrollment features in a 401(k) plan? 2-15

Q 2:37 What is an *automatic contribution arrangement* under PPA? . . . 2-15

Q 2:38 Must employees receive notice of the ACA? 2-15

Q 2:39 Is there any penalty for failing to provide the ACA notice? 2-15

Q 2:40 Why would an employer want to add an ACA to its 401(k) plan? 2-15

Eligible Automatic Contribution Arrangements

Q 2:41 What is an *eligible automatic contribution arrangement*? 2-16

Q 2:42 Must employees receive notice of the EACA? 2-16

Q 2:43 What other requirements must an EACA satisfy? 2-16

Q 2:44 Is an EACA required to be made available to all participants? 2-17

Q 2:45	What does it mean to be a *covered employee* under an EACA?	**2-17**
Q 2:46	Can an EACA be added to a 401(k) plan at any time other than the beginning of the plan year?	**2-17**
Q 2:47	Why would an employer want to add an EACA to its 401(k) plan?	**2-17**
Q 2:48	How do the permissible withdrawal provisions work?	**2-18**
Q 2:49	What are the tax consequences of a permissible withdrawal?	**2-18**
Q 2:50	Is there any other advantage to a 401(k) plan's adopting an EACA?	**2-18**
Q 2:51	What was the effective date of the EACA provisions of the PPA?	**2-19**
	Qualified Automatic Contribution Arrangements	
Q 2:52	What is a *qualified automatic contribution arrangement*?	**2-19**
Q 2:53	Must employees receive notice of the QACA?	**2-19**
Q 2:54	By what date must the automatic deferral percentage be implemented for an employee who fails to make an affirmative election?	**2-20**
Q 2:55	What matters must the notice address?	**2-20**
Q 2:56	Why would an employer want to add a QACA to its 401(k) plan?	**2-20**
Q 2:57	What is meant by the term *qualified percentage* as used in Q 2:52?	**2-20**
Q 2:58	By what date must the initial qualified percentage be increased?	**2-21**
Q 2:59	What is the maximum qualified percentage a QACA can provide?	**2-21**
Q 2:60	Must the employer make contributions to a QACA 401(k) plan?	**2-21**
Q 2:61	Can a 401(k) plan containing a QACA have a safe harbor match formula other than the formula set forth in Q 2:60?	**2-21**
Q 2:62	Can a 401(k) plan containing a QACA require a non-highly compensated employee to be employed on the last day of the plan year and/or complete a specified number of hours of service in the plan year in order to be entitled to a safe harbor contribution?	**2-22**
Q 2:63	Are employer safe harbor contributions made to a 401(k) plan that contains a QACA required to be 100 percent vested?	**2-22**
Q 2:64	Are employer safe harbor contributions to a 401(k) plan containing a QACA subject to the same restrictions on withdrawals as those that apply to employer safe harbor contributions to a safe harbor plan?	**2-22**

Q 2:65	How do the top-heavy rules apply to a 401(k) plan containing a QACA?	2-22
Q 2:66	Is a QACA required to be applied to all participants?	2-22
Q 2:67	How does the definition of compensation in a QACA differ from that for a safe harbor plan?	2-23
Q 2:68	What was the effective date of the QACA provisions of the PPA?	2-23
	Other Elective Deferral Issues and Considerations	
Q 2:69	How frequently must 401(k) plan participants be allowed to make a cash or deferred election?	2-23
Q 2:70	When is compensation considered currently available to an employee?	2-23
Q 2:71	When is an amount considered currently available to a partner in a 401(k) plan sponsored by a partnership?	2-24
Q 2:72	When is a sole proprietor's compensation deemed currently available for purposes of determining the date by which the sole proprietor must make a cash or deferred election?	2-24
Q 2:73	May a self-employed individual defer cash advance payments made during the plan year and before the amount of his or her earned income is finally determined?	2-24
Q 2:74	Are there special limitations that apply to elective contributions?	2-25
Q 2:75	Are elective contributions considered employee contributions?	2-25
Q 2:76	Are there special rules for elective contributions on bonuses?	2-25
Q 2:77	What special rules apply to elective contributions for employees who have veterans' reemployment rights under USERRA?	2-25
	Roth Contributions	
Q 2:78	What is a *Roth contribution*?	2-26
Q 2:79	Under what circumstances will an elective contribution be treated as a Roth contribution?	2-26
Q 2:80	Can a 401(k) plan be designed to offer participants only the Roth option?	2-26
Q 2:81	Can Roth contributions be made part of a 401(k) plan that provides for automatic enrollment?	2-26
Q 2:82	Must Roth contributions be allocated to a separate account?	2-26
Q 2:83	Must Roth contributions meet the same requirements that apply to elective contributions that are not designated as Roth contributions?	2-27
Q 2:84	Are participants able to convert pre-tax elective contributions into Roth contributions?	2-27

Q 2:85 How long have 401(k) plan participants been able to make Roth contributions? . . . 2-27

Matching Contributions

Q 2:86 What is a *matching contribution*? . . . 2-27
Q 2:87 May matching contributions be made on a discretionary basis? . . . 2-28
Q 2:88 May matching contributions be made on a discretionary basis in a SIMPLE 401(k) plan? . . . 2-28
Q 2:89 May matching contributions be made on a discretionary basis in a safe harbor 401(k) plan under Code Section 401(k)(12)? . . . 2-28
Q 2:90 May matching contributions be made on a discretionary basis to a 401(k) plan that contains a qualified automatic contribution arrangement? . . . 2-28
Q 2:91 May matching contributions be made on behalf of self-employed persons who participate in a 401(k) plan maintained by a partnership or sole proprietorship? . . . 2-28
Q 2:92 What special rules apply to matching contributions for employees who have veterans' reemployment rights under USERRA? . . . 2-29
Q 2:93 What special rules apply to matching contributions in the case of a participant who dies or becomes disabled while performing qualified military service? . . . 2-29

Nonelective Contributions

Q 2:94 What is a *nonelective contribution*? . . . 2-29
Q 2:95 What eligibility requirements may be imposed on a 401(k) participant for purposes of receiving a nonelective contribution allocation? . . . 2-30
Q 2:96 What eligibility requirements may be imposed on a 401(k) participant in the case of a SIMPLE 401(k) plan or a safe harbor 401(k) plan under Code Section 401(k)(12)? . . . 2-30
Q 2:97 What eligibility requirements may be imposed on a 401(k) plan that contains a QACA? . . . 2-30
Q 2:98 What are the special concerns of a plan sponsor that imposes minimum hours and/or last day requirements? . . . 2-30
Q 2:99 What special rules apply to nonelective contributions for employees who have veterans' reemployment rights under USERRA? . . . 2-31
Q 2:100 Do special rules apply to nonelective contributions in the case of a participant who dies or becomes disabled while performing qualified military service? . . . 2-31

Allocation Methods

Q 2:101 What methods of allocation of nonelective contributions are available to the sponsor of a 401(k) plan? 2-31

Q 2:102 What are the design-based safe harbor allocation methods? 2-31

Q 2:103 How does the points system allocation method work? 2-32

Q 2:104 What alternative formulas for allocation of discretionary nonelective contributions are available? 2-32

Q 2:105 How does an age-weighted formula differ from a design-based safe harbor formula? 2-34

Q 2:106 How does a new comparability formula differ from a design-based safe harbor formula? 2-34

Q 2:107 How does the conversion from contributions to benefits operate? 2-34

Q 2:108 How are the age-weighting factors determined? 2-35

Q 2:109 How is the contribution allocated to participants under an age-weighted formula? 2-36

Q 2:110 How does an age-weighted formula automatically satisfy the nondiscrimination tests? 2-36

Q 2:111 How is the contribution allocated to participants under a new comparability formula? 2-36

Q 2:112 Will a new comparability formula automatically satisfy the nondiscrimination rules? 2-37

Q 2:113 How does the general nondiscrimination test apply to a new comparability formula? 2-37

Q 2:114 Are there any other restrictions on the use of new comparability formulas in 401(k) plans? 2-37

Q 2:115 When would an age-weighted or new comparability formula be used in lieu of a design-based safe harbor formula or a defined benefit plan? 2-37

Q 2:116 What are the drawbacks of these formulas? 2-38

Q 2:117 In what situations is an age-weighted formula an effective plan design? 2-38

Q 2:118 In what situations is a new comparability formula effective? . . . 2-39

Q 2:119 Will 401(k) plans that contain new comparability formulas that pass the general test always be treated as nondiscriminatory? 2-39

Deemed IRA Contributions

Q 2:120 What is a *deemed IRA contribution*? 2-40

Q 2:121 To what types of IRAs can a deemed IRA contribution be made? 2-40

Q 2:122 What plan document requirements must be met before a 401(k) plan can accept deemed IRA contributions? 2-40

Q 2:123 Must a deemed IRA contribution be kept separate from the other assets of the 401(k) plan? **2-40**

Q 2:124 Are there restrictions on who can serve as trustee of a 401(k) plan that allows for deemed IRA contributions? **2-40**

Q 2:125 How will distribution rules be applied? **2-41**

Q 2:126 Must the 401(k) plan make the deemed IRA contribution feature available to all participants? **2-41**

Q 2:127 Is a 401(k) plan required to accept deemed IRA contributions? **2-41**

Q 2:128 How is the deductibility of IRA contributions to a deemed traditional IRA determined? **2-41**

Q 2:129 What happens if a deemed IRA fails to satisfy qualification requirements applicable to IRAs? **2-41**

Q 2:130 Is a deemed IRA subject to ERISA requirements? **2-41**

Transfer or Rollover of Benefits

Q 2:131 What methods exist for moving benefits from one plan or IRA to a 401(k) plan? **2-42**

Q 2:132 What is a *direct rollover*? **2-42**

Q 2:133 What is a *60-day rollover*? **2-42**

Q 2:134 What is a *transfer*? **2-42**

Q 2:135 What is an *elective transfer*? **2-42**

Q 2:136 What design considerations should govern whether a plan should accept rollover contributions? **2-43**

Q 2:137 If a plan accepts rollover contributions, should any steps be taken to ensure that the contribution is eligible for rollover? **2-43**

Q 2:138 Are plans required to accept transfers? **2-43**

Q 2:139 What considerations are involved in accepting plan transfers? **2-43**

Q 2:140 How are transferred or rolled-over benefits counted for purposes of nondiscrimination testing? **2-44**

Basic Qualification Requirements

Q 2:141 How do basic qualification requirements affect the design of a 401(k) plan? **2-44**

Q 2:142 What advantages accrue to a 401(k) plan that is qualified? **2-44**

Formal Requirements

Q 2:143 Must the 401(k) plan be in writing? **2-45**

Q 2:144 Can a person other than the employer establish and maintain a 401(k) plan for the employees of that employer? **2-45**

Q 2:145 Is there any type of employer that is precluded from sponsoring a 401(k) plan? **2-45**

Q 2:146	Who is considered a *governmental employer*?	2-45
Q 2:147	Are there certain governmental employers that can sponsor a 401(k) plan?	2-46
Q 2:148	Are governmental 401(k) plans subject to the same qualification requirements that apply to 401(k) plans sponsored by nongovernmental employers?	2-46
Q 2:149	Does the plan have to be communicated to employees?	2-46
Q 2:150	How are assets of the plan held?	2-46
Q 2:151	Can a 401(k) plan provide insurance benefits to participants?	2-47
	Continuing Contributions	
Q 2:152	Must the 401(k) plan be a permanent and continuing arrangement?	2-47
Q 2:153	Can the employer take back contributions that have been made to the 401(k) plan?	2-47
Q 2:154	Under what limited circumstances may contributions be returned to the employer without jeopardizing the qualified status of the 401(k) plan?	2-47
	Assignment of Benefits	
Q 2:155	May participants assign or alienate their benefits?	2-48
Q 2:156	What exceptions to the anti-assignment rule are recognized by the IRS?	2-48
Q 2:157	Is there an exception to the anti-assignment rules for bankruptcy of the participant?	2-49
Q 2:158	Is there an exception to the anti-assignment rules for amounts owed to the employer?	2-49
	Merger or Consolidation	
Q 2:159	What protection must participants have in the event of merger or consolidation?	2-49
	Nondiscrimination Rules	
Q 2:160	What is the purpose of the nondiscrimination rules?	2-50
Q 2:161	What are the basic nondiscrimination requirements?	2-50
	Compensation and Benefit Limits	
Q 2:162	How much compensation can be used for calculating plan contributions or benefits?	2-50
Q 2:163	Is there a limit placed on the amount that can be allocated to a participant in a 401(k) plan?	2-50
Q 2:164	What are the annual limits under Code Section 415?	2-51

Q 2:165 Are there special limits that apply to elective contributions? . . . **2-51**

Q 2:166 Do contributions need to be based on business profits?. **2-51**

Distribution Requirements

Q 2:167 Are there basic qualification requirements relating to how benefits must be paid from a 401(k) plan? **2-51**

Q 2:168 Must a participant have the option to make a direct rollover of a distribution to an IRA or other qualified plan? **2-51**

Eligibility Rights

Q 2:169 Can a 401(k) plan place restrictions on which employees may become plan participants? **2-52**

Q 2:170 May a 401(k) plan require employees to reach a certain age before they can become plan participants? **2-52**

Q 2:171 May a 401(k) plan exclude from participation any employee who has reached a specified age? **2-52**

Q 2:172 What length of service requirement may a 401(k) plan impose? **2-52**

Q 2:173 What is a *year of service*? **2-52**

Q 2:174 What is an *eligibility computation period*? **2-52**

Q 2:175 What is an *hour of service*? **2-53**

Q 2:176 Do the regulations provide other methods for determining hours of service?. **2-53**

Q 2:177 Why would an employer decide to use an elapsed time system for calculating service rather than a system based on hours of service? **2-54**

Q 2:178 After an employee has satisfied the minimum age and/or service requirements under a 401(k) plan, when must participation commence? **2-54**

Q 2:179 May an employee waive participation?. **2-55**

Q 2:180 May a 401(k) plan exclude part-time employees from plan participation? **2-55**

Break-in-Service Rules

Q 2:181 If a participant terminates employment and is then rehired at a later date, is the plan allowed to ignore years of service completed by the participant before termination of employment? **2-55**

Q 2:182 What are the break-in-service rules? **2-56**

Q 2:183 How does the one-year break-in-service rule operate?. **2-56**

Q 2:184 What is the *rule of parity*? **2-56**

Q 2:185 How does the two-year, 100 percent vested break-in-service rule operate? **2-56**

Q 2:186 What is a *one-year break in service*? **2-57**

Q 2:187 What computation period is used for determining whether an employee incurs a one-year break in service? **2-57**

Q 2:188 How do maternity or paternity leaves of absence affect the determination of whether an employee incurs a one-year break in service for purposes of eligibility? **2-57**

Q 2:189 What special rules apply for employees who have veterans' reemployment rights under USERRA? **2-58**

Vesting Rules

Q 2:190 What is *vesting*? **2-58**

Q 2:191 Are there circumstances that require a participant's entire interest in a 401(k) plan to be vested? **2-58**

Q 2:192 What does the term *normal retirement age* mean? **2-58**

Q 2:193 What kinds of contributions must always be 100 percent vested? **2-58**

Q 2:194 What kinds of contributions are not subject to the 100 percent vesting requirement? **2-59**

Q 2:195 What is a *year of service*? **2-60**

Q 2:196 What is a *vesting computation period*? **2-60**

Q 2:197 Is a 401(k) plan permitted to disregard any years of service when calculating a participant's vested percentage? **2-60**

Q 2:198 What is a *predecessor plan*? **2-60**

Q 2:199 For purposes of vesting, if a participant terminates employment and is then rehired at a later date, is the plan allowed to ignore years of service completed by the participant before termination of employment? **2-60**

Q 2:200 What special vesting rules apply to an employee who has veterans' reemployment rights under USERRA? **2-61**

Q 2:201 What break-in-service rules may apply in determining an employee's vested percentage? **2-61**

Q 2:202 For purposes of vesting, how does the one-year break-in-service rule operate? **2-61**

Q 2:203 What is the *rule of parity* for vesting purposes? **2-61**

Q 2:204 What is the *five-year rule*? **2-62**

Q 2:205 For purposes of vesting, what is a *one-year break in service*? **2-62**

Q 2:206 How do maternity or paternity leaves of absence affect the determination of whether an employee incurs a one-year break in service for purposes of vesting? **2-62**

Q 2:207 Can a vesting schedule be amended to reduce a participant's vested percentage? **2-63**

Q 2:208 Do any participants have the right to have the vested percentage of their account balances determined under the previous vesting schedule? **2-63**

Q 2:209 What is the election period for selecting the previous vesting schedule? **2-63**

Q 2:210	How do the anti-cutback rules interact with the rules relating to changes in vesting schedules?	2-63
Q 2:211	Under what circumstance will the nonvested portion of a participant's account balance be forfeited?	2-64
Q 2:212	When will the forfeiture occur?	2-64
Q 2:213	What is the *cash out/buy back rule*?	2-64
Q 2:214	How much may be forfeited?	2-64
Q 2:215	What happens to forfeitures under a 401(k) plan?	2-65

Repayment Rights

Q 2:216	What is the *plan repayment provision*?	2-65
Q 2:217	Must the previously forfeited amount that is restored to an employee be credited with interest from the date of the forfeiture?	2-65
Q 2:218	May the plan impose limits on the participant's repayment rights?	2-65
Q 2:219	If repayment rights are exercised, what funds may be used to restore previously forfeited account balances?	2-66

SIMPLE 401(k) Plans

Q 2:220	What is a *SIMPLE 401(k) plan*?	2-66
Q 2:221	Which employers are eligible to sponsor SIMPLE 401(k) plans?	2-66
Q 2:222	Are all employees required to be covered under a SIMPLE 401(k) plan?	2-66
Q 2:223	What dollar limit applies to elective contributions under a SIMPLE 401(k) plan?	2-67
Q 2:224	Under what conditions would the reduced elective deferral limit for SIMPLE 401(k) plans make sense?	2-67
Q 2:225	What employer contributions are required to be made to a SIMPLE 401(k) plan?	2-67
Q 2:226	How do the employer contribution requirements of a SIMPLE IRA compare with those of a SIMPLE 401(k) plan?	2-67
Q 2:227	May an employer contribute more than the amount required to be contributed to a SIMPLE 401(k) plan?	2-68
Q 2:228	May employees eligible for a SIMPLE 401(k) plan also participate in other retirement plans of the sponsoring employer?	2-68
Q 2:229	May employees who are not eligible to participate in a SIMPLE 401(k) plan participate in another qualified plan maintained by the employer?	2-68
Q 2:230	What conditions, if any, can be placed on the receipt of matching contributions in a SIMPLE 401(k) plan?	2-68

Q 2:231	What conditions, if any, can be placed on the receipt of the 2 percent nonelective contribution in a SIMPLE 401(k) plan?	**2-69**
Q 2:232	Can a SIMPLE 401(k) plan have minimum age and service requirements that must be met before an employee can become a participant?	**2-69**
Q 2:233	What special vesting rules apply to SIMPLE 401(k) plans?	**2-69**
Q 2:234	What are the distribution rules for a SIMPLE 401(k) plan?	**2-69**
Q 2:235	How do the minimum distribution rules apply to a SIMPLE 401(k) plan?	**2-70**
Q 2:236	Are SIMPLE 401(k) plans subject to the joint and survivor annuity requirements under Code Sections 401(a)(11) and 417?	**2-70**
Q 2:237	Can an employer suspend contributions to a SIMPLE 401(k) plan during the plan year?	**2-70**
Q 2:238	Are there other differences between SIMPLE 401(k) plans and SIMPLE IRAs?	**2-70**

Safe Harbor 401(k) Plans

Q 2:239	What is a *safe harbor 401(k) plan*?	**2-71**
Q 2:240	Under what circumstances can an employer adopt a safe harbor 401(k) plan?	**2-71**
Q 2:241	What notice must be given to an employee eligible to participate in a safe harbor 401(k) plan?	**2-72**
Q 2:242	Can the safe harbor notice required to be given to each eligible employee be provided through electronic media?	**2-72**
Q 2:243	What information must be contained in a safe harbor notice?	**2-72**
Q 2:244	May a safe harbor plan satisfy the notice requirement by providing an employee with a copy of the plan's summary plan description?	**2-73**
Q 2:245	What are the main advantages and disadvantages of adopting a safe harbor 401(k) plan?	**2-73**
Q 2:246	How is ADP testing avoided with a safe harbor design?	**2-73**
Q 2:247	What employer contributions must be made to a safe harbor 401(k) plan?	**2-73**
Q 2:248	Can other matching contribution formulas satisfy the safe harbor?	**2-74**
Q 2:249	What is a "maybe" safe harbor nonelective contribution?	**2-74**
Q 2:250	How is ACP testing avoided with a safe harbor design?	**2-74**
Q 2:251	In determining whether an HCE receives a rate of match that is not greater than the rate of match of any NHCE, are NHCEs, who terminate during the plan year and who, therefore, do not receive an allocation of matching contribution under the terms of the plan, taken into account?	**2-76**

Q 2:252	May an employer make additional contributions to a safe harbor 401(k) plan?	**2-76**
Q 2:253	May an employer stop safe harbor matching contributions during the plan year?	**2-76**
Q 2:254	May an employer stop safe harbor nonelective contributions during the plan year?	**2-77**
Q 2:255	What special vesting rules apply to safe harbor 401(k) plans?	**2-77**
Q 2:256	Can a safe harbor 401(k) plan have minimum age and service requirements that must be met before an employee can become a participant?	**2-77**
Q 2:257	Can any conditions be placed on the receipt of the safe harbor matching contribution or nonelective contribution in a safe harbor 401(k) plan?	**2-78**
Q 2:258	What restrictions, if any, can be placed on elective contributions made by participants in a 401(k) plan that provides safe harbor contributions?	**2-78**
Q 2:259	What compensation must be used for purposes of the safe harbor contributions?	**2-79**
Q 2:260	By when must safe harbor contributions be made to the 401(k) plan?	**2-79**
Q 2:261	Is the dollar limit on elective deferrals reduced for safe harbor 401(k) plans?	**2-79**
Q 2:262	Are employee after-tax contributions made to a safe harbor 401(k) plan exempt from nondiscrimination testing?	**2-79**
Q 2:263	How do the top-heavy rules apply to a safe harbor 401(k) plan?	**2-80**
Q 2:264	Will a provision allowing an employer to make discretionary nonelective contributions to a safe harbor plan require the employer to make additional employer contributions if the 401(k) plan is top heavy?	**2-80**
Q 2:265	Can the safe harbor nonelective contribution be counted in a cross-tested profit sharing formula or for purposes of permitted disparity?	**2-80**
Q 2:266	Are in-service withdrawals of safe harbor matching and nonelective contributions permitted?	**2-80**
Q 2:267	What are some examples illustrating the various 401(k) safe harbor rules?	**2-80**
Q 2:268	May employees covered by a safe harbor 401(k) plan also participate in other retirement plans of the same employer?	**2-82**
Q 2:269	May a plan's safe harbor provisions be amended mid-year?	**2-83**

Eligible Combined Plans

Q 2:270	What is an *eligible combined plan*?	**2-83**
Q 2:271	Can any employer establish an eligible combined plan?	**2-83**

Q 2:272	What benefits must be provided under an eligible combined plan?	2-83
Q 2:273	What vesting requirements apply to minimum contributions and benefits under an eligible combined plan?	2-84
Q 2:274	From what requirements are eligible combined plans exempt?	2-84

Chapter 3 The 401(k) Plan Document

Plan Document Alternatives

Q 3:1	What plan document alternatives are available to a 401(k) plan sponsor?	3-1

Master and Prototype Plans

Q 3:2	What are *master* and *prototype plans*?	3-2
Q 3:3	What are the requirements for master or prototype plan sponsors?	3-2
Q 3:4	What is a mass submitter master or prototype plan?	3-2
Q 3:5	What is the difference between master and prototype plans?	3-2
Q 3:6	What are the available document options for master and prototype plans?	3-3
Q 3:7	What are the advantages and disadvantages of standardized and nonstandardized plans?	3-3
Q 3:8	Should a plan sponsor use a master or prototype plan?	3-3

Volume Submitter Plan

Q 3:9	What is a *volume submitter plan*?	3-4
Q 3:10	What is a *VS mass submitter*?	3-4
Q 3:11	What is the format of a volume submitter plan?	3-4
Q 3:12	How do volume submitter plans compare with master and prototype plans?	3-4
Q 3:13	What changes were made to the volume submitter plan program in 2011?	3-5

Individually Designed Plans

Q 3:14	What are the advantages and disadvantages of individually designed plans?	3-5

Amendments

Q 3:15	When were 401(k) plans required to be amended for GUST?	3-5

Q 3:16 Did the enactment of the Economic Growth and Tax Relief Reconciliation Act of 2001 require plan documents to be updated? **3-6**

Q 3:17 Did the extended remedial amendment period for updating plans for EGTRRA also apply to plan provisions unrelated to EGTRRA?. **3-7**

Q 3:18 By what date were sponsors of master and prototype 401(k) plans and volume submitter 401(k) (pre-approved plans) required to update their plans for EGTRRA and other plan provisions unrelated to EGTRRA? **3-7**

Q 3:19 What must an employer have done to take advantage of the EGTRRA remedial amendment period available to adopters of pre-approved plans?. **3-8**

Q 3:20 By what date were employers who maintain individually designed 401(k) plans required to update their plans for EGTRRA?. **3-8**

Q 3:21 When were 401(k) plans required to adopt interim good-faith amendments to comply with the Pension Protection Act of 2006? **3-8**

Q 3:22 When were 401(k) plans required to adopt interim good-faith amendments to comply with the Heroes Earnings Assistance and Relief Tax Act of 2008 and the Worker, Retiree, and Employer Recovery Act of 2008?. **3-8**

Q 3:23 By what date were sponsors of master and prototype 401(k) plans and volume submitter 401(k) plans (pre-approved plans) be required to update their plans for PPA, HEART, and WRERA? **3-9**

Q 3:24 By what date will employers who maintain individually designed plans 401(k) plans update be required to update their plans for PPA, HEART, and WRERA? **3-9**

Q 3:25 When will 401(k) plans be required to adopt interim good-faith amendments to comply with IRS guidance issued in connection with the Supreme Court's decision in *United States v. Windsor*, if the terms of the plan are inconsistent with the decision?. **3-9**

Advance IRS Approval

Q 3:26 What is the purpose of securing advance IRS approval of a 401(k) plan? **3-9**

Q 3:27 Is it necessary to secure advance IRS approval of a 401(k) plan document?. **3-10**

Q 3:28 What changes have recently been made in the IRS's determination letter program? **3-10**

Advantages of Qualification and Approval

Q 3:29 What are the advantages of tax qualification? **3-10**

Q 3:30	What is the primary advantage of obtaining IRS approval in advance?	3-11
Q 3:31	What are the other advantages tc obtaining IRS approval in advance?	3-11

Determination Letter Application

Q 3:32	How do plan sponsors obtain IRS approval?	3-11
Q 3:33	Where is the determination letter application sent?	3-11
Q 3:34	Does the IRS charge a fee for reviewing a determination letter application?	3-12
Q 3:35	Must employees be notified of a pending determination letter application?	3-12
Q 3:36	Can a plan obtain the advantages of advance IRS approval without having to apply for a determination letter?	3-13
Q 3:37	What types of provisions or situations will cause the adopter of a nonstandardized prototype or volume submitter plan to fail to have operational reliance?	3-13

Chapter 4 Plan Services and Service Providers

401(k) Plan Services

Q 4:1	What services are needed in operating a 401(k) plan?	4-2
Q 4:2	What is the role of the *named fiduciary*?	4-2
Q 4:3	What is the role of the *plan trustee*?	4-2
Q 4:4	What is the role of the *plan administrator*?	4-3
Q 4:5	What is the role of an *investment manager*?	4-3
Q 4:6	Can the responsibilities of the plan administrator or trustee be delegated to others?	4-4
Q 4:7	What are fiduciary risk management services, and why should a plan sponsor consider buying them?	4-4

Selecting Plan Administration Services

Q 4:8	What choices does an employer have for plan administration services?	4-5
Q 4:9	What factors should an employer focus on when selecting administration services?	4-5
Q 4:10	How has consolidation in the recordkeeping industry impacted the process of selecting administration services?	4-6
Q 4:11	What factors add cost to 401(k) plan administration?	4-7

In-House Administration

Q 4:12	What are the advantages of in-house administration of a 401(k) plan?	4-8

Q 4:13 What are the disadvantages of in-house administration of a 401(k) plan? 4-8

Third-Party Providers

Q 4:14 What are the advantages of using a third-party provider for a 401(k) plan? 4-9

Q 4:15 What are the disadvantages of using a third-party provider for a 401(k) plan? 4-9

Bundled Administration

Q 4:16 What are the advantages of bundled 401(k) administration? . . . 4-9

Q 4:17 What are the disadvantages of bundled 401(k) administration? 4-10

Q 4:18 What questions should a plan sponsor ask before selecting an administrative service provider? 4-10

Q 4:19 What considerations should be taken into account when switching 401(k) plan service providers? 4-11

Selecting Investment Services

Q 4:20 What types of providers offer investment services? 4-11

Q 4:21 What are the key distinctions between brokers and registered investment advisers? 4-12

Q 4:22 What services do investment service providers offer? 4-13

Q 4:23 What is the source for potential conflicts of interest affecting investment service providers of 401(k) plans? 4-13

Q 4:24 What questions should a plan sponsor ask when selecting an investment service provider to help identify potential conflicts of interest? 4-13

Q 4:25 What guidelines has the DOL provided for the selection and monitoring of investment service providers? 4-14

Q 4:26 What other questions should plan sponsors ask to determine the suitability of an investment service provider? 4-15

Q 4:27 How should plan sponsors incorporate answers to these questions into their decision-making process? 4-15

Allocation of Earnings and Expenses

Q 4:28 What are the major methods of allocating earnings and expenses to the accounts of participants? 4-16

Balance Forward Accounting

Q 4:29 How frequently are balance forward accounts valued? 4-17

Q 4:30 What methods are used for allocating earnings and expenses in balance forward accounting? 4-17

Q 4:31 Which balance forward method will provide the most equitable allocation of a plan's earnings and expenses among participants? 4-17

Daily Valuation

Q 4:32 What is *daily valuation*? 4-18
Q 4:33 What are the advantages of daily valuation to the plan sponsor? 4-18
Q 4:34 What are the disadvantages of daily valuation to the plan sponsor? 4-18
Q 4:35 What are the advantages of daily valuation to the participant? 4-19
Q 4:36 What are the disadvantages of daily valuation to the participant? 4-19
Q 4:37 How can some of the disadvantages of daily valuation be avoided? 4-19
Q 4:38 What is a *voice response unit*? 4-19
Q 4:39 What features might a plan sponsor look for in a service provider's participant Web site? 4-20
Q 4:40 What features might a plan sponsor look for in a service provider's plan sponsor Web site? 4-20

Payment of Fees and Expenses

Q 4:41 What expenses are incurred in adopting and maintaining a 401(k) plan? 4-20
Q 4:42 What identifiable costs may be incurred in the operation of a participant directed plan? 4-21
Q 4:43 Who pays a plan's identifiable costs? 4-21
Q 4:44 What are *performance costs*? 4-21
Q 4:45 What performance costs may be incurred in the operation of a participant directed plan? 4-22
Q 4:46 Who pays a plan's performance costs? 4-22
Q 4:47 Why is it important for plan sponsors to calculate total plan costs, especially those borne by participants? 4-22
Q 4:48 Why is it important for plan sponsors to understand the impact of asset-based fees on performance cost? 4-22
Q 4:49 Why are 401(k) plan fees so complicated? 4-24
Q 4:50 How does a plan sponsor calculate the plan's total costs? 4-25
Q 4:51 Who pays for plan costs? 4-26
Q 4:52 How does ERISA treat the use of plan assets to pay administrative expenses? 4-27
Q 4:53 What is the DOL's position on the use of plan assets to pay administrative expenses? 4-27
Q 4:54 What are settlor expenses that cannot be charged to a plan? 4-27

Q 4:55	What plan expenses can be paid out of plan assets?	4-28
Q 4:56	How should expenses be allocated in a plan?	4-29
Q 4:57	What are some examples of how plan expenses can be allocated?	4-29
Q 4:58	What is *fee leveling* and why is it used?	4-31
Q 4:59	What types of expenses may be charged directly to a plan participant?	4-31
Q 4:60	Can a plan sponsor charge fees to the accounts of ex-employees that it is not charging to the accounts of active employees?	4-31
Q 4:61	Can an employer reimburse a plan for expenses paid by the plan?	4-32
Q 4:62	Under what circumstances must an employer break out settlor fees from other fees when they are combined in a single charge?	4-32

Legal and Regulatory Initiatives Concerning 401(k) Plan Fees

Q 4:63	What actions have Congress and the legislative branch taken in the past with regard to 401(k) plan fees?	4-33
Q 4:64	What recent actions has the DOL taken with regard to 401(k) plan fees?	4-34
Q 4:65	What are the changes to Form 5500 that address fee disclosure?	4-34

DOL Final Rule on Service Provider Fee Disclosure

Q 4:66	What is the purpose and scope of the fee disclosure rule?	4-34
Q 4:67	When was the rule effective?	4-35
Q 4:68	Do the required disclosures need to be included in a formal contract?	4-35
Q 4:69	When must the initial disclosure be provided to new customers?	4-35
Q 4:70	Which plans are *covered plans* subject to the rule?	4-35
Q 4:71	Who are *responsible plan fiduciaries* subject to the rule?	4-36
Q 4:72	Who are the *covered service providers* subject to the rule?	4-36
Q 4:73	Do affiliates and subcontractors of a covered service provider have a disclosure obligation?	4-36
Q 4:74	What is the definition of an *affiliate* for purposes of the rule?	4-36
Q 4:75	What is the definition of a *subcontractor* for purposes of the rule?	4-36
Q 4:76	Do service providers to investment products in a plan have a disclosure obligation?	4-37
Q 4:77	How is the $1,000 limit determined?	4-37

Q 4:78	What should a service provider do if it reasonably expects to receive less than $1,000, but receives more than $1,000?	4-37
Q 4:79	How does the rule apply to ERISA fiduciaries and registered investment advisors?	4-37
Q 4:80	How does the rule apply to fiduciaries to plan investment products?	4-38
Q 4:81	How does the rule apply to recordkeepers and brokers?	4-38
Q 4:82	What are *recordkeeping services* under the rule?	4-38
Q 4:83	How does the rule apply to service providers receiving indirect compensation?	4-39
Q 4:84	What information on fees and services must be disclosed?	4-39
Q 4:85	What special disclosure rules apply to all recordkeepers?	4-40
Q 4:86	What special rules apply to some recordkeepers or brokers in participant-directed plans?	4-40
Q 4:87	What is a *designated investment alternative*?	4-40
Q 4:88	What investment-related information must be disclosed?	4-41
Q 4:89	What are the rules for describing plan services?	4-41
Q 4:90	What are the disclosure rules for direct compensation?	4-41
Q 4:91	What are the disclosure rules for indirect compensation?	4-42
Q 4:92	What are the rules for disclosing how compensation is allocated among affiliates and subcontractors?	4-42
Q 4:93	Must potential or actual conflicts of interest be identified?	4-42
Q 4:94	What special rules apply to compensation related to termination of a contract or arrangement?	4-42
Q 4:95	What rules apply to the form or manner in which the disclosure is to be provided?	4-43
Q 4:96	Are covered service providers required to disclose the manner in which compensation will be received?	4-43
Q 4:97	When must the initial disclosure statement be provided?	4-43
Q 4:98	What additional disclosures are required after the initial statement is provided?	4-43
Q 4:99	What happens if disclosures are not provided or if there are errors?	4-44
Q 4:100	What are the consequences to responsible plan fiduciaries and covered service providers if the rule is not followed?	4-45
Q 4:101	What responsibilities do plan sponsors have under the service provider fee disclosure rule?	4-45
Q 4:102	How do plan fiduciaries determine whether a fee is reasonable?	4-46
Q 4:103	How often should fees and services be reviewed?	4-47
Q 4:104	What fee disclosure rules apply when the service provider is not a covered service provider?	4-47
Q 4:105	How are these rules different from the disclosure requirements for Schedule C to Form 550C?	4-47

Q 4:106 Will there be a requirement to provide a guide or index as part of the fee and service disclosure? **4-48**

Q 4:107 Which service providers would be subject to the requirement to provide a guide? **4-48**

Q 4:108 What information needs to be included in the guide? **4-48**

Q 4:109 When would the guide need to be provided? **4-48**

Q 4:110 Could the guide be included as part of the initial disclosure? . . . **4-49**

Q 4:111 When would changes to information referred to in the guide required to be disclosed? **4-49**

Q 4:112 Why is DOL creating a guide requirement? **4-49**

Q 4:113 When would any guide requirement be effective? **4-49**

Other Activity on Fee Disclosure

Q 4:114 Has there been recent litigation involving 401(k) plan fees? **4-49**

Q 4:115 What are some significant rulings from the fee litigation cases? **4-50**

Q 4:116 Have regulatory agencies other than the DOL taken action with respect to plan fees? **4-51**

Q 4:117 What other actions has the DOL taken with regard to 401(k) plan fees? **4-52**

Q 4:118 What tools are available to assist plan sponsors with understanding and evaluating plan fees? **4-53**

Q 4:119 What types of fees are generally of most concern to regulators? **4-53**

Q 4:120 What kinds of plan fees are typically paid from mutual funds? **4-53**

Q 4:121 What types of fees are typically charged by collective funds? **4-54**

Q 4:122 What types of fees are typically charged in insurance company products? **4-54**

Q 4:123 What steps can a plan sponsor take to ensure that using mutual fund revenues to pay service provider fees does not result in paying excess compensation? **4-54**

Q 4:124 What is an ERISA Spending Account? **4-55**

Q 4:125 What are the legal issues involved with using an ERISA Spending Account? **4-55**

Q 4:126 Are revenue-sharing amounts held in an account outside the plan trust "plan assets" for ERISA purposes? **4-56**

Q 4:127 How are payments from an ERISA Spending Account treated for purposes of the new service provider fee disclosure rule? **4-57**

Q 4:128 What is a reasonable amount for a 401(k) plan to pay for plan services? **4-57**

Chapter 5 Fiduciary and Prohibited Transaction Rules

Fiduciary Issues

Who Is and Who Is Not a Fiduciary

Q 5:1	Who is a *fiduciary*?	**5-2**
Q 5:2	What is a 3(21) fiduciary?	**5-3**
Q 5:3	What is a 3(38) fiduciary?	**5-3**
Q 5:4	What is a 3(16) fiduciary?	**5-3**
Q 5:5	What are some examples of services that can be provided to a plan without giving rise to fiduciary status?	**5-4**
Q 5:6	How is *investment advice for a fee* currently defined for the purpose of identifying fiduciary status?	**5-4**

DOL Efforts to Expand Fiduciary Status

Q 5:7	What new guidance is contained in the DOL's 2015 proposal?	**5-5**
Q 5:8	What kind of activity is considered fiduciary activity?	**5-5**
Q 5:9	What is the definition of a "recommendation" for purposes of the rule?	**5-6**
Q 5:10	When is advice provided "for a fee or other compensation"?	**5-6**
Q 5:11	What is the functional test for determining when a person engaged in a fiduciary activity is considered an ERISA fiduciary?	**5-7**
Q 5:12	What are key differences between the current standard and the DOL's 2015 proposal?	**5-7**
Q 5:13	Are there distinctions on how the rule applies based on the type of service provider involved?	**5-7**
Q 5:14	Are there any exceptions or carve-outs?	**5-8**
Q 5:15	What are the conditions for the Seller's Carve-Out?	**5-8**
Q 5:16	Is the "seller's carve-out" available with respect to advice provided to small plans or individuals?	**5-9**
Q 5:17	What is the carve-out for swap transactions?	**5-9**
Q 5:18	What is the carve-out for employees of the plan sponsor?	**5-10**
Q 5:19	What is the carve-out for platform providers?	**5-10**
Q 5:20	What is the carve-out for selection and monitoring assistance?	**5-10**
Q 5:21	What is the carve-out for certain financial reports and valuations?	**5-10**
Q 5:22	What is the carve-out for investment education?	**5-11**
Q 5:23	What other exceptions are contained in the 2015 proposal?	**5-11**
Q 5:24	What other guidance did the DOL issue as part of its 2015 proposal?	**5-11**

Scope of Fiduciary Responsibility

Q 5:25 Will providing help to participants or beneficiaries who are eligible for a distribution create fiduciary risk? 5-12
Q 5:26 What is a *named fiduciary*? 5-12
Q 5:27 Must a person consent to be a fiduciary to be treated as a fiduciary? 5-12
Q 5:28 What is the trustee's responsibility? 5-13
Q 5:29 What is a *directed trustee*? 5-13
Q 5:30 Is a directed trustee a fiduciary? 5-13
Q 5:31 What are the responsibilities of a directed trustee regarding investing plan assets? 5-13
Q 5:32 In light of the DOL's guidance, what steps should directed trustees take to protect themselves from liability for investment decision making? 5-14
Q 5:33 What are the responsibilities of a trustee for ensuring that salary deferral or other plan contributions are deposited in the plan trust in a timely manner? 5-15
Q 5:34 What issues for directed trustees are posed by DOL FAB 2008-01? 5-16
Q 5:35 What steps should directed trustees take to comply with DOL FAB 2008-01? 5-16
Q 5:36 Can a fiduciary perform more than one function? 5-16
Q 5:37 How are fiduciary responsibilities allocated? 5-17
Q 5:38 Which decisions made by plan representatives are fiduciary decisions? 5-17

Funding Policy and Method

Q 5:39 How do fiduciaries decide how to invest plan assets? 5-17
Q 5:40 Who develops the funding policy and method? 5-18
Q 5:41 What might a 401(k) plan investment policy cover? 5-18
Q 5:42 What are the disadvantages of developing, consistently applying, and updating the funding policy and method? 5-18

Fiduciary Selection

Q 5:43 What factors are important in selecting a fiduciary? 5-19
Q 5:44 What procedures should be followed when selecting a fiduciary? 5-19

Fiduciary Duties and Obligations

Q 5:45 What are the basic fiduciary duties and obligations? 5-19
Q 5:46 What is *adequate diversification*? 5-20

ERISA Bond Requirements

Q 5:47	Who must be covered by an ERISA bond?	5-20
Q 5:48	What losses does an ERISA bond cover?	5-21
Q 5:49	Are all plan fiduciaries and service providers required to be covered by an ERISA bond?	5-21
Q 5:50	What constitutes *funds or other property* of a plan?	5-21
Q 5:51	When is a person "handling" funds or other property such that bond coverage is required?	5-21
Q 5:52	Are some persons or organizations exempt from the bonding requirement?	5-22
Q 5:53	Who is responsible for ensuring that all persons who handle funds for a plan are bonded unless exempt?	5-22
Q 5:54	Are there any restrictions on who can issue an ERISA bond?	5-22
Q 5:55	What rules apply regarding the form or terms of the bond?	5-22
Q 5:56	Can a bond be paid for from plan assets?	5-23

Consequences for Breach of Fiduciary Duty

Q 5:57	What happens if fiduciaries breach their duties?	5-23
Q 5:58	Can a fiduciary make a payment directly to the plan to settle a claim for breach of fiduciary duty?	5-23
Q 5:59	What are some issues not addressed by PTE 2003-39?	5-24
Q 5:60	Can nonfiduciaries be held liable for a breach of fiduciary duty?	5-25
Q 5:61	Can a fiduciary be liable for an unwitting violation of ERISA's fiduciary duties?	5-25
Q 5:62	Can a fiduciary be liable for a breach of fiduciary duty that occurred before the fiduciary's appointment?	5-25
Q 5:63	Can a fiduciary be liable for failing to act?	5-26
Q 5:64	Can a nonfiduciary be liable to a plan on non-ERISA grounds?	5-26
Q 5:65	Can a fiduciary be held liable for breaches committed by a co-fiduciary?	5-26
Q 5:66	What should a fiduciary do if a co-fiduciary commits a breach of duty?	5-26
Q 5:67	Does ERISA authorize punitive damages to a beneficiary for breach of fiduciary duty?	5-27
Q 5:68	Does ERISA authorize the recovery of attorneys' fees and costs?	5-27
Q 5:69	What is the impact of the *LaRue* decision on the risk of plan fiduciaries being sued by plan participants for breach of fiduciary duty?	5-27
Q 5:70	What can fiduciaries do to minimize their liability risk?	5-28

Prohibited Transactions

Types of Prohibited Transactions

Q 5:71 What transactions are prohibited? 5-28
Q 5:72 What is a *party in interest* or *disqualified person*? 5-29

Prohibited Transaction Penalties and Corrections

Q 5:73 What penalties may be imposed on a party in interest or disqualified person for engaging in a prohibited transaction? 5-29
Q 5:74 How can a prohibited transaction be corrected? 5-30

Common Prohibited Transactions

Late Deposits of Salary Deferral Contributions

Q 5:75 What is the most likely type of prohibited transaction to occur in a 401(k) plan? 5-30
Q 5:76 Is there any special leniency for multiemployer plans under the DOL's "late deposit" rules? 5-31
Q 5:77 How are late deposits reported to the DOL? 5-31
Q 5:78 How should late deposits be corrected? 5-32
Q 5:79 Why is the DOL concerned with the timeliness of deposits? . . . 5-32
Q 5:80 How should the responsibility for collecting, monitoring, and depositing plan contributions be allocated among plan fiduciaries? 5-32
Q 5:81 What is the safe harbor standard for remitting plan contributions? 5-32

Prohibited Transactions Resulting from Plan Contributions, Plan Design, or the Establishment of a Plan Checking Account

Q 5:82 May a fiduciary accept the contribution of property to a 401(k) plan? 5-33
Q 5:83 How do prohibited transactions occur in the design process? 5-33
Q 5:84 How can prohibited transactions occur in setting up a plan checking account? 5-33
Q 5:85 Can float income be used to pay for plan expenses? 5-34

Prohibited Transactions Resulting from Revenue Sharing and Other Fee Arrangements

Q 5:86 What general guidelines does ERISA provide regarding payment of fees to service providers? 5-35

Q 5:87	What is considered a "reasonable contract or arrangement" allowing service provider fees to be paid from plan assets?	5-35
Q 5:88	Can a fiduciary receive compensation from funds held in the plan without engaging in a prohibited transaction?	5-35
Q 5:89	What are the rules for paying fees to service providers affiliated with fund investment managers?	5-36
Q 5:90	What are the DOL rules for paying fees to nonfiduciaries from mutual funds?	5-36
Q 5:91	What are some DOL rules for paying fees to plan fiduciaries from mutual funds?	5-37
Q 5:92	Why have payments to fiduciaries from mutual funds received so much attention from the DOL in recent years?	5-38
Q 5:93	What has the DOL done to address potential fiduciary or prohibited transaction violations in plan fee arrangements?	5-38
Q 5:94	What responsibilities do plan fiduciaries have under the DOL's final rule on service provider fee disclosure?	5-38

Eligible Investment Advice Arrangements

Q 5:95	What is an *eligible investment advice* arrangement?	5-40
Q 5:96	What relief is available when an EIAA is used?	5-40
Q 5:97	Who can serve as a financial adviser in an EIAA?	5-40
Q 5:98	What are the general conditions that must be satisfied to obtain relief in an EIAA?	5-40
Q 5:99	What additional requirements apply if the computer model approach is used?	5-41
Q 5:100	What are the notice requirements for an EIAA?	5-41
Q 5:101	What is the EIAA audit requirement?	5-41
Q 5:102	What other rules apply to an EIAA?	5-42
Q 5:103	Has the DOL issued guidance on EIAAs?	5-42
Q 5:104	What issues are addressed in the DOL regulation on EIAAs?	5-42
Q 5:105	What is the *scope of the level fee requirement*?	5-42
Q 5:106	What information must be taken into account when providing advice pursuant to an EIAA?	5-43
Q 5:107	What additional information or standards must be taken into account when the computer model approach is used?	5-43
Q 5:108	What are the requirements for obtaining certification of the computer model?	5-44
Q 5:109	What information must be included in the computer model certification?	5-44
Q 5:110	What are the standards for obtaining authorization from an independent fiduciary?	5-44
Q 5:111	What is the annual audit requirement for EIAAs?	5-45

Q 5:112	What additional disclosure standards are in the DOL regulation?	**5-45**
Q 5:113	What other conditions apply to EIAAs?	**5-45**
Q 5:114	Can a fiduciary adviser relying on the computer model exemption provide post-model advice?	**5-46**
Q 5:115	What was the effective date for the final EIAA rule?	**5-46**
Q 5:116	Does the new EIAA exemption change the ability of fiduciaries to rely on prior DOL guidance?	**5-46**

Prohibited Transaction Exemptions

Q 5:117	What is a *prohibited transaction exemption*?	**5-46**
Q 5:118	How will recently proposed DOL guidance change the availability of prohibited transaction class exemptions?	**5-47**
Q 5:119	What kind of relief is available using the Best Interest Contract Exemption?	**5-47**
Q 5:120	What are the general requirements for using the BICE?	**5-47**

Managing Fiduciary Liability in a 401(k) Plan

Fiduciary Insurance

Q 5:121	Can a plan purchase fiduciary liability insurance for itself or for plan fiduciaries?	**5-49**
Q 5:122	Can a fiduciary or an employer purchase insurance for the plan fiduciary to cover liability or losses resulting from the acts or omissions of the plan fiduciary?	**5-49**
Q 5:123	Can a plan fiduciary purchase from the same insurance company that insures the plan against fiduciary breaches a policy that protects the fiduciary from recourse lawsuits that the insurer can bring against the fiduciary?	**5-49**
Q 5:124	What is the purpose of fiduciary liability insurance?	**5-50**
Q 5:125	Who can be covered under a fiduciary liability insurance policy?	**5-50**
Q 5:126	May fiduciary liability insurance policies cover fiduciaries for the 20 percent civil penalty applicable to fiduciary breaches under ERISA Section 502(*l*)?	**5-50**
Q 5:127	How should a plan fiduciary determine which insurance company to use to provide it with fiduciary liability insurance?	**5-50**
Q 5:128	Can a plan purchase insurance to cover any losses to the plan resulting from a prohibited transaction?	**5-51**

Indemnification

Q 5:129	What is *indemnification*?	**5-51**
Q 5:130	May a plan indemnify a fiduciary for liability for breach of duty?	**5-51**

Q 5:131 May an employer who sponsors a plan, or an employee organization whose members are covered by the plan, indemnify a fiduciary? **5-51**

Allocation of Responsibility to an Investment Manager

Q 5:132 Can fiduciary responsibility be delegated? **5-52**

Q 5:133 What are the benefits of delegating fiduciary responsibility to an *investment manager* under ERISA? **5-52**

Participant Direction of Investments—ERISA Section 404(c)

Q 5:134 Can an employer reduce or eliminate its fiduciary liability for investment decision making by giving participants investment control? **5-52**

Q 5:135 Can an employer reduce or eliminate its fiduciary liability for assets deposited in a plan's default fund? **5-53**

Managing Personal Liability

Procedural Due Diligence

Q 5:136 What is *procedural due diligence*? **5-53**

Q 5:137 What are the DOL's expectations concerning the prudent selection and monitoring of service providers offering financial help to participants? **5-54**

Fiduciary Audits

Q 5:138 What is a *fiduciary* audit? **5-55**

The Voluntary Fiduciary Correction Program

Q 5:139 What does the VFCP do? **5-58**

Q 5:140 When is the VFCP effective? **5-58**

Q 5:141 Who can use the VFCP? **5-58**

Q 5:142 What violations can be corrected through the VFCP? **5-59**

Q 5:143 What are the steps to using the VFCP Notice? **5-59**

Q 5:144 What are the general principles for correcting fiduciary violations under the VFCP? **5-60**

Q 5:145 How may a late remittance problem be corrected under the VFCP? **5-61**

Q 5:146 What relief is offered for using the VFCP? **5-61**

Q 5:147 If the fiduciary violation being corrected is a prohibited transaction, will plan fiduciaries be liable for the excise tax? **5-62**

Q 5:148 What are the risks involved in using the VFCP? **5-62**

Q 5:149	Under what circumstances does it make sense to use the VFCP?	5-63
Q 5:150	Under what circumstances should the VFCP not be used?	5-63
Q 5:151	Is there value to reading and understanding the VFCP Notice if the fiduciary does not intend to make a submission?	5-63
Q 5:152	Where can additional information on the DOL's voluntary compliance program be found?	5-64

Fiduciary Concerns Related to Specific Investment Products

Mutual Funds

Q 5:153	What mutual fund practices are of concern?	5-64
Q 5:154	What is *late-day trading* and why is it a concern?	5-64
Q 5:155	What is *market timing*, and why is it a concern?	5-64
Q 5:156	Has the SEC addressed the problem of market timing?	5-65
Q 5:157	How does the SEC rule impact 401(k) plans?	5-65
Q 5:158	What is the current status of the SEC's rule regarding redemption fees?	5-66
Q 5:159	What responsibilities do plan fiduciaries have in relation to market timing activity?	5-66
Q 5:160	What responsibilities do plan fiduciaries have when allocating proceeds received from settlements?	5-67
Q 5:161	How should plan fiduciaries respond to the allegations of improper activity in mutual fund scandals?	5-67

Mutual Fund Revenue Sharing

Q 5:162	What is the responsibility of plan fiduciaries in understanding mutual fund revenue sharing?	5-68

Target Date Funds

Q 5:163	What are unique fiduciary concerns when evaluating target date funds?	5-69
Q 5:164	What has the DOL identified as important steps for plan fiduciaries when selecting and monitoring target date funds?	5-70

Guaranteed Lifetime Income Investments

Q 5:165	What are some unique fiduciary concerns when evaluating investment products that guarantee income for life?	5-71

Chapter 6 Investing Plan Assets

Primary Asset Classes

Stocks

Q 6:1	What is a *stock*?	6-2
Q 6:2	What are *growth stocks*?	6-2
Q 6:3	What are *value stocks*?	6-3
Q 6:4	What are the risks and returns associated with stock ownership?	6-3

Bonds

Q 6:5	What is a *bond*?	6-3
Q 6:6	What are the risks and returns associated with investing in bonds?	6-4
Q 6:7	What types of bonds does the federal government issue?	6-4

Cash Investments

Q 6:8	What is meant by a *cash investment*?	6-4
Q 6:9	What are the risks and returns associated with cash investments?	6-4

Investment Vehicles

Q 6:10	What investment vehicles are offered in 401(k) plans?	6-5

Mutual Funds

Q 6:11	What is a *mutual fund*?	6-5
Q 6:12	What are the advantages associated with offering mutual funds in 401(k) plans?	6-5
Q 6:13	What are some considerations associated with offering mutual funds in 401(k) plans?	6-6

Separately Managed Accounts and Collective Trust Funds

Q 6:14	What is a *separately managed account*?	6-6
Q 6:15	What is a *collective trust fund*?	6-6
Q 6:16	What are common types of investment funds offered in 401(k) plans?	6-7
Q 6:17	What is a *money market fund*?	6-7
Q 6:18	What is a *corporate/government bond fund*?	6-8
Q 6:19	What is a *balanced fund*?	6-8
Q 6:20	What is an *index fund*?	6-8

Q 6:21 What is an *actively managed fund*? **6-9**
Q 6:22 What are *growth and income stock funds*? **6-9**
Q 6:23 What are *growth* and *aggressive growth funds*?. **6-9**
Q 6:24 What are the different types of *international funds*? **6-9**

Asset Allocation and Target Date Funds

Q 6:25 What is an *asset allocation fund*? **6-10**
Q 6:26 What is a *target date fund*?. **6-10**
Q 6:27 What are some regulatory considerations associated with target date funds?. **6-10**
Q 6:28 What guidance have the DOL and IRS released on target date funds? **6-10**
Q 6:29 What other guidance and proposed rules have been set forth by the DOL and SEC?. **6-12**

Real Estate Funds

Q 6:30 What are *real estate funds*? **6-14**

Exchange Traded Funds

Q 6:31 What is an *exchange traded fund*? **6-14**

Group Variable Annuities

Q 6:32 What is a *group variable annuity contract*?. **6-14**

Stable Value Funds

Q 6:33 What is a *stable value fund*? **6-15**

Guaranteed Investment Contracts

Q 6:34 What is a *guaranteed investment contract*? **6-15**

Lifetime Income Products

Q 6:35 What is a *lifetime income product* in the 401(k) context?. **6-16**
Q 6:36 What are some considerations in offering a lifetime income product in a retirement plan?. **6-16**
Q 6:37 What are some regulatory considerations associated with lifetime income products? **6-17**

Life Insurance

Q 6:38 What is a *life insurance contract*? **6-17**

Default Investment Funds

Q 6:39 Is a 401(k) plan required to have a default investment fund? . . . 6-18

Q 6:40 Do investment fiduciaries have fiduciary liability for assets invested in a default fund? . . . 6-18

Q 6:41 What types of funds are typically used as default investment funds? . . . 6-18

Q 6:42 Prior to the Pension Protection Act of 2006, had the DOL provided any guidance on the types of funds that should be used as default funds? . . . 6-18

Q 6:43 How has the Pension Protection Act of 2006 changed the law regarding default funds? . . . 6-19

Q 6:44 What guidance has the DOL provided on the kinds of arrangements that can be qualified default investment alternatives? . . . 6-19

Q 6:45 What notice must participants receive in a default arrangement seeking ERISA Section 404(c) protection? . . . 6-20

Asset Allocation Strategy

Q 6:46 What is *asset allocation*? . . . 6-20

Q 6:47 Why is asset allocation important? . . . 6-20

Q 6:48 What does an asset allocation fund accomplish? . . . 6-21

Managed Account Service

Q 6:49 What is a *managed account service*? . . . 6-21

Employer Securities

Q 6:50 How can a plan sponsor offer employer stock in a 401(k) plan? . . . 6-22

Q 6:51 Do special ERISA fiduciary rules apply to a plan investing in employer securities? . . . 6-22

Qualifying Employer Securities

Q 6:52 What is a *qualifying employer security*? . . . 6-23

Q 6:53 What is an *eligible individual account plan*? . . . 6-24

Q 6:54 What restriction applies to 401(k) plans investing in qualifying employer securities? . . . 6-24

Diversification Requirements

Q 6:55 How does the PPA impact diversification rights in 401(k) plans with respect to employer securities? . . . 6-25

Q 6:56 To what contributions do the diversification rights apply? . . . 6-25

Q 6:57 What options must be offered to a participant in connection with diversifying his or her employer securities? . . . 6-26

Q 6:58	What restrictions or conditions can be placed on investments involving employer securities under the diversification rule?	**6-26**
Q 6:59	What are considered "publicly traded employer securities" subject to the diversification rule?	**6-27**
Q 6:60	What participant notice requirements apply with respect to the diversification requirements?	**6-28**
Q 6:61	What are the penalties for noncompliance with the diversification notice rules?	**6-29**
Q 6:62	When are the diversification rules effective?	**6-29**
	Fair Market Value of Employer Stock	
Q 6:63	What does it mean for a plan to purchase or sell employer securities for *adequate consideration*?	**6-29**
Q 6:64	Why is it important to properly value employer stock when it is offered as a plan investment option?	**6-30**
	Voting Rights for Employer Stock	
Q 6:65	Do companies give participants voting rights with respect to employer stock allocated to their accounts?	**6-31**
	SEC Registration and Reporting Requirements	
Q 6:66	What registration requirements under federal securities laws arise when a 401(k) plan offers employer securities?	**6-31**
Q 6:67	How might the SEC short-swing profits rules apply to transactions involving publicly traded employer stock in a 401(k) plan?	**6-32**
	Sarbanes-Oxley Act of 2002	
Q 6:68	What rules apply to plans invested in employer stock under the Sarbanes-Oxley Act?	**6-32**
Q 6:69	What are the key features of the SEC insider trading prohibitions applicable during blackouts?	**6-33**
	Employer Stock Strategy	
Q 6:70	What are the dangers of being heavily invested in employer stock?	**6-34**
Q 6:71	What are some general considerations for including employer stock as an investment option in a 401(k) plan?	**6-34**

Directed Trustee Considerations

Q 6:72 How does the DOL view a directed trustee's fiduciary responsibilities with respect to investments and in particular with respect to investments in publicly traded employer stock? 6-35

401(k) Stock Ownership Plans

Q 6:73 What is a *401(k) stock ownership plan*? 6-37
Q 6:74 What are the stock bonus rules that apply to KSOPs? 6-37

Self-Directed Options

Q 6:75 What is a *self-directed option*? 6-38
Q 6:76 How can a self-directed option be offered? 6-38

Motivation for Self-Directed Options

Q 6:77 What might motivate an employer to offer a self-directed option or plan to participants? 6-39

Considerations Arising from Self-Directed Options

Q 6:78 What are some considerations when offering a self-directed option?. 6-39
Q 6:79 What administrative complications and costs are sometimes associated with self-directed accounts?. 6-39
Q 6:80 Could some participants become overwhelmed by unlimited investment options in a self-directed environment? 6-40
Q 6:81 When could a self-directed option create discrimination issues under the benefits, rights, and features rules?. 6-40
Q 6:82 What inappropriate or troublesome investments could result in self-directed accounts?. 6-40

Self-Directed Options and ERISA Section 404(c)

Q 6:83 What considerations might arise for a plan sponsor seeking ERISA Section 404(c) protection for a self-directed option? 6-41

Self-Directed Option Strategies

Q 6:84 How can a self-directed option be structured to minimize administrative complications, additional costs, and fiduciary liability exposure? 6-41

Investment Policies

Q 6:85 Is a *written* investment policy statement required under ERISA?. 6-42

Q 6:86 Is a named fiduciary acting as a fiduciary when it adopts an investment policy statement? 6-42

Q 6:87 What provisions may be found in an investment policy? 6-42

Selecting and Monitoring Plan Investments

Q 6:88 What are the major considerations in the investment selection process? 6-43

Q 6:89 What are the investment options typically offered in a 401(k) plan? 6-43

Q 6:90 What are the key elements in an investment monitoring program? 6-44

Q 6:91 Should investment performance be compared with the performance of other similar investments? 6-44

Q 6:92 How often should investment performance be monitored? 6-44

Q 6:93 What is the function of investment fund independent ratings services? 6-44

Mutual Fund Investigations

Q 6:94 How should a plan fiduciary respond if a plan investment is a mutual fund involved in an investigation? 6-44

Investment Fees and Revenue Sharing

Q 6:95 What kinds of fees are typically associated with investments in a 401(k) plan? 6-45

Q 6:96 What particular fees might a mutual fund charge? 6-45

Q 6:97 What are *front-end loads* and *back-end loads*? 6-46

Q 6:98 What is a *12b-1 fee*? 6-46

Q 6:99 What are *management fees*? 6-46

Q 6:100 What are "other" *administrative or operating costs*? 6-47

Q 6:101 What fees are reflected in a mutual fund's expense ratio? 6-47

Q 6:102 How does a plan sponsor determine the fees charged by a particular mutual fund? 6-47

Q 6:103 What particular fees might be charged in a collective trust fund? 6-47

Q 6:104 What particular fees might be charged in a variable annuity? 6-48

Q 6:105 What particular costs are associated with a guaranteed investment contract fund? 6-48

Q 6:106 What types of revenue sharing do 401(k) plan service providers receive from mutual funds? 6-48

Q 6:107 What are the current regulatory developments with regard to the 401(k) plan investments and fees? 6-48

Chapter 7 Participant Direction of Investments—ERISA Section 404(c)

Participant-Directed Plans

Q 7:1	What is a *participant-directed plan*?	7-1
Q 7:2	What is the rule concerning protection from fiduciary liability in participant-directed plans?	7-2
Q 7:3	Are participant-directed plans required to comply with the DOL regulation?	7-2
Q 7:4	What is the effect of having a participant-directed plan that does not comply with the DOL regulation?	7-2
Q 7:5	What are the general requirements of the DOL regulation on a participant-directed plan?	7-2
Q 7:6	Must participants be able to select investments for all their accounts in a participant-directed plan?	7-3
Q 7:7	Must all employees and beneficiaries be given the same rights to direct their accounts?	7-3
Q 7:8	How does a plan become a 404(c) plan?	7-3

Broad Range of Investment Alternatives

Q 7:9	What is considered a broad range of investment alternatives?	7-4
Q 7:10	What is an example of a group of funds that would satisfy the broad-range requirement?	7-4
Q 7:11	Will every plan be able to satisfy the broad-range standard using three funds?	7-4
Q 7:12	Can a fixed-rate investment be one of the three core funds satisfying the broad-range requirement?	7-4
Q 7:13	Can individual stocks or other individual assets be used to satisfy the broad-range requirement?	7-5
Q 7:14	What are the advantages of using look-through funds to satisfy the broad-range requirement?	7-5
Q 7:15	Is ERISA Section 404(c) protection available for investment in employer securities?	7-5
Q 7:16	Are there any restrictions on the types of employer securities that can be offered in an ERISA Section 404(c) plan?	7-5
Q 7:17	Are there special procedures that must be followed in an ERISA Section 404(c) plan that offers employer securities?	7-6

Independent Exercise of Control

Q 7:18	When is a participant's exercise of control considered independent?	7-6
Q 7:19	How do the rules apply to a plan that uses investment managers?	7-7

Q 7:20 How do the rules apply with respect to voting, tender, or similar rights? 7-7

Disclosure Requirements

Q 7:21 In general, what information must be provided to participants about the plan's available investment alternatives? 7-7

Q 7:22 What specific information must be given to participants? 7-7

Q 7:23 Can a mutual fund Summary Prospectus be used to satisfy a requirement to provide a prospectus to participants? 7-8

Q 7:24 What other special requirement must be considered in connection with meeting ERISA disclosure requirements? 7-9

Q 7:25 Are employers obligated to provide investment advice or investment education to 401(k) plan participants? 7-9

Investment Change Frequency

Q 7:26 How frequently must participants be permitted to change their investment choices? 7-9

Q 7:27 How do the investment change-frequency rules apply in a plan offering investment alternatives with different volatility levels (or more frequent change opportunities)? 7-10

Q 7:28 Can a fund with transfer restrictions or transfer fees satisfy the rules concerning transfer frequency? 7-10

Q 7:29 Can actions to limit market timing, such as the imposition of redemption fees, impact a plan's Section 404(c) status? 7-10

Investment Elections

Q 7:30 What procedures must be used to obtain investment elections? 7-11

Q 7:31 Can a default election be used for participants who fail to make an election? 7-11

Q 7:32 May a fiduciary place any restrictions on participant investment rights? 7-11

Q 7:33 May fees associated with investment choices be charged directly to participants' accounts? 7-12

Fiduciary Liability Relief

Q 7:34 What relief from liability is available to fiduciaries in an ERISA Section 404(c) plan? 7-12

Q 7:35 What responsibilities, according to the DOL, can fiduciaries not avoid in participant-directed plans that comply with ERISA Section 404(c)? 7-12

Q 7:36 How do ERISA's fiduciary rules apply to participant-directed plans that do not comply with ERISA Section 404(c)? 7-13

Q 7:37 Is compliance with the DOL's regulation worth the protection offered? 7-13

Q 7:38 How should an ERISA Section 404(c) plan be reported on Form 5500? 7-13

Q 7:39 What was the effective date of the final ERISA Section 404(c) regulation issued by the DOL? 7-14

Qualified Default Investment Arrangements

Q 7:40 Can ERISA Section 404(c) protection be obtained in connection with default investments used when participants fail to make an investment election? 7-14

Q 7:41 What is a *qualified default investment alternative* for purposes of Section 404(c) protection? 7-15

Q 7:42 What other conditions must be met for Section 404(c) protection to extend to default investments? 7-16

Q 7:43 What requirements must a QDIA meet with respect to the participant's ability to transfer out of the QDIA? 7-17

Q 7:44 Would the payment of a fee or expense (such as a redemption fee) by a plan sponsor or service provider that would otherwise be assessed to the account of a participant or beneficiary during the initial 90-day period satisfy the requirements? 7-18

Q 7:45 Does the 90-day period start from the date an investment becomes a QDIA, or does it begin only in reference to a participant who is newly "defaulted" into a QDIA? 7-18

Q 7:46 Is a QDIA prohibited from including any "round-trip" restriction for the first 90 days? 7-19

Q 7:47 Would an investment fund or product with zero fixed income (or, alternatively, zero equity) qualify as one of the so-called long-term QDIAs described in Q 7:41? 7-19

Q 7:48 Can a committee that is established by a plan sponsor and that, pursuant to the documents and instruments governing the plan, is a named fiduciary of the plan be treated as managing a QDIA? 7-19

Q 7:49 Under what conditions can a capital preservation fund be a QDIA (a so-called short-term QDIA)? 7-19

Q 7:50 Under what conditions can a stable value fund be a long-term QDIA (a so-called grandfathered QDIA)? 7-20

Q 7:51 Are plan sponsors required to provide a 120-day capital preservation QDIA? 7-20

Q 7:52 Can a plan sponsor manage the 120-day capital preservation QDIA? 7-21

Q 7:53 Can a variable annuity or common trust fund qualify as a QDIA? 7-21

Q 7:54 What information must be conveyed in notices regarding default investment arrangements? 7-22

Q 7:55	How much information regarding QDIA fees and expenses must be provided in a notice, and can the information be provided by attaching other disclosure documents to the notice?	**7-24**
Q 7:56	Do the electronic distribution rules apply only to the QDIA notice requirement, or more broadly (i.e., to pass-through of investment materials)?	**7-24**
Q 7:57	Do plan sponsors have to combine the QDIA notice required by the regulation with a notice required under a QACA or an EACA?	**7-24**
Q 7:58	Are the timing requirements for the notices required by the QDIA regulation the same as those for the QACA and EACA notices?	**7-24**
Q 7:59	Can the QDIA notice be combined with the safe harbor 401(k) notice in the same manner that it can be combined with QACA and EACA notices?	**7-25**
Q 7:60	Is all the QDIA information required to be furnished automatically without regard to whether, under ERISA Section 404(c), some information can be provided only upon request of a participant or beneficiary?	**7-26**
Q 7:61	Must a plan otherwise comply with Section 404(c) requirements?	**7-26**
Q 7:62	Must a plan's default investment arrangement satisfy the QDIA requirements?	**7-26**
Q 7:63	What relief is not available under a default investment arrangement that qualifies for Section 404(c) protection?	**7-26**
Q 7:64	Must a plan sponsor distribute a notice 30 days before the effective date of the QDIA regulation to obtain relief for prior contributions to a stable value fund or product (so-called grandfathered QDIA)?	**7-26**
Q 7:65	Is relief available under the QDIA regulation for assets invested in a default investment prior to the effective date of the regulation?	**7-27**
Q 7:66	Would a fiduciary obtain the relief referred to above, with respect to assets invested in a QDIA on behalf of participants and beneficiaries who elected to invest in a default investment prior to the effective date of the regulation?	**7-27**
Q 7:67	Is fiduciary relief under the QDIA regulation available if nonelective contributions, such as qualified nonelective contributions, or the proceeds from litigation or settlements, are invested in a QDIA?	**7-28**
Q 7:68	Is QDIA protection available to 403(b) plans?	**7-28**
Q 7:69	Can a plan sponsor use two different QDIAs—for example, one for its automatic contribution arrangement, and another for rollover contributions?	**7-28**
Q 7:70	What was the effective date of the QDIA regulation?	**7-29**

Blackouts and Changes in Investment Options

Q 7:71 Under what circumstances can Section 404(c) protection extend to blackout periods? 7-29

Q 7:72 Under what circumstances would Section 404(c) protection extend to a change in investment options? 7-29

Litigation Involving Participant-Directed Plans

Q 7:73 Has ERISA Section 404(c) been tested as a defense in a lawsuit? 7-30

Q 7:74 What might plan sponsors learn from these cases? 7-30

Q 7:75 What were some issues in the Enron, WorldCom, and other similar cases? 7-30

Q 7:76 What provisions in the Pension Protection Act of 2006 addressed issues in the Enron, WorldCom, and other similar cases? 7-31

Chapter 8 Participant Communication and Education

An Effective 401(k) Communication Program

Q 8:1 Why is initial communication important? 8-2

Content of a Communication Program

Q 8:2 What is important information in a 401(k) plan? 8-3

Q 8:3 What additional information should be communicated if participants choose their own investments in the plan? 8-3

Q 8:4 Why might a 401(k) communications program go beyond the plan's reporting and disclosure requirements? 8-5

Q 8:5 Should a 401(k) communications program present just the facts? 8-5

Implementing a Communication Program

Q 8:6 What are the steps in implementing a 401(k) communications program? 8-5

Q 8:7 What is a method for assessing the information needs of plan participants? 8-6

Q 8:8 What measurable goals might be set for a 401(k) communications program? 8-6

Q 8:9 How might information needs differ among plan participants? 8-6

Q 8:10 What is a way to present retirement planning to the younger, consumption-oriented employee? 8-6

Q 8:11 What may be the best way to move plan participants from a savings orientation to an investing orientation? 8-7

Q 8:12 How can real-life examples introduce the importance of investment return for retirement planning? 8-8
Q 8:13 What is meant by the statement that a 401(k) communications program should have multiple contacts, multiple approaches, and multiple messages? 8-8
Q 8:14 How many yearly contacts are needed for an effective 401(k) communications program? 8-8
Q 8:15 What are some of the multiple approaches in a 401(k) communications program? 8-9
Q 8:16 What are the advantages of computer-based planning tools? 8-9
Q 8:17 What computer-based planning tools and other resources are available online? 8-9
Q 8:18 How can the multiple messages involved in 401(k) communications be structured?. 8-10
Q 8:19 What type of follow-up is needed for an effective 401(k) communications program? 8-10
Q 8:20 What is a participant Retirement Readiness report? 8-10

Department of Labor Guidance on Participant Investment Education

Q 8:21 What guidance has the DOL provided as to whether investment education constitutes investment advice? 8-11

Investment Advice Under ERISA

Q 8:22 How is investment advice characterized under ERISA?. 8-11
Q 8:23 What are the four examples of investment-related information and material that would not, in the view of the DOL, result in the rendering of investment advice under ERISA? 8-12

Plan Information

Q 8:24 What does the DOL mean by *plan information*, and why does it not constitute investment advice? 8-12
Q 8:25 According to the DOL, what information about investment alternatives may be included as plan information?. 8-13

General Financial and Investment Information

Q 8:26 What does the DOL mean by *general financial and investment information*, and why does it not constitute investment advice? 8-13

Asset Allocation Models

Q 8:27 What does the DOL mean by *asset allocation models*, and why does providing them not constitute investment advice?. 8-14

Q 8:28	What conditions must asset allocation models satisfy in order to meet the DOL standard?	8-14

Interactive Investment Materials

Q 8:29	What does the DOL mean by *interactive investment materials*, and why does providing them not constitute investment advice?	8-15
Q 8:30	What are the conditions that interactive investment materials must satisfy in order to meet the DOL standard?	8-15

Investment Education Versus Investment Advice

Q 8:31	Might there be other examples of investment education materials that would not constitute investment advice?	8-17
Q 8:32	Are the four types of investment education materials identified in DOL Interpretive Bulletin 96-1 safe harbors for avoiding the rendering of investment advice as defined by ERISA?	8-17

Investment Education and Fiduciary Liability

Q 8:33	Is the selection by a plan sponsor or fiduciary of a person to provide the types of investment education identified in DOL Interpretive Bulletin 96-1 itself a fiduciary action?	8-17
Q 8:34	In the context of an ERISA Section 404(c) plan, would the designation of a person to provide the types of investment education identified in DOL Interpretive Bulletin 96-1 give rise to fiduciary responsibility for investment losses resulting from a participant's or beneficiary's asset allocation choices?	8-17

Impact of DOL Guidance on Education

Q 8:35	What features of DOL Interpretive Bulletin 96-1 are likely to be of most value to plan sponsors?	8-18

Offering Investment Advice

Q 8:36	Why might a plan sponsor want to provide investment advice from an outside professional?	8-18
Q 8:37	What issues arise under ERISA with respect to offering investment advisory services to participants, and how have the PPA and the DOL's 2015 proposed rule expanded the options available in the investment advice context?	8-18

Individual Retirement Planning

Retirement Planning Scenarios

Q 8:38	What are some economic scenarios involving future salaries and rates of inflation?	8-20

Q 8:39 What is generally meant by salary "falling behind" or "outpacing" inflation? 8-21
Q 8:40 What factors influence whether a person's future salary will fall behind, keep pace with, or outpace inflation? 8-21
Q 8:41 Can historic levels of inflation provide a guide to future inflation? 8-21
Q 8:42 What are some considerations in choosing a planned retirement age? 8-21
Q 8:43 What additional factors are considered in retirement planning tools? 8-21

Replacement Ratios at Retirement

Q 8:44 How is the adequacy of retirement benefits measured? 8-22
Q 8:45 What is a *replacement ratio*? 8-22
Q 8:46 How do individual retirement planners manage the risk of outliving their retirement savings? 8-22

Long-Term Investment Return

Q 8:47 What does experience indicate is a way of increasing the expected return from long-term investments? 8-23
Q 8:48 What is a disadvantage to investing solely in asset classes with higher expected average return on investment? 8-23
Q 8:49 How should a participant interpret the standard deviation of annual return when assessing the riskiness of an asset class? 8-23
Q 8:50 How can long-term 401(k) investors manage the variable return risk that comes with higher-yielding asset classes such as stocks? 8-24
Q 8:51 What is an example of a portfolio that is expected to achieve an investment objective while managing risk? 8-24

Risk Tolerance

Q 8:52 What is meant by *risk tolerance*? 8-25
Q 8:53 How can risk tolerance be measured? 8-25

The Impact of Inflation

Q 8:54 If salaries are likely to keep pace with inflation, is it important to take inflation into account in retirement planning? 8-25
Q 8:55 What does experience show about the ability of various asset classes to keep pace with inflation? 8-25

Other Sources of Retirement Income

Q 8:56 What sources of retirement income besides a 401(k) plan should be considered in planning for retirement? 8-26

Q 8:57 What benefits can be expected from Social Security? 8-26

Managing Longevity Risk

Q 8:58 How does the risk of outliving retirement income decrease for years beyond life expectancy? 8-26

Managing Investment Risk During Retirement

Q 8:59 Why is it important to manage investment risk during retirement? 8-27

Q 8:60 How can the investment risk during retirement be managed? 8-27

Saver's Credit

Q 8:61 What is the *saver's credit* and how can it be communicated to participants? 8-28

Chapter 9 Contribution Limits

Limits on Elective Deferrals

Q 9:1 Is the amount of elective deferrals to a 401(k) plan subject to limitation? 9-2

Q 9:2 For what period does the annual cap apply? 9-2

Q 9:3 What are *elective deferrals*? 9-2

Q 9:4 Are designated Roth contributions treated as elective deferrals? 9-2

Q 9:5 How do the limits on elective deferrals apply to participants who have veterans' reemployment rights under USERRA? 9-3

Excess Deferrals

Q 9:6 What happens if the participant's elective deferrals for the taxable year exceed the annual cap? 9-3

Q 9:7 Does the determination of excess deferrals change if a participant's elective deferrals consist of designated Roth contributions? 9-3

Corrective Distributions

Q 9:8 Is a plan required to permit the distribution of excess deferrals if the excess deferrals arise from elective contributions made to 401(k) plans, SARSEPs, SIMPLE retirement plans, and 403(b) annuity contracts of different employers? 9-4

Q 9:9	If a plan permits the distribution of excess deferrals under the circumstances described in Q 9:8, what conditions can a plan require a participant to meet before permitting a distribution of excess deferrals?	**9-4**
Q 9:10	Must a 401(k) plan wait until after the end of the participant's taxable year before a corrective distribution of excess deferrals can be made?	**9-4**
Q 9:11	If an excess deferral is distributed, must the income allocable to the excess deferrals be distributed as well?	**9-4**
Q 9:12	What is the income allocable to excess deferrals?	**9-4**
Q 9:13	How is income allocable to excess deferrals determined?	**9-5**
Q 9:14	Are excess deferrals still treated as employer contributions?	**9-5**
Q 9:15	How does the distribution or recharacterization of excess contributions affect the amount of excess deferrals that may be distributed to an employee?	**9-6**
Q 9:16	Is employee or spousal consent required for a distribution of excess deferrals and allocable income?	**9-6**
	Tax Treatment	
Q 9:17	What is the tax treatment of corrective distributions to employees?	**9-6**
Q 9:18	Does the tax treatment of corrective distributions change if the distribution consists of designated Roth contributions?	**9-7**
Q 9:19	Are corrective distributions of excess deferrals (plus allocable income) subject to the premature distribution penalty under Code Section 72(t)?	**9-7**
Q 9:20	May a corrective distribution of excess deferrals and allocable income be applied toward an employee's minimum distribution requirement under Code Section 401(a)(9)?	**9-7**
Q 9:21	Is a corrective distribution of excess deferrals and allocable income considered an eligible rollover distribution?	**9-7**
	Failure to Correct	
Q 9:22	What happens if excess deferrals are not corrected?	**9-7**
Q 9:23	What are the consequences of a failure to correct excess deferrals consisting of designated Roth contributions made to plans of unrelated employers?	**9-8**
	Catch-Up Contributions	
Q 9:24	Is there any circumstance under which a participant will be allowed to make elective deferrals in excess of the limitation specified in Q 9:1?	**9-8**
Q 9:25	What is a *plan limit*?	**9-9**
Q 9:26	How is a plan limit determined?	**9-9**

Q 9:27	If a 401(k) plan limits elective deferrals for separate portions of the plan year, are there other ways available to calculate the plan limit?	**9-10**
Q 9:28	What is a *legal limit*?	**9-10**
Q 9:29	What is the *ADP limit*?	**9-10**
Q 9:30	When is it determined whether elective deferrals have exceeded a limit?	**9-11**
Q 9:31	How are catch-up contributions treated for tax purposes?	**9-11**
Q 9:32	Must catch-up contributions be made available to all employees?	**9-12**
Q 9:33	Is the universal availability requirement violated if different limits apply to different groups of participants?	**9-12**
Q 9:34	What happens if a catch-up-eligible individual makes elective deferrals in a calendar year to 401(k) plans of different employers?	**9-12**
Q 9:35	Can catch-up contributions consist of designated Roth contributions?	**9-12**
	SIMPLE 401(k) Plans	
Q 9:36	What is the annual cap on elective deferrals to a SIMPLE 401(k) plan?	**9-13**
Q 9:37	Is there any circumstance under which a participant will be allowed to make elective deferrals in excess of the limitation specified in Q 9:36?	**9-13**
Q 9:38	What happens if a participant's elective deferrals exceed the annual cap on elective deferrals to a SIMPLE 401(k) plan?	**9-14**
	Code Section 415—Annual Addition Limits	
Q 9:39	How does Code Section 415 limit annual additions to a 401(k) plan?	**9-14**
Q 9:40	Will the $40,000 limit be indexed for inflation?	**9-15**
Q 9:41	How are increases in the $40,000 limit applied to limitation years that end on a date other than December 31?	**9-15**
	Annual Additions	
Q 9:42	What are *annual additions*?	**9-15**
Q 9:43	What are not considered annual additions?	**9-16**
Q 9:44	What special rules apply to 401(k) stock ownership plans that have borrowed funds to purchase employer securities of a corporation which, for tax purposes, is considered a C corporation?	**9-16**
Q 9:45	How do the limits on annual additions apply to participants who have veterans' reemployment rights under USERRA?	**9-16**

Compensation Under Code Section 415

Q 9:46 What is considered compensation for purposes of the percentage of compensation limit? 9-17

Q 9:47 Are amounts paid after severance from employment treated as compensation? 9-18

Q 9:48 Are there other definitions of compensation that satisfy Code Section 415? 9-18

Q 9:49 Are elective deferrals treated as compensation for purposes of Code Section 415? 9-18

Q 9:50 What is considered compensation in the case of participants who have veterans' reemployment rights under USERRA? 9-19

Plan Design

Q 9:51 How should a 401(k) plan be designed to ensure that the Section 415 limits are not violated? 9-19

Correcting a Violation

Q 9:52 Can a violation of the Code Section 415 limits be corrected by returning elective deferrals? 9-19

Q 9:53 What are the tax implications of elective deferrals that are returned to a participant to correct a Section 415 violation? 9-20

Maximum Deferral Percentage

Q 9:54 What is the maximum deferral percentage that can be provided for in a 401(k) plan? 9-20

Code Section 404—Deduction Limits

Q 9:55 What deduction limits are applicable to a 401(k) plan? 9-21

Maximum Deductible Amount

Q 9:56 What is the maximum annual deductible amount for a 401(k) plan? 9-21

Q 9:57 How is the deduction limit applied if the employer sponsors two or more profit sharing (including 401(k)) plans? 9-21

Q 9:58 Is the maximum deductible amount determined with respect to each participant, or is it determined on an aggregate basis? 9-21

Q 9:59 Are elective contributions treated as employer contributions for purposes of the deduction limit? 9-21

Q 9:60 What special deduction rules apply to KSOPs maintained by corporations that, for tax purposes, are considered C corporations? 9-21

Compensation Under Code Section 404

Q 9:61	What does the term *compensation* mean?	9-22
Q 9:62	Is there a limit on the amount of compensation that may be taken into account in determining the maximum deductible amount?	9-22
Q 9:63	In determining the maximum deductible amount, may the employer take into account the compensation of all employees, or just those who are plan participants?	9-23
Q 9:64	Is the maximum deductible amount determined on the basis of the plan year or the taxable year of the employer?	9-23

Nondeductible Contributions

Q 9:65	What happens if more than the maximum deductible amount is contributed to a 401(k) plan?	9-23
Q 9:66	May an employer avoid the excise tax on nondeductible contributions by withdrawing them before the end of the taxable year?	9-24

Timing of Deductions

Q 9:67	For what taxable year are contributions to a 401(k) plan deductible?	9-24
Q 9:68	Can an employer deduct elective and matching contributions for a taxable year if they are made before the tax return due date (including extensions for that taxable year) but are attributable to compensation earned by plan participants in the succeeding taxable year?	9-24

Restorative Payments

Q 9:69	Are payments that are made to restore losses resulting from breaches of fiduciary duties considered contributions for purposes of any of the limits discussed in this chapter?	9-25
Q 9:70	What is a *restorative contribution*?	9-25
Q 9:71	What other requirements must be met for such payments to be considered restorative contributions?	9-25

Design Considerations

Q 9:72	How should the deductible limit be taken into account in the design of the plan?	9-26
Q 9:73	What is the deductible limit if the employer also has a defined benefit plan?	9-26
Q 9:74	May an employer with an existing profit sharing plan set up a 401(k) plan?	9-26
Q 9:75	How are the limits coordinated if the employer has a money purchase or target plan?	9-26

Q 9:76	If an employer has an existing money purchase plan in addition to a 401(k) plan, should the employer consider terminating the money purchase plan?	**9-27**
Q 9:77	Will the merger of a money purchase pension plan into a 401(k) plan require 100 percent vesting of the money purchase account balances?	**9-27**

Chapter 10 Data for Nondiscrimination Testing

Who Is the Employer?

Controlled Groups

Q 10:1	Must business entities under common control be treated as a single employer when applying the nondiscrimination and other qualification requirements?	**10-2**
Q 10:2	How many kinds of controlled groups are there?	**10-2**
Q 10:3	What is a *parent-subsidiary controlled group*?	**10-2**
Q 10:4	What is a *controlling interest*?	**10-3**
Q 10:5	What is a *brother-sister controlled group*?	**10-3**
Q 10:6	What constitutes *effective control*?	**10-3**
Q 10:7	What is a *combined group*?	**10-5**
Q 10:8	In determining whether organizations are members of a controlled group, are certain interests disregarded?	**10-5**
Q 10:9	What interests may be disregarded?	**10-5**
Q 10:10	Who is a *principal owner*?	**10-6**
Q 10:11	Who is an *officer*?	**10-6**
Q 10:12	When will an employee's interest in an organization be considered subject to conditions that substantially restrict the right to dispose of that interest?	**10-6**

Constructive Ownership Rules

Q 10:13	What is the *option attribution rule*?	**10-7**
Q 10:14	What is the *entity attribution rule*?	**10-7**
Q 10:15	Under what circumstances will an interest in an organization held by a partnership be attributed to another person?	**10-7**
Q 10:16	Under what circumstances will an interest in an organization held by a corporation be attributed to another person?	**10-8**
Q 10:17	Under what circumstances will an interest in an organization held by an estate or trust be attributed to another person?	**10-8**
Q 10:18	What is the *family attribution rule*?	**10-8**
Q 10:19	When will an interest in an organization owned by a spouse not be attributed to an individual?	**10-8**

Q 10:20 Under what circumstances will an individual's interest in an organization be attributed to a lineal ascendant or descendant? 10-9

Q 10:21 Is there any limit on the number of times an interest in an organization may be attributed? 10-10

Q 10:22 Are there special controlled group rules that apply to organizations that are exempt from tax under Code Section 501(a)? 10-10

Significance of Controlled Groups

Q 10:23 What employee benefit requirements are affected by the controlled group rules? 10-11

Affiliated Service Groups

Q 10:24 What are the types of affiliated service groups? 10-11

Q 10:25 What is a *first service organization*? 10-11

Q 10:26 What is an *organization*? 10-12

Q 10:27 What is a *service organization*? 10-12

Q 10:28 What is an *A-org*? 10-12

Q 10:29 How does one determine whether a service organization regularly performs services for an FSO or is regularly associated with an FSO in performing services for third persons? 10-12

Q 10:30 What is a *B-org*? 10-13

Q 10:31 What constitutes a significant portion of the business of the organization? 10-13

Q 10:32 What is the *service receipts percentage*? 10-13

Q 10:33 What is the *total receipts percentage*? 10-13

Q 10:34 When will services be considered of a type historically performed by employees in the service field of the FSO or A-orgs? 10-14

Q 10:35 Under what circumstances will multiple affiliated service groups be aggregated? 10-15

Q 10:36 What constructive ownership rules apply in determining whether an A-org has an ownership interest in an FSO or whether a 10 percent interest in a B-org is held by the HCEs of the FSO, A-org, or both? 10-15

Q 10:37 In the case of a management-type affiliated service group, when is an organization considered a *management organization*? 10-15

Q 10:38 What are considered *management functions*? 10-15

Q 10:39 What employee benefit requirements are affected by the affiliated service group rules? 10-16

Q 10:40 Can an employer obtain a formal determination as to whether a group of organizations constitutes an affiliated service group? . . . 10-16

Qualified Separate Lines of Business

Q 10:41 What is a *qualified separate line of business*? . . . 10-16
Q 10:42 What is a *line of business*? . . . 10-17
Q 10:43 How does an employer designate LOBs? . . . 10-17
Q 10:44 Must a LOB provide only one type or related types of property and services? . . . 10-17
Q 10:45 Is an employer required to combine within one LOB all property or services of a related type? . . . 10-17
Q 10:46 What is a *separate line of business*? . . . 10-19
Q 10:47 When does a LOB have its own, separate workforce? . . . 10-20
Q 10:48 What is a *substantial-service employee*? . . . 10-20
Q 10:49 When is an employee considered to provide services to a LOB? . . . 10-20
Q 10:50 How does an employer determine what percentage, if any, of an employee's services are provided to a LOB? . . . 10-20
Q 10:51 When does a LOB have its own, separate management? . . . 10-21
Q 10:52 Who are the top-paid employees? . . . 10-21
Q 10:53 How does a SLOB satisfy the administrative-scrutiny requirement? . . . 10-21
Q 10:54 How does a SLOB satisfy the statutory safe harbor? . . . 10-21
Q 10:55 What is the *HCE percentage ratio*? . . . 10-21
Q 10:56 What are the regulatory safe harbors? . . . 10-22
Q 10:57 How are employees allocated to a QSLOB? . . . 10-23
Q 10:58 What is a *residual shared employee*? . . . 10-23

What Is a Plan?

Q 10:59 What is a *separate asset pool*? . . . 10-24
Q 10:60 Is more than one separate asset pool created if participants have the right to direct the investment of their own account balances? . . . 10-24
Q 10:61 What are the mandatory disaggregation rules? . . . 10-24
Q 10:62 Under what circumstances are the mandatory disaggregation rules applied? . . . 10-24

Who Is an Employee?

Q 10:63 Are self-employed individuals considered employees? . . . 10-26
Q 10:64 Are leased employees considered employees? . . . 10-26
Q 10:65 What is the definition of a *leased employee*? . . . 10-27

Q 10:66	Must an agreement between the recipient and a leasing organization be in writing?	10-27
Q 10:67	When is an individual considered to have performed services on a substantially full-time basis for a period of at least one year?	10-27
Q 10:68	Is there an alternative way to determine whether an individual is considered substantially full-time?	10-28
Q 10:69	When will an individual cease to be considered a leased employee?	10-28
Q 10:70	When will services be considered performed under the primary direction or control of the recipient?	10-29
Q 10:71	Must a leased employee be an employee of the leasing organization?	10-29
Q 10:72	If an individual is considered a leased employee, is it necessary to cover the individual under the recipient's 401(k) plan?	10-29
Q 10:73	May leased employees be disregarded if the leasing organization maintains a retirement plan for them?	10-30
Q 10:74	What is a *safe harbor plan*?	10-30
Q 10:75	Who is considered part of the recipient's non-highly compensated workforce?	10-30

Who Is a Highly Compensated Employee?

Q 10:76	Who is a *highly compensated employee*?	10-31
Q 10:77	What are these specified groups of employees?	10-31
Q 10:78	How is the $80,000 threshold adjusted?	10-31
Q 10:79	How is the dollar threshold applied?	10-32
Q 10:80	Is the determination of HCEs limited to the employees of the entity sponsoring the plan?	10-32
Q 10:81	Who are considered employees in the determination of HCEs?	10-32
Q 10:82	Who is a *5 percent owner*?	10-33
Q 10:83	What is the *top-paid group*?	10-33
Q 10:84	How is the number of employees in the top-paid group determined?	10-33
Q 10:85	When is an employee considered to normally work fewer than 17½ hours per week?	10-34
Q 10:86	When is an employee considered to normally work fewer than seven months during the year?	10-34
Q 10:87	How are the particular employees who will make up the top-paid group selected?	10-34
Q 10:88	How does an employer make an election to require membership in the top-paid group?	10-35
Q 10:89	Under what circumstances would an employer want to make the election to require membership in the top-paid group?	10-36

Q 10:90	How is *compensation* defined for purposes of determining the group of HCEs?	10-36
Q 10:91	What are the determination and look-back years?	10-36

What Is Compensation?

Q 10:92	What definitions of compensation will automatically satisfy Code Section 414(s)?	10-38
Q 10:93	Can a definition of compensation that excludes certain deferrals satisfy Code Section 414(s)?	10-38
Q 10:94	If a plan excludes from the definition of compensation any portion of the compensation of an HCE, does the plan's definition of compensation continue to automatically satisfy Code Section 414(s)?	10-38
Q 10:95	If a plan's definition of compensation does not automatically satisfy Code Section 414(s), how does the plan demonstrate that its definition still satisfies Code Section 414(s)?	10-39
Q 10:96	When is a definition of compensation reasonable?	10-39
Q 10:97	Is a definition of compensation considered reasonable if it excludes a specified percentage of each employee's compensation?	10-39
Q 10:98	What is the nondiscrimination requirement?	10-39
Q 10:99	How are average percentages determined?	10-39
Q 10:100	May other methods be used for determining average percentages?	10-40
Q 10:101	How does a plan determine whether the average percentage of total compensation for the HCE group exceeds by more than a de minimis amount the average percentage of total compensation for the NHCE group?	10-41
Q 10:102	Are there special rules that apply to self-employed individuals?	10-41
Q 10:103	Must a plan use a definition of compensation that satisfies Code Section 414(s) in calculating contributions under the plan?	10-41
Q 10:104	Is there a limit on the amount of compensation that may be taken into account?	10-42
Q 10:105	Is the limit on compensation subject to adjustment?	10-42
Q 10:106	What are the situations in which the Section 401(a)(17) limit applies?	10-43

Chapter 11 Minimum Coverage Testing

Minimum Participation

Minimum Participation Rules

Q 11:1	What were the minimum participation rules as they applied to 401(k) plans for plan years beginning before January 1, 1997?	**11-2**

Minimum Coverage

Automatically Satisfying Minimum Coverage

Q 11:2	What types of 401(k) plans automatically satisfy the Code Section 410(b) minimum coverage rules?	**11-2**
Q 11:3	What requirements must a 401(k) plan meet in order to automatically satisfy the minimum coverage rules during the transition period following a change in the employer of the employees in a trade or business?	**11-3**

Ratio Percentage Test

Q 11:4	What is the *ratio percentage test*?	**11-3**
Q 11:5	What does it mean to benefit under a 401(k) plan?	**11-4**
Q 11:6	May 401(k) plans be combined to satisfy the ratio percentage test?	**11-4**
Q 11:7	Is there an exception to the rule that 401(k) plans that are required to be treated as separate plans cannot be combined for purposes of the ratio percentage test?	**11-5**
Q 11:8	If an employer that is divided into QSLOBs maintains a 401(k) plan that is tested on an employer-wide basis, may that plan be combined with any other plan maintained by the employer to demonstrate that the other plan satisfies the ratio percentage test?	**11-6**

Average Benefits Test

Q 11:9	What is the *average benefits test*?	**11-6**

Nondiscriminatory Classification Test

Q 11:10	What is the *nondiscriminatory classification test*?	**11-6**
Q 11:11	What is a *reasonable classification*?	**11-6**
Q 11:12	What is a *nondiscriminatory classification* of employees?	**11-6**
Q 11:13	What is the *safe harbor percentage*?	**11-7**
Q 11:14	What is the *unsafe harbor percentage*?	**11-7**
Q 11:15	What is the *NHCE concentration percentage*?	**11-7**

Q 11:16 What facts and circumstances will be taken into account by the IRS in determining whether a classification under a 401(k) plan will be considered nondiscriminatory? **11-9**

Q 11:17 May 401(k) plans be combined to satisfy the nondiscriminatory classification test? **11-10**

Average Benefit Percentage Test

Q 11:18 What is the *average benefit percentage test*? **11-10**

Q 11:19 How is the average benefit percentage calculated? **11-10**

Q 11:20 How is the actual benefit percentage of each group calculated? **11-10**

Q 11:21 What is the *testing group*? **11-10**

Q 11:22 What is the testing period for the average benefit percentage calculation? **11-11**

Q 11:23 How is an employee's benefit percentage calculated? **11-11**

Disregarding Certain Employees

Q 11:24 Can a 401(k) plan disregard certain employees in applying the minimum coverage rules? **11-12**

Q 11:25 Which employees may be excluded? **11-12**

Testing for Minimum Coverage

Q 11:26 How is a 401(k) plan tested to determine whether it satisfies the minimum coverage rules? **11-14**

Q 11:27 What is the *daily testing method*? **11-14**

Q 11:28 What is the *quarterly testing method*? **11-14**

Q 11:29 What is the *annual testing method*? **11-15**

Q 11:30 Has the IRS developed an alternative to the testing methodologies set forth in the regulations? **11-15**

Correcting Minimum Coverage Failure

Q 11:31 What happens if a 401(k) plan fails to satisfy the minimum coverage rules? **11-15**

Q 11:32 Is there any way to correct retroactively a failure to satisfy the minimum coverage rules? **11-16**

Q 11:33 What level of qualified nonelective contributions must be provided to these NHCEs? **11-16**

Q 11:34 By when must a 401(k) plan be amended to correct retroactively a failure to satisfy the minimum coverage rules? **11-16**

Q 11:35 Does the method of retroactive correction discussed in Qs 11:32–11:34 apply to the nonelective contribution portion of a 401(k) plan? **11-17**

Q 11:36 How does a plan resolve a minimum coverage failure if the plan does not satisfy the retroactive amendment procedure described in Qs 11:32–11:35? 11-17
Q 11:37 May a 401(k) plan be designed to automatically avoid a minimum coverage failure? 11-17

Chapter 12 General Nondiscrimination Testing

Testing of Employer Nonelective Contributions

The Design-Based Safe Harbor

Q 12:1 What is the *design-based safe harbor*? 12-2
Q 12:2 What is a *uniform allocation formula*? 12-2
Q 12:3 What is considered compensation for purposes of applying a uniform allocation formula? 12-2
Q 12:4 What is a *uniform point system plan*? 12-2
Q 12:5 How are an employee's points determined? 12-3
Q 12:6 What nondiscrimination test must be satisfied before a plan can be considered a uniform point system plan? 12-3
Q 12:7 Will an allocation of nonelective contributions that is conditioned on employment on the last day of the plan year cause an allocation formula to lose its status as a design-based safe harbor formula? 12-4
Q 12:8 Will an allocation formula be considered a design-based safe harbor formula if a participant who is a non-key employee receives only a top-heavy minimum contribution? 12-4

The General Nondiscrimination Test

Q 12:9 What is the *general nondiscrimination test*? 12-5
Q 12:10 What is a *rate group*? 12-5
Q 12:11 What is an employee's *allocation rate*? 12-5
Q 12:12 What amounts are taken into account in determining allocation rates? 12-5
Q 12:13 How does a rate group satisfy the minimum coverage rules? 12-5
Q 12:14 Is the general nondiscrimination test required to be satisfied on the basis of allocation rates? 12-7

Permitted Disparity

Basic Permitted Disparity Rules

Q 12:15 What is *permitted disparity*? 12-7
Q 12:16 What is the *integration level*? 12-7

Q 12:17 What is the maximum disparity permitted between the excess contribution percentage and the base contribution percentage? 12-8

Q 12:18 When will a reduction be required in the percentage determined from (1) or (2) of Q 12:17? 12-8

How Permitted Disparity Is Used

Q 12:19 Under what circumstances should permitted disparity be used? 12-9

Q 12:20 Why would an employer use permitted disparity? 12-9

Q 12:21 How does permitted disparity work? 12-10

Permitted Disparity in More Than One Plan

Q 12:22 Can permitted disparity be used in more than one plan of the employer? 12-10

Q 12:23 How is the annual overall limit for permitted disparity computed? 12-10

Q 12:24 What is the *cumulative disparity limit*? 12-11

Q 12:25 What is the practical implication of these limits on the use of permitted disparity? 12-11

Nondiscriminatory Availability of Benefits, Rights, and Features

Q 12:26 What are *benefits, rights, and features*? 12-12

Q 12:27 What is an *optional form of benefit*? 12-12

Q 12:28 What is an *ancillary benefit*? 12-12

Q 12:29 What are *other rights or features*? 12-12

Q 12:30 When are benefits, rights, and features provided on a nondiscriminatory basis? 12-12

Current Availability

Q 12:31 How is the current availability requirement satisfied? 12-13

Q 12:32 When is a benefit, right, or feature considered currently available to an employee? 12-13

Q 12:33 What conditions on the availability of benefits, rights, or features may be disregarded in determining current availability? 12-13

Q 12:34 Are there other conditions that may be disregarded? 12-14

Q 12:35 What happens if a benefit, right, or feature is prospectively eliminated? 12-14

Effective Availability

Q 12:36 What is the *effective availability requirement*? 12-14

Chapter 13 ADP and ACP Testing

Avoiding ADP and ACP Testing

Q 13:1 Can a 401(k) plan avoid ADP and ACP testing? **13-2**

The Actual Deferral Percentage Test

Q 13:2 How do elective contributions to a 401(k) plan satisfy the actual deferral percentage test? **13-2**

Q 13:3 How is the ADP for a group of eligible employees calculated? **13-3**

Prior-Year Versus Current-Year Testing Method

Q 13:4 How is an eligible employee's actual deferral ratio determined? **13-3**

Q 13:5 Can an employer elect to calculate NHCE actual deferral ratios and ADP using current-plan-year data? **13-4**

Q 13:6 Is IRS approval required to use the current-year testing method? **13-4**

Special Adjustments

Q 13:7 Is a 401(k) plan permitted to take into account other types of contributions along with elective contributions in determining actual deferral ratios? **13-4**

Q 13:8 Is the ADP of the NHCEs adjusted if an eligible employee who was an NHCE during the prior plan year is an HCE during the current plan year? **13-4**

Q 13:9 How is the ADP of the NHCEs calculated for the initial plan year of a 401(k) plan? **13-5**

Q 13:10 Is there any circumstance under which the actual deferral ratio of an HCE will be computed differently? **13-5**

Eligible Employees

Q 13:11 Who are considered eligible employees? **13-5**

Calculating Actual Deferral Ratios

Q 13:12 What is considered *compensation* for purposes of calculating actual deferral ratios? **13-5**

Q 13:13 What are *qualified matching contributions* and *qualified nonelective contributions*? **13-6**

Q 13:14 Under what circumstances may QMACs and QNECs be taken into account for purposes of the ADP test? **13-6**

Correcting ADP Test Failures

Q 13:15	What happens if the ADP test for a plan year is not satisfied?	13-8
Q 13:16	Are there correction methods that are not permissible?	13-8

Determining Excess Contributions

Q 13:17	How are excess contributions determined?	13-8
Q 13:18	What is the second step in the determination of excess contributions?	13-9

Recharacterizing Excess Contributions

Q 13:19	What happens when excess contributions are recharacterized?	13-10
Q 13:20	What was the tax treatment of recharacterized excess contributions before the enactment of the Pension Protection Act of 2006?	13-10
Q 13:21	What requirements must be met before recharacterization is permitted?	13-10
Q 13:22	When is recharacterization deemed to have occurred?	13-11

Distributing Excess Contributions

Q 13:23	How does the corrective distribution rule work?	13-11
Q 13:24	What is the income allocable to excess contributions?	13-11
Q 13:25	How is income allocable to excess contributions determined?	13-11
Q 13:26	How was allocable income determined for the gap period for plan years beginning before January 1, 2008?	13-12
Q 13:27	Are excess contributions that are distributed still treated as employer contributions?	13-12
Q 13:28	Is employee or spousal consent required for a distribution of excess contributions and allocable income?	13-12
Q 13:29	What was the tax treatment of corrective distributions made on account of plan years beginning before January 1, 2008?	13-13
Q 13:30	How was the pre-2008 tax treatment of corrective distributions affected if the excess contribution consisted of all or part of Roth deferrals?	13-13
Q 13:31	How does the Pension Protection Act of 2006 affect the tax treatment of corrective distributions?	13-13
Q 13:32	Are corrective distributions of excess contributions (plus income) subject to the additional income tax for distributions made before age 59½?	13-13
Q 13:33	Can a corrective distribution of excess contributions and allocable income be applied toward an employee's minimum distribution requirement under Code Section 401(a)(9)?	13-13

Q 13:34 What happens if excess contributions (plus allocable income) are not distributed within 12 months after the end of the plan year? 13-14

Q 13:35 What happens if excess contributions (plus allocable income) are distributed within 12 months after the end of the plan year but more than 2½ months thereafter? 13-14

Restructuring for ADP Testing

Q 13:36 Under what circumstances can a 401(k) plan be restructured to show that the ADP test is satisfied? 13-14

Q 13:37 How is the 401(k) plan restructured? 13-14

Q 13:38 How does the early participation rule affect the use of restructuring? 13-15

Correcting ADP Test by Making QNECs

Q 13:39 In a 401(k) plan that uses QNECs to correct a failed ADP test, to whom are the QNECs allocated? 13-16

Q 13:40 How did the bottom-up approach to allocating QNECs work? 13-16

Q 13:41 How do the new 401(k) regulations (generally effective for plan years beginning on or after January 1, 2006) affect the use of QNECs in helping to satisfy the ADP test? 13-17

Q 13:42 Why have the Treasury Department and IRS decided to restrict the use of the bottom-up approach for correcting a failed ADP test? 13-18

Q 13:43 Do the new 401(k) regulations allow any type of allocation that is targeted to specific groups of eligible NHCEs? 13-18

Q 13:44 What is a 401(k) plan's *representative contribution rate*? 13-18

Q 13:45 What is the applicable contribution rate of an eligible NHCE? 13-18

Q 13:46 Can QNECs used in correcting a failed ADP test still be allocated on a proportionate basis or per capita basis under the new final 401(k) regulations? 13-20

The Actual Contribution Percentage Test

Q 13:47 How do employer matching and employee after-tax contributions to a 401(k) plan satisfy the actual contribution percentage test? 13-21

Q 13:48 How is the ACP for a group of eligible employees calculated? 13-22

Actual Contribution Ratios

Q 13:49 How is an eligible employee's actual contribution ratio determined? 13-22

Q 13:50	Is there any situation under which matching contributions made on behalf of an NHCE will be disregarded in determining that NHCE's ACR?	**13-23**
Q 13:51	What is a 401(k) plan's *representative matching rate*?	**13-23**
Q 13:52	What is the matching rate of an NHCE?	**13-23**
	Prior-Year Versus Current-Year Testing Method	
Q 13:53	What method is used to determine actual contribution ratios?	**13-23**
Q 13:54	Is IRS approval required to use the current-year testing method?	**13-24**
	Special Adjustments	
Q 13:55	Is the ACP of the NHCEs adjusted if an eligible employee who was an NHCE during the prior plan year is an HCE during the current plan year?	**13-24**
Q 13:56	How is the ACP of the NHCEs calculated for the initial plan year of a 401(k) plan?	**13-24**
Q 13:57	Is there any circumstance under which the actual contribution ratio of an HCE will be computed differently?	**13-24**
	Employee Contributions; Eligible Employees	
Q 13:58	What contributions are considered *employee contributions*?	**13-25**
Q 13:59	Who are considered *eligible employees*?	**13-25**
	Calculating Actual Contribution Ratios	
Q 13:60	What is considered *compensation* for purposes of calculating actual contribution ratios?	**13-25**
Q 13:61	Under what circumstances may elective contributions and QNECs be treated as matching contributions for purposes of the ACP test?	**13-25**
	Correcting ACP Test Failures	
Q 13:62	What happens if the ACP test for a plan year is not satisfied?	**13-27**
Q 13:63	Are there correction methods that are not permissible?	**13-28**
	Determining Excess Aggregate Contributions	
Q 13:64	How are excess aggregate contributions determined?	**13-28**
Q 13:65	What is the second step in the determination of excess aggregate contributions?	**13-28**
Q 13:66	If a 401(k) plan provides for the recharacterization of excess contributions as employee contributions, how will this affect the calculation of excess aggregate contributions?	**13-29**

Distributing Excess Aggregate Contributions

Q 13:67 How does the corrective distribution rule work? **13-29**
Q 13:68 What is the income allocable to excess aggregate contributions? **13-30**
Q 13:69 How is income allocable to excess aggregate contributions determined? **13-30**
Q 13:70 How was allocable income determined for the gap period for plan years beginning before January 1, 2008? **13-30**
Q 13:71 When is a method of distributing excess aggregate contributions considered discriminatory? **13-31**
Q 13:72 How are corrective distributions and forfeited matching contributions treated for tax purposes? **13-31**
Q 13:73 What was the tax treatment of corrective distributions made on account of plan years beginning before January 1, 2008? . . . **13-31**
Q 13:74 How does the Pension Protection Act of 2006 affect the tax treatment of corrective distributions? **13-32**
Q 13:75 Are corrective distributions of excess aggregate contributions (plus income) subject to the additional income tax for distributions made before age 59½? **13-32**
Q 13:76 Can a corrective distribution of excess aggregate contributions and allocable income be applied toward an employee's minimum distribution requirement under Code Section 401(a)(9)? **13-32**
Q 13:77 Is employee or spousal consent required for a corrective distribution of excess aggregate contributions and allocable income? **13-32**
Q 13:78 What happens if a plan fails to make a corrective distribution of excess aggregate contributions and allocable income? **13-32**

Restructuring for ACP Testing

Q 13:79 Under what circumstances can a 401(k) plan be restructured to show that the ACP test is satisfied? **13-33**

Correcting ACP Test by Making QNECs

Q 13:80 How are QNECs used to correct a failed ACP test? **13-33**

Chapter 14 Top-Heavy Rules

Top-Heavy Testing

Q 14:1 What issues must be considered in determining whether a 401(k) plan is top heavy? **14-2**
Q 14:2 How does a plan become top heavy? **14-2**
Q 14:3 Who is considered the *employer*? **14-2**
Q 14:4 Who is considered an *employee*? **14-2**

Aggregation Groups

Q 14:5 What is a *required aggregation group*? 14-2

Q 14:6 What is a *permissive aggregation group*? 14-3

Q 14:7 If more than 60 percent of the sum of the accrued benefits under all plans of the employer in the permissive aggregation group are attributable to key employees, which plans will be considered top heavy? 14-3

Q 14:8 If 60 percent or less of the sum of the accrued benefits under all plans of the employer in the permissive aggregation group is attributable to key employees, will any of the plans required to be aggregated be considered top heavy? 14-4

Key Employee

Q 14:9 Who is considered a *key employee*? 14-4

Q 14:10 Who is a *5 percent owner*? 14-4

Q 14:11 Who is a *1 percent owner*? 14-4

Q 14:12 Who is an *officer*? 14-5

Q 14:13 Who is an *includable officer*? 14-5

Q 14:14 Is there a limit on the number of includable officers who can be considered key employees? 14-6

Q 14:15 How is the number of employees determined? 14-6

Q 14:16 If the number of includable officers is greater than the maximum number of includable officers who can be considered key employees, which includable officers will be treated as key employees? 14-7

Q 14:17 What is considered *compensation* for purposes of determining key employees? 14-7

Determination Date

Q 14:18 When is the top-heavy determination for a plan year made? ... 14-7

Q 14:19 What is the *determination date* for a plan year? 14-7

Present Value of Accrued Benefits

Q 14:20 How is the present value of accrued benefits determined in a defined contribution plan? 14-8

Q 14:21 How is the present value of accrued benefits determined in a defined benefit plan? 14-8

Q 14:22 What actuarial assumptions are used in determining the present value of accrued benefits in a defined benefit plan? 14-9

Q 14:23 Are accrued benefits attributable to employee contributions taken into account? 14-9

Q 14:24 Are catch-up contributions taken into account in determining accrued benefits? 14-9

Q 14:25 What effect do distributions to participants have on the determination of the present value of accrued benefits? 14-9

Q 14:26 What effect do distributions to beneficiaries of deceased participants have on the determination of the present value of accrued benefits? 14-10

Q 14:27 How are rollovers and plan-to-plan transfers handled? 14-10

Q 14:28 Are the accrued benefits of and distributions to certain participants disregarded for purposes of determining whether a plan is top heavy? 14-11

Minimum Vesting

Q 14:29 What special vesting requirements apply to top-heavy plans? 14-11

Q 14:30 What service may be disregarded in determining a participant's vested percentage? 14-12

Q 14:31 Does a top-heavy vesting schedule apply only to that portion of a participant's account balance accrued after a plan becomes top heavy? 14-12

Minimum Contributions

Q 14:32 What special contribution requirements apply to top-heavy plans? 14-12

Q 14:33 What is *compensation* for purposes of determining a non-key employee's minimum contribution? 14-12

Q 14:34 Are allocated forfeitures taken into account in determining whether a non-key employee has received a minimum contribution? 14-13

Q 14:35 Is the top-heavy minimum contribution always 3 percent of compensation? 14-13

Q 14:36 Is there any circumstance under which an employer that sponsors a top-heavy plan must make a contribution in excess of 3 percent of compensation? 14-14

Q 14:37 Are elective contributions made on behalf of key employees taken into account in determining whether a key employee's allocation of contributions and forfeitures constitutes 3 percent of compensation? 14-14

Q 14:38 What amounts are taken into account in determining whether a participant has received a top-heavy minimum? 14-14

Q 14:39 Which non-key employees must receive a minimum contribution? 14-15

Q 14:40 If an employer maintains a 401(k) plan and another defined contribution plan, must both plans provide top-heavy minimums for non-key employees who participate in both? 14-15

Q 14:41 What happens if non-key employees are accruing benefits under both a 401(k) plan and a defined benefit plan? 14-15

Top-Heavy Strategy

Q 14:42 Is there a minimum contribution requirement for a top-heavy 401(k) plan that provides for elective contributions only? 14-16

Q 14:43 Can the top-heavy plan rules be avoided by converting a 401(k) plan to a SIMPLE plan? 14-16

Q 14:44 If an employer makes a discretionary profit sharing contribution, can each non-key employee's allocation of that contribution be credited toward the top-heavy minimum contribution obligation? 14-17

Q 14:45 Can an employer matching contribution be used to satisfy the top-heavy minimum contribution obligation? 14-17

Q 14:46 Is there any other type of employer contribution that can be used to satisfy the top-heavy rules? 14-17

Q 14:47 Can the top-heavy plan rules be avoided by converting a 401(k) plan to a safe harbor 401(k) plan? 14-17

Q 14:48 Can the top-heavy rules be avoided by adding a qualified automatic contribution arrangement to a 401(k) plan? 14-18

Chapter 15 Participant Loans, Hardship Withdrawals, and In-Service Distributions

Participant Loans

Q 15:1 Who may borrow money from his or her 401(k) plan account? 15-2

Department of Labor Regulation of Participant Loans

Q 15:2 What are the purpose and general content of the DOL rules? 15-2

Loan Availability

Q 15:3 When is a loan available to all participants on a reasonably equivalent basis? 15-3

Q 15:4 When are loans made available to highly compensated employees in amounts greater than what is available to other employees? 15-3

Loan Terms and Provisions

Q 15:5 What provisions concerning loans must be in the plan document? 15-4

Q 15:6 What is a reasonable rate of interest for participant loans? 15-4

Q 15:7 Must the plan interest rate be reviewed each time a new loan is taken out? 15-4

Q 15:8 When is a loan considered adequately secured? 15-5

Q 15:9	Can a participant's account balance be used to secure the loan?	15-5
Q 15:10	Must the plan examine the creditworthiness of each borrower in determining whether to approve a loan?	15-5
Q 15:11	Are there any restrictions on how a loan is used by a participant?	15-5
Q 15:12	Can a participant loan be made to a fiduciary involved in administering the loan program?	15-5
Q 15:13	Does the DOL impose any other restrictions on participant loans?	15-5
Q 15:14	What are the consequences of failing to satisfy the DOL loan rules?	15-6

Taxation of Participant Loans

Q 15:15	How may taxation of participant loans be avoided?	15-6
Q 15:16	What constitutes an enforceable agreement for purposes of the loan rules?	15-7
Q 15:17	What documentation should a plan sponsor retain in connection with its loan program?	15-8
Q 15:18	If a loan fails to meet these requirements, what taxes apply?	15-8
Q 15:19	How much of the loan is taxed if the requirements are not met?	15-8
Q 15:20	What is a plan administrator's tax reporting obligation when a deemed distribution occurs?	15-9
Q 15:21	What is the difference between a deemed distribution and a loan offset?	15-9
Q 15:22	Does interest continue to accrue on a deemed distribution?	15-10
Q 15:23	Is the interest that continues to accrue on a deemed loan taxable?	15-10
Q 15:24	What impact does a deemed loan have on a participant's ability to obtain a subsequent loan?	15-11
Q 15:25	How are loan repayments made after a loan is deemed distributed treated for tax purposes?	15-12
Q 15:26	When must a plan apply the final regulations described in Qs 15:23 and 15:25?	15-12
Q 15:27	If some or all of a loan is treated as a deemed distribution, is that portion of the loan still considered outstanding?	15-13
Q 15:28	What special problems can arise under ERISA when a loan is deemed distributed?	15-14
Q 15:29	What are some ways to avoid or minimize the complications associated with deemed loans?	15-14

Other Loan Rules

Q 15:30	What special rules apply to loans from Roth accounts?	15-15

Q 15:31 How do the rollover rules apply to plan loans and loan offsets? 15-15

Q 15:32 How does an employer determine whether a loan is a principal residence loan? 15-16

Q 15:33 Does the level amortization requirement apply when a participant is on a leave of absence? 15-16

Q 15:34 What special loan rules apply when a participant's leave is for military service? 15-17

Q 15:35 Is there any limit on the number of loans that a plan can make to a participant in one year? 15-18

Q 15:36 May a participant refinance (replace with another loan) an outstanding loan? 15-18

Q 15:37 If a participant who has filed bankruptcy has an outstanding loan in the plan, what happens to the loan? 15-20

Q 15:38 Are participant loans subject to federal truth-in-lending disclosure rules? 15-20

Q 15:39 Is interest paid on a participant loan deductible? 15-20

Q 15:40 Can fees incurred to set up and administer a participant loan be charged to that participant's account? 15-21

Q 15:41 Is spousal consent needed to make a participant loan? 15-21

Q 15:42 Can an employer eliminate or change its loan program? 15-22

Q 15:43 When must an employer remit participant loan repayments to the plan? 15-22

Hardship Withdrawals of Elective Contributions

Q 15:44 When is a distribution of elective contributions considered made on account of a hardship? 15-23

The Events Test

Q 15:45 How is the general standard applied to the events test? 15-23

Q 15:46 How is the safe harbor standard applied to the events test? 15-23

The Needs Test

Q 15:47 How is the general standard applied to the needs test? 15-24

Q 15:48 How is the safe harbor standard applied to the needs test? 15-25

Q 15:49 What is meant by the phrase *all other plans maintained by the employer*? 15-25

Safe Harbor Standard Versus General Standard

Q 15:50 What is the best standard to use, and can the standards be combined? 15-25

Plan Sponsor Documentation

Q 15:51 What documentation should a plan sponsor retain when allowing a hardship withdrawal? 15-26

Tax Consequences

Q 15:52 What tax consequences apply to hardship withdrawals of elective contributions? 15-26

Q 15:53 May a plan take into account federal, state, or local income taxes and penalties that may be payable as a result of a hardship withdrawal? 15-27

Other Withdrawal Issues

Q 15:54 Is there a limit on the amount of a hardship withdrawal? 15-27

Q 15:55 Can distributions from employer contribution accounts be made on account of hardship? 15-27

Q 15:56 What special rules apply to hardship withdrawals from Roth elective deferral accounts? 15-28

In-Service Distributions

Q 15:57 In general, when may 401(k) accounts be distributed? 15-29

Q 15:58 Under what circumstances other than death, disability, or severance from employment may employer contribution accounts be distributed? 15-29

Q 15:59 What is considered a *fixed number of years*? 15-30

Q 15:60 Under what circumstances may amounts attributable to elective contributions be distributed? 15-30

Q 15:61 Do the rules that restrict the accessibility of elective contributions apply to other types of contributions made under a 401(k) plan? 15-31

Hurricane Sandy Relief

Q 15:62 What relief was made available to victims of Hurricane Sandy with regard to retirement plan loans and distributions? 15-31

Chapter 16 Distributions Subsequent to Termination of Employment

Optional Forms of Benefit

Q 16:1 What is an *optional form of benefit*? 16-2

Q 16:2 What are not optional forms of benefit? 16-2

Q 16:3 What rules apply to optional forms of benefit? 16-3

Q 16:4 Does an employer have discretion over what optional forms of benefits will be made available to individual participants? . . . 16-3

Q 16:5 Is employer discretion prohibited under all circumstances? 16-3

Anti-Cutback Rules

Q 16:6 Can optional forms of benefits be reduced or eliminated by plan amendment? 16-3

Q 16:7 Are there any exceptions to the anti-cutback rule? 16-4

Q 16:8 May an employer amend a 401(k) plan to eliminate the right to receive an in-kind distribution of a participant's account balance? 16-4

Q 16:9 Can an employer avoid the anti-cutback rules through an employee waiver? 16-5

Q 16:10 What should an employer consider when designing distribution features in a new plan? 16-5

Q 16:11 What should an employer consider in the case of a plan merger or spin-off? 16-5

Q 16:12 Is there any type of plan-to-plan transfer that is not subject to the anti-cutback rules? 16-6

Postponement of Benefits

Q 16:13 How long may a 401(k) plan delay the payment of benefits to a participant? 16-6

Q 16:14 Does an early retirement provision in the 401(k) plan accelerate the payment of benefits? 16-6

Q 16:15 What requirements must be met by a participant who is allowed to elect to delay the payment of benefits? 16-7

Q 16:16 Are there circumstances under which plan provisions delaying the payment of benefits are superseded? 16-7

Q 16:17 What conditions must be satisfied before a participant's consent is considered valid? 16-7

Q 16:18 What must be contained in the notice describing the consequences of failing to defer receipt of distribution? 16-8

Q 16:19 When is the right-to-defer notice required to be given to a participant? 16-8

Q 16:20 Do the regulations offer an alternative to the right-to-defer notice requirement? 16-8

Q 16:21 What information must be included in a summary notice? 16-8

Q 16:22 What form must the right-to-defer notice take? 16-9

Q 16:23 What are the requirements that must be met for a participant to consent electronically to a plan distribution? 16-11

Involuntary Distributions

Q 16:24 Under what circumstances may a 401(k) plan compel a participant to commence receiving benefits? 16-11

Q 16:25 Is a beneficiary's consent required in the event of a participant's death? 16-12

Q 16:26 Is an alternate payee's consent required in the case of a qualified domestic relations order (QDRO)? 16-12

Qualified Reservist Distributions

Q 16:27 Are there any special rules that apply to participants whose employment has been terminated on account of their call to military service? 16-12
Q 16:28 What is a *qualified reservist distribution*? 16-13
Q 16:29 Can a participant who received a QRD pay back the amount that was previously distributed to him? 16-13

Minimum Distribution Requirements

Required Beginning Date

Q 16:30 How long may a participant defer the receipt of benefits in a 401(k) plan? 16-13
Q 16:31 Who is a *5 percent owner* for minimum distribution purposes? 16-14
Q 16:32 Is there any exception to the rules establishing an employee's required beginning date? 16-14
Q 16:33 What happens if a participant revokes an election made under TEFRA Section 242(b)(2)? 16-14
Q 16:34 If a participant dies before his or her required beginning date, what is the date by which post-death benefits must begin? 16-14
Q 16:35 What is the *five-year rule*? 16-15
Q 16:36 Who is a *designated beneficiary*? 16-15
Q 16:37 May an estate or trust be considered a designated beneficiary? 16-15
Q 16:38 What is the *designated beneficiary rule*? 16-16
Q 16:39 What happens if the sole designated beneficiary is the employee's surviving spouse? 16-16
Q 16:40 How did the Worker, Retiree, and Employer Recovery Act of 2008 affect minimum distribution requirements? 16-16

Payment Options

Q 16:41 What payment options may be offered by a 401(k) plan? 16-17
Q 16:42 What requirements must a plan fiduciary meet in selecting an annuity contract that is provided as a payment option under a plan? 16-17
Q 16:43 Must distributions that are made to an employee before the employee's required beginning date satisfy the minimum distribution rules? 16-18

Q 16:44 To satisfy the minimum distribution rules, over what length of time may an employee receive his or her interest in the plan? **16-18**

Q 16:45 If an employee's interest in the plan will be paid out over a period of time not exceeding the employee's life expectancy (or joint life and last survivor expectancy), what amount is required to be paid each calendar year? **16-18**

Q 16:46 What is the value of an employee's interest for purposes of calculating the minimum distribution for a calendar year? . . . **16-19**

Q 16:47 If an employee dies after the required beginning date but before the employee's entire interest has been distributed, how must the remaining interest in the plan be distributed? **16-20**

Q 16:48 How are required minimum distributions reported? **16-21**

Participants Called to Active Military Duty

Q 16:49 Is a 401(k) plan required to permit a participant who is on active military duty for more than 30 days to receive a distribution from the plan? **16-21**

Q 16:50 May a 401(k) plan permit a participant who is receiving differential wage payments to receive a distribution from a 401(k) plan? **16-21**

Q 16:51 If a distribution to a participant who is receiving differential wage payments also qualifies as a qualified reservist distribution, how will the distribution be treated for tax purposes? **16-22**

Rollover Rules

Q 16:52 What is a *rollover*? **16-22**

Q 16:53 How did EGTRRA change the rollover rules? **16-22**

Q 16:54 How has the Pension Protection Act changed the rollover rules? **16-23**

Eligible Rollover Distribution

Q 16:55 What distributions are eligible for tax-free rollover? **16-23**

Q 16:56 What is an *eligible rollover distribution*? **16-23**

Q 16:57 Are there any exceptions to the general rule defining eligible rollover distributions? **16-23**

Q 16:58 How is it determined that a distribution is part of a series of substantially equal periodic payments? **16-24**

Q 16:59 What happens if, while an employee is receiving substantially equal periodic payments that are not eligible rollover distributions, the amount of the payment changes? **16-24**

Q 16:60 When is a distribution considered a minimum distribution under Code Section 401(a)(9) that is not an eligible rollover distribution? **16-25**

Q 16:61	Can property other than cash be rolled over?	16-25
Q 16:62	Is the rollover option available to all distributees?	16-25
Q 16:63	Is a distribution to a participant who has been on active military duty for more than 30 days and who is receiving differential wage payments treated as an eligible rollover distribution?	16-25
	Direct Rollover Option	
Q 16:64	What options must be offered regarding the tax treatment of eligible rollover distributions?	16-26
Q 16:65	What is a *direct rollover*?	16-26
Q 16:66	Are there any restrictions on a distributee's right to elect direct rollover of eligible rollover distributions?	16-26
Q 16:67	What is an *eligible retirement plan*?	16-26
Q 16:68	Are plans required to accept direct rollovers of eligible rollover distributions?	16-27
	Automatic Rollover Rules	
Q 16:69	Is there any circumstance under which a direct rollover would be mandatory?	16-27
Q 16:70	What is a *mandatory distribution*?	16-27
Q 16:71	Must the plan administrator notify plan participants that in the absence of an election, a mandatory distribution will be automatically rolled over?	16-28
Q 16:72	Are amounts attributable to rollover contributions subject to automatic rollover?	16-28
Q 16:73	In the case of a 401(k) plan subject to the joint and survivor rules, is the plan administrator required to obtain the consent of the participant's spouse if the participant's vested account balance does not exceed $5,000?	16-28
Q 16:74	What is considered an individual retirement plan for purposes of the automatic rollover rules?	16-29
Q 16:75	Is the plan administrator allowed to establish an individual retirement plan for a participant who fails to elect to receive or roll over his or her vested account balance?	16-29
Q 16:76	Are employers making fiduciary decisions when they decide which individual retirement plans to establish and how to invest the account balance of a participant who is subject to the automatic rollover rules?	16-29
Q 16:77	Has the Department of Labor provided guidance concerning how an employer can satisfy its fiduciary duties in connection with the automatic rollover of mandatory distributions?	16-29
Q 16:78	Does the DOL safe harbor extend to the automatic rollover of mandatory distributions of $1,000 or less?	16-30

Q 16:79 Can a plan avoid the automatic rollover rules by limiting mandatory distributions to vested accounts of $1,000 or less? 16-30

Rollover of Distributions

Q 16:80 If a distributee elects to receive a cash distribution, can he or she later roll over that distribution? 16-31
Q 16:81 Is there any exception to the 60-day rule? 16-31
Q 16:82 Are there circumstances under which a 60-day rollover option is not available to the distributee of an eligible rollover distribution? 16-31

Direct Rollover Election

Q 16:83 How is a direct rollover elected? 16-32
Q 16:84 Is spousal consent needed on a direct rollover election? 16-32
Q 16:85 Must distributees be given the option to roll over into more than one eligible retirement plan? 16-32
Q 16:86 Must a direct rollover option be offered on a loan offset amount that is an eligible rollover distribution? 16-32
Q 16:87 How is a direct rollover accomplished? 16-32

Direct Rollover Procedures

Q 16:88 May the plan administrator impose procedures or limitations on direct rollover elections? 16-33
Q 16:89 Is notice of the direct rollover option required? 16-33
Q 16:90 What is a reasonable period of time for providing notice? 16-33
Q 16:91 What information must the notice contain? 16-33
Q 16:92 Is there a model notice that can be used to assure compliance with Code Section 402(f)? 16-34
Q 16:93 May the plan administrator establish a cutoff date after which a rollover election cannot be revoked? 16-34
Q 16:94 How do the notice and election rules apply to eligible rollover distributions that are paid in periodic installments? 16-34
Q 16:95 How is a direct rollover distribution reported for income tax purposes? 16-34
Q 16:96 Is a direct rollover considered a transfer of benefits to which the optional form of benefit rules apply? 16-34

Rollovers to Inherited IRAs

Q 16:97 Is a 401(k) plan required to offer a direct rollover of an eligible rollover distribution to a nonspousal beneficiary? 16-35
Q 16:98 Is the direct rollover option available to all nonspousal beneficiaries of a deceased participant? 16-35
Q 16:99 What is an *inherited IRA*? 16-35

Q 16:100 How is an inherited IRA established and titled? 16-35

Q 16:101 If the participant dies before his or her required beginning date, what amount may be rolled over to the inherited IRA? 16-35

Q 16:102 If the participant dies *after* his or her required beginning date, what amount may be rolled over to the inherited IRA? 16-36

Q 16:103 After the deceased participant's account balance has been rolled over to the inherited IRA, how is the minimum distribution determined with respect to the IRA? 16-36

Rollover Strategies

Q 16:104 What are the advantages of a rollover? 16-37

Q 16:105 What are the disadvantages of a rollover? 16-37

Q 16:106 What issues are presented when an eligible rollover distribution includes amounts that were previously taxed like Roth contributions and employee after-tax contributions? 16-37

Withholding on Distributions

Q 16:107 Is withholding required on contributions to a 401(k) plan? 16-38

Q 16:108 Is withholding required on distributions from a 401(k) plan? . . . 16-38

Q 16:109 What is the amount of income tax withholding required on eligible rollover distributions? 16-38

Q 16:110 May a participant elect out of withholding on an eligible rollover distribution? 16-39

Q 16:111 Are hardship withdrawals subject to mandatory withholding? 16-39

Loan Offset Amount

Q 16:112 Are participant loans subject to the new withholding rules? 16-39

Q 16:113 How is the 20 percent withholding requirement applied to a distribution that includes a loan offset amount? 16-39

Q 16:114 Is there any limit on the amount of withholding required for a loan offset amount that is an eligible rollover distribution? . . . 16-40

Other Special Distributions

Q 16:115 How do the 20 percent withholding rules apply to distributions of property? 16-40

Q 16:116 How do the withholding rules apply to the distribution of employer securities? 16-40

Q 16:117 Do the withholding rules apply to distributions from IRAs? 16-40

Responsibility for Withholding

Q 16:118 Who is responsible for enforcing the mandatory 20 percent withholding? 16-41

Q 16:119 Will the plan administrator be responsible for taxes, interest, or penalties if a direct rollover is elected, but the rollover fails? **16-41**

Q 16:120 What constitutes adequate information on which a plan administrator can rely to avoid taxes, interest, and penalties? **16-41**

Distributions Not Eligible for Rollover

Q 16:121 What withholding rules apply to distributions from a qualified plan that are not eligible rollover distributions? **16-41**

Q 16:122 What amounts are subject to withholding under the old rules? **16-42**

Q 16:123 Are there special rules for withholding on distributions of employer securities? **16-42**

Q 16:124 Is aggregation with amounts distributed from another plan of the employer required? **16-42**

Q 16:125 What rate of withholding applies to 401(k) plan distributions under the old rules? **16-42**

Periodic and Nonperiodic Distributions

Q 16:126 What is a *periodic distribution*? **16-42**

Q 16:127 What is the rate of withholding for periodic distributions? **16-43**

Q 16:128 What is a *nonperiodic distribution*? **16-43**

Q 16:129 What is the rate of withholding required on nonperiodic distributions? **16-43**

Electing Out of Withholding

Q 16:130 Who may elect not to have a withholding taken from a 401(k) plan distribution? **16-43**

Q 16:131 Is the plan administrator required to notify payees of their right to elect out of withholding? **16-43**

Q 16:132 What information must be contained in the withholding notice? **16-44**

Q 16:133 When must notice be given on periodic distributions? **16-44**

Q 16:134 When must notice be given for nonperiodic distributions? **16-44**

Q 16:135 What withholding elections should be given effect by the payor? **16-44**

Withholding Procedures and Penalties

Q 16:136 Is withholding required on distributions to participants with foreign addresses? **16-45**

Q 16:137 How are withheld income taxes reported to the IRS? **16-45**

Q 16:138 Are deposits of federal income tax withholding required? **16-45**

Q 16:139 Must withheld amounts be reported to the payee? **16-45**

Q 16:140 Are there penalties for failing to withhold, report, or pay federal taxes? 16-45

Claims for Benefits

Q 16:141 What is considered a claim for benefits? 16-46

Q 16:142 What requirements must a claims procedure meet in order to be considered reasonable? 16-46

Q 16:143 How soon after a benefit claim is filed must the plan administrator make a determination on the claim? 16-46

Q 16:144 If a claim is denied, how must the claimant be notified of the denial? 16-47

Q 16:145 What requirements must the plan's review procedure meet?. 16-47

Q 16:146 If a claim is denied at the appeals stage, how must the claimant be notified of the denial? 16-48

Q 16:147 How soon after an appeal is filed must the plan administrator make a determination on the appeal?. 16-48

Chapter 17 Spousal Rights

Survivor Annuity Requirements

Q 17:1 What plans are subject to the survivor annuity requirements?. 17-1

Q 17:2 What is a *transferee plan*?. 17-2

Q 17:3 If a 401(k) plan is a transferee plan, do the survivor annuity requirements apply to all plan participants? 17-2

Q 17:4 If a 401(k) plan is a transferee plan with respect to a participant, do the survivor annuity requirements apply to that participant's entire account balance? 17-2

Annuity and Other Lifetime Income Products

Q 17:5 What is the issue with applying the survivor annuity rules to deferred annuity contracts?. 17-2

Q 17:6 What guidance has been provided to address this issue?. 17-3

Q 17:7 If the survivor annuity rules are triggered by investment in a deferred annuity contract, do they apply to the participant's entire account balance? 17-3

Q 17:8 How do the survivor annuity rules apply to GLWBs or other similar products? 17-3

Qualified Pre-Retirement Survivor Annuity and Qualified Joint and Survivor Annuity

Q 17:9 What are the survivor annuity requirements? 17-4

Q 17:10 What is a *qualified pre-retirement survivor* annuity? 17-4

Q 17:11 What is a *qualified joint and survivor* annuity? 17-4

Q 17:12 Is a plan required to provide any alternative to the qualified joint and survivor annuity? 17-4

Q 17:13 Is a plan required to provide a qualified pre-retirement survivor annuity that is based on the qualified optional survivor annuity described in Q 17:8? 17-5

Q 17:14 What is the *annuity starting date*? 17-5

Q 17:15 When must payments under a QPSA commence? 17-5

Q 17:16 When must payments under a QJSA commence? 17-5

Q 17:17 What is the *earliest retirement age*? 17-6

Waivers

Q 17:18 May a participant waive the QPSA and/or QJSA? 17-6

Q 17:19 What requirements must be met by a participant's waiver of the QPSA? 17-6

Q 17:20 What requirements must be met by a participant's waiver of the QJSA? 17-6

Q 17:21 When may a participant waive the QPSA? 17-6

Q 17:22 Are there special rules that apply to terminated participants? 17-7

Q 17:23 When may a participant waive the QJSA? 17-7

Written Explanation

Q 17:24 Must a 401(k) plan provide a written explanation of the survivor annuity requirements? 17-7

Q 17:25 How are the financial effects of various forms of benefits provided under the plan described in the written explanation? 17-7

Q 17:26 When must the written explanation of the QPSA be provided to participants? 17-8

Q 17:27 When must the written explanation of the QJSA be provided to participants? 17-8

Q 17:28 Must the written explanations of the survivor annuity requirements be provided on paper? 17-8

Spouse's Consent

Q 17:29 What requirements must a spouse's consent satisfy? 17-8

Q 17:30 If a participant revokes a prior waiver and then elects again during the election period to waive the survivor annuity requirements, must the spouse's consent be obtained again? 17-9

Q 17:31 Is the spouse's consent revocable? 17-9

Q 17:32 Does a spouse's consent to the waiver of the survivor annuity requirements apply to a subsequent spouse? 17-9

Q 17:33 If a participant elects to receive a QOSA in lieu of the QJSA, must the participant's spouse consent to this election? **17-9**

Definition of a "Spouse" for 401(k) Plan Purposes

Q 17:34 How is spousal status determined? **17-10**
Q 17:35 What was the effective date of the *Windsor* decision? **17-11**
Q 17:36 Could plans offer federally created spousal benefits to same-sex spouses prior to the effective date of the *Windsor* decision? **17-11**
Q 17:37 What should a plan do if it did not comply operationally with the *Windsor* decision by the effective date? **17-11**
Q 17:38 When must 401(k) plans be amended to reflect the *Windsor* decision and subsequent IRS guidance? **17-11**
Q 17:39 Can a plan rely on "state of domicile" law to deny benefits to same-sex spouses after September 16, 2013? **17-12**
Q 17:40 Can state laws ban or refuse to offer same-sex marriage? **17-12**
Q 17:41 What plan benefits are affected by the definition of who is a spouse? **17-12**
Q 17:42 What are some remaining questions and concerns for plan sponsors following the Supreme Court's DOMA decision and subsequent guidance? **17-13**
Q 17:43 What steps were required of plan sponsors in response to the Supreme Court's *Windsor* decision? **17-14**
Q 17:44 What additional concerns are raised by the *Obgerfell* decision? **17-14**

Loans

Q 17:45 How do the survivor annuity requirements apply to loans? **17-14**
Q 17:46 Is spousal consent required if, after the loan is obtained, the 401(k) plan becomes subject to the survivor annuity requirements or a single participant marries? **17-15**
Q 17:47 What happens if a secured loan is outstanding at the time the QJSA or QPSA is payable? **17-15**

Special Circumstances

Q 17:48 Is spousal consent required if a plan representative is satisfied that there is no spouse or that the spouse cannot be located? **17-15**
Q 17:49 If a 401(k) plan is not subject to the survivor annuity requirements because it provides that a participant's vested account balance is payable in full, upon the participant's death, to the participant's surviving spouse, when must the participant's account balance be paid to the surviving spouse? **17-15**

Q 17:50 May a participant waive the spousal death benefit applicable to 401(k) plans that are not subject to the survivor annuity requirements? **17-16**

Qualified Domestic Relations Orders

Q 17:51 What is a *qualified domestic relations order*? **17-16**
Q 17:52 What is a *domestic relations order*? **17-16**
Q 17:53 Who can be an *alternate payee*? **17-17**

QDRO Terms

Q 17:54 What terms must be contained in a QDRO? **17-17**
Q 17:55 What terms cannot be contained in a QDRO? **17-17**

Review and Qualification of a Domestic Relations Order

Q 17:56 What is the plan administrator's responsibility when a DRO is received? **17-18**
Q 17:57 Can the plan make payments to a participant while an order is under review? **17-18**

Plan Provisions

Q 17:58 Does a plan need to contain any specific provisions concerning QDROs? **17-18**

Tax Consequences

Q 17:59 What are the tax consequences of distributions to alternate payees? **17-18**

Special Circumstances

Q 17:60 Should a plan administrator distribute benefits to a participant if the administrator knows a QDRO is being drafted, but has not received it? **17-19**
Q 17:61 What rights does an alternate payee have? **17-19**
Q 17:62 If a plan changes administrators, should any QDROs be reapproved by the new administrator? **17-19**
Q 17:63 When can benefits be distributed to an alternate payee? **17-20**
Q 17:64 What is the consequence of making payment pursuant to a domestic relations order that is not qualified? **17-20**
Q 17:65 What happens if the form of benefit specified in a QDRO is no longer available at the time distribution occurs? **17-20**
Q 17:66 Can the administrative expenses associated with reviewing a QDRO be charged to the participant or alternate payee? **17-20**

Q 17:67 Does a DRO fail to be qualified merely because it is issued after or revises a QDRO or merely because of the time at which it is issued? 17-21

Q 17:68 Who is considered to be a "spouse" for purposes of the QDRO rules? 17-21

Chapter 18 Taxation of 401(k) Plans

Payroll Taxes

Federal Insurance Contributions Act

Q 18:1 What is the *FICA tax*? 18-2

Q 18:2 What amounts are subject to FICA withholding? 18-3

Q 18:3 Which employees are subject to FICA tax withholding? 18-3

Q 18:4 How is the FICA tax computed? 18-3

Q 18:5 How is the FICA tax collected? 18-4

Q 18:6 How is the FICA tax paid? 18-4

Q 18:7 How is the FICA tax reported? 18-4

Federal Unemployment Tax Act

Q 18:8 What is the *FUTA tax*? 18-4

Q 18:9 What amounts are subject to FUTA? 18-5

Q 18:10 Which employees' wages are subject to the FUTA tax? 18-5

Q 18:11 How is the FUTA tax computed? 18-5

Q 18:12 How is the FUTA tax reported? 18-5

Q 18:13 How is the FUTA tax paid? 18-5

Taxation and Reporting of Distributions and Pre-Tax Contributions

Lump-Sum Distributions

Q 18:14 How are distributions generally paid from 401(k) plans? 18-6

Q 18:15 How is a *lump-sum distribution* defined? 18-6

Q 18:16 Do distributions as a result of termination of a 401(k) plan qualify for lump-sum treatment? 18-7

Q 18:17 What plans are considered in determining whether a 401(k) distribution qualifies as a lump-sum distribution? 18-7

Q 18:18 What constitutes the *balance to the credit* of a participant? 18-7

Q 18:19 How do subsequent payments affect the lump-sum treatment of a prior distribution? 18-8

Q 18:20	What tax options are available to a participant who qualifies for lump-sum treatment?	**18-8**
Q 18:21	Does an alternate payee in a QDRO qualify for lump-sum treatment?	**18-8**
Q 18:22	How did the Tax Reform Act of 1986 protect favorable treatment for older participants?	**18-8**
Q 18:23	What items can be excluded from taxation in a lump-sum distribution?	**18-9**
Q 18:24	Do small lump-sum distributions qualify for any additional favorable treatment?	**18-9**
Q 18:25	How is the tax on a lump-sum distribution computed?	**18-9**
Q 18:26	What is the impact on future election rights if an individual makes a lump-sum election as a beneficiary?	**18-10**
Q 18:27	How are lump-sum distributions reported?	**18-10**

Employer Securities

Q 18:28	Does a participant in a 401(k) plan receive any favorable treatment when receiving employer securities in a distribution?	**18-10**
Q 18:29	How are *employer securities* defined?	**18-11**
Q 18:30	What options does a participant have after receiving employer securities?	**18-11**
Q 18:31	How are dividends paid on employer securities reported?	**18-11**

Distributions on Death

Q 18:32	How is the beneficiary taxed on proceeds received from a 401(k) plan?	**18-11**
Q 18:33	How are life insurance proceeds treated in a death payout?	**18-12**
Q 18:34	May a spousal beneficiary roll over death proceeds?	**18-12**
Q 18:35	May a nonspousal beneficiary roll over death proceeds to an IRA?	**18-12**

Installment Distributions

Q 18:36	How are installment distributions from a 401(k) plan taxed?	**18-13**
Q 18:37	In the event a participant who is receiving distribution in the form of an annuity has an investment in the contract, how is the portion of the payment that is excluded from gross income determined?	**18-13**
Q 18:38	How are installment distributions reported?	**18-14**

In-Service Withdrawals

Q 18:39	How are withdrawals from a 401(k) plan taxed while a participant is actively employed?	**18-14**

Q 18:40	Will a participant's cost basis from after-tax contributions be excluded from tax in a withdrawal?	18-14
Q 18:41	How did TRA '86 change the basis recovery rules for partial distributions not paid in the form of an annuity?	18-14
Q 18:42	Should employee after-tax contributions be accounted for separately?	18-15
Q 18:43	How did TRA '86 preserve the old basis recovery rules for certain plans?	18-15
Q 18:44	How do the grandfathered basis recovery rules work?	18-15
Q 18:45	How are in-service withdrawals reported?	18-16

Life Insurance

Q 18:46	How is life insurance in a 401(k) plan taxed?	18-16
Q 18:47	How is the taxable cost of life insurance computed?	18-17
Q 18:48	How is survivor whole life taxed?	18-17
Q 18:49	How is the taxable cost of life insurance protection reported?	18-17

Loans

Q 18:50	When do participant loans become taxable to a participant?	18-17
Q 18:51	If a participant loan becomes taxable, does the obligation to the 401(k) plan still exist?	18-18
Q 18:52	May a participant loan ever be converted to a distribution?	18-18
Q 18:53	How is a taxable loan reported?	18-18

Distribution of Excess Deferrals

Q 18:54	What are *excess deferrals*?	18-18
Q 18:55	How are distributions of pre-tax excess deferrals taxed to the participant?	18-19

Distributions of Excess Contributions and Excess Aggregate Contributions

Q 18:56	What are excess contributions and excess aggregate contributions?	18-19
Q 18:57	How are distributions of pre-tax excess contributions and excess aggregate contributions taxed to the participant?	18-20
Q 18:58	How are excess contributions and excess aggregate contributions in a 401(k) plan taxed to the employer?	18-20

Taxation of Roth Distributions and In-Plan Roth Rollovers

Q 18:59	How are distributions from a Roth 401(k) account taxed?	18-20
Q 18:60	What is a *qualified* Roth distribution?	18-21

Q 18:61	Are there certain types of Roth distributions that can never be considered qualified distributions?	**18-21**
Q 18:62	How are partial distributions from a Roth account taxed?	**18-21**
Q 18:63	How are deemed distributions from a Roth account taxed?	**18-22**
Q 18:64	How are hardship distributions from a Roth account taxed?	**18-22**
Q 18:65	How are corrective distributions from a Roth account taxed?	**18-23**
Q 18:66	How are employer securities distributed from a Roth account taxed?	**18-23**
Q 18:67	Are Roth accounts eligible for rollover?	**18-24**
Q 18:68	What conditions apply to in-plan Roth rollovers?	**18-24**
Q 18:69	By when must a plan be amended to adopt an in-plan Roth rollover feature?	**18-25**
Q 18:70	Are both direct and 60-day rollovers eligible for in-plan Roth rollovers?	**18-25**
Q 18:71	Can a participant undo an in-plan Roth rollover?	**18-26**
Q 18:72	Are in-plan Roth rollovers treated as a distribution for all purposes?	**18-26**
Q 18:73	What are the tax consequences of an in-plan Roth rollover?	**18-26**
Q 18:74	What special income tax rules apply to distributions from in-plan Roth rollover accounts?	**18-27**
Q 18:75	How does the 10 percent premature distribution tax apply to distributions from in-plan Roth rollover accounts?	**18-27**
Q 18:76	How is the amount allocable to the taxable portion of an in-plan Roth rollover account determined?	**18-27**
Q 18:77	How is the five-year holding period for qualified distributions calculated when a Roth account has been rolled over?	**18-27**
Q 18:78	How is the five-year holding period for qualified distributions calculated in the case of an in-plan Roth rollover?	**18-28**
Q 18:79	What are some tax planning advantages that the Roth rollover rules offer in the case of a rollover to a Roth IRA?	**18-28**
Q 18:80	How is the five-year holding period tracked, both generally and in the context of a rollover?	**18-28**
Q 18:81	What are the tax consequences of a Roth account set up for an alternate payee or a beneficiary?	**18-29**
Q 18:82	Do excise taxes apply to Roth 401(k) distributions?	**18-29**
Q 18:83	How are distributions from Roth 401(k) plans reported?	**18-29**
Q 18:84	How was the tax treatment of Roth accounts stabilized by the passage of the Pension Protection Act of 2006?	**18-29**

Other Taxes

Premature Distributions

Q 18:85	What is the tax on premature distributions?	18-30
Q 18:86	What are the exceptions to the premature distribution tax?	18-30
Q 18:87	How is the premature distribution penalty reported?	18-31

Required Minimum Distributions

Q 18:88	What is the penalty for failure to distribute minimum distributions as required?	18-31
Q 18:89	How is the minimum distribution penalty reported?	18-32

Federal Estate Tax

Q 18:90	How are 401(k) death distributions treated for federal estate tax purposes?	18-32
Q 18:91	What are the estate tax implications if the spouse is named as beneficiary of the 401(k) plan proceeds?	18-32
Q 18:92	How much is the federal estate tax?	18-33

Filing Requirements for Distributions

Q 18:93	What are the reporting rules for distributions from 401(k) plans?	18-33
Q 18:94	Can a plan provide Form 1099-R to participants in electronic format?	18-33
Q 18:95	What is the penalty for failure to file Form 1099-R?	18-34
Q 18:96	When must a plan administrator file Form 1099-R on magnetic media?	18-34
Q 18:97	What are the rules for filing paper returns?	18-34
Q 18:98	How are 1099-R forms corrected?	18-35

Distribution Planning

Rollovers of Pre-Tax Accounts

Q 18:99	How is a rollover advantageous to an individual?	18-35
Q 18:100	May a rollover be made by an individual who is over age 70½?	18-36
Q 18:101	When may a partial distribution be rolled over?	18-36
Q 18:102	What additional factors should a participant take into account when considering a rollover from a qualified plan to a Roth IRA?	18-36

Rollovers of Roth Accounts

Q 18:103	What should be considered in making a rollover decision with respect to a Roth account?	**18-37**

Lump-Sum Distributions

Q 18:104	What are the tax advantages of a lump-sum distribution?	**18-37**

Avoiding the Premature Distribution Tax

Q 18:105	How may the 10 percent premature distribution tax be avoided if the participant is not deceased or disabled?	**18-37**
Q 18:106	What conditions must be satisfied to avoid the premature distribution tax under the annual installment exception?	**18-38**
Q 18:107	How are equal periodic payments computed?	**18-38**
Q 18:108	What happens when a participant begins receiving equal periodic payments and then changes his or her election?	**18-39**
Q 18:109	Is this exception also available for amounts in an IRA?	**18-39**

Distributions Versus Accumulations

Q 18:110	What are the disadvantages of accelerating the payment of retirement benefits?	**18-39**
Q 18:111	Why may it be advantageous to continue to accumulate funds in a 401(k) plan after they could be withdrawn without penalty?	**18-40**

To Roth or Not to Roth

Q 18:112	What considerations should a plan sponsor take into account when deciding whether to offer Roth deferrals in a plan?	**18-40**
Q 18:113	What factors should a plan participant consider when deciding whether to contribute to a pre-tax 401(k) account or a Roth 401(k) account?	**18-41**

Chapter 19 Reporting and Disclosure

IRS and DOL Form 5500 Reporting

Q 19:1	Who is responsible for reporting information to the IRS and the DOL?	**19-2**
Q 19:2	What is the basic annual reporting requirement?	**19-2**
Q 19:3	For what plans can the simplified Form 5500-SF be filed as opposed to the longer Form 5500?	**19-2**
Q 19:4	For which plans can Form 5500-EZ be filed?	**19-2**
Q 19:5	Is there an audit requirement, and does it apply to small plans?	**19-3**

Q 19:6 What schedules are attached to Form 5500? . . . 19-4
Q 19:7 What is the purpose of Form 8955-SSA? . . . 19-5
Q 19:8 What is the penalty for a late filing of Form 8955-SSA? . . . 19-5
Q 19:9 What type of information is required on Schedule C of the Form 5500? . . . 19-7

EFAST2

Q 19:10 To what extent must Form 5500 be filed and displayed electronically? . . . 19-9
Q 19:11 Where can additional information be obtained regarding the EFAST2 requirements? . . . 19-9
Q 19:12 What items may make a Form 5500 filing particularly challenging? . . . 19-9
Q 19:13 What is the due date for filing the Form 5500 series? . . . 19-10
Q 19:14 What are the penalties for late filing of the Form 5500 series? . . . 19-11
Q 19:15 What is the Delinquent Filer Voluntary Compliance Program? . . . 19-11
Q 19:16 Are incomplete filings subject to these penalties? . . . 19-12
Q 19:17 May late filing penalties be appealed to the DOL? . . . 19-13
Q 19:18 May late filing penalties be appealed to the IRS? . . . 19-13
Q 19:19 Who is responsible for payment of the penalties? . . . 19-13
Q 19:20 Are there any criminal penalties for failure to file annual reports? . . . 19-13

Special Filing Issues

Q 19:21 What filing is required of a plan that is merging, consolidating, or transferring assets? . . . 19-14
Q 19:22 What filing is required of a plan that is terminating? . . . 19-14
Q 19:23 What filing is required to notify the IRS of a change in plan status? . . . 19-14
Q 19:24 What filing is required to report excise taxes? . . . 19-14

Participant Disclosures

Summary Plan Description

Q 19:25 What is a *summary plan description*? . . . 19-17
Q 19:26 What types of information must be included in the SPD? . . . 19-17
Q 19:27 Are there any special requirements if participants do not speak English? . . . 19-18
Q 19:28 Who is entitled to receive an SPD? . . . 19-18
Q 19:29 What is the timing for receipt of the SPD? . . . 19-18
Q 19:30 Should the SPD be filed with the DOL? . . . 19-19

Q 19:31 How should the SPD be distributed to participants? 19-19

Q 19:32 When should an SPD be updated? 19-19

Summary of Material Modifications

Q 19:33 When must participants be notified of any changes in the plan through a summary of material modifications? 19-19

Q 19:34 What information must be provided in the SMM? 19-20

Q 19:35 What are the consequences of failing to provide participants with an SPD or SMM on a timely basis? 19-20

Q 19:36 What are the benefits of including a disclaimer in the SPD? . . . 19-20

Summary Annual Report

Q 19:37 What must be included in a *summary annual report*? 19-20

Q 19:38 When must the SAR be provided to participants? 19-21

Q 19:39 What if the plan has non-English-speaking participants? 19-21

Individual Participant Benefit Statements

Q 19:40 Must a participant receive benefit statements of his or her account balance in a 401(k) plan? 19-21

Q 19:41 What information must be contained in participant benefit statements? 19-22

Q 19:42 How much flexibility is available with respect to providing information on vested benefits? 19-24

Q 19:43 According to the DOL, to what extent can the benefit statement requirements be satisfied in participant-directed plans by using multiple documents or sources for the required information? 19-24

Q 19:44 To what extent can the pension benefit statement requirements be satisfied using electronic media? 19-25

Q 19:45 When must statements be given to participants? 19-25

Q 19:46 Will a plan that does not otherwise provide participants the right to direct the investment of assets in their accounts be required to provide statements quarterly due to a participant loan provision? 19-25

Q 19:47 What types of limitations and restrictions on participant rights to direct investments, if any, need not be included in benefit statements? 19-26

Q 19:48 Is there DOL-approved language for satisfying the requirement to provide information on the importance of diversification and what Web site should participants be referred to for information on investing and diversification? 19-26

Q 19:49 Who is responsible for complying with the benefit statement requirements, and what is the penalty for noncompliance? 19-27

Q 19:50	What are some of the challenges and open questions related to complying with the new benefit statement requirements?	19-27
Q 19:51	Must a terminated participant receive a statement of his or her account balance in the 401(k) plan?	19-28

Information Upon Request

Q 19:52	What other documents may a participant request?	19-28
Q 19:53	May the plan administrator charge for providing the participant with requested reports or documents?	19-28
Q 19:54	What is the time limit for responding to a participant's request for information?	19-28
Q 19:55	What are the consequences of failing to provide requested information in a timely manner?	19-29

Participant Investment and Fee Disclosures

Q 19:56	What must be disclosed to participants under the DOL's participant investment and fee disclosure requirements?	19-29
Q 19:57	What plans are subject to the participant investment and fee disclosure requirements?	19-30
Q 19:58	When must a plan comply with the participant investment and fee disclosure requirements?	19-30
Q 19:59	Who is responsible for complying with the participant investment and fee disclosure requirements?	19-31
Q 19:60	What *plan-related information* must be provided to participants?	19-31
Q 19:61	What *investment-related information* must be provided automatically to participants?	19-33
Q 19:62	In what format must *investment-related information* be provided to participants?	19-36
Q 19:63	What *investment-related information* must be provided to participants subsequent to an investment in a designated investment alternative?	19-37
Q 19:64	What *investment-related information* must be provided to participants upon request?	19-37
Q 19:65	What other information did the DOL set forth in the regulations and other guidance regarding the form and delivery of disclosures?	19-37
Q 19:66	What is meant by a *designated investment alternative* under the DOL regulations?	19-41
Q 19:67	What is meant by the terms *at least annually thereafter* and *at least quarterly* under the DOL regulations?	19-41
Q 19:68	What is meant by the terms *average annual total return* and *total annual operating expenses* under the DOL requirements?	19-42

Q 19:69	With regard to investment-related information listed in Q 19:61, what special rules apply to a designated investment alternative designed to invest in qualifying employer securities?	**19-43**
Q 19:70	With regard to investment-related information listed in Q 19:61, what special rules apply to a designated investment alternative that is an annuity option?	**19-44**
Q 19:71	With regard to investment-related information listed in Q 19:61, what special rules apply to a designated investment alternative that is a fixed-return investment?	**19-45**
Q 19:72	With regard to investment-related information listed in Q 19:61, what additional disclosures would be required regarding target date or similar funds under DOL proposed regulations?	**19-45**
Q 19:73	How do the DOL regulations impact participant disclosure requirements under ERISA Section 404(c)?	**19-46**

DOL Field Assistance Bulletin 2012-02R

Q 19:74	How do the rules apply to a plan that has both participant-directed and trustee-directed investments?	**19-47**
Q 19:75	Do the rules apply to Section 403(b) plans that are ERISA-covered plans?	**19-47**
Q 19:76	If a plan administrator provides plan-related and investment-related information together in a single document, must the plan administrator separately "identify" any designated investment alternatives (as described in Q 19:60) as well as "name" each designated investment alternative (as described in Q 19:61)?	**19-48**
Q 19:77	With regard to plan-related information listed in Q 19:60, how is a "designated investment manager" distinguished from a "designated investment alternative"?	**19-48**
Q 19:78	With regard to plan-related information listed in Q 19:60, what level of detail is required of the explanation of any fees and expenses for general plan administrative services that may be charged against participants' and beneficiaries' accounts and the basis on which such charges will be allocated?	**19-48**
Q 19:79	With regard to plan-related information listed in Q 19:60, how should administrative expense disclosures be handled if revenue sharing payments have exceeded the monthly 2-basis point monthly recordkeeping fee in some, but not all, months?	**19-49**
Q 19:80	With regard to plan-related information in Q 19:60, must a plan's administrative expenses be disclosed if those expenses are paid either from amounts forfeited under the terms of the plan or from the general assets of the employer sponsoring the plan?	**19-50**

Q 19:81 With regard to plan-related information in Q 19:60, must a plan's administrative expenses be disclosed if the plan document provides that administrative expenses shall be paid from individual accounts, from forfeitures, or by the employer (at the discretion of the plan administrator), but administrative expenses have always been paid either from the plan's forfeiture account or by the employer, and the plan has a written commitment from the employer that it will pay administrative expenses not covered by forfeitures? **19-50**

Q 19:82 With regard to plan-related information in Q 19:60, if a plan pays a recordkeeping expense of 10 basis points of its total assets by liquidating shares from participants' and beneficiaries' accounts, does the plan administrator have the discretion to disclose this expense as part of the total annual operating expenses of each of the plan's designated investment alternatives (i.e., as if these recordkeeping expenses actually were being paid from assets of the designated investment alternatives)? **19-51**

Q 19:83 With regard to plan-related information listed in Q 19:60, must the revenue sharing explanation itemize or identify the specific plan administrative expenses being paid from the total annual operating expenses of one or more of the plan's designated investment alternatives?. **19-51**

Q 19:84 With regard to plan-related information listed in Q 19:60, if all of a plan's administrative expenses are paid from revenue sharing received by the plan from one or more of the plan's designated investment alternatives, must the plan administrator provide to participants and beneficiaries the revenue sharing explanation?. **19-52**

Q 19:85 With regard to plan-related information listed in Q 19:60, may the plan include the revenue sharing explanation in each quarterly statement, even though revenue sharing payments to the plan are made by the designated investment alternatives only every other quarter? **19-52**

Q 19:86 With regard to plan-related information listed in Q 19:60, what information must be disclosed about brokerage windows, self-directed brokerage accounts, and other similar plan arrangements that enable participants and beneficiaries to select investments beyond those designated by the plan?. . . **19-52**

Q 19:87 With regard to plan-related information listed in Q 19:60, if only a small percentage of the participants and beneficiaries currently select such a brokerage window, self-directed brokerage account, or similar arrangement, may the plan administrator provide the required annual fee and expense information only to those participants and beneficiaries who have affirmatively elected to use the window, accounts, or arrangement? **19-54**

Q 19:88 With regard to investment-related information listed in Q 19:61, must a plan administrator provide the disclosures for a designated investment alternative that is closed to new investments, but that allows participants and beneficiaries to maintain prior investments in the alternative and to transfer their interests to other plan investment alternatives? **19-54**

Q 19:89 With regard to investment-related information listed in Q 19:61, if a plan administrator furnishes an additional benchmark for a balanced fund by blending more than one appropriate broad-based securities market index, may the plan administrator use the target asset allocation of the fund (e.g., 50 percent stocks, 50 percent bonds) to determine the weightings of the indexes used in creating the additional benchmark? **19-55**

Q 19:90 With regard to investment-related information listed in Q 19:61, what alternatives may be used to comply with the Web site address requirement? **19-55**

Q 19:91 With regard to investment-related information listed in Q 19:61, must the Web site address landing page include all the required supplemental investment information regarding a designated investment alternative?.................... **19-56**

Q 19:92 With regard to investment-related information listed in Q 19:61, what return information for a plan's designated investment alternatives must be available at the required Web site address? **19-56**

Q 19:93 With regard to investment-related information listed in Q 19:61, does the DOL plan to publish a glossary for use in compliance with its regulation? **19-57**

Q 19:94 With regard to investment-related information listed in Q 19:61, must a plan administrator provide a single, unified comparative chart, or may multiple charts, supplied by the plan's various service providers or investment issuers, be furnished to participants and beneficiaries? **19-57**

Q 19:95 With regard to investment-related information listed in Q 19:61, if there is a change to a designated investment alternative's fee and expense information after the plan administrator has provided the annual disclosure (comparative chart) to participants and beneficiaries, does the plan administrator have an obligation to automatically furnish a new comparative chart? **19-58**

Q 19:96 With regard to investment-related information listed in Q 19:61, for designated investment alternatives with variable rates of return, may a plan administrator furnish on the comparative chart average annual total return information that is more recent than the end of the most recently completed calendar year? **19-58**

Q 19:97 With regard to investment-related information listed in Q 19:61, is a plan administrator required to include "since inception" information for all the plan's designated investment alternatives? **19-58**

Q 19:98	What must be provided in terms of a document similar to a prospectus (as described in item 1 of Q 19:64) for designated investment alternatives that are not registered under the Securities Act of 1933 or the Investment Company Act of 1940?	**19-59**
Q 19:99	Must the disclosures required under the regulation be furnished as stand-alone documents?	**19-59**
Q 19:100	If a plan designates a fiduciary investment manager, within the meaning of ERISA Section 3(38), who may be appointed by participants or beneficiaries to allocate the assets in their individual accounts among the plan's designated investment alternatives, is this investment management service a designated investment alternative under the regulation?	**19-60**
Q 19:101	If a plan offers three model portfolios made up of different combinations of the plan's designated investment alternatives, is each model portfolio a designated investment alternative under the regulation?	**19-60**
Q 19:102	Does the regulation cover "brokerage windows"?	**19-61**
Q 19:103	If a plan offers an investment platform that includes a brokerage window, self-directed brokerage account, or similar plan arrangement, and the plan fiduciary did not designate any of the funds on the platform as "designated investment alternatives," is the platform or the brokerage window, self-directed brokerage account, or similar plan arrangement a designated investment alternative?	**19-61**
Q 19:104	If the plan offers a fund-of-funds as a designated investment alternative, and both the acquiring fund and funds in which it invests (acquired funds) are open-end management investment companies registered under the Investment Company Act of 1940, must the acquiring fund's total annual operating expenses reflect the operating expenses of the acquired funds?	**19-62**
Q 19:105	With regard to Q 19:68, how often must an investment alternative not registered under the Investment Company Act of 1940 calculate their net asset values in order to determine their average net asset value for the year?	**19-62**
Q 19:106	If the payment of plan administrative expenses reduces the value of each unit of the designated investment alternative, but has no impact on the number of units owned by participants and beneficiaries or on the share value of the underlying mutual fund, is this designated investment alternative considered "registered" or "unregistered" for purposes of calculating its total annual operating expenses as described in Q 19:68?	**19-63**
Q 19:107	With regard to investment-related information in Q 19:61, if a designated investment alternative purchases insurance to smooth its rate of return, how should the cost of the insurance be disclosed under this regulation?	**19-64**

Q 19:108	Did the *first* initial quarterly statement of fees and expenses need to reflect the fees and expenses deducted prior to the third quarter?	19-64

Blackout Notices

Q 19:109	What is a *blackout period* that triggers the advance notice requirements?	19-65
Q 19:110	What types of plans are subject to the blackout notice requirements?	19-66
Q 19:111	Who is required to give and to receive blackout notices?	19-66
Q 19:112	What additional requirement applies if employer securities are subject to a blackout period?	19-66
Q 19:113	What information must a blackout notice contain?	19-67
Q 19:114	How must the blackout notice be furnished?	19-67
Q 19:115	When must the blackout notice be given?	19-68
Q 19:116	Under what circumstances does the 30-day advance notice requirement not apply?	19-68
Q 19:117	What happens if there is an unexpected change to the duration of the blackout period?	19-69
Q 19:118	What is the effective date of the blackout notice rules?	19-69
Q 19:119	What are the penalties for noncompliance with the blackout notice rules?	19-69
Q 19:120	Has the DOL provided a model blackout notice?	19-69

Diversification Notices

Q 19:121	What notice is required under the Pension Protection Act of 2006 when plan assets are invested in publicly traded employer securities?	19-69

Use of Electronic Technology

Q 19:122	What is meant by *paperless administration*?	19-70
Q 19:123	What are some legal issues associated with paperless administration?	19-70
Q 19:124	What are some issues that arise from ERISA disclosure requirements?	19-70
Q 19:125	What guidance has the DOL issued concerning the use of electronic technologies for complying with ERISA's disclosure requirements?	19-71
Q 19:126	What standards apply to the use of electronic media for the maintenance and retention of records required by ERISA?	19-72
Q 19:127	What standards apply to the use of electronic media for notices and consents required under the Internal Revenue Code?	19-73
Q 19:128	To what types of retirement plans do the standards apply?	19-74

Q 19:129 What general requirements must first be met in connection with using electronic media for Code-based notices, consents, and elections? . . . 19-75

Q 19:130 What are the permissible methods of providing notices using electronic media? . . . 19-75

Q 19:131 What are the requirements for using the "consumer consent method"? . . . 19-76

Q 19:132 What are the requirements of the "alternative method" of providing notices using electronic media? . . . 19-77

Q 19:133 What requirements apply with respect to a participant consent or election made using an electronic system? . . . 19-79

Q 19:134 Can an electronic medium be used in connection with spousal waivers or other elections and consents required to be witnessed by a plan representative or notary public? . . . 19-80

Q 19:135 What is the effective date of the final regulations applicable to Code-based notices and consents in the electronic context? . . . 19-82

Record Retention Under ERISA

Q 19:136 How long must records be retained under ERISA? . . . 19-82

Chapter 20 Correcting 401(k) Plan Qualification Errors

Q 20:1 What is the impact of plan disqualification? . . . 20-1

Employee Plans Compliance Resolution System

Q 20:2 What is the *Employee Plans Compliance Resolution System*? . . . 20-2

Q 20:3 What programs does the IRS offer under EPCRS to avoid plan disqualification? . . . 20-2

Q 20:4 What common features apply to all programs under EPCRS? . . . 20-2

Q 20:5 What principles are taken into account in determining whether full correction is accomplished? . . . 20-2

Q 20:6 Is there only one reasonable and appropriate correction method for a qualification failure? . . . 20-3

Q 20:7 What principles apply in determining corrective allocations and distributions? . . . 20-3

Q 20:8 Are there any exceptions to full correction? . . . 20-6

Q 20:9 Has the IRS prescribed any standard correction methods for common operational errors? . . . 20-7

Q 20:10 Has the IRS provided any other guidance regarding the correction of qualification errors? . . . 20-7

Self-Correction Program

Q 20:11	What qualification defects are covered by SCP?	**20-7**
Q 20:12	Is there a deadline for correcting operational defects under SCP?	**20-9**
Q 20:13	What factors are considered in determining whether or not an operational failure is insignificant?	**20-9**
Q 20:14	Must a plan have a favorable IRS letter in order to take advantage of SCP?	**20-10**
Q 20:15	Is there any other condition that must be met before SCP can be used to correct an operational failure?	**20-10**
Q 20:16	Is SCP available if the plan is being audited by the IRS?	**20-10**
Q 20:17	What procedures are used to take advantage of SCP?	**20-10**
Q 20:18	What is the cost of using SCP?	**20-10**
Q 20:19	Can an operational error be corrected under SCP by retroactively amending the plan to conform its operation to the plan document as amended?	**20-10**

Voluntary Correction Program

Q 20:20	What qualification defects are covered by VCP?	**20-11**
Q 20:21	Is there a deadline for correcting defects under VCP?	**20-11**
Q 20:22	Must a plan have a favorable IRS letter in order to take advantage of VCP?	**20-11**
Q 20:23	Must a plan have established practices and procedures in effect in order to utilize VCP?	**20-11**
Q 20:24	Can operational errors be corrected under VCP by retroactively amending the plan to conform its operation to the plan document as amended?	**20-11**
Q 20:25	Are there other specialized procedures under VCP?	**20-12**
Q 20:26	What procedures are used to take advantage of VCP?	**20-12**
Q 20:27	What is the cost of using VCP?	**20-12**

Audit Closing Agreement Program

Q 20:28	Under what circumstances will Audit CAP be used?	**20-13**
Q 20:29	How is the amount of the Audit CAP sanction determined?	**20-14**

Chapter 21 Plan Terminations, Mergers, Spinoffs, and Abandoned Plans

Plan Terminations

Q 21:1	How is an employer's ability to terminate a 401(k) plan restricted?	**21-1**
Q 21:2	How does an employer terminate its 401(k) plan?	**21-2**

Q 21:3	What is the impact of a plan termination on participants' benefits in the plan?	21-2
Q 21:4	What is the date of termination for purposes of applying the 100 percent vesting rule?	21-3
Q 21:5	How do the nondiscrimination rules apply to plan termination?	21-3
Q 21:6	Under what circumstances can a 401(k) plan not be terminated due to an inability to distribute assets?	21-3
Q 21:7	What is an *alternative defined contribution plan*?	21-3
Q 21:8	How must a distribution on plan termination be paid?	21-3
Q 21:9	What options does an employer have if benefits cannot be distributed in connection with a plan termination?	21-4

Missing Participants

Q 21:10	What steps should a plan administrator take with respect to a participant who cannot be located when the plan is terminated?	21-4
Q 21:11	What are the search methods prescribed under the DOL's guidance for locating missing participants?	21-5
Q 21:12	What distribution methods are acceptable in the missing participant context?	21-6
Q 21:13	What is the additional option created under the Pension Protection Act of 2006 for dealing with missing participants?	21-8

Partial Termination

Q 21:14	What is a *partial termination*?	21-8
Q 21:15	What is the effect of a partial termination?	21-8
Q 21:16	Are there plan events other than termination or partial termination that may require 100 percent vesting?	21-9
Q 21:17	How does an employer decide when a partial termination has occurred?	21-9

Mergers and Spinoffs

Q 21:18	What is a *merger*?	21-10
Q 21:19	What rules apply to the allocation of benefits in a merger?	21-10
Q 21:20	What is a *spinoff*?	21-11
Q 21:21	What rules apply to the allocation of assets in a spinoff?	21-11
Q 21:22	What procedures are involved in a merger or spinoff?	21-11
Q 21:23	What special considerations are involved if a money purchase plan is merged into a 401(k) plan?	21-12
Q 21:24	What plan provisions should be reviewed when merging or spinning off plans?	21-12
Q 21:25	What special distribution concerns are involved in mergers or spinoffs of 401(k) plans?	21-13

Q 21:26 How can the problem of monitoring and harmonizing distribution options be avoided? 21-13

Q 21:27 What relief did the IRS provide from distribution option concerns? 21-13

Plan Considerations During Major Business Transactions

Q 21:28 What types of issues might a 401(k) plan sponsor encounter if it is being acquired by or merged into another company? ... 21-14

Q 21:29 What are some pros and cons of merging the plans? 21-14

Q 21:30 What are some pros and cons of continuing both Company A's and Company B's plans? 21-15

Q 21:31 What are some pros and cons of freezing Company A's plan? 21-15

Q 21:32 What are some pros and cons of terminating Company A's plan? 21-15

Q 21:33 Will Company A be able to distribute 401(k) plan assets to employees who go to work for Company B after the transaction? 21-15

Q 21:34 What is a severance of employment in the context of distributing elective contributions? 21-16

Q 21:35 What special coverage rule applies in the context of an acquisition or disposition? 21-16

Q 21:36 What other guidance is expected from the IRS regarding the application of retirement plan qualification requirements in the context of major business transactions such as mergers and acquisitions? 21-17

Abandoned Plans

Q 21:37 Has the DOL provided guidance regarding abandoned plans? 21-17

Q 21:38 Who can determine whether a plan is abandoned and can terminate an abandoned plan under the DOL regulations? 21-19

Q 21:39 Who is eligible to be a qualified termination administrator? 21-19

Q 21:40 When is a plan considered abandoned according to the DOL's regulations? 21-19

Q 21:41 What information should be contained in the notice to the plan sponsor of an abandoned plan? 21-20

Q 21:42 On what date is a plan considered terminated under the rule? 21-20

Q 21:43 What should the QTA include in the notice of plan abandonment to the DOL? 21-21

Q 21:44 What procedures under the DOL regulations must a QTA follow when terminating and paying out an abandoned plan? 21-21

Q 21:45	What type of final governmental reporting is required of a QTA under the DOL regulation?	21-24
Q 21:46	Is protection from liability provided when guidelines under the DOL regulation are followed?	21-24
Q 21:47	Can a QTA select itself to provide services and be compensated for its services in connection with terminating an abandoned plan?	21-25
Q 21:48	How should distributions to missing participants be handled in a terminated plan (including terminations under the QTA regime)?	21-26
Q 21:49	When do the DOL regulations on terminating abandoned plans become effective?	21-28
Q 21:50	Does the IRS's Employee Plans Compliance Resolution System make provision for abandoned plans?	21-28
Q 21:51	What legal and regulatory developments in the bankruptcy context could impact the prevalence of abandoned plans?	21-28

Chapter 22 401(k) Plan Alternatives

Individual Retirement Arrangements (IRAs)

Traditional IRAs

Q 22:1	What is an *individual retirement account*?	22-3
Q 22:2	What is an *individual retirement annuity*?	22-3
Q 22:3	What is a *Spousal IRA*?	22-3
Q 22:4	What is an *Inherited IRA*?	22-4
Q 22:5	What rules apply when a spouse inherits an IRA?	22-4
Q 22:6	What rules apply to a nonspouse's Inherited IRA?	22-4
Q 22:7	May nonspousal beneficiaries of employer-sponsored retirement plans roll their account balances to an inherited IRA?	22-4
Q 22:8	Are IRA assets subject to bankruptcy?	22-4

Contributions to Traditional IRAs

Q 22:9	What is the maximum IRA contribution by an individual under age 50?	22-5
Q 22:10	What is the maximum IRA contribution by an individual age 50 or over?	22-5
Q 22:11	May individuals age 70½ or older contribute to a traditional IRA?	22-5
Q 22:12	Are contributions to a traditional IRA tax deductible?	22-5
Q 22:13	How is a prorated IRA deduction calculated?	22-7

Q 22:14 How much may be contributed if both spouses are employed? ... **22-7**

Q 22:15 When may nondeductible contributions be made to a traditional IRA? ... **22-7**

Q 22:16 May an employer sponsor an IRA for its employees? ... **22-7**

Distributions, Rollovers, and Transfers

Q 22:17 When may contributions to a traditional IRA be withdrawn? ... **22-8**

Q 22:18 How are distributions from a traditional IRA taxed? ... **22-8**

Q 22:19 What required minimum distribution rules apply to traditional IRAs? ... **22-8**

Q 22:20 May an IRA owner age 70½ or older take tax-free charitable distributions from an IRA to contribute to charity? ... **22-8**

Q 22:21 May an IRA owner make direct transfers between multiple IRAs in one calendar year? ... **22-8**

Q 22:22 May an IRA owner make 60-day rollovers between multiple IRAs in one calendar year? ... **22-9**

Q 22:23 Are rollovers allowed between traditional IRAs and an employer-sponsored plan? ... **22-9**

Roth IRAs

Q 22:24 What is a *Roth IRA*? ... **22-10**

Q 22:25 May a spousal Roth IRA be established? ... **22-10**

Contributions to Roth IRAs

Q 22:26 How much may be contributed to a Roth IRA? ... **22-10**

Q 22:27 May individuals age 70½ or older make Roth IRA contributions? ... **22-11**

Q 22:28 May contributions to a Roth IRA be deducted? ... **22-11**

Distributions from Roth IRAs

Q 22:29 When may contributions to a Roth IRA be withdrawn? ... **22-11**

Q 22:30 What is a qualifying distribution from a Roth IRA? ... **22-11**

Q 22:31 May nonqualifying distributions be made from a Roth IRA? ... **22-12**

Q 22:32 What required minimum distribution rules apply to Roth IRAs? ... **22-12**

Conversions, Rollovers, and Transfers

Q 22:33 May a traditional IRA be converted to a Roth IRA? ... **22-12**

Q 22:34 When are amounts converted to a Roth IRA in 2014 taxed? ... **22-12**

Q 22:35 Should a traditional IRA be converted to a Roth IRA? ... **22-12**

Q 22:36 May distributions from an employer-sponsored retirement plan be rolled directly into a Roth IRA? ... **22-12**

Comparison of Traditional IRAs and Roth IRAs

Q 22:37 Does a Roth IRA provide greater tax savings than a traditional IRA? 22-13
Q 22:38 What are the advantages of a Roth IRA over a traditional IRA? 22-13

Simplified Employee Pensions (SEPs) and Salary Reduction SEPs (SARSEPs)

Q 22:39 What is a *SEP*? 22-14
Q 22:40 What is a *SARSEP*? 22-15
Q 22:41 Could any employer establish a SARSEP? 22-15
Q 22:42 What are the requirements to maintain a SARSEP? 22-15
Q 22:43 What year is used for the 25 or fewer employee rule? 22-15
Q 22:44 Who is an eligible employee for a SEP or SARSEP? 22-15
Q 22:45 Are there employees that may be excluded from a SEP or SARSEP? 22-16
Q 22:46 If an employer has a SEP, can it also have other retirement plans? 22-16

Contributions to SEPs and SARSEPs

Q 22:47 May an employer enroll employees into SEPs and SIMPLE IRAs automatically? 22-16
Q 22:48 How much may the employer contribute to a SEP? 22-16
Q 22:49 Must the same percentage of salary be contributed for all SEP participants? 22-16
Q 22:50 Are there other limits on SEP contributions? 22-17
Q 22:51 May contributions be made to a SEP or SARSEP of a participant over age 70½? 22-17
Q 22:52 How much of the contribution made to employees' SEPs or SARSEPs may be deducted on the employer's tax return? 22-17
Q 22:53 Are employer contributions to a SEP or SARSEP taxable to employees? 22-17
Q 22:54 How much may an employee defer under a SARSEP? 22-17
Q 22:55 Can catch-up contributions be made to a SARSEP? 22-17
Q 22:56 May an employer contribute to the SARSEP for its employees? 22-18
Q 22:57 Can designated Roth contributions be made under a SARSEP? 22-18
Q 22:58 Can loans be taken from a SEP or SARSEP? 22-18

Distributions from SEPs and SARSEPs

Q 22:59 When may funds be withdrawn from a SEP or SARSEP? 22-18

Q 22:60	What required minimum distribution rules apply to SEPs and SARSEPs?	**22-18**
Q 22:61	How are distributions from SEPs and SARSEPs taxed?	**22-18**
Q 22:62	If a SEP or SARSEP fails to meet the applicable requirements, are the tax benefits for the employer and employees lost?	**22-19**
Q 22:63	What IRS guidance is available to assist employers in complying with the SEP and SARSEP rules?	**22-19**

SIMPLE IRAs and SIMPLE 401(k) Plans

Q 22:64	What is a *SIMPLE IRA plan*?	**22-21**
Q 22:65	What is a *SIMPLE 401(k) plan*?	**22-21**
Q 22:66	Can any employer establish a SIMPLE IRA or SIMPLE 401(k) plan?	**22-21**
Q 22:67	May an employer automatically enroll employees into a SIMPLE IRA?	**22-21**
Q 22:68	Which employees are eligible to participate in a SIMPLE IRA or SIMPLE 401(k) plan?	**22-22**
Q 22:69	Are there employees who may be excluded from a SIMPLE IRA?	**22-22**
Q 22:70	Can an employer maintain a SIMPLE IRA and another qualified plan in the same calendar year?	**22-22**
Q 22:71	Can an employer maintain a SIMPLE 401(k) plan and another qualified plan in the same calendar year?	**22-22**

Contributions to SIMPLE IRAs and SIMPLE 401(k) Plans

Q 22:72	What type of contributions may be made to a SIMPLE IRA plan?	**22-22**
Q 22:73	How much may an employee defer under a SIMPLE IRA or SIMPLE 401(k) plan?	**22-23**
Q 22:74	Can catch-up contributions be made to a SIMPLE IRA or SIMPLE 401(k) plan?	**22-23**
Q 22:75	Can contributions made under a SIMPLE IRA be made to any type of IRA?	**22-23**
Q 22:76	May designated Roth contributions be made to a SIMPLE IRA?	**22-23**
Q 22:77	What employer contributions are generally required under a SIMPLE IRA or SIMPLE 401(k) plan?	**22-23**
Q 22:78	How much of the contributions made to employees' SIMPLE IRAs or SIMPLE 401(k) plans may be deducted on the employer's tax return?	**22-24**

Distributions from SIMPLE IRAs and SIMPLE 401(k) Plans

Q 22:79	May amounts held in a SIMPLE IRA or SIMPLE 401(k) be withdrawn at any time?	**22-24**

Q 22:80 What are the tax consequences when amounts are distributed from a SIMPLE IRA? 22-24

Q 22:81 Are loans allowed from a SIMPLE IRA or SIMPLE 401(k)?. 22-25

Q 22:82 Why might an employer choose a SIMPLE IRA rather than a SIMPLE 401(k)? 22-25

Q 22:83 Why might an employer choose a SIMPLE 401(k) plan rather than a SIMPLE IRA? 22-25

Q 22:84 If a SIMPLE IRA or SIMPLE 401(k) plan fails to meet the plan requirements, are the employer and employee tax benefits lost?. 22-25

Q 22:85 What IRS guidance is available to assist employers in complying with the SIMPLE IRA and 401(k) rules? 22-25

Q 22:86 Where can information on retirement plans for small businesses be found? 22-26

Cash Balance Plans

Q 22:87 What is a *cash balance plan*? 22-29

Floor-Offset Plans

Q 22:88 What is a *floor-offset plan*? 22-29

Nonqualified Deferred Compensation (NQDC) Plans

Types of NQDC Plans

Q 22:89 What types of NQDC plans are available? 22-30

Q 22:90 What is a *top-hat plan*? 22-30

Q 22:91 What is an *excess benefit plan*? 22-30

Q 22:92 What is an *unfunded plan*? 22-30

Q 22:93 What is a *funded plan*? 22-31

Tax Aspects of NQDC Plans

Q 22:94 When are amounts deferred under an unfunded NQDC includable in an employee's gross income? 22-31

Q 22:95 What is an example of how the constructive receipt doctrine works?. 22-31

Q 22:96 When are amounts deferred under a funded NQDC includable in an employee's gross income? 22-31

Q 22:97 When are amounts deferred under a NQDC deductible by the employer? 22-32

Q 22:98 When are amounts deferred under a NQDC taken into account for FICA tax purposes? 22-32

Q 22:99 When are amounts deferred under a NQDC taken into account for FUTA tax purposes?. 22-32

Q 22:100	What additional restrictions apply to NQDC plans of tax-exempt organizations?	**22-32**
Q 22:101	Can a NQDC plan be linked to a defined contribution plan?	**22-33**

Advantages and Disadvantages of NQDC Plans

Q 22:102	What are the advantages of a NQDC plan to the employer?	**22-33**
Q 22:103	What are the advantages of an unfunded NQDC plan to employees?	**22-33**
Q 22:104	What are the disadvantages of an unfunded NQDC plan to the employer?	**22-34**
Q 22:105	What are the disadvantages of an unfunded NQDC plan to the employee?	**22-34**

Impact of Code Section 409A

Q 22:106	What is Section 409A?	**22-34**
Q 22:107	When was Section 409A effective?	**22-34**
Q 22:108	Was the Section 409A compliance deadline extended?	**22-34**
Q 22:109	What impact does Code Section 409A have on NQDC plans?	**22-35**
Q 22:110	What are the basic requirements of Code Section 409A?	**22-35**
Q 22:111	How does coverage under Section 409A affect an employee's taxes?	**22-35**
Q 22:112	What are the consequences of noncompliance with Section 409A?	**22-35**
Q 22:113	Is there an IRS correction program for violations of Section 409A?	**22-36**
Q 22:114	What requirements must be satisfied to use the correction program in Notice 2010-06?	**22-36**
Q 22:115	Are penalties reduced or eliminated if an employer corrects a Section 409A violation using the procedures provided in Notice 2010-06?	**22-36**

Benefit Security in Unfunded NQDC Plans

Q 22:116	What is a *rabbi trust*?	**22-37**
Q 22:117	What is the purpose of a rabbi trust?	**22-37**
Q 22:118	Has the IRS issued a model rabbi trust document?	**22-37**

NQDC Plans Versus 401(k) Plans

Q 22:119	When might a NQDC plan be used as an alternative to a 401(k) plan?	**22-38**
Q 22:120	When might a NQDC plan be used to supplement a 401(k) plan?	**22-38**

Section 403(b) Plans—Tax-Sheltered Annuities

Eligible Employers and Funding Rules

Q 22:121 What types of organizations may establish and maintain Section 403(b) plans? 22-38
Q 22:122 What funding vehicles may be used in a Section 403(b) plan? 22-38

Written Plan Document Requirement

Q 22:123 Must a Section 403(b) plan be maintained and operated pursuant to a written plan document? 22-39
Q 22:124 What provisions must be incorporated into Section 403(b) plans? 22-39
Q 22:125 May an employer include a provision in the plan document to terminate the 403(b) plan? 22-40
Q 22:126 Is there a prototype plan program for 403(b) plans? 22-40
Q 22:127 How does the 403(b) Pre-approved Plan Program affect a plan's remedial amendment period? 22-41

Nondiscrimination Rules

Q 22:128 How do the minimum participation and coverage rules apply to Section 403(b) plans? 22-41
Q 22:129 What nondiscrimination rule applies to 403(b) elective deferrals? 22-41
Q 22:130 What categories of employees may be excluded from making elective deferrals? 22-41
Q 22:131 Are there nondiscrimination rules that apply to employer contributions? 22-42

Contributions to Section 403(b) Plans

Q 22:132 Who may make contributions to a Section 403(b) plan? 22-42
Q 22:133 Is there a dollar cap on employee elective deferrals? 22-42
Q 22:134 Are there special catch-up provisions that apply only to 403(b) plans? 22-42
Q 22:135 May employees make age 50 catch-up contributions? 22-42
Q 22:136 May an employee make both the special 403(b) catch-up contribution and the age 50 catch-up contribution in the same year? 22-43
Q 22:137 May employees make Roth contributions to a 403(b) plan? 22-43
Q 22:138 Must Section 403(b) elective deferrals be treated as annual additions? 22-43
Q 22:139 What types of employer contributions are allowed into a 403(b) plan? 22-43

Distributions, Exchanges, and Rollovers

Q 22:140 What distribution restrictions apply to elective deferrals in a 403(b) plan? 22-43
Q 22:141 Are employer contributions subject to distributions restrictions? 22-44
Q 22:142 May Section 403(b) assets be exchanged among annuity contracts issued by different insurers? 22-44
Q 22:143 May distributable amounts in a participant's pre-tax 403(b) account be rolled into a designated Roth account in the same plan? 22-44
Q 22:144 May nondistributable amounts in a participant's pre-tax 403(b) account be transferred into a designated Roth account in the same plan? 22-45
Q 22:145 May pre-tax assets in a 403(b) plan be rolled into a Roth IRA? 22-45

ERISA Title 1 Issues

Q 22:146 Is a Section 403(b) plan subject to Title 1 of ERISA? 22-45
Q 22:147 What rules must be met for a safe harbor exemption from ERISA? 22-45
Q 22:148 What DOL guidance on safe harbor 403(b) plans was issued in conjunction with the IRS final regulations? 22-46
Q 22:149 What activities may employers engage in pursuant to FAB 2007-02 without violating the safe harbor? 22-46
Q 22:150 What types of employer activity may violate the safe harbor? 22-46
Q 22:151 What actions may employers take under the additional guidance provided in Field Assistance Bulletin 2010-01 without violating the safe harbor? 22-47
Q 22:152 What employer actions are outside the safe harbor under FAB 2010-01? 22-47
Q 22:153 Will the safe harbor exemption from ERISA be violated if 403(b) matching contributions are placed in a 401(a) plan? 22-48

Form 5500 Rules Applicable to ERISA 403(b) Plans

Q 22:154 What Form 5500 rules apply to Section 403(b) plans? 22-48
Q 22:155 Which 403(b) contracts or accounts can be excluded for Form 5500 purposes? 22-48
Q 22:156 Which employees can be excluded for Form 5500 purposes? 22-48
Q 22:157 What employer actions could require a pre-2009 contract to be included for Form 5500 purposes? 22-49
Q 22:158 What clarifications did FAB 2010-01 provide with respect to excludable contracts? 22-49

Q 22:159 What guidance has the IRS provided to assist employers in complying with the 403(b) rules? 22-49

Using a Section 403(b) Plan with a Qualified Plan

Q 22:160 How may a Section 403(b) plan be used in conjunction with a qualified plan? 22-50

Section 403(b) Plans Versus 401(k) Plans

Q 22:161 What features of a 403(b) plan might be seen as advantages over 401(k) plans? 22-50

Q 22:162 What features of 401(k) plans might be seen as advantages over 403(b) plans? 22-51

Q 22:163 When might an employer use a 403(b) plan as an alternative to a 401(k) plan? 22-51

Section 457(b) Eligible Deferred Compensation Plans

Eligible Employers and Funding Rules

Q 22:164 What types of organizations are eligible to sponsor a 457(b) plan? 22-52

Q 22:165 Who owns and holds the assets of a Section 457(b) plan? 22-52

Q 22:166 May Section 457(b) plan assets be invested in life insurance policies? 22-53

Section 457(b) Plan Eligibility Requirements

Q 22:167 What are the general eligibility requirements under Section 457(b)? 22-53

Eligible 457(b) Plan Contributions

Q 22:168 Who is eligible to make elective deferrals into a Section 457(b) plan? 22-54

Q 22:169 What are the deferral limits in an eligible Section 457(b) plan? 22-54

Q 22:170 Are special 457(b) catch-up contributions allowed? 22-54

Q 22:171 Are age 50 catch-up contributions allowed? 22-54

Q 22:172 When may the deferrals begin or the deferral amount be changed? 22-55

Q 22:173 May employees make Roth contributions to a 457(b) plan? . . . 22-55

Distributions, Rollovers, and Transfers

Q 22:174 What restrictions apply to Section 457(b) plan distributions? . . . 22-55

Q 22:175 When must distributions from 457(b) plans commence? 22-56

Q 22:176 May distributable amounts in a participant's pre-tax 457(b) account be rolled into a designated Roth account in the same plan? **22-56**

Q 22:177 May amounts in a participant's pre-tax 457(b) account that are *not* eligible for rollover be transferred into a designated Roth account in the same plan? **22-56**

Q 22:178 May pre-tax assets in a governmental 457(b) plan be rolled into a Roth IRA? **22-56**

Q 22:179 May amounts be rolled from a 457(b) plan to another employer's plan? **22-57**

Q 22:180 Are hardship withdrawals from a Section 457(b) plan permitted? **22-57**

Q 22:181 How must unforeseeable emergency be defined in the plan document? **22-57**

Q 22:182 What distribution requirements apply to amounts rolled into a governmental Section 457(b) plan? **22-57**

Q 22:183 When do assets in a 457(b) plan become taxable to the participant? **22-58**

Q 22:184 How are distributions from a Section 457(b) plan taxed? **22-58**

Q 22:185 May a Section 457(b) plan be frozen or terminated? **22-58**

Violations of Code Section 457(b)

Q 22:186 What happens if a Section 457(b) plan does not meet the requirements? **22-60**

Section 457(b) Plans Versus Section 401(k) Plans

Q 22:187 When might an employer use a Section 457(b) plan as an alternative to a 401(k) plan? **22-60**

Chapter 1

Introduction

Over the last four decades, 401(k) plans have evolved into one of the most popular employee benefits. A 401(k) plan may be a stand-alone plan or a feature of a profit sharing or stock bonus plan. When a 401(k) feature is incorporated into a plan, the plan is called a 401(k) plan or a cash or deferred arrangement (CODA). We refer to such arrangements throughout this book as 401(k) plans. A 401(k) plan allows eligible employees the choice between receiving certain amounts in cash or directing the sponsoring employer to contribute these amounts to the qualified plan. Once contributed to the plan, these amounts are fully and immediately vested. However, distributions of these amounts are restricted by law. To retain its qualified status, the 401(k) plan must operate in a nondiscriminatory manner. In other words, the plan must not favor highly compensated over non-highly compensated employees.

This chapter provides an overview of 401(k) plans, including the Roth 401(k) option, their evolution, and pros and cons for employers and employees. It looks at the extent to which 401(k) plans are used today and at the role of 401(k) plans as a benefit into the next century and lists recent legal developments.

History of 401(k) Plans 1-2
Advantages and Disadvantages of 401(k) Plans 1-4
Taxes and 401(k) Plans 1-8
Analyzing the Roth 401(k) Option 1-12
Table 1-1. Base Case—Annual Cash Available 1-13
Table 1-2. Cash Available at Age 65 1-13
Table 1-3. Cash Available at Age 65 If Annual Cash Available ($3,750) Is Invested in Side Fund 1-13
Table 1-4. Roth Contributions Made Net of Tax 1-14
Table 1-5. Lower Post-Retirement Tax Rate 1-14
Table 1-6. Higher Post-Retirement Tax Rate 1-15
Table 1-7. Impact of Higher Earnings Rate 1-15
Table 1-8. Rollover to Roth IRA—Defer Distributions to Age 90 1-16

Table 1-9. Higher Earnings Rate—Defer Distributions to Age 90 1-16
Types of Entities That May Use 401(k) Plans 1-17
When a 401(k) Plan Is Appropriate 1-18
Multiemployer and Multiple-Employer 401(k) Plans 1-20
Multiple-Employer Plans 1-22
Market for and Utilization of 401(k) Plans 1-24
Future of 401(k) Plans 1-25
Legislative and Regulatory Developments Affecting 401(k) Plans 1-27
The Economic Growth and Tax Relief Reconciliation Act of 2001 1-28
The Pension Protection Act of 2006 1-32
The Uniformed Services Employment and Reemployment Rights Act of 1994 1-35
The Heroes Earnings and Assistance Relief Tax (HEART) Act of 2008 1-37
The Worker, Retiree, and Employer Recovery Act of 2008 1-39
The Dodd-Frank Wall Street Reform and Consumer Protection Act of 2010 1-40
The American Taxpayer Relief Act of 2012 1-41
Establishment of MyRA Accounts 1-41
Proposed Legislation and Regulatory Developments 1-41

History of 401(k) Plans

Q 1:1 What was the Internal Revenue Service's position on cash or deferred arrangements prior to the addition of Section 401(k) to the Internal Revenue Code?

A *cash or deferred arrangement* (CODA) was a popular feature in profit sharing plans sponsored by a number of banks in the early to mid-1950s. Under this type of arrangement, an eligible employee could either elect to receive a portion of the profit sharing contribution in cash or to defer it in a profit sharing plan. The Internal Revenue Service (IRS) was somewhat wary of this arrangement but did issue some guidance in 1956. The IRS allowed for this arrangement if two requirements were met:

1. The participant made an irrevocable election to defer the profit sharing contribution before the close of the plan year for which the profit sharing contribution was made.
2. More than half of the participants in the plan (who elected to defer) were among the lowest paid two thirds of all eligible employees.

[Rev. Rul. 56-497, 1956-2 C.B. 284]

The IRS later reaffirmed that this type of arrangement could be a qualified plan. Subsequently, it ruled that if such a plan met the nondiscrimination rules of Revenue Ruling 56-497, the deferred contributions would be exempt from the IRS doctrine of constructive receipt. [Rev. Rul. 63-180, 1963-2 C.B. 189] Further clarification of this position was issued in another revenue ruling in 1968. [Rev. Rul. 68-89, 1968-1 C.B. 402]

Despite these positive rulings, CODAs never became wildly popular. By the early 1970s, there were fewer than 1,000 plans in existence.

The IRS issued proposed regulations in 1972 that dramatically changed its previous position. Under the proposed regulations, salary reduction contributions would have been treated, for tax purposes, as if they had been received by the employee in cash. Although the regulations did not deal directly with the profit sharing deferral arrangements, they cast doubt on these arrangements. Conceptually, the IRS found it difficult to distinguish between the two types of deferrals.

Congress became concerned about the IRS stance in 1974. When Congress passed the Employee Retirement Income Security Act (ERISA), the act contained a provision that froze the existing tax status of CODAs until the end of 1976. Any such arrangements in existence on June 27, 1974, retained their tax-favored status. The moratorium was deferred twice, the last time until the end of 1979.

Q 1:2 How did the passage of Code Section 401(k) influence the growth of cash or deferred arrangements?

Congress followed up in 1978 when it passed the Revenue Act of 1978. Permanent provisions were added to the Internal Revenue Code, Section 401(k), effective for plan years beginning after December 31, 1979. The IRS issued proposed regulations in 1981 that sanctioned the use of salary reductions as a source of plan contributions. The floodgates were opened, as employers responded in 1982 with the adoption of new 401(k) plans and the conversion of existing thrift plans from after-tax contributions to pre-tax contributions.

The Tax Reform Act of 1984 (TRA '84) modified the rules for 401(k) plans in subtle ways. It eliminated the possibility of integrating 401(k) plans with Social Security. Nondiscrimination tests, which previously had been safe harbors with an alternative of testing under the general qualified plan nondiscrimination rules, became mandatory. In addition, certain money purchase pension plans that allowed for salary reductions and were in existence before the passage of ERISA were grandfathered under this law.

Congress and the IRS became seriously concerned about the popularity of these plans in early 1986. The growth of 401(k) plans meant immediate revenue loss to the government, and many in government were concerned about the impact of 401(k) plans on the budget deficit. Some thought was given to repealing Code Section 401(k) entirely. Ultimately, in the Tax Reform Act of 1986 (TRA '86) Congress chose to tighten up the nondiscrimination rules and reduce the maximum annual amount that could be deferred in a 401(k) plan.

In 1991 the IRS issued final regulations that explain the statutory requirements of Section 401(k). In 2004, the IRS issued a comprehensive set of regulations intended to centralize authority for 401(k) plan issues that previously had been scattered among various sources of authority.

On August 17, 2006, the Pension Protection Act (PPA) was signed into law. [Pub. L. No. 109-280, 120 Stat. 780] The PPA makes significant changes to

401(k) plans. Many of the changes are designed to encourage higher savings rates and investment results, reflecting a growing awareness that 401(k) plans will be a major source of retirement income for future retirees.

Advantages and Disadvantages of 401(k) Plans

Q 1:3 How does offering a 401(k) plan benefit the employer?

From the perspective of the sponsoring employer, there are a number of reasons to offer a 401(k) plan to employees. A 401(k) plan is a low-cost means of providing visible and appreciated retirement benefits to employees. It offers employees a real opportunity to participate actively in saving for retirement on a pre-tax basis. A sponsoring employer may use a 401(k) plan as its sole retirement plan or as a supplement to an existing plan. In larger organizations, a 401(k) plan is sometimes used to supplement an existing defined benefit plan. While 401(k) plans were originally viewed as a supplemental source of retirement benefits, in recent years they have become the primary vehicle (in addition to Social Security) for providing those benefits.

For a cash-strapped employer, a 401(k) plan can help the employer address employee pressures for additional cash compensation without significant added cost and without jeopardizing employees' retirement income security. A matching contribution may provide the incentive for employees to save on a pre-tax basis. A discretionary match may be tied to company strategic compensation objectives. A 401(k) plan can also improve the participation and effectiveness of an existing thrift plan.

The plan may also be used as a vehicle to attract and retain qualified employees. To the extent the plan has discretionary employer contributions, the plan can be used to reward employees during years when the employer has reached its profitability objective. The 401(k) plan can improve morale and employee satisfaction, thereby improving productivity. If the 401(k) plan allows for the purchase of employer securities, this can increase an employee's sense of corporate identity.

Because of its inherent flexibility, the 401(k) plan can provide benefits to meet very different employee objectives. At little or no added cost, the 401(k) plan allows employees to take some responsibility for their own retirement savings.

For employers with existing retirement plans, a 401(k) plan can be a very attractive supplement. To the extent that an employer is being pressured to increase benefit levels in a defined benefit plan, the addition of a 401(k) plan can be a low-cost substitute for benefit increases.

Q 1:4 How do competitive pressures motivate an employer to establish a 401(k) plan?

An employer operating in a highly competitive industry will be looking for a way to reduce costs to gain a competitive advantage. Such an employer may view the 401(k) plan as a vehicle for cost sharing, recognizing the need for employees to bear a portion of the cost of saving for their retirement.

In other cases, the benefit plans of competitors may be an employer's primary motivation for adopting a 401(k) plan. The design of a competitor's 401(k) plan can serve as the basis for incorporating features into a new 401(k) plan, including the level of match, the availability of investment options, loan and withdrawal features, and educational services.

Q 1:5 What tax-related objectives may an employer have in establishing a 401(k) plan?

Some employers will set up a 401(k) plan with dual objectives: to provide employees with the opportunity for pre-tax deferral and the employers themselves with significant tax-deductible contributions. Such plans will generally set lower caps on deferral percentages to ensure that sufficient deductible employer contributions may be made and still meet the overall compensation contribution limit (see chapter 8).

Q 1:6 How can a 401(k) plan replace or supplement a defined benefit plan?

Employers with existing defined benefit plans may find that employees do not appreciate or understand the pension plan. Yet employers may be reluctant to terminate the plan out of concern for providing a minimum level of benefit security for their employees. The 401(k) plan in such a situation will need to be a highly visible plan. Attractive features such as a matching contribution, a wide range of investments, and loan or withdrawal options will help the plan to become more visible to employees. Frequent reports will also be an effective tool for maintaining the high profile of the 401(k) plan.

Employers with defined benefit plans may find their retirees dissatisfied with their current level of benefits. Cost-of-living adjustments can help to ease the concern of retirees, but significant benefit increases for existing employees may not be affordable. A 401(k) plan can be designed to supplement an existing defined benefit plan, with the employee and employer jointly bearing the cost. If the employer chooses to freeze the defined benefit plan, establishing a 401(k) plan that offers some type of guaranteed lifetime income investment product may make that decision more palatable to employees.

Q 1:7 What type of employer is most likely to offer both a 401(k) and a defined benefit plan?

Organizations with larger employee populations are more likely to offer both plan types.

Q 1:8 Are there disadvantages to an employer in sponsoring a 401(k) plan?

The 401(k) plan does have some disadvantages from an employer's perspective. The administration of the plan can be costly and complex. Even larger employers who had previously maintained a staff to administer the plan are outsourcing functions to lower-cost providers. If the actual deferral percentage (ADP) test is not passed (see chapter 13), employee relations problems may result when highly compensated employees (HCEs) receive taxable refunds after the close of the plan year.

A 401(k) plan requires intensive communication throughout its life cycle. If the plan is not adequately communicated, the effectiveness of the 401(k) plan as an employee benefit will be lost.

Certain employers may find that the demographics of their employee base preclude the adoption of a 401(k) plan. In certain industries with high turnover, lower-paid employees may prefer cash. Since the success of a 401(k) plan is measured by the degree of participation of lower-paid employees, such a plan may be doomed to failure.

As plan sponsor, the employer must accept some fiduciary responsibility for the management of the plan and its assets. Though many plan functions can be delegated to others, the employer will inevitably be left with some responsibility (and corresponding potential liability) for the plan's operation (see chapter 5).

Q 1:9 How does a 401(k) plan benefit employees?

From the employee's perspective, the 401(k) plan offers a unique opportunity to reduce current federal and state income taxes. The tax-sheltered aspects of the 401(k) plan make it an ideal vehicle for retirement savings. The ultimate tax paid by the employee may be lower, since the employee may find himself or herself in a lower bracket at retirement or when funds are withdrawn.

The 401(k) plan offers an employee a great deal of flexibility and choice: whether or not to defer, how much to defer, where to invest (if allowed by the plan), and when to change the deferral amount or investments. As an employee's circumstances change, different choices may be made. The availability of loans and hardship withdrawals means that invested funds can be used when personal financial circumstances change dramatically. The relative portability of a 401(k) plan allows an employee to change jobs without a significant loss in retirement benefits.

For an employee at a middle or high range of pay, the availability of deductible IRA contributions may be limited because of the existence of an employer's other qualified plan. The 401(k) plan will provide a very attractive option for deductible contributions through periodic savings.

Beginning in 2006, employers with 401(k) plans could offer participants the option to make deferrals to a Roth 401(k). With a Roth 401(k) plan, income tax is paid at the time of deferral, but earnings on the deferred amounts are distributed tax free, provided certain requirements are met (see chapter 18). This option affords participants some significant tax-planning opportunities.

The Pension Protection Act of 2006 [Pub. L. No. 109-280, 120 Stat. 780] (PPA) made a number of changes designed to make automatic enrollment plans more attractive to both employers and employees. This type of plan design, which essentially causes employees to participate in a retirement plan unless they take affirmative action, and to invest in funds with both fixed-income and equity exposure, may increase the number of individuals who are able to retire with substantial 401(k) account balances.

Q 1:10 How may a 401(k) plan supplement an employee's personal savings program?

Employees covered by a qualified plan and at a middle range of pay may be precluded from making a deductible contribution to an IRA and so will find the 401(k) plan an attractive alternative. Even lower-paid employees will find the 401(k) plan an attractive and convenient means of saving through payroll deduction. In these types of plans, matching contributions may be low or nonexistent—the primary objective is providing the opportunity for pre-tax savings.

Q 1:11 How is a 401(k) plan viewed by employees in a competitive environment?

In an era of global competition, layoffs can create tremendous pressure on households relying on dual incomes to maintain their lifestyles. If one spouse is laid off, the spouse who is currently employed will have a greater need for cash compensation and may be reluctant to commit any funds to a 401(k) plan. On the other hand, the presence of hardship withdrawal and loan features may provide the employee with the assurance that the funds are accessible in the event of financial difficulty.

Q 1:12 Are there disadvantages to an employee for participating in a 401(k) plan?

The employee may see some disadvantages in a 401(k) plan. Withdrawal rules will restrict access to funds before retirement or termination of employment. If funds are available before termination of employment, the 10 percent withdrawal penalty may significantly increase taxes on distribution. If the plan allows an employee to make investment choices, the employee may make poor ones and seriously undermine the value of retirement benefits in the 401(k) plan.

Taxes and 401(k) Plans

In considering whether to defer a portion of their current salaries in a 401(k) plan or similar program, employees must decide whether the deferral makes sense from a tax standpoint. If tax rates today are at their lowest point, does it make sense to defer today and pay more taxes tomorrow? The answer depends on a number of factors:

1. Rate of return on assets before taxes;
2. Rate of return on after-tax assets;
3. The increase in tax rates; and
4. The time at which tax rates will change.

This analysis is further complicated by the option to make Roth, or after-tax, contributions and the potential to avoid any tax on earnings. The questions and answers in this section analyze different assumptions in demonstrating that tax deferral is generally the best alternative.

Q 1:13 In a stable tax environment, what are the advantages of accumulating money in a tax-deferred vehicle?

If tax rates remain stable or decline, it inevitably makes sense to accumulate money in a tax-deferred vehicle. Consider an employee who defers $2,000 per year for 20 years in a 401(k) plan or an IRA. The 20-year accumulation after taxes in the tax-deferred vehicle versus after-tax savings is shown below.

28 Percent Tax Bracket

Interest Rate	*401(k) or Traditional IRA*	*After-Tax Savings*	*Difference*
6%	$ 52,971	$ 44,333	$ 8,638
8	65,897	51,625	14,272
10	82,476	60,339	22,137
12	103,756	70,760	32,996

Note: This table assumes that an individual is able to invest after-tax money as effectively as the 401(k) plan or IRA.

Q 1:14 Does it make sense to defer compensation in a rising tax environment?

Consider an employee who participates in a 401(k) plan and has an opportunity to receive a bonus currently or defer the bonus for a fixed number of years. Suppose the employee expects tax rates to rise from 33 percent to 50 percent in 15 years. Should the employee defer a bonus of $5,000 for 15 years?

The employee's alternatives are compared at interest rates of 6, 8, and 12 percent as follows.

At a 6 percent rate of return, there is little difference between after-tax savings and the 401(k) plan:

Year	*401(k) Account*	*After-Tax Savings Account*
0	$ 5,000	$3,350
15	$11,983	$6,051
Tax rate	50%	0%
After taxes	$ 5,991	$6,051

Difference: $60

At 8 percent interest, the 401(k) plan is somewhat more favorable:

Year	*401(k) Account*	*After-Tax Savings Account*
0		
	$ 5,000	$3,350
15	$15,681	$7,331
Tax rate	50%	0%
After taxes	$ 7,930	$7,331

Difference: $599

At 12 percent interest, the 401(k) plan is clearly more favorable:

Year	*401(k) Account*	*After-Tax Savings Account*
0	$ 5,000	$ 3,350
15	$27,368	$10,686
Tax rate	50%	0%
After taxes	$13,684	$10,686

Difference: $2,998

The rate of return on tax-deferred savings is a critical element in determining whether it makes sense to defer money in a period when tax rates rise significantly.

Q 1:15 If an employee chooses to defer salary for a period of ten years, what impact will tax rate changes have?

The employee making a decision to defer a bonus for ten years may want to analyze whether it makes sense to defer if Congress raises tax rates at the end of ten years. Assuming that the employee is currently in a 33 percent tax bracket, tax rates would need to rise to the following levels to destroy the advantage of tax-deferred savings:

Earnings	*Minimum Tax Bracket*
6%	44.50%
8	47.70
10	50.60
12	53.35

If the employee is relatively pessimistic about future tax rates, a decision might be made to take the bonus currently.

Q 1:16 How does a 401(k) plan compare with an after-tax investment in a tax-deferred investment vehicle?

The comparison between a 401(k) plan and an after-tax investment is best illustrated by the following example.

Example. An employee who is 40 years old had the opportunity to defer $13,000 in a 401(k) plan and would like to compare the after-tax accumulation (after 15 years) with a deferred annuity product. The employee is in the 33 percent tax bracket now, intends to retire at age 55, and anticipates that tax rates will increase to 40 percent after 10 years. The scheduled increase to the 401(k) limit is $1,000 per year until 2006 and then assumed to increase at $500 per year thereafter.

Year	*Tax Rate (Percentage)*	*401(k) Contribution*	*401(k) Accumulation*	*After-Tax Contribution*	*After-Tax Accumulation*
1	33	$ 13,000	$ 13,000	$ 8,710	$ 8,710
2	33	14,000	28,040	9,380	18,787
3	33	15,000	45,283	10,050	30,340
4	33	15,500	64,406	10,385	43,152
5	33	16,000	85,558	10,720	57,324
6	33	16,500	108,903	11,055	72,965
7	33	17,000	134,615	11,390	90,192
8	33	17,500	162,884	11,725	109,132
9	33	18,000	193,915	12,060	129,923

Year	Tax Rate (Percentage)	401(k) Contribution	401(k) Accumulation	After-Tax Contribution	After-Tax Accumulation
10	40	18,500	227,928	11,100	151,417
11	40	19,000	265,162	11,400	174,930
12	40	19,500	305,875	11,700	200,624
13	40	20,000	350,345	12,000	228,674
14	40	20,500	398,873	12,300	259,268
15	40	21,000	451,783	12,600	259,268
Total contribution:		$ 261,000		$166,575	292,609
Accumulation subject to tax:		$ 451,783		$126,034	
Tax rate:					
	10%	0			$ 12,603
	40%	$ 180,713			$ 50,414
Total tax due:		$ 180,713			$ 63,017
Available after tax:		$ 271,070			$ 229,592

Assumption:

Annual investment rate of return: 8%

The accumulation in both plans is significant: $451,783 in the 401(k) plan versus $292,609 in the deferred annuity. If the employee retires at age 55 from the company, the 401(k) proceeds will not be subject to a 10 percent premature distribution tax. The accumulation of $451,783, if taken in a lump sum, will be subject to the 40 percent tax rate. The net available for the employee will be $271,070 after taxes.

On the other hand, if the employee puts the same amount (after tax) in a deferred annuity and withdraws the proceeds at age 55, the earnings will be subject to a 10 percent premature distribution tax. The total earnings of $126,034 will be subject to the 40 percent tax rate plus the 10 percent penalty rate. The net proceeds available to the employee from the deferred annuity will be $229,592, or $41,478 less than the amount available from the qualified plan.

If the company makes a matching contribution to the 401(k) plan, the employee will be significantly further ahead by choosing to defer in the 401(k) plan.

Q 1:17 When might a company choose after-tax savings over a 401(k) plan?

In a small, closely held business, an owner may choose after-tax savings if the after-tax amount is greater than the amount that may be deferred in a 401(k) plan.

In the case of a larger business, an after-tax savings plan will make sense only if the 401(k) plan has poor participation and high administrative costs as a percentage of plan assets. Because of the significant economic advantages of accumulating funds in a tax-sheltered environment, it may make more sense to convince the employee group of the value of the 401(k) plan.

Analyzing the Roth 401(k) Option

Employees can be offered the choice of making contributions to a 401(k) plan on an after-tax, or Roth, basis. Earnings on after-tax contributions are distributed tax free if certain requirements are met. (See chapters 2 and 18 for detailed descriptions of the rules governing Roth 401(k) contributions and taxation of distributions from Roth 401(k) plans.)

The decision regarding whether to make contributions on a pre-tax or an after-tax basis is a complicated one. The questions and answers that follow provide some illustrations that may be useful in making an analysis.

Q 1:18 What factors should be considered when deciding whether to contribute on a Roth basis or a before-tax basis?

The decision about whether to contribute to a traditional 401(k) plan or a Roth 401(k) plan is a complicated one that is best made with the help of a personal financial and tax adviser. The following factors are relevant to the decision-making process:

- The participant's ability to maximize deferrals and pay current income tax
- The participant's anticipated pre- and post-retirement income tax rates
- The anticipated earnings rate on investments
- The number of years before distribution of benefits is needed
- The level of concern for tax diversification
- Confidence in the participant's ability to keep Roth money in the plan until "qualified" (i.e., five years in the plan and distribution due to participant's attainment of age 59½ or the participant's death or disability).

Q 1:19 How does ability to maximize deferrals and pay current income tax affect the decision regarding participation in a Roth 401(k) plan?

A participant who maximizes deferrals and pays current income tax on the deferral will generally be better off at retirement age than if he or she makes pre-tax deferrals and invests the money not used to pay current income tax in a taxable side fund.

Example 1. Sam, age 40, earns $50,000 a year. He is in the 25 percent income tax bracket before retirement and will be in the same tax bracket after retirement. He contributes a total of $15,000 annually to a retirement account and earns 7 percent on his investments. As illustrated in Table 1-1, if Sam participates in a Roth 401(k) plan, he would have $51,914 ($948,735 - $896,821) more at retirement age than he would have if he participates in a traditional 401(k) plan.

Table 1-1. Base Case—Annual Cash Available

	Before Tax	*After Tax*
Sam's salary	$50,000	$50,000
Contribution	$15,000	$15,000
Tax rate	25%	25%
Tax	$ 8,750	$12,500
Net annual cash available + $3,750 before taxes		

Table 1-2. Cash Available at Age 65

	Before Tax	*After Tax (Roth)*
Earnings rate	7%	7%
Account at age 65	$ 948,735	$948,735
Tax less 25% tax rate	($237,184)	—
After-tax amount at age 65	$ 711,735	$948,735
Net Cash Available Age 65 + $237,184 in Roth 401(k)		

The Roth advantage is misleading, however, because if Sam made before-tax contributions, he would have $3,750 more in cash each year (representing income tax savings) than he would if he contributed to a Roth 401(k). To make a more meaningful comparison, Table 1-3 looks at the results if Sam invested that extra $3,750 pre-tax money in a taxable side fund.

Table 1-3. Cash Available at Age 65 If Annual Cash Available ($3,750) Is Invested in Side Fund

	Before Tax	*After Tax (Roth)*
Earnings rate	$711,551	$948,735
Side fund after tax	$185,270	—
Total cash at age 65	$896,821	$948,735
Net Cash Available Age 65 + $51,914 in Roth 401(k)		

Example 2. The facts are the same as those in Example 1, except that Sam cannot afford to both contribute the maximum to his 401(k) account and pay

taxes. He reduces the amount of his contribution to the 401(k) plan by the amount of any income taxes due on a Roth contribution. The results would be as shown in Table 1-4.

Table 1-4. Roth Contributions Made Net of Tax

	Before Tax	*After Tax (Roth)*
Annual contribution	$ 15,000	$ 11,250
Account at age 65	948,735	711,551
25% tax	($237,551)	—
Total cash at age 65	$ 711,551	$711,551

In this case, there is no advantage to Sam's choosing the Roth 401(k) option. If the reduced contribution using a Roth results in missing out on any portion of an employer matching contribution, Sam will be worse off with the Roth.

Q 1:20 How do anticipated post-retirement tax rates affect the decision whether to participate in a Roth 401(k)?

Generally speaking, the more that the participant's tax rate is expected to increase after retirement, the more it makes sense to participate in a Roth 401(k), and the more that the participant's tax rate is anticipated to decrease after retirement, the less it makes sense to participate in a Roth 401(k).

In the following example, the assumptions are the same as those in Example 1 in Q 1:19, except that this taxpayer's tax rate is expected to decrease after retirement.

Example 1. Sally, age 40, earns $50,000 a year. Her pre-retirement tax rate is 25 percent. Her tax rate after retirement is expected to drop to 15 percent. By making pre-tax deferrals instead of after-tax deferrals to a Roth 401(k), Sally would have $42,960 more at retirement. Table 1-5 illustrates the break-even point where a decrease in post-retirement tax rates will not generate an advantage in contributing before-tax monies.

Table 1-5. Lower Post-Retirement Tax Rate

	Before Tax	*After Tax (Roth)*
Plan account at age 65	$ 948,735	$948,735
15% tax	($142,310)	—
Side fund after tax	$ 185,270	—
Total cash at age 65	$ 991,695	$948,735

Net Cash Available at Age 65 + $42,960 Before Tax

Example 2. Assume that Sally's pre-retirement tax rate is 25 percent and her post-retirement tax rate is 35 percent. Because Sally's tax rate rises after retirement, the Roth option will give her $146,787 more at age 65 than if she contributed before-tax dollars to a traditional 401(k) plan.

Table 1-6. Higher Post-Retirement Tax Rate

	Before Tax	*After Tax (Roth)*
Plan account at age 65	$ 948,735	$948,735
35% tax	($332,057)	—
Side fund after tax	$ 185,270	—
Total cash at age 65	$ 801,948	$948,735

Net Cash Available at Age 65 + $146,787 in Roth 401(k)

Q 1:21 How does a participant's anticipated earnings rate affect the decision regarding the Roth 401(k) option?

The Roth 401(k) option enables participants to completely avoid, rather than just defer, tax on earnings. Therefore, the higher the earnings rate, the more advantageous the Roth will be. In Q 1:19 (Example 1), it was shown that a participant who invests $15,000 annually in a Roth account earning 7 percent interest would give the participant an advantage in the amount of $51,914 at age 65. As shown in Table 1-7, we assume a 10 percent earnings rate, the Roth advantage would rise to $113,884.

Table 1-7. Impact of Higher Earnings Rate

	Before Tax	*After Tax (Roth)*
Earnings rate	10%	10%
Plan account at age 65	$1,475,206	$1,475,206
25% tax	($ 368,801)	—
After-tax amount at age 65	$1,106,405	$1,475,206
Total cash at age 65	$1,361,322	$1,475,206

Net Cash Available at Age 65 + $113,884 in Roth 401(k)

Q 1:22 How does the number of years until benefits are needed affect the decision regarding a Roth 401(k)?

As a general rule, as long as all contributions remain in the plan, there is no advantage to having a Roth 401(k) because there are no taxes due on earnings. It is only when benefits are distributed and the earnings on pre-tax contributions become taxable that the Roth 401(k) provides a potential advantage. One of the unique characteristics of the Roth 401(k) is that the account can be rolled over to a Roth IRA, thereby avoiding the requirement to begin taking minimum distributions at age 70½. One of the most significant advantages of having a Roth 401(k) is in situations where the participant does not need to take any pre-death distributions from the 401(k) account but can afford to let the assets accumulate past age 70½.

Table 1-8 illustrates the difference between a participant at age 90 who was forced to take minimum distributions at age 70½ and invest the after-tax proceeds from those distributions in a taxable side fund, and a participant who makes Roth contributions and is able to continue accumulating interest without paying any tax on earnings through age 90. The participant who contributed to a Roth is ahead of the game at age 90 by $1,046,921.

Table 1-8. Rollover to Roth IRA—Defer Distributions to Age 90

	Before Tax	*After Tax (Roth)*
Plan account at age 65	$ 948,735	$ 948,735
Plan account at age 90 (after RMDs)	$1,487,435	$5,149,192
25% Tax	($ 371,859)	—
Side fund after tax at age 90	$2,986,695	—
Total cash at age 90	$4,102,271	$5,149,192

Net Cash Available at Age 90 + $1,046,921 Roth

Table 1-9 illustrates that when deferred distribution to age 90 is combined with a 10 percent earnings rate, the advantage of choosing the Roth 401(k) option becomes very significant, over $4 million.

Table 1-9. Higher Earnings Rate—Defer Distributions to Age 90

	Before Tax	*After Tax (Roth)*
Earnings rate	10%	10%
Plan account at age 65	$ 1,475,206	$ 1,475,206
Plan account at age 90 (after RMDs)	$ 4,617,092	$15,983,423
25% Tax	($1,154,273)	—
Side fund after tax at age 90*	$ 8,311,019	—
Total cash at age 90	$11,773,928	$15,983,423

Total Cash at Age 90 + $4,209,495 Roth

* Assumes both $3,750 in annual cash from age 40 to age 65 and all net proceeds of RMDs invested in the side fund.

Q 1:23 How does the level of concern for tax diversification affect the decision regarding the Roth 401(k)?

For participants whose 401(k) plans already have significant amounts that will be subject to tax on earnings and who are uncertain whether their post-retirement tax rate will be higher or lower than their pre-retirement tax rate, contributing to a Roth 401(k) plan is a way to hedge their bet. If the participant accumulates a comparable Roth account balance, then a change in tax rates will hurt the participant in one account but help him or her in the other, thus minimizing the potential negative (and positive) impact of a change in tax rates.

Q 1:24 How does the extension of EGTRRA affect a participant's decision regarding the Roth 401(k)?

The Pension Protection Act of 2006 made EGTRRA permanent as it relates to Roth 401(k) plans and other retirement plans, thus eliminating the concern that Roth 401(k)s might be eliminated.

Q 1:25 How does a participant's confidence that he or she can avoid taking distributions from the Roth account until the account is "qualified" affect the decision regarding a Roth 401(k)?

The tax advantages of a Roth 401(k) account are available only if no distributions are made before the end of the five-year holding period (see chapter 18), and the distributions are due to the participant's attaining age 59½ or the participant's death or disability. If a participant anticipates requiring a distribution prior to the time when his or her account becomes qualified, it generally will not make sense to contribute to a Roth.

Types of Entities That May Use 401(k) Plans

Q 1:26 What entities may adopt a 401(k) plan?

401(k) plans may be adopted by sole proprietorships, partnerships, limited liability companies (LLCs), tax-exempt organizations, or corporations (including Subchapter S corporations). Beginning in 1987 and continuing through 1996, tax-exempt employers were not allowed to adopt 401(k) plans. Beginning in 1987, state and local governments or political subdivisions, agencies, or instrumentalities thereof, other than rural cooperatives, were not allowed to adopt 401(k) plans. A grandfather provision permits employers of tax-exempt entities or government units that maintained a 401(k) plan before 1986 to continue offering 401(k) plans to their current employees. [I.R.C. § 401(k)(4)(B)]

Q 1:27 Can other types of cash or deferred arrangements be offered by governmental or tax-exempt employers?

Yes. Employees of the federal government can contribute to the Federal Thrift Savings Fund, which functions in many respects like a 401(k) cash or deferred arrangement. Employees of public schools or certain charitable or religious entities exempt from tax under Code Section 501(c)(3) may use individual salary reduction agreements to make contributions to an annuity contract (see chapter 21). [I.R.C. §§ 402(g)(3)(C), 403(b)] Employees of state and local governments may be able to use similar salary reduction arrangements (see chapter 22). [I.R.C. § 457]

Q 1:28 What kinds of plans may offer a 401(k) feature?

Profit sharing plans, stock bonus plans (including employee stock ownership plans), rural cooperative plans, or pre-ERISA money purchase plans may include a 401(k) feature. [I.R.C. § 401(k)(1); Treas. Reg. § 1.401(k)-1(a)(1)] Defined benefit plans or post-ERISA target or money purchase plans may not contain a 401(k) feature.

When a 401(k) Plan Is Appropriate

Q 1:29 Does it make economic sense for a small business owner to establish or continue a qualified plan?

A plan design that will maximize the owner's portion of the total plan cost will also maximize the long-term effectiveness of the plan for a small, closely held business. Consider this case study in the following example.

> **Example.** An owner of a small company with three employees set up a profit sharing plan years ago, when the maximum tax bracket was 50 percent. Now that tax rates have declined to 33 percent, the owner is wondering whether it makes sense to continue making tax-deductible contributions to the profit sharing plan.

The current profit sharing plan calls for employees to receive a pro rata share of the contribution based on their compensation. Last year, the company contributed 20 percent of pay to the plan and paid $3,500 in administrative fees:

Employee	*Compensation*	*Contribution*
Owner	$ 220,000	$ 44,000
B	30,000	6,000
C	20,000	4,000
	$ 270,000	$ 54,000

The total cost of the plan is $57,500 ($54,000 in contributions plus $3,500 in administrative fees), $44,000 of which is credited to the owner of the company.

If the owner had dissolved the profit sharing plan and taken a bonus of $57,500 instead, a net after-tax amount of $38,525 would have been available, or approximately $5,500 less than the amount that was deferred in the qualified plan for the owner.

Q 1:30 Are 401(k) plans appropriate for unincorporated businesses?

Yes. Unincorporated businesses may use 401(k) plans as a benefit program for employees. The calculations involved are more difficult, since the compensation of the self-employed individual (either a sole proprietor or partner) is reduced by the contributions made on behalf of common-law employees. Also, the self-employed individual's compensation must be reduced by one half of the Social Security contribution (SECA deduction).

Q 1:31 When is a 401(k) plan appropriate for a sole proprietorship?

Because the cost and complexity of maintaining a 401(k) plan are typically higher than those of a profit sharing plan, it would make sense for a sole proprietor to maintain a 401(k) plan only if he or she wanted to contribute in excess of the defined contribution plan limits but did not want to have the fixed contribution obligation inherent in maintaining a defined benefit plan. Elective deferrals do not count toward the Code Section 404 deduction limit (25 percent of compensation), and that limit is based on compensation before reduction for elective deferrals, so the deductible limit for a sole proprietor with a 401(k) plan that has a profit sharing feature is higher than the limit for a profit sharing plan alone.

Q 1:32 What are the considerations in designing a 401(k) plan for a partnership?

Complex rules govern partnerships that adopt 401(k) plans. In fact, the final regulations under Code Section 401(k) require that any plan that directly or indirectly permits a partner to vary the amount of contributions on his or her behalf will be considered a cash or deferred arrangement. The implications for a partnership are quite significant:

1. The annual contribution for each partner is subject to the 401(k) deferral cap of $18,000 (in 2015).
2. For plan years beginning after December 30, 1997, matching contributions on behalf of each partner are no longer treated as elective deferrals, subject to the 2015 deferral cap of $18,000.
3. Nondiscrimination testing must be performed.

Thus, in designing a plan for a partnership, it is critical that the partners decide whether contributions should be variable for each partner. If contributions will be variable, a 401(k) plan is the only design available, with the resulting reduction in total contributions allocable to the partners. See chapter 2 for more information regarding 401(k) plans for partnerships.

Q 1:33 Can a limited liability company sponsor a 401(k) plan?

Yes. An LLC is a business that operates with the flexibility and informality of a partnership and yet retains the personal liability protection associated with corporation shareholder interests. An LLC is designed to be taxed as a partnership. Members of the LLC (equivalent of partners or shareholders) receive and are taxed on company profits as earned income in the same manner as partners. For 401(k) plan purposes, "members" are treated like partners and nonmembers are treated like partnership employees.

Q 1:34 What are the 401(k) design considerations for a small or professional business?

Many qualified plans designed for small businesses (fewer than 20 employees) and professional firms (e.g., attorneys, accountants, engineers, physicians) will be top heavy (i.e., more than 60 percent of the benefits of the plan will be attributable to key employees—see chapter 14). The impact of top heaviness on a 401(k) plan may be significant, since top-heavy minimum contributions may be required for non-key employees. Thus, the plan design should take into account the fact that fixed employer contributions ranging from 3 percent to 7.5 percent of pay for non-key employees may be required.

Beginning in 1997, 401(k) plans have been able to avoid the top-heavy requirements if they qualify as SIMPLE 401(k) plans. A safe harbor 401(k) plan and a Qualified Automatic Contribution Arrangement (QACA) are other design options for plans that are or are likely to be top heavy (see chapter 2).

Multiemployer and Multiple-Employer 401(k) Plans

The terms of a collective bargaining agreement may call for the establishment or maintenance of a 401(k) plan. If more than one employer is required to contribute to the plan, it is treated as a multiemployer plan. The following section discusses design considerations for multiemployer 401(k) plans.

Negotiated 401(k) plans are generally started for one of two reasons: as a replacement for a terminating defined benefit plan or as a supplement to an existing plan. The design features may be quite different, depending on the reasons behind the start up of the plan.

Q 1:35 Why do multiemployer units consider 401(k) plans?

Multiemployer defined benefit plans lost favor after Congress passed the Multiemployer Pension Plan Amendments Act (MPPAA) in 1980. A major drawback of the defined benefit approach was its withdrawal liability feature: an individual employer attempting to withdraw from a multiemployer defined benefit plan would be assessed a single sum withdrawal charge equal to the individual employer's pro rata share of the unfunded liability. This made withdrawal from an underfunded plan expensive for an employer and discouraged new employers from joining a multiemployer plan.

Favorable investment performance for many defined benefit plans in the mid-1980s caused a number of plans to become well funded, which encouraged the unions to request benefit increases. However, employers were reluctant to grant increases because they feared potential withdrawal liability. This left the union, the employers, and the membership in a difficult situation. In many cases, this was resolved by terminating the defined benefit plan and replacing it with a defined contribution plan.

Q 1:36 In replacing a defined benefit plan, how is the 401(k) plan structured?

The replacement plan often is a profit sharing plan with a 401(k) feature attached to it. The primary emphasis is on replacing benefits lost by the termination of the defined benefit plan. Employer contributions are emphasized, and employee elective contributions are intended merely to supplement the retirement benefits provided by the terminated defined benefit plan and the new profit sharing plan.

Q 1:37 How is a supplemental 401(k) plan structured?

When a multiemployer group institutes a 401(k) plan as a supplement to an existing defined benefit plan, there is much less emphasis on employer contributions. Typically, employers are not interested in making any contributions at all to the 401(k) plan. When employer contributions are made, a common arrangement is that an employer will agree to contribute "x" cents per hour, and this money will be pooled. At the end of the year, the pooled money will be used to match a portion of the deferrals for each contributing employee.

Q 1:38 What design and administration features are unique to a multiemployer 401(k) plan?

There are a number of unique design and administrative features in a multiemployer 401(k) plan:

1. Nondiscrimination testing is performed on a plan-wide basis, making it critical that each employer provide accurate information relative to the plan members who are highly compensated.

2. The mobility of collectively bargained employees in certain industries, such as construction, makes the administration of the plan quite difficult. In a single-employer environment, these employees are simply considered to have terminated employment. In a multiemployer environment, the employees continue to be eligible and earn vesting credit.
3. Investment options may be designed to allow socially responsible investing; that is, "union only" funds may be an option.
4. The collective bargaining agreement will specify the individual employer as responsible for administrative tasks, such as maintaining employee deferral elections, withholding contributions, and forwarding contributions to the plan trustees.
5. Although delinquencies do not have an impact on an employee's benefit in a defined benefit plan, they are of critical importance in a 401(k) plan. Also, delinquencies are more likely to occur in a multiemployer environment.
6. The handling of start-up costs may be difficult; in some cases, the union may borrow money from the bank to cover start-up costs.

Note. If start-up costs are deducted from trust assets, the rate of return on investments in the first year may be negative or extremely low, creating a negative impression of the 401(k) plan on the participants.

Multiple-Employer Plans

Multiple-employer plans (MEPs) are plans where a group of employers participate in a single 401(k) plan, usually with the goal of reducing overall plan cost and minimizing fiduciary exposure. The concept of using MEPs has gained popularity in recent years as a way to encourage more small employers to offer their employees a 401(k) plan; however, the rules regarding MEPs are not as well defined as the rules for traditional 401(k) plans.

Q 1:39 How do multiple-employer plans work?

In a MEP there is a lead employer who generally takes responsibility for administering the plan and acting as the plan's named fiduciary. Historically, the lead employer has been either a trade association or a professional employee organization (PEO)—a company that allows employers to outsource benefits and other employee management costs by becoming the employer of record for tax purposes. Employers that are members of the trade association or customers of the PEO can then join the MEP as participating employers.

Q 1:40 What are the benefits to participating employers of joining a MEP?

The key benefits are reductions in administrative costs and reduction in fiduciary liability. A MEP that is considered a single-employer plan (see Q 1:42) will have a single plan document and file a single Form 5500, and the lead employer generally will handle plan administration activities for all participating employers. Also, the lead employer will typically select and monitor the plan's investments, so that participating employers have limited exposure to fiduciary liability.

Q 1:41 What is an "Open MEP"?

An *open MEP* is a MEP in which there is no common bond or preexisting relationship among the participating employers other than sharing the same service providers for the plan.

Q 1:42 What legal concerns arise with Open MEPs?

Under the Employee Retirement Income Security Act (ERISA), *pension benefit plans* (which include 401(k) plans) must be established or maintained by an employer or an employee organization, such as a labor union. The term "employer" is defined for this purpose to include any person acting directly as an employer, as well as a group or association acting for an employer in relation to a benefit plan. In determining whether such a group or association exists, the Department of Labor (DOL) considers the following factors:

- How members of the association are solicited;
- Who is eligible to participate and who actually participates;
- The process by which the association was formed;
- Preexisting relationships among members; and
- Degree of control that participating employers have over the retirement program.

The DOL has concluded that Open MEPs in which the only commonality among members is the hiring of a common service provider to administer the MEP are *not* single-employer sponsored plans under ERISA. [ERISA §§ 3(2), 3(4), 3(5); DOL Adv. Op. 2012-03A; DOL Adv. Op. 2012-04A]

Q 1:43 What is the practical significance of the DOL's ruling that Open MEPS are not single-employer sponsored plans?

The key significance of the DOL's ruling is that each participating employer in an Open MEP must file a separate Form 5500, including a separate accountant's opinion for large plan filers. It is not clear whether participating employers are required to file amended returns for years prior to 2012 when the status of Open MEPS was not clearly defined.

While not specifically addressed in the Advisory Opinions, treating each participating plan in an Open MEP as a separate plan may also mean that ERISA's bonding requirements (see chapter 5) would need to be met separately for each participating plan.

The 2012 Advisory Opinions did not challenge the tax-qualified status of Open MEPs or the ability to delegate administrative and fiduciary functions to a common service provider, although each participating employer retains fiduciary responsibility for the selection and monitoring of the service provider.

The bottom line is that although the 2012 Advisory Opinions eliminated a key advantage for participating employers in Open MEPS (i.e., the avoidance of filing a separate Form 5500), there are still administrative efficiencies and fiduciary risk management benefits available to employers that participate in an Open MEP.

Market for and Utilization of 401(k) Plans

This section deals with the use of 401(k) plans as employee benefit plans by large and small employers throughout the country.

Q 1:44 How many 401(k) plans and participants are there in the United States?

According to the 2015 SPARK Marketplace Update, there are now more than 526,000 401(k) plans in the United States.

Q 1:45 What are average participation rates in 401(k) plans?

According to a survey by Profit Sharing Council of America, *PSCA's 57th Annual Survey of Profit Sharing and 401(k) Plans*, 80.3 percent of employees eligible to participate in a 401(k) plan in 2013 made contributions to the plan.

Q 1:46 Does the fact that a 401(k) plan offers a matching employer contribution noticeably affect 401(k) participation?

Yes, although the most significant difference occurs between having no match at all versus having some match. Changes in the level of matching contributions do not tend to significantly impact participant behavior. According to the PSCA survey (see Q 1:45), the most common level of match used is $0.50 per $1.00 of salary deferral contributions to a maximum of 6 percent of compensation.

Future of 401(k) Plans

What does the future hold for 401(k) plans? Will they continue to be a popular employee benefit? Will they eventually replace defined benefit plans as the primary employer-sponsored retirement plan vehicle? Will 401(k) plans become available to all employees? The market downturn that began in 2008 had a significant impact on 401(k) plan account balances. Those losses, particularly when combined with the declining ability of either defined benefit plans or Social Security to meet the retirement income needs of employees, have prompted a high level of scrutiny on the value of 401(k) plans. Hearings have been held in Congress and many proposals have been submitted on how to improve savings in 401(k) plans and/or add new retirement savings vehicles to enhance our country's readiness for retirement. It is impossible to know what the outcome of the various proposals will be or how they will impact 401(k) plans. However, by looking at various trends—legislative, economic, and demographic—it is possible to make some reasonable guesses about 401(k) plans in the future.

Q 1:47 How are demographic trends affecting 401(k) plans?

The workforce of today is vastly different from that of earlier decades. Some of the demographic trends that affect 401(k) plans are:

1. *More women, minorities, and foreign-born nationals in the workforce.* As the workforce becomes more diversified, there is greater need for flexible schedules and benefits.
2. *Aging workforce.* The workforce is aging, and with increased age comes an increased cost in benefits, particularly in health and defined benefit plans. The increased life expectancy of the average retiree has staggering implications in terms of future health care costs.
3. *More participant involvement in benefit plans.* The workforce of today wants more choice, and a greater percentage than ever feel that they must bear a portion of the responsibility for providing retirement benefits for themselves. Few employees expect Social Security to be a major source of their retirement income.

Q 1:48 What economic trends are affecting 401(k) plans?

The economic trends that affect 401(k) plans include the following:

1. *Health care costs and reform.* The explosion in health care costs and the structural changes in the health care services industry are forcing many employers to reevaluate their employee benefits. There is a great push to control costs and increase the bottom line while at the same time increasing productivity. Any means of leveraging employee benefits for financial gain will be a possibility for financially strapped companies: cost sharing by employees, reduction of benefits, and consolidation of retirement plans.

2. *Increased utilization of asset allocation funds.* According to the Profit Sharing Council of America's survey, *PSCA's 57th Annual Survey of Profit Sharing and 401(k) Plans,* 66.6 percent of plans offer a target date fund and 15.9 percent of plans offer a target risk fund. This trend is likely to continue with the fiduciary protection available to plan fiduciaries using funds in this category as their default fund option (see chapter 7). Increased exposure to equities and use of age-based formulas to determine asset allocation may increase account balances of 401(k) plan participants over time.
3. *Low retirement savings rates.* In spite of the growth and popularity of 401(k) plans and the efforts of plan sponsors and plan service providers in educating employees about the need to save, a stubborn 25 percent or so of eligible employees still do not participate, and the savings rate for those who do is nowhere near what is needed to generate sufficient income replacement at retirement. This reality has generated a great deal of interest in automatic enrollment and automatic deferral increase plans, whereby employees would end up saving unless they proactively took steps to *avoid* contributing to a 401(k) plan. This type of plan design will become more prevalent in the future.
4. *Increased access to investment options providing guaranteed lifetime income.* Traditionally, 401(k) plans have been viewed more as a savings account than as a source for providing monthly income that is guaranteed for life. However, as participants, plan sponsors, and the government have become more concerned with retirement income adequacy, there has been a growing interest in making guaranteed lifetime income available through 401(k) plan investments. The DOL and the Treasury Department issued a Request for Information in 2010 seeking to understand how these types of investment products might be better integrated into 401(k) plans and/or made available for distributions from 401(k) plans. In 2012 and again in 2014, the Treasury Department issued several pieces of guidance designed to increase the availability and utilization of guaranteed income solutions by defined contribution plan participants. There has also been significant product development by the industry to come up with solutions that provide guaranteed income for life without giving up the flexibility and control most participants are accustomed to having over their account balance in a 401(k) plan. Continued development of regulatory initiatives as well as product enhancement in this area may be expected.

Q 1:49 What are the prospects for 401(k) plans?

With the publicity surrounding 401(k) plans and increased interest in sharing the responsibility for providing retirement benefits, employees of companies who do not sponsor a 401(k) plan have been clamoring for the addition of this plan to the benefits package. To the extent that the maximum 401(k) deferrals remain greater than IRA contributions, middle- and high-income employees will prefer 401(k) plans. Also, the relative availability of funds in a 401(k) plan through hardship withdrawals and loans makes the 401(k) plan an attractive alternative to an IRA.

Congress recognized the need to simplify the retirement plan rules and to some extent did so in the Small Business Job Protection Act of 1996 (SBJPA) and in the Economic Growth and Tax Relief Reconciliation Act of 2001 (EGTRRA). With simplicity will come less flexibility. The availability of special tax treatment on lump-sum distributions will disappear entirely.

The widespread popularity of 401(k) plans has greatly increased the interest of financial institutions in capturing these benefit dollars. The competition for dollars will increase, driving down the cost of administration, as many financial institutions subsidize administrative costs in their full service packages. Larger companies will try to outsource their benefits administration as they critically evaluate the dollars spent for benefits.

Two other employee benefit programs, health insurance and defined benefit plans, will be competing with 401(k) plans for employers' benefit dollars. Health care costs for active employees and retirees will be steadily rising. As the baby boomer generation matures, the demand for defined benefit plans may start to rise and a resurgence of defined benefit plans could occur, for both the small and medium-sized employer.

Legislative and Regulatory Developments Affecting 401(k) Plans

The trend of overall pension policy since the 1990s has been to expand the availability of retirement plans to the workforce. Pension policy, in general, is that the federal government should not subsidize pensions for highly paid employees, and that if highly paid employees are covered, then a fair number of lower-paid employees must also be covered. The Tax Reform Act of 1986 (TRA '86) played a large role by tightening nondiscrimination standards, thus requiring more lower-paid employees to be benefited by employer-sponsored plans. When faster vesting is required, more employees become eligible for retirement plan benefits and expanded coverage is achieved.

Congress has done little to encourage the continuation of defined benefit plans over the last decade. Increased complexity in the form of the Omnibus Budget Reconciliation Acts of 1989 and 1990 (OBRA '89 and OBRA '90) has made plans more costly to administer. The increase in the reversion tax from 0 percent to 15 percent to its present maximum of 50 percent has made it more difficult to terminate defined benefit plans. The increase in the Pension Benefit Guaranty Corporation (PBGC) premiums from $1 per participant after the passage of ERISA in 1974 to an unlimited amount per participant has greatly reduced the attractiveness of these plans. For underfunded defined benefit plans, potential additional premiums have caused many plan sponsors to cease future accruals and look to defined contribution plans as a source of future retirement funds for their employees. Though Congress is currently looking at ways to simplify defined benefit plans, the cost structure of these plans is likely to continue to limit their broad use by employers.

The Pension Protection Act of 2006 continues the trend of encouraging the use of 401(k) plans and makes it potentially more expensive and difficult for an employer to sponsor a defined benefit plan.

The Economic Growth and Tax Relief Reconciliation Act of 2001

EGTRRA [Pub. L. No. 107-16, 115 Stat. 38] was signed into law by President George W. Bush on June 7, 2001. The law contains significant changes affecting 401(k) plans, most of which are designed to expand the use and value of 401(k) plans and to simplify their administration. It also contains many changes to the rules affecting IRAs and changes to the federal estate tax rules, which create planning opportunities.

The enactment of EGTRRA highlighted two legislative trends. One is to make defined contribution plans, including 401(k) plans, more attractive to employers and a potentially more valuable source of retirement savings to employees. The other is to blend the characteristics of individual retirement arrangements (IRAs) and employer-sponsored plans to allow employees maximum flexibility and opportunity to save for retirement.

Q 1:50 What are the key areas of change to 401(k) plans resulting from EGTRRA?

The provisions of EGTRRA affect individual dollar limits for employee contributions to a plan, deduction limits for employer contributions to a plan, the rules governing rollovers, IRA rules, rules designed to encourage use of 401(k) plans by small businesses, and rules simplifying plan administration.

Q 1:51 How has EGTRRA changed plan contribution and benefit limits?

Plan contribution and benefit limits are changed as follows:

- The elective deferral limit for 401(k) plans, 403(b) plans, and 457 plans was raised from $10,500 in 2001 to $11,000 in 2002, to $13,000 in 2004, $14,000 in 2005, and $15,000 in 2006. Thereafter it is adjusted for cost-of-living increases in $500 increments.
- The Section 415 annual additions dollar limit for 401(k) and other defined contribution plans was raised from $35,000 in 2001 to $40,000 in 2002, and to $41,000 in 2004. It has been adjusted for cost-of-living increases in $1,000 increments thereafter. The alternate limit of 25 percent of pay has been increased to 100 percent of pay.
- The SIMPLE plan limit increased from $6,500 in 2001 to $7,000 in 2002, to $9,000 in 2004, and to $10,000 in 2005. It has been adjusted for cost-of-living increases in $500 increments thereafter.

- The amount of compensation that can be taken into account when determining an employee's contribution limit was increased from $170,000 in 2001 to $200,000 in 2002, and is to be adjusted for cost-of-living increases in $500 increments thereafter.
- A special catch-up rule allows people age 50 or older to make additional contributions to a non-SIMPLE 401(k) plan. The catch-up contribution amount went up from $1,000 in 2002 in $1,000 increments through 2006, and it has been adjusted for cost-of-living increases in $500 increments thereafter. These additional contributions are not subject to limitations on contributions such as the ADP test and Code Section 415. However, if matching contributions are made with respect to these catch-up contributions, the match amount would be included in the actual contribution percentage (ACP) test. The catch-up rule in SIMPLE plans allowed for additional contributions of $500 in 2002, increasing in $500 increments until 2006, with adjustment for cost-of-living increases in $500 increments thereafter.
- The deferral limits between 401(k) plans and governmental 457 plans were no longer required to be coordinated beginning in 2002.
- The limit on the annual benefit payable from a defined benefit plan increased from $140,000 in 2001 to $160,000 in 2002 and it has been be adjusted for cost-of-living increases in $5,000 increments thereafter.

See chapter 9 for a more in-depth discussion of contribution limits applicable to 401(k) plans.

Q 1:52 How were employers' deduction limits for plan contributions changed by EGTRRA?

Employers' deduction limits for plan contributions were changed as follows:

- The 15 percent of pay limit on deductibility of employer contributions to a defined contribution plan increased to 25 percent of pay in 2002.
- Beginning with an employer's 2002 taxable year, the 25 percent of pay limit on deductibility is not reduced by any salary deferral contributions made by employees, and participant compensation used to calculate the 25 percent of pay limit is also not reduced by any elective contributions (e.g., salary deferral, cafeteria plans, etc.).
- Beginning with an employer's 2002 tax year, the employer may take a deduction for dividends reinvested in an ESOP pursuant to a participant's election.
- Deductions for contributions to a defined benefit plan are changed in two significant ways. The first relates to an employer's ability to deduct contributions to a defined benefit plan that is considered to be "fully funded." Under prior law, no deduction was available for contributions that exceeded 160 percent of a plan's current liability. With EGTRRA, the contribution limit increased to 165 percent in 2002 and 170 percent in 2003 before being eliminated entirely thereafter, such that the 2003 limit

became the excess of the plan's accrued liability over the plan's asset value. For PBGC covered plans, EGTRRA also eliminates the under-100-participant restriction for making contributions up to the unfunded current liability and, in the case of a terminating plan, the amount necessary to make the plan sufficient.

See chapter 9 for a more in-depth discussion of employer deduction limits.

Q 1:53 How were the rollover rules changed by EGTRRA?

Rollover rules changed as follows:

- Prior to EGTRRA, a rollover could occur from an IRA to a plan only if all the money in the IRA came from a qualified plan. There are also restrictions today on rollovers between plans qualified under Code Sections 401(a), 403(b), and 457. Effective for distributions after December 31, 2001, rollovers can occur between and among qualified plans under Code Section 401(a) (including 401(k) plans), governmental 457 plans, 403(b) annuity plans, and IRAs with individual contributions in them other than Roth IRAs.
- Prior to EGTRRA, any portion of a distribution that was nontaxable could not be rolled over. For distributions after December 31, 2001, after-tax amounts can be rolled from a qualified retirement plan into either an IRA or to a defined contribution plan that provides for separate accounting of the after-tax amounts.
- Prior to EGTRRA, the spouse of a deceased participant was entitled only to roll the death benefit into an IRA. For benefits distributed after December 31, 2001, spouses have the same rollover options as participants.
- EGTRRA created a hardship exception with respect to the 60-day limit on rollovers of cash distributions.
- Involuntary cash-outs in excess of $1,000 are now required to be rolled into an IRA rather than paid in cash. The effective date for this change will be determined after the DOL has prescribed safe harbor investments for this purpose.
- Effective for distributions after December 31, 2001, no portion of a hardship withdrawal, including taxable hardship withdrawals from sources other than salary deferrals, can be rolled over.

See chapter 16 for a more in-depth discussion of the rollover rules.

Q 1:54 How did EGTRRA change the rules for IRAs?

The rules for IRAs are changed as follows:

- The IRA contribution limit is increased from $2,000 in 2001 to $3,000 in 2002 through 2004, to $4,000 in 2005 through 2007, to $5,000 in 2008 and thereafter for cost of living in $500 increments. These limits apply to both Roth and traditional IRA contributions.

- Beginning in 2002, individuals age 50 or older can make an additional IRA contribution of $500 for each year between 2002 and 2005 and $1,000 thereafter.
- Beginning in 2006, qualified plans can be amended to allow for "Roth contributions" (i.e., after-tax contributions for which no tax on the principal or earnings is due at the time of distribution). To avoid tax on the distribution, it must be made after five years and age 59½ or because of death or disability.

See chapter 22 for a more in-depth discussion of IRAs.

Q 1:55 How did EGTRRA encourage the use of qualified plans by small employers?

EGTRRA encouraged the use of qualified plans by small employers as follows:

- Beginning in 2002, the rule that participant loans are not available for partners and S Corporation shareholders is repealed.
- EGTRRA provides for a tax credit for the start-up costs of a retirement plan for small businesses. Employers with no more than 100 employees and with at least one non-highly compensated employee (NHCE) participating in the plan are allowed a credit of up to $500 for the first three years of the plan.
- Small businesses (as defined above) do not need to pay the IRS user fee for determination letter requests made after December 31, 2001, and within the first five years the plan is established.

Q 1:56 How did EGTRRA simplify the rules for plan administration?

EGTRRA simplified the rules for plan administration as follows:

- It revised the rules for top-heavy plans effective in 2002, including eliminating the five-year look-back rule for most purposes (see chapter 14).
- It eliminated the "same desk rule" restricting distributions from 401(k) plans in certain corporate transactions for distributions occurring after December 31, 2001 (see chapter 21).
- It repealed the multiple-use test for 401(k) contributions beginning in 2002 (see chapter 13).
- The rule requiring a 401(k) plan to suspend elective contributions for 12 months following a hardship withdrawal under the safe harbor rules was changed to reduce that period to 6 months beginning in 2002 (see chapter 15).
- Matching contributions in all 401(k) plans, regardless of whether they are top heavy, became subject to the same vesting rules (formerly the top-heavy rules) (see chapters 2 and 14).

Q 1:57 What was unique about the effective dates for EGTRRA?

The provisions of EGTRRA were scheduled to expire for years beginning after December 31, 2010, unless new legislation was passed extending the law. The Pension Protection Act of 2006, which was signed into law on August 17, 2006, made the provisions of EGTRRA affecting retirement plans permanent. (See Qs 1:58–1:64.)

The Pension Protection Act of 2006

The Pension Protection Act of 2006 [Pub. L. No. 109-280, 120 Stat. 780] (PPA) was signed into law by President George W. Bush on August 17, 2006. Well over 900 pages long, the PPA contains many changes for both defined benefit plans and defined contribution plans. One of the most important changes is the permanent extension of the changes to retirement plans and individual retirement arrangements (IRAs) made by EGTRRA in 2001 (see Qs 1:48–1:55). In addition, the PPA contains many changes impacting 401(k) plans. The highlights are discussed in this section (Qs 1:58–1:62).

Q 1:58 What changes did the PPA make to automatic enrollment plans?

The PPA created numerous new definitions, requirements, and opportunities for automatic enrollment plans (i.e., plans in which employees, unless they opt out automatically, become enrolled at deferral rates specified by the plans). The principal changes include:

- ERISA preemption of state wage garnishment laws [ERISA § 514(e)]
- A new nondiscrimination testing safe-harbor available only to automatic enrollment plans [I.R.C. § 401(k)(13)];
- A requirement that the DOL define a category of default funds that can qualify for ERISA Section 404(c) protection [ERISA § 404(c)(5)] (see chapter 7);
- An extension of time for returning excess ACP and ADP contributions [I.R.C. § 4979(f)];
- The option to return salary deferral contributions within 90 days of the first deferral payroll date if so requested by the participant [I.R.C. § 414(w)]; and
- New notice requirements for participants [I.R.C. § 414(w)(4)].

(See chapter 2 for further discussion of these changes and their effective dates.)

Q 1:59 What changes did the PPA make with respect to ERISA's fiduciary and prohibited transaction rules?

The changes made by the PPA to ERISA's fiduciary and prohibited transaction rules include:

- The creation of "Eligible Investment Advice Arrangements" (EIAAs), arrangements that enable participants to receive fiduciary-level investment advice, that allow financial advisors to be paid from the funds for which they are providing advice, and that relieve plan fiduciaries of liability for participant-level investment results [ERISA § 408(g)];
- The addition of statutory exemptions covering block trades, electronic trading, transactions with non-fiduciary service providers, cross trading, foreign exchange transactions, and securities or commodities transactions corrected within 14 days [ERISA § 408(b)(15-20)];
- The expansion of ERISA Section 404(c) protection to certain fund mapping transactions [ERISA § 404(c)(1)]; and
- A mandate that the DOL define, by regulation, default funds qualifying for relief under ERISA Section 404(c) when used in automatic enrollment plans [ERISA § 404(c)(5)].

See chapters 5 and 7 for further discussion of these changes and their effective dates.

Q 1:60 What changes did the PPA make to the rules concerning plan distributions or other withdrawals?

The PPA made a number of changes concerning distributions and other withdrawals from plans, including:

- Allowing a nonspouse beneficiary to roll over a plan distribution into an "inherited" IRA [I.R.C. § 402(c)(11)];
- Allowing rollovers directly from pre-tax 401(k), 403(b), or 457 accounts into Roth IRAs (provided the rollovers satisfy income limit and other rules) [I.R.C. § 408A(e)];
- Allowing rollover of after-tax accounts between different types of qualified plans as long as certain accounting requirements are satisfied [PPA § 824];
- Allowing hardship distributions to be made on account of financial hardship impacting the beneficiary of a participant [PPA § 826];
- Expanding options for distributions to reservists [I.R.C. § 72(t)]; and
- Requiring that plans subject to the joint and survivor annuity rules offer a second survivor annuity option [I.R.C. § 417].

See chapters 15, 16, and 17 for further discussion of these changes and their effective dates.

Q 1:61 What changes did the PPA make to ERISA's notice, reporting, and disclosure requirements?

The PPA made many changes to these requirements, including:

- New rules for the timing and content of participant statements, including a requirement that participants in participant-directed plans receive quarterly statements [ERISA § 105(a)];

- Changes to the distribution notice requirements, extending the time frame from 30 to 90 days, to 30 to 180 days, and requiring the inclusion of certain information that might impact a participant's decision to defer distributions [I.R.C. § 417(a)(6); ERISA § 205(c)(7)(A)];
- New notice requirements for automatic enrollment plans, certain plans offering employer stock as an investment option, plans using a Section 404(c) protected default fund, plans using the new automatic enrollment safe harbor, plans relying on Section 404(c) protection during fund mapping, and plans using the new prohibited transaction exemption for Eligible Investment Advice Arrangements;
- A new requirement for the DOL and plan sponsors to display certain Form 5500 information electronically [ERISA § 104(b)(5)];
- Elimination of the need for non-ERISA plans to provide blackout notices [ERISA § 101(i)(8)(B)];
- Raising the plan asset limit for Form 5500-EZ filing to $250,000 [PPA § 1103]; and
- Requesting the DOL to simplify reporting for plans with 25 or fewer participants [PPA § 1103].

See chapters 8 and 19 for further discussion of these changes and their effective dates.

Q 1:62 What changes did the PPA make to plans offering employer securities as an investment option?

A number of changes effected by the PPA are primarily designed to protect participants whose 401(k) accounts are overly invested in employer securities from having their retirement savings decimated. These changes include:

- Required diversification rights, with different requirements for employee and employer contributions, and including notice of those rights [I.R.C. § 401(a)(35)];
- An increase in the ERISA bond limit for plans holding employer securities [ERISA § 412(a)]; and
- The availability of catch-up IRA contributions (subject to certain conditions and restrictions) in the event the employer becomes bankrupt or is indicted [I.R.C. § 219(b)(5)].

See chapter 6 for further discussion of these changes and their effective dates.

Q 1:63 What other changes did the PPA make that significantly impact 401(k) plans?

Other changes made by the PPA that impact 401(k) plans include:

- Shortened maximum vesting periods for all employer contributions, from 5-year cliff or 7-year graded to 3-year cliff or 6-year graded [I.R.C. § 411(a)(2)] (see chapter 2);

- Creation of a combined defined benefit/401(k) plan design (see chapter 2);
- An enhanced Saver's Credit [I.R.C. § 25B] (see chapters 2 and 8);
- Elimination of the need to calculate gap-period earnings when distributing excess contributions due to failed actual deferral percentage (ADP) tests or actual contribution percentage (ACP) tests for plan years beginning January 1, 2008, or later [I.R.C. §§ 4979(f), 401(k)(8), 401(m)(6)(A)] (see chapter 18);
- Expansion of the rules regarding qualified domestic relations orders (QDROs) in situations where multiple orders are received [PPA § 1001] (see chapter 17);
- Amended contribution deduction limits when an employer maintains both a defined contribution plan and a defined benefit plan [I.R.C. § 404(a)(7)(C)] (see chapter 9).

Q 1:64 What are some changes made by the PPA that impact plans other than 401(k) plans?

Changes made by the PPA that impact plans other than 401(k) plans include:

- Establishment of a simple age discrimination standard for defined benefit plans;
- Elimination of some of the legal uncertainties surrounding cash balance or other hybrid plans;
- Clarification of the status of Indian tribal plans as governmental plans; and
- Exemption of all government plans from nondiscrimination and minimum participation rules.

These changes, along with other changes impacting retirement plans other than 401(k) plans, and effective dates for these changes, are discussed in chapter 22.

The Uniformed Services Employment and Reemployment Rights Act of 1994

Signed into law in 1994, the Uniformed Services Employment and Reemployment Rights Act (USERRA) [38 U.S.C. §§ 4301–4333] establishes certain rights and benefits for employees and duties for employers with regard to the employment, reemployment, and retention in employment of employees who serve or have served in the uniformed services. The key provisions of USERRA as they affect 401(k) plans are discussed in this section. USERRA is also discussed in chapters 9 and 16.

Q 1:65 What action must an employee take in order to secure reemployment rights under USERRA?

Depending on the length of the employee's period of service, the employee is generally entitled to report back to work or apply for reemployment from 1 to 90 days following the end of military service. Upon reemployment, the employee will not be considered to have had a break in service by reason of his or her absence, and the employee's military service will be treated as service for purposes of vesting as well as for meeting any hours worked requirement to accrue a right to share in any employer contribution. [20 C.F.R. § 1002.259]

Q 1:66 Does the rehired employee have the opportunity to make elective deferral contributions with respect to the period of military service?

Yes, the rehired employee must be permitted to make additional elective deferrals up to the maximum amount that he or she could have made during the period of military service had the individual continued to be employed by the employer. The employee has a period of time equal to three times his or her period of military service to make the additional elective deferrals, but in no event can that period of time end later than five years after the employee's date of reemployment. [I.R.C. § 414(u)(2)]

Q 1:67 What compensation is taken into account in determining the rehired employee's additional elective deferrals?

In determining the rehired employee's compensation, the plan will use the rate of pay that the employee would have received but for the period of military service. If the rate of pay he or she would have received is not reasonably certain, the plan will use the average rate of compensation during the 12-month period prior to the period of military service. [I.R.C. § 414(u)(7)]

Q 1:68 What contributions must the employer make?

The employer is required to make all employer contributions the rehired employee would have been entitled to receive had his or her employment not been interrupted by military service and the contributions would be based on compensation as described above (see Q 1:67). In general, the employer must fund those contributions no later than 90 days after the date of reemployment or the date employer contributions are normally due for the year in which the service is performed. The employer is not required to make matching contributions unless the employee elects to make additional elective deferrals. [20 C.F.R. § 1002.262]

Q 1:69 Must employee and employer contributions be adjusted for earnings?

No, contributions are not required to be adjusted for earnings. In addition, the employer is not required to adjust the amount it contributes on behalf of the rehired employee on account of any forfeitures that may have been allocated during the employee's period of military service. [I.R.C. § 414(u)(3)]

Q 1:70 How are employee and employer contributions treated for testing purposes?

Employer and employee contributions are not taken into account for testing purposes for the plan year in which the amounts are actually contributed to the plan. Rather, they are taken into account for the years to which they are attributable; however, any additional elective deferrals and matching contributions made for those years will not cause the plan to fail the actual deferral percentage and actual contribution percentage tests (see chapter 13). [I.R.C. § 414(u)(1)]

The Heroes Earnings and Assistance Relief Tax (HEART) Act of 2008

The Heroes Earnings Assistance and Relief Tax (HEART) Act [Pub. L. No. 110-245, 122 Stat. 1624] was signed into law by President George W. Bush on June 17, 2008. The HEART Act made a number of changes that impact both retirement and welfare plan benefits available to military personnel. The key provisions that impact 401(k) plans are discussed in this section. Plan amendments reflecting HEART provisions were required to be made by the last day of the plan year beginning on or after January 1, 2010.

Q 1:71 How did the HEART Act change the rules regarding differential wage payments?

Differential wage payments are amounts employers voluntarily elect to pay to make up some or all of the difference between an employee's military pay and what they would have received had they not been called to active duty. Under the HEART Act, differential wage payments are treated as W-2 compensation, and the recipient of the payments is treated as being actively employed for most plan purposes (e.g., the ability to make 401(k) deferrals). The IRS issued guidance in 2010 on how differential wage payments should be treated for various purposes. Differential wage payments are counted for purposes of applying the annual additions limit under Code Section 415(c)(3) but need not be counted for purposes of determining contributions and benefits in a plan and can be excluded from the plan's definition of compensation without causing the plan to fall out of a safe harbor definition of compensation. [I.R.C. § 414(u)(12)(A); IRS Notice 2010-15, Qs 9 &10, 17, 2010-6 I.R.B. 390]

Q 1:72 How does the HEART Act impact the qualified reservist distribution rules?

The PPA created a rule allowing reservists called to active duty between September 11, 2001, and December 31, 2007, for a period of 180 days or longer to take a distribution from their 401(k) plan without being subject to the 10 percent early withdrawal penalty tax that applies to distributions made prior to age 59½. For a period of up to two years after returning from active duty, an employee may deposit any amounts distributed under this rule into an IRA without being subject to IRA limits. The HEART Act makes the exemption for qualified reservist distributions permanent. See chapter 16 for more details.

The HEART Act also gives plans the option of allowing persons who are on leave for qualified military service lasting 30 days or more to be treated as having a deemed severance of employment for purposes of the entitlement to receive a distribution from their salary deferral account. An individual who takes a distribution pursuant to this provision is prohibited from making elective deferral contributions for six months following the date of distribution. These deemed severance distributions are considered eligible rollover distributions unless an exception other than the "hardship" exception applies. [I.R.C. § 414(u)(12)(B); IRS Notice 2010-15, Qs 11–16, 2010-6 I.R.B. 390]

Q 1:73 How does the HEART Act change the rules regarding death and disability benefits available to military personnel and their beneficiaries?

Under the HEART Act, plans are required to treat participants who die while performing qualified military service on or after January 1, 2007, as if they had become re-employed on the day prior to their death. This rule allows the deceased participants' beneficiaries to take advantage of any additional benefits, such as accelerated vesting or incidental death benefits, that are available to participants who die while actively employed. Guidance issued by the IRS in 2010 clarified that when determining entitlement to any death benefits as referenced above, the period of the deceased participant's qualified military service is treated as service with the employer for vesting purposes. The 2010 guidance also clarified that if a participant would not have been entitled to reemployment rights if he or she had returned to employment immediately before death, the additional death benefits available under the HEART Act would not be available to the participant's beneficiaries. [I.R.C. § 401(a)(37); IRS Notice 2010-15, Qs 1–4, 2010-6 I.R.B. 390]

The HEART Act also permits plans to credit participants who die or become disabled while performing qualified military service to be credited with their period of military service for purposes of determining benefit accruals. The participant is treated as though he or she had returned to work on the day before his or death or disability and separated from service due to death or disability the next day. The employer would then be allowed to make contributions on behalf of the individual. The amount of any contributions made would be determined based on the employee's actual contributions during the 12-month period immediately preceding his or her period of qualified military service. For example, if an employee whose average deferral had been $200 per month for the requisite period dies after seven months of active duty, and the plan provides a 50 percent match, the employee would receive an additional $350 in matching contributions. In the case of a disabled participant who returns to service and makes elective deferral contributions with respect to periods of military service, plans have the option of using amounts deferred on account of the period of military service as the basis for determining the amount of employer contributions to the participant's account rather than amounts deferred during the 12-month period preceding military service.

This provision may be added to a plan as of any date on or after January 1, 2007, and must be applied in a nondiscriminatory fashion. Applying vesting credit during the period of military service is permitted, but not required, for this purpose. [I.R.C. § 414(u)(9); IRS Notice 2010-15, Qs 5–8, 2010-6 I.R.B. 390]

The Worker, Retiree, and Employer Recovery Act of 2008

The Worker, Retiree, and Employer Recovery Act of 2008 [Pub. L. No. 110-455] (WRERA) was signed into law by President Bush on December 23, 2008. The WRERA includes technical corrections to the Pension Protection Act of 2006 (PPA), as well as provisions designed to provide economic relief to both plan sponsors and plan participants in response to the economic downturn.

Q 1:74 What are the technical corrections to the Pension Protection Act of 2006 included in the WRERA?

The WRERA contained technical corrections to provisions of the PPA that impact 401(k) plans. The key changes are as follows:

Changes to Rollover Rules. The PPA created an option for plans to allow nonspousal beneficiaries to roll their distribution into an inherited IRA. The WRERA requires plans to offer this option for plan years starting on January 1, 2010 or later. The WRERA also provides some clarifications on rolling a Roth account from a qualified plan into a Roth IRA. (See chapter 16.)

QDIA Not Required for 90-Day Permissible Withdrawals. The PPA created new rules for automatic contribution arrangements (ACAs), including the ability for participants to have defaulted contributions returned if requested within 90 days. In order to include this permissible withdrawal feature, a plan had to meet the requirements of an eligible automatic contribution arrangement (EACA), which includes a requirement to use a qualified default investment alternative (QDIA) as the plan default fund. The WRERA eliminated the requirement that a QDIA must be used in plans incorporating the 90-day permissible withdrawal feature. The WRERA also extended the rule to SARSEPs and SIMPLE IRAs and clarified that permissible withdrawals can be disregarded in counting the salary deferral limit under Code Section 402(g). (See chapter 2.)

No Distribution of Gap-Period Earnings on Excess Deferrals. Gap-period earnings are earnings occurring between the end of a plan year for which a corrective distribution is being made and the date of actual distribution. The PPA eliminated the requirement to include gap-period earnings on distributions of excess contributions and excess aggregate contributions. The WRERA extended this relief to distributions of excess deferrals effective for distributions related to plan years starting January 1, 2008 or later. (See chapter 9.)

Synchronization of Definition of a One-Participant Plan. The PPA excluded one-participant plans from certain notice requirements, such as employer stock diversification and blackout notices. The WRERA clarified that the DOL definition of a one-participant plan applies for this purpose. (See chapter 19.)

For rules on when plan documents must be amended for the WRERA, see chapter 3.

Q 1:75 What new rules in the WRERA are designed to provide economic relief to 401(k) plan sponsors and participants?

The WRERA contains several provisions designed to provide economic relief to both plan sponsors and participants. Many of those provisions related to funding requirements for defined benefit plans. A key provision impacting 401(k) plans was the suspension of required minimum distributions (RMDs) or "70 distributions" that otherwise were due to be paid for 2009. Participants whose required beginning date (RBD) occurred in 2008 were still required to take their first payment by April 1, 2009. Payments that would have been RMDs but for the waiver may be eligible for rollover treatment if they otherwise qualify for rollover. (See chapter 16.)

The Dodd-Frank Wall Street Reform and Consumer Protection Act of 2010

The Dodd-Frank Wall Street Reform and Consumer Protection Act [Pub. L. No. 111-203] (Dodd-Frank Act) was signed into law by President Obama on July 21, 2010. The text of the Dodd-Frank Act contains far-reaching changes that affect many aspects of the financial markets. Its impact on 401(k) plans is not entirely clear and may not be apparent until the regulatory agencies complete their work of interpreting its various provisions.

Q 1:76 What impact will the Dodd-Frank Act have on 401(k) plans?

There are many provisions of the Dodd-Frank Act that could impact 401(k) plans, but until further guidance is issued by the regulatory agencies charged with interpreting and implementing the Act, it is too soon to tell what that impact might be. Some concerns that have been raised are:

- Whether the newly created Consumer Financial Protection Agency will exercise any jurisdiction over service providers or activities in the 401(k) marketplace.
- Whether plans that use swaps or other derivatives as a component of any plan investment will be subject to additional requirements that may increase the cost and decrease the efficiency of these investments.
- Whether stable value funds will be characterized as using swaps and therefore are subject to new requirements. They will not be treated as such initially, pending a review by the Securities and Exchange Commission (SEC) and the Commodities Futures Trading Commission (CFTC).

- Whether brokers will be held to the same fiduciary standard as advisors. The SEC is reviewing this issue.

The SEC released a report recommending that a uniform standard of care be implemented. (See Q 1:81 for further information on this report.)

Some guidance was provided in final rules issued by the Commodity Futures Trading Commission (CFTC) on business conduct standards for SWAP dealers, but many questions remain outstanding.

The American Taxpayer Relief Act of 2012

The American Taxpayer Relief Act of 2012 (ACT) [Pub. L. No. 112-240, 126 Stat. 2313] was signed into law by President Obama on January 2, 2013. ACT contained a number of provisions intended to increase tax revenues, including an expansion of Roth in-plan conversions.

Q 1:77 How did ACT expand in-plan Roth conversion opportunities?

ACT allows participants who have a pre-tax retirement account in a 401(k), 403(b), or governmental 457(b) plan to convert some or all of their pre-tax account to a Roth account inside the plan. The plan document would need to permit both Roth contribution accounts and the ability to make these in-plan conversions, but the participant would not need to be eligible for a distribution of the converted amounts. This is an expansion of the prior rule, which allowed for in-plan conversions only of amounts otherwise available for distribution under the terms of the plan. Since the converted amounts would not be eligible for distribution, the tax cost of the conversion would need to be paid from other funds. See chapter 18 for a discussion of this new Roth conversion opportunity.

Establishment of MyRA Accounts

In 2015 President Obama created through Executive Order a new retirement vehicle, the MyRA Account. See chapter 22 for more information about these accounts.

Proposed Legislation and Regulatory Developments

Q 1:78 What proposals are the Obama administration considering?

President Barack Obama's proposed fiscal year 2016 budget contained three key provisions potentially impacting 401(k) plans: setting an accumulation cap, putting a 28 percent cap on tax deductions and exclusions from income, and introducing automatic payroll deduction IRAs.

Cap on Retirement Plan Accumulations

The accumulation cap would limit the amount any individual could accumulate in a tax-favored retirement account, which includes IRAs, defined contribution plans, and defined benefit plans, to the lump-sum amount needed to purchase the maximum annuity benefit available from a defined benefit plan. The current annuity limit is $210,000, but that limit is adjusted annually for inflation. The lump-sum amount needed to purchase this annuity was calculated at $3.4 million in the president's budget but varies as interest rates change. In the current low interest rate environment, an increase in interest rates would decrease the lump-sum cost of purchasing an annuity, thereby effectively decreasing the accumulation limit. Amounts contributed in excess of the accumulation limit would need to be returned under rules similar to the rules that apply to excess deferrals. Excess accumulations that occur solely as the result of investment earnings and gains would not need to be returned.

28 Percent Cap on Deductions and Exclusions

This proposal would limit the value of certain deductions or exclusions from income for taxpayers in the 33 percent, 35 percent, or 39.6 percent tax brackets to 28 percent. For example, if a taxpayer in the 35 percent tax bracket had $100,000 in deductions and exclusions, the value of those tax advantages would be limited to $28,000 instead of the $35,000 they would be worth under current tax law. The types of deductions and exclusions counted toward the 28 percent cap are broad-based and include many non–benefit-related items, such as the mortgage interest rate deduction. They also include contributions to defined contribution plans and IRAs, as well as employer-sponsored health insurance costs paid for by employers.

Automatic IRA Proposal

This proposal would require any employer that has at least 10 employees and has been in business for at least two years to facilitate payroll deduction contributions into IRAs for the employees unless it offered some other type of qualified retirement plan. Contributions would be set at a 3 percent default rate, but employees could opt out or change the contribution rate. Employers could designate a single IRA trustee or custodian or let employees pick their own. A default investment fund, as well as a handful of standard, low-cost investment alternatives in which employees could actively invest, would be specified by statute or regulation. Employers with fewer than 100 employees would receive a tax credit to offset the cost of setting up the automatic IRA arrangement and also could receive a more generous tax credit if they choose to start up a qualified plan instead of offering automatic IRAs.

Q 1:79 What significant new guidance has the Treasury Department issued?

The Department of the Treasury has issued recent guidance in the following areas:

Updating the Employee Plans Compliance Resolution System (EPCRS). The IRS updated its programs allowing plan sponsors to voluntarily correct plan qualification defects (see chapter 20), including making the program available to 403(b) plans (see chapter 22).

The following items are new since the 2015 Edition of this book was published.

Changes to Special Tax Notice. The IRS amended its language in the safe-harbor tax notice given to participants who become eligible for a plan distribution (see chapter 18)

Rules on Allocation of Taxable and Nontaxable Amounts. The IRS clarified how to determine taxable and nontaxable amounts in the context of multiple distributions (see chapter 18).

Deferred Annuities in Target Date Funds. The IRS clarified treatment of deferred annuities as an investment in a target date fund under the "benefits rights and features" rule (see chapter 6).

Substantiation of Hardship Withdrawals. In unofficial guidance, the IRS discussed its views on the process and documentation required to substantiate eligibility to receive a hardship withdrawal (see chapter 15).

Plan Document Issues. The IRS updated its determination letter and submitter programs, including changing its user fees (see chapter 3).

The following items were identified in earlier editions of this book.

Elimination of IRS Letter Forwarding Program. The IRS no longer assists plan sponsors, through its letter forwarding program, to locate plan participants who have plan benefits but who cannot be located at their last known address.

Establishment of Prototype Document Program for 403(b) Plans. Section 403(b) plans were first subject to a written plan document requirement for 2009 plan years. The IRS recently established a prototype program for 403(b) plan documents (see chapter 22 for detailed discussion of this program).

In-Plan Roth Rollovers and Roth Availability in 457 Plans. The IRS issued guidance regarding converting a pre-tax account into a Roth IRA via an in-plan rollover (see chapter 18) and allowing governmental 457 plans to offer Roth accounts (see chapter 22). Additional guidance on in-plan Roth rollover of pre-tax amounts not eligible for distribution was published in 2014 (see chapters 2 and 18).

Other Rollover Guidance. The IRS issued guidance limiting IRA-to-IRA rollovers to one rollover per year per individual (see chapter 22) and provided guidance intended to ease the administrative burden of plan-to-plan rollovers (see chapters 2 and 22).

Guidance on Lifetime Income. The IRS provided guidance on when investment in a deferred annuity contract triggers application of the Qualified Joint and Survivor Annuity and Qualified Preretirement Annuity rules (see chapter 17). It also provided guidance exempting certain longevity annuity contracts from the requirements of the minimum distribution rules (see chapter 16). This guidance was finalized in 2014.

Changes to Savers Credit Rules and Limits. These changes are covered in chapter 8.

Guidance on Treatment of Same-Sex Spouses. The IRS published guidance defining the term "spouse" for purposes of benefits offered under federal law as well as guidance on operational compliance and plan amendment deadlines for compliance with the Supreme Court decision striking down prior law that limited the definition of a spouse to same-sex couples (see chapter 17).

Guidance on Mid-Year Suspension or Elimination of Safe-Harbor Contributions. The IRS published a final rule establishing guidelines for when and how this is permitted without jeopardizing a plan's tax qualified status (see chapter 2).

Q 1:80 What significant new guidance has the Department of Labor issued?

The following items are new since the last edition of this book was published.

Definition of Fiduciary Rule. In April 2015, the DOL published a proposed rule redefining when someone becomes a fiduciary as a result of providing investment advice for a fee (see chapter 5). Along with the proposal the DOL published two new prohibited transaction exemptions (PTEs) and amended a number of existing ones (see chapter 5). The rule contains a number of "carve outs," one of which is for providing information that is considered education, not fiduciary advice (see chapter 8).

Timing for Delivery of Annual Participant Fee and Service Disclosure. In 2015, the DOL published guidance allowing for flexibility in the timing of providing the annual update to the participant fee and investment disclosure (see chapter 19).

Brokerage Window Request for Information. The DOL is seeking information on whether additional guidance is needed to protect participants investing through a brokerage window (see chapters 6 and 19).

Locating Missing Participants. With the elimination of both the IRS and Social Security locater services, the DOL published guidance explaining a plan fiduciary's responsibilities in connection with locating missing participants in terminating plans (see chapter 21).

Annuity as Cash Component of QDIA Fund. In a letter to Treasury, the DOL clarified that an annuity product contained in a target date fund does satisfy the requirement for a QDIA fund to be partially invested in cash (see chapter 7).

The following items were added in prior editions of the book.

Final Rule on Service Provider Fee Disclosure

The DOL issued a final rule on disclosures that prospective service providers must make to the hiring plan fiduciary regarding their fees and services (see chapter 4). The original effective date for the rule was July 16, 2011, but it was extended to July 1, 2012.

Proposed Rule on Service Provider Fee Disclosure Guide. The DOL's final rule on service provider fee disclosure contained a sample guide but did not mandate its use. In 2014 the DOL published a proposed rule that would mandate use of a guide for some disclosures (see chapter 4).

Final Rule on Participant Investment and Fee Disclosures. The DOL issued a final rule on information that must be provided to participants in participant-directed plans regarding fees, services, and investment options. The DOL also issued a Technical Release creating a special electronic delivery rule for the new participant disclosures. In May 2012, the DOL issued a Field Assistance Bulletin providing additional guidance on how to comply with various aspects of the participant disclosure rule (see chapter 19).

Target Date Fund Disclosures. The DOL issued a proposed rule on new disclosures for target date funds in QDIA notices (see chapter 7) and in participant investment and fee disclosures (see chapter 19).

Target Date Fund TIPS for Plan Fiduciaries. The DOL published an educational document designed to assist plan fiduciaries in establishing a prudent process for the selection and monitoring of target date funds (see chapter 5).

Guidance on Open Multiple-Employer Plans. The DOL issued two Advisory Opinions clarifying the circumstances under which a multiple-employer plan can be treated as a single plan for ERISA purposes (see Q 1:39).

Advanced Notice of Proposed Rulemaking on Lifetime Income Illustrations. The DOL published a proposal for including lifetime income illustrations on participant statements (see chapter 19).

Definition of When Revenue Sharing Becomes Plan Assets. The DOL published an Advisory Opinion explaining when revenue sharing payments become plan assets in the context of ERISA Spending Accounts (see chapter 4).

Guidance on Treatment of Same-Sex Couples. The DOL provided guidance on when an individual is considered a spouse for federal law purposes (see chapter 17).

Q 1:81 What other significant guidance has been issued affecting 401(k) plans?

Other significant guidance affecting 401(k) plans include the following:

Participant Disclosures in Non-ERISA Plans. The SEC published guidance allowing for relief from certain securities laws when participant fee and investment disclosures are provided in non-ERISA plans (see chapter 22).

Uniform Fiduciary Standard of Care for Brokers and Advisors. The Dodd-Frank Wall Street Reform and Consumer Protection Act [Pub. L. No. 111-203] (Dodd-Frank Act), which became law in 2010, required the SEC to conduct a study to determine whether a uniform standard of care should apply to both brokers and investment advisers (RIAs) under federal securities law. The SEC released its report on January 22, 2011 (see Q 1:82).

Proposed Rule on Target Date Fund Disclosures. In June 2010, the SEC issued proposed rules on information required in marketing materials for target date funds. In April 2014, the SEC reopened the comment period on this proposed rule in order to evaluate possible amendments to it (see chapter 6).

Proposed Changes to 12b-1 Fees. In July 2010, the SEC issued a proposed rule that would limit 12b-1 fees in mutual funds. The proposed rule contains other options that funds can use to charge investors for marketing, servicing, and ongoing sales expenses (see chapter 6).

Changes to Money Market Funds. The SEC published a rule that would require a floating NAV for some money market funds as well as set limits and/or impose fees on redemptions in certain circumstances (see chapter 6).

Supreme Court Ruling on the Defense of Marriage Act (DOMA). The U.S. Supreme Court ruled that the section in DOMA limiting the definition of marriage to a union of two persons of opposite gender for federal law purposes was unconstitutional and struck it down (see chapter 17).

Q 1:82 What did the SEC report recommend regarding a uniform standard of care for brokers and advisers?

The SEC report concluded that a uniform fiduciary standard of conduct, no less stringent than the standard that currently applies to advisers, should apply to both broker-dealers and investment advisers who provide personalized investment advice to retail investors. The report also recommended that the regulation of financial service providers be harmonized. Further study is required to determine which entity or entities should provide oversight and what rules should apply.

Currently, brokers are regulated by the Financial Industry Regulatory Authority Inc. (FINRA) and RIAs are regulated by the SEC in accordance with the Investment Advisers Act of 1940. RIAs are held to a fiduciary standard, which requires them to put the interests of the client first, and brokers are held to a suitability standard, which requires them to take into account the client's financial status, objectives, and so forth when making recommendations but does not prohibit conflicts of interest. These standards are independent of fiduciary standards under the Employee Retirement Income Security Act of 1974 (ERISA), and the study does not address when a broker or adviser may be considered an ERISA fiduciary.

The next step in the process is for the SEC to conduct rulemaking to implement the recommendations. The report outlined numerous areas where rulemaking would be required, but also stated that the result of any changes should minimize cost and disruption and ensure that retail investors would continue to have access to various investment options, as well as choices for how to pay for investment advice. The SEC has not started a rulemaking process to implement its report.

Chapter 2

401(k) Plan Design

After deciding to establish a 401(k) plan, an employer must consider the design of the plan. Some aspects of plan design involve options that can be chosen by the employer; other aspects, however, are mandated by law if the 401(k) plan is to be considered qualified for favorable tax treatment under the Internal Revenue Code (Code). This chapter considers how employee demographics will affect plan design objectives and considers the design factors that most directly impact plan expenses and participation levels. It details the types of contributions, both employer and employee, that a 401(k) might contain and discusses the basic requirements a 401(k) plan must meet to be qualified. The chapter concludes with an explanation of design options for savings incentive match plans for employees (SIMPLEs), safe harbor 401(k) plans, and eligible combined plans.

Design Options and Objectives 2-2
Options That Impact Plan Expenses 2-3
Options That Impact Plan Participation 2-6
Types of 401(k) Plan Contributions and Automatic
Contribution Arrangements 2-11
Elective Contributions 2-11
Automatic Enrollment Feature 2-14
Automatic Contribution Arrangements Under the Pension
Protection Act of 2006 2-15
Eligible Automatic Contribution Arrangements 2-16
Qualified Automatic Contribution Arrangements 2-19
Other Elective Deferral Issues and Considerations 2-23
Roth Contributions 2-26
Matching Contributions 2-27
Nonelective Contributions 2-29
Allocation Methods 2-31
Deemed IRA Contributions 2-40
Transfer or Rollover of Benefits 2-42
Basic Qualification Requirements 2-44
Formal Requirements 2-45

Continuing Contributions 2-47
Assignment of Benefits 2-48
Merger or Consolidation 2-49
Nondiscrimination Rules 2-50
Compensation and Benefit Limits 2-50
Distribution Requirements 2-51
Eligibility Rights 2-52
Break-in-Service Rules 2-55
Vesting Rules 2-58
Repayment Rights 2-65
SIMPLE 401(k) Plans 2-66
Safe Harbor 401(k) Plans 2-71
Eligible Combined Plans 2-83

Design Options and Objectives

Q 2:1 What elements of employee demographics should be considered in designing a 401(k) plan?

The employee population must be considered in designing a 401(k) plan, including the size of the workforce; the ages, pay levels, and financial status of employees; and the rate of employee turnover. In some cases, the demographics of the workforce may make the 401(k) plan unfeasible. However, in most cases, special features will be incorporated into the 401(k) plan to accommodate the needs of the workforce.

Q 2:2 How does the size of the workforce affect 401(k) plan design?

The size of the workforce is a critical element. If fewer than 100 employees earning over $5,000 will be eligible to participate, a SIMPLE individual retirement account (IRA) plan (discussed in chapter 22) may make the most sense because it will have far fewer administrative requirements than a 401(k) plan or even a SIMPLE 401(k). If the higher employer contribution cost and inflexibility of a SIMPLE IRA plan are not attractive to the smaller employer, a 401(k) plan should be considered. Among the factors for a small company to consider in deciding between a 401(k) and a SIMPLE IRA plan are the possibility of passing the nondiscrimination tests (see chapter 13) and the cost of administration. The start-up costs of a 401(k) plan will be considerably higher on a per-participant basis. Moreover, the sophistication of the employer's payroll system will be a factor. An inadequate payroll system can cause significant administrative problems.

For the small but growing employer, size may not be an issue. If the employer projects significant growth in the workforce in future years, the 401(k) plan will be a good vehicle for attracting new employees. The start-up costs of the 401(k) plan can be a good investment for the future.

Q 2:3 How do the pay levels of employees affect 401(k) plan design?

The relative pay levels of the employee base are also important considerations. If employees generally receive low pay, the employer may have significant difficulty in attaining a sufficient level of participation, and, as a result, limit the ability of highly compensated employees (HCEs) to make substantial deferrals to the plan (although this limitation can be eliminated if the 401(k) plan is a SIMPLE 401(k) or a safe harbor plan (see Qs 2:220–2:269)). If a significant percentage of the employees are highly paid (for example, in a firm employing professionals), the plan should be designed to encourage participation of the lower-paid to allow highly paid professionals a reasonable level of salary deferral.

The pay level of employees is not the only factor, however. If significant numbers of employees are members of dual-income households, even the lower-paid spouse may be interested in making significant contributions. For example, the higher-paid spouse may be working for a company that does not offer a 401(k) plan, while the lower-paid spouse has a 401(k) plan available and may be interested in deferring the maximum allowed in the plan.

Q 2:4 What is the impact of employee turnover on 401(k) plan design?

The amount of employee turnover is another consideration in designing a 401(k) plan. In industries with high turnover, a vesting schedule may be attached to employer contributions. This can also be handled, to some extent, by the use of a one-year waiting period before an employee is eligible to make contributions to the plan. The forfeitures that result when employees leave before becoming fully vested may be used to reduce future employer contributions, to pay administrative expenses, or to be reallocated to the remaining participants. Reallocation can be an attractive feature and can be used to reward employees for long service. Also, the use of vesting schedules can help encourage employees to remain in employment. A design that can help reduce turnover will be welcome, given the high cost of finding and training new employees.

Options That Impact Plan Expenses

Q 2:5 What financial considerations should an employer take into account before adopting a 401(k) plan?

An employer considering the adoption of a 401(k) plan must take its financial impact into account. The biggest portion of the cost of a 401(k) plan is employer contributions to the plan, whether they are matching contributions (see Qs 2:11–2:16, 2:86–2:93), nonelective contributions (see Qs 2:15–2:16, 2:94–2:119), qualified nonelective contributions (QNECs) (see Q 2:17 and chapter 13), SIMPLE 401(k) contributions, or safe harbor contributions (see Qs 2:52–2:68, 2:220–2:269). The employer needs to measure the level of its contributions on both an initial and ongoing basis. The employer will incur other costs as a result of adopting a 401(k) plan, including installation, enrollment, administration, and compliance costs. Estimating these costs will require decisions regarding the design, funding, and reporting frequency of the plan.

Q 2:6 How much will matching contributions cost?

It is useful to look at the cost of the match from two perspectives: the maximum exposure of the employer and the expected cost of the match. The maximum exposure of the employer is the maximum dollar expenditure if 100 percent of eligible employees contribute at least the amount necessary to receive the maximum matching contribution. Generally, the employer will limit the amount of an employee's salary deferral that will be matched; this is called a *match cap*. The maximum exposure of the employer can be computed by the following formula:

Covered payroll × matching percentage × match cap = Maximum exposure

> **Example.** Employer A has covered payroll of $4 million and wishes to provide a matching contribution of 25 percent of elective contributions up to the first 4 percent of pay. The maximum cost Employer A would incur can be calculated as
>
> $4,000,000 × 25% × 4% = $40,000

The maximum exposure of the employer for the matching contribution is, therefore, $40,000, or 1 percent of payroll.

Q 2:7 How is the expected cost of the match computed?

The employer will not generally have experience to draw on, but it can be estimated that the participation rate will be approximately 75 percent if the 401(k) plan has a matching feature. This 75 percent estimate can be adjusted in later years when the actual participation rate is known. The estimated cost can then be obtained by multiplying the maximum exposure by the expected participation rate.

> **Example.** In the example above (see Q 2:6), the expected cost Employer A would incur would be
>
> $4,000,000 × 25% × 4% × 75% = $30,000

Thus, $30,000, or 0.75 percent of payroll, is the expected cost of the employer for the matching contribution. The expected cost of the match will be a useful number for budgeting purposes, since this represents the amount that the employer anticipates spending.

Q 2:8 What other costs may be incurred in conjunction with a 401(k) plan?

In addition to matching contributions, the employer will incur other costs in setting up a 401(k) plan. There may be costs associated with the installation of a 401(k) plan. Installation costs can be reduced if a master or prototype plan or volume submitter plan is used. (See chapter 3.) If the employer uses an outside vendor for payroll processing, it is quite likely that payroll changes to accommodate 401(k) deferrals will be minimal.

Enrollment costs can also be a factor. Although the cost of enrollment materials and a consultant's time may be nominal, there may be costs to the employer of meetings for all employees. Enrollment costs may be highest at the time the plan is installed but will be ongoing as new employees become eligible for the plan. In some cases, re-enrollment meetings will be held to increase the participation of existing participants. Many employers have found that existing participants in the 401(k) plan can do an excellent job of "selling" the plan to their fellow employees.

Ongoing administrative costs should be factored in as well. The cost of participant recordkeeping can vary, depending on the size of the employer, the investment choices allowed the participants, and the frequency of reports. The trustees' fees for trust recordkeeping may be nominal or substantial, depending on the types of investments used in the plan. In some cases, the administrative costs will be deducted from plan assets, thus minimizing the employer's direct costs. However, caution should be used in this approach, as this could have a significant impact on the rate of return realized by employees in a new 401(k) plan. On the other hand, the impact of deducting costs from plan assets in an existing 401(k) plan with substantial assets should be minimal. If the employer chooses to pay fees directly, such costs will be tax deductible.

Finally, the compliance costs should be taken into account. How will ongoing compliance with legislative and regulatory changes be assured? Who will handle 401(k) and 401(m) nondiscrimination and top-heavy testing, and how much will it cost?

Q 2:9 Should plan expenses be paid from plan assets?

If expenses are paid from plan assets, they reduce the rate of return and the value of the participant's account at retirement. If the goal is to maximize retirement values, expenses paid from plan assets should be minimized. On the other hand, there are costs associated with offering a plan, and it is not uncommon for the trust to bear at least some of the cost. See chapter 4 for special considerations under the Employee Retirement Income Security Act of 1974 (ERISA).

Q 2:10 Can plan expenses be used by the employer as a credit against taxes owed by the employer?

Yes. In the case of a new plan sponsored by an employer that has fewer than 100 employees earning over $5,000, 50 percent of the qualified start-up costs for each of the first three years of the plan may be taken as a credit against federal income taxes. However, the credit for each such year cannot exceed $500. Qualified start-up costs are those paid in connection with the establishment or administration of the plan or the retirement-related education of employees who participate in the plan. [I.R.C. § 45E]

Options That Impact Plan Participation

Q 2:11 What is the impact of matching contributions on plan participation?

Surveys consistently confirm that matching contributions can have a significant impact on participation in a 401(k) plan. Once the decision is made to make matching contributions, the employer must choose whether contributions will be fixed or discretionary (see Q 2:12) and whether matching contributions will be ongoing or made at year's end (see Q 2:13). These decisions will affect plan participation.

Q 2:12 Should matching contributions be fixed or discretionary?

The uncertainty as to whether a match will be made or about the level of the match does not provide a good incentive for employees to participate; a matching contribution will be most effective when the level is fixed. It may make sense to start with a modest match (e.g., 25 percent of the first 4 percent of pay) and then increase it in future years. A common fixed matching rate is 50 percent of an employee's deferrals up to 6 percent of pay.

Q 2:13 Should matching contributions be ongoing or made at year's end?

In the majority of plans to which matching contributions are made, the employer makes them on an ongoing (monthly or payroll) basis—that is, at the same time participant deferrals are made. This approach maximizes the visibility of matching contributions, as the employee will see them with each benefit statement. It also becomes a valuable communication tool in encouraging employee participation.

> **Example.** The Fence Post Company is installing a 401(k) plan with a matching contribution of 50 percent on deferrals up to 6 percent of pay. By setting the threshold of the match at 6 percent, the employer is encouraging lower-paid employees to contribute at least 6 percent to the plan. If the matching contributions are made on an ongoing basis, the 50 percent match may be viewed by employees as a guaranteed return of 50 percent on their 6 percent investment. Beyond this "guaranteed return" is the actual investment return, which should further enhance the value of the deferral.

If an employer chooses to have a discretionary match, this match will often occur at or after the end of the plan year, when profits are known.

Q 2:14 Should an employer that makes ongoing match contributions do true-up match contributions after the end of the plan year?

Some participants, nearly always highly compensated employees (HCEs), may reach the annual limit on elective deferrals long before the end of the plan year, and, in that case, match contributions cease for them once the limit is reached. A true-up match contribution is made after the end of the plan year to provide the match contribution that a participant would receive if he or she were to make deferrals throughout the plan year.

> **Example.** Bob, who is under age 50 and has a monthly salary of $20,000, defers $5,000 each month and reaches the 2015 elective deferral annual limit of $18,000 in April. His employer, Big Bucks, LLC, makes an ongoing match contribution of $0.50 for each dollar contributed by a participant, but the match is made only on deferrals up to 6 percent of pay. Bob receives match contributions totaling $2,400 ($600 in each of the months of January, February, March, and April). Big Bucks stops making match contributions when Bob hits the $18,000 limit on deferrals. Had Bob contributed the $18,000 evenly throughout the plan year, he would have received a match contribution of $7,200 (50 percent × $14,400 (Bob's deferrals up to 6 percent of his pay)). If Big Bucks' plan provides for true-up match contributions, Bob would receive a true-up matching contribution of $4,800 ($7,200–$2,400).

It should be noted that a true-up match contribution could also be due in situations other than the one described above. For example, a participant who defers at a high rate during certain portions of the plan year, but at a lower rate or not at all during the remainder of the plan year, might also be due a true-up match contribution.

Q 2:15 Why might an employer choose to make discretionary nonelective contributions to its 401(k) plan?

An employer may choose to supplement the employee elective contributions and employer matching contributions with discretionary nonelective contributions based on profitability or employer performance. More frequently, a 401(k) plan containing only elective contributions will be supplemented by discretionary nonelective contributions. The profit sharing element of discretionary nonelective contributions can provide significant performance incentives to participants. Because the contribution is totally discretionary, the employer can contribute or not, depending on budgetary constraints.

Q 2:16 How does the employer make a choice between allocating funds to matching contributions and allocating them to discretionary contributions?

Matching contributions will be contributed only to participants who choose to make elective contributions, while discretionary nonelective contributions will be allocated to all eligible employees. With limited resources, the employer may opt to direct more dollars to matching contributions (rather than discretionary nonelective contributions) to reward the employees who make elective contributions to the 401(k) plan.

Methods for allocating discretionary nonelective contributions are discussed later in this chapter (see Qs 2:101–2:119).

Q 2:17 How may qualified nonelective contributions be used in a 401(k) plan?

QNECs (discussed in depth in chapter 13) may be a feature in a 401(k) plan for a number of reasons:

1. The employer may wish to allow highly compensated employees (HCEs) the opportunity to defer a greater portion of their compensation by guaranteeing that the actual deferral percentage for non-highly compensated employees (NHCEs) will be equal to at least the level of the QNEC.

> **Example.** The Rolling Mill Corporation is concerned that participation in the 401(k) plan will be low for NHCEs. By making a QNEC equal to 2 percent of pay for all NHCEs, Rolling Mill will enable HCEs to defer at least 4 percent of pay. The 401(k) plan in this example should be able to easily satisfy the actual deferral percentage (ADP) test (discussed in chapter 13).

2. The QNEC may also be used to correct a problem with the ADP test. If it looks likely that the ADP test will not be met, a QNEC may be used to increase the actual deferral percentage for NHCEs. This will be, in some cases, a more viable alternative than refunding excess contributions to HCEs.

3. The QNEC may be used to provide top-heavy minimums for non-key employees in a top-heavy plan. Since non-key participants will generally have to be provided with a 3 percent of pay contribution from the employer, this may be done in the form of a QNEC. Using this approach will have a dual advantage: it will satisfy the top-heavy minimum requirement and assist the plan in passing the ADP test.

Q 2:18 Is access to plan funds important to encourage participation in 401(k) plans?

Probably. Surveys indicate that the vast majority of participants intend to use their 401(k) funds for retirement, but a large percentage also want these funds to be accessible for financial emergencies. To alleviate participants' concerns yet provide employees with incentive to participate, the majority of 401(k) plans provide for hardship withdrawals or loans, or both.

Q 2:19 Are there tax incentives available to lower-paid participants to encourage their participation in 401(k) plans?

Yes. An eligible individual will be allowed a credit against his or her taxes for a specified percentage of the individual's qualified retirement savings contributions up to $2,000 (*the saver's credit*). [I.R.C. § 25B] The IRS has prepared a sample notice explaining the credit that will need to be modified, however, to reflect cost-of-living adjustments (COLAs) in the dollar limits as explained in Q 2:20. [IRS Ann. 2001-106, 2001-44 I.R.B. 416]

Q 2:20 What is the amount of the saver's credit?

The amount of the credit is a function of the eligible individual's adjusted gross income (AGI) and filing status as set forth in the following table, which is the one in effect for calendar 2015.

Joint	*Head of Household*	*Other*	*Credit (Percentage of Retirement Savings Contributions)*
$0–$36,500	$0–$27,375	$0–$18,250	50%
$36,501–$39,500	$27,376–$29,625	$18,251–$19,750	20
$39,501–$61,000	$29,626–$45,750	$19,751–$30,500	10

> **Example.** Don contributes $3,000 of elective deferrals to his employer's 401(k) plan. His AGI for the year is $40,000, and he files a joint return. The amount of his credit against taxes is $300 ($3,000 × 10% = $300).

The dollar limits in the table will be adjusted for increases in the cost of living. [I.R.C. § 25B(b)(3)]

Q 2:21 Is the saver's credit permanent?

The saver's credit was scheduled to expire after 2006. However, the Pension Protection Act of 2006, which was signed into law on August 17, 2006, created new rules making the credit permanent.

Q 2:22 Who is an *eligible individual*?

An *eligible individual* is any individual who has attained age 18 by the end of his or her tax year. However, any person who is a student as defined in Code Section 151(f)(2) or who can be claimed as a dependent on another taxpayer's return is not eligible for the credit. [I.R.C. § 25B(c)]

Q 2:23 What is a *qualified retirement savings contribution*?

A *qualified retirement savings contribution* is the sum of an individual's contributions to a 401(k) plan, 403(b) plan, 457 governmental plan, and IRA.

Also included are voluntary employee contributions made to any qualified plan. [I.R.C. § 25B(d)(1)] The amount of qualified retirement savings contributions is reduced, however, by the amount of any taxable distributions received by the individual (or the individual's spouse, if filing jointly) from a plan or IRA that occur during the two previous tax years, the current tax year, and the period before the due date for filing the individual's tax return for the current year. [I.R.C. § 25B(d)(2)]

Q 2:24 Can an employer establish a 401(k) plan that will cover just one participant?

Nothing in the law prevents an employer from establishing a 401(k) plan that covers only one participant. In fact, because elective deferrals do not count toward the Code Section 404 deduction limit (25 percent of compensation), and because that limit is based on compensation before reduction for elective deferrals, a greater amount can be contributed to a one-person 401(k) plan than can be contributed to a profit sharing plan.

> **Example 1.** In 2015, The Solo Corporation has only one employee, Bill, age 48, who has annual pay of $100,000. If Solo adopts a profit sharing plan, the maximum amount that can be contributed and deducted for Bill is $25,000. Alternatively, Solo can establish a 401(k) plan to which it can contribute the same $25,000, but to which Bill can also contribute $18,000 of elective deferrals for a total contribution of $43,000.

> **Example 2.** The facts are the same as those in Example 1 except that Bill's compensation in 2015 is $40,000. If Solo makes a contribution for Bill to a profit sharing plan, the contribution would be limited to $10,000 (25% × $40,000). Alternatively, Solo can contribute the same amount to a 401(k) plan, which would allow Bill to contribute an additional $18,000.

Q 2:25 What special consideration applies to employers that, under the law, can maintain either a 403(b) plan or a 401(k) plan?

Many of the differences that once existed between these types of plans have been reduced with the issuance of final regulations under Code Section 403(b), especially in the case of a 403(b) plan that is subject to ERISA. For example, starting in 2009, Section 403(b) plans will be required to complete all items in Form 5500 and, if the 403(b) plan covers 100 or more participants at the beginning of the plan year, to have an audit. The big difference between them is that deferrals under a 401(k) plan must be tested for discrimination (see chapter 13) whereas deferrals under a 403(b) plan are not. This means added expense to perform discrimination testing and the possibility of refunds to HCEs unless the 401(k) plan is a SIMPLE 401(k) plan or is a safe harbor plan (see Qs 2:52–2:68, 2:220–2:269). See chapter 22 for more information.

Types of 401(k) Plan Contributions and Automatic Contribution Arrangements

Q 2:26 What types of contributions are generally found in a 401(k) plan?

A 401(k) plan will always include elective contributions (see Q 2:27) and may include bonus deferral contributions (see Q 2:76), matching contributions (see Q 2:86), or discretionary nonelective contributions (see Q 2:94). A 401(k) plan may also allow deemed IRA contributions to be made to the plan (see Q 2:120).

Elective Contributions

Q 2:27 What is an *elective contribution*?

An *elective contribution* is a contribution by an employer pursuant to and after an employee's cash or deferred election is made. [Treas. Reg. §§ 1.401(k)-1(a)(3), 1.401(k)-6] Elective contributions, other than the age 50 catch-up contribution described in chapter 9, are subject to discrimination testing under the ADP test (see chapter 13) unless the 401(k) plan is a SIMPLE 401(k) plan, a safe harbor 401(k) plan, or a 401(k) plan containing a qualified automatic contribution arrangement (QACA) (see Qs 2:52–2:68, 2:220–2:269).

Q 2:28 What is a *cash or deferred election*?

A *cash or deferred election* is any election made by an employee to receive in cash an amount that is not currently available or to have that amount contributed to a 401(k) plan. [Treas. Reg. § 1.401(k)-1(a)(3)(i)]

Q 2:29 Does a cash or deferred election include an arrangement under an employee stock ownership plan, pursuant to which dividends are either distributed or invested pursuant to the election made by the participant in accordance with Code Section 404(k)(2)(A)(iii)?

No. Such an arrangement under an employee stock ownership plan (ESOP) does not constitute a cash or deferred election. [Treas. Reg. § 1.401(k)-1(a)(2)(iii)]

> **Example.** John is a participant in the ESOP maintained by his employer, Marlin Fisheries. Under the terms of the ESOP, a participant may elect to receive dividends from the plan in cash or to reinvest them in employer securities. John elects to reinvest his dividends in additional employer stock. This election is not considered a cash or deferred election.

Q 2:30 May a contribution pursuant to a cash or deferred election be made before the performance of services with respect to which the contribution is made?

In general, any contribution made pursuant to a cash or deferred election must be made *after* the performance of services with respect to which the contribution is made. [Treas. Reg. § 1.401(k)-1(a)(3)(iii)(C)(1)] Presumably, any such anticipatory contribution would be treated as a nonelective (profit sharing-type) contribution.

Example. Computer Plus, Inc., a June 30 fiscal year taxpayer, sponsors a calendar-year 401(k) plan providing for immediate entry into the plan. Emily is hired and becomes a plan participant on May 1, 2015, and on that date elects to contribute 10 percent of her annual salary of $60,000. In anticipation of deferrals that Emily would make through the balance of calendar year 2015, Computer Plus, Inc. contributes $6,000 on behalf of Emily on May 1, 2015. Because the $6,000 contributed by her employer is in anticipation of Emily's future performance of services, that amount is not treated as an elective contribution.

Q 2:31 Is there an exception to the general rule that contributions made pursuant to a cash or deferred election will be treated as elective contributions only if made after the performance of services with respect to which the elective contributions are made?

Yes, there is an exception. It applies if elective contributions for a pay period are occasionally made before the performance of services for bona fide administrative considerations and not for the purpose of accelerating deductions. The regulation refers to the example of the temporary absence of a bookkeeper who is responsible for transmission of elective contributions. [Treas. Reg. § 1.401(k)-1(a)(3)(iii)(C)(2)]

Q 2:32 Is a one-time election to defer a specified amount or percentage of an employee's compensation considered a cash or deferred election?

No. Such an election will not be considered a cash or deferred election if it is irrevocable, is made no later than the employee's first becoming eligible, and has never been made previously with respect to another plan (whether or not terminated) maintained by the employer. The election applies to the plan in question and any other plan of the employer that is currently maintained or adopted in the future. [Treas. Reg. § 1.401(k)-1(a)(3)(v)]

Example. FLO Company sponsors a plan under which each employee, at the commencement of employment, must irrevocably specify what percentage or amount of his or her compensation will be contributed to the plan. Such an election will not be considered a cash or deferred election and the plan will not be considered a 401(k) plan. Contributions made pursuant to such an election will be considered nonelective contributions (see Q 2:94) and will be subject to the nondiscrimination rules applicable to nonelective contributions (see chapter 12).

Q 2:33 Will the dollar equivalent of a participant's unused paid time off that is contributed by an employer to a 401(k) plan be considered an elective deferral contribution?

It may, depending on the design of the arrangement. If the participant elects to receive the dollar equivalent of the unused paid time off (PTO) in cash or to have that amount contributed to the 401(k) plan, any amount contributed to the plan will be considered an elective deferral. On the other hand, if the dollar equivalent of the participant's unused PTO is automatically contributed to the plan, the contribution is considered a nonelective contribution (see Q 2:94). Because not all participants will have unused PTO at the end of the plan year, the latter design can result in a minimum coverage issue (see chapter 11) for the nonelective contribution component of the plan (because participants with no unused PTO may not have any nonelective contributions allocated to their accounts). In addition, allocations of the dollar equivalent of unused PTO will not result in allocations that are a uniform percentage of compensation, and that will require the plan to apply the general nondiscrimination test to determine whether the allocations discriminate in favor of HCEs (see chapter 12). Finally, having the dollar equivalent of unused PTO automatically contributed to the plan will require a plan amendment, and, in the case of prototype plans, could be problematic if the prototype is not sufficiently flexible to accommodate this design. [Rev. Rul. 2009-31, 2009-39 I.R.B. 395] The IRS has issued comparable guidance in the context of a participant who has unused PTO at the time he or she terminates employment. [Rev. Rul. 2009-32, 2009-39 I.R.B. 398]

Example 1. The Oak Leaf Company sponsors a 401(k) plan under which the dollar equivalent of a participant's PTO that is unused on December 31, 2015, under Oak Leaf's PTO plan will be contributed to the 401(k) plan. Kim, an employee of Oak Leaf, has 20 hours of unused PTO and is paid at the rate of $25 per hour. The dollar equivalent of the unused PTO ($500 (20 hours times $25)) is contributed by Oak Leaf on February 28, 2016, and allocated as of December 31, 2015, to Kim's nonelective account. The contribution will be considered an allocation for the 2015 plan year and will be taken into account in determining whether nonelective contributions made by Oak Leaf on account of that plan year meet the Code Section 410(b) minimum coverage requirements, whether the amount of such contributions are nondiscriminatory under Code Section 401(a)(4), and whether annual additions to Kim's account meet the requirements of Code Section 415 (see chapter 9).

Example 2. The facts are the same as those in Example 1, except that Kim can either receive all or part of the dollar equivalent of the unused PTO in cash or elect to defer all or part of it into the 401(k) plan. If the dollar equivalent of the PTO is made available to her on February 28, 2016, any amount she elects to defer will be treated as an elective contribution for 2016, and, as a result, will be taken into account in determining whether her elective contributions for 2016 do not exceed the calendar year 402(g) limit (see chapter 9). In addition, Kim's elective contribution will be considered a 2016 annual addition, and it will be taken into account in performing the 2016 ADP test (see chapter 13).

Automatic Enrollment Feature

Q 2:34 Must an employee's cash or deferred election be affirmative?

No. Since the publication of IRS revenue rulings in 1998 and 2000, it has been clear that a 401(k) plan can be designed to provide that, in the absence of an election by the employee, a fixed percentage of the employee's pay will be contributed to the 401(k) plan. This feature is commonly referred to as a *negative election* or automatic enrollment, and, to distinguish it from automatic contribution arrangements created by the Pension Protection Act of 2006 (PPA), it is sometimes referred to as a pre-PPA automatic contribution arrangement (ACA). [Treas. Reg. § 1.401(k)-1(a)(3)(ii)] There is no specific guidance in the regulations concerning what the maximum automatic election percentage can be. But in a general information letter dated March 17, 2004, the IRS took the position that the automatic election can be as high as the maximum deferral percentage specified in the plan.

The DOL has produced a publication that explains automatic enrollment 401(k) plans of the various types that are described here and later in this chapter. The publication can be accessed online at: *http://www.dol.gov/ebsa/pdf/automaticenrollment401kplans.pdf*. In order to facilitate the adoption of automatic enrollment features, the IRS has made available sample amendments that can be used to add an automatic contribution arrangement, including one that qualifies as an eligible automatic contribution arrangement (see Qs 2:36–2:51). [IRS Notice 2009-65, 2009-39 I.R.B. 413]

Q 2:35 What requirements must an automatic enrollment feature satisfy?

One of the concerns of the IRS is that employees have an effective opportunity to elect to receive in cash the amounts that would otherwise be deferred into their plans under a pre-PPA ACA. According to the IRS, an employee would have an effective opportunity if he or she is notified of the availability of the feature at the time he or she becomes a participant and each year thereafter, and that the employee has a reasonable period of time to elect out of the automatic enrollment feature. The IRS does not specify what constitutes a reasonable period of time, but the notice requirements applicable to safe harbor plans suggest that at least 30 days' notice would likely meet this requirement. [Rev. Rul. 2000-8, 2000-8 I.R.B. 617]

Automatic Contribution Arrangements Under the Pension Protection Act of 2006

Q 2:36 How does the Pension Protection Act of 2006 affect the use of automatic enrollment features in a 401(k) plan?

The enactment of the Pension Protection Act of 2006 (PPA) [Pub. L. No. 109-280, 120 Stat. 780] spurred the use of automatic enrollment features in 401(k) plans. The new law creates the automatic contribution arrangement (ACA), the eligible automatic contribution arrangement (EACA), and the qualified automatic contribution arrangement (QACA) (see Qs 2:37–2:68). [PPA § 902] Note, however, that (as indicated in Qs 2:34 and 2:35) a 401(k) plan can add an ACA that does not satisfy the specific requirements under PPA, but then the benefits of those arrangements will not be available to that 401(k) plan. See Appendix B for an automatic contribution arrangement chart and sample notice templates.

Q 2:37 What is an *automatic contribution arrangement* under PPA?

An *automatic contribution arrangement* (ACA) under PPA is an arrangement whereby an employee who fails to make an election to defer compensation into the 401(k) plan is treated as having elected to defer a plan-specified percentage of his or her compensation into the plan until the employee affirmatively elects to not defer or to defer at a different percentage. An ACA under PPA must also provide that, in the absence of an affirmative investment election, the employee's account will be invested in a default investment meeting the requirements of ERISA Section 404(c)(5). [ERISA § 514(e)(2)]

Q 2:38 Must employees receive notice of the ACA?

Yes. A reasonable period of time before the beginning of each plan year, the employer must provide notice to the participants to whom the ACA applies for that year. The notice must advise employees of their right to not defer or to defer at a different percentage and must explain how the contributions made under the ACA will be invested in the absence of an investment election. [ERISA § 514(e)(3)]

Q 2:39 Is there any penalty for failing to provide the ACA notice?

Yes, the DOL may assess a civil penalty of not more than $1,000 a day for each failure to provide the notice. [ERISA § 502(c)(4)]

Q 2:40 Why would an employer want to add an ACA to its 401(k) plan?

In some states the utilization of automatic enrollment features has been depressed by state laws that require an employee to affirmatively consent to any withholding from his or her wages or salary. State laws of this kind are preempted if an ACA is added to a 401(k) plan. [ERISA § 514(e)(1)]

Note. The DOL takes the position that any state laws that purport to require employee consent to withholding are preempted, regardless of whether an automatic enrollment feature meets the precise definition of an ACA. [DOL Reg. § 2550.404c-5(f)(2)]

Eligible Automatic Contribution Arrangements

Q 2:41 What is an *eligible automatic contribution arrangement*?

An *eligible automatic contribution arrangement* (EACA) under a 401(k) plan is an arrangement whereby an employee who fails to make an election to defer compensation into the plan is treated as having elected to defer a plan-specified percentage of his or her compensation into the plan until the employee affirmatively elects not to defer or to defer at a different percentage. When originally enacted, an EACA was also required to provide that an employee's account, in the absence of investment direction by the employee, be invested in a qualified default investment meeting the requirements of ERISA Section 404(c)(5). This requirement was eliminated by Section 109 of the Worker, Retiree, and Employer Recovery Act of 2008.

Q 2:42 Must employees receive notice of the EACA?

Yes. A reasonable period of time before the beginning of each plan year (and in the year an employee becomes a participant, a reasonable period before an employee becomes eligible), the employer must provide notice to the participants to whom the EACA applies. The timing requirement will be satisfied if the notice is provided at least 30 days (and not more than 90 days) before the beginning of each plan year, or, in the case of a new employee, not more than 90 days before the employee becomes eligible to participate and not later than a date that affords the employee a reasonable period of time after receipt of the notice to make an election. If it is not feasible to provide notice before the date the employee becomes eligible to participate—the plan, for example, provides for immediate entry—the notice will still be considered timely, provided it is given as soon as possible after the employee's eligibility date, and the employee is permitted to elect to defer on any compensation earned beginning on the date he or she becomes eligible. The notice must advise each employee of (1) the level of deferrals that will be made in the absence of an election, (2) the employee's right to not defer or to defer at a different percentage, (3) the investments that will be made in the absence of an election, and (4) if applicable, the procedures for making a permissible withdrawal. The notice must also contain the other information that is required to be provided in a safe harbor notice, and it can be provided electronically (see Q 2:243, Q 2:244). [Treas. Reg. § 1.414(w)-1(b)(3)]

Q 2:43 What other requirements must an EACA satisfy?

An EACA must meet what the regulations refer to as "the uniformity requirement." This means that the EACA must provide that the default election contribution is a uniform percentage of compensation. There are exceptions, however, to this requirement, as enumerated below.

1. The rate of deferral under the 401(k) plan in effect for an employee immediately prior to the effective date of the EACA is not reduced.
2. The rate of deferral is limited to comply with annual limits on the amount of compensation under Code Section 401(a)(17), of elective deferrals under Code Section 402(g), and of annual additions under Code Section 415.
3. The default election does not apply during a period of time an employee is not permitted to make elective contributions (e.g., deferrals are suspended on account of a hardship withdrawal).
4. The percentage, as in a QACA, varies according to the number of years since the date the automatic deferral election is first applied.

[Treas. Reg. § 1.414(w)-1(b)(2)]

Q 2:44 Is an EACA required to be made available to all participants?

No. An EACA is not required to cover all eligible employees. However, if it does not cover all eligible employees, then starting with plan years beginning on or after January 1, 2010, the extension to six months to distribute excess contributions and excess aggregate contributions will not apply (see Q 2:50). [Treas. Reg. § 54.4979-1(c)(1)]

Q 2:45 What does it mean to be a *covered employee* under an EACA?

Under the regulations, a *covered employee* is one who continues to receive the notice described in Q 2:42 even if he or she has made an affirmative election to not defer or to defer at a different percentage or amount. [Treas. Reg. § 1.414(w)-1(e)(3)]

Q 2:46 Can an EACA be added to a 401(k) plan at any time other than the beginning of the plan year?

No. The IRS considered this issue but decided in its final regulation that the Internal Revenue Code compelled the conclusion that an EACA can only be established at the beginning of the plan year in the case of an already existing 401(k) plan.

Q 2:47 Why would an employer want to add an EACA to its 401(k) plan?

A distinct disadvantage of an automatic enrollment feature is that deferrals, once made, cannot be returned to the participant if he or she directs the employer to cease deferrals. If this pattern is repeated on a widespread basis, the plan may be burdened with many small accounts that can add to the plan's administrative expense. A 401(k) plan with an EACA provides a mechanism for employees to have deferrals returned to them if a timely election is made. The returned deferrals are referred to as "permissible withdrawals." [Treas. Reg. § 1.414(w)-1(c)]

Q 2:48 How do the permissible withdrawal provisions work?

A return of deferrals is a permissible withdrawal only if the plan provides for such withdrawals and the election is made no later than 90 days after the date of the first default election contribution made under the EACA. The plan may provide, however, that the election be made earlier than 90 days after the date of the first default contribution, but in no event may the deadline be any sooner than 30 days after such contribution. The effective date of the election cannot be after the earlier of (1) the pay date for the second payroll period that begins after the date the election is made or (2) the first pay date that occurs at least 30 days after the election is made. The election must provide that all deferrals made pursuant to the EACA (plus any earnings attributable thereto) be returned to the participant. Any matching contributions (adjusted for allocable gains and losses) made with respect to the deferrals are forfeited. The amount distributed may be reduced by any generally applicable fees, and must be made in accordance with the plan's ordinary timing procedures for processing and making distributions. [Treas. Reg. § 1.414(w)-1(c)]

Q 2:49 What are the tax consequences of a permissible withdrawal?

Except to the extent attributable to Roth deferrals, the amount of the permissible withdrawal is included in gross income of the employee for the tax year in which it is distributed, the amount will not be subject to the additional income tax imposed under Code Section 72(t) for premature distributions, the amount will be reported on Form 1099-R, and the amount of the withdrawal is not considered an elective deferral for purposes of the actual deferral percentage test (see chapter 13) and the Code Section 402(g) calendar limit on the amount of elective deferrals (see chapter 9). [Treas. Reg. §§ 1.401(k)-2(a)(5)(vi), 1.414(w)-1(d)]

Q 2:50 Is there any other advantage to a 401(k) plan's adopting an EACA?

Yes. A 401(k) plan that adopts an EACA has additional time to distribute excess contributions and excess aggregate contributions that result from the failure to satisfy both the ADP and actual contribution percentage (ACP) tests (see chapter 13). In a 401(k) plan without an EACA, distributions of excess contributions and excess aggregate contributions that are made more than 2½ months after the end of the plan year will subject the employer to the Code Section 4979 excise tax equal to 10 percent of the amount of such contributions. A 401(k) plan containing an EACA that covers (see Q 2:45) all eligible employees will have six months to make such distributions free of the excise tax. [Treas. Reg. § 54.4979-1]

Q 2:51 What was the effective date of the EACA provisions of the PPA?

The EACA provisions became effective starting with plan years beginning on or after January 1, 2008. [PPA § 902(g)]

Qualified Automatic Contribution Arrangements

Q 2:52 What is a *qualified automatic contribution arrangement*?

A *qualified automatic contribution arrangement* (QACA) is an arrangement under which an employee who fails to make an election to defer into the plan is treated as having elected to defer a *qualified percentage* of his or her compensation into the 401(k) plan until the employee affirmatively elects to not defer or to defer at a different percentage. [I.R.C. § 401(k)(13)(B); Treas. Reg. § 1.401(k)-3(j)(1)(i) & (ii)] Although an arrangement that meets the requirements of a QACA may also be, at the same time, an EACA, this is not necessarily the case. Thus, a QACA that is not an EACA could not permit a participant to withdraw deferrals made within 90 days after the arrangement first applies to that participant. (For more information regarding EACAs, see Qs 2:41–2:51.)

Q 2:53 Must employees receive notice of the QACA?

Yes. A reasonable period of time before the beginning of each plan year (and in the year an employee becomes a participant, a reasonable period before an employee becomes eligible), notice must be provided to the participants to whom the QACA applies. The notice timing requirement will be satisfied if the notice is provided at least 30 days (and not more than 90 days) before the beginning of each plan year, or, in the case of a new employee, not more than 90 days before the employee is eligible to participate. If it is not feasible to provide notice before the date the employee becomes eligible to participate (e.g., if the plan provides for immediate entry), the notice will still be considered timely provided if it is given as soon as possible after the employee's eligibility date, and the employee is permitted to elect to defer on any compensation earned beginning on the date he or she becomes eligible. [Treas. Reg. § 1.401(k)-3(k)(4)]

Q 2:54 By what date must the automatic deferral percentage be implemented for an employee who fails to make an affirmative election?

If, after a reasonable period of time after receipt of the notice, an employee fails to make an affirmative election, the employer must implement the automatic deferral percentage no later than the earlier of the following dates:

1. The pay date for the second payroll period that begins after the date the notice is provided or
2. The first pay date that occurs at least 30 days after the notice is provided.

[Treas. Reg. § 1.401(k)-3(k)(4)(iii)]

Q 2:55 What matters must the notice address?

The notice must advise each employee of the level of deferrals that will be made in the absence of an election, the employee's right to not defer or to defer at a different percentage, and, if a participant may elect among two or more investment options, the notice must explain how contributions made under the QACA will be invested in the absence of an investment election. The notice must also contain the information that is required to be provided in a notice applicable to a safe harbor plan (see Q 2:243). [Treas. Reg. § 1.401(k)-3(k)(4)] See Appendix B for an automatic contribution arrangement chart and sample notice templates.

Q 2:56 Why would an employer want to add a QACA to its 401(k) plan?

A 401(k) plan that includes a QACA is not required to perform nondiscrimination testing of elective contributions or matching contributions. [I.R.C. §§ 401(k)(13), 401(m)(12)]

Q 2:57 What is meant by the term *qualified percentage* as used in Q 2:52?

If a participant fails to make an election to defer compensation into the plan, the QACA must provide that no less than 3 percent of the participant's compensation must be deferred into the plan during the plan year in which the employee becomes a plan participant and the following plan year. After that plan year, the QACA must provide that the deferral percentage will increase by at least one percentage point each plan year thereafter until the participant's rate of deferral equals 6 percent of compensation. [Treas. Reg. § 1.401(k)-3(j)(2)]

> **Example 1.** On June 1, 2015, Sylvia becomes a participant in the 401(k) plan, which contains a QACA that is maintained on a calendar year. Sylvia fails to make an election regarding deferral; thus, under the terms of the QACA, an amount equal to 3 percent of her pay is deferred into the plan. That percentage remains in effect during 2015 and 2016 and then increases thereafter by one percentage point each plan year until 2019, when it reaches

6 percent. After 2019, the automatic deferral percentage is no longer required to be increased.

Q 2:58 By what date must the initial qualified percentage be increased?

The 401(k) plan must provide that the initial qualified percentage will be increased no later than the first day of the second plan year following the plan year in which the automatic deferral percentage first becomes effective with respect to a participant as illustrated in the example under Q 2:57. A QACA can be designed to provide for more frequent increases, including increases that occur more frequently than annually. [Treas. Reg. § 1.401(k)-3(j)(2)(ii)]

Q 2:59 What is the maximum qualified percentage a QACA can provide?

A QACA can provide for a qualified percentage of up to 10 percent of compensation. [Treas. Reg. § 1.401(k)-3(j)(2)(i)]

Example 1. The facts are the same as those in the example in Q 2:57, except that after 2016 the deferral percentage increases by 2 percentage points each plan year after 2016 until it reaches 10 percent in 2020. This scheduled increase in the automatic deferral percentage would satisfy the qualified percentage requirement for QACAs.

Q 2:60 Must the employer make contributions to a QACA 401(k) plan?

Yes. The employer must make on behalf of each eligible non-highly compensated employee (NHCE) a safe harbor nonelective contribution equal to 3 percent of compensation or a safe harbor match contribution. The formula under the safe harbor match contribution must match 100 percent of a participant's deferrals up to 1 percent of his or her pay and 50 percent of deferrals between 1 percent and 6 percent of pay. Thus, a participant who is deferring at the rate of 6 percent of pay (whether by reason of the participant's affirmative election or otherwise) will receive a matching contribution equal to 3.5 percent of compensation. The QACA safe harbor matching contribution, as a percentage of pay, is less than the maximum amount that would be provided under a safe harbor plan providing a basic match formula (the match contribution would be 4 percent of pay for a participant who defers 5 percent of his or her compensation). [Treas. Reg. § 1.401(k)-3(k)(2)]

Q 2:61 Can a 401(k) plan containing a QACA have a safe harbor match formula other than the formula set forth in Q 2:60?

Yes. Like a safe harbor plan, a QACA can provide for an alternative match formula as long as the aggregate match contribution produced by that formula at every level of deferral equals or exceeds the amount produced by the formula in Q 2:60. [I.R.C. § 401(k)(13)(D)(ii)]

Q 2:62 Can a 401(k) plan containing a QACA require a non-highly compensated employee to be employed on the last day of the plan year and/or complete a specified number of hours of service in the plan year in order to be entitled to a safe harbor contribution?

No. Just like a safe harbor plan, requirements of this kind cannot be included in a QACA. [I.R.C. § 401(k)(13)(D)(ii)]

Q 2:63 Are employer safe harbor contributions made to a 401(k) plan that contains a QACA required to be 100 percent vested?

No. Unlike a safe harbor plan, employer safe harbor contributions to a 401(k) plan containing a QACA are not required to be 100 percent vested (see Q 2:255). However, the law does require a participant to be vested in those contributions after completing two years of service. [Treas. Reg. § 1.401(k)-3(k)(3)]

Q 2:64 Are employer safe harbor contributions to a 401(k) plan containing a QACA subject to the same restrictions on withdrawals as those that apply to employer safe harbor contributions to a safe harbor plan?

Yes. The same restrictions apply (see Q 2:266). [I.R.C. § 401(k)(13)(D)(iii)(II)]

Q 2:65 How do the top-heavy rules apply to a 401(k) plan containing a QACA?

Like a safe harbor plan, a 401(k) plan containing a QACA under which the only employer contributions are safe harbor contributions is not required to make additional employer contributions to satisfy the top-heavy minimum contribution requirement (see Qs 2:263). [I.R.C. § 416(g)(4)(H)]

Q 2:66 Is a QACA required to be applied to all participants?

No. The default election under a QACA is not required to be applied to an employee who is eligible to participate in the 401(k) plan prior to the effective date of the QACA and has previously elected to defer a specified dollar amount or a percentage of compensation or has elected to not defer at all. Note, however, that a QACA could be designed to apply the default election to those participants whose affirmatively selected deferral percentage is less than the qualified percentage. The preamble to the final regulations also indicates that affirmative elections can be scheduled to expire so that the QACA qualified percentage could, for example, be applied to a participant unless he or she makes another affirmative election. [Treas. Reg. § 1.401(k)-3(j)(1)(iii)]

Q 2:67 How does the definition of compensation in a QACA differ from that for a safe harbor plan?

As pointed out in Q 2:258, in the case of a regular safe harbor plan the employer may limit the types of compensation that may be deferred on by an eligible employee as long as the definition of compensation is reasonable within the meaning of Treasury Regulations Section 1.414(s)-1(d)(2). A reasonable definition, for example, would be one that excludes bonuses. For QACA safe harbor plans, on the other hand, starting with plan years beginning on or after January 1, 2010, the definition of compensation must be one that satisfies a Code Section 414(s) safe harbor definition (see Q 2:259). [Treas. Reg. § 1.401(k)-3(j)(1)]

Q 2:68 What was the effective date of the QACA provisions of the PPA?

The QACA provisions became effective starting with plan years beginning on or after January 1, 2008. [PPA § 902(g)]

Other Elective Deferral Issues and Considerations

Q 2:69 How frequently must 401(k) plan participants be allowed to make a cash or deferred election?

A 401(k) plan must provide employees with an effective opportunity to make or change their cash or deferred election at least once each plan year. Whether an employee has an effective opportunity is determined based on all relevant facts and circumstances, including notice of the availability of the election, the period of time during which the election may be made, and any other condition on elections. [Treas. Reg. § 1.401(k)-1(e)(2)(ii)]

> **Example.** Marble Masons, Inc. maintains a calendar-year 401(k) plan. It allows participants to change their cash or deferred elections only once per year, and the election must be made and turned in on the June 30 before the plan year to which the change is applicable. Marble Masons' requirements for election changes raise a question as to the qualification of the 401(k) arrangement because it is arguable that Marble Masons' employees do not have an effective opportunity to change their cash or deferred elections.

Q 2:70 When is compensation considered currently available to an employee?

An amount is considered currently available if it has been paid to the employee or if the employee is currently able to receive the cash at his or her discretion. [Treas. Reg. § 1.401(k)-1(a)(3)(iv)] A participant's deferral election cannot be applied to compensation that is paid or otherwise available to the participant before the date a participant's deferral election is made.

Example. ABC Company establishes a calendar-year-end 401(k) plan on December 1, 2015. Dennis, a highly paid employee, wishes to defer $6,000 during the month of December. Dennis is compensated at the rate of $12,000 per month; therefore, he elects to defer 5 percent of his compensation, believing that his deferral election will apply to the compensation that he will have received throughout 2015 ($144,000). In fact, his deferral election can apply only to his $12,000 monthly December salary, since that is the only portion of his 2015 annual compensation not currently available. If Dennis wishes to make an elective contribution of $6,000 for 2015, his deferral election percentage for the month of December must be 50 percent.

Q 2:71 When is an amount considered currently available to a partner in a 401(k) plan sponsored by a partnership?

A partner's compensation, which is defined to be his or her earned income under Code Section 401(c), is deemed currently available on the last day of the partnership's taxable year. As a result, a partner's cash or deferred election must be made by the last day of that year. [Treas. Reg. § 1.401(k)-1(a)(6)(iii)]

Example. The XYZ Partnership, which has a November 30 taxable year, sponsors a 401(k) plan with a calendar plan year. For the plan year ending December 31, 2015, a partner's compensation will be his or her compensation from the partnership for its taxable year ending November 30, 2015. A partner must make the cash or deferred election no later than November 30, 2015.

Q 2:72 When is a sole proprietor's compensation deemed currently available for purposes of determining the date by which the sole proprietor must make a cash or deferred election?

A sole proprietor's compensation (earned income) is deemed currently available on the last day of the individual's tax year. As a result, the sole proprietor must make his or her cash or deferred election no later than the last day of the sole proprietor's tax year. [Treas. Reg. § 1.401(k)-1(a)(6)(iii)]

Example. Joan is the sole proprietor of Joan's Hat Shoppe. Her tax year ends December 31. Joan sponsors a 401(k) plan that is administered on a calendar-year basis. She must make a cash or deferred election no later than December 31, if she wishes to defer part of her compensation as an elective contribution for the plan year.

Q 2:73 May a self-employed individual defer cash advance payments made during the plan year and before the amount of his or her earned income is finally determined?

Yes. A self-employed individual, whether a partner in a partnership or a sole proprietor, may defer on cash advance payments made during the plan year and before earned income is finally determined. The cash advance payments must be based on the value of the self-employed individual's services prior to the date of payment and must not exceed a reasonable estimate of earned income for the self-employed individual's taxable year. In addition, the self-employed individual must have made a cash or deferred election before amounts are withheld from the cash advance payments. [Treas. Reg. § 1.401(k)-1(a)(6)(iv)]

> **Example.** Jim is a partner in the Hoppy Brewing Company, which has a calendar tax year. Jim's earned income for the year is estimated to be $120,000; consequently, he receives a monthly advance of $10,000. Jim can elect to defer part of each monthly advance payment as long as he has made a cash or deferred election prior to the date any advance is scheduled to be paid to him.

Q 2:74 Are there special limitations that apply to elective contributions?

Yes. Elective contributions must be 100 percent vested immediately and are subject to the limitations on distributions described in chapter 15. They are also subject to the Code Sections 402(g) and 415 limits explained in chapter 9.

Q 2:75 Are elective contributions considered employee contributions?

No. Elective contributions are treated as employer contributions, not employee contributions, for all purposes under the Code. [Treas. Reg. § 1.401(k)-1(a)(4)(ii)]

Q 2:76 Are there special rules for elective contributions on bonuses?

Yes. Elective contributions may be made on bonus payments, and generally these are treated like any other elective contribution. However, there is a special rule that treats deferrals on bonuses paid within 2½ months after the end of a plan year as having been made within the preceding plan year for purposes of discrimination testing. For this special rule to apply, the bonus must be attributable to services performed within that plan year, and the plan must provide for the allocation of deferrals to that plan year. [Treas. Reg. § 1.401(k)-2(a)(4)] Elective contributions on bonuses are subject to discrimination testing under the ADP test (see chapter 13).

Q 2:77 What special rules apply to elective contributions for employees who have veterans' reemployment rights under USERRA?

An employee who has reemployment rights under USERRA can make elective deferrals up to the maximum amount that he or she would have been permitted to make during the period of military service if the individual had continued to be employed during this period. The make-up deferrals can be made during the period beginning on the date of reemployment and ending on the date which is five years after the date of reemployment or, if earlier, the date that is determined by multiplying the period of military service by three. An employee's compensation for this purpose is deemed to be the compensation he or she would have received during the period of military service had the employee not served or, if the compensation during that period would not be reasonably certain, then the 12-month average immediately preceding that period will be used. [I.R.C. §§ 414(u)(2), 414(u)(7)]

Roth Contributions

Q 2:78 What is a *Roth contribution*?

A *Roth contribution* is an elective contribution (see Q 2:27) that is treated by the employer as includable in the employee's gross income. In other words, it is an elective contribution that is made on an after-tax rather than before-tax basis. [Treas. Reg. § 1.401(k)-1(f)(1)(ii)]

Q 2:79 Under what circumstances will an elective contribution be treated as a Roth contribution?

An elective contribution will be treated as a Roth contribution only if the employee, at the time of making a cash or deferred election, irrevocably designates elective contributions made pursuant to that election as Roth contributions. [Treas. Reg. § 1.401(k)-1(f)(1)(i)]

Q 2:80 Can a 401(k) plan be designed to offer participants only the Roth option?

No. A 401(k) plan must always provide participants with the opportunity to make elective contributions on a pre-tax basis. [Treas. Reg. § 1.401(k)-1(f)(1)(i)]

Q 2:81 Can Roth contributions be made part of a 401(k) plan that provides for automatic enrollment?

Yes. A 401(k) plan can be designed to provide that in the absence of an affirmative election, a participant's elective contributions to the plan are treated as Roth contributions. [Treas. Reg. § 1.401(k)-1(f)(5)(ii)]

Q 2:82 Must Roth contributions be allocated to a separate account?

Yes. Roth contributions to a 401(k) plan must be allocated to a separate account. In addition, the plan must maintain for each employee a record of the undistributed amount of Roth contributions made by that employee. [Treas. Reg. § 1.401(k)-1(f)(3)]

Q 2:83 Must Roth contributions meet the same requirements that apply to elective contributions that are not designated as Roth contributions?

Yes. Roth contributions must meet the same requirements that apply to elective contributions that are not designated as Roth contributions (see Qs 2:74, 2:75). For example, Roth contributions will be taken into account in performing the actual deferral percentage (ADP) test (see chapter 13). [Treas. Reg. § 1.401(k)-1(f)(4)]

Q 2:84 Are participants able to convert pre-tax elective contributions into Roth contributions?

Yes. With the enactment of the Small Business Jobs Act of 2010 [Pub. L. No. 111-240] (SBJA) and the American Taxpayer Relief Act of 2012 [Pub. L. No. 112-240] (ATRA), plan participants are able to convert pre-tax elective contributions as well as other non-Roth accounts in a 401(k) plan by way of an In-Plan Roth Rollover. An *In-Plan Roth Rollover* is a distribution from one or more accounts (other than an account to which Roth contributions have been allocated) under a 401(k) plan that is rolled over to a Roth account in the same 401(k) plan. [I.R.C. § 402A(c)(4); Notice 2010-84, 2010-51 I.R.B. 872, Q&A 1; Notice 2013-74, 2013-52 I.R.B. 819, Q&A 1] See chapter 18 for detailed discussion of the tax and other consequences of doing an in-plan Roth rollover.

Q 2:85 How long have 401(k) plan participants been able to make Roth contributions?

Participants in 401(k) plans have been able to make Roth contributions since 2006.

Matching Contributions

Q 2:86 What is a *matching contribution*?

A *matching contribution* is an employer contribution that is allocated on the basis of a participant's elective contributions or, less typically, a participant's employee after-tax contributions. [I.R.C. § 401(m)(4)(A); Treas. Reg. § 1.401(m)-1(a)(2)] The rate of matching contribution may be specified in the plan document or may be determined at the discretion of the employer. It may be made on an ongoing basis, as elective contributions are paid into the 401(k) plan, or at or after the end of the plan year. Matching contributions, together with employee after-tax contributions, are subject to discrimination testing under the actual contribution percentage (ACP) test (see chapter 13) unless the 401(k) plan is a SIMPLE 401(k) plan or a safe harbor 401(k) plan or a plan containing a QACA (see Qs 2:52–2:68, 2:220–2:268).

Q 2:87 May matching contributions be made on a discretionary basis?

Yes. In some 401(k) plans, the employer will determine each plan year the rate (if any) of matching contributions for that year. If the rate of matching contributions is announced at the beginning of the year, the contributions will usually be made to the 401(k) plan on an ongoing basis and without regard to any minimum hours and/or last day requirements (see Qs 2:95–2:98). On the other hand, if the employer defers the decision until the end of the year or thereafter, the plan may require participants to satisfy either or both of these requirements in order to receive a matching contribution allocation.

Q 2:88 May matching contributions be made on a discretionary basis in a SIMPLE 401(k) plan?

No. Unless an employer elects to make a nonelective contribution of 2 percent of compensation, it is required to make matching contributions to a SIMPLE 401(k) plan on a dollar-for-dollar basis on elective contributions up to 3 percent of compensation. [Treas. Reg. § 1.401(k)-4(e)(3)] An employer cannot require a participant to complete a minimum number of hours of service or to be employed on any particular day of the plan year in order to be entitled to receive matching contributions in a SIMPLE 401(k) plan. (See Qs 2:220–2:238 for further discussion of SIMPLE 401(k) plans.)

Q 2:89 May matching contributions be made on a discretionary basis in a safe harbor 401(k) plan under Code Section 401(k)(12)?

Yes. An employer may elect to make a discretionary matching contribution to a safe harbor 401(k) plan in addition to the safe harbor contribution (whether matching or nonelective). (See Qs 2:239–2:269 for further discussion of safe harbor 401(k) plans.)

Q 2:90 May matching contributions be made on a discretionary basis to a 401(k) plan that contains a qualified automatic contribution arrangement?

Yes. An employer may elect to make a discretionary matching contribution to a 401(k) plan containing a QACA in addition to the safe harbor contribution (whether matching or nonelective). (See Qs 2:52–2:68 for further discussion of QACAs.)

Q 2:91 May matching contributions be made on behalf of self-employed persons who participate in a 401(k) plan maintained by a partnership or sole proprietorship?

Yes, matching contributions may be made with respect to a self-employed person's elective contributions even though the effect of making matching contributions is to indirectly permit a self-employed person, such as a partner in a partnership, to vary the amount of contributions made on his or her behalf. [Treas. Reg. § 1.401(k)-1(a)(6)(ii)]

Q 2:92 What special rules apply to matching contributions for employees who have veterans' reemployment rights under USERRA?

An employee who has veterans' reemployment rights under USERRA is entitled to receive whatever matching contributions would have been made had the make-up deferrals in Q 2:77 been made during the period of military service. [I.R.C. § 414(u)(2)(A)(ii)]

Q 2:93 What special rules apply to matching contributions in the case of a participant who dies or becomes disabled while performing qualified military service?

The plan may, but is not required to, provide matching contributions that would have been made during the period of military service as if the participant had returned to employment in accordance with his or her reemployment rights under USERRA on the day preceding the participant's death or disability. [I.R.C. § 414(u)(9)(A)] For purposes of determining the amount of matching contributions the participant is deemed to have made elective contributions in an amount equal to the actual average elective contributions made by the participant during the 12-month period prior to military service (or, if less than 12 months, the actual length of service). [I.R.S. Notice 2010-15, 2010-6 I.R.B. 390]

Nonelective Contributions

Q 2:94 What is a *nonelective contribution*?

A *nonelective contribution* in a 401(k) plan is an employer contribution that is allocated on the basis of compensation or in some manner other than on the basis of elective contributions or employee after-tax contributions. Nonelective contributions do not need to be included in any of the special nondiscrimination tests for 401(k) plans, but they are subject to the general nondiscrimination rules under Code Section 401(a)(4) (see chapter 12). Nonelective contributions may sometimes be used to help satisfy the ADP and ACP tests (see chapter 13). A participant's right to receive an allocation of a nonelective contribution cannot depend on whether he or she has made elective contributions. [I.R.C. § 401(k)(4)(A); Treas. Reg. § 1.401(k)-1(e)(6)(i)]

Example. Emily earns $35,000 and elects to contribute 10 percent of her compensation for the year. Emily's employer provides a matching contribution of 25 percent of the deferral amount and a nonelective contribution of 5 percent of pay. Emily's total allocation for the year is as follows:

Elective contribution ($35,000 × 10%)	$3,500
Matching contribution ($3,500 × 25%)	875
Nonelective contribution ($35,000 × 5%)	1,750
Total contribution	$6,125

Q 2:95 What eligibility requirements may be imposed on a 401(k) participant for purposes of receiving a nonelective contribution allocation?

A minimum hours requirement of up to 1,000 hours may be imposed. For example, if a plan requires 1,000 hours of service, an active or terminated participant who works fewer than 1,000 hours will not be entitled to an allocation of nonelective contributions.

A requirement that the participant be employed on the last day of the plan year may also be imposed. This requirement would generally preclude any terminated employees from receiving a portion of the nonelective contribution.

Q 2:96 What eligibility requirements may be imposed on a 401(k) participant in the case of a SIMPLE 401(k) plan or a safe harbor 401(k) plan under Code Section 401(k)(12)?

A minimum hours requirement and/or last day requirement may not be imposed in the case of an employer that elects to make the 2 percent of compensation nonelective contribution to a SIMPLE 401(k) plan or the 3 percent of compensation nonelective contribution to a safe harbor 401(k) plan. All participants eligible to make elective contributions are entitled to the nonelective contribution; however, in the case of a SIMPLE 401(k) plan, a participant may be required to receive at least $5,000 of compensation (or such lesser amount designated by the employer) for the plan year. [I.R.C. §§ 401(k)(11), 401(k)(12), 401(m)(10), 401(m)(11)] (SIMPLE and safe harbor 401(k) plans are discussed in Qs 2:220–2:269.)

Q 2:97 What eligibility requirements may be imposed on a 401(k) plan that contains a QACA?

Neither a minimum-hours requirement nor a last-day requirement may be imposed by an employer that elects to make the 3 percent of compensation nonelective safe harbor contribution to a 401(k) plan containing a QACA. [I.R.C. §§ 401(k)(13)(D), 401(m)(12)] (QACAs are discussed in Qs 2:52–2:68.)

Q 2:98 What are the special concerns of a plan sponsor that imposes minimum hours and/or last day requirements?

Because the nonelective contribution portion of the plan is tested separately for coverage (see the definition of *plan* in chapter 10), care must be taken to ensure that the Section 410(b) coverage requirements are met. If a significant number of employees are excluded from an allocation of nonelective contributions, the plan may fail the coverage tests (see chapter 11).

Q 2:99 What special rules apply to nonelective contributions for employees who have veterans' reemployment rights under USERRA?

An employee who has veterans' reemployment rights under USERRA is entitled to receive whatever nonelective contributions would have been made during the period of military service. [I.R.C. § 414(u)(1) and (8)]

Q 2:100 Do special rules apply to nonelective contributions in the case of a participant who dies or becomes disabled while performing qualified military service?

The plan may, but is not required to, provide nonelective contributions that would have been made during the period of military service as if the participant had returned to employment in accordance with his or her reemployment rights under USERRA on the day preceding the participant's death or disability. [I.R.C. § 414(u)(9)(A)]

Allocation Methods

Q 2:101 What methods of allocation of nonelective contributions are available to the sponsor of a 401(k) plan?

The nondiscrimination rules allow plan sponsors the choice of a design-based safe harbor formula or a formula that meets the requirements of the general test for defined contribution plans (see chapter 12). [Treas. Reg. § 1.401(a)(4)-2] Generally, if a safe harbor formula is used, the plan sponsor is assured that the allocation of nonelective contributions will not discriminate in favor of HCEs (see chapter 10).

Q 2:102 What are the design-based safe harbor allocation methods?

There are three basic methods: proportional, integrated, and a points system. The proportional method will provide an allocation that is an equal percentage of pay, an equal dollar amount for each eligible participant, or an equal dollar amount for each uniform unit of service (not to exceed one week) (see chapter 12). The integrated method will allow the plan sponsor to take Social Security contributions into account by providing an allocation that is a greater percentage of pay for more highly paid participants (see chapter 12). The points system is more involved, as a nondiscrimination test must be performed on the allocations to demonstrate that the allocation does not discriminate in favor of HCEs (see chapter 12).

Q 2:103 How does the points system allocation method work?

The plan awards points for age, service, or both. Points may also be given for units of compensation, which cannot exceed $200 in value. Each employee must receive the same number of points for each year of age, for each year of service, and for each unit of compensation. If the plan grants points for years of service, it may limit the number of years of service taken into account. [Treas. Reg. § 1.401(a)(4)-2(b)(3)(i)(A)]

For each plan year, the average of the allocation rates for HCEs cannot exceed the average of the allocation rates for NHCEs (the *average allocation test*). An employee's allocation rate is the amount of contributions and forfeitures allocated to the employee's account for a plan year expressed as either a percentage of compensation or a dollar amount. [Treas. Reg. § 1.401(a)(4)-2(b)(3)(i)(B)]

Q 2:104 What alternative formulas for allocation of discretionary nonelective contributions are available?

Any allocation formula that does not discriminate in favor of HCEs may be used. The general test for nondiscrimination must then be performed on an annual basis (see chapter 12). The employer must weigh the costs of performing this test annually with the results of the allocation to determine the value of using the general test.

For example, a points system formula could be used with compensation units of $1,000. Because each compensation unit exceeds $200, general testing must be performed to use this formula. Similarly, if the points system formula does not satisfy the average allocation test (see Q 2:103), then general testing must also be performed.

Another alternative available to a 401(k) plan sponsor is the age-weighted allocation of nonelective contributions. Although the general test must be applied, an age-weighted allocation formula will, by reason of its nature, usually satisfy the requirements of the general test (see Qs 2:109, 2:110).

Finally, an increasingly popular method of allocation provides for different levels or rates of contribution for plan-defined groups of participants. This method, sometimes referred to as new comparability, also relies on the general test.

> **Example.** The following five illustrations show the results of allocating nonelective contributions under the various methods discussed here. For purposes of these illustrations, a small employer (with three employees) is used, but the concepts are equally applicable to larger employers.
>
> 1. *Proportional method.* ABC Company decides to contribute 10 percent of eligible payroll, or $16,000. Under a proportional allocation, all participants would receive an allocation equal to 10 percent of pay.

Name	*Pay*	*Total Contribution*	*Percentage of Pay*
Alice	$100,000	$10,000	10.00%
Brent	40,000	4,000	10.00
Cathy	20,000	2,000	10.00
Totals	$160,000	$16,000	

2. *Integrated method.* The plan uses an integration level of $55,500 (see chapter 12). If $16,000 is contributed, the formula for allocation is 13.10 percent of compensation in excess of $55,500, plus 8.80 percent of compensation below that amount. The contribution is allocated as follows:

Name	*Pay*	*Excess Pay*	*Excess Contribution*	*Base Contribution*	*Total Contribution*	*Percentage of Pay*
Alice	$100,000	$44,500	$5,830	$ 4,887	$10,717	10.72%
Brent	40,000	0	0	3,522	3,522	8.80
Cathy	20,000	0	0	1,761	1,761	8.80
Totals	$160,000	$44,500	$5,830	$10,170	$16,000	

3. *Points method.* The plan provides one point for each $200 of compensation, one point for each year of age, and five points for each year of service. The total points for all participants amount to 1,000. Each point is, therefore, worth $16 calculated as $16,000/1,000.

Name	*Age*	*Years of Service*	*Pay*	*Pay Points*	*Age Points*	*Service Points*	*Total Points*	*Total Contribution*	*Percentage of Pay*
Alice	50	5	$100,000	500	50	25	575	$ 9,200	9.20%
Brent	40	10	40,000	200	40	50	290	4,640	11.60
Cathy	25	2	20,000	100	25	10	135	2,160	10.80
Totals			$160,000	800	115	85	1,000	$16,000	

4. *Age-weighted method.* $16,000 is contributed, and the plan uses 8.5 percent interest and UP 84 mortality as the basis for age-weighting (see Qs 2:105–2:110).

Name	*Age*	*Pay*	*Total Contributions*	*Percentage of Pay*
Alice	50	$100,000	$13,085	13.09%
Brent	40	40,000	2,315	5.79
Cathy	25	20,000	600	3.00
Totals		$160,000	$16,000	

Note: This plan is top heavy, and top-heavy minimums of 3 percent of compensation are provided for each non-key participant.

5. *New comparability method.* $16,000 is contributed and the plan uses 8.5 percent interest and UP 84 mortality as the basis for testing compliance with the general test. The plan provides for two groups of participants: (1) owners (Alice) and (2) all other employees (see Qs 2:111–2:114).

Name	*Age*	*Pay*	*Total Contributions*	*Percentage of Pay*
Alice	50	$100,000	$13,000	13.00%
Brent	40	40,000	2,000	5.00
Cathy	25	20,000	1,000	5.00
Totals		$160,000	$16,000	

Q 2:105 How does an age-weighted formula differ from a design-based safe harbor formula?

The key difference between an age-weighted formula and a design-based formula is that, in an age-weighted formula, the contributions are allocated to favor older employees. An age-weighted formula tests for nondiscrimination on the basis of benefits; that is, the discretionary nonelective contributions and forfeitures allocated to the accounts of participants are converted to actuarially equivalent benefits at normal retirement age, and testing is performed on the basis of those benefits.

Q 2:106 How does a new comparability formula differ from a design-based safe harbor formula?

The key difference between a new comparability formula and a design-based formula is that, in a new comparability formula, the contributions can be channeled in order to favor select, plan-defined groups of participants. Although the groups favored are typically HCEs, the new comparability formula can still satisfy the general nondiscrimination test on the basis of actuarially equivalent benefits (see chapter 12 for discussion of the general nondiscrimination test).

Q 2:107 How does the conversion from contributions to benefits operate?

The nondiscrimination rules specify that, when testing defined contribution plans on a benefits basis, all allocated contributions and forfeitures must be converted to equivalent benefit accrual rates (EBARs). [Treas. Reg. § 1.401(a)(4)-8] The EBARs represent an annual annuity benefit as a percentage of compensation.

Example. An employer with two employees contributes $12,550 to a defined contribution plan on their behalf, allocating $11,690 to the older employee and $860 to the younger employee. By converting the contribution to a benefit for each employee, it can be demonstrated that the benefits are equivalent as a percentage (5 percent) of pay:

Age	*Salary*	*Contribution*	*Assumed Accumulation at Testing Age*	*Annual Annuity at Testing Age*	*EBAR*
50	$100,000	$11,690	$39,743	$5,000	5%
35	25,000	860	9,940	1,250	5
Totals	$125,000	$12,550	$49,683	$6,250	

Assumptions:

Interest: 8.5%

Mortality: Unisex Pension Table of 1984 (UP 84)

Testing age: 65

Q 2:108 How are the age-weighting factors determined?

A plan document containing an age-weighted formula must contain a table of age-weighting factors or a list of assumptions. The Section 401(a)(4) regulations contain a list of safe harbor mortality tables and specify that interest rates must be in the range of 7.5 percent to 8.5 percent. [Treas. Reg. § 1.401(a)(4)-8(b)(2)]

To ensure that an age-weighted formula satisfies the nondiscrimination tests, a table is set up that defines the contribution, as a percentage of compensation, required to produce at the testing age an annuity benefit equal to 1 percent of compensation. Selected factors from such a table are shown below.

Age	*Factor*
55	3.515%
45	1.555
35	0.688
25	0.304

Assumptions:

Interest: 8.5%

Mortality: UP 84

Testing age: 65

Q 2:109 How is the contribution allocated to participants under an age-weighted formula?

To obtain the contribution allocation for each participant, it is necessary to take the following steps:

1. From the table determine for each participant the factor that applies for an individual of his or her age;
2. Multiply the factor by the participant's compensation; and
3. Allocate the contribution in proportion to each participant's allocation base.

Example. Betty's Basket Weaving Company wishes to make a discretionary nonelective contribution of 10 percent of pay, or $15,000, to its 401(k) plan. Assuming an 8.5 percent interest rate and UP 84 mortality, the contribution would be allocated as follows:

Age	*Compensation*	*Factor*	*Allocation Base (Compensation × Factor)*	*Allocated Contribution (Allocation Base ÷ $3,799 × $15,000)*
55	$ 90,000	3.515%	$3,164	$12,493
45	30,000	1.555	467	1,844
35	20,000	.688	138	545
25	10,000	.304	30	118
Totals	$150,000		$3,799	$15,000

Note: The total contribution of $15,000 is approximately 3.948 times the allocation base of $3,799. This factor can be applied to each individual's allocation base to obtain the allocated contribution.

Q 2:110 How does an age-weighted formula automatically satisfy the nondiscrimination tests?

The EBARs should be an equal percentage of compensation for each participant in the plan. Because the EBARs for all HCEs should be exactly equal to the EBARs for all NHCEs, the plan will comply with the nondiscrimination requirements of Code Section 401(a)(4).

Q 2:111 How is the contribution allocated to participants under a new comparability formula?

In a typical new comparability plan, the employer will determine the amount to be contributed on behalf of each of the different groups specified in the plan. The amount contributed for each group typically will be allocated among the participants in that group in proportion to their compensation.

Example. Jerry's Jeep Repair Company sponsors a 401(k) plan that contains a new comparability formula for allocating employer nonelective contributions under the plan. The plan has two specified groups of participants: owners and all other participants. Under the new comparability formula, Jerry's Jeep Repair decides to contribute an amount equal to 10 percent of compensation for the owners and an amount equal to 4 percent of compensation for all other participants.

Q 2:112 Will a new comparability formula automatically satisfy the nondiscrimination rules?

No. Unlike an age-weighted formula, a new comparability formula does not automatically satisfy the Section 401(a)(4) nondiscrimination rules. In order to satisfy these rules, a new comparability plan must convert allocated contributions and forfeitures to equivalent benefit accruals and must then demonstrate that these equivalent benefits satisfy the general nondiscrimination test (see chapter 12).

Q 2:113 How does the general nondiscrimination test apply to a new comparability formula?

It applies in the same way as explained in chapter 12 except that a rate group is defined with respect to each HCE's EBAR. EBARs are determined using the safe harbor mortality and interest rate assumptions under the Section 401(a)(4) regulations (see Q 2:108).

Q 2:114 Are there any other restrictions on the use of new comparability formulas in 401(k) plans?

Yes. A new comparability formula must meet a minimum allocation gateway test. Under this test, each NHCE must have an allocation rate that is at least one-third of the allocation rate of the HCE with the highest allocation rate. However, the allocation gateway test is considered satisfied if each NHCE has an allocation rate of 5 percent of compensation. A participant's allocation rate is determined by dividing the nonelective contributions and forfeitures allocated to the participant by his or her compensation. [Treas. Reg. § 1.401(a)(4)-8(b)(1)(vi)]

Q 2:115 When would an age-weighted or new comparability formula be used in lieu of a design-based safe harbor formula or a defined benefit plan?

These formulas can be quite advantageous when compared with defined benefit plans or design-based safe harbor formulas for the following reasons:

- The employer has the flexibility to contribute up to 25 percent of total payroll.

- Because these formulas are applied to contributions made to a defined contribution plan, they are much easier to administer than defined benefit plans.
- Participants receive statements reflecting their account balances. This is much easier for employees to understand than accrued benefits in defined benefit plans expressed in terms of benefits commencing at normal retirement age.
- There is no need for an actuary or for filing a Form 5500, Schedule SB. A 401(k) plan containing an age-weighted formula or a new comparability formula is not liable for Pension Benefit Guaranty Corporation (PBGC) premiums. Nor does the plan sponsor have to contend with the complexities of reporting required by Statement of Financial Accounting Standard (FAS) 87, "Employers' Accounting for Pensions."
- Under an age-weighted formula, employer contributions for older HCEs can be significantly higher as a percentage of compensation.
- The contributions under a new comparability formula can be targeted to favored groups of employees.

Q 2:116 What are the drawbacks of these formulas?

Age-weighted and new comparability formulas do have some disadvantages, including the following:

- If the plan is top heavy, care must be taken to ensure that top-heavy minimums are provided, particularly in the case of an age-weighted formula.
- There are some difficult communication issues in replacing a traditional allocation formula with an age-weighted or a new comparability formula because many participants will receive a smaller contribution as a percentage of compensation than in the past.
- These formulas can be more expensive to administer than traditional allocation formulas because of the additional cross-testing necessary to ensure nondiscrimination under Code Section 401(a)(4).
- The employer cannot contribute more than 25 percent of total payroll, or allocate more than the Code Section 415 annual additions limit for any given participant.

Q 2:117 In what situations is an age-weighted formula an effective plan design?

An age-weighted formula can be an effective plan design in a number of situations:

- It is ideal for a business with older, highly paid owners who wish to receive a larger share of the profit sharing plan contribution.

- As a replacement for a terminating defined benefit plan, an age-weighted formula can reduce the benefits lost by older participants as a result of the conversion to a defined contribution plan.
- Age-weighted allocations, the addition of a vesting schedule, and reduced accessibility to funds can be viewed as significant advantages for an employer considering replacing a simplified employee pension (SEP) plan with a 401(k) plan containing an age-weighted formula.

Q 2:118 In what situations is a new comparability formula effective?

Like the age-weighted formula, the new comparability formula can be viewed as having significant advantages over a simplified employee pension. It is also ideal for a business that has a young workforce and that wishes to provide a larger share of the employer's nonelective contributions to targeted groups of favored, older employees.

Q 2:119 Will 401(k) plans that contain new comparability formulas that pass the general test always be treated as nondiscriminatory?

According to the IRS, the answer to this question is no. If the effect of a plan design or an employer's hiring practices is to provide substantial allocations to HCEs and to limit coverage to NHCEs with short periods of service, then the plan will be considered to discriminate in favor of HCEs. [Carol Gold memo dated Oct. 22, 2004] The example below is based on one from that memo.

Example. The Pet Emporium is a corporation that maintains a 401(k) plan. Under its terms, the 401(k) plan provides immediate participation and covers only the HCEs of Pet Emporium and a group of NHCEs defined in the plan. The 401(k) plan provides that the HCEs receive a nonelective contribution of 20 percent of compensation. The other covered employees receive an allocation of 5 percent of compensation.

In 2015, Pet Emporium employs 55 employees. These 55 employees include five HCEs. The remaining 50 employees include 15 employees who are employed on a permanent basis and whose annual compensation ranges from $20,000 to $50,000. These 15 employees are not included in the group of NHCEs covered by the plan. The other 35 employees are temporarily hired for short periods of time and are included in the group of NHCEs covered by the plan. None of the 35 employees receives compensation in excess of $1,000 in 2015 and they all receive allocations under the plan of 5 percent of compensation. The plan intends to satisfy the nondiscrimination in amount general test by using cross-testing under Treasury Regulations Section 1.401(a)(4)-8.

Pet Emporium's plan is discriminatory because it satisfies the general test by covering a group of NHCEs who are hired temporarily for short periods of time and who receive small amounts of compensation while at the same time it excludes all higher-paid, permanent NHCEs and allocates a higher percentage of compensation to the accounts of HCEs than to those of the covered NHCEs.

Deemed IRA Contributions

Q 2:120 What is a *deemed IRA contribution*?

A *deemed IRA contribution*, which is sometimes referred to as "side-car" IRA, is a voluntary participant contribution that is made to a 401(k) plan and considered for tax purposes as if it were a contribution to an IRA. [I.R.C. § 408(q)] The concept of an IRA-type contribution to a qualified plan is not a new one. Between 1982 and 1986, a plan participant could make deductible contributions to a qualified plan. Such contributions were known as *qualified voluntary employee contributions.*

Q 2:121 To what types of IRAs can a deemed IRA contribution be made?

Deemed IRA contributions can be made to traditional IRAs or Roth IRAs, but they cannot be made to IRAs established under a SEP or a SIMPLE plan. [Treas. Reg. § 1.408(q)-1(b)]

Q 2:122 What plan document requirements must be met before a 401(k) plan can accept deemed IRA contributions?

A 401(k) plan must contain provisions allowing for deemed IRA contributions before it can accept deemed IRA contributions. [Treas. Reg. § 1.408(q)-1(d)(1)]. The IRS has issued a model amendment that can be used for this purpose. [Rev. Proc. 2003-13, 2003-4 I.R.B. 317]

Q 2:123 Must a deemed IRA contribution be kept separate from the other assets of the 401(k) plan?

No. The assets of a 401(k) plan and any deemed IRA can be commingled for investment purposes as long as the deemed IRA contributions and earnings credited to them are separately accounted for. [Treas. Reg. §§ 1.408(q)-1(d)(2), 1.408(q)-1(f)(2)(i)]

Q 2:124 Are there restrictions on who can serve as trustee of a 401(k) plan that allows for deemed IRA contributions?

Yes. The rules restricting trusteeship of IRA assets to banks or to other IRS-approved persons means that 401(k) plans allowing for deemed IRA contributions will usually have a financial institution serve as trustee. [Treas. Reg. § 1.408(q)-1(f)(1)]

Q 2:125 How will distribution rules be applied?

Because the deemed IRA and the 401(k) plan are treated as separate entities, the distribution rules applicable to IRAs and qualified plans will be applied separately. For example, whether a participant satisfies the Code Section 401(a)(9) minimum distribution rules under the 401(k) plan will be determined without regard to whether minimum distribution rules applicable to the deemed IRA have been satisfied. [Treas. Reg. § 1.408(q)-1(e)]

Q 2:126 Must the 401(k) plan make the deemed IRA contribution feature available to all participants?

No. The deemed IRA contribution feature is not considered a benefit, right, or feature under the Code Section 401(a)(4) nondiscrimination rules; thus, it is not required to be made available to all participants. [Treas. Reg. § 1.408(q)-1(f)(6)]

Q 2:127 Is a 401(k) plan required to accept deemed IRA contributions?

No. A 401(k) plan is not required to accept deemed IRA contributions. [I.R.C. § 408(q)(1)(A)]

Q 2:128 How is the deductibility of IRA contributions to a deemed traditional IRA determined?

The deductibility of employee contributions to a deemed traditional IRA is determined in the same manner as if the contribution were made to any other traditional IRA. While employee contributions (whether to a traditional or to a Roth deemed IRA) made after the end of a participant's tax year and up to and including the tax return due date for that year can be treated by the employee as having been made for that tax year, the employer will report any withheld employee contributions as income for the year in which the contributions are actually withheld. [Treas. Reg. § 1.408(q)-1(f)(4)]

Q 2:129 What happens if a deemed IRA fails to satisfy qualification requirements applicable to IRAs?

If a deemed IRA fails to satisfy the qualification requirements applicable to an IRA, the qualification of the 401(k) plan will be in jeopardy if the assets of the deemed IRA and 401(k) plan are held in a single trust. Similarly if the 401(k) plan is not qualified, the deemed IRA will no longer qualify as a deemed IRA, and will lose its status as an IRA if the assets of the deemed IRA and 401(k) plan are held in a single trust. [Treas. Reg. § 1.408(q)-1(g)]

Q 2:130 Is a deemed IRA subject to ERISA requirements?

A deemed IRA is subject to the exclusive benefit requirement of ERISA, as well as ERISA's fiduciary and co-fiduciary rules. [ERISA §§ 403(c), 404, and

405] A deemed IRA is also subject to the administration and enforcement rules of ERISA, Part 5.

Transfer or Rollover of Benefits

Q 2:131 What methods exist for moving benefits from one plan or IRA to a 401(k) plan?

Currently, four methods can be used:

- A direct rollover (see Q 2:132)
- A 60-day rollover (see Q 2:133)
- A transfer (see Q 2:134)
- An elective transfer (see Q 2:135)

In-plan Roth rollovers (discussed in chapter 18) do not move benefits from one plan or IRA to a 401(k) plan. A 401(k) plan providing for in-plan Roth rollovers permits a participant to transfer pre-tax moneys held in the participant's account to a Roth account in the same way that an individual can convert a traditional IRA to a Roth IRA.

Q 2:132 What is a *direct rollover*?

A *direct rollover* is a distribution that, at the election of the participant, is transferred directly from the distributing plan or IRA to the receiving plan (see chapter 16).

Q 2:133 What is a *60-day rollover*?

A *60-day rollover* is a distribution that is received by a participant and then deposited into another plan or IRA within 60 days following the participant's receipt of the distribution (see chapter 16).

Q 2:134 What is a *transfer*?

A *transfer* occurs when benefits are distributed directly from one plan trustee to another, and where participants do not have the right to elect immediate distribution. It generally occurs when a group of participants moves from one plan to another as a result of a plan merger, spin-off, or other transaction (see Qs 2:138–2:140).

Q 2:135 What is an *elective transfer*?

An *elective transfer* is the process whereby a participant elects to have his or her account balance transferred into a new plan. An elective transfer typically will be made by an employee who is not entitled to a distribution from the plan but who no longer participates in the plan as a result of an asset or stock acquisition, merger, or similar transaction or as a result of a change in employment status (e.g., union to nonunion). In that case, the employee can elect to transfer his or her entire account balance (both vested and nonvested portions) to another 401(k) plan (see chapter 16). [I.R.C. § 411(d)(6)(D); Treas. Reg. § 1.411(d)-4, Q&A-3(b)]

Q 2:136 What design considerations should govern whether a plan should accept rollover contributions?

Plans are not required to accept rollover contributions. A plan that accepts rollovers will generally need to account separately for rollover contributions and may have different distribution options available with respect to rollover accounts. For example, a plan might permit in-service withdrawal of a participant's rollover account at any time and for any purpose while limiting in-service withdrawals of other 401(k) plan accounts to hardship. Some plans will also permit participants to make their own investment decisions with respect to a rollover account. The only separate treatment for a rollover account that is required as a practical matter is separate accounting of those funds.

One advantage to an employer in accepting rollovers is that it may make the plan more attractive to prospective employees.

Q 2:137 If a plan accepts rollover contributions, should any steps be taken to ensure that the contribution is eligible for rollover?

It makes sense for a plan administrator to obtain some assurance that a rollover contribution is valid—that it came from an eligible plan or IRA and that it was transferred either as a direct rollover or within 60 days after a participant received it. The risk in not taking these precautions is that the contribution will be considered an after-tax contribution subject to nondiscrimination testing under Code Section 401(m) and will be counted as an annual addition under Code Section 415. [Treas. Reg. § 1.401(a)(31)-1, Q&A 14] The IRS has issued a revenue ruling that provides two examples of situations in which a plan administrator is considered to have reasonably concluded that a proposed rollover contribution is valid. [Rev. Rul. 2014-9, 2014-17 I.R.B. 975]

Q 2:138 Are plans required to accept transfers?

No. Accepting transferred benefits is more complicated than accepting rollover contributions (see Q 2:139), and plans are not required to do so.

Q 2:139 What considerations are involved in accepting plan transfers?

The considerations involved in accepting plan transfers depend on the type of transfer (elective versus nonelective). In the case of nonelective transfers, which generally spring from plan mergers or spinoffs, the transferred account balances will carry with them optional forms of benefit, including qualified joint and survivor annuity requirements, and vesting provisions. Thus, an employer accepting account balances as a result of a plan merger may end up essentially operating two separate plans—one for the transferred account balances and another for all other accounts under the plan. In approving the merger, the employer will be required to review the documents of the merged plan in order to identify the protected optional forms of benefit and vesting provisions that apply to the transferred account balances. Recently finalized regulations, however, serve to reduce some of the administrative complexity presented by mergers with the liberalization of the anti-cutback rules. These rules allow certain optional forms of benefit to be eliminated by plan amendment (see chapter 16).

An elective transfer poses far fewer administrative issues for the recipient plan as the optional forms of benefit of the transferor plan are not required to be carried over to the transferee plan. However, the vesting provisions of the transferor plan must be carried forward to the transferee plan (see chapter 16). [Treas. Reg. § 1.411(d)-4, Q&A 3(b)(2)]

Q 2:140 How are transferred or rolled-over benefits counted for purposes of nondiscrimination testing?

Benefits that have been rolled over or transferred pursuant to an elective transfer process (see Q 2:135) are not taken into account in determining whether the amount of contributions or benefits under a plan is nondiscriminatory (see chapter 12). [Treas. Reg. § 1.401(a)(4)-11(b)(1)] Other transferred benefits will be taken into account. For example, benefits transferred as a result of a plan merger will be counted for purposes of Section 401(a)(4) nondiscrimination testing.

Basic Qualification Requirements

Q 2:141 How do basic qualification requirements affect the design of a 401(k) plan?

401(k) plans, like other types of qualified plans, must meet the basic qualification requirements for retirement plans contained in Code Section 401(a). In addition, 401(k) plans must meet qualification rules that apply specifically to cash or deferred arrangements.

Q 2:142 What advantages accrue to a 401(k) plan that is qualified?

The many advantages of having a qualified 401(k) plan include the following:

1. The employer may take a tax deduction for making contributions to the plan.
2. Investment earnings of the plan's assets are exempt from current taxation.

3. Except for Roth contributions, participants avoid current taxation of amounts allocated to their accounts.
4. Participants may roll over plan benefits to other employer-sponsored plans or IRAs on a tax-free basis.

Formal Requirements

Q 2:143 Must the 401(k) plan be in writing?

Yes. Although some states do recognize the existence of an oral trust, a 401(k) plan will not be considered qualified unless it is established and operated in accordance with a definite written program. [Treas. Reg. § 1.401-1(a)(2)] The written document must include all provisions essential for qualification. [Rev. Rul. 74-466, 1974-2 C.B. 131] The plan document serves to define the rights and obligations of the plan sponsor, participants, and beneficiaries. It also forms the basis of any IRS determination that the plan is tax-qualified in form (see chapter 3).

Q 2:144 Can a person other than the employer establish and maintain a 401(k) plan for the employees of that employer?

No. Under Code Section 401(a), a qualified plan is one established and maintained by an employer for the exclusive benefit of its employees. Although this would appear to be a common-sense notion, this issue has received much attention due to the proliferation of professional employment organizations (PEOs) that purport to be the employers or co-employers of individuals who are leased back to a PEO's clients. The IRS has taken the position that, because a PEO may not be the common-law employer of these individuals, any 401(k) plan covering the actual employees of a PEO and the individuals who work for a PEO's clients must be a multiple employer plan. [Rev. Proc. 2002-21, 2002-19 I.R.B. 911]

Q 2:145 Is there any type of employer that is precluded from sponsoring a 401(k) plan?

Yes. In general, a governmental employer cannot sponsor a 401(k) plan. [I.R.C. § 401(k)(4)(B)(ii)] Although most governmental employers cannot sponsor 401(k) plans, they can sponsor Section 457(b) deferred compensation plans, which operate very much like 401(k) plans (see chapter 22).

Q 2:146 Who is considered a *governmental employer*?

A *governmental employer* is a state or local government, or a political subdivision thereof, or any of its agencies or instrumentalities. [I.R.C. § 401(k)(4)(B)(ii)]

Q 2:147 Are there certain governmental employers that can sponsor a 401(k) plan?

Yes, rural cooperatives as well as Indian tribal governments can sponsor 401(k) plans. [I.R.C. § 401(k)(4)(B)(ii), (iii)] Also permitted to sponsor 401(k) plans are governmental employers that adopted 401(k) plans before May 6, 1986. [Treas. Reg. § 1.401(k)-1(e)(4)(iii)]

Q 2:148 Are governmental 401(k) plans subject to the same qualification requirements that apply to 401(k) plans sponsored by nongovernmental employers?

No. Many qualification requirements that apply to nongovernmental 401(k) plans do not apply to 401(k) plans sponsored by governmental employers. Some of the more notable requirements that do not apply are:

- Minimum coverage requirements under Code Section 410(b) (see chapter 11);
- ADP and ACP testing under Code Sections 401(k) and 401(m) (see chapter 13);
- Nondiscrimination testing under Code Section 401(a)(4) (see chapter 12);
- Minimum vesting requirements under Code Section 411 (see Qs 2:190–2:215);
- Minimum participation requirements under Code Section 410(a) (see Qs 2:169–2:189);
- Joint-and-survivor rules under Code Section 401(a)(11) (see chapter 17); and
- Top-heavy rules under Code Section 416 (see chapter 16).

Q 2:149 Does the plan have to be communicated to employees?

Yes. The Code generally requires that a plan be communicated to employees. [Treas. Reg. § 1.401-1(a)(2); Rev. Rul. 71-90, 1971-1 C.B. 115] Department of Labor (DOL) regulations also contain this requirement and detail the content and method for this communication (see chapter 19).

Q 2:150 How are assets of the plan held?

In general, all assets of a qualified plan must be held in a trust that is created and organized in the United States and maintained as a domestic trust. [I.R.C. § 401(a); Treas. Reg. § 1.401-1(a)(3)(i)] DOL provisions generally prohibit a trustee or other fiduciary from maintaining the indicia of ownership of any assets that are not subject to the jurisdiction of the United States district courts. [ERISA § 404(b), 29 U.S.C. § 1104] An exception from the trust requirement is carved out for plans that use custodial accounts held by a bank or other person satisfactory to the IRS, or annuity contracts issued by qualified insurance companies. [I.R.C. § 401(f); ERISA § 403(a)]

Q 2:151 Can a 401(k) plan provide insurance benefits to participants?

A 401(k) plan must be established primarily to offer deferred compensation to employees. The plan will not violate this rule if it provides for incidental life, accident, or health insurance benefits. [Treas. Reg. § 1.401-1(b)(1)(ii)] Insurance benefits in a 401(k) plan will be considered incidental if the aggregate premiums paid for insurance benefits do not exceed 25 percent of the aggregate contributions and forfeitures that have been allocated to that participant. If ordinary life (e.g., whole life) is purchased, the same rule is applied, using a 50 percent limit. The rationale for the increased limit is that only half the premium for ordinary life insurance is used for the purchase of a death benefit. The rest is used to build deferred cash benefits. [Rev. Rul. 61-164, 1961-2 C.B. 99]

Continuing Contributions

Q 2:152 Must the 401(k) plan be a permanent and continuing arrangement?

Yes. A plan will not be considered qualified if it appears from surrounding facts and circumstances that it was established as a temporary program. A profit sharing plan will be considered temporary if substantial and recurring contributions are not made. It will also be considered temporary if it is abandoned within a few years after it is established for reasons other than business necessity. A plan will be considered permanent, however, even though contributions are not made every year. The employer may also reserve the right to terminate the plan or discontinue contributions without jeopardizing its status as a permanent program. [Treas. Reg. § 1.401-1(b)(2)]

The issue of permanency is unlikely to arise in a 401(k) plan because contributions are likely to be made each year and contributions are not dependent on the employer's profits.

Q 2:153 Can the employer take back contributions that have been made to the 401(k) plan?

Under the terms of the trust, it must be impossible for any plan assets to be used for a purpose other than the exclusive benefit of employees and beneficiaries until all the plan's liabilities to employees and beneficiaries have been satisfied. [I.R.C. § 401(a)(2)] This rule generally bars the employer from recapturing any contributions made to the plan or other plan assets.

Q 2:154 Under what limited circumstances may contributions be returned to the employer without jeopardizing the qualified status of the 401(k) plan?

If a contribution is made in the first year of the plan and is contingent on the plan's receiving a favorable determination letter from the IRS, the contribution may be returned if the IRS denies the plan's qualified status and the contribution is returned within one year of that denial. [ERISA § 403(c)(2)(B); Rev. Rul. 91-4, 1991-1 C.B. 57]

If a contribution is made contingent on its tax deductibility and the IRS disallows the deduction, the contribution may be returned within one year of the disallowance. [ERISA § 403(c)(2)(C); Rev. Rul. 91-4, 1991-1 C.B. 57] A contribution may not be returned merely because the IRS could disallow it. An active disallowance by the IRS is required.

If a contribution is made as a result of a good-faith mistake of fact, it may be returned to the employer within one year of when the contribution was made. [ERISA § 403(c)(2)(A); Rev. Rul. 91-4, 1991-1 C.B. 57] Unintentionally making a payment that is in excess of the deductible limit for plan contributions (see chapter 9) is not considered a mistake of fact. [Priv. Ltr. Rul. 9144041]

Assignment of Benefits

Q 2:155 May participants assign or alienate their benefits?

As a general rule, benefits under a 401(k) plan may not be assigned or alienated or be subject to any type of garnishment, levy, or other legal or equitable process. [I.R.C. § 401(a)(13); Treas. Reg. § 1.401(a)-13(b)] ERISA generally preempts state laws relating to employee benefit plans, including state garnishment, levy, or other attachment proceedings. [ERISA § 514(a)] This corresponding ERISA rule helps the plan trustee avoid the situation of being compelled by a state court order to make a distribution to a creditor that would have the effect of disqualifying the entire plan.

Q 2:156 What exceptions to the anti-assignment rule are recognized by the IRS?

- A qualified domestic relations order may award a portion of a participant's benefit to his or her spouse, former spouse, child, or other dependent (see chapter 17).
- Benefits may be pledged as security for a loan from a plan to a plan participant. [Treas. Reg. § 1.401(a)-13(d)(2)]
- A portion of future benefit payments may be assigned by a participant or beneficiary once benefits are in pay status. The assignment must be voluntary and revocable, must not in the aggregate exceed 10 percent of any benefit payments, and must not have the purpose or effect of defraying administrative costs to the plan. [Treas. Reg. § 1.401(a)-13(d)(1)]
- A participant or beneficiary may make a revocable election to pay some or all of his or her benefit to a third party (including his or her employer). The third party must file a statement in writing with the plan administrator stating that he or she has no enforceable rights to any plan benefits that the third party has not already received. [Treas. Reg. § 1.401(a)-13(e)]

- A plan may make payments in response to a federal tax levy or judgment without jeopardizing the qualified status of the plan. [Treas. Reg. § 1.401(a)-13(b)(2)]
- A participant's benefit may be offset by amounts due the plan pursuant to a court order or a settlement agreement with the DOL against the participant for crimes or violations of ERISA involving the plan. [I.R.C. § 401(a)(13)(C)]

Q 2:157 Is there an exception to the anti-assignment rules for bankruptcy of the participant?

No. The U.S. Supreme Court resolved a long-standing question by holding that benefits in a plan subject to Title I of ERISA are not available to pay creditors in a bankruptcy proceeding. [Patterson v. Shumate, 504 U.S. 753 (1992)]

Under bankruptcy law the estate available for distribution to creditors includes all legal and equitable property interests owned by the debtor. There is an exception from this rule for property held in a trust that restricts the transfer of trust property under applicable nonbankruptcy law. The Supreme Court ruled that ERISA's anti-alienation provisions constitute applicable nonbankruptcy law. Therefore, a participant's benefits in a qualified plan are not part of the bankruptcy estate and are thus not available to pay claims of creditors.

Several lower court cases created exceptions to the *Patterson v. Shumate* ruling in cases where the only employees covered by a plan were owner-employees. However, these rulings are likely to have minimal impact in light of the enactment of the Bankruptcy Abuse Prevention and Consumer Protection Act of 2005, which further expands the protections afforded to 401(k) and other retirement plans.

Q 2:158 Is there an exception to the anti-assignment rules for amounts owed to the employer?

There is no exception to the anti-assignment rules that permit an employer to withhold benefit payments otherwise due an employee as security for amounts owed by the employee to the employer. The Supreme Court has ruled that even if an employee embezzles funds from an employer, the employee's benefit in a qualified plan cannot be used to pay back the employer. [Guidry v. Sheet Metal Workers Nat'l Pension Fund, 11 Employee Benefits Cas. (BNA) 2337, 493 U.S. 365 (1990)]

Merger or Consolidation

Q 2:159 What protection must participants have in the event of merger or consolidation?

A plan must provide that upon the merger or consolidation of the plan, each participant is entitled to receive benefits after the merger that are no less than the benefits he or she was entitled to before the merger. [I.R.C. §§ 401(a)(12),

414(*l*); Treas. Reg. § 1.401(a)-12] As a practical matter, this requires that a merging plan allocate any contributions or earnings and identify the account balance of each participant as of the date of the merger. (See chapter 21 for a detailed discussion of plan mergers.)

Nondiscrimination Rules

Q 2:160 What is the purpose of the nondiscrimination rules?

The purpose of the nondiscrimination rules is to limit the extent to which plan sponsors may maintain a 401(k) plan that exclusively or primarily benefits only highly compensated or key employees. The nondiscrimination rules are discussed in detail in chapters 10 through 14.

Q 2:161 What are the basic nondiscrimination requirements?

The Code establishes the following four nondiscrimination requirements:

1. The plan must meet certain minimum standards concerning coverage of employees (see chapter 11).
2. The plan must not discriminate in favor of highly compensated employees with respect to the amount of contributions or benefits, and with respect to the availability of benefits, rights, and features of the plan (see chapter 12).
3. Elective contributions, matching contributions, and employee after-tax contributions must meet special nondiscrimination tests (see chapter 13).
4. A plan that is top heavy must meet additional rules concerning minimum contributions or benefits (see chapter 14).

Compensation and Benefit Limits

Q 2:162 How much compensation can be used for calculating plan contributions or benefits?

There is a limit on the amount of compensation that can be taken into account for computing plan contributions and benefits and for applying nondiscrimination tests. The 2015 limit is $265,000. This limit will subsequently be adjusted for inflation in increments of $5,000 (see chapter 10).

Q 2:163 Is there a limit placed on the amount that can be allocated to a participant in a 401(k) plan?

Yes. Code Section 415 places annual limits on the amount that can be allocated to a plan on behalf of individual plan participants. These limits are discussed in detail in chapter 9.

Q 2:164 What are the annual limits under Code Section 415?

For limitation years beginning in 2015, the amount of annual additions allocated to a participant cannot exceed the lesser of $53,000 or 100 percent of the participant's compensation (see chapter 9). [I.R.C. § 415(c)]

Q 2:165 Are there special limits that apply to elective contributions?

There is an annual limit on the amount of elective contributions that may be made by an individual to the 401(k) plan. In 2015, the annual limit is $18,000. Thereafter, the limit will be adjusted in annual increments of $500 for increases in cost of living. [I.R.C. § 401(a)(30)]

Q 2:166 Do contributions need to be based on business profits?

Contributions to a 401(k) plan do not need to be based on profits or accumulated retained earnings. [I.R.C. § 401(a)(27)]

Distribution Requirements

Q 2:167 Are there basic qualification requirements relating to how benefits must be paid from a 401(k) plan?

Yes. A 401(k) plan must meet certain rules concerning when distributions of benefits must be made available as well as minimum distribution requirements (see chapter 16).

A 401(k) plan must provide for automatic survivor benefits payable to the surviving spouse of a participant in the form of a qualified joint and survivor annuity or a qualified preretirement survivor annuity unless an exception applies (see chapter 17).

Finally, there are restrictions on when elective contributions can be distributed to participants (see chapter 15).

Q 2:168 Must a participant have the option to make a direct rollover of a distribution to an IRA or other qualified plan?

Yes. A 401(k) plan must provide the option for a participant to elect to have an eligible rollover distribution transferred directly to an IRA or other plan of the participant's choice (see chapter 16). [I.R.C. § 401(a)(31)] If a participant elects not to make a direct rollover, the plan administrator is required to withhold 20 percent of the distribution for income tax. [I.R.C. § 3405(c)]

Eligibility Rights

Q 2:169 Can a 401(k) plan place restrictions on which employees may become plan participants?

Many 401(k) plans contain restrictions on who may become plan participants. For example, a plan may restrict participation to employees not covered by a collective bargaining agreement. Plans are free to impose restrictions of this kind; however, the resulting class of eligible employees must satisfy the Section 410(b) coverage rules (see chapter 11). Frequently, 401(k) plans restrict participation to those employees who satisfy minimum age and/or minimum service requirements, but such restrictions are subject to special rules.

Q 2:170 May a 401(k) plan require employees to reach a certain age before they can become plan participants?

Yes. A 401(k) plan may require employees to attain any age up to 21 before they may become participants in the plan. [I.R.C. § 410(a)(1)(A)(i)]

Q 2:171 May a 401(k) plan exclude from participation any employee who has reached a specified age?

No. Maximum age conditions are not permitted. [I.R.C. § 410(a)(2)]

Q 2:172 What length of service requirement may a 401(k) plan impose?

A 401(k) plan may require up to one year of service before allowing employees to make elective contributions. [Treas. Reg. § 1.401(k)-1(e)(5)] This requirement can also be applied to employer contributions under a SIMPLE 401(k) plan and employer safe harbor contributions under either a regular safe harbor plan or a QACA safe harbor plan (see Qs 2:52–2:68, 2:220–2:268). If a 401(k) plan also provides for other types of employer contributions, employees can be required to complete up to two years of service before becoming entitled to receive those contributions. In that case, however, the law requires employees to be 100 percent vested in their accounts attributable to employer contributions. [I.R.C. § 410(a)(1)(B)(i)]

Q 2:173 What is a *year of service*?

A *year of service* is any eligibility computation period during which an employee completes the number of hours of service specified in the plan. Not more than 1,000 hours may be specified for this purpose. [I.R.C. § 410(a)(3)(A)]

Q 2:174 What is an *eligibility computation period*?

The initial *eligibility computation period* is the 12-month period beginning on the date on which an employee is credited with an hour of service (employment commencement date). Subsequent eligibility computation periods may be based on 12-month periods beginning on the anniversaries of the employment commencement date. In the alternative, a plan may base subsequent eligibility computation periods on plan years beginning with the plan year in which occurs the first anniversary of the employment commencement date. [DOL Reg. § 2530.202-2]

> **Example.** The Olive Orchard's 401(k) plan, which is a calendar-year plan with semiannual entry dates, has a one-year minimum service requirement. Janice is hired June 15, 2015. During the initial eligibility computation period (June 15, 2015–June 14, 2016), she does not complete 1,000 hours of service. Under the plan, subsequent eligibility computation periods are based on the plan year, and during the 2016 plan year Janice completes more than 1,000 hours of service. As a result, Janice would become a participant on January 1, 2017. Note that if the plan based subsequent eligibility computation periods on the anniversaries of the employment commencement date, then the earliest Janice could enter the plan would be July 1, 2017, which is the semiannual entry date following the second eligibility computation period (June 15, 2016–June 14, 2017).

Q 2:175 What is an *hour of service*?

Under DOL regulations, an *hour of service* must be credited for each of the following:

1. Each hour for which an employee is paid, or entitled to payment, for the performance of duties;
2. Each hour for which an employee is paid, or entitled to payment, on account of a period of time during which no duties are performed (whether or not employment has been terminated) as a result of vacation, holiday, illness, disability, layoff, jury duty, military duty, or leave of absence (not more than 501 hours of service are required to be credited on account of any single continuous period during which no duties are performed); and
3. Each hour for which back pay, irrespective of mitigation of damages, is either awarded or agreed to by the employer.

[DOL Reg. § 2530.200b-2(a)]

The regulations set forth complicated rules for determining the number of hours of service for reasons other than the performance of duties and for the crediting of hours of service to computation periods. [DOL Reg. §§ 2530.200b-2(b), 2530.200b-2(c)]

Q 2:176 Do the regulations provide other methods for determining hours of service?

Yes. Rather than counting actual hours of service, an employer may elect to use an equivalency method for determining hours of service. There are equivalencies based on hours worked, regular time hours, periods of employment, and earnings. [DOL Reg. §§ 2530.200b-3(c), 2530.200b-3(d), 2530.200b-3(e), 2530.200b-3(f)] In lieu of using hours of service, a 401(k) plan may use an elapsed time system for determining whether an employee has satisfied the plan's length of service requirements. [Treas. Reg. § 1.410(a)-7]

Q 2:177 Why would an employer decide to use an elapsed time system for calculating service rather than a system based on hours of service?

The elapsed time system is simpler than a system based on hours of service because it dispenses with the need to keep track of hours of service during discrete 12-month periods. In the elapsed time system, a year of service is completed when the employee completes 12 months of service or 365 days of service. There are drawbacks, however, to using this system. First, employees who would never complete a year of service (at least 1,000 hours of service in a computation period) under the hours of service system will complete a year of service under the elapsed time system, thus allowing part-time employees to enter the plan. Second, the elapsed time system requires credit to be given during a period of severance from employment that is shorter than one year. No such credit need be given under a 401(k) plan using the hours of service system.

Q 2:178 After an employee has satisfied the minimum age and/or service requirements under a 401(k) plan, when must participation commence?

Participation must commence no later than the earlier of the following dates:

1. The first day of the plan year beginning after the date on which the employee has satisfied the plan's minimum age and/or service requirements; or
2. The date six months after the date such requirements are satisfied.

[Treas. Reg. § 1.410(a)-4(b)(1)]

401(k) plans will generally specify two or more dates on which employees satisfying the minimum age and/or service requirements can enter the plan.

Example. A calendar-year plan provides that an employee may enter the plan on the first semiannual entry date, January 1 or July 1, after the employee has satisfied the plan's minimum age and service requirements. The employee satisfies those requirements on January 15, 2016, and consequently becomes a participant on July 1, 2016. The plan complies with the law because the employee is eligible to participate on July 1, 2016, which is earlier than the date by which the law would require participation to commence, July 15, 2016.

Q 2:179 May an employee waive participation?

Yes. An employee may waive participation if the plan so provides. Unless the waiver is irrevocable, any such waiver provision could attract the scrutiny of the IRS, which might argue that the ability to waive an allocation of profit sharing contribution or to rescind a waiver on a year-by-year basis is tantamount to a cash or deferred election. It should also be noted that unless a waiver is irrevocable and made before an employee's entry date, an employee will be considered an eligible employee for purposes of performing the actual deferral percentage test and the actual contribution percentage test (see chapter 13).

Q 2:180 May a 401(k) plan exclude part-time employees from plan participation?

No. In a field directive issued in November 1994, the IRS takes the position that the exclusion of part-time employees is, in effect, a service requirement that is subject to the limitations described in Q 2:172. According to the field directive, it does not matter that a 401(k) plan will satisfy the minimum coverage requirements (see chapter 11) after excluding part-time employees.

> **Example.** Sally Motor Company sponsors a 401(k) plan that requires one year of service (1,000 or more hours of service in an eligibility computation period) and excludes any employee who is regularly scheduled to work fewer than 30 hours per week. Bob has been a part-time employee (fewer than 30 hours per week) for five years but has completed more than 1,000 hours during each eligibility computation period (see Q 2:174). The 401(k) plan's exclusion of part-time employees has prevented Bob from becoming a plan participant even though he has completed five years of service. Because the part-time employee exclusion is treated as an indirect service requirement, Sally Motor Company's 401(k) plan is subject to disqualification as it contains a length of service requirement in excess of that permitted under Code Section 410(a)(1).

Break-in-Service Rules

Q 2:181 If a participant terminates employment and is then rehired at a later date, is the plan allowed to ignore years of service completed by the participant before termination of employment?

Unless a plan contains a break-in-service rule that applies to the participant, all of an employee's years of service with an employer must be taken into account. (*Employer* is defined in chapter 10.) [Treas. Reg. § 1.410(a)-5(c)(1)]

> **Example 1.** The Cal Cubicle Company sponsors a 401(k) plan that contains no break-in-service rules. Linda, a plan participant, terminates employment on July 15, 2014, and is rehired August 15, 2016. Linda's years of service prior to July 15, 2014, must be taken into account. Accordingly, Linda resumes participation in the plan on her date of rehire, August 15, 2016.

Example 2. The facts are the same as those in Example 1, except that Linda, although satisfying the 401(k) plan's service requirement, was never a participant because she was a member of a collective bargaining unit not covered under the plan. As in Example 1, Linda is rehired, but she is now in a class of employees covered under the plan. Linda commences participation immediately on her date of rehire. Her previous years of service are taken into account even though they were earned while she was not in a class of employees eligible to participate in the plan.

Q 2:182 What are the break-in-service rules?

There are three break-in-service rules:

1. The one-year break-in-service rule (see Q 2:183);
2. The rule of parity (see Q 2:184); and
3. The two-year, 100 percent vested break-in-service rule (see Q 2:185).

Q 2:183 How does the one-year break-in-service rule operate?

Under this rule, a 401(k) plan may disregard years of service completed by a participant before a one-year break in service until the participant completes a year of service after the break. Upon completion of a year of service following the break, the participant's pre-break years of service are retroactively restored. With the restoration of pre-break years of service, the employee's participation commences retroactively to the date of rehire. Although retroactive participation may be feasible in the case of a non-401(k) plan, it is not in a 401(k) plan. This is because an employee cannot make elective contributions with respect to compensation already received. [Treas. Reg. § 1.410(a)-5(c)(3)]

Q 2:184 What is the *rule of parity*?

The *rule of parity* allows a plan to disregard pre-break years of service if a participant does not have a vested account balance and the number of consecutive one-year breaks in service equals or exceeds the greater of five or the number of years of service completed before the break. This rule will generally have little significance in a 401(k) plan as it will not apply to participants who have made 100 percent-vested elective contributions to the 401(k) plan. [I.R.C. § 410(a)(5)(D)]

Q 2:185 How does the two-year, 100 percent vested break-in-service rule operate?

Under this rule, a plan that requires employees to complete two years of service as a condition of participating in employer contributions (other than employer contributions to a SIMPLE 401(k) plan and safe harbor contributions) may, in the case of a participant who has not satisfied this service requirement, disregard a year of service completed before a one-year break in service. [I.R.C.

§ 410(a)(5)(B)] Again, this rule is of little practical significance because the elective contribution portion of a 401(k) plan cannot have a minimum service requirement of greater than one year.

Q 2:186 What is a *one-year break in service*?

A *one-year break in service* is a computation period during which an employee fails to complete more than 500 hours of service. [DOL Reg. § 2530.200b-4(a)(1)]

Q 2:187 What computation period is used for determining whether an employee incurs a one-year break in service?

The computation period used for this purpose is the computation period designated in the plan for measuring years of service after the initial eligibility computation period (see Q 2:174). [DOL Reg. § 2530.200b-4(a)(2)]

Q 2:188 How do maternity or paternity leaves of absence affect the determination of whether an employee incurs a one-year break in service for purposes of eligibility?

Solely for the purpose of determining whether an employee has incurred a one-year break in service, an employee absent from work on account of a maternity or paternity leave of absence must be credited with up to 500 hours of service. The number of hours of service credited during the absence will be the number of hours of service that otherwise would normally have been credited or, if that number cannot be determined, eight hours of service per day. The hours will be credited to the computation period in which the absence begins if an employee would be prevented from incurring a one-year break in service; otherwise, they will be credited to the immediately following computation period. A maternity or paternity leave of absence is any absence from work as a result of the pregnancy of the employee, the birth of the employee's child, the placement of the employee's adopted child, or the caring for the child after its birth or placement. [I.R.C. § 410(a)(5)(E)]

Additional hours are not explicitly required for unpaid leave under the Family and Medical Leave Act of 1993 (FMLA). However, the FMLA regulations do state that any period of unpaid FMLA leave shall not be treated as or counted toward a break in service for purposes of eligibility to participate in a retirement plan. [DOL Reg. § 825.215(d)(4)] In addition to maternity and paternity leave, FMLA leave can include up to 12 weeks during the course of a serious health condition affecting the employee or a family member.

Q 2:189 What special rules apply for employees who have veterans' reemployment rights under USERRA?

An employee who has reemployment rights under USERRA is not treated as having incurred a break in service during his or her period of military service. [I.R.C. § 414(u)(8)(A)]

Vesting Rules

Q 2:190 What is *vesting*?

Vesting refers to the extent to which a participant's interest in a 401(k) plan is nonforfeitable. Any portion of that interest that is not vested is subject to possible forfeiture.

Q 2:191 Are there circumstances that require a participant's entire interest in a 401(k) plan to be vested?

Yes. All of a participant's interest in a 401(k) plan must be 100 percent vested upon the participant's attainment of normal retirement age, upon the termination or partial termination of the plan, or upon the complete discontinuance of contributions to the plan. [Treas. Reg. §§ 1.411(a)-1(a)(1), 1.411(d)-2(a)(1)] Although this is not legally required, nearly all 401(k) plans will provide for 100 percent vesting upon a participant's death or disability. Finally, a participant who dies while performing qualified military service also will become 100 percent vested, as if the participant had returned to employment in accordance with his or her reemployment rights on the day preceding death, and the plan provides for 100 percent vesting of a participant's account upon death. [I.R.C. § 401(a)(37); IRS Notice 2010-15, 2010-6 I.R.B. 390]

Q 2:192 What does the term *normal retirement age* mean?

Normal retirement age means the earlier of:

1. The time specified by the 401(k) plan at which a participant reaches normal retirement age; or
2. The later of:

   The date a participant reaches age 65, or

   The first day of the plan year in which occurs the fifth anniversary of the date a participant commenced participation in the plan.

[I.R.C. § 411(a)(8)]

Q 2:193 What kinds of contributions must always be 100 percent vested?

The following kinds of contributions must always be 100 percent vested:

- Elective contributions (see Q 2:27) [Treas. Reg. §§ 1.401(k)-1(c), 1.401(k)-6]
- Qualified matching contributions (QMACs) (see chapter 13) [Treas. Reg. § 1.401(k)-6]
- Qualified nonelective contributions (QNECs) (see chapter 13) [Treas. Reg. § 1.401(k)-6]
- After-tax employee contributions (see chapter 13) [Treas. Reg. § 1.411(a)-1(a)(2)]
- Deemed IRA contributions (see Qs 2:120–2:130) [I.R.C. § 408(q)]
- Rollover contributions (see Qs 2:131–2:140)
- Nonelective and matching contributions in a SIMPLE 401(k) plan or safe harbor 401(k) plan (see Qs 2:220–2:269)

Q 2:194 What kinds of contributions are not subject to the 100 percent vesting requirement?

In a 401(k) plan that does not qualify as a SIMPLE plan or a safe harbor 401(k) plan, nonelective contributions (see Q 2:94) and matching contributions (see Q 2:86) are not required to be 100 percent vested at all times. Instead, these contributions must become vested under a vesting schedule at least as rapidly as under one of the two schedules below.

Nonelective		*Matching*	
Years of Service	*Vested Percentage*	*Years of Service*	*Vested Percentage*
Fewer than 3	0	Fewer than 2	0
3	20	2	20
4	40	3	40
5	60	4	60
6	80	5	80
7 or more	100	6 or more	100
Fewer than 5	0	Fewer than 3	0
5 or more	100	3 or more	100

As a result of the enactment of the PPA, the vesting schedules above for nonelective contributions no longer apply starting with plan years beginning after December 31, 2006. Nonelective contributions made with respect to plan years beginning after that date must become vested under either of the schedules that apply to matching contributions. Although not required to do so, most 401(k) plans, in the case of a participant who had completed an hour of service on or after the first day of a plan year beginning in 2007 or thereafter, applied the six-year graded and three-year cliff vesting schedules to nonelective contributions made for pre-2007 plan years as that simplified the administration of a

401(k) plan. [I.R.C. § 411(a)(2)(B)] (See Q 2:63 for the special vesting schedule that applies to safe harbor contributions under a 401(k) plan that contains a qualified automatic contribution arrangement.)

Q 2:195 What is a *year of service*?

A *year of service* means any vesting computation period during which an employee completes the number of hours of service specified in the plan. Not more than 1,000 hours may be specified for this purpose. [I.R.C. § 411(a)(5)(A)] (See Q 2:175 for a discussion of the term *hour of service.*)

Q 2:196 What is a *vesting computation period*?

In most 401(k) plans the *vesting computation period* is the plan year. However, any 12-month period may be selected as long as it applies to all participants. [DOL Reg. § 2530.203-2(a)]

Q 2:197 Is a 401(k) plan permitted to disregard any years of service when calculating a participant's vested percentage?

Yes. A 401(k) plan may disregard any years of service completed with respect to vesting computation periods ending before a participant's eighteenth birthday. [I.R.C. § 411(a)(4)(A)] Years of service completed before an employer maintained a 401(k) plan or any predecessor plan may also be disregarded. [Treas. Reg. § 1.411(a)-5(b)(3)]

Q 2:198 What is a *predecessor plan*?

If a 401(k) plan is established within the five-year period immediately preceding or following the date another qualified plan terminates, then the other qualified plan is considered a *predecessor plan* to the 401(k) plan. [Treas. Reg. § 1.411(a)-5(b)(3)(v)]

Example. The Pine Tree Company's qualified defined benefit plan terminated on January 1, 2011. Pine Tree establishes a 401(k) plan on January 1, 2015. The defined benefit plan is a predecessor plan with respect to the 401(k) plan because the 401(k) plan is established within the five-year period immediately following the date the defined benefit plan was terminated.

Q 2:199 For purposes of vesting, if a participant terminates employment and is then rehired at a later date, is the plan allowed to ignore years of service completed by the participant before termination of employment?

Unless a plan contains a break-in-service rule that applies to the participant, all of an employee's prior years of vesting service with an employer must be taken into account. (*Employer* is defined in chapter 10.) [Treas. Reg. § 1.411(a)-5(a)]

Example 1. The Farmlot Feed Company sponsors a 401(k) plan that contains no break-in-service rules and that applies a vesting schedule to the matching contributions made under the plan. Linda, a plan participant, terminates employment on July 15, 2014, and is rehired August 15, 2016. Linda's years of service prior to July 15, 2014, must be taken into account in determining the vested percentage in her account balance attributable to matching contributions.

Example 2. The facts are the same as those in Example 1, except that Linda was never a participant in the 401(k) plan because she was a member of a collective bargaining unit not covered under the plan. As in Example 1, Linda is hired, but is now in a class of employees covered under the 401(k) plan. Linda's years of service completed before July 15, 2014, must be taken into account even though they were earned while she was not in a class of employees eligible to participate in the plan.

Q 2:200 What special vesting rules apply to an employee who has veterans' reemployment rights under USERRA?

In the case of an employee who has reemployment rights under USERRA, each period of qualified military service will be treated as service with the employer for purposes of determining the employee's vesting. [I.R.C. § 414(u)(8)(B)]

Q 2:201 What break-in-service rules may apply in determining an employee's vested percentage?

There are three break-in-service rules:

1. The one-year break-in-service rule (see Q 2:202);
2. The rule of parity (see Q 2:203); and
3. The five-year rule (see Q 2:204).

Q 2:202 For purposes of vesting, how does the one-year break-in-service rule operate?

Under this rule, a 401(k) plan may disregard years of service completed before a one-year break in service until the employee completes a year of service after the break. Upon completion of a year of service following the break, the employee's pre-break years of service are again taken into account in determining the employee's vested percentage. [Treas. Reg. § 1.411(a)-6(c)(1)(i)]

Q 2:203 What is the *rule of parity* for vesting purposes?

The *rule of parity* allows a 401(k) plan to disregard pre-break years of service if a participant does not have a vested account balance under the plan and the number of consecutive one-year breaks in service equals or exceeds the greater of five or the number of years of service completed before the break. This rule will generally have little significance in a 401(k) plan as it will not apply to participants who have made 100 percent-vested elective contributions to the plan. [I.R.C. § 411(a)(6)(D)]

Q 2:204 What is the *five-year rule*?

In the case of a participant who has incurred five consecutive one-year breaks in service, the *five-year rule* permits a 401(k) plan to disregard years of service completed after the break in determining the vested percentage of the participant's account balance attributable to contributions allocated before the break. [I.R.C. § 411(a)(6)(C)]

> **Example.** A 401(k) plan provides for nonelective contributions allocated in proportion to participant compensation. At the time she terminates employment, Betty has completed four years of service and is 60 percent vested in her account balance attributable to nonelective contributions. Betty incurs five consecutive one-year breaks in service and is then rehired. Any service completed after she returns cannot increase the vested percentage of her account balance attributable to nonelective contributions allocated to her account before her termination of employment.

Q 2:205 For purposes of vesting, what is a *one-year break in service*?

A *one-year break in service* is a vesting computation period during which an employee fails to complete more than 500 hours of service. [DOL Reg. §§ 2530.200b-4(a)(1), 2530.200b-4(a)(3)]

Q 2:206 How do maternity or paternity leaves of absence affect the determination of whether an employee incurs a one-year break in service for purposes of vesting?

Solely for the purpose of determining whether an employee has incurred a one-year break in service, an employee absent from work on account of a maternity or paternity leave of absence must be credited with up to 500 hours of service. The number of hours of service credited during the absence will be the number of hours of service that otherwise would normally have been credited or, if that number cannot be determined, 8 hours of service per day. The hours will be credited to the vesting computation period in which the absence begins, if an employee would be prevented from incurring a one-year break in service, or in the immediately following vesting computation period. A maternity or paternity leave of absence is any absence from work as the result of the pregnancy of the employee, the birth of the employee's child, the placement of the employee's adopted child, or the caring for the child after its birth or placement. [I.R.C. § 411(a)(6)(E)]

Additional hours are not explicitly required for unpaid leave under FMLA. However, the FMLA regulations do state that any period of unpaid FMLA leave shall not be treated as or counted toward a break in service for purposes of vesting in a retirement plan. [DOL Reg. § 825.215(d)(4)] In addition to maternity and paternity leave, FMLA leave can include up to 12 weeks for a serious health condition affecting the employee or a family member.

Q 2:207 Can a vesting schedule be amended to reduce a participant's vested percentage?

No. The vested percentage (as determined under the 401(k) plan prior to the amendment) of an employee who is a participant on the later of the date the amendment is adopted or the date the amendment is made effective cannot be reduced by reason of an amendment to the vesting schedule. [Treas. Reg. § 1.411(a)-8(a)]

Q 2:208 Do any participants have the right to have the vested percentage of their account balances determined under the previous vesting schedule?

Yes. Any participant with three or more years of service by the end of an election period has the right to select the previous vesting schedule. This election right, however, need not be provided to any participant whose vested percentage under the amended schedule would never be less than the percentage determined under the previous schedule. [Temp. Treas. Reg. §§ 1.411(a)-8T(b)(1), 1.411(a)-8T(b)(3)]

Q 2:209 What is the election period for selecting the previous vesting schedule?

The election period is a period beginning no later than the date on which the amended vesting schedule is adopted and ending on the latest of the following dates:

1. Sixty days after the amended vesting schedule is adopted;
2. Sixty days after the amended vesting schedule is made effective; or
3. Sixty days after a participant is provided a written notice of the amendment.

[Temp. Treas. Reg. § 1.411(a)-8T(b)(2)]

Q 2:210 How do the anti-cutback rules interact with the rules relating to changes in vesting schedules?

The anti-cutback rules prevent the application of a vesting schedule change to benefits accrued up to the effective date of the amendment making the change even if the change in the vesting schedule complies with the law. [Treas. Reg. § 1.411(d)-3(a)(3)]

Example. A 401(k) plan that applies a 20 percent per year of service vesting schedule to nonelective contributions is amended to apply instead a six-year graded vesting schedule. John has two years of service and is consequently 40 percent vested on the date of the amendment. Though it is acceptable for the plan to apply the amended vesting schedule to John, it can only be applied to benefits accrued after the effective date of the amendment. Thus, after completing three years of service, John will be 60 percent vested in his pre-amendment account balance and 40 percent vested in his post-amendment account balance.

Q 2:211 Under what circumstance will the nonvested portion of a participant's account balance be forfeited?

The forfeiture of a participant's nonvested accounts will ordinarily occur only after the participant's termination of employment.

Q 2:212 When will the forfeiture occur?

The timing of the forfeiture depends on whether the plan has a cash out/buy back rule. For 401(k) plans without this rule, the nonvested portion of a participant's account balance generally is not forfeited until the participant incurs five consecutive one-year breaks in service (see Q 2:204). In the case of a 401(k) plan that contains the cash out/buy back rule, the forfeiture typically occurs at the time the participant receives all or any part of his or her vested interest in the plan.

Q 2:213 What is the *cash out/buy back rule*?

The *cash out/buy back rule* permits the forfeiture of a participant's nonvested account balance upon distribution to the participant of all or part of the vested portion of his or her account balance. This rule will apply, however, only if two conditions are met:

1. The distribution is made no later than the close of the second plan year following the plan year in which the employee's termination of participation occurs; and
2. The plan contains a repayment provision.

[Treas. Reg. § 1.411(a)-7(d)(4)]

Q 2:214 How much may be forfeited?

The amount that may be forfeited depends upon the amount distributed to the participant. If the participant's entire vested account balance is distributed, then the entire nonvested portion of the account balance may be forfeited. If a participant receives less than all of his or her vested account balance, then only a portion of the nonvested account can be forfeited. That portion is determined by multiplying the nonvested account balance by the amount of the distribution and then dividing by the vested account balance. [Treas. Reg. § 1.411(a)-7(d)(4)(iii)]

Q 2:215 What happens to forfeitures under a 401(k) plan?

The disposition of forfeitures depends on the terms of the 401(k) plan. They may, for example, be allocated as if they were additional employer matching and/or nonelective contributions. On the other hand, they can be used to reduce matching and/or nonelective contributions. Some plans provide that forfeitures attributable to nonelective contributions are reallocated and those attributable to matching contributions are used to reduce such contributions. Section 401(k) plans may also direct that forfeitures be used first to pay plan administration expenses. The IRS has recently taken the position, as evidenced by its LRMs (List of Required Modifications) for 401(k) plans, that forfeitures cannot be used by an employer to offset the safe harbor contributions it is required to make under a regular or QACA safe harbor plan.

Repayment Rights

Q 2:216 What is the *plan repayment provision*?

Under the *plan repayment provision,* the nonvested portion of an employee's account balance that was previously forfeited must be restored to the employee upon repayment by the employee of the full amount previously distributed. A plan is not required to extend repayment rights to an employee until the employee is again covered under the plan. [Treas. Reg. § 1.411(a)-7(d)(4)(iv)]

Q 2:217 Must the previously forfeited amount that is restored to an employee be credited with interest from the date of the forfeiture?

No. The previously forfeited amount is not required to be credited with interest. [Treas. Reg. § 1.411(a)-7(d)(4)(v)]

Q 2:218 May the plan impose limits on the participant's repayment rights?

Yes. The 401(k) plan may provide that a participant's repayment rights expire at the earlier of the following:

1. Five years after the day the participant is reemployed; or
2. At the end of a period of five consecutive one-year breaks in service.

[Treas. Reg. § 1.411(a)-7(d)(4)(iv)(C)]

> **Example.** John, a participant in GHI Company's 401(k) plan, receives a distribution of $10,000 following his termination of employment in 2011. The nonvested portion of his interest in the plan, $5,000, is forfeited under the plan's cash out/buy back rule. John is rehired on January 1, 2016, after incurring four consecutive one-year breaks in service. Because he has not incurred five consecutive one-year breaks in service, John's repayment rights are still in effect. His right of payment cannot lapse until January 1, 2021, five years after his date of reemployment.

Q 2:219 If repayment rights are exercised, what funds may be used to restore previously forfeited account balances?

The plan can restore previously forfeited account balances from plan earnings, current forfeitures, or employer contributions. [Treas. Reg. § 1.411(a)-7(d)(6)(iii)(C)]

SIMPLE 401(k) Plans

Q 2:220 What is a *SIMPLE 401(k) plan*?

A *SIMPLE 401(k) plan* is a 401(k) plan under which an eligible employer no longer needs to be concerned with discrimination testing (see chapter 13) or with top-heavy rules (see chapter 14). [I.R.C. §§ 401(k)(11), 401(m)(10)] There is a trade-off, however. SIMPLE 401(k) plans mandate fixed levels of employer contributions, lower the elective deferral limit, and require 100 percent vesting of employer contributions. [I.R.C. § 401(k)(11)]

SIMPLE 401(k) plans are similar to SIMPLE retirement account plans, but they also differ in important ways. (SIMPLE retirement account plans, also called SIMPLE IRA plans, are discussed in chapter 22.)

Q 2:221 Which employers are eligible to sponsor SIMPLE 401(k) plans?

Any employer that has 100 or fewer employees with at least $5,000 of compensation in the preceding calendar year is eligible to sponsor a SIMPLE 401(k) plan. Eligible employers include private tax-exempt organizations but not governmental employers. The Section 414 employer aggregation and leased employee rules apply in determining which employees to count (see chapter 10). An employer that no longer satisfies the 100-employee rule may continue to sponsor a SIMPLE 401(k) plan during a two-year grace period. [Treas. Reg. § 1.401(k)-4(b)]

> **Example.** Because it had only 80 employees earning at least $5,000 during calendar year 2014, Small Company, Inc. decided to establish a SIMPLE 401(k) plan for the 2015 calendar year. During 2015 and 2016, Small Company, Inc. employed fewer than 100 $5,000-per-year employees. In 2017, however, the number of such employees exceeded 100. The grace period during which Small Company, Inc. may continue to maintain its SIMPLE 401(k) plan consists of the years 2018 and 2019.

Q 2:222 Are all employees required to be covered under a SIMPLE 401(k) plan?

No. A SIMPLE 401(k) plan differs from a SIMPLE IRA in that it can exclude groups of employees and employees of other members of a controlled or affiliated service group. The SIMPLE IRA is generally required to cover all employees of the employer (including other members of a controlled or affiliated service group) who meet the eligibility requirements for a SIMPLE IRA (see chapter 22). However, a SIMPLE 401(k) plan that does not cover all non-excludable employees must meet the Section 410(b) minimum coverage rules (see chapter 11).

Q 2:223 What dollar limit applies to elective contributions under a SIMPLE 401(k) plan?

The 2015 dollar limitation on elective contributions is $12,500, a limitation that will be adjusted for cost-of-living increases in increments of $500. There is also a provision for catch-up contributions for participants who have attained age 50, as explained in chapter 9. The age-50 catch-up limit for 2015 is $3,000. [I.R.C. § 414(v)(2); Treas. Reg. § 1.401(k)-4(e)(2)]

Even with these increases in the annual contribution limit, the SIMPLE 401(k) plan dollar limit is significantly less than the dollar limit that applies to a safe harbor 401(k) plan or a 401(k) plan containing a qualified automatic contribution arrangement (QACA).

Q 2:224 Under what conditions would the reduced elective deferral limit for SIMPLE 401(k) plans make sense?

In a 401(k) plan with low participation rates on the part of NHCEs, the nondiscrimination test that applies to elective contributions (see chapter 13) may prevent HCEs from deferring the maximum permitted amount ($18,000 for 2015).

Q 2:225 What employer contributions are required to be made to a SIMPLE 401(k) plan?

An employer is required to provide a dollar-for-dollar match on salary deferrals up to 3 percent of compensation. However, in lieu of making the matching contribution, an employer may elect to make a nonelective contribution of 2 percent of compensation to all eligible employees. [Treas. Reg. § 1.401(k)-4(e)(2) & (3)] This election must be made and communicated to employees within a reasonable time before the 60th day before the beginning of the calendar year for which the election is effective. [Treas. Reg. § 1.401(k)-4(d)] When calculating the required matching or nonelective contributions, a SIMPLE 401(k) plan must cap compensation at the Section 401(a)(17) limit ($265,000 for 2015). (Compensation is not limited by Code Section 401(a)(17) when calculating matching contributions under a SIMPLE IRA plan.)

Q 2:226 How do the employer contribution requirements of a SIMPLE IRA compare with those of a SIMPLE 401(k) plan?

The requirements are basically the same. In the case of a SIMPLE IRA, however, the employer can elect, in no more than two years in any five-year period, to apply the dollar-for-dollar match to deferrals below 3 percent of compensation (but not below 1 percent of compensation). [I.R.C. §§ 408(p)(2)(A)(iii) and (C)(ii)]

Q 2:227 May an employer contribute more than the amount required to be contributed to a SIMPLE 401(k) plan?

No. The limitation on the amount that can be contributed by an employer will make the SIMPLE 401(k) plan unattractive to employers that wish to contribute and deduct the maximum amount permitted under the law (see chapter 9). [Treas. Reg. § 1.401(k)-4(e)(1)] In this respect, a SIMPLE 401(k) plan is similar to a SIMPLE IRA.

Q 2:228 May employees eligible for a SIMPLE 401(k) plan also participate in other retirement plans of the sponsoring employer?

No. The existence of one or more other retirement plans covering any of the same eligible employees would eliminate the SIMPLE 401(k) plan as an option. For example, an employer with a separate profit sharing plan providing a contribution rate of 10 percent of compensation cannot continue to maintain that plan and also provide a SIMPLE 401(k) plan to any of the same group of participants. Nor can the employer terminate the profit sharing plan and provide the same 10 percent nonelective contribution rate under a SIMPLE 401(k) plan, since those contributions would be limited to 2 percent of compensation (see Q 2:225). [Treas. Reg. § 1.401(k)-4(c)]

Q 2:229 May employees who are not eligible to participate in a SIMPLE 401(k) plan participate in another qualified plan maintained by the employer?

Yes. Assuming the other qualified plan satisfies the Section 410(b) minimum coverage requirements (see chapter 11), the employer may maintain that plan for the employees who are not covered by the SIMPLE 401(k) plan. This would not be possible if the employer maintains a SIMPLE IRA, because the SIMPLE IRA must be the only plan maintained by the employer. [I.R.C. § 408(p)(2)(D)]

Q 2:230 What conditions, if any, can be placed on the receipt of matching contributions in a SIMPLE 401(k) plan?

No conditions are allowed just as in the case of a SIMPLE IRA; therefore, an employer must match elective contributions made by all eligible employees. Consequently, a SIMPLE 401(k) plan will not appeal to an employer whose existing 401(k) plan requires an employee to complete a specified number (not more than 1,000) of hours of service during the year and/or to be employed on the last day of the year in order to be entitled to a matching contribution. Of course, if conditions such as these are imposed in a non-SIMPLE 401(k) plan, the employer must be concerned about the 401(k) plan's meeting the Section 410(b) minimum coverage rules (see chapter 11). [Treas. Reg. § 1.401(k)-4(e)(3)]

Q 2:231 What conditions, if any, can be placed on the receipt of the 2 percent nonelective contribution in a SIMPLE 401(k) plan?

As with matching contributions, no hours of service and/or last day requirements are allowed. However, an employer may require a participant to have received $5,000 of compensation during the plan year (or any lesser amount specified by the employer) to be entitled to an allocation of the 2 percent nonelective contribution. [Treas. Reg. § 1.401(k)-4(e)(4)]

Q 2:232 Can a SIMPLE 401(k) plan have minimum age and service requirements that must be met before an employee can become a participant?

Yes. In this respect there is no difference between a regular 401(k) plan and a SIMPLE 401(k) plan (see Qs 2:169–2:178). Hence, employers adopting SIMPLE 401(k) plans can prevent part-time employees (less than 1,000 hours of service in an eligibility computation period) from becoming plan participants. This feature cannot be duplicated in a SIMPLE IRA plan because employees can be kept out of a SIMPLE IRA plan only if their compensation is below $5,000 (see chapter 22).

Q 2:233 What special vesting rules apply to SIMPLE 401(k) plans?

A SIMPLE 401(k) plan must provide that employer contributions as well as elective contributions be 100 percent immediately vested. In a regular 401(k) plan, on the other hand, employer contributions can be made subject to a vesting schedule (see Q 2:194). If an employer has low employee turnover, the 100 percent immediate vesting requirement will probably not be of great concern. High turnover that consistently produces substantial forfeitures will make the SIMPLE 401(k) plan unattractive to employers with a high-turnover workforce. [Treas. Reg. § 1.401(k)-4(f)]

Q 2:234 What are the distribution rules for a SIMPLE 401(k) plan?

The distribution rules that apply to 401(k) plans also apply to SIMPLE 401(k) plans—that is, the plan may allow the withdrawal of elective deferrals only upon the occurrence of certain events (e.g., attainment of age 59, financial hardship, death, disability, severance of employment, or plan termination). These restrictions on distribution do not apply to elective contributions made to a SIMPLE IRA, which can be taken out of the plan at any time.

Matching or nonelective contributions made to a SIMPLE 401(k) plan are not subject to the restrictions that apply to elective deferrals. However, a SIMPLE 401(k) plan can be designed and written to limit access to those contributions as well. In a SIMPLE IRA, on the other hand, employer contributions may be withdrawn at any time.

Q 2:235 How do the minimum distribution rules apply to a SIMPLE 401(k) plan?

The minimum distribution rules apply to a SIMPLE 401(k) plan in the same way that they apply to any other qualified plan. Thus, a currently employed participant who is not a 5 percent owner is not required to receive a minimum distribution until the April 1 following the calendar year in which he or she retires. SIMPLE IRAs, on the other hand, are subject to the IRA minimum distribution rules—in other words, minimum distributions must begin by the April 1 following the calendar year in which the individual attains age 70½.

Q 2:236 Are SIMPLE 401(k) plans subject to the joint and survivor annuity requirements under Code Sections 401(a)(11) and 417?

Because SIMPLE 401(k) plans are qualified plans, they can be subject to these requirements. In most cases, however, SIMPLE 401(k) plans are drafted so that they are exempt from the joint and survivor requirements under Code Sections 401(a)(11) and 417 (see chapter 17). SIMPLE IRAs, because they are not qualified plans, are not subject to the joint and survivor annuity requirements.

Q 2:237 Can an employer suspend contributions to a SIMPLE 401(k) plan during the plan year?

No. Unlike the regulations that govern safe harbor plans, in which there are provisions for mid-year suspension of safe harbor contributions or plan termination, there are no such provisions for SIMPLE 401(k) plans. A SIMPLE 401(k) plan can only be terminated as of December 31. [Treas. Reg. § 1.401(k)-4(g)]

Q 2:238 Are there other differences between SIMPLE 401(k) plans and SIMPLE IRAs?

Yes. Some of the other differences between SIMPLE 401(k) plans and SIMPLE IRAs are as follows:

- In a SIMPLE 401(k) plan, if a participant's vested account balance exceeds the mandatory force-out amount, the participant cannot be forced to take a distribution. In a SIMPLE IRA, the participant always controls the timing of distributions from his or her IRA.
- Account balances in a SIMPLE 401(k) plan are protected from assignment under Code Section 401(a)(13); a SIMPLE IRA does not have the same protections, but with the enactment of the Bankruptcy Abuse Prevention and Consumer Protection Act of 2005, SIMPLE IRAs are now exempt.
- A SIMPLE 401(k) plan can be designed to permit plan loans to participants. In a SIMPLE IRA, loans are prohibited.

- SIMPLE 401(k) plans have more extensive administrative requirements than SIMPLE IRAs (i.e., the plan sponsor must file the Form 5500 annually and distribute SPDs to the plan's participants). These requirements do not apply to SIMPLE IRAs.

Safe Harbor 401(k) Plans

Q 2:239 What is a *safe harbor 401(k) plan*?

A *safe harbor 401(k) plan* is a 401(k) plan under which an employer will no longer be required to perform nondiscrimination testing of elective contributions or matching contributions. [I.R.C. §§ 401(k)(12), 401(m)(11)] To land within the safe harbor, a 401(k) plan must meet certain employer contribution requirements and, like a SIMPLE 401(k) plan, must provide for 100 percent immediate vesting of these contributions. Other limitations that apply to SIMPLE 401(k) plans—reduced elective deferral limits and exclusive plan requirements—do not apply to safe harbor 401(k) plans. This should make safe harbor 401(k) plans more attractive to employers than the SIMPLE 401(k) option. The following questions and answers describe the benefits and myriad requirements of safe harbor 401(k) plans.

Q 2:240 Under what circumstances can an employer adopt a safe harbor 401(k) plan?

The safe harbor design is available for both new and existing plans. In the case of an existing 401(k) plan, the amendment converting the 401(k) plan to a safe harbor plan must be adopted before the plan year the conversion takes effect. This requirement, together with the employee notice requirement (see Q 2:241), makes it necessary for an employer to consider a safe harbor conversion long before the plan year for which the conversion is to be effective. [Treas. Reg. § 1.401(k)-3(e)(1)]

If an existing plan is not a 401(k) plan (for example, a profit sharing plan), the plan can be converted to a safe harbor 401(k) plan after the beginning of a plan year as long as the plan will function as a safe harbor 401(k) plan for at least three months. [Treas. Reg. § 1.401(k)-3(e)(2)]

In the case of a newly established 401(k) plan, the first plan year must be at least three months long (or any shorter period if established soon after the employer comes into existence). [Treas. Reg. § 1.401(k)-3(e)(2)] A safe harbor plan will not be considered "newly established" if it is a successor plan. A plan is a successor plan if 50 percent or more of the eligible employees for the first plan year were eligible under another 401(k) plan of the employer in the prior year. [Treas. Reg. § 1.401(k)-2(c)(2)(iii)] In that situation, the employer would have to wait to adopt 401(k) safe harbor provisions effective as of the next full plan year.

Q 2:241 What notice must be given to an employee eligible to participate in a safe harbor 401(k) plan?

Each eligible employee must be given written notice of rights and obligations under the safe harbor 401(k) plan within a reasonable period before the beginning of the plan year (or, in the year an employee becomes eligible, within a reasonable period before the employee becomes eligible). Giving such notice at least 30 days (and no more than 90 days) before the beginning of each plan year (for employees entering the plan on a day other than the first day of the plan year, during the 90-day period ending on the date of entry) is deemed to satisfy the timing requirement. If it is not feasible to provide notice before the date the employee becomes eligible to participate (e.g., if the plan provides for immediate entry), the notice will still be considered timely if it is given as soon as possible after the employee's eligibility date, and the employee is permitted to elect to defer on any compensation earned beginning on the date he or she becomes eligible. [Treas. Reg. § 1.401(k)-3(d)(3)]

Q 2:242 Can the safe harbor notice required to be given to each eligible employee be provided through electronic media?

Yes. A safe harbor notice can be provided electronically if it meets the requirements of Treasury Regulations Section 1.401(a)-21. These requirements are explained in chapter 16 in the discussion of the right-to-defer notice.

Q 2:243 What information must be contained in a safe harbor notice?

The safe harbor notice must contain the following information:

1. A description of the safe harbor matching or nonelective contribution formula.
2. A description of any other employer contributions under the plan (including the potential for discretionary matching contributions) and the conditions under which these contributions will be made.
3. The identity of the plan to which the safe harbor contributions will be made if it is a plan other than the 401(k) plan.
4. The type and amount of compensation that may be deferred.
5. A description of how a deferral election is made, including any administrative requirements that may apply.
6. The periods during the plan year deferral elections may be made.
7. A description of the plan's withdrawal and vesting provisions.
8. How to obtain additional information about the plan by indicating the telephone numbers, addresses, and electronic addresses of individuals or offices where this information can be obtained.

[Treas. Reg. § 1.401(k)-3(d)(2)(ii)]

See Appendix A for a sample 401(k) safe harbor notice.

Q 2:244 May a safe harbor plan satisfy the notice requirement by providing an employee with a copy of the plan's summary plan description?

No, but the notice may incorporate by reference certain parts of the SPD. The notice can cross-reference those sections of the SPD that address the information required to be disclosed in items 2 through 4 in Q 2:243. [Treas. Reg. § 1.401(k)-3(d)(2)(iii)]

Q 2:245 What are the main advantages and disadvantages of adopting a safe harbor 401(k) plan?

By adopting a safe harbor 401(k) plan, a plan sponsor can avoid ADP testing of elective contributions and ACP testing of matching contributions. The ADP and ACP tests are used to determine whether the amount of elective contributions and matching and after-tax contributions discriminate in favor of HCEs (see chapter 13). The advantage of avoiding certain nondiscrimination testing must be weighed against these disadvantages: the required contributions under a safe harbor 401(k) plan can be costly, and the annual participant notice requirements can be cumbersome. [I.R.C. §§ 401(k)(12), 401(m)(11)]

Generally speaking, employers that might benefit from a safe harbor design include the following:

- Employers with highly paid employees unable to contribute the full 401(k) dollar amount ($18,000 in 2015) because of low participation rates on the part of lower-paid employees
- Employers already making (or planning to make) employer contributions at or near the safe harbor levels
- Employers required to make top-heavy minimum contributions
- Employers with plans using a cross-tested profit sharing formula (i.e., the contribution allocation is tested under the general nondiscrimination test on the basis of projected benefits)
- Employers with relatively low employee turnover

Q 2:246 How is ADP testing avoided with a safe harbor design?

A 401(k) plan will satisfy the ADP test if the prescribed level of employer contributions is made on behalf of all eligible NHCEs and if the employees are provided a timely notice describing their rights and obligations under the plan. The employer contributions must be required under the terms of the plan document. [Treas. Reg. § 1.401(k)-3(b), (c)]

Q 2:247 What employer contributions must be made to a safe harbor 401(k) plan?

Under a safe harbor 401(k) plan, an employer can elect to provide either of the following contributions to its eligible NHCEs:

1. A dollar-for-dollar match on elective contributions up to 3 percent of compensation and a 50 cents-on-the-dollar match on elective contributions between 3 percent and 5 percent of compensation (the *basic matching formula*) [Treas. Reg. § 1.401(k)-3(c)], or
2. A nonelective contribution equal to at least 3 percent of compensation. [Treas. Reg. § 1.401(k)-3(b)]

Q 2:248 Can other matching contribution formulas satisfy the safe harbor?

Yes. If the aggregate amount of matching contributions under an *enhanced matching formula* at any given rate of elective contributions is at least equal to the aggregate amount of matching contributions that would be made under the basic matching formula (see Q 2:247), then the alternative formula will satisfy the safe harbor.

An alternative formula will *not* satisfy the safe harbor, however, if the rate of matching contribution increases as the rate of elective contribution increases or if, at any rate of elective contributions, the rate of matching contributions that would apply with respect to any HCE who is an eligible employee is greater than the rate of matching contributions that would apply with respect to an NHCE who is an eligible employee and who has the same rate of elective contributions. [Treas. Reg. § 1.401(k)-3(c)(3) & (4)]

Q 2:249 What is a "maybe" safe harbor nonelective contribution?

A "maybe" safe harbor nonelective contribution provides a safe harbor nonelective contribution (see Q 2:247), but permits the employer to decide each year whether the contribution will be made. The annual notice provided to participants (see Q 2:243) must indicate that the employer may make a safe harbor nonelective for the upcoming plan year, and, if it elects to do so, participants will be notified no later than 30 days before the end of the plan year of the employer's decision to make the safe harbor nonelective contribution. In each year the employer decides to make the safe harbor nonelective contribution, the plan must be amended no later than the deadline for providing notice to the participants. For plan years in which the safe harbor nonelective contribution will not be made, the plan must provide for current year testing for ADP and ACP testing purposes. [Treas. Reg. § 1.401(k)-3(f)]

Q 2:250 How is ACP testing avoided with a safe harbor design?

A plan that satisfies the ADP test safe harbor will also satisfy the ACP test safe harbor if any of the following is true:

1. The plan provides safe harbor matching contributions using the basic matching formula (see Q 2:247), and no other matching contributions are provided under the plan;

2. The plan provides safe harbor matching contributions using an enhanced matching formula (see Q 2:248) under which matching contributions are made only with respect to elective contributions that do not exceed 6 percent of the employee's compensation, and no other matching contributions are provided under the plan; or
3. The 401(k) plan provides matching contributions, other than safe harbor matching contributions, and (a) the matching contributions are not made with respect to employee contributions or elective contributions that in the aggregate exceed 6 percent of the employee's compensation, (b) the rate of matching contributions does not increase as the rate of employee contributions or elective contributions increases, and (c) at any rate of employee contributions or elective contributions, the rate of matching contributions that would apply with respect to any HCE who is an eligible employee is no greater than the rate of matching contributions that would apply with respect to an NHCE who is an eligible employee and who has the same rate of employee contributions or elective contributions. [Treas. Reg. § 1.401(m)-3(d)]

A plan that satisfies the ADP test safe harbor with matching contributions under the basic matching formula or an enhanced matching formula will not cause the ACP test safe harbor to be failed merely because additional matching contributions may be made at the employer's discretion. The plan will fail to satisfy the ACP test safe harbor, however, if the plan provides for discretionary matching contributions on behalf of any employee that, in the aggregate, could exceed a dollar amount equal to 4 percent of the employee's compensation. [Treas. Reg. § 1.401(m)-3(d)(3)]

The following examples illustrate the requirements of the ACP test safe harbor rules:

Example 1. An employer's only plan, Plan M, satisfies the ADP test safe harbor using safe harbor matching contributions under the basic matching formula. No contributions, other than elective contributions and contributions under the basic matching formula, are made to Plan M. Because Plan M satisfies the ADP test safe harbor using the basic matching formula and Plan M provides for no other matching contributions, Plan M automatically satisfies the ACP test safe harbor.

Example 2. Beginning January 1, 2015, Plan N satisfies the ADP test safe harbor using a 3 percent safe harbor nonelective contribution. Plan N also provides matching contributions equal to 50 percent of each eligible employee's elective contributions up to 6 percent of compensation. Matching contributions under Plan N are fully vested after three years of service. No other matching contributions are provided for under Plan N. The plan is maintained on a calendar-year basis, and all contributions for a plan year are made within 12 months after the end of the plan year. Based on these facts, Plan N satisfies the ACP test safe harbor with respect to matching contributions because the ADP test safe harbor is satisfied and because the matching contribution limitations (described in item 3, above) are not exceeded.

Example 3. The facts are the same as those in Example 2 above, except that Plan N provides matching contributions equal to 50 percent of each eligible employee's elective contributions. Plan N does *not* satisfy the matching contribution limitations because matching contributions are made with respect to elective contributions that exceed 6 percent of compensation. Thus, based on these facts, Plan N fails to satisfy the ACP test safe harbor.

Example 4. The facts are the same as those in Example 2 above, except that Plan N also provides that Employer B, in its discretion, may make additional matching contributions up to 50 percent of each eligible employee's elective contributions that do not exceed 6 percent of compensation. Plan N does not fail to satisfy the ACP test safe harbor on account of discretionary matching contributions, because, under Plan N, the amount of discretionary matching contributions cannot exceed 4 percent of an employee's compensation.

Q 2:251 In determining whether an HCE receives a rate of match that is not greater than the rate of match of any NHCE, are NHCEs, who terminate during the plan year and who, therefore, do not receive an allocation of matching contribution under the terms of the plan, taken into account?

Yes. Any NHCE who is an eligible employee but who does not receive a matching allocation because of the operation of a last-day requirement and/or the 1,000-hours-of-service requirement must be taken into account in determining whether an HCE would receive a greater rate of match than any eligible NHCE. A 401(k) plan with either or both of these requirements for entitlement to a matching contribution allocation will not satisfy the ACP safe harbor.

Q 2:252 May an employer make additional contributions to a safe harbor 401(k) plan?

Yes. An employer that provides a safe harbor matching contribution could, for example, also make a profit sharing contribution to the safe harbor 401(k) plan.

Q 2:253 May an employer stop safe harbor matching contributions during the plan year?

A 401(k) plan using a safe harbor match formula can be amended during the plan year to reduce or eliminate matching contributions. Employees must be notified beforehand of the amendment and be given an opportunity to change their deferral elections. However, starting with plan years beginning on or after January 1, 2015, an employer's freedom to reduce or eliminate safe harbor matching contributions has been cut back. Such an amendment can only be made if the employer is (1) operating at an economic loss as defined in Code Section 412(c)(2)(A) or (2) the safe harbor notice (see Q 2:243) includes a statement that the plan may be amended during the plan year to reduce or eliminate safe harbor matching contributions and that the reduction or elimination will not apply until at least 30 days after all eligible employees are provided notice of the reduction or elimination.

Whether the amendment suspending or reducing safe harbor matching contributions is adopted before, during, or after 2015, the amendment cannot be effective earlier than the date the plan is amended and 30 days after the notice is given. The employer makes the safe harbor match contributions through the effective date of the amendment. ADP and ACP testing, using the current year method (see chapter 13), will apply to all elective and matching contributions (including the safe harbor matching contributions) made during the plan year. [Treas. Reg. §§ 1.401(k)-3(g), 1.401(m)-3(h)] It should be noted that suspending safe harbor contributions (whether match or nonelective as explained in Q 2:254) may result in the employer having to make minimum contributions on behalf of non-key employees if the 401(k) plan is top heavy for the plan year in which the suspension occurs.

Q 2:254 May an employer stop safe harbor nonelective contributions during the plan year?

Yes. For plan years beginning before January 1, 2014, proposed regulations issued in early 2009 permitted the suspension of safe harbor nonelective contributions during the plan year. In addition to meeting the requirements set forth in Q 2:253, the employer must have sustained a substantial business hardship comparable to that described in Code Section 412(c). [Prop. Treas. Reg. §§ 1.401(k)-3(g)(1)(ii), 1.401(m)-3(h)(1)(ii)]

Starting with plan years beginning on or after January 1, 2014, the rules for reducing or eliminating safe harbor nonelective contributions are the same as those that apply starting in 2015 to the reduction or elimination of safe harbor matching contributions. The new rules amount to a liberalization of the circumstances under which a safe harbor nonelective plan is able to eliminate or reduce safe harbor nonelective contributions. These rules have no application to "maybe" safe harbor plans given the nature of their design (see Q 2:249). [Treas. Reg. §§ 1.401(k)-3, 1.401(m)-3(h)]

Q 2:255 What special vesting rules apply to safe harbor 401(k) plans?

A safe harbor 401(k) plan must provide that the safe harbor matching or nonelective contribution be 100 percent immediately vested. Any other employer contributions to a safe harbor 401(k) plan can be made subject to a vesting schedule (see Q 2:194). [I.R.C. § 401(k)(12)(E)(i)]

Q 2:256 Can a safe harbor 401(k) plan have minimum age and service requirements that must be met before an employee can become a participant?

Yes. With regard to minimum age and service requirements, safe harbor 401(k) plans are the same as regular or SIMPLE 401(k) plans (see

Qs 2:169–2:178). As pointed out at Q 2:172, the maximum waiting period that can apply to safe harbor contributions cannot exceed one year of service.

Q 2:257 Can any conditions be placed on the receipt of the safe harbor matching contribution or nonelective contribution in a safe harbor 401(k) plan?

No. Once an employee has satisfied any minimum age and service requirements (see Q 2:256) under the safe harbor 401(k) plan, the employer must make the required contribution (match or nonelective contribution) whether or not the participant is employed on the last day of the plan year or has completed 1,000 hours of service during the plan year.

Q 2:258 What restrictions, if any, can be placed on elective contributions made by participants in a 401(k) plan that provides safe harbor contributions?

In a 401(k) plan that provides safe harbor contributions, elective contributions by NHCEs may not be restricted, *except* in the manner described below:

1. A plan sponsor may limit the frequency and duration of periods in which eligible employees may make or change salary deferral elections under a plan, provided that, after receipt of the safe harbor notice, an employee has a reasonable opportunity (including a reasonable period) to make or change a cash or deferred election for the plan year—for such purposes, a 30-day period is deemed to be a reasonable period;
2. A plan sponsor may limit the amount of elective contributions that may be made by an eligible employee under a plan, provided that each NHCE who is an eligible employee is permitted (unless the employee is restricted under item 4, below) to make elective contributions in an amount that is at least sufficient to receive the maximum amount of matching contributions available under the plan for the plan year and is permitted to elect any lesser amount of elective contributions;
3. A plan sponsor may limit the types of compensation that may be deferred by an eligible employee under a plan, provided that each NHCE who is an eligible employee is permitted to make elective contributions under a definition of compensation that would be a reasonable definition of compensation within the meaning of Treasury Regulations Section 1.414(s)-1(d)(2) (see chapter 10); and
4. A plan sponsor may limit the amount of elective contributions made by an eligible employee under a plan (a) because of the limit on elective deferrals ($18,000 in 2015), or the overall limit on annual additions under Code Section 415 (lesser of 100 percent of compensation or $53,000 in 2015) or (b) because, on account of a hardship distribution, an employee's ability to make elective contributions has been suspended for six months. [Treas. Reg. §§ 1.401(k)-3(c)(6), 1.401(m)-3(d)(6)]

Q 2:259 What compensation must be used for purposes of the safe harbor contributions?

Any definition of compensation that satisfies Code Section 414(s) can be used for purposes of determining safe harbor matching and nonelective contributions; however, a definition of compensation that excludes all compensation in excess of a specified dollar amount cannot be used in the case of NHCEs (see chapter 10). An employer may limit the period used to determine compensation for a plan year to that portion of the plan year in which the employee is an eligible employee, provided that limitation is applied uniformly. [Treas. Reg. § 1.401(k)-3(b)(2)]

Q 2:260 By when must safe harbor contributions be made to the 401(k) plan?

Safe harbor contributions can be made at any time during the plan year and thereafter until 12 months after the end of the plan year. If, however, an employer wants to satisfy the match safe harbor on a basis other than a plan-year basis, the matching contributions must be made no later than the last day of the following plan year quarter. [Treas. Reg. § 1.401(k)-3(c)(5)(ii)]

> **Example.** ABC Company sponsors a calendar-year 401(k) plan that provides a safe harbor basic match formula. Sam, a participant, begins the plan year deferring at the rate of 12 percent. At the end of the first quarter (March 31, 2016), after earning $10,000 of his $40,000 annual pay, he stops deferrals. ABC Company satisfies the match safe harbor on a payroll-by-payroll basis. The match contribution for Sam is $400 and that amount must be contributed by ABC Company no later than June 30, 2016. If ABC Company had decided to satisfy the match safe harbor based on Sam's compensation and deferrals for the entire plan year, the match owed to Sam would be $1,200. That amount would not be required to be contributed by ABC Company until December 31, 2017.

Q 2:261 Is the dollar limit on elective deferrals reduced for safe harbor 401(k) plans?

No. The full elective deferral limit under Code Section 402(g) is available ($18,000 for 2015).

Q 2:262 Are employee after-tax contributions made to a safe harbor 401(k) plan exempt from nondiscrimination testing?

No. In a 401(k) plan that is not a safe harbor 401(k) plan, employer matching contributions and employee after-tax contributions are combined for purposes of the ACP test (see chapter 13). If the 401(k) plan qualifies as a safe harbor 401(k) plan, only matching contributions are exempt from the ACP test. That is, after-tax contributions are still subject to ACP testing. [Treas. Reg. § 1.401(m)-3(j)(6)]

Q 2:263 How do the top-heavy rules apply to a safe harbor 401(k) plan?

A top-heavy safe harbor 401(k) plan under which the only employer contributions that are made are those that satisfy the ADP and ACP safe harbors is no longer required to provide additional employer contributions to satisfy the top-heavy minimum-contribution requirement. Even if the exemption does not apply, because other employer contributions are made or forfeitures are allocated, safe harbor nonelective and matching contributions can be taken into account in determining whether an employer has satisfied its top-heavy minimum-contribution obligation. [I.R.C. § 416(c)(2)(A)]

Q 2:264 Will a provision allowing an employer to make discretionary nonelective contributions to a safe harbor plan require the employer to make additional employer contributions if the 401(k) plan is top heavy?

No. In Revenue Ruling 2004-13 [2004-7 I.R.B. 485], the IRS ruled that the mere existence of a plan provision allowing the employer to make additional nonelective contributions will not cause a safe harbor plan to lose its top-heavy exemption. If, however, nonelective contributions and/or forfeitures are allocated on account of a plan year, then the exemption is lost for that year.

Q 2:265 Can the safe harbor nonelective contribution be counted in a cross-tested profit sharing formula or for purposes of permitted disparity?

The safe harbor nonelective contribution can be counted in a cross-tested profit sharing formula, but cannot be used for purposes of permitted disparity (see chapter 12). [Treas. Reg. §§ 1.401(k)-3(h)(2), 1.401(m)-3(j)(2)]

Q 2:266 Are in-service withdrawals of safe harbor matching and nonelective contributions permitted?

Only in some circumstances may withdrawals be made. Safe harbor matching and nonelective contributions are subject to the withdrawal restrictions of Code Section 401(k)(2)(B). Therefore, in-service withdrawals of safe harbor matching and nonelective contributions may be allowed on or after age 59½. In-service withdrawals of safe harbor contributions on account of financial hardship (or after a specified time period of being made) cannot, however, be permitted. [I.R.C. § 401(k)(12)(E)]

Q 2:267 What are some examples illustrating the various 401(k) safe harbor rules?

The following examples illustrate various rules that apply to safe harbor 401(k) plans.

Example 1. Beginning January 1, 2016, the Adams Axle Company maintains Plan L covering employees (including HCEs and NHCEs) in Divisions D and E. Plan L is a 401(k) plan that provides for a required matching contribution equal to 100 percent of each eligible employee's elective contributions up to 4 percent of compensation. For purposes of the matching contribution formula, compensation is defined as all compensation within the meaning of Code Section 415(c)(3) (a definition that satisfies Code Section 414(s)). Also, each employee is permitted to make elective contributions from all compensation within the meaning of Code Section 415(c)(3) and may change an elective contribution election at any time. Plan L limits the amount of an employee's elective contributions consistent with Code Sections 402(g) and 415, and, in the case of a hardship distribution, suspends an employee's ability to make elective contributions for 6 months. All contributions under Plan L are 100 percent vested and are subject to the withdrawal restrictions of Code Section 401(k)(2)(B). Plan L provides for no other contributions, and Adams Axle maintains no other plans. Plan L is maintained on a calendar-year basis and all contributions for a plan year are made within 12 months after the end of the plan year.

Based on these facts, matching contributions under Plan L are safe harbor matching contributions because they are 100 percent vested, are subject to the withdrawal restrictions of Code Section 401(k)(2)(B), and are required to be made on behalf of each NHCE who is an eligible employee.

Plan L's formula is an enhanced matching formula because each NHCE who is an eligible employee receives matching contributions at a rate that, at any rate of elective contributions, provides an aggregate amount of matching contributions at least equal to the aggregate amount of matching contributions that would have been received under the basic matching formula, and the rate of matching contributions does not increase as the rate of an employee's elective contributions increases.

Plan L would satisfy the safe harbor for purposes of ADP testing if it also satisfied the safe harbor notice requirement. If the ADP test safe harbor applies, Plan L then also satisfies the ACP test safe harbor.

Example 2. The facts are the same as those in Example 1 above, except that instead of providing a required matching contribution equal to 100 percent of each eligible employee's elective contributions up to 4 percent of compensation, Plan L provides a matching contribution equal to 150 percent of each eligible employee's elective contributions up to 3 percent of compensation.

Plan L's formula is an enhanced matching formula, and it satisfies the safe harbor contribution requirement. Plan L would satisfy the ADP test safe harbor if it also satisfied the safe harbor notice requirement. If the ADP test safe harbor applies, Plan L then also satisfies the ACP test safe harbor.

Example 3. The facts are the same as those in Example 1 above, except that instead of permitting each employee to make elective contributions from compensation within the meaning of Code Section 415(c)(3), each employee's elective contributions under Plan L are limited to 15 percent of the employee's "basic compensation." Basic compensation is defined under Plan L as compensation within the meaning of Code Section 415(c)(3), but excluding bonuses and overtime pay. The definition of basic compensation under Plan L is a reasonable definition of compensation within the meaning of Treasury Regulations Section 1.414(s)-1(d)(2).

Plan L will not fail to satisfy the safe harbor contribution requirement merely because Plan L limits the amount of elective contributions and the types of compensation that may be deferred by eligible employees, provided that each NHCE who is an eligible employee may make elective contributions equal to at least 4 percent of the employee's compensation under Code Section 415(c)(3) (i.e., the amount of elective contributions that is sufficient to receive the maximum amount of matching contributions available under the plan).

Example 4. The facts are the same as those in Example 1 above, except that Plan L provides that only employees employed on the last day of the plan year will receive a safe harbor matching contribution. Plan L would not satisfy the safe harbor contribution requirement because safe harbor matching contributions are not made on behalf of all NHCEs who are eligible employees and who make elective contributions.

The result would be the same if, instead of providing safe harbor matching contributions under an enhanced formula, Plan L provides for a 3 percent safe harbor nonelective contribution that is restricted to eligible employees who are employed on the last day of the plan year.

Example 5. The facts are the same as those in Example 1 above, except that instead of providing safe harbor matching contributions under the enhanced matching formula to employees in both Divisions D and E, employees in Division E are provided safe harbor matching contributions under the basic matching formula, while matching contributions continue to be provided to employees in Division D under the enhanced matching formula.

The plan would fail to satisfy the safe harbor contribution requirement because the rate of matching contributions with respect to HCEs in Division D at a rate of elective contributions between 3 percent and 5 percent would be greater than that with respect to NHCEs in Division E at the same rate of elective contributions. For example, an HCE in Division D who would have a 4 percent rate of elective contributions would have a rate of matching contributions of 100 percent while an NHCE in Division E who would have the same rate of elective contributions would have a lower rate of matching contributions.

Q 2:268 May employees covered by a safe harbor 401(k) plan also participate in other retirement plans of the same employer?

Yes. Employees covered by a safe harbor 401(k) plan may also be covered under another qualified retirement plan maintained by their employer. Further, safe harbor contributions may be made to another defined contribution plan as if the contribution were made to the safe harbor 401(k) plan. [Treas. Reg. §§ 1.401(k)-3(h)(4), 1.401(m)-3(j)(4)]

Q 2:269 May a plan's safe harbor provisions be amended mid-year?

According to the regulations, mid-year amendments of safe harbor provisions, a term not defined in the regulations, are permitted only if the IRS issues formal guidance specifying which mid-year amendments are permissible. [Treas. Reg. §§ 1.401(k)-3(e)(1), 1.401(m)-3(f)(1)] Thus far, the only guidance provided by the IRS has been to permit mid-year amendments to add Roth deferral provisions (including in-plan Roth rollovers and conversions—see chapter 18), to permit hardship withdrawals on account of a hardship affecting the beneficiary of a participant, and to revise the definition of spouse if it does not reflect the outcome of the *Windsor* decision. [Ann. 2007-59, 2007-25 I.R.B. 1448; Notice 2013-74, 2013-52 I.R.B. 819; Notice 2014-24 I.R.B. 1100] See Qs 2:253 and 2:254 for rules relating to mid-year amendments to either reduce or eliminate safe harbor contributions.

Eligible Combined Plans

Q 2:270 What is an *eligible combined plan*?

An *eligible combined plan* is a vehicle whereby an employer can maintain both a defined contribution plan and a defined benefit plan on a combined basis, thus reducing the administrative burdens and costs of maintaining separate plans. [I.R.C. § 414(x)] In Notice 2009-71 [2009-35 I.R.B. 262], the IRS requested comments with regard to eligible combined plans, but it has yet to issue guidance with respect to this type of plan, which could only first be established for plan years beginning after December 31, 2009.

Q 2:271 Can any employer establish an eligible combined plan?

No, only a small employer can establish such a plan. In general, a small employer is one that employed, on average, no more than 500 employees on each business day of the preceding calendar year. [I.R.C. § 414(x)(2)(A)]

Q 2:272 What benefits must be provided under an eligible combined plan?

Minimum benefits must be provided under both parts of the plan. The defined benefit part of the plan must be the lesser of 1 percent of the participant's final average pay multiplied by the participant's years of service, or 20 percent of such pay (although there is an alternate minimum benefit for cash balance-type plans). [I.R.C. § 414(x)(2)(B)] The defined contribution part of the plan must contain an automatic contribution feature, and the employer must make a matching contribution equal to 50 percent of an employee's elective contributions that do not exceed 4 percent of compensation. [I.R.C. § 414(x)(2)(C)]

Q 2:273 What vesting requirements apply to minimum contributions and benefits under an eligible combined plan?

All participants must be fully vested in the minimum matching contribution provided under the defined contribution part of the plan and any match contributions that are made in excess of the minimum contribution. Minimum benefits under the defined benefit part of the plan and any nonelective contributions made under the defined contribution part must be fully vested upon completion of three years of service. [I.R.C. § 414(x)(2)(D)]

Q 2:274 From what requirements are eligible combined plans exempt?

The defined contribution part of the plan is exempt from ADP testing, and the minimum matching contribution is treated as a safe harbor contribution for purposes of Code Section 401(m). [I.R.C. § 414(x)(3)] An eligible combined plan is exempt from top-heavy plan requirements. [I.R.C. § 414(x)(4)]

Chapter 3

The 401(k) Plan Document

401(k) plans, like all qualified retirement plans, must be in writing (see chapter 2). The written plan requirement means that a 401(k) plan must be embodied in a formal plan document. This chapter describes the types of documents available to 401(k) plan sponsors and considers the merits of having the plan document reviewed and approved by the Internal Revenue Service (IRS). Additional information regarding plan documents and the IRS approval process can be found at *http://www.irs.gov/Retirement-Plans* and then clicking on the link to Retirement Plans FAQs on the left-hand side of the page.

Plan Document Alternatives 3-1
Master and Prototype Plans 3-2
Volume Submitter Plan 3-4
Individually Designed Plans 3-5
Amendments 3-5
Advance IRS Approval 3-9
Advantages of Qualification and Approval 3-10
Determination Letter Application 3-11

Plan Document Alternatives

Q 3:1 What plan document alternatives are available to a 401(k) plan sponsor?

Currently, a plan sponsor adopting a 401(k) plan has three plan document alternatives:

1. Master or prototype plan;
2. Volume submitter plan; or
3. Individually designed document.

Determining what type of document to use will depend on the sponsor's needs for investment and design flexibility, the costs of document preparation and, if applicable, IRS review, and the costs of ongoing compliance with legislative and regulatory changes.

Master and Prototype Plans

Q 3:2 What are *master* and *prototype plans*?

Master and *prototype plans* are documents that have been reviewed and approved by the IRS. A preapproved document consists of two parts: the basic plan and trust document (the trust document can also be a document wholly separate from the plan document), and the adoption agreement. The basic plan and trust document contains language that cannot be varied and describes the administrative and trust provisions in the plan. The adoption agreement contains choices for the individual plan sponsor. Typical choices include vesting schedules, deferral percentage limitations, level of matching contributions, waiting periods, minimum age requirements, loan and withdrawal options, and distribution provisions. [Rev. Proc. 2011-49, §§ 4.01, 4.02, 2011-44 I.R.B. 608]

Q 3:3 What are the requirements for master or prototype plan sponsors?

A master or prototype plan sponsor is any person who has an established place of business in the United States that is accessible during every business day and has at least 30 clients expected to adopt the sponsor's basic plan document. The 30-client requirement is waived, however, if the plan sponsor is a word-for-word identical adopter or minor modifier adopter of a mass submitter master or prototype plan. [Rev. Proc. 2011-49, § 4.07, 2011-44 I.R.B. 608]

Q 3:4 What is a mass submitter master or prototype plan?

A mass submitter master or prototype plan is a plan approved by the IRS and is to be used by at least 30 unaffiliated sponsors. [Rev. Proc. 2011-49, § 4.08, 2011-44 I.R.B. 608]

Q 3:5 What is the difference between master and prototype plans?

Master and prototype plans are distinguished by the type of trustee used and the funding medium. A prototype plan has a separate funding medium for each adopting employer, and the adopting employer has the ability to designate a trustee or trustees for the plan; a master plan is funded with a single funding medium for the joint use of all adopting employers. The trustee of the master plan is responsible for reporting the trust activity to the adopting employers. [Rev. Proc. 2011-49, §§ 4.01, 4.02, 2011-44 I.R.B. 608]

Q 3:6 What are the available document options for master and prototype plans?

Most master and prototype plan sponsors offer both standardized and nonstandardized plans. The standardized document offers fewer design options. For example, a standardized document must grant a participant employed on the last day of the year an allocation of the employer's contribution without regard to the number of hours completed. Also, a standardized document must provide a terminated participant who works more than 500 hours in a plan year an allocation of the employer's contribution.

A nonstandardized plan allows the employer to vary the plan design to suit its needs more closely. For example, a nonstandardized document may require a participant to be employed on the last day of the year and/or to complete one year of service (up to 1,000 hours of service in a plan year) in order to receive an allocation of employer contributions. In addition, a nonstandardized document gives the employer greater flexibility in defining the employees eligible to participate and the amount of compensation to be taken into account in determining benefits and contributions. [Rev. Proc. 2011-49, §§ 4.09, 4.10, 2011-44 I.R.B. 608]

Q 3:7 What are the advantages and disadvantages of standardized and nonstandardized plans?

The basic advantage of a standardized plan is that it is designed to satisfy automatically the Internal Revenue Code's (Code's) minimum coverage and nondiscrimination requirements (see chapters 11 and 12). It is an ideal choice, therefore, for employers who have few employees and who, consequently, cannot take advantage of the last day and year of service design options available to nonstandardized plans (see Q 3:6). Because it is designed to satisfy the minimum coverage and nondiscrimination requirements, the standardized plan must cover all employees except for collective-bargaining employees and nonresident aliens. This requirement is of little concern to an employer with few employees, but to an employer with a large, multi-location workforce, requiring all employees to participate in a single plan would usually not meet the employer's needs.

Q 3:8 Should a plan sponsor use a master or prototype plan?

The advantages of using a master or prototype document include minimal expense to prepare the document and the ability to rely on the master or prototype plan sponsor for plan amendments to comply with legislative and regulatory changes. In addition, the master or prototype plan sponsor generally provides a summary plan description to be distributed to the participants, so that the adopting employer does not have to bear the expense of drafting this document.

The disadvantages are the loss of design flexibility and the inability to make changes not available on the adoption agreement without loss of prototype/

master plan status. If a master or prototype plan is amended to add provisions not contained in the adoption agreement or to change the provisions of the basic plan document, the plan is considered individually designed, with the consequences described in Q 3:14. [Rev. Proc. 2011-49, § 19.03(3), 2011-44 I.R.B. 608] Also, the terms of the basic plan document may limit the use of funding vehicles to products offered by the master or prototype plan sponsor. A plan sponsor looking for funding flexibility should choose another document type, or at least recognize the need to change documents when funding vehicles are changed.

Volume Submitter Plan

Q 3:9 What is a *volume submitter plan*?

A *volume submitter plan* is generally a single document (although it can be structured, like a master or prototype plan, as a basic plan document and a separate adoption agreement), the format of which is preapproved by the IRS. [Rev. Proc. 2011-49, §§ 13.01, 13.02, 2011-44 I.R.B. 608] Volume submitter plans offer somewhat greater flexibility to the individual plan sponsor. The volume submitter practitioner must certify that at least 30 employers are expected to use the plan document unless the volume submitter practitioner adopts, on a word-for-word basis, the volume submitter plan of a VS mass submitter. [Rev. Proc. 2011-49, § 13.05, 2011-44 I.R.B. 608]

Q 3:10 What is a *VS mass submitter*?

A *VS mass submitter* is a practitioner who submits advisory letter applications on behalf of at least 30 unaffiliated volume submitter practitioners. [Rev. Proc. 2011-49, § 13.06, 2011-44 I.R.B. 608]

Q 3:11 What is the format of a volume submitter plan?

In a volume submitter plan that is not in an adoption agreement-basic plan document format, any plan provisions that do not apply to the individual plan sponsor may be deleted from the individual plan document. However, like a master or prototype plan, any plan provision change not contemplated in the approved volume submitter plan will cause the plan to be considered individually designed. [Rev. Proc. 2011-49, § 19.03, 2011-44 I.R.B. 608]

Q 3:12 How do volume submitter plans compare with master and prototype plans?

Unlike master and prototype plans, a volume submitter plan does not afford the plan sponsor the opportunity to choose a standardized plan. As in the case of master and prototype plans, the adopting employer can rely on the volume submitter practitioner for plan amendments to comply with legislative and regulatory changes.

Q 3:13 What changes were made to the volume submitter plan program in 2011?

Revenue Procedure 2011-49 eliminated what had been an important distinction between volume submitter plans and master/prototype plans. Prior to the issuance of Revenue Procedure 2011-49, volume submitter plans, but not prototype plans, could be designed to accommodate multiple-employer plans. Under Revenue Procedure 2011-49, master/prototype plans can also be designed to accommodate a multiple-employer plan (a plan maintained by two or more employers at least one of which is not a member of the controlled or affiliated service group to which the other participating employers belong). [Rev. Proc. 2011-49, § 3.02(5), 2011-44 I.R.B. 608]

Individually Designed Plans

Q 3:14 What are the advantages and disadvantages of individually designed plans?

Individually designed plans offer the greatest flexibility to the plan sponsor in plan design and availability of investment products. They also require the greatest expense in legal fees and IRS user fees if a determination letter application is to be filed with the IRS. The burden of ongoing compliance with legislative and regulatory changes falls on the plan sponsor, although legal counsel generally handles this function.

Plan amendments are also expensive, as substantial plan changes may need to be submitted to the IRS for approval. Finally, summary plan descriptions and summaries of material modifications require extra effort and expense on the part of the individual plan sponsor.

Amendments

Q 3:15 When were 401(k) plans required to be amended for GUST?

In general, plan amendments for GUST—the acronym used to refer to the General Agreement on Tariffs and Trade (GATT), the Uniformed Services Employment and Re-employment Rights Act of 1994 (USERRA), the Small Business Job Protection Act of 1996 (SBJPA), the Taxpayer Relief Act of 1997 (TRA '97), the Internal Revenue Service Restructuring and Reform Act of 1998 (RRA '98), and the Community Renewal Tax Relief Act of 2000 (CRA)—were required to be made by the later of February 28, 2002, or the last day of the plan year beginning in 2001. [Rev. Proc. 2001-55, 2001-2 C.B. 552] An extension of the GUST remedial amendment period applied, however, to employers who had adopted a master/prototype or volume submitter plan or had certified their intent to adopt such a plan by the last day of the regular GUST remedial amendment period as described in the preceding sentence.

The extended GUST remedial amendment period, in most cases, ended September 30, 2003; however, an extension until January 31, 2004, was available if, by January 31, 2004, the plan filed an application for a determination letter and paid a $250 compliance fee. [Rev. Proc. 2002-73, 2002-49 I.R.B. 932; Rev. Proc. 2003-72, 2003-38 I.R.B. 578] If an employer to which the extended GUST remedial amendment period applied ultimately adopted an individually designed plan, the employer was required to file with the IRS a determination letter application by January 31, 2004. [Rev. Proc. 2003-72, 2003-38 I.R.B. 578] (See chapter 20 for a discussion of the correction procedures available to an employer if its 401(k) plan has not been amended for GUST on a timely basis.)

Q 3:16 Did the enactment of the Economic Growth and Tax Relief Reconciliation Act of 2001 require plan documents to be updated?

Yes, a 401(k) plan was required to be updated to incorporate the changes made by the Economic Growth and Tax Relief Reconciliation Act of 2001 (EGTRRA). The ability to update a plan for EGTRRA was conditioned, however, on the adoption of an interim good-faith EGTRRA plan amendment (see chapter 20 regarding the correction of a failure to timely adopt interim good-faith amendments). Such an amendment should have been adopted by the last day of the plan year beginning in 2002 or, if later, by the last day of the GUST remedial amendment period (see Q 3:15) if the plan was required to implement a provision of EGTRRA for the 2002 plan year, and the plan language was not consistent with that provision. A good-faith amendment must also have been adopted if the employer elected to implement an elective EGTRRA provision and the current language of the plan was inconsistent with operating the plan in accordance with the EGTRRA provision. In general, a good-faith amendment for elective provisions must have been adopted by no later than the last day of the plan year for which the EGTRRA provision was effective. The IRS made available model amendments that employers were able to adopt in order to satisfy the good-faith EGTRRA plan amendment requirement. [IRS Notice 2001-57, 2001-2 C.B. 279; IRS Notice 2001-42, 2001-30 I.R.B. 70]

Because of potential anti-cutback issues under Code Section 411(d)(6), many plans adopted good-faith EGTRRA amendments before they were updated for GUST. An issue had arisen as to whether, in this situation, EGTRRA amendments were considered superseded if the GUST restatements did not incorporate or otherwise previously reflect the previously adopted good-faith EGTRRA amendments. In a December 19, 2003, memorandum, the IRS took the position that an EGTRRA amendment would not be considered superseded by a subsequent GUST update of a plan as long as the plan was operating in accordance with the EGTRRA amendments.

It should be noted that the IRS approach to the process of updating plans for EGTRRA was the opposite of the approach used for GUST. The IRS did not require temporary, good-faith amendments to be adopted as a condition for allowing plans to make retroactive amendments to the various effective dates of the legislation constituting GUST (see Q 3:15).

Q 3:17 Did the extended remedial amendment period for updating plans for EGTRRA also apply to plan provisions unrelated to EGTRRA?

Yes. The EGTRRA remedial amendment period applied to any disqualifying provision of a new plan put into effect after December 31, 2001, and all plan amendments adopted after that date. A *disqualifying provision* is (1) any provision or absence of a provision from a new plan or (2) an amendment to an existing plan that fails to satisfy any qualification requirement, including qualification requirements unaffected by EGTRRA. [Rev. Proc. 2007-44, § 5.03, 2007-28 I.R.B. 54]

The extended remedial amendment period also applied to a disqualifying provision that is caused by a change in plan qualification requirements resulting from changes in the law, regulations, or other IRS guidance. To obtain the remedial amendment period extension an interim good-faith amendment must be adopted by the later of (1) the due date (including extensions) for filing the income tax return for the employer's tax year that includes the date on which the change became effective or (2) the last day of the plan year that includes the effective date of the change. Recent examples of the application of this guidance are the interim good-faith amendments that should have been adopted to reflect the final Code Section 401(a)(9) regulations, the automatic rollover provisions of Code Section 401(a)(31), the final Section 401(k) and Section 401(m) regulations, and the refinalized Section 415 regulations. [Rev. Proc. 2007-44, §§ 2.05, 5.03, 2007-28 I.R.B. 54]

If an amendment is not required as provided above but is simply discretionary, the deadline for adopting the amendment is the last day of the plan year in which the amendment is effective. Note, however, that any discretionary amendment, as well as amendments that are compelled by changes in qualification requirements, must not result in violating the anti-cutback requirements of Code Section 411(d)(6). [Rev. Proc. 2007-44, §§ 5.05(2), 6.05, 2007-28 I.R.B. 54]

Q 3:18 By what date were sponsors of master and prototype 401(k) plans and volume submitter 401(k) (pre-approved plans) required to update their plans for EGTRRA and other plan provisions unrelated to EGTRRA?

The deadline for updating such plans was January 31, 2006. [Rev. Proc. 2007-44, § 2.13, 2007-28 I.R.B. 54] The IRS completed its review of the EGTRRA updates to sponsors' master and prototype 401(k) plans and volume submitter 401(k) plans and issued opinion and advisory letters on or shortly after March 31, 2008. The deadline by which employers must have adopted pre-approved plans was April 30, 2010. [IRS Ann. 2008-23, 2008-14 I.R.B. 731]

Q 3:19 What must an employer have done to take advantage of the EGTRRA remedial amendment period available to adopters of pre-approved plans?

An employer whose pre-approved plan was adopted and made effective before February 16, 2005, was automatically eligible for the extended remedial amendment period. An employer not in that situation could still qualify for the extended remedial amendment period if (1) it adopted a pre-approved plan before the last day of the five-year remedial amendment cycle to which the plan was assigned (see Q 3:20) or (2) it signified its intent to adopt a pre-approved plan by executing Form 8905 by that day. [Rev. Proc. 2007-44, § 17, 2007-28 I.R.B. 54]

Q 3:20 By what date were employers who maintain individually designed 401(k) plans required to update their plans for EGTRRA?

The deadline for updating any individually designed 401(k) plan for EGTRRA depended on which one of the five remedial amendment cycles to which the 401(k) plan was assigned. The assignment was generally based on the tax identification number (TIN) of the 401(k) plan sponsor. Thus, if the last digit of the plan sponsor TIN ended in 1 or 6, its 401(k) plan's cycle and the deadline for completing the EGTRRA update of the 401(k) plan was January 31, 2007. Each subsequent cycle begins on a February 1 and ends on the following January 31. A chart showing the relationship between the plan sponsor's TIN and its 401(k) plan's remedial amendment cycle can be found in Section 9 of Revenue Procedure 2007-44. [2007-28 I.R.B. 54]

Q 3:21 When were 401(k) plans required to adopt interim good-faith amendments to comply with the Pension Protection Act of 2006?

Under PPA Section 1107, 401(k) plans were required to adopt interim good-faith amendments by the last day of the plan year that began on or after January 1, 2009. However, in Notice 2009-97 [2009-52 I.R.B. 972] the IRS extended the deadline to meet the diversification requirements of Code Section 401(a)(35) to the last day of the plan year beginning in 2010.

Q 3:22 When were 401(k) plans required to adopt interim good-faith amendments to comply with the Heroes Earnings Assistance and Relief Tax Act of 2008 and the Worker, Retiree, and Employer Recovery Act of 2008?

Section 401(k) plans were not required to adopt interim good-faith amendments to comply with the Heroes Earning Assistance and Relief Tax Act of 2008 (HEART Act) until the last day of the plan year that began on or after January 1,

2010. [IRS Notice 2010-15, 2010-6 I.R.B. 390] Interim good-faith amendments to reflect the waiver of 2009 minimum distribution requirements provided for in the Worker, Retiree, and Employer Recovery Act of 2008 (WRERA) were required by the last day of the plan year beginning in 2011. [IRS Notice 2009-82, 2009-41 I.R.B. 491]

Q 3:23 By what date were sponsors of master and prototype 401(k) plans and volume submitter 401(k) plans (pre-approved plans) be required to update their plans for PPA, HEART, and WRERA?

The deadline for updating and submitting pre-approved plans to the IRS was originally January 31, 2012, but it was extended to April 2, 2012. [IRS Ann. 2012-3, 2012-4 I.R.B. 335] The IRS completed its review of the PPA, HEART, and WRERA update to sponsors' master and prototype 401(k) plans and volume submitter 401(k) plans and issued opinion and advisory letters on or shortly after March 31, 2014. The deadline for employers to adopt a preapproved plan is April 30, 2016, [IRS Ann. 2014-16, 2014-17 I.R.B 983.]

Q 3:24 By what date will employers who maintain individually designed plans 401(k) plans update be required to update their plans for PPA, HEART, and WRERA?

The deadline for updating individually designed 401(k) plans for these laws depends on the remedial amendment cycle to which the 401(k) plan has been assigned as well as the effective date of the enacted law (see Q 3:20). For example, a Cycle D individually designed plan (TIN ending in 4 or 9) was generally required to be updated for PPA by no later than January 31, 2010. [IRS Notice 2008-108, 2008-50 I.R.B 1275]

Q 3:25 When will 401(k) plans be required to adopt interim good-faith amendments to comply with IRS guidance issued in connection with the Supreme Court's decision in *United States v. Windsor*, if the terms of the plan are inconsistent with the decision?

The deadline for adopting an interim good-faith amendment to a 401(k) plan in which the definition of spouse is inconsistent with the Court's decision in *United States v. Windsor* [570 U.S. 12 (2013)] generally was December 31, 2014. [Notice 2014-19, 2014-10 I.R.B. 619]

Advance IRS Approval

Q 3:26 What is the purpose of securing advance IRS approval of a 401(k) plan?

The purpose is to obtain an IRS determination that the 401(k) plan is qualified in form. IRS approval is sought by filing a determination letter application (see Q: 3:32) and is evidenced by the issuance by the IRS of a favorable determination letter (FDL).

Q 3:27 Is it necessary to secure advance IRS approval of a 401(k) plan document?

It is not necessary to obtain IRS approval to secure the advantages of a tax-qualified 401(k) plan. A 401(k) plan is qualified if, in its form and operation, it meets the various requirements of the Code. Nonetheless, prudence may dictate, particularly in the case of individually designed plans, that IRS approval be obtained through the filing of an application for a determination letter.

Q 3:28 What changes have recently been made in the IRS's determination letter program?

Starting May 1, 2012, the IRS will no longer accept determination letter applications for master/prototype plans and volume submitter plans (pre-approved plans) the terms of which have not been modified. The IRS rationale for its decision is that employers who adopt pre-approved plans can rely on the opinion and advisory letters issued to the pre-approved plans to the same extent they could rely on their own determination letters (see Q 3:36).

In the case of individually designed plans, starting with determination letter applications filed on or after February 1, 2012, the IRS will no longer consider whether an individually designed plan satisfies the minimum coverage rules (see chapter 11) and the Code Section 401(a)(4) nondiscrimination rules (see chapter 12). This change in policy also applies to volume submitter plans the terms of which have been modified. [IRS Ann. 2011-82, 2011-52 I.R.B. 1052]

The IRS announced in July 2015 that, starting January 1, 2017, the agency will accept a determination letter application for an individually designed plan only if it relates to the initial qualification of the plan, a plan's qualification on termination, or other limited circumstances to be determined in the future by the IRS. [IRS Ann. 2015-19, 2015-32 I.R.B. 157]

Advantages of Qualification and Approval

Q 3:29 What are the advantages of tax qualification?

The advantages of tax qualification are as follows:

1. The employer receives a deduction for the taxable year in which contributions are made or are deemed made.
2. The contributions made by the employer and the earnings on those contributions are not includable in the income of employees until received.
3. The earnings generated by the trust are tax exempt.
4. Amounts received by employees may be eligible for special tax treatment.

Q 3:30 What is the primary advantage of obtaining IRS approval in advance?

The primary advantage of obtaining advance IRS approval is that the IRS will not retroactively withdraw its approval of a 401(k) plan if:

1. The determination letter application contains no misstatement or omission of material facts.
2. The facts at any time in the future are not materially different from the facts on which IRS approval was based.
3. There is no change in the applicable law.
4. The employer has acted in good faith in relying on previous IRS approval.

[Rev. Proc. 2015-6, § 21, 2014-1 I.R.B. 194]

Q 3:31 What are the other advantages to obtaining IRS approval in advance?

A 401(k) plan that is timely submitted to the IRS has the opportunity to amend plan provisions that do not comply with the qualification requirements of the Code. It is also believed that IRS approval diminishes the likelihood that the plan will later be audited by the IRS. Finally, certain IRS programs for correcting operational errors are available only to plans with prior IRS approval (see chapter 20).

Determination Letter Application

Q 3:32 How do plan sponsors obtain IRS approval?

Plan sponsors obtain IRS approval by applying for a determination letter. The IRS has developed several application forms, depending upon the type of 401(k) plan being submitted. The following are the most commonly used forms:

- *Form 5300*—used with individually designed plans (including prototype plans that have been modified)
- *Form 5307*—used with volume submitter plans the terms of which have been modified

More detailed information about the determination letter process can be found in Revenue Procedure 2015-6. [2014-1 I.R.B. 194]

Q 3:33 Where is the determination letter application sent?

All applications for determination letters should be sent to Employee Plans Determinations at the following address:

Internal Revenue Service
Attention: EP/EO Determination Letters
Stop 31
P.O. Box 12192
Covington, KY 41012-0192

Applications shipped by express mail or a delivery service should be sent to:

Internal Revenue Service
Attention: EP/EO Determination Letters
Stop 31
201 West Rivercenter Blvd.
Attn: Extracting Stop 31
Covington, KY 41011

[Rev. Proc. 2015-6, § 6.15, 2014-1 I.R.B. 194]

Q 3:34 Does the IRS charge a fee for reviewing a determination letter application?

Yes. The IRS charges a user fee, the amount of which depends on the type of application form. [Rev. Proc. 2015-8, 2015-1 I.R.B. 235] The fees in effect for 2015 are as follows:

Application Form	*User Fee*
5300	$2,500
5307	500

IRS user fees are not charged with respect to an application filed by a small employer. A small employer is one that employed in the previous calendar year not more than 100 employees making over $5,000 of pay and that has at least one non-highly compensated employee (NHCE) participating in the plan. The IRS user fee exemption applies to a small employer only if the employer's application is filed by the end of the plan's fifth plan year or, if later, by the end of any remedial amendment period beginning during the first five plan years of the employer's existence. [I.R.C. § 7528(b)(2); IRS Notice 2002-1, 2002-1 C.B. 283; IRS Notice 2003-49, 2003-32 I.R.B. 294; IRS Notice 2011-86, 2011-45 I.R.B. 698]

Q 3:35 Must employees be notified of a pending determination letter application?

Yes. Employees who are interested parties are entitled to receive notice. In general, an interested party is any employee eligible to participate in the 401(k) plan; however, under certain limited circumstances specified in the regulations, other employees may also be considered interested parties. [Treas. Reg. § 1.7476-1(b)] The notice informs interested parties that the IRS application is pending and that they have a right to comment to the Department of Labor (DOL) and the IRS regarding the qualification of the plan. Rules relating to the content of the notice, its timing, and its manner of distribution can be found in Sections 17 and 18 of Revenue Procedure 2015-6. [2014-1 I.R.B. 194] The regulations also permit the notice to be provided through an electronic medium if it is given under a system that satisfies the requirements set forth in Treas. Reg. § 1.401(a)-21 (see chapter 16). [Treas. Reg. § 1.7476-2(c)]

Q 3:36 Can a plan obtain the advantages of advance IRS approval without having to apply for a determination letter?

Yes. A plan can secure these advantages without having to file a determination letter application with the IRS. Any employer that adopts an IRS-approved master/prototype or volume submitter plan and that chooses only the options permitted under the terms of these plans has automatic reliance. In other words, if an employer adopts an IRS-approved master/prototype or volume submitter plan document and makes no changes to the document, other than those permitted by the plan document, then the employer can rely on the opinion or advisory letter issued to the sponsor of the master/prototype or volume submitter plan to the same extent it could rely on its own favorable determination letter.

Although the employer in this situation has reliance with respect to the plan's provisions, automatic reliance does not generally extend to operational requirements that must be met to ensure plan qualification. However, an employer adopting an IRS-approved nonstandardized master/prototype or volume submitter plan will have operational reliance that its plan satisfies the Code Section 410(b) minimum coverage requirements (see chapter 11) if 100 percent of all nonexcludable employees benefit under the plan. In addition, an employer that adopts one of these plans will have operational reliance with respect to the nondiscrimination requirements of Code Section 401(a)(4) if it adopts a safe harbor allocation formula and uses a definition of compensation that satisfies Code Section 414(s). (See chapters 10 and 12.) Adopters of standardized prototype plans will have automatic reliance with respect to all aspects of plan operation unless the employer currently maintains another plan, in which case reliance does not extend to the requirements of Code Sections 415 and 416. (See chapters 9 and 14.) [Rev. Proc. 2011-49, § 19, 2011-44 I.R.B. 608]

Q 3:37 What types of provisions or situations will cause the adopter of a nonstandardized prototype or volume submitter plan to fail to have operational reliance?

The following provisions or situations would be ones that would typically cause the plan to fail to have operational reliance:

1. The plan requires employment on the last day of the plan year and/or the completion of a specified number of hours in order to be entitled to an allocation of employer contributions (see chapters 11 and 12).

2. In allocating employer contributions or in performing discrimination testing, the plan uses a definition of compensation that does not come within a safe harbor definition under Code Section 414(s) (see chapter 10).
3. The plan covers fewer than all of an employer's non-collective bargaining employees or the plan covers fewer than all the members of a controlled group or affiliated service group (see chapter 11).
4. The plan allocates non-match employer contributions in a manner that is not considered a safe harbor allocation formula (see chapters 2 and 12).

Chapter 4

Plan Services and Service Providers

The proper operation of a 401(k) plan requires both intensive transaction activity in processing ongoing contributions and a working understanding of complex legal rules. The burden on plan sponsors is increased by the fact that they are required to act as experts in matters involving the plan. As a result, most plan sponsors outsource some or all of the services needed to operate the 401(k) plan. This chapter discusses what services a 401(k) plan might need, what types of service providers can fulfill those needs, options for plan accounting, and how to analyze the fees charged by providers.

401(k) Plan Services 4-2
Selecting Plan Administration Services 4-5
In-House Administration 4-7
Third-Party Providers 4-8
Bundled Administration 4-9
Selecting Investment Services 4-11
Allocation of Earnings and Expenses 4-16
Balance Forward Accounting 4-16
Daily Valuation 4-18
Payment of Fees and Expenses 4-20
Table 4-1. Comparisons of Mutual Fund Expense Ratios to Ten-Year Performance Costs 4-23
Figure 4-1. Mismatch Between Plan Revenue and Costs 4-25
Table 4-2. Allocation of Plan Expenses 4-26
Legal and Regulatory Initiatives Concerning 401(k) Plan Fees 4-32
DOL Final Rule on Service Provider Fee Disclosure 4-34
Other Activity on Fee Disclosure 4-49
Table 4-3. Benchmarking Plan Costs 4-57

401(k) Plan Services

Q 4:1 What services are needed in operating a 401(k) plan?

- Named fiduciary services (see Q 4:2)
- Trustee services (see Q 4:3)
- Plan administrator services (see Q 4:4)
- Investment selection and management (see Q 4:5)
- Investment processing (see Qs 4:8–4:38)
- Recordkeeping for trust and financial statements (see Qs 4:8–4:38)
- Recordkeeping for participant statements (see Qs 4:8–4:38)
- Plan design and consultation (see chapter 2)
- Plan Document and Summary Plan Description drafting and maintenance (see chapter 3)
- Legal compliance (see especially chapters 5, 9, 15, and 20)
- Fiduciary risk management (see Q 4:7)
- Qualified domestic relations order (QDRO) review and determination (see chapter 17)
- Participant communication and investment education (see chapter 8)
- Nondiscrimination testing (see chapters 10–14)
- Distribution processing and tax reporting (see chapters 16–18)
- 5500 preparation (see chapter 19)

Many of these functions are typically combined and handled by one service provider.

Q 4:2 What is the role of the *named fiduciary*?

Every plan document must clearly identify one or more persons to be the *named fiduciary* for the plan. [ERISA § 402(a), 29 U.S.C. § 1102 (1974)] If there is only one named fiduciary, that person or entity will be considered a fiduciary for all purposes under the plan. If there is more than one named fiduciary, the named fiduciaries can allocate responsibilities among themselves. The purpose of the named fiduciary designation is to clearly identify to participants and government agencies who is primarily responsible for the plan.

Q 4:3 What is the role of the *plan trustee*?

All plan assets must be held in a trust, and a *plan trustee* must be named. The trustee holds plan assets and is usually responsible for managing the plan's investments, although this function can be subject to the direction of another fiduciary, an investment manager, or plan participants. [ERISA § 403(a), 29 U.S.C. § 1103 (1974)] The plan trustee is usually responsible for processing contributions and investment transactions, preparing financial statements, and disbursing funds to participants or to pay fees and expenses of the trust.

Q 4:4 What is the role of the *plan administrator*?

A *plan administrator* is responsible for determining who is eligible to participate in the plan, determining what benefits are due under the plan, and responding to benefit claims and appeals. Plan administrators also have responsibilities dictated under the Internal Revenue Code (Code) and Employee Retirement Income Security Act of 1974 (ERISA) as follows:

1. Distribution of summary plan description, summary annual reports, and statement of vested benefits to participants and beneficiaries [ERISA §§ 101(a), 105(a), 29 U.S.C. §§ 1021(a), 1025(a) (1974)];
2. Distributing fee and investment information required by ERISA Section 404a-5;
3. Providing other required notices to participants (e.g., EACA, QACA, QDIA) to the extent not provided by the plan sponsor;
4. Engaging an independent qualified public accountant to audit the financial records of the plan as required by ERISA [ERISA § 103(a)(3)(A), 29 U.S.C. § 1023(a)(3)(A) (1974)];
5. Maintenance of plan records for at least six years [ERISA §§ 107, 209, 29 U.S.C. §§ 1027, 1059 (1974)];
6. Determination of whether a domestic relations order is qualified [ERISA § 206(d), 29 U.S.C. § 1056(d) (1974); I.R.C. § 414(p)(6)];
7. Providing a written explanation of rollover and tax withholding election options, as well as an explanation of tax options with respect to distributions to recipients [I.R.C. § 401(f)];
8. Responding to participant claims for additional benefits from a plan. [ERISA § 503, 29 U.S.C. § 1133 (1974)];
9. Providing participants with the right to control investment of their accounts with enough information to permit informed decision making [29 C.F.R. § 2550.404a-5]; and
10. Plan administrators may have additional responsibilities, as defined in the plan document or otherwise allocated to them, such as hiring service providers to assist with plan operations and approving plan distributions and loans.

Q 4:5 What is the role of an *investment manager*?

An *investment manager* for a plan must be a registered investment adviser, bank, or a qualified insurance company. The manager must agree in writing to become a fiduciary with respect to a plan. [ERISA § 3(38), 29 U.S.C. § 1002(38) (1974)] An investment manager has the power to buy, sell, and manage the assets of the plan.

Q 4:6 Can the responsibilities of the plan administrator or trustee be delegated to others?

Yes. ERISA permits fiduciaries to allocate responsibilities among themselves. Nonfiduciaries can also be named to carry out some responsibilities. A common example is the situation in which recordkeeping or other administrative services are provided by a third party to a named plan administrator. [ERISA § 405(c)(1), 29 U.S.C. § 1105(c)(1) (1974)]

The allocation of responsibilities can be described in the plan document, in contracts with service providers, or in records kept by plan officials.

Plan fiduciaries must act prudently when allocating or delegating responsibilities. They remain responsible for monitoring the performance of experts or advisers employed to assist them with their plan responsibilities. The scope of the "monitoring" role is the subject of litigation in several courts following Enron and other similar lawsuits. (See chapter 5 for further discussion of this topic.)

Q 4:7 What are fiduciary risk management services, and why should a plan sponsor consider buying them?

The introduction of fiduciary risk management services by a wide range of 401(k) service providers is a newer trend in the 401(k) marketplace. This development was no doubt prompted by a variety of factors, but certainly two critical factors are the growing reliance of Americans on 401(k) plans for their retirement income and the pending lawsuits that have the potential for significantly raising the bar for what is considered prudent fiduciary conduct.

There are a variety of ways of managing fiduciary risk. (See detailed discussion of this topic in chapter 5.) What is relatively "new" in this area is the offering of fiduciary checklists, audits, reviews, and filing systems designed to ensure that the plan sponsor or other named fiduciary is performing his or her monitoring duty at a level consistent with Department of Labor (DOL) standards. This service may be offered by a 401(k) recordkeeper or trustee, or it may be offered as an independent service. It may cover plan investments, plan operations, or both. For a sample checklist of the types of services that might be covered, see chapter 5. For other checklists, see Appendix C.

Plan sponsors that are already working closely with an ERISA attorney or a consultant knowledgeable about ERISA's fiduciary rules may not need this additional protection. Plan sponsors that do not otherwise have access to this kind of help may want to seriously consider it. The ability to demonstrate and document that all delegated functions have been properly monitored will be extremely valuable in an audit or litigation situation.

Selecting Plan Administration Services

Proper administration is a critical element in the maintenance of an effective 401(k) plan. If participants do not receive statements on a timely basis, their satisfaction with the plan will diminish and they may cease to participate. If nondiscrimination tests are not satisfied, refunds may need to be made to highly compensated employees; worse yet, the plan may lose its qualified status. If fees are excessive and charged to the participants, the impact on the rate of return of their investments will be significant.

Q 4:8 What choices does an employer have for plan administration services?

Employers have many choices for plan administration services and may use any one of them exclusively or in combination with others. Common examples include:

1. In-house administration (see Qs 4:12, 4:13);
2. Third-party providers (see Qs 4:14, 4:15); and
3. Bundled administration (see Qs 4:16, 4:17).

The 401(k) recordkeeping marketplace changes rapidly, so the way services are packaged and offered is in constant flux, but the fundamental considerations for selecting a service provider remain relatively constant.

Q 4:9 What factors should an employer focus on when selecting administration services?

The overall objectives of the employer in choosing an administration method should be the following:

1. Ensuring that data are maintained accurately and processed on a timely basis;
2. Ensuring that participant information is readily accessible to both the employer and the employees;
3. Ascertaining that the recordkeeping is cost-effective and that the fees charged are reasonable (to maximize the earnings credited to participants' accounts);
4. Ensuring that routines are developed that demonstrate ongoing compliance with Internal Revenue Service (IRS) and Department of Labor (DOL) regulations;
5. Maximizing the visibility and usefulness of the 401(k) plan as an employee benefit;
6. Ensuring continuity of services (i.e., the provider is committed to the business and is financially sound);
7. Ensuring that the staff are competent and receive ongoing training to stay informed of changes in the law;

8. Ensuring that the provider's systems and processes are compatible with the plan's funds, the company's payroll system, the level of employee access to the Internet, and so forth;
9. Ensuring that the scope of services offered and the flexibility with which they are packaged meet the needs of the plan;
10. Ensuring that the call center support offered to plan participants will meet their needs in terms of times of operation, languages supported, and quality of help offered;
11. Ensuring that the administrator will work well with your plan's investment consultant and/or other service providers to provide seamless servicing of the plan;
12. Ensuring that the administrator has systems and processes in place to help participants prepare successfully for retirement (i.e., ability to project monthly retirement income, planning tools, and so forth);
13. Ability to handle all investment types contemplated by the plan, including employer stock, exchange traded funds, brokerage windows, insurance products, or other unique assets that may be relevant in a particular plan;
14. Quality of participant communication materials and support in providing education to participants;
15. Flexibility and support with respect to both the content and delivery of required participant notices; and
16. Willingness to act as a 3(16) fiduciary (see chapter 5) if that is an option desired by the plan sponsor.

Q 4:10 How has consolidation in the recordkeeping industry impacted the process of selecting administration services?

There has been significant consolidation in the recordkeeping industry in recent years, primarily due to the high cost of maintaining the technology needed to keep pace with both regulatory requirements and product enhancements. When a plan's recordkeeper is sold, the impact on the plan sponsor can be significant and can include involuntary changes such as:

- Conversion to a new recordkeeping system
- Changes to a plan's investment lineup
- Changes in the plan's customer service contract
- Changes in the role the plan sponsor plays with respect to payroll submissions, distributions, and other plan activity
- Changes in branding

Plan sponsors who are concerned with trying to avoid forced changes due to consolidation may want to ask a prospective recordkeeper the following questions when shopping for services:

1. How many participants are on your system? (Generally the smaller the number, the more vulnerable the provider.)
2. What percentage of your annual budget do you spend on technology upgrades?
3. What has your profit margin been for the last three years?
4. What has your net growth margin been for the last three years?
5. What do you view as your "core" business (e.g., investment management, consulting, recordkeeping)?

Q 4:11 What factors add cost to 401(k) plan administration?

The employer should be aware that certain plan design features can add both complexity and cost to the administration of the 401(k) plan. Such features include different sources of contributions (e.g., after-tax employee contributions, rollovers, mandatory employee contributions), investment options for employees (particularly if unique assets such as real estate, limited partnerships, and closely held stock are used), self-directed brokerage accounts, liberal withdrawal provisions, and loans. The addition of an automatic enrollment feature with automatic escalation can also add complexity and cost to plan administration. Although the employer may not wish to exclude this design flexibility from the plan, it should be aware of the impact on cost.

The structure of the employer may also add to the complexity and cost of plan administration. If the employer has different divisions or different locations, gathering employee data will take more effort. Similarly, employees who transfer from one division or location to another will require special administrative considerations. If the employer has different payroll systems for different locations, this will increase the handling effort. Last, the maintenance of other benefit plans will create additional administrative effort in coordinating the limitations and benefits.

The use of newly developed technology such as on-line investment advice or Internet links to other financial data can also increase 401(k) plan costs.

In-House Administration

Historically, larger employers with more than 1,000 employees have been more likely to choose to administer their 401(k) plans in-house. These employers can typically afford to maintain benefit professionals on their staffs. The employer implementing a 401(k) plan will need to consider whether the management information staff should develop an internal system for 401(k) administration or purchase a package as an adjunct to its payroll system. As the costs of maintaining the technology needed to deliver 401(k) plan services have increased, the trend has been to outsource this function to a third party.

Q 4:12 What are the advantages of in-house administration of a 401(k) plan?

One major advantage is control over the original source data. The employer always maintains certain basic employee information in individual human resources files: name, Social Security number, date of birth, date of employment, and pay information. If this information is passed on to a third party, updates or changes must be handled twice: once by the employer and once by the third party. As a result, errors can occur. The employer also has easiest access to information about the other benefit plans it provides for its employees, making the coordination between plans much simpler. Moreover, an employer who is concerned about the confidentiality of data may be reluctant to pass information on to a third party.

This data control advantage has been somewhat diluted in recent years, as many third-party providers can now access data directly from employers' payroll service providers.

Q 4:13 What are the disadvantages of in-house administration of a 401(k) plan?

Outside recordkeepers have both the expertise and resources to keep abreast of changes in the law. In-house benefit administrators generally have other responsibilities and less ability to assess the impact of these changes on the recordkeeping system, since 401(k) administration will not be the employer's primary business focus. The employer also may find this to be the most expensive option; outside legal and consulting resources need to be retained and consulted with on a regular basis.

In addition to the compliance issues faced by in-house administrators, the increasing use of technology in servicing 401(k) plans makes it more difficult for in-house administrators to offer the types of services and features that many participants want. Features such as daily accounting, investment processing via telephone, Internet access to plan information and transaction activity, and on-line investment advice are often too expensive for an individual employer to invest in.

Third-Party Providers

The employer may consider contracting with a third-party provider to handle the plan recordkeeping. A third-party provider may offer both recordkeeping and compliance services or only one of the two. The third-party provider also may offer investment services as part of a bundled arrangement (see Qs 4:16, 4:17). Thus, the employer may maintain contracts with various vendors for recordkeeping, compliance, investment management, and trustee services.

Q 4:14 What are the advantages of using a third-party provider for a 401(k) plan?

Most established providers have been in the 401(k) administration business for many years. In fact, many providers have worked with defined contribution plan administration since the passage of ERISA in 1974. Thus, providers have considerable expertise. In addition, due to the industry consolidation that has occurred over the past decade, many administrators are able to spread cost over a large number of participants, thus allowing for robust technology enhancements without significant increases in fees.

A relatively new development in 401(k) daily recordkeeping is for providers to outsource high-volume transaction and technology-driven activity while the provider maintains compliance, customer service, and other people-dependent services. The theory is that the customer receives the best of both worlds—cutting-edge technology at reasonable cost and competent compliance work.

Q 4:15 What are the disadvantages of using a third-party provider for a 401(k) plan?

Processing delays may occur, since providers must wait for participant data from the plan sponsor and financial data from the investment adviser or trustee. Also, the provider must rely on the data provided by other parties, increasing the possibility for error to be introduced in the process.

Bundled Administration

Bundled, or "one-stop shopping," services are provided by a single firm, generally an investment firm, a bank, or an insurance company that provides recordkeeping services, investment management, trustee services, compliance and plan document services, and employee communication in one package. The term "bundled" is also sometimes used to refer to any arrangement where multiple services are packaged into a single product offering even if that offering does not include all services required in a 401(k) plan. The idea is to minimize the employer's involvement in the administration of the 401(k) plan.

Q 4:16 What are the advantages of bundled 401(k) administration?

When both the investment management and recordkeeping services are provided at the same place, there is no need to rely on outside parties (other than the employer) for information. The financial institution will have the information necessary to prepare participant statements when it receives payroll data from the employer. Since the financial data are readily available, more frequent reports may be provided to participants than in-house administrators could provide. Some of the larger bundled 401(k) administrators have been in the business for many years and have considerable expertise. One key advantage of a bundled package is often cost, since the packages are frequently designed to reduce or eliminate direct costs by paying administration costs through investment management fees.

Q 4:17 What are the disadvantages of bundled 401(k) administration?

The primary disadvantage is that the employer may not be pleased with the performance of the bundled administrator in all respects. For example, if the investment performance is poor, the employer will have to choose a different administrator to provide employees with different investment opportunities. Similarly, if the employer is pleased with the investment performance but not with the timing of delivery of participant statements, the employer will have to seek another administrator and a new set of plan documents. In some cases, the bundled administrator may subcontract for the recordkeeping functions, and this may delay the delivery of reports.

Moreover, a financial institution's motivation in establishing bundled services often is to manage the assets of 401(k) plans. The administration of 401(k) plans may not be its primary business. It also may be difficult for the employer to ascertain the true cost of administration since certain loads or contract charges may be built into the insurance or investment contract, although this should be easier to ascertain since the new fee disclosure rules that require separate disclosure of administrative services went into effect (see Q 4:82).

Q 4:18 What questions should a plan sponsor ask before selecting an administrative service provider?

The following are questions a plan sponsor should ask when selecting an administrative service provider:

- How has the provider demonstrated a long-term commitment to servicing retirement plans?
- How many clients does the provider have with plans similar to ours? Can we contact those clients?
- Will any services be outsourced? If so, where? What control will we have over those providers?
- What is the total fee the provider will receive for servicing our plan, including direct fees, indirect fees, and any soft-dollar arrangements?
- How does the provider keep abreast of changes in the law?
- Can the provider's services be customized to meet our current and anticipated future needs? At what cost?
- Has the provider been a defendant in litigation relating to the provision of retirement plan services?
- What is the average client duration?
- Is the provider willing to commit to service standards for key plan functions (e.g., statements, distributions), and are those standards market competitive?

- What is the provider's service mode for dealing with questions and issues from our company and/or plan participants?

Q 4:19 What considerations should be taken into account when switching 401(k) plan service providers?

Plan sponsors face something of a quandary when it comes to the issue of switching plan service providers. On the one hand, ERISA's fiduciary rules obligate them to closely monitor both the performance and cost of selected providers and to take action if either is significantly out of line with what the marketplace is currently offering. On the other hand, there are significant costs and risks involved in switching providers, particularly when switching from one bundled provider to another. These include:

- Time and effort involved in performing a due diligence search of alternative providers
- Legal costs in reviewing a new plan document and/or service contract
- Risks involved with liquidating existing plan funds for reinvestment in new fund options
- Risks involved in incurring a "lockdown" or "blackout" period during the conversion during which participants cannot make investment changes or receive distributions
- Time and cost involved in communicating with participants, including providing them with a new Summary Plan Description, educating them about new investment alternatives, and explaining to them how to use new forms and procedures

Industry reports indicate that plan sponsors are looking at changing service providers at rates ranging from 8.5 percent for plans with assets of $1 million to $10 million, to 5.5 percent for plans with more than $1 billion in assets. [Society of Professional Administrators and Recordkeepers (SPARK) 2014 Marketplace Update]

Selecting Investment Services

Investment services are often considered the most critical component of a successful plan and are typically the most expensive component. Due to the complexity of fee payments for investment services, as well as the risk to plan participants from poor performance, both the Department of Labor (DOL) and the Securities and Exchange Commission (SEC) have issued guidance on the proper selection process.

Q 4:20 What types of providers offer investment services?

Investment services are typically provided by either a broker or a registered investment adviser, although other consultants may provide such services.

Q 4:21 What are the key distinctions between brokers and registered investment advisers?

Brokers are regulated by the National Association of Securities Distribution (NASD). Typically, brokers do not exercise discretionary fiduciary control over plan assets, and usually they are paid from revenue generated out of the mutual funds used by the plan (i.e., 12b-1 fees). If investment services are offered by a broker, they may be affiliated with a mutual fund company or they may be independent.

A broker that is affiliated with a mutual fund company will usually want or need to offer some of those funds in a plan's investment lineup.

Registered investment advisers (RIAs) are regulated by the SEC. Typically, RIAs exercise discretion in the selection of the funds to be made available in a plan and are usually paid a specified fee equal to a percentage of the plan's overall assets (e.g., 100 basis points).

There is a difference in the standard of care required of brokers as compared to RIAs. Under the Securities Exchange Act of 1934, brokers are held to a "suitability" standard, meaning generally that they must know the client's financial situation and recommend products suitable for their situation. Brokers are not, however, held to a fiduciary standard under securities law. RIAs, on the other hand, are held to a fiduciary standard under the Investment Advisers Act of 1940. According to that standard they must make the customer's interests paramount, avoid conflicts of interest, comply with disclosure requirements, and act in accordance with a "prudence" standard.

The Dodd-Frank Wall Street Reform and Consumer Protection Act [Pub. L. No. 111-203], which President Obama signed in to law on July 21, 2010, required the Securities and Exchange Commission (SEC) to conduct a study to determine whether a uniform fiduciary standard of care for brokers and advisors should be implemented. The SEC report, which was released on January 22, 2011, concluded that a uniform fiduciary standard of conduct, no less stringent than the standard currently applied to advisers, should apply to both broker-dealers and investment advisers who provide personalized investment advice to retail investors.

The next step is for the SEC to develop rules to implement this recommendation, and it is not clear what the timetable is for writing these rules. In March 2013, the SEC published a request from the public for data about the benefits and costs of the current standards of conduct, as well as the potential costs and benefits of alternative approaches. The original SEC report did state that any changes arising from its recommendation should be designed to minimize cost and disruption in the markets and ensure that retail investors continue to have access to a variety of advice options, as well as methods for paying for the advice.

It should be noted that in addition to the standard of care required under securities law, both brokers and RIAs can be ERISA fiduciaries based on their role in the plan, and then would be held to the standards for ERISA fiduciaries, as discussed in chapter 5.

Q 4:22 What services do investment service providers offer?

The services offered by investment service providers vary from provider to provider, but they may include:

- Assistance with or control over selection of funds to be included in a plan
- Provision of an investment policy statement
- Periodic reviews of investment performance
- Participant education and communication
- Assistance with or control over selection of investment funds by plan participants
- Periodic review of the retirement readiness of plan participants

Q 4:23 What is the source for potential conflicts of interest affecting investment service providers of 401(k) plans?

The rules governing who can be paid what for doing what in the context of distributing mutual funds and other securities are very comprehensive and are beyond the scope of this book. In general, however, mutual fund managers can pay those in the business of distributing their funds (brokers and advisers) for certain services subject to rules regarding the purpose for which the payment is made, the amount of the payment, the type of person or entity the payment is made to, and disclosure of the payment to the purchaser of the fund. The potential for conflict exists because under these rules a broker or adviser may receive higher payments or other benefits from some funds than from others, which could impair their objectivity in making fund recommendations to a plan sponsor.

Q 4:24 What questions should a plan sponsor ask when selecting an investment service provider to help identify potential conflicts of interest?

In 2006, the SEC and the DOL issued a joint release titled "Selecting and Monitoring Pension Consultants—Tips for Plan Fiduciaries," which encourages plan sponsors to obtain answers to the following questions when selecting an investment service provider:

1. Are you registered with the SEC or a state securities regulator as an investment adviser? If so, have you provided me with all the disclosures provided under those laws (including Part II of Form ADV)?
2. Do you or a related company have relationships with money managers that you recommend, consider for recommendation, or otherwise mention to the plan for our consideration? If so, describe those relationships.

3. Do you or a related company receive any payments from money managers you recommend, consider for recommendation, or otherwise mention to the plan for our consideration? If so, what is the extent of these payments in relation to your other income (revenue)?
4. Do you have any policies or procedures to address conflicts of interest or to prevent these payments or relationships from being considered when you provide advice to your clients?
5. If you allow plans to pay for your consulting fees using the plan's brokerage commissions, do you monitor the amount of commissions paid and alert plans when consulting fees have been paid in full? If not, how can a plan make sure it does not overpay its consulting fees?
6. If you allow plans to pay your consulting fees using the plan's brokerage commissions, what steps do you take to ensure that the plan receives best execution for its securities trades?
7. Do you have any arrangements with broker-dealers under which you or a related company will benefit if money managers place trades for their clients with such broker-dealers?
8. If you are hired, will you acknowledge in writing that you have a fiduciary obligation as an investment adviser to the plan while providing the consulting services we are seeking?
9. Do you consider yourself a fiduciary under ERISA with respect to the recommendations you provide the plan?
10. What percentage of your clients use money managers, investment funds, brokerage services, or other service providers from whom you receive fees?

The release is available online at *http://www.sec.gov/investor/pubs/sponsortips.htm.*

Q 4:25 What guidelines has the DOL provided for the selection and monitoring of investment service providers?

In 2007, the DOL issued guidance on Eligible Investment Advice Arrangements (EIAAs), a new prohibited transaction exemption created by the Pension Protection Act of 2006, and included general guidelines for what the agency considers a prudent process for selecting and monitoring financial service providers. (See chapter 5 for discussion of EIAAs.)

The selection process used must be objective (i.e., without any conflicts of interest, self-dealing, or improper influence) and must be designed to elicit information to assess the following:

- The provider's qualifications, including its experience and any state or federal securities law registrations;
- The quality of services offered, including the provider's willingness to assume ERISA fiduciary status, and the extent to which advice will be based on generally accepted investment theories; and

- The reasonableness of the provider's fees.

The monitoring process should include periodic review of the following:

- The extent to which there have been any changes to the information serving as basis for initial selection of the adviser;
- Whether the adviser continues to meet applicable state and federal securities law requirements;
- Whether the advice being furnished is based on generally accepted investment theories;
- Whether the adviser is complying with the contractual terms of the engagement;
- A comparison of the cost of the services to the actual utilization of investment advisory services by participants; and
- Participant comments and complaints about the quality of the advice provided.

[DOL Field Assist. Bull. 2007-01]

Q 4:26 What other questions should plan sponsors ask to determine the suitability of an investment service provider?

Additional questions that plan sponsors should ask to assess the suitability of an investment service provider include:

1. Is the investment advisory business your primary business?
2. What services do you offer to the plan's fiduciaries?
3. What services do you offer to plan participants?
4. What is your theory of investment management?
5. What tools do you use (rating services, etc.) to monitor investment performance?
6. What steps do you go through in the selection and monitoring of funds?
7. What reporting do you provide on fund performance and at what frequency?
8. What do you use to assist plan sponsors with satisfying the rules of ERISA Section 404(c)?
9. What are your credentials and work history?
10. May I see a sample investment policy statement?
11. May I see a sample investment performance report?

Q 4:27 How should plan sponsors incorporate answers to these questions into their decision-making process?

The selection of a plan service provider is a fiduciary act, and having answers to these questions will help plan sponsors make the type of prudent, well-informed decision that ERISA requires (see chapter 5). It is highly likely that many investment service providers are receiving some form of compensation or benefit from the funds they work with because SEC rules allow it, and the mutual fund distribution industry has been built around that structure. Many investment service providers to 401(k) plans will have some degree of conflict of interest. What is critical for plan sponsors to ascertain is whether the total amount the provider is being paid in relation to services being provided to the plan is reasonable, whether the conflict of interest is material enough to impair the provider's judgment, and whether the provider is willing and able to provide full disclosure of all compensation.

Allocation of Earnings and Expenses

In a 401(k) plan, the allocation of plan earnings and expenses to participants may occur as frequently as daily or as infrequently as annually. This allocation process, called a *valuation,* updates a participant's account balance for all activity that has occurred during a valuation period, including contributions, transfers, rollovers, withdrawals, earnings, and expenses.

Historically, a high percentage of 401(k) valuations were performed quarterly, although the current trend is toward daily valuations.

Q 4:28 What are the major methods of allocating earnings and expenses to the accounts of participants?

There are two basic methods: *balance forward accounting* and *daily,* or *on demand, valuation.* Balance forward accounting is a method of approximating a participant's share of gains, losses, and expenses; each participant's account shares proportionately in these. For example, if a participant's account balance represents 1 percent of the plan's assets, then 1 percent of gains, losses, and expenses will be allocated to that participant.

Daily, or on demand, valuation is more precise. Units of securities are allocated to a participant's account; subsequent earnings, gains, losses, and expenses attributable to these units can be directly computed and allocated to the participant by daily revaluing of the units.

Balance Forward Accounting

Historically, balance forward accounting was the traditional method for allocating gains and losses to a participant's account in a defined contribution plan that is not participant directed. This method has provided a reasonable allocation of gains and losses in most defined contribution plans where accounts are valued annually and employer contributions are deposited annually. As 401(k) plans increased in popularity, balance forward accounting was adapted to the increased frequency of valuation and deposits.

Q 4:29 How frequently are balance forward accounts valued?

Balance forward accounts must be valued at least annually, although semi-annual, quarterly, or monthly valuations are common. The terms of the plan document will dictate the frequency of valuation. In some plan documents, accounts may be valued more frequently if a significant event occurs that would result in an inequitable allocation of earnings and expenses (e.g., a stock market crash or a participant's withdrawing a significant portion of the plan's assets). It makes sense to include this flexibility in the document, since an attempt to add it in conjunction with a distribution following a market fluctuation may be considered a violation of fiduciary duty. [Pratt v. Maurice L. Brown Co. Employee Savings Plan, 9 Employee Benefits Cas. (BNA) 2380 (D. Kan. June 30, 1988)] Since the valuation of participant accounts usually occurs in conjunction with the distribution of participant statements, the rules concerning the frequency of participant statements may have an impact on plan valuation dates. See chapter 19 for a full discussion of these rules.

Q 4:30 What methods are used for allocating earnings and expenses in balance forward accounting?

Four basic methods are used in balance forward accounting. Other methods do exist, but they are variations of the methods discussed in the following list. In all cases, an allocation basis is established. Earnings and expenses are then prorated, using the allocation basis. The four methods are described as follows:

1. *Regular defined contribution method.* Allocation basis is the account balance at the beginning of the valuation period.
2. *Adjusted balance method.* Allocation basis is the account balance at the beginning of the valuation period less cash-outs, less transfers, less one half of partial withdrawals, plus one half of contributions.
3. *Ending balance method.* Allocation basis is the account balance at the beginning of the valuation period less cash-outs, less transfers, less withdrawals, plus contributions.
4. *Time-weighted method.* Allocation basis is the account balance at the beginning of the valuation period plus additions (weighted for length of time in the fund), less subtractions (weighted for length of time in the fund).

Q 4:31 Which balance forward method will provide the most equitable allocation of a plan's earnings and expenses among participants?

None of the methods will provide an equitable allocation of earnings (or losses) in the event of dramatic market fluctuations. If the underlying investments in the fund are of the fixed income variety, then methods 2 and 4 will provide a reasonably equitable allocation of earnings.

Daily Valuation

Daily valuation originated with mutual fund companies, which entered the 401(k) recordkeeping business in the mid-1980s. These companies brought with them the facility and expertise to handle daily valuation from their shareholder systems, since mutual funds are valued daily and statements for mutual fund shareholders can be provided as frequently as daily. With the market crash of 1987, 401(k) and other defined contribution plan sponsors began rethinking their approach to allocating gains and losses to participants. Also, the growth of participants' accounts in 401(k) plans has heightened participants' awareness and interest in the following:

- Moving fund balances at will
- Having increased access to current account balances
- Sharing equitably in investment results

The technological advances in automation now make daily valuation available to even small employers.

Q 4:32 What is *daily valuation*?

Daily valuation is a computerized system for tracking trust investment activity at the participant level. In a traditional balance forward system, account balances are tracked in dollars and updated on a periodic basis. In a daily valuation system, account balances are tracked in units, and the number of units allocated is updated whenever a transaction occurs. Participants can determine the value of their accounts on any day by multiplying their allocated number of units by the market price of the unit on that day. Earnings activity (e.g., dividends, capital gains, or market fluctuation) and account activity (e.g., contributions, loans, distributions, or hardship withdrawals) are all incorporated into either the daily market price or the number of units allocated to a participant's account.

Q 4:33 What are the advantages of daily valuation to the plan sponsor?

The plan sponsor has increased flexibility in the number of fund options that may be offered to participants. It can also receive financial reports and participant statements containing information that is days old, instead of two to six weeks old, as is the case under a balance forward system. Because there is no trust reconciliation work (i.e., reconciling fund values to participant allocations) and all activity is tracked as it occurs, a clean report usually can be produced quickly.

Q 4:34 What are the disadvantages of daily valuation to the plan sponsor?

The handling of non-daily priced funds, including guaranteed investment contracts (GICs) and common trust funds, is not easily adapted to daily valuation, and recordkeeping expenses for these types of investment products are generally greater. With daily valuation, there is little error tolerance, as it is more difficult to correct errors than with balance forward accounting, where small errors can generally be absorbed in the gain/loss allocation. There is also a risk that participants may abuse their ability to switch funds daily and that the plan will consequently incur significant transaction charges. Owing to the intensity of transactions, daily valuation can be more costly from a systems usage standpoint.

Q 4:35 What are the advantages of daily valuation to the participant?

The participant enjoys a more equitable allocation of market experience. The participant benefits from more timely investment of elective contributions and timely and accurate exchanges and withdrawals. Account balance information becomes available on a daily basis, compared with a four-to-eight-week lag time for balance forward accounting. Distributions can often be processed more quickly, as the participant will not have to wait for completion of a valuation before benefits can be distributed. Since its appearance in the marketplace, daily valuation has been combined with participant-level investment decision making and Web-based access to retirement planning tools and other helpful information for plan participants.

Q 4:36 What are the disadvantages of daily valuation to the participant?

A 401(k) participant who moves money frequently may make poor choices and adversely affect his or her retirement security. Heightened awareness of the 401(k) investments may discourage a long-term outlook on the plan's investments, and the individual may be less patient in weathering market lows.

Q 4:37 How can some of the disadvantages of daily valuation be avoided?

A plan can provide a daily valuation system that does not permit participants to make investment changes on a daily basis. Participants would still be able to access information about their accounts on a daily basis and distribution processing would be faster, but the employer could limit the number of times during a year that a participant can make investment changes.

Q 4:38 What is a *voice response unit*?

A *voice response unit* is often used as an adjunct to a daily valuation system. It enables participants to access information about their accounts and perform certain types of activity by using a telephone. Participants are generally given a means to access the voice response unit through use of a security code and then can receive information through a recording. In recent years it has become common to provide similar capabilities through a Web site on the Internet.

Q 4:39 What features might a plan sponsor look for in a service provider's participant Web site?

Most daily 401(k) plan recordkeepers offer some level of access to data and transactional capability via the Internet. The features on these Web sites can vary widely, and there is rapid growth and change in the marketplace in this area. Current features might include:

- On-line investment education and/or advice
- Links to other relevant sites such as investment/market information, other benefit plans of the employer, and so forth
- Printable participant statements available online
- Retirement calculations that enable participants to estimate how much they need to save now to have the retirement income they want later

Q 4:40 What features might a plan sponsor look for in a service provider's plan sponsor Web site?

The plan sponsor Web site should:

- Support easy and efficient plan administration (e.g., uploading data, processing payroll files, approval of transactions, and so forth).
- Enable plan sponsors to create and see reports about what is happening in their plan with respect to contribution rates, investment activity, and so forth.
- Support retention of documents demonstrating compliance with both fiduciary and Internal Revenue Code rules.

Payment of Fees and Expenses

Q 4:41 What expenses are incurred in adopting and maintaining a 401(k) plan?

A plan sponsor incurs many expenses in adopting and maintaining a 401(k) plan. Implementing a plan may necessitate legal fees for drafting and submitting plan documents, IRS user fees in requesting a determination letter for the plan, and consulting fees for designing and communicating the plan. An ongoing plan incurs trustee fees, recordkeeping charges, compliance costs, and investment management fees. If the plan is terminated, additional charges may result.

A plan's total cost can be divided into two components: identifiable and performance costs. The plan sponsor may opt to pay those expenses directly and will generally receive a tax deduction for plan-related expenses. Alternatively, the expenses may be paid from plan assets and indirectly borne by plan participants.

Q 4:42 What identifiable costs may be incurred in the operation of a participant directed plan?

Identifiable costs are predictable costs that can be anticipated in the course of plan administration. Identifiable costs generally include the costs of administering the plan and investing plan assets. Administration costs will often include costs related to legal compliance, employee communication, recordkeeping, trust services, consulting, and audits. Because plan assets are typically invested with mutual fund companies, banks, brokerage companies, and insurance companies, investment management costs will include costs such as sales fees, management fees, contract fees, transaction fees, and 12b-1 fees. Costs can be a stated dollar amount or a percentage of plan assets. Stated dollar fees typically include a base fee and per participant fee.

Administration costs will vary depending on the complexity of plan administration. Investment management fees will vary depending on how plan assets are invested. The amount is often expressed as a percentage of assets. Sometimes investment management fees subsidize administration costs under a fee-sharing arrangement. The service provider fee disclosure rules, which went into effect in July 2012, should ensure that all plan sponsors will receive disclosure of any fee sharing arrangements.

Q 4:43 Who pays a plan's identifiable costs?

Administration and investment management costs may be paid by plan sponsors, from plan assets, through payments from one service provider to another, or through a combination of these options. A plan sponsor opting to pay those costs directly will generally receive a tax deduction for the expenses. [Treas. Reg. § 1.404(a)-3(d)] If paid from plan assets, the costs are indirectly borne by plan participants. That is, as costs are shifted to the plan, plan expenses reduce the earnings credited to plan participants' accounts.

Although charging administration costs against plan assets is an attractive option to plan sponsors, they should be aware that participants are paying the costs with money that could otherwise have been compounding on a tax-deferred basis. Administration expenses of a large plan spread over thousands of participants may have little impact on participant accounts; that may not hold true in a smaller plan. Similarly, investment management costs can have a significant impact on participant accounts.

Q 4:44 What are *performance costs*?

Performance costs are unpredictable costs that may or may not occur in the course of plan administration. Obviously, they are not identifiable up front.

Q 4:45 What performance costs may be incurred in the operation of a participant directed plan?

Costs related to legal compliance problems (e.g., additional legal costs needed to avoid plan disqualification and various penalties for noncompliance) and substandard investment performance are examples of performance costs.

Q 4:46 Who pays a plan's performance costs?

Plan sponsors typically pay the costs related to legal compliance problems and operational defects. Plan participants bear costs of substandard investment performance. Careful selection of plan administrators and investment managers can diminish the probability that performance costs will occur.

Q 4:47 Why is it important for plan sponsors to calculate total plan costs, especially those borne by participants?

Years of strong stock market performance in the 1990s made it too easy for plan sponsors to overlook the effect of total costs on participants' investment returns. As we have seen in recent years, however, past performance is no guarantee of future performance. If plan participants are forced to endure a long bear market, plan sponsors may find themselves in court explaining why, as fiduciaries, they neglected the effect of unreasonable plan costs on participants' retirement security.

Examining investment management costs is especially important. Not only are they commonly the largest cost component, but investment management costs are increasingly being paid by plan participants. By relying on mutual funds, for example, the cost of fund management is paid by the plan participant, thus diminishing investment return. A plan sponsor should examine expenses (e.g., sales commissions, management fees, contract fees, transaction fees, 12b-1 fees) of fund options and analyze the impact expenses have on overall investment performance.

Carefully comparing and monitoring plan costs will minimize the potential of being sued for neglect when it comes to plan fees. The DOL regulation on service provider fee disclosure, which became effective on July 1, 2012, defines what information a plan sponsor must review regarding services and fees in order to avoid liability under ERISA's prohibited transaction rules (see chapter 5) when plan assets are used to pay service providers' fees.

Q 4:48 Why is it important for plan sponsors to understand the impact of asset-based fees on performance cost?

It has always been difficult for plan sponsors to understand how much they are paying in internal mutual fund fees. This information is typically buried in a lengthy prospectus and varies by share class. To further complicate matters, it has become increasingly common for mutual funds to include in their internal fund fee a fee to be paid to the recordkeeper to help offset its costs. The total amount of the internal fund fee, called the "expense ratio," can have a dramatic difference on investment performance over time.

Table 4-1 illustrates the dramatic impact that internal fees can have on a plan's investment performance over time. As the table shows, a plan with $1 million in assets is comparing various investment options and service packages. Depending on the types of funds used and the extent to which the service provider is looking to have the plan's funds subsidize the costs of plan administration, the internal fund fees might vary from 0.18 percent or lower to 2.37 percent or higher. The assumption is that all funds have earnings of 8 percent compounded annually over ten years. Comparing a fund with a low expense ratio to one with a high expense ratio, it can be seen that the difference in performance cost paid by participants over ten years is more than $340,000. If the plan sponsor were to pay the expenses out of pocket, that would be the equivalent of spending $34,000 more per year on administrative expenses. Too many plan sponsors are quick to reject out-of-pocket fees, but they fail to calculate or negotiate the impact of internal fund fees.

Table 4-1. Comparisons of Mutual Fund Expense Ratios to Ten-Year Performance Costs

	Low Expense Ratio		*Medium Expense Ratio*		*High Expense Ratio*	
Category	*Expense Ratio*	*10-Year Performance Cost*	*Expense Ratio*	*10-Year Performance Cost*	*Expense Ratio*	*10-Year Performance Cost*
International $100,000	0.65%	$12,648	1.31%	$ 24,803	2.37%	$ 42,962
Aggressive Growth $100,000	0.26%	$ 5,142	1.51%	$ 28,355	2.07%	$ 97,987
Aggressive Value $150,000	0.27%	$ 8,006	1.10%	$ 31,512	2.08%	$ 57,232
Growth $200,000	0.42%	$16,501	1.26%	$ 47,811	2.05%	$ 75,301
Conservative Equity $200,000	0.18%	$ 7,143	1.05%	$ 40,189	1.90%	$ 70,222
Intermediate Bond $150,000	0.22%	$ 8,715	1.10%	$ 42,016	1.67%	$ 62,307
Stable Value $100,000	0.32%	$ 6,313	0.32%	$ 6,313	0.76%	$ 14,721
Total		$64,468		$220,999		$420,732

Q 4:49 Why are 401(k) plan fees so complicated?

There are many reasons why 401(k) fees have gotten so difficult to understand. Some of the key reasons are:

- *The pace of change in the 401(k) marketplace.* There is constant, rapid change in the types of services and features offered.
- *The complexity of the product.* There is a huge variety of services and features available for plan sponsors to consider.
- *The inconsistency of how products and services are packaged.* With all the strategic alliances and outsourcing present in the marketplace, as well as the various types of service providers competing for 401(k) business, no two fee arrangements are likely to include the exact same set of services under their core fee.
- *The variety of ways that fees are expressed.* Fees may be charged on a per participant basis, as a plan level charge, a percentage of assets fee, a cost per service basis, or all of the above—sometimes all within one fee arrangement.
- *The use of fund fees to pay administrative expenses.* Perhaps the most problematic development in 401(k) fees from the standpoint of complexity is the use of mutual fund revenue to pay recordkeeping expenses. It is very difficult for plan sponsors to understand what portion of a fund's expense ratio is being used to pay plan administrative expenses and to convert that cost into dollars. The other problem is that the fee will fluctuate with the volume of investment dollars placed in each fund. As the trend to use mutual fund revenue to pay administrative expenses grows, this becomes more of a concern for regulators. As Figure 4-1 indicates, although almost 70 percent of the cost of a 401(k) plan is related to recordkeeping, less than 30 percent of the revenue generated to pay fees is from recordkeeping fees. The remaining portion comes from mutual fund revenue.
- *The allocation of fees among affiliates or between unrelated service providers.* It is a fairly common practice in the 401(k) marketplace for revenue to be collected at a single source and then used to pay the fees of multiple service providers, both related and unrelated. The new service provider fee disclosure rules will help make these payments more visible to plan sponsors and will also require a more detailed breakout of recordkeeping services and fees.

Figure 4-1. Mismatch Between Plan Revenue and Costs

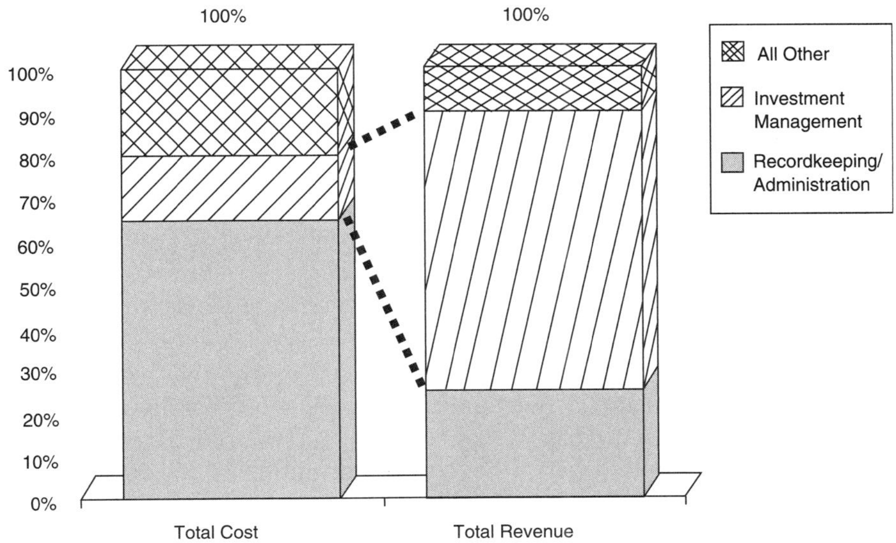

Source: Corporate Executive Board, Retirement Services Roundtable, "Voice of the Participant," July 2002.

Q 4:50 How does a plan sponsor calculate the plan's total costs?

Making an accurate evaluation of plan costs mystifies many plan sponsors. The DOL has attempted to simplify this process for plan sponsors by putting the responsibility on service providers to fully disclose all services and fees. (See Qs 4:66–4:113 for a discussion of the DOL's fee disclosure rules.)

A plan sponsor can determine identifiable costs given the right information. During the provider selection process, a plan sponsor should complete a fee worksheet for each of the various provider options. A fee worksheet can also be used to monitor plan costs on an ongoing basis. To get a sense of whether its plan's costs are higher or lower than industry standards, a plan sponsor should compare them with industry benchmarks. The DOL has developed a tool to assist plan sponsors with identifying and comparing plan costs. It can be found online at *http://www.dol.gov/ebsa/pdf/401ktefm.pdf.*

Because they are not known up front, estimating future performance costs is difficult. A plan sponsor can, however, calculate those costs retrospectively. If, for example, the plan incurred additional costs related to an unintended legal compliance problem, that cost would be included in performance costs.

Though calculating costs is not an exact science, a plan sponsor can estimate costs of substandard investment performance by following these steps:

1. Determining the investment category of each investment option (e.g., money market fund, small-cap growth equity fund);

2. Finding the best-performing fund, or applicable benchmark, in each category (preferably over a three- to five-year period);
3. Comparing each investment option with the best-performing fund, or benchmark, in its investment category;
4. Multiplying the percentage each investment option is performing below the best-performing fund, or benchmark, by the plan assets invested in that option;
5. Finding the total costs of all investment options; and
6. Determining whether comparable levels of risk were taken to achieve the results.

Example. Awesome Company's 401(k) plan offers participants four investment options. Over the past five years, the money market fund has had an average annual return of 3 percent. The benchmark money market fund had an average annual return of 5 percent over the past five years. One million dollars of plan assets are invested in the money market fund. The estimated annual cost of substandard performance for that option is $20,000 (2% × $1,000,000).

Q 4:51 Who pays for plan costs?

According to the Profit Sharing Council of America's (PSCA's) 57th Annual Survey of Profit Sharing and 401(k) Plans, 2013, fees are paid as shown in Table 4-2.

The trend is toward shifting the operational costs of a 401(k) plan from the plan sponsor to the plan. As these costs are shifted to the plan, the plan participants will be affected, as any expenses will reduce the earnings credited to their account. The plan sponsor should be aware of what types of expenses can be shifted to the plan, in keeping with ERISA and the DOL's position (see Qs 4:52–4:61).

Table 4-2. Allocation of Plan Expenses

	Percentage of Plans		
Plan Expenses	*Participant/ Plan Pays*	*Employer Pays*	*Shared Expense*
Audit fees	25.3	70.2	4.6
Internal administrative staff compensation	5.8	90.2	4.0
Employee communication	27.1	53.2	19.7
Investment management	66.9	17.9	15.2
Investment consulting fees	37.7	52.9	9.4
Other Consultant Fees	20.8	69.3	9.9
Legal fees	13.1	78.7	8.1
Trustee fees	45.5	44.8	9.7
Recordkeeping fees	47.9	44.8	9.7

Q 4:52 How does ERISA treat the use of plan assets to pay administrative expenses?

ERISA expressly permits plan assets to be used to defray administrative expenses. [ERISA §§ 403, ERISA §§ 404, 29 U.S.C. §§ 1103, 1104 (1974)] The payment of reasonable administrative expenses from plan assets is an exception to the prohibited transaction rules. The DOL has issued final regulations regarding the conditions for taking advantage of the prohibited transaction exemption. [ERISA § 408(b)(2), 29 U.S.C. § 1108(b)(2) (1974); DOL Reg. § 2550.408b-2]

Q 4:53 What is the DOL's position on the use of plan assets to pay administrative expenses?

The DOL issued a letter in 1987 to Mr. Kirk F. Maldonado, discussing what types of expenses may be appropriate charges against plan assets. [PBA Information Ltr. Mar. 2, 1987] The letter establishes the general principle that payments cannot be made for the employer's benefit or to pay expenses that the employer could reasonably be expected to pay. The DOL opined that expenses related to settlor functions would not be appropriate charges against plan assets. This general principle was reconfirmed in DOL Advisory Opinion Letters 97-03A and 2001-01A.

Q 4:54 What are settlor expenses that cannot be charged to a plan?

The DOL considers certain services provided in conjunction with the establishment, termination, or design of plans to be settlor functions. The DOL has identified the following items as settlor functions which cannot be paid from plan assets:

- Cost of a feasibility or plan design study for a 401(k) plan
- Costs to establish a plan
- Cost of plan amendments that are not required to maintain a plan's tax qualified status
- Fees related to an economic analysis of whether or not to terminate the plan
- Fees for union negotiations concerning plan design and operation
- Fees for disclosure of information that is not plan related, even if included in a document that also contains plan information
- Fees to determine the impact of plan events on an employer's financial statements
- IRS or DOL penalties
- Union negotiations
- Expenses related to plan mergers or spin-offs

- Legal and consulting services provided in connection with the decision to terminate a plan
- Employer responsibilities, such as preparation of FASB Statements 87 and 88

[Employee Benefits Security Administration, Guidance on Settlor Plan Expenses; DOL Adv. Op. 2001-01A, 97-03A]

Q 4:55 What plan expenses can be paid out of plan assets?

The DOL has identified the following items that can be paid from plan assets:

- Fees incurred to amend a plan if the amendment is required to maintain a plan's tax qualified status or to comply with Title I of ERISA
- Fees incurred to implement a change in plan operation resulting from an amendment, regardless of the purpose of the amendment (i.e., maintain tax qualification or other reason)
- Fees for routine nondiscrimination testing
- Fees related to obtaining an IRS determination letter
- Fees related to the disclosure of plan information
- Fees for outsourced plan administration
- Expenses for implementing a plan termination
- Premium payments for an ERISA bond or fiduciary liability insurance if the insurance permits full recourse against a fiduciary who violates his or her fiduciary duties
- Plan administration expenses, including recordkeeping, claims processing, investment management, nondiscrimination testing, and government filings
- Fees for plan accounting
- Legal services related to plan fiduciary issues
- Trustee fees
- Periodic compliance auditing
- Participant communications
- Third-party administration (TPA) services
- Educational seminars and investment advice
- Charges related to plan investments (e.g., sales charges, management fees, contract termination fees)

All expenses and the charges to be reimbursed must be reasonable in amount and necessary for the operation of the plan.

[Employee Benefits Security Administration, Guidance on Settlor Plan Expenses; 29 C.F.R. § 2550.408b-2; DOL Field Assist. Bull. 2003-03; DOL Adv. Op. 2001-01A, 97-03A; 29 C.F.R. § 2509.75-5]

Q 4:56 How should expenses be allocated in a plan?

Once it is determined that an expense may be properly charged to the 401(k) plan, it must then be determined how to allocate the cost to participants. Generally, all appropriate expenses are combined with plan earnings, gains, and losses, resulting in a net gain to be prorated among all participants. However, certain expenses may be directly attributable to an individual participant and should be properly charged to that participant alone.

The DOL has issued guidance regarding the allocation of expenses in a plan. The DOL's position is that plan sponsors have a great deal of discretion regarding how to allocate expenses within the framework of selecting methods that are prudent, are consistent with the requirement to act solely in the interests of participants, and do not constitute a prohibited transaction. A variety of allocation methods may be used, including per capita allocations, utilization allocations, and allocations based on specified categories (e.g., charging terminated participant accounts for administrative expenses without charging active employees for those expenses). [DOL Field Assist. Bull. 2003-3].

One of the challenges plan sponsors face when paying plan expenses through revenue sharing arrangements is that some participants may pay more than others for plan services based on the investments they choose. Some plan sponsors address this challenge by leveling the fees across plan investment options (see Q 4:58).

Q 4:57 What are some examples of how plan expenses can be allocated?

Most service providers offer a variety of methods for paying plan fees so plan sponsors can usually select a method that fits their philosophy and goals. Generally, the available methods include:

1. *Plan Sponsor Pays*. Employers may choose to pay for plan expenses out of company assets instead of plan assets. To the extent plan fees are paid from company assets, employers need not be concerned with the fiduciary risks otherwise associated with the payment and allocation of plan fees. Employers will need to pay for any plan expenses that are considered settlor expenses (see Q 4:54).
2. *Per Head Fee*. Each participant in the plan is charged the same amount (e.g., $100 per participant) to pay for plan expenses. One advantage of this method is that the amount each participant pays does not vary based on the size of his or her account or what investments the participant selects. One disadvantage is that it may discourage employees with low account balances from participating in the plan.

3. *Flat Dollar Fee Assessed at Plan Level.* Employers may choose to take the total cost of plan fees and allocate it across plan assets. For example, if total plan fees are $100,000 and total plan assets are $20 million, a participant with a $100,000 account balance would pay $500 and a participant with a $10,000 account balance would pay $50. Under this approach the amount participants pay varies with the size of their account but does not vary based on their investment selections. One advantage of using a flat dollar fee is that the amount of the fee is fixed and does not vary based on the value of plan assets.
4. *Basis Point Fee Assessed at Plan Level.* Employers can also choose to assess fees across the plan generally as in #3 but set the amount of the fee in basis points rather than dollars. For example instead of charging $100,000 on a plan with $20 million in assets, the charge may be expressed as a 50 basis point fee. It would be allocated the same as in example #3, but amount of the fee would vary as the value of plan assets change. For example, if plan assets grew to $25 million due to additional contributions and earnings, the amount of the fee would grow to $125,000.
5. *Revenue Sharing.* Revenue sharing is a means by which plan fees are taken from plan investments and often reduce earnings on the investment. Typically not all investment options in a plan pay the same amount of revenue sharing so one of the consequences of using revenue sharing is that the amount each participant will pay will vary based on his or her investment selections. For example, if two participants in a plan each have a $50,000 account balance but participant A selects investment funds that pay combined revenue sharing of 10 basis points and participant B selects investments with combined revenue sharing of 20 basis points, participant A will pay $50 and participant B will pay $100.

   Like the methodology described in item 4, the fees paid through revenue sharing will vary as the value of plan assets change. If a plan does not use an ERISA Spending Account (see Qs 4:124–4:127), the fees of the record-keeper or other service provider collecting revenue-sharing payments will vary with the size of plan assets.
6. *Transaction-Based Fees.* For expenses such as loans, distributions, use of investment management services, or other expenses for participant-elected services, many employers choose to charge the participant electing the service and not to spread that cost among participants generally.
7. Most employers use multiple methods for paying fees and most service providers are able to accommodate multiple approaches. For example, within a single plan an employer may choose to pay for investment management fees through revenue sharing, administration fees through a flat dollar fee assessed at the plan level, and transaction-based fees for participant-elected activity.

Q 4:58 What is *fee leveling* and why is it used?

Fee leveling is a mechanism some plans use to ensure that the amount each participant pays for general plan services does not vary based on the investments they choose. For example, let's say a plan offers both a brokerage window and a menu of investment funds all of which have a revenue sharing component that is used to pay for plan administration expenses. Participants investing 100 percent through the brokerage window will not contribute anything toward those expenses, which will be borne disproportionately by participants investing in the other investment funds. Similar issues can arise when a plan offers employer stock, index funds, or other funds that do not have a revenue sharing component along with funds that do.

Fee leveling allocates revenue sharing back to the accounts of participants who generated it so that all participants pay a fair share of the plan's costs. A simpler method of accomplishing that objective is to avoid using funds or share classes that pay revenue sharing, but it is sometimes the case that plan sponsors want to use a particular fund for which that option is not available.

Q 4:59 What types of expenses may be charged directly to a plan participant?

The DOL has issued guidance on this question. Expenses may be allocated to participant accounts as long as the method used is prudent, is consistent with the requirement to act solely in the interests of participants, does not constitute a prohibited transaction, and is disclosed in the plan document and in the summary plan description (SPD). Examples of expenses that can be charged to individual accounts consistent with these standards are:

- Hardship withdrawal fees
- Loan fees
- Distribution processing fees
- Fees to calculate benefits under different distribution options
- Investment-related fees in participant-directed accounts
- Administrative fees for separated participants
- QDRO or qualified medical child support order (QMCSO) processing fees

The DOL rescinded its earlier position, in Advisory Opinion 94-32A, that QDRO processing fees could not be charged to participant accounts. [DOL Field Assist. Bull. 2003-3]

Q 4:60 Can a plan sponsor charge fees to the accounts of ex-employees that it is not charging to the accounts of active employees?

Many employers do not want to have the expense for maintaining terminated participant accounts borne either by the company or by remaining participants. They may, for example, want the plan's recordkeeping expenses paid by the company but then charge terminated participants' accounts for their individual portion of the expense. The concern in doing so in the past was a potential violation of Treasury Regulations Section 1.411(a)-11(c)(2), which prohibits employers from imposing any significant detriment to a participant's right to keep his or her benefits in the plan.

In Field Assistance Bulletin 2003-3, the DOL took the position that it was not an ERISA violation for an employer to impose fees on ex-employees that it did not impose on active employees as long as the fees were reasonable and of a type normally payable by a plan. In 2004, the IRS also supported this right by stating that the imposition of administrative fees was not a significant detriment as long as the allocation method was reasonable (e.g., allocated pro rata) and did not discriminate in favor of highly compensated employees. [Rev. Rul. 2004-10, 2004-8 I.R.B. 484]

Q 4:61 Can an employer reimburse a plan for expenses paid by the plan?

Any reimbursement by an employer of expenses that were previously paid by a plan will be considered an additional contribution subject to both the aggregate deductible limit and the individual limits on allocations (see chapter 9). [Priv. Ltr. Ruls. 9124034, 9124035, 9124036, 9124037]

Q 4:62 Under what circumstances must an employer break out settlor fees from other fees when they are combined in a single charge?

When the employer is clearly combining an objective unrelated to the administration of the plan with one that is, the non-plan related portion of the expenses must be identified or cannot be paid from plan assets. For example, if an employer publishes a booklet that contains both a summary plan description for the 401(k) plan and a description of all other employer provided benefits, the 401(k) plan should not be charged with the expense of the entire booklet.

The fact that the employer will receive an incidental benefit from an activity that would otherwise be considered an activity for which the plan could be charged does not require that a portion of the charge be paid by the employer. For example, the fact that the employer will enjoy a tax benefit attributable to a plan amendment designed to maintain a plan's tax-qualified status does not prevent the entire amendment fee from being chargeable to the plan. [DOL Op. Ltr. 2001-01A]

Legal and Regulatory Initiatives Concerning 401(k) Plan Fees

The topic of 401(k) plan fees is currently receiving a great deal of attention from all sources of government. Congress, regulatory agencies, and the courts have all gotten involved in scrutinizing how fees are paid in the 401(k) marketplace. While the sources of concern vary, the fundamental nature of the concerns is the same. The concerns are: (1) plans paying too much in fees, resulting in lower retirement savings for participants; (2) conflicts of interest in plan fee arrangements, which generally occur in the context of revenue sharing arrangements among plan service providers, negatively impacting the value of investment help participants receive from plan financial advisers; and (3) inadequate disclosure of plan fees to plan sponsors, plan participants, and to the DOL itself.

Q 4:63 What actions have Congress and the legislative branch taken in the past with regard to 401(k) plan fees?

The U.S. Government Accountability Office (GAO) issued a report in November 2006 titled "Changes Needed to Provide 401(k) Plan Participants and the Department of Labor Better Information on Fees." This report recommended that ERISA be amended to require the following:

1. Plan sponsors provide more meaningful fee disclosure to plan participants so that participants can effectively compare investment options on the basis of fees;
2. Service providers should be required to disclose to plan sponsors all sources of compensation received for their work on a plan; and
3. Plan sponsors should be required to provide the DOL with an annual report summarizing all fees paid from plan assets or from participant accounts.

In response to the GAO report, The House Committee on Education and Labor held hearings on March 6, 2007, on the topic of 401(k) plan fees and the adequacy of fee disclosure. Following those hearings, several bills designed to improve disclosure of 401(k) plan fees were introduced in the House and Senate. In January 2011, the GAO produced another report addressing the concern of conflicts of interest in plan fee arrangements. The report recommended improving disclosure in a number of areas to ensure that plan sponsors and plan participants are aware of any potential conflicts of interest when receiving advice or other help from plan service providers.

In the wake of the market downturn in 2008 and 2009, Congress held additional hearings on 401(k) plan fees, as well as on other issues impacting the sufficiency of retirement income generated from 401(k) plan investments. Legislation was introduced in Congress in 2010 setting new standards for fee disclosure. It remains to be seen whether there will be future legislative activity on fee disclosure or whether Congress will be satisfied with the content of the DOL's fee disclosure regulation.

Q 4:64 What recent actions has the DOL taken with regard to 401(k) plan fees?

The DOL has worked on three separate but coordinated initiatives designed to improve fee transparency.

In November 2007, the DOL issued final regulations on changes to the Form 5500 Annual Return/Report of Employee Benefit Plan. Some of those changes involve increased disclosure of plan fees to the DOL. [DOL Reg. § 2520.103-1] Those regulations are effective for plan years starting January 1, 2009, and later. See chapter 19 for a full discussion of fee disclosure requirements for 5500 filings.

The DOL also issued guidance during the second Bush administration on disclosure of service provider fees to plan fiduciaries as well as on fee disclosure to plan participants. This guidance was never finalized and was the subject of criticism from some members of Congress. On July 16, 2010, the DOL issued an interim final rule on fee disclosure requirements for plan service providers that became effective July 1, 2012. On October 20, 2010, the DOL published the final rule on required disclosures to participants in directed plans. That rule is discussed in detail in chapter 7.

Q 4:65 What are the changes to Form 5500 that address fee disclosure?

The DOL has made changes to the Form 5500 that became effective for plan years starting January 1, 2009, and later. These changes include changes to Schedule C that require more detailed disclosure of compensation paid to service providers, including a new requirement to assign codes to various fee and service types. (See chapter 19 for a discussion of the changes to Schedule C.)

DOL Final Rule on Service Provider Fee Disclosure

After years of debate and hearings held by Congress and various regulatory agencies, the DOL has published the final rule on service provider fee disclosure. This section provides an overview of those rules.

Q 4:66 What is the purpose and scope of the fee disclosure rule?

Plan fiduciaries are generally charged with operating plans in the best interests of participants and beneficiaries for the purpose of providing retirement benefits and controlling the costs of the plan. Plan assets can be used to pay service providers only if the contract or arrangement with the service provider is reasonable. The DOL rule defines what disclosures are required in order for certain contracts or arrangements to be considered reasonable. The prohibited transaction rules only apply in situations where trust assets are used so the fee disclosure rules do not apply in situations where fees are paid by the plan sponsor. [ERISA §§ 404, 408(b)(2); 29 C.F.R. § 2550.408b-2(c)]

Q 4:67 When was the rule effective?

The effective date was July 1, 2012. All contracts or arrangements entered into, renewed, or extended on or after July 1, 2012, must be in compliance with the rule. In addition, all existing customers subject to the rule must have received any required written disclosures on or before that date. [29 C.F.R. § 2550.408b-2(c)(1)(xii)]

Q 4:68 Do the required disclosures need to be included in a formal contract?

No. The disclosure must be in writing, but there is no requirement that it be part of a signed contract. This is a change from the proposed rules the DOL published in 2007 and made it much easier to achieve compliance with existing customers.

Q 4:69 When must the initial disclosure be provided to new customers?

There is no specified time period for providing the initial disclosure statement, but the statement must be provided reasonably in advance of the date on which the contract to provide services to the plan is entered into. [29 C.F.R. § 2550.408b-2(c)(1)(v)(A)]

Q 4:70 Which plans are *covered plans* subject to the rule?

A *covered plan* generally includes any retirement plan subject to Title I of the Employee Retirement Security Act of 1974 (ERISA). Plans subject to the rule include defined benefit plans and defined contribution plans (including 401(k) plans and ERISA-covered 403(b) plans), but not governmental plans, simplified employee pension plans (SEPs), individual retirement accounts (IRAs), SIMPLE IRAs, or non-ERISA 403(b) plans.

In the final rule, certain frozen annuity contracts in 403(b) plans were also excluded. If, as of January 1, 2009 (1) the employer ceased making any contributions to the contract and had no contribution obligation, (2) no new contracts were issued after that date, (3) the holders of contracts issued prior to January 1, 2009, have legally enforceable rights against the issuer of the contract without any involvement of the employer, and (4) the owners are fully vested in their contracts, then the contract is not a "covered plan," and no 408(b)(2) disclosure is required. In Field Assistance Bulletin 2012-02R, the DOL clarified that these contracts are also not subject to the investment disclosure requirements under the participant disclosure rules (see chapter 19). The rule does not apply to welfare benefit plans, such as health insurance plans, but the DOL may issue separate fee disclosure rules for welfare plans in the future. [29 C.F.R. § 2550.408b-2(c)(1)(ii)]

Q 4:71 Who are *responsible plan fiduciaries* subject to the rule?

The responsibility for ensuring that required disclosures are made is on the *responsible plan fiduciary* (i.e., the fiduciary with authority to cause the plan to enter into a contract or arrangement with a covered service provider). Generally, the plan document defines who has authority to hire service providers for a plan. [29 C.F.R. § 2550.408b-2(c)(1)(viii)(E)]

Q 4:72 Who are the *covered service providers* subject to the rule?

Not all entities that receive compensation with respect to plan services are subject to the rule, and different disclosure rules apply to different types of service providers. *Covered service providers* subject to the rule are limited to providers that have a contract or arrangement with a covered plan and reasonably expect to receive $1,000 or more in total compensation.

These providers:

- Provide services directly to a plan as a fiduciary or registered advisor;
- Provide services as a fiduciary to an investment vehicle holding plan assets in which the plan has a direct equity investment;
- Provide recordkeeping or brokerage services to a participant-directed plan and make one or more investment alternatives available to participants in connection with those services; or
- Receive indirect compensation and fall within a broad category of service providers.

[29 C.F.R. § 2550.408b-2(c)(1)(iii)]

Q 4:73 Do affiliates and subcontractors of a covered service provider have a disclosure obligation?

No. A person or entity providing services solely as an affiliate of, or subcontractor to, a covered service provider does not have a separate disclosure obligation, although compensation and other information related to their services may need to be disclosed by the covered service provider (see Q 4:92). [29 C.F.R. § 2550.408b-2(c)(1)(iii)(D)(1)]

Q 4:74 What is the definition of an *affiliate* for purposes of the rule?

An *affiliate* is a person or entity that is controlled by, or in common control with, or is an officer, director, employee of, or a partner in a covered service provider. [29 C.F.R. § 2550.408b-2(c)(1)(viii)(A)]

Q 4:75 What is the definition of a *subcontractor* for purposes of the rule?

A *subcontractor* is a person or entity who is not an affiliate of a covered service provider, but provides services that would give rise to covered service provider status if provided directly, and who receives $1,000 or more for providing those services. [29 C.F.R. § 2550.408b-2(c)(1)(viii)(F)]

Q 4:76 Do service providers to investment products in a plan have a disclosure obligation?

A person or entity providing services solely to a mutual fund or other plan investment generally will not have an independent disclosure obligation, although investment-related compensation may need to be disclosed by others (see Qs 4:80, 4:81). However, if the service provider provides fiduciary services to an investment product that holds plan assets in which the plan has a direct equity investment (e.g., investment managers to a collective fund or a pooled separate account), that service provider will have a separate disclosure obligation if it has a contract or arrangement with the plan and receives $1,000 or more in total compensation. [29 C.F.R. § 2550.408b-2(c)(1)(iii)(D)(2)]

Q 4:77 How is the $1,000 limit determined?

The DOL rule does not apply to any service provider who reasonably expects to receive less than $1,000 from sources other than the plan sponsor for providing services to a plan, either directly or through subcontractors or affiliates. Compensation is defined to include money or anything of monetary value, but nonmonetary gifts of less than $250 can be excluded. [29 C.F.R. §§ 2550.408b-2(c)(1)(iii) and (viii)(B)]

Q 4:78 What should a service provider do if it reasonably expects to receive less than $1,000, but receives more than $1,000?

The most prudent course of action probably is to provide any required disclosures within 30 days of learning that the $1,000 limit has been exceeded in accordance with the "good faith error" rule described in Q 4:99.

Q 4:79 How does the rule apply to ERISA fiduciaries and registered investment advisors?

If services as an ERISA fiduciary or as an investment advisor registered under state or federal law are reasonably expected to be provided directly to a plan, the ERISA fiduciary or registered investment advisor (RIA) has a separate disclosure obligation (assuming the contract and $1,000 limit rules do not exclude them). In addition to disclosing their services and compensation, they must also disclose their status as an ERISA fiduciary and/or RIA. They are not required by the rules to identify specifically which services will be provided in a fiduciary capacity, but they may wish to do so in order to clarify which services are subject to fiduciary standards and liability.

If ERISA fiduciary services or RIA services are provided as an affiliate of, or subcontractor to, another covered service provider, then the fiduciary or RIA does not have a disclosure obligation, but the covered service provider must disclose that fiduciary and/or RIA services are provided as part of the contract or arrangement with the plan. [29 C.F.R. §§ 2550.408b-2(c)(1)(iii)(A) and (iv)(F)]

Q 4:80 How does the rule apply to fiduciaries to plan investment products?

If fiduciary services are provided to an investment product that holds plan assets in which the plan has a direct equity investment (e.g., a collective fund), the fund fiduciary has a separate disclosure obligation (assuming the contract and $1,000 limit rules do not exclude it). The fund fiduciary must identify itself as a fiduciary and must disclose services and compensation for that role. For other investments, such as mutual fund investments, the manager of the fund would not be a covered service provider and would not have a disclosure obligation. [29 C.F.R. §§ 2550.408b-2(c)(1)(iii)(A)(2) and (D)(2)]

Fiduciaries to plan investment products that have a disclosure obligation may also be required to disclose investment-related compensation (see Q 4:88) that is not otherwise disclosed by the plan's recordkeeper or broker. [29 C.F.R. § 2550.408b-2(c)(1)(iv)(F)]

Q 4:81 How does the rule apply to recordkeepers and brokers?

If recordkeeping or brokerage services are provided in a participant-directed plan in which one or more funds are made available to participants in connection with the recordkeeping or brokerage services, the service provider has an independent disclosure obligation (assuming the contract and $1,000 limit rules do not exclude them) regardless of whether they are paid with direct or indirect compensation.

If recordkeeping or brokerage services are provided to a plan other than a participant-directed plan as described above, then a disclosure obligation would only apply if these providers are paid with indirect compensation (see Q 4:83).

In addition to the general disclosure requirements, recordkeepers must separately identify amounts paid for recordkeeping services (see Q 4:85).

Recordkeepers and brokers who provide services in a participant-directed plan in which funds are made available in connection with the services also must disclose investment-related compensation (see Q 4:88). This information need not be provided with respect to investments made through a brokerage window or similar arrangement. [29 C.F.R. §§ 2550.408b-2(c)(1)(iii)(B) and (iv)(D)]

Q 4:82 What are *recordkeeping services* under the rule?

Recordkeeping services include services related to plan administration and monitoring of plan, participant, or beneficiary transactions such as enrollment, payroll deductions and contributions, offering of plan investments, loans, withdrawals, and distributions. They also include services related to the maintenance of plan, participant, or beneficiary accounts, records, and statements. [29 C.F.R. § 2550.408b-2(c)(1)(viii)(D)]

Q 4:83 How does the rule apply to service providers receiving indirect compensation?

Indirect compensation is compensation received from a source other than the plan, the plan sponsor, or the reporting covered service provider (including its affiliates or subcontractors). Subject to the contract and the $1,000 limit described in Q 4:72, a service provider who receives indirect compensation is subject to the rule if it provides any of the following services:

- Accounting, auditing, legal
- Banking, custodial, insurance
- Securities or other investment brokerage
- Appraisal, valuation, actuarial
- Recordkeeping or third-party administration (TPA) services
- Investment advice to the plan or plan participants
- Consulting related to the development or implementation of investment policies or objectives, the selection and monitoring or service providers, or the selection of plan investments.

[29 C.F.R. § 2550.408b-2(c)(1)(iii)(C)]

Q 4:84 What information on fees and services must be disclosed?

A covered service provider generally must provide information on compensation received and services provided by itself as well as by any affiliate or subcontractor (if the subcontractor will receive $1,000 or more with respect to a plan). The rules for what must be disclosed vary according to the following:

- whether the service provider is a fiduciary
- whether the service provider is a recordkeeper
- whether the service provider is a recordkeeper or broker to a participant-directed plan
- whether the compensation received is direct or indirect compensation
- whether the compensation is allocated among related parties and is either transaction-based or charged directly against plan investments
- whether the compensation is related to termination of the contract or arrangement.

See Qs 4:79 and 4:80 for discussion of the rules for disclosure by fiduciaries. The rules for other types of disclosure are discussed in Qs 4:85–4:94.

Q 4:85 What special disclosure rules apply to all recordkeepers?

Any covered service provider that provides recordkeeping services (see Q 4:82) must separately identify all direct and indirect compensation they receive in connection with recordkeeping services. If there are not explicit fees charged for recordkeeping services, or if the fees are offset or rebated on the basis of other compensation received, then a reasonable good-faith estimate of the cost of recordkeeping services can be provided. Any estimate must take into account the rates the service provider would charge to, or receive from, a third party, or the prevailing market rates charged for similar recordkeeping services to a comparable plan. The assumptions and methodologies used in calculating the estimate must be described. Also, if an estimate is used, the recordkeeper must explain the recordkeeping services it will provide in detail. [29 C.F.R. § 2550.408b-2(c)(1)(iv)(D)]

Q 4:86 What special rules apply to some recordkeepers or brokers in participant-directed plans?

Service providers who offer recordkeeping or brokerage services to participant directed plans and who make available one or more investment vehicles in connection with these services must disclose their own compensation as well as investment-related compensation (see Q 4:88) on the investments for which they provide such services (other than investments provided through a brokerage window or similar arrangement). This disclosure requirement can be met by passing on current disclosure materials of the issuer of the investment, or information replicated from such materials, as long as the issuer is either a registered investment company (i.e., a mutual fund), an insurance company, an issuer of a publicly traded security, or a financial institution supervised by a state or federal agency. The issuer cannot be an affiliate of the disclosing recordkeeper; the recordkeeper must act in good faith and not know that the materials are incomplete or inaccurate; and the recordkeeper must provide the plan fiduciary with a statement that it is making no representations as to the completeness or accuracy of the materials. [29 C.F.R. § 2550.408b-2(c)(1)(iv)(F)(2)]

Q 4:87 What is a *designated investment alternative*?

A *designated investment alternative* is an investment option that is made available for participants to invest in. It does not include brokerage windows or similar plan arrangements that enable participants and beneficiaries to select investments beyond those designated by the plan. [29 C.F.R. § 2550.408b-2(c)(1)(viii)(C)]

In Field Assistance Bulletin 2012-02R, the DOL clarified when certain types of investments, such as asset allocation models or the designation of fund families (as opposed to individual funds), should be treated as designated investment alternatives. (See chapter 19 for a full discussion of those rules.)

Q 4:88 What investment-related information must be disclosed?

The information that must be disclosed by certain recordkeepers or brokers (see Q 4:81), or to fiduciaries to certain plan investments (see Q 4:80) is as follows:

- Any compensation that will be charged directly against the amount invested in connection with the acquisition, sale, transfer of, or withdrawal from the investment. This includes sales loads and charges, deferred sales charges, redemption fees, surrender charges, exchange fees, surrender charges, exchange fees, account fees, and purchase fees.
- A description of the annual operating expenses of the investment (for example, the expense ratio) for investments other than fixed return investments.
- A description of any ongoing expenses in addition to annual operating expenses. This includes wrap fees as well as mortality and expense fees.
- For any designated investment alternative (see Q 4:87) the total annual operating expense expressed as a percentage and calculated in accordance with the participant investment and fee disclosure rules (see chapter 19).
- For any designated investment alternative (see Q 4:87) any other information or data that is either in the control of, or reasonably available to, the covered service provider and is required for compliance with the participant investment and fee disclosure rules (see chapter 19).

[29 C.F.R. § 2550.408b-2(c)(1)(iv)(E)]

There are limited disclosure requirements for expenses related to investments accessed through a brokerage window or other similar arrangement. [29 C.F.R. § 2550.408b-2(c)(1)(viii)(C)] (See chapter 19.)

Q 4:89 What are the rules for describing plan services?

The general rule is that the level of detail required in describing plan services is left to the judgment of the responsible plan fiduciary (see Q 4:71). [75 Fed. Reg. 41,608 (July 16, 2010)] Special rules apply, however, in the case of recordkeeping services (see Q 4:82), services related to indirect compensation (see Q 4:91), services related to compensation that is transaction based or that directly reduces the value of plan investments (see Q 4:92), or services related to termination of the contract or arrangement (see Q 4:94).

Q 4:90 What are the disclosure rules for direct compensation?

Direct compensation is compensation received directly from the plan. Unless subject to the special rule for recordkeeping services, or related to termination of the contract or arrangement, it can be disclosed either in the aggregate or by service. [29 C.F.R. § 2550.408b-2(c)(1)(iv)(C)(1)]

Q 4:91 What are the disclosure rules for indirect compensation?

Indirect compensation is compensation received from a source other than the plan, the plan sponsor, or the reporting covered service provider (including its affiliates or subcontractors). For all indirect compensation the identity of the payer, the services for which the indirect compensation will be received, and a description of the arrangement between the payer and the covered service provider must be disclosed. [29 C.F.R. § 2550.408b-2(c)(1)(iv)(C)(2)]

Q 4:92 What are the rules for disclosing how compensation is allocated among affiliates and subcontractors?

For compensation other than as described in the following paragraph, there is no requirement to disclose how it is allocated among affiliates and subcontractors.

For compensation that is either set on a transactions basis (e.g., commissions, finder's fees, or other compensation based on business placed or retained), or that is charged directly against plan investments (e.g., 12b-1 or sub-ta fees) disclosure of the allocation among affiliates and subcontractors is required. The disclosure of this compensation must identify the services for which the compensation will be paid, who is paying and receiving it, and the relationship of the payers and recipients to the covered service provider (e.g., affiliate, subcontractor, or other). This rule does not apply to service providers who are employees of the plan sponsor. [29 C.F.R. § 2550.408b-2(c)(1)(iv)(C)(3)]

Q 4:93 Must potential or actual conflicts of interest be identified?

No. In the DOL's proposed rules on service provider fee disclosure published in 2007, service providers were required to describe actual or potential conflicts of interest. The interim final rule does not require service providers to make a determination of whether a conflict of interest does or might exist. The disclosure rules that apply to indirect compensation (see Q 4:91) and to allocation of certain types of compensation among related parties (see Q 4:92) are intended to enable responsible plan fiduciaries to determine where conflicts might exist based on how compensation flows among various service providers to a plan.

Q 4:94 What special rules apply to compensation related to termination of a contract or arrangement?

Compensation that a covered service provider reasonably expects to receive in connection with termination of the contract or arrangement must be separately identified. If there are any prepaid amounts that will be refunded the disclosure must describe how those amounts will be calculated and refunded. A contract will not be considered "reasonable" and therefore exempt from the prohibited transaction rules if it does not permit the plan to terminate the agreement without penalty to the plan on reasonably short notice. Compensation intended to reasonably compensate a service provider for losses due to early termination, such as recoupment of reasonable start-up costs, are not considered a penalty. [29 C.F.R. §§ 2550.408b-2(c)(1)(iv)(C)(4) and -2(c)(1)(iv)(C)(3)]

Q 4:95 What rules apply to the form or manner in which the disclosure is to be provided?

The disclosure must be in writing but does not need to be part of a signed contract. Any description or estimate of compensation must contain sufficient information for the responsible plan fiduciary to evaluate its reasonableness. Compensation may be expressed as a dollar amount, formula, percentage, per capita charge, or any other reasonable method if the compensation cannot reasonably be expressed using any of the specified methods (e.g., float income). [29 C.F.R. § 2550.408b-2(c)(1)(viii)(B)(3)]

The rule also allows covered service providers to cross-reference other documents, such as a prospectus or a service agreement, in order to supply information required to be disclosed. The DOL issued a proposed rule in 2014 (see Qs 4:106–4:113) that may create some type of index or summary requirement to assist plan sponsors with their comprehension of disclosure materials. The current rule does not contain such a requirement, although it does contain a Sample Guide as an appendix to the regulation that covered service providers may choose to use (see Appendix L).

Q 4:96 Are covered service providers required to disclose the manner in which compensation will be received?

Yes. The disclosure must indicate how the compensation will be received, such as billed to the plan or deducted from plan assets. [29 C.F.R. § 2550.408b-2(c)(1)(vi)(G)]

Q 4:97 When must the initial disclosure statement be provided?

For existing customers, the disclosure statement must have been provided on or before July 1, 2012. For customers who enter into, extend, or renew a contract or agreement with a covered service provider after July 1, 2012, the disclosure must be provided reasonably in advance of the date the contract is entered into. [29 C.F.R. § 2550.408b-2(c)(1)(v)]

Q 4:98 What additional disclosures are required after the initial statement is provided?

There are four circumstances that would require additional disclosures to be provided:

1. The plan adds a new investment vehicle. Information regarding the new investment must be provided as soon as practical, but in any event no

later than the date the investment becomes a designated investment alternative (see Q 4:87).

2. An investment vehicle that did not hold plan assets is later determined to hold plan assets. The information required to be disclosed (see Q 4:80) must be provided as soon as practical, but no later than 30 days from the date the service provider knows the investment holds plan assets.
3. There is a change to the information required in the initial disclosure. If that occurs disclosure of the change must generally be provided as soon as practicable but no more than 60 days after the provider learns of the change. However, changes to investment-related information (see Q 4:88) need only be disclosed on an annual basis.
4. A plan representative requests in writing additional compensation information needed to comply with ERISA's disclosure requirements (e.g., for 5500 Schedule C reporting purposes, or to comply with participant fee disclosure rules). This information must generally be provided reasonably in advance of the date the plan representative indicates it must comply with the disclosure requirement.

[29 C.F.R. §§ 2550.408b-2(c)(1)(v)(A) and (vi) and (B)(2)]

Q 4:99 What happens if disclosures are not provided or if there are errors?

The rule allows good-faith errors to be corrected without penalty to either party as long as reasonable diligence was exercised in providing the disclosure and the service provider corrects the information within 30 days after learning of the error. This 30-day grace period also applies to errors that occur in the context of communicating changes to any of the required disclosures. For other errors or failures to disclose, protection against the consequences of violating ERISA's prohibited transaction rules is available to responsible plan fiduciaries, but not to covered service providers. Plan fiduciaries can obtain relief if the following conditions are satisfied:

- The fiduciary did not know the service provider failed or would fail to provide the required information and reasonably believed the provider complied with its disclosure obligations.
- Upon discovering the failure, the fiduciary requested a correction in writing.
- The fiduciary notified the DOL if the service provider did not provide the correction within 90 days of the request. A form for providing this notification is available at *www.dol.gov/ebsa/DelinquentServiceProviderDisclosureNotice.doc*.
- The plan fiduciary made a determination of whether to terminate the arrangement consistent with the duty of prudence. If the requested information relates to future services and it is not disclosed promptly after

the end of the 90-day period, the arrangement must be terminated as expeditiously as possible consistent with the duty of prudence.

[29 C.F.R. §§ 2550.408b-2(c)(1)(vii) and (ix)]

Q 4:100 What are the consequences to responsible plan fiduciaries and covered service providers if the rule is not followed?

Both the responsible plan fiduciary and the covered service provider are "parties in interest" (see chapter 5) subject to ERISA's prohibited transaction rules and therefore could be charged an excise tax equal to 15 percent of the amount involved, which can escalate to 100 percent if the transaction is not corrected. A plan fiduciary's failure to collect, review, and assess service provider fees and services may also be a breach of fiduciary duty (see chapter 5).

Q 4:101 What responsibilities do plan sponsors have under the service provider fee disclosure rule?

Plan sponsors are responsible for understanding from whom they should be receiving disclosures and what should be in those disclosures. They are responsible for understanding the information and making a determination that the fees are reasonable in light of the quantity and quality of services offered. The goal is not to find the lowest-cost provider, but to determine that the fees fit within a range of reasonableness. Plan sponsors may want to use benchmarking services or consult with experts in making this determination. Plan sponsors are also held accountable for determining whether there are any conflicts of interest based on how service providers are paid.

Following is a checklist that plan sponsors may find helpful in responding to service provider disclosures:

1. Determine who is responsible for collecting and reviewing disclosures from the plan's service providers (see Q 4:71) and document that decision.
2. Make a list of the plan's covered service providers (see Q 4:72) and ensure that disclosures have been received from all of them.
3. If the disclosures received require the plan sponsor to look at other documents in order to determine fees and services, such as a prospectus or service agreement, gather that information and include it in the review.
4. If the information received is incomplete or does not contain enough information for the plan sponsor to determine reasonableness, make a written request for additional information.
5. If a current service provider does not provide a disclosure or does not respond to the plan sponsor's request for additional information, the plan sponsor should take steps necessary to protect itself from an ERISA violation (see Q 4:99).
6. Identify all service providers that will be providing services as an ERISA fiduciary or registered investment adviser.

7. Review all disclosures in accordance with ERISA's fiduciary standards (see chapter 5), ensure that the plan sponsor understands what it is paying for plan services, including any compensation paid through revenue sharing, and make a determination as to whether the fees fit within a range of reasonableness based on the quality and quantity of services offered.
8. If the plan sponsor determines that compensation being paid is not reasonable, take steps to either adjust the compensation or service level or to end the service arrangement.
9. In the event there are changes to be disclosed (see Q 4:98), ensure that a new disclosure is provided and reviewed.
10. Before hiring a new service provider, ensure that a disclosure is provided reasonably in advance of the date a contract is entered into.
11. Keep in the plan fiduciary file copies of all disclosure documents, as well as notes describing what was reviewed and what the ultimate determination was regarding reasonableness.

Q 4:102 How do plan fiduciaries determine whether a fee is reasonable?

There are two parts to this analysis, both of which are equally important. The first part is to understand the quality and quantity of services offered.

Example. Assume a fiduciary is looking at proposals from two plan consultants. Provider A charges 25 basis points and provider B charges 15 basis points. It is not consistent with the role of a hiring fiduciary to simply pick Provider B because B is the lowest-cost provider. Rather, the fiduciary must understand any differences in the level of service being offered. If Provider A offers more frequent or more robust consulting opportunities or has demonstrated past results in improving core success metrics in plans it has consulted on, then Provider A may be the better choice.

The second part of the equation is to look at fees paid to the provider. It is critical that the hiring fiduciary understand all fees being paid from all sources, as well as how those fees may increase over time as assets of the plan grow. Fees should be considered on a per provider basis, as well as in total. There are various ways to measure fees (e.g., as a dollar amount per participant or a percentage of total plan assets) and some plans analyze fees by category of plan service (e.g., compliance, administration, and investing).

Once fees have been calculated the plan fiduciary must compare the provider fees against the marketplace. Many plans use consultants to assist with this process. Some plans use fee benchmarking services or data. There is a great deal of variety in the types of benchmarking services available. The least expensive data to obtain are usually generic in nature, so there may be ranges of fees for plans of certain sizes that do not take into account differences in plan design, investment offerings, or other factors that may influence cost. There are also benchmarking services that take a more granular approach and can therefore provide more relevant data, but those services are typically more expensive.

There is not a single approach that is the right one. What's critical is that plan fiduciaries understand what they're paying and what they're getting, that they follow a prudent process for determining reasonableness, and that they have some basis for concluding that fees are reasonable.

Q 4:103 How often should fees and services be reviewed?

There is no rule dictating how frequently fees and services need to be evaluated. According to PSCA's 57th Annual Survey of Profit Sharing and 401(k) Plans (2013), the majority of plan sponsors (58.5%) conduct a review annually. Many consultants recommend that a complete review and benchmarking process be undertaken once every three years. As a general rule, larger plans tend to conduct this review more frequently than smaller plans.

Q 4:104 What fee disclosure rules apply when the service provider is not a covered service provider?

Service providers to a plan who are not covered service providers do not have a disclosure obligation under the DOL's interim final rule. This may include, for example, a consultant who is paid directly from the plan, an attorney who is paid by the plan sponsor, or a custodian who receives less than $1,000 in total compensation. However, both service providers to a plan and the fiduciaries selecting them remain subject to the general rule that the services must be necessary and the compensation must be reasonable (see Q 4:66).

Q 4:105 How are these rules different from the disclosure requirements for Schedule C to Form 5500?

The Section 408(b)(2) disclosure rules vary in many respects from the fee disclosure rules pertaining to Schedule C to Form 5500, which are discussed in chapter 19. Some key differences are as follows:

- The Schedule C rules generally only apply to plans with 100 or more participants, while the 408(b)(2) rules apply to all ERISA-covered plans.
- The maximum compensation a provider can receive without being subject to the disclosure requirement is less than $5,000 annually for Schedule C and less than $1,000 total for 408(b)(2).
- For Schedule C purposes, the disclosure obligation is on the plan administrator or plan sponsor, whereas for 408(b)(2) purposes the obligation is on plan service providers.
- The categories of compensation are defined differently. For example, in the 408(b)(2) rules, "indirect compensation" is defined more narrowly and there is no separate category for "eligible indirect compensation."
- The 408(b)(2) rules do not contain guidance for how compensation received with respect to multiple plans should be allocated, whereas the Schedule C rules do address this issue.

Q 4:106 Will there be a requirement to provide a guide or index as part of the fee and service disclosure?

In March 2013, the DOL published a proposed rule that would require some service providers to provide a guide or index with their initial disclosure. [DOL Prop. Reg. § 2550.408b-2(c)(1)(iv)(H). See discussion of the contents of the DOL's proposal in Qs 4:107–4:113.

Q 4:107 Which service providers would be subject to the requirement to provide a guide?

A guide would be required as part of the initial disclosure if that disclosure either cross-references other documents, such as a prospectus or service agreement, or exceeds a specified number of pages. The DOL is seeking comment on the number of pages that should trigger a guide requirement. A guide would not be required in circumstances where all the information required to be disclosed is contained in a single document that does not exceed the page count.

Q 4:108 What information needs to be included in the guide?

The guide would need to identify both the document being referred to (if a cross-referenced document) and a page number, or other sufficiently specific locator, such as a section number, where the relevant information can be found. If the disclosure is provided electronically, a link to the page or section (not just to the document generally) could be used in place of a descriptive reference. In either case, the standard is that the locator method must enable the plan fiduciary to quickly and easily find the relevant information.

The guide must provide locator information for all principal disclosure elements, which include:

- A description of services to be provided;
- A statement concerning status as a fiduciary or Registered Investment Advisor;
- A description of all direct and indirect compensation, compensation paid among related parties, compensation for termination of the agreement, and compensation for recordkeeping services; and
- Investment related compensation—a description of shareholder fees and annual operating expenses.

The guide must also include the name and contact information for the person or entity the plan sponsor can contact for questions about the disclosure.

Q 4:109 When would the guide need to be provided?

The guide would need to be provided with the initial disclosure. It is not clear whether a guide would be required to be delivered only to clients receiving their initial disclosure after the effective date of the guide requirement, or whether it would also be required to be delivered to clients who had previously received their initial disclosure document.

Q 4:110 Could the guide be included as part of the initial disclosure?

No. The guide would need to be delivered with the initial disclosure but must be contained in a separate document. The DOL is seeking comment on whether this is necessary.

Q 4:111 When would changes to information referred to in the guide required to be disclosed?

In addition to the current rules regarding disclosure of changes (see Q 4:98), changes to any of the information for which the guide must contain locator information (see Q 4:108) would need to be disclosed at least annually.

Q 4:112 Why is DOL creating a guide requirement?

Based on anecdotal evidence, the DOL believes that small plan fiduciaries in particular have difficulty obtaining required fee and service information in understandable format. The agency will be conducting focus groups to confirm whether a guide is needed and, if so, what it should contain.

Q 4:113 When would any guide requirement be effective?

The proposed effective date is 12 months after a final rule is published.

Other Activity on Fee Disclosure

Q 4:114 Has there been recent litigation involving 401(k) plan fees?

Yes. Beginning in 2006, a number of class action lawsuits have been filed against plan sponsors and plan service providers claiming that participants suffered damages in the form of reduced account balances as a result of improper plan fee arrangements. The claims against plan sponsors have been made against large companies, generally Fortune 500 companies, as well as against service providers to 401(k) plans. The following claims were raised in a number of these complaints:

- Plan fiduciaries did not select share classes with lower expense ratios that are available to large investors (e.g., by investing in retail funds instead of institutional funds), thus causing the plan to pay excessive fees.
- Plan fiduciaries did not utilize revenue sharing opportunities that could have reduced plan expenses.
- Plan fiduciaries selected actively managed funds with higher expenses than passively managed funds (e.g., index funds).

- Plans with employer stock failed to take appropriate action when the value of the stock dropped.
- Plan fiduciaries failed to adequately disclose fees to plan participants.

Some of the cases have been settled; some claims and/or cases have been dismissed without requiring a trial; and many remain open. Since these cases are being resolved in courts all over the country, a ruling on one case does not create a general rule applicable to all ERISA plans—that would only happen in the event of a ruling by the Supreme Court. A key question over which there has been a disparity of opinion by the courts is whether there is a requirement under ERISA's general fiduciary rules to disclose fees to plan participants, or whether the only fee disclosure requirements are those arising from specific notice and disclosure rules and regulations. [See, e.g., ruling on defendant's motion to dismiss in Kanawi v. Bechtel Corp., 590 F. Supp. 2d 1213 (N.D. Cal. 2008); Hecker v. Deere & Co., 556 F.3d 575 (7th Cir. 2009).] The fact that there are so many unresolved cases on 401(k) fee issues in the federal court system at this time, and the disparity of interpretations applied by different courts, contributes to the general uncertainty about what actions plan fiduciaries need to take to avoid liability related to plan fees.

Q 4:115 What are some significant rulings from the fee litigation cases?

The courts have been relatively consistent in ruling that the selection of certain types of funds (for example, actively managed instead of passively managed, or retail instead of institutional shares) is not an automatic violation of ERISA's prudence requirement and that plan fiduciaries are not required to find the cheapest possible fund. [Hecker v. Deere & Co., 556 F.3d 575 (7th Cir. 2009); Abbot v. Lockheed Martin Corp., 2009 U.S. Dist. LEXIS 26878 (S.D. Ill. Mar. 31, 2009)] However, a 2010 ruling held that the duty of prudence under ERISA Section 404(a) was breached when a plan fiduciary selected retail shares over institutional shares where, based on the facts of the case, there was no identifiable advantage to the retail shares and no evidence that the fiduciaries gave consideration to offering the less expensive institutional shares. [Tibble v. Edison Int'l, C.A. No. 2:07-CV-05359, 2010 WL 2757153 (C.D. Cal. July 8, 2010)]

The courts have been split on the question of whether there is a duty to disclose revenue sharing information to participants in participant-directed plans, particularly if ERISA Section 404(c) is being claimed as a defense in the litigation. [*Hecker,* 556 F.3d 575; Braden v. Wal-Mart Stores, Inc., 588 F.3d 585 (8th Cir. 2009)]

There have been a number of rulings on the question of whether a service provider who has the authority to add or delete the investment options available to their plan sponsor customers is a fiduciary. The rulings on this question are not consistent and are generally tied to the specific facts involved. [*Hecker*, 556 F.3d 575; Columbia Air Servs., Inc. v. Fidelity Mgmt. Trust Co., 2008 WL 4457861 (D. Mass. Sept. 30, 2008); Charters v. John Hancock Life Ins. Co., 583 F. Supp. 2d 189 (D. Mass. 2008); Haddock v. Nationwide Fin. Servs., Inc., 419 F. Supp. 2d 156 (D. Conn. 2006)]

The DOL has filed amicus briefs in a number of the fee litigation cases aimed at clarifying the scope of the defense available under ERISA Section 404(c). It is concerned that some of the rulings in fee litigation cases may be interpreted to mean that the 404(c) defense can be used as a shield against improper selection and monitoring of plan investments. Courts have been split on the question of whether the 404(c) defense extends to a plan fiduciary's exercise of discretion in selecting and monitoring investments available for participant investment in a plan that complies with Section 404(c). [See, e.g., Howell v. Motorola, Inc., 2011 WL 183966 (7th Cir. Jan. 21, 2011); DiFelice v. U.S. Airways, Inc. 497 F. 3d 410 (4th Cir. 2007); Langbecker v. Electronic Data Sys., 479 F. 3d 299 (5th Cir. 2007).]

One of the most damaging cases from a service provider's perspective is *Tussey v. ABB, Inc.* [No. 2:06-CV-04305-NKL (W.D. Mo. 2006).] In March 2012, the court in *Tussey* awarded $37 million in damages to plan participants for fiduciary breaches related to plan fees. The breaches included failure to negotiate and monitor reasonable fees, failure to follow the terms of the plan's Investment Policy Statement when mapping funds, engaging in a conflict of interest whereby the plan sponsor benefited from fees paid by the plan, and unauthorized retention of float income to pay for plan fees. It is important to note that the *Tussey* court did not disapprove of revenue sharing generally or attempt to define what level of fee is reasonable. Rather, it was the process used by plan fiduciaries (e.g., failure to calculate revenue-sharing fees and monitor available share classes) that created the liability. The *Tussey* ruling was appealed and in March of 2014 the 8th Circuit issued an opinion upholding the $13.4 million in damages for failure to prudently negotiate and monitor fees, reversed the $1.7 million for unauthorized retention of float, and sent the mapping issue back to the trial court to reconsider. [Tussey v. ABB, Inc., No. 12-2056, 2014 WL 1044831 (8th Cir. Mar. 19, 2014)]

None of the cases filed under ERISA has resulted in rulings on what the standard should be for determining whether plan fees are reasonable. However, there was a Supreme Court decision on a case brought under the Investment Company Act of 1940 claiming that a mutual fund advisor charged excessive fees to individual mutual fund investors as compared to institutional investors. The Court ruled that the charging of fees does not constitute a breach of fiduciary duty under the Investment Company Act of 1940 unless they are so disproportionately large that they bear no reasonable relationship to the services offered and could not have been the result of an arm's-length transaction. [Jones v. Harris Assocs. L.P., No. 08-586, 130 S. Ct. 1418 (2010)] It remains to be seen whether courts will apply this same standard when reviewing excessive fee claims brought under ERISA's fiduciary rules.

Q 4:116 Have regulatory agencies other than the DOL taken action with respect to plan fees?

Yes. The Securities and Exchange Commission (SEC) has a number of initiatives relating to mutual fund fees and fee disclosure that could impact 401(k) plans. The challenge will be to coordinate the activities of all the interested agencies and components of government to achieve meaningful controls and disclosure at a reasonable cost.

Q 4:117 What other actions has the DOL taken with regard to 401(k) plan fees?

The DOL has engaged in a number of initiatives around the issue of plan fees. In May 1998, it conducted an extensive study of plan fees and expenses. One of the key findings of that study was that plan sponsors and participants did not fully understand how 401(k) plan fees are charged, and, as a result, may be paying more than they should in fees. The study relied on a report which concluded that 78 percent of plan sponsors did not know what they were paying for plan services and that this is in part a function of the fact that there are over 80 different ways that vendors charge fees for the same services. The DOL study quoted results from a 1997 survey conducted by Stephen J. Butler of Pension Dynamics, which obtained quotes from 17 different providers on a 401(k) plan with 100 participants and $2 million in assets. The quotes for annual fees ranged from $11,375 to $42,775.

The DOL's study made the following observations:

1. Total plan costs are determined substantially by investment-related expenses. Investment expenses typically constitute 75 to 90 percent of total plan expenses.
2. There are significant variations in observed investment fees across the spectrum of 401(k) plan service providers. For a given amount of assets in a plan, expensive providers can generate fees several times higher than the lower-cost providers.
3. Plan sponsors control overall investment-related expenses. Within a diverse marketplace with thousands of available funds, there is substantial opportunity to pursue fee reduction strategies. To some extent, the literature suggests that one problem sponsors face is the appeal of "name brand" retail mutual funds to many participants. This appeal is often reinforced by the free or low-cost communication and education services that sponsors can obtain from these providers.
4. The other major expense categories—recordkeeping and administration, processing of loans, and trustees' fees—exhibit wide variations in the level of providers' fees and the manner in which those fees are structured. Some providers charge relatively high per capita or per transaction fees for certain services, while charging low or no fees for other services. Plan sponsors shopping for the best price for a given package of services must assess the total effect of all the components of the fee structure.
5. Larger plans enjoy potentially significant economies of scale. In the case of investment expenses, they have access to more providers offering a wide range of investment vehicles at lower cost. Very large plans may be able to reduce investment expenses even more through fee-reduction negotiations with the providers or use of lower-cost institutional accounts. In other expense categories, the combination of flat (or nearly

flat) fees regardless of plan size, plus declining per capita charges in the basic administration fee, reduces per participant administrative costs among larger plans.

Q 4:118 What tools are available to assist plan sponsors with understanding and evaluating plan fees?

The DOL's Web site offers various resources designed to assist plan sponsors with understanding and evaluating plan fees. They include the report titled "A Look at 401(k) Plan Fees," a document titled "Understanding 401(k) Plan Fees and Expenses," and a model fee disclosure form. (See *http://dol.gov/ebsa.*) Many service providers, if asked, will also provide fee comparisons when bidding for plan services. The DOL's new fee disclosure rules should also be of great help to plan sponsors in obtaining information needed for evaluating plan fees.

Q 4:119 What types of fees are generally of most concern to regulators?

Fees paid through revenue sharing arrangements, most commonly from mutual funds, are generally the types of fees receiving the most scrutiny. These fees are difficult to disclose in meaningful terms because they typically vary with the volume and nature of plan assets, and they carry the potential for creating conflicts of interest.

Q 4:120 What kinds of plan fees are typically paid from mutual funds?

Typically, two categories of revenue sharing are paid from internal mutual fund expense charges:

1. *12b-1 fees*. The distribution fee paid to the broker-dealer, generally for fund distribution services. These fees must be disclosed in the fund's prospectus and generally range from .25 percent to 1.0 percent of assets.
2. "Sub-transfer agency" *(Sub-ta) fee*. This fee is paid to the plan's recordkeeper for participant-level recordkeeping services. It is not itemized separately in the plan's prospectus, but is contained in the "other expenses" category in the prospectus. If the recordkeeper is retaining the sub-ta fee, the amount of the fee should be disclosed to the plan sponsor. Most sub-ta fees are asset-based and might range from 0.10 to 0.50 percent of assets. Some are paid on a "per participant" basis, and those typically range from $3 to $15 per participant.

Both 12b-1 and sub-ta fees are paid from the fund itself and are therefore borne by individual plan participants and have the impact of reducing the fund's earnings rate.

In addition to the 12b-1 and Sub-ta fees that a mutual fund might pay to unrelated service providers, mutual fund expense ratios typically also include fees for operation of the fund. The fees typically include an investment management fee as well as administrative fees. If multiple mutual funds are combined into a single "fund of funds" (for example, in a target date fund), there typically will be an expense for managing the portfolio of funds in addition to the individual fund fees. See chapter 6 for more information on fees charged by mutual funds.

Q 4:121 What types of fees are typically charged by collective funds?

Collective investment trust funds are funds managed by a bank or trust company that operate in a manner very similar to a mutual fund, but which are not subject to the same securities act rules regarding registration and disclosure as a mutual fund. The types of fees charged by a collective fund are similar to those charged by a mutual fund and typically include investment management fees, fund administration fees, and potentially revenue sharing amounts paid to third parties. There is typically more flexibility in determining fee levels in collective funds as compared to mutual funds.

Q 4:122 What types of fees are typically charged in insurance company products?

There are several types of insurance company products used in 401(k) plans. In general account products or GICs there is no stated expense ratio. Rather, the insurance company generates revenue from the spread between the guaranteed rate of return and the earnings on the underlying investments. There may be additional fees for early withdrawals from these types of funds.

In variable annuity contracts offered by insurance companies, there are typically two layers of fees. There are fees for whatever the underlying funds are, as well as a variable asset charge, or wrapper fee, to pay for administration and other expenses associated with offering the portfolio of funds.

Some variable annuity contracts also provide a guarantee, such as a guarantee to pay income for life at a specified rate. In those products there will be a fee for the guarantee in addition to the underlying fund expenses and the wrapper fee.

Q 4:123 What steps can a plan sponsor take to ensure that using mutual fund revenues to pay service provider fees does not result in paying excess compensation?

When mutual fund revenues such as 12b-1 or sub-ta fees are used to pay service providers, the fee is usually expressed as a percentage of assets in the mutual fund (e.g., 25 basis points or .0025 percent of assets vested in the fund). As assets invested in the fund grow over time with new deposits or investment earnings, the amount paid out as a fee also grows without there necessarily being any corresponding increase in services provided or other justification for raising the fee paid to the service provider. There are a number of mechanisms that plan sponsors can use to avoid this result. They include:

- Negotiating a cap on fees paid to the service provider from mutual fund revenues at the beginning of the arrangement with any excess amounts going back to the plan.
- Reviewing fees and services on a periodic basis and renegotiating fees if they are determined to be excessive or unreasonable.
- Setting up what is sometimes referred to as an "ERISA Spending Account" and using mutual fund revenues to pay the fees of all service providers and/or otherwise used for the benefit of the plan.

Q 4:124 What is an ERISA Spending Account?

An *ERISA Spending Account,* sometimes known as an *ERISA Budget Account* or some other name, is a mechanism that some plans use to maximize the potential of using payments received from investment funds to cover a broad array of plan expenses. This mechanism can be set up in a number of different ways. In some situations, a bookkeeping account may be set up independent of the plan trust to collect all mutual fund revenues and use them to pay plan expenses submitted for payment and approved by a plan fiduciary. In other cases, the mutual fund revenues are held in the plan trust in an unallocated account that is used to pay plan expenses during the year. At the end of the year, any unused revenues are allocated to participant accounts as additional earnings.

An ERISA Spending Account can be an effective tool for tracking and managing plan expenses. However, owing to the complexity of the arrangement and the legal issues involved in how such an account is structured, an ERISA attorney should be consulted in connection with setting up the account.

> **Example.** The XYZ Plan has $10 million in assets from which mutual fund revenues are paid out at an average of 25 basis points, for a total annual payment of $25,000. If that revenue is being collected by a single service provider whose actual invoiced fee amount would be $20,000, if converted to dollars, the excess $5,000 is retained by that service provider as additional profit. If an ERISA Spending Account is used for revenue payments, the $5,000 could be tracked and used to either pay the fees of other service providers or allocated among plan participants as additional investment earnings.

Q 4:125 What are the legal issues involved with using an ERISA Spending Account?

Using an ERISA Spending Account can help plan fiduciaries fulfill their duty to ensure that fees paid to service providers are reasonable. There are rules clarifying the types of expenses that can be paid from the account, as well as proper methods for allocating amounts that are leftover after expenses are paid. However, there are some unresolved legal issues surrounding these accounts.

The first question is whether the money in ERISA Spending Accounts constitutes "plan assets." If they do, then fiduciary standards of conduct apply in dealing with the funds and they must be included in the plan's financial statements for 5500 reporting purposes. It is pretty clear that if funds are deposited in the plan trust they are plan assets. See Q 4:126 for a discussion of whether funds deposited in a separate account are plan assets.

Another key issue is that the revenue generated to pay fees comes from plan investments, typically in unequal amounts. Therefore, participants will pay more or less of their share of plan fees based on their investment choices. While this reality exists in all types of revenue sharing payments, it could be exacerbated in the context of ERISA Spending Accounts.

There is also a lack of certainty regarding how to handle any amounts remaining in the account at the end of the year after all eligible plan expenses have been paid. While these accounts are not forfeiture accounts subject to the requirement that all funds be allocated at year end, most plans do not allow for carryover to the next year. Typically plans will either purchase additional services, such as an education campaign, or allocate any remaining funds to participants.

Q 4:126 Are revenue-sharing amounts held in an account outside the plan trust "plan assets" for ERISA purposes?

In July 2013, the DOL published Advisory Opinion 2013-03A on this issue, clarifying that revenue-sharing payments to a bookkeeping account held outside of the plan trust are generally not considered plan assets for ERISA purposes. The opinion was based on general rules regarding property rights, so if payments are made to an account inside the plan, or to an outside account in the name of the plan, or if there is documentation saying the funds belong to the plan, then the payments would be considered plan assets.

Even though these payments are not considered plan assets, plan sponsor fiduciaries have an obligation to ensure that the fees are reasonable, and they must determine that the formula, methodology, and assumptions used in allocating funds is in the best interest of participants. The financial institution receiving the funds has an obligation to disclose them under the service provider fee disclosure rules.

Advisory Opinion 2013-03A also clarified that while the funds themselves are not plan assets, a plan's contractual right to make a claim to those funds is a plan asset. For example, if there is an agreement to use the funds to pay expenses and to allocate any remaining funds at year-end to plan participants, and the financial institution fails to make those payments, the plan sponsor fiduciary would have the right to bring a legal claim against the financial institution, and that claim would be a plan asset for ERISA purposes.

Q 4:127 How are payments from an ERISA Spending Account treated for purposes of the new service provider fee disclosure rule?

Another issue that has arisen recently is how payments from an ERISA Spending Account should be treated under the new fee disclosure rules. For example, are these payments "indirect compensation" (see Q 4:91), the receipt of which can trigger a disclosure obligation (see Q 4:83) under the service provider fee disclosure rules, or are they "direct compensation" (see Q 4:90), the receipt of which does not trigger a disclosure obligation? The answer may vary based on how the account is operated. It seems clear that if the ERISA Spending Account is maintained inside the plan trust, any payments would be direct compensation, which would not trigger a disclosure obligation. That conclusion is less clear when amounts are collected from a mutual fund and held in a non-plan account.

Q 4:128 What is a reasonable amount for a 401(k) plan to pay for plan services?

The most meaningful way to compare 401(k) plan costs is to look at total cost either on a per participant basis or according to the number of basis points on total plan assets. As a rule, the smaller the plan, the higher the relative cost. One of the challenges in comparing costs is to standardize the level of services provided, as there can be wide disparity in the scope and level of services offered among providers.

Data that can provide help in benchmarking include the following results from a survey conducted by HR Investment Consultants and published in *401(k) Averages Book, 13th Edition*, comparing costs on both a per participant and percentage of assets basis.

Table 4-3. Benchmarking Plan Costs

	Average Plan Cost Per Participant			
Plan Size & Plan Assets	*Investment*	*Recordkeeping & Administration*	*Trustee*	*Total Bundled*
100 Participants $5 million in assets	$610	$30.00	$3.00	$643.00

	Average Plan Cost as a Percentage of Assets			
Plan Size & Plan Assets	*Investment*	*Recordkeeping & Administration*	*Trustee*	*Total Bundled*
100 Participants $5 million in assets	1.22%	0.06%	0.01%	1.29%

Source: *401(k) Averages Book, 13th Edition*, available from 401kSource.com. Reprinted with permission.

Chapter 5

Fiduciary and Prohibited Transaction Rules

The establishment and management of a 401(k) plan involves numerous fiduciary responsibilities. Certain types of investment transactions carry such fiduciary risk that they are prohibited altogether. There are important steps that plan sponsors and other fiduciaries can take to manage the fiduciary liability arising out of the administration of a 401(k) plan.

Fiduciary Issues 5-2
- Who Is and Who Is Not a Fiduciary 5-2
- DOL Efforts to Expand Fiduciary Status 5-5
- Scope of Fiduciary Responsibility 5-12
- Funding Policy and Method 5-17
- Fiduciary Selection 5-19
- Fiduciary Duties and Obligations 5-19
- ERISA Bond Requirements 5-20
- Consequences for Breach of Fiduciary Duty 5-23

Prohibited Transactions 5-28
- Types of Prohibited Transactions 5-28
- Prohibited Transaction Penalties and Corrections 5-29
- Common Prohibited Transactions 5-30
- Late Deposits of Salary Deferral Contributions 5-30
- Prohibited Transactions Resulting from Plan Contributions, Plan Design, or the Establishment of a Plan Checking Account 5-33
- Prohibited Transactions Resulting from Revenue Sharing and Other Fee Arrangements 5-35
- Eligible Investment Advice Arrangements 5-40
- Prohibited Transaction Exemptions 5-46

Managing Fiduciary Liability in a 401(k) Plan 5-48
- Fiduciary Insurance 5-48
- Indemnification 5-51
- Allocation of Responsibility to an Investment Manager 5-52
- Participant Direction of Investments—ERISA Section 404(c) 5-52

Managing Personal Liability 5-53
- Procedural Due Diligence 5-53
- Fiduciary Audits 5-55

The Voluntary Fiduciary Correction Program 5-58
Fiduciary Concerns Related to Specific Investment Products 5-64
Mutual Funds 5-64
Mutual Fund Revenue Sharing 5-68
Target Date Funds 5-69
Guaranteed Lifetime Income Investments 5-71

Fiduciary Issues

Retirement plans are managed for the exclusive benefit of participants by plan officials called fiduciaries. A critical phase in the establishment of a 401(k) plan is the definition and allocation of plan responsibilities among the various fiduciaries. A typical 401(k) plan will involve the following fiduciaries

- Named fiduciary
- Trustee
- Investment fiduciary
- Plan administrator

Note that a plan may have more than one person or entity perform each of these fiduciary functions. For example, if a plan has an Investment Committee composed of the plan sponsor's employees working with an outside Registered Investment Advisor when selecting funds for a plan, both the RIA and the Investment Committee members would be fiduciaries.

Who Is and Who Is Not a Fiduciary

Q 5:1 Who is a *fiduciary*?

There are several ways a person can acquire fiduciary status. The fiduciaries easiest to identify are those who acquire that status by virtue of their title. Every plan document will name a Trustee, a Plan Administrator, and a Named Fiduciary, and all the individuals or entities that fulfill those roles are plan fiduciaries. In addition, if a plan uses an Investment Manager (see Q 5:3), that person or entity also is a fiduciary.

Fiduciary status can also be acquired by function. In the past it may have been difficult for plan sponsors to determine whether a service provider who was not a fiduciary by title was providing fiduciary or nonfiduciary services. The service provider fee disclosure rules (see chapter 4) now require all service providers who offer fiduciary services to disclose their fiduciary status, so it makes it easier for plan sponsors to identify which service providers are also plan fiduciaries.

Q 5:2 What is a 3(21) fiduciary?

There are four ways in which fiduciary status can be acquired based on the role a person or an entity plays with respect to fiduciary decision making:

1. Exercising discretion or control over management of the plan (e.g., someone with authority to hire and fire service providers for a plan)
2. Exercising discretion or control over plan administration (e.g., someone with authority to approve of loans or benefit distributions, and so forth)
3. Exercising authority or control with respect to the management and disposition of plan assets (e.g., members of the Investment Committee that selects and monitors funds to make available in a 401(k) plan)
4. Rendering investment advice for a fee or other compensation (see Q 5:6 for a detailed description of how one becomes this type of fiduciary)

[ERISA § 3(21), 29 U.S.C. § 1002(21) (1974)]

A *3(21) fiduciary* generally works with the plan sponsor when making fiduciary decisions and shares responsibility with the plan sponsor in the event of a fiduciary breach. [ERISA § 3(21)]

Q 5:3 What is a 3(38) fiduciary?

In addition to being a fiduciary by virtue of ERISA Section 3(21), a service provider may also be an investment manager fiduciary pursuant to ERISA Section 3(38). An investment manager is a fiduciary who

- has the power to manage, acquire, or dispose of plan assets;
- is either a registered adviser under state or federal law or is exempt from registration; and
- acknowledges in writing that he or she is a plan fiduciary.

Investment manager fiduciaries are often named in the plan document and, unlike many 3(21) fiduciaries, have the authority to execute transactions independently without prior approval from the plan sponsor or other plan fiduciary. In addition, while investment managers must be prudently selected and monitored, plan trustees generally are not liable for the acts or omissions of an investment manager. [ERISA §§ 3(38), 405(d)]

Q 5:4 What is a 3(16) fiduciary?

A *3(16) fiduciary* is the person or entity identified in the plan document as the named plan administrator. If the document does not name a plan administrator, the plan sponsor is automatically the plan administrator. [ERISA § 3(16)] A plan administrator's responsibilities include both fiduciary and nonfiduciary functions (see Q 4:4). Historically, it has been common for plan administrators to delegate nonfiduciary functions to recordkeepers, third-party administrator (TPAs), or other service providers. More recently, some providers have begun to offer service arrangements that include accepting fiduciary responsibility for certain plan administrator functions, such as the approval of loans, distributions, and/or qualified domestic relations orders (QDROs). It is important for plan sponsors to review providers' fee and service disclosures to understand the level of service being offered, because a service provider offering fiduciary services must declare that in its disclosure.

Q 5:5 What are some examples of services that can be provided to a plan without giving rise to fiduciary status?

Typically, service providers such as attorneys, actuaries, accountants, brokers, or recordkeepers are not plan fiduciaries. Persons performing mere ministerial functions within guidelines established by others are not plan fiduciaries. DOL regulations list the following job functions as ministerial:

- Applying rules to determine eligibility for participation or benefits;
- Calculating service and pay for benefit purposes;
- Preparing account statements or communications to employees;
- Maintaining participants' work records;
- Preparing reports required by government agencies;
- Calculating benefits;
- Explaining the plan to new participants and advising participants of their rights and options under the plan;
- Collecting contributions and applying them according to plan provisions;
- Preparing reports covering participants' benefits;
- Processing claims; and
- Making recommendations to others for decisions with respect to plan administration.

[DOL Reg. § 2509.75-8, D-2]

Q 5:6 How is *investment advice for a fee* currently defined for the purpose of identifying fiduciary status?

Under current law a person will become a fiduciary under the "investment advice for a fee" standard if the person either:

- Renders advice as to the value of securities or other property or
- Makes recommendations regarding the purchase, sale, or retention of plan assets; and either
  - Has discretionary authority or control regarding the purchase or sale of plan assets; or
  - Meets all of the conditions of the following five-part test:
    1. Renders advice to a plan regarding the value of property or makes a recommendation regarding the purchase, retention or sale of property;
    2. On a regular basis;

3. Pursuant to a mutual agreement, arrangement, or understanding (written or verbal);
4. The advice will serve as the primary basis for the investment decision; and
5. The advice is individualized to the needs of the plan.

[DOL Reg. § 2510.3-21(c)]

DOL Efforts to Expand Fiduciary Status

The DOL has been working on a multi-year project to expand the definition of when a person or entity is a fiduciary as a result of providing investment advice for a fee (see Q 5:6). It published a proposed rule in 2010, which it subsequently withdrew in 2011. In April 2015, it published a new proposed rule (see Qs 5:7–5:24). The proposed effective date of the new rule is 60 days after a final rule is published. There is a separate "applicability" date of eight months after a final rule is published. In addition to the new proposal, the DOL simultaneously published two new prohibited transactions and amended existing ones (see Qs 5:118–5:120).

Q 5:7 What new guidance is contained in the DOL's 2015 proposal?

The 2015 proposal contains four key components:

1. A definition of what type of activity is considered fiduciary activity
2. A description of the functional test for when communications offered in the context of fiduciary activity is considered fiduciary advice
3. Carve-outs or exceptions for certain people or activities
4. New prohibited transaction exemptions and revisions to existing ones

Q 5:8 What kind of activity is considered fiduciary activity?

The following activities would be considered fiduciary activities if provided to a plan, plan fiduciary, plan participant or beneficiary, IRA, or IRA owner in exchange for a fee or other compensation:

- A recommendation regarding the purchase, retention, sale or exchange of securities or other property, including a recommendation to take a distribution from a plan or recommendations regarding the investment of assets to be distributed or rolled over from a plan or IRA.
- A recommendation regarding the management of plan or IRA assets (e.g., a recommendation regarding how to vote a proxy), including assets to be rolled over or distributed.
- An appraisal, fairness opinion, or similar statement (written or verbal) concerning the value of property if provided in connection with a purchase, sale, or exchange (but see Q 5:21 regarding exceptions).

- A recommendation of a person who will receive a fee or other compensation for providing any of the services described above.

Note: For fiduciary status to apply, the person engaged in the activity also must meet the conditions described in Q 5:11.

[DOL Prop. Rule § 2510.3-21(a)(1)]

The DOL's 2015 proposal broadens the current definition in many respects. One of the most significant changes is that providing advice to an IRA or IRA owner will be considered fiduciary activity and can subject the advice provider to the consequences of being an ERISA fiduciary if the conditions described in Q 5:11 are met. It is also significant that a recommendation to take a distribution or rollover (as distinct from a recommendation about how to invest funds received in a distribution or rollover) would be considered fiduciary activity. This is a reversal of the position the DOL took in DOL Advisory Opinion Letter 2005-23A, which will be superseded by this new rule if and when it is finalized.

Q 5:9 What is the definition of a "recommendation" for purposes of the rule?

A "recommendation" is defined as a communication that, based on its content, context, and presentation, would reasonably be viewed as a suggestion that the advice recipient engage in, or refrain from, taking a particular course of action. [DOL Prop. Rule § 2510.3-21(f)(1)]

Q 5:10 When is advice provided "for a fee or other compensation"?

Advice is considered provided for a fee or other compensation if the person providing advice, or an affiliate, receives from any source any direct or indirect compensation incident to the transaction in which the investment advice is or will be rendered. The term specifically includes, but is not limited to, brokerage fees and mutual fund and insurance sales commissions. [DOL Prop. Rule § 2510.3-21(f)(6)] An "affiliate" is defined for this purpose as any person directly or indirectly, through one or more intermediaries, controlling, controlled by, or under common control with such person, as well as any officer, director, partner, employee, or relative of such person and any corporation or partnership of which such person is an officer, director, or partner. [DOL Prop. Rule § 2510.3-21(f)(7)] "Control" for purposes of this definition means the power to exercise a controlling influence over the management or policies of a person. [DOL Prop. Rule § 2510.3-21(f)(8)]

In the preamble to the proposal, the DOL provides an example that states: If a fiduciary adviser recommends that a participant or IRA owner invests in a mutual fund that is offered by an affiliated company, and if the fund manager receives a fee from the fund, the receipt by the affiliate of advisory fees from the mutual fund is indirect compensation received in connection with the rendering of investment advice to the participant.

Q 5:11 What is the functional test for determining when a person engaged in a fiduciary activity is considered an ERISA fiduciary?

A person engaged in a "fiduciary activity" as defined in Q 5:7 will be considered an ERISA fiduciary if the person either:

1. Represents or acknowledges that he or she is acting as a fiduciary with respect to the advice provided; or
2. Renders advice pursuant to a written or verbal agreement, arrangement, or understanding that the advice is individualized to, or specifically directed to, the advice recipient for consideration in making investment or management decisions with respect to assets in the plan or IRA.

[DOL Prop. Rule § 2510.3-21(a)(2)]

Q 5:12 What are key differences between the current standard and the DOL's 2015 proposal?

There are significant differences between the DOL's current five-part test (see Q 5:6) and its 2015 proposal, all of which are likely to broaden the scope of when a communication made in connection with a fiduciary activity will be considered fiduciary advice.

- The advice would no longer need to be provided *on a regular basis.* Even if a recommendation was made solely in the context of a sales conversation, it could be considered fiduciary advice if all the other conditions are satisfied.
- The advice would not need to serve as the *primary basis* for an investment or management decision—it need only be *considered* in the decision.
- The advice could be *either* individualized (as is the current standard) *or* specifically directed to the advice recipient.
- There would no longer need to be a *mutual understanding* regarding the intended purpose of the advice. One of the intended impacts of removing the mutuality component is to prevent advisers from avoiding fiduciary status by including disclaimers of fiduciary status in their written materials.

Q 5:13 Are there distinctions on how the rule applies based on the type of service provider involved?

No. The DOL's 2010 proposal would have automatically assigned fiduciary status to certain types of providers, such as Registered Investment Advisers. The 2015 proposal does not contain this provision and applies the same standards to all types of service providers, including call center representatives.

Q 5:14 Are there any exceptions or carve-outs?

Yes. The 2015 proposal contains exceptions or carve-outs (in other words, even if someone is engaged in a fiduciary activity and meets the functional test, that person will not be considered an ERISA fiduciary) for the following activities:

- Counterparty transactions with plan fiduciaries with financial expertise—the "Seller's Carve-Out"
- Swap transactions
- Advice provided by an employee of the plan sponsor
- Platform providers offering investment menus
- Selection and monitoring assistance offered by platform providers
- Some financial reports and valuations
- Investment education

Q 5:15 What are the conditions for the Seller's Carve-Out?

This carve-out is available for advice provided by an adviser to a plan if the following conditions are met:

- The advice is provided by a person as a counterparty (or seller) to an employee benefit plan;
- The advice is provided to a plan fiduciary who is independent of the seller and who exercises authority or control over plan investments or plan management;
- The transaction for which the incidental advice is provided is an arm's-length sale, purchase, loan, or bilateral contract between the plan and the seller, or a proposal to enter into such a transaction;
- Before providing any recommendation, the seller satisfies one of the two following requirements:
  1. <u>Plan With 100 or More Participants</u>
     - The seller must obtain a written representation from the independent plan fiduciary stating that s/he has authority to manage plan assets, that the plan has 100 or more participants, and that the independent fiduciary is not relying on the adviser to act in the best interests of the plan, provide impartial advice, or give advice in a fiduciary capacity;
     - The seller informs the independent plan fiduciary of the existence and nature of his or her personal financial interest in the transaction;
     - The seller does not receive a fee or other compensation directly from the plan or plan fiduciary for providing investment advice (the seller can still be compensated for other services); and
     - The seller reasonably believes that the independent plan fiduciary has sufficient expertise to evaluate the transaction to determine whether it is prudent and in the best interests of plan participants.

Alternatively, a seller may rely on this carve-out if the following requirements are met:

2. Plans With $100 Million or More in Assets
    - The seller reasonably believes that the independent plan fiduciary has responsibility for managing at least $100 million in employee benefit plan assets. The adviser can rely on the most recently filed 5500 report or, if the fiduciary manages assets for multiple plans, on a representation from the fiduciary.
    - The seller informs the independent fiduciary that s/he is not providing impartial investment advice or providing advice in a fiduciary capacity.
    - The seller does not receive a fee or other compensation directly from the plan or plan fiduciary for providing investment advice (they can still be compensated for other services).

[DOL Prop. Rule § 2510.3-21(b)(1)(i)]

Q 5:16 Is the "seller's carve-out" available with respect to advice provided to small plans or individuals?

No. The 2010 version of the proposal contained a seller's carve-out that was available regardless of the size of the plan measured by either assets or participants, but the 2015 proposal limits the exception to large plans being managed by knowledgeable plan fiduciaries as more fully described in Q 5:15. The carve-out is also not available with respect to advice provided to plan participants or IRA owners.

Q 5:17 What is the carve-out for swap transactions?

The 2015 proposal carves out transactions involving the sale to a plan in connection with a swap or security-based swap if the following conditions are met:

1. The plan is represented by a fiduciary independent of the seller;
2. The seller is a swap dealer, security-based swap dealer, major swap participant, or major security-based swap participant;
3. The person (if a swap dealer or security-based swap dealer) is not acting as an advisor to the plan as defined by the SEC or CFTC; and
4. In advance of providing any recommendations, the seller obtains a written representation from the independent plan fiduciary that the fiduciary will not be relying on the seller's recommendations.

[DOL Prop. Rule § 2510.3-21(b)(1)(ii)]

Q 5:18 What is the carve-out for employees of the plan sponsor?

This exception to fiduciary status applies to persons who provide advice to a plan fiduciary in their capacity as employees of the plan sponsor and receive no compensation in addition to their normal compensation for the advice. Notably this carve-out is available only with respect to advice provided to plan sponsors, not to plan participants or beneficiaries. [DOL Prop. Rule § 2510.3-21(b)(2)]

Q 5:19 What is the carve-out for platform providers?

This exception is available to people who market and make available to plans a platform from which a plan fiduciary can select and monitor investment alternatives to be made available in a participant directed plan as long as the platform is provided without regard to the individualized needs of the plan. It includes making available a platform of investments that can serve as a Qualified Default Investment Alternative (QDIA). The platform provider must disclose in writing to the plan fiduciary that they are not providing impartial or fiduciary advice. This carve-out is not available for advice provided to plan participants or IRA owners. [DOL Prop. Rule § 2510.3-21(b)(3)]

Q 5:20 What is the carve-out for selection and monitoring assistance?

In connection with providing a platform of investments as described in Q 5:19, a person will not be a fiduciary if the person:

- Merely identifies investment alternatives that meet objective criteria specified by the plan fiduciary (e.g., based on expense ratio, size, etc.), *or*
- Merely provides objective financial data and comparisons with independent benchmarks.

[DOL Prop. Rule § 2510.3-21(b)(4)]

Q 5:21 What is the carve-out for certain financial reports and valuations?

Persons providing appraisals, fairness opinions, or statements of value will not be fiduciaries if the information is provided to:

- An ESOP regarding employer securities, or
- An investment fund, such as a collective fund, in which multiple unaffiliated plans are invested, or
- A plan, plan participant or beneficiary, or IRA owner solely for the purposes of complying with legally required reporting or disclosures.

[DOL Prop. Rule § 2510.3-21(b)(5)]

Q 5:22 What is the carve-out for investment education?

The 2015 proposal preserves all the categories of what is considered "education" and not "advice" as defined in prior guidance (DOL Interpretive Bulletin 96-1), but makes this guidance part of the regulation that will supersede its prior guidance. Following are some key changes from prior guidance:

- Clarification that the carve-out applies regardless of whether the information is provided to a plan, a participant or beneficiary, or an IRA owner. The DOL's prior guidance referenced information provided to participants only.
- Expanded to include information about distribution options, including information about the respective advantages and disadvantages; estimates of future retirement income needs and retirement related risks; and general strategies for managing assets in retirement.
- Restricted to prohibit reference to any specific investments in asset allocation models.

[DOL Prop. Rule § 2510.3-21(b)(6)]

For further information about the carve-out for investment education, see chapter 8.

Q 5:23 What other exceptions are contained in the 2015 proposal?

The proposal clarifies that mere "order taking" or execution of a securities transaction is not fiduciary activity as long as:

- The person executing the order is not a plan sponsor fiduciary of the plan involved.
- There are specific instructions regarding the identity of the security to be purchased, the acceptable price range, a time span for the purchase or sale of not more than 5 business days, and the minimum or maximum quantity of shares to be purchased or sold.

[DOL Prop. Rule § 2510.3-21(d)]

Q 5:24 What other guidance did the DOL issue as part of its 2015 proposal?

In addition to redefining who is an "investment advice for a fee" fiduciary and creating carve-outs, the DOL also created two new prohibited transaction exemptions and advice on numerous existing ones. These exemptions allow persons who are fiduciaries and who receive compensation that would otherwise be prohibited from continuing to receive the compensation if certain conditions are satisfied. The most notable addition is a new "Best Interest Contract Exemption" (see Qs 5:118–5:120).

Scope of Fiduciary Responsibility

Generally speaking, each plan fiduciary only has fiduciary responsibility for the functions over which they have accepted fiduciary responsibility and/or exercised fiduciary authority. For example, a fiduciary responsible for selecting plan investments would not be responsible for decisions regarding benefit determinations. This next section analyzes specific fiduciary roles and the type of liability associated with those roles.

Q 5:25 Will providing help to participants or beneficiaries who are eligible for a distribution create fiduciary risk?

Under current law, there is potential risk under both ERISA's fiduciary and prohibited transaction rules for financial service providers who offer distribution assistance to participants. The DOL is concerned that service providers will use their influence with plan participants to cause them to roll assets into an IRA or other account where the service provider may receive an increased fee and/or the services offered to the participant may be less robust than those in a 401(k) plan. Under existing authority, a current service provider to a 401(k) plan who advises participants to roll their accounts into IRAs from which the service provider will receive fees may be participating in a prohibited transaction. [DOL Adv. Op. Ltr. 2005-23A)] The DOL's recent proposal redefining "investment advice for a fee" fiduciaries (see Qs 5:7–5:24) would (1) make the mere recommendation to take a distribution or rollover a fiduciary act, (2) extend ERISA fiduciary status to advice provided to IRA owners, and (3) make it more difficult to provide investment help to IRA owners without crossing the line between education or information and fiduciary advice.

Q 5:26 What is a *named fiduciary*?

A *named fiduciary* is one who has the ultimate authority to control and manage the operation and administration of the plan. This fiduciary must be specifically named or clearly identifiable in the plan document so that participants or other interested parties such as the Internal Revenue Service (IRS) or the DOL will be able to identify who is responsible for the plan and will be able to address issues to that person. [ERISA § 402(a), 29 U.S.C. § 1102(a) (1974)]

Q 5:27 Must a person consent to be a fiduciary to be treated as a fiduciary?

No. A person who has or actually exercises discretionary management or control will have fiduciary responsibility, regardless of whether that person explicitly consents to becoming a fiduciary. It should be noted, however, that an investment manager or a qualified professional asset manager (QPAM) must explicitly consent to be a fiduciary in order to be appointed as one. Such explicit appointment or qualification is necessary to protect other fiduciaries and to enable the use of certain prohibited-transaction class exemptions. If an investment manager or a QPAM does not acknowledge that it is a fiduciary, it will not be an ERISA-qualified investment manager or QPAM. It will, however, still be a fiduciary and thus will be subject to liability under the Employee Retirement Income Security Act of 1974 (ERISA) if it performs fiduciary functions (e.g., invests plan assets using discretion). [ERISA § 3(38)(C); PTE 84-14]

Q 5:28 What is the trustee's responsibility?

The trustee collects and holds plan assets in trust for the participants. The trustee will also be responsible for managing the plan investments unless the plan expressly provides that the trustee is subject to direction from a named fiduciary or an investment manager. [ERISA § 403(a), 29 U.S.C. § 1103(a) (1974)]

Q 5:29 What is a *directed trustee*?

A *directed trustee* is a person or entity who has been named as trustee in the plan document but who does not have discretion over management of the plan's assets. Directed trustees are usually required by the terms of the plan document to follow investment directions given to them by the plan sponsor, plan participants, or an investment manager. [ERISA § 403(a), 29 U.S.C. § 1103(a) (1974)]

Q 5:30 Is a directed trustee a fiduciary?

Yes. The DOL's position is that certain positions in a plan, including those of trustee and plan administrator, inherently contain discretion over plan matters and therefore are always considered fiduciary roles. [DOL Reg. § 2509.75-8, Q-D-3; DOL Field Assist. Bull. 2004–03] However, while a directed trustee may be a fiduciary with respect to some matters and always subject to the rules of co-fiduciary responsibility, a directed trustee will generally not be considered a fiduciary with respect to investment decision making.

Q 5:31 What are the responsibilities of a directed trustee regarding investing plan assets?

The DOL has defined its position on the role of directed trustees with respect to the investment of plan assets. The agency reinforced its earlier position that a directed trustee will always be considered a plan fiduciary subject to ERISA's co-fiduciary responsibilities (see Q 5:65). It also clarified when a directed trustee is and is not protected from liability for following the directions of a fiduciary with investment discretion:

1. *Direction must be properly given.* The person providing direction must be authorized under the terms of the plan document to do so.
2. *The direction must not be contrary to the terms of the plan document.* The term "plan document" is used here in its broad sense to include not only the plan and trust document but also the investment policy statement or

any other document governing the plan. Directed trustees are required to request and review all such documents relevant to their role as trustee and are held to a standard of liability if they "knew or should have known" that a transaction was prohibited by the plan. If the documents are ambiguous with respect to a particular transaction, the directed trustee must request clarification from the investing fiduciary.

3. *The direction must not be contrary to ERISA's prohibited transaction rules.* With respect to ERISA's prohibited transaction rules, directed trustees must follow a process designed to avoid prohibited transactions. (See Qs 5:71–5:72 for a discussion of the prohibited transaction rules.) This can be accomplished by getting a written statement from the investment fiduciary stating that the plan maintains and follows procedures for identifying prohibited transactions and, if relevant, identifying any class exemption applicable to a transaction.
4. *The direction must not be contrary to ERISA's prudence rules.* With respect to the prudence requirement, a directed trustee generally does not have responsibility to independently investigate the prudence of every transaction or to second-guess the decisions of the investment fiduciary. However, a directed trustee is not relieved of liability under the prudence standard if it:
   - Has material nonpublic information regarding a security that is relevant to the transaction (e.g., knows that misrepresentations have been made in financial statements). Knowledge of nonpublic information is not imputed across the organization.
   - Ignores clear and compelling public indicators, such as an SEC 8-K filing, a bankruptcy, or the initiation of charges by regulators against the company in which plan assets are to be invested.

If either of these situations exists, the directed trustee must bring this information to the attention of the investment fiduciary and must also conduct an independent assessment of the transaction. [DOL Field Assist. Bull. 2004-3]

The DOL's guidance has already impacted the outcome of directed trustee litigation. In *In re WorldCom Inc. ERISA Litigation* [354 F. Supp. 2d 423 (S.D.N.Y. 2005)], charges against the directed trustee of WorldCom's plan, Merrill Lynch Trust Co., were dismissed on the grounds that Merrill Lynch did not possess nonpublic information that would have required it to refuse to follow the direction to invest in WorldCom stock.

Q 5:32 In light of the DOL's guidance, what steps should directed trustees take to protect themselves from liability for investment decision making?

Directed trustees should consider taking the following steps to protect themselves from liability for investment decision making:

- Review plan documents and signature cards to make sure it is clear who is authorized to provide investment direction and ensure internal procedures are in place so direction will be accepted only from those individuals.
- Review the investment policy statements, trust provisions, and any other plan documentation that might limit a plan's investment options and make sure any limitations are communicated to any representative of the directed trustee who has authority to execute investment transactions.
- Obtain a statement from the plan's investment fiduciary regarding its procedures for ensuring that no prohibited transactions will occur and identifying any relevant class exemptions.
- If acting as directed trustee for any publicly traded individual securities, monitor for public information regarding any bankruptcies, 8-K filings, or charges brought against company representatives. (See chapter 6 for a discussion of investments in employer stock.)
- Review insurance coverages, any other protections, and trustee fees to assess whether the risks of acting as directed trustee are being adequately covered and compensated.

Q 5:33 What are the responsibilities of a trustee for ensuring that salary deferral or other plan contributions are deposited in the plan trust in a timely manner?

Typically, the plan document defines who is responsible for ensuring that plan contributions are timely deposited in the plan trust. That responsibility usually is retained by the plan sponsor, and most plan and trust documents do not delegate this responsibility to a directed trustee.

The DOL, which has been concerned with the timeliness of deposits, issued two pieces of guidance in 2008 on this topic. In an amendment to DOL Regulation Section 2510.3-102, the DOL created a safe harbor for plans having 100 or fewer participants that remit plan contributions within seven business days (see Q 5:81).

In Field Assistance Bulletin (FAB) 2008-01, the DOL addressed the role of various plan fiduciaries in ensuring that deposits are made timely. The responsibility to collect and remit plan contributions must be assigned to a discretionary trustee, an investment manager, or a directed trustee subject to direction from a named fiduciary. In circumstances where a directed trustee is to act at the direction of a named fiduciary, the directed trustee has a responsibility under ERISA's co-fiduciary rules (see Qs 5:65, 5:66) for taking steps to remedy the situation if it knows that contributions have not been timely made. These steps may include alerting the named fiduciary and the DOL of the breach, reporting the breach to other named fiduciaries, taking direct action to enforce the contribution obligation on behalf of the plan, amending the plan, or seeking a court order. A directed trustee cannot avoid these co-fiduciary obligations through plan document or contractual provisions. [DOL Field Assist. Bull. 2008-01 (Feb. 1, 2008)]

Q 5:34 What issues for directed trustees are posed by DOL FAB 2008-01?

FAB 2008-1 posed a number of issues for directed trustees. One key issue is, What does it mean to have "knowledge" that contributions are not being timely made? Does it mean knowledge of the facts as a result of a phone call from a disgruntled participant? If there is information in the directed trustee's database for the plan from which a late deposit can be identified, does the trustee have an affirmative obligation to extract that data, run reports, and build processes to respond to information in the reports? The only guidance provided in FAB 2008-01 is that "knowledge" is a facts and circumstances determination.

Another critical issue for the directed trustee is determining when a late deposit should be considered a breach. For example, is any deposit by a plan with 100 or fewer participants made after the seven business day safe harbor a breach (see Q 5:81), or does it not become a breach until after the outside limit of 15 business days into the month following the payroll month?

A third critical issue is how should a directed trustee respond upon discovering a breach. Some of the options identified by the DOL, such as notifying plan fiduciaries and the DOL, seem reasonable. Others, such as amending the plan document or seeking a court order, are either beyond the scope of authority for most directed trustees or are prohibitively expensive.

Q 5:35 What steps should directed trustees take to comply with DOL FAB 2008-01?

The first step, assuming the directed trustee does not want fiduciary responsibility for collecting, monitoring, and depositing contributions, is to ensure that the terms of the plan and trust agreement specify that the directed trustee does not have discretion for these functions and that they are allocated to a specified plan fiduciary. Absent further direction from the DOL, directed trustees may also want to define their interpretation of what constitutes "knowledge" of a breach, at what point in time late deposits are considered to be a breach, and what steps they will take upon discovering a breach. Reasonable interpretations of these requirements consistently applied may assist in satisfying the DOL, as well as explaining to the plan sponsor's customers why a directed trustee is taking certain actions with respect to late deposits of plan contributions.

Q 5:36 Can a fiduciary perform more than one function?

All of the fiduciary functions can be performed by one individual. It is sometimes the case with plans sponsored by smaller businesses that all discretionary actions and authority will be given to one person, usually the business owner. It is rare, however, for one person to have the necessary skills and knowledge to perform all of these functions at the standard to which fiduciaries are held. Often, such individual fiduciaries will engage experts to advise them in these various areas. In fact, if the fiduciary lacks the required expertise in an area, he or she must seek expert advice. The fiduciary will remain responsible for the quality of the decision.

Q 5:37 How are fiduciary responsibilities allocated?

Major functions are defined in the plan and trust document. Specific, detailed responsibilities are often developed and limited in service contracts or management agreements, or in the minutes and records of meetings of plan officials. These side letters and documents must not conflict with the express terms of the plan and trust. [ERISA §§ 402, 404(a)(1)(D), 29 U.S.C. §§ 1102, 1104(a)(1)(D) (1974)]

The new rules on service provider fee disclosure, which went into effect on July 1, 2012, should make it easier for plan sponsors to determine which service providers are offering fiduciary services and what their responsibilities are. (See chapter 4 for a full discussion of the new rules.)

Q 5:38 Which decisions made by plan representatives are fiduciary decisions?

Every decision related to a retirement plan is not a fiduciary decision, and the distinction is significant because fiduciary liability only attaches to decisions that are fiduciary in nature. The DOL has issued a number of opinion letters regarding which decisions are or are not fiduciary in nature, and consolidated those opinions in guidance available on its Web site at *http://www.dol.gov/ebsa/regs/AOs/settlor_guidance.html.* Decisions about a plan that are not fiduciary in nature are referred to as "settlor" functions, meaning they are more in the nature of business decisions than fiduciary decisions. Following are examples of plan decisions that are considered settlor, or nonfiduciary, decisions:

- Plan design decisions (e.g., whether or not to offer loans)
- The decision to terminate a plan
- The decision to make discretionary amendments to a plan (e.g., to reduce or eliminate an employer match)

[DOL Adv. Op. 97-03A; DOL Adv. Op. 2001-01A; Letter to Kirk Maldonado (Mar. 2, 1987)]

Funding Policy and Method

Q 5:39 How do fiduciaries decide how to invest plan assets?

Every plan is required to establish and carry out a funding policy and method consistent with the objectives of the plan. The funding policy and method serves as a guide to the fiduciary for evaluating a specific investment opportunity. [ERISA § 402(b)(1), 29 U.S.C. § 1102(b)(1) (1974)] At a minimum, the fiduciary also gives appropriate consideration to the following questions:

1. How is the investment, as part of the portfolio, reasonably designed to further the purposes of the plan?
2. What is the risk of loss, and the opportunity for gain?
3. How does the investment affect the diversification of the portfolio?

4. Are the liquidity and current return sufficient to meet the expected cash flow needs of the plan?
5. What is the projected return of the portfolio compared with the funding objectives of the plan?

Q 5:40 Who develops the funding policy and method?

Typically, the funding policy is developed by a team. The investment manager brings knowledge of investment opportunities and a sense of realistic long-term market performance goals. The plan administrator or actuary brings information about the projected need to provide cash for anticipated benefit payments, as well as projections about the cash flow of future contributions. The named fiduciary usually has detailed knowledge about the employer's business objectives and resources, including a feel for what benefits are needed to attract and retain employees. In addition, legal advice helps to ensure that the policy says what it is intended to mean and documents the prudent actions of the fiduciary.

Q 5:41 What might a 401(k) plan investment policy cover?

Investment policies need to be flexible enough to adapt to an employer's specific situation and reflect the fiduciaries' attitudes and philosophies. For a typical 401(k) plan that allows participants a choice among investment funds, the policy should also recognize the participants' needs and goals. Further, the policy should deal with the number and types of funds to be made available. How many choices are enough? How many choices are too many? What types of investments are acceptable/unacceptable? What benchmarks will be used to monitor performance? How frequently will performance be measured and by whom? Are the asset classes selected consistent with identified risk and return tolerances and time horizon? (See chapter 6 for more information on investment policies.)

The policy may also cover how any loan program will affect investments and whether the withdrawal program is consistent with the types of funds selected. For example, if participants are expected to access funds through loans or withdrawals, do the investment funds allow for such withdrawals without penalty?

Finally, the policy may deal with the regulatory issues, specifically the requirements of ERISA Section 404(c), discussed in chapter 7.

Q 5:42 What are the disadvantages of developing, consistently applying, and updating the funding policy and method?

There are none.

Fiduciary Selection

Q 5:43 What factors are important in selecting a fiduciary?

The selection of a fiduciary is, in itself, a fiduciary decision subject to the fiduciary standard of care. The selecting fiduciary should document the investigation and selection of a potential fiduciary or service provider. Answers to the following questions should be gathered and reviewed:

1. What are the candidate's qualifications with respect to relevant experience, education, credentials, licensing and registration, and reputation?
2. How will the candidate be compensated? Are the fees reasonable?
3. What specific services are covered in the service contract?
4. What provisions are made for monitoring and documenting performance?
5. Does the candidate have proper bonding and insurance coverage?
6. Are the financial and organizational resources of the candidate consistent with the scale and needs of the plan?

The new rules on service provider fee disclosure, which went into effect on July 1, 2012, should make it easier for plan sponsors to evaluate the services and fees of prospective service providers. (See chapter 4 for a full discussion of the new rules.)

Q 5:44 What procedures should be followed when selecting a fiduciary?

Each fiduciary should acknowledge acceptance of fiduciary status in writing. The plan document and service agreement should detail the specific authority and responsibility of the fiduciary. Fiduciary performance should be monitored, and the appointment should be reviewed regularly.

Fiduciary Duties and Obligations

Q 5:45 What are the basic fiduciary duties and obligations?

A fiduciary must

1. Act in the exclusive retirement benefit interest of participants and control expenses of administration [ERISA § 404(a), 29 U.S.C. § 1104(a) (1974)];
2. Make decisions with the level of care that a prudent person familiar with retirement plans would use under the same circumstances [ERISA § 404(a)(1)(B), 29 U.S.C. § 1104(a)(1)(B) (1974)];
3. Diversify investments to minimize the risk of large losses [ERISA § 404(a)(1)(C), 29 U.S.C. § 1104(a)(1)(C) (1974)];
4. Use care to prevent co-fiduciaries from committing breaches and rectify the actions of others [ERISA § 405, 29 U.S.C. § 1105 (1974)];
5. Hold plan assets within the jurisdiction of U.S. courts [ERISA § 404(b), 29 U.S.C. § 1104(b) (1974)];

6. Be bonded in the amount of 10 percent of funds handled up to a $500,000 maximum bond ($1 million for plans holding employer securities) [ERISA § 412, 29 U.S.C. § 1112 (1974)];
7. Act according to the terms of written plan documents unless the documents are in conflict with the provisions of ERISA [ERISA § 404(a)(1)(D), 29 U.S.C. § 1104(a)(1)(D) (1974)]; and
8. Not engage in prohibited transactions. [ERISA § 406, 29 U.S.C. § 1106 (1974)]
9. In plans where participants have investment control over their accounts, provide enough information to permit informed decision making. [DOL Reg. § 2550.404a-5]

Q 5:46 What is *adequate diversification*?

Adequate diversification cannot be reliably defined by a fixed percentage or allocation. The standard turns on a plan's facts and circumstances. Courts have upheld high concentrations of assets in a single investment or asset category where the concentration is consistent with a particular preplanned written investment policy or philosophy. General issues for fiduciaries to consider are

- Portfolio composition with respect to diversification
- Portfolio liquidity, current return, and anticipated cash flow
- Projected return of the portfolio relative to the funding objectives

The fiduciary should also consider the possible risk of loss of an investment, as well as the financial soundness of any insurance company or bank that issues an investment. Real estate loans should be documented with a credit check on the borrower as well as an appraisal of the borrower's property. [DOL Reg. § 2550.404b-1]

ERISA Bond Requirements

Q 5:47 Who must be covered by an ERISA bond?

Every fiduciary of a plan and anyone else (plan official) who handles or has authority to handle plan assets must be bonded. [ERISA § 412(a), 29 U.S.C. § 1112(a) (1974)] The bond must provide a direct right of access in favor of the plan in the event the insured plan official takes plan assets. The bond coverage amount must be at least 10 percent of plan assets up to a maximum bond amount of $500,000 per plan and a minimum amount of $1,000 per covered plan official. It is unlawful for anyone who is required to be bonded to handle plan assets without a bond. Likewise, it is unlawful for any fiduciary to allow another plan official to handle plan assets without being properly bonded. [ERISA § 412(b), 29 U.S.C. § 1112(b) (1974)]

The Pension Protection Act enacted on August 17, 2006 [Pub. L. No. 109-280, 120 Stat. 780] (PPA) increased the bond limit for any plan holding employer securities to a $1 million maximum for plan years beginning after December 31, 2007. (See chapter 6 for a definition of employer securities.)

Q 5:48 What losses does an ERISA bond cover?

An ERISA bond protects plans from losses due to fraud or dishonesty such as theft, embezzlement, or forgery. It does not cover losses due to breach of fiduciary duty where the breach does not involve fraud or dishonesty. [DOL Field Assist. Bull. 2008-04, Qs 1 & 2] Protection for losses due to breach of fiduciary duty can be obtained by purchasing fiduciary liability insurance (see Qs 5:116–5:126).

Q 5:49 Are all plan fiduciaries and service providers required to be covered by an ERISA bond?

No. Only persons who handle funds or other property of the plan are required to be bonded. For example, a service provider who assists with plan design and prepares the Form 5500 Annual Report but who has no contact with plan assets would not need to be bonded. [DOL Field Assist. Bull. 2008-04, Qs 5, 7, & 8]

Q 5:50 What constitutes *funds or other property* of a plan?

The term *funds or other property* includes contributions from any source that are received by the plan or segregated from the employer's assets or otherwise paid out or used for plan purposes. It also includes all items in the nature of quick assets such as cash, checks, other negotiable instruments, government obligations, marketable securities, and any other property that is convertible into cash or has a cash value that is held or acquired for the ultimate purpose of distribution to plan participants or beneficiaries. [DOL Field Assist. Bull. 2008-04, Q 17]

Q 5:51 When is a person "handling" funds or other property such that bond coverage is required?

A person is considered to be "handling" funds whenever his or her duties with respect to plan funds are such that there is a risk the funds could be lost in the event of fraud or dishonesty of the person either acting alone or in collusion with others. This would include:

- Physical contact (or power to exercise physical contact or control) with cash, checks, or other similar property;
- Power to transfer funds or other property from the plan to oneself or to a third party, or to negotiate such property for value (e.g., mortgages, title to land or buildings, or securities);
- Disbursement authority or authority to direct disbursement;
- Authority to sign checks or other negotiable instruments; and

- Supervisory or decision-making responsibility related to activities that require bonding (factors considered are the system of fiscal controls, the closeness and continuity of the supervision, and who exercises final authority for the activity involving plan funds).

Bonding is not required where the risk of loss to the plan is negligible, such as where physical contact with checks is clerical in nature and subject to close supervision and control. If the handling activity involved is done by a plan committee with final decision-making authority, then all members of the committee must be bonded. [DOL Field Assist. Bull. 2008-04, Qs 18–21]

Q 5:52 Are some persons or organizations exempt from the bonding requirement?

Yes. Certain types of financial institutions such as banks, insurance companies, trust companies, and registered broker dealers, as well as directors, officers, or employees of these entities may be exempt from the bond requirement. Unique rules apply to each type of entity seeking an exemption, but the common theme is that the entity is subject to state or federal oversight or examination. [ERISA § 412; 29 C.F.R. § 2580.412; DOL Field Assist. Bull. 2008-04, Q 15]

Q 5:53 Who is responsible for ensuring that all persons who handle funds for a plan are bonded unless exempt?

This responsibility is shared by the person who is required to be bonded as well as the person (or persons) hiring or delegating functions to that person. [DOL Field Assist. Bull. 2008-04, Q 6]

Q 5:54 Are there any restrictions on who can issue an ERISA bond?

Yes. ERISA bonds must be issued by an insurance company or reinsurer that is named on the Department of the Treasury's Listing of Approved Sureties. This list is in Department Circular 570, which can be accessed at *www.fms.treas.gov/c570/c570.html*. Neither the plan nor a party in interest with respect to the plan (see Q 5:72) may have any control or significant financial interest in the insurer or in any agent or broker through which the bond is obtained. [DOL Field Assist. Bull. 2008-04, Q 4]

Q 5:55 What rules apply regarding the form or terms of the bond?

The plan must be the named insured on the bond. The bond can be a standalone document or be attached as a rider to an employer's existing bond or insurance policy. A plan can purchase a single bond to cover all service providers, or separate bonds can be purchased for each person handling funds of the plan. The persons covered under the bond may be identified by name or position, or the plan may buy a blanket bond. A single bond may be purchased to provide coverage for more than one plan as long as the amount of the bond is sufficient to provide for the minimum coverage required for each plan. An ERISA bond cannot contain a deductible for any amount of coverage required by ERISA. The bond can be written for a period of more than one year as long as the coverage meets the minimum amounts for all periods of time covered by the bond. [DOL Field Assist. Bull. 2008-04, Qs 3, 22, 23, 30, 31, & 33]

Q 5:56 Can a bond be paid for from plan assets?

Yes. The bond serves to protect the plan, not the service provider or other plan official, and therefore the bond can be purchased using plan assets. [DOL Field Assist. Bull. 2008-04, Q 11]

Consequences for Breach of Fiduciary Duty

Q 5:57 What happens if fiduciaries breach their duties?

Fiduciaries who breach their duties may be personally liable to make a plan whole for losses caused by their breaches. Losses can include lost-opportunity costs and, possibly, attorneys' fees and court costs. Co-fiduciaries may be jointly liable with a breaching fiduciary if the co-fiduciary knew of or should have known of the breach and failed to take steps to protect the plan. Fiduciaries can be removed from responsibility and barred from acting in a future fiduciary capacity with respect to any plan. [ERISA §§ 409, 502, 29 U.S.C. §§ 1109, 1132 (1974)]

In addition to liability for plan losses, the IRS and the DOL can levy civil penalties. The IRS can levy a 15 percent prohibited transaction excise tax on a fiduciary who is party to a prohibited transaction—increased from 10 percent effective August 5, 1997, by the Taxpayer Relief Act of 1997 (TRA '97). This tax is reported on Form 5330. The DOL can levy a civil penalty of 20 percent of the amount recovered with respect to a plan. [I.R.C. § 4975; ERISA § 502(*l*), 29 U.S.C. § 1132(*l*) (1974)]

Effective August 5, 1997, a participant's benefit may be offset by a settlement involving fiduciary violations. [I.R.C. § 401(a)(13)(C)]

Q 5:58 Can a fiduciary make a payment directly to the plan to settle a claim for breach of fiduciary duty?

No. The payment by a fiduciary to a plan to settle a claim against the fiduciary in exchange for a release of that claim generally would be considered a violation of ERISA's prohibited transaction rules. The DOL has issued Prohibited Transaction Exemption (PTE) 2003-39 [68 Fed. Reg. 75,632 (2003)], which allows fiduciaries to settle claims by making a payment to the plan under certain circumstances without running afoul of the prohibited transaction rules.

The exemption has separate rules for claims generally and for settlements entered into after January 30, 2004. Following are the rules for all claims under PTE 2003-39:

- There is a genuine controversy involving the plan. (A genuine controversy is deemed to exist when a court has certified the case as a class action.)
- The settlement is authorized by an independent fiduciary.
- The settlement is reasonable in light of the plan's likelihood of full recovery, the risks and costs of litigation, and the value of claims forgone.
- The terms and conditions of the transaction are not less favorable to a plan than comparable arm's-length terms and conditions that would have been agreed to by unrelated parties under similar circumstances.
- The transaction is not part of an agreement designed to benefit a party in interest.
- Any extension of credit involved in the settlement between the plan and a party in interest is done on reasonable terms, taking into account the creditworthiness of the borrower and the time value of money.
- The settlement does not involve claims for delinquent contributions to a multiple-employer plan.

Additional rules for settlements entered into after January 30, 2004, are as follows:

- Except in cases where litigation has been certified as a class action, an attorney for the plan who has no relationship to any party other than the plan determines that there is a genuine controversy involving the plan.
- All terms of the settlement are specifically described in a written settlement or consent decree.
- Payment to the plan must be in the form of cash unless (1) use of other assets is necessary to rescind the transaction at issue; (2) the assets used are securities for which there is a generally recognized market; or (3) the transaction at issue involved employer securities, and employer securities are used to correct it.
- To the extent that assets other than cash are used, such assets must be specifically described in the settlement agreement and must be valued at fair market value.
- The settlement may contain requirements to make future contributions to the plan, amend the plan, or provide additional employee benefits.
- The fiduciary acting on behalf of the plan must acknowledge on behalf of the plan that it is a fiduciary with respect to the settlement.
- Records must be kept and must be made available to participants and government agencies that would allow them to determine the plan's compliance with the terms of the exemption.

Q 5:59 What are some issues not addressed by PTE 2003-39?

One of the most problematic questions for fiduciaries is understanding when a dispute is likely to be a "genuine controversy" warranting hiring an attorney to designate the dispute as such. There are disputes within a plan all the time—disputes involving trading errors, miscommunication between participants and plan representatives, and benefits disputes, to name a few. Many such disputes are resolved today by paying an amount into a plan that is much less than the amount one would pay for a legal opinion.

Another issue not addressed by PTE 2003-39 relates to the allocation of payments made within a plan. These payments typically are not intended to be allocated in the same manner as employer contributions or earnings, but there is no guidance from the DOL regarding what an appropriate allocation methodology would be.

Q 5:60 Can nonfiduciaries be held liable for a breach of fiduciary duty?

The United States Supreme Court has held that outside service providers, such as attorneys, actuaries, and other consultants, are not liable for fiduciary breach damages even where the nonfiduciary participated in the breach. [Mertens v. Hewitt Assocs., 948 F.2d 607 (9th Cir. 1991), *aff'd,* 508 U.S. 248 (1993)] Service providers who are parties in interest under ERISA's prohibited transaction rules (see Qs 5:71–5:73) may, however, be liable for the return of funds involved in such a transaction, as well as the prohibited transaction excise tax, even if they are not fiduciaries.

Q 5:61 Can a fiduciary be liable for an unwitting violation of ERISA's fiduciary duties?

Yes. Even if a fiduciary is unaware that he or she is violating ERISA's fiduciary duties, the fiduciary can still be liable for the violation. The ERISA standard of conduct is an objective one: good faith is not sufficient. [Donovan v. Cunningham, 716 F.2d 1455 (5th Cir. 1983), *cert. denied,* 467 U.S. 1251 (1984)]

Similarly, a fiduciary will be liable under ERISA for engaging in a prohibited transaction if he or she knew or should have known that the transaction was prohibited. [ERISA § 406(a)(1), 29 U.S.C. § 1106(a)(1) (1974)] Under the Internal Revenue Code, excise taxes will be imposed on a fiduciary for engaging in certain transactions as a disqualified person, even if the fiduciary does not satisfy the "knows or should have known" standard. [I.R.C. §§ 4975(c)(1)(E), 4975(c)(1)(F)]

Q 5:62 Can a fiduciary be liable for a breach of fiduciary duty that occurred before the fiduciary's appointment?

No. A fiduciary cannot be held liable for a breach of fiduciary duty that was committed before the fiduciary became a fiduciary. Although the fiduciary may not be liable for the original breach, if the fiduciary knows about it, he or she should take steps to remedy the situation. Failure to do so may constitute a subsequent independent breach of fiduciary duty by the successor fiduciary. [ERISA § 409(b); Morrisey v. Curran, 567 F.2d 546 (2d Cir. 1977)]

Q 5:63 Can a fiduciary be liable for failing to act?

Yes. A breach of fiduciary duty can occur by reason of omission as well as commission. Some fiduciary duties are affirmative in nature, and a fiduciary who fails to execute them risks liability. Similarly, a co-fiduciary can be liable for failing to take reasonable steps to correct another fiduciary's breach of duty. [Bussian v. RJR Nabisco, 223 F.3d 286 (5th Cir. 2000)]

Q 5:64 Can a nonfiduciary be liable to a plan on non-ERISA grounds?

Yes. Nonfiduciaries may be liable to a plan under various statutes or state-law negligence theories. For example, a plan may have a malpractice claim against an attorney who erred in representing the plan. Or a plan may have a securities fraud claim against a nonfiduciary broker who excessively trades or churns a plan account or misrepresents an investment sold to the plan. Some state law claims, however, are barred by ERISA's preemption clause, which preempts all state laws that relate to an employee benefit plan. [ERISA § 514(a), 29 U.S.C. § 1144(a) (1974)]

Q 5:65 Can a fiduciary be held liable for breaches committed by a co-fiduciary?

Yes. A fiduciary can be liable for the acts of a co-fiduciary if the fiduciary does any of the following:

1. Knowingly participates in or tries to conceal a co-fiduciary's breach;
2. Enables a co-fiduciary to commit a breach by failing to meet his or her specific fiduciary responsibilities; or
3. Knowing of a co-fiduciary's breach, fails to make a reasonable effort to remedy it.

[ERISA § 405(a), 29 U.S.C. § 1105(a) (1974)]

Q 5:66 What should a fiduciary do if a co-fiduciary commits a breach of duty?

A fiduciary must try to remedy a breach of duty by a co-fiduciary. For example, if an improper investment was made, the fiduciary might consider disposing of the asset. Alternatively, the fiduciary might notify the company or the plan participants of the breach, institute a lawsuit against the co-fiduciary, or bring the matter before the DOL. The fiduciary's resignation as a protest against the breach, without making reasonable efforts to prevent it, will not relieve the fiduciary of liability. [ERISA § 405(a)(3), 29 U.S.C. § 1105(a)(3) (1974); DOL Reg. § 2509.75-5, FR-10]

Q 5:67 Does ERISA authorize punitive damages to a beneficiary for breach of fiduciary duty?

No. The United States Supreme Court has held that punitive damages are not available to a beneficiary in an action against the plan fiduciary for an alleged breach of fiduciary duty. Remedies available to the beneficiary in such instances would include only recovery of the benefits owed, clarification of the beneficiary's right to present or future benefits, or removal of the breaching fiduciary. [Massachusetts Mut. Life Ins. Co. v. Russell, 473 U.S. 134 (1985)]

Q 5:68 Does ERISA authorize the recovery of attorneys' fees and costs?

Yes. A court may in its discretion award reasonable attorneys' fees and costs to either party in an action by a participant, beneficiary, or fiduciary. [ERISA § 502(g), 29 U.S.C. § 1132(g) (1974)] The award of attorneys' fees is the exception rather than the rule.

Courts weigh the following factors in deciding whether to award fees and costs:

- Opponent's bad faith
- Opponent's ability to pay
- Deterrent effect on others in similar circumstances
- Whether action benefited all plan participants
- Relative merits of parties' positions

[Eddy v. Colonial Life Ins. Co. of Am., 59 F.3d 201 (D.C. Cir. 1995)]

Q 5:69 What is the impact of the *LaRue* decision on the risk of plan fiduciaries being sued by plan participants for breach of fiduciary duty?

The ERISA statute contains a very comprehensive set of rules governing litigation concerning such issues as who has the right to sue, based on what claims, in what court, and for what types of damages. It is beyond the scope of this book to cover ERISA's litigation provisions.

In a 1985 case involving a defined benefit plan, *Massachusetts Mutual Life Insurance Company v. Russell* [473 U.S. 134 (1985)], the U.S. Supreme Court ruled that breach of fiduciary claims under ERISA could only be brought on behalf of the plan as a whole and could not be brought to address losses impacting an individual participant.

In 2008, in a case involving a defined contribution plan, the Court ruled that the "whole plan" standard established in *Russell* did not apply to defined contribution plans, and that participants in a defined contribution plan can bring fiduciary breach claims for losses suffered in their individual accounts. The claimant in *LaRue* alleged that he lost $150,000 in his account due to the fact that the plan fiduciary had failed to follow his investment instructions. [LaRue v. DeWolff, Boberg & Assocs., Inc., 128 S. Ct. 1020 (2008)]

In the wake of the *LaRue* decision, there has been much concern about the risk of participant litigation. There is a concern not only that participants can bring claims that were not perceived as available to them before, but also that some of the steps participants are required to take before bringing claims for additional plan benefits (e.g., first using the plan's claims review procedure) may be avoided by casting the claim as a fiduciary breach claim. These concerns may be tempered somewhat by the reality that using litigation to resolve disputes is a very expensive option for all concerned and individual account losses may not justify that expense in many situations.

Q 5:70 What can fiduciaries do to minimize their liability risk?

Fiduciaries should accept only the responsibilities that they can carry out faithfully, exercise procedural due diligence in executing their duty, and document all their actions and decisions. Although fiduciaries are not expected to be clairvoyant when selecting investments or carrying out their other functions, they are expected to follow a process that ensures that their decisions are well informed and consistent with the plan's stated objectives at the time the decision is made.

A plan may not agree in advance to excuse a fiduciary from liability or indemnify the fiduciary. Fiduciary insurance may be provided by an errors-and-omissions policy or by indemnification by the sponsoring employer. [ERISA § 410, 29 U.S.C. § 1110 (1974)]

Responsibility for investment decisions can be shifted to an investment manager or to plan participants where the participants are allowed to direct the investments in their accounts (see chapter 7). [ERISA §§ 401(c)(3), 405(d), 404(c), 29 U.S.C. §§ 1101(c)(3), 1105(d), 1104(c) (1974)]

Prohibited Transactions

There are certain investment transactions that the DOL considers so fraught with potential to run afoul of the fiduciary requirement to act exclusively in the interests of plan participants that it prohibits the transaction altogether. It is important to bear in mind that these transactions are prohibited regardless of whether they prove to be good or bad investments for a plan, and regardless of the actual motive of the fiduciary making the investment decision.

Types of Prohibited Transactions

Q 5:71 What transactions are prohibited?

The Code and ERISA contain outright prohibitions against direct or indirect economic transactions involving plan assets and parties related to the plan unless the transaction is covered by an exemption. The Code calls related parties *disqualified persons*. Under ERISA, they are referred to as *parties in interest*.

Prohibited transactions cover the direct or indirect sale, exchange, or lease of property; extension of credit; provision of goods or services; transfer or use of plan assets; and the investment in employer securities or employer real estate in excess of the legal limits. In addition, ERISA specifically prohibits fiduciaries from dealing with plan assets where the fiduciary has a conflict of interest. This includes self-dealing, acting on behalf of a party whose interest is adverse to the interests of the plan, or receiving a kickback from any other person in connection with a transaction involving plan assets. [ERISA § 406, 29 U.S.C. § 1106 (1974)]

Q 5:72 What is a *party in interest* or *disqualified person*?

The definitions for both *party in interest* and *disqualified person* are complex and include plan fiduciaries, service providers, sponsoring employers, and those who control the employer, as well as individuals who are related to the foregoing by family or business ties.

Under ERISA, the following are parties in interest with respect to a plan (the Code definition for disqualified person is nearly identical):

1. Any fiduciary, counsel, or employee of the plan;
2. A person providing services to the plan;
3. An employer, any of whose employees are covered by the plan, and any direct or indirect owner of 50 percent or more of such employer;
4. A relative, namely, the spouse, ancestor, lineal descendant, or spouse of a lineal descendant of any of the persons described in items 1, 2, or 3 of this list;
5. An employee organization, any of whose members are covered by the plan;
6. A corporation, partnership, estate, or trust of which at least 50 percent is owned by any person or organization described in items 1, 2, 3, 4, or 5 of this list;
7. Officers, directors, 10 percent-or-more shareholders, and employees of any person or organization described in items 2, 3, 5, or 6 of this list; and
8. A 10 percent-or-more partner of or joint venturer with any person or organization described in items 2, 3, 5, or 6 of this list.

[ERISA § 3(14), 29 U.S.C. § 1002(14) (1974)]

Prohibited Transaction Penalties and Corrections

Q 5:73 What penalties may be imposed on a party in interest or disqualified person for engaging in a prohibited transaction?

Under ERISA, a prohibited transaction is a breach of fiduciary duty. Any fiduciary who engages in a prohibited transaction is therefore personally liable for any losses to the plan and must restore to the plan any profit made by the fiduciary through the use of the plan's assets. Also, a 20 percent civil penalty imposed by the DOL for certain breaches of fiduciary duty applies to prohibited transactions; however, the penalty is reduced by any penalty tax imposed under Code Section 4975. [ERISA §§ 409(a), 502(*l*), 29 U.S.C. §§ 1109(a), 1132(*l*) (1974)]

Under the Code, a penalty tax is imposed on a disqualified person for each year or part thereof that the transaction remains uncorrected. For prohibited transactions occurring before August 20, 1996, the tax is 5 percent. For prohibited transactions occurring after August 20, 1996, the tax is increased from 5 percent to 10 percent. For transactions occurring after August 5, 1997, the tax is increased to 15 percent. An additional tax equal to 100 percent of the amount involved is imposed if the prohibited transaction is not timely corrected. [I.R.C. §§ 4975(a), 4975(b)]

Q 5:74 How can a prohibited transaction be corrected?

A prohibited transaction can be corrected by undoing the transaction to the extent possible but in any event by placing the plan in a financial position no worse than the position it would have been in had the party in interest acted under the highest fiduciary standards. [I.R.C. § 4975(f)(5)]

The correction of certain prohibited transactions can be done using the DOL's Voluntary Fiduciary Compliance Program (VFCP). (See Qs 5:139–5:152 for a description of the program and the relief offered.)

Common Prohibited Transactions

The questions in the following sections (Qs 5:75-5:94) discuss types of prohibited transactions that occur frequently in 401(k) plans.

Late Deposits of Salary Deferral Contributions

Q 5:75 What is the most likely type of prohibited transaction to occur in a 401(k) plan?

An employer's failure to timely remit salary deferral contributions to the plan trustee is the most frequent type of prohibited transaction to occur in a 401(k) plan.

Salary deferrals must be held in trust as soon as they become plan assets. Amounts paid by participants or withheld by the employer from participants' wages as contributions to a plan will be considered plan assets as of the earliest date on which the contributions can reasonably be segregated from the general assets of the employer. In any event, that date can be no later than 15 business days after the end of the month in which the contributions are received by the employer or would have been paid to the employee in cash if not withheld from wages. [DOL Reg. § 2510.3-102(a) (effective Feb. 3, 1997)] Furthermore, if contributions can reasonably be segregated from general company assets prior to this time limit, then the employer should place the assets in trust at such earlier time. Once salary deferral contributions become plan assets, their retention by the employer is treated by the IRS as a prohibited transaction. This transaction is treated as a prohibited loan from the plan to the employer. [Rev. Rul. 2006-38, 2006-29 I.R.B. 80] The DOL will require that the delinquent payments, plus interest, be returned to the trust.

The DOL has created a safe harbor for plans with 100 or fewer participants, allowing them 7 business days to turn over plan contributions. See Q 5:81 for a discussion of this safe harbor.)

Q 5:76 Is there any special leniency for multiemployer plans under the DOL's "late deposit" rules?

Multiemployer plans face some unique challenges in complying with the DOL's regulation. They often are collecting salary deferral contributions from a variety of locations and may have language in a collective bargaining or other agreement specifying when contributions should be sent. The DOL provided guidance in this area. Multiemployer plans are subject to the same standard as other plans regarding the timing for remitting contributions. However, the time frames contained in any agreement can be taken into account in determining when assets can reasonably be segregated. As long as those time frames reflect an appropriate balancing of the administrative effort involved versus the benefit of early investment, and as long as deposits are made within the 15th business day standard, remitting in accordance with the contract language is acceptable. [DOL Field Assist. Bull. 2003-2]

Q 5:77 How are late deposits reported to the DOL?

The DOL has required for several years that employers report late deposits of salary deferral contributions on Form 5500, Annual Return/Report of Employee Benefit Plan. The instructions for Form 5500 not only require the employer to report whether or not late deposits have been made, but also require the plan's auditor to confirm the accuracy of the employer's response. [*See* Frequently Asked Questions About Reporting Delinquent Participant Contributions on the Form 5500 at *www.dol.gov/ebsa/faqs/faq_compliance_5500.html.*] Plans with fewer than 100 participants are generally exempt from the audit requirement, but they are not exempt from the requirement to accurately report late deposits. If a plan does have late deposits, it must report them on IRS Form 5330, Return of Excise Taxes Related to Employee Benefit Plans, and pay the prohibited transaction excise tax.

Substantial changes have been made to the 5500 reporting rules for plan years beginning on or after January 1, 2009 (see chapter 19). For all plans except one-participant plans, delinquent contributions must be reported. For plans with 100 or more participants, or plans with fewer than 100 participants that do not meet the asset requirements enabling reporting on Form 5500 SF, a separate schedule must also be completed with detail regarding correction efforts undertaken and use of the Department of Labor's Voluntary Fiduciary Correction Program (see Qs 5:139–5:152).

Q 5:78 How should late deposits be corrected?

The option providing a plan with the greatest protection against future DOL action is to file under the Voluntary Fiduciary Correction Program (VFCP) (see Qs 5:139–5:152). As the excise tax liability on prohibited transactions is generally small, and the costs of using VFCP can be significant, many employers correct late deposits by following the methodology of VCFP but do not file under the program. This methodology requires the plan sponsor to pay back the amount of the missed contributions, with earnings at rates described in the VCFP for the period of time the funds were late.

Q 5:79 Why is the DOL concerned with the timeliness of deposits?

More frequent deposits allow the plan to maximize the benefits of dollar cost averaging and reduce investment purchase risk. In addition, increased deposit frequency puts contributions to work sooner, earning in the tax-free trust.

Q 5:80 How should the responsibility for collecting, monitoring, and depositing plan contributions be allocated among plan fiduciaries?

In DOL Field Assistance Bulletin (FAB) 2008-01, the DOL took the position that the responsibility for collecting, monitoring, and timely depositing participant contributions to the plan must be assigned to (1) a discretionary trustee, (2) a directed trustee acting at the direction of a named fiduciary, or (3) an investment manager. (See Qs 5:33–5:35 for more information on DOL FAB 2008-01.)

Q 5:81 What is the safe harbor standard for remitting plan contributions?

In an amendment to DOL Regulation Section 2510.3-102, the DOL created a safe harbor rule for plans with no more than 100 participants as of the beginning of the plan year. The safe harbor rule provides that deposits to a 401(k) plan made within seven business days of the payroll date (or, for contributions received other than via payroll—for example, participant loan repayments made via check, received within seven business days of receipt by the employer) are considered timely.

The safe harbor rule was effective as of January 14, 2010, although the DOL had stated in a proposed amendment published on February 29, 2008, that it would not assess penalties for deposits made consistent with the proposed safe harbor rule from that date forward.

The final rule makes it clear that the safe harbor is not the exclusive means by which small employers can comply with the deposit timing rule. In other words, if a deposit is made later than seven business days after the payroll date, it will not be a prohibited transaction as long as the deposit was made as soon as the salary deferrals could reasonably be segregated from employer assets and was not made later than 15 business days into the month following the payroll month. [DOL Reg. § 2510.3-102(a)(2)]

Prohibited Transactions Resulting from Plan Contributions, Plan Design, or the Establishment of a Plan Checking Account

Q 5:82 May a fiduciary accept the contribution of property to a 401(k) plan?

A transfer of property to a pension plan that is used to satisfy a contribution obligation is a prohibited transaction. Further, a contribution of encumbered property to a plan is also a prohibited transaction. [Commissioner v. Keystone Consol. Indus. Inc., 508 U.S. 152 (1993)] However, a wholly discretionary contribution to a profit sharing plan may be made in the form of unencumbered property. [DOL Adv. Op. Ltrs. 81-69A, 90-05A]

In a 401(k) plan, "in-kind" contributions may be made to the employer discretionary account. Strong arguments can be made that both salary deferral and matching contributions are employer obligations (except perhaps for a truly discretionary match) and that in-kind contributions made to satisfy these obligations would result in prohibited transactions.

Q 5:83 How do prohibited transactions occur in the design process?

The following are examples of situations where prohibited transactions occur during plan design:

- The plan hires the owner's spouse as paid investment adviser for the plan assets.
- The broker for the insurance contract used to fund the plan is the son of the sole director of the sponsoring employer.
- An insurance agent sells a contract without disclosing specific information about the payment of commissions required under the applicable class exemption.
- The plan contracts with a person to provide administrative services and agrees to pay him or her more than reasonable compensation.

Care should be taken during the plan design stage to avoid selection of fiduciaries, service providers, or investment structures that might result in prohibited transactions. Plans may wish to identify significant parties in interest from the outset and use the list to screen prospective investments for conflicts.

Q 5:84 How can prohibited transactions occur in setting up a plan checking account?

Most banks, trust companies, and other financial institutions run disbursement checks through a master controlled disbursement account. The master account generates collected balances from uncashed checks. The collected balances are invested in short-term interest-bearing securities. The institution keeps the earnings generated on the account as a fee. (The funds are generally not able to be precisely allocated back to the plan from which the check was cut.) In 1993, the DOL advised Tennessee banking regulators that such a practice is a prohibited transaction. [DOL Adv. Op. Ltr. 93-24A]

The DOL has provided guidance regarding how financial institutions can avoid a prohibited transaction from occurring through retention of this float income by providing proper disclosure. The disclosure to the plan fiduciary selecting the financial institution should include the following information:

- The specific circumstances under which float is earned and retained.
- For float earned on contributions pending investment direction, the specific time frames within which investment will occur following receipt of direction, as well as any exceptions.
- For float earned on distributions, the event prompting the generation of float (e.g., check request date, check mailing date) as well as the event causing generation of float income to cease (e.g., check presentment). The disclosure should also state time frames for mailing and other administrative practices that could affect the duration of float income.
- The rate of float or how such rate is determined.

Plan fiduciaries selecting financial services are cautioned to take the following steps to ensure that the plan is paying no more than reasonable compensation after taking into account float income:

1. Review comparable arrangements to determine whether other providers credit float to the plan rather than the provider. If selecting a provider who retains float, verify that it makes sense given the total cost and quality of services.
2. Review the circumstances under which float may be retained by the provider and the rate of float earnings.
3. Ask for language in the service contract setting standards for investing cash and distributing checks to avoid unnecessary float.
4. Periodically monitor transactions generating float (e.g., cash awaiting investment instructions, distribution checks awaiting presentment) to ensure that administrative practices are in place to minimize float income.

[DOL Field Assist. Bull. 2002-3]

Q 5:85 Can float income be used to pay for plan expenses?

Yes, it is not uncommon for float income to be used to pay for plan banking or other fees but great care must be taken to ensure compliance with the rules described in Q 5:84 and general fiduciary obligations. For example, in the case of *Tussey v. ABB, Inc.* [No. 2:06-cv-04305-NKL (W.D. Mo 2006)], a service provider used float income to pay for overnight bank transfer charges, which is a fairly common practice. The court in *Tussey* found this practice to be a breach of fiduciary duty because the service provider's agreement with the plan said the provider would be paid solely through revenue sharing and did not disclose the fact that float income was an additional fee. In March 2014 the Eighth Circuit reversed the district court's ruling on the float issue on the grounds that float income is not a plan asset. [Tussey v. ABB, Inc., No. 12-2056, 2014 WL 1044831 (8th Cir. Mar. 19, 2014)]

Prohibited Transactions Resulting from Revenue Sharing and Other Fee Arrangements

It is a common practice in the 401(k) marketplace for plan service providers to receive some or all of their compensation for services to a plan in the form of some type of revenue sharing. Examples of common revenue sharing arrangements include payment of 12b-1 fees and front- or back-end loads from a mutual fund to a broker in exchange for distribution or other services and payment of a subtransfer agency fee from a mutual fund to a recordkeeper in exchange for participant-level recordkeeping services. The payment of such fees can result in a prohibited transaction because service providers are "parties in interest" unless a specific exemption applies.

Q 5:86 What general guidelines does ERISA provide regarding payment of fees to service providers?

Plan fiduciaries are obligated to operate the plan for the exclusive purpose of providing benefits to participants and defraying reasonable expenses of administering the plan. [ERISA § 404(a)(1)(A)] Generally, using plan assets to compensate service providers is a prohibited transaction because service providers are parties in interest to the plan. There is a statutory exemption that allows plan assets to be used to pay service providers as long as the services are necessary and the contract and compensation are reasonable. [ERISA § 408(b)(2)] If the service provider is a fiduciary (e.g., the investment manager) for the plan, there are additional rules requiring the service provider to avoid conflicts of interest in its compensation arrangements—basically, to avoid any arrangements whereby the method of payment may improperly influence the services provided to the plan. [ERISA § 406] The DOL has issued a number of rulings outlining how these standards may be satisfied in the context of plan revenue sharing arrangements.

Q 5:87 What is considered a "reasonable contract or arrangement" allowing service provider fees to be paid from plan assets?

The DOL has issued regulations under ERISA Section 408(b)(2) defining what constitutes a reasonable contract or arrangement for purposes of fitting within the prohibited transaction exemption. See chapter 4 for further discussion of these rules.

Q 5:88 Can a fiduciary receive compensation from funds held in the plan without engaging in a prohibited transaction?

Yes, but there are many rules and restrictions governing these transactions depending on the scope of the fiduciary's role, the type of fee being paid and the connection between the fiduciary receiving the fee and the fund paying the fee. It is not within the scope of this book to cover all possible variations and the rules applicable to them, but the following questions address some common scenarios.

Q 5:89 What are the rules for paying fees to service providers affiliated with fund investment managers?

One common situation involves the retention of fees from mutual funds when the investment adviser of the fund is an affiliate of the trustee or other fiduciary of the plan investing in the fund. For example, in a bundled product offered by a bank, the bank might act as trustee and the plan might invest in funds managed by an affiliate of the bank. In this situation, the trustee can be paid a fee from the fund and the fund manager can be paid an investment management fee if the following conditions are met:

- The plan does not pay a sales commission for buying shares of the fund.
- The plan does not pay a redemption fee unless it is paid to the investment company and is disclosed at the time of sale.
- The plan does not pay an investment management fee to the plan fiduciary with respect to plan assets invested in the affiliated funds.
- A plan fiduciary independent of the affiliated fiduciary receives a current prospectus disclosing investment advisory and other fees.
- The independent plan fiduciary approves of the fees in writing prior to the plan's investment in the affiliated fund.
- The independent fiduciary approves in writing any changes in the fees prior to their effective date.

[DOL PTE 77-4, 42 Fed. Reg. 18,732 (1977)].

It should be noted that when the DOL published its proposal redefining "investment advice for a fee" fiduciaries (see Qs 5:7–5:24), it also published proposed amendments to numerous prohibited transaction exemptions, including this one, to add a "best interests" standard of care as a condition for receiving relief.

Q 5:90 What are the DOL rules for paying fees to nonfiduciaries from mutual funds?

Another common situation involves the payment of fees to a service provider from a nonaffiliated mutual fund. It has become a fairly common practice in the 401(k) marketplace for mutual fund companies to enter into agreements with recordkeepers or other service providers whereby the mutual fund company will pay a fee for plan level accounting, participant communication, or other services. In 1997, the DOL expressed its opinion indicating that the service provider could retain fees in this situation only if:

- It did not have fiduciary authority to cause the plan to select the fund paying the fee.
- The fee was disclosed to and approved by an independent fiduciary.
- The services provided for the fee were reasonable and necessary for operation of the plan.

[DOL Adv. Op. Ltr. 97-16A]

Q 5:91 What are some DOL rules for paying fees to plan fiduciaries from mutual funds?

In its 1997 guidance, the DOL's position was that if the fiduciary receiving the fee had investment discretion with respect to selecting the fund paying the fee, it could not retain the fee and must credit any fees received from the fund back to the plan. The credit could be used to offset fees due to the fiduciary or another service provider or could simply be allocated to participants. [DOL Adv. Op. Ltr. 97-15A]

In a separate opinion, the DOL clarified that a service provider who retains the right to add or delete funds from their platform, and correspondingly from investment line-ups chosen by a fiduciary containing that fund, does not become a fiduciary by virtue of that substitution right as long as plan sponsor fiduciaries receive adequate notice and have a reasonable period of time to switch to a new provider if they choose not to accept the change. This allows the service provider to receive fees from funds on the platform without violating ERISA's prohibited transaction rules as long as a notice and other requirements are satisfied. [DOL Adv. Op. Ltr. 97-15A]

In 2001, the DOL issued an advisory opinion that appeared to relax the position it took in 1997. [DOL Adv. Op. Ltr. 2001-09A] In the 2001 Advisory Opinion, the DOL allowed the fiduciary, SunAmerica, to retain fees from funds offered as part of a discretionary asset allocation program. The asset allocation models were designed by a fiduciary selected by, but independent of, SunAmerica. The fees received by SunAmerica from the funds varied based upon the advice offered, a condition that was prohibited in the DOL's earlier opinion letter. Participants were permitted to disregard the advice and make their own choices, and full disclosure was made to plan fiduciaries regarding the relationship of the parties. SunAmerica did not have authority to override any of the investment decisions or programs made by the investment fiduciary it selected. [DOL Adv. Op. Ltr. 2001-09A]

In Advisory Opinion Letter 2003-09A, the DOL extended its position in Advisory Opinion Letters 97-15A and 97-16A to include the receipt of 12b-1 and subtransfer agency fees by a directed trustee from an affiliated fund. The facts involved a directed trustee that offered a bundled product including both affiliated and nonaffiliated mutual funds. Customers selecting the product were required to select at least one affiliated fund, and the trustee was paid fees from that fund as well as from the nonaffiliated funds.

The DOL took the position that the requirement to include an affiliated fund did not cause the trustee to have discretionary authority with respect to selecting that fund because the plan sponsor had the option of rejecting the bundled product altogether. It also took the position that, as long as the appropriate notice and disclosure requirements were satisfied, there was no reason to treat fees paid from affiliated funds differently from fees paid from nonaffiliated funds. [DOL Adv. Op. Ltr. 2003-09A]

More recently, the DOL issued a final rule on eligible investment advice arrangements (EIAAs) that offers two options allowing plan fiduciaries to be paid from funds on which they offer advice. (See Qs 5:95–5:116 for a detailed discussion of these arrangements.)

Q 5:92 Why have payments to fiduciaries from mutual funds received so much attention from the DOL in recent years?

Over the past 15 years, as 401(k) plans have become the retirement savings vehicle of choice and mutual funds have become the investment of choice in 401(k) plans, there has been a gradual shift away from having the plan sponsor pay fees to service providers toward having those fees offset by payments from mutual funds held in the plan.

There are two main problems with this development. The first is that fees paid from mutual funds are generally borne by participants because the fund charge used to generate that fee will have the impact of lowering participants' rate of the return in the fund. (See chapter 4 for an illustration of the impact of fee payments on plan participants over time.) The second problem is that even with the disclosure requirements the DOL has put in place, it often is difficult for the plan sponsor to fully understand and appreciate what fees it is paying for what services when a portion of those fees is paid by mutual funds. The rates paid by each fund vary, and the disclosure is expressed in terms of basis points, not dollars, so it is difficult for plan sponsors to have a full picture of what they are paying.

The new rules on service provider fee disclosure, which went into effect on July 1, 2012, have made it easier for plan sponsors to understand fees paid from mutual funds or from one service provider to another. (See chapter 4 for a full discussion of the new rules.)

Q 5:93 What has the DOL done to address potential fiduciary or prohibited transaction violations in plan fee arrangements?

The DOL has mandated greater disclosure of plan fee arrangements and, in particular, greater disclosure of revenue sharing arrangements. (See chapter 19 for a discussion of the new fee disclosure rules related to Form 5500 filings and rules on participant fee disclosures; see chapter 4 for a discussion of the new service provider fee disclosure rules.)

Q 5:94 What responsibilities do plan fiduciaries have under the DOL's final rule on service provider fee disclosure?

The DOL has defined the information that service providers must give to the fiduciary that is hiring them in order to fit within the prohibited transaction exemption that allows plan assets to be used to pay for plan services. These rules, which became effective on July 1, 2012, are discussed in detail in chapter 4. The steps that plan fiduciaries must take to comply with the rule and avoid engaging in prohibited transaction in the hiring process are the following:

1. Determine who is the "responsible plan fiduciary" (see chapter 4) in the hiring process. This person should have primary responsibility for ensuring that all the requirements of the prohibited transaction exemption have been met.
2. Identify which service providers are "covered service providers" (see chapter 4) with a disclosure obligation and the extent of their disclosure obligation, which will be based on both the type of services they provide and the nature of the compensation they receive.
3. Verify that all "covered service providers" have provided the requisite information and that the level of detail is sufficient to enable the responsible plan fiduciary to determine that the compensation is reasonable for the services being offered.
4. Review the disclosure information to identify any potential conflicts of interest that may exist based on how service providers are paid and the relationships among service providers. If a conflict is identified, exercise procedural due diligence to confirm whether hiring the service provider is still in the best interests of plan participants and beneficiaries.
5. If any missing or incorrect information is discovered, request in writing that the missing information be supplied and the incorrect information be corrected. The correction should occur within 30 days of the request. If the correction does not occur within 90 days of the request, notify the DOL using the form available at *www.dol.gov/ebsa/*DelinquentServiceProviderDisclosureNotice*.doc.*
6. If the information is not provided within 90 days of a written request, make a prudent decision about whether to terminate the arrangement. If the requested information relates to future services and is not provided after the end of the 90-day period, the provider's services must be terminated as soon as possible consistent with the duty of prudence.
7. If additional information is needed in order to comply with any ERISA Title I requirements, such as Schedule C reporting on Form 5500, or to comply with participant fee disclosure rules expected in the near future, provide a written request for this information. The information should be provided within 30 days of the request.
8. If a service provider is not a "covered service provider" but its fees are paid out of plan assets, use general fiduciary standards of care to determine whether the plan is providing reasonable fees for necessary services.

[29 C.F.R. § 2550.408b-2(c)]

Note that the rule is generally effective for contracts entered into on or after July 1, 2012, but service providers were also required to provide disclosure information to current customers on or before July 1, 2012, to the extent it has not already been provided.

Eligible Investment Advice Arrangements

Q 5:95 What is an *eligible investment advice* arrangement?

An *eligible investment advice arrangement* (EIAA) is an exemption to the prohibited transaction rules created by the PPA that provides fiduciary and prohibited transaction relief in certain situations where fiduciary-level investment advice is made available to plan participants. The new rules are contained in new ERISA Sections 408(b)(14) and 408(g).

Q 5:96 What relief is available when an EIAA is used?

Both plan sponsors and financial advisors can receive relief when an EIAA is used. Plan sponsors will remain responsible for the prudent selection and monitoring of the financial adviser, but will not have fiduciary liability for the individual advice provided to participants. Financial advisers will be able to receive compensation from funds on which they are providing fiduciary-level investment advice without violating ERISA's prohibited transaction and conflict of interest rules. [ERISA § 405(g)(1) and (g)(10)]

Q 5:97 Who can serve as a financial adviser in an EIAA?

The financial adviser to an EIAA must be (1) a registered investment adviser; (2) a bank or similar institution; (3) an insurance company; (4) a broker or broker-dealer; or (5) an affiliate, employee, representative, or agent of any of the aforementioned entities. [ERISA § 408(g)(11)]

Q 5:98 What are the general conditions that must be satisfied to obtain relief in an EIAA?

The adviser to an EIAA must use one of two options to avoid potential conflicts of interest. The first option is to receive level compensation from all funds so that the amount the adviser is paid does not vary based on the investment options selected by participants.

The second option is to use a computer model approach whereby a computer program determines the actual asset allocation to be used by the participant. Under either option, the conditions are:

1. The plan sponsor or other fiduciary must expressly authorize the arrangement;
2. The arrangement must be audited annually; and
3. Certain notice and other requirements must be satisfied.

[ERISA § 408(g)(11)]

See Q 5:99 for additional requirements that apply if the computer model approach is used.

Q 5:99 What additional requirements apply if the computer model approach is used?

If the computer model approach is used, the following additional requirements apply:

- The computer program must apply generally accepted investment theories, must take into account individual participant information, must consider all investment options available under the plan and not be biased toward affiliated funds, and must apply objective criteria to develop asset allocation portfolios.
- The computer program must be certified by an independent investment expert.

[ERISA § 408(g)(3)]

Q 5:100 What are the notice requirements for an EIAA?

The notice to participants in an EIAA must be provided in advance and updated annually or upon request of the participant. It must disclose the following information:

- Any affiliated party in the development of the advice program or the selection of investment options;
- Past performance and historical rates of return for the available investment options;
- Any fees the adviser or an affiliate will receive (the DOL provided a model fee disclosure form for this purpose);
- Any affiliation between the adviser and any of the available investment options;
- How participant information will be used or disclosed;
- Services to be provided by the adviser;
- A statement that the adviser is a fiduciary; and
- An explanation that the participant has the option to arrange for advice from an unaffiliated adviser.

[ERISA § 408(g)(6)]

Q 5:101 What is the EIAA audit requirement?

An audit of an EIAA must satisfy the following requirements:

- It must be conducted annually by a person or entity that is independent of both the adviser and the funds.
- The person conducting the audit must have appropriate technical training or experience and must indicate that in writing.
- The purpose of the audit is to verify compliance with the terms of the exemption.

- A written report must be provided to the plan sponsor.

[ERISA § 408(g)(5)]

Q 5:102 What other rules apply to an EIAA?

Other rules that apply to an EIAA include:

- The compensation received by the adviser must be reasonable, and the terms of the transaction must be at least as favorable to participants as those of an arm's-length transaction.
- The EIAA must comply with all securities law disclosure rules.
- The person who develops or markets the advice program or computer model will be a fiduciary, although the DOL is given latitude to narrow the scope of this rule.

[ERISA §§ 408(g)(7), (11)]

Q 5:103 Has the DOL issued guidance on EIAAs?

Yes. In 2009, the DOL issued final regulations that also incorporated a class exemption related to EIAAs. The class exemption was to become effective in March 2009. [DOL Reg. § 2550.408g, 76 Fed. Reg. 66,136 (Oct. 25, 2011)] The final regulation and class exemption were first delayed and ultimately rescinded by the Obama administration. The DOL issued new proposed regulations on EIAAs in March 2010 and finalized the regulation in October 2011.

Q 5:104 What issues are addressed in the DOL regulation on EIAAs?

The DOL regulation provides clarity on:

- The scope of people or entities subject to the level fee requirement
- The types of information which must be taken into account when providing advice
- The requirements for obtaining certification of the computer model
- Standards for obtaining authorization by an independent fiduciary
- Standards for conducting the annual audit
- Disclosure requirements, including a model disclosure form
- Other conditions applicable to the exemption

[DOL Reg. § 2550.408g-1]

Q 5:105 What is the *scope of the level fee requirement*?

The scope of the level fee requirement was a provision that was debated extensively. In the final rule, the requirement applies to the fiduciary advisor and any employee, agent, or registered representative of the advisor, but does not apply to affiliates of the advisor. For example, if an advisor works for an organization that has an investment company as an affiliate, and the advisor includes mutual funds issued by that investment company in its plans, the EIAA rules would not prevent the investment company from receiving non-level compensation from the plan's investments. The rule also defines compensation subject to the level fee requirement to include fees, commissions, salary, bonuses, awards, promotions or other things of value that are based in whole or in part on a participant's or beneficiary's selection of an investment option. The rule specifically includes payments from affiliates as part of the compensation that must be level. The purpose of this inclusion is to prohibit the use of bonuses or other rewards designed to favor certain investments. Broad-based bonuses or other things of value can be paid as long as investments in retirement plans and IRAs are either excluded from, or constitute a negligible portion of, the calculation. [DOL Reg. § 2550.408g-1(b)(3)(i)(D)]

Q 5:106 What information must be taken into account when providing advice pursuant to an EIAA?

Under either the level fee or computer model approach the advice provided must be based on generally accepted investment theories that take into account historic risks and returns of different asset classes. The advice must also take into account investment management or other fees attendant to the investment. It must take into account personal participant information to the extent furnished by the plan such as age, life expectancy, risk tolerance, other assets, or investment preferences. One change in the final rule is that under either the fee-leveling approach or the computer model approach, this information must be requested from participants, although there is no penalty for providing advice in the absence of this information if participants do not respond to the request. Also, information in addition to that required to be requested can be requested from participants and taken into account in the advice. [DOL Reg. § 2550.408g-1(b)(3) and (4)].

Q 5:107 What additional information or standards must be taken into account when the computer model approach is used?

In addition to the information described in Q 5:106, the computer model must be designed to:

- Utilize appropriate objective criteria to provide asset allocation portfolios comprised of investment options under the plan.
- Avoid investment recommendations that inappropriately favor options offered by the fiduciary adviser (or someone with whom they have a material affiliation or contractual relationship), that may generate greater income for the adviser (or for someone with whom they have a material affiliation or contractual relationship), or that inappropriately distinguish among investment options within a single asset class on a basis of a factor that cannot confidently be expected to persist in the future.
- Take into account all the designated investment options available in the plan without giving inappropriate weight to any investment option.

However, the model is not required to take into account annuity options or any investment option a participant has requested to exclude.

[DOL Reg. § 2550.408g-1(b)(4)(i)(F) and (G)]

Q 5:108 What are the requirements for obtaining certification of the computer model?

Prior to using a computer model or implementing a modification that impacts its eligibility to satisfy EIAA requirements, the fiduciary adviser must obtain a written certification from an eligible investment expert stating that all requirements have been met. An eligible investment expert is a person who, through employees or otherwise, has the appropriate technical training or experience and proficiency to analyze, determine and certify whether the model meets the requirements. The expert cannot have any material affiliation or contractual relationship with the fiduciary adviser of any employee, agent, or registered representative of the adviser and must not have participated in developing the computer model. [DOL Reg. § 2550.408g-1(b)(4)(ii) and (iii)] The final rule also clarified that the selection of the eligible investment expert is a fiduciary function. [DOL Reg. § 2550.408g-1(b)(4)(v)]

Q 5:109 What information must be included in the computer model certification?

The certification must include the following information:

- Identification of the methodology used in determining whether the computer model meets EIAA requirements as defined in Qs 5:106 and 5:107.
- An explanation of how the applied methodology demonstrated compliance with the requirements.
- A description of any limitations imposed by any person on the eligible investment expert's selection or application of methodologies used to determine compliance.
- A representation that the methodology was applied by a person with the educational background, technical training, or experience necessary to determine compliance.
- A signed statement certifying that the eligible investment expert has determined that the computer model is compliant.

This statement must be signed by the eligible investment expert. [DOL Reg. § 2550.408g-1(b)(4)(iv)]

Q 5:110 What are the standards for obtaining authorization from an independent fiduciary?

All EIAAs, regardless of whether they use the level fee or computer model approach, must be expressly authorized by a plan fiduciary who is not the person offering the EIAA, any person providing designated investments under the plan, or an affiliate of either. If the plan sponsor is also the entity providing the advice, it can authorize the arrangement as long as the same arrangement is offered to participants and beneficiaries of unaffiliated plans in the ordinary course of business. Offering employer securities as a plan investment will not cause the plan sponsor to lose its status as an independent fiduciary. [DOL Reg. § 2550.408g-1(b)(5)].

Q 5:111 What is the annual audit requirement for EIAAs?

All EIAAs must be audited annually by an independent auditor who represents in writing that it has the appropriate technical training, experience or proficiency to determine compliance with all EIAA requirements. An auditor is independent if it does not have any material affiliation or contractual relationship with the person providing the advice or with any of the plan's designated investment options. The process for the audit in a 401(k) plan is as follows:

- The selection of the auditor is a fiduciary decision.
- The auditor must review sufficient relevant information to determine compliance, although sampling methods may be used.
- Within 60 days of completing the audit a written report must be issued to the fiduciary adviser and to each fiduciary that authorized use of the EIAA.
- The report must set forth specific findings regarding compliance with EIAA rules.

[DOL Reg. § 2550.408g-1(b)(6)]

Q 5:112 What additional disclosure standards are in the DOL regulation?

The general rules for disclosure to plan participants in EIAAs are described in Q 5:98. The regulation clarifies that the compensation to be disclosed includes fees or other compensation of the adviser or any affiliate in connection with the provision of the advice, the sale, acquisition or holding of any security or property pursuant to the advice, or any rollover of distribution of assets pursuant to such advice. A model disclosure form was also provided (see Appendix H). The notice can be provided in either paper or electronic form. The fiduciary adviser must maintain current, accurate information on all of the required disclosure items and disclosure must be provided without charge annually, or upon request of a participant. [DOL Reg. § 2550.408g-1(b)(7)]

Q 5:113 What other conditions apply to EIAAs?

The DOL regulation contains other requirements for EIAAs as follows:

- The fiduciary adviser must provide all disclosures required by applicable securities laws.
- The sale, purchase or holding of an investment must occur solely at the direction of the recipient of the advice.

- The compensation received by the adviser and affiliates must be reasonable.
- The terms of the sale, purchase or holding of the investment must be at least as favorable to the plan as an arm's-length transaction would be.
- The adviser provides the authorizing fiduciary with a notice stating that he or she intends to comply with the EIAA rules, that the arrangement will be audited annually, and that the auditor's report will be provided within 60 days following the completion of the audit.
- The fiduciary adviser must maintain any records necessary to verify compliance with the rule for a period of six years.

[DOL Reg. §§ 2550.408g-1(b)(8) and (9) and 2550.408g-1(d)]

Q 5:114 Can a fiduciary adviser relying on the computer model exemption provide post-model advice?

No. Prior versions of the EIAA rule did allow for post-model advice under certain conditions, but the final rule does not allow for it. Advice can only be provided if it falls within either the level fee or computer model rules.

Q 5:115 What was the effective date for the final EIAA rule?

The final rule applied to transactions occurring on or after December 27, 2011.

[DOL Reg. § 2550.408g-1(f)]

Q 5:116 Does the new EIAA exemption change the ability of fiduciaries to rely on prior DOL guidance?

Pre-PPA guidance issued by the DOL on how fiduciaries can participate in revenue sharing without violating ERISA remains valid and can be relied on. [DOL Field Assist. Bull. 2007-01] The DOL's final rule also acknowledged that prior guidance relating to the ability of advisors to be paid from funds on which they provide advice remains valid. [DOL Reg. § 2550.408g-1(a)(3)].

Prohibited Transaction Exemptions

Q 5:117 What is a *prohibited transaction exemption*?

There are three kinds of exemptions from the prohibited transaction rules

1. *Statutory exemption.* This is an exemption for routine transactions with low risk of abuse. For example, a plan may pay benefits to a fiduciary who is also a participant in accordance with the terms of the plan, or plan service providers may be paid fees from the plan as long as no more than reasonable compensation is paid. [ERISA § 408(b), 29 U.S.C. § 1108(b) (1974)]

2. *Class exemption.* The DOL has granted class exemptions for transactions that were not specifically defined in ERISA but are of a similar low-risk character. For example, insurance policies may be transferred between the plan and a party in interest if detailed procedural requirements are adhered to. [ERISA § 408(a), 29 U.S.C. § 1108(a) (1974)]
3. *Individual exemption.* An individual may apply to the DOL for an individual prohibited transaction exemption if he or she is able to demonstrate that an intended prohibited transaction is in the best interests of the plan. [ERISA § 408(a), 29 U.S.C. § 1108(a) (1974)]

Q 5:118 How will recently proposed DOL guidance change the availability of prohibited transaction class exemptions?

When the DOL published its proposed rule redefining "investment advice for a fee" fiduciaries (see Qs 5:7–5:24), it also published two new prohibited transaction class exemptions and amended numerous existing ones. The amendments to existing exemptions primarily made distinctions between different types of investors receiving services (plans, IRA owners, etc.) and added a "best interest" standard of care as a condition for receiving relief. The most significant new class exemption is the "Best Interest Contract Exemption" (BICE).

Q 5:119 What kind of relief is available using the Best Interest Contract Exemption?

The BICE is available to allow for certain forms of compensation, the receipt of which would otherwise be a violation of ERISA's prohibited transaction rules. It is available when advice is provided to plan participants, IRA owners, and plan sponsors of nonparticipant-directed plans that have fewer than 100 participants. Note that the BICE is not available for compensation received in connection with providing services to plan sponsors in participant-directed plans. The exemption is also limited to cover only compensation received with respect to investments commonly used in plans and IRAs, such as mutual funds, collective funds, etc., and does not cover compensation received with respect to futures or puts or other specialty investments. The BICE is not available if the person providing the advice is the plan sponsor or a named fiduciary to the plan. It is also not available if advice is generated exclusively through a computer-generated program ("robo advice").

Q 5:120 What are the general requirements for using the BICE?

It is beyond the scope of this book to cover in detail the numerous requirements for reliance on the BICE, since this exemption is not available for providing advice to participant-directed plans (although it may be used when providing advice to participants in those plans). The following are some key conditions that must be satisfied by the advice provider.

1. A written contract entered into prior to providing the advice that:
   a. Acknowledges the fiduciary status of the adviser,
   b. Commits to adhering to defined Impartial Conduct Standards,
   c. Commits to adhering to a Best Interest standard of care—which is generally an ERISA fiduciary standard;
2. Provision of written warranties, including:
   a. Compliance with all applicable state and federal laws,
   b. Adoption of written policies and procedures designed to mitigate potential conflicts of interest and ensure compliance with the Impartial Conduct Standards;
3. Satisfaction of numerous disclosure requirements, including:
   a. Publicly available Web-based information about compensation received in the last year,
   b. Point-of-sale disclosures with fee detail displayed in a chart format,
   c. An annual disclosure showing transactions and fees;
4. Notification to the DOL and retention of specified data:
   a. Must tell DOL of intent to use the BICE before using it,
   b. Must maintain specified data elements for six years to be made available in the event of an audit.

Managing Fiduciary Liability in a 401(k) Plan

There are a number of ways that fiduciaries and plans can protect themselves from the failure of a fiduciary to perform at the required level of skill and competence. Two major strategies are to insure against the risk and to limit or shift responsibility through allocation of duties to others. Insurance can be achieved through a formal insurance policy or by means of indemnification provisions in plan documents and service contracts. In participant directed plans, shifting the responsibility of asset allocation decisions to the plan participants is often a major objective. The use of a designated investment manager can also help to reduce investment risk. Finally, understanding the scope of the fiduciary role and practicing procedural due diligence in fulfilling that role can substantially reduce risk.

Fiduciary Insurance

It is beyond the scope of this book to provide a detailed discussion of the intricacies of fiduciary liability insurance policies. For an in-depth discussion of fiduciary liability insurance, including an analysis of common policy provisions and limitations, see T. Ferrera, *ERISA Fiduciary Answer Book* (New York: CCH, Inc.).

Plan sponsors should consider engaging an insurance agent with experience in writing this type of coverage and should also have the policies reviewed by ERISA counsel. Although many policy provisions are required by state insurance law, there is still significant opportunity to negotiate optional terms of coverage. Care should be taken to ensure that a policy covers the activities in which the plan and its fiduciaries in fact intend to engage.

Q 5:121 Can a plan purchase fiduciary liability insurance for itself or for plan fiduciaries?

Yes. The insurance contract must, however, permit recourse by the insurer against the fiduciary for the loss resulting from a breach of a fiduciary obligation by such fiduciary. [ERISA § 401(b), 29 U.S.C. § 1101(b) (1974)] Whether fiduciary liability insurance may cover fiduciaries for the 20 percent excise tax for fiduciary breaches under ERISA Section 502(*l*) is a matter of state law.

A fiduciary can purchase a nonrecourse rider to the policy. (A fiduciary should ensure that plan funds are not used for such purpose.) The nonrecourse rider provides that the insurance company waives its rights to proceed against the fiduciary. The fiduciary involved in purchasing insurance against fiduciary breaches for the plan must do his or her best to secure the most suitable coverage for the plan at no greater expenditure of plan assets than is necessary. [DOL News Rel. 75-127 (Mar. 4, 1975)]

Q 5:122 Can a fiduciary or an employer purchase insurance for the plan fiduciary to cover liability or losses resulting from the acts or omissions of the plan fiduciary?

Yes. A fiduciary can purchase insurance to cover his or her liability resulting from a breach of fiduciary duties, and an employer or an employee organization can purchase insurance for the plan fiduciary. [Mazur v. Gaudet, 826 F. Supp. 188 (E.D. La. 1992)] Here, in contrast with the situation in which the plan purchases the policy, the policy need not provide for recourse against the fiduciary. [ERISA § 410(b), 29 U.S.C. § 1110(b) (1974)]

Q 5:123 Can a plan fiduciary purchase from the same insurance company that insures the plan against fiduciary breaches a policy that protects the fiduciary from recourse lawsuits that the insurer can bring against the fiduciary?

Yes. A *linked* insurance policy—one that links low-cost insurance for an individual fiduciary purchased by a fiduciary (which protects the fiduciary against recourse lawsuits that the insurer can bring against the fiduciary) with high-cost insurance (which protects the plan against a fiduciary's breach) purchased by the plan—is legal as long as the plan fiduciary purchases the insurance policy prudently and solely in the interest of plan participants and beneficiaries. [DOL News Rel. 75-127 (Mar. 4, 1975)] The plan may not pay for such coverage.

Q 5:124 What is the purpose of fiduciary liability insurance?

Fiduciary liability insurance is designed to protect fiduciaries who, although acting in good faith, violate the complex fiduciary rules as expressed in federal rules, regulations, and court rulings. Fiduciaries also need additional protection from liability for acts of co-fiduciaries, especially where a fiduciary should have known of the breach by a co-fiduciary and failed to remedy the breach.

Q 5:125 Who can be covered under a fiduciary liability insurance policy?

Fiduciary liability insurance policies generally protect a wide range of plan fiduciaries (e.g., administrators, trustees, committees), the company sponsoring the plan (and, in many cases, its employees), and the plan itself from certain claims brought against it based on alleged fiduciary breaches. The fiduciaries covered are typically past, present, and future trustees of the trust under the plan, in-house plan administrators, and all plan and trust fund employees who are fiduciaries. In some cases, third-party plan administrators, arbitrators, and attorneys may also be protected by fiduciary liability insurance with respect to employee benefit issues arising under the plan.

Q 5:126 May fiduciary liability insurance policies cover fiduciaries for the 20 percent civil penalty applicable to fiduciary breaches under ERISA Section 502(*l*)?

ERISA Section 502(*l*) provides that a penalty of 20 percent of the amount payable pursuant to a court order or settlement agreement with the DOL may be assessed by the DOL for a breach of fiduciary duty. State insurance law must be reviewed to ascertain whether the 20 percent penalty may be covered by insurance.

Q 5:127 How should a plan fiduciary determine which insurance company to use to provide it with fiduciary liability insurance?

In recommending or choosing fiduciary liability insurance protection for the plan, a fiduciary must act prudently and solely in the interest of plan participants and beneficiaries. [DOL News Rel. 75-127 (Mar. 4, 1975)] A fiduciary involved in purchasing insurance against fiduciary breaches for the plan must therefore do his or her best to secure the most suitable coverage for the plan at no greater expenditure of plan assets than is necessary. In order to satisfy ERISA's requirements, the fiduciary should ascertain that the insurance company from which he or she wishes to purchase the policy has a satisfactory rating from a reputable rating agency.

Q 5:128 Can a plan purchase insurance to cover any losses to the plan resulting from a prohibited transaction?

Yes. A plan can carry insurance to protect itself from losses it incurs as the result of the misconduct of a fiduciary, including participation in a prohibited transaction. A plan may not, however, contain a provision that would relieve a fiduciary of liability for a prohibited transaction. [ERISA § 410, 29 U.S.C. § 1110 (1974)]

Indemnification

Q 5:129 What is *indemnification*?

Indemnification is a promise to reimburse or hold a person harmless for acting in good faith. It can be important because fiduciary liability can attach to a fiduciary who acted on behalf of a plan in good faith. A plan fiduciary may wish to consider obtaining an indemnity from the plan sponsor in lieu of, or in addition to, fiduciary liability insurance. Indemnification is only as good as the financial viability of the company providing the indemnity.

Q 5:130 May a plan indemnify a fiduciary for liability for breach of duty?

No. ERISA prohibits the indemnification and exculpation of a fiduciary by a plan. Therefore, the plan may not agree to excuse the fiduciary from responsibility for fiduciary breaches. Similarly, plan assets may not be used to reimburse a fiduciary for liability it is found to have for its actions. A plan may, however, provide for indemnification of expenses of a fiduciary who successfully defends against a claim of breach of fiduciary duty. [Packer Eng'g, Inc. v. Kratville, 965 F.2d 174 (7th Cir. 1992)]

Q 5:131 May an employer who sponsors a plan, or an employee organization whose members are covered by the plan, indemnify a fiduciary?

Yes. ERISA permits the indemnification of a fiduciary by an employer who sponsors a plan or by an employee organization whose members are covered by a plan. The indemnification does not relieve the fiduciary of responsibility or liability for fiduciary breaches. Rather, it leaves the fiduciary fully responsible and liable, but permits another party to satisfy any liability incurred by the fiduciary. [DOL Reg. § 2509.75-4]

The DOL has taken the position that it may be prudent for a plan fiduciary to accept limitation of liability and/or indemnification provisions in a service provider contract as long as they apply only to acts of negligence or unintentional malpractice. The DOL's position is that any such provision that purports to apply to acts of fraud or willful misconduct would be void as against public policy and therefore not prudent. [DOL Op. Ltr. 2002-08A]

Allocation of Responsibility to an Investment Manager

Q 5:132 Can fiduciary responsibility be delegated?

Yes. For example, the trust instrument can provide that one trustee has responsibility for one half of the plan assets and a second trustee has responsibility for the other half. Neither trustee would be liable for the acts of the other except under the co-fiduciary liability rule of ERISA Section 405(a). [ERISA § 405(b), 29 U.S.C. § 1105(b) (1974)] Fiduciary responsibility for selecting and monitoring plan investments can also be delegated to an investment manager (see Q 5:3).

Q 5:133 What are the benefits of delegating fiduciary responsibility to an *investment manager* under ERISA?

An ERISA *investment manager* is a bank, insurance company, or registered investment adviser under the Investment Advisers Act of 1940 (Advisers Act) that acknowledges in writing that it is a fiduciary with respect to the plan and accepts the power to manage plan assets. [ERISA § 3(38), 29 U.S.C. § 1002(38) (1974)]

In selecting a registered investment adviser as an investment manager, therefore, a plan sponsor or fiduciary should ask about the adviser's registration status and inquire as to the amount of securities the adviser has under management.

A key benefit in delegating to an investment manager is that, as long as the person is properly selected and monitored and acts in accordance with his or her role, plan trustees or other fiduciaries do not share in liability for the consequences of the investment manager's decisions. [ERISA §§ 3(38), 405(d)]

Participant Direction of Investments—ERISA Section 404(c)

Q 5:134 Can an employer reduce or eliminate its fiduciary liability for investment decision making by giving participants investment control?

ERISA Section 404(c) says that if a participant is given control over the investment of his or her account, plan fiduciaries will not be held responsible for investment losses resulting from that exercise of control. There are very specific requirements, discussed more fully in chapter 7, that must be met before ERISA Section 404(c) can be claimed as a defense.

Even if a plan satisfies the requirements of ERISA Section 404(c), plan fiduciaries cannot completely eliminate liability for investment decision making. Plan fiduciaries in a Section 404(c) plan typically remain responsible for the selection and monitoring of funds available for investment, for prompt and accurate execution of transactions, and for providing adequate disclosure. See chapter 7 for a detailed discussion of Section 404(c).

Q 5:135 Can an employer reduce or eliminate its fiduciary liability for assets deposited in a plan's default fund?

Yes. Prior to enactment of the Pension Protection Act of 2006 (PPA) and the issuance of DOL Regulation Section 2550.404c-5, amounts deposited in a default fund were not eligible for relief under ERISA Section 404(c) because participants did not affirmatively elect to invest in the fund, which is a requirement of Section 404(c). This changed with the creation of ERISA Section 404(c)(5) under the PPA and the issuance of regulations by the DOL.

Deposits into a default fund meeting the requirements of a qualified default investment alternative (QDIA) are now eligible for fiduciary relief. This relief is available in any participant-directed plan or account satisfying the terms of the DOL's regulation. Plan fiduciaries remain responsible for the prudent selection and monitoring of the QDIA fund.

Generally speaking, the fund must be within an investment category defined by the QDIA rules, proper notice and opportunity to make an affirmative election must be provided to participants, certain fund information must be disclosed, and there are restrictions on the type of fees that can be charged in a QDIA. The types of investments that can qualify as a QDIA include managed account services, target date funds, and balanced funds. Not all funds in these investment categories will qualify; the fund or service must meet specific criteria defined in the regulation. The DOL also authorized the use of certain capital preservation type funds as QDIA funds, but only for 120 days after the initial deposit. Certain guaranteed funds also can serve as QDIA funds, but only with respect to deposits made on or before December 23, 2007.

See chapter 7 for further discussion of QDIAs.

Managing Personal Liability

All plan fiduciaries will be left with some degree of responsibility for decision making, and for some the scope of that responsibility will be broad. It is essential for any fiduciary to review the plan document, service agreements with other providers, and any other documents necessary to understanding the exact scope and nature of the fiduciary role. Once that is understood, procedural due diligence should be applied to all decision making within that role. In addition, plan sponsors or named fiduciaries may want to consider conducting fiduciary audits of their plans on a regular basis.

Procedural Due Diligence

Q 5:136 What is *procedural due diligence*?

Procedural due diligence is a process for making high-quality, prudent fiduciary decisions and documenting the decision-making process. In addition, use of procedural due diligence will help to ensure that the fiduciary is in a good position to defend himself or herself in the event that the prudent decision results in a bad outcome. Procedural due diligence in analyzing plan investment alternatives involves the following:

- Reading the investment documents, prospectus, proposed contracts, and disclosure materials and highlighting the costs (including fees or penalties for early liquidation), level of risk, and expected return;
- Determining whether the fees associated with the investment are reasonable;
- Demonstrating that the investment is reasonably designed to further the purposes of the plan and that it is consistent with the plan's funding policy and method;
- Reviewing investment alternatives and, where appropriate, obtaining competitive bids;
- Reviewing the historical performance of the investment and its sponsor, including checking any information available from a ratings service that covers the individual stock, mutual fund, or insurance company;
- If necessary, hiring an expert to help in the decision-making process and consulting with advisers;
- Having a qualified appraiser value investments in real estate, closely held stock, or other assets for which a market is not readily available to establish fair market value as of the date of purchase;
- Making arrangements to receive regular information about the performance of the investment, reviewing the information promptly, and following up on material discrepancies; and
- Documenting all of the above and maintaining a file of reports, meeting notes, analyses, and legal documents.

Q 5:137 What are the DOL's expectations concerning the prudent selection and monitoring of service providers offering financial help to participants?

The DOL has provided many tools designed to assist plan sponsors with the selection of service providers and the analyses of plan fees (see chapter 4 for detailed discussion of this topic). In 2007, the DOL published guidelines on what constitutes a prudent process for selecting service providers that will be providing investment help to plan participants.

The selection process used must be *objective* (i.e., without any conflicts of interest, self-dealing, or improper influence) and must be designed to elicit information to assess the following:

- The provider's qualifications, including its experience and any state or federal securities law registrations;
- The quality of services offered, including the provider's willingness to assume ERISA fiduciary status, and the extent to which advice will be based on generally accepted investment theories; and
- The reasonableness of fees.

The monitoring process should include periodic review of the following:

- The extent to which there have been any changes to the information serving as the basis for initial selection of the adviser;
- Whether the adviser continues to meet applicable state and federal securities law requirements;
- Whether the advice being furnished is based on generally accepted investment theories;
- Whether the adviser is complying with the contractual terms of the engagement;
- A comparison of the cost of the services to the actual utilization of investment advice services by participants; and
- Participants' comments and complaints about the quality of the advice.

[DOL Field Assist. Bull. 2007-01]

Fiduciary Audits

Q 5:138 What is a *fiduciary* audit?

In light of the growing reliance of employees on 401(k) plans to fund their retirement years, there is increased scrutiny from both regulators and the public on the activities of plan fiduciaries. One way for plan fiduciaries to identify and control risk is to develop and implement a fiduciary audit of their plan on an annual or other routine basis. The purpose of a fiduciary audit is to examine all aspects of a plan's operation that involve any kind of fiduciary decision making or risk, and verify that each area of operations adheres to fiduciary standards of care.

Following is a checklist of common items to be reviewed in a fiduciary audit:

1. Plan Documents and Records
   a. Do you have a complete, current set of Plan and Trust documents that have received IRS approval and that are up to date with law changes?
   b. Have summary plan descriptions (SPDs) and summaries of material modifications (SMMs) been timely distributed to all required recipients?
   c. Do you have copies of summary annual reports (SARs) and Form 5500 filings for the past seven years?
   d. Do you have a current copy of the plan's fidelity bond and any other insurance protecting the plan or its fiduciaries? Do you know who is covered under those policies? Is the coverage adequate?
   e. Do you have an Investment Policy Statement that reflects current practices and investment needs?
   f. Do you have service contracts with all of the plan's service providers? Are the contracts adequate and accurate?

g. Have you received and reviewed appropriate disclosures from all of the plan's Covered Service Providers?

h. Do you have committee minutes or other documentation of all fiduciary decisions made for the prior period (e.g., hiring of service providers, selection and ongoing monitoring of investments, changes in plan benefits).

2. Service Providers

    a. Do you have clear documentation of the responsibilities of each of the plan's service providers?

    b. Have all service providers been selected in accordance with the plan's written procedures, and is it clear who is responsible for ongoing monitoring of each provider?

    c. Do you know which providers are fiduciaries for what purposes, and have the providers agreed to such fiduciary status in writing?

    d. Do you have a defined and documented process for selecting and monitoring service providers, and have those processes been followed?

    e. Do you know what fees you are paying for what services, and have you documented the process you followed to determine that those fees were reasonable?

    f. For reporting years beginning January 1, 2009, or later, do you have all the information you need from your service provider to complete the required disclosures on Schedule C of Form 5500? (See chapter 19.)

    g. Beginning on July 1, 2012, do you know which service providers are obligated to provide you with service provider fee disclosures under the DOL's new rule, and have you received all these disclosures? (See chapter 4.)

3. Investments

    a. Are the plan's investments reviewed within the time frames and according to the procedures outlined in the plan's Investment Policy Statement?

    b. Are decisions regarding the selection, retention, and deletion of an investment option properly documented (including comparisons with comparable funds) and consistent with the Investment Policy Statement?

    c. Do the investment options offered by your current service provider satisfy the needs of the plan, and are they consistent with the standards contained in your Investment Policy Statement?

    d. To the extent participants are responsible for investment decision making, have they received adequate communication, education, and fund alternatives to support that role? (Note that if a plan intends to comply with ERISA Section 404(c), additional items should be reviewed; see chapter 7.)

e. Have participants received all the required disclosures under the DOL's new participant disclosure rule? (See chapter 19.)

f. If you intend to use a qualified default investment alternative (QDIA), have you provided the required notice and disclosures and otherwise complied with the terms of the DOL Regulation on QDIAs? (See chapter 7.)

g. If your plan invests in employer securities, have legal experts in the securities and ERISA areas been consulted to address particular issues surrounding investment in employer securities, particularly in light of developments in the *Enron* and *WorldCom* litigation (e.g., securities registration and reporting, special fiduciary issues; see also chapters 6 and 7)?

4. Prohibited Transactions

a. Have you identified all persons or entities involved with the plan who are parties in interest?

b. To the extent you are paying a party in interest with funds from plan assets, have you verified that such payments are exempt from the prohibited transaction rules?

c. Do you have reliable people and processes in place to ensure that all salary deferral contributions are remitted timely to the plan trustee?

5. Plan Operations

a. Is the plan being operated in accordance with the terms of the plan and trust document?

b. Do your service providers keep you informed of plan activity and escalate matters that require corporate involvement?

c. Are the reports you receive from your service providers timely and accurate?

d. When mistakes are made, are they identified and addressed in a timely and accurate manner?

e. Is the process of communication (electronic, verbal, or otherwise) used to integrate services among various providers timely, accurate, and cost-efficient?

f. Are your employees adequately educated about plan features?

6. Retirement Readiness (It should be noted that employers do not have a fiduciary responsibility to ensure that their employees save enough for a comfortable retirement, but promoting retirement readiness can result in many benefits, including more satisfied employees who are less likely to sue their employer.)

a. Do you monitor participation and savings rates, selected investments, and other factors that illustrate the success of the plan over time?

b. If the plan is not achieving desired retirement readiness targets, do you review plan design alternatives such as automatic enrollment and automatic escalation; education and disclosure initiatives such as illustration of lifetime income benefits or targeted communication initiatives; and investment options that promote long-term investment strategies?

(See Appendix C for a sample Plan Sponsor Fiduciary Manual and Checklist.)

The Voluntary Fiduciary Correction Program

On March 16, 2000, the Pension and Welfare Benefits Administration (PWBA) section of the DOL released a notice describing how certain fiduciary violations can be voluntarily corrected. The PWBA, now renamed the Employee Benefits Security Administration (EBSA), is trying to emulate the IRS's approach to achieving broad-based compliance through voluntary initiatives (see chapter 20). In 2002, the DOL finalized its program, titled the Voluntary Fiduciary Correction Program (VFCP). On April 6, 2005, significant proposed changes to the program were issued, and additional changes were made in an amendment published on April 19, 2006. These proposed changes to the program may be found online at *www.dol.gov/ebsa/compliance_assistance.html#section8*. [*See also* 65 Fed. Reg. 20,135, 20,262 (Apr. 19, 2006).]

Q 5:139 What does the VFCP do?

The VFCP allows certain violations of ERISA to be voluntarily corrected in accordance with guidelines defined by the PWBA. Upon submission to the PWBA, the applicant can obtain relief from any further action by the DOL, as well as certain other relief, if the correction is satisfactorily made. [65 Fed. Reg. 14,164 (Mar. 5, 2000)]

Q 5:140 When is the VFCP effective?

The VFCP is effective as of April 29, 2002. The latest changes to the program are effective as of May 19, 2006.

Q 5:141 Who can use the VFCP?

A VFCP submission can be made by any "plan official," which includes a plan sponsor, any plan fiduciary, a party in interest, or any other person who is in a position to correct a breach. Since relief under the VFCP is available only to individuals who join in the application, it makes sense to join all individuals who might otherwise be at risk for liability in the submitted transaction. A submission will not be accepted by the EBSA if either the plan or the applicant is under investigation by the DOL, the IRS, or the SEC, or if the application contains evidence of potential criminal violations. A plan is considered to be "under investigation" upon receipt of notification of the federal agency's intent to conduct an investigation. However, recent amendments to the VFCP mean that only investigations involving the plan or a plan transaction will preclude use of the VFCP.

Q 5:142 What violations can be corrected through the VFCP?

There are 19 specific financial transactions that can be corrected. They are:

1. Delinquent participant contributions and participant loan repayments to pension plans;
2. Delinquent participant contributions to insured welfare plans;
3. Delinquent participant contributions to welfare plan trusts;
4. Fair market value interest rate loans with parties in interest;
5. Below market interest rate loans with parties in interest;
6. Below market interest rate loans with nonparties in interest;
7. Below market interest rate loans due to delay in perfecting security interest;
8. Participant loans failing to comply with plan provisions for amount, duration, or level amortization;
9. Defaulted participant loans;
10. Purchase of assets by plans from parties in interest;
11. Sale of assets by plans to parties in interest;
12. Sale and leaseback of property to sponsoring employers;
13. Purchase of assets from nonparties in interest at more than fair market value;
14. Sale of assets to nonparties in interest at less than fair market value;
15. Holding of an illiquid asset previously purchased by the plan;
16. Benefit payments based on an improper valuation of plan assets;
17. Payment of duplicative, excessive, or unnecessary compensation;
18. Improper payment of expenses by the plan; and
19. Payment of dual compensation to plan fiduciaries.

Q 5:143 What are the steps to using the VFCP Notice?

The first step is for the applicant to make sure that the plan and the applicant are eligible for the program. In other words, the violation must be one of the 19 violations described in Q 5:142, neither the plan nor the applicant can be under investigation by the DOL, the IRS, or the SEC, and there must be no criminal violations involved.

The next step is to correct the violation. The notice is very specific in describing how to correct each of the 19 violations covered.

An application must then be completed and filed with the applicant's regional EBSA office.

In its 2005 and 2006 amendments to the VCP, the DOL simplified the application requirements. A model application form, which is designed to eliminate common errors and deficiencies and expedite review, can be downloaded from the agency's Web site. In addition, the amount of detail required for some transactions has been reduced. For example, for submissions to address delinquent filings of salary deferral contributions where the delinquent deposits either total less than $50,000 or are corrected in less than 180 days, summary information can now be provided in lieu of detailed data and payroll records.

In the DOL's original notice, applicants were also required to notify all plan participants of the application and collection. This notice requirement was eliminated in the final notice. Participants are expected to be given an explanation of any corrections made to their accounts and they retain the right to receive copies of any VFCP application and supporting documentation upon request.

The following supporting documentation must be provided to the EBSA office:

- Copies of relevant portions of the plan and related documents;
- Documents supporting the transaction at issue, such as leases and loan documents;
- Documentation of lost earnings amounts;
- Documentation of restored profits, if applicable;
- Proof of payment of required amounts;
- Specific documents required for certain transactions;
- Signed checklist; and
- Penalty of perjury statement.

Q 5:144 What are the general principles for correcting fiduciary violations under the VFCP?

The general standard for correcting errors is that participants and beneficiaries must be restored to the condition they would have been in had the breach not occurred, and the applicant must provide proof of payment. In determining the proper amount to restore, the following guidelines apply:

1. Any valuation of plan assets must use generally recognized markets for the assets or, if no such market exists, appraisal reports from qualified professionals that are based on generally accepted appraisal standards.
2. Restorations to the plan must include the principal amount involved, plus the greater of lost earnings, starting at the date of loss and extending to the recovery date, or profits resulting from the use of the principal and earnings starting on the date of the loss and extending to the date the profit is realized. There is an on-line calculator (see *http://askebsa.dol.gov/VFCPCalculator/WebCalculator*) that can be used for this purpose.
3. The applicant must pay the expenses associated with correcting the transaction(s), such as appraisal costs or fees for recalculating participant account balances.
4. The applicant must make supplemental distributions when appropriate to former employees, beneficiaries, or alternate payees and provide proof of such payments.

Q 5:145 How may a late remittance problem be corrected under the VFCP?

The following example illustrates how a late remittance problem can be corrected under the VFCP.

> **Example.** Employer B generally deposits salary deferral contributions into the plan trust within two business days of each payday. Because of a payroll processing error, participant contributions in the amount of $10,000 from a January 31 payroll date were not deposited until March 2. The amount to be restored to the plan is $10,000, plus lost earnings for the period of February 2 (the date they should have been deposited) through March 2 (the date of actual deposit).
>
> Because the amount of late deposits was less than $50,000, the new simplified method for calculating lost earnings can be used. This is done by calculating the corporate underpayment rate under Code Section 6621(a)(2) for each quarter involved in the transaction (first quarter in this example). Assuming the rate was 9 percent for the period in question, the lost profit would be $75 ($10,000 × 9% × 1/12 of the year).

Other methods may be required depending on the amount of the late deposit, the amount of earnings due using the above method to calculate, or the time delay between the delinquency and the correction. To assist plans with calculating the amount of lost earnings due, the DOL has provided an on-line calculator, at *www.dol.gov/ebsa/calculator/main.html.*

If the $75 in lost earnings is not paid into the plan on March 2, additional earnings are due on the $75 from March 2 until the date the lost earnings are paid to the plan trust.

The program also provides a de minimis exception for allocation collections to participant accounts. If the amount due is less than $20 and the individual no longer has an account in the plan, the applicant can demonstrate in its submission that the cost of making the submission exceeds the amount of the payment and allocate those amounts to the plan generally as earnings.

Q 5:146 What relief is offered for using the VFCP?

The DOL generally has the authority to hold fiduciaries personally accountable for restoring losses to a plan resulting from fiduciary violations, as well as paying a 20 percent settlement penalty to the DOL on any amounts recovered. [ERISA § 502 (*l*), 29 U.S.C. § 1132(*l*) (1974)] In addition, the DOL can bring criminal charges against fiduciaries and can enjoin or prohibit them from acting in a fiduciary capacity to a plan. The result of a successful VFCP submission is that the applicant receives a "no-action" letter from the DOL that in essence says that the DOL will not take any action against the fiduciary for the violation contained in the submission. In effect, since full correction is required to use the program, the applicant avoids the 20 percent penalty and the threat of injunction.

In the DOL's revisions to the program, correction under the VFCP also constitutes correction of any prohibited transaction involved in the violation under Code Section 4975. Also, to the extent the correction fixes operation failures eligible for correction under the IRS correction programs (see chapter 20), correction under the VCFP program is also deemed a correction under the IRS's program.

Q 5:147 If the fiduciary violation being corrected is a prohibited transaction, will plan fiduciaries be liable for the excise tax?

One of the concerns people had about using the VFCP was the possibility of having the IRS impose the 15 percent excise tax on prohibited transactions based on VFCP applications forwarded to the agency. This concern was addressed by the issuance of a DOL prohibited transaction exemption, PTE 2002-51, which provided excise tax relief for the following transactions if cured through the VFCP:

1. Late remittance of salary deferral contributions;
2. Participant loans at less than fair market interest;
3. Purchase or sale of an asset between a plan and party in interest; and
4. Sale and leaseback of property between a plan and employer.

In 2006, the DOL revised PTE 2002-51 to cover the following transactions:

- Prohibited transaction violations involved in the purchase of an asset by a plan when the asset has been determined to be illiquid and/or the subsequent sale of the illiquid asset by the plan;
- Use of plan assets to pay expenses to a service provider for services that are characterized as "settlor expenses," provided such payments were not expressly prohibited in the plan documents; and
- Elimination of the notice requirement for de minimis situations involving delinquent participant contributions and/or the failure to transmit participant loan repayments.

To receive this relief, the fiduciary must have received a "no action" letter in response to its VFCP application and must provide notice to interested parties of the event. "Interested parties," under the program, are not defined.

It should be noted that, due to the reciprocity available under both VFCP and the Treasury Department's Employee Plans Compliance Resolution System (EPCRS) (see chapter 20), there may be a choice for correcting a prohibited transaction through either program, and plan representatives may wish to compare the correction methods and relief offered to select the best option.

Q 5:148 What are the risks involved in using the VFCP?

There are some risks involved in using the VFCP:

- Relief is available only to the applicant, who must identify all parties involved in the transaction. The DOL is free to take action against any party other than the applicant.
- Action can be taken against the applicant if the submission contains any potential criminal violations. In many states, failure to timely remit salary deferral contributions falls within the definition of criminal embezzlement. Since submissions cannot be made on an anonymous basis, there is no way to know in advance whether the DOL will take this position.
- If the DOL does not agree with the correction method used by the applicant, the applicant may have to pay an additional negotiated amount, plus the 20 percent settlement penalty.
- The requirement to make the detailed application available to participants upon request may prompt participant dissatisfaction and lawsuits.

Q 5:149 Under what circumstances does it make sense to use the VFCP?

The VFCP may be most helpful in the context of mergers and acquisitions as a means of cleaning up potential plan liabilities. Similarly, it may be useful to a successor fiduciary to clean up breaches committed by a prior fiduciary.

Q 5:150 Under what circumstances should the VFCP not be used?

Use of the VFCP may not be the right choice to correct a violation if any of the following conditions exist:

- There are violations involved in the transaction in addition to the 18 violations covered under the program.
- Providing copies of the application to participants is likely to occur and to create problems.
- There are correction methods available consistent with ERISA principles that are less expensive than the method required by the VFCP.
- Not all fiduciaries involved in the transaction are willing to join in the application.
- There are potential criminal violations involved.

Q 5:151 Is there value to reading and understanding the VFCP Notice if the fiduciary does not intend to make a submission?

Yes. The VFCP Notice provides a great deal of information on how the DOL views various violations and what it considers to be acceptable correction methods. A fiduciary who corrects a violation using the methods described in the notice may still be vulnerable to the 20 percent settlement penalty, but will probably not be required to take additional corrective measures if the violation is discovered on audit.

Q 5:152 Where can additional information on the DOL's voluntary compliance program be found?

There is a great deal of information about the VFCP program on the DOL's Web site at *http://www.dol.gov/ebsa/compliance_assistance.html.*

Fiduciary Concerns Related to Specific Investment Products

The area of greatest fiduciary concern to most plan sponsors is the selection of appropriate investment alternatives to make available to participants. Different types of investments require different types of analysis by plan fiduciaries to determine their appropriateness for a plan. This section looks at common and evolving types of investments in 401(k) plans and unique fiduciary considerations when selecting these investment products.

Mutual Funds

Mutual funds are the most common type of investment found in 401(k) plans. Following are some issues unique to mutual fund investments that plan fiduciaries may wish to consider.

Q 5:153 What mutual fund practices are of concern?

The practices that have received the most attention both in the press and from regulators are late-day trading, market timing, and revenue sharing.

Q 5:154 What is *late-day trading* and why is it a concern?

Late-day trading is the practice of buying or selling mutual fund shares after the time at which funds calculate their net asset value (NAV), which is usually 4:00 P.M. EST. This practice is a concern because investors who are allowed to trade after the NAV has been calculated have a clear advantage over investors who must make their investment decisions without knowing the price at which the trade will be executed.

Late trading is illegal under the Investment Company Act of 1940. The allegations involving late trading have generally involved fund insiders either trading themselves or giving preference to other individual or institutional investors. The allegations have not involved any 401(k) plan investors.

Q 5:155 What is *market timing*, and why is it a concern?

Market timing refers to the practice of excessive trading in mutual funds in order to exploit the inefficiencies in mutual fund pricing, primarily between U.S. and non-U.S. markets. Market timing favors short-term investors over long-term investors, but it is not specifically prohibited by law. However, mutual fund advisers have an obligation to ensure that no group of shareholders is preferred over another, and many fund prospectuses state that market timing will be discouraged.

Q 5:156 Has the SEC addressed the problem of market timing?

Yes. The SEC released a rule in 2005 that approved the use of redemption fees as a means of curbing market timing. [SEC Rel. No. IC-26 782 (Mar. 11, 2005)] The rule does the following:

1. Permits, but does not require, a mutual fund to impose a redemption fee of up to 2 percent of the amount involved in a transaction involving a purchase and sale within seven or fewer calendar days. All fees collected are to be retained by the fund.
2. Requires mutual fund boards to consider whether a redemption fee is necessary and appropriate and, if it is, what the holding period and amount of the fund should be.
3. Requires funds to enter into written agreements with intermediaries, such as recordkeepers, requiring such intermediaries to provide shareholder identity and transaction information upon request of the fund, and further requiring the intermediary to implement any instructions from the fund to impose trading restrictions to prevent violations of the fund's market timing policies.

Certain types of funds, such as money market funds, exchange traded funds, and funds specifically designed for market timers are exempt from the rules. [SEC Rel. No. IC-26 782 (Mar. 11, 2005)]

Q 5:157 How does the SEC rule impact 401(k) plans?

The SEC rule (see Q 5:156) impacts recordkeepers because it requires them to develop mechanisms for identifying and implementing prohibited market timing activities and any attendant redemption fees. A critical challenge here is the fact that the SEC rule does not impose a uniform standard, which means that a variety of rules must be accommodated in every recordkeeping system. Not only will funds differ with respect to the amount of any redemption fee and the applicable holding period, but they may also differ with respect to the types of transactions affected. For example, some funds may distinguish between participant initiated transactions, such as investment transfers, and plan initiated transactions, such as fee payments.

The impact on plan financial advisers is that they must consider the possibility of redemption fee charges or other market timing restrictions as part of their due diligence analysis in selecting funds. There will also be some concern about the need to communicate and explain mutual fund trading restrictions and redemption fees to plan sponsors and participants.

Plan sponsors have a fiduciary responsibility to ensure that some participants do not engage in market timing activity to the disadvantage of other participants. The SEC rule assists plan sponsors in ensuring that this obligation is met. Plan participants may be unpleasantly surprised when trying to execute certain transactions to learn either that they are barred from doing so or that they must pay a fee if they engage in the transaction.

Q 5:158 What is the current status of the SEC's rule regarding redemption fees?

The SEC issued proposed amendments to Rule 22c-2 on March 7, 2006. The rule contained a number of helpful clarifications:

- The definition of a "financial intermediary" is limited to those institutions that trade directly with the fund, or "first-tier" institutions. The SEC is still seeking comments on how to ensure that those first-tier institutions are empowered to obtain whatever data they need from downstream institutions in order to comply with Rule 22c-2. This clarification is helpful, however, in that it limits the number of institutions that must enter into written agreements with mutual fund companies.
- The definition of "financial intermediary" does not include any financial intermediary that the fund treats as an individual investor. For example, if redemption fees would be applied against a plan, as opposed to plan participants, that plan would not be considered a financial intermediary.
- The SEC clarified that if a fund fails to enter into a written agreement with an intermediary, no purchase transactions can occur between the fund and that financial intermediary.

On September 27, 2006, the SEC published additional changes to Rule 22c-2, extending the dates for compliance. The deadline for entering into shareholder information agreements was extended from October 16, 2006, to April 16, 2007, with an additional extension for implementation of those agreements until October 16, 2007. [SEC Rel. No. IC-27255 (Mar. 7, 2006); SEC Rel. No. IC-27504 (Sept. 27, 2006)]

Q 5:159 What responsibilities do plan fiduciaries have in relation to market timing activity?

There have been a number of lawsuits alleging that plan fiduciaries breached their fiduciary duty by continuing to invest in mutual funds that allowed market timing to occur, thereby potentially diminishing the returns of long-term investors. A Maryland district court issued a series of opinion letters on February 27, 2006, that essentially refused to dismiss claims brought against plan representatives (including directed trustees, plan committee members, mutual fund companies, and plan financial consultants) based on market timing activity. [*See* Zarate v. Bank One Corp., Civ. JFM-04-0830, 2006 WL 735095 (D. Md. Feb. 27, 2006); Corbett v. Marsh & McLennan Cos., Civ. JFM-04-0883, 2006 WL 734560 (D. Md. Feb. 27, 2006); Walsh v. Marsh & McLennan Cos., Civ.

JFM-04-0888, 2006 WL 734899 (D. Md. Feb. 27, 2006); Walker v. Massachusetts Fin. Servs. Co., Civ. JFM-04-1758, 2006 WL 734796 (D. Md. Feb. 27, 2006); Calderon v. Amvescap PLC, Civ. JFM-04-0824, 2006 WL 735006 (D. Md. Feb. 27, 2006).] The bottom line is that plan investment fiduciaries do have some responsibility for ensuring that market timing and/or late-day trading activity will not harm the earnings opportunity for plan participants, who are generally long-term investors.

Q 5:160 What responsibilities do plan fiduciaries have when allocating proceeds received from settlements?

Settlement amounts that are received by a plan representative from a settlement fund for distribution among omnibus account holders are considered "plan assets." In some instances the methodology for allocating the settlement will be predetermined. In other instances it will not be, and plan fiduciaries must have a reasonable method for allocating the proceeds, although a precise allocation is not required. The method used must be reasonable, fair, and objective. For example, proceeds could be allocated among omnibus account holders according to the average share or dollar balance of each participant's balance in the fund during the relevant period. If a plan entitled to proceeds has terminated, reasonable efforts must be made to find the plan sponsor or other representative who could distribute the proceeds to former plan participants. If no such representative can be located after a reasonable and diligent search, the proceeds may be distributed to other omnibus account holders of the funds. Any fees charged for implementing the allocation must be approved by an independent fiduciary. [DOL Field Assist. Bull. 2006-01]

Q 5:161 How should plan fiduciaries respond to the allegations of improper activity in mutual fund scandals?

On February 17, 2004, Assistant Secretary of Labor Ann L. Combs released guidance regarding the duties of plan fiduciaries in response to mutual fund investigations. [DOL Rel. No. 04-207-NAT] In situations where a fund held by the plan has been identified as under investigation by government agencies, fiduciaries are requested to consider the following information in determining how to respond:

- The nature of the alleged abuses;
- The potential economic impact of the alleged abuse on the plan's investments;
- The steps taken by the fund to limit such abuses in the future; and
- Any remedial action taken or considered by the fund to make investors whole.

Fiduciaries are encouraged to contact funds directly if necessary to obtain the information they need to make their evaluation. They may need to consider the costs and benefits of participating in settlements or litigation involving the fund. Fiduciaries are also encouraged to review funds for which no government investigation has been initiated if the fiduciary deems that to be appropriate or necessary to protect the interests of plan participants.

The DOL also addressed questions raised by taking actions to limit market timing at the plan level and the availability of ERISA Section 404(c) protection. Actions to limit market timing include placing limits on the number of times a participant may move in and out of a fund within a particular time frame and/or imposing redemption fees. According to the DOL, such actions should not, in and of themselves, affect Section 404(c) protection, provided that such restrictions are "reasonable," allowed under the terms of the plan, and clearly disclosed to participants. Trading restrictions not contemplated under the terms of the plan, according to the DOL, raise issues under Section 404(c) and could trigger a "blackout period" requiring advance notice.

The DOL guidance is available online at *www.dol.gov/ebsa/newsroom/pr021704.html.*

Other commentators have suggested that plan fiduciaries take the following steps in response to the mutual fund scandals:

- Make sure that you are, at a minimum, following the terms of your Investment Policy Statement for investment review.
- Determine whether a fund company that is the subject of allegations has acknowledged the impropriety, responded quickly, terminated any person involved in improper conduct, and instituted new procedures to prevent future abuses.
- Document due diligence efforts in this area and consider sharing information obtained in the process with participants.

The DOL, as well as other commentators, caution plans against divesting their portfolios of a mutual fund without the benefit of an informed decision-making process.

Mutual Fund Revenue Sharing

Q 5:162 What is the responsibility of plan fiduciaries in understanding mutual fund revenue sharing?

It is common for mutual funds to make payments to plan service providers in the form of revenue sharing. The types of fees charged by mutual funds are described in chapter 6. The employer's responsibility to understand revenue sharing payments and the services received for them are described in chapter 4. The legal rules for determining when a service provider may receive compensation from the plan's investments without violating ERISA's prohibited transaction rules are described earlier in chapter 5.

Target Date Funds

Q 5:163 What are unique fiduciary concerns when evaluating target date funds?

Target date funds are an age-based type of asset allocation fund. Since they were identified as an available qualified default investment alternative (QDIA) in 2008, they have been added to many 401(k) plans (see chapter 7). When the financial markets collapsed in 2008 and 2009 many investors in target date funds suffered losses, which caused Congress and the regulatory agencies to conduct a review of these types of funds. Following are some of the issues regulators have identified related to fiduciary review of target date funds:

- *Adequacy of Performance History:* Many of these funds are relatively new and do not have extended performance histories to review.
- *Quality of Underlying Investments:* The quality of the mutual funds making up the target date fund should be reviewed and the level of proprietary funds should be considered.
- *Type of Glide Path Utilized:* The glide path of a target date fund refers to the manner in which asset allocations change over time. One of the concerns expressed by regulators was that funds with the same target date varied dramatically in the extent to which they had equity exposure on the targeted date. Plan fiduciaries should understand how the balance between stocks and bonds adjusts over time. There is not necessarily a "right" answer to what the allocation should be, but fiduciaries should understand the level of risk they are accepting in a chosen glide path.
- *Understanding the Fee Structure:* In most target date funds there is a fee for the underlying mutual fund investments, and an additional fee for managing the asset allocations in those investments. Plan fiduciaries need to understand both levels of fees and ensure that they are reasonable.
- *Level of Participant Education Needed:* Target date funds are designed to be the sole investment in a participant's account since they automatically apply an appropriate asset allocation based on age and adjust that allocation over time. However, many participants do not understand this and will invest a portion of their account in a target date fund and a portion in other funds, which has the result of skewing the appropriate asset allocation. Participants need education to understand how to use these funds in an effective retirement income planning strategy.

In response to these concerns, regulators have taken the following actions:

- The DOL issued a proposed rule requiring greater disclosure to participants regarding target date funds in the new participant disclosure rules and when a target date fund is used as a qualified default investment alternative (QDIA). (See chapters 6, 7, and 19.)
- The SEC issued a proposed rule on required disclosures in target date fund marketing materials. (This rule is discussed in chapter 6.)

- The DOL and SEC jointly published information designed to help plan participants make decisions about investing in target date funds. This material is available on the DOL's Web site at *http://www.dol.gov/ebsa/pdf/TDFInvestorBulletin.pdf*.

In February 2013 the DOL issued an educational document titled "Target Date Funds—Tips for ERISA Plan Fiduciaries," which is available at *http://www.dol.gov/ebsa/newsroom/fsTDF.html*.

Q 5:164 What has the DOL identified as important steps for plan fiduciaries when selecting and monitoring target date funds?

The DOL's document titled "Target Date Retirement Funds—Tips for ERISA Fiduciaries" provides an overview of what target date funds are and how they work. The agency recommended that plan fiduciaries take the following steps in choosing a target date fund:

- Establish a prudent process for comparing and selecting target date funds. Include a comparison of performance, fees, and compatibility with the plan's employee population.
- Establish a prudent process for periodic review of selected target date funds. Review any changes in the fund, such as a change in the investment manager, and any inconsistency with stated objectives, as well as any changes to the plan's objectives for offering the fund.
- Understand the fund's underlying investments and how they will change over time. Review the principal strategies and risks as defined in the prospectus. Understand the glide path and whether the fund will reach its most conservative allocation at or after the target date. Understand what the most conservative allocation is and what degree of equity exposure and risk remains at that allocation.
- Understand all the fees associated with the fund, including fees for the underlying funds as well as fees for the target date fund itself, and any sales loads or other expenses.
- Inquire as to whether it is better to use a "pre-packaged" target date fund consisting of the vendor's proprietary funds, or a custom fund offering the ability to use the plan's core funds as the underlying investments in the target date fund.
- Develop an effective employee communication program that includes both legally required disclosures as well as general education about target date funds.
- Take advantage of commercially available sources of information that may assist in the evaluation of the target date fund.
- Document the selection and review proves, including how individual investment decisions were reached.

Guaranteed Lifetime Income Investments

Traditionally, 401(k) plans have been viewed like a savings account and most participants receive their distribution in the form of a lump-sum distribution. As baby boomers have aged, Social Security has become less reliable, and we have recently confronted the volatility of the financial markets, interest has grown in using 401(k) plans to provide annuities or other types of guaranteed lifetime income to participants. For example, the DOL and the Treasury Department issued a joint Request for Information (RFI) exploring ways in which the agencies can facilitate the use of lifetime income investments in defined contribution plans. In 2013 the DOL published an Advanced Notice of Proposed Rulemaking that would require participant benefits statements to include a projection of monthly lifetime income benefits at retirement and it is in the DOL's 2014 regulatory agenda to publish a proposed rule on this topic. There has also been product innovation, with providers designing products that can offer guaranteed lifetime payments but that are more compatible with defined contribution plans than a traditional annuity.

Q 5:165 What are some unique fiduciary concerns when evaluating investment products that guarantee income for life?

There are a wide variety of lifetime income products available to 401(k) plans, some of which are offered as a distribution option only and some of which are available as an ongoing investment. When looking at an option designed as an ongoing investment in a plan, following are factors to consider:

- Does offering a lifetime income investment option make sense based on the demographics of the employee population? If so, what type of product is best suited to employees? (See chapter 6.)
- What is the strength of the insurance company providing the guarantee? There are guidelines in DOL Regulations Section 2550.404a-4 that might be helpful to this analysis, although they are focused solely on annuity products.
- How solid is the performance of the investments underlying the product (if applicable)?
- What degree of control, if any, will the participant have over his or her account balance once they make the investment? Will they be able to take loans or other withdrawals, transfer money in or out of the investment, leave a death benefit if they die before hitting their life expectancy date, and so forth?
- What type of protection does the investment offer against outliving your assets (longevity risk), inflation risk (or the inability to participate in future market earnings), cognitive risk (or the risk that an investor will need to make critical financial decisions at an age where there is a significant risk of cognitive deterioration), or the risk that a market loss at or near the retirement date of the participant will substantially reduce the amount of retirement income available to them?

- What fees are associated with the investment and who pays them?
- Is the investment portable or transferable in the event a participant separates from service or the plan changes recordkeepers?
- Will the plan document need to be amended in order to accommodate the investment?
- Is there sufficient educational support provided to help participants make well-informed decisions?

It is on the DOL's regulatory agenda for 2014 to update its guidance on selecting annuity products and, in particular, to address the information a plan fiduciary should review when assessing the long-term solvency of the insurance company or other entity providing the guarantee.

Chapter 6

Investing Plan Assets

Most 401(k) plans give participants some degree of investment control over the assets in their accounts. The most common method is for the employer to designate a limited number of investment alternatives among which participants can elect to invest some or all of their accounts. An alternative is the fully directed plan in which participants can elect from a virtually unlimited universe of investments. A brief description of the characteristics of different investment alternatives is contained in this chapter. See chapters 5 and 7 for information on fiduciary issues related to investment of plan assets.

Primary Asset Classes 6-2
- Stocks 6-2
- Bonds 6-3
- Cash Investments 6-4

Investment Vehicles 6-5
- Mutual Funds 6-5
- Separately Managed Accounts and Collective Trust Funds 6-6
- Asset Allocation and Target Date Funds 6-10
- Real Estate Funds 6-14
- Exchange Traded Funds 6-14
- Group Variable Annuities 6-14
- Stable Value Funds 6-15
- Guaranteed Investment Contracts 6-15
- Lifetime Income Products 6-16
- Life Insurance 6-17
- Default Investment Funds 6-18

Asset Allocation Strategy 6-20

Managed Account Service 6-21

Employer Securities 6-21
- Qualifying Employer Securities 6-23
- Diversification Requirements 6-25
- Fair Market Value of Employer Stock 6-29
- Voting Rights for Employer Stock 6-31
- SEC Registration and Reporting Requirements 6-31
- Sarbanes-Oxley Act of 2002 6-32

Employer Stock Strategy 6-34
Directed Trustee Considerations 6-35
401(k) Stock Ownership Plans 6-37
Self-Directed Options 6-38
Motivation for Self-Directed Options 6-39
Considerations Arising from Self-Directed Options 6-39
Self-Directed Options and ERISA Section 404(c) 6-41
Self-Directed Option Strategies 6-41
Investment Policies 6-42
Selecting and Monitoring Plan Investments 6-43
Mutual Fund Investigations 6-44
Investment Fees and Revenue Sharing 6-45

Primary Asset Classes

The three primary asset classes are stocks, bonds, and cash investments. Those broad asset classes are commonly divided into more narrow categories: for example, large-cap and small-cap stocks and corporate and government bonds. International stock and bond investments and real estate are also important asset classes. It is the primary asset classes that underlie most investment options in 401(k) plans. As in any long-term investment portfolio, which asset classes are included and how much is allocated to each asset class will generally dominate the return, with such factors as investment selection and market timing tending to be less significant.

Stocks

Q 6:1 What is a *stock*?

A *stock* is a security that represents part ownership, or equity, in a corporation. Each share of stock is a claim on its proportionate stake in the company, some of which may be paid out as dividends. Of the three major asset classes, only stocks have historically provided both an income component and a significant long-term growth component. Investment professionals use the terms *equity* and *stock* interchangeably to refer to financial instruments that represent ownership interests in a company.

Q 6:2 What are *growth stocks*?

Growth stocks are stocks of companies whose earnings are expected to grow faster than average. Because of its potential for strong growth, a growth stock tends to be expensive relative to current earnings.

Q 6:3 What are *value stocks*?

Value stocks are stocks that tend to be inexpensive based on such various measures as current earnings, current cash flow, and book value. They appear to be undervalued for some reason. A value investor seeks to identify companies that are favorably priced and/or poised for a turnaround that will result in rising earnings and higher stock prices.

Q 6:4 What are the risks and returns associated with stock ownership?

Historically, stocks have had the highest long-term average rate of return of the three major asset classes. To achieve such long-term results, investors are exposed to a degree of risk, which means that returns can vary greatly from year to year and that there is a chance of a significant loss of market value in any one year. Stocks have a higher expected risk than do bonds or cash investments.

The most significant risks associated with stock investing are market risk (i.e., losing money in a market downturn) and business risk (i.e., company whose stock was purchased will experience financial difficulty, causing the investment to lose value). An investor can, however, reduce inflation risk by having a portion of his or her portfolio invested in stocks. That is because stocks have over time outperformed inflation by a greater margin than other asset classes.

Bonds

Q 6:5 What is a *bond*?

A *bond* is a debt instrument issued by a corporation, government (federal, state, or local), or government agency interested in raising money. As fixed income investments, bonds pay stated interest at regular intervals until they mature, at which time investors receive the face value of the bond. Since bonds are issued with a fixed coupon rate and a fixed face value, their market value or purchase price must change to reflect changes in the interest climate—the market value must fall to return a higher yield and must increase to reflect a lower yield. Bonds that are purchased to yield a higher return than their coupon rate are said to be purchased *below par* or *at a discount,* while bonds that are purchased to yield a lower return than their coupon rate are said to be purchased *above par* or *at a premium.* Some corporate bonds are secured by a pledge of collateral; unsecured corporate bonds are called *debentures.*

For most bonds, the interest rate that the issuer promises to pay the bondholder is called the *coupon rate.* The coupon rate on a bond is closely tied to its maturity, the credit quality of the issuing entity, and the general level of interest rates at the date of issue. Bondholders have a lending, or creditor, interest in the issuer as opposed to an ownership or equity interest.

Q 6:6 What are the risks and returns associated with investing in bonds?

Of the three major asset classes, bonds fall between cash investments and stocks on the risk and return spectrum. The risks most associated with bond investing are inflation risk (i.e., investment will not sufficiently outperform the rate of inflation), credit risk (i.e., company whose bonds were purchased will not make promised payments), and interest rate risk (i.e., investment will lose relative value because interest rates rise). It is important to remember that since bonds provide a fixed payment stream, their market value must fall when interest rates rise and must increase when interest rates decline. Thus, even the most secure of bonds—say, those issued by the United States Government—are subject to a loss in market value due to interest rate risk even if they present a negligible business risk of default.

Q 6:7 What types of bonds does the federal government issue?

The federal government issues four basic types of bonds:

1. *Treasury bills* with original maturities of 1 year or less;
2. *Treasury notes* with original maturities of more than 1 year, but not more than 10 years;
3. *Treasury bonds* with maturities longer than 10 years; and
4. *Treasury Inflation-Protected Securities* with a face value (and hence coupon payments) that changes with inflation.

Cash Investments

Q 6:8 What is meant by a *cash investment*?

A *cash investment* is a very short-term loan to a borrower with a very high credit rating. Examples of cash investments are short-term bank certificates of deposit (CDs), Treasury bills (T-bills), and commercial paper (i.e., short-term obligations of corporations with the highest credit ratings). Money market funds, which hold bank CDs, T-bills, and commercial paper, are also considered cash investments.

Q 6:9 What are the risks and returns associated with cash investments?

Cash investments generally have lower expected risk and return than bonds and stocks. The risk of losing principal in a cash investment is low because the borrowers are creditworthy and the loans are so short, typically one year or less. Having relatively low returns, however, exposes long-term investors to significant inflation risk (i.e., investment will not sufficiently outperform the rate of inflation).

Investment Vehicles

With the exception of employer securities and plans with a self-directed option, investment options in 401(k) plans seldom include individual stocks and bonds directly. Rather, they include investment vehicles that invest in a number of securities. The growth market for the financial services industry continues to be retirement plan assets, including those in 401(k) plans.

Q 6:10 What investment vehicles are offered in 401(k) plans?

Investment vehicles offered in 401(k) plans may include, but are not limited to, mutual funds, variable annuity contracts, guaranteed investment contracts (GICs), stable value funds, life insurance contracts, and employer stock. It is less common for 401(k) plans to offer individual securities and exchange traded funds (ETFs) as investment options.

Mutual Funds

Q 6:11 What is a *mutual fund*?

A *mutual fund* is an investment company that pools the resources of many investors to purchase a portfolio of individual securities. The mutual fund is merely a structure, a "wrapper," containing various investments such as stocks, bonds, and cash. By owning shares (or units) of a mutual fund, shareholders own a fraction of each security purchased by that mutual fund.

Q 6:12 What are the advantages associated with offering mutual funds in 401(k) plans?

There are many advantages to offering mutual funds in a 401(k) plan:

1. *Diversification.* Because the money of a participant is pooled with money from thousands of other investors, a mutual fund can invest in a wide array of securities.
2. *Professional management.* Decisions about buying and selling securities in a mutual fund are overseen by a professional investment manager.
3. *Liquidity.* Shares in most mutual funds may be sold whenever an investor chooses.
4. *Convenience.* Shares can be conveniently purchased under many different arrangements.
5. *Information.* Performance and other information is available from fund houses, Web sites, and fund rating services.
6. *Flexibility.* A mutual fund has the ability to accommodate large numbers of individual investors and accept cash inflows at irregular intervals.

Q 6:13 What are some considerations associated with offering mutual funds in 401(k) plans?

The following are some considerations to mutual fund investing in 401(k) plans:

1. *No guarantees.* Unlike bank deposits (such as CDs), mutual funds generally are not insured or guaranteed by the Federal Deposit Insurance Corporation (FDIC) or any other federal agency. Even though mutual funds are regulated by the SEC and state securities regulators, they do not protect a fund from the risk of losing value.
2. *Manager risk.* For actively managed funds, finding star performers in advance may be difficult to do on a consistent basis. Even if a good manager is on board, there is still the danger that the investment manager will change his or her investment style or leave the fund altogether.
3. *Fees.* Although mutual funds can offer lower costs than would arise from buying individual securities through brokers, the combination of fees charged by mutual funds should be considered.

Separately Managed Accounts and Collective Trust Funds

Q 6:14 What is a *separately managed account*?

Some plan sponsors offer alternative investment vehicles such as separately managed accounts and collective trust funds (see Q 6:15). Fees may be lower than those for mutual funds, in part because these investments are not sold to the retail public. Separately managed accounts and collective trust funds may not provide name-brand recognition and communication materials typical of mutual funds.

A *separately managed account* is a customized portfolio maintained by an investment manager to meet the needs of a particular investor or group of similar investors. It is unlike a mutual fund, which pools the assets of many investors into a common portfolio. Independently managed, a separately managed account may be managed by a registered investment adviser, a bank trust company, or a mutual fund company.

Q 6:15 What is a *collective trust fund*?

A *collective trust fund* is a trust fund exempt from taxation under Internal Revenue Code (Code) Section 501(a) in which assets of qualified plans, generally sponsored by unrelated employers, can be pooled for investment purposes. [Rev. Rul. 81-100, 1981-1 C.B. 326 as amended] In general, collective funds are operated by the trust departments of financial institutions, whereas mutual funds are operated by independent investment companies (which may be subsidiaries or affiliates of banks or insurance companies). In both collective funds and mutual funds, however, the net effect is to pool assets into a single fund that is invested in a diversified portfolio of securities.

Q 6:16 What are common types of investment funds offered in 401(k) plans?

- Money market funds (see Q 6:17)
- Corporate/government bond funds (see Q 6:18)
- Balanced funds (see Q 6:19)
- Indexed funds (see Q 6:20)
- Actively managed funds (see Q 6:21)
- Growth and income stock funds (see Q 6:22)
- Growth stock funds (see Q 6:23)
- Aggressive growth stock funds (see Q 6:23)
- International stock funds (see Q 6:24)

Two other types of funds that are found in 401(k) plans are asset allocation funds (including target date and lifecycle funds) (see Qs 6:25, 6:26) and real estate funds (see Q 6:30).

Q 6:17 What is a *money market fund*?

A *money market fund* is a fund that invests in very short-term, high-quality instruments such as Treasury bills, CDs, and commercial paper. Because money market funds are constantly buying and selling such instruments, they earn a fluctuating rate of interest. The original investment, or principal, remains stable, though strictly speaking it is not guaranteed since there is always some business risk from the underlying investments.

In July 2014, the Securities and Exchange Commission (SEC) adopted amendments to the rules that govern money market mutual funds (money market funds) designed to reform the way those funds operate in order to make them less susceptible to runs that could harm investors. The need for reform, according to the SEC, was triggered when such funds "broke the buck" during the financial crisis in September 2008. The rules are designed to manage and mitigate potential redemption runs and increase transparency of risk while preserving the benefits of money market funds as much as possible.

Under the amended rules that govern money market funds under the Investment Company Act of 1940:

- The SEC is removing the valuation exemption that permitted institutional non-government money market funds (whose investors historically have made the heaviest redemptions in times of stress) to maintain a stable net asset value per share (NAV), and is requiring those funds to sell and redeem shares based on the current market-based value of the securities in their underlying portfolios rounded to the fourth decimal place (e.g., $1.0000), i.e., transact at a "floating" NAV.
- The SEC is giving the boards of directors of money market funds new tools to stem heavy redemptions by giving them discretion to impose a liquidity fee if a fund's weekly liquidity level falls below the required regulatory

threshold, and giving them discretion to suspend redemptions temporarily (i.e., to "gate" funds) under the same circumstances. These amendments will require a non-governmental money market fund to impose a liquidity fee if the fund's weekly liquidity level falls below a designated threshold, unless the fund's board determines that imposing such a fee is not in the best interests of the fund.

- There are requirements designed to make money market funds more resilient by increasing the diversification of their portfolios, enhancing their stress testing, and improving transparency by way of additional reporting to the SEC and to investors.
- Investment advisers to certain large unregistered liquidity funds, which can have many of the same economic features as money market funds, are required to provide additional information about those funds to the SEC.

The rules become effective 60 days after their publication in the Federal Register and provide a two-year transition period to enable both funds and investors time to fully adjust their systems, operations, and investing practices. More details on the final rules are available at *www.sec.gov/rules/final/2014/33-9616.pdf*.

Q 6:18 What is a *corporate/government bond fund*?

A *corporate/government bond fund* is a fund that invests mainly in bond issues of various companies and bonds issued by the U.S. government, one of its agencies, or both.

Q 6:19 What is a *balanced fund*?

A *balanced fund* is a fund that invests in a relatively fixed combination of both stocks and bonds. Balanced funds can offer both income and growth, a first step in controlling risk through diversification. The discretion an investment manager has to change the percentage of assets invested in stocks and bonds depends on the individual fund. The fund's prospectus may provide some insight into the leeway a manager has to change those percentages. If a manager has considerable freedom, participants trying to maintain specific asset allocation strategies (e.g., 80 percent stocks and 20 percent bonds) should be mindful of that when investing in such a fund.

Q 6:20 What is an *index fund*?

An *index fund*, or passively managed fund, is one for which its manager, with the aid of computer software, structures a diversified portfolio whose holdings replicate those of a particular securities universe (i.e., a bond or stock index). An index fund essentially invests in all the stocks or bonds in the same proportion as they are represented in a market index. For example, an S&P 500 index fund buys the 500 stocks that make up the index. Other major indexes include the Russell 2000, which tracks the performance of the stocks of 2,000 small companies, and the Barclay's Capital Aggregate Bond Index, which tracks the performance of investment-grade bonds.

Q 6:21 What is an *actively managed fund*?

An *actively managed fund* is one for which its manager actively analyzes individual holdings in an attempt to outperform a selected market index. Actively managed funds typically involve higher fees than index funds. Some critics will suggest that, on average, actively managed funds do not outperform index funds sufficiently to cover the higher fees, though others support the opposite conclusion, particularly where there is a selection process for actively managed funds.

Q 6:22 What are *growth and income stock funds*?

Growth and income stock funds are funds that invest mainly in stocks of large and medium-sized companies with a long history of steady growth and reliable dividends. Such funds seek to provide a balance between current dividend income and long-term growth. They tend to grow less rapidly, however, than pure growth funds (see Q 6:23). Growth and income funds are sometimes *value funds* if they trade at a price less than fundamentals (e.g., dividends, earnings).

Q 6:23 What are *growth* and *aggressive growth funds*?

A *growth fund* is a fund that invests in stock of companies whose earnings are expected to grow faster than average—that is, growth stocks. An *aggressive growth fund* is a fund that typically invests in smaller, less established companies having high growth potential but higher than average risk. Both types of funds are quite vulnerable to short-term market fluctuations.

Growth stocks tend to carry high price tags relative to current earnings. The market is willing to pay more for growth stocks because they are from companies with the potential for strong, consistent earnings growth that may be worth considerably more in the future. A growth stock fund manager determines if a stock's price is justified based on the company's potential for growth.

Q 6:24 What are the different types of *international funds*?

Funds that hold only non-U.S. securities are known as *international funds*; those that invest in both U.S. and non-U.S. securities are known as *global funds*. Funds that target a small group of neighboring foreign countries are called *regional funds,* and those that specialize in newer, less established markets are called *emerging market funds*. Within those broad categories, risks and returns will vary widely.

International funds can provide a source of diversification since markets outside the United States often move independently of the domestic markets. In general, they also tend to be riskier for the same levels of return because of currency risk and higher risk of political instability and corruption within less regulated markets. International funds also tend to carry higher investment fees than do domestic funds.

Asset Allocation and Target Date Funds

Q 6:25 What is an *asset allocation fund*?

An *asset allocation fund* blends various funds into broad-based asset allocations that are appropriate for predefined investor profiles. Such blending is an investor-friendly attempt to match an investor with a fund that delivers an appropriate mix of risk and return. The goal of asset allocation funds is to offer participants a convenient way to get both professional asset allocation and broad diversification from one investment.

Q 6:26 What is a *target date fund*?

A *target date fund* or *lifecycle fund* is a type of asset allocation fund where the participant's age over time is taken into account in determining which funds will be invested in. The use of these types of funds has steadily increased over the years, perhaps in part because they are an option under a QDIA (see chapter 7). There is a wide array of target date funds in the marketplace, including collective trust and mutual fund options. Another option, typically at the large end of the market, is customized funds. A custom series of funds, managed in a separate account or other structure, can be tailored to a particular company's preferences and demographics.

Q 6:27 What are some regulatory considerations associated with target date funds?

Because of their increasing popularity, there may be more regulatory oversight of these funds, in particular, the proportion of investment in equities and the rules surrounding investor disclosures. (See chapter 5 for fiduciary aspects of evaluating a target-date fund.)

The name of a target date fund often includes a date that reflects the year an investor plans to retire (e.g., Retirement Date Fund 2030). Concerns have been raised regarding investor understanding of risks and the differences among target date funds.

Q 6:28 What guidance have the DOL and IRS released on target date funds?

In 2013, the U.S. Department of Labor (DOL) released a fact sheet with general guidance on selecting and monitoring target date funds in 401(k) plans. The DOL emphasized the importance of understanding the fund's glide path and whether the glide path uses a "to retirement" approach (i.e., reduces equity exposure over time to its most conservative point at the target date) or "through retirement" approach (i.e., reduces equity exposure through the target date so it does not reach its most conservative point until years later).

Because there are considerable differences in target date fund offerings (e.g., investment strategies, glide paths), the DOL set forth the following guidance when choosing target date funds:

- Establish a process for comparing and selecting target date funds.
- Establish a process for the periodic review of selected target date funds.
- Understand the fund's investments, the allocation in different asset classes (stocks, bonds, cash), individual investments, and how these will change over time.
- Review the fund's fees and investment expenses.
- Inquire about whether a custom or non-proprietary target date fund would be a better fit for a plan.
- Develop effective employee communications.
- Take advantage of available sources of information to evaluate the target date fund and recommendations received regarding the fund selection.
- Document the process.

Additional information on the above criteria is available on the DOL Web site at: *www.dol.gov/ebsa/newsroom/fsTDF.html.*

In 2014, both the IRS and the DOL released guidance on offering a series of target date funds that include deferred annuities. In Notice 2014-66, the IRS addressed whether such an offering could satisfy nondiscrimination requirements as they apply to plan rights and features (see chapter 12 for additional information on those requirements). Each such fund is invested in a manner appropriate for a particular age group. As each group's age advances, an increasing portion is applied to purchase deferred annuities. Questions arose as to whether the use of age-restricted target date funds could violate nondiscrimination rules (because, as a group, older employees are often higher paid than younger employees).

The IRS set forth a special rule that, if certain conditions are satisfied in the Notice, a series of target date funds offered by a plan is treated as a single right or feature for purposes of the nondiscrimination requirements. This permits the offering to satisfy those nondiscrimination requirements as they apply to rights or features even if one or more of the funds considered on its own would not satisfy those requirements.

The conditions that must be satisfied generally include the following:

1. The series of target date funds is designed to serve as a single integrated investment program under which the same investment manager manages each fund and applies the same generally accepted investment theories across the series of funds. Thus, the only difference across the funds is the mix of assets selected by the investment manager, which difference results solely from the intent to achieve the level of risk appropriate for the age-band of individuals participating in each fund.

2. Some of the funds available to participants in older age-bands include deferred annuities, and none of the deferred annuities provide a guaranteed lifetime withdrawal benefit (GLWB) or guaranteed minimum withdrawal benefit (GMWB) feature.
3. The funds generally do not hold employer securities.
4. Each fund in the series is treated in the same manner with respect to rights or features other than the mix of assets. For example, the fees and administrative expenses for each target date fund are determined in a consistent manner, and the extent to which those fees and expenses are paid from plan assets (rather than by the employer) is the same.

[IRS Notice 2014-66]

The DOL also released guidance indicating this type of target date fund offering could satisfy the requirements of a QDIA (see chapter 7).

Q 6:29 What other guidance and proposed rules have been set forth by the DOL and SEC?

Prior to the DOL's 2013 guidance discussed in Q 6:28, both the SEC and DOL released guidance and proposed rules regarding target date funds starting in 2010. Final rules in this area are pending as this edition goes to press.

On May 6, 2010, the DOL and the Securities Exchange Commission (SEC) released guidance to help investors better understand and evaluate target date funds. The guidance discusses variations in funds and general considerations such as:

- Where will money in the fund be invested and what are the fund's strategy and risks?
- How do the fund's investments change over time?
- When will the fund reach its most conservative investment mix relative to the target date?
- How does the investment mix match up to an investor's plan to withdraw money for retirement?

The guidance is available on the DOL's Web site at *www.dol.gov/ebsa/pdf/TDFInvestorBulletin.pdf*.

On June 16, 2010, the SEC proposed rule amendments designed to (1) clarify the meaning of a date in a target date fund's name, and (2) enhance the information provided to target date fund investors. Most target date funds are designed to automatically change the fund's mix of investments (e.g., stocks, bonds, and cash) in a way that is intended to become more conservative as the target date approaches. This automatic allocation is referred to as a "glide path."

The SEC's proposal is designed to enable investors to better assess a fund's anticipated glide path and risk profile by, for example, requiring marketing materials for a target date fund to include:

- Information with the first use of the fund's name that discloses the asset allocation of the fund among types of investments (at a current date and at the target date).
- Graphic depictions (table, chart, or graph) of asset allocations that clearly depict the allocation of assets among types of investments over the entire life of the fund, along with a statement explaining that the asset allocation changes over time, and information on the target allocation ("target date") and final allocation ("landing point").
- Disclosures to the effect that a target date fund should not be selected solely on age and retirement date, is not a guaranteed investment, and that stated asset allocations may be subject to change.

[75 Fed. Reg. 35,920 (June 23, 2010)]

Additional information on the proposed rule amendments is available on the SEC's Web site (*www.sec.gov*).

On November 29, 2010, the DOL released a proposed rule that would amend:

- The QDIA regulations to provide more specificity as to the information that must be disclosed in the required notices to participants regarding target date or similar investments (see chapter 7); and
- The participant investment and fee disclosure requirements, applicable to all participant-directed plans, to require the same additional information when a plan offers a target date or similar investment (see chapter 19).

Supplemental information that would be required under the proposed rules includes:

- A narrative explanation of how the target date fund's asset allocation will change over time and the point in time when it will reach its most conservative position;
- A graphical illustration of how the target date fund's asset allocation will change over time; and
- For a target date fund that refers to a particular date (e.g., "Retirement 2015 Fund"), an explanation of the relevance of the date.

[75 Fed. Reg. 73,987 (Nov. 30, 2010)]

Some general comments on the proposed rule being made by those in the industry include:

- Would there be enough time to comply after the rule becomes effective?
- Should certain clarifications be made to improve disclosures and enhance certainty regarding compliance?
- Should the DOL's requirements be consistent with those being set forth by the SEC?
- Should the various disclosures be consolidated and streamlined?

Given the importance of asset allocation decisions, offering asset allocation funds in 401(k) plans clearly has its advantages. That is especially true if participants lack the time or investment savvy to make proper asset allocation decisions. The drawback of such funds is that they may have additional fees: fees of the underlying funds plus fees related to operating and managing the asset allocation fund. But any additional fees associated with these products may be worth it if better asset allocation decisions are being made at the participant level.

Real Estate Funds

Q 6:30 What are *real estate funds*?

Real estate funds are funds that invest primarily in real estate investment trusts (REITs), which are publicly traded securities representing ownership interests in real estate. Some REITs spread their holdings across a variety of properties—apartment buildings, offices, hotels, and so forth. Others concentrate in a single real estate category.

Exchange Traded Funds

Q 6:31 What is an *exchange traded fund*?

An *exchange traded fund* (ETF) is a security that tracks an index, a commodity, or a basket of assets like an index fund but trades like a stock on an exchange, thus experiencing price changes throughout the day as it is bought and sold. Because an ETF trades like a stock whose price fluctuates, it does not have its net asset value calculated daily like a mutual fund. When buying or selling an ETF, an investor pays a brokerage commission the same as it would with a stock transaction. ETFs tend to have lower expense ratios than the average mutual fund. The nature of the trading may not be compatible with some retirement plan recordkeeping systems unless offered through a self-directed option.

Group Variable Annuities

Q 6:32 What is a *group variable annuity contract*?

Some sponsors of 401(k) plans offer participants a menu of investment options under a variable annuity contract sold by an insurance company. Investments provided under such a contract may include a selection of proprietary investment portfolios, nonproprietary funds, or both. A variety of features and fees are associated with a variable annuity contract.

A group variable annuity contract typically offers a number of investment options. Some insurance companies manage their own investment portfolios. In addition, mutual fund groups have funds that are offered through variable annuity contracts.

Unlike those under a fixed annuity contract, payments under a variable annuity contract will depend on the performance of the underlying investment portfolios. Variable annuity contracts are also offered on an individual basis.

The insurance-like feature of a variable annuity is the death benefit, which guarantees that a minimum amount will be left to one's survivors regardless of market conditions. Death benefit provisions will vary depending on the contract.

A plan sponsor should ask the following questions when analyzing a group variable annuity contract for its 401(k) plan:

- Is there an opportunity to provide participants a fund lineup that allows them to construct portfolios that fit their investment goals and risk profiles?
- How do the performance records of the underlying funds compare with those of other mutual funds in their peer groups?
- Have managers of the underlying funds employed consistent investment styles?
- What are the fees of the underlying funds?
- What is the annual insurance contract charge?
- Is there a surrender charge?
- Are there any fees for switching investment choices?
- What are the death benefits?
- How do the sponsoring insurance company's financial stability and claims-paying ability rate?
- What other services are being provided under the contract (e.g., administration, education, recordkeeping)?
- How do the cost and quality of overall services compare with those of other available options?

Stable Value Funds

Q 6:33 What is a *stable value fund*?

A *stable value fund* generally is a fund that seeks to protect principal while offering a higher rate of return than money market funds. These funds generally invest in bonds and then use bank or insurance-company contracts to protect against interest rate volatility. Such funds are not risk-free—they are impacted by the performance of underlying funds and the financial situation of the contract issuers.

A stable value fund is generally structured either as a separately managed account, which is a stable value fund managed for one specific 401(k) plan, or as a collective fund, which pools together assets from many 401(k) plans.

Guaranteed Investment Contracts

Q 6:34 What is a *guaranteed investment contract*?

A *guaranteed investment contract* (GIC) is a contract sold by an insurance company that guarantees the payment of a specified rate of interest on the amount of money invested for a specified period of time.

Lifetime Income Products

Q 6:35 What is a *lifetime income product* in the 401(k) context?

A *lifetime income product* generally refers to a product or other arrangement that provides a stream of income during retirement. One of the goals of these products is to reduce the chances that individuals will run out of money during their retirement years.

These offerings include those that are offered in connection with a distribution, as well as those that are investment options. In the distribution context, a plan could make available an annuity form of payment that is purchased with a participant's account balance.

Guaranteed benefit products (e.g., a guaranteed lifetime withdrawal benefit, guaranteed minimum income benefit) are another option that, generally speaking, combine a method of guaranteeing a payout of a participant's account value over their lifetime with the potential of upside returns from investment market experience.

A guaranteed lifetime withdrawal benefit, for example, could provide a "floor" to the benefit amount that a participant could withdraw from at some point in the future. It does not guarantee a specific return or account value for lump-sum withdrawal; rather, it guarantees that a certain percentage of the benefit amount may be paid out over a person's lifetime (e.g., 5 percent of the benefit amount for life). The guaranteed lifetime withdrawal balance would increase as deposits are made. It could also periodically adjust upward to the current account value (e.g., on an annual basis) for market gains. However, if the account value drops due to poor market performance, the amount of the payout that is guaranteed remains intact. These types of products vary greatly in terms of structure, features, and fees.

Participants invested in guaranteed benefit products typically have access to defined investment options. Although product features may vary, participants often maintain the flexibility to take loans or other withdrawals, transfer funds into or out of the product, and maintain an account balance that can be passed to a beneficiary to the extent it is not depleted through funding of guaranteed payments.

Another option would be offering a deferred fixed annuity or longevity annuity contracts in the plan. Under this type of option, for example, a participant could take a portion of his or her account balance and purchase a Qualifying Longevity Annuity Contract (QLAC) that provides a set stream of payments starting no later than age 85. If specified requirements are met, the QLAC rules provide the participant an exemption to the minimum distribution requirements with respect to QLAC-invested amounts (see chapter 16 for more information on QLACs as they relate to RMDs).

Q 6:36 What are some considerations in offering a lifetime income product in a retirement plan?

Some considerations for plan sponsors in the lifetime income product context are:

- Financial strength of the insurance company offering the product
- Product features and costs
- Portability of the features (e.g., if the plan sponsor changes providers, if a participant changes jobs, if a participant rolls over his or her account)
- Participant education offered by the insurance company regarding the product

Q 6:37 What are some regulatory considerations associated with lifetime income products?

On February 2, 2010, the DOL and IRS jointly issued a Request for Information (RFI) regarding lifetime income options for participants and beneficiaries. The purpose of the request was to obtain information from the industry and general public to assess the use of lifetime income or other arrangements designed to provide a lifetime stream of income after retirement. (See chapter 5 for additional information regarding the RFI and fiduciary aspects involving lifetime products.)

The IRS released the following guidance in this area:

- A revenue ruling clarifying when deferred annuity contracts are subject to the survivor annuity requirements (see chapter 7).
- Final regulations that would exempt certain longevity annuity contracts (contracts with delayed initial payment dates, such as at age 80 or 85) from the age 70½ required minimum distribution rules (see chapter 16).

The IRS also released guidance regarding lifetime income options in the defined benefit plan context.

Both IRS and the DOL released guidance regarding target date funds that invest in deferred annuity contracts. The IRS guidance related to the nondiscrimination requirements applicable to plan rights and features perspective (see Q 6:28). The DOL guidance related to whether such funds could satisfy the requirements of a QDIA (see chapter 7).

See chapters 16 and 17 for additional information on annuity selection and spousal consent rules.

Life Insurance

Q 6:38 What is a *life insurance contract*?

A *life insurance contract* is a contract in which an insurance company agrees to pay the contract owner a sum of money when the insured person dies. Although the primary purpose of a retirement plan is to pay retirement benefits, a plan may also provide incidental life insurance coverage for participants. (See chapters 2 and 18 for more information on life insurance in retirement plans.) No part of an individual retirement account (IRA) can be invested in life insurance contracts, so life insurance contracts held in a 401(k) plan cannot be rolled over into an IRA upon distribution. [I.R.C. § 408(a)(3)]

Default Investment Funds

A *default investment fund* is a vehicle, chosen by the plan's investment fiduciary, in which to place assets for which no investment direction has been given. This typically occurs when an employee joins a 401(k) plan but does not provide investment instructions for his or her account. Default investment funds have received increased attention since the advent of "automatic enrollment" plans, since employees in such plans can become active participants, and deferrals can take place, without their taking any action (see chapter 2).

Q 6:39 Is a 401(k) plan required to have a default investment fund?

There is no legal requirement for a 401(k) plan to offer a default investment fund. As a practical matter, however, trustees and plan administrators should have a designated fund in which to place assets when no investment direction has been provided. Absent the designation of a default fund, the trustee or other investment fiduciary would need to make a separate investment decision for each occurrence of undirected funds.

Q 6:40 Do investment fiduciaries have fiduciary liability for assets invested in a default fund?

If the fiduciary is deemed to have selected the default fund, then the fiduciary has potential liability for assets that are invested on behalf of a participant in the default fund. Providing notice to participants in advance of where their money will go if they do not provide directions (essentially using a "negative consent" approach) does not necessarily shift fiduciary responsibility to the participant. [Preamble to DOL Reg. § 2550.404c-1] (See Q 6:43.)

Q 6:41 What types of funds are typically used as default investment funds?

Historically, most default investment funds have been "cash" type funds because they are the safest alternative from the point of view of preservation of principal. Because of the risk that returns on cash investments may not outpace inflation, investment professionals may suggest that balanced funds, target date funds, or managed accounts be considered for default fund options.

Q 6:42 Prior to the Pension Protection Act of 2006, had the DOL provided any guidance on the types of funds that should be used as default funds?

Prior to the enactment of the Pension Protection Act of 2006 [Pub. L. No. 109-280, 120 Stat. 780] (PPA), the only direction from the DOL on default funds was in the context of the automatic rollover rules (see chapter 16). In DOL Regulations Section 2550.404a-2(c), the DOL had stated that a default fund should have the goal of preserving principal consistent with a reasonable rate of return and liquidity, should maintain a dollar value equal to the amount of the individualized investment, must be offered by a state or federally regulated institution, and must charge no more than the market rate in fees.

Q 6:43 How has the Pension Protection Act of 2006 changed the law regarding default funds?

The PPA extends fiduciary relief under ERISA Section 404(c) to investments in certain types of default arrangements in the absence of participants' investment direction. To obtain protection, two conditions must be met: (1) participant contributions must be invested in accordance with DOL regulations in a "qualified default investment alternative" (QDIA) and (2) participant notice requirements must be met. [ERISA § 404(c)(5)]

See chapter 7 for further information regarding default funds in the context of ERISA Section 404(c).

Q 6:44 What guidance has the DOL provided on the kinds of arrangements that can be qualified default investment alternatives?

On October 24, 2007, the DOL released final regulations regarding types of arrangements that would be considered QDIAs. A QDIA may not (1) hold employer securities (subject to certain exceptions) or (2) impose penalties or restrictions on participants' ability to transfer out of a fund to another plan investment option.

Types of arrangements that are eligible to be QDIAs include:

- Target date or lifecycle funds that hold a mix of stocks and bonds that shift from riskier assets to more conservative assets as a participant nears retirement;
- Balanced funds that maintain a mix of equity and fixed-income instruments with a target level of risk appropriate for participants in the plan as a whole, rather than each participant;
- Managed account service under which assets in a participant's account are invested in a mix of equities and fixed income investments, taking into account the participant's age, target retirement date or life expectancy, where the asset allocation of the account becomes more conservative as the participant grows older and closer to retirement; and
- A capital preservation product for only the first 120 days of participation.

[DOL Reg. § 2550.404c-5]

See chapter 7 for additional information on QDIAs.

Q 6:45 What notice must participants receive in a default arrangement seeking ERISA Section 404(c) protection?

Each participant must receive initial and annual notices of the QDIA arrangement. The notices must satisfy the following requirements:

1. Describe the circumstances under which assets will be invested in a QDIA (and, if applicable, provide certain information regarding a plan's automatic enrollment feature);
2. Explain the right of participants to direct the investment of assets in their accounts;
3. Describe the QDIA, including a description of its investment objectives, risk and return characteristics (if applicable), and fees and expenses;
4. Describe the right to direct investment of assets into any other investment alternative under the plan, including any applicable restrictions, fees, or expenses in connection with such transfer; and
5. Explain where participants can obtain investment information concerning the plan's other investment alternatives.

[ERISA § 404(c)(5)(B)(i); DOL Reg. § 2550.404c-5]

See chapter 7 for additional information on QDIAs.

Asset Allocation Strategy

The allocation of assets across different asset classes (e.g., stocks, bonds, and cash investments) has been shown to be a major factor in the variation of portfolio returns. In 401(k) plans, the importance of asset allocation cannot be overemphasized.

Q 6:46 What is *asset allocation*?

Asset allocation is the process of allocating assets across broad asset classes (e.g., stocks, bonds, and cash investments). Those broad asset classes can be further divided into more narrow categories. In the stocks category, for example, there may be large-cap stocks, small-cap stocks, and international stocks. The bond category might have long-term and short-term bonds and corporate and government bonds. Asset allocation differs from investment selection, which is selecting specific investments to hold within a particular asset class.

Q 6:47 Why is asset allocation important?

Asset allocation decisions can account for much of the variation in a portfolio's performance. In other words, investment selection and market timing can have far less impact than asset allocation decisions. Participants in 401(k) plans should dedicate much of their investment decision making to arriving at an appropriate asset allocation. That decision should not be obscured or downplayed because of its seeming simplicity.

Q 6:48 What does an asset allocation fund accomplish?

An asset allocation fund (e.g., lifecycle fund, target date fund) invests in several different types of assets normally invested in separate funds. With an asset allocation fund, a portfolio manager makes the asset allocation decisions. In 401(k) plans, such funds can provide some assurance that participants, especially those ill equipped to make asset allocation decisions, will meet their investment objectives (see Qs 6:25, 6:26).

Managed Account Service

To assist participants with asset allocation decisions, some plans offer participants a managed account service option. Under a managed account service, a participant's individual account is automatically invested in the plan's investment alternatives and periodically rebalanced, based on methodologies and tools employed by the entity providing the service.

Q 6:49 What is a *managed account service*?

A *managed account service* automatically allocates assets in a participant's individual account between and among the plan's investment alternatives based on certain factors (e.g., age, target retirement date, life expectancy, risk tolerance). Other services may be offered under a managed account product (e.g., participant-level online investment guidance), and the actual delivery of services may vary depending on the arrangement. (See chapters 5 and 8 for additional information concerning investment advice in the 401(k) plan context.)

Employer Securities

The decision to offer employer securities as an investment option in a 401(k) plan is quite different from a decision to offer other investment options. Although offering employer securities can help align participants' interests with those of the company, plan sponsors have special factors to consider with such an arrangement. One consideration will be ensuring that the fiduciary rules of ERISA are met. Complying with diversification requirements under the PPA also must be addressed. If ERISA Section 404(c) protection is intended to extend to an employer stock option, special conditions must be satisfied. Whether participant assets are adequately diversified—that is, not overly invested in employer stock—may also be a consideration.

Federal and state securities law issues also arise whenever a plan invests in employer securities. Liquidity, voting, valuation, and other unique issues may surface as a result of a decision to offer employer stock in a 401(k) plan. Because of the complexities involved, a plan sponsor considering employer stock for its plan should consult attorneys specializing in ERISA and securities law.

Q 6:50 How can a plan sponsor offer employer stock in a 401(k) plan?

There are two ways employer stock is generally offered to plan participants:

1. Participants are given the option to direct the investment of their accounts in, among other investment options, employer stock. Depending on the plan, the option may be available to only certain accounts, including elective contribution, match, profit sharing, after-tax, and rollover accounts.
2. Employer contributions (i.e., match and profit sharing contributions) may be made, or automatically invested, in employer stock. Under such an arrangement, participants are typically given the ability to transfer out of (and back into) employer stock allocated to their accounts. (see Qs 6:55–6:62 for information on employer stock diversification requirements applicable to 401(k) plans.)

Other basic design considerations may include:

- Whether the plan will (or must) allow distributions in employer stock
- Whether participant investment in employer stock will be limited to a certain percentage
- What voting rights participants will (or must) be given with respect to employer stock
- Whether ERISA Section 404(c) protection will be sought for participant investment in employer stock (see chapter 7)
- Whether some portion of the plan will be designated an employee stock ownership plan (ESOP) or a stock bonus plan
- Whether to have a pass-through dividend feature
- Whether to include a money market fund in the employer stock option to generate liquidity for payouts
- What method of accounting will be used (share or unit)

Q 6:51 Do special ERISA fiduciary rules apply to a plan investing in employer securities?

Yes. A plan fiduciary engages in a prohibited transaction (see chapter 5) if he or she causes a plan to acquire or hold employer securities and does not follow all of these requirements:

1. The plan may invest only in qualifying employer securities (see Q 6:52). [ERISA § 407(a)(1)(A)]

2. The plan may not have more than 10 percent of its assets invested in employer securities. [ERISA § 407(a)(2)] An eligible individual account plan (see Q 6:53) may, however, invest more than 10 percent if the plan explicitly provides for the acquisition and holding of employer securities. [ERISA §§ 407(b)(1), 407(d)(3)(B)] No more than 10 percent of a participant's elective contributions can be required to be invested in employer securities. [ERISA § 407(b)(2)]
3. The plan's sale or acquisition of employer securities involving a party in interest must be for adequate consideration (see Q 6:63), and no commission may be charged. [ERISA § 408(e)]

[ERISA §§ 406(a)(1)(E), 406(a)(2)]

As a general rule, a plan fiduciary must also act prudently and for the exclusive benefit of plan participants and beneficiaries. [ERISA § 404(a)] So, although the responsible plan fiduciary might not engage in a prohibited transaction by offering employer stock, he or she might still violate ERISA's fiduciary duty requirements by, for example, offering the stock when it is no longer appropriate to do so. Plan fiduciaries responsible for selecting plan investments should seek independent legal and investment advice to ensure compliance with ERISA's fiduciary standards. (See chapters 5 and 7.)

Qualifying Employer Securities

Q 6:52 What is a *qualifying employer security*?

A *qualifying employer security* is a security issued by an employer (or an affiliate) of employees covered by the plan that is stock, a marketable obligation, or an interest in certain publicly traded partnerships. [ERISA §§ 407(d)(1), 407(d)(5)]

The term *marketable obligation* means a bond, debenture, note, certificate, or other evidence of indebtedness where the following conditions are met:

1. The obligation is acquired on the market either at the price prevailing on a national securities exchange (registered with the SEC) or, if not traded on such exchange, at a price not less favorable to the plan than the offering price as established by the current bid and asked prices (quoted by persons independent of the issuer), from an underwriter at a price not in excess of the public offering price and at which a substantial portion of the same issue is acquired by persons independent of the issuer, or directly from the issuer at a price not less favorable to the plan than the price paid currently for a substantial portion of the same issue by persons independent of the issuer;
2. Immediately after the obligation is acquired, no more than 25 percent of the aggregated amount of obligations issued in such issue and outstanding is held by the plan, and at least 50 percent of the aggregated amount is held by persons independent of the issuer; and

3. Immediately after the obligation is acquired, no more than 25 percent of the assets of the plan are invested in obligations of the employer or its affiliate.

[ERISA § 407(e)]

Stock interests acquired by a plan (other than an eligible individual account plan) after December 17, 1987, will be a qualifying employer security only if, immediately following the acquisition of such stock:

1. No more than 25 percent of the aggregate amount of stock of the same class issued and outstanding at the time of acquisition is held by the plan; and
2. At least 50 percent of such aggregate amount is held by persons independent of the issuer.

[ERISA § 407(f)(1)]

Note. *Qualifying employer security* has a more restricted definition in the ESOP context. [I.R.C. §§ 4975(e)(8), 409(*l*)]

Q 6:53 What is an *eligible individual account plan*?

An *eligible individual account plan* is an individual account plan (i.e., a defined contribution plan) that is one of the following:

1. A profit sharing, stock bonus, thrift, or savings plan (including a 401(k) plan);
2. An ESOP; or
3. A pre-ERISA money purchase pension plan invested primarily in employer securities.

The term does not include an individual retirement account or annuity. [ERISA § 407(d)(3)(A)] A plan will be treated as an eligible individual account plan only if such plan explicitly provides for the acquisition and holding of qualifying employer securities. [ERISA § 407(d)(3)(B)]

Q 6:54 What restriction applies to 401(k) plans investing in qualifying employer securities?

Eligible individual account plans, which would include 401(k) plans, are generally not subject to the 10 percent limit on investment in employer securities. However, the portion of a 401(k) plan consisting of employee salary deferrals, and earnings thereto, that is *required* to be invested in employer stock under the terms of the plan or at the direction of a person other than the participant will be treated as a separate plan subject to the 10 percent limit.

The restriction will not apply to 401(k) plans that permit participant investment of salary deferral contributions or to ESOPs. It also will not apply if the fair market value of all the employer's individual account plans is no more than 10 percent of the fair market value of all the employer's retirement plans, and it will not apply if no more than 1 percent of the employee's eligible compensation is required to be invested in employer securities. [ERISA § 407(b)]

Diversification Requirements

Q 6:55 How does the PPA impact diversification rights in 401(k) plans with respect to employer securities?

Under the PPA, participants in defined contribution plans (other than certain employee stock ownership plans (ESOPs)) must have the right to divest employer securities in their accounts and reinvest those amounts in certain diversified investments. Only plans that hold publicly traded securities (see Q 6:59) are subject to the diversification rules.

The rules do not apply to an ESOP if: (1) there are no contributions held in the plan (or earnings thereunder) that are (or ever were) subject to Code Section 401(k) or 401(m) (i.e., elective deferrals, employee after-tax contributions, or matching contributions), and (2) the plan is, for purposes of Section 414(*l*) (see chapter 10), a separate plan from any other plan maintained by the employer. Thus, an ESOP is subject to the rules if either the ESOP holds any contributions to which either Section 401(k) or 401(m) applies (or earnings thereon) or the ESOP is a portion of a plan that holds any amounts that are not part of the ESOP. A plan is not considered to hold amounts ever subject to Section 401(k) or Section 401(m) merely because it receives a rollover of amounts from another plan that are held in a separate account, even if those amounts were attributable to contributions that were subject to 401(k) or 401(m) in the other plan. A one-participant retirement plan is also not subject to these rules. [ERISA § 204(j); I.R.C. § 401(a)(35); Treas. Reg. § 1.401(a)(35)-1(f)(2)]

Q 6:56 To what contributions do the diversification rights apply?

The diversification rights apply to elective deferrals and employee contributions (and earnings thereon) and must be available to (1) any participant, (2) any alternate payee who has an account under the plan, and (3) any beneficiary of a deceased participant. For this purpose, employee contributions include both employee after-tax contributions and rollover contributions held under the plan.

The diversification rights also apply to employer contributions (and earnings thereon) and must be available to (1) a participant who has completed at least three years of service, (2) an alternate payee who has an account under the plan with respect to a participant who has completed at least three years of service, or (3) a beneficiary of a deceased participant.

The date on which a participant completes three years of service occurs immediately after the end of the third vesting computation period provided for under the plan that constitutes the completion of a third year of service. However, for a plan that uses the elapsed time method of crediting service for vesting purposes (or that provides for immediate vesting without using a vesting computation period), a participant completes three years of service on the day immediately preceding the third anniversary of the participant's date of hire.

For employer securities acquired in a plan year beginning before January 1, 2007, a plan could phase in diversification rights over a three-year period ("transition rule"). The applicable percentage is 33 percent for the first plan year to which the diversification rule applies, 66 percent for the second plan year, and 100 percent for all subsequent plan years. If a plan holds more than one class of securities, the transition rule applies separately with respect to each class. This transition rule did not apply to a participant who, before the first plan year beginning after December 31, 2005, had attained age 55 and completed at least three years of service. A plan sponsor may not have taken advantage of the transitional rule due to administrative complexity. [ERISA § 204(j); I.R.C. § 401(a)(35); Treas. Reg. § 1.401(a)(35)-1]

Q 6:57 What options must be offered to a participant in connection with diversifying his or her employer securities?

The plan must offer at least three investment options, other than employer securities, to which a participant can direct the proceeds from the divestment of employer securities, each of which is diversified and has materially different risk and return characteristics.

Q 6:58 What restrictions or conditions can be placed on investments involving employer securities under the diversification rule?

A plan cannot (directly or indirectly) impose restrictions or conditions with respect to the investment of employer securities that are not imposed on the investment of other assets of the plan. A restriction or condition in this context means:

- A restriction on a participant's right to divest an investment in employer securities that is not imposed on an investment that is not employer securities; and
- A benefit that is conditioned on the investment in employer securities.

A plan will not fail to meet the requirements because it limits the time for divestment and reinvestment to periodic, reasonable opportunities occurring no less frequently than quarterly.

Following are examples of prohibited restrictions or conditions:

- A plan allows applicable individuals the right to divest employer securities on a periodic basis (such as quarterly), but permits divestiture of another investment on a more frequent basis (such as daily).
- A plan under which a participant who divests his or her account of employer securities receives less favorable treatment (such as a lower rate of matching contributions) than a participant whose account remains invested in employer securities.

- A plan provides that a participant who divests his or her account balance with respect to employer securities is not permitted for a period of time thereafter to reinvest in employer securities is a restriction that is prohibited. This limitation takes into account a prior exercise of rights to divest employer securities.

The following are examples of restrictions or conditions that are not prohibited, provided that the limitations apply without regard to a prior exercise of rights to divest employer securities:

- A provision that limits the extent to which an individual's account balance can be invested in employer securities. Thus, a provision that does not allow more than 10 percent of an individual's account balance to be invested in employer securities is permitted.
- A provision under which an employer securities investment fund is closed or frozen, but only if the plan does not permit additional contributions or other investments to be invested in employer securities. Dividends paid on employer securities can be reinvested in employer securities. Allocations from leveraged ESOP suspense accounts are permitted under special transitional rules.

A plan is also permitted to impose reasonable restrictions on the timing and number of investments in employer securities, provided that the restrictions are designed to limit short-term trading in the employer securities (e.g., a prohibition on the ability to invest in employer securities if the employee has selected to divest employer securities within a short period of time, such as seven days).

Other permitted restrictions and conditions include, for example, those imposed by the application of securities laws (e.g., limiting divestiture rights of certain participants under Section 16(b) of the Securities Exchange Act of 1934), the imposition of fees on other investment options under the plan that are not imposed with respect to investments in employer securities, and the imposition of a reasonable fee for the divestment of employer securities. Under certain conditions, a plan can permit more frequent transfers into or out of a stable value fund or similar fund than other funds (including funds invested in employer securities) and out of a qualified default investment alternative (QDIA). A plan can delay the application of the diversification rules for up to 90 days after it becomes subject to the rules (e.g., the date on which the employer securities held under the plan become publicly traded). [ERISA § 204(j); I.R.C. § 401(a)(35); Treas. Reg. § 1.401(a)(35)-1]

Q 6:59 What are considered "publicly traded employer securities" subject to the diversification rule?

Publicly traded employer securities are employer securities that are readily tradable on an established securities market. For this purpose, if a plan holds employer securities that are not publicly traded, those employer securities are nevertheless treated as publicly traded employer securities if any employer corporation, or any member of the controlled group of corporations that includes an employer corporation, has issued a class of stock that is a publicly traded employer security. For this purpose, an employer corporation means any corporation that is an employer maintaining the plan and a controlled group of corporations has the meaning given under Section 1563(a), except that 50 percent is substituted for 80 percent wherever it occurs in Section 1563. (See chapter 10 for discussion of controlled groups.)

However, a plan is not treated as holding employer securities with respect to any securities held indirectly as part of a broader fund that is one of the following:

- a regulated investment company described in Code Section 851(a);
- a common or collective trust fund or pooled investment fund maintained by a bank or trust company supervised by a state or federal agency;
- a pooled investment fund of an insurance company that is qualified to do business in a state;
- an investment fund managed by an investment manager under ERISA Section 3(38) for a multiemployer plan; or
- other investment fund designated under guidance published by the IRS.

This exception only applies if the investment in employer securities is held in a fund under which there are stated investment objectives and the investment is independent of the employer and any affiliate thereof (the aggregate value of the employer securities held by the fund is not to exceed 10 percent of the total value of all the fund's investments). [ERISA § 204(j); I.R.C. § 401(a)(35); Treas. Reg. § 1.401(a)(35)-1]

Q 6:60 What participant notice requirements apply with respect to the diversification requirements?

Not later than 30 days before the first date on which a participant is eligible to exercise his or her diversification rights, the plan administrator must provide to such participant a notice that: (1) describes his or her diversification rights and (2) contains information on the importance of diversifying retirement plan investments.

The notice required by this subsection must be written in a manner calculated to be understood by the average plan participant and may be delivered in written, electronic, or other appropriate form to the extent that such form is reasonably accessible to the participant.

The IRS released a model notice for purposes of complying with the diversification notice requirements. The notice must be adapted to reflect particular plan provisions, for example, to reflect whether a plan provides the same diversification rights without regard to the three-year vesting rule. (See Appendix G for the model notice.)

With regard to plans that already provided participants diversification rights that satisfied the diversification rules as of January 1, 2007, the DOL indicated that if the plan complied with the participant benefit statement requirements (i.e., timely sends periodic benefit statements with specified information), it was not required to also send a separate stand-alone notice regarding diversification of employer securities. Doing so may cause confusion and result in unnecessary costs since both the notice and statements would contain similar information. (See chapter 19 for information on the benefit statement requirements.) [ERISA Section 101(m); Notice 2006-107; FAB 2006-03]

Q 6:61 What are the penalties for noncompliance with the diversification notice rules?

Failure to provide timely notice of diversification rights can result in civil penalties of up to $100 per participant per day computed from the date that is 30 days before the first date on which diversification rights become exercisable under the rules to the date such a notice is furnished. The amount of the penalty is determined by the DOL, taking into consideration the degree and/or willfulness of the failure or refusal to provide the notice of diversification rights. [DOL Reg. § 2560.502c-7]

Q 6:62 When are the diversification rules effective?

The diversification and notice requirements are generally effective for plan years beginning after December 31, 2006 (certain special effective date rules apply to plans maintained by a collective bargaining agreement). [ERISA §§ 191(m), 204(j); I.R.C. § 401(a)(35)]

Final Treasury regulations under Section 401(a)(35), issued on May 19, 2010, are effective for plan years beginning on or after January 1, 2011. Until those regulations went into effect, plans could apply guidance under Notice 2006-107 or the final regulations. Plans also were permitted to apply the proposed regulations for plan years before the final regulations went into effect. The proposed regulations generally follow and expand the guidance in Notice 2006-107. [Treas. Reg. § 1.401(a)(35)-1; Notice 2006-107, 2006-51 I.R.B. 1114]

See chapter 3 for information regarding the deadline to amend plan documents for these diversification requirements.

Fair Market Value of Employer Stock

Q 6:63 What does it mean for a plan to purchase or sell employer securities for *adequate consideration*?

The acquisition or sale of qualifying employer securities is exempt from the prohibited transaction rules only if the acquisition or sale is for adequate consideration and no commission is charged. [ERISA § 408(e)] In the case of a security for which there is a generally recognized market, *adequate consideration* means the price of the security prevailing on a national securities exchange registered under Section 6 of the Securities Exchange Act of 1934 (the 1934 Act), or, if the security is not traded on such a national securities exchange, a price not less favorable to the plan than the offering price for the security as established by the current bid and asked prices quoted by persons independent of the issuer and any party in interest. [ERISA § 3(18)(A)]

In the case of a security not freely tradable, *adequate consideration* means the fair market value of the security as determined in good faith by the fiduciary, pursuant to the terms of the plan and the regulations promulgated by the Department of Labor (DOL). For such purpose, fair market value is the price at which an asset would change hands between a willing buyer and a willing seller in an arm's-length transaction determined as of the applicable date and reflected in a written document meeting the requirement of the DOL regulations. The good-faith component requires:

1. Objective standards of conduct;
2. Prudent investigation of circumstances prevailing at the time of the valuation;
3. Application of sound business principles of valuation; and
4. That the fiduciary making the valuation either be independent of all parties (other than the plan) or be reliant on the report of an appraiser who is independent of all parties (other than the plan).

[Prop. DOL Reg. § 2510.3-18]

Q 6:64 Why is it important to properly value employer stock when it is offered as a plan investment option?

An accurate assessment of the fair market value is essential to a plan's ability to comply with the requirements set forth in the Code and ERISA. For instance, a prohibited transaction exemption may not apply unless the fair market value of assets is accurately determined.

Although most investments held by a plan present minimal valuation problems (e.g., publicly traded employer stock and mutual funds), some investments such as closely held employer stock, real estate, and limited partnerships may receive special scrutiny. The Internal Revenue Service (IRS) monitors compliance with the valuation standards on Form 5500, which requires a statement of plan assets valued at fair market value (see chapter 19). A valuation problem may exist, according to the IRS, if a plan reports assets with level values in successive years or if there is a sudden jump in plan asset values in the same year a large distribution is made to highly compensated employees.

Because amounts allocated or distributed to participants in a defined contribution plan must be ascertainable, such a plan must value its assets at least once a year in accordance with a method consistently followed and uniformly applied. [Rev. Rul. 80-155] Furthermore, employer securities must be valued at the time of the transaction whenever acquired or sold. [Rev. Rul. 69-494]

Voting Rights for Employer Stock

Q 6:65 Do companies give participants voting rights with respect to employer stock allocated to their accounts?

Some companies pass through voting of shares to participants to enforce the awareness of ownership. Some do not; instead, the plan trustee typically controls how shares are voted in its own discretion or at the direction of a named fiduciary. Alternatively, a properly appointed ERISA investment manager may control voting of shares. [ERISA § 404(a); DOL Reg. § 2509.94-2(1)] If ERISA Section 404(c) protection is desired, however, voting, tender, and similar rights with respect to the employer stock must be passed through to the participants. [DOL Reg. § 2550.404c-1(d)(2)(ii)(E)(4)(vi)] (See chapter 7.)

Special rules under the Code govern when voting must be passed through to participants in an ESOP. If an employer has securities that are readily tradable on an established securities exchange, voting on allocated shares must be passed through to plan participants. [I.R.C. § 409(e)(2)] If the employer has securities that are not readily tradable, voting on allocated shares must be passed through to participants only with respect to major corporate matters (e.g., merger, recapitalization, liquidation, sale of substantially all of the assets). [I.R.C. § 409(e)(3)]

It should be noted that tender decisions may be considered investment decisions as opposed to voting decisions. The plan and trust document should be carefully reviewed to determine who has the power with respect to voting and tender issues.

SEC Registration and Reporting Requirements

Q 6:66 What registration requirements under federal securities laws arise when a 401(k) plan offers employer securities?

Under federal securities law, each offer or sale of an employer's stock must be registered with the SEC, or there must be an applicable exemption from the registration requirement. [Securities Act of 1933, §§ 2(1), 3–4, 5, 15 U.S.C. §§ 77b(1), 77c–77d, 77e] The rule applies whether or not the employer's stock is publicly traded.

The SEC has taken the position that when a plan allows voluntary employee contributions including salary deferrals to be invested in employer stock, an individual employee's interest in that plan is a security. That may subject the plan to securities registration, prospectus, and antifraud requirements, although, depending on the employer and plan structure, there may be exemptions from some of those requirements. If registration requirements apply, the *plan* must be registered for SEC purposes. It is not enough that the stock itself is registered. The plan is typically registered by means of an abbreviated S-8 filing. [SEC Rel. 33-6188, 45 Fed. Reg. 8,960 (Feb. 11, 1980)] If interests in the plan itself must be registered, annual financial reports on the plan may also need to be filed with the SEC. [SEC Rule 15d-21, 17 C.F.R. § 240.15d-21]

If a plan does not permit investment of voluntary employee contributions, registration may not be required even if participants have the right to direct investment of employer contributions and earnings among various investments, including employer stock. Even though employee interests in the plan may not be securities, however, the underlying employer stock may be considered a security that must be either registered or offered pursuant to an available exemption from registration. Further, although a distribution of unregistered stock from a plan to a participant in satisfaction of a benefit obligation does not require SEC registration, the participant may not be able then to sell the stock unless it is registered or falls within a securities law exemption. [SEC Rel. 33-6188, Part V, C, and Part VI, B, 45 Fed. Reg. 8,976, 8,977 (Feb. 11, 1980)]

A registration exemption may not, however, provide an exemption from disclosure (antifraud) requirements and, in some cases, state registration. Whatever the situation, it is best to seek advice from a securities law expert before offering employer stock.

Q 6:67 How might the SEC short-swing profits rules apply to transactions involving publicly traded employer stock in a 401(k) plan?

The 1934 Act imposes reporting requirements and liability on transactions in publicly traded employer stock by directors, executive officers, and more-than-10-percent shareholders of the employer (i.e., corporate insiders). [Securities Exchange Act of 1934 § 16, 15 U.S.C. § 78p] Section 16(a) requires corporate insiders to file certain periodic reports with the SEC of their ownership, including changes to that ownership. Under Section 16(b), liability is imposed on insiders for any profit derived from any purchase and sale (or sale and purchase) during the same six-month period; this is known as *short-swing profit liability*. The provisions were intended to prevent the misuse of insider information prohibited under Section 10(b) and SEC Rule 10b-5.

Example. To avoid short-swing profit liability, a participant insider electing into an employer stock alternative on January 1, 2012, would not be allowed to transfer shares out of that employer stock until July 1, 2012.

Transactions in employer stock should also be analyzed under other SEC trading rules, such as the prohibition on market manipulation.

Sarbanes-Oxley Act of 2002

Q 6:68 What rules apply to plans invested in employer stock under the Sarbanes-Oxley Act?

As a result of the enactment of the Sarbanes-Oxley Act of 2002 [Pub. L. No. 107-204, 116 Stat. 745] (SOX), the following rules apply to plans invested in employer stock:

- Directors and executive officers are prohibited from buying or selling employer stock held by them during a retirement plan blackout period. [SOX § 306(a)]

- Plan administrators are required to give the issuer of employer stock offered under the plan (i.e., the employer or plan sponsor) a notice similar to that given to plan participants in advance of a blackout period if the employer stock will be subject to the blackout period (see chapter 19). [SOX § 306(b)(1)(i)(2)(E)]
- After the issuer receives notice of a blackout period from the plan administrator, the issuer of employer stock is required to give directors and executive officers and the SEC advance notice of the blackout within specified time frames. [SOX § 306(a)(6); SEC Rel. 34-47225, 68 Fed. Reg. 4,338 (2003)]
- Plan administrators should include special language in a blackout notice if investments in employer stock will be subject to the blackout period (see chapter 19 and Appendix F). [SOX § 306(b)(1)(i)(2)(A)]
- Section 16 of the 1934 Act [15 U.S.C. § 78p] was amended to shorten the deadline for reporting employer stock transactions of corporate insiders to within two business days. A 30-day time frame generally applied under prior rules. [SOX § 403]

Q 6:69 What are the key features of the SEC insider trading prohibitions applicable during blackouts?

The insider trading restrictions applicable during blackouts were designed to eliminate the inequities that may result when retirement plan participants are temporarily prevented from trading employer stock in their plan accounts at a time when certain corporate higher-ups can trade in employer stock, including stock that is held outside the plan. As a result of the rules, interests of directors and executive officers will be more aligned with the interests of rank-and-file employees in blackout situations. Key features of the SEC insider trading rules include the following:

- The rules generally apply to "directors" and "executive officers" as defined under Section 16 of the 1934 Act. [15 U.S.C. § 78p]
- Directors and executive officers are prohibited from directly or indirectly purchasing or selling employer stock "acquired in connection with service or employment as a director or executive officer," which is defined broadly to include, among other things, stock acquired under any compensatory arrangement such as incentive and bonus plans or as an inducement to service or employment.
- A blackout period is generally defined as any period of more than three consecutive business days during which the ability of not fewer than 50 percent of the participants or beneficiaries under all individual account plans to purchase, sell, or otherwise acquire or transfer employer stock is temporarily suspended.
- The rules generally apply to companies that file periodic reports and/or are registered with the SEC under the 1934 Act.
- The effective date of the rules was January 26, 2003.

[SOX § 306(a); SEC Rel. 34-47225, 68 Fed. Reg. 4,338 (2003)]

The rules above are described in very general terms. Onerous penalties and sanctions are applicable if the rules are violated. It is essential that a securities law expert be consulted to ensure compliance.

Employer Stock Strategy

Q 6:70 What are the dangers of being heavily invested in employer stock?

Being heavily invested in a single security can carry risk. If both job and retirement security are tied to the performance of the same company, the risk could be magnified. Proper diversification by participants applies to investment in employer stock. Information that must be conveyed in participant benefit statements includes the importance of having a well-diversified portfolio (see chapter 19 for further discussion of participant benefit statement requirements).

Q 6:71 What are some general considerations for including employer stock as an investment option in a 401(k) plan?

The following are some general considerations for including an employer stock investment alternative in a 401(k) plan:

1. If stock is publicly traded, consider ERISA Section 404(c) protection for participant-directed investments in employer stock.
2. If stock is publicly traded, allow full diversification of investments across all contribution sources.
3. If the stock is not registered, offer the option of investing in employer stock only for matching or profit sharing accounts—not salary deferral, rollover, or after-tax accounts.
4. If the stock is not registered, make all distributions from the plan in the form of cash, not stock, when permissible.
5. If the stock is not publicly traded, include a money market fund in the employer stock fund to generate the liquidity necessary to make payouts.
6. Work closely with the plan administrator to create a plan design that will match the type of stock and goals of the employer with the purchase availability and distribution options made available to participants under the plan.
7. Provide adequate education to participants on the role of diversification in mitigating investment risk.
8. Consider hiring an outside, independent fiduciary to oversee investments in employer stock.
9. In all situations, consult a securities law attorney and an ERISA attorney to ensure that all SEC filings, state and federal securities requirements, and other compliance issues are addressed.

(See also chapters 5 and 7.)

Directed Trustee Considerations

Q 6:72 How does the DOL view a directed trustee's fiduciary responsibilities with respect to investments and in particular with respect to investments in publicly traded employer stock?

In 2004, the DOL issued Field Assistance Bulletin 2004-03 on the duties of a directed trustee with respect to investments and in particular investments in publicly traded employer stock. Under ERISA, a directed trustee is subject to the proper directions of a named fiduciary. A directed trustee may not, however, follow a direction that the trustee knows or should know is inconsistent with the terms of the plan or contrary to ERISA. [ERISA § 403(a)(1)] Within that broad context, DOL Field Assistance Bulletin 2004-03 provided the following guidance to directed trustees regarding the investment of plan assets:

- It is permissible to follow a direction that is not prohibited under the terms of the plan. If the terms are ambiguous, the directed trustee should seek clarification from the fiduciary responsible for interpreting the terms of the plan and the directed trustee may rely on that interpretation.
- A directed trustee must follow processes that are designed to avoid prohibited transactions. A directed trustee could satisfy its obligation by obtaining appropriate written representations from the directing fiduciary that the plan maintains and follows procedures for identifying prohibited transactions and, if any are prohibited, identifying the individual or class exemption applicable to the transaction. A directed trustee may rely on the representations of the directing fiduciary unless the directed trustee knows that the representations are false.
- With respect to the prudence of a particular investment transaction, a directed trustee does not have an independent obligation to determine the prudence of every transaction. Nor does a directed trustee have an obligation to duplicate or second-guess the work of the plan fiduciaries that have discretionary authority over the management of plan assets.
- If a directed trustee has material nonpublic information that is necessary for a prudent decision, the directed trustee has a duty to inquire about the named fiduciary's knowledge and consideration of the information with respect to the direction. For example, if a directed trustee has nonpublic information indicating that a company's public financial statements contain material misrepresentations that significantly inflate the company's earnings, the trustee could not simply follow a direction to purchase that company's stock at an artificially inflated price.
- The possession of nonpublic information by one part of an organization will generally not be imputed to the organization as a whole (including personnel providing directed trustee services) where the organization maintains procedures designed to prevent the illegal disclosure of such information under securities, banking, or other laws. If, despite such procedures, the individuals responsible for the directed trustee services have actual knowledge of material nonpublic information, the directed

trustee, prior to following a direction that would be affected by such information, has a duty, as indicated above, to inquire about the named fiduciary's knowledge and consideration of the information with respect to the direction. Similarly, if the directed trustee performs an internal analysis in which it concludes that the company's current financial statements are materially inaccurate, the directed trustee would have an obligation to disclose this analysis to the named fiduciary before making a determination whether to follow a direction to purchase the company's security. The directed trustee would not have an obligation to disclose reports and analyses that are available to the public.

- Absent material nonpublic information, a directed trustee, given its limited fiduciary duties as determined by statute, will rarely have an obligation under ERISA to question the prudence of a direction to purchase publicly traded securities at the market price solely on the basis of publicly available information.
- In limited, extraordinary circumstances, where there are clear and compelling public indicators, as evidenced by an 8-K filing with the Securities and Exchange Commission (SEC), a bankruptcy filing, or similar public indicator, that call into serious question a company's viability as a going concern, the directed trustee may have a duty not to follow the named fiduciary's instruction without further inquiry. A directed trustee's actual knowledge of media or other public reports or analyses that merely speculate on the continued viability of a company does not, in and of itself, constitute knowledge of clear and compelling evidence concerning the company sufficient to give rise to a directed trustee's duty to act. With respect to 8-K filings, not all 8-K filings regarding a company would trigger a duty on the part of a directed trustee to question a direction to purchase or hold securities of that company. Only those relatively few 8-Ks that call into serious question a company's ongoing viability may trigger a duty on the part of the directed trustee to take some action.
- If a company filed for bankruptcy under circumstances which made it unlikely that there would be any distribution to equity holders, or otherwise publicly stated that it was unlikely to survive the bankruptcy proceedings in a manner that would leave current equity holders with any value, the directed trustee would have an obligation to question whether the named fiduciary had considered the prudence of the direction. Even under such circumstances, it might not be imprudent to purchase or hold stock in a distressed company in bankruptcy. There may be situations in which the plan's fiduciaries could reasonably conclude that the stock investment makes sense, even for a long-term investor, in light of the proposed restructuring of the company's debts or other factors.
- In situations where a fiduciary who is a corporate employee gives an instruction to buy or hold stock of his or her company after the company and its officers or directors have been formally charged by state or federal regulators with financial irregularities, the directed trustee, taking such facts into account, may need to decline to follow the direction or may need to conduct an independent assessment of the transaction in order to assure

itself that the instruction is consistent with ERISA. If, however, an independent fiduciary was appointed to manage the plan's investment in company stock, a directed trustee could follow the proper directions of the independent fiduciary without having to conduct its own independent assessment of the transaction. The DOL noted, however, that a directed trustee would not have a heightened duty whenever a regulatory body opened an investigation of a company whose securities were the subject of a direction, merely based on the bare fact of the investigation.

- A directed trustee does not become primarily responsible for the prudence of an investment by providing information to a named fiduciary as described above and/or if a named fiduciary changes a direction in response to a directed trustee's inquiries or information.
- If a directed trustee has knowledge of a fiduciary breach, the directed trustee may be liable as a co-fiduciary unless the directed trustee takes reasonable steps to remedy the breach.

See chapter 5 for more detailed information on responsibilities of plan fiduciaries.

401(k) Stock Ownership Plans

Q 6:73 What is a *401(k) stock ownership plan*?

A *401(k) stock ownership plan,* commonly called a *KSOP*, is a stock bonus plan in which salary deferrals and/or employer contributions (usually matching contributions) may be invested in employer stock. A KSOP must comply with all the stock bonus plan rules as well as the 401(k) rules. [I.R.C. § 401(k)(*1*)]

Q 6:74 What are the stock bonus rules that apply to KSOPs?

The following regulatory and Code provisions generally govern KSOPs:

1. If the plan or a portion of the plan is designated to be an ESOP, it must be designed to invest primarily in employer securities and satisfy other special ESOP rules. [I.R.C. § 4975(e)(7)]
2. With few exceptions, benefit payments must be distributable in employer stock. The plan may provide a cash distribution option as long as the participants have the right to demand that a distribution be made in stock. [I.R.C. § 409(h)]
3. Distribution of non-publicly traded securities from a plan are subject to the participants' right to sell the stock back to the employer. [I.R.C. § 409(h)]
4. Participants in an ESOP have certain voting rights on employer stock. [I.R.C. § 409(e)]
5. An ESOP may be designed to allow the plan to borrow funds to purchase employer securities. [I.R.C. § 4975(e)(7)]

6. Distributions must begin by the end of the plan year after the year a participant stops work because of normal retirement, death, or disability. Other distributions generally must be made by the end of the sixth plan year after the year the participant terminates employment; however, the plan may allow for the delay of payment for large account balances consisting of securities acquired with ESOP loans. [I.R.C. § 409(o)]
7. An ESOP plan that invests in non-publicly traded employer securities must have the valuation of those securities made by an independent appraiser at least annually. [I.R.C. § 401(a)(28)(C)]
8. Special rules apply under Code Sections 404 and 415 (see chapter 9).

Self-Directed Options

A majority of employers find a menu of investment options adequate for most participants. Some employers are offering participants a wider range of investment options, however, through a self-directed option (also known as a self-directed brokerage account). That number appears to be slowly rising. See chapter 19 for special rules in the Form 5500 and participant disclosure contexts.

Q 6:75 What is a *self-directed option*?

A *self-directed option* is an option permitting participants to invest their plan assets in an unlimited number of investment options.

Q 6:76 How can a self-directed option be offered?

A self-directed option can be set up in two ways:

1. A *full brokerage account,* which allows participants to invest in any mutual fund, stock, or bond made available through the account; or
2. A *mutual fund window,* which allows participants to invest in any mutual fund made available but not in individual securities.

These accounts are set up with designated brokers or a broker of the participant's choice.

Self-directed accounts are often an added feature of a plan that already has a broad menu of investment options. For instance, the first level of a plan will consist of standard core options, and the second level will include self-directed accounts. In such an arrangement, the plan may or may not limit investment in the self-directed account to a certain percentage of plan assets. Alternatively, the plan can be entirely self-directed (i.e., a self-directed or open-ended plan). Participants typically pay an annual fee to maintain a self-directed account, as well as broker fees and commissions on trades. Historically, self-directed accounts have appealed to only a small portion of an employee population—for example, senior-level executives—though this appears to be changing as 401(k) balances grow larger.

Motivation for Self-Directed Options

Q 6:77 What might motivate an employer to offer a self-directed option or plan to participants?

An employer may choose to offer a self-directed plan, or add a self-directed option to a current plan, for the following reasons:

- To respond to employees who are demanding more and varied investment offerings;
- To balance competing needs of employees who might need more investment options with those who might be confused by an unlimited number of investment offerings; and/or
- To avoid or minimize fiduciary liability associated with the selection of plan investment alternatives.

Considerations Arising from Self-Directed Options

Q 6:78 What are some considerations when offering a self-directed option?

Following are considerations that plans may have with providing a self-directed option to employees:

- Administrative impact and costs
- Participants being overwhelmed by unfettered investment options
- Discrimination issues under the "benefits, rights, and features" rules (see Q 6:81)
- Participant investment in inappropriate or troublesome assets
- Satisfying certain ERISA Section 404(c) requirements (see Q 6:83)

Q 6:79 What administrative complications and costs are sometimes associated with self-directed accounts?

Self-directed accounts have the potential to impact plan administration and costs. All trading is done at the participant level, rather than aggregated at the plan level as is done with menu plans. When participants use their own brokerage firms to custody their accounts, assets are fragmented, thus complicating the plan's aggregate recordkeeping and reporting functions. Investment in assets that create valuation issues, such as limited partnerships, can also be problematic. Plan sponsors and trustees will require fair values for those types of assets to comply with requirements under the Code and ERISA.

As for costs, there are fees charged for each brokerage account and additional costs for administration services. Although the additional costs are often passed through to participants, the costs should be reasonable in light of services being provided.

Q 6:80 Could some participants become overwhelmed by unlimited investment options in a self-directed environment?

In the self-directed environment, there is a potential that participants will be overwhelmed by the sheer volume of investment possibilities. 401(k) plans with a menu of investment options provide a more manageable investment decision-making forum for some participants and a reasonable framework for an ongoing investment education program. They may not, however, satisfy all the investment desires of a diverse workforce.

Q 6:81 When could a self-directed option create discrimination issues under the benefits, rights, and features rules?

Offering employees the option to self-direct investments could present discrimination issues under Code Section 401(a)(4). Under that section each benefit, right, or feature must be made available to employees on a nondiscriminatory basis. A right or feature would include a self-directed option because it can reasonably be expected to be of meaningful value to an employee. Therefore, the option must be available to non-highly compensated employees (NHCEs) in a manner that satisfies the *current availability* and *effective availability* tests (see chapter 11). [I.R.C. § 401(a)(4); Treas. Reg. § 1.401(a)(4)-4(a)]

The current availability test is generally satisfied if, under the terms of the plan document, the option's availability to NHCEs satisfies the Code Section 410(b) coverage test. [Treas. Reg. § 1.401(a)(4)-4(b)] The effective availability test is a facts-and-circumstances determination as to whether availability substantially favors highly compensated employees (HCEs). [Treas. Reg. § 1.401(a)(4)-4(c)]

Problems arise if only HCEs are given the option to self-direct. If instead all employees are given the option, a plan may still fail to satisfy the effective availability test if NHCEs do not receive information about the option (including how to use it). [Treas. Reg. § 1.401(a)(4)-4(c)(2), Ex. 2] Requiring a minimum account balance or minimum investment amount could also cause problems under the effective availability test.

Q 6:82 What inappropriate or troublesome investments could result in self-directed accounts?

Self-directed accounts can complicate an employer's ability to oversee plan investments. Unless certain safeguards are in place, there is the potential that participants will invest in inappropriate or troublesome assets. For example, a participant investment decision could result in a prohibited transaction, contravene the plan document, or cause the indicia of ownership of plan assets to be outside U.S. jurisdiction. [ERISA §§ 406, 404(a)(1)(D), 404(b); DOL Reg. § 2550.404-1]

Free rein to invest in any asset, such as real estate and limited partnerships, could also create valuation problems. To comply with various requirements under ERISA and the Code, plan assets must be valued at least annually. If no fair market value is readily available, the assets will have to be appraised—a process that could be both costly and time consuming. [ERISA § 103; Rev. Rul. 80-155, 1980-1 C.B. 84]

Participant investment in collectibles (i.e., works of art, rugs, antiques, metals, gems, stamps, coins, and other tangible personal property specified by the IRS) should also be avoided. Certain types of investment could result in unrelated business taxable income (UBTI) for the plan. [I.R.C. § 512]

Self-Directed Options and ERISA Section 404(c)

Q 6:83 What considerations might arise for a plan sponsor seeking ERISA Section 404(c) protection for a self-directed option?

With access to unlimited investment options, a self-directed option may satisfy the broad-range-of-investment-alternatives requirement automatically or through its core fund menu.

The market volatility rule generally provides that participants must be permitted to make investment changes with a frequency appropriate to market volatility. Allowing participants to switch their investments quarterly may be acceptable in a menu plan; it may not be for a plan with a self-directed option where there is access to investments with volatilities all over the board. Such a plan typically permits investment transfers on a daily basis to satisfy the volatility rule.

Special considerations may be necessary to ensure that participants are receiving the requisite ERISA Section 404(c) disclosure information (see chapter 7).

Self-Directed Option Strategies

Q 6:84 How can a self-directed option be structured to minimize administrative complications, additional costs, and fiduciary liability exposure?

To minimize administrative complications, additional costs, and fiduciary liability exposure, careful consideration should be given to the following:

- Prohibiting investment in certain types of investments such as limited partnerships, collectibles, and real estate
- Selecting one or more brokers to serve as the plan's *designated brokers,* who agree to provide certain information to participants and investment oversight

- Selecting brokers and service providers performing consolidated reporting functions that can be electronically linked
- Permitting daily investment transfers
- Offering the option to participants in a manner that will not create discrimination issues and communicating how to use the option
- Conducting a cost/benefit analysis of a self-directed option and monitoring its costs on an ongoing basis

See also chapter 19 for discussion on self-directed accounts under the topic of the participant investment and fee disclosure requirements.

In 2014, the DOL released a Request for Information (RFI) to help it determine whether, and to what extent, additional regulatory standards or other guidance is needed in order to protect participants in plans that offer a self-directed feature.

Investment Policies

Q 6:85 Is a *written* investment policy statement required under ERISA?

Technically, no. Plans are required to have a funding policy (see chapter 5); ERISA does not, however, explicitly require that plans have *written* investment policy statements. Nonetheless, the maintenance of such a statement designed to further the purposes of the plan and its funding policy will help ensure that investments are made in a prudent and rational manner consistent with the fiduciary standards. [DOL Reg. § 2509.08-2]

Q 6:86 Is a named fiduciary acting as a fiduciary when it adopts an investment policy statement?

According to the DOL, a named fiduciary's determination of the terms of a statement of investment policy represents an exercise of fiduciary responsibility. Such statements need to consider factors such as the plan's funding policy and its liquidity needs, as well as issues of prudence, diversification, and other fiduciary requirements. [DOL Reg. § 2509.08-2]

Q 6:87 What provisions may be found in an investment policy?

Investment policies may have the following sections:

- Purpose of the Plan
- Regulatory Environment
- Responsible Parties
- Investment Options
- Investment Selection Criteria

- Investment Monitoring
- Default Fund Selection

(See chapter 5 for more information on investment policies.)

Selecting and Monitoring Plan Investments

A key criterion for selecting and monitoring plan investments is to ensure that each plan investment is generating sufficient returns given its risk level. That includes evaluating the effects fees have on returns. In addition, plan sponsors will want to analyze investment manager style and monitor changes that may occur in that style.

Plan sponsors have many sources of information for evaluating plan investments, including those that track investment performance, rate mutual funds, and identify trends in the marketplace. Some sources of information entail little or no expense—for example, mutual fund prospectuses and financial publications; others may involve more costs—for example, independent ratings services and consultants.

Q 6:88 What are the major considerations in the investment selection process?

The ultimate goal in the investment selection process is to offer a menu of funds that give participants the ability to construct portfolios that fit their investment goals and risk profiles. To do that requires having several investment options with varying risk and return characteristics. It also means offering a variety of funds across different investment styles.

Offering several investment options can provide more investment opportunity; however, each option must be reviewed against others to determine that it is clearly distinct. Too many funds with similar risk and reward characteristics may not provide participants adequate opportunity to diversify. Participants faced with an overwhelming array of investment options may also experience unnecessary confusion.

The investment options selected should have solid performance records and reasonable fees. Among other things, a plan's investment policy should have guidelines about the investment options to be made available, the selection criteria, including acceptable risk and return characteristics, and the monitoring process. (See Q 6:87 for additional discussion of a plan's investment policy.)

Q 6:89 What are the investment options typically offered in a 401(k) plan?

The average employer offers participants ten or more investment options. A plan designed to comply with ERISA Section 404(c) must provide a minimum of three funds (see chapter 7). The typical mix might include funds investing mainly in stocks, bonds, or cash; a balanced stock and bond fund; funds that mirror an index such as the S&P 500; GIC or stable value investment; an international stock fund; and, in some cases, shares of employer stock.

Q 6:90 What are the key elements in an investment monitoring program?

The key elements in an investment monitoring program are setting performance objectives for each investment option, establishing a review procedure, and incorporating those objectives and procedures in a written investment policy.

Q 6:91 Should investment performance be compared with the performance of other similar investments?

Investment performance is typically compared with the performance of other investments with similar risk characteristics (and/or applicable market index). That means, for example, comparing the performance of an aggressive growth fund with that of other aggressive growth funds. That is of particular importance in the case of actively managed portfolios. "Peer group"-type data can help put performance in the context of other actively managed portfolios. It is available from independent rating services such as Morningstar (see Q 6:93), software products, and various consulting firms.

Q 6:92 How often should investment performance be monitored?

Investment performance is typically monitored at least quarterly. Nonetheless, absent clear changes in investment management style or objectives, decisions to change funds are typically based on performance over a longer period of time.

Q 6:93 What is the function of investment fund independent ratings services?

Several independent ratings services provide comprehensive information about funds, such as expense ratios, risk analysis, and performance figures. Morningstar is a prominent source of comprehensive mutual fund information.

Mutual Fund Investigations

Q 6:94 How should a plan fiduciary respond if a plan investment is a mutual fund involved in an investigation?

A few years back, a number of mutual funds had been the subject of investigations for potential late trading and market timing abuses. (See chapters

4 and 5 for DOL guidance and SEC rules issued in response to the alleged abuses with respect to 401(k) plans.)

Investment Fees and Revenue Sharing

Q 6:95 What kinds of fees are typically associated with investments in a 401(k) plan?

Fees that may be charged with respect to investment options in a 401(k) plan include:

- Sales charges (also known as loads or commissions) in connection with buying and selling of securities;
- Management fees (also known as investment advisory fees) for managing the assets of the investment fund;
- Other administrative or operating fees for such services as recordkeeping, furnishing statements, toll-free telephone numbers, and investment advice in connection with the day-to-day management of investment products.

Transaction costs also may be incurred in connection with the buying and selling of securities. The greater the volume of buying and selling by the mutual fund, for example, the greater is the transaction fees. Transaction costs are not reflected in sales commissions or management fees. An investment's portfolio turnover rate is an indicator of the potential impact of transaction costs on returns. A turnover rate of 100 percent, for example, indicates that the investment manager sold and replaced securities valued at 100 percent of assets within a one-year period.

Sales commissions or loads are charged when an investment is purchased or sold. These are onetime expenses. Management, administrative/operating, and transaction fees are ongoing fees. Both onetime expenses and ongoing expenses are deducted from an investment's assets and reduce the investment's return.

> **Note.** The material on fees in this section is, in part, from the DOL's publications: "Understanding Retirement Plan Fees and Expenses," available online at *www.dol.gov/ebsa/publications/undrstndgrtrmnt.html,* and "A Look at 401(k) Fees," available online at *www.dol.gov/ebsa/publications/401k_employee.html.* Another tool on the DOL's Web site, "401(k) Plan Fee Disclosure Form," helps employers compare administrative and investment fees of competing plan service providers. The form is available at *www.dol.gov/ebsa/pdf/401kfefm.pdf.*

Q 6:96 What particular fees might a mutual fund charge?

The following are common types of mutual fund fees:

- Sales charges (front-end or back-end loads) (see Q 6:97)
- 12b-1 fees (see Q 6:98)

- Management fees (see Q 6:99)
- "Other" administrative costs (see Q 6:100)
- Transaction costs (see Q 6:95)

A mutual fund may have several share classes reflecting varying fees and fee structures.

Q 6:97 What are *front-end loads* and *back-end loads*?

A *front-end load* is a sales commission charged up front when an investor purchases an investment. If a fund has a 6 percent front-end load, for example, $94,000 out of a $100,000 investment is actually used to purchase shares.

A *back-end load* is a sales commission charged at the time fund shares are redeemed. Back-end loads may be assessed either as a percentage of the value of assets being redeemed or as a flat fee. Some back-end loads decrease over time and are eliminated after a period; they are referred to as contingent deferred sales loads.

Q 6:98 What is a *12b-1 fee*?

A *12b-1 fee* is a charge to cover ongoing marketing and distribution expenses. Unlike onetime sales loads, 12b-1 fees are assessed annually. The fees can range from about 0.25 percent to 1 percent of average net assets.

On July 21, 2010, the SEC proposed a new framework for 12b-1 fees designed to improve the regulation of these fees and provide better disclosures to investors. Under the SEC proposal, generally speaking, the new rules would:

- Place limits on the amount of asset-based sales charges, or "ongoing sales charges," an investor would pay over time.
- Place a limit (e.g., 25 basis points per year) that may be deducted from fund assets for distribution or "marketing and service fees" such as advertising, sales compensation, and services.
- Require disclosure of any "ongoing sales charges" and any "marketing and service fees" in the fund's prospectus, shareholder reports, and investor transaction confirmations. Transaction confirmations also would have to describe the total sales charge rate that an investor would pay.
- Permit funds to sell shares through intermediaries at negotiated rates.
- Eliminate the need for fund directors to explicitly approve and re-approve fund distribution arrangements.

Additional information on the proposed new framework is available on the SEC's Web site (*www.sec.gov*).

Q 6:99 What are *management fees*?

Management fees compensate the investment manager for providing services to the fund. These fees can range from about 0.50 percent to 1.50 percent or more of average fund assets.

Q 6:100 What are "other" *administrative or operating costs*?

Other administrative costs generally include the costs of administering the portfolio, and are incurred principally through the provision of recordkeeping and transaction services to fund shareholders.

Q 6:101 What fees are reflected in a mutual fund's expense ratio?

A mutual fund's expense ratio comprises 12b-1 fees, management fees, and other administrative costs. This ratio usually represents the most significant cost of mutual fund ownership.

Q 6:102 How does a plan sponsor determine the fees charged by a particular mutual fund?

A mutual fund is required to disclose in its prospectus the fees paid by investors. Each fund is also required to estimate the impact of such fees over a number of years. Thus, if a mutual fund has a 1.03 percent expense ratio, its prospectus may contain, for example:

> The following examples are intended to help you compare the cost of investing in the fund with the cost of investing in other funds. The examples assume that you invest $10,000 in the fund for the time periods indicated and then redeem all your shares at the end of those periods. The examples also assume that your investment yields a 5 percent return each year, that all distributions are reinvested, and that the fund's operating expenses remain the same. Although your actual costs may be higher or lower, based on these assumptions your costs would be:

1 Year	*3 Years*	*5 Years*	*10 Years*
$105	$328	$569	$1,259

To assist plan participants in analyzing mutual fund fees, the SEC's Office of Investor Education and Assistance provides a variety of tools that can be found on the SEC's Web site (*www.sec.gov*); see, for example, the Mutual Fund Cost Calculator.

Q 6:103 What particular fees might be charged in a collective trust fund?

In a collective trust fund, a bank or trust company pools and invests monies of various investors. There are typically no front-end or back-end fees; however, there are trustee/investment management fees, administrative fees, and transaction costs.

Q 6:104 What particular fees might be charged in a variable annuity?

A *variable annuity* is a group annuity contract "wrapped" around investment alternatives, often various mutual funds, and may include one or more insurance elements. In addition to fees of underlying investments, the following fees may also be charged:

- Insurance-related charges associated with annuity features, interest and expense guarantees, and death benefits; and
- Surrender and transfer charges if the plan sponsor terminates the contract before the term of the contract expires, similar to a back-end load charged by a mutual fund.

Q 6:105 What particular costs are associated with a guaranteed investment contract fund?

Investment management, administrative, and transaction costs are associated with a guaranteed investment fund (GIC). The guaranteed rate may be net of these costs. The cost to an investor could include a penalty fee for early withdrawal.

Q 6:106 What types of revenue sharing do 401(k) plan service providers receive from mutual funds?

The types of compensation often referred to as revenue sharing, which service providers typically receive from investments, include:

- Mutual fund 12b-1 fees: Service providers such as brokers and retirement plan recordkeepers receive these fees in connection with the distribution (i.e., marketing) and servicing of the mutual fund's shares to plans.
- Subtransfer agency (sub-ta) or administration fees: Retirement plan recordkeepers receive these fees for recordkeeping services provided to investment providers in connection with the buying and selling of fund shares in plans. Fees shared vary and are calculated based on assets and/or on number of participant accounts.
- Some mutual fund companies provide other types of payments to service providers with whom they have a relationship. So-called finders' fees paid by mutual fund companies to brokers fall into this category.

The legal framework surrounding revenue-sharing arrangements and the importance of determining overall fees being paid by participants to 401(k) service providers are discussed in chapters 4 and 5.

Q 6:107 What are the current regulatory developments with regard to the 401(k) plan investments and fees?

The SEC conducted a study on payments made by mutual fund companies to investment consultants. In response, the SEC and the DOL jointly issued a guide for selecting investment consultants that is designed to identify potential conflicts of interest resulting from fee arrangements. (See chapter 4.)

The DOL has recently issued new rules to enhance fee disclosures in the 401(k) marketplace at both the plan level and the participant level. (See chapters 4 and 19 for further information on the new rules.)

See Q 6:28 and Q 6:98, respectively, regarding developments in the target date fund and 12b-1 fee areas.

Chapter 7

Participant Direction of Investments—ERISA Section 404(c)

Many 401(k) plans include an option for participants to choose how to invest the money in their plan accounts. A key reason why participant direction is often offered is the protection from fiduciary liability that is available in participant-directed plans. This chapter discusses regulations and other guidance issued under ERISA Section 404(c) by the Department of Labor (DOL) on how a participant-directed plan must be designed and operated in order to take advantage of this fiduciary relief.

Participant-Directed Plans 7-1
Broad Range of Investment Alternatives 7-4
Independent Exercise of Control 7-6
Disclosure Requirements 7-7
Investment Change Frequency 7-9
Investment Elections 7-11
Fiduciary Liability Relief 7-12
Qualified Default Investment Arrangements 7-14
Blackouts and Changes in Investment Options 7-29
Litigation Involving Participant-Directed Plans 7-30

Participant-Directed Plans

Q 7:1 What is a *participant-directed plan*?

A *participant-directed plan* is a plan in which each participant chooses how to invest the assets held in his or her account. Some of these plans are open-ended or have an open-ended feature; that is, a participant can invest in an unlimited array of investments. (See chapter 6 and chapter 19 for a discussion of self-directed, open-ended plans and features and ERISA Section 404(c).)

Most participant-directed plans offer participants a choice among a limited group of funds designated by the employer. This type of arrangement is the type of plan design that the ERISA Section 404(c) regulation focuses on. [DOL Reg. § 2550.404c-1]

Q 7:2 What is the rule concerning protection from fiduciary liability in participant-directed plans?

ERISA Section 404(c) states that if a participant in a defined contribution plan exercises control over the assets in his or her account, the participant will not be considered a fiduciary by reason of that control, and no other fiduciary shall be held responsible for losses resulting from that control. [ERISA § 404(c)] This general rule has been interpreted by the DOL in a 1992 DOL regulation. [DOL Reg. § 2550.404c-1]

Q 7:3 Are participant-directed plans required to comply with the DOL regulation?

No. Compliance with the DOL regulation is optional. Participant direction may be offered in a plan that does not satisfy the DOL regulation. [DOL Reg. § 2550.404c-1(a)(2)]

Q 7:4 What is the effect of having a participant-directed plan that does not comply with the DOL regulation?

According to the DOL, the DOL regulation sets the standard for obtaining relief under ERISA Section 404(c), but such standards are not intended to be applied in determining whether a noncompliant plan satisfies fiduciary duties. [DOL Reg. § 2550.404c-1(a)(2)]

Q 7:5 What are the general requirements of the DOL regulation on a participant-directed plan?

Under the DOL regulations, fiduciary protection is available to a participant-directed plan only if it meets the following requirements:

1. It permits participants to choose from a broad range of investment alternatives that meet certain criteria (see Q 7:9);
2. It provides an opportunity for participants to exercise control over the assets in their accounts. For this opportunity to exist, the following conditions must be present:
    a. Participants can give investment instructions to an identified plan fiduciary who is obligated to comply with those instructions (see Q 7:30).
    b. Participants are provided with sufficient information to permit informed investment decision making (see Qs 7:21–7:22).

c. Participants are permitted to make transfers among investment alternatives with a frequency commensurate with the volatility of the investments (see Qs 7:26–7:29).

[DOL Reg. § 2550.404c-1(b)]

Q 7:6 Must participants be able to select investments for all their accounts in a participant-directed plan?

No. It is not required that participants be given the option to choose their own investments with respect to all accounts in a plan. However, the protection from liability exists only in those accounts that permit participant investment direction. The right to direct investments is a protected benefit under Section 401(a)(4) of the Internal Revenue Code (Code), so if this right is offered only with respect to certain accounts, it cannot be offered in a way that results in discrimination in favor of highly compensated employees. [Treas. Reg. § 1.401(a)(4)-4(e)(3)]

Q 7:7 Must all employees and beneficiaries be given the same rights to direct their accounts?

Not necessarily. The protection from fiduciary liability is available with respect to investment decisions made by any person with a benefit under the plan. That includes participants, beneficiaries, and alternate payees. The plan can limit investment control to categories of people. [Preamble to DOL Reg. § 2550.404c-1] However, the right to direct investments is a protected benefit under Code Section 401(a)(4). Therefore, if this right is limited to a particular category of people, it cannot be limited in a way that discriminates in favor of highly compensated employees. [Treas. Reg. § 1.401(a)(4)-4(e)(3)]

Q 7:8 How does a plan become a 404(c) plan?

No notice is required to be filed with the IRS or the DOL concerning a plan's intent to comply with the Section 404(c) regulation. The plan must simply comply with the requirements of the regulation. (See Appendix C for a sample Section 404(c) compliance checklist.) This includes giving notice to plan participants that the plan is designed to comply with ERISA Section 404(c) and that plan fiduciaries may be relieved of liability for investment losses (see Q 7:22). This notice may be considered the "trigger" establishing the date when Section 404(c) protection becomes available. Although perhaps not the "trigger," the plan document may be drafted to reflect a plan's intent to comply with Section 404(c).

Broad Range of Investment Alternatives

Q 7:9 What is considered a broad range of investment alternatives?

The broad-range requirement is satisfied if the following conditions are met:

1. Participants are given a reasonable opportunity to materially affect the level of return and degree of risk to which their accounts are subject.
2. Participants are given the opportunity to choose from at least three investment alternatives that satisfy the following:
   a. Each alternative is diversified.
   b. Each alternative is materially different in terms of risk and return characteristics.
   c. In the aggregate, the alternatives enable participants to achieve a portfolio with aggregate risk and return characteristics at any point within a range normally appropriate for the participants.
   d. Each alternative, when combined with other alternatives, tends to minimize through diversification the overall risk of loss.
3. Participants must have the opportunity to diversify so as to minimize the risk of large losses, taking into account the nature of the plan investments and the size of participant accounts.

[DOL Reg. § 2550.404c-1(b)(3)(i)]

Q 7:10 What is an example of a group of funds that would satisfy the broad-range requirement?

The number and types of funds needed to satisfy the broad-range standard will vary depending on the age and income level of participants, the size of the participants' accounts and the nature of the funds. A typical group of funds that meets the broad-range standard might include a money market or stable value fund, a bond fund, and an equity fund.

Q 7:11 Will every plan be able to satisfy the broad-range standard using three funds?

No. Three funds are the minimum for any plan. If a plan covers a group of employees diversified in terms of age or income levels, uses funds at either end of the volatility spectrum, or uses small or specialized funds, it may be required to offer more than three funds to satisfy the broad-range standard.

Q 7:12 Can a fixed-rate investment be one of the three core funds satisfying the broad-range requirement?

Yes. The regulation specifically permits fixed-rate investments to serve as core funds. [DOL Reg. § 2550.404c-1(e)(1)]

Q 7:13 Can individual stocks or other individual assets be used to satisfy the broad-range requirement?

As a practical matter, no. The regulation requires that all participants in the plan, regardless of the dollar amounts of their accounts and/or years to retirement, must have an opportunity to diversify. Therefore, the required diversification is typically achieved by using either an open-ended approach or designated look-through funds (see Q 7:14).

Q 7:14 What are the advantages of using look-through funds to satisfy the broad-range requirement?

If a look-through fund (e.g., a mutual fund, a collective investment fund, or a fixed-rate insurance contract) is used, the underlying assets held in the fund will be considered for purposes of determining whether the diversification requirement is met. [DOL Reg. § 2550.404c-1(b)(3)(ii)] Therefore, in a new plan or any plan in which participants have relatively small account balances, look-through funds will be the only means of achieving diversification under a designated investment approach. [DOL Reg. § 2550.404c-1(b)(3)(i)(C)]

Q 7:15 Is ERISA Section 404(c) protection available for investment in employer securities?

Yes. Employer securities may be offered in a 401(k) plan, and ERISA Section 404(c) protection can extend to those investments. An employer security cannot function as one of the minimum three core funds, however, since it is not a diversified investment. [Preamble to DOL Reg. § 2550.404c-1] As with any investment option offered to participants, plan fiduciaries with investment responsibility must select and monitor the employer stock offering (see chapter 6).

Q 7:16 Are there any restrictions on the types of employer securities that can be offered in an ERISA Section 404(c) plan?

Yes. The securities offered must be qualifying securities under ERISA Section 407(d)(5). In addition, they must meet all of the following requirements:

1. The securities must be publicly traded and traded with sufficient frequency to permit prompt execution of participants' investment instructions.
2. Participants and beneficiaries investing in employer securities must receive all information that is provided to the shareholders.
3. All voting, tender, and similar rights with respect to the securities must be passed through to participants.

[DOL Reg. § 2550.404c-1(d)(2)(ii)(E)(4)]

Q 7:17 Are there special procedures that must be followed in an ERISA Section 404(c) plan that offers employer securities?

Yes. The following procedures must all be followed:

1. The plan must have procedures in place concerning the purchase and sale of employer securities as well as the exercise of any voting, tender, or other rights that are designed to ensure the confidentiality of these transactions.
2. The plan must designate a fiduciary to ensure that the procedures are being followed and that, when required (as in procedure 3), an independent fiduciary is designated.
3. An independent fiduciary must be appointed in connection with any transaction involving employer securities whenever there is a potential for undue influence (e.g., in a tender offer situation or when there is competition for board of directors' positions). [DOL Reg. § 2550.404c-1(d)(2)(ii)(E)(4)]

The plan must offer participants the ability to transfer funds out of employer securities and into any of the core funds with certain frequency (see Q 7:27).

It should be noted that limiting investment in employer securities to some specified percentage (e.g., 25 percent of a participant's account balance) does not affect the availability of Section 404(c) relief inasmuch as it does not relate to core funds. [DOL Reg. § 2550.404c-1(f)(4)]

Independent Exercise of Control

Q 7:18 When is a participant's exercise of control considered independent?

The determination as to whether a participant has exercised independent control, in order for ERISA Section 404(c) protection to apply, is made through a facts-and-circumstances analysis. The exercise of control will fail to be independent if any of the following conditions exists:

1. A plan fiduciary uses improper influence with respect to a transaction (e.g., a plan fiduciary offers some type of incentive to participants selecting a particular investment alternative).
2. A fiduciary has concealed material, nonpublic facts that he or she is not prohibited from revealing under any federal or state law not preempted by ERISA.
3. A fiduciary accepts instructions from a participant knowing him or her to be legally incompetent.

[DOL Reg. § 2550.404c-1(c)(2)]

Q 7:19 How do the rules apply to a plan that uses investment managers?

The individual investment decisions of an investment manager, who is designated directly by a participant or who manages a look-through investment vehicle selected by the employer, will not be considered the direct and necessary result of the designation of the investment manager or of the decision to invest in the look-through investment vehicle. In either situation, the investment manager will remain responsible for its decisions, and the employer or other plan fiduciary will not lose the protection it would otherwise have under ERISA Section 404(c) with respect to those decisions. [DOL Reg. § 2550.404c-1(d)(2)(iii)]

Q 7:20 How do the rules apply with respect to voting, tender, or similar rights?

Section 404(c) protection is available with respect to voting, tender, or similar rights associated with an investment alternative passed through to participants. Protection is available if (1) the participant's investment in the alternative was itself an exercise of control; (2) the participant was provided a reasonable opportunity to give instructions with respect to such rights, including being provided with any materials provided to the plan relating to the exercise of such rights; and (3) the participant has not failed to exercise independent control due to circumstances described in Q 7:18. [DOL Reg. § 2550.404c-1(c)(1)(ii); 75 Fed. Reg. 64,946 (Oct. 20, 2010)]

Disclosure Requirements

Q 7:21 In general, what information must be provided to participants about the plan's available investment alternatives?

In general, participants must be given sufficient information about the investment alternatives to make meaningful investment choices. If the plan uses designated funds, plan fiduciaries have an affirmative obligation to provide participants with information about those fund options. This obligation is not limited to just those investments intended to satisfy the broad-range requirement (see Q 7:9). Participants must be given information on all available alternatives. Participants must also be given sufficient information to permit informed decision making with respect to any voting rights or other incidents of ownership that are passed on to them in connection with an investment. [DOL Reg. § 2550.404c-1(b)(2)(i)(B)]

Q 7:22 What specific information must be given to participants?

The disclosure requirements under ERISA Section 404(c) regulations were amended when the participant disclosure requirements under DOL Regulation Section 2550.404a-5, applicable to participant-directed plans regardless of

404(c) status, were finalized (see chapter 19). Under the amended regulations, the disclosure requirements applicable to participant-directed plans generally were integrated into the 404(c) requirements, thus avoiding the need to follow two sets of disclosure rules. [75 Fed. Reg. 64,910 (Oct. 20, 2010)]

As a result of this integration, the only two additional disclosure requirements applicable solely to 404(c) plans after the participant disclosure requirements went into effect are: (1) the explanation that the plan is intended to comply with Section 404(c), and (2) if the plan offers an employer securities alternative, a description of the procedures for maintaining confidentiality when a participant invests in employer securities and the name, address, and telephone number of the plan fiduciary responsible for monitoring compliance with the procedures. Another key change was the elimination of the automatic prospectus delivery requirement.

For plan years beginning on or after November 1, 2011, a plan fiduciary (or a person designated by the plan fiduciary to act on his or her behalf) must provide participants with the following information:

1. An explanation that the plan is an ERISA Section 404(c) plan, and that plan fiduciaries may be relieved of liability for any losses that are the direct and necessary result of the participant's investment instructions;
2. The information required pursuant to the participant disclosure requirements applicable to participant-directed plans under DOL Regulation Section 2550.404a-5 (see section on Participant Investment and Fee Disclosures in chapter 19); and
3. If the plan permits investment in employer securities, a description of the procedures for maintaining confidentiality of transactions, as well as the name, address, and telephone number of the plan fiduciary responsible for monitoring compliance with the procedures.

[DOL Reg. § 2550.404c-1(b)(2)(i)(B); 75 Fed. Reg. 64,910 (Oct. 20, 2010)]

The DOL provided transition rules extending the applicability date of the participant disclosure requirements under DOL Regulations Section 2550.404a-5 (see chapter 19). In May 2012, the DOL clarified that a fiduciary of a 404(c) plan does not have to provide information required under that regulation before that information must be provided under the participant disclosure requirements, taking into account the regulation's transition rules. [DOL Field Assist. Bull. 2012-02R]

See chapter 19 for a discussion of using electronic media for complying with ERISA's disclosure requirements.

Q 7:23 Can a mutual fund Summary Prospectus be used to satisfy a requirement to provide a prospectus to participants?

Under a recent SEC rule, mutual fund prospectus delivery requirements can be satisfied by the delivery of a Summary Prospectus and providing the full prospectus ("statutory prospectus") on an Internet Web site. The requirements applicable to Summary Prospectuses are detailed in the final rule. [74 Fed. Reg. 4,546 (Jan. 26, 2009)]

According to the DOL, the delivery of a Summary Prospectus by an identified plan fiduciary or designee satisfies the prospectus delivery requirements under ERISA Section 404(c). [DOL Field Assist. Bull. 2009-03] The DOL confirmed this position with regard to the requirement to provide a prospectus upon request under the participant disclosure requirements (under DOL Regulations Section 2550.404a-5) that were integrated into the ERISA Section 404(c) requirements. (See Q 7:22 and chapter 19.) [DOL Reg. § 2550.404a-5(d)(4)(i)]

Q 7:24 What other special requirement must be considered in connection with meeting ERISA disclosure requirements?

Under DOL requirements, the SPD of a plan intending to comply must specifically state that the plan is an ERISA Section 404(c) plan. If Section 404(c) is intended to apply to only certain aspects of the plan, or if participants have the right to direct only certain investments in their accounts, such information should be communicated in the SPD in a clear, understandable manner. [DOL Reg. § 2520.102-3(d)]

Q 7:25 Are employers obligated to provide investment advice or investment education to 401(k) plan participants?

No. The DOL regulation specifically states that plan fiduciaries are not obligated to provide investment advice [DOL Reg. § 2550.404c-1(c)(4)], nor is there a general requirement to provide investment education. An employer may have good reasons for wanting to give participants general information about long-term investing, however. This type of information may help participants achieve their investment goals and thereby reduce the possibility for participant claims in the future. However, there is nothing in the DOL regulation that requires employers or other plan fiduciaries to provide this type of education to participants.

In DOL Bulletin 96-1 [DOL Reg. § 2509.96-1] (discussed in detail in chapter 8), the DOL offers guidance on how employers can provide meaningful investment education to participants without giving investment advice under ERISA.

Investment Change Frequency

Q 7:26 How frequently must participants be permitted to change their investment choices?

The general standard is that participants must be permitted to make investment changes with a frequency that is appropriate in light of the volatility of the investment. Participants must be permitted to make investment changes at least once within any three-month period among at least three of the investment alternatives made available under the plan that satisfy the broad-range requirement. [DOL Reg. § 2550.404c-1(b)(2)(ii)(C)(1)]

Q 7:27 How do the investment change-frequency rules apply in a plan offering investment alternatives with different volatility levels (or more frequent change opportunities)?

If a plan offers quarterly changes for its three core funds and then adds a fund with a higher level of volatility, the plan must permit participants to move out of the more volatile fund and into at least one of the core funds, or an income-producing, low-risk, liquid fund, with the same degree of frequency that is available for the more volatile investment. [DOL Reg. § 2550.404c-1(b)(2)(ii)(C)(2)]

In the case of employer securities, the participants must be able to transfer into any one of the core investment alternatives intended to satisfy the broad-range requirement or, alternatively, into an income-producing, low-risk, liquid fund as frequently as they are permitted to give instructions with respect to employer securities. If the income-fund method is used, participants must be able to make transfers out of the income fund and into any one of the core funds as frequently as they are permitted to give instructions with respect to each core fund. [DOL Reg. § 2550.404c-1(b)(2)(ii)(C)(3)]

Q 7:28 Can a fund with transfer restrictions or transfer fees satisfy the rules concerning transfer frequency?

Yes. A fund that contains early withdrawal penalties, back-end commissions, or other restrictions on transfer will not automatically lose Section 404(c) protection because of the change-frequency requirement. However, the charges or other restrictions must be reasonable in light of the investment and cannot have the effect of limiting a participant's actual ability to make investment changes in accordance with the regulation. [Preamble to DOL Reg. § 2550.404c-1] (See also Q 7:33.)

Q 7:29 Can actions to limit market timing, such as the imposition of redemption fees, impact a plan's Section 404(c) status?

It depends. Some mutual funds have limits on transfers in and out of a fund and redemption fee policies to prevent improper market timing activity. Such restrictions, according to the DOL, should not impact a plan's Section 404(c) status, as long as:

- The restrictions are "reasonable";
- The restrictions are allowed under the terms of the plan; and
- The restrictions are clearly disclosed to participants.

See chapter 5 for more information on market timing and redemption fees.

Investment Elections

Q 7:30 What procedures must be used to obtain investment elections?

A participant must have a reasonable opportunity to give investment instructions, in writing or otherwise, to an identified plan fiduciary obligated to comply with those instructions. The participant also must have the opportunity to receive confirmation of the transaction in writing. [DOL Reg. § 2550.404c-1(b)(2)(i)(A)]

Q 7:31 Can a default election be used for participants who fail to make an election?

Yes, but the protection offered under ERISA Section 404(c) may not be available for investments not made as a result of a participant's affirmative election. Therefore, if a default option is used in a plan, the employer may remain responsible for transactions into that default fund (see Q 7:40). Once an affirmative election has been made by a participant, it may be given effect until affirmatively revoked. [Preamble to DOL Reg. § 2550.404c-1]

Q 7:32 May a fiduciary place any restrictions on participant investment rights?

Yes. Fiduciaries may decline to implement any of the following types of instructions:

1. Any instruction that would result in a prohibited transaction under ERISA;
2. Any instruction that would generate taxable income to a plan;
3. Any instruction that would be contrary to the plan document;
4. Any instruction that would cause the plan to maintain the indicia of ownership of assets held outside the jurisdiction of United States courts;
5. Any investment that would jeopardize the plan's tax-qualified status; and
6. Any instruction that could result in a loss to the participant in excess of the participant's account balance.

[DOL Reg. §§ 2550.404c-1(d)(2)(ii), 2550.404c-1(b)(2)(ii)(B)]

A plan may also impose reasonable restrictions on a participant's ability to make transfers. For example, it may require a minimum transfer of $100 or 5 percent of the amount to be invested. Any such restriction, however, must bear a reasonable relationship to the administrative costs attendant to such transactions and be applied on a reasonable and consistent basis. A plan cannot place a maximum limit on the amount to be transferred to any investment alternative that is necessary to satisfy the broad range requirement. [Preamble to DOL Reg. § 2550.404c-1]

Q 7:33 May fees associated with investment choices be charged directly to participants' accounts?

Yes. A plan may charge participants' accounts with any reasonable expenses of carrying out their investment instructions. The plan must periodically inform participants of the actual expenses incurred in their individual accounts. [DOL Reg. § 2550.404c-1(b)(2)(ii)(A)]

Fiduciary Liability Relief

Q 7:34 What relief from liability is available to fiduciaries in an ERISA Section 404(c) plan?

Two consequences result from maintaining a complying Section 404(c) plan. One is that the participants and beneficiaries making investment decisions will not be considered plan fiduciaries simply by reason of controlling investment of their accounts. The second, more significant result is that plan fiduciaries will not be held responsible for any loss that is a direct and necessary result of a participant's exercise of control. [DOL Reg. § 2550.404c-1(d)(2)] Generally, relief is offered from the prudence and diversification requirements of ERISA.

To take advantage of this fiduciary relief, two conditions must be present:

1. The plan must be designed as a Section 404(c) plan—in other words, it must offer a broad range of investment alternatives, offer change dates at least quarterly for its three core funds, provide the disclosure required in the regulation, and so forth.
2. The participant must have actually exercised control with respect to whatever transaction is at issue.

The responsible fiduciary must also ensure that the requirements are met on an ongoing basis.

Q 7:35 What responsibilities, according to the DOL, can fiduciaries not avoid in participant-directed plans that comply with ERISA Section 404(c)?

According to the DOL, ERISA Section 404(c) does not relieve a fiduciary from its duty to prudently select and monitor any service provider or designated investment alternative offered under the plan. [DOL Reg. § 2550.404c-1(d)(2)(iv); 75 Fed. Reg. 64,946 (Oct. 10, 2010)] Relief is also not available for transactions described in Q 7:32.

Fiduciaries will also remain responsible for maintaining procedures to comply with the information disclosure requirements, as well as the special procedures required in the event employer securities are offered as an investment alternative. There is also no relief from the IRS prohibited transaction rules. [DOL Reg. § 2550.404c-1(d)(3)]

Special requirements must be met for Section 404(c) protection to apply to investments in a default fund and during a blackout or change in investment options (see Qs 7:40–7:72) and to investments in employer securities (see Qs 7:15–7:17).

Q 7:36 How do ERISA's fiduciary rules apply to participant-directed plans that do not comply with ERISA Section 404(c)?

A participant's investment decision in a plan that does not comply with ERISA Section 404(c) may be judged according to ERISA's general fiduciary rules.

According to the U.S. Court of Appeals for the Seventh Circuit, ERISA Section 404(c) is not the only means by which a fiduciary can avoid liability for participant-directed investments. If investment decision-making authority is properly delegated to participants, ERISA will not require plan fiduciaries to review each participant's investment directions for appropriateness. According to the court, fiduciaries must communicate material facts affecting the interests of plan participants and beneficiaries even if the participants and beneficiaries do not ask for the information. [Jenkins v. Yager, 444 F.3d 916 (7th Cir. 2006)]

Q 7:37 Is compliance with the DOL's regulation worth the protection offered?

If a plan already offers three or more funds that satisfy the broad-range requirement, permits quarterly transfers, and is capable of implementing procedures to satisfy the disclosure requirements, it makes sense to comply, particularly after the disclosure requirements applicable to participant-directed plans, regardless of 404(c) status, were integrated into the ERISA Section 404(c) disclosure requirements (see Q 7:22).

Q 7:38 How should an ERISA Section 404(c) plan be reported on Form 5500?

Form 5500, Annual Return/Report of Employee Benefit Plan, requires that the preparer indicate, in item 8a, whether a plan is participant-directed and whether it is intended to meet the requirements of ERISA Section 404(c). More specifically, item 8a requires a disclosure of "Plan Characteristic Codes," which include, among others, the following options:

Code	*Plan Characteristic*
2F	ERISA Section 404(c) Plan—This plan, or any part, is intended to meet the conditions of 29 C.F.R. § 2550.404c-1.
2G	Total participant-directed account plans—Participants have the opportunity to direct the investment of all the assets allocated to their individual accounts, regardless of whether 29 C.F.R. § 2550.404c-1 is intended to be met.

Code	*Plan Characteristic*
2H	Partial participant-directed account plan—Participants have the opportunity to direct the investments of a portion of the assets allocated to their individual accounts, regardless of whether 29 C.F.R. § 2550.404c-1 is intended to be met.

Q 7:39 What was the effective date of the final ERISA Section 404(c) regulation issued by the DOL?

The final ERISA Section 404(c) regulation was effective with respect to transactions occurring on or after the first day of the second plan year beginning after October 12, 1992 (or January 1, 1994, for a calendar-year plan). For collectively bargained plans, the regulation became effective on the later of the general effective date or the date the last collective bargaining agreement ratified before October 13, 1992, terminated. [DOL Reg. § 2550.404c-1(g)] Because compliance with the regulation is optional, a plan sponsor can elect to comply at a later time and receive ERISA Section 404(c) protection from the date compliance is achieved.

In October 2010, the DOL issued amendments to the ERISA Section 404(c) regulation to integrate new participant disclosure requirements (i.e., fee and investment disclosures) applicable to participant-directed plans (see Q 7:22 and chapter 19). The amendments also clarified the DOL's position regarding fiduciary responsibilities with respect to selecting and monitoring service providers or designated investment alternative offered under the plan (see Q 7:35).

Qualified Default Investment Arrangements

Q 7:40 Can ERISA Section 404(c) protection be obtained in connection with default investments used when participants fail to make an investment election?

The protection available under ERISA Section 404(c) is generally available for investments made as a result of a participant's affirmative election.

The Pension Protection Act of 2006 extends fiduciary relief under Section 404(c) to investments in certain types of default arrangements in the absence of participant investment direction. To obtain protection, two conditions must be met:

1. Participant contributions must be invested in accordance with DOL regulations (i.e., in a qualified default investment alternative (QDIA)) (see Q 7:41); and
2. Participant notice requirements must be met (see Q 7:54).

[ERISA § 404(c)(5)]

The extended relief was crafted to increase plan participation through the adoption of automatic enrollment provisions and increase in retirement savings through use of default investments that are more likely to increase retirement savings for participants who do not direct their own investments. (See chapter 2 for discussion of automatic enrollment designs.)

Q 7:41 What is a *qualified default investment alternative* for purposes of Section 404(c) protection?

According to DOL regulations, a *qualified default investment alternative* (QDIA) is an investment that meets all of the following requirements:

1. It does not hold or permit the acquisition of employer securities, unless the employer securities are either
   a. held or acquired by a mutual fund or a similar pooled investment vehicle regulated and subject to periodic examination by a state or federal agency in accordance with stated investment objectives, independent of the plan sponsor or an affiliate thereof, or
   b. acquired as a matching contribution from the employer/plan sponsor or were acquired by the participant prior to management by the investment management service, provided the investment management service can exercise discretion over such securities.
2. It satisfies the requirement that a participant may transfer, in whole or in part, his or her investment from the QDIA to any other investment alternative available under the plan (see Q 7:43).
3. It is:
   a. managed by an investment manager, within the meaning of ERISA Section 3(38); a trustee of the plan that meets the requirements of ERISA Section 3(38)(A), (B), and (C); or the plan sponsor who is a named fiduciary within the meaning of ERISA Section 402(a)(2);
   b. an investment company registered under the Investment Company Act of 1940; or
   c. an investment product or fund described in Q 7:49 or Q 7:50 (a so-called short-term or grandfathered QDIA).
4. It constitutes one of the following types of investment products (a so-called long-term QDIA):
   a. An investment fund product or model portfolio that applies generally accepted investment theories, is diversified so as to minimize the risk of large losses, and is designed to provide varying degrees of long-term appreciation and capital preservation through a mix of equity and fixed-income exposures based on the participant's age, target retirement date (e.g., normal retirement age under the plan) or life expectancy. Such products and portfolios change their asset allocations and associated risk levels over time with the objective of becoming more conservative (i.e., decreasing risk of losses) with increasing age. It is not required to take into account risk tolerances, investments,

or other preferences of an individual participant. An example of such a fund or portfolio may be a "life cycle" or "targeted-retirement-date" fund or account.

b. An investment fund product or model portfolio that applies generally accepted investment theories, is diversified so as to minimize the risk of large losses, and is designed to provide long-term appreciation and capital preservation through a mix of equity and fixed-income exposures consistent with a target level of risk appropriate for participants of the plan as a whole. It is not required to take into account an individual participant's age, risk tolerance, investments, or other preferences (but should take in account the plan's demographics as a whole). An example of such a fund or portfolio may be a "balanced" fund.

c. An investment management service with respect to which an investment manager, applying generally accepted investment theories, allocates the assets of a participant's individual account to achieve varying degrees of long-term appreciation and capital preservation through a mix of equity and fixed income exposures, offered through investment alternatives available under the plan, based on the participant's age, target retirement date (e.g., normal retirement age under the plan), or life expectancy. Such portfolios are diversified so as to minimize the risk of large losses and change their asset allocations and associated risk levels for an individual account over time with the objective of becoming more conservative (i.e., decreasing risk of losses) with increasing age. It is not required to take into account an individual participant's risk tolerance, investments, or other preferences. An example of an investment management service may be a "managed account."

[DOL Reg. § 2550.404c-5(e)]

Q 7:42 What other conditions must be met for Section 404(c) protection to extend to default investments?

In addition to investing in a QDIA, a default investment arrangement must meet the following requirements to receive Section 404(c) protection:

1. Participants and beneficiaries had the opportunity to direct the investment of assets but did not do so. No relief is available, for example, when a participant or beneficiary has provided affirmative investment direction concerning the assets invested on the participant's or beneficiary's behalf.
2. Participants and beneficiaries receive a notice at least 30 days in advance of the date of plan eligibility, or the first such investment in the QDIA; or on or before the date of plan eligibility if participants can take a 90-day permissible withdrawal under an EACA (see chapter 2); and within a reasonable period of time at least 30 days in advance of each subsequent plan year. (See Q 7:54 for notice content requirements.)

3. Participants and beneficiaries receive the following material relating to the investment in a QDIA:
   - If the QDIA is subject to the Securities Act of 1933, a copy of the most recent prospectus provided to the plan (immediately before or after a participant's or beneficiary's initial investment in the QDIA, i.e., automatic prospectus delivery requirement);
   - Any materials provided to the plan relating to the exercise of voting, tender, or similar rights to the extent such rights are passed through to participants and beneficiaries under the plan, as well as a description of or reference to plan provisions relating to the exercise of those rights; and
   - Information that must be provided under ERISA Section 404(c) *upon request* (see Q 7:22).
4. The plan offers participants and beneficiaries the opportunity to invest in a broad range of investment alternatives consistent with Section 404(c) standards (see Q 7:9).

(See also Q 7:43 regarding the transferability requirement.)

[DOL Reg. § 2550.404c-5(c)]

The automatic prospectus delivery requirement under the Section 404(c) regulations was eliminated under amended rules that go into effect for plan years beginning on or after November 1, 2011 (see Q 7:22).

In November 2010, the DOL issued proposed amendments to the QDIA requirements that would change the requirements in item 3 above to clarify the requirements under amended rules (see Q 7:22). Under the amended rules, participants and beneficiaries must receive the following information relating to the QDIA:

- Subsequent to investment, any materials provided to the plan relating to the exercise of voting, tender, and similar rights, to the extent such rights are passed through to participants under the terms of the plans.
- Information that must be provided upon request under the new participant disclosure requirements applicable to participant-directed plans (i.e., copies of prospectuses or similar documents; copies of financial statements, shareholder reports or similar information; statement of value; and underlying asset information) (see chapter 19).

[75 Fed. Reg. 73,987 (Nov. 30, 2010)]

See also chapter 19 for information on required participant investment and fee disclosures applicable to designated investment alternatives under the plan.

Q 7:43 What requirements must a QDIA meet with respect to the participant's ability to transfer out of the QDIA?

A participant must be able to transfer all or part of the assets in the QDIA to any other investment alternative under the plan with a frequency that is afforded participants who elected to invest in the QDIA, but not less frequently than once within any three-month period.

Any transfers or withdrawals made during the 90-day period beginning on the date of the participant's first elective contribution, a date determined by Code Section 414(w)(2) applicable to EACAs (see chapter 2), or other first investment shall not be subject to any restrictions, fees, or expenses (including surrender charges, liquidation or exchange fees, redemption fees, and similar expenses charged in connection with the liquidation of, or transfer from, the investment). This would not include fees and expenses charged on an ongoing basis for the operation of the investment itself (e.g., investment management fees, distribution and/or service fees, 12b-1 fees, or legal, accounting, transfer agent and similar administrative expenses), and are not imposed, or do not vary, based on a participant's decision to withdraw, sell, or transfer assets out of the QDIA.

After the 90-day period, any transfer or permissible withdrawal shall not be subject to restrictions, fees, or expenses not otherwise applicable to a participant who elected to invest in the QDIA. [DOL Reg. § 2550.404c-5(c)(5)]

Q 7:44 Would the payment of a fee or expense (such as a redemption fee) by a plan sponsor or service provider that would otherwise be assessed to the account of a participant or beneficiary during the initial 90-day period satisfy the requirements?

Yes. To the extent that any such fees or expenses otherwise assessed to the account of a participant or beneficiary are paid by the plan sponsor or a service provider, and not by the participant or beneficiary or the plan generally, such fees or expenses would not inhibit a participant's or beneficiary's decision to opt out of the investment alternative and the policy objective of the requirement would be satisfied. It is unclear how these payments would be treated for the purposes of the Internal Revenue Code. [DOL Field Assist. Bull. 2008-03]

Q 7:45 Does the 90-day period start from the date an investment becomes a QDIA, or does it begin only in reference to a participant who is newly "defaulted" into a QDIA?

The 90-day condition on restrictions, fees, or expenses does not apply to participants or beneficiaries who have "existing" assets invested in the plan as of the effective date of the QDIA regulation. For example, if a plan, prior to the effective date of the QDIA regulation, used a balanced fund as its default investment, and the balanced fund qualifies as a QDIA under the QDIA regulation, the plan sponsor may wish to continue to use this fund as its default investment and obtain relief under the regulation.

If a new participant is enrolled in the plan on or after the effective date of the QDIA regulation, the 90-day restriction will apply with respect to the first elective contribution or other investment that is made into the balanced fund QDIA on behalf of that participant. [DOL Field Assist. Bull. 2008-03]

Q 7:46 Is a QDIA prohibited from including any "round-trip" restriction for the first 90 days?

No. According to the DOL, "round-trip" restrictions, unlike fees and expenses assessed directly upon liquidation of, or transfer from, an investment, generally affect only a participant's ability to reinvest in the QDIA for a limited period of time. However, to the extent that a "round-trip" restriction would affect a participant's or beneficiary's ability to liquidate or transfer from a QDIA or restrict a participant's or beneficiary's ability to invest in any other investment alternative available under the plan, it would be impermissible for purposes of the QDIA regulation. [73 Fed. Reg. 23,349 (Apr. 30, 2008)]

Q 7:47 Would an investment fund or product with zero fixed income (or, alternatively, zero equity) qualify as one of the so-called long-term QDIAs described in Q 7:41?

No. Each of the so-called longer-term QDIAs described in Q 7:41 requires that the investment fund product, model portfolio, or investment management service be "diversified so as to minimize the risk of large losses" and be designed to provide varying degrees of long-term appreciation and capital preservation through a mix of equity and fixed-income exposures. Although an investment option with no fixed-income component may be appropriate for certain individuals actively directing their own investments, a QDIA must have some fixed-income exposure. Similarly, a fund, product, or service with no equity exposure cannot qualify as a QDIA for the purposes of the QDIA regulation.

The regulation does not establish minimum fixed income or equity exposures necessary to satisfy the requirement for a mix within a QDIA. [DOL Field Assist. Bull. 2008-03]

Q 7:48 Can a committee that is established by a plan sponsor and that, pursuant to the documents and instruments governing the plan, is a named fiduciary of the plan be treated as managing a QDIA?

Yes. A committee of the plan sponsor may manage a qualified default investment alternative. [DOL Reg. § 2550.404c-5(e)(3)(i)(C)]

Q 7:49 Under what conditions can a capital preservation fund be a QDIA (a so-called short-term QDIA)?

An investment product or fund designed to preserve principal and provide a reasonable rate of return, whether or not such return is guaranteed, consistent with liquidity can qualify as a QDIA, provided:

- It seeks to maintain, over the term of the investment, the dollar value that is equal to the amount invested in the product; and
- It is offered by a state-regulated or federally regulated financial institution.

A capital preservation fund can qualify as a QDIA for not more than 120 days after the date of the participant's first elective contribution, as determined under Code Section 414(w)(2)(B). (See chapter 2 for discussion of how the date of a participant's first elective contribution under EACA is determined.) [DOL Reg. § 2550.404c-5(e)(4)(iv)]

The 120-day capital preservation QDIA is intended to provide administrative flexibility to plans that satisfy the EACA requirements and allow employees to make permissible withdrawals (see chapter 2). According to the DOL, the use of the 120-day capital preservation QDIA for the investment of assets other than assets contributed pursuant to an EACA will not obtain fiduciary relief under the regulation. For example, use of the 120-day capital preservation QDIA for a rollover from an IRA or other plan would not relieve a plan sponsor from liability under the QDIA regulation (unless the rollover was made during the 120-day period following a participant's first EACA contribution). [DOL Field Assist. Bull. 2008-03]

Q 7:50 Under what conditions can a stable value fund be a long-term QDIA (a so-called grandfathered QDIA)?

An investment product or fund designed to (1) preserve principal, (2) provide a rate of return generally consistent with that earned on intermediate investment grade bonds, and (3) provide liquidity for withdrawals, including for transfers to other investment alternatives, can qualify as a QDIA if:

- There are no fees or surrender charges imposed in connection with withdrawals initiated by a participant or beneficiary; and
- It invests primarily in investment products that are backed by state-regulated or federally regulated financial institutions.

A stable value fund can qualify as a QDIA only with respect to assets invested in the product or fund before December 24, 2007. [DOL Reg. § 2550.404c-5(e)(4)(v)]]

Q 7:51 Are plan sponsors required to provide a 120-day capital preservation QDIA?

No. A plan sponsor is not required to use any of the QDIAs described in the regulation for its plan, including the 120-day capital preservation QDIA. The 120-day capital preservation QDIA was included in the regulation to afford plan sponsors the flexibility of using a capital preservation investment alternative for the investment of contributions during the period when employees are most likely to opt out of plan participation. [DOL Field Assist. Bull. 2008-03]

Q 7:52 Can a plan sponsor manage the 120-day capital preservation QDIA?

Generally, no. The investment fund or product must be offered by a State or federally regulated financial institution as required in the QDIA regulation. [DOL Field Assist. Bull. 2008-03]

Q 7:53 Can a variable annuity, collective trust fund, or unallocated deferred annuity contract qualify as a QDIA?

Yes. An investment product or model portfolio that otherwise meets the QDIA requirements and is offered though a variable annuity or similar contract or through common or collective trust funds or pooled investment funds can qualify as a QDIA. [DOL Reg. § 2550.404c-5(e)(4)(vi)]

In an Information Letter released in 2014, the DOL indicated that a series of target date funds that invest in unallocated deferred annuity contracts could satisfy the requirements of a QDIA, provided that:

1. The series of funds is as described in IRS Notice 2014-66 relating to satisfying the nondiscrimination requirements applicable to plan rights and features (see chapter 6);
2. The fund's designated investment manager satisfies ERISA prudence requirements in selecting annuity contracts (see chapter 16); and
3. The plan sponsor, as the appointing fiduciary, prudently selects and monitors the investment manager.

The DOL provided the following additional information on the funds:

- An "unallocated deferred annuity contract" is an insurance contract that promises to pay income to covered plan participants at some future date (possibly far into the future) on a regular basis for a period of time or for life. The annuity is written on behalf of a group of participants and not issued to and owned by a specific individual. As such, unallocated deferred annuity contracts do not ordinarily require the insurance company to have or maintain any personal information on individuals in the group. Rather, units of the unallocated annuity generally are largely interchangeable among members of the covered group, which facilitates transferability and allocation within the group—for example, at the dissolution date of each fund.
- Each fund within the series is available only to participants who will attain normal retirement age within a limited number of years around the fund's target date. For example, the 2020 Fund is restricted to participants who will attain normal retirement age within a limited number of years (e.g., 3 years) around 2020.
- Each fund dissolves at its target date, and participants with an interest in the fund will receive an annuity certificate providing for immediate or deferred commencement of annuity payments. The certificate represents the participant's interest in the unallocated deferred annuity contracts held

by the fund. For instance, if a fund's asset mix contains a 50 percent investment in unallocated deferred annuity contracts, half of each participant's individual account balance will be reflected in the certificate. The remaining portion of each such participant's interest in the fund will be reinvested by the participant or plan fiduciary in other plan investment alternatives.

[DOL Information Letter (Oct. 23, 2014)]

Q 7:54 What information must be conveyed in notices regarding default investment arrangements?

Notices to participants regarding default investment arrangements must be written in a manner calculated to be understood by the average plan participant and contain the following:

1. A description of the circumstances under which assets in the individual account of a participant or beneficiary may be invested on behalf of the participant and beneficiary in a QDIA, and, if applicable, an explanation of the circumstances under which elective contributions will be made on behalf of a participant, the percentage of such contributions, and the right of the participant to elect not to have such contributions made on his or her behalf (or to elect to have such contributions made at a different percentage);
2. An explanation of the right of the participants and beneficiaries to direct the investment of their individual accounts;
3. A description of the QDIA, including a description of the investment objectives, risk and return characteristics (if applicable), and fees and expenses attendant to the investment alternative;
4. A description of the right of the participants and beneficiaries on whose behalf assets are invested in a QDIA to direct the investment of those assets to any other investment alternative under the plan, including a description of any applicable restrictions, fees, or expenses in connection with such transfer; and
5. An explanation of where the participants and beneficiaries can obtain investment information concerning the other investment alternatives available under the plan.

[DOL Reg. § 2550.404c-5(d)]

If the plan has both automatic enrollment (QACA and/or EACA) and QDIA features, required notices under both features can be satisfied with a single notice. [Preamble to DOL Reg. § 2550.404c-5; 72 Fed. Reg. 60,452 (Oct. 24, 2007)] See Appendixes B and C for sample notices.

In November 2010, the DOL proposed amendments to the QDIA regulation to provide more specificity as to the information that must be provided concerning investments in QDIAs, including target date or similar investments. (With respect to information regarding target-date investments, the additional information must be provided to all participants under the participant disclosure requirements applicable to participant-directed plans (see chapter 19).)

More specifically, requirements 3, 4, and 5 above would be changed as set forth below.

3. A description of the QDIA, including:
   - The name of the investment's issuer
   - The investment's objectives or goals
   - The investment's principal strategies (including a general description of the types of assets held by the investment) and principal risks'
   - The investment's historical performance data and a statement indicating that an investment's past performance is not necessarily an indication of how the investment will perform in the future; and, if applicable, a description of any fixed return, annuity, guarantee, death benefit, or other ancillary features
   - The investment's fees and expenses, including:
     a. Any fees charged directly against the amount invested in connection with acquisition, sale, transfer of, or withdrawal (e.g., commissions, sales loads, sales charges, deferred sales charges, redemption fees, surrender charges, exchange fees, account fees, and purchase fees);
     b. Any annual operating expenses (e.g., expense ratio); and
     c. Any ongoing expenses in addition to annual operating expenses (e.g., mortality and expense fees).
   - For an investment fund product or model portfolio intended to be a QDIA under item 4.a. in Q 7:41 (e.g., target date fund):
     a. An explanation of the asset allocation, how the asset allocation will change over time, and the point in time when the qualified default investment alternative will reach its most conservative asset allocation; including a chart, table, or other graphical representation that illustrates such change in asset allocation over time and that does not obscure or impede a participant's or beneficiary's understanding of the information;
     b. If the QDIA is named, or otherwise described, with reference to a particular date (e.g., a target date), an explanation of the age group for whom the investment is designed, the relevance of the date, and any assumptions about a participant's or beneficiary's contribution and withdrawal intentions on or after such date; and
     c. If applicable, a statement that the participant or beneficiary may lose money by investing in the QDIA, including losses near and following retirement, and that there is no guarantee that the investment will provide adequate retirement income.
4. A description of the right of the participants and beneficiaries on whose behalf assets are invested in a QDIA to direct the investment of those

assets to any other investment alternative under the plan and, if applicable, a statement that certain fees and limitations may apply in connection with such transfer.

5. An explanation of where the participants and beneficiaries can obtain additional investment information concerning the QDIA and the other investment alternatives available under the plan.

[75 Fed. Reg. 73,987 (Nov. 30, 2010)]

Q 7:55 How much information regarding QDIA fees and expenses must be provided in a notice, and can the information be provided by attaching other disclosure documents to the notice?

According to the DOL, participants and beneficiaries generally should be provided information concerning: (1) the amount and a description of any shareholder-type fees (such as sales loads, sales charges, deferred sales charges, redemption fees, surrender charges, exchange fees, account fees, purchase fees, and mortality and expense fees) and (2) for investments with respect to which performance may vary over the term of the investment, the total annual operating expenses of the investment expressed as a percentage (e.g., expense ratio).

It would be permissible to use separate, but simultaneously furnished, documents to satisfy the notice requirements. [DOL Field Assist. Bull. 2008-03]

Q 7:56 Do the electronic distribution rules apply only to the QDIA notice requirement, or more broadly (i.e., to pass-through of investment materials)?

According to the DOL, plans that wish to use electronic means to satisfy their notice requirements may rely on guidance issued either by the DOL or the IRS (see chapter 19). Absent other guidance, that reliance extends only to the QDIA regulation's notice requirements. [DOL Field Assist. Bull. 2008-03]

Q 7:57 Do plan sponsors have to combine the QDIA notice required by the regulation with a notice required under a QACA or an EACA?

No. Plan sponsors are not required to combine these notices and can choose to satisfy these notice requirements independently. [DOL Field Assist. Bull. 2008-03]

Q 7:58 Are the timing requirements for the notices required by the QDIA regulation the same as those for the QACA and EACA notices?

Not exactly, so care must be taken to ensure timing requirements are met if a plan has both QDIA and automatic enrollment features. Under the DOL's QDIA regulation, an initial notice generally must be provided at least 30 days in advance of a participant's date of plan eligibility or any first investment in a QDIA, or on or before the date of plan eligibility (if the participant has the opportunity to make a permissible withdrawal under an EACA). An annual notice also must be provided at least 30 days in advance of each subsequent plan year.

Under the IRS regulations on QACAs and EACAs, a notice must be provided within a reasonable period of time before the beginning of each plan year or a reasonable period of time before an employee first becomes eligible under the plan. A notice is deemed to satisfy these timing requirements if it is provided at least 30 days (and not more than 90 days) before the beginning of each plan year or, if an employee did not receive the annually required notice because it was provided before his or her date of eligibility for the plan, at least by the employee's eligibility date or, if that is not practicable, as soon a practicable after that date under certain conditions (and not more than 90 days before the employee's eligibility date). (See chapter 2 for more details regarding notice timing.)

Although the timing provisions for these notices are not identical, a plan sponsor can satisfy the annual notice requirements under the QDIA regulation and the IRS regulations if it provides notices at least 30 days, but not more than 90 days, before the beginning of each plan year. For example, the sponsor of a calendar year plan may choose to distribute a notice on November 1 of each year. A notice distributed on September 1 would not necessarily satisfy the IRS rules, because September 1 is more than 90 days before the first day of the subsequent plan year.

A plan that includes an EACA and permits an employee to withdraw default contributions during the initial 90-day period can satisfy the QDIA initial notice requirement, as well as the IRS requirements, by providing a notice on or before, but no more than 90 days before, an employee's date of plan eligibility. For example, if a new employee is eligible for participation on his or her first day of employment, which is June 1, the distribution of a notice to that employee on June 1 would satisfy both regulations. [DOL Field Assist. Bull. 2008-03]

If an immediate entry plan chooses not to offer a permissible withdrawal option, the plan's QDIA fiduciary relief would start 30 days after the delivery of notice instead of immediately.

Q 7:59 Can the QDIA notice be combined with the safe harbor 401(k) notice in the same manner that it can be combined with QACA and EACA notices?

Yes. While the QDIA regulation generally provides for disclosure through a separate notice, the DOL views the information required to be disclosed in the safe harbor 401(k) notice sufficiently related to the information required to be disclosed in the QDIA notice, such that combining the notices would improve rather than complicate the disclosure of plan information to participants and beneficiaries (see chapter 2 for information on safe harbor 401(k) plans). [DOL Field Assist. Bull. 2008-03]

Q 7:60 Is all the QDIA information required to be furnished automatically without regard to whether, under ERISA Section 404(c), some information can be provided only upon request of a participant or beneficiary?

No. According to the DOL, the QDIA informational requirements were not meant to create a lower or higher threshold in that regard. [DOL Field Assist. Bull. 2008-03]

Q 7:61 Must a plan otherwise comply with Section 404(c) requirements?

No. Fiduciary relief under ERISA Section 404(c) for default investment arrangements is not contingent on a plan being an "ERISA 404(c) plan" and is therefore available to fiduciaries in any participant-directed plan that meets applicable requirements. [DOL Reg. § 2550.404c-5(a)]

Q 7:62 Must a plan's default investment arrangement satisfy the QDIA requirements?

The standards set forth under the QDIA requirements, according to the DOL, are not intended to be the exclusive means of satisfying ERISA fiduciary standards with respect to investment of participant assets. Money market funds and stable value products, for example, may be prudent investments for some participants and beneficiaries. [DOL Reg. § 2550.404c-5(a)(2)].

Q 7:63 What relief is not available under a default investment arrangement that qualifies for Section 404(c) protection?

According to the DOL, Section 404(c) does not provide relief:

1. To a fiduciary from its duties to prudently select and monitor any QDIA or from any liability that results from a failure to satisfy those duties;
2. To any fiduciary managing investments in a QDIA for its fiduciary duties under ERISA or from any liability that results from a failure to satisfy those duties; and
3. To any fiduciary from the prohibited transaction rules of ERISA Section 406 (see chapter 5) or from any liability that results from a violation of those provisions.

[DOL Reg. § 2550.404c-5(b)]

Q 7:64 Must a plan sponsor distribute a notice 30 days before the effective date of the QDIA regulation to obtain relief for prior contributions to a stable value fund or product (so-called grandfathered QDIA)?

No, but the relief provided by the QDIA regulation generally will not take effect until 30 days after the initial notice is furnished to participants and beneficiaries. For example, if a plan sponsor distributed the initial notice on January 1, 2008, to participants and beneficiaries who were defaulted into a stable value fund prior to the effective date of the regulation, and, assuming all other requirements of the regulation have been satisfied, the fiduciary relief provided by the regulation would be available to the plan sponsor on January 31, 2008 (i.e., 30 days later). Regardless of the date on which fiduciary relief is available to the plan sponsor, the relief will extend only to assets that were invested in the stable value product or fund on or before the effective date of the final regulation. [DOL Field Assist. Bull. 2008-03]

Q 7:65 Is relief available under the QDIA regulation for assets invested in a default investment prior to the effective date of the regulation?

Yes, if all conditions of the QDIA regulation are satisfied with respect to such assets. The relief available under the QDIA regulation is not limited to assets that are invested in a QDIA on or after the effective date of the regulation. If the notice and other requirements for relief under the QDIA regulation are satisfied, the fiduciary will, except to the extent otherwise limited by the regulation, be relieved of liability with respect to all assets invested in the QDIA, without regard to whether the assets were contributed prior to the effective date of the regulation.

The fiduciary will have the benefit of the relief under the QDIA regulation for fiduciary decisions made on or after the date that all requirements of the QDIA regulation have been satisfied. However, relief is not available for fiduciary decisions made prior to the effective date of the QDIA regulation, such as decisions by a fiduciary to invest assets in a default investment. [DOL Field Assist. Bull. 2008-03]

Q 7:66 Would a fiduciary obtain the relief referred to above, with respect to assets invested in a QDIA on behalf of participants and beneficiaries who elected to invest in a default investment prior to the effective date of the regulation?

Yes. The relief available under the QDIA regulation would extend to all assets invested in a QDIA on behalf of participants and beneficiaries who, on or after the effective date of the regulation, fail to give investment direction after being provided the required notice, regardless of whether the participant or beneficiary made an earlier affirmative election to invest in the default investment. This provision may be significant when plan records cannot establish that an investment was the direct and necessary result of a participant's or beneficiary's exercise of control for purposes of the QDIA regulation.

Example. Default A was used as the default investment for its plan, an investment that would not qualify as a QDIA under the regulation. Following publication of the QDIA regulation, the Default A is changed to Default B, an investment that would qualify as a QDIA under the regulation, but the plan sponsor is unable to distinguish between those participants and beneficiaries who directed that their assets be invested in Default A and those participants and beneficiaries who were defaulted into Default A. If a new investment election form is distributed to all participants and beneficiaries invested in Default A, relief under the QDIA regulation would be available with respect to assets that are moved into Default B and held in the plan accounts of participants and beneficiaries who failed to respond to the investment election form, if all of the requirements of the regulation are otherwise satisfied with respect to such participants and beneficiaries. Alternatively, if Default A is an investment that would qualify as a QDIA under the regulation and plan sponsor complies with the notice and other requirements necessary to establish Default A as a QDIA, relief from liability under the QDIA regulation would apply with respect to all assets invested in Default A, without regard to whether the assets were the result of a default investment. [DOL Field Assist. Bull. 2008-03]

Q 7:67 Is fiduciary relief under the QDIA regulation available if nonelective contributions, such as qualified nonelective contributions, or the proceeds from litigation or settlements, are invested in a QDIA?

If participants and beneficiaries are not provided the opportunity to direct the investment of plan assets that result from qualified nonelective contributions (QNECs) or the proceeds from litigation or other settlements, at least one of the conditions for fiduciary relief will not have been satisfied, and relief would not be available under the QDIA regulation. To the extent a participant or beneficiary is, in fact, given the opportunity to direct the investment of such contributions, or after such amounts are allocated to a participant's or beneficiary's plan account and the participant or beneficiary is subsequently provided the opportunity to direct the investment of those assets, QDIA protection would be available, provided the other requirements are met. [DOL Field Assist. Bull. 2008-03]

Q 7:68 Is QDIA protection available to 403(b) plans?

Yes. The fiduciary relief provided under the QDIA regulation is available to a 403(b) plan subject to Title I of ERISA. [DOL Field Assist. Bull. 2008-03]

Q 7:69 Can a plan sponsor use two different QDIAs—for example, one for its automatic contribution arrangement, and another for rollover contributions?

Yes. Nothing in the QDIA regulation limits the ability of a plan sponsor to use more than one QDIA, so long as all requirements of the regulation are satisfied with respect to each QDIA. [DOL Field Assist. Bull. 2008-03]

Q 7:70 What was the effective date of the QDIA regulation?

The DOL's final regulation implementing QDIAs came into effect December 24, 2007. [72 Fed. Reg. 60,452 (Oct. 24, 2007)]

Blackouts and Changes in Investment Options

Q 7:71 Under what circumstances can Section 404(c) protection extend to blackout periods?

During a blackout period (see chapter 19), participant access to 401(k) accounts is temporarily suspended or restricted. Blackouts can occur in connection with a service provider change, a change to investment offerings, or a plan merger or spin-off.

The PPA extends protection to plan fiduciaries under Section 404(c) during a blackout if:

1. The plan complied with Section 404(c) requirements prior to the blackout; and
2. Plan fiduciaries complied with ERISA requirements in connection with authorizing and implementing the blackout period.

The rule generally applies to plan years beginning after December 31, 2007 (later for plans maintained pursuant to a collectively bargaining agreement). [ERISA § 404(c)(1)]

Q 7:72 Under what circumstances would Section 404(c) protection extend to a change in investment options?

The PPA extends protection for plan fiduciaries under Section 404(c) in connection with a change in investment offerings (a "qualified change in investment options") in the following circumstances:

1. The plan complied with Section 404(c) requirements prior to the effective date of the change;
2. Participants are given 30 to 60 days' prior written notice of the change, including information comparing the new and existing investment options, and explaining what will happen if they do not make an affirmative election;
3. The account is mapped to reasonably similar funds with similar risk and return characteristics; and
4. The participants or beneficiaries do not make affirmative elections contrary to the change before the effective date of the change.

The rule generally applies to plan years beginning after December 31, 2007 (later for plans maintained pursuant to a collective bargaining agreement). [ERISA § 404(c)(1)]

Litigation Involving Participant-Directed Plans

Q 7:73 Has ERISA Section 404(c) been tested as a defense in a lawsuit?

Yes. Over the years ERISA Section 404(c) has been asserted as a defense in a number of lawsuits, some of which were settled out of court. Some lawsuits in which Section 404(c) has been raised as a defense are in connection with actions involving employer stock investments and investment-related fees.

Q 7:74 What might plan sponsors learn from these cases?

Strategies that might be used to manage fiduciary liability exposure with respect to investments may include the following:

- Document the investment policy, procedure, and selection and monitoring process.
- Compare and analyze investment alternatives.
- Identify and document the basis for decisions.
- Keep participant disclosure data up to date.
- Exercise regular oversight according to a documented procedure and process.
- Use independent experts when needed to make prudent decisions.

Q 7:75 What were some issues in the Enron, WorldCom, and other similar cases?

In 2001, participants in Enron Corporation's 401(k) plan saw their retirement savings decline significantly as a result of Enron Corporation's collapse. Participants in WorldCom Corporation's 401(k) plan similarly suffered in the aftermath of WorldCom's bankruptcy. Some of questions in those cases include the following:

- Did plan fiduciaries breach their duties to be loyal, to invest prudently, and/or to diversify investments by continuing to hold employer stock?
- To what extent were plan fiduciaries acting in an individual or corporate capacity?
- Did the employer fail to properly select and monitor plan fiduciaries?
- Did the plan comply with ERISA Section 404(c) requirements and, if so, what protections are afforded the plan as a result of its compliance?
- What are the responsibilities of plan fiduciaries with respect to the timing and duration of a blackout period?
- What are the responsibilities of plan fiduciaries with respect to investments during a blackout period?
- When is it appropriate to consult an independent fiduciary when conflicts of interest arise?

- What responsibilities do directed trustees have with respect to plan investments?

See chapters 5 and 6 for information on directed trustees in the context of employer stock.

Q 7:76 What provisions in the Pension Protection Act of 2006 addressed issues in the Enron, WorldCom, and other similar cases?

The following provisions in the Pension Protection Act of 2006 addressed issues involved in the Enron, WorldCom, and other similar cases:

- Expanding participants' rights to diversify assets invested in employer stock (stand-alone employer stock ownership plans and plans with closely held employer stock excluded).
- Requiring benefit statements to be provided at least quarterly to plan participants in plans where participants direct investments.
- Providing that protection under ERISA Section 404(c) is available with respect to a loss occurring during a blackout period if the loss is a result of a participant's exercise of control over assets prior to the blackout period, and plan fiduciaries satisfy their obligations during the blackout period (e.g., length of blackout period is reasonable, adequate notice of blackout was given to participants, and determination to enter into the blackout period was reasonable).
- Encouraging plan sponsors to offer third-party investment advice by limiting plan sponsor fiduciary responsibilities to the selection and periodic review of the third-party adviser.
- Requiring that information on diversifying investments in employer stock be given to participants.
- Increasing maximum ERISA bonding limit for plans invested in employer stock.

Chapter 8

Participant Communication and Education

In a 401(k) plan, employees are asked to choose to give up current income in exchange for a future benefit. Depending on the demographics of the employee group, this may appear an unattractive choice. Lower-paid or younger employees may be less interested in tax benefits or retirement planning than they are in the availability of current income. For this reason, it is important to have an employee communication strategy that enables employees to understand the ways in which a 401(k) plan can benefit them. It is also important that employees understand the basics of setting a retirement planning goal and be able to assess their progress in reaching that goal.

For participant-directed plans, investment education is an important part of an effective communications program. Some plan sponsors are choosing to go beyond offering investment education and offer participants fiduciary investment advice.

An Effective 401(k) Communication Program 8-2
  Content of a Communication Program 8-3
  Table 8-1. Advantages of Saving in a 401(k) Plan Versus an IRA 8-3
  Implementing a Communication Program 8-5
Department of Labor Guidance on Participant Investment Education 8-10
  Investment Advice Under ERISA 8-11
  Plan Information 8-12
  General Financial and Investment Information 8-13
  Asset Allocation Models 8-14
  Interactive Investment Materials 8-15
  Investment Education Versus Investment Advice 8-17
  Investment Education and Fiduciary Liability 8-17
  Impact of DOL Guidance on Education 8-18
  Offering Investment Advice 8-18
Individual Retirement Planning 8-20
  Retirement Planning Scenarios 8-20
  Replacement Ratios at Retirement 8-22

Long-Term Investment Return 8-23
Risk Tolerance 8-25
The Impact of Inflation 8-25
Other Sources of Retirement Income 8-26
Managing Longevity Risk 8-26
Table 8-2. Years (Male/Female) Needed for Each Risk Level of Outliving Retirement Income 8-27
Managing Investment Risk During Retirement 8-27
Saver's Credit 8-28
Table 8-3. Saver's Credit: Credit Rates (2015) 8-28

An Effective 401(k) Communication Program

This chapter begins with employee communication strategy as it relates to an employee's general understanding of a 401(k) plan. It then provides a broader view of 401(k) communications as it relates to individual retirement planning. This chapter does not address communication required under the disclosure rules of the Employee Retirement Income Security Act (ERISA). That subject is discussed in detail in chapter 19. Nor does this chapter address notice requirements associated with certain plan design features (e.g., safe harbor 401(k) feature, automatic enrollment feature, ERISA Section 404(c) feature) and certain plan events (e.g., plan distributions). Those topics are covered in other chapters. See chapter 19 for a table with key participant disclosure requirements and cross-references for additional information.

Q 8:1 Why is initial communication important?

Employees who do not understand the benefits of a 401(k) plan are less likely to participate in and appreciate the value of the plan. The benefits of a 401(k) plan are not as obvious as those of a profit sharing or other type of plan that is funded entirely by employer contributions. Where employees are being asked to sacrifice current income by contributing to a 401(k) plan, it is critical that they understand how this sacrifice will benefit them in the long run.

Better communication can increase participation of lower-paid employees in the plan and permit the higher-paid employees to put in greater dollar amounts without violating the actual deferral percentage (ADP) test (see chapter 13). This result often serves an employer's goal of rewarding key executives.

Employees who understand how a 401(k) plan works are also more likely to plan realistically for their retirement. Since a 401(k) plan is designed to encourage employees to take some responsibility for their own retirement planning, it is important that they understand the relationship between current contributions and future retirement income.

Content of a Communication Program

Q 8:2 What is important information in a 401(k) plan?

It is essential to communicate key plan provisions such as eligibility, the availability of funds through loans or hardship withdrawals, and any limits on contributions. A short plan summary can be helpful in getting employees to focus on key provisions.

The benefits of investing in a 401(k) plan, particularly when the plan is compared with individual retirement accounts (IRAs) or after-tax savings accounts could also be explained. Table 8-1 demonstrates the advantages of saving in a 401(k) plan versus a traditional or Roth IRA. The table reflects limits in effect in 2014.

Table 8-1. Advantages of Saving in a 401(k) Plan Versus an IRA

	IRA	*401(k)*
Limits	$5,500 annual limit (2015) on contributions and $1,000 annual limit (2015) on age 50 contributions	$18,000 annual limit (2015) on employee contributions and $6,000 annual limit (2015) on age 50 contributions (subject to any additional plan limits)
Company match	None	Company match is common
Deposits	Usually single deposit	Deposits through convenient payroll deduction
Penalty-Free Early Access	Penalty-free access is limited	Depending on plan design can access through participant loans without paying penalty
Timing of tax savings on contributions	Tax deduction when return is filed for traditional IRA	Immediate tax reduction (tax withholding is reduced)
Use with other company plans	Traditional IRA may not be available on a tax-deductible basis if participating in a company plan at the same time; Roth IRA not available to higher-income employees (special rules apply to Roth IRA conversions)	Available even if participating in another company plan; Roth feature may be available, depending on plan design

Q 8:3 What additional information should be communicated if participants choose their own investments in the plan?

Most plans let participants choose their own investments, particularly for their elective and rollover contributions. Plans that offer this option limit the investment choices to an array of designated funds. However, the number of options that can be offered is generally unlimited, and a plan may offer an open-ended investment choice. Participant directed plans are discussed in more detail in chapters 6 and 7.

Often, one of the goals in letting participants choose their own investments is to protect the employer from legal liability for the investment performance of participants' accounts. The information required to be provided to participants in a plan that intends to comply with the Department of Labor (DOL) regulation under ERISA Section 404(c) is described in chapter 7.

In 2010, the DOL issued regulations that require certain investment- and fee-related information be provided to participants in participant-directed plans (see chapter 19).

Participants may become discouraged with the investment performance of their accounts if they do not understand the risks and benefits of the available funds or how to match those risks and benefits with their individual goals. Employees may find the following information useful in making appropriate investment decisions:

1. The factors an individual should consider when making investment decisions (e.g., risk tolerance) (see Qs 8:52–8:53);
2. The effect of a participant's age, income, years to retirement, and other individual factors on his or her investment decisions;
3. How to estimate income needed for retirement;
4. An explanation of basic investment concepts (e.g., risk, return, diversification, inflation) (see chapter 6);
5. A historical analysis showing how different asset types (e.g., stocks, bonds, fixed income funds) have performed when measured in 5-, 10-, or 20-year cycles;
6. The attributes of each investment option (e.g., risk characteristics, performance data) (see chapter 6);
7. The importance of asset allocation decisions (see chapter 6); and
8. An explanation of the saver's credit (see Q 8:61).

Employers who offer 401(k) plans are not necessarily investment experts and are often reluctant to discuss investment strategies with participants, particularly in a written format. Participants with no investment information may be more likely to follow the market (i.e., buy high and sell low) or to limit unnecessarily the investment growth of their accounts by investing all of it in the most conservative fund choice available. Given these tendencies, basic information on investment planning may be useful so that the 401(k) plan will become an effective retirement savings vehicle for employees. If the employer is uncomfortable providing this information directly, it can bring in outside expertise.

The Financial Industry Regulatory Authority (FINRA) launched "Smart 401(k) Investing," which provides information on investing in 401(k) plans. The information is accessible at *http://www.finra.org/investors/smartinvesting/retirement/smart401kinvesting/introduction.*

Q 8:4 Why might a 401(k) communications program go beyond the plan's reporting and disclosure requirements?

Following the government's reporting and disclosure requirements is important, but fulfilling these requirements alone may not produce an effective employee benefit communications program. The summary plan description is at best a communications starting point. Plan administrators must provide benefit statements to participants and, in plans with participant-directed investments, certain investment- and fee-related information. Information in these documents could help fill some of the gaps in the communication and education process. (See chapter 19 for detailed information on requirements for participant benefit statements and other reporting and disclosure requirements.)

Q 8:5 Should a 401(k) communications program present just the facts?

Although many facts about the design and operation of the 401(k) plan must be part of a communications program, the program may go beyond the facts in a number of ways. It could put the facts in a context that relates to the perceived needs, wants, and even fears of the participants. It could do this in a way that both attracts and maintains their attention. A question and answer format with examples is a way to put facts into a context that participants can easily understand and use.

Just the facts would provide account balances and a list of investment options. But participants may need to know more than this in order to use the plan effectively to provide for their retirements. Retirement planning involves future uncertainties and difficult decision making.

Implementing a Communication Program

Q 8:6 What are the steps in implementing a 401(k) communications program?

A 401(k) communications program may involve the following steps:

1. Assess the information needs of the participants (see Q 8:7).
2. Set a measurable goal for the program (see Q 8:8).
3. Keep in mind the differing information needs among plan participants (see Q 8:9).
4. Structure the program to have:
   a. Multiple contacts (see Q 8:13),
   b. Multiple approaches (see Q 8:15), and
   c. Multiple messages (see Q 8:18).
5. Evaluate the effectiveness of the program (see Q 8:20).

Q 8:7 What is a method for assessing the information needs of plan participants?

A way to assess information needs for an existing plan is to obtain plan data or metrics on, for example, the plan's participation and deferral rates, investment positions, outstanding loans, withdrawal activity, and account balances. This type of assessment could be part of a plan success measurement and/or a participant Retirement Readiness report (see Q 8:20).

Q 8:8 What measurable goals might be set for a 401(k) communications program?

A goal might be increased understanding as evidenced by a follow-up assessment. Often the goal will be an increased number of participants, or participation at a higher level, or an increased number participating at levels above a company match. Greater diversity among investment choices or greater understanding of investments might also be set as goals.

Q 8:9 How might information needs differ among plan participants?

Information needs may well differ by age groups, or by management versus nonmanagement, or by salary level, or by education level, or by the type of work and other experience. As participants learn more about their 401(k) plan and how it can meet their retirement needs, their interests typically move along the spectrum: consumption, savings, investing, planning. A communications program could have at least these two aims: to present material relevant to the location of the participant along this spectrum, and to present material that will move the participant's interest along the spectrum.

Q 8:10 What is a way to present retirement planning to the younger, consumption-oriented employee?

Younger participants without prior experience with a 401(k) plan are often focused on consumption rather than saving, investing, or planning. It may seem to them that their salary levels are not adequate to permit saving or they may be newly independent, focused on immediate wants, and feel that they have plenty of time "in the future" for retirement saving. For this group, it may be important to emphasize the immediate tax advantages of a 401(k) plan and the gain from an employer match. Accessibility of 401(k) funds through loan or hardship withdrawal provisions will also be of interest.

Even a consumption-oriented group will have experience with the monthly budgeting needed to pay the rent or mortgage. Many will know teachers who are paid only nine months of the year but soon learn to budget for the year's fourth quarter. Most people have careers that are like that: individuals are paid for about three quarters of their adult life and need to budget for necessities during retirement in order to do well during life's fourth quarter. The impact of beginning retirement savings during life's first quarter rather than delaying until the second or third quarter will be an important concept for this group.

The following table illustrates the approximate amount of monthly savings needed to produce $10,000 annual income in today's dollars at age 65, and how the amount of savings varies by the age at which the savings begin:

Age When Savings Begin	*Monthly Savings Needed*
25	$406
35	693
45	1,276
55	2,997

As shown in the table, monthly retirement savings must be more than 70 percent greater if savings begin at age 35 rather than age 25.

The assumptions involved in this case are as follows:

- Inflation is 3 percent annually.
- Tax-sheltered investments average 8 percent returns before retirement and 6 percent after retirement.
- The participant lives until age 90.
- Retirement spending is designed to allow for a 10 percent chance of outliving retirement savings.

The lesson is that budgeting for retirement is much easier to achieve if begun during life's first quarter. The follow-up discussion of assumptions may set the stage for investment education and retirement planning at a later time or later in the same presentation.

Some plan sponsors are implementing automatic contribution features to further enhance plan participation. (See chapter 2 for information on automatic contribution features.)

Q 8:11 What may be the best way to move plan participants from a savings orientation to an investing orientation?

Use concrete examples of the significance that investment earnings have on retirement income, and then follow up with information on basic investment classes and the returns that historically have been achieved with each. This approach can also serve as an introduction to a retirement planning tool such as a computer-based retirement planning tool.

Q 8:12 How can real-life examples introduce the importance of investment return for retirement planning?

Often a participant will be ready to move from a saving orientation to an investing orientation after a few years of plan participation when he or she has an account balance to invest.

> **Example.** Sally, at age 40, has a 401(k) account about twice her annual salary. Assume her salary will keep pace with 3 percent inflation and that she will live to age 90. Sally plans to retire at age 65. In retirement, she can expect to replace about 19.5 percent of her salary with income from what she has saved to date if she earns 6 percent on her investments.

It may be important to follow up this example by showing the impact that higher rates of return would have, typically through computer-based models. If Sally could earn 8 percent pre-retirement instead of 6 percent over the next 25 years, she would be able to replace about 31 percent of her income at retirement. An increase in investment return from 6 percent to 8 percent leads to more than a 60 percent increase in retirement income, but those numbers must be balanced with information on investment risk.

This is a natural lead-in to a discussion of what asset classes might be expected to return 6 to 8 percent rather than 3 to 5 percent over a 25-year investment horizon. Good investment education should also include a discussion of investment risk (variability) and how it relates to investment horizon. Discussion of risk addresses the trade-off between investment risk (which decreases significantly for investment horizons over ten years) and the risk of insufficient retirement income.

Retirement planning tools will be complex because of the number of assumptions that must be taken into account. A discussion could begin with simple explorations that focus the participants' attention on the tools and leave for later a detailed consideration of all the factors needed to develop a complete individual plan.

Q 8:13 What is meant by the statement that a 401(k) communications program should have multiple contacts, multiple approaches, and multiple messages?

Repetition is important for learning, and a 401(k) communications program may cover a number of complex concepts. This can be accomplished through a program with multiple contacts through the year that reinforce one another and build upon the material presented earlier. The use of a variety of approaches reinforces the message for each person.

Q 8:14 How many yearly contacts are needed for an effective 401(k) communications program?

It depends. Most 401(k) plans are required to provide quarterly statements to participants, which supplies a yearly base of four contacts. Another three or four contacts can provide a well-rounded program. This could involve benefit statement stuffers using brochures that emphasize a key retirement planning or investing concept. Short articles in company newsletters can also introduce and reinforce these messages. Where the goal is a sizable increase in participation, face-to-face presentations and discussions could be considered.

Q 8:15 What are some of the multiple approaches in a 401(k) communications program?

Material presented in person can get participants' attention and dramatize messages in ways participants can remember. Written material also can be used to convey important information and allows for reference at a later time.

In order to move participants along the spectrum of consumption, savings, investing, and planning, it is important to give them tools that they can apply to answer questions they already have as well as to answer questions suggested by the material. Computer tools that provide for planning as well as investment education are available, and many Internet sites now make similar tools available online. Many retirement plan service providers provide access to these types of programs online along with other retirement plan information.

Q 8:16 What are the advantages of computer-based planning tools?

Individuals may find a computer software approach to planning and education attractive since it is more interactive and allows the illustration of many calculations in a short period of time.

Q 8:17 What computer-based planning tools and other resources are available online?

Many retirement plan service providers offer direct access through participant Web sites to on-line retirement planning tools. Such Web sites may provide access to retirement readiness-type calculations based on various underlying assumptions such as rates of return. Retirement plan providers may also offer specific advice involving the particular investments in the plan (see Q 8:36).

Retirement planning packages are also available from most software retailers. Many Internet sites provide interactive retirement planning tools. Other tools offered by the American Savings Education Council (ASEC), such as The Ballpark Estimate, are available at *www.asec.org*. An on-line retirement planning resource developed by the DOL for individuals approaching retirement is available at *www.dol.gov/ebsa/publications/nearretirement.html*.

Q 8:18 How can the multiple messages involved in 401(k) communications be structured?

No one structure will work for all plans. The traditional enrollment meeting may cover the operation of the plan and introduce consumer-oriented employees to the benefits of tax-deferred retirement savings. A follow-up contact may concentrate on the factors needed to develop a retirement income plan (importance of starting early; importance of investment return; retirement age, life expectancy, and the impact of inflation). A third type of contact may go into more detail about investment concepts (asset classes and their associated rewards and risks, risk measurement such as standard deviation, investment horizon, and asset allocation).

Q 8:19 What type of follow-up is needed for an effective 401(k) communications program?

A communications program over a period of several months can achieve the immediate goals that were set for it. However, after a few months or a year has passed, participants may no longer remember many of the concepts they had begun to learn during the program. For example, the goal may have been to discuss the risks and rewards of equity investments. Participants may need to be reeducated yearly about the risks and rewards involved with equity investments. Otherwise, a year or two with a changing market will lead them to question or even reverse sound investment decisions they made earlier.

Follow-up communications can be less extensive than the initial communications program, but the important messages should be recommunicated periodically. Core elements of a 401(k) communications program may be redone after a number of years, especially as the investment climate changes, as new participants enter, or as changes are made in plan design or investment options.

Q 8:20 What is a participant Retirement Readiness report?

Some service providers are offering Retirement Readiness reports to plan sponsors that display plan data and information to help identify trends and analyze participants' retirement readiness. These reports might be used to assess educational needs and provide information on aligning plan design, services, and products toward improving participants' retirement readiness.

Department of Labor Guidance on Participant Investment Education

Under ERISA anyone who provides investment advice for a fee with respect to any moneys or property of an employee benefit plan becomes a fiduciary with respect to that plan (see chapter 5). With the growth of participant directed individual account plans sponsors have increasingly relied upon ERISA Section 404(c) to avoid fiduciary liability and have looked to the DOL for guidance as to when investment education does not constitute investment advice. In light of the importance of investment education and the uncertainty related to the fiduciary implications of providing investment information to participants, the DOL clarified the circumstances under which participant investment education will not give rise to fiduciary status under ERISA by issuing Interpretive Bulletin 96-1. In 2015, the DOL published a proposed rule modifying the definition of nonfiduciary investment education. [DOL Prop. Rul. § 2510.3-21(b)(6)] If and when finalized, the new rule will supersede Interpretive Bulletin 96-1. The DOL's proposed rule is discussed in detail in chapter 5.

Q 8:21 What guidance has the DOL provided as to whether investment education constitutes investment advice?

Plan sponsors and service providers were reluctant to provide any investment-related information because it was unclear when investment education crossed the line and became advice. ERISA imposes fiduciary duties and potential liability on those who provide "investment advice." (See chapter 5.) [ERISA § 3(21), 29 U.S.C. § 1002(21); DOL Reg. § 2510.3-21(c)]

The DOL in June 1996 issued Interpretive Bulletin 96-1, titled Participant Investment Education. [DOL Reg. § 2509.96-1] This bulletin provides guidance as to which activities that have been designed to educate and assist participants and beneficiaries in making informed investment decisions will not, as such, cause persons engaged in such activities to become plan fiduciaries. This guidance was updated in a proposed rule published in 2015. One significant change is that it now covers education provided not only to plan participants and beneficiaries, but also to plans, IRAs, and IRA owners. [DOL Prop. Rul. § 2510.3-21(b)(6)]

Investment Advice Under ERISA

Q 8:22 How is investment advice characterized under ERISA?

In the context of providing investment-related information to participants and beneficiaries of participant directed individual account plans, a person will be considered to be rendering investment advice only if both of the following items are true:

1. The person either renders advice as to the value of securities or other property, or makes recommendations as to the advisability of investing in, purchasing, or selling securities or other property; and
2. The person either has discretionary authority or control with respect to purchasing or selling securities or other property for the participant or beneficiary, or renders advice on a regular basis, pursuant to a mutual agreement that the person will render individualized advice based on the particular needs of the participant or beneficiary and that such advice will serve as a primary basis for the participant's or beneficiary's investment decisions with respect to plan assets.

[DOL Reg. § 2510.3-21(c)]

See chapter 5 for proposed DOL rule change in the context of fiduciary investment advice.

Q 8:23 What are the four examples of investment-related information and material that would not, in the view of the DOL, result in the rendering of investment advice under ERISA?

The DOL has determined that the furnishing of any of four categories of information and materials to a participant or beneficiary in a participant directed individual account retirement plan will not, as such, constitute investment advice under ERISA, irrespective of

- Who provides the information
- The frequency with which the information is shared
- The form in which the information and materials are provided (e.g., individual or group basis, in writing or orally, or via video or computer software)
- Whether the information in any one category is furnished alone or in combination with the other categories

The four categories of information are as follows:

1. Plan information (see Q 8:24);
2. General financial and investment information (see Q 8:26);
3. Asset allocation models (see Q 8:27); and
4. Interactive investment materials (see Q 8:29).

[DOL Reg. § 2509.96-1(d)]

The DOL's 2015 proposed rule would modify this definition by:

- Clarifying that it applies to both information and materials;
- Adding education provided via a call center to the list of examples of acceptable forms for providing education; and
- Adding a requirement that the information and materials provided do not include, either standing alone or with other materials, recommendations regarding specific investment products or specific plan or IRA alternatives, or any recommendations regarding investment, management, or value of a particular investment.

[DOL Prop. Rul. § 2510.3-21(b)(6)]

Plan Information

Q 8:24 What does the DOL mean by *plan information*, and why does it not constitute investment advice?

By *plan information*, the DOL means information or materials that inform plan participants or beneficiaries about any of the following:

- Benefits of plan participation
- Benefits of increasing plan participation
- Impact of preretirement withdrawals on retirement income
- Terms of the plan
- Operation of the plan
- Investment alternatives under the plan (see Q 8:25)

Since this information relates to plan participation without reference to the appropriateness of any individual investment option for a particular participant or beneficiary, furnishing the information does not constitute rendering investment advice within the meaning of ERISA. [DOL Reg. § 2509.96-1(d)(1)]

The DOL's 2015 proposed rule would modify this definition by:

- Expanding it to include information about IRAs
- Adding retirement income needs as a category of information
- Adding information related to distributions, such as information about varying forms of distribution (including rollovers), and information about annuitization and other forms of lifetime income payment options (e.g., immediate or deferred annuities or incremental purchase of a deferred annuity) and the advantages, disadvantages, or risks of different forms of distributions.

[DOL Prop. Rul. § 2510.3-21(b)(6)(i)]

Q 8:25 According to the DOL, what information about investment alternatives may be included as plan information?

According to the DOL, information about investment alternatives may include descriptions of investment objectives and philosophies, risk and return characteristics, historical return information, and related prospectuses. [DOL Reg. § 2509.96-1(d)(1)(ii)]

General Financial and Investment Information

Q 8:26 What does the DOL mean by *general financial and investment information*, and why does it not constitute investment advice?

By *general financial and investment information*, the DOL means information or materials that inform plan participants or beneficiaries about any of the following:

- General financial and investment concepts such as risk and return, diversification, dollar-cost averaging, compounded return, and tax-deferred investment
- Historic differences in rates of return among different asset classes (e.g., equities, bonds, or cash) based on standard market indices
- Effects of inflation

- Estimating future retirement income needs
- Determining investment time horizons
- Assessing risk tolerance

Since this general financial and investment information has no direct relationship to the investment alternatives available to participants and beneficiaries, furnishing it would not constitute rendering investment advice within the meaning of ERISA. [DOL Reg. § 2509.96-1(d)(2)]

The DOL's 2015 proposed rule would modify this definition by:

- Adding information about retirement-related risks, such as longevity, market/interest risks, inflation, health care and other expenses.
- Adding information about general methods and strategies for managing assets in retirement (e.g., systematic withdrawal payments, annuitization, or guaranteed minimum withdrawal benefits), including those offered outside the plan or IRA.

[DOL Prop. Rul. § 2510.3-21(b)(6)(ii)]

Asset Allocation Models

Q 8:27 What does the DOL mean by *asset allocation models*, and why does providing them not constitute investment advice?

According to the DOL, *asset allocation models* are information and materials (such as pie charts, graphs, or case studies) made available to all plan participants and beneficiaries that provide asset allocation portfolios of hypothetical individuals with different time horizons and risk profiles. Because the asset allocation models would enable a participant or beneficiary to assess the relevance of any particular model to his or her individual situation, furnishing the models would not constitute a recommendation and thus would not be investment advice within the meaning of ERISA. [DOL Reg. § 2509.96-1(d)(3)]

Q 8:28 What conditions must asset allocation models satisfy in order to meet the DOL standard?

In order to meet the safe harbor of DOL Interpretive Bulletin 96-1, asset allocation models must meet the following four conditions:

1. Such models must be based on generally accepted investment theories that take into account the historic returns of different asset classes (e.g., equities, bonds, or cash) over defined periods of time [DOL Reg. § 2509.96-1(d)(3)(i)];
2. All material facts and assumptions on which such models are based must accompany the models (e.g., retirement ages, life expectancies, income levels, financial resources, replacement income ratios, inflation rates, and rates of return) [DOL Reg. § 2509.96-1(d)(3)(ii)];

3. To the extent that an asset allocation model identifies any specific investment alternative available under the plan, the model must be accompanied by a statement indicating that other investment alternatives having similar risk and return characteristics may be available under the plan and identifying where information on those investment alternatives may be obtained [DOL Reg. § 2509.96-1(d)(3)(iii)]; and
4. The asset allocation models must be accompanied by a statement indicating that in applying particular asset allocation models to their individual situations, participants or beneficiaries should consider their other assets, income, and investments (e.g., equity in a home, IRA investment, savings accounts, and interests in other qualified and nonqualified plans) in addition to their investments in the plan. [DOL Reg. § 2509.96-1(d)(3)(iv)]

However, the status of the asset allocation model would not, in the view of the DOL, be affected by the fact that a plan offers only one investment alternative in a particular asset class identified in the model.

The DOL's 2015 proposed rule would modify this definition by:

- Prohibiting reference in the model to any specific investment available under the plan or IRA (basically eliminating item 3 above).
- Eliminating the language stating that the status of allocation models as nonfiduciary education would not be affected by the fact that a plan offers only one investment alternative in a particular asset class identified in the model.

[DOL Prop. Rul. § 2510.3-21(b)(6)(iii)]

Interactive Investment Materials

Q 8:29 What does the DOL mean by *interactive investment materials*, and why does providing them not constitute investment advice?

According to the DOL, *interactive investment materials* include questionnaires, worksheets, software, and similar materials that provide a participant or beneficiary the means to estimate future retirement income needs and assess the impact of different asset allocations on retirement income. Because these materials enable participants and beneficiaries independently to design and assess asset allocation models, but otherwise do not differ from asset allocation models based on hypothetical assumptions, they would not constitute a recommendation and hence would not be investment advice within the meaning of ERISA. [DOL Reg. § 2509.96-1(d)(4)]

Q 8:30 What are the conditions that interactive investment materials must satisfy in order to meet the DOL standard?

In order to meet the safe harbor of DOL Interpretive Bulletin 96-1, interactive investment materials must meet the five following conditions:

1. Such interactive materials must be based on generally accepted investment theories that take into account the historic returns of different asset classes (e.g., equities, bonds, or cash) over defined periods of time. [DOL Reg. § 2509.96-1(d)(4)(i)]
2. There must be an objective correlation between the asset allocation generated by the materials and the information and data supplied by the participant or beneficiary. [DOL Reg. § 2509.96-1(d)(4)(ii)]
3. All material facts and assumptions that may affect a participant or beneficiary's assessment of the different asset allocations must either accompany the interactive materials or be specified by the participant or beneficiary (e.g., retirement ages, life expectancies, income levels, financial resources, replacement income ratios, inflation rates, and rates of return). [DOL Reg. § 2509.96-1(d)(4)(iii)]
4. To the extent an asset allocation generated by the materials identifies any specific investment alternative available under the plan, the asset allocation must be accompanied by a statement indicating that other investment alternatives having similar risk and return characteristics may be available under the plan and identifying where information on those investment alternatives may be obtained. [DOL Reg. § 2509.96-1(d)(4)(iv)]
5. The interactive materials must either take into account or be accompanied by a statement indicating that, in applying particular asset allocation models to their individual situations, participants or beneficiaries should consider their other assets, income, and investments (e.g., equity in a home, IRA investment, savings accounts, and interests in other qualified and nonqualified plans) in addition to their investments in the plan. [DOL Reg. § 2509.96-1(d)(4)(v)]

The DOL's 2015 proposed rule would modify this definition by:

- Adding a requirement that there be an objective correlation between the income stream generated by the materials and data supplied by the participant or IRA owner.
- Adding to the list of material facts and assumptions (item #3 above) any other features and rates specific to income annuities or a systematic withdrawal plan. Item #3 above was also expanded to include information relevant to a participant or IRA owner's assessment of different income streams.
- The interactive materials can no longer include reference to any specific investment or distribution option available to the participant or IRA owner unless specified by them.
- The list of other assets to be either taken into account or accompanied by a statement indicating the participant or IRA owner should consider it is expanded to include Social Security benefits. Item #5 above was also expanded to specify that other assets should be considered not only in applying asset allocations, but also in assessing the adequacy of an estimated income stream.

[DOL Prop. Rul. § 2510.3-21(b)(6)(iv)]

Investment Education Versus Investment Advice

Q 8:31 Might there be other examples of investment education materials that would not constitute investment advice?

Yes. According to the DOL, there may be many other examples of investment education materials that would not constitute investment advice. Determination of whether any such information constitutes investment advice must be made by reference to the criteria set forth in DOL Regulations Section 2510.3-21(c)(1) and discussed in Q 8:22. [DOL Reg. § 2509.96-1(d)]

Q 8:32 Are the four types of investment education materials identified in DOL Interpretive Bulletin 96-1 safe harbors for avoiding the rendering of investment advice as defined by ERISA?

Only in a limited sense. The four types of investment education identified in DOL Interpretive Bulletin 96-1 will not in themselves constitute investment advice. However, any of them could be used in a context that could cross the line to become investment advice if they were accompanied by particular recommendations or otherwise interfered with a participant's or beneficiary's exercise of independent control in the selection of asset allocations under the plan.

Investment Education and Fiduciary Liability

Q 8:33 Is the selection by a plan sponsor or fiduciary of a person to provide the types of investment education identified in DOL Interpretive Bulletin 96-1 itself a fiduciary action?

Yes. As with any designation of a service provider to a plan, the designation of a person to provide investment education is an exercise of discretionary authority or control with respect to the management of the plan. Thus, the persons making the designation must act prudently and solely in the interest of the plan participants and beneficiaries both in making the designation and in continuing it. [DOL Reg. § 2509.96-1(e)] While Interpretive Bulletin 96-1 will be superseded in its entirety if and when the DOL's 2015 proposed rule is finalized, in the preamble to the 2015 proposal, the DOL noted that this portion of the bulletin merely applies generally understood and accepted principles that will continue to apply regardless of the status of the bulletin.

Q 8:34 In the context of an ERISA Section 404(c) plan, would the designation of a person to provide the types of investment education identified in DOL Interpretive Bulletin 96-1 give rise to fiduciary responsibility for investment losses resulting from a participant's or beneficiary's asset allocation choices?

No. According to the DOL, the designation of a person to provide investment education (or even the designation of a fiduciary to provide investment advice) would not by itself give rise to fiduciary responsibility for investment loss that was the direct and necessary result of a participant's or beneficiary's independent control over his or her asset allocation choices. [DOL Reg. § 2509.96-1(e)] The DOL's 2015 proposal does not contain this specific language, but indicates the agency's position on this issue has not changed.

Impact of DOL Guidance on Education

Q 8:35 What features of DOL Interpretive Bulletin 96-1 are likely to be of most value to plan sponsors?

In Interpretive Bulletin 96-1 the DOL has clarified that use of model portfolios and interactive materials for generating model portfolios can generally be used in investment education without crossing the line into investment advice. Moreover, these tools can be used in individual counseling sessions as well as in group presentations and can be used on a continuing basis. The DOL's 1996 guidance made it clear that providing investment education will not conflict with the protection from liability for loss provided by ERISA Section 404(c). The DOL's 2015 proposal does not contain this specific language, but indicates the agency's position on this issue has not changed.

Offering Investment Advice

Q 8:36 Why might a plan sponsor want to provide investment advice from an outside professional?

Even with investment education, participants may continue to make inappropriate investment selections and asset allocation decisions. An adviser can offer participants professional investment advice. The person or entity offering investment advice may or may not be affiliated with the plan's investment offerings. Should the investment adviser be deemed to be a fiduciary, the advice must satisfy ERISA's fiduciary duty provisions. The plan fiduciary who selects the investment adviser, who in most cases is the plan sponsor, must act prudently and solely in the interest of participants both in making the selection and in continuing it (see Q 8:37).

Q 8:37 What issues arise under ERISA with respect to offering investment advisory services to participants, and how have the PPA and the DOL's 2015 proposed rule expanded the options available in the investment advice context?

An investment provider that sponsors and manages various investment options that are offered to participants could be seen as violating ERISA's self-dealing provisions if it advises participants to invest in its investments that charge higher fees. [ERISA § 406(b), 29 U.S.C. § 1106(b)] To sidestep fiduciary liability issues, investment providers have enlisted independent consultants to provide advice which is typically computer-generated. The DOL has granted a number of individual exemptions from ERISA's fiduciary provisions for such arrangements.

In 2001, the DOL approved of a SunAmerica program in the form of an advisory opinion, rather than an exemption, based on its finding that the program did not trigger a *per se* violation of ERISA Sections 406(b)(1) and (3) and therefore did not warrant an exemption. The DOL's opinion was based on the following main conditions:

1. Plan fiduciaries responsible for selecting the program are fully informed about, and approve the program;
2. The program under which investment advisory services are provided is facilitated by an independent third-party financial expert;
3. The financial expert retains sole control and discretion over the development and maintenance of program methodologies and advice is based solely on input of participant information into computer programs using those methodologies; and
4. The financial expert's compensation is not related to the fee income the investment provider will receive from investments made under the program.

[DOL Adv. Op. 2001-09A]

The Pension Protection Act of 2006 [Pub. L. No. 109-280, 120 Stat. 780] (PPA) added a statutory exemption for the provision of investment advice under an "eligible investment advice arrangement" (EIAA). Under an EIAA, the investment advice, the investments entered into pursuant to the advice, and the advisor's receipt of fees are exempt from the prohibited transaction rules. This exemption granted to EIAAs under the PPA does not invalidate or otherwise affect prior guidance. So, for example, the following guidance and opinions continue to represent the views of the DOL:

- DOL Interpretive Bulletin 96-1, in which the DOL identified categories of investment-related information and materials that do not constitute investment advice (see Qs 8:21–8:35);
- Advisory Opinion Nos. 97-15A and 2005-10A, in which the DOL explained that a fiduciary investment adviser could provide investment advice with respect to investment funds that pay it or an affiliate additional fees without engaging in a prohibited transaction if those fees are offset against fees that the plan otherwise is obligated to pay to the fiduciary (see chapter 5); and
- Advisory Opinion 2001-09A, in which the DOL concluded that the provision of fiduciary investment advice, under circumstances where the advice provided by the fiduciary with respect to investment funds that pay additional fees to the fiduciary is the result of the application of methodologies developed, maintained, and overseen by a party independent of the fiduciary, would not result in a prohibited transaction (see above).

Whether or not advice is provided pursuant to an EIAA, a plan sponsor has a fiduciary duty to select and monitor the investment advice provider. According to the DOL, a plan sponsor or other fiduciary that prudently selects and monitors an investment advice provider will not, however, be liable for the specific advice given to participants by the advisor.

With regard to the selection process, the plan sponsor should engage in an objective process that is designed to elicit information necessary to assess the provider's qualifications, quality of services offered, and reasonableness of fees charged for the service. Assessing the adviser's registration with applicable federal and/or state securities laws and the adviser's willingness to assume the status of fiduciary with respect to the advice should also be part of the process.

In the monitoring process, fiduciaries should assess the extent to which there have been any changes in the information that served as the basis for the initial selection of the advisor, adherence to contractual provisions of the engagement, utilization of the advisory services by the participants relative to costs, and participant comments and complaints about the quality of the furnished advice. [ERISA §§ 408(b)(14), 408(g); DOL Field Assist. Bull. 2007-1]

The DOL's 2015 proposed rule defining when a person becomes a fiduciary as a result of providing investment advice for a fee is likely to have an impact on advice provided to participants, particularly in the context of distribution or rollover advice. Simultaneous with the publication of the proposed rule, the DOL published a new prohibited transaction exemption, the "Best Interest Contract Exemption," which can be used to allow for fee arrangements that would otherwise by prohibited when providing advice to participants or IRA owners. Both the 2015 proposed rule and the new exemption, as well as more detailed information on EIAAs and related topics in the investment advice area, are covered in chapter 5.

Individual Retirement Planning

This section describes and illustrates key retirement planning concepts. Because retirement planning involves many unknown factors, it may take into consideration a variety of economic scenarios concerning the relationship of an individual's future salary, inflation, and investment choices. Retirement planning may also take into consideration a range of possible retirement ages and provide for different life expectancies at retirement. (See Qs 8:16 and 8:17.)

Retirement Planning Scenarios

Q 8:38 What are some economic scenarios involving future salaries and rates of inflation?

Some sample scenarios involving expectations for future salaries and inflation are:

- Level salary and no inflation
- Salary keeps pace with mild 3 percent inflation
- Salary outpaces mild 3 percent inflation

Q 8:39 What is generally meant by salary "falling behind" or "outpacing" inflation?

Salary falling behind inflation means a person's salary increases on average less than inflation over his or her working life. Similarly, *salary outpacing inflation* means a person's salary increases on average more than inflation over his or her working life.

Q 8:40 What factors influence whether a person's future salary will fall behind, keep pace with, or outpace inflation?

Salary increases are generally regarded to have two components: the increase in salary levels for the entire workforce and increases due to an individual's increased productivity (as evidenced by greater job skill or promotion).

Q 8:41 Can historic levels of inflation provide a guide to future inflation?

Since 1970, inflation has varied greatly from year to year. During the period 1971 to 2005, low to moderate inflation, averaging 2.7 percent, occurred 55 percent of the time, and rapid inflation, averaging 7.2 percent, occurred 45 percent of the time. During a more recent ten-year period (1995 to 2005), inflation averaged 2.8 percent annually. The average during the previous ten-year period (1985 to 1995) was 4.4 percent annually. In 2014, inflation averaged 0.8 percent.

Q 8:42 What are some considerations in choosing a planned retirement age?

At age 59½, qualified retirement plan savings and IRA savings can be withdrawn without a 10 percent early withdrawal penalty. Age 65 has for many years been considered "normal retirement age" under many retirement plans.

Retirement after age 70 should also be considered. Since retirement is no longer mandatory for most workers, more workers are retiring later. This is both practical, since more people are remaining healthy and productive later in life, and necessary, as longer life expectancies require greater amounts for retirement. Although workers traditionally received full Social Security benefits at age 65, current law calls for normal retirement age under Social Security to increase gradually for workers born after 1937 until it reaches age 67 for workers born after 1959.

Q 8:43 What additional factors are considered in retirement planning tools?

Retirement planning tools may take into account probable life expectancy at retirement, expected return on 401(k) assets before and after retirement, and the expected number of years of retirement. Many electronic tools also take into account other available assets (e g., spousal assets or retirement assets held outside the plan), Social Security benefits, and the individual's health.

Replacement Ratios at Retirement

Q 8:44 How is the adequacy of retirement benefits measured?

Replacement ratios are sometimes used to measure the adequacy of retirement benefits. A replacement ratio can be used to measure the adequacy of current benefits.

Q 8:45 What is a *replacement ratio*?

A *replacement ratio* is a ratio obtained by dividing total projected retirement income (including Social Security) by current pay at the time of retirement. Typical adequacy standards vary by income level and decline as income increases.

Example. Company W has a defined benefit plan providing a benefit equal to 25 percent of pay. The company is concerned about the adequacy of its benefits programs. By reviewing the company benefits and projected Social Security benefits at normal retirement age, the company finds shortfalls at all thresholds of income:

Gross Pay	*Defined Benefit Plan*	*Social Security*[a]	*Replacement Ratio (percentage)*	*Target Replacement Ratio (percentage)*	*Shortfall (percentage)*
$ 20,000	$ 5,000	$ 6,000	55%	75%	20%
25,000	6,250	7,500	55	70	15
40,000	10,000	12,000	55	65	10
60,000	15,000	12,000	45	65	20
80,000	20,000	12,000	40	65	25
100,000	25,000	12,000	33	55	22
150,000	37,500	12,000	33	55	22

[a] *Note:* For illustration only—not intended to reflect current levels of Social Security.

Company W might consider installing a 401(k) plan with employer matching contributions to supplement the existing defined benefit plan and make up for the projected shortfalls in replacement income at retirement.

Q 8:46 How do individual retirement planners manage the risk of outliving their retirement savings?

Traditionally, the answer to this problem was to work for a large company that provided a defined benefit plan. However, for most workers, this is not an option. The best way to manage the risk of outliving the savings from a 401(k) is to plan conservatively. For retirement at age 65, using conservative life expectancies—such as more than 20 years for a man and 25 years for a woman—minimizes the risk of outliving retirement savings.

More conservative investment return assumptions may also be used to manage risk. Some 401(k) plans offer annuities or other types of investment options that provide guaranteed payments for life, which is another strategy for managing the risk of outliving one's retirement savings.

Long-Term Investment Return

Q 8:47 What does experience indicate is a way of increasing the expected return from long-term investments?

Experience indicates that different asset classes on average yield significantly different average return on investments. For long-term investments (at least 10 to 20 years), common stocks average an annual return of about 9 to 10 percent, and bonds average an annual return of about 5 to 6 percent.

Q 8:48 What is a disadvantage to investing solely in asset classes with higher expected average return on investment?

Experience shows that asset classes with higher average return on investment are also much riskier in the sense that the investment gain or loss varies more from year to year than does the gain or loss on lower-yielding investment classes.

A common way to measure the risk of variable return from year to year is with the statistic called *standard deviation*. For example, a report on various asset classes over a 20- to 25-year period might show results as follows:

Asset Class	*Average Annual Return*	*Annual Standard Deviation*
Short-term Treasuries	3.0%	3.0%
Intermediate bonds	4.5	5.5
Long-term bonds	5.5	8.3
Real estate	7.0	13.5
Large stocks	10.5	15.5
Small stocks	11.0	19.0

Q 8:49 How should a participant interpret the standard deviation of annual return when assessing the riskiness of an asset class?

About 68 percent of the time, the annual return can be expected to lie within one standard deviation of the average. About 95 percent of the time, the return should lie within two standard deviations, and over 99 percent of the time, the return should lie within three standard deviations. In other words, there is about a one in six chance that the return in any one year will be less than the average return by at least one standard deviation. Since this is the same odds as getting a one when rolling a single die, it is easy to understand that this would not be a very unlikely or surprising outcome.

There is about a 1 in 40 chance any year's return will be as much as 2 standard deviations below the average. Another way to illustrate risk is to show the lowest return over the last 40 or more years—this is often close to the average less 2 standard deviations.

Based on the table above (see Q 8:48), even though large stocks are expected to average 10.5 percent return, there is a 1 in 6 chance that any given year will have a return as low as (or lower than) negative 5 percent (10.5 percent average, less 15.5 percent standard deviation). There is also a 1 in 6 chance that the return in any given year will equal or exceed 26 percent, but most investors do not lie awake nights worrying that their stock investments will earn more than expected.

Q 8:50 How can long-term 401(k) investors manage the variable return risk that comes with higher-yielding asset classes such as stocks?

As return is measured over longer periods of time, the variability decreases substantially. For example, an annual standard deviation of return measuring 7.2 percent may fall to 4.6 percent after 10 years and may fall even further, to 3.8 percent, after 15 years.

Investing across different asset classes can also lower variability of return because of diversification (see chapter 6).

Q 8:51 What is an example of a portfolio that is expected to achieve an investment objective while managing risk?

Suppose that the goal is to achieve an expected return of 7 percent. Given the expected returns seen above (see Q 8:48), a portfolio consisting of 100 percent real estate would have this expected return, but would have a high standard deviation (13.5 percent).

Computer programs are available that can calculate an optimum portfolio given the historical returns of each available asset class, optimum in the sense that it will have the desired expected return but will have a lower variability than any other possible asset mix for that group of asset classes. Such a portfolio for this example might contain 1 percent treasuries, 30 percent intermediate bonds, 16 percent long-term bonds, 27 percent real estate, 18 percent large stocks, and 8 percent small stocks. Such a portfolio may then have the required 7 percent expected return, but would typically have a standard deviation of about 7.2 percent, significantly lower than the real estate class standard deviation of 13.5 percent.

Risk Tolerance

Q 8:52 What is meant by *risk tolerance*?

Risk tolerance refers to the comfort level an investor feels in dealing with different degrees of risk. As discussed above, an asset mix with a higher expected long-term rate of return will also have higher risk in the sense of greater variation of return on a year-by-year basis. How well any investor can or should tolerate this risk depends on a number of factors ranging from the investor's overall economic well-being and the time period before he or she may need to draw on the investment to more psychological factors. It is an important part of investment education to help plan participants relate their risk tolerance to an appropriate asset class mix.

Q 8:53 How can risk tolerance be measured?

Risk tolerance can be measured on a simple scale of low, moderate, or high via computer-based programs and be an underlying component in computer-based retirement planning tools.

The Impact of Inflation

Q 8:54 If salaries are likely to keep pace with inflation, is it important to take inflation into account in retirement planning?

Yes, for two reasons. First, salaries keep pace with inflation only while the employee is working, while inflation continues into retirement. Second, during periods of inflation, more of an employee's investment may be based on higher salaries late in his or her career, and there is less time for compound returns to build substantial retirement assets.

Q 8:55 What does experience show about the ability of various asset classes to keep pace with inflation?

When investing for retirement, investments should keep up with if not outpace inflation over time. Investors can put too much focus on nominal returns that may be reported for an investment. Returns that take inflation into account are real returns. Thus, if the inflation rate is 3 percent and an investment returns 6 percent, its real rate of return is 3 percent.

For the period 1900 to 2011, in the United States, the nominal return on stocks was 9.3 percent and the real return was 6.2 percent, while the nominal return on bonds was 5 percent and the real return was 2 percent. During periods of high inflation, real returns for stock and bonds have been significantly lower than during periods of low inflation.

Other Sources of Retirement Income

Q 8:56 What sources of retirement income besides a 401(k) plan should be considered in planning for retirement?

For the most part, there are three major sources of retirement income: Social Security, employer-provided retirement plans, and personal savings (e.g., IRAs, savings accounts). Home ownership has also been an important source of income during retirement. Retirees have often been able to sell a larger house for much more than they paid for it. After buying a smaller retirement house, they have been able to use the difference to provide income during retirement. As with a qualified retirement plan, the government provides significant tax savings for home ownership.

As indicated above (see Q 8:55), housing has historically been a good investment during periods of inflation. The demand in the housing market has contributed to higher yields. However, the country has experienced a period when housing has done less well.

Q 8:57 What benefits can be expected from Social Security?

Social Security benefits are designed to replace a portion of income lost as a result of retirement, disability, or death. Plan participants should be made well aware that Social Security will not ensure them complete financial security in retirement.

In January 2013, the Social Security Administration announced that individuals now have the ability to access benefit estimates, earnings record, and other information using an online account on the Internet at *www.ssa.gov.* Benefit statements are not automatically mailed annually to most individuals.

Future Social Security levels will be subject to both political and economic forces. As the baby boomers move into retirement, retirees will continue to be a potent political lobby for continuing Social Security payments at historic levels. However, as the percentage of the population that is retired increases, the taxes needed to continue Social Security at historic levels will also increase.

Managing Longevity Risk

Q 8:58 How does the risk of outliving retirement income decrease for years beyond life expectancy?

One way for an individual to manage this risk is to build a measured amount of safety into his or her plan. Table 8-2 starts with a sample 50 percent risk "life expectancy" for retirement ages ranging from 59 to 71, then indicates the payment years needed to reduce the risk of outliving retirement income to 25 percent, 10 percent, 5 percent, and 1 percent. The two numbers shown are for average male mortality and average female mortality, respectively. For example, a male of average health retiring at age 65 would need to plan for payments for 32 years to reduce his risk to 5 percent. A female of average health retiring at age 68 and willing to settle for a 10 percent risk of outliving her retirement income would need to plan for 30 years of payments.

If a person considers himself or herself to be of better than average male/female health, he or she can add three years; if worse than average male/female health, he or she can subtract three years. It should be noted that females on average have better than average male health and need to plan for about three to four more years of income.

Table 8-2. Years (Male/Female) Needed for Each Risk Level of Outliving Retirement Income*

Retirement Age	*50% Risk*	*25% Risk*	*10% Risk*	*5% Risk*	*1% Risk*
59	22/26	29/33	35/38	37/41	42/46
62	20/24	26/30	32/35	35/38	39/43
65	18/21	24/27	29/32	32/35	36/40
68	15/18	20/23	27/30	29/32	33/37
71	13/16	19/22	24/27	26/29	30/34

* For illustration only.

Managing Investment Risk During Retirement

Q 8:59 Why is it important to manage investment risk during retirement?

A retiree withdraws fixed amounts to live on rather than adding fixed amounts as he or she did while saving before retirement. A market downturn before retirement results in more shares being purchased for that fixed dollar savings, and in the long term that results in greater accumulations. After retirement the situation is in effect reversed. Market downturns early in retirement result in a greater permanent reduction in assets as fixed amounts are withdrawn. Even if the average investment return during retirement meets expectations, a pattern of low or negative returns earlier in retirement can seriously affect how long savings will last, and these early low returns may not be offset by higher returns later on.

This illustrates that the length of time savings will last during retirement depends not only on the average rate of return during the period of withdrawal but also on the pattern of those returns during withdrawal.

Q 8:60 How can the investment risk during retirement be managed?

The investment risk during retirement can be managed in a variety of ways. Some of those ways are: saving more before retirement, using more conservative rate of return assumptions in the various planning phases, lowering amounts of postretirement withdrawals in certain time periods, and forgoing potentially higher returns with more conservative investment portfolios near or during retirement. Having access to information on the probabilities or likeliness that any given plan will reach its objective could be helpful in this type of analysis.

Another method for managing risk may be to consider investing in products with certain guaranteed income or withdrawal benefits (e.g., fixed annuities, lifetime income products) (See chapter 6.)

Saver's Credit

Q 8:61 What is the *saver's credit* and how can it be communicated to participants?

Participants who make contributions to a 401(k) plan (or to an IRA) may be eligible for a tax credit called the *saver's credit*. The credit reduces, dollar-for-dollar, federal income taxes payable by the participant. The amount of the credit depends on the contributions made by the participant, the participant's adjusted gross income, and the participant's filing status. The credit rate ranges from 10 to 50 percent of contributions depending on adjusted gross income (AGI). (See Table 8-3.) The maximum contribution taken into account for the credit for an individual is $2,000 ($4,000 if married filing jointly). Thus, the maximum credit is $1,000 ($2,000 if filing jointly). The credit is available to any individual who meets all of the following criteria:

- Is 18 years of age or older
- Is not a full-time student

Table 8-3. Saver's Credit: Credit Rates (2015)

If Income Tax Filing Status Is "Married Filing Jointly" and AGI is	*Credit Rate*
$ 0–$36,500	50% of contribution
$36,501–$39,500	20% of contribution
$39,501–$61,000	10% of contribution
Over $ 61,000	Credit not available
If Income Tax Filing Status Is "Head of Household" and AGI is	***Credit Rate***
$ 0–$27,375	50% of contribution
$27,376–$29,625	20% of contribution
$29,626–$45,750	10% of contribution
Over $45,750	Credit not available
If Income Tax Filing Status Is "Single," "Married Filing Separately," or "Qualifying Widow(er)" and AGI Is	***Credit Rate***
$ 0–$18,250	50% of contribution
$18,251–$19,750	20% of contribution
$19,751–$30,500	10% of contribution
Over $30,500	Credit not available

- Is not claimed as a dependent on someone else's tax return
- Has AGI not exceeding:
  - $50,000 (indexed) if married filing jointly
  - $37,500 (indexed) if head of household with a qualifying person
  - $25,000 (indexed) if single or married filing separately

The PPA made permanent the saver's credit and the applicable AGI limits subject to cost-of-living adjustments after 2006. [PPA §§ 812, 833; I.R.C. § 25B(b)]

The IRS released two sample notices to help employers communicate the saver's credit to employees—one in English and one in Spanish. [IRS Anns. 2001-106, 2001-44 I.R.B. 416; 2001-120, 2001-50 I.R.B. 583] The sample notices must be updated for the applicable adjusted AGI limits. For additional information on the saver's credit, see IRS Publication 590, *Individual Retirement Arrangements (IRAs)*, IRS Publication 4703, *Retirement Savings Contributions Credit*, and IRS Form 8880, Credit for Qualified Retirement Savings Contributions (to claim the saver's credit).

Chapter 9

Contribution Limits

401(k) plans, like other qualified plans, are subject to restrictions on the amounts that can be contributed to them. These restrictions apply at both the employer level and the participant level. At the employer level the restriction takes the form of a limitation on the maximum amount of plan contributions that are deductible by the employer. At the participant level the law limits the total amounts—*annual additions*—that can be allocated to a participant under all plans maintained by the employer. The law also caps the amount of elective deferrals that can be made by an employee during any calendar year, whether to the plans of a single employer or to the plans of more than one employer. This chapter explains these restrictions and their often complex interrelationships.

Limits on Elective Deferrals 9-2
- Excess Deferrals 9-3
- Corrective Distributions 9-4
- Tax Treatment 9-6
- Failure to Correct 9-7
- Catch-Up Contributions 9-8
- SIMPLE 401(k) Plans 9-13

Code Section 415—Annual Addition Limits 9-14
- Annual Additions 9-15
- Compensation Under Code Section 415 9-17
- Plan Design 9-19
- Correcting a Violation 9-19
- Maximum Deferral Percentage 9-20

Code Section 404—Deduction Limits 9-21
- Maximum Deductible Amount 9-21
- Compensation Under Code Section 404 9-22
- Nondeductible Contributions 9-23
- Timing of Deductions 9-24
- Restorative Payments 9-25
- Design Considerations 9-26

Limits on Elective Deferrals

Q 9:1 Is the amount of elective deferrals to a 401(k) plan subject to limitation?

Yes. The law imposes an annual cap on the amount of elective deferrals (see Q 9:3) that can be made by any individual. By 2001, the year before the changes made by the Economic Growth and Tax Relief Reconciliation Act of 2001 (EGTRRA) took effect, the annual cap had risen to $10,500. As a result of EGTRRA, the annual limitation was increased to $11,000 in 2002, with scheduled increases in $1,000 increments thereafter until 2006, at which time the annual cap hit $15,000. After 2006, the dollar cap on elective deferrals has been adjusted periodically in increments of $500 to reflect cost-of-living increases. [I.R.C. § 402(g)(1)] The annual cap for 2015 is $18,000. (See Q 9:36 for a discussion of the lower annual cap for 401(k) plans that are considered SIMPLE 401(k) plans.)

Q 9:2 For what period does the annual cap apply?

The annual cap applies to the participant's taxable year, which, in most cases, will be the calendar year. Thus, a participant's elective deferrals for the taxable year cannot be greater than the annual cap in effect for that year. [I.R.C. § 402(g)(1); Treas. Reg. § 1.402(g)-1(d)(1)]

Q 9:3 What are *elective deferrals*?

Elective deferrals consist of elective contributions made to 401(k) plans, to salary reduction simplified employee pensions (SARSEPs) under Code Section 408(k)(6), and to Section 408(p) SIMPLE retirement plans. Salary reduction contributions made to a Section 403(b) annuity contract are also considered elective deferrals, but salary reduction contributions made to a Section 457 plan are not. (See chapter 22.) [I.R.C. § 402(g)(3); Treas. Reg. § 1.402(g)-1(b)] Finally, permissible withdrawals from an eligible automatic contribution arrangement are not treated as elective deferrals. [Treas. Reg. § 1.414(w)-1(d)(1)(iv)]

> **Example.** From January 1, 2015, to June 30, 2015, when he terminated his employment with a not-for-profit hospital, John contributed $7,000 to a 403(b) annuity contract. On July 1, 2015, he became an employee of ABC Company, which sponsors a 401(k) plan. His participation in the 401(k) plan commenced August 1, 2015. The maximum amount of elective contribution he can make to ABC Company's 401(k) plan for the balance of 2015 is $11,000 ($18,000 minus $7,000 of contributions made to the 403(b) annuity).

Q 9:4 Are designated Roth contributions treated as elective deferrals?

Yes. Designated Roth contributions are treated as elective deferrals for purposes of the annual cap. [I.R.C. § 402A(c)(2); Treas. Reg. § 1.402(g)-1(b)(5)]

Q 9:5 How do the limits on elective deferrals apply to participants who have veterans' reemployment rights under USERRA?

Elective deferrals made by participants with veterans' reemployment rights are treated as elective deferrals with respect to the tax year to which they relate and not to the tax year in which they are actually made. [I.R.C. § 414(u)(1)]

Excess Deferrals

Q 9:6 What happens if the participant's elective deferrals for the taxable year exceed the annual cap?

If a participant has *excess deferrals* (the amount by which a participant's elective deferrals exceed the annual cap) based only on the elective contributions made to a single 401(k) plan, then the plan must return the excess deferrals to the participant by April 15 of the following year. [I.R.C. § 401(a)(30); Treas. Reg. § 1.402(g)-1(e)(1)] It could happen, however, that a participant has excess deferrals as a result of making elective contributions to 401(k) plans, SARSEPs, SIMPLE retirement plans, and 403(b) annuity contracts of different employers. If the 401(k) plan so provides, the participant may notify the plan of the amount of excess deferrals allocated to it no later than April 15 (but typically an earlier date specified in the plan). The plan is then required to distribute to the participant no later than April 15 the amount of the excess deferrals allocated to the 401(k) plan by the participant. [Treas. Reg. § 1.402(g)-1(e)(2)]

> **Example.** Steve is age 43 and participates in Employer Y's 401(k) plan. From January through September, Steve defers $1,600 per month. On October 1, Steve leaves Employer Y and becomes employed by Employer Z (unrelated to Y). During the remainder of 2015, Steve defers $4,000 under Z's 401(k) plan. In January 2016, Steve realizes that he has deferred a total of $18,400 in 2015 and therefore has a $400 excess deferral ($18,400 minus $18,000, the applicable limit for 2015). Assuming at least one of the 401(k) plans permits corrective distributions, Steve has until April 15, 2016 (or such earlier date specified in the plan) to request a distribution of excess deferrals.

Q 9:7 Does the determination of excess deferrals change if a participant's elective deferrals consist of designated Roth contributions?

The determination of excess deferrals does not change if a participant's elective deferrals consist entirely or only partly of designated Roth contributions. [Treas. Reg. § 1.402(g)-1(a)] If a participant has made both pre-tax elective contributions and designated Roth contributions to the same 401(k) plan, the participant must identify the extent to which the excess deferrals consist of designated Roth contributions. If excess deferrals are made to one or more plans maintained by the same employer, and the participant does not identify what portion, if any, of the excess deferral consists of designated Roth contributions, then the plan may provide what portion of the deferral will consist of designated Roth contributions. [Treas. Reg. § 1.402(g)-1(e)(2)(i)]

Corrective Distributions

Q 9:8 Is a plan required to permit the distribution of excess deferrals if the excess deferrals arise from elective contributions made to 401(k) plans, SARSEPs, SIMPLE retirement plans, and 403(b) annuity contracts of different employers?

No, a plan is not required to permit distributions of excess deferrals arising from elective contributions made to 401(k) plans, SIMPLE retirement plans, SARSEPs, and 401(b) annuity contracts of different employers. [Treas. Reg. § 1.402(g)-1(e)(4)]

Q 9:9 If a plan permits the distribution of excess deferrals under the circumstances described in Q 9:8, what conditions can a plan require a participant to meet before permitting a distribution of excess deferrals?

A plan can require that any request by a participant to refund excess deferrals be in writing. It may also require the participant to certify or otherwise establish that the requested refund is an excess deferral. [Treas. Reg. § 1.402(g)-1(e)(4)]

Q 9:10 Must a 401(k) plan wait until after the end of the participant's taxable year before a corrective distribution of excess deferrals can be made?

No. A plan may provide that an individual with excess deferrals can receive a corrective distribution during the taxable year in which the excess deferral occurs. The corrective distribution must occur after the excess deferral is made and must be treated by both the employer and the participant as a corrective distribution. [Treas. Reg. § 1.402(g)-1(e)(3)]

Q 9:11 If an excess deferral is distributed, must the income allocable to the excess deferrals be distributed as well?

Yes. Any income allocable to the excess deferrals must be distributed. [Treas. Reg. § 1.402(g)-1(e)(2)(ii)]

Q 9:12 What is the income allocable to excess deferrals?

The income allocated to excess deferrals is the amount of the allocable gain or loss for the taxable year of the participant. For tax years beginning in 2007 only, it also included the allocable gain or loss for the *gap period* that was the period between the end of the participant's tax year and the date of distribution, if the excess deferrals would have been credited with gain or loss after the end of the tax year and prior to distribution if the participant's total account balance were distributed. As a practical matter, this meant that a gap-period gain or loss calculation was required in the case of a daily valued plan, but was not required in a plan valued less frequently than daily if the excess deferrals were distributed before the first valuation date following the end of the participant's tax year. [Treas. Reg. § 1.402(g)-1(e)(5)(i)] Gap-period income allocations are not required for tax years beginning on or after January 1, 2008, on account of the enactment of Section 109(b)(3) of the Worker, Retiree, and Employer Recovery Act of 2008 [Pub. L. No. 110-458 (Dec. 23, 2008)] (WRERA).

Q 9:13 How is income allocable to excess deferrals determined?

Any reasonable method may be used, provided that the method is not discriminatory, is consistently used for all participants and for all corrective distributions, and is used by the plan for allocating income to participants' accounts. In lieu of devising its own method for allocating income to excess deferrals, a plan may use a method prescribed by the regulations. Under the regulatory method, the income allocable to excess deferrals is determined by multiplying the income allocable for the tax year to elective deferrals by a fraction. The numerator of the fraction is the amount of excess deferrals; the denominator is the amount of the account balance attributable to elective deferrals as of the beginning of the tax year plus the employee's elective deferrals for the tax year. [Treas. Reg. § 1.402(g)-1(e)(5)(ii) and (iii)]

Example. Omicron Company sponsors a daily-valued 401(k) plan. Linda, an employee who has not attained age 50, has an excess deferral of $1,000 for the 2015 calendar year. To determine the amount of income allocable to the excess deferral, Omicron will use the allocation method contained in the regulations. Following are the data needed to calculate the income for the calendar year allocable to Linda's excess deferral.

Income allocated to Linda's elective deferral account for 2015:	$ 6,000
Value of elective deferral account on January 1, 2015:	$75,000
Amount of elective deferrals made during 2015:	$19,000

The income for 2015 allocable to Linda's excess deferral is $63.83, calculated as $1,000 ÷ $94,000 ($95,000 + $19,000) × $6,000.

Q 9:14 Are excess deferrals still treated as employer contributions?

In general, excess deferrals are treated as employer contributions. However, if a non-highly compensated employee (NHCE) makes elective deferrals in excess of the annual cap to one or more plans of the same employer (see definition of *employer* in chapter 10), then the excess deferrals are not taken into account in calculating that NHCE's actual deferral ratio (see chapter 13). Also, excess deferrals that are distributed timely to a participant, including a participant who is a highly compensated employee (HCE), will not be considered annual additions under Code Section 415 (see Q 9:43). [Treas. Reg. §§ 1.402(g)-1(e)(1)(ii), 1.415(c)-1(b)(2)(ii)(D)] This contrasts with the distribution of excess contributions, which continue to be treated as Section 415 annual additions (see chapter 13). (As explained in chapter 13, *excess contributions* are the amounts by which elective contributions for an HCE exceed the amounts permitted by the actual deferral percentage (ADP) nondiscrimination test of Code Section 401(k).)

Q 9:15 How does the distribution or recharacterization of excess contributions affect the amount of excess deferrals that may be distributed to an employee?

The amount of excess deferrals that may be distributed to an employee is reduced by any excess contributions previously distributed or recharacterized with respect to the employee for the plan year beginning with or within the participant's tax year (see chapter 13). In the event of a reduction, the amount of excess contributions includable in the gross income of the employee and reported as a distribution of excess contributions is in turn reduced by the amount of the reduction. [Treas. Reg. § 1.402(g)-1(e)(6)]

Example. Beth, age 35, is an HCE who makes elective contributions of $18,000 to Employer Z's 401(k) plan during the plan year ending December 31, 2015. To satisfy the ADP test for the 2015 plan year, Beth receives a $2,500 distribution of excess contributions in January 2016. In February, Beth notifies Employer Z that she made elective deferrals of $2,200 in 2015 under the 401(k) plan of a different employer and requests distribution of the excess deferral from the 401(k) plan of Employer Z. Since a $2,500 excess contribution has already been distributed to Beth, no additional amount needs to be distributed to her. When reporting these distributions, Employer Z must treat $2,200 of the $2,500 distributed as a distribution of excess deferrals and, as a result, taxable to her in 2015; the $300 balance is treated as a distribution of excess contributions taxable to her in 2016.

Q 9:16 Is employee or spousal consent required for a distribution of excess deferrals and allocable income?

No, consent for a distribution of excess deferrals and allocable income from a 401(k) plan is not required of either the participant or the spouse. [Treas. Reg. § 1.402(g)-1(e)(7)]

Tax Treatment

Q 9:17 What is the tax treatment of corrective distributions to employees?

Because the amount of excess deferrals is includable in the participant's gross income for the calendar year in which the excess deferral is made, a timely corrective distribution of excess deferrals is not included in the participant's gross income for the distribution year. However, the income or loss allocable to excess deferrals is taken into account in determining the participant's gross income for the taxable year in which the distribution of excess deferrals occurs. [Treas. Reg. § 1.402(g)-1(e)(8)(i)]

Q 9:18 Does the tax treatment of corrective distributions change if the distribution consists of designated Roth contributions?

No. The tax treatment is the same because all designated Roth contributions, including a contribution that is considered an excess deferral, are includable in the gross income for the calendar year in which the designated Roth contributions are made. [Treas. Reg. § 1.402(g)-1(e)(8)(i)]

Q 9:19 Are corrective distributions of excess deferrals (plus allocable income) subject to the premature distribution penalty under Code Section 72(t)?

No, corrective distributions are not subject to the premature distribution penalty. [Treas. Reg. § 1.402(g)-1(e)(8)(i)]

Q 9:20 May a corrective distribution of excess deferrals and allocable income be applied toward an employee's minimum distribution requirement under Code Section 401(a)(9)?

No, corrective distributions of excess deferrals and allocable income cannot be used to satisfy an employee's required minimum distributions under Code Section 401(a)(9). [Treas. Reg. § 1.402(g)-1(e)(9)]

Q 9:21 Is a corrective distribution of excess deferrals and allocable income considered an eligible rollover distribution?

A corrective distribution cannot be considered an eligible rollover distribution. [Treas. Reg. §§ 1.402(c)-2, Q&A 4(a), 1.402(g)-1(e)(8)(iv)]

Failure to Correct

Q 9:22 What happens if excess deferrals are not corrected?

It depends on how they arise. If excess deferrals arise out of elective deferrals made to one or more plans maintained by the same employer (see definition of *employer* in chapter 10), then the qualification of the plan is at risk. This is because Code Section 401(a)(30) provides that a plan cannot accept elective deferrals in excess of the annual cap. If, on the other hand, the excess deferrals arise out of elective deferrals made to plans maintained by unrelated employers, the excess deferral will be included in gross income twice: in the calendar year in which the excess deferral was contributed, and in the calendar year in which the excess deferral is ultimately distributed to the participant. [Treas. Reg. § 1.402(g)-1(e)(8)(iii) and (iv)]

Q 9:23 What are the consequences of a failure to correct excess deferrals consisting of designated Roth contributions made to plans of unrelated employers?

If a designated Roth account contains excess deferrals that were not timely distributed, any subsequent distribution from the account will be treated as first coming from the excess deferrals (and attributable income) and will be includable in the gross income of the participant at the time of distribution. Thus, the excess deferral will be includable in income at the time the excess deferral was contributed and at the time it is subsequently distributed. An excess deferral that is not timely distributed cannot be treated as a qualified distribution within the meaning of Code Section 402A(d)(2). [Treas. Reg. § 1.402(g)-1(e)(8)(iv)]

Catch-Up Contributions

Q 9:24 Is there any circumstance under which a participant will be allowed to make elective deferrals in excess of the limitation specified in Q 9:1?

Yes. If a participant will reach age 50 by the end of the year and is unable to make additional deferrals because of a legal, plan, or ADP limit, then the participant can make catch-up contributions. The amount of catch-up contributions that can be made is set forth in the following table.

Year	*Catch-Up Contribution*
2002	*$1,000*
2003	*$2,000*
2004	*$3,000*
2005	*$4,000*
2006	*$5,000*
2007	*$5,000*
2008	*$5,000*
2009	*$5,500*
2010	*$5,500*
2011	*$5,500*
2012	*$5,500*
2013	*$5,500*
2014	*$5,500*
2015	*$6,000*

After 2006, the amount of catch-up contributions is adjusted periodically in increments of $500 to reflect cost-of-living increases. [Treas. Reg. § 1.414(v)-1(c)(2)(i) and (iii)]

Example 1. Alice, an HCE over age 50, participates in a Section 401(k) plan sponsored by her employer. Alice's compensation for the year is $120,000. The maximum annual deferral limit for the year is $18,000. Under the terms of the 401(k) plan, the maximum permitted deferral is 10 percent of compensation or, in Alice's case, $12,000, the amount Alice actually contributes to the plan. After application of the special nondiscrimination rules that govern Section 401(k) plans, the maximum elective deferral Alice may make for the year is $8,000. Alice is able to treat the amount by which her deferrals ($12,000) exceed the amount permitted under the ADP test ($8,000) as a catch-up contribution.

Example 2. Bruce, an NHCE over age 50, is a participant in a Section 401(k) plan. Bruce's compensation for the year is $30,000. The maximum annual deferral limit for the year is $18,000. Under the terms of the 401(k) plan, the maximum permitted deferral is 10 percent of compensation or, in Bruce's case, $3,000. Bruce can contribute up to $9,000 for the year ($3,000 under the normal operation of the plan and an additional $6,000 under the catch-up contribution provision).

Q 9:25 What is a *plan limit*?

A *plan limit* is a limit contained under the terms of the plan but which is not required by the Code. An example would be a plan provision that limits a participant to a deferral percentage of 15 percent of pay. [Treas. Reg. § 1.414(v)-1(b)(1)(ii)] The preamble to the final regulations makes clear that a plan limit would include any limit administratively imposed by the plan administrator pursuant to the provisions of the plan.

Q 9:26 How is a plan limit determined?

Generally, the plan limit is determined as of the end of the plan year by comparing elective deferrals for the plan year with the plan-imposed limit for that year. Alternatively, a plan may provide for separate limits on elective deferrals for separate portions of the plan year. In that case, the plan limit for the plan year is the sum of the amounts determined for each of the separate portions of the plan year. [Treas. Reg. § 1.414(v)-1(b)(2)(i)(A)]

Example. The Dairy Barn Company sponsors a 401(k) plan that provides that participants may defer up to 15 percent of their compensation for each month during the plan year. The plan is amended six months into the plan year to reduce the maximum deferral percentage to 10 percent. Bob, who is over age 50 and makes $4,000 per month, defers the maximum amount permitted each month. The plan limit for Bob is $6,000 ((15% × $4,000 × 6) + (10% × $4,000 × 6)).

Q 9:27 If a 401(k) plan limits elective deferrals for separate portions of the plan year, are there other ways available to calculate the plan limit?

Yes. The regulations permit the calculation of the plan limit to be done on a time-weighted average basis. Thus, the plan limit for any participant is the participant's plan year compensation multiplied by the time-weighted average of the deferral percentage limits in effect during the plan year. [Treas. Reg. § 1.414(v)-1(b)(2)(i)(B)(1)]

Example 1. Phil, age 53, is an HCE participating in his company's 401(k) plan. The plan provides for separate limits on elective deferrals made for each month. At the start of the plan year, the plan administrator, pursuant to the terms of the plan, sets the maximum deferral percentage for HCEs at 10 percent. After two months, the maximum deferral percentage is reduced by the plan administrator to 6 percent. Finally, with two months left in the plan year, the maximum deferral percentage is increased to 8 percent. The time-weighted average for determining Phil's plan limit is 7 percent, calculated as follows:

$$(10\% \times 2) + (6\% \times 8) + (8\% \times 2) \div 12$$

If Phil's pay for the plan year is $120,000, the plan limit for Phil would be $8,400.

The regulations also permit a plan to calculate a participant's plan limit by using compensation as defined for ADP testing purposes (see chapter 13). This alternative can be used even if no changes are made to the deferral percentage limit during the plan year.

Example 2. The facts are the same as those in Example 1, except that for ADP testing purposes, the plan defines compensation to mean compensation net of elective deferrals made to the plan. If Phil contributed $8,000 to the 401(k) plan, his plan limit for the plan year would be $7,840, or ($120,000 – $8,000) × 7%.

Q 9:28 What is a *legal limit*?

A *legal limit* is one imposed by the law. An example would be the annual cap ($18,000 for 2015) on elective deferrals or the limit on annual additions under Code Section 415. [Treas. Reg. § 1.414(v)-1(b)(1)(i)]

Q 9:29 What is the *ADP limit*?

The *ADP limit* is the amount of excess contributions that can be retained in the plan rather than refunded to or recharacterized with respect to an HCE (see Example 1 in Q 9:24). [Treas. Reg. § 1.414(v)-1(b)(1)(iii)]

Q 9:30 When is it determined whether elective deferrals have exceeded a limit?

The timing of this determination depends on the limit in question:

- Plan limits, ADP limits, and some legal limits (Code Section 415, for example) are based on the plan year, and whether or not elective deferrals exceed a limit is determined at the end of the plan year.
- Legal limits not based on the plan year—specifically, the annual cap on elective deferrals (see Q 9:1)—are based on the employee's tax year and are determined as elective deferrals are being made.

Example 1. Joe, an HCE, has elective deferrals of $18,000 for the plan year ending December 31, 2015. The plan fails the ADP test, and an excess contribution of $5,000 is allocated to him. Because the amount of the excess contributions ($5,000) is not greater than the 2015 limit on catch-up contributions ($6,000), no refund is made to Joe.

Example 2. The facts are the same as those in Example 1, except that Joe's allocated excess contribution is $6,500. Because the amount of the excess contribution ($6,500) is greater than the 2015 limit on catch-up contributions ($6,000), Joe must receive a refund of $500.

Example 3. The facts are the same as those in Example 1, except that Joe's elective deferrals reach the annual cap by October 1, 2015. He then makes an additional ($6,000) elective deferral before December 31, 2015. Joe exceeds the legal limit on October 1, 2015, so the $6,000 he contributes thereafter is considered a catch-up contribution. The $6,000 of excess contribution allocated to him as a result of the failed ADP test must be refunded to him.

Q 9:31 How are catch-up contributions treated for tax purposes?

Basically, catch-up contributions are disregarded for tax purposes:

- They are not taken into account in determining a participant's actual deferral ratio for purposes of the ADP test (see Example 3 in Q 9:30).
- They are not treated as annual additions under Code Section 415.
- They do not count toward the annual limitation on the amount of elective deferrals under Code Section 402(g).
- They cannot trigger a top-heavy minimum contribution obligation under Code Section 416; however, in determining whether a plan is top heavy they are taken into account in determining a participant's accrued benefit as of any determination date.
- They are not taken into account for purposes of the average benefit percentage test under Code Section 410(b) if the calculation of the benefit percentages is based on current-year contributions.

[I.R.C. § 414(v)(3) & (4); Treas. Reg. § 1.414(v)-1(d)]

Q 9:32 Must catch-up contributions be made available to all employees?

A 401(k) plan is not required to provide for catch-up contributions, but if a 401(k) plan does contain a catch-up provision, then catch-up contributions must be made available to all employees age 50 or over who are not covered by collective bargaining agreements and who participate in any 401(k) plan maintained by the employer (see chapter 10 for the definition of *employer*). An exception to this rule, which is referred to as the universal availability requirement, applies if a 401(k) plan that does not offer catch-up contributions is acquired by an employer through a merger or similar transaction. In such a case, catch-up contributions would not have to be made available until the second plan year beginning after the plan year in which the merger or similar transaction occurs. [Treas. Reg. § 1.414(v)-1(e)(2) and (4)]

Q 9:33 Is the universal availability requirement violated if different limits apply to different groups of participants?

The universal availability requirement is not violated if different limits apply to different groups of participants. (See also Qs 9:25–9:29.) However, a plan may not provide lower plan limits for catch-up eligible participants. [Treas. Reg. § 1.414(v)-1(e)(1)(i)]

Q 9:34 What happens if a catch-up-eligible individual makes elective deferrals in a calendar year to 401(k) plans of different employers?

If an individual makes contributions in excess of the 402(g) limit for his or her taxable year, the excess (up to the maximum catch-up contribution limit for the year) will be treated as a catch-up contribution. This is the case even if the individual does not exceed any plan, legal, or ADP limit under any of the plans in which he or she participates. [Treas. Reg. § 1.402(g)-2(b)]

> **Example.** Jim, an NHCE who is over age 50, participates in Company A's 401(k) plan during the first six months of 2015 and contributes $9,000. Starting July 1, 2015, he commences participation in Company B's 401(k) plan and contributes $10,000 to that plan. Both plans provide that the maximum elective deferral amount is the current Code Section 402(g) limit ($18,000 in 2015). Even though Jim did not exceed the plan limit in either plan, the $1,000 he contributes in excess of the 2015 Section 402(g) limit is considered a catch-up contribution.

Q 9:35 Can catch-up contributions consist of designated Roth contributions?

Yes. The operation of the catch-up contribution rules does not change if a participant's deferrals are designated Roth contributions.

SIMPLE 401(k) Plans

Q 9:36 What is the annual cap on elective deferrals to a SIMPLE 401(k) plan?

As a result of the enactment of EGTRRA, the annual cap for 2002 was $7,000. It has increased since then as set forth in the table below.

Year	*Annual Cap*
2003	$ 8,000
2004	$ 9,000
2005	$10,000
2006	$10,000
2007	$10,500
2008	$10,500
2009	$11,500
2010	$11,500
2011	$11,500
2012	$11,500
2013	$12,000
2014	$12,000
2015	$12,500

The dollar cap on elective deferrals will be adjusted periodically in increments of $500 to reflect cost-of-living increases. [I.R.C. § 408(p)(2)(E)]

Q 9:37 Is there any circumstance under which a participant will be allowed to make elective deferrals in excess of the limitation specified in Q 9:36?

Yes. If a participant has reached age 50 by the end of the year and is unable to make additional elective deferrals because of a legal or a plan restriction (see Qs 9:25, 9:28), then the participant can make catch-up contributions. The annual limit on the amount of catch-up contributions is set forth in the following table.

Year	*Catch-Up Contribution*
2002	$ 500
2003	$1,000
2004	$1,500
2005	$2,000
2006	$2,500

Year	*Catch-Up Contribution*
2007	$2,500
2008	$2,500
2009	$2,500
2010	$2,500
2011	$2,500
2012	$2,500
2013	$2,500
2014	$2,500
2015	$3,000

The annual limit on catch-up contributions will be adjusted periodically in increments of $500 to reflect cost-of-living increases. [I.R.C. § 414(v)(2)(B)(ii)]

Q 9:38 What happens if a participant's elective deferrals exceed the annual cap on elective deferrals to a SIMPLE 401(k) plan?

The law is at present unclear about what happens if a participant has excess deferrals based only on the elective deferrals made to a single SIMPLE 401(k) plan. The mechanism for returning excess deferrals, as explained in Q 9:6, does not appear to apply to SIMPLE 401(k) plans. Perhaps, in this situation, the 401(k) plan will lose its SIMPLE status and will be required to satisfy the actual deferral percentage test (see chapter 13) and to provide for top-heavy minimum contributions. However, excess deferrals resulting from elective deferrals to 401(k) plans, SARSEPs, SIMPLE retirement plans, and 403(b) annuity contracts of different employers can be returned as explained above in Q 9:6.

Example. Joan, age 48, who is a participant in the Lydell Corporation's 401(k) plan, defers $10,000 between January 1, 2015, and June 30, 2015. On July 1, 2015, Joan leaves Lydell and commences employment with the Silo Company (unrelated to Lydell). Joan is allowed to participate immediately in Silo's SIMPLE 401(k) plan, and she defers $9,000 during the last six months of 2015. In January 2016, Joan realizes that she has deferred a total of $19,000 in 2015 and therefore has a $1,000 excess deferral ($19,000 minus $18,000, the applicable limit for 2015). Assuming that the Lydell plan permits corrective distributions, Joan has until April 15, 2016, to receive a distribution of excess deferrals plus allocable income.

Code Section 415—Annual Addition Limits

Q 9:39 How does Code Section 415 limit annual additions to a 401(k) plan?

Code Section 415 limits the annual additions that may be allocated to an individual's account in any limitation year. The limitation year is the calendar year unless another 12-month period is designated in the plan document. (Nearly every plan will designate the plan year as its limitation year.) The maximum annual addition is the lesser of 100 percent of compensation or $40,000. [I.R.C. § 415(c)(1)]

Q 9:40 Will the $40,000 limit be indexed for inflation?

Yes, the $40,000 limit will be indexed for inflation in increments of $1,000. [I.R.C. § 415(d)] The limit in effect for 2015 is $53,000.

Q 9:41 How are increases in the $40,000 limit applied to limitation years that end on a date other than December 31?

Any increase in the $40,000 limit is applied to any limitation year that ends in the calendar year for which the increase is effective. [Treas. Reg. § 1.415(d)-1(b)(2)(iii)]

> **Example.** The Glendale Corporation sponsors a 401(k) plan that has a March 31 limitation year. For the limitation year that ended March 31, 2015, the Section 415 dollar limitation on annual additions was $53,000.

Annual Additions

Q 9:42 What are *annual additions*?

Annual additions consist of the following:

1. Elective contributions (including designated Roth contributions) but not including elective contributions that are catch-up contributions for participants who have reached age 50 (see Qs 9:24, 9:37);
2. Employer matching contributions;
3. Employer nonelective contributions;
4. Employee mandatory and voluntary after-tax contributions;
5. Employer contributions to other defined contribution plans, including money purchase plans, ESOPs, and profit sharing plans;
6. Forfeitures allocated to a participant's account from nonvested or partially vested terminated participants;
7. Amounts allocated to a Section 401(h) individual medical account, which is part of a qualified pension plan maintained by the employer; and
8. Employer contributions for a key employee allocated to a separate account under a welfare benefit plan for post-retirement medical benefits.

[Treas. Reg. § 1.415(c)-1(b)]

The annual additions described at (7) and (8) count only toward the dollar limit. They do not count toward the percentage of compensation limit. [Treas. Reg. § 1.415(c)-1(e)] When determining an employee's annual additions, contributions to all defined contribution plans maintained by the same employer must be aggregated. [Treas. Reg. § 1.415(f)-1(a)(2)] (See chapter 10 for the definition of *employer*.)

Q 9:43 What are not considered annual additions?

The items listed below are not considered annual additions:

1. A direct transfer of funds from one defined contribution plan to another;
2. ESOP dividends that are reinvested in employer securities at the election of the participant;
3. Amount paid by the employer to restore the previously forfeited account balance of a participant;
4. Amounts paid to the plan to restore losses to a plan resulting from the actions of a fiduciary for which there is a reasonable risk of liability for breach of ERISA fiduciary duties (see Q 9:69);
5. Excess deferrals that are distributed on or before April 15;
6. Rollover contributions;
7. Loan repayments;
8. Amounts paid by a participant to buy back the portion of his or her account that was previously forfeited; and
9. Catch-up contributions.

[Treas. Reg. §§ 1.415(c)-1(b)(1)(iii) & (iv), 1.415(c)-1(b)(2)(ii), 1.415(c)-1(b)(3)]

Q 9:44 What special rules apply to 401(k) stock ownership plans that have borrowed funds to purchase employer securities of a corporation which, for tax purposes, is considered a C corporation?

If no more than one-third of an employer's contributions to a 401(k) stock ownership plan (KSOP) is allocated to HCEs (see chapter 10), the following will not be considered annual additions:

1. Forfeitures of employer securities that were acquired with borrowed funds; and
2. Contributions that are applied to the payment of interest on funds borrowed to acquire employer securities.

[I.R.C. § 415(c)(6); Treas. Reg. § 1.415(c)-1(f)]

Q 9:45 How do the limits on annual additions apply to participants who have veterans' reemployment rights under USERRA?

Employer and employee contributions allocated to the account of a participant with veterans' reemployment rights are treated as annual additions for the limitation year to which they relate and not to the limitation year in which they are actually made and allocated. [I.R.C. § 414(u)(1)]

Compensation Under Code Section 415

Q 9:46 What is considered compensation for purposes of the percentage of compensation limit?

Generally, total compensation earned during the limitation year from the employer maintaining the plan is considered. Specifically, the following items are included in the general definition of compensation under Code Section 415:

1. The employee's wages, salaries, fees for professional services, and other amounts received for personal services, to the extent that such amounts are includable in gross income;
2. For a self-employed individual, earned income;
3. Taxable amounts that result from employer-provided accident and health insurance benefits and medical reimbursement plan benefits;
4. Moving expenses paid by the employer that are not expected to be deductible by the employee;
5. The value of a nonstatutory stock option granted to an employee to the extent includable in gross income for the taxable year in which granted;
6. The amount includable in gross income upon making an election under Section 83(b) to be taxed on the value of restricted property;
7. Amounts includable in gross income under the rules for nonqualified deferred compensation plans under Code Section 409A or because such amounts are constructively received; and
8. Differential wage payments as defined in Code Section 3401(h)(2).

[Treas. Reg. § 1.415(c)-2(b); Notice 2010-15, Q&A 10, 2010-6 I.R.B. 390]

The following items are specifically excluded from the general definition of compensation:

1. Employer contributions to a deferred compensation plan (other than elective contributions as explained in Q 9:49) to the extent not includable in gross income;
2. Distributions from a deferred compensation plan, unless such distributions are from an unfunded nonqualified plan (in which case they may be treated as compensation);
3. Amounts realized from the exercise of a nonstatutory stock option or when restricted stock or property held by an employee either becomes freely transferable or is no longer subject to a substantial risk of forfeiture;
4. Amounts realized from the sale, exchange, or other disposition of stock acquired under a statutory stock option; and
5. Amounts that receive special tax benefits, such as premiums for group term life insurance, but only to the extent that such benefits are not includable in gross income of the employee.

[Treas. Reg. § 1.415(c)-2(c)]

Q 9:47 Are amounts paid after severance from employment treated as compensation?

Certain types of remuneration will be treated as compensation if paid within 2½ months after severance or, if later, by the end of the limitation year in which the severance from employment occurs. Payments on account of services rendered by the employee before termination that would have been paid to the employee had employment not terminated are treated as compensation. Also included, if the plan so provides, are payments for unused accrued bona fide sick, vacation, or other leave or pursuant to a nonqualified unfunded deferred compensation plan provided the employee would have been able to use the leave or receive the deferred compensation payments if his or her employment had not terminated. In addition, salary continuation payments for disabled participants and military continuation payments that are not differential wage payments may also be treated as compensation if the plan so provides. All other types of post-severance compensation are not considered compensation for purposes of Code Section 415. [Treas. Reg. § 1.415(c)-2(e)(3) & (4)]

Q 9:48 Are there other definitions of compensation that satisfy Code Section 415?

Yes. The regulations provide for three alternatives:

1. The short list definition, which treats as compensation for Section 415 purposes only the items included in (1) and (2) of the first paragraph in Q 9:46 [Treas. Reg. § 1.415(c)-2(d)(2)];
2. The W-2 definition, under which compensation for Section 415 purposes is generally the amount of compensation that would be reported on Form W-2 [Treas. Reg. § 1.415(c)-2(d)(4)]; and
3. The federal income tax withholding definition, under which compensation for Section 415 purposes is generally the amount of compensation subject to federal income tax withholding under Code Section 3401(a). [Treas. Reg. § 1.415(c)-2(d)(3)]

Table 10-1 in chapter 10 shows which items of remuneration are treated as Section 415 compensation under these various definitions.

Q 9:49 Are elective deferrals treated as compensation for purposes of Code Section 415?

Elective deferrals are treated as compensation for purposes of Code Section 415. Also treated as compensation are amounts that employees elect to defer to SARSEPs under Code Section 408(k)(6), and to Section 408(p) SIMPLE retirement plans (see Q 9:3), as well as amounts deferred into Section 125 cafeteria plans, Section 132(f) qualified transportation fringe plans, and Section 457 plans. [I.R.C. § 415(c)(3); Treas. Reg. §§ 1.415(c)-2(b)(1), 1.415(c)-2(d)(3) & (4)]

Q 9:50 What is considered compensation in the case of participants who have veterans' reemployment rights under USERRA?

A participant with veterans' reemployment rights will be treated as receiving compensation during his or her period of military service equal to the compensation the participant would have received during that period if he or she had not been in military service, based on the rate of pay the participant would have received but for his or her absence. However, if the compensation the participant would have received is not reasonably certain, then the participant's average compensation for the 12-month period (or, if shorter, the period of employment) immediately preceding military service is used in determining the participant's compensation during his or her military service. [I.R.C. § 414(u)(7)]

Plan Design

Q 9:51 How should a 401(k) plan be designed to ensure that the Section 415 limits are not violated?

The plan should contain some fail-safe language, such as the following, that provides for inadvertent violations of this limit:

> Amounts in excess of this limit will be reallocated to the remaining participants. To the extent that every participant in the plan has reached his or her limit, any remaining amounts shall be placed in a suspense account and reallocated in the next year.

If the 401(k) plan is designed carefully, there should be little chance that the annual additions limitation will be violated in a limitation year. With the enactment of EGTRRA and its increase in the defined contribution Section 415(c) limits, potential violations will usually be confined to those whose annual additions approach the $40,000 (as indexed) limitation.

Correcting a Violation

Q 9:52 Can a violation of the Code Section 415 limits be corrected by returning elective deferrals?

Yes. If the violation of Code Section 415 results from annual additions attributable to elective deferrals, Section 6.06(2) of Revenue Procedure 2013-12 [2013-4 I.R.B.313] provides that the violation will be corrected in the following order:

1. Unmatched employee after-tax contributions are distributed.
2. Unmatched elective deferrals are distributed.
3. Matched employee after-tax contributions are distributed and the associated match contributions are forfeited and placed in a suspense account.
4. Matched elective deferrals are distributed and the associated match contributions are forfeited and placed in a suspense account.
5. Nonelective contributions are forfeited.

The amounts to be distributed or forfeited are adjusted for earnings. Amounts held in a suspense account are used to reduce employer contributions in the current and succeeding years, the suspense account is to be adjusted for earnings, and, while amounts remain in the suspense account, the employer is not permitted to make contributions (other than elective deferrals) to the plan.

Q 9:53 What are the tax implications of elective deferrals that are returned to a participant to correct a Section 415 violation?

The tax consequences of returned elective deferrals are as follows:

1. The distribution, to the extent it does not consist of Roth deferrals, is includable in income for the taxable year distributed.
2. The distribution cannot carry out any basis (after-tax contributions, PS-58 costs, etc.) a participant may have in the 401(k) plan.
3. The distribution is not subject to the additional income tax on premature distributions under Code Section 72(t).
4. The distribution is not considered wages for Federal Insurance Contributions Act (FICA) and Federal Unemployment Tax Act (FUTA) purposes.
5. No consent (by either the participant or the spouse) is required.
6. The distribution is subject to voluntary withholding under Code Section 3405. Thus, it is not considered an eligible rollover distribution.
7. The returned elective deferrals are not counted toward the annual limit on elective deferrals (see section dealing with limits on elective deferrals in this chapter) and are not treated as elective contributions for purposes of the actual deferral percentage test. (See section on actual deferral percentage test in chapter 13.)

[Rev. Proc. 92-93, 1992-2 C.B. 505]

Maximum Deferral Percentage

Q 9:54 What is the maximum deferral percentage that can be provided for in a 401(k) plan?

Subject only to the annual cap on elective deferrals (see Q 9:1), the maximum deferral percentage can be 100 percent in a 401(k) plan that provides for elective contributions only. Two changes under EGTRRA make this possible. First, elective contributions are no longer counted in determining the maximum deductible contribution under Code Section 404. Second, the Section 415(c) percentage limit on annual additions is now 100 percent of compensation. In a 401(k) plan that provides for other types of contributions (e.g., match, nonelective, or both) the maximum deferral percentage would need to be reduced only by such other contributions (expressed as an anticipated percentage of compensation).

Code Section 404—Deduction Limits

Q 9:55 What deduction limits are applicable to a 401(k) plan?

Because a 401(k) plan is usually a type of profit sharing plan, contributions will be subject to the deductibility rules for profit sharing plans. [I.R.C. § 404(a)(3)]

Maximum Deductible Amount

Q 9:56 What is the maximum annual deductible amount for a 401(k) plan?

The maximum deductible amount is 25 percent of the compensation paid during the taxable year to the participants under the plan. [I.R.C. § 404(a)(3)(A)]

Q 9:57 How is the deduction limit applied if the employer sponsors two or more profit sharing (including 401(k)) plans?

If an employer maintains two or more profit sharing plans, they are treated as a single plan for purposes of applying the 25 percent limit. [I.R.C. § 404(a)(3)(A)(iv)]

Q 9:58 Is the maximum deductible amount determined with respect to each participant, or is it determined on an aggregate basis?

The maximum deductible amount is determined on an aggregate basis. Thus, it does not matter that a particular participant's allocation of contributions in a 401(k) plan is greater than 25 percent of his or her compensation. What does matter is that the total amount contributed to the 401(k) plan not exceed the maximum percentage of the aggregate compensation of the participants benefiting under the plan. [Treas. Reg. § 1.404(a)-9(c)]

Q 9:59 Are elective contributions treated as employer contributions for purposes of the deduction limit?

Elective contributions are not treated as employer contributions for purposes of the deduction limit. Thus, elective contributions are always fully deductible. [I.R.C. § 404(n)]

Q 9:60 What special deduction rules apply to KSOPs maintained by corporations that, for tax purposes, are considered C corporations?

Employer contributions that are used to repay interest on funds borrowed by the KSOP to acquire employer securities are deductible without limitation.

[I.R.C. § 404(a)(9)] In addition, cash dividends paid by the corporation are deductible if any one of the circumstances below applies:

1. The dividend is used to make payments on amounts borrowed by the KSOP to acquire employer securities;
2. The dividend is paid in cash to the participants;
3. The dividend is paid to the plan and is distributed in cash to the participants no later than 90 days after the end of the plan year in which the dividend is paid; or
4. At the election of the participant, the dividend is paid as provided in 2 or 3 above or is paid to the KSOP and reinvested in employer securities.

[I.R.C. § 404(k); IRS Notice 2002-2, 2000-2 I.R.B. 285]

Compensation Under Code Section 404

Q 9:61 What does the term *compensation* mean?

According to the regulations, *compensation* means all compensation paid or accrued during the taxable year. Compensation includes elective contributions and other amounts contributed by employees on a pre-tax basis. [I.R.C. § 404(a)(12)] Finally, the plan's definition of compensation is not relevant in determining the maximum deductible amount. [Rev. Rul. 80-145, 1980-1 C.B. 89]

> **Example.** Under a 401(k) plan, participants are not allowed to defer any portion of a bonus, and bonuses are not taken into account in allocating nonelective contributions. Compensation not including bonuses is $1 million; bonuses for the year are $500,000. The maximum deductible amount for the taxable year is $375,000 ($1,500,000 × 25%).

Q 9:62 Is there a limit on the amount of compensation that may be taken into account in determining the maximum deductible amount?

Yes. Under Code Section 404(*l*), the amount of compensation that may be taken into account with respect to any participant is limited to $200,000. The $200,000 limit will be adjusted for future cost-of-living increases in increments of $5,000. [I.R.C. § 404(*l*)] The following table shows the compensation limit in effect for taxable years beginning in the following years:

Year	*Compensation Limit*
2002	$200,000
2003	$200,000
2004	$205,000
2005	$210,000
2006	$220,000

2007	$225,000
2008	$230,000
2009	$245,000
2010	$245,000
2011	$245,000
2012	$250,000
2013	$255,000
2014	$260,000
2015	$265,000

Q 9:63 In determining the maximum deductible amount, may the employer take into account the compensation of all employees, or just those who are plan participants?

Only the compensation of those participants who benefit under the 401(k) plan may be taken into account. [Rev. Rul. 65-295, 1965-2 C.B. 148] The cited revenue ruling does not deal specifically with a 401(k) plan. It has always been assumed that the compensation of a participant who elects not to make contributions would be taken into account in determining the maximum deductible amount, but in Private Letter Ruling 201229012 the IRS took the opposite view.

Q 9:64 Is the maximum deductible amount determined on the basis of the plan year or the taxable year of the employer?

The maximum deductible amount is determined with reference to compensation paid or accrued during the taxable year of the employer, not the plan year.

Nondeductible Contributions

Q 9:65 What happens if more than the maximum deductible amount is contributed to a 401(k) plan?

If contributions to a 401(k) plan exceed the maximum deductible amount for the taxable year, the employer is obligated to pay an excise tax equal to 10 percent of the nondeductible amount. [I.R.C. § 4972] Any excess amount can be deducted in a succeeding taxable year if the excess amount and the contributions made in the succeeding taxable year do not exceed the maximum deductible limit in the succeeding taxable year. [I.R.C. § 404(a)(3)(A)(ii)]

> **Example.** For its tax year beginning July 1, 2014, Alpha contributed $300,000 (not including elective contributions) to its 401(k) plan. Aggregate participant compensation for the year was $1 million. As a result, Alpha made a nondeductible contribution of $50,000 ($300,000 − (25% × $1,000,000)), which resulted in an excise tax liability of $5,000 (10% × $50,000). In the succeeding tax year, beginning July 1, 2015, aggregate

compensation was $1.5 million and contributions (not including elective contributions) for that year again totaled $300,000. The $50,000 nondeductible contribution was fully deductible because $350,000 ($50,000 + $300,000) was less than $375,000 ($1,500,000 × 25%), the maximum deductible amount for the tax year beginning July 1, 2015.

Q 9:66 May an employer avoid the excise tax on nondeductible contributions by withdrawing them before the end of the taxable year?

No. Absent a good-faith mistake of fact (see chapter 2), contributions made to a plan cannot be returned without jeopardizing its qualified status. [I.R.C. § 401(a)(2); Rev. Rul. 91-4, 1991-1 C.B. 57]

Timing of Deductions

Q 9:67 For what taxable year are contributions to a 401(k) plan deductible?

As a general rule, contributions are deductible for the taxable year in which they are paid. The fact that an employer may be an accrual basis taxpayer is not relevant. The one exception to the general rule treats contributions as having been paid on the last day of the taxable year if the contributions are paid no later than the tax return due date (including extensions) for that taxable year. [I.R.C. § 404(a)(6)]

Q 9:68 Can an employer deduct elective and matching contributions for a taxable year if they are made before the tax return due date (including extensions for that taxable year) but are attributable to compensation earned by plan participants in the succeeding taxable year?

No. According to the IRS, these contributions are not deductible in the previous taxable year because they do not relate to compensation paid in that taxable year. [Rev. Rul. 90-105, 1990-2 C.B. 69; Rev. Rul. 2002-46, 2002-29 I.R.B. 117]

Example. SRT Company, which is a June 30 taxpayer, sponsors a 401(k) plan that is administered on a calendar-year basis. SRT Company makes elective contributions and matching contributions in July 2015. These contributions are attributable to compensation paid to participants in that month. Although these contributions were paid before the tax return due date for the tax year ending June 30, 2015, they are not deductible for that year. They are deductible for the tax year ending June 30, 2016, because they relate to compensation paid in that year.

Restorative Payments

Q 9:69 Are payments that are made to restore losses resulting from breaches of fiduciary duties considered contributions for purposes of any of the limits discussed in this chapter?

No. Such payments are not considered contributions for purposes of any of the limits discussed in this chapter. In addition, restorative payments are not considered contributions for applying the nondiscrimination rules that apply to contributions made to a 401(k) plan. [Treas. Reg. § 1.415(c)-1(b)(2)(ii)(C); Rev. Rul. 2002-45, 2002-29 I.R.B. 116]

Q 9:70 What is a *restorative contribution*?

A *restorative contribution* is a payment made to restore losses to the plan resulting from actions by a fiduciary where there is a reasonable risk of liability for breach of fiduciary duty under ERISA or other federal or state law. [Treas. Reg. § 1.415(c)-1(b)(2)(ii)(C); Rev. Rul. 2002-45, 2002-29 I.R.B. 116]

> **Example 1.** An employer maintaining a 401(k) plan caused the plan to invest 75 percent of its assets in a limited partnership that is later determined to be worthless. A group of participants files suit against the employer, the result of which is a settlement in which the employer does not admit liability but does make payments to the plan in the amount of loss. The payment made by the employer is considered a restorative contribution and, accordingly, is not considered a contribution for tax purposes.

> **Example 2.** An employer maintaining a 401(k) plan caused an annuity contract to be surrendered as part of the process of changing to a different plan recordkeeper. The annuity contract has surrender charges; thus, the employer proposes to make payments to the plan equal to the amount of the surrender charges. Because the loss to the plan does not involve a breach of fiduciary duty, the employer's proposed payment will not be considered a restorative contribution.

> **Example 3.** The facts are the same as those in Example 2, except that the surrender charges are paid by a different insurance company, which issues an annuity contract to replace the one that was previously surrendered. The replacement annuity contract also contains surrender charges in the event the contract is terminated prematurely. In this situation, the IRS has ruled that the restoration of the surrender charges by the insurance company is considered a restorative contribution. [Priv. Ltr. Rul. 200404050]

Q 9:71 What other requirements must be met for such payments to be considered restorative contributions?

For payments to be considered restorative contributions, plan participants who are similarly situated must be treated similarly with respect to the payment. However, this rule will not be violated if the participant who is the fiduciary responsible for the loss is not made whole by the payment. In addition, other than adjustments to reflect lost earnings, the restorative contribution must be limited to the amount actually lost. [Treas. Reg. § 1.415(c)-1(b)(2)(ii)(C); Rev. Rul. 2002-45, 2002-29 I.R.B. 116]

Design Considerations

Q 9:72 How should the deductible limit be taken into account in the design of the plan?

For tax years beginning after December 31, 2001, the deduction limit is not as important a design factor as it was for previous years. Its diminished importance results from the increase in the deduction limit from 15 percent to 25 percent of compensation, from the treatment of elective contributions and other pre-tax deferred amounts (see Q 9:61) as compensation for purposes of computing the maximum deductible amount, and from not counting elective contributions toward the new 25 percent of compensation limit. Even in the case of an employer that maintains another profit sharing plan, it is unlikely that nonelective contributions (both discretionary profit sharing and match) under both plans will approach the 25 percent of compensation limit.

Q 9:73 What is the deductible limit if the employer also has a defined benefit plan?

Generally speaking, deductibility is limited to 25 percent of pay, or, if greater, the amount necessary to satisfy the defined benefit plan's minimum funding requirements. But this combined limit only applies if at least one employee is covered by both a 401(k) plan and a defined benefit plan. However, the combined 25 percent limit does not apply at all when the only contributions to the 401(k) plan are elective deferrals and does not apply to the 401(k) plan if the amount of employer matching and nonelective contributions to the 401(k) plan does not exceed 6 percent of the compensation of the participants in the 401(k) and defined benefit plans. If the amount of employer matching and nonelective contributions to the 401(k) plan exceeds 6 percent of compensation of the participants in the plans, the combined limit only applies to the amount of such contributions in excess of 6 percent. [I.R.C. § 404(a)(7)]

Q 9:74 May an employer with an existing profit sharing plan set up a 401(k) plan?

An employer that regularly makes an annual contribution equal to 25 percent of pay into a profit sharing plan can still set up a 401(k) plan since elective contributions do not count toward the 25 percent-of-pay deduction limit.

Q 9:75 How are the limits coordinated if the employer has a money purchase or target plan?

Coordination of a money purchase plan or target plan with a 401(k) plan presents a situation that is no different from the situation of an employer that wants to add a 401(k) feature to its existing profit sharing plan (see Q 9:74). The situations are the same because money purchase and target plans are, for deduction purposes, subject to the same deduction limit as are profit sharing plans. [I.R.C. § 404(a)(3)(A)(v)]

Q 9:76 If an employer has an existing money purchase plan in addition to a 401(k) plan, should the employer consider terminating the money purchase plan?

Before the enactment of EGTRRA, most employers with a 401(k) plan needed to maintain a money purchase plan in order to provide fully deductible contributions up to the pre-EGTRRA Code Section 415 annual additions limitation (lesser of $35,000 or 25 percent of pay in 2001). Because money purchase plans are now subject to the same deduction limitations as 401(k) plans, in most cases there is no need for an employer to maintain both plans to achieve its retirement plan objectives. As a result, many employers have terminated their money purchase plans or have merged them into their 401(k) plans.

An employer considering a merger of its money purchase plan into its 401(k) plan must be aware of the issues that such a merger presents. First, the employer must provide advance notice of the merger because it will be considered a significant reduction in the rate of future benefit accrual as defined in ERISA Section 204(h) and Code Section 4980F. Second, a participant's vested percentage in his or her account balance cannot be reduced as a result of the merger and those participants with three or more years of vesting service have the right to have their vested percentages determined under the vesting schedule that was contained in the money purchase plan. Third, the money purchase account balances, even after the merger, retain their character as pension plan-type funds. Thus, those balances remain subject to Code Section 417 joint and survivor rules; and in-service distribution provisions, which may be available to account balances under the 401(k) plan (for example, hardship withdrawals), in most cases cannot be extended to the money purchase account balances.

Q 9:77 Will the merger of a money purchase pension plan into a 401(k) plan require 100 percent vesting of the money purchase account balances?

No. The IRS has made clear that 100 percent vesting is not required in the case of a merger of a money purchase pension plan into a 401(k) plan. [Rev. Rul. 2002-42, 2002-28 I.R.B. 76]

Chapter 10

Data for Nondiscrimination Testing

This chapter, along with chapters 11 through 13, sets forth the nondiscrimination tests a 401(k) plan must pass to ensure that the plan does not unduly favor highly compensated employees (HCEs). The data for performing these tests must be assembled correctly. Crucial to the data collection are certain terms and concepts that are explained in this chapter.

Because 401(k) plans are established and maintained by employers, the chapter starts by discussing who is considered to be the employer when the Internal Revenue Code's nondiscrimination rules are applied. The chapter then defines the term *plan,* which, for purposes of applying the nondiscrimination rules, differs from the commonsense notion of what a 401(k) plan is. Following that, the chapter defines and discusses other terms that will be important in applying the Code's nondiscrimination rules:

- Who are considered *employees*?
- Which employees are considered *HCEs*?
- What is *compensation*?

Who Is the Employer? 10-2
Controlled Groups 10-2
Constructive Ownership Rules 10-7
Significance of Controlled Groups 10-11
Affiliated Service Groups 10-11
Qualified Separate Lines of Business 10-16
Flowchart 10-1. Qualified Separate Lines of Business (QSLOBs) 10-18
What Is a Plan? 10-23
Who Is an Employee? 10-26
Who Is a Highly Compensated Employee? 10-30
Worksheet 10-1. How to Determine Membership in the Top-Paid Group 10-35
Flowchart 10-2. Determination of HCEs 10-37

What Is Compensation? 10-37
Table 10-1. Compensation Definitions That Satisfy Code Section 414(s) 10-44

Who Is the Employer?

To prevent taxpayers from avoiding nondiscrimination and other qualification requirements through the use of multiple entities, rules have been developed that require certain related entities to be treated as a single employer for purposes of these requirements. Where there is sufficient common ownership to form a *controlled group* of corporations, employees are treated as employed by a single employer. Similar controlled group rules also apply to groups consisting of at least one noncorporate employer. Even where there may not be sufficient common ownership to form a controlled group, other rules require the aggregation of members of an *affiliated service group.* Although aggregation of related entities is the general rule, it is possible for multiple entities (and even parts of a single entity) to be treated as separate employers if the *qualified separate lines of business* (QSLOB) rules are satisfied.

Controlled Groups

Q 10:1 Must business entities under common control be treated as a single employer when applying the nondiscrimination and other qualification requirements?

Yes, provided the entities meet the definition of a *controlled group* as set forth in either Code Section 414(b) or 414(c).

Q 10:2 How many kinds of controlled groups are there?

In general, there are three kinds of controlled groups:

1. A parent-subsidiary controlled group;
2. A brother-sister controlled group; and
3. A combined group.

[Treas. Reg. §§ 1.414(c)-2(a), 1.1563-1(a)]

Q 10:3 What is a *parent-subsidiary controlled group*?

A *parent-subsidiary controlled group* consists of one or more chains of organizations in which a controlling interest in each of the organizations, except for the common parent, is owned by another organization. [Treas. Reg. §§ 1.414(c)-2(b)(1), 1.1563-1(a)(2)(i)]

Q 10:4 What is a *controlling interest*?

For a corporation, a *controlling interest* means ownership of stock possessing at least 80 percent of the total combined voting power of all classes of stock entitled to vote, or at least 80 percent of the total value of shares of all classes of stock. In the case of a trust or estate, it means ownership of an actuarial interest of at least 80 percent of the trust or estate. Finally, in the case of a partnership, a controlling interest means ownership of at least 80 percent of the profits or capital interest of the partnership. [Treas. Reg. §§ 1.414(c)-2(b)(2), 1.1563-1(a)(2)(i)]

> **Example.** The Cheese Factory Partnership owns stock possessing 80 percent of the total combined voting power of all the classes of stock of Dairy Farm Corporation entitled to vote. Dairy Farm Corporation owns 80 percent of the profits interest in the Holstein Partnership. The Cheese Factory Partnership is the common parent of a controlled group consisting of the Cheese Factory Partnership, Dairy Farm Corporation, and the Holstein Partnership. The result would be the same if the Cheese Factory Partnership, rather than Dairy Farm Corporation, owned 80 percent of the profits interest in the Holstein Partnership.

Q 10:5 What is a *brother-sister controlled group*?

A *brother-sister controlled group* consists of two or more organizations satisfying two requirements:

1. The same five or fewer persons who are individuals, estates, or trusts own a controlling interest (see Q 10:4) in each organization; and
2. Taking into account the ownership of each such person only to the extent ownership is identical with respect to each organization, such persons are in effective control of each such organization.

The persons whose ownership is considered for purposes of the controlling-interest requirement in (1) above must be the same persons whose ownership is considered for purposes of the effective-control requirement in (2) above. Consequently, a person who, for example, has an ownership interest in just one of two organizations will not be taken into account in determining whether those organizations form a controlled group. [Treas. Reg. §§ 1.414(c)-2(c)(1), 1.1563-1(a)(3)(i)]

Q 10:6 What constitutes *effective control*?

In the case of a corporation, *effective control* means owning stock possessing more than 50 percent of the total combined voting power of all classes of stock entitled to vote, or more than 50 percent of the total value of shares of all classes of stock. For a trust or estate, it means owning an actuarial interest of more than 50 percent of the trust or estate. Finally, in the case of a partnership, effective control means owning more than 50 percent of the profits or capital interest of the partnership. [Treas. Reg. §§ 1.414(c)-2(c)(2), 1.1563-1(a)(3)(i)]

Example 1. The outstanding stock of corporations P, Q, R, S, and T, each of which has only one class of stock outstanding, is owned by the following unrelated individuals:

	Corporations				
Individuals	*P (Percentage)*	*Q (Percentage)*	*R (Percentage)*	*S (Percentage)*	*T (Percentage)*
A	55%	51%	55%	55%	55%
B	45	49			
C			45		
D				45	
E					45
Totals	100%	100%	100%	100%	100%

Corporations P and Q are members of a brother-sister controlled group. Although the effective-control requirement is met for all five corporations (A owns more than 50 percent of each corporation), corporations R, S, and T are not members of the controlled group because a controlling interest (80 percent or more) in each of those corporations is not owned by the same five or fewer persons whose stock ownership is considered for purposes of the effective-control requirement.

Example 2. The outstanding stock of corporations U and V, which have only one class of stock outstanding, is owned by the following unrelated individuals:

	Corporations	
Individuals	*U (Percentage)*	*V (Percentage)*
A	12%	12%
B	12	12
C	12	12
D	12	12
E	13	13
F	13	13
G	13	13
H	13	13
Totals	100%	100%

Any group of five shareholders will have effective control of the stock in each corporation. However, U and V are not members of a brother-sister controlled group because a controlling interest (80 percent or more) in each corporation is not owned by the same five or fewer persons.

Q 10:7 What is a *combined group*?

A *combined group* consists of three or more organizations satisfying two requirements:

1. Each organization is a member of either a parent-subsidiary controlled group or a brother-sister controlled group; and
2. At least one organization is the common parent of a parent-subsidiary controlled group and is a member of a brother-sister controlled group.

[Treas. Reg. §§ 1.414(c)-2(d), 1.1563-1(a)(4)]

Q 10:8 In determining whether organizations are members of a controlled group, are certain interests disregarded?

Yes. In the case of a corporation, for example, treasury stock and nonvoting stock that is limited and preferred as to dividends are disregarded. [Treas. Reg. §§ 1.414(c)-3(a), 1.1563-2(a)] Other interests are disregarded only if certain conditions are satisfied first.

Q 10:9 What interests may be disregarded?

All the following interests may be disregarded:

1. An interest held by a plan of deferred compensation covering certain U.S. citizens and residents who are employees of a foreign affiliate. [I.R.C. § 406(a)(3)] This exclusion applies to parent-subsidiary controlled groups only. [Treas. Reg. §§ 1.414(c)-3(b)(3), 1.1563-2(b)(2)(i)]
2. An interest held by a qualified plan. This exclusion applies to brother-sister controlled groups only. [Treas. Reg. §§ 1.414(c)-3(c)(2), 1.1563-2(b)(4)(i)]
3. An interest held by an individual who is a principal owner (see Q 10:10), officer (see Q 10:11), partner, or fiduciary of the parent. This exclusion applies to parent-subsidiary controlled groups only. [Treas. Reg. §§ 1.414(c)-3(b)(4), 1.1563-2(b)(2)(ii)] (See the example at the end of this answer.)
4. An interest held by an employee if the interest is subject to conditions that run in favor of the organization or a common owner of the organization and that substantially restrict or limit the employee's right to dispose of the interest. This exclusion applies to both parent-subsidiary and brother-sister controlled groups. [Treas. Reg. §§ 1.414(c)-3(b)(5), 1.414(c)-3(c)(3), 1.1563-2(b)(2)(iii), 1.1563-2(b)(4)(ii)]
5. An interest held by a controlled organization exempt from tax under Code Section 501(c)(3). This exclusion applies to both parent-subsidiary and brother-sister controlled groups. [Treas. Reg. §§ 1.414(c)-3(b)(6), 1.414(c)-3(c)(4), 1.1563-2(b)(2)(iv), 1.1563-2(b)(4)(iii)]

For purposes of determining whether a group of organizations is a parent-subsidiary controlled group, these interests are disregarded only if such group would be considered a parent-subsidiary controlled group if the test for a controlling interest (see Q 10:4) is based on 50 percent rather than 80 percent. [Treas. Reg. §§ 1.414(c)-3(b)(1), 1.1563-2(b)(1)] For purposes of determining whether a group of organizations is a brother-sister controlled group, these interests are disregarded only if the same five or fewer persons who are individuals, estates, or trusts own a controlling interest in each organization based on 50 percent rather than 80 percent. [Treas. Reg. §§ 1.414(c)-3(c)(1), 1.1563-2(b)(3)]

Example. ABC Partnership owns 70 percent of both the capital and profits interests in the DEF Partnership. The remaining capital and profits interests in DEF are owned as follows: 4 percent by A (a general partner in ABC) and 26 percent by D (a limited partner in ABC). On first impression, ABC and DEF do not form a parent-subsidiary controlled group because ABC does not own at least 80 percent of DEF. But ABC does own at least 50 percent of DEF; thus, as explained in (3) above, the capital and profits interests in DEF owned by A and D, who are partners in ABC, are disregarded for purposes of determining whether ABC and DEF are members of a parent-subsidiary controlled group. By disregarding A's and D's interests in DEF, ABC is considered to own 100 percent of the capital and profits interests in DEF. Accordingly, ABC and DEF are members of a parent-subsidiary controlled group.

Q 10:10 Who is a *principal owner*?

A *principal owner* is an individual who owns 5 percent or more of the parent organization. [Treas. Reg. §§ 1.414(c)-3(d)(2), 1.1563-2(b)(2)(ii)]

Q 10:11 Who is an *officer*?

An *officer* is an individual who serves in any one of the following capacities for the parent organization: president, vice president, general manager, treasurer, secretary, comptroller, or any other individual who performs duties corresponding to those performed by individuals in those capacities. [Treas. Reg. §§ 1.414(c)-3(d)(3), 1.1563-2(b)(2)(ii)]

Q 10:12 When will an employee's interest in an organization be considered subject to conditions that substantially restrict the right to dispose of that interest?

Substantial restrictions exist if another person has preferential rights to the acquisition of the employee's interest. A right of first refusal in favor of the other person is an example of such a restriction. However, in some cases, an employee's interest in an organization will not be considered substantially restricted if the conditions apply to all owners of the organization. [Treas. Reg. §§ 1.414(c)-3(d)(6), 1.1563-2(b)(4)(ii)]

Constructive Ownership Rules

In determining whether organizations are members of a controlled group, a plan must take into account not only the interests in an organization that are directly owned, but also those that are indirectly or constructively owned. Under the constructive ownership rules, an interest held by a person in an organization will, under certain circumstances, be attributed to another person. There are three basic forms of attribution: (1) option, (2) entity, and (3) family.

Q 10:13 What is the *option attribution rule*?

Under the *option attribution rule*, a person who has an option to acquire an outstanding interest in an organization will be considered to own that interest. [Treas. Reg. §§ 1.414(c)-4(b)(1), 1.1563-3(b)(1)] The option attribution rule takes precedence over all other attribution rules. (See Example 3 in Q 10:21.) [Treas. Reg. §§ 1.414(c)-4(c)(3), 1.1563-3(c)(3)]

Q 10:14 What is the *entity attribution rule*?

Under the *entity attribution rule*, a person will be treated as the owner of an interest in an organization held by a partnership, estate, trust, or corporation.

Q 10:15 Under what circumstances will an interest in an organization held by a partnership be attributed to another person?

An interest in an organization owned, directly or indirectly, by a partnership will be considered owned by any partner having an interest of 5 percent or more in either the profits or capital interest of the partnership. A partner's attributed ownership will be in proportion to the partner's interest in the profits or capital of the partnership, whichever proportion is larger. [Treas. Reg. §§ 1.414(c)-4(b)(2), 1.1563-3(b)(2)]

Example. A, B, and C, unrelated individuals, are partners in the Big Bus Partnership. The partners' interests in the capital and profits of Big Bus are as follows:

Partner	*Capital (Percentage)*	*Profits (Percentage)*
A	36%	25%
B	60	71
C	4	4

The Big Bus Partnership owns the entire outstanding stock (100 shares) of Small Trolley Corporation. A is considered to own the stock of Small Trolley owned by the Big Bus Partnership in proportion to his interest in capital (36 percent) or profits (25 percent) of the Big Bus Partnership, whichever proportion is larger. Therefore, A is considered to own 36 shares (100 × 36%) of Small Trolley stock. Since B has a greater interest in the profits of Big

Bus than in its capital, B is considered to own Small Trolley stock in proportion to his interest in such profits. Therefore, B is considered to own 71 shares (100 × 71%) of Small Trolley stock. Because C does not have an interest of 5 percent or more in either the capital or profits of the Big Bus Partnership, C is not considered to own any shares of Small Trolley stock.

Q 10:16 Under what circumstances will an interest in an organization held by a corporation be attributed to another person?

An interest in an organization owned, directly or indirectly, by a corporation will be considered owned by a shareholder owning 5 percent or more in value of the stock of the corporation. The shareholder's ownership will be proportionate to the value of the stock owned by the shareholder relative to the total value of all stock in the corporation. [Treas. Reg. §§ 1.414(c)-4(b)(4), 1.1563-3(b)(4)]

Q 10:17 Under what circumstances will an interest in an organization held by an estate or trust be attributed to another person?

An interest in an organization owned, directly or indirectly, by an estate or trust will be considered owned by a beneficiary of the estate or trust if the beneficiary has an actuarial interest of 5 percent or more in the estate or trust. A beneficiary's attributed ownership in the organization will be in proportion to the beneficiary's actuarial interest in the estate or trust. [Treas. Reg. §§ 1.414(c)-4(b)(3), 1.1563-3(b)(3)]

Q 10:18 What is the *family attribution rule*?

Under the *family attribution rule,* an interest held by the spouse of an individual will generally be attributed to that individual. [Treas. Reg. §§ 1.414(c)-4(b)(5)(i), 1.1563-3(b)(5)(i)] The family attribution rule also deals with children, grandchildren, parents, and grandparents. Note that this family attribution rule (and the spousal attribution rule discussed in Q 10:19) applies only for the purpose of determining controlled groups. A separate family attribution rule applies when determining who is an HCE by reason of being a 5 percent owner (see Q 10:82).

Q 10:19 When will an interest in an organization owned by a spouse not be attributed to an individual?

Spousal attribution will not occur if four conditions are satisfied:

1. The individual does not, at any time during the year, directly own any interest in the organization;
2. The individual is not a member of the board of directors, a fiduciary, or an employee of the organization, and does not participate in the management of the organization at any time during the year;

3. Not more than 50 percent of the organization's gross income is derived from unearned income; and
4. The spouse's interest in the organization is not subject to conditions that substantially restrict or limit the spouse's right to dispose of the interest and that run in favor of the individual or the individual's children who have not attained age 21.

[Treas. Reg. §§ 1.414(c)-4(b)(5)(ii), 1.1563-3(b)(5)(ii)]

Q 10:20 Under what circumstances will an individual's interest in an organization be attributed to a lineal ascendant or descendant?

An individual will be considered to own an interest in an organization owned, directly or indirectly, by his or her child who has not reached age 21. Similarly, if an individual has not reached age 21, that individual will be considered to own an interest in an organization owned, directly or indirectly, by his or her parents. [Treas. Reg. §§ 1.414(c)-4(b)(6)(i), 1.1563-3(b)(6)(i)]

If an individual has effective control of an organization (see Q 10:6), then that individual will be considered to own any interest in the organization owned, directly or indirectly, by his or her parents, grandparents, grandchildren, and children regardless of age. [Treas. Reg. §§ 1.414(c)-4(b)(6)(ii), 1.1563-3(b)(6)(ii)]

Example. F owns directly 40 percent of the profits interest of the High Tech Partnership. His son, M, age 20, owns directly 30 percent of the profits interest of High Tech, and his other son, A, age 30, owns directly 20 percent of the profits interest. The remaining 10 percent of the profits interest and 100 percent of the capital interest of High Tech are owned by an unrelated person. The attribution of ownership for each individual is determined as follows: F owns 40 percent of the profits interest in High Tech directly and is considered to own the 30 percent of profits interest owned directly by M. Consequently, F is treated as owning 70 percent of the profits interest of High Tech and, as a result, is in effective control of High Tech. With effective control of High Tech, F is also considered to own the 20 percent profits interest of High Tech owned by his adult son, A. Accordingly, F is considered to own a total of 90 percent of the profits interest in High Tech.

Minor son, M, owns 30 percent of the profits interest in High Tech directly and is considered to own the 40 percent profits interest owned directly by his father, F. However, M is not considered to own the 20 percent profits interest of High Tech owned directly by his brother, A, and owned constructively by F, because an interest constructively owned by F by reason of family attribution is not considered as owned by him for purposes of making another member of his family the constructive owner of such interest (see Q 10:21). Therefore, M is considered to own a total of 70 percent of the profits interest of the High Tech Partnership.

Adult son, A, owns 20 percent of the profits interest in High Tech directly. A is not in effective control of High Tech because F's profits interest is not attributed to A. Accordingly, A is considered to own only the 20 percent profits interest in High Tech that he owns directly.

Q 10:21 Is there any limit on the number of times an interest in an organization may be attributed?

In general, no. Consequently, an interest constructively owned by a person will be treated as actually owned by the person for the purpose of attributing that ownership to another. However, an interest constructively owned by an individual as a result of the operation of the family attribution rules cannot be reattributed to another family member. [Treas. Reg. §§ 1.414(c)-4(c)(1), 1.414(c)-4(c)(2), 1.1563-3(c)(1), 1.1563-3(c)(2)]

Example 1. A, 30 years of age, has a 90 percent interest in the capital and profits of the Giant Oil Partnership. Giant Oil owns all the outstanding stock of Corporation X, and X owns 60 shares of the 100 outstanding shares of Corporation Y. The 60 shares of Y constructively owned by Giant Oil by reason of the corporation attribution rule are treated as actually owned by Giant Oil for purposes of applying the partnership attribution rule. Therefore, A is considered as owning 54 shares of the Y stock (90 percent of 60 shares).

Example 2. The facts are the same as those in Example 1, except that B, who is 20 years of age and the brother of A, directly owns 40 shares of Y stock. Although the stock of Y owned by B is considered as owned by C (the father of A and B), under the family attribution rule, such stock may not be treated as owned by C for purposes of making A the constructive owner of such stock.

Example 3. The facts are the same as those in Examples 1 and 2, except that C has an option to acquire the 40 shares of Y stock owned by his son, B. In this case, the 40 shares owned by B may be attributed to A because under the precedence given to the option attribution rule (see Q 10:13), C is considered to own the 40 shares by reason of option attribution and not by reason of family attribution. Because A is in effective control of Y, the 40 shares of Y stock constructively owned by C are reattributed to A. A is therefore considered to own a total of 94 shares of Y stock.

Q 10:22 Are there special controlled group rules that apply to organizations that are exempt from tax under Code Section 501(a)?

Yes, there are special rules in addition to the rules explained in the previous questions. Under the special rules, an exempt organization will be treated as under common control with another if at least 80 percent of the directors or trustees of one of the exempt organizations are either representatives of, or directly or indirectly controlled by, the other organization. A trustee or director is treated as a representative of another exempt organization if he or she also is a trustee, director, agent, or employee of the other exempt organization. A trustee or director is considered controlled by another organization if the other organization has the general power to remove that trustee or director and designate a new trustee or director. [Treas. Reg. § 1.414(c)-5(b)]

Significance of Controlled Groups

Q 10:23 What employee benefit requirements are affected by the controlled group rules?

If two or more organizations are members of the same controlled group, then the employees of all such members will be treated as if they were employed by a single employer when applying the following qualification requirements:

1. General qualification requirements under Code Section 401;
2. Minimum participation and coverage standards under Code Section 410;
3. Minimum vesting standards under Code Section 411;
4. Limitations on benefits and contributions under Code Section 415; and
5. Special rules for top-heavy plans under Code Section 416.

[I.R.C. §§ 414(b), 414(c)]

It should be noted that for purposes of applying Code Section 415, a controlling interest in a parent-subsidiary controlled group will be based on ownership of more than 50 percent rather than 80 percent (see Q 10:4). [I.R.C. § 415(h)]

Affiliated Service Groups

Even in cases where there may not be sufficient common ownership to form a controlled group, the employees of an *affiliated service group* are treated, for various employee benefit requirements, as if they were employed by a single employer.

Q 10:24 What are the types of affiliated service groups?

There are three types of affiliated service groups. One type consists of a first service organization (FSO) and one or more A-organizations (A-orgs). [I.R.C. § 414(m)(2)(A)] The second consists of an FSO and one or more B-organizations (B-orgs). [I.R.C. § 414(m)(2)(B)] The third variety is composed of a management organization and any organization that is the recipient of the management-type services provided by the management organization. [I.R.C. § 414(m)(5)]

Q 10:25 What is a *first service organization*?

A *first service organization* (FSO) is a service organization (see Q 10:27). [Prop. Treas. Reg. § 1.414(m)-2(a)] However, a corporation that is not a professional service corporation under state law cannot be treated as an FSO with respect to any A-orgs. [Prop. Treas. Reg. § 1.414(m)-1(c)]

Q 10:26 What is an *organization*?

An *organization* includes a sole proprietorship, partnership, corporation, or any other type of entity regardless of its ownership format. [Prop. Treas. Reg. § 1.414(m)-2(e)]

Q 10:27 What is a *service organization*?

An organization will be considered a *service organization* if capital is not a material income-producing factor for the organization. Generally, capital will be considered a material income-producing factor if a substantial portion of the gross income of the business is attributable to the employment of capital in the business, as reflected in substantial investments in inventories, plant, and equipment. However, capital is not a material income-producing factor if the gross income of the business consists primarily of fees, commissions, and other compensation for personal services rendered. Any organization engaged in any one of the following fields will be deemed a service organization: health, law, engineering, architecture, accounting, actuarial science, performing arts, consulting, and insurance. [Prop. Treas. Reg. §§ 1.414(m)-2(f)(1), 1.414(m)-2(f)(2)]

Q 10:28 What is an *A-org*?

An *A-org* is a service organization that is a partner or shareholder in an FSO (regardless of the percentage interest it owns, or constructively owns, in the FSO) and regularly performs services for the FSO or is regularly associated with the FSO in performing services for third persons. [Prop. Treas. Reg. § 1.414(m)-2(b)(1)]

Example. Attorney N is incorporated, and his corporation is a partner in a law firm. Attorney N and his corporation are regularly associated with the law firm in performing services for third persons. Considering the law firm as an FSO, the corporation is an A-org because it is regularly associated with the law firm in performing services for third persons. Accordingly, the corporation and the law firm constitute an affiliated service group.

Q 10:29 How does one determine whether a service organization regularly performs services for an FSO or is regularly associated with an FSO in performing services for third persons?

This determination is made on the basis of all relevant facts and circumstances. The proposed regulations indicate that one relevant factor is the amount of income derived by the service organization from performing services for the FSO or from performing services for third persons in association with the FSO. [Prop. Treas. Reg. § 1.414(m)-2(b)(2)]

Q 10:30 What is a *B-org*?

An organization will be considered a *B-org* if three requirements are satisfied:

1. A significant portion of the business of the organization is the performance of services for the FSO, for one or more A-orgs determined with respect to the FSO, or for both;
2. The services are of a type historically performed by employees in the service field of the FSO or the A-orgs; and
3. Ten percent or more of the interest in the organization is owned, directly or indirectly, in the aggregate by persons who are HCEs (see Qs 10:76–10:91) of the FSO or the A-orgs.

A B-org is not required to be a service organization (see Q 10:27).

[I.R.C. § 414(m)(2)(B); Prop. Treas. Reg. § 1.414(m)-2(c)(1)]

Q 10:31 What constitutes a significant portion of the business of the organization?

The performance of services for an FSO, for one or more A-orgs, or for both, will be considered a significant portion of the business of an organization if the total receipts percentage is 10 percent or more. On the other hand, the performance of services for an FSO, for one or more A-orgs, or for both will not be considered a significant portion of the business of an organization if the service receipts percentage is less than 5 percent. If neither of these mechanical tests applies, then the determination will be based on all relevant facts and circumstances. [Prop. Treas. Reg. §§ 1.414(m)-2(c)(2)(i), 1.414(m)-2(c)(2)(ii), 1.414(m)-2(c)(2)(iii)]

Q 10:32 What is the *service receipts percentage*?

The *service receipts percentage* is the ratio of the gross receipts of the organization derived from performing services for an FSO, for one or more A-orgs, or for both, to the total gross receipts of the organization derived from performing services. This ratio is the greater of the ratio for the year for which the determination is being made, or for the three-year period including that year and the two preceding years. [Prop. Treas. Reg. § 1.414(m)-2(c)(2)(iv)]

Q 10:33 What is the *total receipts percentage*?

The *total receipts percentage* is calculated in the same manner as the service receipts percentage, except that gross receipts in the denominator of the ratio are determined without regard to whether such gross receipts are derived from performing services. [Prop. Treas. Reg. § 1.414(m)-2(c)(2)(v)]

Example. The income of the Back Office Corporation is derived from both performing services and other business activities. The amount of its receipts derived from performing services for the Physician Plus Corporation and the total receipts for all other customers are set forth below.

Origin of Income		*Physician Plus*	*All Customers*
Year 1	Services	$ 4,000	$100,000
	Other		20,000
	Total		120,000
Year 2	Services	9,000	150,000
	Other		30,000
	Total		180,000
Year 3	Services	42,000	200,000
	Other		40,000
	Total		240,000

In year 1 (the first year of existence of Back Office), the service receipts percentage for Back Office (for its business with Physician Plus) is less than 5 percent ($4,000/$100,000, or 4 percent). Thus, performing services for Physician Plus will not be considered a significant portion of the business of Back Office.

In year 2, the service receipts percentage is the greater of the ratio for that year ($9,000/$150,000, or 6 percent) or for years 1 and 2 combined ($13,000/ $250,000, or 5.2 percent), which is 6 percent. The total receipts percentage is the greater of the ratio for that year ($9,000/$180,000, or 5 percent) or for years 1 and 2 combined ($13,000/$300,000, or 4.3 percent), which is 5 percent. Because the service receipts percentage is greater than 5 percent and the total receipts percentage is less than 10 percent, whether performing services for Physician Plus constitutes a significant portion of the business of Back Office is determined by the facts and circumstances.

In year 3, the service receipts percentage is the greater of the ratio for that year ($42,000/$200,000, or 21 percent) or for years 1, 2, and 3 combined ($55,000/$450,000, or 12.2 percent), which is 21 percent. The total receipts percentage is the greater of the ratio for year 3 ($42,000/$240,000, or 17.5 percent) or for years 1, 2, and 3 combined ($55,000/$540,000, or 10.1 percent), which is 17.5 percent. Because the total receipts percentage is greater than 10 percent and the service receipts percentage is not less than 5 percent, a significant portion of the business of Back Office is considered to be the performance of services for Physician Plus.

Q 10:34 When will services be considered of a type historically performed by employees in the service field of the FSO or A-orgs?

Services will be considered of a type historically performed by employees in a particular service field if it was not unusual for the services to be performed by employees of organizations in that service field (in the United States) on December 13, 1980. [Prop. Treas. Reg. § 1.414(m)-2(c)(3)]

Q 10:35 Under what circumstances will multiple affiliated service groups be aggregated?

Multiple affiliated service groups will be aggregated and treated as one affiliated service group if the affiliated service groups have a common FSO. [Prop. Treas. Reg. § 1.414(m)-2(g)]

Q 10:36 What constructive ownership rules apply in determining whether an A-org has an ownership interest in an FSO or whether a 10 percent interest in a B-org is held by the HCEs of the FSO, A-org, or both?

The constructive ownership rules of Code Section 318(a) apply for this purpose. [I.R.C. § 414(m)(6)(B)] These constructive ownership rules are not identical to the constructive ownership rules that apply in the determination of controlled groups.

Q 10:37 In the case of a management-type affiliated service group, when is an organization considered a *management organization*?

An organization will be considered a *management organization* if the principal business of the organization is to perform, on a regular and continuing basis, management functions for a recipient organization. [I.R.C. § 414(m)(5)] Proposed regulations, which were withdrawn in April 1993, contained complicated rules for determining whether the principal business of the organization was the performance of management functions. [Prop. Treas. Reg. § 1.414(m)-5(b)]

Q 10:38 What are considered *management functions*?

The Code does not define management functions. According to the now defunct proposed regulations, *management functions* included only those activities and services historically performed by employees such as determining, implementing, or supervising (or providing advice or assistance in accomplishing) any of the following:

1. Daily business operations;
2. Personnel;
3. Employee compensation and benefits; or
4. Organizational structure and ownership.

[Prop. Treas. Reg. § 1.414(m)-5(c)(1)]

Q 10:39 What employee benefit requirements are affected by the affiliated service group rules?

If two or more organizations are members of the same affiliated service group, the employees of all such members will be treated as if they were employed by a single employer when applying any of the following employee benefit requirements:

1. Minimum participation and coverage standards under Code Section 410;
2. The nondiscrimination requirements under Code Section 401(a)(4);
3. Minimum vesting standards under Code Section 411;
4. Limitations on benefits and contributions under Code Section 415;
5. The $200,000 (as adjusted) cap on compensation under Code Section 401(a)(17); and
6. Special rules for top-heavy plans under Code Section 416.

[I.R.C. § 414(m)(4)]

Q 10:40 Can an employer obtain a formal determination as to whether a group of organizations constitutes an affiliated service group?

Yes. A formal determination can be obtained from the IRS by filing Form 5300, Application for Determination for Employee Benefit Plan.

Qualified Separate Lines of Business

Generally, all employees of corporations that are members of the same controlled group of corporations and all employees of trades or businesses under common control are treated as employed by a single employer for purposes of applying nondiscrimination and other qualification requirements (see Q 10:23). Similarly, all employees of members of an affiliated service group are considered employed by a single employer. (see Q 10:39). Generally, the minimum coverage rules (see chapter 11) are applied only after the application of these controlled group and affiliated service group provisions. There is an exception to this general rule, however, in the case of the controlled group rules. If an employer operates two or more qualified separate lines of business (QSLOBs), the minimum coverage rules can be applied separately to each QSLOB. Flowchart 10-1 outlines the operation of the QSLOB rules.

Q 10:41 What is a *qualified separate line of business*?

A *qualified separate line of business* (QSLOB) is a line of business (see Q 10:42) that is also a separate line of business (see Q 10:46) and that meets all of the following requirements:

1. The separate line of business has 50 employees [Treas. Reg. § 1.414(r)-1(b)(2)(iv)(B)];

2. The employer notifies the IRS on Form 5310-A that it is applying the QSLOB rules [Treas. Reg. § 1.414(r)-1(b)(2)(iv)(C)]; and
3. The separate line of business passes administrative scrutiny. [Treas. Reg. § 1.414(r)-1(b)(2)(iv)(D)]

Q 10:42 What is a *line of business*?

A *line of business* (LOB) is a portion of the employer identified by the property and services sold to customers in the ordinary course of the conduct of a trade or business. [Treas. Reg. §§ 1.414(r)-2(a), 1.414(r)-2(b)(2)]

Q 10:43 How does an employer designate LOBs?

An employer must first identify all property and services provided to customers. Then the employer may designate which property and services will be provided by each LOB. [Treas. Reg. § 1.414(r)-2(b)(1)] All such property and services must be assigned to a LOB. [Treas. Reg. § 1.414(r)-2(b)(3)(i)]

Q 10:44 Must a LOB provide only one type or related types of property and services?

No. The employer may combine dissimilar types of property or services within one LOB. [Treas. Reg. § 1.414(r)-2(b)(3)(ii)]

> **Example.** AlphaOmega Corporation is a domestic conglomerate engaged in the manufacture and sale of consumer food and beverage products and the provision of data processing services to private industry. AlphaOmega also owns and operates a regional commuter airline, a professional basketball team, a pharmaceutical manufacturer, and a leather-tanning company. AlphaOmega apportions all the property and services it provides to its customers among three LOBs, one providing all its consumer food and beverage products, a second providing all its data processing services, and a third providing all the other property and services provided to customers through AlphaOmega's regional commuter airline, professional basketball team, pharmaceutical manufacturer, and leather-tanning company. Even though the third LOB includes dissimilar types of property and services that are otherwise unrelated to one another, AlphaOmega is permitted to combine these in a single LOB. Thus, AlphaOmega has three LOBs.

Q 10:45 Is an employer required to combine within one LOB all property or services of a related type?

No. An employer may designate two or more LOBs that provide related or the same types of property or services. However, the employer's designation must be reasonable. Designations would be reasonable, for example, if the product or services of related types or the same type are manufactured, prepared, or provided in different geographic areas, in different levels in the chain of

Flowchart 10-1. Qualified Separate Lines of Business (QSLOBs)

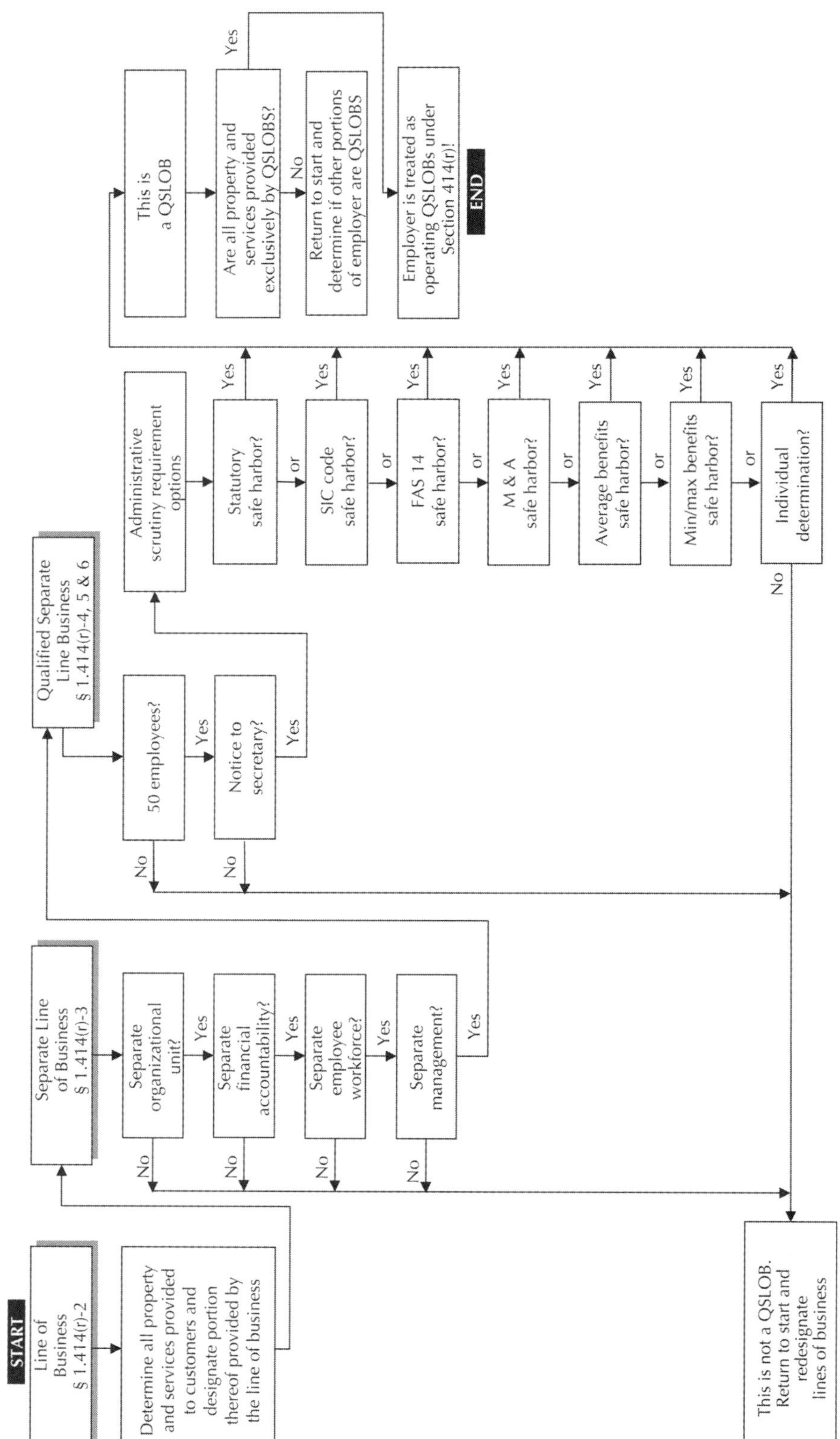

commercial distribution (wholesale or retail), in different types of transactions (sale or lease), or for different types of customers (government or private). A designation would be unreasonable, for example, if two types of related property or services are not provided separately to customers, or if one type of property or service is ancillary to another. [Treas. Reg. § 1.414(r)-2(b)(3)(iii)]

Example 1. Slide Rule Corporation is a diversified engineering firm offering civil, chemical, and aeronautical engineering services to government and private industry. Slide Rule provides no other property or services to its customers. Slide Rule operates the aeronautical engineering services portion of its business as two separate divisions, one serving federal government customers and the other serving customers in private industry. Slide Rule apportions all the property and services it provides to its customers among four LOBs, one providing all its civil engineering services, a second providing all its chemical engineering services, a third providing aeronautical engineering services to federal government customers, and a fourth providing aeronautical engineering services to customers in private industry. Even though the third and fourth LOBs include the same type of service (i.e., aeronautical engineering services), Slide Rule is permitted to separate its aeronautical engineering services into two LOBs, since they are provided to different types of customers.

Example 2. Among its other business activities, the Piston Corporation manufactures industrial diesel generators. At no additional cost to its buyers, Piston warrants the proper functioning of its diesel generators for a one-year period following sale. Pursuant to its warranty, Piston provides labor and parts to repair or replace any components that malfunction within the one-year warranty period. Because Piston does not provide the industrial diesel generators and the warranty repair services and replacement parts separately to its customers, it would be unreasonable for Piston to separate them into different LOBs.

Q 10:46 What is a *separate line of business*?

A *separate line of business* (SLOB) is a LOB that is organized and operated separately from the remaining businesses of the employer. [Treas. Reg. § 1.414(r)-3(a)] A SLOB must meet all four of the following requirements:

1. The LOB must be formally organized as a separate organizational unit or group of separate organizational units. An organizational unit is a corporation, partnership, division, or other unit having a similar degree of organizational formality [Treas. Reg. § 1.414(r)-3(b)(2)];
2. The LOB must be a separate profit center or group of separate profit centers [Treas. Reg. § 1.414(r)-3(b)(3)];
3. The LOB must have its own, separate workforce [Treas. Reg. § 1.414(r)-3(b)(4)]; and
4. The LOB must have its own, separate management. [Treas. Reg. § 1.414(r)-3(b)(5)]

Q 10:47 When does a LOB have its own, separate workforce?

A LOB has its own, separate workforce only if at least 90 percent of the employees who provide services to the LOB are substantial-service employees (see Q 10:48) with respect to the LOB and are not substantial-service employees with respect to any other line of business. [Treas. Reg. § 1.414(r)-3(b)(4)]

Q 10:48 What is a *substantial-service employee*?

An employee is a *substantial-service employee* with respect to an LOB if at least 75 percent of the employee's services are provided to that LOB. In addition, if an employee provides at least 50 percent of his or her services to a LOB, the employer may treat the employee as a substantial-service employee. [Treas. Reg. § 1.414(r)-11(b)(2)]

Q 10:49 When is an employee considered to provide services to a LOB?

An employee is considered to provide services to a LOB if more than a negligible portion of the employee's services contribute to the production of the property or services provided by the LOB. [Treas. Reg. § 1.414(r)-3(c)(5)(i)]

Q 10:50 How does an employer determine what percentage, if any, of an employee's services are provided to a LOB?

The most recent version of the final regulations does not provide any guidance. The initial version of the regulations provided that the employer must make these determinations in a manner that is reasonably reliable with respect to all employees and uniform with respect to similarly situated employees.

Example. OmegaAlpha's first LOB manufactures and sells construction machinery, its second LOB manufactures and sells agricultural equipment, and its third LOB manufactures and sells tires. As part of these LOBs, OmegaAlpha operates construction machinery, agricultural equipment, and tire factories on the same site. OmegaAlpha's facilities at this site include a health clinic and a fitness center that serve the employees of the construction machinery, agricultural equipment, and tire factories. Employee O is a nurse in the health clinic and Employee P is a fitness instructor in the fitness center. Both employees therefore provide services to OmegaAlpha's construction machinery LOB, agricultural equipment LOB, and tire factory LOB. In addition, OmegaAlpha determines that approximately 33 percent of the services of Employee O and Employee P are provided to each of OmegaAlpha's LOBs. As a result, neither Employee O nor Employee P provides at least 75 percent of their respective services to any of OmegaAlpha's LOBs. Therefore, Employee O and Employee P are not substantial-service employees with respect to any of OmegaAlpha's three LOBs.

Q 10:51 When does a LOB have its own, separate management?

A LOB has its own, separate management if at least 80 percent of the employees who are top-paid employees with respect to a LOB are substantial-service employees (see Q 10:48). [Treas. Reg. § 1.414(r)-3(b)(5)]

Q 10:52 Who are the top-paid employees?

An employee is a top-paid employee with respect to a LOB if the employee is not a substantial-service employee with respect to any other LOB and is among the top 10 percent by compensation of those employees who provide services to that LOB. In determining top-paid employees, an employer must disregard all employees who provide less than 25 percent of their services to the LOB. [Treas. Reg. § 1.414(r)-11(b)(3)]

Example. The Big Tool Corporation operates four LOBs. One of its LOBs is a machine toolshop. Sixty of Big Tool's employees provide at least 25 percent of their services to the machine tool shop. Of the 6 employees who constitute the top 10 percent by compensation of those 60 employees, 4 are substantial-service employees with respect to the LOB. Only 67 percent (4/6) of the top-paid employees with respect to the machine tool shop LOB are substantial-service employees with respect to that LOB. Therefore, the machine tool shop LOB does not satisfy the separate management requirement because less than 80 percent of the top-paid employees are substantial-service employees.

Q 10:53 How does a SLOB satisfy the administrative-scrutiny requirement?

A SLOB satisfies the administrative-scrutiny requirement if it satisfies a statutory safe harbor or one of several regulatory safe harbors. A SLOB that does not satisfy a safe harbor may still satisfy the administrative-scrutiny requirement if the IRS so determines. [Treas. Reg. §§ 1.414(r)-5(a), 1.414(r)-6]

Q 10:54 How does a SLOB satisfy the statutory safe harbor?

A SLOB satisfies the statutory safe harbor if the HCE percentage ratio of a SLOB is at least 50 percent and not more than 200 percent. [Treas. Reg. § 1.414(r)-5(b)(1)] A SLOB is deemed to satisfy the statutory safe harbor if at least 10 percent of all HCEs provide services to the SLOB and do not provide services to any other SLOBs. [Treas. Reg. § 1.414(r)-5(b)(4)]

Q 10:55 What is the *HCE percentage ratio*?

The *HCE percentage ratio* is a fraction, the numerator of which is the percentage of employees of the SLOB who are HCEs and the denominator of which is the percentage of all employees of the employer who are HCEs. [Treas. Reg. § 1.414(r)-5(b)(2)] (For the definition of HCE see Qs 10:76–10:91.)

Example. The Conglomerate Corporation operates three SLOBs: a dairy products manufacturer, a candy manufacturer, and a chain of housewares stores. Conglomerate employs a total of 1,000 employees, 100 of whom are HCEs. Thus, the percentage of all employees of Conglomerate who are HCEs is 10 percent. The distribution of HCEs and non-highly compensated employees (NHCEs) among Conglomerate's SLOBs is as follows.

	Employer-wide	*Dairy Products*	*Candy Mfg*	*Housewares Stores*
Number of employees	1,000	200	500	300
Number of HCEs	100	5	50	45
Number of NHCEs	900	195	450	255
HCE percentage	10	2.5	10	15
	(100/1,000)	(5/200)	(50/500)	(45/300)
HCE percentage ratio	N/A	25	100	150
		(2.5/10)	(10/10)	(15/10)

Because the HCE percentage ratio for the dairy products LOB is less than 50 percent, it does not satisfy the requirements of the statutory safe harbor. However, because Conglomerate's other two SLOBs (candy manufacturing and housewares stores) each employ more than 10 percent of all HCEs, they each satisfy the statutory safe harbor. To qualify its dairy products SLOB as a QSLOB, Conglomerate may be able to apply one of the regulatory safe harbors or seek an individual determination by the IRS. Conglomerate could also combine the dairy products LOB with either of its other LOBs.

Q 10:56 What are the regulatory safe harbors?

There are five regulatory safe harbors:

1. *The different industries safe harbor.* This safe harbor applies if the products and services of the SLOB fall exclusively within one or more industry categories established by the IRS. [Treas. Reg. § 1.414(r)-5(c)]
2. *The mergers and acquisitions (M&A) safe harbor.* This safe harbor applies if an employer acquires a LOB that, after the acquisition, constitutes a SLOB. This safe harbor may be used for up to four years after the acquisition. [Treas. Reg. § 1.414(r)-5(d)]
3. *The industry segments safe harbor.* This safe harbor applies if a SLOB is reported as one or more industry segments (SIC code) on annual reports required to be filed under U.S. securities laws. [Treas. Reg. § 1.414(r)-5(e)]
4. *The average benefits safe harbor.* This safe harbor applies in two situations. If a SLOB has an HCE percentage ratio of less than 50 percent, the safe harbor applies if the average benefits provided to the SLOB's NHCEs are not less than the average benefits provided to other NHCEs. If a SLOB has an HCE percentage ratio of more than 200 percent, the safe

harbor applies if the average benefits provided to the SLOB's HCEs are not greater than the average benefits provided to other HCEs. [Treas. Reg. § 1.414(r)-5(f)]

5. *The minimum or maximum benefits safe harbor.* This safe harbor operates to provide minimum benefits to NHCEs of a SLOB with an HCE percentage ratio of less than 50 percent. On the other hand, if a SLOB's HCE percentage ratio is greater than 200 percent, the safe harbor operates to place maximums on the benefits accrued by HCEs of the SLOB. [Treas. Reg. § 1.414(r)-5(g)]

Q 10:57 How are employees allocated to a QSLOB?

All substantial-service employees of a QSLOB must be assigned to that QSLOB. [Treas. Reg. § 1.414(r)-7(b)(2)(i)] All residual shared employees (see Q 10:58) must be assigned to a QSLOB under one of the following three allocation methods:

1. *Dominant line of business method of allocation.* Under this method, all residual shared employees are assigned to the QSLOB to which at least 50 percent of the substantial-service employees of the employer are allocated. In some circumstances, this percentage can be reduced to 25 percent. [Treas. Reg. § 1.414(r)-7(c)(2)]
2. *Pro rata method of allocation.* Under this method, the number of residual shared employees to be assigned to a QSLOB will be in proportion to the substantial-service employees allocated to that QSLOB. This determination is done separately for HCEs and NHCEs. After the number of residual shared employees to be assigned to the QSLOB is determined, the employer may choose which residual shared employees will be allocated to the QSLOB. [Treas. Reg. § 1.414(r)-7(c)(3)]
3. *HCE percentage ratio method of allocation.* This method is similar to the pro rata method except that the number of residual shared employees to be assigned to a QSLOB is determined solely with reference to the percentage of the employer's HCEs that have already been assigned to a QSLOB. [Treas. Reg. § 1.414(r)-7(c)(4)]

Q 10:58 What is a *residual shared employee*?

A *residual shared employee* with respect to a LOB is an employee who provides services to a LOB but who is not a substantial-service employee with respect to any LOB. [Treas. Reg. § 1.414(r)-11(b)(4)]

What Is a Plan?

Nondiscrimination rules are applied to plans. The word *plan* in this context is a term of art and may differ from the commonsense notion of what a plan is.

The determination of a plan for purposes of applying the nondiscrimination rules is a two-step process. First, separate asset pools are identified. Second, each separate asset pool is broken into two or more parts under the mandatory disaggregation rules. Each of the resulting parts is considered a plan.

Q 10:59 What is a *separate asset pool*?

Under the regulations, a *separate asset pool* exists if all assets in the pool are available to pay benefits to participants and their beneficiaries. A separate asset pool exists even though there are several distinct benefit structures or multiple documents. A separate asset pool is not affected by the fact that two or more employers—whether affiliated or not—make contributions or that assets are invested in several trusts or annuity contracts. [Treas. Reg. § 1.414(*l*)-1(b)(1)]

> **Example.** Company A sponsors a 401(k) plan covering its two divisions, C and D. The contributions made by Division C's employees are invested in a trust separate from the trust maintained for employees of Division D. Benefits are payable only from the trust established for the division for which an employee works. In this example, Company A would be treated as maintaining two separate asset pools.

Q 10:60 Is more than one separate asset pool created if participants have the right to direct the investment of their own account balances?

No. Also, multiple asset pools are not created merely because assets are invested in individual insurance or annuity contracts. [Treas. Reg. §§ 1.401(k)-1(b)(4)(iii)(A), 1.410(b)-7(b)]

Q 10:61 What are the mandatory disaggregation rules?

The mandatory disaggregation rules operate to divide a separate asset pool into two or more parts. Each resulting part is considered a plan to which the nondiscrimination rules are applied.

Q 10:62 Under what circumstances are the mandatory disaggregation rules applied?

The mandatory disaggregation rules are applied under any of the six circumstances described below.

1. *Plans benefiting collective bargaining employees.* A plan that benefits both collective bargaining employees and employees not included in a collective bargaining unit is treated as two plans. If more than one collective bargaining unit is covered, a separate plan is deemed to exist for each collective bargaining unit. Under the Section 401(k) regulations, however, at the employer's option, two or more collective bargaining units may be treated as a single collective bargaining unit as long as the combination of units is determined on a basis that

is reasonable and is reasonably consistent from year to year. [Treas. Reg. §§ 1.401(k)-1(b)(4)(v)(B), 1.410(b)-7(c)(4)(ii)(B)]

Example. The Hampton Corporation sponsors a 401(k) plan that covers employees who are members of collective bargaining units X, Y, and Z. The plan also covers nonunion employees of Hampton. For purposes of applying the Section 410(b) minimum coverage requirements, the plan is considered to be four separate plans. In applying the special nondiscrimination rules that apply to elective contributions, Hampton may treat the plan as four separate plans or may combine two or all three collective bargaining units so that the combined units are treated as a single plan.

2. *Plans benefiting employees of qualified separate lines of business.* If an employer is treated as operating QSLOBs, a plan covering the employees of two or more QSLOBs will be treated as consisting of as many plans as the employer has QSLOBs (see Q 10:41). [Treas. Reg. §§ 1.401(k)-1(b)(4)(iv)(A), 1.410(b)-7(c)(4)(ii)(A)] This mandatory disaggregation rule does not apply, however, if the plan is tested under the special rule for employer-wide plans (see chapter 11).

3. *Multiple-employer plans.* A plan that is maintained by two or more employers that are not members of the same controlled group or affiliated service group and that benefits only non-collective bargaining employees is subdivided into as many plans as there are employers maintaining the plan. [Treas. Reg. §§ 1.401(k)-1(b)(4)(iv)(A), 1.410(b)-7(c)(4)(ii)(C)]

Example. Alpha and Omega maintain a 401(k) plan for their nonunion employees. There is a certain amount of common ownership but not enough to cause Alpha and Omega to be considered part of the same controlled group. For purposes of applying all nondiscrimination rules, the 401(k) plan will be treated as two plans, one maintained by Alpha and the other by Omega.

4. *Multiemployer plans.* A plan maintained by multiple, unrelated employers for the benefit of their collective bargaining employees will be treated as a single plan. However, if the plan also covers non-collective bargaining employees, the portion of the plan covering those employees will be treated as a separate plan. [Treas. Reg. § 1.401(k)-1(b)(4)(v)(C)]

5. *Plans of different contribution types.* A plan must be disaggregated on the basis of the types of contributions made to it. The part of a plan that provides for elective contributions under Code Section 401(k) will be treated as a separate plan for purposes of the minimum coverage and nondiscrimination rules. The part of a plan that provides for employer matching contributions, employee after-tax contributions, or both, is similarly treated as a separate plan. Finally, if a plan provides for nonelective contributions (for example, discretionary profit-sharing contributions), that portion of the plan will also be treated as a separate plan. [Treas. Reg. § 1.410(b)-7(c)(1)]

Example. The Evergreen Company sponsors a 401(k) plan under which elective contributions made by employees are matched by the company.

Evergreen also makes discretionary profit sharing contributions. For purposes of the minimum coverage and nondiscrimination requirements, this plan is treated as three separate plans.

6. *ESOPs and non-ESOPs.* The portion of a plan that is an employee stock ownership plan (ESOP) and the portion of a plan that is not are treated as separate plans. [Treas. Reg. § 1.410(b)-7(c)(2)] However, for purposes of ADP and ACP testing (see chapter 13) there is no mandatory disaggregation. [Treas. Reg. §§ 1.401(k)-1(b)(4)(v)(A), 1.401(m)-1(b)(4)(v)]

Who Is an Employee?

401(k) plans, like all other qualified plans, are established and maintained by employers for the exclusive benefit of employees. Since 1962, the advantages of qualified plans have been extended to self-employed individuals—partners in entities taxed as partnerships and sole proprietors. The potential pool of qualified plan participants was expanded in 1982 to require employers, under certain circumstances, to cover individuals who were not its employees as a result of the leased-employee rules.

Q 10:63 Are self-employed individuals considered employees?

Yes. Self-employed individuals (owners treated as partners for income tax purposes and sole proprietors) are deemed employees of the businesses they own under Code Section 401(c).

Q 10:64 Are leased employees considered employees?

During the late 1970s and early 1980s, Congress became concerned about employers who excluded employees from retirement plans through leased-employee arrangements. Under these arrangements, employers would dismiss their employees, who would then become employees of leasing organizations. Leasing organizations would then contract with those employers for the services of their former employees.

In response to these arrangements, Congress passed the leased-employee rules. In general, these rules require employers to take into account leased employees for various employee benefit requirements. For example, an individual who is a leased employee must be treated as an employee when the minimum coverage rules are applied (see chapter 11). Also, a leased employee will be considered an employee for purposes of identifying an employer's HCEs.

Example. The Landmark Company, which sponsors a 401(k) plan for its employees, has made the top-paid group election described in Q 10:88. During the look-back year ending December 31, 2015, Landmark has 40 employees and 80 leased employees who cannot be excluded under the provisions described in Q 10:84. The maximum number of employees in the top-paid group is 24 (120 × 20%) because leased employees must be treated as if they were employees for this purpose. If the leased employees were not considered employees, the maximum number of employees in the top-paid group would be 8 (40 × 20%).

Starting in 1988, the primary guidance in the leased employee area was provided through proposed regulations. In April 1993, those regulations were withdrawn. In this section, reference will be made to the now-withdrawn proposed regulations where the law or IRS Notice 84-11 [1984-2 C.B. 469] (which is the sole IRS guidance in this area) fails to elaborate upon certain employee leasing rules.

Q 10:65 What is the definition of a *leased employee*?

A *leased employee* is any individual who provides services to a recipient in a capacity other than as an employee of the recipient and with respect to whom the following three requirements are all met:

1. The services of the individual are provided pursuant to one or more agreements between the recipient and a leasing organization;
2. The individual has performed services for the recipient on a substantially full-time basis for a period of at least one year; and
3. The individual's services are performed under the primary direction or control of the recipient. [I.R.C. § 414(n)(2)]

Q 10:66 Must an agreement between the recipient and a leasing organization be in writing?

The agreement need not be in writing. According to the now-withdrawn proposed regulations, an agreement includes any mutual understanding that the leasing organization will provide individuals to perform services for the recipient. The regulation also stated that an agreement was deemed to exist with respect to an individual if a leasing organization received or was entitled to receive payment from the recipient in exchange for making the individual's services available to the recipient. [Prop. Treas. Reg. § 1.414(n)-1(b)(5); IRS Notice 84-11, 1984-2 C.B. 469, Q&A 6]

Q 10:67 When is an individual considered to have performed services on a substantially full-time basis for a period of at least one year?

An individual is considered to have performed services on a substantially full-time basis for a period of at least one year if the individual is credited with

1. At least 1,500 hours of service; or
2. At least 75 percent of the average number of hours of service credited during the same period to employees of the recipient who perform similar services for the recipient.

In determining whether this requirement is satisfied, Notice 84-11 looks to any period of 12 consecutive months. The withdrawn regulation was more specific. Under it the period for determining hours of service was based on the 12-month period beginning on the date an individual first performed services for the recipient or any subsequent plan year of the recipient's plan as illustrated in the example below. [Prop. Treas. Reg. § 1.414(n)-1(b)(10)(i); IRS Notice 84-11, 1984-2 C.B. 469, Q&A 7]

> **Example.** Dr. Jones employs three nurses—Richard, Sue, and Bob—who work 2,000, 1,800, and 1,200 hours, respectively, per year. Thus, the average number of hours of service performed by Dr. Jones's nurse-employees is 1,667. On July 15, 2015, Dr. Jones contracts with a leasing organization for the services of nurse Jane. During the 12-month period ending July 15, 2016, Jane completes 1,200 hours of service. Jane is not a leased employee at the end of this initial 12-month period because 1,200 hours of service is less than 1,500 hours and is also less than 75 percent of the average number of hours of service worked by employee nurses in Dr. Jones's office (1,667 hours × 75% = 1,250 hours). Dr. Jones's 401(k) plan has a calendar plan year. During calendar year 2016, Jane completes 1,400 hours of service. On December 31, 2016, Jane is considered a leased employee because 1,400 hours of service is greater than 75 percent of the average number of hours of service worked by the employee nurses.

Q 10:68 Is there an alternative way to determine whether an individual is considered substantially full-time?

Under the withdrawn proposed regulations, a recipient could treat any individual who had more than 1,000 hours of service during the period for determining hours of service (see Q 10:67) as substantially full-time. Using this alternative eliminated the need to determine who, if any, of the employees of the recipient were performing services similar to those provided by the individual. [Prop. Treas. Reg. § 1.414(n)-1(b)(10)(ii)]

Q 10:69 When will an individual cease to be considered a leased employee?

The withdrawn proposed regulations (but not Notice 84-11, 1984-2 C.B. 469, which does not deal with this question) provided that an individual would cease to be considered a leased employee if the number of consecutive nonqualifying years equals or exceeds the greater of five or the total number of qualifying years. A nonqualifying year was a year during which the individual worked fewer than 501 hours of service for the recipient. [Prop. Treas. Reg. § 1.414(n)-1(b)(13)]

> **Example.** Larry has performed services for Dr. Bob substantially full-time since May 1, 2008. On December 31, 2013, Larry ceases to perform services for Dr. Bob, who maintains a calendar-year plan. As of December 31, 2013, Larry has six qualifying years (2009–2013, plus the period May 1, 2008–May 1, 2009). Larry resumes performing services for Dr. Bob on

January 1, 2016. Larry is considered a leased employee on January 1, 2016, because the number of qualifying years (six) exceeds the number of non-qualifying years (two: 2014 and 2015).

Q 10:70 When will services be considered performed under the primary direction or control of the recipient?

According to the committee reports to SBJPA Section 1454, whether services are performed by an individual under the primary direction or control of the recipient depends on the facts and circumstances. In general, primary direction or control means that the recipient exercises the majority of direction or control over the individual. Factors that are relevant in determining whether primary direction or control exists include whether the individual is required to comply with instructions of the recipient about when, where, and how he or she is to perform the services, whether the services must be performed by a particular person, whether the individual is subject to the supervision of the recipient, and whether the individual must perform services in the order or sequence set by the recipient.

Factors that generally are not relevant in determining whether direction or control exists include whether the recipient has the right to hire or fire the individual and whether the individual also works for others.

Q 10:71 Must a leased employee be an employee of the leasing organization?

According to the withdrawn proposed regulations, the answer to this question was no. For example, an independent contractor who performed services for a recipient could be considered a leased employee. [Prop. Treas. Reg. § 1.414(n)-1(b)(1)] Some commentators have suggested, however, that an independent contractor cannot be a leased employee because the language of the statute requires the leased employee and the leasing organization to be two different persons.

Q 10:72 If an individual is considered a leased employee, is it necessary to cover the individual under the recipient's 401(k) plan?

It is not necessary to cover a leased employee under the recipient's 401(k) plan. However, unless the leased employee is covered by a safe harbor plan (see Q 10:74), he or she must be taken into account for various employee benefit requirements, including minimum coverage. [I.R.C. § 414(n)(3)]

Example. ABC Company sponsors a 401(k) plan covering its 10 HCEs and 200 NHCEs. ABC Company also uses the services of 40 leased employees, all of whom are considered NHCEs. Although the leased employees are not covered by ABC Company's 401(k) plan, they must be taken into account in determining whether the 401(k) plan satisfies the minimum coverage requirements. Accordingly, the percentage of NHCEs benefiting under the plan is 83.33 percent (200/240). The 401(k) plan satisfies the ratio percentage test because the percentage of NHCEs benefiting under the 401(k) plan (83.33 percent) is greater than 70 percent of the percentage of HCEs benefiting under the plan (100 percent).

Q 10:73 May leased employees be disregarded if the leasing organization maintains a retirement plan for them?

Leased employees may be disregarded by the recipient if the leased employees are covered by a safe harbor plan, and they do not constitute more than 20 percent of the recipient's non-highly compensated workforce. [I.R.C. § 414(n)(5)]

Q 10:74 What is a *safe harbor plan*?

A *safe harbor plan* is a money purchase plan (see Glossary), maintained by the leasing organization, that meets all the following requirements:

1. The plan provides for immediate participation;
2. Contributions are provided at a rate of at least 10 percent of compensation as defined for purposes of Code Section 415 (see chapter 9);
3. Contributions are provided to an individual whether or not the individual is employed by the leasing organization on the last day of the plan year and regardless of the number of hours of service completed during the plan year; and
4. The plan provides for immediate vesting.

[I.R.C. § 414(n)(5); Prop. Treas. Reg. § 1.414(n)-2(f)(1)]

Q 10:75 Who is considered part of the recipient's non-highly compensated workforce?

A recipient's non-highly compensated workforce consists of NHCEs who are either leased employees or employees of the recipient who have performed services for the recipient on a substantially full-time basis for at least one year. [I.R.C. § 414(n)(5)(C)(ii)]

Who Is a Highly Compensated Employee?

The application of nondiscrimination rules requires employees to be categorized as either highly compensated or non-highly compensated pursuant to objective rules.

Q 10:76 Who is a *highly compensated employee*?

An employee is a *highly compensated employee* (HCE) for a plan year only if the employee performs services for the employer during the determination year (see Q 10:91). In addition, the employee must be a member of at least one specified employee group (see Q 10:77). [I.R.C. § 414(q)(1)]

Q 10:77 What are these specified groups of employees?

There are two separate groups of employees. Membership in either of these groups will cause an employee to be an HCE:

1. The employee is a 5 percent owner at any time during the determination year or look-back year (see Q 10:91); or
2. The employee receives compensation in excess of $80,000 (indexed) during the look-back year and, at the election of the employer, is a member of the top-paid group during the look-back year.

Example. ABC Company sponsors a 401(k) plan with a plan year beginning each April 1. For the look-back year ending March 31, 2015, Joe received $120,000 in compensation. For the plan year beginning April 1, 2015, Joe is considered an HCE because his compensation for the look-back year ending March 31, 2015, exceeded $115,000 (indexed amount for look-back years beginning in 2014).

Q 10:78 How is the $80,000 threshold adjusted?

The $80,000 threshold will be indexed at the same time and in the same manner as the limits under Code Section 415(d). This dollar threshold will always be a multiple of $5,000 and will always be rounded to the next lowest multiple of $5,000. The base period for the indexation of the $80,000 threshold is the calendar quarter ending September 30, 1996. [I.R.C. § 414(q)(1)] The following table shows the dollar thresholds in effect since 1997.

Year	*$80,000 Threshold*
1997	$ 80,000
1998	80,000
1999	80,000
2000	85,000
2001	85,000
2002	90,000
2003	90,000
2004	90,000
2005	95,000
2006	100,000

Year	*$80,000 Threshold*
2007	100,000
2008	105,000
2009	110,000
2010	110,000
2011	110,000
2012	115,000
2013	115,000
2014	115,000
2015	120,000

Q 10:79 How is the dollar threshold applied?

The indexed threshold amount for a look-back year is determined with reference to the calendar year in which the look-back year begins. [Temp. Treas. Reg. § 1.414(q)-1T, Q&A 3(c)(2)]

> **Example.** The look-back year of a plan begins on December 1, 2014. The $80,000 threshold amount for this look-back year is $115,000 because that amount is the threshold amount in effect for the calendar year in which the look-back year begins.

Q 10:80 Is the determination of HCEs limited to the employees of the entity sponsoring the plan?

No. All employers required to be aggregated under the controlled group and affiliated service group are treated as a single employer. [Temp. Treas. Reg. § 1.414(q)-1T, Q&A-6(a)] For example, if John receives $65,000 from Alpha Corporation and $65,000 from its affiliate, Omega Corporation, during a look-back year beginning in 2015, John will be considered an HCE even though only Alpha sponsors a 401(k) plan. HCEs are determined before applying the QSLOB rules (see Q 10:41). [Temp. Treas. Reg. § 1.414(q)-1T, Q&A 6(c)]

Q 10:81 Who are considered employees in the determination of HCEs?

Employees are any individuals who perform services for the employer and include both common-law employees and self-employed individuals treated as employees under Code Section 401(c)(1). [Temp. Treas. Reg. § 1.414(q)-1T, Q&A-7(a)] Leased employees must also be treated as employees unless the leased employee is covered by a safe harbor plan (see Q 10:74) and is not otherwise covered by a qualified plan maintained by the employer. [Temp. Treas. Reg. § 1.414(q)-1T, Q&A 7(b)]

Q 10:82 Who is a *5 percent owner*?

An employee is considered a *5 percent owner* if at any time during a look-back year or a determination year an employee owns or is considered to own (applying attribution rules under Code Section 318) more than 5 percent of the value of the outstanding stock of a corporation or stock having more than 5 percent of the total combined voting power of all stock of the corporation. If the employer is not a corporation, a 5 percent owner is any employee owning more than 5 percent of the capital or profits interest of the employer. The controlled group and affiliated service group rules are disregarded in determining a 5 percent owner. [Temp. Treas. Reg. § 1.414(q)-1T, Q&A 8]

Note that the attribution rules described in Qs 10:13–10:21 do not apply in determining who is a *5 percent owner*. Those rules are used only for the purpose of determining whether two or more employers are members of the same controlled group.

> **Example.** An affiliated service group consists of a law firm partnership with 100 partners, each of which is a professional corporation owned by a single attorney. Although each professional corporation, and, by attribution, each attorney-owner, has only a 1 percent interest in the law partnership, each attorney-owner will be treated as a 5 percent owner because each attorney-owner owns 100 percent of his or her professional corporation.

Q 10:83 What is the *top-paid group*?

The *top-paid group* is the highest paid 20 percent of the employer's nonexcludable employees (see Q 10:84). [Temp. Treas. Reg. § 1.414(q)-1T, Q&A 9(a)]

Q 10:84 How is the number of employees in the top-paid group determined?

The starting point is to determine the total number of employees who perform services for the employer during the year, not taking into account, however, the number of employees who are nonresident aliens with no U.S.-source earned income. From that number, the employer may subtract the number of employees who are in any of the following categories:

1. Employees who have not completed six months of service by the end of the year (for this purpose, service in the immediately preceding year is taken into account);
2. Employees who normally work fewer than 17½ hours per week during the year;
3. Employees who normally work fewer than seven months during the year;
4. Employees who are not age 21 by the end of the year; and
5. Employees who are covered by a collective bargaining agreement. This exclusion applies, however, only if 90 percent or more of the employees are covered under collective bargaining agreements and the plan does not benefit employees covered under such agreements.

An employer may elect to modify these exclusions by requiring shorter periods of service or a lower age. In fact, these exclusions may be eliminated altogether. Also, the employer may ignore the collective bargaining employee exclusion. The ability to modify or ignore these exclusions must be provided for in the plan document. Exclusions must also be uniformly applied to all other retirement plans with plan years beginning in the same calendar year. [Temp. Treas. Reg. § 1.414(q)-1T, Q&A 9(b)]

Q 10:85 When is an employee considered to normally work fewer than 17½ hours per week?

An employee is deemed to normally work fewer than 17½ hours per week if the employee works fewer than 17½ hours per week for 50 percent or more of the total weeks worked by the employee. Any week during which an employee does not work is not taken into account. [Temp. Treas. Reg. § 1.414(q)-1T, Q&A 9(e)]

Q 10:86 When is an employee considered to normally work fewer than seven months during the year?

The determination as to whether an employee normally works fewer than seven months during the year is based on the employer's customary experience in prior years. An employee who works on one day during a month is deemed to have worked that month. [Temp. Treas. Reg. § 1.414(q)-1T, Q&A 9(f)]

Q 10:87 How are the particular employees who will make up the top-paid group selected?

After the number of employees in the top-paid group has been determined, those employees with the highest compensation are identified. The exclusions (other than the exclusion for collective bargaining employees) used in determining the number of employees in the top-paid group are not applicable. [Temp. Treas. Reg. § 1.414(q)-1T, Q&A-9(c)]

> **Example.** Mix-Max Company sponsors a 401(k) plan and, for purposes of determining HCEs, requires membership in the top-paid group. Jane is hired on July 15, 2015, and makes $125,000 during the look-back year ending December 31, 2015. Because she has worked fewer than six months as of December 31, 2015, Jane is excluded in determining the number of employees in the top-paid group. However, as long as her compensation places her in the top 20 percent of employees for the look-back year when ranked on the basis of compensation, she is considered an HCE for the plan year beginning January 1, 2016.

Worksheet 10-1 can be used to identify the employees who are in the top-paid group.

Q 10:88 How does an employer make an election to require membership in the top-paid group?

Code Section 414(q) does not prescribe a procedure for making this election. The IRS has indicated that an election to require membership in the top-paid group is not irrevocable and may be changed without prior IRS approval. According to the IRS, however, the plan document must reflect the election, and any change in the election must be accomplished through a plan amendment. [IRS Notice 97-45, 1997-2 C.B. 296]

Worksheet 10-1. How to Determine Membership in the Top-Paid Group

TOP-PAID GROUP: Highest-paid 20 percent of employees.

EMPLOYEES: Anyone (other than nonresident aliens with no U.S.-source income) who performed services during the look-back year. May exclude any of the following:

- Employees employed fewer than six months at the end of the year
- Employees who normally work fewer than 17½ hours per week
- Employees who normally work fewer than seven months
- Employees who have not attained age 21 at the end of the year
- Employees covered by collective bargaining agreements (but only if such employees make up 90 percent or more of the employees and no such employees are covered by the plan)

Plan Year 12/31/2015	Look-back Year 12/31/2014 Dollar Limitation $115,000
Total employees	75
Employed < 6 months	− 8
Work < 17½ hours/week	− 2
Work < 7 months	− 0
Not age 21	− 3
Collective bargaining	− 0
Employees subject to test	= 62
	× 20%
Number of employees who can be in the top-paid group (rounding down)	= 12

EMPLOYEES WHO EARN MORE THAN THE DOLLAR LIMITATION DURING THE LOOK-BACK YEAR RANKED IN ORDER OF TOTAL COMPENSATION (includes any employee—other than any employee excluded as a collective bargaining employee—who may have been excluded in determining number of employees in top-paid group):

Worksheet 10-1. How to Determine Membership in the Top-Paid Group (*cont'd*)

Look-back Year

Mary	$130,000
Bill	122,000
Tom	116,000

The employees who are considered HCEs are those employees (not more than the number of employees who can be in the top-paid group, as determined above) whose total compensation is the highest.

Q 10:89 Under what circumstances would an employer want to make the election to require membership in the top-paid group?

The election to require membership in the top-paid group may be advantageous to a company with a large number of HCEs.

Example. Mega Law Firm employs 200 nonexcludable employees, 100 of whom are attorneys consisting of 20 shareholders and 80 associates. Each attorney in the firm has compensation in excess of $115,000, the dollar threshold currently in effect. Without an election to require membership in the top-paid group, all 100 attorneys would be considered HCEs. If, however, the election is made, only the highest-paid 40 attorneys would be treated as HCEs (assuming that all shareholders would be among this top-paid 40).

Q 10:90 How is *compensation* defined for purposes of determining the group of HCEs?

Compensation means compensation as defined for purposes of Code Section 415. (See chapter 9.) It also includes elective contributions to 401(k) plans, SIMPLE retirement plans, and salary reduction simplified employee pension (SARSEP) plans and elective deferrals under a cafeteria plan. [I.R.C. § 414(q)(4)]

Q 10:91 What are the determination and look-back years?

Generally, the determination year is the plan year and the look-back year is the 12-month period immediately preceding the plan year. An employer also can elect to treat the calendar year beginning in the look-back year as the look-back year. [IRS Notice 97-45, 1997-2 C.B. 296] According to IRS Notice 97-45, this election applies only to the $80,000 (indexed) test.

Example. A 401(k) plan has a plan year that ends on March 31. For the plan year ending March 31, 2016, the employer makes the calendar-year-calculation election. As a result, the look-back year for determining whether an employee is an HCE by reason of having compensation in excess of

$120,000 (the $80,000 threshold amount indexed for 2015) is the calendar year ending December 31, 2015. The calendar-year-calculation election does not apply in determining whether an employee is an HCE by reason of being a 5 percent owner. Thus, an employee will be a 5 percent owner if he or she owns more than 5 percent of the employer at any time during the look-back year ending March 31, 2015, or the determination year ending March 31, 2016.

A calendar-year election is not irrevocable and may be changed without IRS approval. However, according to IRS Notice 97-45, the plan document must reflect the election, and any change in the election must be accomplished by plan amendment.

Flowchart 10-2. Determination of HCEs

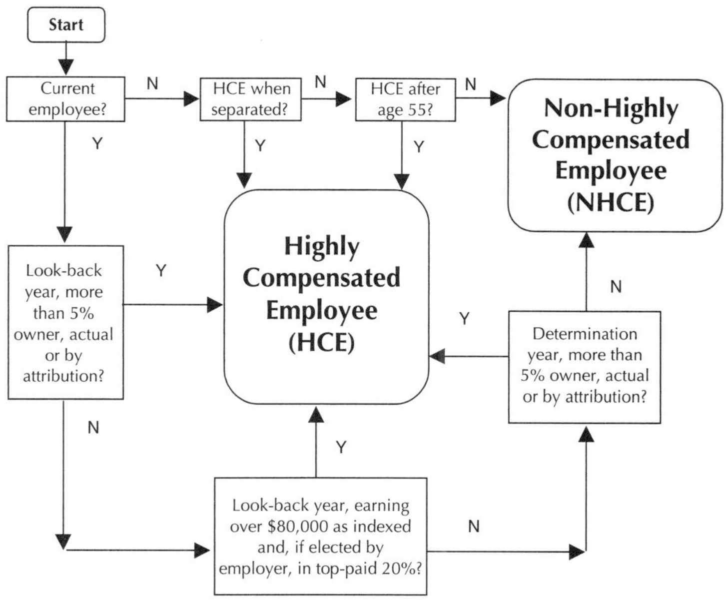

What Is Compensation?

An employee's compensation is a key factor in the application of the Section 401(a)(4) nondiscrimination rules. In applying these rules to elective contributions and to employer matching and employee after-tax contributions, a plan must calculate ratios for each employee, which are based, in part, on the employee's compensation. (See chapter 13.) The amount of nonelective contributions allocated to an employee, expressed as a percentage of compensation, is the basis for determining whether the allocation is nondiscriminatory. (See chapter 12.) A plan is not free to use any definition of compensation when applying the Section 401(a)(4) nondiscrimination rules. In applying these rules, the plan must use a definition of compensation that is nondiscriminatory under Code Section 414(s).

For the definition of compensation to be used under Code Sections 404 and 415, see chapter 9.

Q 10:92 What definitions of compensation will automatically satisfy Code Section 414(s)?

Any definition of compensation that satisfies Code Section 415(c)(3) will automatically satisfy Code Section 414(s)—see chapter 9 for the definition of compensation under Code Section 415(c)(3). The regulations under Code Section 414(s) also provide for a safe harbor alternative definition. Under the safe harbor, a plan starts with a definition of compensation that satisfies Code Section 415(c)(3), reduced by all of the following categories of compensation:

1. Reimbursements or other expense allowances;
2. Cash and noncash fringe benefits;
3. Moving expenses;
4. Deferred compensation; and
5. Welfare benefits.

[Treas. Reg. §§ 1.414(s)-1(c)(2), 1.414(s)-1(c)(3)]

See Table 10-1 at the end of this chapter for a comparison of the definitions of compensation that automatically satisfy Code Section 414(s).

Q 10:93 Can a definition of compensation that excludes certain deferrals satisfy Code Section 414(s)?

Yes. A definition of compensation will satisfy Code Section 414(s) even though it is modified to exclude all the following amounts contributed pursuant to a salary reduction agreement:

1. Cafeteria plan deferrals under Code Section 125;
2. Elective contributions under a 401(k) plan;
3. Elective contributions under a salary reduction SEP, a SIMPLE retirement account, or a 403(b) tax-sheltered annuity; and
4. Elective contributions under a Code Section 132(f) qualified transportation fringe benefit program.

[I.R.C. § 414(s)(2)]

Q 10:94 If a plan excludes from the definition of compensation any portion of the compensation of an HCE, does the plan's definition of compensation continue to automatically satisfy Code Section 414(s)?

Yes. The plan's definition of compensation automatically satisfies Code Section 414(s) whether the exclusion applies to some or all HCEs. [Treas. Reg. § 1.414(s)-1(c)(5)]

Q 10:95 If a plan's definition of compensation does not automatically satisfy Code Section 414(s), how does the plan demonstrate that its definition still satisfies Code Section 414(s)?

A definition of compensation will satisfy Code Section 414(s) if the definition meets three requirements:

1. The definition does not by design favor HCEs;
2. The definition is reasonable; and
3. The definition is nondiscriminatory.

[Treas. Reg. § 1.414(s)-1(d)(1)]

The regulations address only the last two requirements; they are silent with respect to the first requirement.

Q 10:96 When is a definition of compensation reasonable?

A definition of compensation is considered reasonable if it would otherwise automatically satisfy Code Section 414(s) except that it excludes certain types of irregular or additional compensation. According to the regulations, these types of compensation include overtime pay, shift differential and call-in premiums, bonuses, and any one of the categories of compensation excludable in determining the alternative safe harbor definition (see Q 10:92).

Q 10:97 Is a definition of compensation considered reasonable if it excludes a specified percentage of each employee's compensation?

No. However, a definition of compensation is not considered unreasonable merely because it excludes all compensation in excess of a specified dollar amount. [Treas. Reg. § 1.414(s)-1(d)(2)(iii)]

Q 10:98 What is the nondiscrimination requirement?

A definition of compensation is nondiscriminatory if the average percentage of total compensation included under the plan's definition of compensation for HCEs as a group does not exceed by more than a de minimis amount the average percentage calculated in the same way for NHCEs. [Treas. Reg. § 1.414(s)-1(d)(3)(i)]

Q 10:99 How are average percentages determined?

The first step is to determine a compensation percentage for each employee in a group by dividing that employee's compensation, as defined in the plan, by the employee's total compensation. Total compensation is an amount determined under any definition of compensation that satisfies Code Section 415(c)(3), with or without the modification described at Q 10:93, but which does not exceed the Section 401(a)(17) limit (see Q 10:104). Total compensation for an HCE does not include any amount excluded as described in Q 10:94 unless the exclusion applies consistently in defining the compensation of all HCEs. The average of the separately calculated individual compensation percentages is the average percentage for a group. [Treas. Reg. §§ 1.414(s)-1(d)(3)(ii), 1.414(s)-1(d)(3)(iv)(A)]

Example. ABC Company sponsors a plan under which bonuses and overtime pay are excluded. Is this plan's definition of compensation nondiscriminatory on the basis of these facts?

Employee	*Plan Compensation*	*Total Compensation*	*Inclusion Percentage*
HCE 1	$ 100,000	$ 120,000	83.3%
HCE 2	95,000	110,000	86.4
HCE 3	95,000	105,000	90.5
NHCE 1	30,000	35,000	85.7
NHCE 2	25,000	30,000	83.3
NHCE 3	24,000	25,000	96.0
NHCE 4	22,000	24,000	91.7
NHCE 5	22,500	23,000	97.8
NHCE 6	19,000	20,000	95.0

The average percentage for the HCE group is 86.7 percent, and the average percentage for the NHCE group is 91.6 percent. Because the average percentage of the NHCE group is greater, the plan's definition of compensation is considered nondiscriminatory.

Q 10:100 May other methods be used for determining average percentages?

Yes. Other reasonable methods to determine average percentages for either or both groups are permitted. The regulations point out, however, that any other method cannot be used if it can be reasonably expected to create a significant variance from the average percentage determined under the method described in Q 10:99. A significant variance could occur, for example, if several employees in a group have significantly higher compensation. [Treas. Reg. § 1.414(s)-1(d)(3)(iv)(B)]

Example. The facts are the same as those in the example in Q 10:99, except that ABC Company computes the average percentage for NHCEs by aggregating the plan compensation for the members of this group and dividing that number by the aggregate total compensation of the NHCEs.

$$\frac{(35{,}000 + 30{,}000 + 25{,}000 + 24{,}000 + 23{,}500 + 20{,}000)}{(30{,}000 + 25{,}000 + 24{,}000 + 22{,}000 + 22{,}500 + 19{,}000)} = 90.8\%$$

Because 90.8 percent is not significantly different from 91.6 percent (as computed in the example in Q 10:99), the method illustrated in this example for determining the average percentage is reasonable.

Q 10:101 How does a plan determine whether the average percentage of total compensation for the HCE group exceeds by more than a de minimis amount the average percentage of total compensation for the NHCE group?

According to the regulations, a plan may take into account the differences between the percentages in prior periods in determining whether the difference in percentages for the current period is more than a de minimis amount. In addition, a plan may ignore an isolated instance of more than a de minimis amount between percentages that occurs because of an extraordinary unforeseeable event (for example, overtime payments to employees of a public utility on account of a major hurricane). A de minimis amount is not quantified by the regulations. Rather, it is the result of a determination made by the plan and based on the applicable facts and circumstances. [Treas. Reg. § 1.414(s)-1(d)(3)(v)]

Q 10:102 Are there special rules that apply to self-employed individuals?

If a plan uses a definition of compensation that does not satisfy Code Section 415(c)(3), a self-employed individual's compensation for purposes of Code Section 414(s) is the total earned income of the self-employed individual multiplied by the average percentage of total compensation included under the plan's definition of compensation for common-law NHCEs as a group. [Treas. Reg. § 1.414(s)-1(g)(1)]

Q 10:103 Must a plan use a definition of compensation that satisfies Code Section 414(s) in calculating contributions under the plan?

A plan is not required to use a definition of compensation that satisfies Code Section 414(s) in determining contributions under the plan. However, whether contributions allocated under a plan satisfy the Section 401(a)(4) nondiscrimination rules must be tested on the basis of a compensation definition that does satisfy Code Section 414(s). [Treas. Reg. § 1.414(s)-1(a)(2)]

Example. Omega Corporation sponsors a 401(k) plan that allows employees to defer a specified percentage of their compensation. Lynn, an NHCE, elects to defer 5 percent ($2,000) of her base pay of $40,000. Her deferral percentage does not apply, however, to the $4,000 of overtime pay received by Lynn, because the plan's definition of compensation does not allow deferrals with respect to overtime pay. Bob, an HCE, also elects to defer 5 percent, but his deferral percentage applies to his total compensation of $200,000, including a bonus of $20,000. Because it excludes overtime pay, the plan's definition of compensation favors HCEs by design, does not satisfy Code Section 414(s), and cannot be used in performing the actual deferral percentage (ADP) test (see chapter 13). Consequently, in order to perform the ADP test, the plan must use a definition of compensation meeting the requirements of Code Section 414(s). If total compensation is used for this purpose, then Lynn's deferral ratio is 4.55 percent ($2,000/$44,000).

Q 10:104 Is there a limit on the amount of compensation that may be taken into account?

Under Code Section 401(a)(17), the amount of compensation that may be taken into account is limited to $200,000. [I.R.C. § 401(a)(17)(A)]

Q 10:105 Is the limit on compensation subject to adjustment?

Yes. The compensation limit will be indexed at the same time and in the same manner as the limits under Code Section 415(d). The compensation limit will always be a multiple of $5,000 and will always be rounded to the next lowest multiple of $5,000. The base period for the indexation of the compensation limit is the calendar quarter that ended September 30, 2001. An adjustment in the compensation limit is effective as of January 1, and it applies to any plan years beginning in that calendar year. [I.R.C. § 401(a)(17)(B); Treas. Reg. § 1.401(a)(17)-1(a)(3)(i)]

The following table shows the Section 401(a)(17) limit in effect since 1994:

Year	*Section 401(a)(17) Limit*
1994	$ 150,000
1995	150,000
1996	150,000
1997	160,000
1998	160,000
1999	160,000
2000	170,000
2001	170,000
2002	200,000
2003	200,000
2004	205,000
2005	210,000
2006	220,000
2007	225,000
2008	230,000
2009	245,000

Year	*Section 401(a)(17) Limit*
2010	245,000
2011	245,000
2012	250,000
2013	255,000
2014	260,000
2015	265,000

Q 10:106 What are the situations in which the Section 401(a)(17) limit applies?

The Section 401(a)(17) limit applies in four situations:

1. A plan may not base the allocation of contributions on compensation in excess of the Section 401(a)(17) limit [Treas. Reg. § 1.401(a)(17)-1(b)(1)];
2. The amount of compensation taken into account in applying nondiscrimination rules cannot exceed the Section 401(a)(17) limit [Treas. Reg. § 1.401(a)(17)-1(c)(1)];
3. An employer may not determine the maximum deductible amount to a 401(k) plan by taking into account compensation in excess of the Section 401(a)(17) limit [I.R.C. § 404(*l*)]; and
4. The amount of compensation taken into account in applying the annual additions limitations of Section 415(c) cannot exceed the Section 401(a)(17) limit. [Treas. Reg. § 1.415(c)-2(f)]

Table 10-1. Compensation Definitions That Satisfy Code Section 414(s)

	"Long List" Code Section 415	*"Short List" Code Section 415*	*Code Section 3401(a)*	*W-2*	*Section 414(s) Safe Harbor Exclusion*[a]
Direct pay (e.g., wages and salaries, including overtime pay, bonuses, and commissions)	Yes	Yes	Yes	Yes	
Expense reimbursements under a non-accountable plan and taxable fringes	Yes	Yes	Yes	Yes	Exclude
Section 911 earned income	Yes	Yes	Yes[b]	Yes	
Includable Section 105(h)	Yes	No	Yes	Yes	Exclude
Short-term disability pay (sick pay) and long-term disability pay	Yes	No	Yes	Yes	Exclude[c]
Deductible moving expense	No	No	No	No	
Nondeductible moving expense	Yes	No	Yes	Yes	Exclude
Nonqualified stock option at grant (if taxable on option privilege)	Yes	No	Yes	Yes	
Nonqualified stock option taxable at exercise	No	No	Yes	Yes	
Qualified stock option—grant or exercise	No	No	No	No	
Section 83(b) elections	Yes	No	Yes	Yes	
Section 83 property vesting	No	No	Yes	Yes	
Unfunded deferred compensation payouts while employed (if plan so provides)	Yes	Yes	Yes	Yes	Exclude
Taxable group-term life insurance	Yes	Yes	No	Yes	Exclude

Nontaxable dependent care, education assistance, Section 132 fringe benefits	No	No	No	No
Meals or lodging under Code Section 119	No	No	No	No

[a] The Section 414(s) safe harbor can be used with any of the preceding safe harbor definitions, but with the adjustments noted. Note that all of the adjustments must be made; an employer cannot elect to exclude only some of the excludable items.
[b] Section 3401(a)(8) excludes certain Section 911 earned income from "wages," but the regulation disregards exclusions based on the nature or location of work.
[c] The short-term disability is disregarded only if it is deemed to constitute a "welfare benefit."

Chapter 11

Minimum Coverage Testing

To qualify for tax-favored status, a 401(k) plan must meet standards of minimum coverage. (See definition of *plan* in chapter 10.) For plan years beginning before 1997, 401(k) plans were also required to meet the minimum participation rules.

Minimum Participation 11-1
  Minimum Participation Rules 11-2
Minimum Coverage 11-2
  Automatically Satisfying Minimum Coverage 11-2
  Ratio Percentage Test 11-3
  Average Benefits Test 11-6
  Nondiscriminatory Classification Test 11-6
    Table 11-1. Safe and Unsafe Harbor Percentages 11-7
  Average Benefit Percentage Test 11-10
  Disregarding Certain Employees 11-12
  Testing for Minimum Coverage 11-14
Correcting Minimum Coverage Failure 11-15

Minimum Participation

The minimum participation rules were added to the Internal Revenue Code (Code) effective with plan years beginning in 1989. Before 1989, an employer was free to establish different plans for different groups of employees as long as the plans were comparable to one another. Congress believed, however, that the comparability rules were unduly complex and unevenly applied and that they permitted benefit disparities that too greatly favored highly compensated employees (HCEs). After 1989, many plans were terminated or merged with other plans of employers to satisfy the minimum participation rules.

For plan years beginning after 1996, the minimum participation rules no longer apply to defined contribution plans, including 401(k) plans, although they continue to apply to defined benefit plans and, in some cases, have even been strengthened.

Minimum Participation Rules

Q 11:1 What were the minimum participation rules as they applied to 401(k) plans for plan years beginning before January 1, 1997?

A 401(k) plan satisfied the minimum participation rules for plan years beginning before 1997 only if it benefited at least the lesser of 50 employees of the employer or 40 percent of the employees of the employer. [Treas. Reg. § 1.401(a)(26)-2(a)]

Minimum Coverage

The minimum coverage rules require employers to make a 401(k) plan available to a cross-section of employees. Certain plans automatically satisfy the coverage rules, but most others must meet either of two tests: the ratio percentage test or the average benefits test. The minimum coverage rules are applied to each plan as that term is defined in chapter 10. There are rules, however, that permit or require plans to be combined before the minimum coverage rules are applied. The employer, for purposes of the coverage rules, is considered to be the entity sponsoring the plan and all other entities required to be aggregated with it, as explained in greater detail in chapter 10.

Automatically Satisfying Minimum Coverage

Q 11:2 What types of 401(k) plans automatically satisfy the Code Section 410(b) minimum coverage rules?

Four types of 401(k) plans automatically satisfy the minimum coverage rules:

1. A plan maintained by an employer that has no non-highly compensated employees (NHCEs) at any time during the plan year [Treas. Reg. § 1.410(b)-2(b)(5)];
2. A plan that benefits no HCEs during the plan year [Treas. Reg. § 1.410(b)-2(b)(6)];
3. A plan that benefits only collective bargaining employees [Treas. Reg. § 1.410(b)-2(b)(7)]; and
4. A plan of an employer involved in an asset or stock acquisition or disposition, merger, or other similar transaction involving a change in the employer of the employees of a trade or business for the transition period beginning on the date of the acquisition or disposition and ending on the last day of the plan year following the plan year in which the acquisition or disposition occurs. [Treas. Reg. § 1.410(b)-2(f)]

Example. Acme maintains a 401(k) plan that covers both collective and non-collective bargaining employees. The 401(k) plan provides for elective contributions only. For purposes of the minimum coverage rules, the 401(k) plan is treated as two plans, one covering the collective bargaining employees and the other covering the non-collective bargaining employees. The plan covering the collective bargaining employees automatically satisfies the coverage rules. Note that if the 401(k) plan also provided for matching contributions and employer nonelective contributions, the 401(k) plan would be treated as if it consisted of six separate plans. The three plans covering the collective bargaining employees would automatically satisfy the minimum coverage rules.

Q 11:3 What requirements must a 401(k) plan meet in order to automatically satisfy the minimum coverage rules during the transition period following a change in the employer of the employees in a trade or business?

To satisfy the minimum coverage rules during the transition period following an asset or stock acquisition or disposition, merger, or other transaction involving a change in the employer of the employees of a trade or business (see Q 11:2), a 401(k) plan must meet the following two conditions:

1. The plan of the employer involved in the acquisition, disposition, merger, or similar transaction must have satisfied the minimum coverage rules immediately before the acquisition, disposition, merger, or similar transaction; and
2. Coverage under the 401(k) plan must not significantly change during the transition period.

[Rev. Rul. 2004-11, 2004-7 I.R.B. 480]

Example. Feedlots, a wholly owned subsidiary of Pastureland Corp., sponsors a 401(k) plan maintained on a calendar-year basis. On April 15, 2015, Pastureland sells the stock of Feedlots to Milk Machine, Inc. Immediately prior to the sale, Feedlots' 401(k) plan satisfies the minimum coverage rules. If Feedlots makes no significant change to its 401(k) plan, the plan automatically satisfies the minimum coverage rules until December 31, 2016.

Ratio Percentage Test

Q 11:4 What is the *ratio percentage test*?

The *ratio percentage test* is a test that requires that the percentage of NHCEs benefiting under the plan be at least 70 percent of the percentage of HCEs benefiting under the plan. [Treas. Reg. § 1.410(b)-2(b)(2)]

Example 1. ABC Company maintains a 401(k) plan that benefits 78 percent of its NHCEs and 90 percent of its HCEs. The 401(k) plan satisfies the ratio percentage test because the percentage of NHCEs benefiting under the plan (78 percent) is 86.67 percent of the percentage of HCEs benefiting under the plan (90 percent).

Example 2. XYZ Company maintains a 401(k) plan that benefits 40 percent of its NHCEs and 60 percent of its HCEs. The 401(k) plan does not satisfy the ratio percentage test because the percentage of NHCEs benefiting under the plan (40 percent) is 66.67 percent of the percentage of HCEs benefiting under the plan (60 percent).

Q 11:5 What does it mean to benefit under a 401(k) plan?

The definition of benefiting depends on the portion of the 401(k) plan being tested. In the case of the portion of the 401(k) plan attributable to elective contributions, benefiting means being eligible to make elective contributions. Similarly, being eligible to make employee contributions or to receive an allocation of matching contributions constitutes benefiting under the Section 401(m) portion of the plan. Employees are considered eligible even though eligibility to make elective contributions and employee contributions and to receive matching contributions has been suspended owing to a hardship distribution, a loan, or an election not to participate. [Treas. Reg. § 1.410(b)-3(a)(2)(i)] With respect to that portion of a 401(k) plan attributable to nonelective contributions, the minimum coverage rules require employees to actually receive an allocation of contributions or forfeitures before they are considered to be benefiting. [Treas. Reg. § 1.410(b)-3(a)(1)] An employee who would otherwise benefit under a 401(k) plan but for the limits imposed by Code Section 415 is still treated as benefiting. [Treas. Reg. § 1.410(b)-3(a)(2)(ii)]

Example. Joe, an employee of B&H Video, Inc., is eligible to participate in his employer's 401(k) plan under which B&H Video will match salary deferral contributions made by plan participants. B&H Video's 401(k) plan also provides for employer nonelective contributions for those participants employed on the last day of the plan year. Joe elects not to make salary deferrals and, because he terminates employment during the year, is not entitled to an allocation of his employer's nonelective contributions. Under the minimum coverage rules, Joe is considered benefiting for purposes of the Section 401(k) (elective contributions) and Section 401(m) (matching contributions) components of the plan, but is not considered benefiting for purposes of the employer nonelective contribution component of the plan.

Q 11:6 May 401(k) plans be combined to satisfy the ratio percentage test?

401(k) plans may be combined only if they have the same plan year. Generally, portions of plans that are required to be treated as separate plans cannot be combined (nor can an employer combine two or more plans that would be disaggregated if they were portions of the same plan). If an employer treats two or more plans as a single plan for purposes of the ratio percentage test, it must treat them as a single plan for purposes of applying all other nondiscrimination rules. [Treas. Reg. § 1.410(b)-7(d)]

Example 1. Bon-Ton Shoes maintains a 401(k) plan covering its salaried and office clerical employees and maintains a defined benefit plan for its collective bargaining employees. No plan is maintained for Bon-Ton's noncollective bargaining hourly employees. The 401(k) plan cannot be aggregated with the defined benefit plan for purposes of satisfying the ratio percentage test. Aggregation is not allowed because plans established for collective bargaining employees cannot be aggregated with plans established for employees who are not covered by a collective bargaining agreement.

Example 2. Fox Head Company maintains two 401(k) plans, one for its salaried employees and the other for its non-collective bargaining hourly employees, and both plans have the same plan year and use the same testing methods. Fox Head decides to treat the two plans as a single plan for purposes of satisfying the ratio percentage test. Because the plans have been aggregated, they must be treated as one plan in applying the nondiscrimination rules. (See chapters 12 and 13.) Consequently, the actual deferral percentage (ADP) test for determining whether elective contributions are discriminatory in amount will be applied as if the two 401(k) plans were one. If both plans provide for matching and/or employee contributions, the actual contribution percentage (ACP) test will be applied as if the two plans were one. Any nonelective contributions to the plans will be tested under the Section 401(a)(4) nondiscrimination rules as if the two plans were one. Finally, the benefits, rights, or features provided under the plans will be tested as if the plans were one plan.

Q 11:7 Is there an exception to the rule that 401(k) plans that are required to be treated as separate plans cannot be combined for purposes of the ratio percentage test?

Yes. Normally, a 401(k) plan covering the employees of two or more qualified separate lines of business (QSLOBs) must be treated as consisting of as many plans as there are QSLOBs. (See chapter 10.) However, this disaggregation rule may be ignored and the ratio percentage test satisfied if the plan, when tested on an employer-wide basis, benefits 70 percent of the employer's NHCEs. If a plan is tested on an employer-wide basis, other nondiscrimination rules are also applied on that basis. [Treas. Reg. § 1.414(r)-1(c)(2)(ii)]

Example. Weber Company maintains a 401(k) plan covering all three of its QSLOBs. Tested on an employer-wide basis, the plan benefits more than 70 percent of Weber's NHCEs; thus, the rules requiring the plan to be treated as three separate plans (one for each QSLOB) may be ignored. Because the plan is tested on an employer-wide basis, the nondiscrimination rules are also applied on that basis. For example, the ADP test, used to determine whether elective contributions are discriminatory in amount, will take into account all Weber employees. If the 401(k) plan had not been tested on an employer-wide basis, an ADP test would have to be conducted separately with respect to each QSLOB.

Q 11:8 If an employer that is divided into QSLOBs maintains a 401(k) plan that is tested on an employer-wide basis, may that plan be combined with any other plan maintained by the employer to demonstrate that the other plan satisfies the ratio percentage test?

No. Plans cannot be combined under these circumstances. [Treas. Reg. § 1.410(b)-7(d)(4)]

Example. Mega Corporation is divided into two QSLOBs. Mega maintains a 401(k) plan that benefits all of its employees and that is considered to satisfy the ratio percentage test on an employer-wide basis. Mega also maintains a defined benefit plan that benefits the salaried and office clerical employees of QSLOB 1. The defined benefit plan does not benefit 70 percent of Mega's NHCEs when tested on an employer-wide basis. In determining whether the defined benefit plan satisfies the ratio percentage test, the defined benefit plan may not be combined with that portion of the 401(k) plan that benefits the employees of QSLOB 1.

Average Benefits Test

Q 11:9 What is the *average benefits test*?

The *average benefits test* consists of two separate tests, both of which must be satisfied. The two tests are the nondiscriminatory classification test (see Qs 11:10–11:17) and the average benefit percentage test (see Qs 11:18–11:23). [Treas. Reg. § 1.410(b)-2(b)(3)]

Nondiscriminatory Classification Test

Q 11:10 What is the *nondiscriminatory classification test*?

The *nondiscriminatory classification test* is a test that requires the 401(k) plan to benefit a class of employees established by the employer that is both reasonable and nondiscriminatory. [Treas. Reg. § 1.410(b)-4(a)]

Q 11:11 What is a *reasonable classification*?

A *reasonable classification* is one established under objective business criteria that identify in the plan document the group of employees who are eligible to participate in the 401(k) plan. Reasonable classifications include job categories, nature of compensation (salaried or hourly), and geographic location. A list of named employees eligible to participate in the plan would not be considered a reasonable classification. [Treas. Reg. § 1.410(b)-4(b)]

Q 11:12 What is a *nondiscriminatory classification* of employees?

A *classification* is automatically considered *nondiscriminatory* if the 401(k) plan's ratio percentage (the percentage determined by dividing the percentage of NHCEs benefiting under the plan by the percentage of HCEs benefiting under the plan) is greater than or equal to the safe harbor percentage. [Treas. Reg. § 1.410(b)-4(c)(2)] If the plan's ratio percentage is less than the safe harbor percentage, a classification can still be considered nondiscriminatory if

1. The plan's ratio percentage is greater than or equal to the plan's unsafe harbor percentage; and
2. The classification, based on all relevant facts and circumstances, is determined by the IRS to be nondiscriminatory (see Q 11:16).

[Treas. Reg. § 1.410(b)-4(c)(3)]

Q 11:13 What is the *safe harbor percentage*?

A 401(k) plan's *safe harbor percentage* is 50 percent reduced by three quarters of a percentage point for each whole percentage point by which the NHCE concentration percentage is greater than 60 percent. [Treas. Reg. § 1.410(b)-4(c)(4)(i)]

Q 11:14 What is the *unsafe harbor percentage*?

A 401(k) plan's *unsafe harbor percentage* is 40 percent reduced by three quarters of a percentage point for each whole percentage point by which the NHCE concentration percentage is greater than 60 percent. In no event, however, can the unsafe harbor percentage be less than 20 percent. [Treas. Reg. § 1.410(b)-4(c)(4)(ii)]

Q 11:15 What is the *NHCE concentration percentage*?

An employer's *NHCE concentration percentage* is the percentage of all employees of the employer who are NHCEs. This percentage is determined by taking into account only nonexcludable employees (see Q 11:24). [Treas. Reg. § 1.410(b)-4(c)(4)(iii)]

Table 11-1 shows the safe and unsafe harbor percentages for any given NHCE concentration percentage.

Table 11-1. Safe and Unsafe Harbor Percentages

NHCE Concentration Percentage	*Safe Harbor Percentage*	*Unsafe Harbor Percentage*
0–60%	50.00%	40.00%
61	49.25	39.25
62	48.50	38.50
63	47.75	37.75
64	47.00	37.00
65	46.25	36.25

Table 11-1. Safe and Unsafe Harbor Percentages (*cont'd*)

NHCE Concentration Percentage	*Safe Harbor Percentage*	*Unsafe Harbor Percentage*
66	45.50	35.50
67	44.75	34.75
68	44.00	34.00
69	43.25	33.25
70	42.50	32.50
71	41.75	31.75
72	41.00	31.00
73	40.25	30.25
74	39.50	29.50
75	38.75	28.75
76	38.00	28.00
77	37.25	27.25
78	36.50	26.50
79	35.75	25.75
80	35.00	25.00
81	34.25	24.25
82	33.50	23.50
83	32.75	22.75
84	32.00	22.00
85	31.25	21.25
86	30.50	20.50
87	29.75	20.00
88	29.00	20.00
89	28.25	20.00
90	27.50	20.00
91	26.75	20.00
92	26.00	20.00
93	25.25	20.00
94	24.50	20.00
95	23.75	20.00
96	23.00	20.00
97	22.25	20.00
98	21.50	20.00
99	20.75	20.00

Q 11:16 What facts and circumstances will be taken into account by the IRS in determining whether a classification under a 401(k) plan will be considered nondiscriminatory?

The regulations cite several examples of facts and circumstances that will be taken into account in determining whether a classification is nondiscriminatory:

1. The underlying business reason for the classification. The greater the business reason for the classification, the more likely the classification is nondiscriminatory. Reducing the employer's cost of providing retirement benefits is not considered a relevant business reason.
2. The percentage of the employer's employees benefiting under the plan. The higher the percentage, the more likely the classification is nondiscriminatory.
3. Whether the number of employees benefiting under the plan in each salary range is representative of the number of employees in each salary range of the employer's workforce. In general, the more representative the percentages of employees benefiting under the plan in each salary range, the more likely the classification is nondiscriminatory.
4. The difference between the plan's ratio percentage and the safe harbor percentage. The smaller the difference, the more likely the classification is nondiscriminatory.
5. The extent to which the plan's average benefit percentage exceeds 70 percent (see Q 11:19).

[Treas. Reg. § 1.410(b)-4(c)(3)(ii)]

Example 1. The Madison Company has 130 nonexcludable employees. Of those employees, 120 are NHCEs and 10 are HCEs. Madison maintains a 401(k) plan that benefits 60 NHCEs and 9 HCEs. Thus, the plan's ratio percentage is 55.56 percent [(60/120)/(9/10) = 0.5556], which is below the percentage (70 percent) necessary to satisfy the ratio percentage test.

Madison's NHCE concentration percentage is 92.3 percent (120/130); thus, Employer A's safe harbor percentage is 26 percent, and its unsafe harbor percentage is 20 percent. (See Table 11-1.) Because the plan's ratio percentage is greater than the safe harbor percentage, the plan's classification is considered nondiscriminatory.

Example 2. Great-East has 10,000 nonexcludable employees. Of those employees, 9,600 are NHCEs and 400 are HCEs. Great-East maintains a 401(k) plan that benefits 500 NHCEs and 100 HCEs. Thus, the plan's ratio percentage is 20.83 percent [(500/9,600)/(100/400) = 0.2083], which is below the percentage necessary (70 percent) to satisfy the ratio percentage test.

Great-East's NHCE concentration percentage is 96 percent (9,600/10,000); thus, the plan's safe harbor percentage is 23 percent, and its unsafe harbor percentage is 20 percent. Because the plan's ratio percentage (20.83 percent) is above the unsafe harbor percentage (20 percent) and below the safe harbor percentage (23 percent), the IRS may determine that the classification is nondiscriminatory after considering all the facts and circumstances.

Q 11:17 May 401(k) plans be combined to satisfy the nondiscriminatory classification test?

Yes, 401(k) plans may be combined in the same way as they are for purposes of satisfying the ratio percentage test (see Q 11:6). [Treas. Reg. § 1.410(b)-7(d)]

Average Benefit Percentage Test

Q 11:18 What is the *average benefit percentage test*?

The *average benefit percentage test* is one that requires the average benefit percentage of the 401(k) plan for the plan year to be at least 70 percent. [Treas. Reg. § 1.410(b)-5(a)]

Q 11:19 How is the average benefit percentage calculated?

The average benefit percentage is determined by dividing the actual benefit percentage of the NHCEs in plans in the testing group for the testing period by the actual benefit percentage of the HCEs in plans in the testing group for the testing period. (See Qs 11:21 and 11:22 for the definitions of testing group and testing period.) [Treas. Reg. § 1.410(b)-5(b)]

Q 11:20 How is the actual benefit percentage of each group calculated?

The actual benefit percentage of a group of employees (HCEs or NHCEs) for a testing period is the average of the employee benefit percentages, calculated separately with respect to each employee of the group, for the testing period. If nonexcludable employees are not benefiting under any plan in the testing group, their employee benefit percentages are zero. [Treas. Reg. § 1.410(b)-5(c)]

Q 11:21 What is the *testing group*?

The *testing group* consists of the 401(k) plan being tested and all other plans that could be combined with the plan for purposes of satisfying the ratio percentage test or the nondiscriminatory classification test (the same-plan-year requirement does not apply, however). (See Qs 11:6, 11:17.) The rules requiring disaggregation on the basis of types of contributions are also ignored. Consequently, elective contributions and matching contributions (but not employee after-tax contributions) are included in determining an employee's benefit percentage. In addition, the rules requiring disaggregation of the ESOP (employee stock ownership plan) and non-ESOP portions of a plan are not taken into account. Finally, the portions of plans benefiting the employees of the same QSLOB are combined even though one or more of the plans may have been tested on an employer-wide basis. (See Q 11:8.) [Treas. Reg. §§ 1.410(b)-5(d)(3)(i), 1.410(b)-7(e)(1)]

Example. The Big-Deal Corp. is treated as operating two QSLOBs: QSLOB 1 and QSLOB 2. Big-Deal maintains the following plans:

1. Plan A, the portion of Big-Deal's employer-wide 401(k) plan that benefits all non-collectively bargained employees of QSLOB 1;
2. Plan B, the portion of Big-Deal's employer-wide 401(k) plan that benefits all non-collectively bargained employees of QSLOB 2;
3. Plan C, a defined benefit plan that benefits all hourly, non-collectively bargained employees of QSLOB 1;
4. Plan D, a defined benefit plan that benefits all collectively bargained employees of QSLOB 1;
5. Plan E, an ESOP that benefits all non-collectively bargained employees of QSLOB 1; and
6. Plan F, a profit sharing plan that benefits all salaried, non-collectively bargained employees of QSLOB 1.

Assume that Plan F does not satisfy the ratio percentage test but satisfies the nondiscriminatory classification test when tested on both an employer-wide basis and a separate line of business basis. Therefore, to satisfy the minimum coverage rules, Plan F must satisfy the average benefit percentage test. The plans in the testing group used to determine whether Plan F satisfies the average benefit percentage test are Plans A, C, E, and F. Plan B is not included in the testing group because it is maintained for the benefit of the non-collectively bargained employees of QSLOB 2. Plan D is not included in the testing group because it is maintained for the benefit of collective bargaining employees. [Treas. Reg. §§ 1.410(b)-7(e)(2), 1.414(r)-8(b)(2)]

Q 11:22 What is the testing period for the average benefit percentage calculation?

An employee's benefit percentage (see Q 11:20) is determined on the basis of plan years ending in the same calendar year. These plan years, in the aggregate, are considered the testing period. [Treas. Reg. § 1.410(b)-5(d)(3)(ii)]

Q 11:23 How is an employee's benefit percentage calculated?

The rules for determining an employee's benefit percentage can be quite complicated, especially if defined benefit and defined contribution plans are in the same testing group. In general, an employee's benefit percentage is calculated by dividing employer-provided contributions by a participant's compensation for a plan year ending in the testing period. If there are both defined benefit and defined contribution plans in the testing group, the normal procedure is either to convert contributions to equivalent benefits or to convert benefits to equivalent contributions. [Treas. Reg. § 1.401(b)-5(d)(5)] The regulations do contain an option, however, to test defined contribution plans and defined benefit plans separately. [Treas. Reg. § 1.410(b)-5(e)(3)]

> **Example.** Randy is a participant in a 401(k) plan that must show that it satisfies the average benefit percentage test. Randy's compensation for the plan year is $50,000 and the following amounts of contributions are allocated to his account: (1) elective, $6,000; (2) match, $2,000; and (3) profit sharing, $4,000. Randy's benefit percentage for purposes of the average benefit percentage test is 24 percent ([$6,000 + $2,000 + $4,000]/$50,000).

Disregarding Certain Employees

Q 11:24 Can a 401(k) plan disregard certain employees in applying the minimum coverage rules?

Yes. In applying the minimum coverage rules, the plan may exclude certain employees. These exclusions are applied with reference to the 401(k) plan that is being tested. If, for example, two or more plans are combined, whether permissively, as in the case of the ratio percentage or nondiscriminatory classification tests, or mandatorily, as in the case of the average benefit percentage test, the exclusions are applied to this deemed-single plan. [Treas. Reg. § 1.410(b)-6(a)(2)]

Q 11:25 Which employees may be excluded?

The employees described below may be excluded in applying the minimum coverage rules:

1. *Age and service conditions.* A 401(k) plan may exclude all employees who have not satisfied the plan's age and service eligibility conditions until the date on which employees enter the plan. This exclusion is available, however, only if no employee who does not satisfy these conditions is benefiting under the plan. [Treas. Reg. § 1.410(b)-6(b)(1)] If a plan has two or more age and service eligibility conditions, only those employees who fail to satisfy all the different sets of age and service conditions are excludable. [Treas. Reg. § 1.410(b)-6(b)(2)]

> **Example.** Badger Tanning maintains Plan A for salaried employees and Plan B for hourly employees. Plan A has no minimum age or service condition. Plan B has no minimum age condition but requires one year of service. Badger Tanning treats Plans A and B as a single plan for purposes of the ratio percentage test. Because Plan A does not impose minimum age and service conditions, all employees of Badger Tanning automatically satisfy the minimum age and service conditions of Plan A. Therefore, no employees can be excluded for purposes of satisfying the ratio percentage test.

2. *Air pilots and nonresident aliens.* Air pilots covered by collective bargaining agreements and nonresident aliens who have no U.S. source earned income are considered excludable employees. Also, certain nonresident aliens who

have U.S.-source earned income may be excluded if a treaty so provides. [I.R.C. § 410(b)(3)(B); Treas. Reg. § 1.410(b)-6(c)]

3. *Collective bargaining employees.* Employees who are covered by a collective bargaining agreement are treated as excludable employees when testing a plan covering only noncollective bargaining employees. [Treas. Reg. § 1.410(b)-6(d)] A collective bargaining employee is an employee who is included in a unit of employees covered by an agreement that the Secretary of Labor finds to be a collective bargaining agreement between employee representatives and one or more employers, provided there is evidence that retirement benefits were the subject of good-faith bargaining between employee representatives and the employer or employers. [Treas. Reg. § 1.410(b)-6(d)(2)(i)] However, an employee will not be considered a collective bargaining employee if 50 percent or more of the membership of the organization to which he or she belongs consists of owners, officers, or executives of employers. [I.R.C. § 7701(a)(46)] In addition, an employee will not be considered covered under a collective bargaining agreement if more than 2 percent of the employees who are covered under the agreement are professionals. [Treas. Reg. §§ 1.410(b)-6(d)(2)(iii)(B)(1), 1.410(b)-9]

4. *Employees of QSLOBs.* When applying the minimum coverage rules to a 401(k) plan that benefits the employees of a QSLOB, the employees of other QSLOBs are considered excludable employees. This exclusion does not apply, however, in determining whether a plan satisfies the nondiscriminatory classification test (see Q 11:10). [Treas. Reg. § 1.410(b)-6(e)] Also, this exclusion is disregarded if a plan is tested on an employer-wide basis (see Q 11:7).

5. *Certain terminating employees.* An employee may be treated as an excludable employee for a plan year with respect to a plan if all of the following requirements are met:

- The employee does not benefit under the plan for the plan year.
- The employee is eligible to participate in the plan.
- The plan has a minimum service requirement or a requirement that an employee be employed on the last day of the plan year (last-day requirement) for an employee to receive an allocation for the plan year.
- The employee fails to receive an allocation under the plan solely because of the failure to satisfy the minimum service or last-day requirement.
- The employee is not employed on the last day of the plan year and is credited with no more than 500 hours of service.

[Treas. Reg. § 1.410(b)-6(f)]

Example. Abe's Books has 30 employees who are eligible to participate under a 401(k) plan that also provides for employer nonelective contributions. The plan requires 1,000 hours of service to receive an allocation of nonelective contributions. Ten employees do not receive an allocation because of their failure to complete 1,000 hours of service. Three of the ten employees who fail to satisfy the minimum service requirement complete 500 or fewer hours of service and terminate their employment. Two of the employees complete more than 500 but fewer than 1,000 hours of service and terminate their employment. The remaining five employees do not terminate employment. The three terminated employees who complete 500 or fewer hours of service are treated as excludable employees for the portion of the plan year they are employed. The other seven employees who do not receive an allocation are taken into account for purposes of the minimum coverage rules, but are treated as not benefiting under the nonelective contribution portion of the plan.

6. *Employees of a Section 501(c)(3) tax-exempt organization.* Any such employees who participate in a Section 403(b) plan are excluded if they do not participate in a 401(k) plan and at least 95 percent of the employees who are not employed by the tax-exempt organization are eligible to participate in a 401(k) plan. This exclusion applies only for purposes of the 401(k) and 401(m) components of a 401(k) plan; it does not apply to that part of a 401(k) plan providing for nonelective contributions. [Treas. Reg. § 1.410(b)-6(g)]

Testing for Minimum Coverage

Q 11:26 How is a 401(k) plan tested to determine whether it satisfies the minimum coverage rules?

The regulations set forth three methods for determining whether a 401(k) plan satisfies the minimum coverage rules:

1. The daily testing method;
2. The quarterly testing method; and
3. The annual testing method.

The last of these methods must be used by those portions of a 401(k) plan attributable to elective contributions and to matching and employee contributions. The annual testing method must also be used to apply the average benefit percentage test. [Treas. Reg. § 1.410(b)-8(a)]

Q 11:27 What is the *daily testing method*?

The *daily testing method* is a method under which the employer must show that a plan satisfies the ratio percentage or nondiscriminatory classification test on each day of the plan year. Only individuals employed on that day are taken into account. [Treas. Reg. § 1.410(b)-8(a)(2)]

Q 11:28 What is the *quarterly testing method*?

The *quarterly testing method* is a method under which the employer must show that the plan satisfies the ratio percentage test or nondiscriminatory classification test on at least one day in each quarter of the plan year. The days selected must be reasonably representative of the plan's coverage over the entire plan year. Only individuals employed on the dates selected are taken into account. [Treas. Reg. § 1.410(b)-8(a)(3)]

Q 11:29 What is the *annual testing method*?

The *annual testing method* is a method under which the employer must show that the minimum coverage rules are satisfied on the last day of the plan year, taking into account all individuals who were employed on any day during the plan year. [Treas. Reg. § 1.410(b)-8(a)(4)]

> **Example.** The Bell Company sponsors a calendar-year 401(k) plan that provides for matching and nonelective contributions. In performing minimum coverage testing of the elective contribution and matching contribution components of the plan, Bell is required to use the annual testing method, but it decides to use the quarterly testing method for purposes of testing the nonelective contribution portion of the plan. Bell selects March 31, April 1, September 30, and October 1 as the testing dates. These dates are acceptable as long as they are reasonably representative of the plan's coverage over the entire plan year.

Q 11:30 Has the IRS developed an alternative to the testing methodologies set forth in the regulations?

Yes. Under Revenue Procedure 93-42 [1993-2 C.B. 260] an employer may substantiate that a 401(k) plan complies with the minimum coverage rules on the basis of the employer's workforce on a single day during the plan year as long as that day is reasonably representative of the employer's workforce and the 401(k) plan coverage during the plan year. That revenue procedure also permits an employer to establish a three-year testing cycle. Under this cycle, an employer that demonstrates that its 401(k) plan complies with the minimum coverage rules in a plan year can rely on this demonstration for the two following plan years if the employer reasonably concludes that there are no significant changes in coverage since the initial plan year.

Correcting Minimum Coverage Failure

Q 11:31 What happens if a 401(k) plan fails to satisfy the minimum coverage rules?

The sanction for failing to satisfy the minimum coverage rules is directed at HCEs. In the case of a failure, an HCE must include in gross income the value of the HCE's vested account balances (other than any value attributable to the HCE's own basis in the plan resulting from employee after-tax contributions, PS-58 costs, and taxable loans) as of the close of the plan year in which the failure occurs. [I.R.C. § 402(b)(4)]

Q 11:32 Is there any way to correct retroactively a failure to satisfy the minimum coverage rules?

Yes. Regulations under Code Section 401(a)(4) allow plans to be amended retroactively to satisfy the minimum coverage rules. In the case of the portion of the plan attributable to elective contributions, retroactive correction is accomplished by making qualified nonelective contributions to nonexcludable NHCEs who were not considered eligible employees for the plan year in question (see chapter 13). Similarly, if the portion of a 401(k) plan attributable to matching contributions and employee contributions does not satisfy the minimum coverage rules, qualified nonelective contributions can be made on behalf of nonexcludable NHCEs who were not considered eligible employees for the plan year in question. [Treas. Reg. § 1.401(a)(4)-11(g)(3)(vii)]

Example. Jersey Dairy maintains an elective-contribution-only 401(k) plan for the employees of Division A. For its plan year ending December 31, 2015, the 401(k) plan does not cover the employees of Division B. The QSLOB rules do not apply. After the end of the 2015 plan year, the plan administrator determines that the 401(k) plan can satisfy neither the ratio percentage test nor the nondiscriminatory classification test. To satisfy the minimum coverage rules, Jersey Dairy amends the 401(k) plan to provide for qualified nonelective contributions on behalf of the nonexcludable Division B NHCEs.

Q 11:33 What level of qualified nonelective contributions must be provided to these NHCEs?

The amount to be provided to each nonexcludable NHCE equals his or her compensation for the plan year in question multiplied by the ADP and/or the ACP (see chapter 13), as the case may be, of the group of NHCEs who were eligible employees under the 401(k) plan. [Treas. Reg. § 1.401(a)(4)-11(g)(3)(vii)]

Example. In the example in Q 11:32, the actual deferral percentage of the NHCE group for the 2015 plan year was 4 percent. Hence, Jersey Dairy must provide to each nonexcludable Division B NHCE an amount equal to 4 percent of his or her 2015 compensation.

Q 11:34 By when must a 401(k) plan be amended to correct retroactively a failure to satisfy the minimum coverage rules?

The 401(k) plan must be amended, and the amendment must be implemented, no later than the fifteenth day of the tenth month after the close of the plan year. [Treas. Reg. § 1.401(a)(4)-11(g)(3)(iv)] For example, in the case of a plan year ending December 31, 2015, the corrective amendment must be made and implemented by October 15, 2016.

Q 11:35 Does the method of retroactive correction discussed in Qs 11:32–11:34 apply to the nonelective contribution portion of a 401(k) plan?

Yes. In this case, however, correction does not require that qualified nonelective contributions be made on behalf of NHCEs. All that is required is a timely amendment (see Q 11:34) that brings in and provides an allocation of nonelective contributions to a sufficient number of employees to satisfy the minimum coverage rules.

Q 11:36 How does a plan resolve a minimum coverage failure if the plan does not satisfy the retroactive amendment procedure described in Qs 11:32–11:35?

If a plan does not satisfy the retroactive amendment procedure, it is considered to have a demographic failure. To correct this failure, the plan needs to file a VCP application with the IRS (see chapter 20). [Rev. Proc. 2013-12, § 4.01(2), 2013-4 I.R.B. 313]

Q 11:37 May a 401(k) plan be designed to automatically avoid a minimum coverage failure?

Yes. In the case of a 401(k) plan that requires a participant to be employed on the last day of the plan year and/or to have completed a specified number of hours of service during the plan year in order to receive an allocation of employer nonelective and matching contributions, the 401(k) plan may contain what is often referred to as a "fail safe" provision. This provision comes into play if the plan's allocation conditions cause the nonelective and/or matching portions of the plan to fail minimum coverage. Fail safe provisions operate by waiving the conditions for a number of participants sufficient to cause the plan to pass one of the minimum coverage tests. The identity of the participants who receive allocations under the fail safe provision is determined under a procedure defined in the plan document.

Chapter 12

General Nondiscrimination Testing

Like other qualified plans, a 401(k) plan will retain its qualified status only if the contributions or benefits under the plan do not discriminate in favor of highly compensated employees (HCEs). This chapter discusses what tests are applied in determining whether the amount of employer nonelective contributions (such as profit sharing contributions) is discriminatory. The special tests that apply to elective (deferral) contributions, matching contributions, and employee after-tax contributions are covered in chapter 13. This chapter also explains the interaction of the permitted disparity rules with the antidiscrimination requirement. Finally, this chapter addresses the rules for determining whether benefits, rights, and features under the plan discriminate in favor of HCEs.

Testing of Employer Nonelective Contributions 12-1
The Design-Based Safe Harbor 12-2
The General Nondiscrimination Test 12-5
Permitted Disparity 12-7
Basic Permitted Disparity Rules 12-7
How Permitted Disparity Is Used 12-9
Permitted Disparity in More Than One Plan 12-10
Nondiscriminatory Availability of Benefits, Rights, and Features 12-11
Current Availability 12-13
Effective Availability 12-14

Testing of Employer Nonelective Contributions

The actual deferral percentage (ADP) and actual contribution percentage (ACP) tests are used to determine whether the amount of elective (deferral) contributions, matching contributions, and employee after-tax contributions (both mandatory and voluntary) made under a 401(k) plan discriminates in favor of HCEs (see chapter 13). Employer nonelective contributions other than matching contributions must also be nondiscriminatory in amount. Profit sharing contributions are a common example of such nonelective contributions.

Under the Section 401(a)(4) regulations, a plan may be designed to ensure that nonelective contributions to a 401(k) plan are allocated on a nondiscriminatory basis (see Qs 12:1–12:8). However, if a plan does not contain a design-based safe harbor formula for allocating nonelective contributions, the plan must satisfy the Section 401(a)(4) general test on either a contributions or an equivalent benefits basis (see Qs 12:9–12:14).

The Design-Based Safe Harbor

Q 12:1 What is the *design-based safe harbor*?

A 401(k) plan will satisfy the *design-based safe harbor* for nonelective contributions if the plan contains a uniform allocation formula (see Q 12:2) or the plan is a uniform point system plan (see Q 12:4). [Treas. Reg. § 1.401(a)(4)-2(b)(1)]

Q 12:2 What is a *uniform allocation formula*?

A *uniform allocation formula* is a formula that allocates the same percentage of compensation or the same dollar amount to each employee in the plan. A plan that determines allocations based on the same dollar amount for each uniform unit of service (not to exceed one week) will also be considered to have a uniform allocation formula. An allocation formula is still considered uniform even if the plan takes into account permitted disparity under Internal Revenue Code (Code) Section 401(*l*) (see Qs 12:15–12:18). [Treas. Reg. § 1.401(a)(4)-2(b)(2)]

Q 12:3 What is considered compensation for purposes of applying a uniform allocation formula?

A uniform allocation formula that takes into account compensation must use a definition of compensation that is nondiscriminatory under Code Section 414(s). (See the discussion of *compensation* in chapter 10.) Generally, compensation paid during the plan year will be used for this purpose, but the regulations do permit the use of compensation paid during any 12-month period ending within the plan year. The plan may also provide that only compensation paid during the portion of a plan year that an employee is a participant will be taken into account. [Treas. Reg. § 1.401(a)(4)-12]

Q 12:4 What is a *uniform point system plan*?

A *uniform point system plan* is a plan under which each employee's allocation of nonelective contributions is determined by multiplying the contribution to be allocated by a fraction. The numerator of the fraction is the employee's points for the year, and the denominator of the fraction is the points of all employees entitled to an allocation. A uniform point system plan must also satisfy a nondiscrimination test (see Q 12:6). [Treas. Reg. § 1.401(a)(4)-2(b)(3)]

Q 12:5 How are an employee's points determined?

The plan must award points for either age or service and may award points for both. Points may also be granted for units of compensation. Each employee must receive the same number of points for each year of age, for each year of service, and for each unit of compensation. The unit of compensation must be the same for all employees and cannot exceed $200. If a plan grants points for years of service, the plan may impose a limit on the number of years of service taken into account. [Treas. Reg. § 1.401(a)(4)-2(b)(3)(i)(A)]

Q 12:6 What nondiscrimination test must be satisfied before a plan can be considered a uniform point system plan?

For each plan year, the average of the allocation rates for HCEs cannot exceed the average of the allocation rates for non-highly compensated employees (NHCEs). An employee's allocation rate is the amount allocated to the employee's account for a plan year expressed as either a percentage of compensation or a dollar amount. [Treas. Reg. § 1.401(a)(4)-2(b)(3)(i)(B)]

Example. A 401(k) plan provides for profit sharing contributions that are allocated pursuant to a uniform point system formula. The plan grants each employee ten points for each year of service and one point for each $100 of compensation. For the plan year, total allocations are $74,700, and total points for all employees in the plan are 7,470. Each employee's allocation for the plan year is set forth in the following table.

Employee	*Years of Service*	*Plan Year Compensation*	*Points*	*Amount of Allocation*	*Rate*
H1	10	$150,000	1,600	$16,000	10.7
H2	5	150,000	1,550	15,500	10.3
H3	30	120,000	1,500	15,000	12.5
H4	3	120,000	1,230	12,300	10.3
N1	10	50,000	600	6,000	12.0
N2	5	35,000	400	4,000	11.4
N3	3	30,000	330	3,300	11.0
N4	1	25,000	260	2,600	10.4
Total			7,470	$74,700	

For the plan year, the average allocation rate for the HCEs in the plan (H1–H4) is 10.95 percent [(10.7% + 10.3% + 12.5% + 10.3%)/4], and the average allocation rate for NHCEs in the plan (N1–N4) is 11.2 percent [(12.0%

+ 11.4% + 11.0% + 10.4%)/4]. Because the average of the allocation rates for the HCEs in the plan does not exceed the average of the allocation rates for the NHCEs, the plan will be treated as a uniform point system plan for the plan year.

Q 12:7 Will an allocation of nonelective contributions that is conditioned on employment on the last day of the plan year cause an allocation formula to lose its status as a design-based safe harbor formula?

No. A 401(k) plan that contains a last-day requirement for sharing in an allocation of nonelective contributions will still be considered a design-based safe harbor formula. Similarly, a plan requiring a minimum number of hours of service in order to obtain an allocation will not affect the formula's safe harbor status. [Treas. Reg. § 1.401(a)(4)-2(b)(4)(iii)] However, 401(k) plans containing these requirements may find it more difficult to pass the minimum coverage rules because participants not receiving allocations on account of these requirements are likely to be treated as non-excludable. (See chapter 11.)

Q 12:8 Will an allocation formula be considered a design-based safe harbor formula if a participant who is a non-key employee receives only a top-heavy minimum contribution?

Yes, but only if the nonelective contribution component of the 401(k) plan satisfies the Section 410(b) coverage rules when the non-key employee who receives only a top-heavy minimum contribution is treated as not benefiting (see the discussion of the minimum coverage rules in chapter 11). [Treas. Reg. § 1.401(a)(4)-2(b)(4)(vi)(D)(3)] If the 401(k) plan cannot satisfy the minimum coverage rules under these circumstances, the allocation formula loses its status as a design-based safe harbor formula, and the nonelective contribution portion of the 401(k) plan must satisfy the general nondiscrimination test (see Q 12:9).

> **Example.** Somba Corporation sponsors a top-heavy 401(k) plan that provides for nonelective contributions allocated in proportion to the compensation paid to all those participants who are employed on the last day of the plan year and who complete 1,000 or more hours of service during the plan year. Somba makes a nonelective contribution equal to 6 percent of pay. All of its HCEs receive a 6 percent allocation, and each of 12 NHCEs receives a 6 percent allocation. The remaining 3 NHCEs receive only a top-heavy minimum contribution equal to 3 percent of pay because they have not completed 1,000 or more hours of service during the year. The plan's allocation formula is considered a design-based safe harbor because the 401(k) plan, after treating the participants who receive only a top-heavy minimum contribution as not benefiting, has a ratio percentage of 80 percent, a percentage that is in excess of the ratio percentage (70 percent) necessary to satisfy the ratio percentage test under Code Section 410(b). (See chapter 11.)

The General Nondiscrimination Test

Q 12:9 What is the *general nondiscrimination test*?

The *general nondiscrimination test* is a test requiring that each rate group under the plan satisfy the minimum coverage rules (see chapter 11) as if the rate group were a separate plan. [Treas. Reg. § 1.401(a)(4)-2(c)(1)]

Q 12:10 What is a *rate group*?

A *rate group* exists for each HCE and consists of that HCE and all other employees who have allocation rates greater than or equal to the allocation rate for that HCE. [Treas. Reg. § 1.401(a)(4)-2(c)(1)]

Q 12:11 What is an employee's *allocation rate*?

An employee's *allocation rate* is the amount allocated to an employee's account for the plan year expressed as either a percentage of compensation (as illustrated at Q 12:13) or a dollar amount. [Treas. Reg. § 1.401(a)(4)-2(c)(2)(i)]

Q 12:12 What amounts are taken into account in determining allocation rates?

The amounts taken into account are the nonelective contributions (other than matching contributions) allocated to an employee's account for the plan year. Forfeitures are also included if allocated in the same way as nonelective contributions. Earnings, expenses, gains, and losses allocable to an account are not taken into account. [Treas. Reg. § 1.401(a)(4)-2(c)(2)(ii)]

Q 12:13 How does a rate group satisfy the minimum coverage rules?

Each rate group must satisfy the minimum coverage rules as if the rate group were a separate plan. However, in applying these rules, the following exceptions apply:

1. A rate group cannot be permissibly aggregated with another rate group for purposes of satisfying the ratio percentage test or the nondiscriminatory classification test.
2. If the rate group is being tested under the nondiscriminatory classification test, the rate group is deemed to satisfy the reasonable classification requirement. (See chapter 11.)
3. If the rate group is being tested under the nondiscriminatory classification test, there will not be a facts-and-circumstances determination in the event that the rate group's ratio percentage (see chapter 11) is less than the safe harbor percentage but greater than or equal to the unsafe harbor percentage. Instead, the facts and circumstances requirement will be

considered satisfied if the ratio percentage of the rate group is greater than or equal to the lesser of:

a. The ratio percentage of the plan; or
b. The midpoint between the safe and unsafe harbor percentages for the plan. (See chapter 11.)

4. If a rate group is being tested under the average benefit percentage test, the rate group will be treated as satisfying this test if the plan of which it is a part satisfies this test.

[Treas. Reg. § 1.401(a)(4)-2(c)(3)]

Example. Employer Y has six nonexcludable employees, all of whom benefit under its 401(k) plan, which also provides for nonelective profit sharing contributions. The HCEs in the plan are H1 and H2, and the NHCEs are N1–N4. For the plan year, H1 and N1–N3 have an allocation rate of 5 percent of compensation. For the same plan year, H2 has an allocation rate of 7.5 percent of compensation, and N4 has an allocation rate of 8 percent of compensation.

The plan has two rate groups. Rate group 1 consists of H1 and all those employees who have an allocation rate greater than or equal to H1's allocation rate (5 percent). Thus, rate group 1 consists of H1, H2, and N1–N4. Rate group 2 consists of H2 and all those employees who have an allocation rate greater than or equal to H2's allocation rate (7.5 percent). Thus, rate group 2 consists of H2 and N4.

Rate group 1 satisfies the ratio percentage test under the minimum coverage rules because the ratio percentage of the rate group is 100 percent—that is, 100 percent (the percentage of all NHCEs who are in the rate group) divided by 100 percent (the percentage of all HCEs who are in the rate group).

Rate group 2 does not satisfy the ratio percentage test because the ratio percentage of the rate group is 50 percent—that is, 25 percent (the percentage of all NHCEs who are in the rate group) divided by 50 percent (the percentage of all HCEs who are in the rate group).

However, rate group 2 satisfies the nondiscriminatory classification test under the minimum coverage rules because the rate group is deemed to satisfy the reasonable classification requirement and the ratio percentage of the rate group (50 percent) is greater than the safe harbor percentage applicable to the plan—safe harbor percentage from Table 11-1 would be 45.5 percent based on an NHCE concentration percentage of 66.7 percent (4/6).

If the plan satisfies the average benefit percentage test (see chapter 11), rate group 2 will also be treated as satisfying that test. In that case, the plan satisfies the general nondiscrimination test because each rate group under the plan satisfies the minimum coverage rules as if each rate group were a separate plan.

Q 12:14 Is the general nondiscrimination test required to be satisfied on the basis of allocation rates?

No. In applying the general nondiscrimination test, a plan may substitute equivalent accrual rates for allocation rates. Equivalent accrual rates are determined by converting nonelective contributions and forfeitures allocated to employees into actuarially equivalent benefits. The ability to convert nonelective contributions into benefits is the basis for age-weighted and other types of cross-tested profit sharing plans (see chapter 2). [Treas. Reg. § 1.401(a)(4)-8(b)]

Permitted Disparity

The permitted disparity rules allow higher retirement plan allocations on behalf of higher-paid employees as a way of recognizing that lower-paid employees receive relatively higher Social Security benefits. This section presents the basic permitted disparity rules, considers how permitted disparity can be used, and ends with the rules covering use of permitted disparity in more than one plan.

Basic Permitted Disparity Rules

Q 12:15 What is *permitted disparity*?

Permitted disparity is the allocation of nonelective contributions at different rates on compensation above and below the plan's integration level. [Treas. Reg. § 1.401(*l*)-2(a)(1)] It is allowed under Code Section 401(*l*) as a way of recognizing the Social Security contributions made by the employer on behalf of the plan's participants. Traditionally, permitted disparity was known as integration with Social Security, or simply integration. The rate of contribution on compensation below the integration level is called the *base contribution percentage.* [Treas. Reg. § 1.401(*l*)-1(c)(4)] The rate of contribution on compensation above the integration level is the *excess contribution percentage.* [Treas. Reg. § 1.401(*l*)-1(c)(15)]

Q 12:16 What is the *integration level*?

The *integration level* is a dollar amount that is either specified in the plan or determined under a formula contained in the plan. The integration level cannot exceed the Social Security taxable wage base in effect at the beginning of the plan year. [Treas. Reg. § 1.401(*l*)-2(d)]

Q 12:17 What is the maximum disparity permitted between the excess contribution percentage and the base contribution percentage?

The excess contribution percentage may not be more than two times the base contribution percentage. In no event, however, may the excess contribution percentage exceed the base benefit percentage by the greater of:

1. 5.7 percent; or
2. The percentage rate of tax under Code Section 3111(a), in effect as of the beginning of the plan year, that is attributable to the old age insurance portion of the Old Age, Survivors and Disability Insurance provisions of the Social Security Act (currently less than 5.7 percent).

[Treas. Reg. § 1.401(*l*)-2(b)]

The percentage determined from (1) or (2) above may need to be reduced, as described at Q 12:18.

> **Example.** The Ultraviolet Company sponsors a 401(k) plan under which it may make nonelective contributions that are allocated taking into account the permitted disparity rules. The integration level of the plan is the Social Security taxable wage base. Ultraviolet makes a nonelective contribution for the 2015 plan year. If the allocation results in an excess contribution percentage of 6 percent, then the base contribution percentage must be no less than 3 percent. (The excess contribution percentage cannot be more than two times the base contribution percentage.) If the allocation results in an excess contribution percentage of 12 percent, the base contribution percentage must be no less than 6.3 percent. (The excess contribution percentage cannot exceed the base contribution percentage by more than 5.7 percentage points.)

Q 12:18 When will a reduction be required in the percentage determined from (1) or (2) of Q 12:17?

A reduction will be required unless the integration level of the plan is either of the following:

1. The Social Security taxable wage base; or
2. A dollar amount that is equal to or less than 20 percent of the Social Security taxable wage base.

If the integration level is otherwise, then the excess contribution percentage cannot exceed the base contribution percentage by more than the percentage determined from the following table.

Integration Level	*Percentage*
Greater than 20 percent of the taxable wage base, but not more than 80 percent of the taxable wage base	4.3%
Greater than 80 percent of the taxable wage base, but less than the taxable wage base	5.4

[Treas. Reg. § 1.401(*l*)-2(d)(4)]

Example. The facts are the same as those in the example in Q 12:17, except that the integration level is 40 percent of the Social Security taxable wage base. If the allocation results in an excess contribution percentage of 6 percent, the base contribution percentage must be no less than 3 percent. (The excess contribution percentage cannot be more than twice the base contribution percentage.) If the allocation results in an excess contribution percentage of 12 percent, then the base contribution percentage must be no less than 7.7 percent. (The excess contribution percentage cannot exceed the base contribution percentage by more than 4.3 percentage points.)

How Permitted Disparity Is Used

Q 12:19 Under what circumstances should permitted disparity be used?

Whether the employer should use permitted disparity in allocating nonelective contributions depends on two issues: the objectives of the employer and the degree to which permitted disparity is or was used in other plans of the employer.

Q 12:20 Why would an employer use permitted disparity?

Employers who wish to make a larger contribution (as a percentage of pay) for higher-paid employees than for lower-paid employees will want to use permitted disparity. Permitted disparity takes into account the regressive Social Security taxes under which the employer contributes a larger percentage of pay for employees earning less than the maximum taxable wage base ($118,500 in 2015).

Example. John and Jim earn $40,000 and $200,000, respectively. The 2015 contributions made by their employer for old age, survivors, and disability insurance under Social Security are as follows:

Employee	*Pay*	*FICA*	*Percentage of Pay*
John	$ 40,000	$ 2,480	6.20%
Jim	200,000	7,347	3.67

As a percentage of pay, Jim is credited with a contribution of 3.67 percent, which is far less than John's contribution of 6.20 percent.

Q 12:21 How does permitted disparity work?

The operation of permitted disparity is best illustrated by example.

Example. Ajax Company wishes to make a profit sharing contribution equal to approximately 4.30 percent of pay of all participants. Employees H, J, and K are the only participants in the plan. The plan's integration level is 81 percent of the maximum taxable wage base of $118,500. In this case, the formula for allocating the profit sharing contribution is equal to 3 percent of pay up to $95,985 plus 6 percent of pay in excess of $95,985. The profit sharing contribution is allocated as follows:

Employee	*Total Compensation*	*Excess Compensation*	*Excess 6%*	*Base 3%*	*Total Contribution*	*Percentage of Pay*
J	$200,000	$104,015	$6,241	$2,880	$ 9,121	4.56%
K	36,000	0	0	1,080	1,080	3.00
H	20,000	0	0	600	600	3.00
Totals	$256,000	$104,015	$6,241	$4,560	$10,801	

J is thus receiving a greater contribution as a percentage of pay than K or H, making up partially for the fact that Ajax makes larger Social Security contributions (as a percentage of pay) on behalf of H and K.

Permitted Disparity in More Than One Plan

Q 12:22 Can permitted disparity be used in more than one plan of the employer?

Yes. However, if an employee is covered by two or more plans, each of which uses permitted disparity, an annual overall limit prevents the overuse of permitted disparity in the plans.

Q 12:23 How is the annual overall limit for permitted disparity computed?

For each employee a fraction is computed for each plan in which the employee is a participant. The fraction is computed as follows:

$$\frac{\text{Actual disparity in the plan}}{\text{Maximum permitted disparity}}$$

The fractions are then summed for each employee. The annual overall limit is met if the sum of these fractions does not exceed 1. [Treas. Reg. § 1.401(*l*)-5(b)]

Example. The Morgan Company has a money purchase plan with a formula equal to 3 percent of pay plus 3 percent of pay in excess of the maximum taxable wage base. The disparity fraction for the money purchase plan is:

$$\frac{\text{Actual disparity in the plan}}{\text{Maximum permitted disparity}} = \frac{3\%}{5.7\%} = 0.5263$$

If Morgan wishes to use permitted disparity in allocating a profit sharing contribution to the 401(k) plan, the sum of the disparity fractions cannot exceed 1.0. Since 0.5263 is "used up," 0.4737 is the allowable disparity fraction in the 401(k) plan.

$$\frac{\text{Actual disparity}}{\text{Maximum permitted disparity}} = 0.4737$$

$$\frac{\text{Actual disparity}}{5.7\%} = 0.4737$$

$$\begin{aligned}\text{Actual disparity} &= 0.4737 \times 5.7\% \\ &= 2.7\%\end{aligned}$$

Morgan could use a formula of 2.7 percent of total pay plus 2.7 percent of pay in excess of the maximum taxable wage base to allocate the profit sharing contribution in the 401(k) plan.

Q 12:24 What is the *cumulative disparity limit*?

The *cumulative disparity limit* is a limit providing that the sum of an employee's annual disparity fractions cannot exceed 35. This limit applies, however, only in the case of an employee who benefits after 1993 in a defined benefit plan that uses permitted disparity. [Treas. Reg. § 1.401(*l*)-5(c)(1)]

Q 12:25 What is the practical implication of these limits on the use of permitted disparity?

The practical implication of these limits is that an employer designing a 401(k) plan will generally not be able to use permitted disparity in the 401(k) plan if the employer has other defined benefit or defined contribution plans that use permitted disparity.

Nondiscriminatory Availability of Benefits, Rights, and Features

Until now we have been concerned with whether employer nonelective contributions under the plan are nondiscriminatory in amount. The focus of this section of the chapter shifts to the question of whether benefits, rights, and features under the 401(k) plan are provided on a nondiscriminatory basis. To resolve this question, it is necessary to examine the "availability" to employees of a benefit, right, or feature.

Q 12:26 What are *benefits, rights, and features*?

Benefits, rights, and features consist of all optional forms of benefits, ancillary benefits, and other rights and features. [Treas. Reg. § 1.401(a)(4)-4(a)]

Q 12:27 What is an *optional form of benefit*?

An *optional form of benefit* is a distribution alternative available for the payment of an employee's account balance. A distribution alternative is different from another distribution alternative if the difference results from variations in payment schedule, timing, commencement, medium of distribution, election rights, or the portion of the benefit to which the distribution alternative applies. [Treas. Reg. § 1.401(a)(4)-4(e)(1)(i)]

Q 12:28 What is an *ancillary benefit*?

In the case of a 401(k) plan, an *ancillary benefit* means any incidental life insurance or health insurance benefits provided under the plan. [Treas. Reg. § 1.401(a)(4)-4(e)(2)]

Q 12:29 What are *other rights or features*?

Other rights or features are those that are not part of optional forms of benefits or ancillary benefits and that can reasonably be expected to have more than insignificant value. (The term *insignificant value* is not defined in the regulations.) The regulations provide examples of other rights or features:

- Plan loan provisions (other than a provision relating to a distribution of an employee's account balance upon loan default, which is considered an optional form of benefit)
- The right to direct investments
- The right to a particular form of investment
- The right to purchase additional ancillary benefits
- The right to make each rate of elective contributions
- The right to make each rate of employee contributions
- The right to receive each rate of matching contributions
- The right to make rollover contributions

[Treas. Reg. § 1.401(a)(4)-4(e)(3)]

Q 12:30 When are benefits, rights, and features provided on a nondiscriminatory basis?

Benefits, rights, and features under the plan are provided on a nondiscriminatory basis when they satisfy the current availability requirement and the effective availability requirement. [Treas. Reg. § 1.401(a)(4)-4(a)]

Current Availability

Q 12:31 How is the current availability requirement satisfied?

The current availability requirement is satisfied if the benefit, right, or feature is currently available to a group of employees that satisfies either the ratio percentage test or the nondiscriminatory classification test. (See discussion of minimum coverage rules in chapter 11.) [Treas. Reg. § 1.401(a)(4)-4(b)(1)]

Q 12:32 When is a benefit, right, or feature considered currently available to an employee?

Whether or not a benefit, right, or feature is currently available to an employee is based on the current facts and circumstances with respect to the employee. Unless an exception applies, the fact that an employee may, in the future, be eligible for a benefit, right, or feature does not cause the benefit, right, or feature to be currently available. [Treas. Reg. § 1.401(a)(4)-4(b)(2)]

Q 12:33 What conditions on the availability of benefits, rights, or features may be disregarded in determining current availability?

For purposes of determining the current availability of optional forms of benefits (but not ancillary benefits or other rights or features), age and service conditions may be disregarded. However, age and service conditions cannot be ignored if they must be met within a certain period. In that case, the plan is allowed to project the age and service of employees to the last date by which the conditions must be satisfied. [Treas. Reg. § 1.401(a)(4)-4(b)(2)(ii)(A)]

Example 1. The Acme Corporation maintains a 401(k) plan for its sole HCE and nine NHCEs. The HCE is age 65, and all of the NHCEs are under age 50. The plan provides that elective contributions may be withdrawn on or after the attainment of age 59½. The plan satisfies the current availability requirement because the optional form of benefit (the right to withdraw elective contributions at age 59½) is considered currently available to all employees. The age 59½ condition is disregarded.

Example 2. The facts are the same as those in Example 1, except that the right to withdraw will be available only for a period of one year. The plan does not satisfy the current availability requirement because none of the NHCEs will meet the age 59½ condition by the end of the one-year period.

Example 3. The facts are the same as those in Example 1, except that it is the right to direct investments that is made available to any employee who reaches age 59½. The plan does not satisfy the current availability requirement because the age 59½ condition cannot be disregarded in the case of other rights or features.

Q 12:34 Are there other conditions that may be disregarded?

Any conditions on the availability of a benefit, right, or feature such as termination of employment, death, satisfaction of a specified health condition (or failure to meet such condition), disability, hardship, or family status are disregarded. Also disregarded are plan provisions requiring mandatory payouts for employees whose vested account balances are not greater than $5,000 (or a lesser specified amount), plan provisions requiring an employee's vested account balance to be less than a specified dollar amount, and plan provisions requiring vested account balances large enough to support a minimum participant loan amount. It should be noted that these conditions may be disregarded whether they apply to optional forms of benefits, ancillary benefits, or other rights or features. [Treas. Reg. §§ 1.401(a)(4)-4(b)(2)(ii)(B), 1.401(a)(4)-4(b)(2)(ii)(C), 1.401(a)(4)-4(b)(2)(ii)(D), 1.401(a)(4)-4(b)(2)(ii)(E)]

Q 12:35 What happens if a benefit, right, or feature is prospectively eliminated?

A benefit, right, or feature that is prospectively eliminated but that is retained with respect to benefits accrued prior to the date of elimination will satisfy the current availability requirement in the future as long as the current availability requirement is met as of the date of elimination. This rule applies, however, only if there are no changes in the terms of the benefit, right, or feature after the elimination date. In addition, in the case of optional forms of benefit that are considered protected benefits under Code Section 411(d)(6), the employee's accrued benefit as of the elimination date must be credited with gains or losses subsequent to the elimination date. [Treas. Reg. § 1.401(a)(4)-4(b)(3)]

> **Example.** A 401(k) plan provides for in-service withdrawals at age 59½. The employer sponsoring the 401(k) plan amends the plan to eliminate the in-service withdrawal option for benefits accruing after the elimination date. The age 59½ in-service withdrawal right is a protected benefit; therefore, the pre-elimination date benefit must be adjusted for subsequent gains and losses.

Effective Availability

Q 12:36 What is the *effective availability requirement*?

The *effective availability requirement* is the requirement that a 401(k) plan, in light of all facts and circumstances, not substantially favor HCEs as the group of employees to whom the benefit, right, or feature is effectively available. [Treas. Reg. § 1.401(a)(4)-4(c)]

> **Example.** The Zolon Corporation amends its 401(k) plan on June 30, 2015, to provide for a single-sum optional form of benefit for employees who terminate employment with Zolon after June 30, 2015, and before January 1, 2016. The availability of this single-sum optional form of benefit is conditioned on the employee's having a particular disability at the time of termination of

employment. The only employee of Zolon who meets this disability requirement at the time of the amendment and thereafter through December 31, 2015, is an HCE. The disability condition is disregarded in determining the current availability of the single-sum optional form of benefit. Nevertheless, under these facts, the only employee to whom the single-sum optional form of benefit is effectively available is an HCE.

Chapter 13

ADP and ACP Testing

As explained in chapter 11, a 401(k) plan must satisfy a minimum coverage test. In addition, the amount of contributions or benefits under a 401(k) plan must not discriminate in favor of highly compensated employees (HCEs). The amount of elective (deferral) contributions under a 401(k) plan is not considered discriminatory if the plan satisfies the *actual deferral percentage* (ADP) test. Similarly, any employer matching contributions and employee after-tax contributions (both voluntary and mandatory) are not discriminatory in amount if the plan meets the *actual contribution percentage* (ACP) test. (For a comparison of the ADP and ACP tests, see Table 13-1 at the end of this chapter.) Note that employer matching contributions are often referred to simply as matching contributions and that employee after-tax contributions are often referred to simply as employee contributions.

Avoiding ADP and ACP Testing 13-2
The Actual Deferral Percentage Test 13-2
- Prior-Year Versus Current-Year Testing Method 13-3
- Special Adjustments 13-4
- Eligible Employees 13-5
- Calculating Actual Deferral Ratios 13-5
- Correcting ADP Test Failures 13-8
- Determining Excess Contributions 13-8
- Recharacterizing Excess Contributions 13-10
- Distributing Excess Contributions 13-11
- Restructuring for ADP Testing 13-14
- Correcting ADP Test by Making QNECs 13-16

The Actual Contribution Percentage Test 13-21
- Actual Contribution Ratios 13-22
- Prior-Year Versus Current-Year Testing Method 13-23
- Special Adjustments 13-24
- Employee Contributions; Eligible Employees 13-25
- Calculating Actual Contribution Ratios 13-25

Correcting ACP Test Failures 13-27
Determining Excess Aggregate Contributions 13-28
Distributing Excess Aggregate Contributions 13-29
Restructuring for ACP Testing 13-33
Correcting ACP Test by Making QNECs 13-33
Table 13-1. Comparison of ADP and ACP Tests 13-34

Avoiding ADP and ACP Testing

Q 13:1 Can a 401(k) plan avoid ADP and ACP testing?

A 401(k) plan can avoid ADP testing and ACP testing if it qualifies as a SIMPLE 401(k) plan (see chapter 2). [I.R.C. §§ 401(k)(11), 401(m)(10)] ADP testing and ACP testing of matching contributions can also be avoided if the 401(k) plan qualifies as a safe harbor 401(k) plan (see chapter 2). [I.R.C. §§ 401(k)(12), 401(m)(11)] Finally, ADP testing and ACP testing of matching contributions can be avoided if the 401(k) plan contains a qualified automatic contribution arrangement (QACA) (see chapter 2). [I.R.C. §§ 401(k)(13), 401(m)(12)]

The Actual Deferral Percentage Test

Q 13:2 How do elective contributions to a 401(k) plan satisfy the actual deferral percentage test?

Elective contributions under a 401(k) plan will satisfy the ADP test if at least one of the following tests is met:

1. The ADP of the group of eligible HCEs is not more than 125 percent of the ADP of the eligible non-highly compensated employees (NHCEs); or
2. The ADP of the eligible HCEs is not more than two percentage points greater than the ADP of the eligible NHCEs, and the ADP of the eligible HCEs is not more than two times the ADP of the eligible NHCEs.

[Treas. Reg. § 1.401(k)-2(a)(1)]

The following table combines these two tests to show the maximum ADP for HCEs, given an ADP for NHCEs:

ADP for NHCEs	*ADP for HCEs*	*Rule Used*
1	2	Times 2
2	4	Plus 2
3	5	Plus 2

ADP for NHCEs	*ADP for HCEs*	*Rule Used*
4	6	Plus 2
5	7	Plus 2
6	8	Plus 2
7	9	Plus 2
8	10	Times 1.25
9	11.25	Times 1.25
10	12.50	Times 1.25

Example 1. If the ADP of the NHCEs is 1.23 percent, the ADP of the HCEs can be no greater than 1.23 times 2, or 2.46 percent.

Example 2. If the ADP of the NHCEs is 7.43 percent, the ADP of the HCEs can be no greater than 7.43 plus 2, or 9.43 percent.

Example 3. If the ADP of the NHCEs is 9.87 percent, the ADP of the HCEs can be no greater than 9.87 times 1.25, or 12.34 percent.

Q 13:3 How is the ADP for a group of eligible employees calculated?

The ADP for a group of eligible employees (see Q 13:11) is the average of the actual deferral ratios of the eligible employees in that group. The ADP and actual deferral ratios are calculated to the nearest hundredth of a percentage point. [Treas. Reg. § 1.401(k)-2(a)(2) and (3)]

Prior-Year Versus Current-Year Testing Method

Q 13:4 How is an eligible employee's actual deferral ratio determined?

The actual deferral ratio of an eligible employee who is an HCE is the amount of his or her elective contributions for the current plan year divided by the eligible employee's compensation for the current plan year. However, unless the election in Q 13:5 is made, the actual deferral ratios and the ADP of NHCEs are based on the elective contributions and compensation for the preceding plan year. A 401(k) plan that performs the ADP test using NHCE data from the preceding plan year is using the *prior-year testing method.* [Treas. Reg. § 1.401(k)-2(a)(2)(ii)]

Actual deferral ratios, whether calculated for HCEs or NHCEs, do not include age 50 catch-up contributions. [Treas. Reg. § 1.414(v)-1(d)(2)] They also do not include additional elective contributions under USERRA made by a participant after his or her reemployment following qualified military service, and elective contributions made under an eligible automatic contribution arrangement (EACA) that are returned to the participant as a permissible withdrawal. [Treas. Reg. § 1.401(k)-2(a)(5)(v) and (vi)]

Q 13:5 Can an employer elect to calculate NHCE actual deferral ratios and ADP using current-plan-year data?

Yes. An employer that makes this election is using the *current-year testing method*. Once made, this election generally cannot be revoked unless the current-year testing method has been used for each of the five plan years preceding the plan year of revocation (or, if fewer, for the number of plan years the 401(k) plan has been in existence). [Treas. Reg. §§ 1.401(k)-2(a)(2)(ii), 1.401(k)-2(c)(1)]

> **Example.** Tip Top Corporation sponsors a 401(k) plan administered on a December 31 plan year. For the plan year ending December 31, 2014, the ADP of the NHCEs was 5.2 percent. Unless Tip Top elects to use the current-year testing method, the ADP of the NHCEs for the 2015 plan year will be 5.2 percent (regardless of whether the composition of the NHCE group had changed for 2015). Thus, the maximum ADP of the HCEs (based on NHCE elective contributions and compensation for the 2014 plan year) is 7.2 percent for the plan year ending December 31, 2015.

Q 13:6 Is IRS approval required to use the current-year testing method?

IRS approval is not required for either making or revoking an election to use the current-year testing method. Nor is there any IRS filing requirement. According to the IRS, however, the plan document must reflect the election and any change in the election must be accomplished through a plan amendment. [IRS Notice 98-1, 1998-1 C.B. 327]

Special Adjustments

Q 13:7 Is a 401(k) plan permitted to take into account other types of contributions along with elective contributions in determining actual deferral ratios?

Under the regulations, *qualified matching contributions* (QMACs) and *qualified nonelective contributions* (QNECs) may be treated as elective contributions for purposes of the ADP test (see Q 13:13). [Treas. Reg. § 1.401(k)-2(a)(3)(i)] However, elective contributions treated as matching contributions for purposes of the ACP test (see Q 13:61) are not taken into account in calculating an eligible employee's actual deferral ratio. [Treas. Reg. § 1.401(k)-2(a)(5)(iv)]

Q 13:8 Is the ADP of the NHCEs adjusted if an eligible employee who was an NHCE during the prior plan year is an HCE during the current plan year?

No. An adjustment is not required in this situation. In addition, an adjustment is not required if an eligible employee who was an NHCE during the prior plan year is not an eligible employee during the current plan year. [Treas. Reg. § 1.401(k)-2(a)(2)(ii)]

Q 13:9 How is the ADP of the NHCEs calculated for the initial plan year of a 401(k) plan?

For the initial year, the ADP of the NHCEs is deemed to be 3 percent unless the employer elects to calculate the actual deferral ratios and ADP of the NHCEs using the current-year testing method. An employer is free to revoke this election for the plan year following the initial year. [Treas. Reg. § 1.401(k)-2(c)(2)(i)]

Q 13:10 Is there any circumstance under which the actual deferral ratio of an HCE will be computed differently?

Yes. A different method of computation applies if an HCE is eligible to participate in two or more 401(k) plans in which the HCE can make elective contributions. In that case, the actual deferral ratio of the HCE will be calculated by treating all the 401(k) plans as one plan. [Treas. Reg. § 1.401(k)-2(a)(3)(ii)]

> **Example.** The Wondrous Widget Company maintains two 401(k) plans, one covering its salaried and office clerical employees and the other covering all its employees. Mary, an HCE, elects in each plan to defer 4 percent of her $200,000 in total compensation. For purposes of each 401(k) plan, Mary's actual deferral ratio is 8 percent, calculated as ($8,000 + $8,000) ÷ $200,000.

Eligible Employees

Q 13:11 Who are considered eligible employees?

Employees are considered eligible if they are directly or indirectly eligible to make elective contributions under the 401(k) plan for all or any portion of the plan year. Employees are considered eligible even if their right to make elective contributions has been temporarily suspended on account of a plan loan or distribution, or because of an election not to participate in the plan. However, an employee is not considered an eligible employee if, before first becoming eligible to participate in the plan, an employee makes a one-time election not to participate in the plan or any other 401(k) plan maintained (whether presently or in the future) by the employer. [Treas. Reg. § 1.401(k)-6]

Calculating Actual Deferral Ratios

Q 13:12 What is considered *compensation* for purposes of calculating actual deferral ratios?

The definition of *compensation* used in determining actual deferral ratios must be one that is nondiscriminatory under Internal Revenue Code (Code) Section 414(s). (See discussion of compensation in chapter 10.) Generally, compensation paid during the plan year with respect to which the actual deferral ratio is being calculated will be used for this purpose, but the regulations do permit the use of compensation paid during the calendar year ending within the plan year. The plan may also provide that only compensation paid during the portion of a plan year or calendar year that an employee is an eligible employee will be taken into account. [Treas. Reg. § 1.401(k)-6]

Example. Joe becomes eligible to participate in his employer's 401(k) plan on July 1, 2015, which is one of two entry dates for the plan year ending December 31, 2015. Joe elects to contribute 4 percent of his compensation to the plan. He makes $20,000 during the final six months of the year, and $18,000 during the first six months. If the plan provides that compensation will be counted from the entry date, Joe's actual deferral ratio will be 4 percent. On the other hand, if the plan uses compensation for the entire plan year, Joe's actual deferral ratio will be 2.11 percent calculated as (20,000 × 4%) ÷ 38,000.

Q 13:13 What are *qualified matching contributions* and *qualified nonelective contributions*?

Qualified matching contributions (QMACs) are matching contributions that are 100 percent vested at all times and that are subject to the same restrictions on distributability as are elective contributions. *Qualified nonelective contributions* (QNECs) are employer nonelective contributions, other than matching contributions, that satisfy these same requirements. These requirements must be satisfied by QMACs and QNECs even though they are not taken into account for purposes of the ADP test and, in the case of QNECs, for purposes of the ACP test. [Treas. Reg. § 1.401(k)-6] To be taken into account in determining actual deferral ratios and ADPs, QMACs and QNECs must be made no later than 12 months after the plan year to which they relate. [Treas. Reg. § 1.401(k)-2(a)(6)(i)] This rule applies even in the case of a 401(k) plan using the prior-year testing method, as illustrated in the following example.

Example. Bill's Bread Company maintains a 401(k) plan with a calendar plan year. In performing the ADP test for the plan year ending December 31, 2015, Bill's Bread is using the prior-year testing method. In the preceding plan year ending December 31, 2014, the ADP of the NHCEs was 5 percent. Thus, the maximum ADP of the HCE group for the plan year ending December 31, 2015, is 7 percent. Because Bill's Bread failed to monitor the salary deferral elections of its HCEs, Bill's Bread discovers in late December 2015 that the 2015 ADP of its HCEs is 8 percent. If Bill's Bread decides to correct the failed ADP test by making QNECs on behalf of its NHCEs, the QNEC contributions must be made by December 31, 2015. Note that if the 401(k) plan uses the current-year testing method, the QNEC deadline will be December 31, 2016.

Q 13:14 Under what circumstances may QMACs and QNECs be taken into account for purposes of the ADP test?

All or any portion of the QMACs and QNECs made with respect to employees who are eligible to make elective contributions may be treated as elective contributions for purposes of the ADP test. As a condition of using QNECs for purposes of the ADP test, the allocation of nonelective contributions, including QNECs used for this purpose and the ACP test, must be nondiscriminatory. Also, the allocation of nonelective contributions, excluding QNECs used to satisfy the ADP test and the ACP test, must be nondiscriminatory. [Treas. Reg. § 1.401(k)-2(a)(6)(ii)] QMACs that are treated as elective contributions for purposes of the ADP test may not be taken into account in determining whether the ACP test is satisfied. [Treas. Reg. § 1.401(m)-2(a)(5)(iii)]

Example. Bob's Biscuit Company maintains a profit sharing plan under which employees may make elective contributions. The following amounts are contributed under the plan:

1. Six percent of each employee's compensation. These contributions are not QNECs.
2. Two percent of each employee's compensation. These contributions are QNECs.
3. Elective contributions, if any, made by the employees.

Bob's Biscuit elects to use the current-year testing method in performing the ADP test. For the 2015 plan year, the compensation, elective contributions, and actual deferral ratios of employees M through S are as follows:

Employee	*Compensation*	*Elective Contributions*	*Actual Deferral Ratio*
M	$ 150,000	$ 4,500	3%
N	150,000	3,000	2
O	60,000	1,800	3
P	40,000	0	0
Q	30,000	0	0
R	20,000	0	0
S	20,000	0	0

Both types of nonelective contributions are made for all employees.

The elective contributions alone do not satisfy the ADP test because the ADP for the HCE group, consisting of Employees M and N, is 2.5 percent calculated as (3% + 2%) ÷ 2, and the ADP for the NHCE group is 0.6 percent calculated as (3% + 0% + 0% + 0% + 0%) ÷ 5. However, the 2 percent QNECs may be taken into account in applying the ADP test. The 6 percent nonelective contributions may not be taken into account because they are not QNECs.

If the 2 percent QNECs are taken into account, the ADP for the HCE group is 4.5 percent calculated as (5% + 4%) ÷ 2, and the ADP for the NHCE group is 2.6 percent calculated as (5% + 2% + 2% + 2% + 2%) ÷ 5. Because 4.5 percent is not more than two percentage points greater than 2.6 percent, and not more than two times 2.6, the ADP test is satisfied.

Correcting ADP Test Failures

Q 13:15 What happens if the ADP test for a plan year is not satisfied?

If the ADP test for a plan year is not satisfied, the portion of the 401(k) plan attributable to elective contributions—and, most likely, the plan in its entirety—will no longer be qualified. The regulations, however, provide several mechanisms for correcting an ADP test that does not meet the requirements of the law. These mechanisms are as follows:

1. Excess contributions are recharacterized.
2. Excess contributions and allocable income are distributed.
3. The portion of the 401(k) plan attributable to elective contributions is restructured.
4. The employer makes QNECs or QMACs that are treated as elective contributions for purposes of the ADP test and that, when combined with elective contributions, cause the ADP test to be satisfied.

A plan may use any one or more of these correction methods. [Treas. Reg. §§ 1.401(k)-2(b)(1), 1.410(b)-7(c)(3)]

Q 13:16 Are there correction methods that are not permissible?

It is impermissible for excess contributions to remain unallocated or to be placed in a suspense account for allocation in future plan years. [Treas. Reg. § 1.401(k)-2(b)(1)(iii)]

Determining Excess Contributions

Q 13:17 How are excess contributions determined?

The determination of excess contributions is a two-step process. The first step is to determine the aggregate amount by which HCE elective contributions must be reduced so that the ADP of HCEs will satisfy the ADP test. This is done by first reducing the actual deferral ratio of the HCE with the highest deferral ratio. If, after reducing this HCE's actual deferral ratio to the actual deferral ratio of the HCE with the second-highest actual deferral ratio, the ADP test is still not satisfied, then the actual deferral ratio of both HCEs must be further reduced. This process is repeated until the ADP test is satisfied. [Treas. Reg. § 1.401(k)-2(b)(2)(ii)]

Example. Yard Sign Corporation maintains a 401(k) plan. The plan year is the calendar year and Yard Sign has elected to use the current-year testing method to calculate the actual deferral ratios and ADP of its NHCEs. For the 2015 plan year, all 12 of Yard Sign's employees are eligible to participate in the plan. The employees' compensation, elective contributions, and actual deferral ratios are shown in the following table.

Employee	*Compensation*	*Elective Contributions*	*Actual Deferral Ratios*
A	$ 200,000	$ 8,000	4.00%
B	180,000	9,000	5.00
C	140,000	14,000	10.00
D	120,000	12,000	10.00
E	60,000	3,000	5.00
F	45,000	4,500	10.00
G	40,000	4,000	10.00
H	40,000	4,000	10.00
I	24,000	800	3.33
J	21,000	0	0
K	21,000	0	0
L	20,000	0	0

Employees A–D are HCEs. Employees E–L are NHCEs. The ADP for the HCE group is 7.25 percent calculated as (4% + 5% + 10% + 10%) ÷ 4, and the ADP for the NHCE group is 4.79 percent calculated as (5% + 10% + 10% + 10% + 3.33% + 0% + 0% + 0%) ÷ 8. The ADP test is not met. Yard Sign will not contribute QMACs or QNECs to the plan.

The ADP for the HCE group must be reduced to 6.79 percent. This is done by reducing the actual deferral ratios of the HCEs with the highest actual deferral ratios (Employees C and D) to 9.08 percent since (9.08% + 9.08% + 4% + 5%) ÷ 4 = 6.79%. The aggregate amount of excess contributions that must be either distributed or recharacterized is $1,242, determined as follows:

Employee C $14,000 – (9.08% × $140,000)	=	$1,288
Employee D $12,000 – (9.08% × $120,000)	=	$1,104
Excess contributions	=	$2,392

Q 13:18 What is the second step in the determination of excess contributions?

The second step in the determination of excess contributions is to allocate the excess contributions to the HCEs. This allocation is done on the basis of the amount of elective contributions, starting with the HCE with the largest amount of elective contributions. [Treas. Reg. § 1.401(k)-2(b)(2)(iii)]

Example. The facts are the same as those in the example in Q 13:17. The total excess contributions for the plan year are $2,392 (Employee C's $1,288 plus Employee D's $1,104). The first $2,000 of excess contributions is allocated to Employee C, who has $14,000 of elective contributions. After the initial allocation, $392 of excess contributions remains to be allocated. This remaining amount is allocated equally between Employees C and D. After this second allocation, all excess contributions will have been allocated in the following amounts:

Employee	*Allocated Excess Contributions*
A	$ 0.00
B	0.00
C	2,196
D	196
	$ 2,392

The amount of excess contributions as allocated above must then be distributed or recharacterized.

Recharacterizing Excess Contributions

Q 13:19 What happens when excess contributions are recharacterized?

Except as noted in Q 13:20, excess contributions that are recharacterized, to the extent they do not consist of Roth deferrals, are includable in the employee's gross income for the tax year in which recharacterization is deemed to have occurred (see Q 13:22). [I.R.C. § 4979(f)(2); Treas. Reg. § 1.401(k)-2(b)(3)(ii)]. Although includable in gross income, recharacterized excess contributions are generally treated as employer contributions. However, they will be treated as employee contributions for purposes of the ACP test. [Treas. Reg. § 1.401(k)-2(b)(3)(ii)] It should be noted that the recharacterization of excess contributions as employee contributions will often result in a failure to satisfy the ACP test. Consequently, these recharacterized excess contributions may ultimately be distributed to correct the ACP test.

Q 13:20 What was the tax treatment of recharacterized excess contributions before the enactment of the Pension Protection Act of 2006?

For plan years beginning before January 1, 2008, excess contributions, to the extent they did not consist of Roth deferrals, were includable in the employee's gross income on the earliest date any elective contributions would have been received had the employee elected to receive the elective contributions in cash. This tax rule, in some cases, would have required HCEs to amend their income tax returns for the tax year in which the excess contributions were made.

Q 13:21 What requirements must be met before recharacterization is permitted?

A plan must not only provide for recharacterization as a correction method for excess contributions but must also provide for employee contributions. The regulations indicate that the amount of recharacterized excess contributions plus the amount of employee contributions actually made cannot exceed the maximum amount of employee contributions permitted under the plan. [Treas. Reg. § 1.401(k)-2(b)(3)(iii)(B)]

Q 13:22 When is recharacterization deemed to have occurred?

Recharacterization is deemed to have occurred on the date on which the last of the HCEs with excess contributions is notified that his or her excess contributions are to be recharacterized. Excess contributions may not be recharacterized more than 2½ months after the plan year to which the excess contributions relate. [Treas. Reg. § 1.401(k)-2(b)(3)(iii)(A)]

Distributing Excess Contributions

Q 13:23 How does the corrective distribution rule work?

The corrective distribution rule requires that excess contributions and income allocable to those contributions be distributed to the appropriate HCEs after the close of the plan year, but no later than 12 months thereafter. [Treas. Reg. § 1.401(k)-2(b)(2)(v)]

Q 13:24 What is the income allocable to excess contributions?

The income allocable to excess contributions is the amount of the allocable gain or loss for the plan year. Before the enactment of the Pension Protection Act of 2006 and for plan years beginning before January 1, 2008, it also included the allocable gain or loss for the *gap period*, which was the period between the end of the plan year and the date of distribution, if the excess contributions would have been credited with gain or loss after the end of the plan year and prior to distribution if the participant's total account balance were distributed. As a practical matter, this meant that a gap-period gain or loss calculation was required in the case of a plan that was valued daily, but was not required in a plan valued less frequently than daily if the excess contribution was distributed before the first valuation date following the end of the plan year. [Treas. Reg. § 1.401(k)-2(b)(2)(iv)(D)]

Q 13:25 How is income allocable to excess contributions determined?

Any reasonable method may be used to allocate income to excess contributions, provided the method is not discriminatory, is consistently used for all participants and for all corrective distributions, and is used by the plan for allocating income to participants' accounts. In lieu of devising its own method for allocating income to excess contributions, a plan may use a method of allocating income to excess contributions prescribed by the regulations. Under the regulatory method, the income allocable to excess contributions is determined by multiplying the income allocable for the plan year to elective contributions by a fraction. The numerator of the fraction is the amount of excess contributions, and the denominator is the account balance attributable to elective contributions as of the beginning of the plan year plus the employee's elective contributions for the plan year. [Treas. Reg. § 1.401(k)-2(b)(2)(iv)(B) and (C)]

Example. Omicron Company sponsors a 401(k) plan. Linda, an HCE, will receive an excess contribution of $1,000 for the plan year ending June 30, 2015. To determine the amount of income allocable to the excess contribution, Omicron will use the allocation method contained in the regulations. The following data elements are needed to calculate the income for the plan year allocable to her excess contribution:

1.	Income allocated to Linda's elective contribution account for the plan year ending June 30, 2015:	$ 5,000
2.	Value of elective contribution account on July 1, 2014:	$75,000
3.	Amount of elective contributions for the plan year ending June 30, 2015:	$ 8,000

The income for the plan year ending June 30, 2015, allocable to Linda's excess contribution is $60.24 calculated as $1,000 ÷ ($75,000 + $8,000) × $5,000.

Q 13:26 How was allocable income determined for the gap period for plan years beginning before January 1, 2008?

Gap-period income allocable to excess contributions was determined under the methods described in Q 13:25 or was determined pursuant to a safe harbor method. Under the safe harbor method, income on excess contributions for the gap period was equal to 10 percent of the income allocable to excess contributions for the preceding plan year under the regulatory method described in Q 13:25 times the number of calendar months that had elapsed since the end of the plan year. A corrective distribution made on or before the 15th day of a month was treated as made on the last day of the preceding month. A distribution made after the 15th day was treated as made on the first day of the next month. [Treas. Reg. § 1.401(k)-2(b)(2)(iv)(D)]

Q 13:27 Are excess contributions that are distributed still treated as employer contributions?

Yes. For example, a distributed excess contribution continues to be treated as an annual addition for purposes of Code Section 415. [Treas. Reg. §§ 1.415(c)-1(b)(1)(ii), 1.401(k)-2(b)(2)(vii)(B)] This contrasts with the distribution of excess deferrals that are not considered Section 415 annual additions (see chapter 9).

Q 13:28 Is employee or spousal consent required for a distribution of excess contributions and allocable income?

No. Employee or spousal consent is not required for a distribution of excess contributions and allocable income. [Treas. Reg. § 1.401(k)-2(b)(2)(vii)(A)]

Q 13:29 What was the tax treatment of corrective distributions made on account of plan years beginning before January 1, 2008?

The tax treatment of a corrective distribution depended on when the distribution was made. A corrective distribution made within 2½ months after the end of the plan year was includable in the employee's gross income on the earliest dates any elective contributions made by the employee during the plan year would have been received by the employee had the employee originally elected to receive cash. A corrective distribution made more than 2½ months after the end of the plan year was includable in gross income for the taxable year in which it was distributed. The same rules applied to any income allocable to excess contributions. However, if the total amount of excess contributions and excess aggregate contributions (see Q 13:64) for a plan year was less than $100, the amount of any corrective distribution was includable in the year distributed, regardless of whether it was made within 2½ months after the end of the plan year. [Treas. Reg. § 1.401(k)-2(b)(2)(vi)(A) and (B)]

Q 13:30 How was the pre-2008 tax treatment of corrective distributions affected if the excess contribution consisted of all or part of Roth deferrals?

That portion of a corrective distribution consisting of Roth deferrals was not includable in gross income. Any allocable income, however, was includable in gross income as provided in Q 13:29. [Treas. Reg. § 1.401(k)-2(b)(2)(vi)(C)]

Q 13:31 How does the Pension Protection Act of 2006 affect the tax treatment of corrective distributions?

Starting with plan years beginning on or after January 1, 2008, excess contributions, to the extent they do not consist of Roth deferrals, and any allocable income are includable in gross income for the tax year in which they are distributed. [Treas. Reg. § 1.401(k)-2(b)(2)(vi)(A)]

Q 13:32 Are corrective distributions of excess contributions (plus income) subject to the additional income tax for distributions made before age 59½?

No, corrective distributions of excess contributions (plus income) are not subject to additional income tax for distributions made before age 59½. [Treas. Reg. § 1.401(k)-2(b)(2)(vi)(A)]

Q 13:33 Can a corrective distribution of excess contributions and allocable income be applied toward an employee's minimum distribution requirement under Code Section 401(a)(9)?

No, corrective distributions cannot be applied toward an employee's minimum distribution requirement under Code Section 401(a)(9). [Treas. Reg. § 1.401(k)-2(b)(2)(vii)(C)]

Q 13:34 What happens if excess contributions (plus allocable income) are not distributed within 12 months after the end of the plan year?

If excess contributions and allocable income are not distributed within the 12-month period following the plan year in which the excess contributions arose, the portion of the plan attributable to elective contributions will no longer be qualified for that plan year and all later plan years during which the excess contribution is not corrected. Pre-tax elective contributions, in this case, would be includable in an employee's gross income at the time the cash would have been received but for the employee's election. For all other purposes, elective contributions would be treated as employer nonelective contributions subject to the separate nondiscrimination rules that apply to nonelective contributions. [Treas. Reg. § 1.401(k)-2(b)(5)(ii)] The adverse consequences indicated above may be avoided, however, if this error is corrected (see chapter 20).

Q 13:35 What happens if excess contributions (plus allocable income) are distributed within 12 months after the end of the plan year but more than 2½ months thereafter?

In this case, the employer will be subject to a 10 percent excise tax on the amount of excess contributions. [I.R.C. § 4979] The excise tax can be avoided, however, if the employer makes QMACs or QNECs, or both, thereby enabling the plan to satisfy the ADP test. [Treas. Reg. § 1.401(k)-2(b)(5)(i)] As pointed out in Q 13:13, in 401(k) plans using the prior-year testing method in performing the ADP test, QMACs and QNECs must be made no later than 12 months after the end of the prior plan year.

Starting with plan years beginning on or after January 1, 2008, a distribution of excess contributions (plus allocable income) will not be subject to the 10 percent excise tax if the distribution is made within six months after the end of the plan year, the 401(k) plan contains an eligible automatic contribution arrangement, and for plan years beginning on or after January 1, 2010, the arrangement covers all eligible employees (see chapter 2). [Treas. Reg. § 1.401(k)-2(b)(5)(iii)]

Restructuring for ADP Testing

Q 13:36 Under what circumstances can a 401(k) plan be restructured to show that the ADP test is satisfied?

A 401(k) plan that does not use the statutory minimum age or service eligibility conditions (age 21 and one year of service) under Code Section 410(a) may be restructured. [Treas. Reg. § 1.401(k)-2(a)(1)(iii)]

Q 13:37 How is the 401(k) plan restructured?

Restructuring is accomplished by treating the portion of the 401(k) plan attributable to elective contributions as two component plans for ADP testing purposes. The first component plan consists of those eligible employees who have met the statutory minimum age and service eligibility conditions; the second consists of those eligible employees who have not met the statutory minimum conditions but who have met the 401(k) plan's less restrictive age and service conditions. By segregating the younger and shorter-service eligible employees (typically NHCEs who defer at lower rates) from the remaining eligible employees, the 401(k) plan may be able to demonstrate that the ADP test is satisfied by showing that each component plan satisfies this test.

Example. A 401(k) plan with no age and service requirements allows any employee to begin participating on his or her date of hire. The ADP of the eligible HCEs, all of whom have met the statutory minimum age and service conditions, is 6 percent, and that of the eligible NHCEs is 3 percent, as calculated below using the current-year testing method:

Eligible NHCEs	*Actual Deferral Ratio*	*Met Statutory Minimum Age and Service Conditions*
A	6	Yes
B	5	Yes
C	4	Yes
D	3	Yes
E	4	No
F	0	No
G	2	No
H	0	No

Without the benefit of restructuring, the 401(k) plan does not satisfy the ADP test because the ADP of the NHCEs, which is 3 percent [(6% + 5% + 4% + 3% + 4% + 0% + 2% + 0%) ÷ 8], is less than 4 percent, the minimum percentage necessary to pass the ADP test. However, with restructuring, only the NHCEs who have met the statutory minimum age and service conditions need be taken into account. The ADP of that group (NHCEs A-D) is 4.5 percent [(6% + 5% + 4% + 3%) ÷ 4], a percentage large enough to cause the 401(k) plan to satisfy the ADP test.

Q 13:38 How does the early participation rule affect the use of restructuring?

The early participation rule eliminates the need to test the group of employees who meet only a 401(k) plan's more liberal age and service requirements (otherwise excludable employees). The need for testing of this group is eliminated because all HCEs, regardless of whether they have completed the minimum age and service conditions permitted under the law, are ADP-tested with the group of eligible employees who have met these conditions. [Treas. Reg. § 1.401(k)-2(a)(1)(iii)(A)] Note, however, that the early participation rule applies for ADP testing purposes only. For Section 410(b) minimum coverage purposes (see chapter 11), HCEs who have not met the statutory minimum age and service conditions are tested with the otherwise excludable employees.

Example. Gary's Oil Corp. maintains a 401(k) plan that provides for immediate entry regardless of age or length of service. The following table shows the distribution of HCEs and NHCEs between those employees who have met the statutory minimum age and service requirements (age 21 and one year of service) and those who have not.

	Have Met Statutory Minimums	*Have Not Met Statutory Minimums*
HCEs	5	1
NHCEs	50	10

Gary's Oil decides to disaggregate on the basis of otherwise excludable employees as permitted under the Section 410(b) minimum coverage rules. Having made that decision, Gary's Oil can administer its ADP test in one of two ways. First, Gary's Oil can test separately the five HCEs and 50 NHCEs who have met the statutory minimums and the one HCE and 10 NHCEs who have not met them. Alternatively, Gary's Oil can apply the early participation rule to test all six HCEs (the five HCEs who have met the statutory minimums and the one HCE who has not) and the 50 NHCEs who have met the statutory minimums. The ten NHCEs who have not met the statutory minimums need not be tested, because there is no HCE in that group of otherwise excludable employees.

Correcting ADP Test by Making QNECs

Q 13:39 In a 401(k) plan that uses QNECs to correct a failed ADP test, to whom are the QNECs allocated?

Typically, QNECs will be allocated only to NHCEs. The manner in which they are allocated depends on the plan document. In some cases, the plan provides that QNECs are to be allocated among all NHCEs in proportion to their compensation. A 401(k) plan can also provide that QNECs be contributed as an equal dollar amount to each NHCE (referred to as the per capita approach). Finally, for plan years beginning before January 1, 2006, a plan could provide for a bottom-up approach to allocating QNECs to NHCEs.

Q 13:40 How did the bottom-up approach to allocating QNECs work?

The bottom-up approach targeted QNECs to certain NHCEs in order to reduce the total QNEC contributions that had to be allocated to NHCEs in order to correct the ADP test. Under the bottom-up approach, the employer made a QNEC to the extent permitted by the Section 415 limits to the NHCE with the lowest compensation during the plan year in order to raise that NHCE's actual deferral ratio (ADR). If the 401(k) plan still failed to pass the ADP test after this initial QNEC allocation, the employer expanded the group of NHCEs that received QNECs starting with the next lowest-paid NHCE and continuing until the ADP test was satisfied. By using the bottom-up approach, the employer could pass the ADP test by allocating small amounts to NHCEs who had very low compensation for the plan year (e.g., an eligible NHCE who terminated employment in the first week of the plan year with $300 of compensation). The bottom-up approach worked so efficiently to raise the ADP of the eligible NHCEs because the ADP test is based on an unweighted average of ADRs, and a small dollar (but high percentage of compensation) contribution to a terminated or other partial-year NHCE had a larger impact on the ADP test than a more significant contribution to a full-time, full-year NHCE.

Example. For the plan year ending December 31, 2005, the HCE group in Employer T's 401(k) plan has an ADP of 8 percent. The compensation, elective contributions, and the ADRs of the eligible NHCEs for that plan year are shown in the following table:

Employee	*Compensation*	*Elective Contribution*	*ADR*
A	$ 60,000	$3,600	6%
B	45,000	0	0
C	30,000	0	0
D	20,000	0	0
E	15,000	0	0
F	500	0	0

The ADP of the NHCE group is 1 percent ((6% + 0% + 0% + 0% + 0% + 0%) ÷ 6). The ADP of the NHCE group (1 percent) must be raised to 6 percent if Employer T uses QNECs to correct the failed ADP test.

Employer T decides to use the bottom-up approach, as provided in the plan document, in order to correct the failed ADP test. Under this approach, Employer T will allocate a QNEC to the eligible NHCE with the least amount of compensation (Employee F). In order to raise the ADP of the eligible NHCE group to 6 percent, Employer T makes a QNEC of $150 on Employee F's behalf, thereby raising Employee F's ADR to 30 percent. With this allocation, the ADP of the NHCE is increased to 6 percent, and the failed ADP test is corrected ((6% + 0% + 0% + 0% + 0% + 30%) ÷ 6).

Q 13:41 How do the new 401(k) regulations (generally effective for plan years beginning on or after January 1, 2006) affect the use of QNECs in helping to satisfy the ADP test?

The new 401(k) regulations severely restrict the use of the so-called bottom-up approach in the allocation of QNECs to NHCEs in order to correct a failed ADP test.

Q 13:42 Why have the Treasury Department and IRS decided to restrict the use of the bottom-up approach for correcting a failed ADP test?

The Treasury Department and IRS are concerned that the use of the bottom-up approach enables employers to pass the ADP test by making high-percentage QNECs to a small number of employees with low compensation rather than providing contributions to a broader group of NHCEs. In addition, the legislative history of EGTRRA expresses a congressional intent that the Secretary of the Treasury use his or her existing authority to address situations where QNECs are targeted to certain participants with lower compensation in order to increase the ADP of the NHCEs. [*See* EGTRRA Conference Report, H.R. Conf. Rep. 107-84, 240.]

Q 13:43 Do the new 401(k) regulations allow any type of allocation that is targeted to specific groups of eligible NHCEs?

The new 401(k) regulations do allow a certain amount of disproportion in the targeting of QNEC contributions to eligible NHCEs. Under the new regulations, a QNEC made to an eligible NHCE will be taken into account to the extent that it does not exceed the product of the NHCE's compensation and the greater of (1) 5 percent or (2) two times the 401(k) plan's representative contribution rate. [Treas. Reg. § 1.401(k)-2(a)(6)(iv)(A)]

Q 13:44 What is a 401(k) plan's *representative contribution rate*?

A 401(k) plan's *representative contribution rate* is the lowest applicable contribution rate of any eligible NHCE among a group of eligible NHCEs that consists of half of all eligible NHCEs for the plan year. However, if greater, the representative contribution rate will be based on the lowest applicable contribution rate among those eligible NHCEs who are employed by the employer on the last day of the plan year. [Treas. Reg. § 1.401(k)-2(a)(6)(iv)(B)]

Q 13:45 What is the applicable contribution rate of an eligible NHCE?

The applicable contribution rate for an eligible NHCE is the sum of any QMACs taken into account in calculating an eligible NHCE's ADR for the plan year and the QNECs made for that eligible NHCE for the plan year divided by his or her compensation for the plan year. [Treas. Reg. § 1.401(k)-2(a)(6)(iv)(C)]

Example 1. In Plan P, a calendar-year 401(k) plan, QMACs as a percentage of compensation of the eligible NHCEs A through F for the 2015 plan year are shown in the following table:

Employee	*Percentage*
A	6%
B	4
C	0
D	0
E	0
F	0

The lowest applicable contribution rate among a group of eligible NHCEs that consists of half of all eligible NHCEs for the plan year is 0 percent. (Employees A, B, and C would constitute one half of the eligible NHCEs, and the Employee C has lowest applicable contribution rate in that group.)

Example 2. The facts are the same as those in Example 1, except that Employees C and D are not employed on December 31, 2015. In that case, the lowest applicable contribution rate is based on those NHCEs who are employed on the last day of the plan year because it is greater than the lowest applicable rate based on all eligible NHCEs during the year (0 percent from Example 1). Consequently, the lowest applicable contribution rate is 4 percent, which is the percentage determined for Employee B.

Example 3. Plan Q is a calendar-year 401(k) plan that uses the current-year testing method. The compensation, elective contributions, and ADRs of employees M through S for the 2015 plan year, all of whom are employed on the last day of the plan year, are shown in the following table:

Employee	*Compensation*	*Elective Contributions*	*ADR*
M	$ 200,000	$ 11,200	5.6%
N	200,000	7,200	3.6
O	60,000	1,800	3.0
P	40,000	0	0
Q	30,000	0	0
R	5,000	0	0
S	20,000	0	0

The ADP of the eligible HCE group (Employees M and N) is 4.6 percent. The ADP of the eligible NHCE group (Employees O through S) is .6 percent. To correct the failed ADP test with QNECs, the ADP of the eligible NHCEs must be raised to 2.6 percent. To correct the failed ADP test, the employer makes a QNEC of $500 on Employee R's behalf.

With the bottom-up approach permitted by the previous 401(k) regulations, under which Employee R would receive a QNEC of $500, the ADP for the NHCEs would be 2.6% ((3% + 0% + 0% + 10% + 0%) ÷ 5) and the 401(k) plan would satisfy the ADP test. However, under the new 401(k) regulations, the QNEC is disproportionate and cannot be taken into account to the extent that it exceeds the greater of 5 percent and two times the plan's representative contribution rate (0 percent), multiplied by Employee R's compensation. The plan's representative contribution rate is 0 percent because it is the lowest applicable contribution rate among a group of NHCEs that is at least half of all NHCEs. Therefore, the QNEC made on R's behalf may be taken into account under the ADP test only to the extent it does not exceed 5 percent times Employee R's compensation (or $250), and the 401(k) plan consequently fails to satisfy the ADP test.

Q 13:46 Can QNECs used in correcting a failed ADP test still be allocated on a proportionate basis or per capita basis under the new final 401(k) regulations?

Yes, these methods are still permissible, but the per capita method may still result in a disproportionate QNEC.

Example 1. The facts are the same as those in the example in Q 13:40, except that Employer T decides to allocate its QNEC contribution in proportion to the compensation of the eligible NHCEs. Using that method, Employer T would contribute a QNEC equal to 5 percent of each NHCE's compensation in order to correct the failed ADP test.

NHCE	*Compensation*	*Elective Contributions*	*QNEC*	*ADR*
A	$ 60,000	$3,600	$ 3,000	11%
B	45,000	0	2,250	5
C	30,000	0	1,500	5
D	20,000	0	1,000	5
E	15,000	0	750	5
F	500	0	25	5

The total amount required to be contributed under this approach for correcting a failed ADP test ($8,525) is much higher than the QNEC that Employer T would need to contribute under the bottom-up approach ($150) illustrated in the example in Q 13:40.

Example 2. The facts are the same as those in the example in Q 13:40, except that instead of using the proportional QNEC allocation method illustrated in Example 1, Employer T decides to allocate QNECs among the eligible NHCEs on a per capita basis (i.e., each eligible NHCE will be allocated a QNEC of the same dollar amount). Under this method, approximately $137 would be allocated to each eligible NHCE. As that would result in an allocation to Employee F of a QNEC in excess of 20 percent of his compensation, that QNEC contribution would be considered disproportionate under the new final 401(k) regulations.

The Actual Contribution Percentage Test

Q 13:47 How do employer matching and employee after-tax contributions to a 401(k) plan satisfy the actual contribution percentage test?

The employer matching and employee contributions to a plan must satisfy either of the following tests:

1. The ACP of the group of eligible HCEs cannot be more than 125 percent of the ACP of the eligible NHCEs; or
2. The ACP of the eligible HCEs cannot be more than two percentage points greater than the ACP of the eligible NHCEs, and the ACP of the eligible HCEs cannot be more than two times the ACP of the eligible NHCEs.

[Treas. Reg. § 1.401(m)-2(a)(1)]

The following table combines these rules to show the maximum ACP for HCEs, given an ACP for NHCEs:

ACP for NHCEs	*ACP for HCEs*	*Rule Used*
1	2	Times 2
2	4	Plus 2
3	5	Plus 2
4	6	Plus 2
5	7	Plus 2
6	8	Plus 2
7	9	Plus 2
8	10	Times 1.25
9	11.25	Times 1.25
10	12.50	Times 1.25

See Table 13-1, at the end of this chapter, for a comparison of the ACP and ADP tests.

Example 1. If the ACP of the NHCEs is 1.23 percent, the ACP of the HCEs can be no greater than 1.23 times 2, or 2.46 percent.

Example 2. If the ACP of the NHCEs is 7.87 percent, the ACP of the HCEs can be no greater than 7.87 plus 2, or 9.87 percent.

Example 3. If the ACP of the NHCEs is 10.98 percent, the ACP of the HCEs can be no greater than 10.98 times 1.25, or 13.73 percent.

Q 13:48 How is the ACP for a group of eligible employees calculated?

The ACP for a group of eligible employees is the average of the actual contribution ratios (ACRs) of the eligible employees in that group. The ACP, as well as ACRs, must be calculated to the nearest hundredth of a percentage point. [Treas. Reg. § 1.401(m)-2(a)(2) and (3)]

Actual Contribution Ratios

Q 13:49 How is an eligible employee's actual contribution ratio determined?

In general, an eligible employee's ACR is the sum of employer matching and employee contributions allocated to the employee's account divided by the employee's compensation. Recharacterized excess contributions (see Q 13:19) are also taken into account in determining an employee's ACR. [Treas. Reg. § 1.401(m)-2(a)(4)(ii)] However, matching contributions treated as elective contributions for purposes of the ADP test are disregarded (see Q 13:7) as are matching contributions that are forfeited because the elective contributions to which they relate are permissibly withdrawn by a participant under an EACA (see chapter 2). Also disregarded are employee and matching contributions under USERRA that are made by or on behalf of a participant after his or her reemployment following qualified military service. [Treas. Reg. § 1.401(m)-2(a)(5)(iii), (v), and (vi)]

In addition, matching contributions that are forfeited because the elective or employee contributions to which they relate are treated as excess contributions, excess aggregate contributions, or excess deferrals (see chapter 9) are not taken into account (see Q 13:71). [Treas. Reg. § 1.401(m)-2(a)(5)(v)] It should be noted, however, that if the ACP test is not satisfied, plan provisions calling for the distribution and/or forfeiture of excess aggregate contributions (see Q 13:62) are implemented first before determining whether matching contributions must be forfeited. [Treas. Reg. § 1.401(a)(4)-4(e)(3)(iii)(G)]

> **Example.** Fred's Food Company maintains a 401(k) plan that provides for a fully vested matching contribution. Under the plan, Fred's Food will contribute 50 cents for each $1 of elective contributions. Tom, whose compensation is $200,000, is the only HCE of Fred's Food. Tom makes elective contributions of $14,000 and, consequently, receives a matching contribution of $7,000. Because the plan does not satisfy the ADP test, Tom's actual deferral ratio must be reduced to 5 percent. The plan does, however, satisfy the ACP test.
>
> The plan provides for the distribution of excess contributions in order to correct a failed ADP test; hence, $4,000 (plus allocable income) is distributed to Tom. After the distribution of excess contributions, the effective rate of matching contribution for Tom is 70 percent ($7,000 of matching contributions divided by $10,000, the amount of elective contributions remaining after distribution of the excess contributions). Tom's rate of matching contributions is discriminatory because it is higher than the rate of matching

contributions provided to NHCEs under the plan (50 percent). To achieve nondiscrimination, $2,000 of the $7,000 of matching contributions made on Tom's behalf must be forfeited.

Q 13:50 Is there any situation under which matching contributions made on behalf of an NHCE will be disregarded in determining that NHCE's ACR?

Under the new 401(k) regulations, which were generally effective with plan years beginning on or after January 1, 2006, matching contributions are not taken into account in determining an NHCE's ACR to the extent they exceed the greatest of the following amounts:

- 5 percent of compensation,
- the NHCE's elective contributions for the plan year, or
- the product of 2 times the plan's representative matching rate and an employee's elective contributions for the plan year.

The purpose of this rule is to prevent the targeting of disproportionate matching contributions to eligible NHCEs with low levels of compensation. [Treas. Reg. § 1.401(m)-2(a)(5)(ii)]

Q 13:51 What is a 401(k) plan's *representative matching rate*?

A 401(k) plan's *representative matching rate* is the lowest matching rate of any eligible NHCE among a group of eligible NHCEs that consists of half of all NHCEs who make elective contributions for the plan year. However, if greater, the representative matching rate will be based on the lowest matching rate among those eligible NHCEs who are employed by the employer on the last day of the plan year and who make elective contributions for the plan year. [Treas. Reg. § 1.401(m)-2(a)(5)(ii)(B)]

Q 13:52 What is the matching rate of an NHCE?

The NHCE's matching rate generally is the result of dividing the NHCE's matching contributions by the NHCE's elective contributions for the plan year. If the matching rate is not the same at all levels of elective contributions for an NHCE, the matching rate is determined assuming that the NHCE's elective contributions are equal to 6 percent of compensation. [Treas. Reg. § 1.401(m)-2(a)(5)(ii)(C)]

Prior-Year Versus Current-Year Testing Method

Q 13:53 What method is used to determine actual contribution ratios?

The ACRs and the ACP of HCEs will be based on contributions and compensation for the current plan year, whereas, in the absence of an election, the ACRs and the ACP of NHCEs will be based on contributions and compensation for the preceding plan year (the prior-year testing method). Alternatively, an employer may elect to use current plan year data for the NHCE group (the current-year testing method). Once made, however, this election generally cannot be revoked unless the current-year testing method had been used for each of the five plan years preceding the plan year of revocation (or, if fewer, for the number of plan years the 401(k) plan has been in existence). [I.R.C. § 401(m)(2)(A); Treas. Reg. § 1.401(m)-2(c)(1)]

Q 13:54 Is IRS approval required to use the current-year testing method?

No. IRS approval is not required for either making or revoking an election to use the current-year testing method. Nor is there any IRS filing requirement. According to the IRS, however, the plan document must reflect the election, and any change in the election must be accomplished through a plan amendment. [IRS Notice 98-1, 1998-1 C.B. 327]

Special Adjustments

Q 13:55 Is the ACP of the NHCEs adjusted if an eligible employee who was an NHCE during the prior plan year is an HCE during the current plan year?

No. An adjustment is not required in this situation. Also, an adjustment is not required if an eligible employee who was an NHCE during the prior plan year is not an eligible employee during the current plan year. [Treas. Reg. § 1.401(m)-2(a)(2)(ii)]

Q 13:56 How is the ACP of the NHCEs calculated for the initial plan year of a 401(k) plan?

For the initial plan year, the ACP of the NHCEs is deemed to be 3 percent unless the employer elects to calculate the ACRs and ACP of the NHCEs using the current-year testing method. An employer is free to revoke this election for the plan year following the initial plan year. [Treas. Reg. § 1.401(m)-2(c)(2)]

Q 13:57 Is there any circumstance under which the actual contribution ratio of an HCE will be computed differently?

Yes. A different method of computation applies if an HCE is eligible to participate in two or more plans of an employer to which matching and employee contributions are made. In that case, the ACR of an HCE will be calculated by treating all plans in which the HCE is eligible to participate as one plan (see Q 13:10). [Treas. Reg. § 1.401(m)-2(a)(3)(ii)]

Employee Contributions; Eligible Employees

Q 13:58 What contributions are considered *employee contributions*?

An *employee contribution* is either a mandatory or a voluntary contribution that is treated as an after-tax employee contribution. Recharacterized excess contributions are treated as employee contributions (see Q 13:19). Employee contributions do not include loan payments, buybacks to restore previously forfeited amounts, transfers directly from another plan, or designated Roth IRA contributions (see chapter 2). [Treas. Reg. § 1.401(m)-1(a)(3)]

Q 13:59 Who are considered *eligible employees*?

Eligible employees are employees who are directly or indirectly eligible to make employee contributions or to receive an allocation of matching contributions for a plan year. Employees are considered eligible even if their right to make employee contributions or to receive matching contributions has been temporarily suspended on account of a plan loan or distribution, or because of an election not to participate in the plan. However, an employee is not considered an eligible employee if, before first becoming eligible to participate in the plan, the employee makes a one-time election not to participate in the plan or any other plan maintained (whether presently or in the future) by the employer. [Treas. Reg. § 1.401(m)-5]

Calculating Actual Contribution Ratios

Q 13:60 What is considered *compensation* for purposes of calculating actual contribution ratios?

The definition of *compensation* used in determining ACRs must be one that is nondiscriminatory under Code Section 414(s). (See discussion of *compensation* in chapter 10.) Generally, compensation paid during the plan year with respect to which the ACR is being calculated will be used for this purpose, but the regulations do permit the use of compensation paid during the calendar year ending within the plan year. The plan may also provide that only compensation paid during the portion of a plan year or calendar year that an employee is eligible will be taken into account (see Q 13:12). [Treas. Reg. § 1.401(m)-5]

Q 13:61 Under what circumstances may elective contributions and QNECs be treated as matching contributions for purposes of the ACP test?

Elective contributions and QNECs made with respect to employees who are eligible employees under the plan may be treated as matching contributions for purposes of the ACP test. If QNECs are treated as matching contributions, two requirements must be met. First, the allocation of the nonelective contributions, including QNECs treated as matching contributions for purposes of the ACP test and as elective contributions for purposes of the ADP test, must be nondiscriminatory. Second, the allocation of nonelective contributions, excluding

QNECs treated as matching contributions for purposes of the ACP test and as elective contributions for purposes of the ADP test, must be nondiscriminatory. [Treas. Reg. § 1.401(m)-2(a)(6)(iii)] Elective contributions can be used in the ACP test but only if the 401(k) plan is required to satisfy the ADP test and the ADP test is satisfied, including the elective contributions taken into account under the ACP test. [Treas. Reg. § 1.401(m)-2(a)(6)(ii)]

Example 1. The Fast Park Company maintains a 401(k) plan to which elective contributions, QNECs, employee contributions, and matching contributions are made and with respect to which the current-year testing method is employed. The contributions for the plan year are shown in the following table.

	QNECs	*Elective Contributions*	*Employee/Matching Contributions*
HCE	0%	6%	6%
NHCE	3	3	3

The QNECs may be used in the ADP test, the ACP test, or a combination of the two. If Fast Park treats one third of the QNECs as elective contributions and two thirds as matching contributions, the ADPs for the HCEs and NHCEs are 6 percent and 4 percent, respectively, and satisfy the 200 percent/2 percentage point part of the ADP test. Similarly, the ACPs for the two groups are 6 percent and 5 percent, respectively, and also satisfy the 200 percent/2 percentage point part of the ACP test.

Example 2. Ned's Tree Nursery maintains a 401(k) plan to which elective contributions, QNECs, employee contributions, and matching contributions are made and with respect to which the current-year testing method is employed. The QNECs, elective contributions, and employee and matching contributions for the plan year are shown in the following table:

	QNECs	*Elective Contributions*	*Employee/Matching Contributions*
HCE	3%	5%	6%
NHCE	3	4	2

The elective contributions satisfy the ADP test. The employee and matching contributions, however, do not meet the ACP test. Ned's Tree Nursery may not use any QNECs of the NHCEs to meet the ACP test because the remaining QNECs would discriminate in favor of the HCEs. However, Ned's Tree Nursery could make additional QNECs or matching contributions of 2 percent of compensation on behalf of the NHCEs. Alternatively, Ned's Tree Nursery could treat all QNECs for all employees and elective contributions equal to 1 percent of compensation for NHCEs as matching contributions and make additional QNECs of 1 percent of compensation on behalf of NHCEs. The ACPs for HCEs and NHCEs would then be 9 percent and 7 percent, respectively, thus satisfying the 200 percent/2 percentage point part of the

ACP test. The ADPs for the two groups would be 5 percent and 3 percent, respectively, which would satisfy the same test.

Correcting ACP Test Failures

Q 13:62 What happens if the ACP test for a plan year is not satisfied?

If the ACP test for a plan year is not satisfied, the plan will no longer be qualified. However, the regulations provide the following five mechanisms for correcting an ACP test that does not meet the requirements of the law:

1. The employer makes QNECs that are treated as matching contributions for purposes of the ACP test and that, when combined with employee and matching contributions, cause the ACP test to be satisfied.
2. Elective contributions are treated as matching contributions for purposes of the ACP test and, when combined with employee and matching contributions, cause the ACP test to be satisfied.
3. Excess aggregate contributions and allocable income are distributed.
4. If the plan so provides, excess aggregate contributions, to the extent attributable to nonvested matching contributions and allocable income, are forfeited.
5. The portion of the 401(k) plan attributable to employee and matching contributions is restructured.

A plan may use any one or more of these correction methods. [Treas. Reg. §§ 1.401(m)-2(b)(1), 1.401(m)-2(a)(6), 1.401(m)-2(a)(1)(iii)]

Example. An employer maintains a 401(k) plan under which elective contributions up to 8 percent of compensation are matched on a dollar-for-dollar basis. The plan provides for the vesting of matching contributions at the rate of 20 percent per year of service. It also provides for the distribution of excess contributions plus allocable income. Mary, who is under age 50 and whose compensation for the plan year is $200,000, is the only HCE, and she is 60 percent vested in matching contributions at the end of the plan year, which began January 1, 2015. The ADPs and ACPs for Mary and the NHCE group are as follows:

	ADP	*ACP*
Mary	8%	8%
NHCEs	4	4

To satisfy the ADP test, Mary's actual deferral ratio must be reduced to 6 percent, resulting in a corrective distribution of $4,000 calculated as (8% − 6%) × $200,000 plus any allocable income. To satisfy the ACP test, Mary's actual contribution ratio must also be reduced to 6 percent. The amount of Employee A's excess aggregate contribution is $4,000 calculated as (8% − 6%) × $200,000. The plan has two options available in disposing of Mary's excess aggregate contribution of $4,000:

1. The plan may provide for the distribution to Mary of $2,400, which represents the vested portion of her matching contribution, and for the forfeiture of the $1,600 balance. These amounts are in proportion to her vested and nonvested interests in all matching contributions.
2. The plan may provide for the distribution to Mary of $4,000, thus leaving the nonvested matching contributions in the plan. If this option is selected, the plan would have to apply one of the formulas contained at Treasury Regulations Section 1.411(a)-7(d)(5) in determining the vested percentage of her remaining matching contributions.

Q 13:63 Are there correction methods that are not permissible?

It is impermissible for excess aggregate contributions to remain unallocated or to be placed in a suspense account for allocation in future plan years. Also, excess aggregate contributions may not be corrected by forfeiting vested matching contributions, recharacterizing matching contributions, or not making matching contributions required under the terms of the plan. [Treas. Reg. § 1.401(m)-2(b)(1)(iii)] Finally, any method of distributing excess aggregate contributions must not be discriminatory. [Treas. Reg. § 1.401(m)-2(b)(3)(v)(B)]

Determining Excess Aggregate Contributions

Q 13:64 How are excess aggregate contributions determined?

The determination of excess aggregate contributions is a two-step process. The first step is to determine the aggregate amount by which HCE matching and employee contributions must be reduced so that the ACP of the HCE group will satisfy the ADP test. This is done by first reducing the ACR of the HCE with the highest ratio. If, after reducing this HCE's ACR to that of the HCE with the second-highest ACR, the ACP test is still not satisfied, then the ACRs of both HCEs must be reduced further. This process is repeated until the ACP test is satisfied. [Treas. Reg. § 1.401(m)-2(b)(2)(ii)]

Q 13:65 What is the second step in the determination of excess aggregate contributions?

The second step in the determination of excess aggregate contributions is to allocate them to the HCEs. This allocation is done on the basis of the amount of matching contributions and employee contributions starting with the HCE with the largest amount of these contributions (see Q 13:18). [I.R.C. § 401(m)(6)(C); Treas. Reg. § 1.401(m)-2(b)(2)(iii)]

Q 13:66 If a 401(k) plan provides for the recharacterization of excess contributions as employee contributions, how will this affect the calculation of excess aggregate contributions?

The amount of excess aggregate contributions for an HCE is calculated after determining the amount of excess contributions recharacterized as employee contributions. [Treas. Reg. § 1.401(m)-1(a)(3)(i)(C)]

Example. Adam, who is not yet age 50, is the only HCE in a 401(k) plan maintained by his employer. The 401(k) plan provides a fully vested matching contribution equal to 50 percent of elective contributions. The 401(k) plan is a calendar-year plan and corrects excess contributions by recharacterization. For the 2015 plan year, Adam's compensation is $116,667, Adam's elective contributions are $14,000, and Adam's matching contributions are $7,000. The ADPs and ACPs of Adam and the NHCEs are shown below:

	ADP	*ACP*
Adam	12%	6%
NHCEs	8	4

In February 2016, it is determined that Adam's actual deferral ratio must be reduced to 10 percent to satisfy the ADP test. As a result, $2,333 calculated as $14,000 – (10% × $116,667) of Adam's elective contributions is recharacterized as employee contributions. After recharacterization, Adam's ACR is 8 percent ($7,000 in matching contributions plus $2,333 in recharacterized elective contributions, divided by $116,667 in compensation). Since Adam's ACR must be limited to 6 percent to satisfy the ACP test, the plan must distribute $2,333 calculated as ($7,000 + $2,333) – (6% × $116,667) or all of Adam's recharacterized excess contributions. Because Adam's elective contributions after recharacterization total $11,667, the amount of Adam's matching contribution allocation must be reduced to $5,833 calculated as $11,667 × 50% to avoid discrimination. The $1,167 difference between the matching contributions initially allocated ($7,000) and the amount permitted thereafter ($5,833) must be forfeited.

Distributing Excess Aggregate Contributions

Q 13:67 How does the corrective distribution rule work?

The corrective distribution rule requires that excess aggregate contributions and the income allocable to those contributions be distributed to the appropriate HCEs after the close of the plan year, but not later than 12 months thereafter. [Treas. Reg. § 1.401(m)-2(b)(2)(v)]

Q 13:68 What is the income allocable to excess aggregate contributions?

The income allocable to excess aggregate contributions is the amount of the allocable gain or loss for the plan year. Before the enactment of the Pension Protection Act of 2006 and for plan years beginning before January 1, 2008, it also included the allocable gain or loss for the gap period, which was the period between the end of the plan year and the date of distribution, if the excess aggregate contributions would have been credited with gain or loss after the end of the plan year and prior to distribution if the participant's total account balance were distributed. As a practical matter, this meant that a gap-period gain or loss calculation was required in the case of a plan that was valued daily, but was not required in a plan valued less frequently than daily if the excess aggregate contribution was distributed before the first valuation date following the end of the plan year. [Treas. Reg. § 1.401(m)-2(b)(2)(iv)(D)]

Q 13:69 How is income allocable to excess aggregate contributions determined?

Any reasonable method may be used to allocate income to excess aggregate contributions, provided the method is not discriminatory, is consistently used for all participants and for all corrective distributions, and is used by the plan for allocating income to participants' accounts. In lieu of devising its own method for allocating income to excess aggregate contributions, a plan may use a method of allocating income to excess aggregate contributions prescribed by the regulations. Under the regulatory method, the income allocable to excess aggregate contributions is determined by multiplying the income allocable for the plan year to employee contributions and matching contributions by a fraction. The numerator of the fraction is the amount of excess aggregate contributions. The denominator of the fraction is the sum of the account balances attributable to employee contributions and matching contributions as of the beginning of the plan year plus employee contributions and matching contributions for the plan year (see Q 13:25). [Treas. Reg. § 1.401(m)-2(b)(2)(iv)(B) and (C)]

Q 13:70 How was allocable income determined for the gap period for plan years beginning before January 1, 2008?

Gap-period income allocable to excess aggregate contributions was determined under the methods described in Q 13:69 or was determined pursuant to a safe harbor method. Under the safe harbor method, income on excess aggregate contributions for the gap period was equal to 10 percent of the income allocable to excess aggregate contributions for the preceding plan year under the regulatory method times the number of calendar months that had elapsed since the end of the plan year. A corrective distribution made on or before the 15th day of a month was treated as made on the last day of the preceding month. A distribution made after the 15th day was treated as made on the first day of the next month. [Treas. Reg. § 1.401(m)-2(b)(2)(iv)(D)]

Q 13:71 When is a method of distributing excess aggregate contributions considered discriminatory?

If excess contributions are recharacterized or distributed, a 401(k) plan must be sure that the level of matching contributions is nondiscriminatory. For example, if a plan matches elective contributions on a dollar-for-dollar basis, each dollar of elective contribution that is distributed or recharacterized must result in a forfeiture of a dollar of matching contribution. On the other hand, if the match is made only on elective contributions up to 6 percent of compensation, no matching contributions are required to be forfeited if an HCE receives a distribution of excess contributions which results in the reduction of the HCE's actual deferral ratio from 8 percent to 7 percent. [Treas. Reg. § 1.401(m)-2(b)(3)(v)(B)] However, as pointed out in Q 13:49, the IRS takes the position that whether the level of matching contributions is discriminatory is determined only after giving effect to distributions and/or forfeitures required in order to satisfy the ACP test.

Q 13:72 How are corrective distributions and forfeited matching contributions treated for tax purposes?

To the extent attributable to matching contributions, excess aggregate contributions, including forfeited matching contributions, are treated as employer contributions for purposes of Code Section 404. A forfeited matching contribution is considered an annual addition under Code Section 415 with respect to the HCE whose excess aggregate contribution includes the forfeited matching contribution. That same forfeited matching contribution, when allocated to the accounts of other participants, will also be considered a Section 415 annual addition with respect to those other participants. [Treas. Reg. § 1.401(m)-2(b)(3)(ii)]

Q 13:73 What was the tax treatment of corrective distributions made on account of plan years beginning before January 1, 2008?

The tax treatment of corrective distributions to employees depended on when the distribution was made. A corrective distribution made within 2½ months after the end of the plan year was includable, to the extent attributable to matching contributions, in the employee's gross income for the taxable year of the employee ending with or within the plan year in which the excess aggregate contribution arose. A corrective distribution made more than 2½ months after the end of the plan year was includable, to the extent attributable to matching contributions, in gross income for the taxable year in which it was distributed. The same rules applied to any income allocable to excess aggregate contributions. However, if the total amount of excess contributions and excess aggregate contributions for a plan year was less than $100, excess aggregate contributions and any allocated income were includable in the year distributed regardless of when the corrective distribution was actually made. [Treas. Reg. § 1.401(m)-2(b)(2)(vi)(B)]

Q 13:74 How does the Pension Protection Act of 2006 affect the tax treatment of corrective distributions?

Under the PPA, starting with plan years beginning on or after January 1, 2008, excess aggregate contributions, to the extent attributable to matching contributions, and any allocable income are includable in gross income for the tax year in which they are distributed. [Treas. Reg. § 1.401(m)-2(b)(2)(vi)(A)]

Q 13:75 Are corrective distributions of excess aggregate contributions (plus income) subject to the additional income tax for distributions made before age 59½?

No, corrective distributions of excess aggregate contributions (plus income) are not subject to the additional income tax for distributions made before age 59½. [Treas. Reg. § 1.401(m)-2(b)(2)(vi)(A)]

Q 13:76 Can a corrective distribution of excess aggregate contributions and allocable income be applied toward an employee's minimum distribution requirement under Code Section 401(a)(9)?

No, corrective distributions cannot be applied toward an employee's minimum distribution requirement under Code Section 401(a)(9). [Treas. Reg. § 1.401(m)-2(b)(3)(iii)]

Q 13:77 Is employee or spousal consent required for a corrective distribution of excess aggregate contributions and allocable income?

No. Employee or spousal consent is not required [Treas. Reg. § 1.401(m)-2(b)(3)(i)]

Q 13:78 What happens if a plan fails to make a corrective distribution of excess aggregate contributions and allocable income?

If a plan fails to make a corrective distribution during the 12-month period following the plan year in which the excess aggregate contribution arose, the plan will be disqualified for that plan year and for all subsequent plan years in which the excess aggregate contribution remains in the plan. (But see chapter 20, which describes procedures for avoiding these consequences by correcting the error.) If a corrective distribution is made before the end of the 12-month period but more than 2½ months after the end of the plan year, the employer will be subject to a 10 percent excise tax on the amount of the excess aggregate contributions. The excise tax can be avoided, however, if the employer makes QNECs enabling the plan to satisfy the ACP test. [Treas. Reg. § 1.401(m)-2(b)(4)] To be taken into account in performing the ACP test, QNECs must be made no later than 12 months after the plan year to which they relate. [Treas. Reg. § 1.401(m)-2(a)(6)] Thus, in 401(k) plans using the prior-year testing method in performing the ACP test, QNECs must be made no later than 12 months after the end of the prior plan year (see Q 13:13).

Starting with plan years beginning on or after January 1, 2008, a distribution of excess aggregate contributions (plus allocable income) will not be subject to the 10 percent excise tax if the distribution is made within six months after the end of the plan year, the 401(k) plan contains an eligible automatic contribution arrangement, and for plan years beginning on or after January 1, 2010, the arrangement covers all eligible employees (see chapter 2). [Treas. Reg. § 1.401(m)-2(b)(4)(iii)]

Restructuring for ACP Testing

Q 13:79 Under what circumstances can a 401(k) plan be restructured to show that the ACP test is satisfied?

The portion of the 401(k) plan attributable to employee and matching contributions can be restructured in the same way as the elective contribution portion of the 401(k) plan, as explained in Qs 13:36–13:38.

Correcting ACP Test by Making QNECs

Q 13:80 How are QNECs used to correct a failed ACP test?

QNECs can be used to correct a failed ACP test in the same way in which they are used to correct a failed ADP test. The issues presented by the new 401(k) regulations, as explained in Qs 13:39 through 13:46, also apply in using QNECs to correct a failed ACP test.

Table 13-1. Comparison of ADP and ACP Tests

Feature	*ADP Test*	*ACP Test*
Name of test Required by Code Section	Actual deferral percentage 401(k)(3)	Actual contribution percentage 401(m)(2)
When applicable—the tests do not apply to 401(k) plans that qualify as SIMPLE plans under Code Section 401(k)(11), to 401(k) plans that are considered safe harbor plans under Code Section 401(k)(12), and, starting with plan years beginning on or after January 1, 2008, to 401(k) plans containing a QACA.	Any 401(k) plan year when both HCEs and NHCEs are eligible to make elective contributions (i.e., deferrals)	Any plan year when both HCEs and NHCEs are eligible either to receive employer matching contributions or to make after-tax contributions
Which contributions to test—use NHCE contributions for the preceding plan year unless the employer elects to use data for the current year (note that QNECs and QMACs are employer nonelective and matching contributions, respectively, fully vested, and subject to Section 401(k) distribution restrictions)	• Include elective contributions (deferrals) allocated as of a date within the plan year • For HCEs, include elective contributions to all other plans of the employer for which the HCE is eligible • Include any QNECs or QMACs treated as elective contributions (QNECs and QMACs used to pass the ADP test may not also be used to pass the ACP test) • Exclude any elective contributions used to satisfy the ACP test	• Include employer matching contributions • Include employee after-tax contributions (including any excess contributions under the ADP test recharacterized as employee after-tax contributions) • For HCEs, include matching and employee after-tax contributions to all other plans of the employer for which the HCE is eligible

	• Exclude contributions under a onetime, irrevocable election made at the time of first eligibility	• Include any elective contributions or QNECs treated as matching contributions and any QMACs not used to satisfy the ADP test
What compensation to test against—use NHCE compensation for the preceding plan year unless the employer elects to use compensation for the current year	By employer choice: • Can use either plan-year compensation or compensation for the calendar year ending within the plan year • May elect to exclude compensation earned when the participant was not yet eligible	Same choices as ADP
Calculation of each employee's actual deferral or contribution ratio	The *actual deferral ratio* is the sum of the employee's elective contributions and any other included amounts, divided by the employee's compensation, rounded to the nearest hundredth of a percentage point	The *actual contribution ratio* is the sum of the employee's matching and after-tax contributions and any other included amounts, divided by the employee's compensation, rounded to the nearest hundredth of a percentage point
Calculation of actual deferral or contribution percentage for the HCE group and for the NHCE group	For the group of HCEs and for the group of NHCEs, calculate the ADP as the average of each group's individual actual deferral ratios (in the average, remember to include eligible employees with a zero ratio)	For the group of HCEs and for the group of NHCEs, calculate the ACP as the average of each group's individual actual contribution ratios (in the average, remember to include eligible employees with a zero ratio)

(*Continued*)

Table 13-1. Comparison of ADP and ACP Tests (*cont'd*)

Feature	*ADP Test*	*ACP Test*
Primary and alternative limit	• If ADP of NHCEs exceeds 8 percent, ADP of HCEs must not exceed 1.25 times ADP of NHCEs (primary limit) • If ADP of NHCEs is between 2 percent and 8 percent, ADP of HCEs must not exceed ADP of NHCEs plus 2 percent (part of the alternative limit) • If ADP of NHCEs is less than 2 percent, ADP of HCEs must not exceed two times ADP of NHCEs (other part of the alternative limit)	• If ACP of NHCEs exceeds 8 percent, ACP of HCEs must not exceed 1.25 times ACP of NHCEs (primary limit) • If ACP of NHCEs is between 2 percent and 8 percent, ACP of HCEs must not exceed ACP of NHCEs plus 2 percent (part of the alternative limit) • If ACP of NHCEs is less than 2 percent, ACP of HCEs must not exceed two times ACP of NHCEs (other part of the alternative limit)
Determination of excess amounts	Beginning with the HCE with the largest actual deferral ratio, reduce deferral ratios until the test is passed; the amounts identified by this leveling process are called *excess contributions*—these amounts are allocated beginning with the HCE who has the largest deferral amount	After any excess contributions have been recharacterized and beginning with the HCE with the largest actual contribution ratio, reduce contribution ratios until the test is passed; the amounts identified by this levelling process are called *excess aggregate contributions*—these amounts are allocated beginning with the HCE who has the largest contribution amount

Permissible methods to correct initial failure of the test	• Distribute excess contributions • Recharacterize excess contributions as employee after-tax contributions • Treat QNECs or QMACs as elective contributions • Restructure the 401(k) plan if eligibility requirements are less restrictive than allowed under law OR • Any combination of the above (an HCE can be allowed to choose between recharacterization and distribution)	• Forfeit nonvested excess aggregate contributions if permitted by the plan • Treat elective contributions and QNECs as matching contributions • Distribute vested excess aggregate contributions • Restructure the 401(k) plan if eligibility requirements are less restrictive than allowed under law OR • Any combination of the above
Impermissible methods to correct initial feature of the test	• Cannot place excess contributions in a suspense account	• Cannot recharacterize excess aggregate contributions • Cannot place excess aggregate contributions in a suspense account • Cannot fail to make required matching contributions to HCEs • Cannot forfeit vested contributions of HCEs

(*Continued*)

Table 13-1. Comparison of ADP and ACP Tests (*cont'd*)

Feature	*ADP Test*	*ACP Test*
Failure to correct within 2½ months after close of tested plan year	Employer penalty of 10 percent of the excess contributions (unless additional QNECs or QMACs are treated as eligible, even if made more than 2½ months after close of tested plan year). Beginning in 2010, excise tax will not apply if the 401(k) plan contains an EACA that covers all eligible employees and correction is made within 6 months after close of tested year.	Same as ADP except that penalty is based on amount of excess aggregate contributions
Failure to correct within 12 months after close of tested plan year	Disqualification of the 401(k) cash or deferred arrangement for the tested plan year and for any following year until corrected	Disqualification of the plan for the tested plan year and for any following year until corrected
Limits on recharacterization of excess contributions as employee after-tax contributions	• Must be recharacterized within 2½ months after close of tested plan year • The plan must allow for employee after-tax contributions • Amounts recharacterized, when combined with employee contributions actually made by the HCE, may not exceed the maximum amount of employee contributions permitted under the plan	Not applicable

Distribution of excess amounts	• Must include fund earnings • Still treated as employer contributions under Code Section 404 and as annual additions under Code Section 415 • No spousal consent is required • Do not count as early distributions under Code Section 72(t) • Do not count toward the required minimum distributions under Code Section 401(a)(9)	Same as ADP
When distributions must be included in income	• For plan years beginning before January 1, 2008, if distributed within $2\frac{1}{2}$ months of close of tested plan year, include as income in the year deferred; however, if the sum of excess contributions and excess aggregate contributions is less than $100, include as income in the year of distribution. If distributed more than $2\frac{1}{2}$ months after close of tested plan year, include as income in the year of distribution • For 2008 plan year and thereafter, distributions will always be included in the year distributed	• For plan years beginning before January 1, 2008, if distributed within $2\frac{1}{2}$ months of close of tested plan year, include as income for employee's tax year ending with or within tested plan year; however, if the sum of excess contributions and excess aggregate contribution is less than $100 include as income in the year of distribution. If distributed more than $2\frac{1}{2}$ months after close of tested plan year, include as income in the year of distribution • For 2008 plan year and thereafter, distributions will always be included in the year distributed

Chapter 14

Top-Heavy Rules

When more than 60 percent of the benefits of a 401(k) plan are attributable to key employees, the plan will become a top-heavy plan and, as a result, will be required to provide minimum contributions to non-key employees. While a top-heavy plan is also required to provide for accelerated vesting of employer contributions, the impact of this requirement is increasingly limited due to recent changes in the law that require vesting at a more rapid rate. However, 401(k) plans that are considered SIMPLE plans (see chapter 2) are not subject to top-heavy minimum contribution and vesting requirements. These requirements also do not apply to certain safe harbor plans and, starting with plan years beginning after December 31, 2007, 401(k) plans containing qualified automatic contribution arrangements (see chapter 2). Finally, after 2009, Section 903 of the Pension Protection Act of 2006 will exempt certain combined defined benefit/401(k) plans from the top-heavy rules.

Top-Heavy Testing 14-2
  Aggregation Groups 14-2
  Key Employee 14-4
  Determination Date 14-7
  Present Value of Accrued Benefits 14-8
Minimum Vesting 14-11
Minimum Contributions 14-12
Top-Heavy Strategy 14-16

Top-Heavy Testing

Q 14:1 What issues must be considered in determining whether a 401(k) plan is top heavy?

In determining whether a 401(k) plan is top heavy, the employer must consider the following issues:

1. Who is the *employer*?
2. What is the top-heavy determination date for the plan year?
3. Which employees are key employees or former key employees?
4. Which former employees have not performed services during the past year?
5. Which plans of the employer must be aggregated or may be aggregated?
6. What is the value of accrued benefits under the plan?

[I.R.C. § 416(g)(4)(E); Treas. Reg. § 1.416-1, Q&A T-1(a)]

Q 14:2 How does a plan become top heavy?

A plan becomes top heavy if the present value of accrued benefits for key employees is more than 60 percent of the present value of accrued benefits of all employees. A plan that is part of a required aggregation group (see Q 14:5) will also be considered top heavy if the sum of the accrued benefits for key employees under all plans of the employer in the required aggregation group is more than 60 percent of the sum of the accrued benefits for all employees. [Treas. Reg. § 1.416-1, Q&As T-1(c), T-9]

Q 14:3 Who is considered the *employer*?

For purposes of the top-heavy rules, the *employer* is considered to be the entity sponsoring the 401(k) plan and all other entities that are aggregated with it under Internal Revenue Code (Code) Sections 414(b), 414(c), and 414(m) (discussed in chapter 10). [Treas. Reg. § 1.416-1, Q&A T-1(b)]

Q 14:4 Who is considered an *employee*?

An *employee* is an individual currently or formerly employed by the employer. [Treas. Reg. § 1.416-1, Q&A T-1(d)] Leased employees (see chapter 10) are also treated as employees. [I.R.C. § 414(n)(3)(B)]

Aggregation Groups

Q 14:5 What is a *required aggregation group*?

A *required aggregation group* includes each plan of the employer in which a key employee participates during the plan year containing the determination date (see Q 14:19). This plan year is referred to as the *determination period*. Also included in a required aggregation group is any plan in which a key employee does not participate but which, during the determination period, enables another plan in which a key employee participates to satisfy the Code Section 410(b) minimum coverage rules (see chapter 11). [Treas. Reg. § 1.416-1, Q&A T-6]

Q 14:6 What is a *permissive aggregation group*?

A *permissive aggregation group* consists of all plans of the employer that are required to be aggregated, plus any other plan of the employer that is not part of the required aggregation group. A plan or plans cannot be added to form a permissive aggregation group unless such plan (or plans) and the plans required to be aggregated together satisfy the nondiscrimination requirements of Code Section 401(a)(4). [Treas. Reg. § 1.416-1, Q&A T-7]

Example. ABC Company has three divisions, each of which sponsors a 401(k) plan. Key employees participate in the plans maintained by Divisions X and Y, but no key employees are participants in the 401(k) plan for Division Z employees. The 401(k) plans maintained by Divisions X and Y form a required aggregation group. The 401(k) plan for Division Z employees is part of the required aggregation group if this plan enables the 401(k) plans of Divisions X and Y to satisfy the minimum coverage rules of Code Section 410(b). If the 401(k) plans of Division X and Y satisfy Code Section 410(b) without the assistance of the Division Z 401(k) plan, then the 401(k) plans of Divisions X, Y, and Z can form a permissive aggregation group as long as the plans together satisfy the nondiscrimination requirements of Code Section 401(a)(4).

Q 14:7 If more than 60 percent of the sum of the accrued benefits under all plans of the employer in the permissive aggregation group are attributable to key employees, which plans will be considered top heavy?

Only those plans that are part of the required aggregation group are considered top heavy. [Treas. Reg. § 1.416-1, Q&A T-11]

Example. Plans W, X, Y, and Z form a permissive aggregation group, but only plans Y and Z are required to be aggregated. It is determined that more than 60 percent of the sum of the accrued benefits under the four plans forming the permissive aggregation group is attributable to key employees. As a result, plans Y and Z are considered top heavy. Plans W and X will not be considered top heavy; consequently, the special minimum contribution rules for top-heavy plans will not apply to them.

Q 14:8 If 60 percent or less of the sum of the accrued benefits under all plans of the employer in the permissive aggregation group is attributable to key employees, will any of the plans required to be aggregated be considered top heavy?

No. None of the plans in the permissive aggregation group will be considered top heavy. [Treas. Reg. § 1.416-1, Q&A T-11]

Key Employee

Q 14:9 Who is considered a *key employee*?

A *key employee* is any employee (including any deceased employee) who at any time during the determination period is:

1. An includable officer (see Q 14:13);
2. A 5 percent owner (see Q 14:10); or
3. A 1 percent owner (see Q 14:11) having annual compensation from the employer greater than $150,000.

[I.R.C. § 416(i)(1)(A)]

Q 14:10 Who is a *5 percent owner*?

An employee is considered a *5 percent owner* if at any time during the determination period (see Q 14:5) an employee owns or is considered to own (applying attribution rules under Code Section 318 as modified under Code Section 416(i)(1)(B)(iii)(I)) more than 5 percent of the value of the outstanding stock of a corporation, or stock having more than 5 percent of the total combined voting power of all stock of the corporation. If the employer is not a corporation, a 5 percent owner is any individual owning more than 5 percent of the capital or profits interest of the employer. [Treas. Reg. § 1.416-1, Q&A T-17] The controlled group and affiliated service group rules are disregarded in determining a 5 percent owner as illustrated in the following example. [I.R.C. § 416(i)(1)(C); Treas. Reg. § 1.416-1, Q&A T-20]

> **Example.** An affiliated service group consists of a law firm partnership with 100 partners, each of which is a professional service corporation owned by a single attorney. Although each professional service corporation, and, by attribution, each attorney-owner, has only a 1 percent interest in the law firm partnership, each attorney-owner will be treated as a 5 percent owner because each attorney-owner owns 100 percent of his or her professional service corporation.

Q 14:11 Who is a *1 percent owner*?

A *1 percent owner* is determined in exactly the same way as a 5 percent owner, except that 1 percent is substituted for 5 percent. [Treas. Reg. § 1.416-1, Q&A T-16] Although the controlled group and affiliated service group rules are disregarded in determining a 1 percent owner, they are taken into account in determining whether an employee has $150,000 in compensation for the determination period. [Treas. Reg. § 1.416-1, Q&A T-20]

> **Example.** Tom owns 2 percent of the value of a professional service corporation, which in turn owns a 10 percent interest in a partnership. The entities are part of an affiliated service group. Tom performs services for the professional service corporation and for the partnership. He receives compensation of $125,000 from the professional service corporation and $26,000 from the partnership. Tom is considered a key employee because he has a 2 percent interest in the professional service corporation and because his combined compensation from both the professional service corporation and the partnership is more than $150,000.

Q 14:12 Who is an *officer*?

In general, an *officer* is an administrative executive who is in regular and continued service. The determination of whether an employee is an officer is based on all the facts and circumstances, including, for example, the source of authority, the term for which appointed or elected, and the nature and extent of duties. Titles are not relevant. An individual's status as an officer will be determined on the basis of the responsibilities to the employer for which the individual is directly employed. The fact that an officer's employer may be a member of a controlled group or an affiliated service group is disregarded. [Treas. Reg. § 1.416, Q&A T-13]

Q 14:13 Who is an *includable officer*?

An *includable officer* is an employee who, at any time during the determination period, is an officer and receives compensation in excess of $130,000. The $130,000 floor will be increased by increments of $5,000 to reflect cost-of-living adjustments. [I.R.C. § 416(i)(1)(A)]

An adjustment in the $130,000 floor is effective for any determination period ending in the calendar year in which the adjustment occurs.

The following table shows the floor in effect since 2002.

Year	*Floor*
2002	$ 130,000
2003	130,000
2004	130,000
2005	135,000
2006	140,000
2007	145,000
2008	150,000

Year	*Floor*
2009	160,000
2010	160,000
2011	160,000
2012	165,000
2013	165,000
2014	170,000
2015	170,000

Q 14:14 Is there a limit on the number of includable officers who can be considered key employees?

Yes. Depending on the number of employees (including leased employees), the limit is determined as follows:

Number of Employees	*Maximum Number of Includable Officers*
500 or more employees	50
30 or more employees, but fewer than 500 employees	10% of the number of employees
Fewer than 30 employees	3

[I.R.C. § 416(i)(1)(A)]

Q 14:15 How is the number of employees determined?

The number of employees is determined only after excluding the following categories of employees:

1. Employees who have not completed six months of service by the end of the year (for this purpose, service in the immediately preceding year is taken into account);
2. Employees who normally work fewer than 17½ hours per week during the year (see Q 10:85);
3. Employees who normally work fewer than seven months during the year (see Q 10:86);
4. Employees who are not age 21 by the end of the year;
5. Employees who are nonresident aliens with no U.S.-source earned income; and
6. Employees who are covered by a collective bargaining agreement. This exclusion applies, however, only if 90 percent or more of the employees are covered under collective bargaining agreements and the plan does not benefit employees covered under such agreements.

[I.R.C. §§ 414(q)(8), 416(i)(1)(A); Temp. Treas. Reg. § 1.414(q)-1T, Q&A 9(b); Treas. Reg. § 1.416-1, Q&A T-14]

Q 14:16 If the number of includable officers is greater than the maximum number of includable officers who can be considered key employees, which includable officers will be treated as key employees?

The includable officers who will be treated as key employees will be those who have the greatest amount of compensation during the determination period. [Treas. Reg. § 1.416-1, Q&A T-14]

> **Example.** Elven Company is testing its 401(k) plan to see whether it is top heavy for the plan year beginning January 1, 2016. During the determination period (January 1, 2015, to December 31, 2015), Elven Company had 40 employees who could not be disregarded for purposes of determining the number of includable officers who can be considered key employees (see Q 14:15). In 2015, Elven Company had six officers who each received compensation in excess of $170,000. The maximum number of includable officers who can be considered key employees is limited to four (10% × 40). Thus, the officers who are treated as key employees for the 2016 plan year are those four officers who received the greatest amount of compensation during the determination period.

Q 14:17 What is considered *compensation* for purposes of determining key employees?

Compensation means compensation as defined for purposes of Code Section 415. [I.R.C. § 415(c)(3)] It also includes elective contributions to 401(k) plans, SARSEPs, SIMPLE retirement accounts, and elective deferrals under a cafeteria plan. [I.R.C. § 416(i)(1)(D)]

Determination Date

Q 14:18 When is the top-heavy determination for a plan year made?

The top-heavy determination for a plan year is made on the determination date. When two or more plans constitute an aggregation group, the plan years taken into account are those whose determination dates fall within the same calendar year. [Treas. Reg. § 1.416-1, Q&As T-22, T-23]

Q 14:19 What is the *determination date* for a plan year?

The *determination date* for a plan year is the last day of the preceding plan year. In the case of a plan's initial plan year, however, the determination date is the last day of such plan year. [Treas. Reg. § 1.416-1, Q&A T-22]

Example. Beta Corporation maintains Plan A and Plan B, each containing a key employee. Plan A's plan year commences July 1 and ends June 30. Plan B's plan year is the calendar year. For Plan A's plan year commencing July 1, 2015, the determination date is June 30, 2015. For Plan B's plan year commencing January 1, 2016, the determination date is December 31, 2015. These plans are required to be aggregated (see Q 14:5). For each plan, as of their respective determination dates, the present values of the accrued benefits for key employees and all employees are separately determined. Since the two determination dates, June 30, 2015, and December 31, 2015, fall within the same calendar year, the present values of accrued benefits as of each of these dates are combined to determine whether the group is top heavy. If, after combining the two present values, the required aggregation group is top heavy, Plan A will be top heavy for the plan year commencing July 1, 2015, and Plan B will be top heavy for the 2016 calendar year.

Present Value of Accrued Benefits

Q 14:20 How is the present value of accrued benefits determined in a defined contribution plan?

The present value of accrued benefits as of the determination date for any individual is the participant's account balance as of that date. (Technically, the regulations provide that account balances are determined as of the most recent valuation date occurring within the 12-month period ending on the determination date. For most plans, however, the determination date, because it is the last day of a plan year, will be a valuation date.) Under the regulations, contributions made after the determination date but allocated as of that date are not taken into account unless either of these conditions exists:

1. The plan is a money purchase, target benefit, or other defined contribution plan subject to minimum funding requirements under Code Section 412; or
2. The plan is a 401(k) plan or other profit sharing or stock bonus plan, and a top-heavy determination is being made for the initial plan year.

[Treas. Reg. § 1.416-1, Q&A T-24]

The IRS has informally indicated that contributions made after the determination date but allocated as of that date could be taken into account even if the conditions above do not apply.

Q 14:21 How is the present value of accrued benefits determined in a defined benefit plan?

In general, the present value of accrued benefits as of the determination date for any individual is determined as of the most recent valuation date occurring within the 12-month period ending on the determination date. It should be noted that if a defined benefit plan's valuation date is the first day of a plan year, the determination of whether a plan is top heavy for a plan year is based on a valuation date occurring one year before the plan year begins.

Example. An employer sponsors a defined benefit plan maintained on a calendar-year basis and valued annually on the first day of the plan year. The determination date for the plan year beginning January 1, 2016, is December 31, 2015. The determination of the present value of accrued benefits will be based on the valuation that occurred on January 1, 2015.

Special rules apply for determining the present value of accrued benefits for the first two plan years of a defined benefit plan. [Treas. Reg. § 1.416-1, Q&A T-25]

Q 14:22 What actuarial assumptions are used in determining the present value of accrued benefits in a defined benefit plan?

The actuarial assumptions must be set forth in the defined benefit plan and they must be reasonable, but they need not be the same as those used for minimum funding purposes or for determining actuarially equivalent optional forms of benefit. The present value of a participant's accrued benefit must be computed using an interest rate assumption and a post-retirement mortality assumption. A pre-retirement mortality assumption may be used, but withdrawal and salary scale assumptions may not. [Treas. Reg. § 1.416-1, Q&A T-26]

Q 14:23 Are accrued benefits attributable to employee contributions taken into account?

Yes; however, account balances attributable to deemed IRAs are disregarded. [Treas. Reg. § 1.408(q)-1(c)]

Q 14:24 Are catch-up contributions taken into account in determining accrued benefits?

Yes, except for the initial plan year of a 401(k) plan, catch-up contributions are taken into account in determining account balances as of the determination date. [Treas. Reg. § 1.414(v)-1(d)(3)]

Q 14:25 What effect do distributions to participants have on the determination of the present value of accrued benefits?

In general, distributions made during the determination period are added to the present value of accrued benefits. Distributions occurring after the most recent valuation date but before the determination date are disregarded for this purpose. (This is likely to be an issue only for defined benefit plans). Also disregarded are certain distributions that are rolled over or transferred to a related plan (see Q 14:27). Distributions include all distributions, even those of an employee's own contributions. [I.R.C. § 416(g)(3)(A); Treas. Reg. § 1.416-1, Q&A T-30]

Distributions made for a reason other than severance from employment, death, or disability will be added to the present value of accrued benefits if they are made during the determination period or the four-plan-year period preceding the determination period. [I.R.C. § 416(g)(3)(B)]

Q 14:26 What effect do distributions to beneficiaries of deceased participants have on the determination of the present value of accrued benefits?

Distributions made during the determination period and paid by reason of death are also taken into account; however, the distribution is taken into account only to the extent of the present value of the participant's accrued benefit determined immediately before death. [Treas. Reg. § 1.416-1, Q&A T-31]

> **Example.** AMO Company maintains a defined benefit plan on a calendar-year basis. The plan provides a pre-retirement death benefit equal to 100 times a participant's projected monthly normal retirement benefit. In 2015, Doug's widow, Sara, receives a death benefit of $200,000. Immediately prior to his death, the present value of Doug's accrued benefit under the plan is $100,000. For purposes of determining whether the plan is top heavy, only $100,000 will be treated as having been distributed to Sara.

Q 14:27 How are rollovers and plan-to-plan transfers handled?

It depends on whether they are related. A rollover or plan-to-plan transfer is considered related if it is not initiated by the participant or if it is made between plans of the same employer (see definition of *employer* in chapter 10); it is considered unrelated if it is initiated by the employee and is made between plans maintained by different employers.

If a rollover or plan-to-plan transfer is related, then it will not be treated as a distribution from the transferor plan. Instead, the rollover or plan-to-plan transfer will become part of a participant's present value of accrued benefits under the transferee plan. If a rollover or plan-to-plan transfer is unrelated, then it will be treated as a distribution from the transferor plan, but it will not be taken into account under the transferee plan. [Treas. Reg. § 1.416-1, Q&A T-32]

> **Example.** John terminates his employment with the High Plains Company. At his request, the 401(k) plan in which John participated makes a direct rollover to the 401(k) plan of his new employer, Cattlepens Corp., which is unrelated to High Plains. This rollover is unrelated; consequently, it will be treated as a distribution from the 401(k) plan of High Plains and will not be treated as part of John's accrued benefit under the 401(k) plan of Cattlepens.

Q 14:28 Are the accrued benefits of and distributions to certain participants disregarded for purposes of determining whether a plan is top heavy?

There are two occasions when accrued benefits are disregarded:

1. The participant is a former key employee; that is, he or she was previously a key employee but is now a non-key employee. [I.R.C. § 416(g)(4)(B)]
2. The participant has not performed services for the employer during the determination period. [I.R.C. § 416(g)(4)(E)]

Example. Joan has been a key employee for many years, including the plan year ending December 31, 2014. For the 2015 plan year, however, Joan ceased to be a key employee. As a result, in determining whether the plan is top heavy for the 2016 plan year, the plan will not take into account Joan's accrued benefit as of December 31, 2015, the determination date for the 2016 plan year, because she is a former key employee.

Minimum Vesting

Q 14:29 What special vesting requirements apply to top-heavy plans?

If a 401(k) plan becomes top heavy, account balances attributable to employer nonelective contributions must vest at a rate that is at least as rapid as one of the following schedules:

Schedule 1

Years of Service	*Vested Percentage*
Fewer than 2	0%
2	20
3	40
4	60
5	80
6 or more	100

Schedule 2

Years of Service	*Vested Percentage*
Fewer than 3	0%
3 or more	100

Employer match contributions made on account of plan years beginning after December 31, 2001, are required to comply with these top-heavy vesting schedules whether or not the plan is top heavy. [I.R.C. § 411(a)(2)(B)] Following the enactment of the Pension Protection Act of 2006 [Pub. L. No. 109-280, 120 Stat. 780] (PPA), employer nonelective contributions made on account of plan years beginning after December 31, 2006, must also comply with these schedules regardless of the plan's top-heavy status. [PPA § 904] Account balances attributable to elective contributions, qualified nonelective contributions (QNECs), and qualified matching contributions (QMACs) are always 100 percent vested. In addition, safe harbor employer contributions under a 401(k) safe harbor plan and all employer contributions under a SIMPLE 401(k) plan are 100 percent vested at all times (see chapter 2). Thus, the above schedules are relevant only if a 401(k) plan provides for employer match and nonelective contributions, and the employer decided not to apply either of the top-heavy vesting schedules to match contributions made on account of plan years beginning before January 1, 2002, and to nonelective contributions made on account of plan years beginning before January 1, 2007.

Q 14:30 What service may be disregarded in determining a participant's vested percentage?

Any service permitted to be disregarded under the regular vesting rules (see chapter 2) may be disregarded in determining a participant's vested percentage in a top-heavy plan. [Treas. Reg. § 1.416-1, Q&A V-2]

Q 14:31 Does a top-heavy vesting schedule apply only to that portion of a participant's account balance accrued after a plan becomes top heavy?

No. The top-heavy vesting schedule applies to the participant's entire account balance. However, a top-heavy vesting schedule will not apply to a participant who does not have an hour of service after the plan becomes top heavy. [Treas. Reg. § 1.416-1, Q&A V-3]

Minimum Contributions

Q 14:32 What special contribution requirements apply to top-heavy plans?

If a 401(k) plan becomes top heavy, non-key employees must be provided with a minimum contribution. In general, the minimum contribution will be equal to 3 percent of compensation. [Treas. Reg. § 1.416-1, Q&A M-7]

Q 14:33 What is *compensation* for purposes of determining a non-key employee's minimum contribution?

For this purpose, *compensation* has the same meaning as it does for purposes of determining who is a key employee (see Q 14:17). The minimum contribution is generally based on compensation for the entire plan year, although the regulations permit the use of compensation for the calendar year ending within the plan year. [Treas. Reg. § 1.416-1, Q&A M-7]

Example. The Mayfair Company sponsors a top-heavy 401(k) plan that provides for employer nonelective contributions. Diane first enters the plan, which is administered on a calendar-year basis, on July 1, 2015, one of the plan's two entry dates. Mayfair makes a nonelective contribution for the plan year ending December 31, 2015, that is allocated in proportion to compensation received while an employee is a participant; thus, Diane's share of the nonelective contribution is based on the pay that she received on or after July 1, 2015. However, because the plan is top heavy and is required to provide a 3 percent of compensation top-heavy contribution, Mayfair will have met its top-heavy contribution obligation with respect to Diane only if her allocation is at least 3 percent of her compensation for the entire 2015 plan year.

Q 14:34 Are allocated forfeitures taken into account in determining whether a non-key employee has received a minimum contribution?

Yes. Forfeitures are taken into account in determining whether a non-key employee has received a minimum contribution. [Treas. Reg. § 1.416-1, Q&A M-7]

Q 14:35 Is the top-heavy minimum contribution always 3 percent of compensation?

No. A lower minimum is permitted when the allocation of contributions and forfeitures on behalf of any key employee is less than 3 percent of compensation. In that event, the minimum contribution is the largest percentage of compensation allocated to any key employee. There is, however, an exception to this rule. The top-heavy minimum remains at 3 percent of compensation if the 401(k) plan enables a defined benefit plan in the same required aggregation group to satisfy the minimum coverage rules under Code Section 410(b). [Treas. Reg. § 1.416-1, Q&A M-7]

Example 1. ABC Company maintains a top-heavy 401(k) plan that provides for elective contributions only. Michael is the only key employee to defer more than 3 percent of compensation. The top-heavy minimum contribution for non-key employees is 3 percent of compensation.

Example 2. The facts are the same as those in Example 1, except that Michael defers only 2 percent of his compensation, which is the highest rate of deferral by any key employee in the plan. The top-heavy minimum contribution for non-key employees is 2 percent of compensation.

Example 3. The facts are the same as those in Example 2, except that ABC Company sponsors a defined benefit plan that is required to be aggregated with the 401(k) plan (see Q 14:5) and that satisfies the minimum coverage rules under Code Section 410(b) only when aggregated with the 401(k) plan. The top-heavy minimum contribution for non-key employees is 3 percent of compensation.

Q 14:36 Is there any circumstance under which an employer that sponsors a top-heavy plan must make a contribution in excess of 3 percent of compensation?

Yes, this can happen if an employer also maintains a defined benefit plan and elects to make the top-heavy minimum contribution in the 401(k) plan (see Q 14:41). This can also happen in the case of an employer that sponsors a plan containing a new comparability formula (see chapter 2) that must meet a minimum allocation gateway test. That test provides that each NHCE must have an allocation rate that is at least one third of the allocation rate of highly compensated employees, but in no event is that rate required to be greater than 5 percent of compensation. A participant who ordinarily would be entitled to only a top-heavy minimum contribution (see Q 14:39) may be required to receive a larger allocation to satisfy the gateway test. [Treas. Reg. § 1.401(a)(4)-8(b)(1)(vi)]

Q 14:37 Are elective contributions made on behalf of key employees taken into account in determining whether a key employee's allocation of contributions and forfeitures constitutes 3 percent of compensation?

Yes, elective contributions are taken into account for this purpose. [Treas. Reg. § 1.416-1, Q&A M-20] The examples in Q 14:35 illustrate this point.

Q 14:38 What amounts are taken into account in determining whether a participant has received a top-heavy minimum?

Except as noted below, all employer contributions and forfeitures allocated to a participant are taken into account. [Treas. Reg. § 1.416-1, Q&A M-7] Such contributions include QNECs, QMACs, matching contributions, and safe harbor contributions under a 401(k) plan. [I.R.C. § 416(c)(2)(A)] However, elective contributions made by non-key employees cannot be applied toward top-heavy minimums. [Treas. Reg. § 1.416-1, Q&A M-20]

As pointed out at the beginning of this chapter, safe harbor plans, including qualified automatic contribution arrangements (QACAs), to which no non-safe harbor employer contributions are made or forfeitures are allocated will be deemed to satisfy the top-heavy rules. [I.R.C. § 416(g)(4)(H); Rev. Rul. 2004-13, 2004-7 I.R.B. 485]

> **Example.** The Rocky Mountain Corporation sponsors a safe harbor 401(k) plan that does not provide for employer contributions other than a basic safe harbor match contribution. Joe, a plan participant, elects not to make elective deferrals to the plan. Even if the plan is top heavy, Rocky Mountain is not required to make a top-heavy minimum contribution on Joe's behalf because the 401(k) plan is a safe harbor plan that provides for no employer contributions other than the basic safe harbor match contribution.

Q 14:39 Which non-key employees must receive a minimum contribution?

Those non-key employees who are participants in a 401(k) plan and who are employed on the last day of the plan year must receive a top-heavy minimum. A non-key employee is entitled to a minimum contribution even if the non-key employee fails to complete the number of hours of service (typically 1,000) required by the plan for an allocation of employer contributions. [Treas. Reg. § 1.416-1, Q&A M-10]

> **Example.** Arborway Company sponsors a top-heavy 401(k) plan. It also provides for a discretionary profit sharing contribution that is allocated in proportion to pay among those participants who have completed at least 1,000 hours of service and are employed on the last day of the plan year. Joan, a plan participant, is employed on the last day of the plan year but is credited with fewer than 1,000 hours of service for the plan year. Dana, also a plan participant, completed 1,850 hours of service during the plan year but terminated her employment one week before the end of the plan year. Because Joan is employed on the last day of the plan year, she must receive a top-heavy minimum contribution. Dana, on the other hand, is not entitled to any share of the company's profit sharing contribution, including a top-heavy minimum contribution, because she is not employed by Arborway on the last day of the plan year.

Q 14:40 If an employer maintains a 401(k) plan and another defined contribution plan, must both plans provide top-heavy minimums for non-key employees who participate in both?

No. As long as one plan provides the top-heavy minimum contribution for a non-key employee who participates in both plans, the other plan does not have to provide a minimum contribution. [Treas. Reg. § 1.416-1, Q&A M-8]

Q 14:41 What happens if non-key employees are accruing benefits under both a 401(k) plan and a defined benefit plan?

As noted in Q 14:40, two top-heavy minimums are not required. The regulations provide four different methods for determining top-heavy minimums in this situation:

1. Provide for the defined benefit top-heavy minimum (generally a benefit at normal retirement age equal to 2 percent of average annual compensation per year of service up to a maximum of 20 percent of average annual compensation);
2. Provide that the defined benefit top-heavy minimum will be offset by the benefits provided under the 401(k) plan [Rev. Rul. 76-259, 1976-2 C.B. 111] (presumably, account balances attributable to elective contributions cannot be used as an offset);

3. Demonstrate that benefits under the defined benefit plan and the 401(k) plan are providing benefits in the aggregate that are comparable to the defined benefit minimums (as explained in (2) above, elective contributions cannot be taken into account); or
4. Provide for a top-heavy minimum contribution of 5 percent of compensation in the 401(k) plan.

[Treas. Reg. § 1.416-1, Q&A M-12]

Top-Heavy Strategy

A newly established 401(k) plan may be top heavy from its inception, possibly to the surprise and chagrin of an employer who had viewed the plan as a vehicle for elective contributions only. Top heaviness can result, for example, from the requirement that distributions from a terminated plan be taken into account in testing the new 401(k) plan (see Q 14:25). It can also result in plans maintained by employers who have few employees and low rates of deferral on the part of non-key employees. This section explains how an employer may cope with the resulting top-heavy minimum contribution requirements or avoid them altogether. In the end, however, there is no substitute for careful monitoring of the top-heavy status of a plan and for the employer being aware of the consequences of "top heaviness" before top-heavy contributions must actually be made.

Q 14:42 Is there a minimum contribution requirement for a top-heavy 401(k) plan that provides for elective contributions only?

Yes, there can be a minimum contribution requirement if a key employee makes elective contributions to the 401(k) plan (see Q 14:37). Consequently, if no key employee makes elective contributions, there will be no top-heavy minimum contribution obligation. The lack of participation by key employees may also hasten the day the 401(k) plan is no longer top-heavy because the present value of accrued benefits attributable to key employees will decline relative to that of non-key employees (see Q 14:2).

Q 14:43 Can the top-heavy plan rules be avoided by converting a 401(k) plan to a SIMPLE plan?

Yes. Although a SIMPLE 401(k) plan is not subject to the top-heavy plan rules, their nonapplication comes at a cost. First, eligible employers under a SIMPLE 401(k) plan must provide either a dollar for dollar matching contribution on elective contributions up to 3 percent of pay or a 2 percent of pay nonelective contribution. Second, any employer contribution must be 100 percent vested immediately. Note that, in theory, an employer could avoid matching contributions if no non-key employee elected to participate in the SIMPLE 401(k) plan. Also, the 2 percent nonelective contribution, if elected by the employer, is less than the minimum contribution (generally 3 percent of pay) under the top-heavy plan rules. (See chapter 2 for a discussion of SIMPLE 401(k) plans.)

Q 14:44 If an employer makes a discretionary profit sharing contribution, can each non-key employee's allocation of that contribution be credited toward the top-heavy minimum contribution obligation?

Yes. If the allocation of the profit sharing contribution results in each non-key employee's receiving the top-heavy minimum (see Qs 14:32–14:35), no additional amount need be contributed.

Q 14:45 Can an employer matching contribution be used to satisfy the top-heavy minimum contribution obligation?

Yes. Matching contributions can be used to satisfy the top-heavy minimum contribution obligation (see Q 14:38).

Q 14:46 Is there any other type of employer contribution that can be used to satisfy the top-heavy rules?

Yes. 401(k) plans that fail the ADP test, the ACP test, or both will sometimes satisfy these tests by making QNECs as defined in chapter 13. In addition to performing that function, QNECs that are allocated to non-key employees will count toward fulfilling the employer's top-heavy minimum contribution obligation.

Q 14:47 Can the top-heavy plan rules be avoided by converting a 401(k) plan to a safe harbor 401(k) plan?

A 401(k) plan that is a safe harbor plan and to which no non-safe harbor employer contributions are made (including forfeitures allocated as if additional non–safe harbor employer contributions) will automatically satisfy the top-heavy plan rules. Consequently, in a safe harbor match contribution plan, a non-key employee with no deferrals would receive no employer contribution for the plan year even though the plan is top heavy. (See chapter 2 for a discussion regarding safe harbor 401(k) plans.) However, there are costs to the use of safe harbor contributions. First, the safe harbor contributions must be 100 percent vested at all times. Second, if the employer makes a safe harbor nonelective contribution in lieu of a safe harbor matching contribution, it must provide the safe harbor nonelective contribution for any employee who is a participant at any time during the plan year, even if the participant does not defer. Finally, the number of hours of service completed during the plan year and employment on the last day of the plan year are irrelevant in determining whether a participant is entitled to a safe harbor contribution.

Q 14:48 Can the top-heavy rules be avoided by adding a qualified automatic contribution arrangement to a 401(k) plan?

Starting with plan years beginning after December 31, 2007, a 401(k) plan that contains a QACA and to which no non-QACA safe harbor contributions are made (including forfeitures allocated as additional non-safe harbor contributions) will automatically satisfy the top-heavy plan rules. Thus, in the case of a QACA that provides for a safe harbor QACA match contribution, a participant who affirmatively declines to make deferrals into the plan will receive no employer contribution for the plan year even though the plan is top heavy. (See chapter 2 for a discussion of QACAs.)

As in the case of regular safe harbor plans, there are costs associated with adding a QACA to a 401(k) plan. First, although they are not required to be 100 percent vested when made, as is the case with regular safe harbor plans, QACA safe harbor contributions must become 100 percent vested after the employee completes two years of service. Second, if the employer makes a QACA safe harbor nonelective contribution in lieu of a matching contribution, it must be provided to any employee who is a participant at any time during the plan year, even if the participant does not defer. Finally, like regular safe harbor plans, the number of hours of service completed during the plan year and whether the participant was employed on the last day of the plan year are not relevant in determining whether the participant is entitled to a QACA safe harbor contribution.

Chapter 15

Participant Loans, Hardship Withdrawals, and In-Service Distributions

In the case of most companies, a successful 401(k) plan requires significant participation from lower-paid employees. Many employees, however, may be reluctant to commit funds to the 401(k) plan if they have no savings or other resources with which to respond to unanticipated financial demands. One common way to address that concern is to provide access to funds in the 401(k) plan through loans, hardship withdrawals, or other distributions while a participant is actively employed. This chapter discusses the rules and design considerations involved when including loans, hardship withdrawals, and in-service distribution provisions in a 401(k) plan.

Participant Loans 15-2
  Department of Labor Regulation of Participant Loans 15-2
  Loan Availability 15-3
  Loan Terms and Provisions 15-4
  Taxation of Participant Loans 15-6
  Other Loan Rules 15-15
Hardship Withdrawals of Elective Contributions 15-23
  The Events Test 15-23
  The Needs Test 15-24
  Safe Harbor Standard Versus General Standard 15-25
  Plan Sponsor Documentation 15-26
  Tax Consequences 15-26
  Other Withdrawal Issues 15-27
In-Service Distributions 15-29
Hurricane Sandy Relief 15-31

Participant Loans

Participant loans provide a means for participants to access their 401(k) account balances without incurring tax liability. There are two sets of rules that must be complied with when designing and implementing a participant loan program. The Department of Labor (DOL) provisions of the Employee Retirement Income Security Act of 1974 (ERISA) dictate how loans must be structured to avoid treatment as a prohibited transaction. The Internal Revenue Code (Code) dictates how loans must be structured to avoid treatment as a taxable distribution. This section discusses both the DOL and the Code rules, as well as other issues related to participant loans.

Q 15:1 Who may borrow money from his or her 401(k) plan account?

A plan generally may permit participants to borrow against their 401(k) plan accounts. Many plan sponsors include this option in their 401(k) plans to encourage a higher rate of participation by lower-paid employees.

Prior to 2002, participant loans could not be made to any owner-employee, which includes a sole proprietor, a 5 percent shareholder of a Subchapter S corporation, or a partner with an ownership interest of at least 10 percent. Any loan to an owner-employee was a prohibited transaction.

Effective beginning January 1, 2002, the rule treating plan loans from 401(k) plans to owner-employees as prohibited transactions was eliminated. That means plan loans can be made available to owner-employees in 401(k) plans. This change was made by the Economic Growth and Tax Relief Reconciliation Act of 2001 (EGTRRA). [I.R.C. § 4975(f)(6)(B)(iii); ERISA § 408(d)(2)(C), 29 U.S.C. § 1108(d)(2)(C)]

Department of Labor Regulation of Participant Loans

Q 15:2 What are the purpose and general content of the DOL rules?

A loan from a plan to a participant falls within the definition of a prohibited transaction under ERISA. [ERISA § 406(a)(1)(B), 29 U.S.C. § 1106(a)(1)(B)] (The prohibited transaction rules are discussed more fully in chapter 5.) A statutory exemption provides the means to avoid treatment as a prohibited transaction as long as certain conditions are met. To qualify for this exemption, loans must satisfy all of the following:

- Be made available to all participants and beneficiaries on a reasonably equivalent basis (see Q 15:3)
- Not be made available to highly compensated employees in an amount greater than the amount available to other employees (see Q 15:4)
- Be made in accordance with specific provisions that are set forth in the plan (see Q 15:5)
- Bear a reasonable rate of interest (see Qs 15:6, 15:7)

- Be adequately secured (see Qs 15:8, 15:9)

[ERISA § 408(b)(1), 29 U.S.C. § 1108(b)(1); DOL Reg. § 2550.408b-1]

Loan Availability

Q 15:3 When is a loan available to all participants on a reasonably equivalent basis?

The plan sponsor can place some restrictions on loan availability without running afoul of the reasonably equivalent rule. The following are some examples of acceptable restrictions:

1. A plan can effectively make loans available to active employees without making them available to terminated participants or plan beneficiaries. This can be done by making loans available only to parties in interest to the plan. [Treas. Reg. § 1.401(a)(4)-10(c); DOL Adv. Op. 89-30A]
2. The availability of loans can be restricted to particular purposes, such as hardship. However, the restriction must be consistent with the interest of participants and cannot operate in a way that makes loans unavailable to large numbers of participants. Also, any such restrictions cannot be designed to benefit the employer, fiduciary, or other party in interest. For example, a plan cannot restrict the availability of loans to situations where the loan proceeds must be used to make a capital investment in the plan sponsor. [DOL Reg. § 2550.408b-1(a)(4), Ex. 2]
3. A sponsor can limit loans to a minimum dollar amount up to $1,000. [Treas. Reg. § 1.401(a)(4)-4(b)(2)(ii)(E); DOL Reg. § 2550.408b-1(b)(2)]

A plan sponsor cannot restrict loans based on factors upon which a commercial lender would not rely. For example, the sponsor may not take into account race, color, religion, sex, age, national origin, or other factors unrelated to the creditworthiness of the employee. [DOL Reg. § 2550.408b-1(b)(1)]

Q 15:4 When are loans made available to highly compensated employees in amounts greater than what is available to other employees?

This is a facts-and-circumstances determination. The general rule is that the loan program cannot exclude large numbers of employees. [DOL Reg. § 2550.408b-1(c)(1)] For example, if the sponsor sets a minimum service limit that results in only 20 percent of employees qualifying for a loan, most of whom are highly compensated, the loan program will be considered to favor highly compensated employees (HCEs) improperly. It is permissible to vary the loan amount with the size of account balances. For example, a plan might limit loans to 50 percent of an employee's vested account balance. [DOL Reg. § 2550.408b-1(c)(2)]

Loan Terms and Provisions

Q 15:5 What provisions concerning loans must be in the plan document?

The plan document must include the following provisions:

1. The identity of the person authorized to administer the participant program;
2. The procedure for applying for loans;
3. The standards for approving or denying loans;
4. Any limitations on loan types or loan amounts;
5. The procedures used to determine a reasonable rate of interest;
6. The types of collateral that can be used to secure participant loans; and
7. The events constituting default and the steps necessary to preserve plan assets in the event of default.

This information may be contained either in the plan document itself or in a written document forming part of the plan. [DOL Reg. § 2550.408b-1(d)]

Q 15:6 What is a reasonable rate of interest for participant loans?

The interest rate chosen must be consistent with interest rates charged by commercial lenders for a loan made under similar circumstances. [DOL Reg. § 2550.408b-1(e)] The DOL's view is that there is no justification for using below-market interest rates on participant loans. The DOL has not provided a safe harbor for determining what is a reasonable interest rate for plans secured by a participant's account balance. Plans commonly use a "prime + " standard.

In 2011, an IRS representative indicated in a phone forum that a rate set below "prime" plus 2 percent may not meet the reasonable requirement. This information is not in any published guidance. Subsequent to the phone forum, the IRS in its Winter 2012 publication, "Retirement News for Employers" (available at *http://www.irs.gov/pub/irs-tege/rne_win12.pdf*), set forth the DOL's general guidelines and several examples based on those guidelines.

Q 15:7 Must the plan interest rate be reviewed each time a new loan is taken out?

Yes. The DOL regulations state that the reasonable rate of interest standard must be looked at each time a loan is originated, renewed, renegotiated, or modified. [DOL Reg. § 2550.408b-1(a)(3)(ii)] Therefore, a plan sponsor cannot simply choose a rate at the time the plan is set up and use that rate continuously. Rates must be reviewed and updated as often as necessary to ensure that they remain consistent with commercial lending practices.

Q 15:8 When is a loan considered adequately secured?

The general rule is that the security must be adequate to ensure that all principal and interest on the loan will be paid. The type and amount of collateral must be comparable to what a commercial lender would require in an arm's-length transaction between unrelated parties. [DOL Reg. § 2550.408b-1(f)(1)]

Q 15:9 Can a participant's account balance be used to secure the loan?

Yes. Up to 50 percent of the present value of a participant's vested account balance can be used to secure a loan. This is measured at the time the loan is made. [DOL Reg. § 2550.408b-1(f)(2)] Therefore, if a participant borrows one half of his or her account balance and then takes a hardship distribution before the loan is repaid, he or she will still be in compliance with this rule.

Q 15:10 Must the plan examine the creditworthiness of each borrower in determining whether to approve a loan?

No. The DOL does not require plan sponsors to review financial statements or other indications of creditworthiness of each participant who wants a loan.

Q 15:11 Are there any restrictions on how a loan is used by a participant?

No. In fact, as long as the employer does not place any restrictions on use of the loan that would benefit itself, a fiduciary, or other party in interest, there is no reason why a participant cannot independently make the decision to use loan proceeds in a way that would benefit the employer or other restricted party. [DOL Reg. § 2550.408b-1(a)(4), Ex. 6]

Q 15:12 Can a participant loan be made to a fiduciary involved in administering the loan program?

Yes, but the loan must be made according to strict objective criteria. When the fiduciary borrows from his or her own account, an independent plan representative could approve the loan to ensure objectivity. For example, if the plan trustee is the person authorized to approve participant loans and he or she is seeking approval for a loan, that approval could come from the plan administrator or some other authorized representative of the plan.

Q 15:13 Does the DOL impose any other restrictions on participant loans?

Yes. The parties to a loan agreement must intend to repay the loan. [DOL Reg. § 2550.408b-1(a)(3)(i)] For this reason, it is important that the plan be diligent in collecting amounts due on participant loans. Many employers use payroll deductions for loan repayments to avoid collection problems.

Furthermore, the general fiduciary rules concerning plan investments that require prudence and diversification must be adhered to when making an investment in a participant loan. [DOL Adv. Op. 81-12A]

Q 15:14 What are the consequences of failing to satisfy the DOL loan rules?

The loan will be considered a prohibited transaction (see chapter 5). Also, if the loan results in a loss to the plan, the fiduciary responsible for plan investments may be held personally liable to the plan for the loss. [ERISA § 409(a), 29 U.S.C. § 1109(a)] A disqualifying loan may also disqualify the plan by violating the anti-alienation rule (see chapter 2). [Treas. Reg. § 1.401(a)-13(d)(2); Rev. Rul. 89-14, 1989-1 C.B. 111]

Taxation of Participant Loans

Q 15:15 How may taxation of participant loans be avoided?

Loans from a plan to a plan participant would generally be treated as distributions and are taxable in whole or in part under Code Section 72(p). [Treas. Reg. § 1.72(p)-1, Q&A 3] The following three conditions must be met in order to avoid taxation of a participant loan at the time the loan is made:

1. The loan must be paid in full within five years, unless the loan is used to acquire a principal residence of the participant (see Q 15:32). [I.R.C. § 72(p)(2)(B)]
2. The loan must require substantially level amortization of principal and interest, with payments required at least quarterly (see Q 15:33). For example, a loan for a five-year term that requires payments of interest only until the end of the term, and a balloon payment at the end, does not qualify. [I.R.C. § 72(p)(2)(C)]
3. The loan is evidenced by a legally enforceable agreement (see Q 15:16) and the loan is limited to a dollar limit equal to the lesser of (a) or (b):
   (a) $50,000, reduced by:The highest outstanding balance of loans during the one-year period ending on the day before the date a loan is to be made less The outstanding balance of loans on the date the loan is to be made.
   (b) The greater of:One half of a participant's vested accrued benefit; or $10,000.

[I.R.C. § 72(p)(2)(A)]

The rules were generally effective for loans made after August 13, 1982 [Treas. Reg. § 1.72(p)-1, Q&A 22]

Generally, if no other plan loans are outstanding, a participant may borrow up to the following amounts:

Vested Account Balance	*Maximum Loan Amount*
$10,000 or less	Entire vested account balance*
$10,001–$20,000	$10,000*
$20,001–$100,000	50% of vested account
Over $100,000	$50,000

* A loan may not be secured by more than 50 percent of the vested account balance (see Q 15:9). As a result, additional collateral would be required if a loan exceeds 50 percent of the vested account balance under the $10,000 minimum rule. Most plans therefore limit loans to 50 percent of the vested amount.

If the participant has a loan outstanding and wants a new loan, or has repaid a loan within the 12 months preceding his or her request for a new loan, the loan amount is determined as demonstrated in the following example.

> **Example.** Michael, whose vested accrued benefit is $150,000, has a $20,000 loan balance currently. The highest outstanding loan balance for the prior 12-month period is $28,000. Michael's nontaxable loan limit is calculated as follows:
>
> Limited to lesser of (a) or (b):
>
> (a) $50,000, reduced by:
> Highest outstanding balance for prior 12 months ($28,000) less Outstanding balance on date of new loan ($20,000) = $42,000
>
> (b) Greater of:
> One half of vested accrued benefit (½ × $150,000 = $75,000) or $10,000 = $75,000
>
> Since (a) = $42,000 and (b) = $75,000, the nontaxable loan limit—the lesser of (a) or (b)—is $42,000.
>
> Michael could borrow up to $22,000, calculated as $42,000 – $20,000.

In determining the dollar limit, the employer must aggregate all vested accrued benefits and all loans from any other plans of the employer or related company under Code Sections 414(b), 414(c), and 414(m). (For the definition of *employer,* see chapter 10.) Also, a deemed loan is considered outstanding for purposes of the dollar limit calculation (see Q 15:22). For the limit on the value of a participant's account balance that can be used as collateral to secure a loan, see Q 15:9. For special rules applicable to loans from Roth accounts, see Q 15:30.

Q 15:16 What constitutes an enforceable agreement for purposes of the loan rules?

The loan agreement must specify the amount and date of the loan and the repayment schedule. The agreement does not have to be signed if it is enforceable under applicable law without being signed. The agreement must be set forth either:

1. In a written paper document; or
2. In a document that is delivered through an electronic medium under an electronic system that satisfies the requirements of Treasury Regulations Section 1.401(a)-21. [Treas. Reg. § 1.72(p)-1, Q&A 3]

See chapter 19 for details regarding the requirements applicable to notices and consents in an electronic environment. See also Q 15:41 for information on obtaining spousal consents in an electronic loan process.

Q 15:17 What documentation should a plan sponsor retain in connection with its loan program?

The IRS indicated in "Retirement News for Employers" published April 2, 2015 (available at *http://www.irs.gov/pub/irs-tege/rne_0415.pdf*) that a plan sponsor should retain the following records, in paper or electronic format, for each plan loan granted to a participant:

- Evidence of the loan application, review, and approval process;
- An executed plan loan note;
- If applicable, documentation verifying that the loan proceeds were used to purchase or construct a primary residence;
- Evidence of loan repayments; and
- Evidence of collection activities associated with loans in default and the related Forms 1099-R, if applicable.

With regard to a loan with a repayment period of more than five years for the purpose of purchasing or constructing a primary residence, the plan sponsor must obtain documentation of the home purchase before the loan is approved. Allowing participants to self-certify their eligibility would not suffice.

Q 15:18 If a loan fails to meet these requirements, what taxes apply?

A loan that fails to meet these requirements is treated as a deemed distribution and under these rules will be subject to regular income tax as well as the 10 percent additional tax imposed by Code Section 72(t) on premature distributions. (See chapter 18.) However, if the participant has a cost basis, all or a portion of the deemed distribution may not be taxable. [Treas. Reg. § 1.72(p)-1, Q&A 11] It should be noted that the premature distribution tax does not apply to distributions to participants who have attained age 59½. A loan that becomes taxable but that is not offset against a participant's account balance is not an eligible rollover distribution and therefore is not subject to the 20 percent withholding requirement. [Treas. Reg. § 1.402(c)-2, Q&A 4(d)]

Q 15:19 How much of the loan is taxed if the requirements are not met?

The answer depends on which rule is violated and when the violation occurs. If a loan by its terms does not require repayment within five years or does not call for quarterly payments of principal and interest, then the entire amount of the loan will be deemed a distribution at the time the loan is made. [Treas. Reg. § 1.72(p)-1, Q&A 4(a)] If the loan exceeds the dollar limit, then only the amount in excess of the limit is deemed distributed at the time the loan is made. [Treas. Reg. § 1.72(p)-1, Q&A 4(a)] If the loan terms are in compliance but the loan goes into default, then the amount of principal and interest remaining upon default or, if later, at the end of any cure period allowed by the plan administrator is deemed distributed. A cure period can continue up to the last day of the calendar quarter following the calendar quarter in which a default occurs. [Treas. Reg. § 1.72(p)-1, Q&A 10]

Example. On August 1, 2015, Sam has a vested account balance of $45,000 and borrows $20,000 from his plan to be repaid over five years in level monthly installments due at the end of each month. After making all monthly payments due through July 31, 2016, Sam fails to make the payment due on August 31, 2016, or any other monthly payments due thereafter. The plan allows a three-month cure period.

Because Sam failed to satisfy the requirement that the loan be repaid in level installments, he has a deemed distribution on November 30, 2016, which is the last day of the three-month cure period for the August 31, 2016, installment. The amount of the deemed distribution is $17,157, which is the outstanding loan balance on November 30, 2016. Alternatively, if the plan allowed a cure period through the end of the next calendar quarter, there would be a deemed distribution on December 31, 2016, equal to $17,282, which is the outstanding loan balance on December 31, 2016.

Q 15:20 What is a plan administrator's tax reporting obligation when a deemed distribution occurs?

The amount includable in income as a result of a deemed distribution must be reported on Form 1099-R. [Treas. Reg. § 1.72(p)-1, Q&A 14]

Q 15:21 What is the difference between a deemed distribution and a loan offset?

Plan loans can give rise to two types of taxable distributions: (1) a loan offset and (2) a deemed distribution under Code Section 72(p).

In a loan offset, the plan reduces the participant's account balance by the amount of the outstanding loan balance. This theoretical distribution is treated as a repayment of the loan and the loan is eliminated. A loan offset could occur in a variety of situations, such as when the terms of the plan require that a loan be repaid immediately upon termination or upon default. A loan offset, however, will not always be available for the repayment of loans made from 401(k) plans because of restrictions on the distributability of salary deferrals. Offsetting a participant's account balance is considered an actual distribution under the Code, not a deemed distribution under Code Section 72(p); thus, any distribution of salary deferrals that occurs for reasons other than separation of service, hardship, disability, or attainment of age 59½ disqualifies the plan. Therefore, in a 401(k) plan, if the participant's non-salary deferral dollars are insufficient to offset the loan, the plan must typically wait until a distribution event occurs before it can offset salary deferral dollars.

Unlike a loan offset, a deemed distribution under Code Section 72(p) is treated as a distribution for tax purposes only. Consequently, the plan will not violate any prohibition against in-service withdrawals by deeming a loan distributed because, although a loan deemed distributed constitutes a distribution for tax purposes, the participant's account balance is not reduced by the amount of the loan and the loan remains an asset of the plan. [Treas. Reg. § 1.72(p)-1, Q&A 13]

Q 15:22 Does interest continue to accrue on a deemed distribution?

Yes. Once a loan is deemed distributed it essentially "disappears" for tax purposes, but remains outstanding. Interest continues to accrue, and the outstanding obligation must be taken into account in making and in calculating the maximum permissible amount of any subsequent loan. The unpaid amount of the loan, including accrued interest, is considered outstanding for purposes of determining the maximum dollar amount of any subsequent loan (see Q 15:15). [Treas. Reg. § 1.72(p)-1, Q&A 19] This of course becomes relevant only if a participant is able to borrow additional funds from the plan.

Q 15:23 Is the interest that continues to accrue on a deemed loan taxable?

No. Once a loan is deemed distributed, the interest continues to accrue but is not includable in income. Further, under the regulations to Code Section 72(p), neither the income that resulted from the deemed distribution nor the interest that accrues thereafter increases the participant's tax basis. In preparing the participant's Form 1099-R for an actual distribution, the plan should ignore the amount of the prior "deemed distribution" and report only the value of the nonloan asset distributed. [Treas. Reg. § 1.72(p)-1, Q&As 19, 22]

> **Example.** After a loan was made to Bill from his 401(k) plan, a deemed distribution in the amount of $10,000 (the amount of unpaid principal and interest at the time of default) occurred as a result of Bill's failure to make timely loan repayments. The plan cannot offset the loan at that time because of restrictions on the distributability of Bill's 401(k) dollars. As a result of the deemed distribution, the plan reports, in Box 1 of Form 1099-R, a gross distribution of $10,000 and, in Box 2 of Form 1099-R, a taxable amount of $10,000 (Bill has no tax basis). Thereafter, the plan disregards, for purposes of Code Section 72, the interest that accrues on the loan after the deemed distribution.
>
> At separation from employment, Bill receives a distribution of the total account balance under the plan consisting of $60,000 in cash and the loan receivable. At that time, the plan's records reflect an offset of the loan amount against the loan receivable in Bill's account and a distribution of $60,000 in cash.

Bill would have a taxable distribution of $60,000 reflecting the nonloan assets that are distributed in a lump sum. There is no tax basis attributed to the prior deemed distribution of the loan amount. The offset of the loan would be disregarded for tax purposes because it was already deemed distributed as a result of the failure to make timely payments.

Q 15:24 What impact does a deemed loan have on a participant's ability to obtain a subsequent loan?

Some plans permit participants to have only a single loan outstanding at one time. In those plans, a participant who received a deemed distribution of a prior loan (which would still be considered outstanding) would not be permitted to take out another plan loan until the loan is satisfied either by offset or repayment.

Along the same lines, a plan may have a loan procedure prohibiting new loans to participants who are in arrears on any existing loan. Therefore, even though the participant's account balance may provide sufficient collateral to support the new loan, the participant would not be permitted to borrow from the plan until payments on the existing loan are made current (or the loan is satisfied). Such a procedure demonstrates that a participant intends to repay his or her loans and that the new loan is bona fide, and not a disguised distribution, for purposes of Code Section 72(p).

Some plans do not formally prohibit a participant who has a deemed loan outstanding from obtaining a subsequent loan. Under the final regulations, which apply to loans made on or after January 1, 2004, the subsequent loan must satisfy one of the following conditions to avoid being a taxable distribution:

1. There must be an enforceable arrangement under which loan repayments are made by payroll withholding; or
2. The plan must receive security from the participant that is in addition to his or her vested benefit under the plan. [Treas. Reg. § 1.72(p)-1, Q&A 19(b)(2)]

For purposes of the first condition, the arrangement will not fail to be enforceable because a party has the right to revoke the arrangement prospectively.

If the conditions set forth above are no longer satisfied with respect to the second loan (e.g., if the loan recipient revokes consent to payroll withholding), the amount then outstanding on the second loan is treated as a deemed distribution. [Treas. Reg. § 1.72(p)-1, Q&A 19(b)(3)]

Under the preamble to the final regulations, plan sponsors must inquire about other loans made from the plan or any other plan of the employer before extending a loan. Because it may sometimes be difficult to determine whether a participant has an existing deemed loan, the plan can condition a new loan on a participant's disclosure of prior loans and, for this purpose, can rely on a participant's certification concerning the status of prior loans, assuming the plan has no reason to doubt the participant's certification.

Because a deemed loan is considered an outstanding loan obligation, it will reduce the maximum dollar limit of any subsequent loan (see Qs 15:15, 15:22).

Q 15:25 How are loan repayments made after a loan is deemed distributed treated for tax purposes?

If a participant makes any cash repayments on the loan after it is deemed distributed, the participant's tax basis increases by the amount of the cash repayments. The loan repayments will not, however, be treated as after-tax contributions for other purposes, including for purposes of Code Sections 401(m) and 415. [Treas. Reg. § 1.72(p)-1, Q&A 21]

> **Example.** Amy receives a $20,000 loan on January 1, 2011, to be repaid in 20 quarterly installments of $1,245 each. On December 31, 2011, the outstanding loan balance ($19,179) is deemed distributed as a result of Amy's failure to make quarterly installment payments that were due on September 30, 2011, and December 31, 2011. On June 30, 2012, Amy repays $5,147 (which is the sum of the three installment payments that were due on September 30, 2011, December 31, 2011, and March 31, 2012, with interest thereon to June 30, 2012, plus the installment payment that was due on June 30, 2012). Thereafter, Amy resumes making the installment payments of $1,245 from September 30, 2012, through December 31, 2015. The loan repayments made after December 31, 2011, through December 31, 2015, total $22,577.
>
> Because Amy repaid $22,577 after the deemed distribution that occurred on December 31, 2011, she has an investment in the contract (tax basis) equal to $22,577 (14 payments of $1,245 each plus a single payment of $5,147) as of December 31, 2015.

Q 15:26 When must a plan apply the final regulations described in Qs 15:23 and 15:25?

The final regulations apply to loans made on or after January 1, 2002. Plans were generally permitted to apply the final regulations (see Qs 15:23, 15:25) to loans made before the regulatory effective date; however, a special consistency rule applied to loans that were deemed distributed before the new rules were implemented.

According to the consistency rule, generally, a plan could determine a participant's taxable income under the new rules if a gross distribution that is at least equal to the *initial default amount* was reported on Form 1099-R. The *initial default amount,* under the regulations, is the amount that would be reported as a gross distribution (see Q 15:19). In addition, tax basis must not be attributed to the participant based on the deemed distribution of the loan. A plan that increased a participant's tax basis based on the deemed distribution of the loan could, however, comply with the consistency rule by reducing the participant's tax basis by the appropriate amount. The regulations include several examples applying the consistency rule. [Treas. Reg. § 1.72(p)-1, Q&A 22(c)]

> **Example.** After Robert took a loan from his 401(k) plan, a deemed distribution in the amount of $20,000 occurred in 1999 when Robert failed to make timely loan repayments. For 1999, the plan reported, in Box 1 of Form 1099-R, a gross distribution of $20,000 and, in Box 2 of Form 1099-R, a taxable amount of $20,000. The plan then recorded an increase in Robert's tax basis for the same amount ($20,000). Thereafter, the plan disregarded, for purposes of Code Section 72(p), the interest that accrued on the loan after the 1999 deemed distribution. Thus, as of December 31, 2001, the total taxable amount reported by the plan as a result of the deemed distribution was $20,000 and Robert's tax basis was the same amount ($20,000). As of January 1, 2002, the plan decided to apply the new rules under Code Section 72(p). To apply the new rules, the plan had to reduce Robert's tax basis by the initial default amount of $20,000, so that his tax basis in the plan is zero. Thereafter, the amount of the outstanding loan was not treated as part of the account balance under the new rules. Robert attained age 59½ in 2003 and received a distribution of the full account balance under the plan, consisting of $60,000 in cash and the loan receivable. At that time, the plan's records reflect an offset of the loan amount against the loan receivable in Robert's account and a distribution of $60,000 in cash.

A plan likely wanted to apply the new rules to all loans (deemed both pre- and post-regulation) for ease and consistency. Fully complying with the consistency rule may have been difficult if not impossible (e.g., when there were prior deemed loans and the initial default amount was not reported properly); therefore, many plans may have been forced to employ different methods of determining a participant's taxable income upon actual distribution depending on how a prior deemed loan was reported and tracked for tax purposes—a predicament plan administrators may have found to be less than pleasant.

Q 15:27 If some or all of a loan is treated as a deemed distribution, is that portion of the loan still considered outstanding?

Yes. Until it is repaid or distributed from the plan as a loan offset, a participant loan that was deemed distributed remains an outstanding obligation of the participant and an asset of the plan. The loan will still be considered effective and a trustee's obligation to preserve the asset represented by the plan loan will remain in effect even though some or all of the loan amount is taxed to the participant. In addition, a deemed loan is still considered outstanding for purposes of determining the maximum amount of any subsequent loan to the participant or beneficiary (see Q 15:15).

Q 15:28 What special problems can arise under ERISA when a loan is deemed distributed?

The IRS specifically provides that no inference should be drawn from the regulations or examples that such a loan would not result in a prohibited transaction or would be consistent with ERISA fiduciary standards. [Treas. Reg. § 1.72(p)-1] Although the IRS has spoken as to tax treatment of deemed loans, it is unclear how deemed loans (and post-default interest accruals) are to be handled from an ERISA standpoint. Special challenges under ERISA can arise when those loans are "pooled" in a fund and many participants share in the fund's investment performance (or nonperformance).

When a participant is allowed to borrow from a plan, plan assets are liquidated and those assets are replaced with a note (or loan receivable), which then becomes an asset of the plan. When plan loans are maintained as investments of an individual participant's account (i.e., earmarked or segregated assets), only that participant is affected by that asset's investment experience. An alternative approach is to pool participant loans in a fund, and as participants make loan payments, the payments are made to that fund (e.g., separate loan fund or money market fund). Under the pooled approach, all participants invested in that fund share in its investment experience.

If a participant's loan is segregated, whether the participant makes payments on a deemed loan has no effect on other participants. If the loan remained in a pooled fund, all participants invested in the fund (and not just the participant who defaulted on a loan) would suffer the investment loss associated with a deemed loan. In that situation, a plan fiduciary may have a duty to preserve that asset and thus continue to accrue interest on that loan and recoup that interest at the time of actual distribution. Should a plan administrator then continue to accrue interest on a deemed loan even after its maturity date? The answer may be yes. What happens if accrued interest exceeds the value of the participant's nonloan assets? The answer may be that the loan should be earmarked or segregated before accrued interest exceeds the value of nonloan assets. The DOL, however, has yet to weigh in on those issues.

Q 15:29 What are some ways to avoid or minimize the complications associated with deemed loans?

The following are some ways to avoid or minimize the complications associated with deemed loans:

1. Limit participants to having only one outstanding loan at a time so that a participant is forced to repay any outstanding loan balance (which would include a deemed loan) before being able to borrow additional amounts;
2. Require that the repayment of loans be made through payroll deduction to minimize the potential for default and necessity to deem a loan distributed;

3. Segregate participant loans instead of pooling loans whenever possible so that other participants are not affected when one participant defaults on a loan;
4. Do not allow participants to refinance an existing loan (see Q 15:36); and
5. Limit the ability of participants to borrow from Roth accounts (see Q 15:30).

Other Loan Rules

Q 15:30 What special rules apply to loans from Roth accounts?

A plan can permit participant loans from Roth accounts. Roth amounts can be used to calculate the maximum loan limit and as a money source for a participant loan. IRS final regulations provide the following additional guidance applicable to loans from Roth accounts:

1. Amounts borrowed from Roth and non-Roth accounts are aggregated for purposes of the maximum loan amount (see Q 15:15). [Treas. Reg. § 1.402A- 1, Q&A 12] The maximum loan amount may not be applied separately to amounts borrowed from Roth and non-Roth accounts.
2. The requirement that the loan be paid back in substantially level payments at least quarterly (see Q 15:15) must be satisfied separately with respect to loans from Roth and non-Roth accounts. [Treas. Reg. § 1.402A-1, Q&A 12] Loan repayments must be proportionally credited to Roth and non-Roth accounts.
3. A deemed distribution of a loan (see Q 15:19) from a Roth account is a *nonqualified* distribution for tax purposes even if the deemed distribution occurs after the employee attains age 59½ and the five-taxable-year period of participation was satisfied. [Treas. Reg. § 1.402A-1, Q&A 11] Thus, the portion of the deemed distribution that is allocable to earnings on Roth elective contributions is includable in income. The portion allocable to Roth deferrals is not includable in income. Therefore, a pro rata calculation (sub-account balances on the date of default are used for purposes of the calculation) will be necessary to determine the taxable portion of a deemed loan from a Roth account. A separate Form 1099-R is required for reporting amounts distributed from a Roth account, including the taxable portion of such a distribution.

The extent to which Roth accounts are available for loans should be covered in the plan's loan policy and will impact how loan repayments must be credited to participant accounts and the taxation of deemed loans. (See chapters 2 and 18 for additional information on Roth 401(k) plans.)

Q 15:31 How do the rollover rules apply to plan loans and loan offsets?

Distributed loans and loan offsets are eligible rollover distributions. (See chapter 16.) When a participant terminates employment and receives a distribution, the note representing the participant loan may be directly rolled over to another qualified plan (not an IRA), avoiding the triggering of a loan offset. However, a plan is not required to offer a direct rollover option for loans, and a recipient plan is not required to accept a rolled over loan. Further, a plan may provide that loan notes are immediately due and payable upon termination of employment. In that case, a participant must pay the note in full upon termination to avoid triggering a loan offset. [Treas. Reg. § 1.401(a)(31)-1, Q&A 16] When a loan offset occurs, whether or not that occurs at the time of a termination distribution, a participant can roll over the taxable amount by contributing to an IRA (or to another qualified plan) cash equal to the loan offset amount within 60 days after the date of the offset. [Treas. Reg. § 1.402(c)-2, Q&A 9] A previously taxed deemed loan is not eligible for rollover at the time of an offset.

Q 15:32 How does an employer determine whether a loan is a principal residence loan?

A plan loan must be repaid within five years unless the loan is used, within a reasonable period of time, to acquire a principal residence of the participant. A so-called principal residence loan need not be secured by the participant's principal residence to satisfy the requirements. A refinancing generally cannot qualify as a principal residence plan loan. However, a loan from a plan used to repay a loan from a third party will qualify as a principal residence loan. [Treas. Reg. § 1.72(p)-1, Q&As 5–8]

Example. On July 1, 2015, Claire obtains a $50,000 plan loan to be repaid in level monthly installments over 15 years. On August 1, 2015, she acquires a principal residence and pays a portion of the purchase price with a $50,000 bank loan. On September 1, 2015, the plan lends Claire $50,000 to repay the bank loan. The loan qualifies as a principal residence loan.

There is no formal guidance as to what level of proof is required before an employer can extend the five-year term.. The IRS indicated in "Retirement News for Employers" published on April 2, 2015 (available at *http://www.irs.gov/pub/irs-tege/rne_0415.pdf*) that if a participant requests a loan with a repayment period in excess of five years for the purpose of purchasing or constructing a primary residence, the plan sponsor must obtain documentation of the home purchase before the loan is approved. Allowing participants to self-certify their eligibility would not suffice.

Q 15:33 Does the level amortization requirement apply when a participant is on a leave of absence?

A plan may permit a participant to suspend loan payments under certain circumstances, during a leave of absence, including leave for military service (see Q 15:34). In those plans, the level amortization requirement does not apply for a period, not to exceed one year (or such longer period of time as may apply if leave is due to military service), that a participant is on a bona fide leave of absence. The leave of absence must be either without pay from the employer or at a rate of pay (after employment tax withholdings) that is less than the amount of the installment payments required under the terms of the loan. The loan, including interest that accrues during the leave of absence, must be repaid by the latest date permitted under the rules (i.e., the suspension cannot extend the term of the loan beyond five years, in the case of loan that is not a principal residence loan), and the amount of the installments must not be less than the amount required under the terms of the original loan. [Treas. Reg. § 1.72(p)-1, Q&A 9] By referencing the latest date under the rules, a plan can extend the term of the loan if the original term was less than the statutory maximum.

> **Example.** On July 1, 2011, Peter, who had a vested account balance of $80,000, borrowed $40,000 to be repaid in level monthly installments of $825 each over five years. The loan was not a principal residence plan loan. Peter makes 9 monthly payments and commences an unpaid leave of absence that lasts for 12 months. He does not perform military service during the leave. Thereafter, he resumes active employment and resumes making repayments on the loan until the loan is repaid in full (including interest that accrued during the leave of absence). The amount of each monthly installment is increased to $1,130 in order to repay the loan by June 30, 2016. There is no violation of the level amortization requirement. Alternatively, Peter could continue the monthly installments of $825 after resuming active employment and, on June 30, 2016, repay the full balance remaining due.

Q 15:34 What special loan rules apply when a participant's leave is for military service?

A plan may permit a participant to suspend loan repayments during a leave of absence for military service (as defined in Chapter 43 of Title 38, United States Code). When repayments are suspended, the level amortization requirement will not be violated even if the suspension exceeds one year and even if the term of the loan is extended beyond the statutory maximum. Loan repayments must resume upon completion of military service, the frequency and amount of periodic installments may not be less than what was required under the terms of the original loan, and the loan must be repaid in full (including interest that accrues during the period of military service) by the latest date permitted under the rules (i.e., five years, assuming the loan is not a principal residence loan, plus the period of such military service). [Treas. Reg. § 1.72(p)-1, Q&A 9(b)]

> **Example.** On July 1, 2009, Jim, who has a vested account balance of $80,000, borrowed $40,000 to be repaid in level monthly installments of $825 over five years. The loan is not a principal residence loan. Jim goes on military leave for two years. After his military service ends on April 2, 2012, Jim resumes active employment on April 19, 2012, continues the monthly installments of $825 thereafter, and, on June 30, 2016, repays the full balance remaining due. There is no violation of the level amortization rule. Alternatively, the amount of each monthly installment after April 19, 2012, is increased to $930 in order to repay the loan by June 30, 2016 (without any balance remaining due then).

Under the Servicemembers Civil Relief Act of 2003 (SCRA) [Pub. L. No. 108-189], a maximum rate of 6 percent interest may be charged on a loan during a period of military service. The SCRA replaced the Soldiers' and Sailors' Civil Relief Act of 1940 and provides expanded guidance in the area of loans to the military. A loan is subject to the interest rate limitation if

- The loan was incurred prior to the military service, and
- The participant provides to the plan a written notice and a copy of the military orders not later than 180 days after the date of the participant's release or termination from military service.

Upon receipt of the written notice and orders, the plan shall limit the interest rate to 6 percent, effective as of the date the participant was called to military service. Interest in excess of the 6 percent must be forgiven. Under the SCRA, interest includes service charges, renewal charges, fees, and any other charges (except bona fide insurance). [50 U.S.C. App. § 527]

If loan repayments are suspended during military leave, the plan must make an appropriate interest adjustment to the beginning of the military service. If, at the time notice is given, payments at a higher rate have already been made during the participant's period of service, the plan must make an appropriate adjustment (such as considering any excess payments as a prepayment of future interest).

Q 15:35 Is there any limit on the number of loans that a plan can make to a participant in one year?

No. Under proposed regulations issued on July 31, 2000, a loan would have been treated as a taxable distribution if a plan previously made two or more loans to the participant during the year. This restriction was not included in the final regulations that, in effect, eliminate a barrier to credit card loans that otherwise meet the loan rules.

Q 15:36 May a participant refinance (replace with another loan) an outstanding loan?

Yes. However, under the final regulations, if a loan is replaced by a loan, and the term of the replacement loan ends after the latest permissible term of the replaced loan (i.e., five years, assuming that the replaced loan is not a principal residence loan, and that no additional period of suspension due to military service applied under the replaced loan), both the replacement loan and replaced loan are treated as outstanding on the date of the transaction. The term of the replaced loan is determined under the terms of that loan in effect immediately prior to the making of the replacement loan. So, for example, the replacement loan results in a deemed distribution if the sum of the amount of the replacement loan plus the outstanding balance of all other loans on the date of the transaction, including the replaced loan, exceeds the dollar limitation (see Q 15:15).

The above restriction will not apply if the replacement loan is structured to satisfy the loan rules as two separate loans, the replaced loan (amortized in substantially level payments over a period ending not later than the last day of the latest permissible term of the replaced loan) and a new loan based on the difference between the amount of the replacement loan and the amount of the replaced loan (also amortized in substantially level payments over a period ending not later than the last day of the latest permissible term of the replaced loan). [Treas. Reg. § 1.72(p)-1, Q&A 20]

Example. Dana's vested account balance exceeded $100,000. She borrowed $40,000 from the plan on January 1, 2011, to be repaid in 20 quarterly installments of $2,491 each. The term of the loan ends on December 31, 2015. On January 1, 2012, when the outstanding balance on the loan was $33,322, the loan was refinanced and replaced by a new $40,000 loan from the plan to be repaid in 20 quarterly installments. Under the terms of the refinanced loan, the loan was to be repaid in level quarterly installments (of $2,491 each) over the next 20 quarters. The term of the new loan ended on December 31, 2016.

The amount of the new loan, when added to the outstanding balance of all other loans from the plan, was not to exceed $50,000 reduced by the excess of the highest outstanding balance of loans from the plan during the one-year period ending on December 31, 2011, over the outstanding balance of loans from the plan on January 1, 2012, with such outstanding balance to be determined immediately prior to the new $40,000 loan. Because the term of the new loan ended later than the term of the loan it replaced, both the new loan and the loan it replaced had to be taken into account for purposes of applying the dollar limitation. The amount of the new loan is $40,000, the outstanding balance on January 1, 2012, of the loan it replaced was $33,322, and the highest outstanding balance of loans from the plan during 2011 was $40,000. Accordingly, the sum of the new loan and the outstanding balance on January 1, 2012, of the loan it replaced must not exceed $50,000 reduced by $6,678 (the excess of the $40,000 maximum outstanding loan balance during 2011 over the $33,322 outstanding balance on January 1, 2012, determined immediately prior to the new loan) and thus must not exceed $43,322. The sum of the new loan ($40,000) and the outstanding balance on January 1, 2012, of the loan it replaced ($33,322) was $73,322. Since $73,322 exceeds the $43,322 limit by $30,000, there was a deemed distribution of $30,000 on January 1, 2012.

However, no deemed distribution would have occurred if, under the terms of the refinanced loan, the amount of the first 16 installments on the refinanced loan was equal to $2,907, which is the sum of the $2,491 originally scheduled quarterly installment payment amount under the first loan, plus $416 (which is the amount required to repay, in level quarterly installments over five years beginning on January 1, 2012, the excess of the refinanced loan over the January 1, 2012, balance of the first loan—$40,000 minus $33,322 equals $6,678), and the amount of the four remaining installments was equal to $416. The refinancing would not have resulted in a deemed distribution because the new loan is determined to consist of two loans, one of which is in the amount of the first loan ($33,322) and is amortized in substantially level payments over a period ending December 31, 2015 (the last day of the term of the first loan), and the other of which is in the additional amount ($6,678) borrowed under the new loan. Similarly, the loan also would not have resulted in a deemed distribution if the terms of the refinanced loan provided for repayments to be made in level quarterly installments (of $2,990 each) over the next 16 quarters.

Q 15:37 If a participant who has filed bankruptcy has an outstanding loan in the plan, what happens to the loan?

The Bankruptcy Code generally prohibits creditors from attempting to collect any payment from a debtor once the bankruptcy has been filed. [Bankruptcy Code § 362] A plan administrator may be required to cease all efforts at collecting the plan loan while a bankruptcy is pending.

On April 20, 2005, Congress enacted the Bankruptcy Abuse Prevention and Consumer Protection Act of 2005. [Pub. L. No. 109-8, 119 Stat. 23] Among other things, this law clarified that participant loans in a 401(k) plan are not discharged in bankruptcy, and ongoing loan repayments by payroll deduction are permitted to avoid a loan default and resulting taxation. The rules under the Bankruptcy Abuse Prevention and Consumer Protection Act of 2005 apply to participants who file for bankruptcy on or after October 17, 2005.

The rules concerning the taxability of participant loans continue to apply in bankruptcy. That is, if a required payment is not made by the end of the cure period, if any (see Q 15:19), the entire principal and interest will be deemed distributed for tax purposes.

Q 15:38 Are participant loans subject to federal truth-in-lending disclosure rules?

Effective July 1, 2010, a 401(k) plan is not required to comply with the truth-in-lending disclosure requirements, provided the loans are made from fully vested funds in the participant accounts and the loans comply with the requirements under the Internal Revenue Code. [12 C.F.R. § 226.3(g)] Prior to that date, the disclosure requirements applied to a plan that made 25 or more plan loans in the current or prior calendar year (or 5 or more loans secured by a dwelling).

Q 15:39 Is interest paid on a participant loan deductible?

Generally, no. Interest paid on a participant loan is generally not deductible. If the loan is secured by the participant's principal residence, the interest may be deductible if the participant is not a key employee (see chapter 14). [I.R.C. § 72(p)(3)] Because securing a loan with real property is complicated, few plans offer this option.

Q 15:40 Can fees incurred to set up and administer a participant loan be charged to that participant's account?

Yes, as long as the fee is reasonable and permitted under the terms of the plan document. (See chapter 4 for more information on fees.)

Q 15:41 Is spousal consent needed to make a participant loan?

If the plan is subject to spousal annuity requirements (see chapter 17), the employee's spouse must give written consent to any loan secured by the employee's account balance. This rule does not apply if the total account balance serving as security for the loan does not exceed $5,000. If consent is required, it must be given a specified number of days before the date the loan is made. [Treas. Reg. § 1.401(a)-20, Q&A 24(a)(1)]

IRS regulations extend the availability of electronic media to the consent rules applicable to plans subject to the survivor annuity requirements, provided:

1. The signature is witnessed in the physical presence of the plan representative or notary public;
2. An electronic notarization acknowledging a signature is in accordance with federal and state law applicable to notary publics; and
3. The electronic system has the same safeguards for participant elections as are provided through physical requirements.

[Treas. Reg. § 1.401(a)-21(d)(6)]

Example. Company A's qualified money purchase pension plan permits a married participant to request a plan loan through the company Web site with the notarized consent of the spouse. Under the plan's system for requesting a plan loan, a participant must enter his or her account number, PIN, and his or her e-mail address. The information entered by the participant must match the information in the plan's records in order for the transaction to proceed. Lisa, a married plan participant, is effectively able to access the Web site available to apply for a plan loan. The plan requires the participant applying for a loan to enter his or her account number and PIN in order to prevent any person other than the participant from making the election. Lisa completes the loan application on the plan's Web site.

Within a reasonable period of time after submitting the plan loan application, the plan administrator sends Lisa an e-mail containing the loan application, including all attachments, setting forth the terms of the loan agreement and all other required information. In the e-mail, the plan administrator also notifies Lisa that, upon request, the loan application may be provided to her as a written paper document at no charge. The plan administrator instructs Lisa that, in order for the loan application to proceed, she must submit to the plan administrator a notarized spousal consent form. Lisa and her husband, Peter, go to a notary public and the notary witnesses Peter signing the spousal consent for the loan agreement on an electronic signature capture pad with adequate security.

After witnessing Peter signing the spousal consent, the notary public sends an e-mail with an electronic acknowledgment that is attached to or logically associated with Peter's signature to the plan administrator. The electronic acknowledgment is in accordance with Section 101(g) of the Electronic Signatures in Global and National Commerce Act (E-SIGN) [Pub. L. No. 106-229, 114 Stat. 464 (2000)] and the relevant state law applicable to notary publics.

After the plan receives the e-mail, the plan administrator sends an e-mail to Lisa giving her a reasonable period to review and confirm the completed loan application and to determine whether the loan application should be modified or rescinded. In addition, the e-mail also provides that Lisa may request the completed loan application as a written paper document and that, if she requests the written paper document, it will be provided at no charge. The plan retains an electronic copy of the loan agreement, including the spousal consent, in a form that is capable of being retained and accurately reproduced for later reference by all parties.

By requiring that the spousal consent be signed on an electronic signature capture pad in the physical presence of a notary public, according to the IRS, the electronic system satisfies the requirement that the system be reasonably designed to preclude any person other than the appropriate individual from making the election and provides the necessary safeguards.

See chapter 19 for further information on satisfying notice and consent requirements using electronic media.

Q 15:42 Can an employer eliminate or change its loan program?

The features of an employer's loan program are not protected optional forms of benefits subject to the anti-cutback rules of Code Section 411(d)(6). [Treas. Reg. § 1.411(d)-4, Q&As 1(d)(4), 2(b)(2)(vii)] The features of a loan program are subject to the rule prohibiting discrimination in favor of HCEs. Therefore, a plan can freely change or eliminate its loan program as long as the changes do not cause the features of the loan program to become less available to non-highly compensated employees (NHCEs).

Q 15:43 When must an employer remit participant loan repayments to the plan?

Similar to salary deferral contributions, according to the DOL, participant loan repayments made to the employer or withheld by the employer from wages become plan assets (and must be transmitted to the plan) as of the earliest date such repayments can reasonably be segregated from the employer's general assets—but no later than 15 business days after the end of the month in which the contributions are received by the employer or would have been paid to the employee in cash if not withheld from wages (see chapter 5). According to the DOL, the holding of participant loan repayments beyond such maximum period would raise serious questions as to whether the employer forwarded the repayments to the plan as soon as they could reasonably be segregated from its general assets. [DOL Reg. § 2510.3-102(a)(1); DOL Adv. Op. 2002-02A] See chapter 5 for information on the safe harbor standard for small plans.

Hardship Withdrawals of Elective Contributions

Participants in a 401(k) plan may be permitted to withdraw their elective deferral contributions because of hardship without otherwise becoming eligible for a distribution from the plan (see Q 15:60). Hardship withdrawals are an optional plan feature.

Many sponsors choose to include this feature in their plans because of a belief that it encourages higher levels of participation by lower-paid employees, which will help the plan pass the actual deferral percentage (ADP) test (see chapter 13).

An FAQ on hardship distributions is available on the IRS Web site at *www.irs.gov/retirement/article/0,,id = 162416,00.html.*

Q 15:44 When is a distribution of elective contributions considered made on account of a hardship?

A distribution is considered made on account of a hardship if it is made in response to an immediate and heavy financial need (the *events test*), and it is necessary to satisfy that need (the *needs test*). [Treas. Reg. § 1.401(k)-1(d)(3)] The regulation provides two different standards for determining whether these tests are satisfied: the *general standard* (also called the facts-and-circumstances standard) and the *safe harbor standard.* It is not necessary to use the same standard to determine whether both tests are satisfied.

Plan administrators should obtain and file documentation supporting the type and amount of each hardship distribution (see Q 15:51). [I.R.C. § 6001] See Q 15:55 for information on hardship distributions from employer accounts.

The Events Test

Q 15:45 How is the general standard applied to the events test?

The regulation's guidance on this question is limited to a direction that all relevant facts and circumstances be considered. The regulations do point out that whether a need can be foreseen or the fact that it is voluntarily incurred is generally not relevant. [Treas. Reg. § 1.401(k)-1(d)(3)(iii)(A)]

Q 15:46 How is the safe harbor standard applied to the events test?

The events test is deemed satisfied if a distribution is made for any of the following reasons:

1. Payment of medical care expenses that would be deductible under Code Section 213(d) without regard to whether expenses exceed 7.5 percent of the participant's adjusted gross income;
2. Costs related to the purchase of a participant's principal residence (not including mortgage payments);
3. Payment of tuition, related educational fees, and room and board expenses for the next 12 months of post-secondary education for the participant or the participant's spouse, children, or dependents;
4. Payments necessary to prevent eviction from or foreclosure on a mortgage on the participant's principal residence;
5. Payments for burial or funeral expenses for the participant's deceased parent, spouse, children, or dependents; and
6. Expenses for repairing damages to the participant's principal residence that would qualify for a casualty deduction under Code Section 165 without regard to whether the loss exceeds 10 percent of the participant's adjusted gross income.

[Treas. Reg. § 1.401(k)-1(d)(3)(iii)(B)]

The fifth and sixth events are effective for plan years beginning on or after January 1, 2006. Beginning August 17, 2006, a plan may also permit distributions for expenses described in items 1, 3, and 5 above (relating to medical, tuition, and funeral expenses, respectively) for a "primary beneficiary under the plan." A *primary beneficiary under the plan* is the individual who is named as a beneficiary under the plan and has an unconditional right to all or a portion of the participant's account balance under the plan upon the death of the participant. A plan is permitted but not required to adopt these expanded hardship provisions. If a plan adopts these provisions, it must still satisfy all the other requirements applicable to hardship distribution, such as the requirement that the distribution be necessary to satisfy the financial need. [PPA § 826; Notice 2007-7, 2007-5 I.R.B. 395]

See chapter 3 for information on when plans must be amended for the PPA provisions.

The Needs Test

Q 15:47 How is the general standard applied to the needs test?

The needs test is satisfied if, based on all the facts and circumstances, a distribution is needed to relieve the participant's financial need. In determining whether that need exists, the plan is required to consider whether the need can be relieved through other resources reasonably available to the employee. This determination, however, would require intruding into the personal financial circumstances of employees. As a result, the regulations offer an escape hatch. Under the regulations, the needs test is deemed satisfied if the employer, in the absence of actual knowledge to the contrary, relies on the participant's written statement that his or her financial need cannot be satisfied through any of the following:

1. Reimbursement or compensation by insurance or otherwise;
2. Liquidation of the participant's assets;
3. Ceasing contributions under the plan;
4. Other distributions or nontaxable loans from plans maintained by the employer or any other employer; or
5. Borrowing from commercial sources on reasonable commercial terms.

None of the actions listed above will be deemed necessary if the effect would be to increase the amount of the need.

[Treas. Reg. § 1.401(k)-1(d)(3)(iv)(B), (C), and (D)]

Q 15:48 How is the safe harbor standard applied to the needs test?

The needs test is deemed satisfied if the following requirements are met:

1. The participant has obtained all distributions (other than hardship distributions) and all nontaxable loans from all plans maintained by the employer; and
2. The participant does not make elective contributions and employee contributions to the plan and all other plans maintained by the employer (see Q 15:49) for at least six months after the hardship distribution is received.

[Treas. Reg. § 1.401(k)-1(d)(3)(iv)(E)]

Q 15:49 What is meant by the phrase *all other plans maintained by the employer*?

All other plans maintained by the employer means all qualified and nonqualified plans of deferred compensation including stock option, stock purchase or similar plans, or a cash or deferred arrangement that is part of a Section 125 cafeteria plan. However, the phrase does not include defined benefit plans or health and welfare benefit plans to which participants make mandatory contributions. [Treas. Reg. § 1.401(k)-1(d)(3)(iv)(F)]

Safe Harbor Standard Versus General Standard

Q 15:50 What is the best standard to use, and can the standards be combined?

Each plan sponsor must reach its own conclusion as to what standard will work best. The advantage to using the safe harbor standard rather than the general standard is that the employer avoids needing to dig into a participant's personal financial situation. The disadvantage is that it is less flexible in terms of when hardship distributions will be available, making the feature somewhat restrictive. Some employers may feel that the inability to make salary deferral contributions for six months following a hardship withdrawal under the safe harbor rules is a deterrent to using the safe harbor method (see Q 15:48).

It is possible to use a combination of the safe harbor and the general facts-and-circumstances standards. It is also possible for an employer to use the safe harbor standard for one part of the test (e.g., the circumstances creating a financial need) and the general facts-and-circumstances standard for the other part of the test. For example, an employer may specify the circumstances creating a financial need and include all the safe harbor events but also include additional events. If an employer uses this combined method, it will not have to review independently requests for hardship withdrawals where the event is one of the six contained in the safe harbor rules. However, for additional events that do not fall within the safe harbor rules, it will have to do an independent review under the general facts-and-circumstances test.

Plan Sponsor Documentation

Q 15:51 What documentation should a plan sponsor retain when allowing a hardship withdrawal?

As indicated in the IRS's publication "Retirement News for Employers" published April 2, 2015 (available at *http://www.irs.gov/pub/irs-tege/rne_0415.pdf*), a plan sponsor must retain the following records, in paper or electronic format, for a hardship withdrawal:

1. Documentation of the hardship request, review, and approval;
2. Financial information and documentation that substantiates the employee's immediate and heavy financial need;
3. Documentation to support that the hardship distribution was properly made in accordance with the applicable plan provisions and the Internal Revenue Code; and
4. Proof of the actual distribution made and related Forms 1099-R.

Self-certification is allowed to show that a withdrawal was the only way to alleviate a hardship (i.e., need), but is not allowed to show the nature of a hardship (i.e., event). A plan sponsor must request and retain additional documentation to show the nature of the hardship.

Tax Consequences

Q 15:52 What tax consequences apply to hardship withdrawals of elective contributions?

Hardship distributions are subject to ordinary income tax and to the 10 percent additional income tax on distributions prior to age $59\frac{1}{2}$. For this reason, it is often more advantageous for a participant to access his or her account through a plan loan rather than a hardship withdrawal.

Any distribution on account of hardship—whether it consists of elective contributions and/or employer contributions—is not subject to the 20 percent withholding and direct rollover rules (and thus cannot be rolled over in an IRA or other qualified plan). [I.R.C. § 402(c)(4)(C)] Distributees can elect out of the 10 percent withholding that applies to taxable distributions not eligible for rollover. (See chapter 16.)

See Q 15:56 for special rules applicable to hardship withdrawals from Roth accounts.

Q 15:53 May a plan take into account federal, state, or local income taxes and penalties that may be payable as a result of a hardship withdrawal?

Yes. Income taxes and penalties may be taken into account for the purpose of determining whether the needs test is satisfied. [Treas. Reg. § 1.401(k)-1(d)(3)(iv)]

Other Withdrawal Issues

Q 15:54 Is there a limit on the amount of a hardship withdrawal?

Yes. A hardship distribution cannot exceed the participant's withdrawal basis, which is the participant's total elective contributions as of the date of withdrawal reduced by the amount of previous distributions of elective contributions. The maximum distributable amount does not include earnings, QNECs, or QMACs. If the plan so provides, a participant's withdrawal basis may be increased by the amount of income attributable to elective contributions, the amount of qualified matching contributions (QMACs) and qualified nonelective contributions (QNECs), and the amount of income attributable to such QMACs and QNECs. These amounts include only those credited to a participant's account during any plan year ending before July 1, 1989. [Treas. Reg. § 1.401(k)-1(d)(3)(ii)(B)]

Safe harbor contributions (including those in a qualified contribution arrangement (QACA)) are not available for a hardship withdrawal (see chapter 2). See Q 15:55 for information on hardship withdrawals of other employer contributions. See Q 15:56 for special rules applicable to hardship withdrawals from Roth accounts.

Q 15:55 Can distributions from employer contribution accounts be made on account of hardship?

Yes. Although not specified in the regulations, the IRS has allowed a plan provision permitting withdrawal of amounts attributable to employer contributions on account of hardship. According to the IRS, the term *hardship* must be defined, the rules relating to hardship distributions must be uniformly and consistently applied, and the portion distributed cannot exceed the participant's vested account. [Rev. Rul. 71-224, 1971-1 C.B. 124] This revenue ruling would not apply to a 401(k) plan that is part of a pre-ERISA money purchase plan.

See Q 15:54 for special rules applicable to QNECs, QMACs, and safe harbor contributions.

Q 15:56 What special rules apply to hardship withdrawals from Roth elective deferral accounts?

Roth elective deferral accounts are subject to the same distribution restrictions, including those applicable to distributions on account of hardship, as pre-tax elective deferral accounts (see Q 15:60). The maximum amount available for a hardship distribution is the participant's total elective contributions (after-tax and pre-tax) minus the amount of previous distributions of elective contributions. Earnings on elective contributions are not available for a hardship withdrawal.

Unless the plan document restricts hardship withdrawals to non-Roth accounts, a participant can be given the option to take a hardship withdrawal from his or her Roth account. IRS regulations provide additional guidance in the event a participant chooses to take a hardship withdrawal from his or her Roth accounts:

1. Although earnings on Roth contributions are not available for hardship, a pro rata portion of a hardship withdrawal taken from a Roth account must be treated as earnings for tax purposes. [Treas. Reg. § 1.402A-1, Q&As 7 & 8] If not a qualified Roth distribution (see chapter 18), the amount allocable to earnings will be includable in income and subject to the 10 percent penalty tax on premature distributions (see chapter 18). A separate Form 1099-R is required for reporting amounts distributed from a Roth account including the taxable portion of such a distribution.
2. When a participant applies for a future hardship withdrawal from a Roth account, both earnings and Roth contributions will be used to limit the maximum amount available for a hardship withdrawal. [Treas. Reg. § 1.402A-1, Q&A 8]

Example 1. Jane, age 45, has contributed to both a pre-tax account and a Roth account, and Jane's plan allows her to elect a certain account or accounts for hardship withdrawals.

Jane's Accounts

	Contributions	*Earnings*	*Total*
Roth	$ 9,000	$1,000	$10,000
Pre-tax	$17,000	$3,000	$20,000
Total	$26,000	$4,000	$30,000

Assume Jane elects a hardship withdrawal of $5,000 from her Roth account. The taxable portion is the amount allocable to earnings or 10 percent ($1,000 ÷ $10,000). Thus $500 (1/10) is includable in income and subject to the 10 percent premature distribution penalty under Code Section 72(t). The amount available for future hardship withdrawals is $21,000 ($26,000 – $5,000).

Example 2. The facts are the same as those in Example 1, except that Jane elects a hardship withdrawal of $5,000 from her non-Roth, pre-tax account. The amount includable in income and subject to the 10 percent premature distribution penalty is $5,000. The amount available for future hardship withdrawals is $21,000 ($26,000 – $5,000).

Example 3. The facts are the same as those in Example 1, except that Jane takes a hardship withdrawal of $10,000, of which $5,000 is from her Roth account and $5,000 is from her non-Roth, pre-tax account. The amount includable in income and subject to the 10 percent premature distribution penalty is $5,500 ($500 allocable to the Roth account, and $5,000 allocable to the non-Roth account). The amount available for future hardship withdrawals is $16,000 ($26,000 – $10,000).

See chapters 2, 16, and 18 for additional information on Roth 401(k) plans.

In-Service Distributions

Q 15:57 In general, when may 401(k) accounts be distributed?

A 401(k) plan is subject to rules that restrict a participant's access to his or her 401(k) plan accounts. All 401(k) plans may provide that a participant's accounts may be distributed upon death, disability, or severance from employment. [Treas. Reg. § 1.401(k)-1(d)] Whether accounts are accessible in other situations depends on the type of contribution used to fund a particular account. In general, accounts attributable to elective contributions (including Roth contributions) and safe harbor contributions are, under the law, less accessible to participants than accounts funded with other types of employer contributions.

See chapter 2 for information on safe harbor plans.

Q 15:58 Under what circumstances other than death, disability, or severance from employment may employer contribution accounts be distributed?

According to the regulations, employer contribution accounts may be distributed after a fixed number of years, the attainment of a stated age, or upon the occurrence of some event such as layoff, illness, disability, retirement, death, or severance from employment. [Treas. Reg. § 1.401-1(b)(1)(ii)] These regulations apply to a 401(k) plan that is part of a profit sharing or stock bonus plan. A 401(k) plan that is part of a pre-ERISA money purchase plan may not allow distributions under these circumstances.

See Qs 15:54–15:55 and 15:61 for information on hardship withdrawals of employer contributions and special rules applicable to QNECs, QMACs, and safe harbor contributions.

Q 15:59 What is considered a *fixed number of years*?

The IRS believes that contributions must be held in a plan for two years before they can be considered held for a fixed number of years. [Rev. Rul. 71-295, 1971-2 C.B. 184] According to the IRS, this two-year period runs from the date contributions are actually made and not from the date as of which they are deemed made under Code Section 404(a)(6).

> **Example.** ABC Company maintains a 401(k) plan administered on a calendar-year basis. ABC makes a nonelective contribution on March 1, 2014, which is deemed made and allocated as of December 31, 2013, under Code Section 404(a)(6). Under the plan, participants are allowed on January 10, 2015, to withdraw employer contributions allocated to them on December 31, 2013. According to the IRS, the plan provision violates the two-year rule because the contributions are withdrawn less than two years after they are actually made.

The IRS has indicated that the two-year rule can be disregarded if there has been a significant deferral of compensation. In a revenue ruling, the IRS permitted the withdrawal of all funds (even contributions made within two years of the withdrawal) where the right to withdraw was extended only to employees who had been participants for 60 months. [Rev. Rul. 68-24, 1968-1 C.B. 150]

The above-referenced IRS guidelines are collectively referred to as the two-year/five-year rule.

Q 15:60 Under what circumstances may amounts attributable to elective contributions be distributed?

Amounts attributable to elective contributions (including Roth contributions) may be distributed under the following circumstances:

1. Death, disability, or severance from employment;
2. Attainment of age 59½ (profit sharing or stock bonus plan only);
3. Hardship as discussed in Qs 15:44–15:56 (profit sharing or stock bonus plan only); or
4. Termination of the plan (see chapter 21).

[Treas. Reg. § 1.401(k)-1(d)(1)]

A severance from employment occurs when a participant ceases to be employed by the employer that maintains the plans. An employee does not have a severance from employment if, in connection with a change of employment, the employee's new employer maintains the plan by continuing or assuming sponsorship of the plan or by accepting a transfer of plan assets and liabilities with respect to the employee. [Treas. Reg. § 1.401(k)-1(d)(2)]

Special rules apply to elective contributions distributed within a specified time frame under certain automatic enrollment plan designs (permissible withdrawals under an eligible automatic contribution arrangement (EACA)) (see chapter 2).

See chapter 16 for discussion of qualified reservist distributions (QRDs)—distribution rights that may be available to reservists called to active duty.

From time to time, the IRS sets forth special rules regarding the availability and tax treatment of distributions and loans to individuals affected by disasters such as hurricanes or floods (see Q 15:62).

Q 15:61 Do the rules that restrict the accessibility of elective contributions apply to other types of contributions made under a 401(k) plan?

Yes. QNECs and QMACs (see chapter 13) and safe harbor contributions (see chapter 2) are subject to the same withdrawal restrictions as elective contributions. Therefore, in-service withdrawals of these contributions are only allowed on or after age 59½. In-service withdrawals on account of hardship, however, are not permitted (see Q 15:54 for limited exception applicable to QNECs and QMACs).

Hurricane Sandy Relief

Q 15:62 What relief was made available to victims of Hurricane Sandy with regard to retirement plan loans and distributions?

A 401(k) plan sponsor was permitted to make a loan or hardship distribution on or after October 26, 2012 through February 1, 2013, to a participant for a need arising from Hurricane Sandy. A plan that does not provide for loans or hardship distributions must be amended to provide for them, as applicable, no later than the end of the first plan year beginning after December 31, 2012.

The amount available for a hardship distribution was limited to the maximum amount that would have been permitted to be available for a hardship distribution under the plan and applicable regulations. The special relief applied to any hardship of the employee, not just the types enumerated in the regulations, and no post-distribution contribution restrictions were required. For example, the safe harbor hardship distribution standards are met only for certain enumerated events, and after receipt of the hardship amount, the participant is prohibited from making contributions for at least six months. Plans need not follow these rules with respect to hardship distributions under this relief. The hardship distribution must have been made on account of a hardship resulting from Hurricane Sandy.

A plan will not be treated as failing to follow procedural requirements for loans or hardship distributions if the plan administrator made a good-faith diligent effort under the circumstances to comply with those requirements. However, as soon as practicable, the plan administrator must make a reasonable attempt to assemble any forgone documentation. [IRS Ann. 2012-44]

Hurricane Sandy FAQs are available on the IRS Web site at *www.irs.gov/Retirement-Plans/Hurricane-Sandy-Relief-FAQs-Retirement- Plan-Loans-&-Distributions*. Information available on the site includes locations that qualified for relief and taxation rules.

Chapter 16

Distributions Subsequent to Termination of Employment

A 401(k) plan participant who terminates employment with a vested account balance wants the answers to three questions: (1) When can I receive my benefits? (2) How will those benefits be paid to me? (3) Can tax deferral be maintained? The answers to the first two questions depend upon what optional forms of benefit are available under the plan. In large part, what is available is decided by the employer at the time the plan is established. The employer's decisions, however, must be made within a legal framework that places limits on the employer's ability to dictate when and how benefits will be paid. The answer to the third question depends on the rules relating to the rollover of 401(k) plan distributions to employer retirement plans and to individual retirement accounts. Although this chapter concentrates on distributions subsequent to termination of employment, it also points out cases where the distribution rules have special significance for hardship withdrawals. (For additional information on hardship withdrawals and other in-service distributions, see chapter 15.)

Optional Forms of Benefit 16-2
Anti-Cutback Rules 16-3
Postponement of Benefits 16-6
Involuntary Distributions 16-11
Qualified Reservist Distributions 16-12
Minimum Distribution Requirements 16-13
Required Beginning Date 16-13
Payment Options 16-17
Table 16-1. Divisor Amounts for Determining the Amount To Be Paid Each Calendar Year 16-18
Participants Called to Active Military Duty 16-21
Rollover Rules 16-22
Eligible Rollover Distribution 16-23
Direct Rollover Option 16-26
Automatic Rollover Rules 16-27

Rollover of Distributions 16-31
Direct Rollover Election 16-32
Direct Rollover Procedures 16-33
Rollovers to Inherited IRAs 16-35
Rollover Strategies 16-37
Withholding on Distributions 16-38
Loan Offset Amount 16-39
Other Special Distributions 16-40
Responsibility for Withholding 16-41
Distributions Not Eligible for Rollover 16-41
Periodic and Nonperiodic Distributions 16-42
Electing Out of Withholding 16-43
Withholding Procedures and Penalties 16-45
Claims for Benefits 16-46

Optional Forms of Benefit

Q 16:1 What is an *optional form of benefit*?

An *optional form of benefit* is a distribution alternative available under a plan. It includes any plan provision that affects the timing of a distribution, the payment schedule for a distribution, the medium of distribution (e.g., cash or in kind), any election rights related to distributions, and when distributions commence. [Treas. Reg. §§ 1.411(d)-3(g)(6)(ii), 1.411(d)-4, Q&A 1(b)(1)]

Example 1. The Video Rental Company has a 401(k) plan that permits employees, upon termination of employment, to receive distributions in the form of a lump sum, joint and survivor annuity, or installments. The payment of any vested account in excess of $10,000 is deferred until normal retirement age. In-service hardship withdrawals of elective contributions are permitted. Distribution can be made in the form of cash or employer stock. Each one of these distribution features is a separate optional form of benefit subject to the rules discussed in Q 16:3.

Example 2. ABC Company's plan requires the payment of benefits to Division A employees with vested accounts in excess of $10,000 to be deferred until normal retirement age. The payment of benefits to Division B employees, regardless of the value of the vested account, is to be deferred until normal retirement age. These are two separate optional forms of benefits, because they differ as to the portion of the benefit to which the option applies.

Q 16:2 What are not optional forms of benefit?

The following are examples of plan features that are not optional forms of benefit:

- Ancillary life insurance protection

- Accident or health insurance benefits
- The availability of loans
- The right to make elective deferrals or after-tax employee contributions
- The right to direct investments
- The right to a particular form of investment
- Contribution, valuation, and allocation dates
- Procedures for distributing benefits
- Rights that derive from administrative and operational provisions

[Treas. Reg. §§ 1.411(d)-3(b)(3)(i), 1.411(d)-4, Q&A 1(d)]

Q 16:3 What rules apply to optional forms of benefit?

The availability of optional forms of benefit cannot discriminate in favor of highly compensated employees [Treas. Reg. § 1.401(a)(4)-4] (see chapter 12) and cannot be subject to employer discretion. [Treas. Reg. § 1.411(d)-4, Q&A-4(a)] Also, but for the exceptions discussed in Q 16:7, optional forms of benefit cannot be reduced or eliminated with respect to benefits that have already been accrued. [Treas. Reg. §§ 1.411(d)-3(b)(1)(i), 1.411(d)-4, Q&A 2(a)(1)]

Q 16:4 Does an employer have discretion over what optional forms of benefits will be made available to individual participants?

No. The availability of any optional form of benefit cannot be subject to employer discretion. For example, a plan cannot permit some participants to take an immediate lump-sum distribution while prohibiting others from doing so based on a subjective determination made by the employer. [Treas. Reg. § 1.411(d)-4, Q&A 4]

Q 16:5 Is employer discretion prohibited under all circumstances?

No. A plan can apply objective criteria as a condition for a distribution option and permit the employer the limited discretion of determining whether these criteria are met. [Treas. Reg. § 1.411(d)-4, Q&As 4(b), 6(a)] For example, a plan may permit distributions in the event of disability and let the plan administrator decide whether a participant is disabled based on a written definition of disability contained in the plan.

Anti-Cutback Rules

Q 16:6 Can optional forms of benefits be reduced or eliminated by plan amendment?

The general rule is that an employer cannot eliminate or reduce optional forms of benefits with respect to benefits that have already been accrued. [Treas. Reg. §§ 1.411(d)-3(b)(1)(i), 1.411(d)-4, Q&A 2(a)] For example, if an employer maintains a plan that permits immediate lump-sum distributions and wants to amend the plan to require deferral of any lump-sum distributions until normal retirement age, the employer will not be able to apply the deferral provision to any benefits that had accrued while the older, more liberal plan provision was in place. The deferral provision can apply only to benefits that accrue after the later of the date the amendment is adopted or the date it becomes effective. This is known as the anti-cutback rule. [Treas. Reg. § 1.411(d)-4, Q&A 2(a)(1)]

Q 16:7 Are there any exceptions to the anti-cutback rule?

Yes. The regulations include a number of exceptions to the anti-cutback rule. A plan may add or delete a provision requiring the cash-out of vested benefits with a present value of $5,000 or less. [Treas. Reg. § 1.411(d)-4, Q&A 2(b)(2)(v)] A plan may also amend or eliminate its hardship distribution provisions without violating the anti-cutback rule. [Treas. Reg. § 1.411(d)-4, Q&A 2(b)(2)(x)] Perhaps the most significant exception allows a 401(k) plan sponsor to eliminate optional forms of benefit as long as the participant can receive his or her account balance as a single sum that is otherwise identical to the optional forms of benefit that have been eliminated. [Treas. Reg. § 1.411(d)-4, Q&A 2(e)]

> **Example 1.** Acme Corporation sponsors a 401(k) plan under which a participant's account balance will be paid immediately after termination of employment in the form of a lump sum, installments from the plan, or an annuity contract purchased from an insurance company. The plan is subject to the joint and survivor annuity rules under Internal Revenue Code (Code) Section 401(a)(11). Acme amends its 401(k) plan to eliminate the installment and annuity payout methods, including the joint and survivor annuity provisions. This amendment does not violate the anti-cutback rule.

> **Example 2.** The facts are the same as those in Example 1, except that a participant must wait until one year after termination to receive his or her account balance in the form of a lump sum, in contrast to the installment and annuity payout methods, which can be used immediately after termination of employment. An amendment eliminating the installment and annuity payout methods violates the anti-cutback rules because the lump-sum payout method is not otherwise identical to the payout methods being eliminated.

Q 16:8 May an employer amend a 401(k) plan to eliminate the right to receive an in-kind distribution of a participant's account balance?

Yes. A plan may be amended to eliminate the right to receive a participant's account balance in the form of marketable securities other than securities of the employer. A right to receive payment in the form of nonmarketable securities can be effectively eliminated if the plan amendment provides that the participant's right to receive nonmarketable securities is limited to those securities held by the plan at the time of the amendment and if, subsequent to the amendment, these securities are then sold or otherwise disposed of by the plan. [Treas. Reg. § 1.411(d)-4, Q&A 2(b)(2)(iii)]

Q 16:9 Can an employer avoid the anti-cutback rules through an employee waiver?

No. An employee cannot waive the protection afforded under the anti-cutback rules. [Treas. Reg. § 1.411(d)-4, Q&A 3(a)(3)]

Q 16:10 What should an employer consider when designing distribution features in a new plan?

An employer's main concern at the time a plan is established should be to avoid including distribution options or other protected features of a plan that it may want to eliminate later. For example, an employer may be concerned that once accounts in a plan build up to a substantial level, the immediate availability of those funds to a terminated participant would enable that participant to set up a competing business. Consequently, the employer may want to include a deferral provision at the time the plan is established, even though the concern is not an immediate one. A plan can always be amended to liberalize distribution options without running afoul of the anti-cutback rules. It is far more problematic to eliminate or reduce these options, as it will require the plan to have a dual tracking system that applies the more permissive features for benefits accrued prior to the date of the reduction and applies the more restrictive features to benefits accrued after the amendment becomes effective.

Example. ABC Company sponsors a 401(k) plan that allows a terminated participant to receive his or her account balance at any time after termination of employment. Because a number of employees have terminated employment simply because they wish to have access to their 401(k) accounts, ABC Company would like to amend the 401(k) plan to require a two-year deferral period before a participant's account balance can be paid out. Although such an amendment can be made, it can only apply to that portion of a participant's account balance attributable to contributions allocated after the later of the adoption or effective date of the amendment.

Q 16:11 What should an employer consider in the case of a plan merger or spin-off?

The anti-cutback rules cannot be avoided simply by transferring benefits to another plan in connection with a plan merger, spin-off, or other type of plan-to-plan transfer. For example, if a profit sharing plan that provides for an immediate, lump-sum payment option on termination of employment merges into a 401(k) plan, participants' rights to retain this optional form of benefit with respect to their profit sharing plan account balances cannot be eliminated. The rules concerning protected benefits in mergers and spin-offs, as well as ways to avoid a dual tracking system for transferred benefits, are discussed in chapter 21.

Q 16:12 Is there any type of plan-to-plan transfer that is not subject to the anti-cutback rules?

The law allows a participant who is not entitled to receive benefits under a 401(k) plan to voluntarily elect to transfer his or her account balance from the 401(k) plan to any other defined contribution plan. [I.R.C. § 411(d)(6)(D)] The regulations also permit a participant to voluntarily elect to transfer his or her account balance to another 401(k) plan if the transfer is made in connection with a change in the employer of the participant as a result of an asset or stock acquisition, merger, or similar transaction, or if it results from a participant's change in employment status that renders him or her no longer eligible to participate in the 401(k) plan. Under either elective transfer rule, the participant's account balance can be transferred without preserving the benefits that would otherwise be protected by the anti-cutback rules. [Treas. Reg. § 1.411(d)-4, Q&A 3(b)]

> **Example.** John, who is covered under a collective bargaining agreement, participates in a 401(k) plan that covers only union employees. He is transferred to a position that is not covered by the agreement. John, pursuant to the terms of the union 401(k) plan, elects to transfer his account balance to the non-union 401(k) plan maintained by the employer. Any protected benefits that are eliminated as a result of the transfer of his account balance to the non-union 401(k) plan will not violate the anti-cutback rules.

Postponement of Benefits

Q 16:13 How long may a 401(k) plan delay the payment of benefits to a participant?

A 401(k) plan may be designed to delay the payment of benefits until 60 days after the close of the plan year in which the latest of the following events occurs:

1. The participant's attainment of age 65 or, if earlier, the normal retirement age specified in the plan;
2. The tenth anniversary of the date an employee's participation in the plan commenced;
3. The participant's termination of service with the employer; or
4. If permitted in the plan, the date specified in an election by the participant.

[Treas. Reg. § 1.401(a)-14(a)]

Q 16:14 Does an early retirement provision in the 401(k) plan accelerate the payment of benefits?

Yes. If the plan provides for the payment of benefits upon satisfying the requirements for early retirement, a participant who terminates employment before satisfying the age requirement for early retirement, but after satisfying the service requirement, if any, must be allowed to begin receiving benefits at the time the participant satisfies the age requirement. [Treas. Reg. § 1.401(a)-14(c)]

Example. DEF Company maintains a 401(k) plan that permits participants to retire early and receive benefits at age 60 after completing 5 years of service. Joe terminates employment at age 40 after completing 15 years of service. The 401(k) plan must allow Joe to commence receiving benefits when he reaches age 60.

Q 16:15 What requirements must be met by a participant who is allowed to elect to delay the payment of benefits?

The election must be in writing, must be signed by the participant, and must describe when benefits will begin and in what form they will be paid. Any election must not violate the Section 401(a)(9) minimum distribution rules discussed in Qs 16:30–16:48. [Treas. Reg. § 1.401(a)-14(b)]

Q 16:16 Are there circumstances under which plan provisions delaying the payment of benefits are superseded?

Yes. The payment of benefits must commence by the required beginning date under the Section 401(a)(9) minimum distribution rules even if the required beginning date is earlier than the date determined under Q 16:13. Also, benefits cannot begin without the consent of the participant if the date determined under Q 16:13 occurs when benefits are considered immediately distributable under Code Section 411(a)(11) (see Q 16:24). [Treas. Reg. § 1.411(a)-11(c)]

Example. QRS Company sponsors a 401(k) plan that is administered on a calendar-year basis and that has a normal retirement age of 60. Jane retires in 2015 upon attaining age 60 and after having participated in the plan for more than ten years. Although Code Section 401(a)(14) requires the payment of benefits to commence by March 2, 2016, the participant consent rules in Code Section 411(a)(11) take precedence. Accordingly, benefits may not be paid to Jane on March 2, 2016, without her previous consent. Her consent would be required until she reaches age 62, when benefits are no longer considered immediately distributable under Code Section 411(a)(11).

Q 16:17 What conditions must be satisfied before a participant's consent is considered valid?

A participant's consent is not considered valid unless a participant receives the following:

1. A general description of the material features of the forms of benefit provided under the plan; and
2. A notice of his or her right to defer payment of benefits.
3. A description of the consequences of failing to defer receipt of a distribution.

[Treas. Reg. § 1.411(a)-11(c)(2)(i); Prop. Treas. Reg. § 1.411(a)-11(c)(2)(i)]

Q 16:18 What must be contained in the notice describing the consequences of failing to defer receipt of distribution?

The notice must describe the federal tax consequences of a failure to defer receipt. It must also contain a statement that currently available investment options may not generally be available on the same terms outside the plan and that the fees and expenses outside the plan may be different from the fees and expenses currently charged by the plan. [Prop. Treas. Reg. § 1.411(a)-11(c)(2)(vi)]

Q 16:19 When is the right-to-defer notice required to be given to a participant?

This notice must be provided no less than 30 days and no more than 180 days before the date on which benefits are to be paid. In the case of a 401(k) plan that is not subject to the Section 401(a)(11) joint and survivor rules, the 30-day requirement will be considered satisfied, even if benefits are paid less than 30 days after the notice is provided, as long as the notice makes clear that the participant has 30 days after the notice is provided to make a decision (see Q 16:90). [Treas. Reg. § 1.411(a)-11(c)(2)(iii)(A)] The immediately preceding sentence also applies to a 401(k) plan that is subject to the Section 401(a)(11) joint and survivor rules as long as benefits are not paid until 7 days after the date notice is given. [Treas. Reg. § 1.417(e)-1(b)(3)(ii)] A participant's consent must not be given before the participant receives the notice and must not be given more than 180 days before the date the distribution begins. [I.R.C. § 417(a)(6)(A)]

Q 16:20 Do the regulations offer an alternative to the right-to-defer notice requirement?

Yes. A 401(k) plan is allowed to provide the notice more than 180 days before the distribution begins if the 401(k) plan provides a summary notice within 180 days of the distribution. [Treas. Reg. § 1.411(a)-11(c)(2)(iii)(B)]

Q 16:21 What information must be included in a summary notice?

The summary notice must advise the participant of the right, if any, to defer receipt of the distribution and the consequences of failing to defer receipt; must set forth a summary of the distribution options under the plan; must refer the participant to the most recent occasion on which the full notice was provided (and, in the case of a full notice provided in any document containing information in addition to the full notice, must identify that document and must indicate where that notice may be found in that document); and must advise the participant that, upon request, a copy of the full notice will be provided without charge. [Treas. Reg. § 1.411(a)-11(c)(2)(iii)(B)(3); Prop. Treas. Reg. § 1.411(a)-11(c)(2)(iii)(B)(3)]

Q 16:22 What form must the right-to-defer notice take?

The notice may be provided either on a written paper document or through an electronic medium reasonably accessible to the participant. The information in the notice must be provided under an electronic system that satisfies the following requirements:

1. The electronic system must be reasonably designed to provide the information in the notice in a manner that is no less understandable to the participant than a written paper document.
2. The electronic system must be designed to alert the participant, at the time the notice is provided, of the significance of the information in the notice (including identification of the subject matter of the notice) and provide any instructions needed to access the notice in a manner that is readily understandable.

Unless consent is not required as explained below, the notice may be provided to a participant through an electronic medium only with the consent of the participant. The consent requirements will be satisfied if the following conditions are satisfied.

1. The participant must affirmatively consent to the delivery of the notice using an electronic medium. This consent may be made electronically in a manner that reasonably demonstrates that the participant has access to the notice in the electronic medium through which the notice will be provided. Alternatively, consent may be made using a paper document, but only if the participant confirms the consent electronically in a manner that reasonably demonstrates that the participant has access to the electronic medium through which the medium will be provided.
2. The participant must be provided with a clear and conspicuous statement that contains the following disclosures:
   a. The participant has the right to receive any notice in the form of a paper document, either before the notice is provided electronically or afterwards;
   b. The participant has the right to withdraw consent to receive electronic delivery of the notice in the future and to an explanation of how to withdraw consent and the conditions, consequences, and fees for doing so;
   c. Whether the consent to electronic delivery applies to a particular transaction or other identified transactions that may occur in the future;
   d. The procedures for updating the information needed to contact the participant electronically; and
   e. The hardware and software requirements needed to access and retain the notice.
3. If, after the participant provides consent to receive electronic delivery, there is a change in the hardware or software requirements and such change creates a material risk that the participant will not be able to

access or retain the notice, then the participant must receive a statement indicating the revised hardware or software requirements and setting forth the participant's right to withdraw consent to electronic delivery of notices. In addition, the participant must affirm, in accordance with item 1 above, his or her consent to electronic delivery.

The above consent requirements are not required to be satisfied if the electronic medium used to provide the notice is a medium that the participant has access to, and, at the time the notice is provided, the participant is advised that he or she may request a copy of the notice on a paper document at no charge. [Treas. Reg. § 1.401(a)-21(a), (b) & (c)]

Example 1. E-Mail Consent and Confirmation. Plan A, a qualified plan, permits participants to request benefit distributions from the plan on Plan A's Internet Web site. Under Plan A's system for distributions, a participant must enter his or her account number and personal identification number (PIN), and his or her e-mail address to which the notice is to be sent. The participant's PIN and account number must match the information in Plan A's records in order for the distribution to proceed. Tom, an employee who is single, requests a distribution from Plan A on Plan A's Internet Web site. The plan administrator provides Tom with the notice in an attachment to the e-mail. Plan A sends the e-mail with a request for a computer-generated notification that the message was received and opened. The e-mail instructs Tom to read the attachment for important information regarding the request for a distribution. In addition, the e-mail states that Tom may request the notice on a written paper document, and if he so requests the notice on a written paper document will be provided at no charge. Plan A receives notification that the e-mail was received and opened by Tom. Plan A's delivery of the notice satisfies the notice and consent requirements of Code Section 411(a)(11).

Example 2. Automated Phone System. A qualified plan (Plan C) permits participants to request distributions through its automated telephone system. Under Plan C's system for such transactions, a participant must enter his or her account number and PIN; this information must match that in Plan C's records in order for the transaction to proceed. Plan C provides only the following distribution options: a lump sum or annual installments over 5, 10, or 20 years. Shelley, a participant who is single, requests a distribution from Plan C by following the applicable instructions on the automated telephone system. After Shelley has requested a distribution, the automated telephone system reads the notice to her. The automated telephone system also advises Shelley that she may request the notice on a written paper document and that, if she so requests, the written paper document will be provided at no charge. Because Plan C's distribution options are relatively few and simple, the notice delivered through the automated telephone system is not less understandable to Shelley than a written paper notice and thus satisfies the notice and consent requirements of Code Section 411(a)(11).

Q 16:23 What are the requirements that must be met for a participant to consent electronically to a plan distribution?

For a participant to consent to a plan distribution through an electronic medium, the following requirements must be met:

1. The electronic medium through which consent to a distribution will be provided must be a medium the participant is effectively able to access.
2. The electronic medium used by the participant is reasonably designed to preclude any other person from providing consent.
3. The electronic system used by the participant provides him or her with a reasonable opportunity to review, confirm, modify, or rescind his or her election before it becomes effective.
4. The participant receives within a reasonable time a confirmation of the effect of his or her election through either a written paper document or an electronic medium.

[Treas. Reg. § 1.401(a)-21(d)]

> **Example.** Tom (the employee in Example 1 under Q 16:22) requests a benefit distribution from Plan A, receives the notice as an attachment to e-mail, and enters his account number and PIN to preclude another person from making the election. After Tom's identity has been authenticated, Tom completes a distribution form on Plan A's Web site. After the form is completed, the Web site provides a summary of the information entered on the form and gives Tom the opportunity to review and modify the information. Within a reasonable time after Tom provides his consent, the plan administrator, by e-mail, confirms the terms of the distribution to Tom and advises him that he may request that the confirmation be provided to him on a written paper document at no charge. Plan A retains an electronic copy of the consent form, which can be retained and accurately reproduced by Tom for later reference. Plan A's system for obtaining Tom's consent to the distribution through an electronic medium satisfies the notice and consent requirements of Code Section 411(a)(11).

See chapter 19 for further information on using electronic media for required notices and consents under the Internal Revenue Code.

Involuntary Distributions

Q 16:24 Under what circumstances may a 401(k) plan compel a participant to commence receiving benefits?

Under the law, a 401(k) plan may provide that a participant's vested account balance be paid immediately and in the form of a single sum if the vested account balance does not exceed $5,000. If the participant's vested account balance is greater than $5,000, a participant's consent is required for any distribution that is immediately distributable. In the case of a 401(k) plan subject to the joint and survivor annuity rules, participant consent is also required, even if the value of a participant's vested account balance no longer exceeds $5,000, as long as it exceeded $5,000 at the time distributions to the participant commenced. [Treas. Reg. § 1.417(e)-1(b)(2)(i)] A distribution is considered immediately distributable at any time before the later of the following dates:

1. The date on which the participant attains the plan's normal retirement age; or
2. The date on which the participant attains age 62.

[Treas. Reg. § 1.411(a)-11(c)(4)]

> **Example.** XYZ Company sponsors a 401(k) plan that has a normal retirement age of 65. Frank terminates employment when he is 55 years old. His vested account balance exceeds $5,000. Any distribution to Frank is considered immediately distributable until he reaches his normal retirement age of 65 (since this is later than age 62); consequently, Frank's consent is required if distribution is made before he reaches age 65.

In determining whether participant consent is required, a 401(k) plan can provide that the value of a participant's rollover account be ignored when determining whether the vested account balance is greater than $5,000. [I.R.C. §§ 411(a)(11)(D), 417(e)(1)]

Starting March 28, 2005, it has no longer been possible to cash out a participant whose vested account balance exceeds $1,000 but is not greater than $5,000. In the absence of a direction from the participant, the plan will be required to transfer the participant's account balance to an individual retirement plan (see Q 16:69).

Q 16:25 Is a beneficiary's consent required in the event of a participant's death?

No. A 401(k) plan is not required to provide that the consent of a participant's beneficiary be obtained before benefit payments commence. [Treas. Reg. § 1.411(a)-11(c)(5)]

Q 16:26 Is an alternate payee's consent required in the case of a qualified domestic relations order (QDRO)?

The consent of the alternate payee is not required unless the QDRO itself requires the alternate payee's consent. [Treas. Reg. § 1.411(a)-11(c)(6)]

Qualified Reservist Distributions

Q 16:27 Are there any special rules that apply to participants whose employment has been terminated on account of their call to military service?

Yes. A participant, regardless of age, who is a member of the reserves and who is ordered or called to active duty after September 11, 2001, for a period in excess of 179 days or for an indefinite period is not required to pay the additional

10 percent income tax under Code Section 72(t) on any distribution that is a qualified reservist distribution (see Q 16:28). [I.R.C. § 72(t)(2)(G)] This exception from the application of Code Section 72(t) was enacted into law by the Pension Protection Act of 2006 (PPA) and was originally designed to expire with respect to reservists called or ordered to active duty on or after December 31, 2007. However, the exception has been made permanent as a result of the enactment of Section 107(a) of the Heroes Earnings Assistance and Relief Tax (HEART) Act of 2008.

Q 16:28 What is a *qualified reservist distribution*?

A *qualified reservist distribution* (QRD) is a distribution consisting of elective deferrals that is made during the period beginning on the date of the order or call to active duty and ending at the close of the active duty period. A plan that wishes to permit QRDs must contain provisions that allow such distributions to be made. (See chapter 3 for the deadline for amending plans to comply with the PPA.) [I.R.C. § 72(t)(2)(G)(iii)]

Q 16:29 Can a participant who received a QRD pay back the amount that was previously distributed to him?

Yes. During the two-year period beginning on the day after the end of active duty period, a participant may make one or more contributions to an IRA in an amount not greater than the amount of the QRD. The contributions are not subject to any dollar limitations applicable to IRAs, and no deduction will be allowed for any such contributions. [I.R.C. § 72(t)(2)(G)(ii)]

Minimum Distribution Requirements

Payment of benefits cannot be postponed indefinitely. Whether or not the plan grants a participant the right to determine when benefits are payable, benefits from a 401(k) plan must commence no later than the participant's required beginning date.

Required Beginning Date

Q 16:30 How long may a participant defer the receipt of benefits in a 401(k) plan?

The required beginning date (RBD) for a participant who is not a 5 percent owner is April 1 of the calendar year following the later of the calendar year in which he or she reaches age 70½ or the calendar year in which the participant retires. In the case of a participant who is a 5 percent owner, the RBD is April 1 of the calendar year following the calendar year in which the participant attains age 70½. [I.R.C. § 401(a)(9)(C)] A plan can provide, however, that the rule applicable to 5 percent owners will also apply to participants who are not 5 percent owners. [Treas. Reg. § 1.401(a)(9)-2, Q&A 2(e)]

Q 16:31 Who is a *5 percent owner* for minimum distribution purposes?

A participant is considered a *5 percent owner* if he or she is a 5 percent owner for the plan year ending in the calendar year in which he or she attains age 70½. According to the law, a 5 percent owner is to be determined for this purpose in the same way as it is determined for top-heavy purposes. Note that a 5 percent owner must own more than 5 percent of the company (see chapter 14). [I.R.C. § 401(a)(9)(C)(ii)(I)]

Q 16:32 Is there any exception to the rules establishing an employee's required beginning date?

Yes. If an employee made an election under Section 242(b) of the Tax Equity and Fiscal Responsibility Act of 1982 (TEFRA), then that employee's required beginning date is the date established under the TEFRA election. An IRS notice sets forth the requirements that must have been satisfied for a valid TEFRA election. [Treas. Reg. § 1.401(a)(9)-8, Q&A 13; Notice 83-23, 1983-2 C.B. 418]

Q 16:33 What happens if a participant revokes an election made under TEFRA Section 242(b)(2)?

If a participant revokes an election made under TEFRA Section 242(b)(2) by electing to receive a distribution earlier than provided in the election form, then any "catch-up" distributions must be made by December 31 of the calendar year following the calendar year of revocation. [Treas. Reg. § 1.401(a)(9)-8, Q&A 16]

> **Example.** Sal, who owns 50 percent of the stock of his employer, had made an election under TEFRA Section 242(b) to defer receipt of benefits until age 80. In 2015, at age 75, Sal elects to receive a partial distribution of $10,000. Since Sal effectively revoked his election, he must catch up for any distributions not made after reaching age 70½. Sal turned 70½ in 2010 and should have received distributions for the years 2010 through 2014. The revocation rules require that catch-up distributions for those years be made by December 31, 2016.

Q 16:34 If a participant dies before his or her required beginning date, what is the date by which post-death benefits must begin?

The required beginning date for post-death benefits depends on whether the plan employs either or both of two rules permitted under the law:

1. The five-year rule (see Q 16:35); or
2. The designated beneficiary rule (see Q 16:38).

[Treas. Reg. § 1.401(a)(9)-3, Q&A 1(a)]

Q 16:35 What is the *five-year rule*?

The *five-year rule* is a rule by which the employee's entire interest in a 401(k) plan must be distributed no later than December 31 of the calendar year containing the fifth anniversary of the employee's death. [Treas. Reg. § 1.401(a)(9)-3, Q&As 1, 2] The five-year rule always applies to a beneficiary that is not a designated beneficiary. A designated beneficiary may also be subject to the five-year rule if the plan so provides, or if the designated beneficiary elects the five-year rule pursuant to an election permitted under the plan. [Treas. Reg. § 1.401(a)(9)-3, Q&A 4]

Q 16:36 Who is a *designated beneficiary*?

A *designated beneficiary* is an individual who is entitled, upon the death of an employee, to all or any portion of the employee's interest in the plan, and who is designated as a beneficiary under the plan either by the plan's terms or, if the plan so provides, by an election of the employee. A designated beneficiary need not be specified by name in order to be a designated beneficiary as long as the individual who is to be the beneficiary can be ascertained. [Treas. Reg. § 1.401(a)(9)-4, Q&A 1]

> **Example.** Gamma Corporation's 401(k) plan permits a participant to designate a beneficiary to receive the participant's account balance upon his or her death. In the absence of a valid designation, the plan provides that the participant's spouse will be the beneficiary. Bob, who, at the time of his death, was married to Jane, died without having designated a beneficiary. Under the plan's terms, Jane will be the beneficiary. Even though Jane is not specifically named as Bob's beneficiary, she is considered a designated beneficiary for purposes of the minimum distribution rules because at the time of Bob's death it is possible to ascertain that Jane is the beneficiary under the terms of the plan.

Q 16:37 May an estate or trust be considered a designated beneficiary?

An estate cannot be a designated beneficiary. [Treas. Reg. § 1.401(a)(9)-4, Q&A 3] A trust itself cannot be a designated beneficiary, but individuals who are beneficiaries of the trust are treated as designated beneficiaries if the trust meets the following requirements:

1. It is valid under state law or would be valid but for the fact that there is no trust corpus;
2. It is irrevocable, or it will, by its terms, become irrevocable on the participant's death;
3. Its beneficiaries are identifiable under the trust instrument; and
4. A copy of the trust instrument or a certified list of beneficiaries is provided to the plan.

[Treas. Reg. § 1.401(a)(9)-4, Q&A 5]

Q 16:38 What is the *designated beneficiary rule*?

The *designated beneficiary rule* provides that payment of the employee's interest in the plan must begin no later than December 31 of the calendar year immediately following the calendar year in which the employee dies. The designated beneficiary rule is available only to designated beneficiaries or trusts whose beneficiaries are treated as designated beneficiaries (see Q 16:37). The designated beneficiary rule requires that the employee's interest be paid over a period not exceeding the designated beneficiary's life expectancy determined using the beneficiary's age as of the beneficiary's birthday in the calendar year following the calendar year of the employee's death. [Treas. Reg. § 1.401(a)(9)-5, Q&A 5(b)] Life expectancies are determined under the single life table in the Section 401(a)(9) regulations, available on the IRS Web site, *www.irs.gov*. [Treas. Reg. § 1.401(a)(9)-5, Q&A 6]

Q 16:39 What happens if the sole designated beneficiary is the employee's surviving spouse?

If the surviving spouse is the sole beneficiary, the RBD under the designated beneficiary rule is determined differently. The RBD is the later of:

1. December 31 of the calendar year immediately following the calendar year in which the employee died; or
2. December 31 of the calendar year in which the employee would have attained age $70^1/_2$.

[Treas. Reg. § 1.401(a)(9)-3, Q&A 3(b)]

Q 16:40 How did the Worker, Retiree, and Employer Recovery Act of 2008 affect minimum distribution requirements?

The Worker, Retiree, and Employer Recovery Act of 2008 [Pub. L. No. 110-458] (WRERA) was signed into law on December 23, 2008. Section 201 of the WRERA waived any RMD that was due for 2009. It did not waive, however, any 2008 RMD that an individual elected to delay until April 1, 2009.

Example 1. Joe turned age $70^1/_2$ in 2009. Under the WRERA he was not required to receive an RMD for 2009. His first RMD was due no later than December 31, 2010.

Example 2. Mary turned age $70^1/_2$ in 2008. Under the WRERA she was not required to receive an RMD for 2009, but her 2008 RMD must have been paid to her no later than April 1, 2009.

Example 3. Ellen is the beneficiary of a deceased participant who died in 2004 before his required beginning date (RBD). Ellen elected to apply the five-year rule in determining the timing of her RMDs. Under that rule the deceased participant's account balance would ordinarily have been paid out in its entirety no later than December 31, 2009. However, under the WRERA waiver provision, the deadline for paying out the account was postponed until December 31, 2010.

Calendar 2009 RMDs that were waived are not taken into account in determining the amount to be distributed in 2010 and later years.

> **Example 4.** The facts are the same as those in Example 1. Joe's RMD for 2010 was based on the value of his account on December 31, 2009. Joe was not required to receive any additional amount owing to any decision by him not to take a distribution in 2009.

In late 2009 the IRS issued guidance relating to the waiver of 2009 RMDs, including sample amendments that could have been adopted by employers to reflect how the waiver was implemented by the employer. [IRS Notice 2009-82, 2009-41 I.R.B. 491] The deadline for adopting an amendment reflecting the waiver is discussed in chapter 3.

Payment Options

Q 16:41 What payment options may be offered by a 401(k) plan?

Except as otherwise required by the Section 401(a)(11) joint and survivor rules (see chapter 17), a 401(k) plan is free to offer as few or as many payment options as desired. For example, a 401(k) plan may provide that benefits are payable as a single sum only. On the other hand, a 401(k) plan can provide a whole panoply of payment options from single sums to annuity contracts. No matter which payment options are offered, the amounts paid under these distribution options must satisfy the minimum distribution rules.

Q 16:42 What requirements must a plan fiduciary meet in selecting an annuity contract that is provided as a payment option under a plan?

A plan fiduciary will satisfy the prudence requirement of ERISA in its selection of an annuity contract if the following requirements are met:

1. The fiduciary engages in an objective, thorough, and analytical search of annuity providers.
2. The fiduciary considers information sufficient to assess the annuity provider's ability to make the payouts under the annuity contract.
3. The fiduciary considers the cost of the annuity in relation to the benefits and administrative services to be provided under the annuity contract.
4. At the time an annuity provider is selected, the fiduciary concludes that the annuity provider is financially able to make all future payments under the annuity contract and the cost of the annuity contract is reasonable in relation to the benefits and services provided under the contract.
5. If necessary, the fiduciary consults with an appropriate expert or experts for purposes of complying with the above requirements.

The regulation has raised questions regarding how to apply the "time of selection" standard. To clarify how this standard interacts with a fiduciary's duty to monitor and review the selection of annuity providers, the DOL has issued additional guidance in FAB 2015-2. The guidance also addresses the application of limitations rules on fiduciary liability for the selection of annuity providers and annuity contracts. [20 C.F.R. § 2550.404a-4]

Q 16:43 Must distributions that are made to an employee before the employee's required beginning date satisfy the minimum distribution rules?

No. Distributions made to an employee before his or her RBD are not required to satisfy the minimum distribution rules. [Treas. Reg. § 1.401(a)(9)-2, Q&A 4]

Q 16:44 To satisfy the minimum distribution rules, over what length of time may an employee receive his or her interest in the plan?

An employee's interest in the plan may be paid over the life of the employee (or the joint lives of the employee and a designated beneficiary), or over a period not extending beyond the life expectancy of the employee (or the joint life and last survivor expectancy of the employee and designated beneficiary). [I.R.C. § 401(a)(9)(A)] It should be noted, however, that an election made under TEFRA Section 242 can provide for a longer period of payment (see Q 16:32).

Q 16:45 If an employee's interest in the plan will be paid out over a period of time not exceeding the employee's life expectancy (or joint life and last survivor expectancy), what amount is required to be paid each calendar year?

The amount required to be paid each calendar year must at least equal the quotient obtained by dividing the value of the employee's interest in the plan by the applicable divisor amount from Table 16-1. If the participant's spouse is the sole beneficiary, the divisor amount is their joint life expectancy if that amount is larger than the amount from the table. Life expectancies are based on the joint and last survivor table in the Section 401(a)(9) regulations (available on the IRS Web site, *www.irs.gov*). [Treas. Reg. § 1.401(a)(9)-5, Q&A 4(b)] The first calendar year for which a distribution is required is the calendar year immediately preceding the calendar year containing the employee's RBD. The minimum distribution for that calendar year must be made by the RBD (see Q 16:30). The minimum distribution for any subsequent calendar year must be made by December 31 of that year. [Treas. Reg. § 1.401(a)(9)-5, Q&As 1, 4]

Table 16-1. Divisor Amounts for Determining the Amount To Be Paid Each Calendar Year

Age of the Employee	*Divisor Amount*	*Age of the Employee*	*Divisor Amount*
70	27.4	74	23.8
71	26.5	75	22.9
72	25.6	76	22.0
73	24.7	77	21.2

Table 16-1. Divisor Amounts for Determining the Amount To Be Paid Each Calendar Year *(cont'd)*

Age of the Employee	*Divisor Amount*	*Age of the Employee*	*Divisor Amount*
78	20.3	97	7.6
79	19.5	98	7.1
80	18.7	99	6.7
81	17.9	100	6.3
82	17.1	101	5.9
83	16.3	102	5.5
84	15.5	103	5.2
85	14.8	104	4.9
86	14.1	105	4.5
87	13.4	106	4.2
88	12.7	107	3.9
89	12.0	108	3.7
90	11.4	109	3.4
91	10.8	110	3.1
92	10.2	111	2.9
93	9.6	112	2.6
94	9.1	113	2.4
95	8.6	114	2.1
96	8.1	115 and older	1.9

Example. Diane, a 5 percent owner, single, and a participant in a 401(k) plan, reaches age 70½ during the last half of 2015. The minimum distribution for calendar year 2015 must be made on or before April 1, 2016, her RBD. The minimum distribution for calendar year 2016 is due no later than December 31, 2016. The applicable divisors for 2015 and 2016 are 27.4 and 26.5, respectively.

Q 16:46 What is the value of an employee's interest for purposes of calculating the minimum distribution for a calendar year?

The value of an employee's interest is the employee's account balance as of the last valuation date in the calendar year (valuation calendar year) immediately preceding the calendar year for which a minimum distribution is being made, with the following adjustments:

1. The account balance is increased by contributions or forfeitures allocated as of dates in the valuation calendar year after the valuation date (but contributions actually made after the valuation calendar year may be disregarded for this purpose); and

2. The account balance is decreased by distributions made in the valuation calendar year after the valuation date. [Treas. Reg. § 1.401(a)(9)-5, Q&A 3]
3. The value of a participant's account balance is decreased by the value of any Qualifying Longevity Annuity Contract (QLAC). A QLAC is a deferred life annuity contract that is purchased with not more than the lesser of $125,000 or 25 percent of the participant's account and which guarantees a lifetime income to a participant starting no later than age 85. [Treas. Reg. §§ 1.401(a)(9)-5, Q&A 3, 1.401 (a)(9)-6, Q&A 17]

Example. FGH Company maintains a 401(k) plan that has an annual valuation date of May 31. On May 31, 2015, the value of Judy's account balance under the plan is $50,000. Between June 1, 2015, and December 31, 2015, Judy, who is age 73 and who is not a 5 percent owner, makes elective contributions of $2,000. She also withdraws $10,000 on November 15, 2015. Judy retires during calendar year 2016; thus, her RBD date is April 1, 2017. The value of her interest in the 401(k) plan for purposes of calculating her 2016 RMD is $42,000, calculated as ($50,000 + $2,000) – $10,000.

Q 16:47 If an employee dies after the required beginning date but before the employee's entire interest has been distributed, how must the remaining interest in the plan be distributed?

The period of time over which the participant's remaining interest in the plan must be distributed depends on the identity of the beneficiary. If the participant does not have a designated beneficiary (see Q 16:36) as of September 30 of the calendar year following the calendar year of death, then the distribution period is based on the participant's remaining life expectancy using the participant's age as of the participant's birthday in the calendar year of his or her death. If the participant has a designated beneficiary as of September 30 of the calendar year following the calendar year of death, then the distribution period is based on the beneficiary's life expectancy using the beneficiary's age as of his or her birthday in the calendar year following the calendar year of the participant's death or, if longer, it is based on the participant's remaining life expectancy. In subsequent calendar years, the distribution period is reduced by one for each year after the calendar year in which life expectancy was originally determined. However, if the spouse is the participant's sole beneficiary, then the spouse's life expectancy is recalculated each year based on his or her birthday for the year in which a minimum distribution is required. For this purpose, life expectancies are based on the single life table in the Section 401(a)(9) regulations. [Treas. Reg. § 1.401(a)(9)-5, Q&As 5, 6]

Example 1. John, who had been receiving RMDs from a 401(k) plan with a December 31 plan year-end, dies on April 5, 2015, at age 75. His 76th birthday would have been July 15, 2015. His beneficiary, as of September 30, 2016, is John's estate. The minimum amount required to be distributed to John's estate by December 31, 2016, is the value of John's 401(k) account balance as of December 31, 2015, divided by 11.7 (John's life expectancy in the year of death reduced by one).

Example 2. The facts are the same as those in Example 1, except that John's sole beneficiary on September 30, 2016, is his daughter Betty, who turns age 45 on November 9, 2016. The minimum amount required to be distributed to Betty by December 31, 2016, is the value of John's account balance as of December 31, 2015, divided by 38.8, Betty's life expectancy based on her attained age in 2016. In 2017, the divisor for minimum distribution purposes will be 37.8.

Example 3. The facts are the same as those in Example 2, except that John's beneficiary is his wife, Doris. The minimum amount required to be distributed by December 31, 2016, is the same as that in Example 2. In 2017, the divisor for minimum distribution purposes will be 37.9, which is Doris's life expectancy for that year based on her attained age in 2017.

Q 16:48 How are required minimum distributions reported?

RMDs are taxable as ordinary income and reported on Form 1099-R. They are not eligible rollover distributions (see Q 16:57). To the extent the participant has a cost basis, the exclusion ratio would be applied unless the minimum distribution is a qualified distribution from a designated Roth account (see chapter 18).

Distributions to actively employed participants who are over age 70½ and who are not 5 percent owners are no longer considered required minimum distributions. As a result, distributions to participants in this category are considered eligible rollover distributions (see Q 16:57) unless they fall within another exception to that rule. [IRS Notice 97-75, 1997-2 C.B. 337]

Participants Called to Active Military Duty

Q 16:49 Is a 401(k) plan required to permit a participant who is on active military duty for more than 30 days to receive a distribution from the plan?

No, a 401(k) plan is not required to provide for a distribution to such a participant even though the participant has a severance from employment and is not receiving differential wage payments under Code Section 3401(h)(2). [IRS Notice 2010-15, Q&As 11–14, 2010-6 I.R.B. 390]

Q 16:50 May a 401(k) plan permit a participant who is receiving differential wage payments to receive a distribution from a 401(k) plan?

Yes, a 401(k) plan may provide that a participant, who is on active military duty for more than 30 days, receive a distribution from the plan. If a participant who is receiving differential wage payments receives a distribution from the plan, he or she may not make elective deferrals or employee contributions during the six-month period beginning on the date of the distribution. [IRS Notice 2010-15, Q&As 11–14, 2010-6 I.R.B. 390]

Q 16:51 If a distribution to a participant who is receiving differential wage payments also qualifies as a qualified reservist distribution, how will the distribution be treated for tax purposes?

A distribution to any participant who is receiving differential wage payments and that also qualifies as a qualified reservist distribution will be treated as a qualified reservist distribution (see Qs 16:27–16:29) [IRS Notice 2010-15, Q&A 15, 2010-6 I.R.B. 390]

Rollover Rules

Q 16:52 What is a *rollover*?

A *rollover* is a tax-free transfer of cash or other property from a 401(k) plan into an individual retirement account or annuity (IRA), including a Roth IRA, another qualified plan, a 403(b) plan, or a governmental 457 plan. A participant in a 401(k) plan defers the tax on a distribution by rolling it over. [I.R.C.§ 402(c)(1)] A rollover into a 401(k) plan is permitted only if the plan document allows for rollovers. A rollover chart prepared by the IRS is shown in Appendix I.

See chapter 18 for a discussion of the rules relating to the rollover of distributions from a designated Roth account and to in-plan Roth rollovers.

Q 16:53 How did EGTRRA change the rollover rules?

EGTRRA, which has been in effect for all distributions occurring on or after January 1, 2002, expands rollover options for participants. Expansion of these options is accomplished in a number of different ways:

1. Under prior law, an eligible rollover distribution could be transferred only to another qualified plan or to an IRA. Starting in 2002, rollovers can also be made to 403(b) and governmental 457 plans.
2. Before EGTRRA, a rollover to a qualified plan could only come from another qualified plan or from a conduit IRA. Under the new law, rollovers can also come from 403(b) and governmental 457 plans.
3. Prior to EGTRRA, a rollover from an IRA to a qualified plan could come only from a conduit IRA. With EGTRRA, any amount from a traditional IRA, except for amounts representing nondeductible IRA contributions, can be rolled into a qualified plan.

4. Under prior law, any portion of a distribution not included in gross income could not be rolled over. Starting in 2002, nontaxable amounts can be rolled over to a qualified plan or to an IRA.

[I.R.C. §§ 402(c)(2), 402(c)(8), 403(b)(8), 408(d)(3), 457(e)(16)]

Q 16:54 How has the Pension Protection Act changed the rollover rules?

The Pension Protection Act of 2006 [Pub. L. No. 109-280, 120 Stat. 780] (PPA) increased rollover options as follows:

1. Any portion of an eligible rollover distribution not included in gross income can be rolled over to a Section 403(b) plan (see item 4 in Q 16:53).
2. Eligible rollover distributions can be rolled over to a Roth IRA.
3. A distribution to a designated beneficiary who is not the spouse of a deceased participant can, under certain circumstances, be an eligible rollover distribution that can be rolled over directly to an inherited IRA.

Options 1 and 3 apply to eligible rollover distributions occurring after December 31, 2006. Option 2 applies to distributions occurring after December 31, 2007. [PPA §§ 822, 824, 829]

Eligible Rollover Distribution

Q 16:55 What distributions are eligible for tax-free rollover?

Any distribution that fits within the definition of an eligible rollover distribution (see Qs 16:56, 16:57) can be rolled over.

Q 16:56 What is an *eligible rollover distribution*?

An *eligible rollover distribution* is a distribution of all or any portion of the balance to the credit of an employee's account in a qualified plan. [I.R.C. § 402(c)(4); Treas. Reg. § 1.402(c)-2, Q&A 3]

Q 16:57 Are there any exceptions to the general rule defining eligible rollover distributions?

Yes. The following distributions are not considered eligible rollover distributions:

1. Any distribution to the extent it is required under the minimum distribution rules of Code Section 401(a)(9) (see Q 16:60);
2. Any distribution that is part of a series of substantially equal periodic payments made not less frequently than annually over the life (or life expectancy) of the employee, the joint lives (or joint life and last survivor expectancy) of the employee and his or her designated beneficiary, or for a period of ten years or more (see Q 16:58);

3. Section 401(k) elective contributions that are returned as a result of Section 415 limitations (see chapter 9);
4. Corrective distributions of excess contributions, excess deferrals, or excess aggregate contributions, as well as the income allocable to those corrective distributions (see chapters 9 and 13);
5. Loans that are considered deemed distributions by reason of default (see chapter 15);
6. Dividends on employee stock ownership plan (ESOP) stock either paid to participants or used to repay an ESOP loan [I.R.C. § 404(k)];
7. Any distribution made on account of the hardship of the employee;
8. Any permissible withdrawal from an eligible automatic contribution arrangement (EACA); and
9. Any other item designated by the IRS in any revenue ruling, notice, or other guidance of general applicability.

[I.R.C. §§ 402(c)(2), 402(c)(4); Treas. Reg. § 1.402(c)-2, Q&A 4]

Note that any amount that would have been treated as an RMD but for the waiver of this requirement in 2009 under Section 201 of WRERA would have been considered an eligible rollover distribution [IRS Notice 2009-82, 2009-41 I.R.B 491]

Q 16:58 How is it determined that a distribution is part of a series of substantially equal periodic payments?

The determination that a payment is part of a series of substantially equal periodic payments is made at the time payments begin without taking into account contingencies that have not yet occurred. For example, if payment is being made in the form of a joint and survivor annuity, whereby the amount of the payment will increase in the event the beneficiary predeceases the participant, those payments are still considered a series of payments that are not eligible rollover distributions. [Treas. Reg. § 1.402(c)-2, Q&A 5(a)]

Q 16:59 What happens if, while an employee is receiving substantially equal periodic payments that are not eligible rollover distributions, the amount of the payment changes?

If there is a change in the amount of the payment, a new determination must be made whether the remaining payments are eligible rollover distributions, without taking into account payments that were made prior to this change. [Treas. Reg. § 1.402(c)-2, Q&A 5(c)] If the payment is an isolated payment that is substantially smaller or larger than other payments in the series, that payment may be considered an eligible rollover distribution even though all prior and subsequent distributions are not eligible rollover distributions. [Treas. Reg. § 1.402(c)-2, Q&A 6]

Q 16:60 When is a distribution considered a minimum distribution under Code Section 401(a)(9) that is not an eligible rollover distribution?

For each calendar year, all distributions will be treated as required distributions under Code Section 401(a)(9) until the total minimum distribution amount has been met for that calendar year. If the full amount of an RMD is not distributed in a calendar year, the amount that was required but which was not distributed is added to the RMD for the next calendar year. [Treas. Reg. § 1.402(c)-2, Q&A 7]

> **Example.** A participant's RMD in a given calendar year is $1,000, and the participant receives four quarterly distributions of $400 each. The first two distributions and $200 of the third distribution are not eligible rollover distributions. However, $200 of the third distribution and the final $400 distribution are eligible rollover distributions unless these distributions are part of a series of substantially equal payments (see Q 16:58).

Q 16:61 Can property other than cash be rolled over?

Yes. Property generally is eligible for rollover. The only restriction arises from the ability of the recipient plan or IRA to accept the property. For example, insurance policies cannot be rolled into an IRA.

A distributee has two choices with regard to rolling over property other than cash: he or she may simply transfer title to the new trustee, or the distributee may sell the property and transfer the proceeds to the new trustee. [I.R.C. § 402(c)(6)]

Q 16:62 Is the rollover option available to all distributees?

For the most part, yes. All plan participants, as well as the spouses of deceased participants, have the option to roll over eligible rollover distributions. A former spouse who is an alternate payee under a qualified domestic relations order also has a rollover option. Nonspouse beneficiaries who are designated beneficiaries (see Q 16:36) of deceased participants may roll over the distribution directly to an inherited IRA (see Q 16:97). Finally, a rollover to a Roth IRA before January 1, 2010, was available to an individual only if his or her adjusted gross income was no greater than $100,000 or, if the taxpayer was married, he or she did not file a separate tax return. (These limitations on rollovers to IRAs were eliminated as of January 1, 2010.) [I.R.C. §§ 402(c)(9), (11); 402(e)(1); Notice 2007-7, § V, 2007-5 I.R.B. 395]

Q 16:63 Is a distribution to a participant who has been on active military duty for more than 30 days and who is receiving differential wage payments treated as an eligible rollover distribution?

Yes, such a distribution will be considered an eligible rollover distribution. [IRS Notice 2010-15, Q&A 16, 2010-6 I.R.B. 390]

Direct Rollover Option

Q 16:64 What options must be offered regarding the tax treatment of eligible rollover distributions?

An individual receiving an eligible rollover distribution must be given the option to have the distribution paid directly to an eligible retirement plan (see Qs 16:83–16:96). This is referred to as the *direct rollover option*, and a 401(k) plan is required to offer this option in order to maintain its tax-qualified status. [I.R.C. § 401(a)(31)(A); Treas. Reg. § 1.401(a)(31)-1, Q&A 1] Additionally, with a distribution of $500 or more, the distributee must be given the opportunity to have a portion of the distribution rolled over to an eligible retirement plan and the remainder distributed in cash, subject to withholding. [Treas. Reg. § 1.401(a)(31)-1, Q&A 9] Although a distribution to a participant that would have been treated as an RMD, but for the waiver of this requirement in 2009 under Section 201 of WRERA, was treated as an eligible rollover distribution, the plan was not required to offer or to provide notice of the direct rollover option to the participant (see Q 16:89).

Q 16:65 What is a *direct rollover*?

A *direct rollover* is a distribution that is made directly from the distributing plan to the recipient eligible retirement plan. The distribution does not pass through the participant or other distributee. [Treas. Reg. § 1.401(a)(31)-1, Q&A 3]

Q 16:66 Are there any restrictions on a distributee's right to elect direct rollover of eligible rollover distributions?

Yes. If the amount of all eligible rollover distributions during a year is reasonably expected to total less than $200, the distributee need not be offered the option of a direct rollover. The plan may simply cash out the participant, and no withholding is required. [Treas. Reg. §§ 1.401(a)(31)-1, Q&A 11, 31.3405(c)-1, Q&A 14] In applying the $200 rule, eligible rollover distributions to Roth accounts are treated as being distributed from a separate plan. [Treas. Reg. § 1.401(k)-1(f)(4)(ii)]

If the amount of the eligible rollover distribution is less than $500, a plan may also require that the distribution cannot be divided. In other words, the entire amount distributed must be either rolled over or distributed. If an eligible rollover distribution is divided, the plan may also require that the amount directly rolled over be at least $500. [Treas. Reg. § 1.401(a)(31)-1, Q&A 9] Like the $200 rule, the $500 rule is applied as if the Roth accounts constituted a separate plan. [Treas. Reg. § 1.401(k)-1(f)(4)(ii)]

Q 16:67 What is an *eligible retirement plan*?

An eligible retirement plan can be (1) an individual retirement account or an individual retirement annuity, including a Roth IRA; (2) an annuity plan described in Code Section 403(a); or (3) a qualified plan. [I.R.C. § 401(a)(31);

Treas. Reg. § 1.402(c)-2, Q&A 2] An eligible retirement plan can also be a 403(b) plan or a governmental 457 plan. However, with respect to that portion of an eligible rollover distribution attributable to a Roth account, only 401(k) and 403(b) plans that provide for Roth contributions or Roth IRAs are considered eligible retirement plans. [I.R.C. § 402(c)(8)]

Q 16:68 Are plans required to accept direct rollovers of eligible rollover distributions?

No. A plan can refuse to accept rollovers altogether or limit the circumstances under which it will accept rollovers. For example, a plan may accept rollovers only from certain types of plans or assets or may refuse to accept any portion of an eligible rollover distribution that consists of after-tax contributions. [Treas. Reg. § 1.401(a)(31)-1, Q&A 13] The plan administrator may also refuse a rollover because of concerns regarding the validity of the proposed rollover. To encourage plans to accept rollover contributions, the regulations provide that a rollover will not jeopardize the qualification of the receiving plan if the plan administrator reasonably concludes that the distributing plan is an eligible rollover plan even if that plan does not have a favorable determination letter from the IRS. [Treas. Reg. § 1.401(a)(31)-1, Q&A 14(a)]

Automatic Rollover Rules

Q 16:69 Is there any circumstance under which a direct rollover would be mandatory?

Yes. In the case of a 401(k) plan that provides for mandatory distributions to participants whose vested account balances do not exceed $5,000, an eligible rollover distribution that exceeds $1,000 must be directly rolled over to an individual retirement plan if the participant fails to elect to receive the distribution directly or to do a direct rollover. [I.R.C. § 401(a)(31)(B); IRS Notice 2005-5 Q&A 3, 2005-3 I.R.B. 337] In general, these rules, known as the automatic rollover rules, became effective for distributions made on or after March 28, 2005. [IRS Notice 2005-5, Q&A 4, 2005-3 I.R.B. 337]

Q 16:70 What is a *mandatory distribution*?

A *mandatory distribution* is a distribution that is made without the consent of the participant and before the participant attains the later of age 62 or normal retirement age (see Q 16:24). However, distributions made to surviving spouses, alternate payees, and nonspousal designated beneficiaries of deceased participants are not considered mandatory distributions and are, therefore, not subject to automatic rollover. [IRS Notice 2005-5, Q&A 2, 2005-3 I.R.B. 337; IRS Notice 2007-7, Q&A 15, 2007-5 I.R.B. 395]

> **Example 1.** Joe, age 50 and a participant in his employer's 401(k) plan, terminates employment with a vested account balance of $4,000. The plan provides for the payment, without participant consent, of any vested account

balance of $5,000 or less. Joe fails to elect to receive or roll over his account balance. In the absence of direction, Joe's employer must roll over Joe's vested account balance to an individual retirement plan.

Example 2. The facts are the same as those in Example 1, except that Joe is age 66. Because he has attained the normal retirement age (65) under his employer's 401(k) plan, the distribution to be made to Joe is not considered a mandatory distribution. Consequently, the employer, in the absence of direction from Joe, is not required to roll over the vested account balance to an individual retirement plan.

Q 16:71 Must the plan administrator notify plan participants that in the absence of an election, a mandatory distribution will be automatically rolled over?

Yes, the plan administrator must notify participants in writing (or through electronic media) that in the absence of an election, a mandatory distribution will be automatically rolled over. The notice can be made part of the model notice described in Q 16:92. The notice must also identify the issuer of the individual retirement plan. The notice requirement will be treated as satisfied even if the notice is returned as undeliverable. [IRS Notice 2005-5, Q&A 15, 2005-3 I.R.B. 337]

Q 16:72 Are amounts attributable to rollover contributions subject to automatic rollover?

Although rollover accounts can be disregarded in determining whether a participant's account balance can be distributed without his or her consent (see Q 16:24), they are taken into account in applying the automatic rollover rules. [IRS Notice 2005-5 Q&A 14, 2005-3 I.R.B. 337]

Example. Evelyn, age 40, terminates employment with an elective deferral account of $4,000 and a rollover account of $50,000. The 401(k) plan in which she participates disregards rollover accounts in determining whether a distribution can be made without the consent of the participant. Evelyn fails to elect to receive or roll over her total account balance of $54,000. In view of that failure, her employer will be required to roll over her total account to an individual retirement plan.

Q 16:73 In the case of a 401(k) plan subject to the joint and survivor rules, is the plan administrator required to obtain the consent of the participant's spouse if the participant's vested account balance does not exceed $5,000?

No. The consent of the spouse is not required in that case. [IRS Notice 2005-5, Q&A 13, 2005-3 I.R.B. 337]

Example. On termination of employment, Bob's vested account balance is $3,000. The 401(k) plan in which he participates is subject to the joint and survivor rules. It also provides for distributions without participant consent if the vested account balance does not exceed $5,000. Bob fails to elect either to receive or to roll over the balance in his account. His employer must roll over Bob's total vested account to an individual retirement plan, and the automatic rollover can be performed without the consent of Bob's wife.

Q 16:74 What is considered an individual retirement plan for purposes of the automatic rollover rules?

An individual retirement plan means an individual retirement account or annuity (IRA). Automatic rollovers can also be accomplished by transferring the mandatory distribution to a deemed IRA under Code Section 408(q), or to an individual retirement account that meets the requirements of Code Section 408(c). [IRS Notice 2005-5, Q&A 11, 2005-3 I.R.B. 337]

Q 16:75 Is the plan administrator allowed to establish an individual retirement plan for a participant who fails to elect to receive or roll over his or her vested account balance?

Yes, the plan administrator can establish an individual retirement plan under these circumstances. [IRS Notice 2005-5, Q&A 10, 2005-3 I.R.B. 337]

Q 16:76 Are employers making fiduciary decisions when they decide which individual retirement plans to establish and how to invest the account balance of a participant who is subject to the automatic rollover rules?

Yes, decisions made under these circumstances are decisions of a fiduciary that should be made in a manner consistent with his or her fiduciary duties under ERISA Section 404(a).

Q 16:77 Has the Department of Labor provided guidance concerning how an employer can satisfy its fiduciary duties in connection with the automatic rollover of mandatory distributions?

Yes. The DOL has issued final regulations that establish a safe harbor to protect fiduciaries who decide how to invest the automatic rollover funds. To come within the safe harbor, the following conditions must be met:

1. The amount to be rolled over must be covered by the automatic rollover rules.
2. The automatic rollover must be to an individual retirement plan, including deemed IRAs under Code Section 408(q).
3. The plan administrator must enter into a written agreement with the individual retirement plan, which provides that:

- The funds rolled over will be invested with the goal of preserving principal and providing a reasonable rate of return (whether or not guaranteed) consistent with liquidity;
- The selected investment should, over the term of the investment, maintain a dollar value equal to the amount initially invested;
- The investment must be offered by a state or federally regulated institution;
- Fees and expenses cannot be greater than those normally charged for comparable individual retirement plans established for reasons other than automatic rollover; and
- The participant on whose behalf the automatic rollover is established can enforce the terms of the written agreement.

[29 C.F.R. § 2550.404a-2(c)]

In connection with the release of its guidance, the DOL also issued a prohibited transaction class exemption that allows a plan sponsor that is a financial institution to establish automatic rollover accounts using its financial products. [PTCE 2004-16]

Q 16:78 Does the DOL safe harbor extend to the automatic rollover of mandatory distributions of $1,000 or less?

If a plan elects to apply the automatic rollover rules to mandatory distributions of $1,000 or less, the safe harbor protections will apply. [29 C.F.R. § 2550.404a-2(d)]

Q 16:79 Can a plan avoid the automatic rollover rules by limiting mandatory distributions to vested accounts of $1,000 or less?

Yes, the automatic rollover rules can be effectively avoided if mandatory distributions are limited to participants with vested accounts of $1,000 or less. A plan amendment reducing the mandatory distribution amount from $5,000 to $1,000 will not be considered a cutback of an optional form of benefit in violation of Code Section 411(d)(6) [IRS Notice 2005-5, Q&A 12, 2005-3 I.R.B. 337]

Example 1. The 401(k) plan in which John participates provides for distributions without participant consent so long as the vested account balance does not exceed $1,000. Upon termination, John's total vested account is $800. In this case, the plan can cash out John even though he fails to elect either to receive or to roll over the funds in his account.

Example 2. The facts are the same as those in Example 1, except that John already has a rollover account of $5,000. The 401(k) plan provides that rollover accounts are disregarded in determining whether a distribution can be made without participant consent. In this case, the plan will be required to do an automatic rollover because the value of the rollover account is taken into account in determining whether the automatic rollover rules apply (see Q 16:72).

Rollover of Distributions

Q 16:80 If a distributee elects to receive a cash distribution, can he or she later roll over that distribution?

Yes. The old rules concerning rollover availability within 60 days following receipt of a distribution continue to apply. Under these rules, the rollover must be accomplished within 60 days of the date of receipt of the distribution. [Treas. Reg. § 1.402(c)-2, Q&A 11] The amount that is actually rolled over will be exempt from income tax. However, if the distributee does not make up the amount that was withheld from the plan distribution, that amount will be subject to income tax and, if applicable, the additional income tax on early distributions.

> **Example.** Gary receives a distribution of $10,000 and elects to receive it in cash. The plan withholds 20 percent, or $2,000, and pays Gary $8,000. Within 60 days of receiving the $8,000, Gary decides to deposit the amount into an IRA. The $8,000 deposited will not be subject to income tax. The $2,000 withheld will be included in Gary's taxable income. Gary can avoid taxation on the $2,000 by depositing a total of $10,000 in the IRA, using assets other than the plan distribution to make up the $2,000 difference.

Q 16:81 Is there any exception to the 60-day rule?

Yes. The requirement that a rollover be accomplished in 60 days can be waived by the IRS if failure to meet the requirement would be against equity or good conscience, and the inability to complete the rollover is due to casualty, disaster, or other event beyond the participant's reasonable control. [I.R.C. § 402(c)(3)(B)]

In many cases, waiver of the requirement will require the taxpayer to obtain a private letter ruling from the IRS. In determining whether to grant a waiver, the IRS will consider all relevant facts and circumstances, including the taxpayer's inability to complete a rollover due to death, disability, hospitalization, incarceration, or postal error, whether the distribution check was cashed, and the amount of time that has elapsed since the distribution occurred.

No ruling is required in the event a financial institution receives the rollover before the 60-day period expires and, solely due to an error on the part of the financial institution, the funds are not deposited into an eligible retirement plan within the 60 days. However, automatic approval applies only if the funds are deposited to the eligible retirement plan within one year from the beginning of the 60-day rollover period. [Rev. Proc. 2003-16, 2003-4 I.R.B. 359]

Q 16:82 Are there circumstances under which a 60-day rollover option is not available to the distributee of an eligible rollover distribution?

Yes, there are circumstances under which the 60-day rollover option is not available. The portion of any eligible rollover distribution that consists of after-tax contributions must be directly rolled over to a qualified plan or a 403(b) plan. The same is true for all or any portion of a distribution from a designated Roth account that is not includable in gross income. In addition, the rollover of a deceased participant's account to an inherited IRA for the benefit of a nonspousal designated beneficiary's inherited IRA can only be accomplished by way of a direct rollover. [I.R.C. §§ 402(c)(2), (11)]

Direct Rollover Election

Q 16:83 How is a direct rollover elected?

The plan administrator is required to notify recipients of their right to a direct rollover and to provide forms and procedures to accomplish the rollover. (See Qs 16:88–16:96.)

Q 16:84 Is spousal consent needed on a direct rollover election?

Yes. If the distribution is subject to the survivor annuity rules (see chapter 17), then spousal consent is needed on a direct rollover election.

Q 16:85 Must distributees be given the option to roll over into more than one eligible retirement plan?

No. A plan administrator is not required (but is permitted) to allow distributees to divide eligible rollover distributions into more than one plan. [Treas. Reg. § 1.401(a)(31)-1, Q&A 10]

Q 16:86 Must a direct rollover option be offered on a loan offset amount that is an eligible rollover distribution?

No. A plan need not offer participants the option of rollover for a loan offset amount (see Q 16:112). [Treas. Reg. § 1.401(a)(31)-1, Q&A 16]

Q 16:87 How is a direct rollover accomplished?

A trustee can transfer benefits in a direct rollover using any reasonable means. Reasonable means include wire transfers and mailing a check to the new trustee. If there is no trustee (such as in an individual retirement annuity), the check or wire should be directed to the custodian of the plan or the issuer of the contract. [Treas. Reg. § 1.401(a)(31)-1, Q&A 3] A direct rollover can also be accomplished by sending a check to the distributee with instructions to deliver it to the trustee of the eligible retirement plan. If this method is used, the check must be made payable to the named trustee as trustee of the named plan. The check must also indicate for whose benefit it is. [Treas. Reg. § 1.401(a)(31)-1, Q&A 4]

Direct Rollover Procedures

Q 16:88 May the plan administrator impose procedures or limitations on direct rollover elections?

The plan administrator may prescribe reasonable procedures for electing a direct rollover. These procedures may include a requirement that the recipient provide adequate information or documentation that the distribution is being directed to an eligible retirement plan. However, the plan administrator cannot require information or documentation that would effectively eliminate the distributee's ability to elect a direct rollover. For example, the plan administrator cannot require an attorney's opinion that the plan receiving the rollover is an eligible retirement plan. [Treas. Reg. § 1.401(a)(31)-1, Q&A 6]

Q 16:89 Is notice of the direct rollover option required?

Yes. Plan administrators must provide distributees with a written explanation of their right to elect a direct rollover and the tax consequences of not doing so. Certain other tax information is also required. This notice must be provided within a reasonable period of time before a distributee makes an eligible rollover distribution. [Treas. Reg. § 1.402(f)-1, Q&A 1] The term *distributee* includes any person who is able to roll over a deceased participant's account to an inherited IRA (see Qs 16:97–16:103). [WRERA § 108(f)(2)(B)]

Q 16:90 What is a reasonable period of time for providing notice?

Notice must be provided no less than 30 days and no more than 180 days before a distribution is made. For distributions not subject to spousal consent requirements, however, if, after receiving the notice, a distributee makes an affirmative election, the distribution may be made immediately without violating the reasonable time requirement. The plan administrator must clearly indicate to the distributee that he or she has an opportunity to consider a decision regarding rollover for at least 30 days after notice is provided. [Treas. Reg. § 1.402(f)-1, Q&A 2(a); Prop. Treas. Reg. § 1.402(f)-1] For distributions subject to the spousal consent requirements of Code Sections 401(a)(11) and 417, the 30-day notice period can be waived as long as benefits are not paid until 7 days after the date notice is given. [Treas. Reg. § 1.417(e)-1(b)(3)(ii)] The notice requirement may be provided through an electronic medium (see Q 16:22). [Treas. Reg. § 1.401(a)-21(b), (c)]

Q 16:91 What information must the notice contain?

The notice must explain the rules under which the distributee may have the distribution paid in a direct rollover to an eligible retirement plan, the rules requiring the withholding of income tax if it is not paid in a direct rollover, the rules under which the distributee will not be subject to tax if the distribution is rolled over to an eligible retirement plan within 60 days of the distribution, and any other special tax rules that might apply. Also, if the payment is one in a series and the plan administrator intends to apply the initial election to subsequent payments, this must be explained in the notice. [Treas. Reg. §§ 1.402(f)-1, Q&As 1, 3; 1.401(a)(31)-1, Q&A 12] Finally, a participant whose distribution is potentially subject to the automatic rollover rules must receive the information described in Q 16:71.

Q 16:92 Is there a model notice that can be used to assure compliance with Code Section 402(f)?

Yes. The IRS recently issued two model notices titled "Your Rollover Options." One notice deals with distributions from Roth accounts and the other from non-Roth accounts. A participant who has accounts with both types of funds should receive both notices. [IRS Notice 2014-74, 2014-5 I.R.B. 937] A plan administrator who provides the model notices will be deemed to have complied with the requirements of Code Section 402(f). [Treas. Reg. § 1.402(f)-1, Q&A 1(b)]

Q 16:93 May the plan administrator establish a cutoff date after which a rollover election cannot be revoked?

Yes; however, the deadline must not be more restrictive than the deadline used in the plan for permitting changes in electing a form of distribution. [Treas. Reg. § 1.401(a)(31)-1, Q&A 8]

Q 16:94 How do the notice and election rules apply to eligible rollover distributions that are paid in periodic installments?

A plan may treat a participant's rollover election with respect to the initial payment in a series of periodic payments as applying to all subsequent payments. The employee must be permitted to revoke that election at any time and must receive an explanation that the election will apply to all future payments unless revoked. [Treas. Reg. § 1.401(a)(31)-1, Q&A 12] The employee must be provided with a notice concerning his or her right to a direct rollover prior to the first payment and then annually for as long as payments continue. [Treas. Reg. § 1.402(f)-1, Q&A 3]

Q 16:95 How is a direct rollover distribution reported for income tax purposes?

A direct rollover distribution must be reported on Form 1099-R. For purposes of 1099-R reporting, it is treated as a distribution that is immediately rolled over. [Treas. Reg. § 31.3405(c)-1, Q&A 16]

Q 16:96 Is a direct rollover considered a transfer of benefits to which the optional form of benefit rules apply?

No. A direct rollover is treated as though the employee elected a cash distribution and later rolled it over. Therefore, the rule requiring the carryover of certain distribution rights (see Qs 16:1–16:12) on transferred benefits does not apply to amounts directly rolled over. [Treas. Reg. § 1.401(a)(31)-1, Q&A 15]

Rollovers to Inherited IRAs

Q 16:97 Is a 401(k) plan required to offer a direct rollover of an eligible rollover distribution to a nonspousal beneficiary?

Before January 1, 2010, a 401(k) plan was not required to offer a direct rollover option. [Notice 2007-7 Q&A 11, 2007-5 I.R.B. 395] After December 31, 2009, a 401(k) plan is required to provide this option as a result of the enactment of the WRERA.

Q 16:98 Is the direct rollover option available to all nonspousal beneficiaries of a deceased participant?

No. Only nonspousal beneficiaries who are *designated beneficiaries* (see Q 16:36) may make a direct rollover. Thus, a direct rollover is not available to the estate of a deceased participant. However, a direct rollover can be made with respect to a trust that meets the requirements set forth in Q 16:37. [IRS Notice 2007-7, Q&A 16, 2007-5 I.R.B. 395]

Q 16:99 What is an *inherited IRA*?

An *inherited IRA* is any individual retirement account (including a Roth IRA) that is acquired by a person by reason of the death of the IRA owner, and the person acquiring the IRA is not the spouse of the deceased owner. [I.R.C. § 408(d)(3)(C); IRS Notice 2008-30, Q&A 7, 2008-12 I.R.B. 638]

Q 16:100 How is an inherited IRA established and titled?

The IRA must be established in a manner that identifies it as an IRA with respect to a deceased individual and also identifies the deceased individual and the beneficiary. [IRS Notice 2007-7, Q&A 13, 2007-5 I.R.B. 395]

Q 16:101 If the participant dies before his or her required beginning date, what amount may be rolled over to the inherited IRA?

The amount that may be rolled over depends on which rule—the five-year rule or the life expectancy rule—applies and when the rollover occurs.

If distribution is made in the calendar year of the participant's death, the entire account balance may be rolled over to the inherited IRA no matter which rule applies. If distribution occurs in the year following the calendar year of the participant's death, the account balance less the required minimum distribution (RMD) under the life expectancy rule for that year may be rolled over. Again, it does not matter which rule applies. If distribution occurs in a subsequent year, and the plan provides for the life expectancy rule or the beneficiary is allowed to elect that rule, then the account balance less the RMD for the year of distribution can be rolled over to the inherited IRA. If, instead, the five-year rule applies, the entire account balance can be rolled over through the calendar year containing the fourth anniversary of the participant's death. After the end of the fourth calendar year, a rollover to an inherited IRA is not permitted. [IRS Notice 2007-7, Q&As 17 & 19, 2007-5 I.R.B. 395]

Q 16:102 If the participant dies *after* his or her required beginning date, what amount may be rolled over to the inherited IRA?

If death occurs after the participant's RBD, the amount that can be rolled over to the inherited IRA is the account balance less any amount that would have been required to be distributed to the participant in the calendar year of his or her death or to any beneficiary in the calendar year subsequent to the participant's death. [IRS Notice 2007-7, Q&A 18, 2007-5 I.R.B. 395]

Q 16:103 After the deceased participant's account balance has been rolled over to the inherited IRA, how is the minimum distribution determined with respect to the IRA?

The RMD rules that apply to the 401(k) plan from which the rollover originates apply to the inherited IRA. However, even if the five-year rule applies, the designated beneficiary may elect to use the life expectancy rule if the rollover occurs in the calendar year of the participant's death or the calendar year thereafter. [IRS Notice 2007-7, Q&As 17(c)(2) & 19, 2007-5 I.R.B. 395]

Example 1. John dies in 2015 before his RBD. Sue, John's nonspousal beneficiary, elects, after receiving the RMD for 2016, to roll over John's remaining account balance in that year. Even though the plan applies the five-year rule in the case of deaths occurring before a participant's RBD, Sue can have the minimum distributions from the inherited IRA determined under the life expectancy rule.

Example 2. The facts are the same as those in Example 1, except that Sue elects to do the rollover in 2017. Because the plan applies the five-year rule, Sue is able to roll over John's entire account balance to an inherited IRA. The five-year rule also applies in determining the minimum distribution from the inherited IRA; therefore, the balance in the inherited IRA must be paid out to Sue no later than December 31 of the calendar year containing the fifth anniversary of John's date of death (i.e., no later than December 31, 2020).

Example 3. The facts are the same as those in Example 1, except that Sue does not take any distribution from the plan before January 1, 2020. Sue will not be able to roll over John's account balance to an inherited IRA because the deadline for doing so (December 31 of the calendar year containing the fourth anniversary of John's date of death) will have passed.

Rollover Strategies

Q 16:104 What are the advantages of a rollover?

The major advantage of a rollover is the postponement of tax, since the distribution will accumulate earnings on a tax-deferred basis. When distributions are ultimately paid from the eligible retirement plan, the distributee may be in a lower tax bracket, or tax rates may be lower, which would maximize the ultimate benefits received.

Another advantage of rollover to an IRA is that a distribution from an IRA is not subject to the mandatory 20 percent income tax withholding requirement (see Q 16:109). Recipients of distributions from an IRA can generally elect out of income tax withholding.

Q 16:105 What are the disadvantages of a rollover?

If a distribution with respect to a participant who was born before January 2, 1936, is rolled over, the recipient loses the ability to elect the special tax treatment available for lump-sum distributions. There is no opportunity, therefore, to elect capital gains treatment for a portion of the distribution or to use income averaging (see chapter 18).

An additional disadvantage to distributees who are alternate payees pursuant to a QDRO (see chapter 17) is the potential imposition of the 10 percent additional income tax on early distributions (see chapter 18). Distributions from a qualified plan to an alternate payee are exempt from this tax, but distributions from an IRA are not.

Q 16:106 What issues are presented when an eligible rollover distribution includes amounts that were previously taxed like Roth contributions and employee after-tax contributions?

The law provides that if a participant's account includes both pre-tax and after-tax amounts, then distributions from the account are considered to include a pro rata share of each amount. [I.R.C. § 72(e)(8)(D)]

Example 1. George has an account balance of $100,000 consisting of $80,000 in pre-tax amounts and $20,000 in after-tax amounts. George requests a distribution of $50,000, of which $40,000 would be considered a distribution of pre-tax amounts and $10,000 of after-tax amounts.

Until issuance of IRS Notice 2014-54 [2014-41 I.R.B. 670], the IRS treated any distribution from a retirement plan that was rolled over to multiple destinations as separate distributions to each destination, with each separate distribution containing pro rata portions of the pre-tax and after-tax amounts.

Example 2. In Example 1 above, George elects to roll over half of the $50,000 distribution to a traditional IRA and the other half to a Roth IRA. Each IRA is deemed to receive $20,000 and $5,000 of pre-tax and after-tax amounts respectively.

IRS Notice 2014-54 changes this result by providing that all distributions from a plan scheduled to be made at the same time will be treated as a single distribution even if the distributions are sent to multiple destinations. As a result, George could transfer through direct rollover $40,000 to a traditional IRA, thus avoiding taxation on the pre-tax amount, and transfer $10,000 of the after-tax amount to a Roth IRA.

Withholding on Distributions

Most 401(k) plan distributions are subject to income tax withholding. This section discusses these withholding rules, including procedures for notifying recipients and for reporting and paying withheld taxes.

Q 16:107 Is withholding required on contributions to a 401(k) plan?

No. Federal income tax withholding is not required on elective contributions or any other type of 401(k) plan contribution. However, elective contributions are subject to withholding for Social Security (FICA) and unemployment (FUTA) tax purposes. [I.R.C. §§ 3121(v)(1)(A), 3306(r)(1)(A)]

Q 16:108 Is withholding required on distributions from a 401(k) plan?

Yes. Federal income tax withholding is required on distributions from a 401(k) plan that are considered eligible rollover distributions. [I.R.C. §§ 3405(a), 3405(b), 3405(c)] Until January 1, 2010, withholding was not required on any eligible rollover distribution that could have been but was not rolled over to an inherited IRA. Starting January 1, 2010, federal income tax withholding applies to any eligible rollover distribution that a person elects not to roll over to an inherited IRA. Finally, for withholding purposes, any distribution that would have been treated as an RMD in 2009 under WRERA Section 201 was not treated as an eligible rollover distribution for withholding purposes. [IRS Notice 2009-82, Q&A 7, 2009-41 I.R.B 491]

Q 16:109 What is the amount of income tax withholding required on eligible rollover distributions?

The amount of withholding on all eligible rollover distributions is 20 percent of the sum of the cash and the fair market value of other property received in a distribution. [Treas. Reg. § 31.3405(c)-1, Q&A 1] This is true regardless of whether the distribution is made in a single sum or in a series of periodic payments that are still considered eligible rollover distributions. Beginning in 2011, most plans will need to remit income taxes electronically using the IRS's Electronic Federal Tax Payment System (EFTPS). [Treas. Reg. § 31.6302-1(h)(2)(iii)]

Q 16:110 May a participant elect out of withholding on an eligible rollover distribution?

No. The only way to avoid income tax withholding on an eligible rollover distribution is to have it transferred in a direct rollover. [Treas. Reg. § 31.3405(c)-1, Q&A 2] Income tax withholding is avoided even if an eligible rollover distribution is directly rolled over to a Roth IRA. [IRS Notice 2008-30, Q&A 6, 2008-12 I.R.B. 638]

Q 16:111 Are hardship withdrawals subject to mandatory withholding?

Hardship withdrawals are not subject to mandatory withholding. [I.R.C. § 402(c)(4)(C)]

Loan Offset Amount

Q 16:112 Are participant loans subject to the new withholding rules?

A participant loan that complies with the requirements of Code Section 72(p) is not considered a taxable distribution and therefore is not an eligible rollover distribution subject to withholding. The regulations also indicate that in the event a participant loan becomes taxable because of a default or failure to comply with Code Section 72(p), the amount of the outstanding loan is still not considered an eligible rollover distribution. [Treas. Reg. § 1.402(c)-2, Q&A 4(d)]

When a loan is distributed as an offset to the participant's account balance, the amount of the offset is considered an eligible rollover distribution subject to 20 percent withholding. [Treas. Reg. § 1.402(c)-2, Q&A 9] This is true regardless of whether the participant's employment is terminated at the time the offset occurs. For example, if the plan document permits an offset upon loan default such that the participant's account is actually reduced by the amount of the outstanding loan, that offset will be considered an eligible rollover distribution.

Q 16:113 How is the 20 percent withholding requirement applied to a distribution that includes a loan offset amount?

The amount of the cash and property distributed, plus the amount of the loan offset, is subject to 20 percent withholding. Any amount that the employee elects to have directly rolled over to an eligible retirement plan is not subject to 20 percent withholding. [Treas. Reg. § 31.3405(c)-1, Q&A 11]

> **Example.** Jim has an account balance of $10,000, of which $3,000 is invested in a plan loan. Jim elects to receive $2,000 as a cash distribution and to have $5,000 rolled to an eligible retirement plan. The amount subject to withholding is $5,000 (the amount of the loan offset plus the amount of the cash distribution). Therefore, the amount of the withholding is $1,000 and Jim will receive only $1,000 in cash.

Q 16:114 Is there any limit on the amount of withholding required for a loan offset amount that is an eligible rollover distribution?

Yes. The amount withheld cannot exceed the sum of cash and the fair market value of any property (other than employer securities) received by a participant. [Treas. Reg. § 31.3405(c)-1, Q&A 11]

> **Example.** Martha has an account balance of $10,000, of which $3,000 is invested in a plan loan. Martha elects to have her entire $7,000 distribution directly rolled over to an eligible retirement plan. Even though the $3,000 loan offset amount is considered an eligible rollover distribution, no withholding is required since Martha received no cash or property from which to withhold the tax.

Other Special Distributions

Q 16:115 How do the 20 percent withholding rules apply to distributions of property?

If property other than employer securities is distributed as part of an eligible rollover distribution, the fair market value of the property is subject to 20 percent withholding. If the distribution does not include enough cash to satisfy the withholding requirement, the plan has two options: it can sell part of the property prior to the distribution to satisfy withholding, or it can permit the payee to remit to the plan administrator enough cash to satisfy the withholding requirement. [Treas. Reg. § 31.3405(c)-1, Q&A 9; Temp. Treas. Reg. § 35.3405-1T, Q&A F-2]

Q 16:116 How do the withholding rules apply to the distribution of employer securities?

The maximum amount that can be withheld in a distribution is the sum of the cash distributed and the fair market value of property, other than employer securities, received in the distribution. [Treas. Reg. § 31.3405(c)-1, Q&A 11] Therefore, if only employer securities are distributed, no withholding is required.

If employer securities and cash are received in a single distribution, then the cost basis of those securities will be subject to 20 percent withholding, assuming there is sufficient cash to pay that withholding. For example, if an employee receives a distribution consisting of employer securities with a cost basis of $3,000 and $5,000 in cash, 20 percent withholding will be applied against an amount equal to $8,000. The employee will receive the employer securities plus $3,400 in cash. [Treas. Reg. § 31.3405(c)-1, Q&As 11, 12]

Q 16:117 Do the withholding rules apply to distributions from IRAs?

No. The 20 percent withholding requirement applies only to eligible rollover distributions. [I.R.C. §§ 402(c)(8), 3405(c)(3)] Therefore, a participant has the ability to avoid the 20 percent withholding requirement by electing a direct rollover to an IRA and then taking a distribution from that IRA. The IRA distribution would be subject to regular income tax, the early distribution tax if the recipient is under age 59½, and, possibly, fees associated with the transaction.

Responsibility for Withholding

Q 16:118 Who is responsible for enforcing the mandatory 20 percent withholding?

The plan administrator is generally responsible for satisfying the notice requirement and for withholding 20 percent of any eligible rollover distribution that is not directly rolled over. The plan administrator can shift this responsibility to the payor. [Treas. Reg. § 31.3405(c)-1, Q&As 4, 5]

Q 16:119 Will the plan administrator be responsible for taxes, interest, or penalties if a direct rollover is elected, but the rollover fails?

The plan administrator will be liable in this circumstance only if its reliance on the information provided by the distributee is not reasonable. The plan administrator is not required to independently verify the accuracy of information, as long as it is not clearly erroneous on its face. [Treas. Reg. § 31.3405(c)-1, Q&A 7(a)]

Q 16:120 What constitutes adequate information on which a plan administrator can rely to avoid taxes, interest, and penalties?

To avoid tax liability on a direct rollover that fails, the plan administrator must have been furnished with the name of the eligible retirement plan to receive the distribution; a representation from the distributee that the recipient plan is an eligible retirement plan (see Q 16:67); and any information necessary to permit the plan administrator to accomplish the direct rollover (i.e., the name and address of the recipient trustee). [Treas. Reg. § 31.3405(c)-1, Q&A 7(b)]

Distributions Not Eligible for Rollover

Q 16:121 What withholding rules apply to distributions from a qualified plan that are not eligible rollover distributions?

Distributions that are not eligible rollover distributions are subject to the old withholding rules described in this section (Qs 16:121–16:135). [Treas. Reg. § 31.3405(c)-1, Q&A 1] Therefore, distributees can elect out of withholding altogether. Also, the rate of withholding varies depending on the type of distribution involved.

Q 16:122 What amounts are subject to withholding under the old rules?

No withholding is required on nonperiodic distributions (see Q 16:128) of $200 or less. [Temp. Treas. Reg. § 35.3405-1T, Q&A F-7] For other distributions, any cash and the value of any property distributed from a plan are subject to withholding unless the payor reasonably believes that an amount is not includable in gross income. [I.R.C. § 3405(e)] For example, if the payor knows that a portion of the distribution represents after-tax employee contributions, those amounts are not subject to withholding.

If the distribution is of property other than cash, the payor must use a valuation made within one year of the distribution as the basis for determining the withholding amount. If the employee does not elect out of withholding, he or she can simply pay the amount of tax to the payor in lieu of selling a portion of the property. [Treas. Reg. § 35.3405-1T, Q&As F-1, F-2]

Q 16:123 Are there special rules for withholding on distributions of employer securities?

Yes. A distribution of employer securities is not subject to withholding. [I.R.C. § 3405(e)(8)] The appreciation on employer securities distributed from a qualified plan is not subject to income tax until the securities are sold. Relief from the withholding provisions protects payees from being forced to sell securities that would otherwise qualify for this income tax deferral just to pay the withholding amount.

Q 16:124 Is aggregation with amounts distributed from another plan of the employer required?

No. The payor is not required to aggregate 401(k) plan distributions with distributions from other plans when computing and reporting withholding. The payor may elect to aggregate; however, the payee has a separate right to elect out of withholding for each plan distribution. [I.R.C. § 3405(e)(9)]

Q 16:125 What rate of withholding applies to 401(k) plan distributions under the old rules?

The rate of withholding depends on the type of distribution involved as well as the elections made by the payee. There are separate rules for periodic and nonperiodic distributions (see Qs 16:126–16:129).

Periodic and Nonperiodic Distributions

Q 16:126 What is a *periodic distribution*?

Any distribution that is paid under an annuity contract or is one of a series of payments payable over a period of more than one year is a *periodic distribution.* [Temp. Treas. Reg. § 35.3405-1T, Q&As A-9, B-8] It is not necessary that the payments be of equal amounts or that they be made at regular intervals.

However, a payment cannot be treated as a periodic distribution unless the frequency of payments is known. [Treas. Reg. § 35.3405-1T, Q&A B-7]

Q 16:127 What is the rate of withholding for periodic distributions?

The rate of withholding on periodic distributions is determined by the payee on a withholding certificate, Form W-4. If the payee does not submit a withholding certificate, the rate of withholding should be determined as if the payee were married and claiming three exemptions. [I.R.C. § 3405(a)(4)]

Q 16:128 What is a *nonperiodic distribution*?

A *nonperiodic distribution* is any taxable distribution from a plan that is not a periodic distribution (see Q 16:126). [I.R.C. § 3405(e)(3)]

Q 16:129 What is the rate of withholding required on nonperiodic distributions?

The rate of withholding on nonperiodic distributions is 10 percent. [I.R.C. § 3405(b)]

Electing Out of Withholding

Q 16:130 Who may elect not to have a withholding taken from a 401(k) plan distribution?

Any payee who receives a distribution in the United States that is not an eligible rollover distribution (see Qs 16:55, 16:56) may elect out of withholding. The right to make this election applies whether the distribution is periodic or nonperiodic. The only payees who cannot elect out of withholding are those with foreign addresses. (For the rules concerning withholding on distributions to foreign payees, see Q 16:136.)

Q 16:131 Is the plan administrator required to notify payees of their right to elect out of withholding?

Yes. Payees must be notified of their right to elect out of the withholding requirement. The time for providing this notification varies depending on the type of distribution (see Qs 16:133, 16:134). Payees of periodic distributions must also be notified of their right to renew or revoke a withholding election at least once per calendar year. [I.R.C. § 3405(e)(10)(B)] Any election not to have withholding apply will remain in effect until revoked. [Treas. Reg. § 35.3405-1T, Q&A D-1] Notice can also be provided through an electronic medium (see Qs 16:22–16:23). [Treas. Reg. § 35.3405-1, Q&A d-35]

Q 16:132 What information must be contained in the withholding notice?

The notice must inform payees of their right to elect out of withholding and tell them how to revoke any prior election. It must inform the payee that any prior election will continue to apply until it is revoked and must also advise the payee that penalties could be incurred if the amount of tax withheld is less than that required under the estimated tax payment requirements of Code Section 6654. [Treas. Reg. § 35.3405-1T, Q&A D-18]

Q 16:133 When must notice be given on periodic distributions?

Payees receiving periodic distributions must receive notice of their right to elect out of withholding not earlier than six months before the first payment and not later than the date of the first payment. After the initial notification, notice must also be provided at least once each calendar year thereafter. [I.R.C. § 3405(e)(10)(B)(i)] Failure to provide timely notice will subject the plan administrator to a penalty tax of $10 per failure, not to exceed $5,000 for any calendar year. [I.R.C. § 6652(h)]

If the amount of the annual payment is expected to be less than $5,400, the payor can notify the payee that no tax will be withheld unless a withholding certificate is filed. [Treas. Reg. § 35.3405-1T, Q&A D-5]

Q 16:134 When must notice be given for nonperiodic distributions?

Notice of withholding on nonperiodic distributions must be given no earlier than six months before the distribution and no later than a time that gives the payee a reasonable period within which to elect not to have withholding apply. [Treas. Reg. § 35.3405-1T, Q&A D-9] The "reasonable period of time" requirement is met if notice is given at the time the application for benefits is provided to the payee. [Treas. Reg. § 35.3405-1T, Q&A D-10] Failure to provide timely notice will subject the plan administrator to a penalty tax of $10 per failure, not to exceed $5,000 for any calendar year. [I.R.C. § 6652(h)]

Q 16:135 What withholding elections should be given effect by the payor?

Any time a participant clearly indicates his or her desire to elect out of the withholding requirement, that election should be given effect. [Treas. Reg. § 35.3405-1T, Q&As D-22, D-26]

The payor of a periodic distribution may require the payee to elect out of withholding up to 30 days before the first payment is due. [Temp. Treas. Reg. § 35.3405-1T, Q&A D-11] However, if the payment is a nonperiodic one, the payor must honor any election made up to the time of distribution. [Treas. Reg. § 35.3405-1T, Q&A D-12] If the payment is a periodic one, any withholding election or revocation of a prior election must be given effect no more than 30 days after it is received, if periodic payments have not yet begun. If the payments have begun, it must be given effect on the January 1, May 1, July 1, or October 1 that is at least 30 days after the request is received. [Treas. Reg. § 35.3405-1T, Q&A B-3]

A withholding election will not be given effect if the taxpayer does not properly disclose his or her taxpayer identification number. [I.R.C. § 3405(e)(12)]

Withholding Procedures and Penalties

Q 16:136 Is withholding required on distributions to participants with foreign addresses?

Yes. A flat 30 percent rate of withholding is required on distributions to payees with foreign addresses, and those payees may not elect out of this withholding requirement. However, if the payee certifies under penalty of perjury that he or she is not a U.S citizen, resident alien, or tax-avoiding expatriate, withholding can be avoided. [I.R.C. § 3405(e)(13); IRS Notice 87-7, 1987-1 C.B. 420]

Q 16:137 How are withheld income taxes reported to the IRS?

Withheld income taxes are reported on IRS Form 945. In general, the return is due one month after the end of each calendar year. However, if deposits have been made on time in full payment of the withheld income taxes, the return may be filed by February 10. [Treas. Reg. § 31.6071(a)-1(a)(1)]

Q 16:138 Are deposits of federal income tax withholding required?

Yes. Withheld income taxes must be deposited with either a financial institution qualified as a depository for federal taxes or a federal reserve bank. Deposits must be made monthly or semiweekly, depending on the amount of tax reported on Form 945 in the previous year. If the accumulated withheld income tax reaches $100,000 within the deposit period, the withheld income taxes must be deposited by the close of the next banking day. [I.R.C. § 6302(g)] Payors with income and employment tax obligations are required to electronically deposit all such taxes using the Electronic Federal Tax Payment System beginning January 1, 2011. [Treas. Reg. § 31.6302-1(h)(2)(iii)]

Q 16:139 Must withheld amounts be reported to the payee?

Yes. Payees must be informed of any amounts withheld on Form 1099-R.

Q 16:140 Are there penalties for failing to withhold, report, or pay federal taxes?

Yes. Civil penalties may apply for late filing of a return [I.R.C. § 6651(a)], failing to deposit taxes when due [I.R.C. § 6656], or failing to pay tax due after payment has been demanded by the IRS. [I.R.C. § 6651(d)] Additional penalties may apply if a failure is willful or due to fraud. [I.R.C. §§ 6663, 6672] If the violation is done with a corrupt motive or an intent to disobey the law, criminal penalties may also apply. [I.R.C. §§ 7201, 7202, 7203, 7204, 7205, 7206, 7207]

Claims for Benefits

To receive his or her benefits under a 401(k) plan, a participant must file a claim for benefits. Like other employee benefit plans, a 401(k) plan is required by ERISA to establish and maintain reasonable procedures relating to the filing of benefit claims, notification of benefit determinations, and appeal of adverse benefit determinations.

Q 16:141 What is considered a claim for benefits?

Under the regulations, a claim for benefits is a request for a plan benefit made by a participant or a beneficiary pursuant to a plan's reasonable procedures for filing benefit claims. [29 C.F.R. § 2560.503-1(e)]

Q 16:142 What requirements must a claims procedure meet in order to be considered reasonable?

A claims procedure will be deemed reasonable if it meets the following requirements:

1. It is described in the summary plan description.
2. It does not contain any provision and is not administered in a way that unduly inhibits or hampers the initiation or processing of benefit claims.
3. It does not prevent a benefit claimant from using an attorney or other representative to act on the claimant's behalf.
4. It contains administrative processes and safeguards designed to ensure and verify that decisions on benefit claims are consistent with the governing plan documents and with prior determinations in similar situations.

[29 C.F.R. § 2560.503-1(b)]

Q 16:143 How soon after a benefit claim is filed must the plan administrator make a determination on the claim?

In general, the plan administrator has up to 90 days to make a determination. If the plan administrator believes more time is necessary to process the claim, it can require an additional 90 days to consider the claim. To obtain an extension of time to consider the claim, the plan administrator is required to notify the claimant in writing before the end of the initial 90-day period. [29 C.F.R. § 2560.503-1(f)(1)]

In the case of a claim based on disability, the plan administrator has 45 days to make a decision unless additional time is required to consider the claim, in which case two 30-day extensions are available. To obtain an extension, the plan administrator must notify the claimant and explain the standards for entitlement to a disability benefit, the unresolved issues that prevent a decision, and the additional information needed to resolve those issues. [29 C.F.R. § 2560.503-1(f)(3)]

Q 16:144 If a claim is denied, how must the claimant be notified of the denial?

The plan administrator is required to provide written or electronic notification of the denial. It must be written in a manner calculated to be understood by the claimant and must contain the following:

1. The specific reason for the denial;
2. A reference to the specific plan provisions upon which the denial is based;
3. A description of the additional material or information needed to perfect the claim and an explanation of their relevance;
4. A description of the plan's review procedures and their applicable time limits, including a statement of the claimant's right to sue under ERISA Section 502(a); and
5. In the case of disability claims, a description of any internal rule, guideline, protocol, or similar criterion relied on in denying the claim.

[29 C.F.R. § 2560.503-1(g)]

Q 16:145 What requirements must the plan's review procedure meet?

The review procedure must provide the claimant a reasonable opportunity for a full and fair review of the claim denial and also meet the following requirements:

1. Provide the claimant at least 60 days (180 days for disability claims) to appeal the denial of the claim;
2. Provide the claimant an opportunity to submit written comments, documents, records, and other information relating to the claim;
3. Provide the claimant, upon request and free of charge, reasonable access to and copies of, all documents, records, and other information relevant to his or her claim; and
4. Provide a review that takes into account all comments, documents, records, and other information submitted by the claimant even if such matters were not considered in the initial benefit determination.

[29 C.F.R. § 2560.503-1(h)(1), (2)]

Additional requirements designed to ensure fairness and objectivity apply in the case of disability claims. [29 C.F.R. § 2560.503-1(h)(4)]

Q 16:146 If a claim is denied at the appeals stage, how must the claimant be notified of the denial?

The plan administrator is required to provide written or electronic notification of the denial. It must be written in a manner calculated to be understood by the claimant and must contain the following:

1. The specific reason for the denial;
2. A reference to the specific plan provisions on which the denial is based;
3. A statement that the claimant is entitled to receive, upon request and free of charge, copies of all documents, records, and other information relevant to his or her claim;
4. A statement describing any voluntary appeals procedures offered by the plan, a statement of the claimant's right to sue under ERISA Section 501(a), and, in the case of a disability claim, a statement advising the claimant of the availability of other voluntary dispute resolution options; and
5. In the case of a disability claim, the internal rule, guideline, protocol, or other criteria relied on in denying the claim.

[29 C.F.R. § 2560.503-1(j)]

Q 16:147 How soon after an appeal is filed must the plan administrator make a determination on the appeal?

In general, the plan administrator has 60 days to make a determination unless the plan administrator believes more time is required to consider the appeal, in which case an additional 60 days is available if the claimant is notified beforehand. In the case of disability claims, however, the plan administrator has only 45 days to consider the appeal. [29 C.F.R. § 2560.503-1(i)]

Chapter 17

Spousal Rights

This chapter deals with the legal protections that are extended to the spouse of a 401(k) plan participant and includes a discussion of who is considered a "spouse" for 401(k) plan purposes. Protection is afforded in two contexts. First, benefits are provided upon death to a surviving spouse unless, during the participant's lifetime, those benefits are waived by the participant with the consent of his or her spouse. Second, a spouse can be awarded all or any part of a participant's interest in a 401(k) plan upon the dissolution of the marriage.

Survivor Annuity Requirements 17-1
Annuity and Other Lifetime Income Products 17-2
Qualified Pre-Retirement Survivor Annuity and Qualified Joint and Survivor Annuity 17-4
Waivers 17-6
Written Explanation 17-7
Spouse's Consent 17-8
Definition of a "Spouse" for 401(k) Plan Purposes 17-10
Loans 17-14
Special Circumstances 17-15
Qualified Domestic Relations Orders 17-16
QDRO Terms 17-17
Review and Qualification of a Domestic Relations Order 17-18
Plan Provisions 17-18
Tax Consequences 17-18
Special Circumstances 17-19

Survivor Annuity Requirements

Q 17:1 What plans are subject to the survivor annuity requirements?

A 401(k) pre-ERISA money purchase plan is always subject to these requirements. A 401(k) profit sharing or stock bonus plan is subject to the survivor annuity requirements unless all of the following conditions are satisfied:

1. The plan provides that upon death the participant's entire vested account balance is payable to the participant's surviving spouse unless the surviving spouse consents to the designation of another beneficiary.
2. The participant does not elect to have his or her account balance paid over the participant's lifetime. (This requirement does not apply if the plan does not offer life annuities as payment options.)
3. The 401(k) plan is not a transferee plan as to the participant.

[Treas. Reg. § 1.401(a)-20, Q&A 3(a)]

Q 17:2 What is a *transferee plan*?

A 401(k) plan is considered a *transferee plan* if it receives—through merger, spin-off, or other similar transfer—benefits from a plan subject to the survivor annuity requirements. However, a 401(k) plan is not considered a transferee plan if these benefits come into the 401(k) plan as a result of a rollover contribution. [Treas. Reg. §§ 1.401(a)-20, Q&A 5(a); 1.411(d)-4, Q&A 3(b)]

Q 17:3 If a 401(k) plan is a transferee plan, do the survivor annuity requirements apply to all plan participants?

No. The survivor annuity requirements apply only to the participants whose benefits are transferred to the 401(k) plan. [Treas. Reg. § 1.401(a)-20, Q&A 5(a)]

Q 17:4 If a 401(k) plan is a transferee plan with respect to a participant, do the survivor annuity requirements apply to that participant's entire account balance?

The general rule is that a participant's entire account balance is subject to the survivor annuity requirements. However, if a separate account is maintained for the benefits transferred to the plan, then the survivor annuity requirements apply only to the transferred benefits. [Treas. Reg. § 1.401(a)-20, Q&A 5(b)]

Annuity and Other Lifetime Income Products

Q 17:5 What is the issue with applying the survivor annuity rules to deferred annuity contracts?

Many 401(k) plans offer participants the option of investing their plan account in a deferred annuity contract. The way these investments generally work is that during the accumulation phase investments are made in mutual funds or similar products and, upon reaching their annuity starting date (see Q 17:14), participants either have an option to be paid in the form of an annuity, or automatically receive their benefit in that form. In plans offering this type of product that take advantage of the 100 percent spousal death benefit option (see Q 17:1) there is a question as to whether, and when, investment in a deferred annuity contract is considered the election of a life annuity triggering application of the survivor annuity rules. This issue is of concern to both plan sponsors and plan recordkeepers because plans that are designed to avoid application of the survivor annuity rules by providing for a 100 percent spousal death benefit may not have either the plan document provisions, or the administrative support, necessary to support the survivor annuity rules.

Q 17:6 What guidance has been provided to address this issue?

In 2012, the IRS issued guidance that partially addresses the issue by drawing conclusions based on specific factual scenarios.

In the first scenario, the participant invests in an annuity contract where, at any time prior to the annuity starting date, he or she can transfer funds out of the annuity contract and in to other plan investments. Participants can also elect an alternate form of distribution, such as a lump sum. In this scenario the survivor annuity rules are not triggered by investing in the annuity contract, but are only triggered in the event the participant does not elect a non-annuity form of benefit prior to their annuity starting date.

In the second scenario, participants do not have the option of transferring funds out of the deferred annuity contract or of electing a form of benefit other than a life annuity. In this scenario the survivor annuity rules are triggered with the participant's first investment in the annuity contract.

The third scenario is the same as scenario number two except participants can elect to have amounts invested in the annuity contract that are attributable to matching contributions paid in a different form of distribution, such as a lump sum. The result here is the same as in scenario two and the survivor annuity rules are triggered with the participant's first investment in the annuity contract.

[Rev. Rul. 2012-3, 2012-8 I.R.B. 383]

Q 17:7 If the survivor annuity rules are triggered by investment in a deferred annuity contract, do they apply to the participant's entire account balance?

If the plan separately accounts for the deferred annuity contract then the survivor annuity rules will not apply to the remainder of the plan. [Rev. Rul. 2012-3, 2012-8 I.R.B. 383]

Q 17:8 How do the survivor annuity rules apply to GLWBs or other similar products?

A *guaranteed lifetime withdrawal benefit* (GLWB) is an investment option allowing participants who reach their annuity starting date to begin receiving guaranteed lifetime income payments while still maintaining their account balance. The guaranteed payments are funded from the participant's account balance until it is depleted, at which time payments are funded by the insurer who issued the product. A key distinction between GLWBs and other similar products from deferred annuity contracts is that the spousal protection offered by the 100 percent spousal death benefit option continues to have value even after lifetime payments to the participant commence.

The IRS has not yet issued guidance on how the survivor annuity rules apply to these types of investments but it is anticipated that they will do so as part of their overall initiative to facilitate use of lifetime income options in defined contribution plans.

Qualified Pre-Retirement Survivor Annuity and Qualified Joint and Survivor Annuity

Q 17:9 What are the survivor annuity requirements?

If a participant dies before the annuity starting date, benefits must be paid to the surviving spouse in the form of a qualified pre-retirement survivor annuity. If a participant survives until the annuity starting date, the participant's account balance must be used to purchase a qualified joint and survivor annuity. [Treas. Reg. § 1.401(a)-20, Q&A 8(a)]

Q 17:10 What is a *qualified pre-retirement survivor* annuity?

A *qualified pre-retirement survivor annuity* (QPSA) is an immediate annuity for the life of the surviving spouse purchased with not less than 50 percent and not more than 100 percent of the value of the participant's vested account balance determined as of the date of death. [Treas. Reg. § 1.401(a)-20, Q&A 20] The percentage of the participant's account balance used to purchase the QPSA is specified in the plan document.

Q 17:11 What is a *qualified joint and survivor* annuity?

In the case of a married participant, a *qualified joint and survivor annuity* (QJSA) is an annuity for the life of the participant with a survivor annuity for the life of the spouse. The amount of the survivor annuity is a plan-specified percentage that is not less than 50 percent and not more than 100 percent of the amount of the annuity that is payable during the joint lives of the participant and spouse. [I.R.C. § 417(b)] In the case of an unmarried participant, the QJSA is an annuity for the life of the participant. [Treas. Reg. § 1.401(a)-20, Q&A 25(a)]

Q 17:12 Is a plan required to provide any alternative to the qualified joint and survivor annuity?

Under the Pension Protection Act of 2006 [Pub. L. No. 109-280, 120 Stat. 780] (PPA), starting with plan years beginning on or after January 1, 2008, a plan is required to offer a qualified optional survivor annuity (QOSA) in the event a participant waives the QJSA. If the survivor annuity under the QJSA is less than 75 percent of the amount of the annuity that is payable during the joint lives of the participant and spouse, then the QOSA is 75 percent of the amount that is payable during their joint lives. If the survivor annuity under the QJSA is equal to or greater than 75 percent, the QOSA is 50 percent. [I.R.C. § 417(g); IRS Notice 2008-30, Q&A-8, 2008-12 I.R.B 638]

Q 17:13 Is a plan required to provide a qualified pre-retirement survivor annuity that is based on the qualified optional survivor annuity described in Q 17:8?

No. A plan is not required to provide a QPSA that is based on the QOSA. [IRS Notice 2008-30, Q&A-13, 2008-12 I.R.B. 638]

> **Example.** A 401(k) plan that is subject to survivor annuity requirements provides for a qualified joint and 50 percent survivor annuity. The plan, as a result, must offer to a participant who waives the QJSA a QOSA that provides a survivor annuity of 75 percent of the amount of the annuity payable during the joint lives of the participant and the spouse. The 401(k) plan also provides for a QPSA that is purchased with 50 percent of a deceased participant's account. Because the QOSA requirements do not apply in the case of the QPSA, the plan is not required to offer a QPSA that is purchased with 75 percent of the deceased participant's account balance.

Q 17:14 What is the *annuity starting date*?

The *annuity starting date* is the first day of the first period for which an account is payable as an annuity or any other form. [Treas. Reg. § 1.401(a)-20, Q&A 10(b)]

> **Example.** Alex retires and elects to receive his 401(k) account balance in the form of a life annuity commencing April 1. Because of administrative delays, Alex's April 1 payment is not received until April 15. April 1 is still considered the annuity starting date.

Q 17:15 When must payments under a QPSA commence?

The 401(k) plan must permit the surviving spouse to begin receiving payments under a QPSA within a reasonable time after the participant's death. [Treas. Reg. § 1.401(a)-20, Q&A 22(b)]

Q 17:16 When must payments under a QJSA commence?

The 401(k) plan must permit the participant to begin receiving payments under a QJSA when the participant attains the earliest retirement age under the plan. [Treas. Reg. § 1.401(a)-20, Q&A 17(a)] Payments under a QJSA, however, cannot be made while benefits are considered immediately distributable (see chapter 16), unless the participant's consent is obtained. [Treas. Reg. § 1.417(e)-1(b)(1)]

Q 17:17 What is the *earliest retirement age*?

The *earliest retirement age* under a 401(k) plan is the earliest age at which a participant may elect to receive benefits under the plan. [Treas. Reg. § 1.401(a)-20, Q&A 17(b)]

> **Example.** Beta Corporation sponsors a 401(k) plan under which participants who separate from service cannot receive benefits until they reach age 50. Fred, age 40, terminates employment with a vested account balance under the plan. The earliest retirement age under the plan with respect to Fred is age 50, the age at which he can elect to receive benefits.

Waivers

Q 17:18 May a participant waive the QPSA and/or QJSA?

Yes. With the consent of the participant's spouse, a participant may waive either or both of these benefits during the election period applicable to each benefit. [Treas. Reg. § 1.401(a)-20, Q&A 8(b)] A participant's waiver may be made either on a paper document or through an electronic medium that satisfies the requirements of Treasury Regulations Section 1.401(a)-21(d) (see chapter 16).

Q 17:19 What requirements must be met by a participant's waiver of the QPSA?

A participant's waiver of the QPSA must specify the nonspouse beneficiaries who will receive benefits upon the participant's death. [Treas. Reg. § 1.401(a)-20, Q&A 31(a)]

Q 17:20 What requirements must be met by a participant's waiver of the QJSA?

A participant's waiver of the QJSA must specify the nonspouse beneficiaries who will receive benefits upon the participant's death. In addition, the waiver must specify the form of benefit the participant will receive in lieu of the QJSA. [Treas. Reg. § 1.401(a)-20, Q&As 31(a), 31(b)]

Q 17:21 When may a participant waive the QPSA?

In general, a participant may waive the QPSA only after the first day of the plan year in which the participant reaches age 35. A plan may allow a participant to waive the QPSA before then if the previous waiver becomes invalid at the beginning of the plan year in which the participant reaches age 35. A participant must then execute a new waiver in order to avoid the QPSA requirement. [Treas. Reg. § 1.401(a)-20, Q&A 33(b)]

Q 17:22 Are there special rules that apply to terminated participants?

Yes. A participant who separates from service before age 35 is allowed to waive the QPSA any time after the date of separation. [I.R.C. § 417(a)(6)] In this case, the rule described in Q 17:21 that automatically revokes a previously made waiver does not apply.

> **Example.** Ethan is 27 when he separates from service. The 401(k) plan in which he participates and which is subject to the survivor annuity requirements does not allow the payment of benefits until a participant reaches 45. Ethan can waive the QPSA even though he is not yet 35. In addition, when Ethan reaches age 35, his waiver will not be automatically revoked.

Q 17:23 When may a participant waive the QJSA?

A participant may waive the QJSA no earlier than 180 days before the annuity starting date. [I.R.C. § 417(a)(6)(A)]

Written Explanation

Q 17:24 Must a 401(k) plan provide a written explanation of the survivor annuity requirements?

Yes. A plan must provide to each participant a written explanation containing the following information:

1. A general description of the QJSA or QPSA and the circumstances under which they will be paid;
2. The participant's right to make, and the effect of, an election to waive the QJSA or QPSA;
3. The spouse's right to consent to the participant's waiver;
4. The participant's right to make, and the effect of, a revocation of a previously made election to waive the QJSA or QPSA; and
5. A general description of the eligibility conditions and other material features of the plan's other forms of benefit, including the QOSA, and their financial effects.

[I.R.C. § 417(a)(3); Treas. Reg. § 1.401(a)-20, Q&A 36; Treas. Reg. § 1.417(a)(3)-1; IRS Notice 2008-30, Q&A 12, 2008-12 I.R.B. 638]

Q 17:25 How are the financial effects of various forms of benefits provided under the plan described in the written explanation?

The written explanation is required to set forth the benefit amounts that would be payable under an annuity contract purchased with the participant's account balance. If the benefit amounts are determined using estimates rather than actual quotes from an insurance company, the written explanation must state that the benefit amounts are based on estimates. [Treas. Reg. § 1.417(a)(3)-1(c)(3) and (4)]

Q 17:26 When must the written explanation of the QPSA be provided to participants?

The answer to this question depends on the particular circumstance of each participant. For most participants, this explanation must be given sometime during the period beginning on the first day of the plan year in which the participant reaches age 32 and ending on the last day of the plan year in which the participant reaches age 34. If an individual becomes a participant after this period, then the period runs from the date one year before the individual becomes a participant until the date one year after participation commences. In the case of an individual who separates from service before age 35 (see Q 17:22), the explanation must be given during the one-year period following the participant's separation from service. [Treas. Reg. § 1.401(a)-20, Q&A 35]

Q 17:27 When must the written explanation of the QJSA be provided to participants?

The written explanation must be provided no less than 30 days and no more than 180 days before the annuity starting date. The 30-day requirement may be waived if the explanation clearly indicates that the participant has the right to at least 30 days to consider whether to waive the QJSA. In no event, however, can distribution of the participant's benefit begin until 7 days after the date the written explanation is given to the participant. [I.R.C. § 417(a)(6)(A); Treas. Reg. § 1.417(e)-1(b)(3)]

Q 17:28 Must the written explanations of the survivor annuity requirements be provided on paper?

No. Written explanations of the survivor annuity requirements may be provided either on a paper document or through an electronic medium that satisfies the requirements of Treasury Regulations Section 1.401(a)-21(c) (see chapter 16).

Spouse's Consent

Q 17:29 What requirements must a spouse's consent satisfy?

The spouse's consent must be in writing, must acknowledge the effect of a participant's waiver, and must be witnessed by a plan representative or notary public. [I.R.C. § 417(a)(2)(A)] The consent must specify the nonspouse beneficiaries who will receive benefits upon the participant's death. It must also specify, in the case of a participant's waiver of a QJSA, the particular optional form of benefit selected by the participant. [Treas. Reg. § 1.401(a)-20, Q&As

31(a), 31(b)] The spouse's consent to the waiver may be made either on a paper document or through an electronic medium that satisfies the requirements of Treasury Regulations Section 1.401(a)-21(d)(6) (see chapter 16).

Q 17:30 If a participant revokes a prior waiver and then elects again during the election period to waive the survivor annuity requirements, must the spouse's consent be obtained again?

In general, the answer is yes. The spouse's consent is also required if, during the election period, the participant changes the beneficiary to whom benefits are payable on death or if the participant selects an optional form of benefit different from the one selected when the QJSA was originally waived. [Treas. Reg. § 1.401(a)-20, Q&A 31(a), 31(b)] Spousal consent may not be required, however, if the spouse's original consent permits the participant to change beneficiaries or other forms of benefit without further consent of the spouse. The spouse's relinquishment of consent rights may be total or limited. [Treas. Reg. § 1.401(a)-20, Q&A 31(c)]

Example. Darlene waives the QPSA and names her mother, Joan, as her beneficiary. Darlene's husband, Jim, consents to the waiver and to the naming of any other beneficiary as long as that beneficiary is a child of Darlene's. At a later date, Darlene names her father as beneficiary. This change can be made only if Jim consents.

Q 17:31 Is the spouse's consent revocable?

Whether the spouse's consent is revocable depends on the provisions of the plan. [Treas. Reg. § 1.401(a)-20, Q&A 30] Most 401(k) plans that are subject to the survivor annuity requirements provide that a spouse's consent cannot be revoked.

Q 17:32 Does a spouse's consent to the waiver of the survivor annuity requirements apply to a subsequent spouse?

Except in the case of a loan secured by a participant's account balance, the answer is no. [Treas. Reg. § 1.401(a)-20, Q&A 29]

Q 17:33 If a participant elects to receive a QOSA in lieu of the QJSA, must the participant's spouse consent to this election?

No. The spouse of a participant who elects to receive a QOSA in lieu of the QJSA is not required to consent to that election. [IRS Notice 2008-30, Q&A-11, 2008-12 I.R.B. 638]

Example. A 401(k) plan that is subject to survivor annuity requirements provides for a qualified joint and 50 percent survivor annuity. The plan, as a result, must offer to a participant who waives the QJSA a QOSA that provides a survivor annuity of 75 percent of the amount of the annuity payable during the joint lives of the participant and the spouse. The participant waives the QJSA and elects instead to receive a QOSA. This election can be made by the participant without obtaining the consent of his or her spouse.

Definition of a "Spouse" for 401(k) Plan Purposes

In recent years, there have been significant legal developments in defining the term "spouse," particularly in the context of same-sex legal relationships. This section discusses those developments and their impact on 401(k) plans.

Q 17:34 How is spousal status determined?

In 1996, Congress enacted the Defense of Marriage Act [Pub. L. No. 104-199, 110 Stat. 2419 (1996), Sect. 3, 1 U.S.C. 7], which states that federal law recognizes only a marriage between a man and a woman. DOMA also allowed individual states to refuse to recognize same-sex marriages performed in other states. On June 26, 2013, the Supreme Court held that Section 3 of DOMA limiting the definition of marriage to a union between persons of opposite gender was a violation of the Fourteenth Amendment right to equal protection under the law and struck it down. [United States v. Windsor, 570 U.S. 12 (2013)] The Court did not strike down the part of DOMA allowing individual states to decide whether or not to recognize same-sex marriages performed in other states. However, the Supreme Court has subsequently held that state laws prohibiting same-sex marriage also are in violation of the Fourteenth Amendment right to equal protection. The ruling in *Obgerfell v. Hodges* [576 U.S. __ (2015)] has broad application; it applies not only to rights offered under federal law but to any right that may be available based on spousal status.

On August 29, 2013, the IRS published Revenue Ruling 2013-17, which provided much-needed guidance on how the *Windsor* decision should be implemented in the context of federal tax law. The ruling clarified that same-sex couples will be treated as married for all federal tax purposes, including employee benefit provisions, if the marriage was legal in the state in which it was celebrated, regardless of the legality of the marriage in the state where the couple resides. The ruling also clarified that terms such as "spouse," "husband," and "wife," as used in the Internal Revenue Code shall be interpreted to include same-sex spouses. Among the reasons cited by the IRS in support of this ruling were the need for uniformity and efficiency in the application of federal tax law. Revenue Ruling 2013-17 does not apply to domestic partnerships, civil unions, or other legal relationships that are not a marriage under state law. The effective date of the ruling was September 16, 2013. The ruling applies only to tax code provisions and does not govern the definition of marriage for purposes of Department of Labor (DOL) or other rules. [Rev. Rul. 2013-17, 2013-38 I.R.B. 1]

On September 18, 2013, the DOL published Technical Release No. 2013-04 providing guidance on how the *Windsor* decision should be implemented in the context of ERISA. The DOL followed the IRS's lead in establishing a "state of celebration" rule but applying it only to marriage and not to other legal relationships. On April 4, 2014, the IRS published additional guidance addressing operational compliance with the *Windsor* decision as well as plan amendment issues. [IRS Notice 2014-19, 2014-17 I.R.B. 979 and corresponding FAQ document]

These regulatory rulings have effectively been superseded by the recent *Obgerfell* decision, which invalidates state laws banning same-sex marriage. The rulings may still have validity in making a distinction between marriage and other legal relationships.

Q 17:35 What was the effective date of the *Windsor* decision?

Generally, plans must have begun compliance with the *Windsor* decision (i.e., offering spousal benefits created by federal law (see Q 17:41) to both same-sex and opposite-sex married couples) as of June 26, 2013, the date *Windsor* was published. Since the effective date of the guidance clarifying that marital status is determined solely by the legality of the marriage in the state it was celebrated and not by the state of domicile was September 16, 2013, plans will not be at risk of disqualification if they applied a "state of domicile" rule for the period between June 26, 2013 and September 16, 2013.

Q 17:36 Could plans offer federally created spousal benefits to same-sex spouses prior to the effective date of the *Windsor* decision?

Plans may be operated to reflect the outcome of *Windsor* prior to June 16, 2013 for either all or limited purposes (for example, plans could be amended for purposes of the QJSA and QPSA rules only), but the IRS cautions that there may be unintended consequences that raise issues under other plan qualification rules if such amendments are enacted.

Q 17:37 What should a plan do if it did not comply operationally with the *Windsor* decision by the effective date?

If a plan did not comply operationally by the specified effective date (see Q 17:35), it should follow the rules contained in the IRS's Employee Plans Compliance Resolution System (see chapter 20) to correct any operational errors. For example, if a participant in a plan subject to the QJSA rules died after June 26, 2013, and the same-sex spouse did not receive the benefit or waive the right to receive it, the plan could seek a waiver from the same-sex spouse.

Q 17:38 When must 401(k) plans be amended to reflect the *Windsor* decision and subsequent IRS guidance?

If the plan's current definitions of "spouse" and "marriage" are consistent with the *Windsor* decision and subsequent IRS guidance, and if the operational effective dates are consistent with IRS rules (see Qs 17:35, 17:36), no amendment is required. Some plan sponsors may choose to amend their plans anyway to provide more clarity on the definitions, but it is not required in this circumstance.

If either the plan's definitions are not consistent with current law or the plan is using earlier effective dates than what's required, then the plan must be amended by the later of:

- December 31, 2014, *or*
- The end of the plan year in which the amendment is first effective, *or*
- The due date of the employer's tax return for the year in which the amendment is first effective.

Q 17:39 Can a plan rely on "state of domicile" law to deny benefits to same-sex spouses after September 16, 2013?

No. Any plan provisions that rely on state of domicile law for determining who is considered married must be amended, and plan operations must be changed, if a plan is to maintain its tax- qualified status. This is the rule for any spousal benefits created under federal law (see Q 17:41). For other benefits that a plan may voluntarily offer to spouses, relying on the law of the state of domicile does not create a plan qualification issue but may create other legal issues, either immediately or in the future, based on the legal reasoning of the *Windsor* decision (i.e., that denying benefits to spouses on the basis of gender is a violation of the Fourteenth Amendment's right to equal protection under the law).

Q 17:40 Can state laws ban or refuse to offer same-sex marriage?

Based on the reasoning of the *Obgerfell* decision (576 U.S. __ (2015)], it would appear that any state law that treats same-sex marriage or spouses differently than opposite-sex relationships would no longer be valid.

Q 17:41 What plan benefits are affected by the *Windsor* definition of who is a spouse?

The definition of who is a spouse is relevant for the following plan purposes:

- *QJSA and QPSA Rules* (see Qs 17:9–17:33). In plans subject to these rules, death benefits must be paid to the surviving spouse in the form of a survivor annuity unless the spouse waives that benefit.
- *100% Death Benefit Rule* (see Q 17:1). In plans that rely on the profit-sharing plan exception to the QJSA and QPSA rules, a participant's spouse must receive 100 percent of any death benefit (unless waived).
- *Qualified Domestic Relations Orders* (see Qs 17:50–17:67). Spouses have the right to be awarded benefits pursuant to a QDRO and also are treated differently for tax purposes under the QDRO rules.
- *Eligible Rollover Distributions* (see chapter 16). A spouse may roll over a death benefit to his or her own IRA or qualified plan account whereas a nonspouse beneficiary is limited to rolling the benefit to an inherited IRA.

- *Minimum Required Distributions* (see chapter 16). Spousal beneficiaries in some cases have the option to defer taking these distributions for a longer period of time than can nonspouse beneficiaries.
- *Hardship Distributions* (see chapter 15). Under the safe harbor events test, these distributions can be made for medical, tuition, or funeral expenses of a participant's spouse.
- *Loans Subject to Spousal Consent* (see chapter 15). In plans subject to the survivor annuity rules, spousal consent must be obtained for participant loans.
- *One Participant Plans* (see chapter 19). Plans covering only the owner and his or her spouse may be exempt from ERISA reporting and other requirements.
- *Family Member Attribution* (see chapters 5 and 10). The status of spouse is relevant both for determining who is a party in interest under ERISA's prohibited transaction rules, as well as for determining who is the "employer" under controlled group rules.
- *Employee Stock Ownership Plans (ESOPs)*. Status as a spouse is relevant for applying certain allocation and accrual limits.

Spousal status may also be relevant for purposes of required ERISA disclosures, the right to bring benefit claims, and prohibited transaction class exemptions.

Q 17:42 What are some remaining questions and concerns for plan sponsors following the Supreme Court's DOMA decision and subsequent guidance?

Critical questions for plan sponsors concern the following:

1. *Treatment of People in Domestic Partnerships or Civil Unions.* The *Windsor* decision did not address legal relationships other than marriage, and Revenue Ruling 2013-17 did not extend to those relationships, so the rules have not changed in terms of how plans address them. For example, if a participant in a defined contribution plan dies, and the plan requires that 100 percent of any death benefit be paid to the surviving spouse, a same-sex spouse from a marriage that is legal in the state where it was celebrated would automatically be entitled to the death benefit. But if the participant was in a registered domestic partnership or some other non-marriage legal relationship, the surviving partner would not automatically be entitled to the death benefit. However, the plan document provisions could state that a participant's domestic partner is the default death beneficiary, in which case the partner would receive the benefit as long as the participant had not elected a different beneficiary. Given that same-sex marriages must be recognized and made available in all states, there may be changes to state laws providing for legal relationships that are not a marriage.
2. *The Risk of Participant Claims.* IRS guidance deals with protecting the tax-qualified status of 401(k) plans but does not address the risk of claims

brought against plan fiduciaries. For example, assume a same-sex spouse was denied a death benefit during the period June 26, 2013 and September 16, 2013 based on a state of domicile interpretation of the *Windsor* rule. The plan would not be subject to disqualification under IRS rules pursuant to IRS Notice 2014-19, but the spouse still may have a legal argument that he or she is entitled to receive the benefit.

Q 17:43 What steps were required of plan sponsors in response to the Supreme Court's *Windsor* decision?

Pending further guidance from the regulatory agencies, plans sponsors were advised to take the following initial steps:

- Review the plan document to ensure that its current definition of "spouse" is in compliance with the *Windsor* decision, Revenue Ruling 2013-17, and IRS Notice 2014-19. If not, amend the plan within the deadline.
- Review your practices for determining the marital status of employees and revise as needed.
- Review your administrative practices for the functions described in Q 17:41 or any other function where spousal status is relevant. Update and educate internal staff and/or outside vendors as needed.
- Consider whether additional employee communication is needed regarding the *Windsor* decision. The implications of the decision extend to health benefits, general taxation, and other matters beyond retirement plan benefits.

Q 17:44 What additional concerns are raised by the *Obgerfell* decision?

The *Obgerfell* decision will mainly impact plan sponsors that previously were denying spousal status in same-sex marriages based on the law of the state of celebration and/or were recognizing spousal status for purposes of federally provided benefits (see Q 17:41) but not for purposes of other plan benefits. These practices will need to change, and it is unclear at the time of this writing what the effective date of those changes will need to be and whether the changes need to be retroactive.

Loans

Q 17:45 How do the survivor annuity requirements apply to loans?

If a 401(k) plan is subject to the survivor annuity requirements at the time of the loan and the participant's account balance is pledged as security for the loan, then spousal consent must be obtained. Spousal consent must be obtained no earlier than 180 days before the participant's account balance is pledged. The spouse's consent must be in writing, must acknowledge the effect of the loan, and must be witnessed by a plan representative or notary public. [Treas. Reg. § 1.401(a)-20, Q&A 24(a)] The spouse's consent to the waiver may be made either on a paper document or through an electronic medium that satisfies the requirements of Treasury Regulations Section 1.401(a)-21(d)(6) (see chapter 16).

Q 17:46 Is spousal consent required if, after the loan is obtained, the 401(k) plan becomes subject to the survivor annuity requirements or a single participant marries?

No. In addition, the consent of a former spouse is effective with respect to any subsequent spouse. [Treas. Reg. § 1.401(a)-20, Q&A 24(b)]

Q 17:47 What happens if a secured loan is outstanding at the time the QJSA or QPSA is payable?

If a secured loan is outstanding at the time the QJSA or QPSA is payable, the participant's account balance usually will be reduced by the outstanding amount of the loan. [Treas. Reg. § 1.401(a)-20, Q&A 24(d)]

> **Example.** At the time of her death, Karen was an active participant in a 401(k) plan with an account balance of $40,000. There was also outstanding a $10,000 loan secured by her account balance. The QPSA was not waived prior to her death; accordingly, Karen's husband, Dan, is entitled to a QPSA with a value of no less than $15,000, calculated as ($40,000 – $10,000) × 50%.

Special Circumstances

Q 17:48 Is spousal consent required if a plan representative is satisfied that there is no spouse or that the spouse cannot be located?

No. Spousal consent is also not required if the participant is legally separated or the participant has been abandoned (within the meaning of local law) and the participant has a court order to that effect. If a spouse is legally incompetent, the spouse's legal guardian, including the participant, may give consent. [Treas. Reg. § 1.401(a)-20, Q&A 27]

Q 17:49 If a 401(k) plan is not subject to the survivor annuity requirements because it provides that a participant's vested account balance is payable in full, upon the participant's death, to the participant's surviving spouse, when must the participant's account balance be paid to the surviving spouse?

The participant's account balance must be available to the participant's spouse within a reasonable period of time after the participant's death; availability within 90 days will be deemed reasonable. If benefits are not available within this 90-day period, reasonableness, according to the regulations, will be based on the particular facts and circumstances, unless, under the plan, the surviving spouse is treated less favorably than other participants entitled to distributions. In that event, availability is deemed unreasonable. [Treas. Reg. § 1.401(a)-20, Q&A 3(b)(1)]

Q 17:50 May a participant waive the spousal death benefit applicable to 401(k) plans that are not subject to the survivor annuity requirements?

Yes. A participant may waive the spousal death benefit at any time, including any point in time prior to the first day of the plan year in which the participant reaches age 35. A participant's waiver is effective, however, only if the spouse consents to the waiver. A spouse's consent must satisfy the same requirements that apply to the consent of a participant's waiver of the QPSA (see Q 17:29). [Treas. Reg. § 1.401(a)-20, Q&As 32, 33]

Qualified Domestic Relations Orders

Qualified domestic relations orders (QDROs) are an exception to the general rule that prohibits benefits in a qualified plan from being assigned or alienated under Code Section 401(a)(13). The QDRO rules grew out of a recurring controversy between state courts, which were attempting to award qualified plan benefits in divorce proceedings, and plan trustees, who were concerned that compliance with these orders would place them in violation of the anti-assignment rules and disqualify the plan. Enacted in 1984, the QDRO rules now make clear what a plan administrator's or trustee's obligations are when an order dividing benefits is received. This section discusses those rules.

Q 17:51 What is a *qualified domestic relations order*?

A *qualified domestic relations order* (QDRO) is a court order that creates a right for an alternate payee to receive some or all of a participant's benefits in a qualified plan. [I.R.C. § 414(p)(1)(A)]

Q 17:52 What is a *domestic relations order*?

A *domestic relations order* (DRO) is a judgment, decree, or other order made pursuant to a state domestic relations law that relates to the provision of child support, alimony, or marital property rights (including the division of community property). [I.R.C. § 414(p)(1)(B)] For example, a stipulation signed by both parties in a divorce attempting to award retirement plan benefits is not a DRO. However, a court order incorporating and approving that stipulation is a DRO subject to the QDRO rules.

Q 17:53 Who can be an *alternate payee*?

An *alternate payee* must be the spouse, former spouse, child, or other dependent of a participant. [I.R.C. § 414(p)(8)] For example, a QDRO cannot award benefits to a participant's grandchild who is not living with the participant.

QDRO Terms

Q 17:54 What terms must be contained in a QDRO?

A QDRO must clearly specify the following information:

1. The name and last known mailing address of the participant and each alternate payee awarded benefits in the order. However, if the plan administrator has independent knowledge of this information, the order cannot be rejected for failing to provide it. [S. Rep. No. 98-575, 98th Cong., 2d Sess. 20 (1984)]
2. The amount or percentage of benefits to be paid the alternate payee, or the manner in which such amount or percentage is to be determined. This requirement generally prohibits a QDRO from using plan benefits as collateral for a separate obligation, as opposed to being the primary source of payment. For example, a QDRO can require payment in the amount of $5,000 to an alternate payee; it cannot, however, require that a participant's benefit serve as collateral in the event of default on a promissory note in the amount of $5,000 from a participant to the alternate payee. In the latter situation, there is simply no way for the plan administrator to determine how much of the participant's benefit is affected by the order at any given point in time.
3. The number of payments or the period to which the order applies. This generally requires that the order specify whether payments will be paid as a lump sum, as an annuity, in installments, and so forth.
4. The plan to which the order applies.

[I.R.C. § 414(p)(2)]

Q 17:55 What terms cannot be contained in a QDRO?

A QDRO cannot contain any provision that requires a plan to provide any type or form of benefit or any option not otherwise provided under the plan. For example, a QDRO cannot require that a segregated, self-directed account be established for an alternate payee if the plan does not permit participants and beneficiaries to segregate and direct the investments of their accounts.

A QDRO cannot contain a provision that would require the plan to pay increased benefits. For example, a QDRO cannot award an alternate payee a dollar amount that is in excess of a participant's vested account balance.

Finally, a QDRO cannot require a plan to pay to one alternate payee benefits that have already been awarded to another alternate payee in a separate QDRO. [I.R.C. § 414(p)(3)]

Review and Qualification of a Domestic Relations Order

Q 17:56 What is the plan administrator's responsibility when a DRO is received?

The plan administrator must promptly notify the participant and alternate payee that an order has been received and inform them of the plan's procedures for reviewing orders. Within a reasonable period of time, the plan administrator must determine whether the order is qualified. This determination must also be communicated to the participant and alternate payee. [I.R.C. § 414(p)(6)]

Q 17:57 Can the plan make payments to a participant while an order is under review?

A plan administrator cannot pay to a participant any amounts that would be payable to an alternate payee if the order were qualified. These amounts must be separately accounted for and must be held back from distribution for an 18-month period beginning on the date the first payment would be required under the order. [I.R.C. § 414(p)(7)]

Plan Provisions

Q 17:58 Does a plan need to contain any specific provisions concerning QDROs?

No. A plan must have reasonable procedures for reviewing DROs, but this information need not be contained in the plan document. No other plan documentation is required to achieve compliance with the QDRO rules. [Treas. Reg. § 1.401(a)-13(g)(2)] A plan may want to include a provision permitting immediate payment to alternate payees (see Q 17:63). This avoids the administrative task of maintaining alternate payee accounts and providing disclosure to alternate payees.

Tax Consequences

Q 17:59 What are the tax consequences of distributions to alternate payees?

If the alternate payee is the spouse or former spouse of a participant, the distribution is taxed to the alternate payee. [I.R.C. § 402(e)(1)(A)] If the alternate payee is not a spouse or former spouse, the distribution is taxed to the participant.

The 10 percent additional income tax that generally applies to distributions made before a participant attains age 59½ does not apply to distributions made to a spousal alternate payee. [I.R.C. § 72(t)(2)(C)]

An alternate payee who is the spouse or former spouse of a participant may roll over his or her distribution. [I.R.C. § 402(e)(1)(B)]

Special Circumstances

Q 17:60 Should a plan administrator distribute benefits to a participant if the administrator knows a QDRO is being drafted, but has not received it?

This situation can present a dilemma for a plan administrator since the optional form of benefit rules (see chapter 16) and the plan document may require the immediate lump-sum payment of benefits to the participant. In many circumstances where an order might be pending, the participant will not have a divorce decree yet and therefore will not be able to take a lump sum without his or her spouse's consent because of the survivor annuity rules. However, if this is not the case, the decision is a difficult one. The legislative history of the QDRO rules suggests that whenever a plan administrator is on notice that a QDRO is being sought, payment to a participant may be delayed for a reasonable period of time. [Conf. Rep. No. 99-841, 99th Cong., 2d Sess. II-858 (1986)] If a "hold" procedure will be used, it should be reflected in the plan's written QDRO procedures. [Schoonmaker v. Employee Sav. Plan of Amoco Corp., 987 F.2d 410 (7th Cir. 1993)]

Q 17:61 What rights does an alternate payee have?

An alternate payee is generally treated as a plan beneficiary and is entitled to receive a summary plan description, benefit statements, and other information available under ERISA's disclosure rules (see chapter 19). [ERISA § 206(d)(3)(J)] A QDRO may also award survivor annuity rights to an alternate payee. [I.R.C. § 414(p)(5)] To the extent such rights are awarded, the rights of any subsequent spouse of a participant will be limited.

It is not always clear from the plan document whether an alternate payee is entitled to receive loans and/or hardship distributions or to direct the investment of his or her account to the same extent participants are given these rights. Many plan sponsors avoid this issue by providing for immediate distribution to alternate payees. If an alternate payee's benefit will remain in a plan, it makes sense to give investment control to the alternate payee to the same extent it is available to plan participants.

Q 17:62 If a plan changes administrators, should any QDROs be reapproved by the new administrator?

No. Once a determination has been made by a plan administrator that an order is qualified, any successor plan administrator is bound by that determination. [S. Rep. No. 98-575, 98th Cong., 2d Sess. 20 (1984)]

Q 17:63 When can benefits be distributed to an alternate payee?

The answer to this question will vary depending on the terms of the plan and the QDRO. A 401(k) plan may contain a provision permitting immediate distribution to alternate payees once an order is approved. If this provision is in the plan and the order calls for immediate distribution, benefits may be paid right away. [Treas. Reg. § 1.401(a)-13(g)(3)]

If the plan does not contain this special provision, an order can still require payment to be made to an alternate payee when a participant attains age 50, even if the participant has not terminated employment. [I.R.C. § 414(p)(4)] It is not necessary for there to be any special provision in the plan to permit this distribution; it is only necessary that this language be contained in the QDRO.

It is possible that an order will not take advantage of either of these early distribution options. In that event, payment will be permitted at whatever point called for in the order after the participant becomes eligible for a distribution.

Q 17:64 What is the consequence of making payment pursuant to a domestic relations order that is not qualified?

Any such payment will be considered a violation of the anti-assignment and alienation rules contained in Code Section 401(a)(13) and will provide a basis for disqualifying the entire plan.

Q 17:65 What happens if the form of benefit specified in a QDRO is no longer available at the time distribution occurs?

The Report of the Senate Committee on Finance on the Tax Reform Act of 1986 suggests that if an alternate payee is awarded a right to a particular form of benefit in a QDRO that is later eliminated either through plan amendment or change of law, the alternate payee is still entitled to receive that form of benefit unless it would adversely affect a participant's right to his or her benefits. [S. Rep. No. 99-313, 99th Cong., 2d Sess. 20 (1986)]

Q 17:66 Can the administrative expenses associated with reviewing a QDRO be charged to the participant or alternate payee?

Yes. Previously, the DOL had taken the position that QDRO expenses could be paid only from general plan assets. [DOL. Adv. Op. 94-32A] Several years ago, the DOL changed its position so that these expenses can now be charged to the participant and alternate payee. [Field Serv. Bull. 2003-3]

Q 17:67 Does a DRO fail to be qualified merely because it is issued after or revises a QDRO or merely because of the time at which it is issued?

No, a DRO does not fail to become a QDRO merely because it is issued after or revises a QDRO or merely because of the time at which it is issued. [DOL Reg. § 2530.206]

Example 1. Bruce, a married plan participant, and his spouse, Betty, divorce. The plan administrator determines that the DRO submitted to the plan is a QDRO. The QDRO allocates a portion of Bruce's account balance to Betty as alternate payee. Subsequently, before benefits have commenced, Bruce and Betty seek a second DRO that reduces the portion of the account balance payable to Betty. The second DRO does not fail to be a QDRO simply because it is issued after the first QDRO.

Example 2. The facts are the same as those in Example 1, except that the plan administrator determines that the DRO is not a QDRO. Shortly thereafter, Bruce dies while employed. A second DRO correcting the defects of the first order is submitted to the plan administrator. The DRO does not fail to be a QDRO solely because it is issued after Bruce's death.

Q 17:68 Who is considered to be a "spouse" for purposes of the QDRO rules?

The term "spouse" was defined under federal tax law for QDRO purposes in Revenue Ruling 2013-17. The term included any person in a same-sex or opposite-sex marriage that is valid under the law of the state where the marriage was celebrated. It did not include partners in civil unions, domestic partnerships, or other non-marriage legal relationships; it also did not include same-sex couples who were married in a state that does not recognize same-sex marriages (see Qs 17:34, 17:40). The revenue ruling has since been superseded by the Supreme Court's decision in *Obgerfell v. Hodges* [(576 U.S. __ (2015)] such that a married person of either the same or opposite sex will be treated as a spouse regardless of any state law.

Chapter 18

Taxation of 401(k) Plans

This chapter focuses on the tax reporting and payment requirements of 401(k) plans. Federal withholding is covered, from both a contribution and a distribution standpoint. Internal Revenue Service (IRS) forms are discussed, including tax reporting of distributions from 401(k) plans. Also covered are some planning strategies for reducing or eliminating income tax on 401(k) distributions.

Payroll Taxes 18-2
Table 18-1. Type of Tax Due and Deadlines for Collecting, Paying, and Reporting Federal Taxes 18-2
Federal Insurance Contributions Act 18-2
Federal Unemployment Tax Act 18-4
Taxation and Reporting of Distributions and Pre-Tax Contributions 18-6
Lump-Sum Distributions 18-6
Employer Securities 18-10
Distributions on Death 18-11
Installment Distributions 18-13
In-Service Withdrawals 18-14
Life Insurance 18-16
Loans 18-17
Distribution of Excess Deferrals 18-18
Distributions of Excess Contributions and Excess Aggregate Contributions 18-19
Taxation of Roth Distributions and In-Plan Roth Rollovers 18-20
Other Taxes 18-29
Premature Distributions 18-30
Required Minimum Distributions 18-31
Federal Estate Tax 18-32
Filing Requirements for Distributions 18-33
Distribution Planning 18-35
Rollovers of Pre-Tax Accounts 18-35
Rollovers of Roth Accounts 18-37
Lump-Sum Distributions 18-37
Avoiding the Premature Distribution Tax 18-37
Distributions Versus Accumulations 18-39

To Roth or Not to Roth 18-40
Table 18-2. Estimated Break-Even Point of Tax Rate After Retirement (Retirement Age: 65) 18-42

Payroll Taxes

Employers that maintain 401(k) plans are subject to a number of requirements concerning the withholding, reporting, and payment of federal taxes. Some of these requirements apply at the time elective contributions to a plan are made, some apply at the time distributions from the plan are made, and others must be attended to on a quarterly and/or annual basis. Table 18-1 provides an overview of what federal taxes are due and the deadlines for collecting, paying, and reporting those taxes.

Table 18-1. Type of Tax Due and Deadlines for Collecting, Paying, and Reporting Federal Taxes

	FICA	*FUTA*	*FIT*
Roth elective contributions	Taxable	Taxable	Taxable
Pre-tax elective contributions	Taxable	Taxable	Exempt
Employer contributions	Exempt	Exempt	Exempt
Pre-tax distributions	Exempt	Exempt	Taxable
Qualified Roth distributions	Exempt	Exempt	Exempt
Withholding on distributions	None	None	Required unless payee elects a rollover
IRS reporting	Quarterly on Form 941	Annually on Form 940	Annually on Form 1099-R
Participant reporting of withheld amounts	Annually on Form W-2	None	Annually on Form W-2

Federal Insurance Contributions Act

Q 18:1 What is the *FICA tax*?

The *FICA tax* is a tax authorized by the Federal Insurance Contributions Act (FICA) an offshoot of the Social Security Act, enacted in 1935. Its purpose is to provide retirement and welfare benefits to people who are no longer employed. [21 U.S.C. §§ 3101–3128 (subtitle C)] The employer and the employee each pay equal portions of the FICA tax, which is collected by the IRS.

Q 18:2 What amounts are subject to FICA withholding?

Elective contributions to a 401(k) plan (both pre-tax and Roth) are subject to FICA withholding at the time the contributions are made. [I.R.C. § 3121(v)(1)(A)] However, matching contributions or profit sharing contributions are not subject to FICA withholding, either at the time the contributions are made or at the time a distribution is made to a participant. [I.R.C. § 3121(a)(5)(A)]

> **Example.** Erin earns $30,000 and elects to contribute $2,000 annually to her 401(k) plan. Erin's employer makes a matching contribution to her account of $1,000. Although Erin's obligation for payment of federal income tax will be based on earnings of $28,000, her FICA tax obligation will be based on $30,000. She will, however, avoid both federal income and FICA tax on the $1,000 matching contribution made to her account.

Q 18:3 Which employees are subject to FICA tax withholding?

Generally, FICA tax is due on amounts paid to any common-law employee or corporate officer for services performed in the United States. [I.R.C. § 3121(d)] Since the Employee Retirement Income Security Act of 1974 (ERISA) requires that qualified plans be offered for the benefit of employees, as a general rule, anyone who is a plan participant will be subject to FICA tax. Self-employed individuals are subject to the Self-Employment Contributions Act (SECA), which imposes taxes similar to those imposed on common-law employees under FICA. [I.R.C. § 1401]

Q 18:4 How is the FICA tax computed?

The FICA tax is composed of two elements: Old-Age, Survivor, and Disability Insurance (OASDI) and Hospital Insurance (HI). The employer and employee are each taxed for OASDI at the rate of 6.2 percent of wages up to the Social Security Taxable Wage Base in effect for the year. With respect to HI, the employer and employee are each taxed at the rate of 1.45 percent on all wages. [I.R.C. §§ 3101(a), 3101(b), 3111(a), 3111(b)]

> **Example.** The employee's wages subject to FICA tax are $1,000. The total FICA tax owed is $153, and the portion paid by the employer and the employee is the same: $76.50 ($1,000 × 7.65 percent), broken down as follows:

FICA Tax	*Employer Portion*	*Employee Portion*
OASDI	$62.00	$62.00
HI	14.50	14.50
Total	76.50	76.50

Starting in 2013, individuals, but not employers, will pay HI tax of 2.35 percent of compensation in excess of $200,000 ($250,000 for married individuals filing jointly or half that amount for any married individual filing separately). [I.R.C. § 3101(b)(2)]

Q 18:5 How is the FICA tax collected?

The employee portion of the FICA tax on elective contributions is deducted from an employee's pay at the time the payment is issued. [I.R.C. § 3102(a)] The employer will be liable for the employee portion of the tax, in addition to the employer portion, whether or not the tax is collected from the employee. [I.R.C. § 3102(b); Treas. Reg. § 31.3102-1(d)]

Q 18:6 How is the FICA tax paid?

Deposits of collected FICA withholdings must be made to a financial institution qualified as a depository for federal taxes or to a federal reserve bank. The frequency of required deposits depends on the amount of tax withheld by the employer: the larger the amount withheld, the more frequently deposits are required. Some employers are required to make deposits daily, while others may do so as infrequently as quarterly. From 2011, most employers have been remitting FICA taxes electronically using the IRS's Electronic Federal Tax Payment System (EFTPS). [Treas. Reg. § 31.6302-1(h)(2)(iii)]

Q 18:7 How is the FICA tax reported?

FICA taxes are reported quarterly on IRS Form 941. Employees who have FICA tax withheld must be furnished with IRS Form W-2, Wage and Tax Statement, on an annual basis. [I.R.C. § 6051(a); Treas. Reg. § 31.6051-1(a)(*1*)(i)]

Federal Unemployment Tax Act

Q 18:8 What is the *FUTA tax*?

The *FUTA tax* is a tax imposed by the Federal Unemployment Tax Act (FUTA) on employers to fund cash benefits to former employees undergoing temporary periods of unemployment. [23 U.S.C. §§ 3301–3311] Like the FICA tax, these amounts are paid to the IRS. Unlike FICA, this tax is collected from employers only, so there is no withholding requirement on amounts paid to employees.

The Unemployment Insurance Program is a joint federal and state program. As such, credits may be available on amounts due the federal government under FUTA for payments that have been made to state unemployment funds. [I.R.C. § 3302(a)(1)]

Q 18:9 What amounts are subject to FUTA?

As with FICA, elective contributions to a 401(k) plan (both pre-tax and Roth) are subject to FUTA tax, but matching or profit sharing contributions and plan distributions are not. [I.R.C. §§ 3306(b)(5)(A), 3306(r)(1)(A)]

Q 18:10 Which employees' wages are subject to the FUTA tax?

The first $7,000 of wages paid to a common-law employee who performs services within the United States or outside the United States, if the employee is a U.S. citizen employed by a U.S. employer, are subject to the FUTA tax. [I.R.C. § 3306(c)] There is no tax comparable to FUTA that applies to net employment income earned by self-employed individuals.

Q 18:11 How is the FUTA tax computed?

The FUTA tax rate decreased from 6.2 percent to 6 percent as of July 1, 2011. [I.R.C. § 3301(1) and (2)] Credits against the FUTA tax may be available for payments made to a state unemployment fund, as well as for employers with a historically low incidence of unemployment. [I.R.C. §§ 3302(a)(1), 3302(b)]

Q 18:12 How is the FUTA tax reported?

FUTA taxes are reported annually to the IRS on Form 940, which is due by the end of January of the following calendar year. If all deposits have been timely made, the due date is extended to February 10.

Because there is no obligation for employees to pay any portion of the FUTA tax, there is also no corresponding obligation on the part of employers to collect FUTA tax from wages.

Q 18:13 How is the FUTA tax paid?

If the employer's FUTA tax liability exceeds $500 in any calendar quarter, deposits must be made to an authorized financial institution or a federal reserve bank. [Treas. Reg. § 31.6302(c)-3(a)(2)] In calculating the $500 limit, the employer may assume that the maximum credit is available. From 2011, most employers have been remitting FUTA taxes electronically using the IRS's Electronic Federal Tax Payment System (EFTPS). [Treas. Reg. §§ 31.6302-1(h); 31.6302(c)-3(b)]

Taxation and Reporting of Distributions and Pre-Tax Contributions

One of the major advantages of a qualified plan is that contributions are generally not taxed when made to the plan, only when distributed to the participant. In some cases, the distribution may not be in cash; the participant will then generally be taxed on the value of the property distributed. This section deals with the federal tax treatment of distributions from 401(k) plans and how such distributions are reported. Most distributions are reported on Form 1099-R, but certain excise taxes are reported on personal or estate tax returns. If the distribution is an eligible rollover distribution, tax may be deferred by rolling it over to an eligible retirement plan or annuity. Additional information concerning the tax treatment of eligible rollover distributions can be found in chapter 16.

The tax consequences and rules of distributions from a Roth 401(k) account are different from those of pre-tax account distributions. The tax consequences of distributions from a Roth account are discussed at Qs 18:59–18:84.

Lump-Sum Distributions

Q 18:14 How are distributions generally paid from 401(k) plans?

Distributions from most 401(k) plans are generally made in the form of a single sum. If a single sum qualifies as a lump-sum distribution, then favorable tax treatment may be available to the participant. If the distribution does not qualify as a lump-sum distribution, the entire distribution is taxable as ordinary income in the year of receipt. Prior to the passage of the Small Business Job Protection Act of 1996 (SBJPA), the definition of a lump-sum distribution was relevant to all plan participants due to the availability of five-year forward averaging, a technique designed to lower the tax rate on plan distributions. For distributions occurring after December 31, 1999, five-year averaging is no longer available and the definition of a lump-sum distribution is only relevant to plan participants who were 50 years of age or older on January 1, 1986, or who receive a distribution in the form of employer securities (see Qs 18:22, 18:28).

Q 18:15 How is a *lump-sum distribution* defined?

A distribution will qualify as a *lump-sum distribution* if it meets the following requirements:

1. The distribution or distributions are made within one year (the recipient's taxable year is used for purposes of these rules);
2. The distribution represents the balance to the credit of the employee;
3. The distribution is made on account of death, attainment of age 59½, separation from service (applicable only to common-law employees), or disability (applicable only to self-employed individuals) [I.R.C. § 402(e)(4)(D)]; and

4. The participant has participated in the plan for five or more taxable years. (Beneficiaries of death proceeds are exempt from this requirement.) The number of tax years of participation in the plan completed prior to the taxable year of termination is counted for this purpose. [IRS Publication 575, *Pension and Annuity Income*]

Q 18:16 Do distributions as a result of termination of a 401(k) plan qualify for lump-sum treatment?

A notable omission from the list of qualified lump-sum distribution events is a distribution on account of termination of the plan. These distributions are not entitled to favorable treatment for purposes of the lump-sum distribution rules unless the participant has attained age 59½.

Q 18:17 What plans are considered in determining whether a 401(k) distribution qualifies as a lump-sum distribution?

All similar plans of the employer are aggregated for lump-sum purposes, including all 401(k) and profit sharing plans of the employer. [I.R.C. § 402(e)(4)(D)(ii)] Defined benefit, money purchase, and target plans need not be considered when determining whether a single-sum distribution from a 401(k) plan constitutes a lump-sum distribution.

Q 18:18 What constitutes the *balance to the credit* of a participant?

The definition of the *balance to the credit* of a participant is critical in the determination of whether a distribution qualifies as a lump sum. The general meaning of *balance to the credit* in a 401(k) plan is the vested account balance. However, all 401(k) and profit sharing plans of the employer must be treated as one plan. [I.R.C. § 402(e)(4)(D)(ii)] Thus, if an employee receives a distribution of his or her vested balance from a 401(k) plan but not from the profit sharing plan, the 401(k) distribution does not qualify as the balance to the credit of the employee.

The balance to the credit does not include amounts payable to an alternate payee under a qualified domestic relations order (QDRO). [I.R.C. § 402(e)(4)(D)(v)] The balance to the credit includes all amounts in the participant's account as of the time of the first distribution received after the event that triggers the distribution. A participant receiving installment payments after separation from service may elect a single sum in a later year, but the single sum will not qualify as a lump-sum distribution because the balance to the credit of the participant has not been paid within one taxable year of the participant. [Prop. Treas. Reg. § 1.402(e)-2(d)(1)(ii)(C)]

Q 18:19 How do subsequent payments affect the lump-sum treatment of a prior distribution?

After a participant's account has been distributed, incidental amounts may be credited to the account as a result of calculation errors, additional earnings, forfeiture reallocations, or year-end contributions. These incidental payments do not destroy the lump-sum treatment of amounts received in a prior taxable year. However, the incidental payment itself is taxable as ordinary income in the calendar year received. [Prop. Treas. Reg. § 1.402(e)-2(d)(1)(ii)(B)]

Q 18:20 What tax options are available to a participant who qualifies for lump-sum treatment?

In certain grandfathered cases, special tax treatment may still be available (see Qs 18:22, 18:25). For most participants, however, whether a distribution qualifies as a lump-sum distribution is irrelevant and their options are the following:

1. Pay ordinary income tax on the entire distribution.
2. Roll over the distribution to an IRA or another retirement plan, deferring taxation until funds are withdrawn.
3. Roll over to a Roth IRA or, if the plan permits, convert a pre-tax account into a Roth account inside the 401(k) plan. Pay ordinary income tax on the rolled over or converted amounts.
4. Roll over a portion of the distribution and receive the remainder in cash, which is subject to ordinary income tax.

These options are available with respect to the taxable portion of a participant's distribution. Some or all of a distribution may be distributed tax free, such as a qualified Roth distribution or distribution of a participant loan that was previously taxed (see Q 18:23).

Q 18:21 Does an alternate payee in a QDRO qualify for lump-sum treatment?

If lump-sum treatment is available to a participant, a payment to an alternate payee, who is the spouse or former spouse of a participant under a QDRO, of the total sum due under the terms of the QDRO will also qualify as a lump-sum distribution. [I.R.C. § 402(e)(4)(D)(vii)]

Q 18:22 How did the Tax Reform Act of 1986 protect favorable treatment for older participants?

The Tax Reform Act of 1986 (TRA '86) grandfathered certain participants who were born before January 2, 1936. These participants may elect ten-year forward income averaging based on 1986 rates. Capital gains treatment is available at a flat 20 percent rate on any pre-1974 accumulation.

Q 18:23 What items can be excluded from taxation in a lump-sum distribution?

If the participant has an investment in the contract (cost basis), certain items are excluded from taxation. These items would include after-tax voluntary or mandatory employee contributions (including contributions to Roth accounts), PS-58 costs (see Q 18:47), the net unrealized appreciation in employer securities, and repayments of any loans that were taxable under Internal Revenue Code (Code) Section 72(p). [*See* IRS Publication 575, *Pension and Annuity Income.*] However, earnings related to after-tax employee contributions and Roth contributions are taxable items unless the earnings attributable to the Roth contributions are distributed as part of a qualified Roth distribution, in which case they are excluded. To the extent 401(k) excess deferrals have remained in the plan and have been previously taxed, that money is once again taxed when distributed.

Q 18:24 Do small lump-sum distributions qualify for any additional favorable treatment?

To the extent ten-year income averaging is available (see Q 18:22), the minimum distribution allowance (MDA) will serve to further reduce the amount of tax on a lump-sum distribution. This applies to distributions of less than $70,000. The MDA is calculated in two steps:

1. The lesser of $10,000 or 50 percent of the taxable distribution,
2. Minus 20 percent of the excess over $20,000.

[IRS Form 4972]

An example of the calculation of the MDA is shown below.

Example. Emily receives a lump-sum distribution of $50,000. The amount of this distribution that is not subject to federal income tax is the MDA. The allowance is:

1. Lesser of
   $10,000 or ($\frac{1}{2}$ × $50,000) = $25,000
   ($10,000 is the result)
2. Reduced by 20 percent of ($50,000 – $20,000) = $6,000
   (1) – (2) = MDA
   $10,000 – $6,000 = $4,000

As a result, $4,000 will not be subject to federal income tax; the remaining $46,000 will be subject to federal tax.

Q 18:25 How is the tax on a lump-sum distribution computed?

The following steps are taken in computing the tax with ten-year income averaging:

1. Subtract the MDA from the total taxable amount.

2. Divide the net result by 10.
3. Compute the tax using the tax table for single individuals.
4. Multiply the result by 10.

An example of the calculation is shown below.

1. Distribution: $45,000
   MDA:
   Lesser of (a) $10,000 or
   (b) $1/2 \times$ $45,000 = $22,500
   Reduced by 20% × ($45,000 – $20,000) = $5,000
   MDA = $10,000 – $5,000 = $5,000
   Taxable distribution: $45,000 – $5,000 = $40,000
2. Divide by 10:
   $40,000/10 = $4,000
3. Calculate tax on $4,000 per Form 4972: $503
4. Multiply result by 10:
   10 × $503 = $5,030

If ordinary income tax is paid on the distribution without applying income averaging or the MDA, the total tax is $7,113 (2014, single return tax rates). The tax savings from the special treatment results in a savings of $2,083 to the taxpayer.

Q 18:26 What is the impact on future election rights if an individual makes a lump-sum election as a beneficiary?

If an individual receives a lump-sum distribution as a beneficiary of a participant in a qualified plan, any election made in the capacity of a beneficiary does not affect a subsequent election by the individual in his or her capacity as a participant in a qualified plan.

Q 18:27 How are lump-sum distributions reported?

Lump-sum distributions are reported on Form 1099-R. If the participant has a cost basis, such basis will be reported on this form. In addition, any portion of the distribution attributable to pre-1974 participation will also be reported on Form 1099-R.

Employer Securities

Q 18:28 Does a participant in a 401(k) plan receive any favorable treatment when receiving employer securities in a distribution?

Yes. The net unrealized appreciation (the difference between the market value of the security at the time distributed from the plan and the cost basis of the security) is not subject to tax until the employer securities are sold. In the case of a distribution other than a lump-sum distribution (determined without regard to the five-year participation rule described in Q 18:15), this treatment applies only to employer securities attributable to employee after-tax contributions. The cost basis of the securities is included in taxable income at the time of the distribution. [I.R.C. § 402(e)(4)(A)& (B)]

Q 18:29 How are *employer securities* defined?

Employer securities are shares of stock, bonds, or debentures issued by a corporation sponsoring the plan. Employer securities include securities of a parent or subsidiary corporation. [I.R.C. § 402(e)(4)(E)]

Q 18:30 What options does a participant have after receiving employer securities?

A participant who receives employer stock in a distribution has four options:

1. Roll the stock into an individual retirement account or annuity (IRA);
2. Sell the stock and roll the proceeds into the IRA;
3. Keep the stock, pay tax on the cost basis, and sell the stock later for potential capital gains treatment; and
4. Keep the stock and pay tax on the market value of the stock at the time of distribution.

The participant may not keep the stock and substitute its value with cash to roll over to an IRA.

Q 18:31 How are dividends paid on employer securities reported?

Dividends paid by a C corporation on employer securities held by an employee stock ownership plan (ESOP) are subject to special distribution and tax rules. [I.R.C. § 404(k)] These distributions are not subject to the 10 percent early distribution excise tax (see Qs 18:85–18:87), are not eligible rollover distributions (see chapter 16), are not subject to withholding, and are not taken into account in determining required minimum distributions (RMDs). (See chapter 16.)

Originally, these dividend distributions were required to be reported on Form 1099-DIV. However, distributions made in 2009 or later must be reported on Form 1099-R. If the recipient receives any distributions from the plan in addition to the distribution of dividend income, he or she must receive a separate 1099-R for reporting of the dividend income. [IRS Ann. 2008-56, 2008-26 I.R.B. 1192]

Distributions on Death

Q 18:32 How is the beneficiary taxed on proceeds received from a 401(k) plan?

Death benefits are generally paid to the beneficiary of a deceased participant in a lump sum. In effect, the tax treatment available to the participant is extended to the beneficiary. The investment in the contract (cost basis) will not be taxable to the beneficiary. If the participant is eligible for capital gains and ten-year income averaging treatment, this treatment is also available to the beneficiary. The five-year participation requirement does not apply to the beneficiary.

Q 18:33 How are life insurance proceeds treated in a death payout?

If part of the death benefit includes the proceeds of a life insurance policy, a portion of the proceeds is income tax free to the beneficiary. The difference between the face amount of the life insurance and the cash surrender value is treated as life insurance proceeds and is not subject to tax. The cash surrender value of the policy, minus the aggregate PS-58 costs that have been previously reported (see Qs 18:47, 18:49), plus any side fund proceeds, will be taxable to the beneficiary. [Treas. Reg. § 1.72-16(c)]

Q 18:34 May a spousal beneficiary roll over death proceeds?

Yes. If the beneficiary is the participant's spouse, and the distribution is an eligible rollover distribution, rollover treatment is available and may be made in the form of either a direct rollover or a 60-day rollover (see chapter 16). [I.R.C. § 402(c)(9)]

Q 18:35 May a nonspousal beneficiary roll over death proceeds to an IRA?

Yes. The Pension Protection Act of 2006 [Pub. L. No. 109-280, 120 Stat. 780] (PPA) added Code Section 402(c)(11), allowing nonspousal beneficiaries to roll over plan benefits to an inherited IRA (see chapter 16) and receive tax treatment as an eligible rollover distribution. The rollover must be in the form of a trustee-to-trustee transfer, not a 60-day rollover where benefits first pass through the hands of the beneficiary. The PPA made this feature optional, allowing individual plans to decide whether or not to offer it. The Worker, Retiree, and Employer Recovery Act of 2008 [Pub. L. No. 110-458 (2008)] (WRERA), which contained technical corrections to the PPA, requires plans to allow nonspousal rollovers for plan years beginning after December 31, 2009. [WRERA § 108(f); I.R.C. § 402(c)(11)]

The IRS has issued guidance further interpreting this new rule. It clarified that the IRA title must contain the names of both the decedent and the beneficiary (e.g., Jean Mettler as beneficiary of Rollin Mettler). A nonspousal beneficiary cannot roll over any portion of a distribution that is a required minimum distribution (RMD) (see chapter 16 for more information on RMDs). [IRS Notice 2009-82, 2009-41 I.R.B. 491; IRS Notice 2007-7, 2007-5 I.R.B. 395]

Installment Distributions

Q 18:36 How are installment distributions from a 401(k) plan taxed?

Installment distributions (made over a fixed period of time or in a fixed amount) are generally taxable as ordinary income when received. Likewise, payments in annuity form are treated as ordinary income when received. To the extent that a participant has a cost basis (investment in the contract) in the plan, a portion of each installment will be excluded from gross income. If the installment distribution is an eligible rollover distribution (see chapter 16), it can be rolled over to an eligible retirement plan and thus avoid current income taxation.

Q 18:37 In the event a participant who is receiving distribution in the form of an annuity has an investment in the contract, how is the portion of the payment that is excluded from gross income determined?

Generally, the portion of the payment that is excluded from gross income is determined by dividing the investment in the contract by the total number of anticipated monthly payments. For payments that are payable for the life of the participant (or participant and beneficiary), the total number of anticipated monthly payments is determined from the tables below and is based on the age of the participant and, if applicable, the age of the beneficiary. For other types of annuities this number is based on the number of scheduled monthly payments. [I.R.C. § 72(d)(1)(B)]

Age of Participant on Start Date	*Number of Anticipated Payments*
Not over 55	360
Over 55, not over 60	310
Over 60, not over 64	260
Over 65, not over 70	210
Over 70	160

Combined Ages of Participant and Beneficiary on Start Date	*Number of Anticipated Payments*
Not more than 110	410
More than 110 but not more than 120	360
More than 120 but not more than 130	310
More than 130 but not more than 140	260
More than 140	210

Example. Rosemary retires at age 62 with an account balance of $150,000 and opts to receive distributions of $1,000 per month until her account balance is completely paid out. Her investment in the contract is $30,000, the amount of her after-tax voluntary contributions. Using the exclusion ratio calculation above, the portion of each annual installment that is free of income tax is computed as follows:

$$\$30{,}000 \div 260 = \$115.38$$

The method described above is not available to participants who are age 75 or over and are entitled to five or more years of guaranteed payments. For those participants the portion of any payment excluded from gross income is determined using the exclusion ratio method under Code Section 72(b). [I.R.C. § 72(d)(1)(E)]

Q 18:38 How are installment distributions reported?

Installment distributions are reported on Form 1099-R.

In-Service Withdrawals

Q 18:39 How are withdrawals from a 401(k) plan taxed while a participant is actively employed?

In-service withdrawals are taxable as ordinary income when received and generally are treated as installment distributions. If the participant is under age 59½ and does not qualify for any of the exceptions, the participant is subject to a 10 percent premature withdrawal penalty (see Q 18:85). [I.R.C. § 72(t)]

Q 18:40 Will a participant's cost basis from after-tax contributions be excluded from tax in a withdrawal?

If the participant's account balance includes voluntary or mandatory after-tax contributions, the basis recovery rules will allow a portion of the in-service withdrawal to be treated as a nontaxable item. Before TRA '86, employee after-tax contributions could be recovered first in an in-service withdrawal; once the employee contributions were recovered, the balance would be treated as taxable.

Q 18:41 How did TRA '86 change the basis recovery rules for partial distributions not paid in the form of an annuity?

In an attempt to discourage the use of retirement plans for purposes other than retirement, TRA '86 changed the basis recovery rules, effective for withdrawals made after July 1, 1986. The rules provide a pro rata recovery of the employee's cost basis. The following ratio is applied to each withdrawal to determine the nontaxable amount:

$$\frac{\text{Investment in contract}}{\text{Vested account balance}} \times \text{withdrawal amount} = \text{Amount not taxed}$$

Example. Clare has a vested account balance in a 401(k) plan of $5,000. Voluntary after-tax contributions (exclusive of earnings) of $1,000 have been made. If Clare withdraws $2,000 for hardship purposes, it will be taxed as follows:

$$\frac{\$1{,}000}{\$5{,}000} \times \$2{,}000 = \$400$$

$400 is recovered tax free, and the balance of $1,600 is taxable as ordinary income. [I.R.C. § 72(e)(8)]

Q 18:42 Should employee after-tax contributions be accounted for separately?

The taxable amount can be minimized if employee after-tax contributions are accounted for separately from employer contributions and elective contributions. The reason for favorable treatment is that the account balance considered in the recovery ratio would then consist only of the after-tax employee contributions plus earnings. [I.R.C. § 72(d)(2)]

Example. James has an account balance of $5,000. It consists of $2,700, representing voluntary after-tax contributions plus earnings, and $2,300, representing elective contributions plus earnings. Voluntary after-tax contributions of $1,000 have been made. If James withdraws $2,000 from his voluntary account, the basis recovery rules are applied as follows:

$$\frac{\text{Investment in contract}}{\text{Vested account balance}} \times \text{withdrawal amount} = \text{Amount not taxed}$$

$$\frac{\$1{,}000}{\$2{,}700} \times \$2{,}000 = \$740.74$$

$740.74 is tax free, and the remaining $1,259.26 is taxable as ordinary income.

Q 18:43 How did TRA '86 preserve the old basis recovery rules for certain plans?

TRA '86 provided a grandfather rule to exempt certain plans from the new basis recovery rules. If a plan contained voluntary or mandatory after- tax contributions and, on May 5, 1986, allowed for withdrawal of these contributions before separation from service, then the basis recovery rules do not apply to pre-1987 after-tax contributions. [I.R.C. § 72(e)(8)(D)]

Q 18:44 How do the grandfathered basis recovery rules work?

The following steps would be taken to determine the taxable amount of an in-service withdrawal under the grandfather rules:

Step I. Grandfather rule:

1. Determine current amount of pre-1987 after-tax contributions, exclusive of earnings.
2. If distribution is less than or equal to the current balance of pre-1987 after-tax contributions, the entire amount is not taxable.
3. If distribution is more than the current balance of pre-1987 after-tax contributions, taxation of excess is determined in Steps II and III.

Step II. Pro rata taxation of remaining distribution, if any (up to the amount of total post-1986 after-tax contributions plus earnings thereon):

1. Remaining portion of distribution (up to the amount of total post-1986 after-tax contributions plus earnings thereon), multiplied by
2. Post-1986 after-tax contributions, exclusive of earnings, divided by
3. Post-1986 after-tax contributions, plus earnings equals
4. Amount that is not taxable.

[IRS Notice 87-13, 1987-1 C.B. 432]

Assume:

$10,000 distribution

$8,000 pre-1987 after-tax contributions, exclusive of earnings

$4,000 post-1986 after-tax contributions, exclusive of earnings

$1,250 earnings on after-tax contributions

Step I. Grandfather rule (not taxable): $8,000

Step II. Amount subject to pro rata rule:

$$\$2{,}000 \times \frac{\$4{,}000 \text{ (post-1986 after-tax contributions)}}{\$5{,}250 \text{ (post-1986 after-tax contributions plus earnings)}} = \$1{,}524 \text{ not taxable; } \$476 \text{ taxable}$$

Q 18:45 How are in-service withdrawals reported?

In-service withdrawals are reported on Form 1099-R.

Life Insurance

Q 18:46 How is life insurance in a 401(k) plan taxed?

If life insurance benefits are provided in a 401(k) plan, the cost of the life insurance protection is includible annually in the employee's gross income. This treatment applies for each year deductible employer contributions or trust income is applied to purchase life insurance protection. [Treas. Reg. § 1.72-16(b)(2)] The types of contracts included in a 401(k) plan that are subject to this treatment would include term, whole life, and universal life. The employee will be taxed on the cost of the insurance protection if the proceeds are payable to the estate or designated beneficiary or they are payable to the trustee but the trustee is required to pay the proceeds to the employee's estate or designated beneficiary. [Treas. Reg. § 1.72-16(b)(1)]

Q 18:47 How is the taxable cost of life insurance computed?

The taxable cost of life insurance is determined by subtracting the cash value at the end of the policy year from the face amount of life insurance. One-year term premium rates are then applied at the insured's age to this difference, otherwise known as the *amount at risk.* The PS-58 rates published in IRS Notice 2002-8 [2002-4 I.R.B. 398] are the applicable rates for purposes of this calculation. However, if the insurance company rates for individual one-year term policies available to all standard risks are lower, these insurance company rates may be used. [Rev. Rul. 2003-105, 2003-40 I.R.B. 696]

Q 18:48 How is survivor whole life taxed?

A number of 401(k) plans use a special type of life insurance protection called *survivor whole life,* or *second-to-die,* life insurance. This type of life insurance protection pays death proceeds only after the death of the surviving spouse. Since the payment of proceeds is contingent upon the deaths of two individuals, premium rates are substantially lower, and greater life insurance protection can be provided. Likewise, in determining the current taxation of these contracts, a government table with lower rates can be used, the US Life Table 38. [Information letter from Norman Greenberg, Chief of the Actuarial Branch, Department of Treasury] If the participant's spouse dies while the policy is held in the 401(k) plan, the PS-58 rates would be applicable thereafter.

Q 18:49 How is the taxable cost of life insurance protection reported?

The taxable cost of life insurance must be reported annually on Form 1099-R.

Loans

Q 18:50 When do participant loans become taxable to a participant?

Participant loans in 401(k) plans can generate taxable income to the participant if principal and interest payments are not made on a timely basis. Furthermore, if a participant loan exceeds the maximum loan limits (the lesser of 50 percent of the vested account balance or $50,000, as discussed in chapter 15), or if it fails to satisfy the requirements of Code Section 72(p) by its terms, immediate taxation can result. [I.R.C. § 72(p)] See chapter 15 for an in-depth discussion of taxation of participant loans.

Q 18:51 If a participant loan becomes taxable, does the obligation to the 401(k) plan still exist?

Yes. From the trustee's perspective, the fact that all or a portion of the loan is taxed to the participant does not remove the participant's obligation to the plan. The participant is still responsible for paying interest on the loan and repaying principal.

Q 18:52 May a participant loan ever be converted to a distribution?

Yes. If the plan permits withdrawals after age 59½ and the participant is older than age 59½, the outstanding loan may be converted to a distribution and no further obligation to the plan will exist. Similarly, if the loan was taken from an account other than a salary deferral account, foreclosure and distribution can occur at that time if the plan so provides. If the loan is still outstanding at the time of retirement or severance of employment, the obligation may be extinguished by reducing the participant's account balance by the outstanding loan. It is important to note that the loan will not be taxed twice.

Q 18:53 How is a taxable loan reported?

A loan or any portion of a loan that becomes taxable for any reason is reported on Form 1099-R. If the loan becomes taxable due to a default, it is taxable for the year in which the default occurs. If the loan or a portion of the loan becomes taxable due to failure to satisfy the conditions of Code Section 72(p) (see Q 18:50), it is taxable in the year the loan is issued.

Distribution of Excess Deferrals

Q 18:54 What are *excess deferrals*?

Excess deferrals are elective deferrals made in excess of the annual limit established pursuant to Code Section 402(g). For 2015 the excess deferral limit is $18,000. The limit is adjusted for inflation in $500 increments. In order for a 401(k) plan to maintain its tax-qualified status (see chapter 2), any excess deferrals resulting from elective deferrals made only to that 401(k) plan must be returned to the participants who made them. The amount returned is the amount of the excess deferral adjusted for earnings. Excess deferrals must be returned by April 15 of the year following the year the excess deferral was made. (See chapter 9 for more information on deferral limits.)

Excess deferrals can consist of either pre-tax or after-tax (Roth) contributions. For the tax treatment of excess deferrals that are Roth deferrals, see Q 18:65.

Q 18:55 How are distributions of pre-tax excess deferrals taxed to the participant?

Distribution of an excess deferral is taxed to the participant in the year in which the excess deferral is made. However, the income or loss allocable to the excess deferral is taken into account in the taxable year in which the distribution occurs. [Treas. Reg. § 1.402(g)-1(e)(8)(i)] For taxable years prior to 2008, these distributions were required to include gap-period earnings, or earnings generated between the end of the plan year in which the excess deferral was made and the date it was distributed. For plan years beginning on or after January 1, 2008, gap-period earnings are no longer required to be included in these distributions. [WRERA § 109(b)(3); I.R.C. § 402(g)(2)(A)(ii)] There is no penalty tax for distribution of pre-tax excess deferral amounts made to participants who are under age 59½. [Treas. Reg. § 1.402(g)-1(e)(8)(i)]

Distributions of Excess Contributions and Excess Aggregate Contributions

Q 18:56 What are excess contributions and excess aggregate contributions?

Excess contributions result from plans that fail to satisfy the actual deferral percentage (ADP) test, which generally compares the elective contribution rates of non-highly compensated employees (NHCEs) to highly compensated employees (HCEs). *Excess aggregate contributions* result from plans that fail to satisfy the actual contribution percentage (ACP) test, which makes a similar comparison taking into account employer matching and employee after-tax contributions. (See chapter 13 for detailed discussion of ADP and ACP testing.)

Several mechanisms are available for correcting ADP and ACP test failures. A method commonly used is to return excess contributions and excess aggregate contributions (to the extent vested) to HCEs. Any forfeited excess aggregate contributions are reallocated to the accounts of other participants. The amounts distributed must consist of the excess contributions and excess aggregate contributions made, adjusted for earnings.

For plan years beginning January 1, 2008, or later, there is no longer a requirement to calculate and distribute gap-period earnings on excess contributions and excess aggregate contributions. In order for a plan to maintain its tax-qualified status (see chapter 2), these excess amounts must be distributed no later than 12 months after the close of the plan year.

Excess contributions can consist of either pre-tax or after-tax (Roth) contributions. For the tax treatment of excess contributions that are Roth deferrals, see Q 18:65.

Q 18:57 How are distributions of pre-tax excess contributions and excess aggregate contributions taxed to the participant?

For plan years starting on or after January 1, 2008, excess contributions and excess aggregate contributions (adjusted for earnings) are taxed to the participants in the year they are distributed regardless of when during the year they are distributed. This PPA-enacted rule simplifies the process for plan participants, since they no longer are at risk of having to file an amended return in the event such contributions are returned to them after they have filed their prior year's tax return. [I.R.C. § 4979(f)(2)] There is no penalty tax for distribution of these amounts to participants who are under age 59½. [Treas. Reg. §§ 1.401(k)-2(b)(2)(v), 1.401(m)-2(b)(2)(vi)]

Q 18:58 How are excess contributions and excess aggregate contributions in a 401(k) plan taxed to the employer?

If excess contributions or excess aggregate contributions are distributed more than 2½ months following the close of the plan year (but before the close of the next plan year), the employer is subject to a 10 percent excise tax. Beginning with plan years starting after December 31, 2007, for plans that are "eligible automatic contribution arrangements" (see chapter 2), corrective distributions can be made up to six months following the end of a plan year without incurring the 10 percent excise tax. [I.R.C. § 4979(f)(1)] If excess contributions are not distributed within 12 months following the close of the plan year, the plan is subject to disqualification. [Treas. Reg. §§ 1.401(k)-2(b)(5)(ii), 1.401(m)-2(b)(4)(ii)]

Taxation of Roth Distributions and In-Plan Roth Rollovers

For plan years beginning January 1, 2006, or later, elective contributions to a 401(k) plan can be made on an after-tax basis as part of a participant's total elective contribution amount. Since these contributions are made on an after-tax basis (i.e., subject to FICA, FUTA, and federal income tax at the time contributed), their tax treatment when coming out of the plan is different from that afforded to distributions from pre-tax accounts. This section discusses the taxation of distributions from a Roth 401(k) account. For a discussion on whether it is advantageous to elect to contribute to a Roth 401(k) plan, see Q 18:113. (For the rules governing Roth 401(k) plans, see I.R.C. §§ 402A, 402(g); Treas. Reg. §§ 1.401(k)-1(f), 1.402A-1.)

Q 18:59 How are distributions from a Roth 401(k) account taxed?

If the distribution is a "qualified" distribution (see Q 18:60), no tax is due on either the contributions or earnings distributed from the Roth account. If the distribution is not a qualified distribution, income tax will generally be due on the portion of the distribution attributable to earnings. [I.R.C. § 402A(d)(1)]

Q 18:60 What is a *qualified* Roth distribution?

A distribution from a Roth 401(k) account will be considered qualified if it meets the following conditions:

1. The distribution is made on account of the participant's death, disability, or attainment of age 59½, *and*
2. The distribution is made after the five-year period beginning on January 1 of the first year that the participant made a Roth contribution into the plan.

Example. Betty, who was born on September 14, 1956, made her first contribution to a Roth 401(k) plan on October 1, 2008. The earliest date on which Betty could receive a nontaxable distribution of her Roth account would be March 14, 2016, when she attains age 59½. If Betty had been born on September 14, 1951, she could receive a nontaxable distribution of her Roth account on January 1, 2013, when her five-year holding period ended.

[I.R.C. § 402A(d)(2); Treas. Reg. § 1.402A-1, Q&A 4]

Note. If the only contributions to a participant's Roth account during a year consist of excess deferrals, excess contributions, or amounts returned to the participant in an eligible automatic contribution arrangement using the 90-day permissible withdrawal feature (see chapter 2), the five-year tracking period will not begin. [Treas. Reg. § 1.402A-1, Q&A 4(a)]

Q 18:61 Are there certain types of Roth distributions that can never be considered qualified distributions?

Yes. The following types of distributions can never be treated as qualified distributions, so tax will always be due on the amount of the distribution attributable to earnings:

- Deemed distributions on defaulted loans under Code Section 72(p)
- Corrective distributions of amounts exceeding the limits of Code Section 415 or 402(g) (see chapter 9)
- Corrective distributions of excess contributions or excess aggregate contributions (see chapter 13)
- Dividends paid out of the plan on employer stock

[Treas. Reg. § 1.402A-1, Q&As 2 and 11]

Q 18:62 How are partial distributions from a Roth account taxed?

If the partial distribution is a qualified distribution, no tax is due. If it is not a qualified distribution, then tax will be due on the portion of the distribution attributable to earnings. The rules for determining what portion of a distribution consists of taxable earnings are the same as those that apply to after-tax distributions from a 401(k) plan generally (see Q 18:41), using a pro rata approach.

Example. Ryan has a $50,000 balance in his Roth 401(k) account, which consists of $40,000 in contributions and $10,000 in earnings. If Ryan takes a $10,000 distribution that is not a qualified distribution, he will owe income tax on $2,000.

[Treas. Reg. § 1.402(A)-1, Q&A 3]

Q 18:63 How are deemed distributions from a Roth account taxed?

If a participant takes a loan from a Roth account and there is a default resulting in a deemed distribution, the earnings portion of the deemed distribution will be taxed just like any other partial distribution. A deemed distribution can never be considered a qualified distribution; thus, even if the participant has a qualifying event and has met the five-year holding requirement, he or she will be taxed on the earnings. For this reason, plans may want to limit participant loans to pre-tax accounts. [Treas. Reg. § 1.402A-1, Q&A 11]

Q 18:64 How are hardship distributions from a Roth account taxed?

Hardship withdrawals are not specifically included in the list of types of distributions that can never be considered qualified. However, as a practical matter, given the list of qualifying events (death, disability, attainment of age 59½), a hardship distribution will almost never be a qualified distribution, because most 401(k) plans allow for normal distribution of benefits upon the occurrence of those events.

Hardship distributions that are not qualified distributions are treated like any other partial distributions for tax purposes (see Q 18:62). However, the method of accounting for hardship availability does not follow the tax treatment of the hardship distribution. While hardship distributions are treated as pro rata distributions of contributions and earnings for tax purposes, they are treated as coming 100 percent from contributions for purposes of calculating future hardship withdrawal availability.

Example. Bob's $30,000 Roth 401(k) account consists of $24,000 in contributions and $6,000 in earnings. Bob's hardship withdrawal limit is the amount of his elective deferrals, or $24,000. If he takes a $10,000 hardship distribution, it will be treated for tax purposes as though $2,000 were attributable to earnings, which will be taxed, and the remaining $8,000 is attributable to elective deferrals, which are not taxed. For purposes of determining the amount available for future hardship withdrawal, however, the entire $10,000 will be treated as coming from Bob's elective deferral account, and his future withdrawal limit will be $14,000.

[Treas. Reg. § 1.402(A)-1, Q&A 8]

Q 18:65 How are corrective distributions from a Roth account taxed?

If contributions are made to a Roth 401(k) account in excess of the Section 402(g) limit, but are removed from the account by April 15 of the following year, the portion of the distribution attributable to earnings will be taxed in the year of distribution. The portion attributable to Roth contributions will not be taxed since those amounts were already subject to tax in the year contributed. If the excess is removed after April 15 of the following year, because the excess deferral arose from elective deferrals to a single plan, the entire amount will be taxed, resulting in double taxation of the Roth elective deferral amounts. Excess deferrals that arise from elective deferrals made to plans of unrelated employers and that are not removed by April 15 of the following year cannot, when ultimately distributed, be treated as a qualified distribution (see Q 18:60). [Treas. Reg. § 1.402(g)-1(e)(8)(iv)] See chapter 9 for a full discussion of the rules regarding corrective distributions.

A refund of excess contributions is treated like any other partial distribution, with taxation of the portion of the distribution attributable to earnings.

If a participant has contributed to both a Roth and a pre-tax 401(k) plan during the year for which a corrective distribution is made, the plan may allow the participant to choose the source of the corrective distribution. As a practical matter, however, given the data collection and accounting complexities involved with allowing each participant to choose a source, it is likely that plans adopting the Roth feature will define the source for corrective distributions.

If a participant does an in-plan Roth rollover (including in-plan Roth transfers or conversions of accounts not otherwise distributable) of his or her entire account, excess deferrals, excess contributions, and excess aggregate contributions must be refunded to the participant even if the in-plan Roth rollover consists of amounts that were not otherwise distributable. [IRS Notice 2013-74, Q&A 11, 2013-52 I.R.B. 819]

Q 18:66 How are employer securities distributed from a Roth account taxed?

If the securities are distributed as part of a qualified distribution (see Q 18:60), no tax is due and the employee's basis is the fair market value of the stock at the time of distribution.

If employer securities are distributed as part of a nonqualified distribution, there is no tax due on the net unrealized appreciation at the time of distribution, but the employee's basis does not include the net unrealized appreciation on the stock, which will be subject to capital gains tax when the stock is sold (see Q 18:28).

Any dividends paid out of the plan are taxable and cannot be considered a qualified distribution. However, if dividends from an ESOP (see chapter 6) are reinvested in the plan and later distributed as part of a qualified distribution, the dividend amounts are not subject to tax and are treated the same as the rest of the qualified distribution for tax purposes. [Treas. Reg. § 1.402A-1, Q&As 10 and 11]

Q 18:67 Are Roth accounts eligible for rollover?

Yes, although the rules are slightly different from those for pre-tax accounts. A Roth 401(k) account may be rolled over to a Roth 401(k), a Roth 403(b), or a Roth IRA. If the account is rolled over to a Roth 401(k) in a 60-day rollover instead of a direct rollover (see chapter 16), only the earnings in the Roth account may be rolled over, not the elective contributions to the account. A Roth IRA account may not be rolled into a Roth 401(k). [I.R.C. § 402A(c)(3); Treas. Reg. § 1.402A-1, Q&A 5] The Small Business Jobs Act of 2010 [Pub. L. No. 111-240] (SBJA) and the American Taxpayer Relief Act of 2012 [Pub. L. No. 112-240, 126 Stat. 2313] (ATRA) allow participants to convert pre-tax accounts into Roth accounts inside their 401(k) plan. This conversion is done by way of an *in-plan Roth rollover*, which is a distribution from one or more accounts (other than an account to which Roth contributions have been allocated) under a 401(k) plan that is rolled over to a Roth account in the same 401(k) plan. Before 2013 only accounts that were otherwise eligible to be distributed could be the subject of an in-plan Roth rollover. With the enactment of ATRA, starting January 1, 2013, accounts not otherwise eligible to be distributed can also be the subject of an in-plan Roth rollover or, as commonly referred to in the retirement plan industry, an in-plan Roth transfer or conversion. [I.R.C. § 402A(c)(4); IRS Notice 2010-84, Q&A 1, 2010-51 I.R.B. 872, and IRS Notice 2013-74, 2013-52 I.R.B. 819]

Q 18:68 What conditions apply to in-plan Roth rollovers?

For a participant to take advantage of an in-plan Roth rollover, the following conditions must apply:

- The plan document must allow for Roth elective deferrals.
- The plan document must allow for in-plan Roth rollovers.
- The amounts to be rolled over must be fully vested.
- Before January 1, 2013, the account to be rolled over must have been eligible for distribution under the terms of the Code and must have qualified as an eligible rollover distribution as defined in Code Section 402(c)(4) (see chapter 16).
- Only participants, surviving spouse beneficiaries, and alternate payees who are the spouse or former spouse of a participant may elect in-plan Roth rollovers.
- In the case of in-plan Roth rollovers of otherwise distributable accounts, the Special Tax Notice required under Code Section 402(f) (see chapter 16) must be provided and must include a description of the in-plan Roth rollover feature. A safe harbor notice including this description is available.

- An in-plan Roth rollover of an otherwise distributable account could not occur before September 28, 2010. An in-plan Roth rollover of an account not otherwise distributable could not occur before January 1, 2013.

[IRS Notice 2010-84, 2010-51 I.R.B. 872; IRS Notice 2013-74, 2013-52 I.R.B. 819]

Q 18:69 By when must a plan be amended to adopt an in-plan Roth rollover feature?

Generally, an amendment to add an in-plan Roth rollover feature is a discretionary amendment that must be adopted by the last day of the plan year in which the amendment is effective. In the case of a 401(k) plan that decided to permit in-plan Roth rollovers of accounts that are otherwise distributable in 2010, an extension was available such that an amendment was effective for 2010 plan years if adopted by the later of the last day of the plan year or by December 31, 2011. In safe-harbor plans (regular or QACA), the deadline for 2010 plan years was the later of December 31, 2011, or the last day of the plan year prior to the plan year for which the amendment is effective. For example, a 401(k) safe-harbor plan that had a plan year beginning July 1 could allow in-plan Roth rollovers during the plan year (July 1, 2010 to June 30, 2011) without having to amend for this change in operation until December 31, 2011.

In the case of a 401(k) plan that decided to permit in-plan Roth rollovers of accounts that are not otherwise distributable in 2013, an extension was available such that an amendment was effective for 2013 plan years if adopted by the later of the last day of the plan year or by December 31, 2014. With safe harbor plans, the deadline for amending the plan was December 31, 2014. [IRS Notice 2013-74, Q&A 5, 2013-52 I.R.B. 819]

Although a plan may be amended retroactively to provide for Roth contributions and in-plan Roth rollovers, the rollover feature cannot be made available prior to the date that employees had an opportunity to elect to make Roth contributions to the plan. [IRS Notice 2010-84, Q&As 15, 17, 18, and 19, 2010-51 I.R.B. 872]

Q 18:70 Are both direct and 60-day rollovers eligible for in-plan Roth rollovers?

Yes. In the case of an in-plan Roth rollover of an otherwise distributable account, an in-plan Roth rollover can be accomplished by either a direct rollover or a distribution to a participant who then rolls the funds back into a Roth account in the plan within 60 days. [IRS Notice 2010-84, Q&A 1, 2010-51 I.R.B. 872] In the case of an in-plan Roth rollover of accounts that are not otherwise distributable, the 60-day rollover option is not available. [IRS Notice 2013-74, Q&A 1, 2013-52 I.R.B. 819]

Q 18:71 Can a participant undo an in-plan Roth rollover?

No. Roth rollovers to an IRA can be recharacterized if done timely but once an in-plan Roth rollover occurs, the funds must remain in the Roth account until distributed, and the transaction cannot be undone. [IRS Notice 2010-84, Q&A 6, 2010-51 I.R.B. 872]

Q 18:72 Are in-plan Roth rollovers treated as a distribution for all purposes?

No. An in-plan Roth rollover changes the tax character of the funds but is not treated as a distribution for other plan purposes. For example:

- A plan loan transferred in an in-plan Roth rollover without changing the payment schedule is not treated as a new loan.
- A married participant in a plan subject to spousal annuity requirements is not required to obtain spousal consent in order to make an in-plan Roth rollover.
- All optional forms of benefit protected under Code Section 411(d)(6) (see chapter 16) that were available in the participant's pre-tax account must remain available in the in-plan Roth rollover account after the rollover.
- Amounts transferred in an in-plan Roth rollover must be taken in to account in determining whether a participant's vested accrued benefit exceeds $5,000.
- A notice of the right to defer receipt of distribution is not triggered by an in-plan Roth rollover that is a direct rollover.
- In the case of an in-plan Roth rollover of accounts not otherwise distributable, the accounts rolled over remain subject to the distribution restrictions that applied prior to the in-plan Roth rollover.

[IRS Notice 2010- 84, Q&A 3, 2010-51 I.R.B. 872; IRS Notice 2013-74, Q&A 3, 2013-52 I.R.B. 819]]

Q 18:73 What are the tax consequences of an in-plan Roth rollover?

The taxable amount of the in-plan Roth rollover must be included in the participant's gross income. If an outstanding loan is included in the rollover, the taxable amount is the balance due on the loan. Mandatory 20 percent withholding does not apply; however, a participant electing an in-plan Roth rollover may need to increase his or her withholding or make estimated tax payments in order to avoid a penalty for underpayment.

Generally, the tax on an in-plan rollover is due in the tax year in which the rollover occurs. For in-plan rollovers made in 2010, the tax liability was deferred such that half of the tax was due in 2011 and the other half was due in 2012. Participants who did not want the tax deferred could have elected to pay it all in 2010. [IRS Notice 2010-84, Q&As 7–10, 2010-51 I.R.B. 872; IRS Notice 2013-74, Q&A 4, 2013-52 I.R.B. 819]

Q 18:74 What special income tax rules apply to distributions from in-plan Roth rollover accounts?

Generally, the same tax rules that apply to all distributions from Roth accounts also apply to distributions from in-plan Roth rollover accounts. There are, however, some special tax rules that apply.

If a participant who elected to make an in-plan Roth rollover in 2010 took advantage of the two-year tax deferral (see Q 18:73), and then took a distribution of an amount allocable to the taxable amount of the 2010 in-plan Roth rollover that otherwise would not be includable in income until 2011 or 2012, his or her taxable income in the year of distribution was increased by the amount of the distribution that otherwise would not be included until a later year.

> **Example.** If Mike made an $8,000 in-plan Roth rollover in 2010 and took a $3,000 distribution from his Roth account in 2011, there was no change in income tax consequences: he would pay tax on $4,000 in 2011 and on another $4,000 in 2012. However, if Mike took a distribution of $5,000 in 2011, he would pay tax on $5,000 in 2011 and on $3,000 in 2012.

[IRS Notice 2010-84, Q&A 11, 2010-51 I.R.B. 872]

Q 18:75 How does the 10 percent premature distribution tax apply to distributions from in-plan Roth rollover accounts?

The premature distribution tax generally does not apply to an in-plan Roth rollover that occurs while the participant is under age 59½. However, if an amount allocable to the taxable portion of an in-plan Roth rollover account is distributed within the five-year period beginning with the first day of the year in which the rollover was made and ending on the last day of the fifth year, the amount distributed would be subject to the 10 percent early distribution tax. [IRS Notice 2010-84, Q&A 12, 2010-51 I.R.B. 872]

Q 18:76 How is the amount allocable to the taxable portion of an in-plan Roth rollover account determined?

For purposes of applying the income acceleration rule (see Q 18:74) or the five-year recapture rule (see Q 18:75), the amount allocable to the taxable portion of an in-plan Roth rollover account is generally determined using the basis recovery rules (see Qs 18:37 and 18:41). If a participant has both a regular Roth 401(k) account and an in-plan Roth rollover account, there are allocation rules for determining how to allocate the taxable and nontaxable portions of a distribution to each account. [IRS Notice 2010-84, Q&A 13, 2010-51 I.R.B. 872]

Q 18:77 How is the five-year holding period for qualified distributions calculated when a Roth account has been rolled over?

The answer depends on the type of rollover involved. If a Roth 401(k) is rolled into another Roth 401(k) or a Roth 403(b) in a direct rollover, the trigger date for the five-year holding period will be the earlier of the trigger date in the distributing plan or the trigger date in the receiving plan.

If Roth 401(k) earnings are rolled into another Roth 401(k) within 60 days, the trigger date is determined solely with respect to the receiving plan.

> **Example.** Freddy makes his first Roth 401(k) contribution to the Circuit-Wise plan on April 9, 2008, and a subsequent contribution to the Mettler Realty plan on January 2, 2009. Freddy then rolls his Circuit-Wise Roth account into the Mettler Realty plan on March 17, 2010, in a direct rollover. The trigger date for the five-year holding period for Freddy's entire Roth account in the Mettler Realty plan, both the rolled amounts and the already existing account, would be January 1, 2008. If Freddy rolled over his Circuit-Wise account in a 60-day rollover, rather than a direct rollover, he would be able to roll over only the earnings, and the five-year trigger date for Freddy's entire Roth account in the Mettler Realty plan would be January 1, 2009.

[Treas. Reg. § 1.402A-1, Q&As 4(b), 5(c)]

If a Roth 401(k) is rolled into a Roth IRA as a direct rollover or as an indirect rollover, the trigger date for the five-year holding period is based on the date of the first contribution to the Roth IRA. [Treas. Reg. § 1.408A-10, Q&A 4]

Q 18:78 How is the five-year holding period for qualified distributions calculated in the case of an in-plan Roth rollover?

If a participant has not previously made Roth contributions, the five-year holding period begins on the first day of the participant's taxable year in which the participant makes the in-plan Roth rollover. [IRS Notice 2013-74, Q&A 8, 2013-52 I.R.B. 819]

Q 18:79 What are some tax planning advantages that the Roth rollover rules offer in the case of a rollover to a Roth IRA?

Roth rollover rules offer three possible advantages: (1) the ability to get a step-up in the five-year holding period if the rollover is made to a Roth IRA with an earlier five-year holding period beginning date; (2) the ability to avoid taking required minimum distributions (RMDs) at age 70½ (see chapter 16), as minimum distributions from a Roth IRA are not required as long as the participant is still alive; and (3) the ability to take advantage of the tax rules on Roth IRA distributions, which allow participants to withdraw 100 percent of the nontaxable amounts in the account before withdrawing the taxable amounts.

Q 18:80 How is the five-year holding period tracked, both generally and in the context of a rollover?

Third-party administrators are required to maintain separate accounts for Roth contributions and earnings and to track the aggregate amount of undistributed Roth contributions and the date of the first Roth deposit. In a direct rollover, the administrator must provide the recipient institution with information on whether or not the distribution is qualified and, if it is not, the first year of the five-year holding period for that account and the amount of the rollover attributable to contributions and to earnings. If benefits are paid directly to a participant, this same information must be provided to the participant upon his or her request. [Treas. Reg. § 1.402A-2, Q&As 1 and 2]

Q 18:81 What are the tax consequences of a Roth account set up for an alternate payee or a beneficiary?

If a Roth account is allocated in part to an alternate payee pursuant to a qualified domestic relations order or it is split among multiple beneficiaries, each account established will be allocated a proportionate share of contributions and earnings. The participant's five-year holding period will apply to any alternate payee or beneficiary account. [Treas. Reg. § 1.402A-1, Q&A 9(b)]

Q 18:82 Do excise taxes apply to Roth 401(k) distributions?

Yes. For example, if a distribution from a Roth account is taken before the participant is age 59½ and none of the exceptions to the 10 percent premature distribution penalty applies, the taxable amount of the distribution will be subject to the 10 percent penalty.

Q 18:83 How are distributions from Roth 401(k) plans reported?

Distributions from a Roth 401(k) plan are reported using the same forms as pre-tax distributions—that is, a Form 1099-R to report income tax and a Form 5329 to report any excise taxes.

Q 18:84 How was the tax treatment of Roth accounts stabilized by the passage of the Pension Protection Act of 2006?

Roth 401(k) plans were created as part of the Economic Growth and Tax Relief and Reconciliation Act of 2001 (EGTRRA), which was scheduled to sunset on December 31, 2010, unless Congress took action to extend it. Since the first qualified distribution from a Roth account could not have occurred before January 1, 2011, because of the five-year holding period, it was possible that none of the tax benefits of a Roth 401(k) would have ever been realized. This uncertainty was eliminated with the enactment of the Pension Protection Act of 2006 (PPA).

Other Taxes

Up to this point, the focus has been on federal income tax on distributions from 401(k) plans. Certain distributions from 401(k) plans may be subject to additional income tax if distributions occur before age 59½. Other distributions may be subject to excise tax if they are delayed beyond age 70½ (see, however, the section on minimum distributions requirements in chapter 16). Even if distributions commence on a timely basis at age 70½, excise taxes may be levied if distributions are too small. This section deals with the rules relating to the computation of these taxes, the exceptions to those rules, and how the taxes are paid.

Premature Distributions

Q 18:85 What is the tax on premature distributions?

Distributions received from a 401(k) plan before the participant reaches age 59½ may be subject to a 10 percent additional income tax. [I.R.C. § 72(t)] If the distribution is rolled over to an IRA or other eligible retirement plan, this additional tax will not apply.

Q 18:86 What are the exceptions to the premature distribution tax?

There are a number of exceptions to the general rule:

1. *Death.* Distribution made to a beneficiary or estate of the participant after the participant's death [I.R.C. § 72(t)(2)(A)(ii)];
2. *Disability.* If the participant meets a special definition of disability by virtue of being unable to "engage in any substantial gainful activity by reason of a medically determinable physical or mental impairment which can be expected to result in death or to be of long-continued and indefinite duration" [I.R.C. §§ 72(m)(7), 72(t)(2)(A)(iii)];
3. *Substantially equal periodic payments.* If payments are made after a participant's separation from service, in at least annual installments over the life (or life expectancy) of the participant or the joint lives of the participant and designated beneficiary (discussed in more detail in Qs 18:105–18:108) [I.R.C. § 72(t)(2)(A)(iv), 72(t)(3)(B)];
4. *Attainment of age 55.* If the participant separates from service during or after the year in which he or she attains age 55 [I.R.C. § 72(t)(2)(A)(v)];
5. *Medical expenses.* If payments are made for medical care, but not in excess of amounts allowable as a deduction under Code Section 213 [I.R.C. § 72(t)(2)(B)];
6. *QDRO.* If payments are made to an alternate payee under a QDRO [I.R.C. § 72(t)(2)(C)];
7. *401(k) excesses.* If excess deferrals, excess contributions, or excess aggregate contributions plus earnings are refunded to a participant on a timely basis [Treas. Reg. §§ 1.402(g)-1(e)(8), 1.401(m)-2(b)(2)(vi), 1.401(k)-2(b)(2)(vi)];
8. *ESOP dividends.* If dividends are distributed in cash to ESOP participants [I.R.C. § 72(t)(2)(A)(vi)];
9. *PS-58 costs.* If the taxable cost of life insurance is reported annually by a participant [IRS Notice 89-25, 1989-1 C.B. 662];

10. *Permissible withdrawals from an EACA.* If a permissible withdrawal of a default contribution is made from an eligible automatic contribution plan (EACA) (see chapter 2) [Treas. Reg. § 1.414(w)-1(d)(1)(ii)];
11. *Qualified reservist distributions.* If the distribution is made to an individual called to active military duty (see chapter 1) [I.R.C. § 72(t)(2)(G)]; and
12. *IRS levies.* If the amounts are distributed on account of an IRS levy on the plan under authority of Code Section 6331. [I.R.C. § 72(t)(2)(A)(vii)]
13. *Post-2015 distributions to qualified public safety employees.* If the participant is a qualified public safety employee who separates from service during or after the year in which he or she attains age 50. A qualified public safety employee is a federal government employee who is a law enforcement officer, a customs and borders protection officer, a firefighter, or an air traffic controller. Also included in this category are employees of state or local governments who provide police protection, firefighting services, or emergency medical services. [I.R.C. § 72(t) (10)]

These exceptions apply to distributions from qualified retirement plans only. Additional exceptions apply to distributions from individual retirement accounts or annuities.

In addition to these more permanent exceptions, temporary exceptions are occasionally enacted in response to temporary economic conditions. For example, the Emergency Economic Stabilization Act of 2008 [Pub. L. No. 110-343] offered relief from the 10 percent early distribution excise tax for victims of weather-related disasters occurring in certain states between May 20 and August 1, 2008, if the distribution was a qualified disaster recovery assistance distribution.

Q 18:87 How is the premature distribution penalty reported?

If none of the exceptions listed above (see Q 18:86) applies, the distribution is reported on Form 1099-R as a premature distribution and is subject to a 10 percent additional income tax. The employer is not responsible for withholding this tax. The participant computes the 10 percent penalty by completing Form 5329 (Part I), if required, and entering the result on Form 1040 under "Additional tax on IRAs, other qualified retirement plans, etc."

Required Minimum Distributions

Q 18:88 What is the penalty for failure to distribute minimum distributions as required?

If a 401(k) plan sponsor fails to distribute the required minimum distribution to a participant who is over age 70½ and who is a 5 percent owner or has terminated employment, an excise tax of 50 percent of the shortfall is imposed on the participant (see chapter 16). The tax is imposed on the participant during the taxable year that begins with or within the calendar year for which the distribution is required. [I.R.C. § 4974(a); Treas. Reg. § 54.4974-2, Q&A 1] The excise tax may be waived if it is established that the shortfall was due to reasonable error and that reasonable steps are being taken to remedy it. [I.R.C. § 4974(d)]

> **Note.** The Worker, Retiree, and Economic Recovery Act of 2008 [Pub. L. No. 110-458] (WRERA) suspended the requirement to take minimum distributions due for the 2009 calendar year. See chapters 1 and 16 for more detailed discussion of this change.

Q 18:89 How is the minimum distribution penalty reported?

The excise tax is reported on Form 5329 (Part VIII) and entered on Form 1040 under "Additional tax on IRAs, other qualified retirement plans, etc."

Federal Estate Tax

Q 18:90 How are 401(k) death distributions treated for federal estate tax purposes?

The treatment of qualified plan assets for federal estate tax purposes has varied considerably over the years. Prior to the passage of the Tax Equity and Fiscal Responsibility Act of 1982 (TEFRA) in 1982, amounts attributable to employer contributions enjoyed an unlimited estate tax exclusion.

The Deficit Reduction Act of 1984 (DEFRA) removed the estate tax exclusion completely. DEFRA provided for the grandfathering of certain estates in pay status as of December 31, 1984. To avail themselves of a $100,000 exclusion, beneficiaries had to make an irrevocable election to receive benefits before July 18, 1984.

The Economic Growth and Tax Relief Reconciliation Act of 2001 (EGTRRA) changed the estate tax rules by increasing the value of a decedent's estate eligible for the unified credit against the estate tax and by reducing the rate of tax. EGTRRA also repealed the estate tax for decedents who died in 2010. The changes made by EGTRRA were scheduled to expire in 2010, but on December 17, 2010, the Tax Relief, Unemployment Insurance Reauthorization, and Job Creation Act was signed into law. [Pub. L. No. 111-312, 124 Stat. 3296] This law set new rates and exemption amounts for decedents dying in 2011 and 2012. On January 2, 2013, the American Taxpayer Relief Act (ATRA) was enacted into law, establishing new estate tax rules for persons dying after December 31, 2012.

Q 18:91 What are the estate tax implications if the spouse is named as beneficiary of the 401(k) plan proceeds?

From a practical standpoint, the proceeds of a 401(k) plan resulting from the death of a participant are subject to federal estate tax. However, if the spouse is named as the beneficiary of the proceeds, there is an unlimited marital deduction. Upon the death of the spouse, the proceeds would then be subject to federal estate tax.

Q 18:92 How much is the federal estate tax?

In general, the federal estate tax will apply only to those decedents whose estates exceed $5 million, an amount that is adjusted for inflation ($5.43 million for 2015). The rate of estate tax is 40 percent. [I.R.C. §§ 2001, 2010]

Filing Requirements for Distributions

Q 18:93 What are the reporting rules for distributions from 401(k) plans?

All taxable distributions from 401(k) plans are reported on Form 1099-R. If the distribution is less than $10, Form 1099-R does not need to be filed. If a plan pays dividends on employer securities held by an ESOP that are reportable under Code Section 404(k) and it makes another plan distribution in the same taxable year, separate Forms 1099-R must be used. [IRS Ann. 2008-56, 2008-26 I.R.B. 1192] The instructions to Form 1099-R permit (but do not require) the payor to include only the last four digits of the recipient's Social Security number on the form. The individual who receives Form 1099-R must attach it to Form 1040 if federal income tax is withheld. Copy B is used for this purpose. The reporting of distributions from 401(k) plans is also required in some states.

Distributions consisting of permissible withdrawals from an EACA (see chapter 2) are reported in the year of distribution. [Treas. Reg. § 1.414(w)-1(d)]

Q 18:94 Can a plan provide Form 1099-R to participants in electronic format?

Yes, as long as certain notice, consent, and other requirements are met. Before providing Form 1099-R electronically to participants, the trustee must:

- Ensure that the electronic format contains all the required information and complies with Revenue Procedure 2014-27 [2014-27 I.R.B. 41], the applicable revenue procedure for substitute payments to recipients.
- Post the applicable statement, on or before the January 31 due date, on a Web site that is accessible to the participant through October 15 of that year.
- Inform the participant, electronically or by mail, of the posting and how to access and print the statement.
- Obtain the participant's consent, which must be made electronically, in a way showing that he or she can access the statement in the electronic format in which it will be furnished.
- Notify the participant of any hardware or software changes and obtain new consent after any such hardware or software is put into service.
- Prior to furnishing the electronic statement, provide the participant with a statement prominently displaying the following information:
  - — The participant has a right to receive a paper statement;

- — Information regarding the intended scope and duration of the consent;
- — How to obtain a paper copy after giving consent;
- — How participants may withdraw consent (participants must be allowed to withdraw consent at any time by notification in writing (electronic or paper) and must be sent a written confirmation of the withdrawal);
- — The conditions under which electronic statements will no longer be provided to the participant;
- — Procedures that will be used to update the recipient's information; and
- — A description of the hardware and software required to access, print, and retain a statement and the date when the statement will no longer be available on the Web site.

[IRS Notice 2004-10, 2004-6 I.R.B. 433]

Q 18:95 What is the penalty for failure to file Form 1099-R?

The penalty for failure to file depends on when the Form 1099-R is filed.

- If the form is correctly filed within 30 days after the due date, the penalty is $30 per return up to a maximum of $250,000 per year.
- If the form is correctly filed more than 30 days after the due date but by August 1, the penalty is $60 per return up to a maximum of $500,000 per year.
- If the form is filed after August 1, the penalty is $100 per return up to a maximum of $1,500,000 per year.

The maximum penalties are reduced for small businesses as defined in the general instructions to Form 1099. [I.R.C. § 6721]

Q 18:96 When must a plan administrator file Form 1099-R on magnetic media?

A payor that prepares more than 250 1099-R forms must submit the information to the IRS electronically. It is necessary to obtain approval of the particular electronic format from the IRS 30 days before the due date of the return. Form 4419 is used for these purposes. It is not necessary to reapply for approval each year. If filing electronically presents a hardship, the payor may request a waiver on Form 8508 filed 45 days before the due date of the return. Failure to file electronically may result in a penalty of $100 per return.

Q 18:97 What are the rules for filing paper returns?

For payors filing fewer than 250 forms, certain requirements must be met. The forms themselves are printed by the IRS. The first copy is headlined in red. Photocopies may not be used. The forms are two to a sheet and should not be cut or separated, and no stapling, tearing, or taping is allowed. Pinfeed holes on the forms are not allowed. Copy A is submitted to the IRS. When providing the paper return to the payee, a statement should be provided that indicates the following: "This information is being furnished to the IRS." Form 1096 is used to transmit paper copies to the IRS.

Q 18:98 How are 1099-R forms corrected?

If it becomes necessary to correct a Form 1099-R, the payor must complete the entire form, not just the corrected items. If 250 or more corrections are needed, the payor must file electronically. If fewer than 250 corrections are done, the corrections should be submitted with Form 1096.

Distribution Planning

Employees who are about to retire will need to make a number of important decisions about the payment of their retirement benefits. Some of the decisions will be tax motivated, since the employee wishes to maximize the amount left after paying federal and state taxes. Other decisions will be driven by the individual's family and financial situation, health, and established retirement objectives. The individual's view of the future will enter into the decisions as well: the health of the economy, the impact of budget deficits, and anticipated changes in future tax laws. The broad range of investment opportunities available to the individual at retirement also can be a significant factor in the decision-making process.

Distribution planning is not just for the wealthy trying to avoid federal income and estate taxes. As 401(k) plans grow in popularity and the funds in these plans accumulate, many individuals will find their 401(k) plan the most significant part of their retirement savings program. This section is concerned with techniques that may prove useful in deferring, minimizing, or avoiding taxes on 401(k) plan distributions.

The availability of Roth 401(k) accounts creates additional opportunities and complexities in the distribution planning process.

Rollovers of Pre-Tax Accounts

Q 18:99 How is a rollover advantageous to an individual?

An individual who receives an eligible rollover distribution (see the section on eligible rollover distributions in chapter 16) from a 401(k) plan may choose to defer taxation on all or a portion of the distribution by rolling over the proceeds. Once the distribution is rolled over, no funds will be required to be withdrawn until the individual reaches age 70½ (if from a traditional IRA or from a qualified plan sponsored by a company in which the individual has more than a 5 percent ownership interest), or separates from service (if from a qualified plan of the employer and the individual is not a 5 percent owner). If the individual dies before reaching age 70½, his or her beneficiary may opt to roll over the benefit. The rules concerning the types of available rollovers and the application of the minimum distribution rules vary depending on whether the beneficiary is or is not the spouse. (See chapter 16 for further discussion of the eligible rollover and minimum distribution rules.)

Q 18:100 May a rollover be made by an individual who is over age 70½?

Yes, but if the individual is subject to the minimum distribution requirements, the minimum distribution amount for that year must first be paid out to the participant before the balance of his or her account may be rolled over (see chapter 16). This option may prove to be useful for an older participant in a 401(k) plan who has retired but does not wish to receive 401(k) plan proceeds in a lump sum.

Q 18:101 When may a partial distribution be rolled over?

If a distribution is not a life annuity or is not in installments extending past ten years, there is no longer any relevant distinction between partial distributions and total distributions as they affect the ability to roll over the distribution. The payment of any portion of a participant's account can constitute an eligible rollover distribution that can be rolled into an IRA or another qualified plan. [Treas. Reg. § 1.402(c)-2, Q&A 3]

Q 18:102 What additional factors should a participant take into account when considering a rollover from a qualified plan to a Roth IRA?

Prior to the enactment of the Pension Protection Act of 2006 (PPA), participants in pre-tax retirement plans could not roll over amounts directly into a Roth IRA. The PPA changed that rule to allow eligible rollover distributions (see chapter 16) from qualified plans to a Roth IRA either directly or in a 60-day rollover. For taxable years beginning prior to January 1, 2010, the ability to roll over a pre-tax eligible rollover distribution into a Roth IRA was subject to the Roth IRA adjusted gross income limits. The plan administrator was not responsible for assuring that the participant's rollover into a Roth IRA qualified under the income limit rules. For taxable years beginning January 1, 2010, and later the income limits no longer apply. In addition, for rollovers of this type occurring in 2010, the taxpayer could elect to pay income taxes due on the rollover amount over a two-year period beginning in 2011. [I.R.C. § 408A(d)(3)(A)(iii); IRS Notice 2008-30, 2008-12 I.R.B. 638; IRS Notice 2009-75, 2009-39 I.R.B. 436] After September 27, 2010, an in-plan Roth rollover option may be available, and after December 31, 2012, an in-plan Roth conversion also may be available (see Qs 18:67–18:76.)

Rollovers of Roth Accounts

Q 18:103 What should be considered in making a rollover decision with respect to a Roth account?

A Roth 401(k) can be rolled into another Roth 401(k), a Roth 403(b), or a Roth IRA.

If the Roth distribution is not a qualified distribution (see Q 18:60) and the participant does not need the money currently, it makes sense to roll the Roth and wait until the earnings in the account can be received tax free.

If a participant has a choice between rolling into a Roth 401(k), a Roth 403(b), or a Roth IRA, he or she needs to understand the implications, if any, of the five-year holding period. For example, if the money being rolled over is two years into its five-year holding period, the Roth IRA would be a new account, so the rollover would not carry forward the two-year period. (See Qs 18:77 and 18:78 for a more detailed discussion of tackling periods for Roth rollovers.)

If the participant intends to leave the moneys in his or her Roth 401(k) account for beneficiaries, then it makes sense to roll the Roth 401(k) into a Roth IRA to avoid taking RMDs prior to death. Minimum distributions are required from Roth 401(k) plans and from traditional IRAs during the participant's lifetime, but they are not required from Roth IRAs.

Lump-Sum Distributions

Q 18:104 What are the tax advantages of a lump-sum distribution?

A 401(k) plan may allow a participant to choose whether the account balance is to be paid in a single sum or installments. If a single sum is chosen, the participant must determine whether favorable tax treatment is available. If the participant was at least age 50 on January 1, 1986, he or she can choose ten-year income averaging. If the individual participated in the plan before 1974, a portion of the distribution may be entitled to capital gains treatment. Currently, the capital gains portion would be taxed at a 20 percent rate. Depending on the amount of the distribution, it may be more advantageous to income average the entire distribution. However, as the amount of the distribution increases, the tax advantage of continuing deferrals may outweigh the tax advantage of income averaging.

Avoiding the Premature Distribution Tax

Q 18:105 How may the 10 percent premature distribution tax be avoided if the participant is not deceased or disabled?

The 10 percent additional income tax penalty on distributions taken before age $59^1/_2$ may be avoided if the participant separates from service during or after the year in which he or she attains age 55. For a younger participant, the tax may be avoided after severing employment by beginning to take distributions in annual installments. For other exceptions to the premature distribution penalty, see Q 18:86.

Q 18:106 What conditions must be satisfied to avoid the premature distribution tax under the annual installment exception?

A number of requirements need to be met to satisfy the annual installment exception noted above (see Q 18:105):

1. Each distribution must be part of a series of substantially equal periodic payments made over the life (or joint lives) of the participant (and participant's beneficiary).
2. Distributions must commence after separation from service.
3. Distributions may not be later modified (other than by reason of death or disability) before the later of:
   a. The end of the five-year period after benefits commence; or
   b. After attainment of age 59½.

[I.R.C. §§ 72(t)(2)(A)(iv), 72(t)(3)(B), 72(t)(4)]

Q 18:107 How are equal periodic payments computed?

The requirement that distributions be part of a series of substantially equal periodic payments can be met by using one of three possible methods:

1. The principles used for determining the amount of minimum distributions can be applied (see chapter 16);
2. The annual payment can be determined by amortizing the individual's account balance over the number of years equal to his or her life expectancy or joint life expectancy using the IRS tables prescribed under the Section 401(a)(9) regulations and using a reasonable interest rate (see chapter 16); or
3. The annual payment can be determined by dividing the individual's account balance by an annuity factor (using reasonable interest and mortality factors).

[Rev. Rul. 2002-62, 2002-42 I.R.B. 710; IRS Notice 89-25, 1989-1 C.B. 662]

Example. Dan, age 50, is single. He leaves his employer in 2015, when he has a vested account balance of $1,278,000. Dan wishes to receive annual installments from the 401(k) plan without incurring the 10 percent premature distribution penalty. He can choose one of three methods of distribution:

1. Use the IRS tables with single life expectancy factor of 34.2 (see the IRS's Web site: *www.irs.gov*). A joint life expectancy factor could also be used if Dan had a designated beneficiary. The 2014 distribution would be equal to:

$$\frac{\$1{,}278{,}000}{34.2} = \$37{,}368$$

2. Amortize the account balance over 33 years at 8 percent:

$$\frac{\$1{,}278{,}000}{12.435} = \$102{,}774$$

3. Annuitize the account balance, using 8 percent interest and the widely used UP-1984 Mortality Table:

$$\frac{\$1{,}278{,}000}{10.6509} = \$119{,}990$$

Since Dan is looking to maximize the distribution, he would probably choose option 3.

Q 18:108 What happens when a participant begins receiving equal periodic payments and then changes his or her election?

The general rule is that if any change is made to the method of payment before the later of the participant's attainment of age 59½ or five years from the date of the first payment, the 10 percent additional income tax applies to all payments. An exception applies if the change is made due to the participant's death or disability. [I.R.C. § 72(t)(4)(A)(ii)] In 2002, the IRS made additional relief available out of concern that, with the poor performance of the equity markets, participants who elected a method that resulted in payments in fixed dollar amounts would deplete their retirement account prematurely and might not have sufficient assets to make all required payments. The IRS has stated that if assets are depleted before all required payments are made, the cessation of payments will not be treated as a modification and no additional income tax will be due. The IRS also will allow a one-time change to a minimum distribution method for participants who initially elected either the fixed annuitization or fixed amortization methods (see the example in Q 18:107). Participants may elect to switch to the required minimum distribution (RMD) method but must then follow that method for all subsequent years. The RMD method allows the current value of a participant's account to be factored into the required payment amount. [Rev. Rul. 2002-62, 2002-42 I.R.B. 710]

Q 18:109 Is this exception also available for amounts in an IRA?

Yes. The participant can qualify for the annual installment exception even though the 401(k) plan may not allow for installment payments. The participant would elect a lump-sum distribution, roll the proceeds into the IRA, and commence distributions under the above rules.

Distributions Versus Accumulations

Q 18:110 What are the disadvantages of accelerating the payment of retirement benefits?

By taking larger distributions earlier, the participant may be incurring a larger ongoing tax liability, since the earnings on the funds withdrawn from the 401(k) plan will be subject to income tax. However, the current tax liability could be reduced through the use of tax-sheltered accumulation vehicles such as municipal bonds, real estate, life insurance, or annuity products.

Q 18:111 Why may it be advantageous to continue to accumulate funds in a 401(k) plan after they could be withdrawn without penalty?

In general, it is advantageous to keep assets accumulating on a tax-deferred basis for as long as possible, although an individual should compare the use of a qualified plan or IRA with other investment alternatives. The examples below all assume a net tax rate of 33 percent and a pre-tax rate of investment return of 9 percent (6 percent after tax).

Example 1. Linda retires at age 60 with $750,000 in a 401(k) plan. If she takes a distribution and pays the income tax due, she can invest the money on an after-tax basis. If none of the money has been spent by age 85, she will have accumulated $2,156,665.

Example 2. Judy also retires at age 60 with $750,000 in a 401(k) plan. She rolls over the entire amount into a traditional IRA, thus preserving its tax-deferred status. At age 70½ she begins receiving required minimum distributions, always investing the after-tax amount of the distribution on an after-tax basis. At age 85, if Judy withdraws the remainder from her IRA and pays tax on it, she will have a total after-tax accumulation of $3,604,670, which is significantly more than Linda's accumulation.

Example 3. Like Linda in Example 1 and Judy in Example 2, Fred also retires at age 60 with $750,000 in a 401(k) plan. He also rolls over the entire amount into a traditional IRA but then transfers the amount to a Roth IRA (see chapter 22). Fred must pay income tax at the time of the transfer. He can do this out of the transferred amount. Fred need not commence taking minimum distributions from the Roth IRA at age 70½ and by age 85 will have accumulated within the Roth IRA an after-tax balance of $4,333,098, which is significantly more than the amount either Linda or Judy accumulated.

To Roth or Not to Roth

Whether or not to take advantage of Roth 401(k) accounts is a complicated decision at both the plan sponsor level and participant level. Roth 401(k) accounts have not been adopted as broadly as originally anticipated, and there is speculation that the complexity of the decision making is a factor delaying more broad-based adoption.

Q 18:112 What considerations should a plan sponsor take into account when deciding whether to offer Roth deferrals in a plan?

A plan sponsor should consider the following issues when making a decision about whether to offer a Roth 401(k) plan:

1. Will a significant number of participants be likely to benefit from and take advantage of Roth deferrals?

2. Can the plan sponsor's payroll vendor and plan recordkeeper handle the data collection, reporting, and separate accounting requirements of the Roth?
3. Can the plan's service provider accommodate the Roth with respect to plan amendments and changes to administrative forms?
4. Who will handle communications at the participant level and to what extent will planning at the individual participant level be offered?
5. Will the plan also allow for in-plan Roth rollovers?
6. What is the cost of all of the above?

Q 18:113 What factors should a plan participant consider when deciding whether to contribute to a pre-tax 401(k) account or a Roth 401(k) account?

To answer this question, some extensive individual financial and tax planning is required. There are, however, some general guidelines that can help guide the decision. Contributing to a Roth 401(k) instead of a pre-tax 401(k) account will generally be more advantageous to participants who:

- Believe they will be in a higher tax bracket in retirement than they are now (see Table 18-2 for an illustration of what level of tax differential it takes at what age to create an advantage with a pre-tax account);
- Are deferring the maximum amount allowed;
- Want to avoid taking lifetime distributions at age 70½ (this feature is only available in Roth IRA accounts);
- Are seeking tax diversification (i.e., a balance between taxable and nontaxable income upon retirement); or
- Believe that inflation will impact significantly the amount of money they will need to withdraw from the plan in retirement to support their current lifestyle.

Contributing to a Roth over a pre-tax account will generally be less advantageous to participants who:

- Believe they will be in a significantly lower tax bracket at retirement;
- Expect to take money out of the plan before it is qualified (see Q 18:60); or
- Will contribute less and/or lose match dollars as a result of having to pay income tax currently on contributions.

Table 18-2 may help participants and their advisers in making the decision "to Roth or not to Roth."

Table 18-2. Estimated Break-Even Point of Tax Rate After Retirement (Retirement Age: 65)

Current Age	*50*		*40*		*30*	
Current Tax Rate	*Est. Break-Even Tax Rate After Retirement**	*% of Decrease*	*Est. Break-Even Tax Rate After Retirement**	*% of Decrease*	*Est. Break-Even Tax Rate After Retirement**	*% of Decrease*
25.00%	22.00%	12.00%	19.50%	22.00%	17.20%	31.20%
26.00%	22.50%	13.46%	20.10%	22.69%	17.65%	32.12%
27.00%	23.50%	12.96%	20.60%	23.70%	18.05%	33.15%
28.00%	24.00%	14.29%	21.20%	24.29%	18.40%	34.29%
29.00%	25.00%	13.79%	21.80%	24.83%	18.80%	35.17%
30.00%	25.50%	15.00%	22.40%	25.33%	19.20%	36.00%
31.00%	26.50%	14.52%	22.90%	26.13%	19.60%	36.77%
32.00%	27.00%	15.63%	23.40%	26.88%	19.90%	37.81%

* The tax rate after retirement will need to go down to this level before a traditional 401(k) will outperform a Roth 401(k), assuming that contributions are equal and all other factors stay the same.

Source: Lawrence Johnson & Associates, Inc.

Chapter 19

Reporting and Disclosure

This chapter discusses the reporting requirements under the Employee Retirement Income Security Act of 1974 (ERISA) and the Internal Revenue Code (I.R.C.) applicable to 401(k) plans, as well as certain requirements for providing information to participants. Other disclosure and notice requirements applicable to certain plan design features (e.g., automatic enrollment, ERISA Section 404(c) protection, safe harbor 401(k)) are covered in other chapters.

IRS and DOL Form 5500 Reporting 19-2
Table 19-1. Summary of Form 5500 Components 19-6
EFAST2 19-9
Special Filing Issues 19-14
Participant Disclosures 19-15
Table 19-2. Key Required Participant Disclosures/Notices 19-15
Summary Plan Description 19-17
Summary of Material Modifications 19-19
Summary Annual Report 19-20
Individual Participant Benefit Statements 19-21
Information Upon Request 19-28
Participant Investment and Fee Disclosures 19-29
DOL Field Assistance Bulletin 2012-02R 19-46
Blackout Notices 19-65
Diversification Notices 19-69
Use of Electronic Technology 19-70
Record Retention Under ERISA 19-82

IRS and DOL Form 5500 Reporting

Q 19:1 Who is responsible for reporting information to the IRS and the DOL?

The plan administrator who is designated in the plan document is responsible for IRS and DOL reporting. If the plan document does not designate a plan administrator, the plan sponsor must handle the reporting. [ERISA § 3(16)(A); Treas. Reg. § 1.414(g)-1(b)(1)]

Q 19:2 What is the basic annual reporting requirement?

The 5500 series (5500, 5500-SF, or 5500-EZ) must be filed for each year in which the plan has assets. Plan administrators who comply with the instructions for the applicable Form 5500 generally will satisfy the annual reporting requirements for the IRS and DOL.

Q 19:3 For what plans can the simplified Form 5500-SF be filed as opposed to the longer Form 5500?

Form 5500-SF is a simplified annual reporting form available to certain small plans. Eligibility requirements to use the Form 5500-SF are detailed in the form's instructions. Most notably, the plan must generally have fewer than 100 participants at the beginning of the plan year.

A plan that is required to file an annual report but is not eligible to file Form 5500-SF must file Form 5500, Annual Return/Report of Employee Benefit Plan, with all the required schedules and attachments, unless the plan is eligible to file the Form 5500-EZ (see Q 19:4).

Q 19:4 For which plans can Form 5500-EZ be filed?

A "one-participant plan" is eligible to file Form 5500-EZ, Annual Return of One-Participant (Owners and Their Spouses) Retirement Plan. If a plan is eligible to file Form 5500-EZ, no reporting is necessary as long as plan assets at the end of the plan year do not exceed $250,000. All plans of the employer must be aggregated for purposes of the $250,000 limit.

A Form 5500-EZ should be filed for the final plan year whether or not the plan was required to file a Form 5500-EZ for any prior year.

A *one-participant plan* for this purpose is a retirement plan that (a) covered only the individual (and his or her spouse), and the individual (and his or her spouse) owned the entire business (whether or not incorporated) or (b) covered only one or more partners (and their spouses) in the plan sponsor, and (c) does not provide benefits for anyone except the person(s) identified in (a) or (b).

Form 5500-EZ is filed on paper with the IRS. As an alternative to filing Form 5500-EZ, a one-participant plan may be eligible to file Form 5500-SF (see Q 19:3). Such a plan could elect to file Form 5500-SF electronically using EFAST2 rather than filing a Form 5500-EZ on paper with the IRS (see Q 19:9).

Q 19:5 Is there an audit requirement, and does it apply to small plans?

For any plan with 100 or more participants as of the beginning of the plan year (large plan filer), a certified public accountant or licensed public accountant must conduct an audit of the plan's financial statements and schedules. [ERISA § 103(a)(3)(A), 29 U.S.C. § 1023(a)(3)(A)] The accountant must not have a financial interest in the plan or the plan sponsor, and the audit must express an opinion on the financial statements and schedules, as well as the accounting principles and practices used by the plan. [DOL Reg. § 2520.103-1(b)(5)] There is a special rule whereby if a plan has between 80 and 120 participants as of the beginning of the plan year, the plan may elect to file under the same filing status as in the prior year. [DOL Reg. § 2520.103-1(d)]

The Form 5500 instructions provide a detailed definition of a participant for 5500 purposes (line 5) and should be carefully reviewed when determining filer status. Generally speaking, a participant includes any individual eligible to participate in the plan (including, in a 401(k) plan, an individual who is eligible to make a salary deferral election even if he or she elects not to defer) and certain retired or separated participants.

The opinion of the auditor need not extend to any statement or information prepared and certified by a bank or similar institution or an insurance carrier. [DOL Reg. § 2520.103-8]

Plans with fewer than 100 participants at the beginning of the plan year must also obtain an accountant's opinion unless the following conditions are met:

1. As of the last day of the preceding plan year, at least 95 percent of the plan's assets are invested in qualifying plan assets (see definition below) *or* the assets that are not qualifying plan assets must be covered by a bond meeting the requirements of ERISA Section 412; *and*
2. With the exception of qualifying plan assets described in items 1, 4, and 6 below, the summary annual report (SAR) for the plan includes disclosure of the name of each institution holding (or issuing) qualifying plan assets, the amount of assets held as of the end of the plan year, and notification of the participants' right to receive financial statements describing these assets without charge; information about any surety company issuing a bond as required by item 1 above and advising participants of their right to receive a copy of the bond without charge; and notification of the participants' right to contact the DOL's Employee Benefits Security Administration (EBSA) if they are unable to obtain any of these documents.

Qualifying plan assets include:

1. Qualifying employer securities;
2. Shares issued by a mutual fund that is registered under the Investment Company Act of 1940;

3. Assets held by a regulated financial institution, which includes banks, registered broker-dealers, insurance companies, and any other organization authorized to act as an IRA trustee under Internal Revenue Code (Code) Section 408;
4. Participant loans that satisfy the prohibited transaction exemption requirements of ERISA Section 408(b)(1);
5. Investment and annuity contracts issued by an insurance company; and
6. Assets held in the individual account of a participant or beneficiary over which the participant or beneficiary has the right to exercise control and with respect to which the participant or beneficiary is furnished with an annual statement from a regulated financial institution describing the assets.

[DOL Reg. §§ 2520.104-41(c), 2520.104-46(b)(1), 2520.104-46(d)]

Example. An employer-directed plan with 75 participants and for which the employer is trustee has the following assets as of the end of its December 31, 2014 plan year:

$ 610,000 —	Registered mutual funds
65,000 —	Annuity contracts
29,000 —	Participant loans
96,000 —	Limited partnerships
$ 800,000	Total

For the plan year ending December 31, 2015, the plan is subject to the audit requirement because the limited partnership interest, which constituted 12 percent of plan assets, is not a qualified plan asset. To avoid the audit requirement the plan can obtain an ERISA bond for the $96,000 and comply with special SAR requirements described above.

The DOL issued frequently asked questions (FAQs) on the small-plan audit waiver and a sample SAR disclosure (available on the Web at *www.dol.gov/ebsa/faqs/faq_auditwaiver.html*).

Q 19:6 What schedules are attached to Form 5500?

Short descriptions of the Form 5500 schedules are shown in Table 19-1. This table also identifies which schedules have recently been revised. Social Security numbers should not appear on the Form 5500 or any schedule unless specifically required by the form, schedule, or instructions. Filings can be rejected if the forms include Social Security numbers or any attachment that is open to public inspection.

In connection with the move to the electronic filing system EFAST2, filers will no longer attach Schedule SSA to the Form 5500. Instead, a standalone Form 8955-SSA must be separately filed with the IRS (see Q 19:7).

The Form 5500 and its instructions are available on the IRS Web site at *www.irs.gov/Forms-&-Pubs.*

For more information, visit the DOL's Web site at *www.dol.gov/ebsa/compliance_assistance.html* under "Reporting and Filing." For additional information concerning Form 5500 filing requirements, see *5500 Preparer's Manual for 2014 Plan Years* (Wolters Kluwer Law & Business).

Q 19:7 What is the purpose of Form 8955-SSA?

Form 8955-SSA is a standalone form used to report information relating to separated participants who have deferred vested benefits that was previously reported on Schedule SSA to Form 5500. It is filed directly with the IRS, and not filed with the DOL through EFAST2.

In general, as with Schedule SSA, if a Form 8955-SSA must be filed for a plan year, it must be filed by the last day of the seventh month following the last day of that plan year (plus extensions). Thus, for calendar-year plans, any 2013 Form 8955–SSA must be filed with the IRS by July 31, 2014.

The rules applicable to the extension of time for filing Form 8955-SSA are the same as those applicable to the extension of time for filing Schedule SSA (Form 5500). Therefore, Form 5558 may be used to file for an extension for a Form 8955-SSA filing. The IRS revised the Form 5558 to enable filers to obtain extensions of the time to file Form 8955-SSA. Moreover, plan administrators are granted an automatic extension of time to file Form 8955-SSA (without filing a Form 5558) until the due date of the federal income tax return of the employer if certain conditions are satisfied.

For 2013 and prior years, filers had the option of filing Form 8955-SSA electronically. Beginning with the 2014 Form 8955-SSA, some filers are now required to file the form electronically. The new requirements are detailed in the form's instructions.

See IRS Web site for FAQs regarding Form 8955-SSA at *www.irs.gov/Retirement-Plans/ FAQs-Regarding-Form-8955-SSA*.

Q 19:8 What is the penalty for a late filing of Form 8955-SSA?

The IRS may impose a penalty for failure to file Form 8955-SSA (including failure to include all required participants). The penalty is $1 for each participant not reported and for each day multiplied by the number of days the failure continues. The penalty, up to a maximum of $5,000, is imposed on the person failing to so file unless it is shown the failure is due to reasonable cause.

Table 19-1. Summary of Form 5500 Components

5500 Filing Component	*Type of Information Collected*	*Description of Changes in 2014*
Form 5500	Overview information on type of annual return/report, type of plan, and schedules attached	New line item for Active Participants Information; new informational requirements for multiple-employer plans.
Schedule A	Information on contracts with insurance companies	No material revisions.
Schedule C	Information on service providers for large plans	No material revisions.
Schedule D	Information on participation in certain pooled investment/insurance arrangements (CCTs, PSAs, MTIAs, and 103-12 1Es) or direct filing entity (DFE)	No material revisions.
Schedule G	Information on nonexempt transactions and on loans, leases, and fixed income investments in default or uncollectable for large plans	No material revisions.
Schedule H	Financial statements and related information for large plans	Instructions enhanced with regard to the description of a registered investment company.
Schedule I	Financial statements and related information for small plans not eligible to file Form 5500-SF	No material revisions.
Schedule R	Information on pension plans, including plan distributions and funding requirements, as well as certain information on employee stock ownership plans (ESOPs)	No material revisions.
Schedules MB and SB	Actuarial information on pension plans	Updates/clarifications applicable to defined benefit plans.
Form 8955-SSA	Information on separated participants with deferred vested benefits.	No longer attached to Form 5500; a standalone form (see Q 19:7).

Q 19:9 What type of information is required on Schedule C of the Form 5500?

Large plans (generally, plans with 100 or more participants) are required to report, in more detail, compensation of service providers that received, directly or indirectly, $5,000 or more in reportable compensation on Schedule C. Reportable compensation includes money and any other items of value received, directly or indirectly, from the plan (including fees charged as a percentage of assets and deducted from investment returns) in connection with services rendered to the plan. Payments made directly by the plan sponsor that are not reimbursed by the plan are not subject to Schedule C reporting requirements. Compensation that is reportable is disclosed on Schedule C in the following categories:

1. *Direct Compensation*. Payments made directly by the plan (e.g., direct payments by the plan out of a plan account, charges to plan forfeitures, charges to trust, and direct charges to plan participant individual accounts).
2. *Indirect Compensation*. Compensation received from sources other than directly from the plan or plan sponsor, including:
    - Fees and expense reimbursement payments received by mutual funds, bank-commingled trusts, insurance company pooled separate accounts, and other investment funds in which the plan invests that are charged against the fund or account and reflected in the value of the plan's investment (e.g., management fees paid by a mutual fund to its adviser, sub-transfer fees, shareholder servicing fees, account maintenance fees, 12b-1 fees);
    - Finders' fees, float revenue, brokerage commissions, and other transaction-based fees received in connection with transactions or services involving the plan.
3. *Eligible indirect compensation (EIC)*. Fees or expense reimbursements charged to investment funds and reflected in the net value of the investment or return such as finders' fees, soft dollars, float, brokerage commissions or other transaction-based fees involving the plan that were not paid directly by the plan or plan sponsor and for which the plan received written disclosures describing (a) the existence of the indirect compensation, (b) the services provided for the indirect compensation or the purpose of the payment of the indirect compensation, (c) the amount (or estimate) of the compensation or description of the formula used to calculate or determine the compensation, and (d) the identity of the party receiving the compensation. The written disclosures for a bundled arrangement must separately disclose and describe each element of indirect compensation that would be required to be separately reported to rely on this alternative reporting option.

The information that must be provided for reportable compensation includes the service provider entity name and employer identification number (EIN) or address, all codes that describe services and compensation received (a list of over 50 codes is provided, as many codes that apply must be entered), the service provider's relationship to the plan sponsor or any person known to be a party in interest, and the total amount of compensation by category.

For compensation in category 3, above, an alternative reporting option is available. Certain detailed reporting is not required for EIC.

Special additional disclosure requirements may apply with respect to indirect compensation received by a service provider who (1) is a fiduciary or (2) provides one or more of the following services—contract administration, consulting, investment advisory (to plan or participants), investment management, securities brokerage, or recordkeeping. The source from which the indirect compensation was received by the service provider and other information must be provided if: (1) the amount of the compensation was $1,000 or more, or (2) the plan was given a formula or other description of the method used to determine the indirect compensation rather than an amount or estimated amount of the indirect compensation.

A plan's direct payments to a bundled service provider need not be allocated among affiliates or subcontractors and also reported as indirect compensation, unless the amount paid is set on a per transaction basis (e.g., brokerage fees and commissions). Fees charged to the plan's investment and reflected in the net value of the investment, such as management fees paid by mutual funds to their advisers, float revenue, commissions (including soft dollars), finders' fees, 12b-1 fees, account maintenance fees, and shareholder servicing fees, must be treated as separate compensation.

Certain nonmonetary compensation (such as gifts or meals of insubstantial value) is not reportable if value does not reach defined threshold limits. Also included in Schedule C is a section for reporting service providers who failed or refused to provide requisite information for the filing.

The DOL released two sets of Frequently Asked Questions (FAQs) relating to the Form 5500 Schedule C reporting requirements. [See the DOL's Web site at *www.dol.gov/ebsa/compliance_assistance.html* under "Reporting and Filing."] The FAQs address various technical aspects of the reporting requirements, such as:

- The availability of the EIC alternative reporting option for certain types of compensation
- Guidelines for using a formula for reporting indirect compensation
- Reporting reimbursements to a plan sponsor for fees paid to a third-party service provider
- Fees charged against an investment fund that will and will not be considered reportable indirect compensation
- The reporting requirements involving nonmonetary compensation

For information on service provider and participant fee-related disclosure requirements, see chapters 4 and 19, respectively.

EFAST2

Q 19:10 To what extent must Form 5500 be filed and displayed electronically?

Effective for plan years beginning on or after January 1, 2009, the DOL is requiring that Form 5500 and Form 5500-SF be filed electronically under the wholly electronic filing system known as EFAST2. EFAST2 is Internet-based and compatible with a variety of third-party software products. Under the new regime:

- There are a few limited options for entering data and filing reports (e.g., EFAST2-approved third-party software application, the DOL's Web-based IFILE system).
- Different credentials (e.g., filing/schedule author, signer, transmitter) must be obtained from the DOL to effectuate the online filings.
- Attachments are provided via text files or PDF (required format for attachments needing signatures).
- Plan administrators will need Internet access and EFAST2 credentials to sign/submit Form 5500.
- The electronic mandate does not apply to Form 5500-EZ, which is to be filed on paper with the IRS.

Q 19:11 Where can additional information be obtained regarding the EFAST2 requirements?

Additional information on the EFAST2 requirements is available on the DOL's Web site (*www.efast.dol.gov*). On the Web site are links to EFAST2 Frequently Asked Questions (FAQs), User Guides, and Tutorials. Topics covered include, but are not limited to:

- Filings of pre-2010 reports after January 1, 2014
- Filing software options
- Registering for EFAST2 credentials
- Completing and submitting Forms 5500 and attachments
- Checking on filing status
- Option for service providers to transmit filings on behalf of a plan administrator under specified conditions

Q 19:12 What items may make a Form 5500 filing particularly challenging?

Following are some items that may require special attention in connection with filing Form 5500:

- For plan years beginning after November 15, 2007, requirements under FASB, Fair Value Measurements (ASC 820, formerly FAS 157) impact fair market measurements in a plan's financial statements. Generally speaking, the requirements enhance the plan sponsor's responsibility to understand and display fair value information according to specified guidelines. A plan sponsor will need to work with its auditor and service providers in connection with satisfying its responsibilities in this area. Additional information is available on the Web site of the American Institute of Certified Public Accountants (AICPA) at *www.aicpa.org*.

- Late deposits of participant contributions must be reported on Schedule H and Schedule I (line 4a). According to the instructions, all late deposits, including those for which VFCP requirements are met, must be reported. Late deposits should be carried forward and reported again on line 4a for each subsequent year until the year after the violation is fully corrected, which includes the payment of any lost earnings or profits. A failure to timely deposit participant contributions according to the rules can result in adverse consequences, including the imposition of penalties and taxes. (See chapter 5.) Information on reporting late deposits is available on the DOL's Web site (*www.dol.gov/ebsa/faqs/faq_compliance_5500.html*).
- Various *plan characteristic codes* must be listed in Form 5500 to identify plan features such as participant-directed investments, ERISA Section 404(c) status, and automatic enrollment. If a plan offers self-directed brokerage accounts, a plan characteristic code must be included in the Form 5500 to identify that feature. There are options for reporting investments in assets made through self-directed brokerage accounts on Schedule H (see the Form 5500 instructions for details).
- Under IRS regulations governing tax return preparers, a preparer is required to obtain a Preparer Tax Identification Number (PTIN) and may be subject to mandatory competency exams and continuing education requirements if he or she prepares certain tax forms. IRS Notice 2011-6 (available at *www.irs.gov*)) provides guidance regarding the implementation of the requirements. Notice 2011-6 and other guidance (e.g., *www.irs.gov/for-Tax-Pros*) in this area should be carefully reviewed by service providers that prepare tax forms. Certain forms (e.g., Form 5500) are exempt from the registration and PTIN system, while others (e.g., Form 5330) are not.

The DOL has posted on its Web site (*www.dol.gov/ebsa/compliance_assistance.html*) information regarding required disclosures on Form 5500. The Web site offers links to filing tips, frequently asked questions (FAQs) about the small plan audit waiver, and other information.

Q 19:13 What is the due date for filing the Form 5500 series?

The plan must file the Form 5500 series and accompanying schedules by the last day of the seventh month following the close of the plan year. An extension of 2½ months may be obtained by filing Form 5558 before the due date of the Form 5500 series. For Form 5500 filings for taxable years beginning after December 31, 2015, the maximum extension is 3½ months (ending on November 15 for calendar-year plans. [The Surface Transportation and Veterans

Health Care Choice Improvement Act of 2015 (H.R. 3236), § 2006(b)(3). [Pub. L. No. 113-41, signed into law on July 31, 2015]

Form 5500 may be automatically extended (without filing Form 5558) if the following requirements are met:

1. The plan year and the employer's tax year are the same;
2. The employer has been granted an extension of time to file its federal income tax return to a date later than the normal due date for filing Form 5500; and
3. A copy of the application for extension of time to file the federal income tax return is maintained with the filer's records.

In this case, the extension is to the extended due date of the federal income tax return.

A terminating plan must continue to file Form 5500 until assets are fully distributed, and the due date for the final 5500 filing is the last day of the seventh month following distribution of the plan's last asset.

The IRS clarified that a Form 5558 filed for a Form 5500 extension and Form 8955-SSA extension does not require a signature. [77 Fed. Reg. 37,352 (June 21, 2012)] If, however, the Form 5558 is filed for a Form 5330 extension (e.g., to report a delinquent contribution), a signature is required. Those who can sign the Form 5558 include employers, plan sponsors, plan administrators, or other individual or authorized representative permitted to sign the Form 5330.

See Appendix J for a 401(k) Compliance Calendar.

Q 19:14 What are the penalties for late filing of the Form 5500 series?

The DOL has authority to assess penalties of up to $1,100 per day. [ERISA § 502(c)(2), 29 U.S.C. § 1132(c)(2); Form 5500 Instructions] The DOL's Employee Benefits Security Administration (EBSA) maintains an enforcement program for the assessment of civil penalties for noncompliance with ERISA's annual reporting requirements.

The penalty period begins from the due date of filing, regardless of any extensions obtained, and generally continues to the date a satisfactory return is filed. The penalty could reflect the materiality of the failure and may also take into account the willfulness of the failure and the good faith and diligence exercised by the plan administrator. [DOL Reg. § 2560.502c-2]

The IRS may assess a penalty of $25 per day up to $15,000. The penalty begins to run on the due date of the return. If an extension has been filed, the penalty begins to run on the extended due date. [I.R.C. § 6652(e)] Late Form 5500-EZ filings are only subject to IRS penalties.

Q 19:15 What is the Delinquent Filer Voluntary Compliance Program?

The DOL's Delinquent Filer Voluntary Compliance (DFVC) Program is for late filers or nonfilers of Form 5500 returns. For employers who participate in the DFVC program, the late filing penalty is $10 per day with an annual cap of $750 for small plans and $2,000 for large plans. If there are delinquencies for multiple plan years, the per plan cap is $1,500 for small plans and $4,000 for large plans. Small plans are plans with fewer than 100 participants at the beginning of the plan year or that filed as a small plan pursuant to the "80–120" participant rule.

In order to obtain this relief, a complete annual report including all required statements and schedules for each plan year for which relief is sought must be submitted. Once a plan administrator has been notified by the DOL of a failure to file, the DFVC program is no longer available.

In January 2013, the DOL announced technical updates to the DFVC program. Those include:

- Incorporating an existing voluntary online penalty calculator and Web payment system into the DFVC program.
- Fully integrating the DFVC Program into the EFAST2 electronic filing system and making available a Form 5500 Version Selection Tool, available at *www.dol.gov/ebsa/5500selectorinstructions.html*, which helps filers determine which forms they must use when filing electronically for prior years.

Further information on DFVC can be obtained from the DOL by calling (202) 693-8360 or by visiting *www.dol.gov/ebsa/faqs/faq_dfvc.html*.

If a late filer satisfies the requirements of the DFVC program, including paying the reduced civil penalty, relief from IRS penalties is also available. The late filer need not file a separate application with the IRS. The IRS will coordinate with the DOL in determining which late filers are eligible for relief from IRS penalties. The IRS will not impose penalties provided (1) the requirements of the DFVC program are met with respect to a delinquent Form 5500 series return for such year and (2) a Form 8955-SSA is filed separately with the IRS for the year to which the DFVC filing relates (to the extent that the information has not previously been provided to the IRS). Any Form 8955-SSA required to be filed must be filed by the later of 30 calendar days after the filer completes the DFVC filing or December 1, 2014. [IRS Notice 2014-35, 2014-23 I.R.B. 1072] Additional information is available on the IRS Web site at *www.irs.gov/Retirement-Plans/Changes-to-IRS-Penalty-Relief-for-DOL-DFVC-Filers-of-Late-Annual-Reports*.

The above IRS relief is available only to the extent that a Form 5500 series return is required to be filed under ERISA. Therefore, for example, Form 5500-EZ and Form 5500-SF filers for plans without employees (e.g., one-participant plans) would not be eligible. On June 2, 2014, the IRS established a one-year pilot program to provide penalty relief for delinquent Form 5500 filers for non-ERISA plans. [Rev. Proc. 2014-32; 2014-23 I.R.B. 1073] Additional information is available on the IRS Web site at *www.irs.gov/Retirement-Plans/New-Penalty-Relief-Program-for-Form-5500-EZ-Late-Filers*.

Q 19:16 Are incomplete filings subject to these penalties?

Yes. An annual report that has been rejected for lack of material information will be treated as having not been filed. However, under the DOL rules, once the plan administrator is notified that a filing has been rejected for lack of material information, it has 45 days in which to cure the problem by filing a satisfactory report. If such a report is filed, no penalty will be assessed. [DOL Reg. § 2560.502c-2(b)(3)]

Q 19:17 May late filing penalties be appealed to the DOL?

Yes. Under DOL rules, the plan administrator has 30 days from the date it is served with a notice of assessment in which to file a statement of reasonable cause. It must be a written statement setting forth all the facts alleged to support a claim of reasonable cause and must declare that the statement is being made under penalty of perjury. [DOL Reg. § 2560.502c-2(e)]

The DOL will take into account the degree of willfulness involved and any facts indicating good faith and diligence on the part of the plan administrator.

Q 19:18 May late filing penalties be appealed to the IRS?

Yes. The IRS rules also contain a reasonable-cause exception. The IRS should generally recognize as reasonable cause filing in the wrong district, reliance on erroneous information provided by an IRS employee, serious illness or death of the taxpayer or someone in the immediate family, unavoidable absence of the taxpayer, destruction by fire or casualty of the taxpayer's business records, or failure of the IRS to provide assistance by means of blank forms or advice following a written or in-person request by the taxpayer. If none of the above situations applies, the standard will be whether a reasonable person of ordinary prudence and intelligence would consider that the facts show a reasonable cause for delay and clearly indicate no willful intent to disobey the filing requirement. The IRS released frequently asked questions (FAQs) regarding responding to a proposed IRS penalty assessment (Notices from IRS (CP 403 and CP 406 Notices)—Delinquency Notices). This guidance is available online at *www.irs.gov/Retirement-Plans/Understanding-Your-CP-403-or-CP-406—Notice.* If a plan is contacted by the IRS regarding a late filing, the plan administrator can still submit a filing under the DFVP (see Q 19:15).

Q 19:19 Who is responsible for payment of the penalties?

The DOL penalty is assessed against the plan administrator. [DOL Reg. § 2560.502c-2(a)] The IRS penalty is assessed against the plan administrator or employer. [Treas. Reg. § 301.6652-3(a)(3)] In both cases, the penalty is the personal liability of the plan administrator or employer and therefore is not deductible from plan assets as an administrative expense.

Q 19:20 Are there any criminal penalties for failure to file annual reports?

Yes. Criminal penalties may be imposed for willful violations of the reporting requirements: $100,000 for an individual and $500,000 for any other type of entity. [ERISA § 501, 29 U.S.C. § 1131] In addition, up to ten years' imprisonment could be imposed.

Special Filing Issues

Q 19:21 What filing is required of a plan that is merging, consolidating, or transferring assets?

Form 5310-A must be filed with the IRS for some plans involved in a transfer of assets or liabilities, or any merger or consolidation. The filing is due no later than 30 days prior to the date of the transfer. [I.R.C. § 6058(b)] The penalty for failure to file is $25 per day, with a maximum penalty of $15,000. [I.R.C. §§ 6058, 6652(e)] No filing is generally required if the transaction involves plans of the same type (i.e., two or more defined contribution plans or two or more defined benefit plans) and the requirements of Treasury Regulations Section 1.414(*l*)-1 are met.

Q 19:22 What filing is required of a plan that is terminating?

No special filing is required. The plan sponsor must indicate on the Form 5500 series filing that it is a final return. It is possible to get an IRS determination that a plan is qualified upon termination. This is done by filing IRS Form 5310. Requesting an IRS determination may involve some delay in the termination process, if payments are held up pending the IRS determination, and it does not prevent the IRS from auditing the plan or disqualifying it for years prior to the termination. It is a procedure that may be used when large account balances are rolled or transferred to an IRA or another qualified plan. An IRS determination in this circumstance provides additional assurance that the transfer or rollover will be considered a nontaxable event.

Q 19:23 What filing is required to notify the IRS of a change in plan status?

If a plan changes its name or if the name or address of the plan administrator changes, the IRS must be notified on the filing for the year the change occurred. [I.R.C. § 6057(b)] Failure to comply with this rule may result in a penalty of $1 per day of delinquency, up to a maximum of $1,000. [I.R.C. § 6652(d)(2)]

Notification of a change in the status of the plan or a change in the name or address of the plan administrator occurs when the plan sponsor or administrator completes Form 5500, 5500-SF, or 8955-SSA, and, at that time, identifies any changes to the plan on the form.

Q 19:24 What filing is required to report excise taxes?

Form 5330, Return of Excise Taxes Related to Employee Benefit Plans, is filed to report any prohibited transactions or excise taxes. Among the events reported on Form 5330 are prohibited transactions, nondeductible contributions, failure to file a 204(h) notice, excess contributions to 401(k) plans, and certain ESOP dispositions. The penalty tax is computed and should be remitted when the form is filed. The due date, generally, is the same date for filing the Form 5500 series.

However, in the case of 401(k) excess contributions, Form 5330 is due on the last day of the fifteenth month after the close of the plan year. A separate Form 5558 must be filed to request an extension of time for filing Form 5330, and an estimated excise tax payment must accompany it.

The IRS clarified that a Form 5558 filed for a Form 5330 extension requires a signature (see Q 19:13). (A signature is not required on the Form 5558 filed for a Form 5500 extension.)

Participant Disclosures

There are a number of requirements under the Code and ERISA for providing disclosures and notices to participants. This section covers some of the requirements applicable to 401(k) plans under ERISA. Table 19-2 lists key participant disclosure and notice requirements under both the Code and ERISA, with cross-references to the chapters in this book for more detailed information.

Table 19-2. Key Required Participant Disclosures/Notices

*Participant Disclosure/Notice**	*General Purpose*	*Chapters Addressed*
Summary Plan Description/ Summary of Material Modifications	Description of Plan Provisions	Chapter 19
Summary Annual Report	Information on Plan Financials	Chapter 19
Periodic Benefit Statements	Periodic statement of accounts	Chapter 19
Investment/Fee Disclosures	Information on investments and fees in a participant-directed plan	Chapter 19
Blackout Notice	Required if participant's ability to direct investments or obtain loans or distributions is suspended for more than three (3) consecutive business days.	Chapter 19
404(c) Notice/Disclosures	Required for protection under ERISA Section 404(c)	Chapter 7
Safe Harbor 401(k) Plan Notice	Notice of safe harbor 401(k) feature	Chapter 2
Auto-enrollment Notices (Pre-PPA, EACA, QACA)	Notices of auto-enrollment feature	Chapter 2

Table 19-2. Key Required Participant Disclosures/Notices (*cont'd*)

*Participant Disclosure/Notice**	*General Purpose*	*Chapters Addressed*
Qualified Default Investment Arrangement (QDIA) Notices	Required if ERISA Section 404(c) protection desired for default investment	Chapter 7
Eligible Investment Advice Arrangement (EIAA) Notice	Required notices under an EIAA	Chapter 5
Employer Stock Diversification Notice	Notice of right to diversify investment of plan assets in employer stock	Chapters 6, 19
Distribution-Related Notices/Forms (right-to-defer notice, rollover election/special tax/402(f) notice, notice of survivor annuity rights, 1099-R, etc.)	Various notices/forms in connection with a termination of employment/ plan distribution	Chapters 16, 17, 18
Notice to Interested Parties	Informs certain parties of pending IRS letter of determination	Chapter 3
Qualified Domestic Relations Order (QDRO) Notices	Notifications involving QDROs	Chapter 17
Claim for Benefits Notifications	Notifications Involving Participant Benefit Claims	Chapter 16
Special notifications involving electronic medium	Notifications to meet DOL and/or IRS requirements for electronic delivery of consents, notices, disclosures	Chapter 19
Notice of Reduction of Future Benefits or Contributions	Certain benefit reductions require notice (e.g., safe harbor match, money purchase contribution (204(h))	Chapters 2, 21

* Certain documents must be provided to participants upon written request—such as the plan and trust document and the latest Form 5500 filing (see Q 19:52).

See also Appendix J for a 401(k) Compliance Calendar.

Summary Plan Description

Q 19:25 What is a *summary plan description*?

A *summary plan description* (SPD) describes the provisions of the plan as well as the participants' rights under the plan. The SPD must be written in a style and format that are comprehensible to the average participant. The level of comprehension and education of the typical plan participant should be taken into account. Technical jargon should be avoided, as well as long, complex sentences. Including clarifying examples and illustrations, clear cross-references, and a table of contents should be considered. [DOL Reg. § 2520.102-2]

Q 19:26 What types of information must be included in the SPD?

The SPD must provide the following information:

1. The name of the plan and type of plan;
2. The name and address of the employer, the employer identification number (EIN), and the identification number of the plan;
3. The identification and address of the plan administrator and trustee(s), including identification of agents for service of legal process, and a statement that service of legal process may be made upon the plan administrator or trustee(s), and the telephone number of the plan administrator;
4. A description of the eligibility, vesting, and benefit accrual features;
5. A description of the break-in-service rules;
6. The plan's normal retirement age;
7. The plan's provisions describing any conditions that must be met before a participant is eligible to receive benefits;
8. If the plan provides joint and survivor benefits, any requirements necessary to reject these benefits;
9. Any circumstances under which benefits may be denied, lost, or forfeited;
10. The sources of contributions to the plan and the method by which the contribution is calculated;
11. The funding media used for the accumulation of assets;
12. The procedures to be used in making a claim for benefits;
13. The plan's fiscal year end;
14. For plans that intend to comply with ERISA Section 404(c), a statement that the plan is an ERISA Section 404(c) plan;
15. A description of the plan's procedures for dealing with qualified domestic relations orders (QDROs) or, alternatively, notice that these procedures can be obtained without charge from the plan administrator;

16. A statement identifying circumstances that may result in disqualification, ineligibility, denial, loss, forfeiture, or suspension of benefits, including plan amendments, and plan termination;
17. Information on any fees or charges that a participant or beneficiary must pay as a condition of receiving benefits under the plan;
18. Information on whether the plan is covered by insurance from the PBGC;
19. A statement of ERISA rights;
20. Information on whether the plan is maintained pursuant to a collective bargaining agreement; and
21. The type of plan administration.

[DOL Reg. § 2520.102-3]

Q 19:27 Are there any special requirements if participants do not speak English?

Yes. If a significant number of participants are literate only in the same non-English language, the plan administrator must attach a notice to the English-language SPD. This notice, written in the non-English language common to these participants, must offer assistance to participants in their own language. The notice must clearly set forth procedures to obtain assistance (i.e., include the name of a contact at the office of the plan administrator). This requirement is applicable in the following situations:

1. If the plan covers fewer than 100 participants and at least 25 percent of all plan participants are literate only in the same non-English language; or
2. If the plan covers 100 or more participants and the lesser of:
   a. 500 or more participants, or
   b. 10 percent or more of all plan participants are literate only in the same non-English language.

[DOL Reg. § 2520.102-2(c)]

Q 19:28 Who is entitled to receive an SPD?

All plan participants and beneficiaries entitled to receive benefits must receive an SPD. [ERISA § 102, 29 U.S.C. § 1022]

Q 19:29 What is the timing for receipt of the SPD?

The SPD must be distributed no later than 120 days after the plan becomes subject to the reporting and disclosure requirements of Title I of ERISA. If a new plan does not become effective until the IRS issues a favorable determination letter, then the SPD must be distributed within 120 days following receipt of the favorable determination letter. [DOL Reg. § 2520.104b-2(a)]

Future participants must receive an SPD within 90 days after becoming participants. In the case of beneficiaries entitled to death benefits, the SPD must be received within 90 days after commencement of benefits. [DOL Reg. § 2520. 104b-2(a)]

Q 19:30 Should the SPD be filed with the DOL?

No. TRA '97 eliminated the requirement to file the SPD with the DOL. The SPD must be made available to the DOL upon request.

Q 19:31 How should the SPD be distributed to participants?

The plan administrator must be reasonably sure that participants and beneficiaries actually receive the SPD. The SPD may be hand-delivered at the workplace or mailed using first-class mail. If second or third-class mail is used, return and forwarding postage should be guaranteed and address correction requested. Any returns should be sent back by first-class mail or personally delivered at the workplace.

Another option is to include the SPD as a special insert in a company periodical or publication, if the distribution list is current and comprehensive. A prominent notice should be placed on the front page of the periodical advising readers that the issue contains important information about rights under the plan. The notice should also advise the reader that the SPD should be read and retained for future reference.

It is not acceptable merely to place copies of the material in a location frequented by plan participants. [DOL Reg. § 2520.104b-1(b)(1)] (See Q 19:125 for information regarding SPD delivery via electronic media.)

Q 19:32 When should an SPD be updated?

If the plan has been amended, an updated SPD should be provided no later than five years after the date of the most recent SPD. There is a 210-day grace period to complete the updated SPD. [DOL Reg. § 2520.104b-2(b)(1)]

If the plan has not been amended, an updated SPD should be provided no later than ten years after the date of the most recent SPD. There is also a 210-day grace period for the completion of this updated SPD. [DOL Reg. § 2520.104b-2(b)(2)]

Summary of Material Modifications

Q 19:33 When must participants be notified of any changes in the plan through a summary of material modifications?

A summary of material modifications (SMM) must be provided to participants and beneficiaries within 210 days after the close of the plan year in which the sponsor adopts the amendment. [DOL Reg. § 2520.104b-3(a)] The definition of *material* cannot be found in ERISA or the regulations. However, the general view is that any amendment that changes the information found in the SPD is material and must be disclosed in the SMM.

An SMM does not need to be prepared if an updated SPD is prepared and distributed within 210 days after the close of the plan year in which a material modification occurred. [DOL Reg. § 2520.104b-3(b)]

See Q 19:31 regarding delivery requirements.

Q 19:34 What information must be provided in the SMM?

The SMM has no prescribed format. Like the SPD, the information must be in simple, understandable language comprehensible to the average participant. [DOL Reg. § 2520.104b-3(a)]

Q 19:35 What are the consequences of failing to provide participants with an SPD or SMM on a timely basis?

No specific penalty applies for failing to provide participants with an SPD or SMM on a timely basis. However, when participants are not provided with this information, a court may hold them not bound to the terms of the SPD or SMM. A plan administrator could face penalties of up to $110 per day for failing to furnish an SPD within 30 days of a participant's request. [ERISA § 502(c)]

Q 19:36 What are the benefits of including a disclaimer in the SPD?

The SPD is only an outline of the governing plan document and as such does not contain all the terms and conditions affecting the operation of the plan. Some SPDs contain a disclaimer stating that the plan document is the controlling authority as to the terms of the plan. A disclaimer may be useful in situations where there may be a conflict between the SPD or SMM and the plan document. However, use of the disclaimer may not provide complete protection to the plan where such a conflict exists. The best protection is to make sure that SPDs are accurate and that any changes that may affect participants' rights or benefit amounts are communicated in a timely fashion in an SMM or updated SPD.

Summary Annual Report

Q 19:37 What must be included in a *summary annual report*?

The basic information provided in the summary annual report (SAR) must include:

1. The plan's name and EIN;
2. The period covered by the annual report;
3. A basic financial statement of the plan; and
4. A notice advising the participant that a copy of the full annual report is available on request, that the individual may obtain additional information

regarding the annual report, and that the individual may inspect the annual report at a designated location of the employer or at the DOL.

[DOL Reg. § 2520.104b-10(d)(3)]

See Q 19:5 for requirements if an audit waiver is desired in the case of a small plan.

A SAR must be furnished annually to each participant.

Q 19:38 When must the SAR be provided to participants?

The SAR must be provided to all participants and to all beneficiaries receiving benefits by the later of nine months after the plan year or two months after the due date of the plan administrator's 5500 filing, including extensions.

See Q 19:31 regarding delivery requirements.

Q 19:39 What if the plan has non-English-speaking participants?

As in the case of the SPD requirements (see Q 19:27), notice that assistance is available must be provided in the non-English language. [DOL Reg. § 2520. 104b-10(e)]

Individual Participant Benefit Statements

Q 19:40 Must a participant receive benefit statements of his or her account balance in a 401(k) plan?

Yes. Effective for plan years beginning after 2006, the plan administrator of an individual account plan must provide benefit statements as follows:

1. At least once each calendar quarter to a participant or beneficiary who has the right to direct the investment of assets in his or her account under the plan;
2. At least once each calendar year to a participant or beneficiary who has his or her own account under the plan but does not have the right to direct the investment of assets in that account; and
3. Upon written request from a plan beneficiary not described in clause 1 or 2.

In the case of a plan maintained pursuant to one or more collectively bargained agreements ratified on or before the PPA's enactment, the effective date of the participant benefit statement rules was the earlier of

1. The later of December 31, 2007, or the date on which the last collectively bargained agreement terminates (without regard to any extension after the PPA's enactment) or
2. December 31, 2008.

A "one-participant retirement plan" is exempt from the participant statement requirements. A *one-participant retirement plan* is a retirement plan that meets the following conditions:

On the first day of the plan year, the plan (a) covered only the individual (and his or her spouse), and the individual (and his or her spouse) owned the entire business (whether or not incorporated) or (b) covered only one or more partners (and their spouses) in the plan sponsor.

[ERISA § 105(a)]

Q 19:41 What information must be contained in participant benefit statements?

A benefit statement must contain all of the following:

1. Based on the latest available information, the total benefit accrued and the vested benefits, if any, that have accrued or the earliest date on which benefits will become vested (see Q 19:42);
2. An explanation of any permitted disparity provisions (see chapter 12) or any floor-offset arrangement (whereby defined contribution plan account balances are used to offset benefits under a defined benefit plan) that may be applied in determining accrued benefits;
3. The value of each investment to which assets in the individual account have been allocated, determined as of the most recent valuation date under the plan (including the value of any assets held in the form of employer securities, without regard to whether such securities were contributed by the plan sponsor or acquired at the direction of the plan, the participant, or the beneficiary); and
4. If the plan allows participants and beneficiaries to direct plan investments (a) an explanation of any limitations or restrictions on any right of the participant or beneficiary under the plan to direct an investment, (b) an explanation, written in a manner calculated to be understood by the average plan participant, of the importance, for the long-term retirement security of participants and beneficiaries, of a well-balanced and diversified investment portfolio, including a statement of the risk that holding more than 20 percent of a portfolio in the security of one entity (such as employer securities) may not be adequately diversified; and (c) a notice directing the participant or beneficiary to the Internet Web site of the DOL for sources of information on individual investing and diversification.

Statements must be written in a manner calculated to be understood by the average plan participant, and may be delivered in written, electronic, or other appropriate form that is reasonably accessible to the participant and beneficiary. [ERISA § 105(a)].

The DOL has indicated that it is considering adding a requirement that participants' statements carry retirement income projections (e.g., a snapshot of what a participant current balance would give that person through retirement or a projection of what a participant's balance would be when he or she retires).

In May 2013, the DOL published an advanced notice of proposed rulemaking (ANPRM) requesting comments on whether, and how, a participant benefit statement could present a participant's accrued benefit as an estimated lifetime stream of payments in addition to being presented as an account balance. Doing so, according to the DOL, would help participants in defined contribution plans better prepare for retirement.

As part of its request for comments on the ANPRM, the DOL set forth the following proposed language and concepts:

- A participant's benefit statement would show his or her current account balance and an estimated lifetime income stream of payments based on such balance. The lifetime income illustration would assume the participant had reached normal retirement age as of the date of the benefit statement, even if he or she is much younger.
- For a participant who has not yet reached normal retirement age, his or her benefit statement also would show a projected account balance and the estimated lifetime income stream based on such balance. A participant's current account balance would be projected to normal retirement age based on assumed future contributions and investment returns. The projected account balance would be converted to an estimated lifetime income stream of payments, assuming that the person retires at normal retirement age. This account balance and the related lifetime income payment would be expressed in current dollars.
- Both lifetime income streams (i.e., the one based on the current account balance and the one based on the projected account balance) would be presented as estimated monthly payments based on the expected mortality of the participant. In addition, if the participant has a spouse, the lifetime income streams would be based on the joint lives of the participant and spouse.
- Participant benefit statements would contain an understandable explanation of the assumptions behind the lifetime income stream illustrations, as well as a statement that projections and lifetime income stream illustrations are estimates and not guarantees.

The lifetime income illustrations contemplated by the ANPRM depend on the use of certain assumptions. For example, contribution and investment return assumptions are needed to project an account balance to a person's retirement age, and mortality and interest rate assumptions are needed to convert an account balance (whether current or projected) into a lifetime income stream. The ANPRM requires that plan administrators use only reasonable assumptions taking into account certain professional standards when developing lifetime income illustrations. The ANPRM, however, provides two safe harbors under which certain assumptions are deemed reasonable. As part of the release of the ANPRM, the DOL made available an interactive calculator that computes lifetime income streams in accordance with the proposed regulatory framework on its Web site at *www.dol.gov/ebsa/regs/lifetimeincomecalculator.html.*

Additional information on the ANPRM is available on the DOL's Web site (*www.dol.gov/ebsa*) under Lifetime Income Illustrations in the "New and Noteworthy" section.

Q 19:42 How much flexibility is available with respect to providing information on vested benefits?

The requirement to provide information on vested benefits is satisfied if the plan:

1. Updates vested benefit information contained in statements at least annually, or
2. Provides a separate statement, at least annually, containing information that would enable a participant or beneficiary to determine his or her vested benefits.

[ERISA § 105(a)(2)(C)]

Q 19:43 According to the DOL, to what extent can the benefit statement requirements be satisfied in participant-directed plans by using multiple documents or sources for the required information?

On December 20, 2006, pending its release of final regulations, the DOL released guidance on complying with the benefit statement requirements. The guidance was in the form of a Field Assistance Bulletin (FAB) that outlines what would be considered "good faith" compliance in the interim. [DOL Field Assist. Bull. 2006-03]

In FAB 2006-03, the DOL recognized that information required in benefit statements will, in many instances, involve multiple service providers, each of whom is a source for some, but not all, of the required information. For example, the plan administrator may be the source for information on vesting, whereas the plan's recordkeeper or brokerage firm may be the source for investment-related account information. Compiling all the required information for disclosure in a single document, according to the DOL, may be impractical for plans.

Under the DOL's good-faith compliance standard, multiple documents or sources for benefit statement information may be used, provided that participants and beneficiaries have received notification explaining how and when the required information will be provided to participants and beneficiaries. Such notification should be written in a manner calculated to be understood by the average plan participant and provided in advance of the date on which a plan is required to provide the first pension benefit statement under the rules.

Q 19:44 To what extent can the pension benefit statement requirements be satisfied using electronic media?

In Field Assistance Bulletin (FAB) 2006-03, the DOL indicated that a plan administrator could satisfy its obligation using established standards under ERISA or the Internal Revenue Code regarding acceptable use of electronic media (see Qs 19:125, 19:127).

With regard to pension plans that provide participants continuous access to benefit statement information through one or more secure Web sites, the availability of benefit statement information through such media will constitute good faith compliance with the requirement to provide benefit statement information, provided that participants and beneficiaries have been provided notification that explains the availability of the required pension benefit statement information and how such information can be accessed by the participants and beneficiaries. In addition, the notification must apprise participants and beneficiaries of their right to request and obtain, free of charge, a paper version of the benefit statement information.

Such notification should be written in a manner calculated to be understood by the average plan participant and provided in advance of the date on which a plan is required to provide the first pension benefit statement as well as annually thereafter. [DOL Field Assist. Bull. 2006-03]

Q 19:45 When must statements be given to participants?

With regard to plans that permit participants and beneficiaries to direct the investment of assets in their account, benefit statements must be provided at least once each calendar quarter. Plans that do not give participants and beneficiaries the right to direct their investments are required to provide benefit statements at least once each calendar year.

Pending the issuance of further guidance, the DOL's good-faith compliance standard requires plan administrators to provide benefit statement information (if plan permits participants to direct investments) not later than 45 days following the end of the period (calendar quarter or calendar year). [DOL Field Assist. Bull. 2006-03] For plans that do not allow for participant direction of investments, the DOL's good-faith compliance standard requires plan administrators to provide benefit statement information on or before the date on which the Form 5500 is filed by the plan (but in no event later than the date, including extensions, on which the Form 5500 is required to be filed by the plan) for the plan year to which the statement relates. [DOL Field Assist. Bull. 2007-03]

Q 19:46 Will a plan that does not otherwise provide participants the right to direct the investment of assets in their accounts be required to provide statements quarterly due to a participant loan provision?

Under Field Assistance Bulletin (FAB) 2006-03, the DOL indicates a participant loan feature does not, on its own, cause a plan to be considered to have participant-directed investments and trigger quarterly statement requirements. [DOL Field Assist. Bull. 2006-03]

Q 19:47 What types of limitations and restrictions on participant rights to direct investments, if any, need not be included in benefit statements?

Under Field Assistance Bulletin (FAB) 2006-03, benefits statements must include limitations and restrictions on participants' or beneficiaries' rights imposed "under the plan," but need not include limitations and restrictions imposed by investment funds, other investment vehicles, or by state or federal securities laws.

Q 19:48 Is there DOL-approved language for satisfying the requirement to provide information on the importance of diversification and what Web site should participants be referred to for information on investing and diversification?

In the absence of a model benefit statement, the DOL provided the following language in FAB 2006-03 to comply with the requirement to provide information on the importance of diversification:

> To help achieve long-term retirement security, you should give careful consideration to the benefits of a well-balanced and diversified investment portfolio. Spreading your assets among different types of investments can help you achieve a favorable rate of return, while minimizing your overall risk of losing money. This is because market or other economic conditions that cause one category of assets, or one particular security, to perform very well often cause another asset category, or another particular security, to perform poorly. If you invest more than 20% of your retirement savings in any one company or industry, your savings may not be properly diversified. Although diversification is not a guarantee against loss, it is an effective strategy to help you manage investment risk.
>
> In deciding how to invest your retirement savings, you should take into account all of your assets, including any retirement savings outside of the Plan. No single approach is right for everyone because, among other factors, individuals have different financial goals, different time horizons for meeting their goals, and different tolerances for risk.
>
> It is also important to periodically review your investment portfolio, your investment objectives, and the investment options under the Plan to help ensure that your retirement savings will meet your retirement goals.

Pursuant to the FAB, plan administrators may reference the following document on the DOL Web site for information on investing and diversification: *www.dol.gov/ebsa/investing.html.*

With regard to plans invested in employer securities, the DOL indicated in the FAB that a plan administrator's compliance with the periodic benefit statement requirements would satisfy special diversification notice requirements applicable to plans invested in employer securities if, prior to January 1, 2007, the plan provided participants and beneficiaries diversification rights at least equal to those required under the PPA. (See chapter 6 for detailed information on the diversification requirements).

[DOL Field Assist. Bull. 2006-03]

Q 19:49 Who is responsible for complying with the benefit statement requirements, and what is the penalty for noncompliance?

The plan administrator is responsible for complying with the benefit statement requirements and, if he or she fails to comply, could face noncompliance penalties up to $110 per day per participant per failure to comply.

Q 19:50 What are some of the challenges and open questions related to complying with the new benefit statement requirements?

At the time this book went to press, the DOL had not yet released final regulations for participant benefit statement requirements. Some of the challenges and questions involved in complying with the rules include:

- How will timing and informational requirements be met if several providers service the plan?
- What is meant by "latest available information" with respect to vested and accrued benefits? (For example, can a plan use information that is available in its recordkeeping system at the time statements are prepared if more current information cannot be obtained?)
- If a plan provides for both employer-directed and participant-directed investment portions, are quarterly statements required for both portions? Can quarterly statements be provided on the participant-directed portion and annual statements on the employer-directed portion?
- Does the 45-day deadline run only from calendar quarters (March 31, June 30, September 30, and December 31) for participant-directed plans or from a calendar year-end (December 31) for employer-directed plans? In other words, if a participant-directed plan's quarter falls on February 28, does the 45-day deadline for that period end in May (45 days from March 31) or April (45 days from February 28)?
- The requirement to provide information on the value of each investment to which assets are allocated presents challenges in the following circumstances:
  - In employer-directed plans with pooled investments, is each participant given a listing of all the assets in the pool?

— If a participant-directed plan offers model or target pooled-investment options, to what extent must underlying assets in the pool be reflected on statements?

Q 19:51 Must a terminated participant receive a statement of his or her account balance in the 401(k) plan?

Under proposed DOL regulations that were not finalized, a plan administrator is to furnish a benefit statement to a terminated participant within 180 days after the close of the plan year in which the participant terminates employment. [Prop. DOL Reg. § 2520.105-2(b)] With the new PPA requirements (see Q 19:40), benefit statements must be provided to participants automatically on a periodic basis (i.e., not just upon certain events such as termination or upon request). The DOL is expected to issue new regulations for participant benefit statements that will replace the previously proposed regulations and will take into account the new PPA requirements.

Information Upon Request

Q 19:52 What other documents may a participant request?

The participant may request a copy of the latest annual report, terminal report, collective bargaining agreements, trust agreements, or any other document under which the plan is established or operated. [ERISA § 104(b)(4)]

Q 19:53 May the plan administrator charge for providing the participant with requested reports or documents?

The plan administrator may not charge participants or beneficiaries for providing the SPD, updated SPD, SAR, SMM, or individual benefit statements. However, the plan administrator may impose a reasonable charge (for actual costs incurred for the least expensive means of acceptable reproduction) of up to 25 cents per page for furnishing additional copies of the SPD, updated SPD, or SMM, or for requested copies of the latest annual report, terminal report, collective bargaining agreements, trust agreements, or any other document under which the plan is established or operated. [DOL Reg. § 2520.104b-30]

Q 19:54 What is the time limit for responding to a participant's request for information?

A plan administrator must supply information required to be disclosed under ERISA within 30 days of when a request for the information is received. [ERISA § 502(c)(1), 29 U.S.C. § 1132(c)(1)]

Q 19:55 What are the consequences of failing to provide requested information in a timely manner?

The plan administrator may be required to pay the requesting participant an amount up to $110 per day from the date of the request. This penalty will not be imposed if the reason for delay is reasonably beyond the control of the plan administrator. [ERISA § 502(c), 29 U.S.C. § 1132(c)]

Participant Investment and Fee Disclosures

In October 2010, the DOL issued final regulations that require fiduciaries of participant-directed individual account plans to provide specific disclosures to participants (and beneficiaries) concerning plan investment options and fees. This is the third regulatory initiative involving fee disclosures. The other initiatives involve enhanced fee disclosures in the Form 5500 context (see Q 19:9) and contractual arrangements with plan service providers under ERISA Section 408(b)(2) (see chapter 4). [75 Fed. Reg. 64,910 (Oct. 20, 2010)]

Q 19:56 What must be disclosed to participants under the DOL's participant investment and fee disclosure requirements?

Under the final regulations, the fiduciary of a 401(k) plan (and other plans subject to ERISA) must disclose certain investment- and fee-related information to each participant who has the right to direct investments in his or her individual account, regardless of whether the plan elected to comply with ERISA Section 404(c) (see chapter 7). Under ERISA Section 404(a), a fiduciary must meet certain requirements to act prudently and solely in the interest of participants and beneficiaries (see chapter 5). The regulations would attach to those general duties a requirement to provide certain information to participants in a participant-directed plan.

A plan administrator must take steps to ensure participants on a regular and periodic basis are made aware of their rights and responsibilities with respect to the investment of assets in their accounts and are provided sufficient information regarding the plan and designated investment alternatives (including fees and expenses) to make informed decisions regarding the management of their accounts. [DOL Reg. Sec. 2550.404a-5(a)]

The disclosure requirements under the DOL regulations fall into two categories:

1. Plan-related information (see Q 19:60), which includes:
    - Initial and annual disclosures of general plan information, plan administrative expenses, and individual expenses; and
    - Quarterly disclosures of actual plan administrative and individual expenses; and
2. Initial and annual investment-related information (see Q 19:61).

See Appendix C for a Sample ERISA Section 404(a) Participant Disclosure Checklist.

In 2012, the IRS launched a Web site that offers participants information about the disclosures, particularly the fee and expense component: *www.dol.gov/ebsa/publications/understandingretirementfees.html.*

Q 19:57 What plans are subject to the participant investment and fee disclosure requirements?

The disclosure requirements apply to any participant-directed defined contribution plan (including 401(k) plans) that are subject to ERISA, except individual retirement accounts or individual retirement annuities described in Section 408(k) ("simplified employee pensions") or 408(p) ("simple retirement accounts") of the Code. [DOL Reg. § 2550-404a-5(b)(2)]

Q 19:58 When must a plan comply with the participant investment and fee disclosure requirements?

The new requirements apply to plan years beginning on or after November 1, 2011. For calendar-year plans, compliance was required as of January 1, 2012. The DOL provided a transitional rule with respect to initial disclosures required on or before the date on which a participant can first direct investments. Those disclosures must have been provided no later than 60 days after the plan's applicability date or 60 days after the effective date of the service provider fee disclosure regulations under ERISA Section 408(b)(2) (that effective date was July 1, 2012).

The DOL also provided a transitional rule for when the first quarterly disclosures must have been provided under the rules. The first quarterly disclosures must be provided no later than 45 days after the end of the quarter in which the initial disclosures are required to be provided under the transitional rule described above.

According to the DOL in the preamble, the transitional rules ensure that the disclosures under Section 408(b)(2) became effective first, as well as preserve the sequencing of disclosures by preventing the first quarterly disclosure from being due before the first initial disclosure.

Following is an illustration of the application of the transitional rules to a calendar-year plan:

The plan must have provided the first set of initial disclosures (all disclosures other than those required at least quarterly) no later than August 30, 2012, which is 60 days after the July 1, 2012 effective date of the Section 408(b)(2) regulation. The quarterly disclosures (e.g., the quarterly statement of fees/expenses actually deducted) must have been provided no later than November 14, 2012, which is the 45th day after the end of the third quarter (July–September) in which the initial disclosure was required.

For plan years beginning before October 1, 2021, if a plan administrator reasonably and in good faith determines that it does not have the information on expenses necessary to calculate average annual total return the 5-year and 10-year periods (see Q 19:61) for an alternative that is not registered under the Investment Company Act of 1940, the plan administrator may use a reasonable estimate of such expenses or the most recently reported total annual operating expenses of the alternative as a substitute for such expenses. A plan administrator that uses either a reasonable estimate or the most recently reported total annual operating expenses as a substitute is required to inform participants of the basis on which the returns were determined. There is no requirement to disclose returns for periods before the inception of a designated investment alternative. [DOL Reg. § 2550.404a-5(j)]

In July 2012, the DOL released Field Assistance Bulletin (FAB) 2012-02R with more detailed guidance relating to the disclosure requirements (see Qs 19:74–19:108).

Q 19:59 Who is responsible for complying with the participant investment and fee disclosure requirements?

The plan administrator is responsible for complying with the disclosure requirements with respect to each participant (or beneficiary) that, pursuant to the terms of the plan, has a right to direct the investment of assets in his or her account. In the preamble to the regulation, the DOL indicated that disclosures must be made to all employees eligible to participate under the terms of the plan, without regard to whether the participant has actually enrolled in the plan.

Compliance with the disclosure requirements will satisfy the duty to make the regular and periodic disclosures described in Q 19:56, provided the information contained in such disclosures is complete and accurate. A plan administrator will not be held liable for the completeness and accuracy of information used to satisfy the requirements when the plan administrator reasonably and in good faith relies on information received from or provided by a plan service provider or the issuer of a designated investment alternative. [DOL Reg. § 2550.404a-5(b)(1)]

According to the DOL, compliance with the disclosure requirements does not relieve a fiduciary from its duty to prudently select and monitor plan service providers or designated investment alternatives offered under the plan. [DOL Reg. § 2550.404a-5(f)]

Q 19:60 What *plan-related information* must be provided to participants?

Under the DOL regulations, the following plan-related information must be provided to participants based on the latest information available to the plan:

1. *General Information*

   On or before the date on which a participant (or beneficiary) can first direct his or her investments and at least annually thereafter:

   - An explanation of the circumstances under which participants may give investment instructions;
   - An explanation of any specified limitations on such instructions under the terms of the plan, including any restrictions on transfer to or from a designated investment alternative (see Q 19:66);
   - A description of or reference to plan provisions relating to the exercise of voting, tender, and similar rights pertaining to an investment in a designated investment alternative, as well as any restrictions on such rights;
   - An identification of any designated investment alternatives offered under the plan;
   - An identification of any designated investment managers; and
   - A description of any "brokerage windows," "self-directed brokerage accounts," or similar plan arrangements that enable participants to select investments beyond those designated by the plan.

     If there is a change to the information described above, each participant (and beneficiary) must be provided a description of such change at least 30 days, but not more than 90 days, in advance of the effective date of such change, unless the inability to provide such advance notice is due to events that were unforeseeable or circumstances beyond the control of the plan administrator, in which case notice of such change must be provided as soon as reasonably practicable.

2. *Administrative Expenses*

   On or before the date on which a participant (or beneficiary) can first direct his or her investments and at least annually thereafter:

   - An explanation of any fees and expenses for general plan administrative services (e.g., legal, accounting, recordkeeping) that, to the extent not otherwise reflected in the total annual operating expenses of any designated investment alternative, may be charged against the individual participant accounts and the basis on which such charges will be allocated (e.g., pro rata, per capita) to, or affect the balance of, each individual account.

     If there is a change to the information described above, each participant (and beneficiary) must be provided a description of such change at least 30 days, but not more than 90 days, in advance of the effective date of such change, unless the inability to provide such advance notice is due to events that were unforeseeable or circumstances beyond the control of the plan administrator, in which case notice of such change must be provided as soon as reasonably practicable.

     At least quarterly, a statement that includes:

   - The dollar amount of fees and expenses actually charged during the preceding quarter to the participant's account for administrative services;

- A description of the services provided to the participant for such amount (e.g., recordkeeping); and
- If applicable, an explanation that, in addition to the fees and expenses disclosed above, some of the plan administration expenses for the preceding quarter were paid from the total annual operating expenses of one or more of the plan's designated investment alternatives (e.g., through revenue-sharing arrangements, Rule 12b-1 fees, sub-transfer agent fees).

3. *Individual Expenses*

   On or before the date on which a participant (or beneficiary) can first direct his or her investments and at least annually thereafter:

   - An explanation of any fees that may be charged against the participant's account for services provided on an individual basis rather than a plan-wide basis (e.g., fees to process plan loans or QDROs or for investment advice, fees for brokerage windows, commissions, front- or back-end loads or sales charges, redemption fees, transfer fees and similar expenses, and optional rider charges in annuity contracts) and which are not reflected in the total annual operating expenses of any designated investment alternative.

     If there is a change to the information described above, each participant (and beneficiary) must be provided a description of such change at least 30 days, but not more than 90 days, in advance of the effective date of such change, unless the inability to provide such advance notice is due to events that were unforeseeable or circumstances beyond the control of the plan administrator, in which case notice of such change must be provided as soon as reasonably practicable. At least quarterly, a statement that includes:

     - The dollar amount of fees and expenses actually charged during the preceding quarter to the participant's account for individual services; and
     - A description of the services provided to the participant (e.g., fees to process plan loans).

The requirement to provide information on or before the date on which a participant (or beneficiary) can first direct his or her investments may be satisfied by providing the most recent annual disclosure plus any updates to the information provided to participants for informational changes (as described above). [DOL Reg. § 2550.404a-5(c)]

Q 19:61 What *investment-related information* must be provided automatically to participants?

Under the DOL regulations, on or before the date on which a participant (or beneficiary) can first direct his or her investments and at least annually thereafter, the following investment-related information (based on the latest information available to the plan) must be provided automatically to participants with respect to designated investment alternatives (see Q 19:66) offered under the plan:

1. *Identifying information*
   - The name of the designated investment alternative; and
   - The type or category of the investment (e.g., money market fund, balanced fund, large cap fund stock fund, employer stock fund, employer securities).
2. *Performance Data*
   - For designated investments for which the return is not fixed, the average annual total return of the investment for 1, 5, and 10 calendar-year periods (or for the life of the alternative, if shorter) ending on the date of the most recently completed calendar year; as well as a statement indicating that an investment's past performance is not necessarily an indication of future performance.
   - For designated investments for which the return is fixed, both the fixed or stated annual rate of return and the term of the investment. If, with respect to such a designated investment alternative, the issuer reserves the right to adjust the fixed or stated rate of return prospectively during the term of the contract or agreement, the current rate of return, the minimum rate guaranteed under the contract, if any, and a statement advising participants that the issuer may adjust the rate of return prospectively and how to obtain (e.g., telephone or Web site) the most recent rate of return required under the rules.
3. *Benchmarks*
   - For designated investments for which the return is not fixed, the name and returns of an appropriate broad-based securities market index over the 1, 5, and 10 calendar-year periods (or for the life of the alternative, if shorter) comparable to the performance data periods provided under the preceding "Performance Data" section, and which is not administered by an affiliate of the investment issuer, its investment adviser, or principal underwriter, unless the index is widely recognized and used.
4. *Fee and Expense Information*
   - For designated investment alternatives for which the return is not fixed:
     - — The amount and description of each shareholder-type fee (fees charged directly against a participant's investment, such as commissions, sales loads, sales charges, deferred sales charges, redemption fees, surrender charges, exchange fees, account fees, and purchase fees, which are not included in the total annual operating expenses of any designated investment alternative) and a description of any restriction or limitation that may be applicable to a purchase, transfer, or withdrawal of the investment in whole or in part (such as round trip, equity wash, or other restrictions);
     - — The total annual operating expenses of the investment expressed as a percentage (expense ratio);
     - — The total annual operating expenses of the investment for a one-year period expressed as a dollar amount for a $1,000 investment

  (assuming no returns and based on the total annual operating expenses percentage);
  - A statement indicating that fees and expenses are only one of several factors that participants should consider when making investment decisions; and
  - A statement that the cumulative effect of fees and expenses can substantially reduce the growth of a participant's retirement account and that participants can visit the Employee Benefit Security Administration's Web site for an example demonstrating the long-term effect of fees and expenses.
- For designated investments for which the return is fixed, the amount and a description of any shareholder-type fees and a description of any restriction or limitation that may be applicable to a purchase, transfer, or withdrawal of the investment in whole or in part.

5. *Internet Web Site Address*
   - An Internet Web site address that is sufficiently specific to provide participants access to the following information regarding the designated investment alternative:
     - The name of the alternative's issuer;
     - The alternative's objectives or goals in a manner consistent with SEC Form N-1A or N-3, as appropriate;
     - The alternative's principal strategies (including a general description of the types of assets held by the investment) and principal risks in a manner consistent with SEC Form N-1A or N-3, as appropriate;
     - The alternative's portfolio turnover rate in a manner consistent with SEC Form N-1A or N-3, as appropriate;
     - The alternative's performance data described in item 2 above on at least a quarterly basis, or more frequently if required by other applicable law; and
     - The alternative's fee and expense information described in item 4 above.

6. *Glossary*
   - A general glossary of terms to assist participant in understanding the designated investment alternatives, or an Internet Web site address that is sufficiently specific to provide access to such a glossary along with a general explanation of the purpose of the address. (The DOL was considering, but did not provide, a sample or model glossary of terms in the regulation.)

7. *Annuity Options*
   - If a designated investment alternative *is part of* a contract, fund, or product that permits participants to allocate contributions toward the future purchase of a stream of retirement income payments guaranteed by an insurance company (e.g., annuity feature in a variable annuity

contract), the additional information described in Q 19:70 with respect to the annuity option, to the extent not otherwise included in investment-related fees and expenses described in item 4 above.

The requirement to provide the investment-related information set forth above to participants on or before the date on which a participant (or beneficiary) can first direct his or her investments may be satisfied by providing the most recent annual disclosure provided to participants.

[DOL Reg. § 2550.404a-5(d)]

In the preamble to the regulation, the DOL indicated that the fixed-return provisions of the regulation are limited to alternatives that provide a fixed or stated return to the participant for a standard duration, and with respect to which investment risks are borne by an entity other than the participant (e.g., an insurance company). Examples provided include certificates of deposit, guaranteed insurance contracts, variable annuity fixed accounts, and similar interest-bearing contracts from banks or insurance companies. Even though they routinely hold fixed-return investments and generally aim to preserve principal, money market and stable value funds, according to the DOL, are subject to the variable-return provisions of the regulation because they are not free of investment risk to the investor.

Q 19:62 In what format must *investment-related information* be provided to participants?

The investment-related information set forth above (see Q 19:61) must be provided in a chart or similar format that is designed to facilitate comparison of designated investment options under the plan and prominently displays the date, as well as:

- A statement indicating the name, address, and telephone number of the plan administrator (or designee) to contact for information available upon request (see Q 19:64); and
- A statement that additional investment-related information (including more current performance information) is available at the listed Internet Web site (see Q 19:61); and
- A statement explaining how to request and obtain, free of charge, paper copies of the information required to be made available on a Web site (described in Q 19:61, and Qs 19:70 and 19:71, as applicable).

A plan administrator may include additional information that it determines is appropriate for such comparisons, provided such information is not inaccurate or misleading.

[DOL Reg. § 2550.404a-5(d)(2)]

The DOL provided a Model Comparative Chart in the regulations. (See Appendix K.)

A plan administrator that uses and accurately completes the model chart will be deemed to have satisfied the investment-related disclosure requirements. [DOL Reg. § 2550.404a-5(e)(3)]

Q 19:63 What *investment-related information* must be provided to participants subsequent to an investment in a designated investment alternative?

In addition to meeting the other disclosure requirements, participants must be provided, subsequent to an investment in a designated investment alternative, any materials provided to the plan relating to voting, tender, and similar rights pertaining to the investment, to the extent that such rights are passed through to participants under the terms of the plan. [DOL Reg. § 2550.404a-5(d)(3)]

Q 19:64 What *investment-related information* must be provided to participants upon request?

Investment-related information relating to designated investment alternatives must be provided to participants upon request. Such information includes:

1. Copies of prospectuses (or any short form or summary prospectus, the form of which has been approved by the SEC) for the disclosure of information on investments registered under either the Securities Act of 1933 or the Investment Company Act of 1940, or similar documents for investments not registered under either Act;
2. Copies of financial statements or reports, such as statements of additional information and shareholder reports, and of any other similar materials relating to the plan's designated investment alternatives, to the extent that such materials are provided to the plan;
3. A statement of the value of a share or unit of each designated investment alternative as well as the date of the valuation; and
4. A list of assets comprising the portfolio of each designated investment alternative and the value of each such asset (or the proportion of the investment that it comprises).

Q 19:65 What other information did the DOL set forth in the regulations and other guidance regarding the form and delivery of disclosures?

Under the DOL regulations, *plan-related information* (see Q 19:60) that must be provided to participants on or before the date on which a participant can first direct his or her investments and at least annually thereafter may be provided as part of the plan's summary plan description (SPD) or participant benefit statement (if such document is provided with the frequency that meets the requirements). Since SPDs typically are not provided annually to participants, it is expected that most plan administrators will use participant benefit statements or another vehicle to deliver this information. Plan-related information that must be provided at least quarterly (i.e., certain plan administrative and individual expense information) may be included as part of a participant benefit statement.

Disclosures under the regulations must be written to be understood by average plan participant and, pending further guidance, provided in a manner consistent with ERISA disclosure requirements, including those relating to electronic disclosures (see Qs 19:124, 19:125).

In December 2011, the DOL issued Technical Release 2011-03R, which sets forth temporary guidance for the use of electronic media to satisfy the participant disclosure requirements under ERISA Section 404(a). The release was intended to establish a temporary DOL enforcement policy regarding the circumstances under which the disclosures can be provided to participants electronically and otherwise.

According to the DOL, plan-related disclosures (see Q 19:60) that are included in a participant benefit statement may be provided in the same manner that the other information included in the same participant benefit statement is provided. For example, if the statement is provided through a secure continuous access Web site in accordance with FAB 2006-03 (see Q 19:44), then the disclosures included as part of the statement also may be provided electronically in the same manner. Disclosures not provided as part of a participant benefit statement as permitted under the regulations may not be provided electronically under the guidance of FAB 2006-03.

Investment-related disclosures can be provided as part of, or along with, participant benefit statements, either in paper form (see Q 19:124 for information on general delivery requirements) or electronically in accordance with the following options.

The options for providing participant investment and fee disclosures electronically under Technical Release 2011-03R:

- By using the safe harbor method described in Q 19:125 or
- By using electronic media (including a continuous access Web site) if all the conditions of paragraphs 1 through 6 below are satisfied (except as provided under the Special Transition Provision in paragraph 7 below):
  1. *Provide E-mail Address Voluntarily.* Participants and beneficiaries must voluntarily provide the employer, plan sponsor, or plan administrator (or its designee) with an e-mail address for the purpose of receiving the disclosures. The e-mail address must be provided in response to a request accompanied by an Initial Notice, as described in paragraph 2 below. If giving an e-mail address is a condition of employment or participation in the plan, such e-mail address will not be treated as being provided voluntarily. If, however, a participant is required to provide an e-mail address electronically in order to access a secure continuous access Web site housing the required disclosure, the provision of such e-mail address is considered voluntary where an Initial

Notice is provided in accordance with paragraph 2 below. The mere establishment or assignment of an e-mail address by an employer for a participant will not be treated as being voluntarily provided.

2. *Initial Notice.* The Initial Notice must be clear and conspicuous, provided contemporaneously and in the same medium as the request for the e-mail address, and contain the following information:
   a. A statement that providing an e-mail address for the receipt of the required disclosures is entirely voluntary, and that as the result of providing the e-mail address, the required disclosures will be made electronically;
   b. Identification or a brief description of the information that will be furnished electronically and how it can be accessed by participants and beneficiaries;
   c. A statement that the participant or beneficiary has the right to request and obtain, free of charge, a paper copy of any of the information provided electronically and an explanation of how to exercise that right;
   d. A statement that the participant or beneficiary has the right, at any time, to opt out of receiving the information electronically and an explanation of how to exercise that right; and
   e. An explanation of the procedure for updating the participant's or beneficiary's e-mail address.
3. *Annual Notice.* Commencing with the year beginning after the year in which the participant or beneficiary voluntarily provided his or her e-mail address in accordance with paragraph 1 above, and annually thereafter, the plan administrator must provide an Annual Notice to each such participant or beneficiary. For purposes of this paragraph 3, "year" means a calendar year, plan year, or any other 12-month period selected by the plan administrator.

   The Annual Notice must contain the information in b. through e. of paragraph 2 above. The Annual Notice must be furnished on paper (see Q 19:124 for information on general delivery requirements). Alternatively, the plan may furnish the Annual Notice electronically by sending it to the e-mail address on file for the participant or beneficiary if there is evidence that such participant or beneficiary interacted electronically with the plan after the date the Annual Notice for the preceding year was furnished (or in the case of the first Annual Notice, after the date the Initial Notice was furnished). Examples of electronic interaction include, but are not limited to, the participant or beneficiary updating, resubmitting, or confirming his or her e-mail address to the plan; the participant or beneficiary sending an electronic message to the plan; logging onto a secure continuous access Web site housing plan information; or the receipt and opening of an electronic message sent by the plan to the participant or beneficiary. Electronic interaction described in this paragraph 3 is not a substitute for the condition of paragraph 1 above relating to voluntarily providing an e-mail address.

4. *Delivery.* The plan administrator takes appropriate and necessary measures reasonably calculated to ensure that the electronic delivery system results in actual receipt of transmitted information (e.g., using return receipt or notice of undelivered electronic mail features, conducting periodic reviews or surveys to confirm receipt of transmitted information, etc.).
5. *Confidentiality.* The plan administrator takes appropriate and necessary measures reasonably calculated to ensure that the electronic delivery system protects the confidentiality of personal information.
6. *Calculated to be Understood.* Notices furnished to participants and beneficiaries shall be written in a manner calculated to be understood by the average plan participant.
7. *Special Transition Provision.* With respect to e-mail addresses of participants and beneficiaries that are on file with the employer, plan sponsor, or plan administrator (or its designee) on the date specified in b. below (the "Transition Group"), the conditions in paragraphs 1 and 2 above shall be deemed to be satisfied if a Transition Group Initial Notice, described below, is furnished to the Transition Group as follows:
    a. The Transition Group Initial Notice must contain the information set out in subparagraphs b. through e. of paragraph 2 above;
    b. The Transition Group Initial Notice must be furnished no earlier than 90 nor later than 30 days prior to the date the initial disclosures are required to be provided under the regulations to the Transition Group;
    c. The Transition Group Initial Notice must be furnished on paper (see Q 19:124 for information on general delivery requirements). Alternatively, the plan may furnish the Transition Group Initial Notice electronically by sending it to an e-mail address on file for a participant or beneficiary if there is evidence of electronic interaction with the plan, within the meaning of paragraph 3 above during the 12-month period preceding the date the Transition Group Initial Notice is furnished in accordance with b. of this paragraph 7.

This Special Transition Provision is not available for an e-mail address established or assigned by the employer, plan sponsor, or its or their designee unless there is evidence that such e-mail address was used by the participant or beneficiary for plan purposes during the 12-month period preceding the date the Transition Group Initial Notice is furnished in accordance with b. of this paragraph 7. For this purpose, examples of using e-mail address for plan purposes include, but are not limited to, the participant or beneficiary sending an electronic message to the plan from such e-mail address; receiving and opening an electronic message sent by the plan to such e-mail address; or logging onto a secure continuous access Web site housing plan information, using such e-mail address as the username.

Except as otherwise specified, fees and expenses may be expressed in terms of a monetary amount, formula, percentage of assets, or per capita charge. [DOL Reg. § 2550.404a-5(e)]

Q 19:66 What is meant by a *designated investment alternative* under the DOL regulations?

A *designated investment alternative*, under the regulations, means any plan-designated investment wherein participants may direct the investment of assets in their individual accounts. It does not include brokerage windows, self-directed brokerage accounts, or similar plan arrangements that enable participants to select investments beyond those designated by the plan. [DOL Reg. § 2550.404a-5(h)(4)]

Q 19:67 What is meant by the terms *at least annually thereafter* and *at least quarterly* under the DOL regulations?

Effective for disclosures made on or after June 17, 2015, *at least annually thereafter* means *at* least once in any 14-month period regardless of whether the plan operates on a calendar-year or fiscal-year basis. [80 Fed. Reg. 14,301 (Mar. 19, 2015)] Prior to that date, *at least annually thereafter* means at least once in any 12-month period, regardless of whether the plan operates on a calendar- or fiscal-year basis. *At least quarterly* means at least once in any 3-month period, regardless of whether the plan operates on a calendar-year basis or fiscal-year basis. [DOL Reg. § 2550.404a-5(h)(1),(2)]

In 2013, the DOL provided a one-time "re-set" with respect to the *at least annually thereafter* requirement. The guidance, in the form of a temporary enforcement policy, was in response to concerns regarding having to provide a 2013 disclosure within 12 calendar months of the initial disclosure that had a deadline of August 30, 2012 (see Q 19:58). For example, a plan administrator that provided a disclosure on August 25, 2012, must provide the next disclosure no later than August 25, 2013—a date that may not correlate to the timing of any other annual participant disclosures. If there was more flexibility, the disclosure could be distributed at times more likely to attract attention and minimize costs (e.g., distributed at the year-end during enrollment periods or with individual benefit statements).

Under FAB 2013-02, the DOL permitted a one-time 18-month "re-set" of the timing requirement as set forth below. The guidance specifically refers to the investment disclosures required to be provided in a comparative chart format (see Qs 19:61, 19:62).

- A plan administrator may provide the "2013 comparative chart" no later than 18 months after the prior comparative chart was provided. For example, if a plan administrator provided the first comparative chart on August 25, 2012, the "2013 comparative chart" was due no later than August 25, 2013. However, the DOL would take no enforcement action based on timeliness if the plan administrator provided the "2013 comparative chart" by February 25, 2014.

- If a plan administrator provided the "2013 comparative chart" by the original regulatory deadline, those plan administrators were permitted to provide the "2014 comparative chart" no later than 18 months after furnishing the prior comparative chart. For example, if a plan administrator provided the first comparative chart on August 25, 2012, and provided the second comparative chart on August 25, 2013, the DOL would take no enforcement action based on timeliness if the plan administrator furnished the "2014 comparative chart" by February 25, 2015. This gave these plan administrators the same opportunity for the one-time "re-set."

According to the DOL, this special one-time "re-set" is limited to the required annual disclosures of information (see Qs 19:60, 19:61). It did not provide relief related to other obligations to timely provide information under the requirements.

[DOL Field Assist. Bull. 2013-02]

Q 19:68 What is meant by the terms *average annual total return* and *total annual operating expenses* under the DOL requirements?

Average annual total return means the average annual compounded rate of return that would equate an initial investment alternative in a designated investment alternative to the ending redeemable value of that investment calculated with the before-tax methods of computation prescribed in SEC N-1A, N-3, or N-4, as appropriate, except that such method of computation may exclude any front-end, deferred, or other sales loads that are waived for the participants of the covered individual account plan.

Total annual return operating expenses means:

- In the case of an alternative that is registered under the Investment Company Act of 1940, the annual operating expenses and other asset-based charges before waivers and reimbursements (e.g., investment management fees, distribution fees, service fees, administrative fees, separate account expenses, mortality, and expense risk fees) that reduce the alternative's rate of return, expressed as a percentage, calculated in accordance with the required SEC form—e.g., Form N-1A (open-end management investment companies) or Form N-3 or N-4 (separate accounts offering variable annuity contracts).
- In the case of an alternative that is not registered under the Investment Company Act of 1940, the sum of the fees and expenses described below before waivers and reimbursements, for the alternative's most recently completed fiscal year, expressed as a percentage of the alternative's average net asset value for that year:
  - Management fees as described in the SEC Form N-1A that reduce the alternative's rate of return;

- Distribution and/or servicing fees as described in SEC Form N-1A that reduce the alternative's rate of return; and
- Any other fees and expenses not identified above that reduce the alternative's rate of return (e.g., externally negotiated fees, custodial expenses, legal expenses, accounting expenses, transfer agent expenses, recordkeeping fees, administrative fees, separate account expenses, mortality and expense risk fees), excluding brokerage costs described in Item 21 of the SEC Form N-1A.

[DOL Reg. § 2550.404a-5(h)(3), (5)]

Q 19:69 With regard to investment-related information listed in Q 19:61, what special rules apply to a designated investment alternative designed to invest in qualifying employer securities?

The following requirements apply to qualifying employer securities (within the meaning of ERISA Section 407 (see chapter 6)):

- In lieu of providing principal strategies/risks information under item 5, provide an explanation of the importance of a well-balanced and diversified investment portfolio.
- The requirements under item 5 relating to portfolio turnover rate do not apply.
- The requirements under item 5 relating to fee/expense information do not apply, unless the employer stock is a fund with respect to which participant acquire units rather than shares.
- The requirements under item 4 relating to total annual operating expense expressed as a percentage do not apply, unless the employer stock is a fund with respect to which participant acquire units rather than shares.
- The requirements under item 4 relating to total annual operating expense expressed as a dollar amount per $1,000 do not apply, unless the employer stock is a fund with respect to which participant acquire units rather than shares.
- With respect to the requirement under item 2 relating to performance data for 1-, 5-, and 10-year periods, unless the employer stock is a fund with respect to which participants acquire units rather than shares, there is a special definition for "average annual total return" that generally applies:

  > The change in value of an investment in one share of stock on an annualized basis over a specified period, calculated by taking the sum of the dividends paid during the measurement period, assuming reinvestment, plus the difference between the stock price at the end and at the beginning of the measurement period; reinvestment of dividends is assumed to be in stock at market prices at approximately the same time actual dividends are paid.

[DOL Reg. § 2550.404a-5(i)(1)]

Q 19:70 With regard to investment-related information listed in Q 19:61, what special rules apply to a designated investment alternative that is an annuity option?

In the case of a contract, fund, or product that permits participants to allocate contributions toward the current purchase of a stream of retirement income payments guaranteed by an insurance company, the plan administrator must, in lieu of the information in items 1 through 5, provide participants the following information with respect to each such option:

- The name of the contract, fund, or product;
- The option's objectives or goals (e.g., to provide a stream of fixed income payments for life);
- The benefits and factors that determine the price (e.g., age, interest rates, form of distribution) of the guaranteed payments;
- Any limitations on the ability of a participant to withdraw or transfer amounts (e.g., lock-ups) and any fees or charges applicable to such withdrawals or transfers;
- Any fees that will reduce the value of amounts allocated by participants to the option, such as surrender charges, market value adjustments, and administrative fees;
- A statement that guarantees of an insurance company are subject to its long-term strength and claims-paying ability; and
- An Internet Web site address that is sufficiently specific to provide participants access to the following information:
    - The name of the option's issuer and of the contract, fund, or product;
    - Description of the option's objectives and goals;
    - Description of the option's distribution alternatives/guaranteed income payments (e.g., payments for life, payments for a specified term, joint and survivor payments, optional rider payments), including any limitations on the right of a participant to receive such payments;
    - Description of costs and/or factors taken into account in determining the price of benefits under an option's distribution alternative/ guaranteed income payments (e.g., age, interest rates, other annuitization assumptions);
    - Description of any limitations on the right of a participant or beneficiary to withdraw or transfer amounts allocated to the option and any fees or charges applicable to a withdrawal or transfer; and
    - Description of any fees that will reduce the value of amounts allocated by participants to the option (e.g., surrender charges, market value adjustments, administrative fees).

[DOL Reg. § 2550.404a-5(i)(2)]

Q 19:71 With regard to investment-related information listed in Q 19:61, what special rules apply to a designated investment alternative that is a fixed-return investment?

In the case of an alternative where the return is fixed for the term of the investment, the plan administrator must, in lieu of complying with the requirements under item 5, provide an Internet Web site address that is sufficiently specific to provide participants access to the following information:

- The name of the alternative's issuer;
- The alternative's objectives or goals (e.g., to provide stability of principal and guarantee a minimum rate of return);
- The alternative's performance data described under item 2 for a fixed-rate investment, updated on at least a quarterly basis, or more frequently if required by other applicable law; and
- The alternative's fees and expense information described under item 4 for a fixed-rate investment.

[DOL Reg. § 2550.404a-5(i)(3)]

Q 19:72 With regard to investment-related information listed in Q 19:61, what additional disclosures would be required regarding target date or similar funds under DOL proposed regulations?

In November 2010, the DOL issued a proposed rule that would amend the participant investment and fee disclosure requirements concerning investments in target date funds.

The plan administrator must provide, in addition to other required disclosures, the following information as an appendix (or appendices) to the chart or similar documents described in Q 19:62:

1. An explanation of the alternative's asset allocation, how the asset allocation will change over time, and the point in time when the alternative will reach its most conservative asset allocation; including a chart, table, or other graphical representation that illustrates such change in asset allocation over time and that does not obscure or impede a participant's or beneficiary's understanding of the information explained herein;
2. If the alternative is named, or otherwise described, with reference to a particular date (e.g., a target date), an explanation of the age group for whom the alternative is designed, the relevance of the date, and any assumptions about a participant's contribution and withdrawal intentions on or after such date; and
3. A statement that the participant may lose money by investing in the alternative, including losses near or following retirement, and that there is no guarantee that the alternative will provide adequate retirement income.

[75 Fed. Reg. 73,987 (Nov. 30, 2010)]

See chapter 7 for a similar proposed amendment to the disclosure requirements applicable to investments in target date funds under a qualified default investment arrangement (QDIA).

Q 19:73 How do the DOL regulations impact participant disclosure requirements under ERISA Section 404(c)?

The DOL regulations integrate the new participant disclosure requirements into the disclosure requirements under ERISA Section 404(c), thereby establishing a more uniform disclosure framework for participant-directed plans. (See chapter 7 for information on Section 404(c) requirements.) Disclosure requirements under the regulations replace most disclosure requirements under the Section 404(c) regulations. A Section 404(c) plan is required to meet participant disclosure requirements under the regulations, in addition to any special requirements applicable to Section 404(c) plans. With the exception of two requirements, the DOL applied the myriad participant disclosure requirements to participant-directed plans regardless of 404(c) status. The only two additional disclosure requirements applicable solely to 404(c) plans after the participant disclosure requirements went into effect are: (1) the explanation that the plan is intended to comply with Section 404(c); and (2) if the plan offers an employer securities alternative, a description of the procedures for maintaining confidentiality when a participant invests in employer securities, and the name, address, and telephone number of the plan fiduciary responsible for monitoring compliance with the procedures.

The requirement to automatically provide prospectuses immediately before or after a participant's initial investment in a fund no longer applies.

Now that the DOL has broadly applied the disclosure requirements to participant-directed plans, plan sponsors that declined to seek 404(c) protection due to the disclosure requirements may want to reconsider that decision. Very little remains to be disclosed to qualify for 404(c) protection after the participant investment and fee disclosure requirements applicable to all participant-directed plans are met.

DOL Field Assistance Bulletin 2012-02R

In May 2012, the DOL released Field Assistance Bulletin (FAB) 2012-02 with more detailed guidance relating to the disclosure requirements. That guidance was subsequently revised and released in July 2012 in the form of DOL Field Assistance Bulletin (FAB) 2012-02R. Questions 19:74 through 19:108 below reflect that guidance. The deadline for compliance was not extended in connection with the release of the additional guidance. The DOL indicated, however, that for enforcement purposes it would take into account whether plan administrators acted in good faith based on a reasonable interpretation of the new regulations. If they have acted in good faith based on a reasonable interpretation of the new regulations, enforcement actions generally would be unnecessary if the plan administrator also establishes a plan for complying with the requirements of the FAB in future disclosures. The DOL also clarified that a fiduciary of a 404(c) plan did not have to provide information required under the regulation before it must be provided under the participant disclosure requirements, taking into account the regulation's transitional rules (see Qs 19:58, 19:73). [DOL Field Assist. Bull. 2012-02R]

Q 19:74 How do the rules apply to a plan that has both participant-directed and trustee-directed investments?

The plan administrator must provide the plan-related disclosures in Q 19:60 and the investment-related disclosures in Q 19:61. However, the plan administrator is not required to provide the investment-related disclosures for the trustee-directed investments. The plan administrator's obligation with respect to the investment-related disclosures is limited to the plan's designated investment alternatives. [DOL Field Assist. Bull. 2012-02R]

Q 19:75 Do the rules apply to Section 403(b) plans that are ERISA-covered plans?

Yes. However, the DOL indicated that it will not take enforcement action against any plan administrator who reasonably determines it would be impracticable, or impossible, to obtain the information necessary to meet the investment-related disclosure requirements in Q 19:61 with respect to any designated investment alternative that is an annuity contract or custodial account if:

1. The contract or account was issued to a current or former employee before January 1, 2009;
2. The employer ceased to have any obligation to make contributions (including employee salary reduction contributions), and in fact ceased making contributions to the contract or account for periods before January 1, 2009;
3. All the rights and benefits under the contract or account are legally enforceable against the insurer or custodian by the individual owner of the contract or account without any involvement by the employer; and
4. The individual owner is fully vested in the contract or account.

In general, a plan's election to take advantage of similar relief under the 5500 requirements and service provider disclosure rules are evidence of the impracticability of obtaining the necessary information (see chapters 4 and 22). The regulation does not apply to tax-sheltered annuities that are not ERISA-covered plans. [DOL Field Assist. Bull. 2012-02R]

Q 19:76 If a plan administrator provides plan-related and investment-related information together in a single document, must the plan administrator separately "identify" any designated investment alternatives (as described in Q 19:60) as well as "name" each designated investment alternative (as described in Q 19:61)?

No. The rule does not require that the same information be disclosed twice when plan-related and investment-related disclosures are furnished in a single document. If the plan-related information is provided separate from the investment-related information, in which case the designated investment alternatives would have to be identified (as described in Q 19:60) and named (as described in 19:61) in each respective disclosure document. [DOL Field Assist. Bull. 2012-02R]

Q 19:77 With regard to plan-related information listed in Q 19:60, how is a "designated investment manager" distinguished from a "designated investment alternative"?

A *designated investment manager* (DIM) is a Section 3(38) investment manager who is designated by a plan fiduciary and made available to participants and beneficiaries to manage all or a portion of the assets held in, or contributed to, their individual accounts. When participants appoint a DIM to manage all or a portion of their individual accounts, the DIM becomes responsible for investing their accounts on a participant-by-participant basis. The regulation does not impose any limitations on the investment alternatives that a DIM may use for investing participants' and beneficiaries' accounts. However, a plan may impose limitations by its terms or in its agreement with the DIM (e.g., the DIM may only invest in a plan's designated investment alternatives). [DOL Field Assist. Bull. 2012-02R]

Q 19:78 With regard to plan-related information listed in Q 19:60, what level of detail is required of the explanation of any fees and expenses for general plan administrative services that may be charged against participants' and beneficiaries' accounts and the basis on which such charges will be allocated?

The necessary level of detail for any particular explanation, and whether it is written in a manner calculated to be understood by the average plan participant, depends on the specific facts and circumstances of the particular service and the particular fee or expense.

When fees for a given service are known at the time of the disclosure, the explanation must clearly identify the service (e.g., recordkeeping), the cost of the services (e.g., .12 percent of the participant's account balance or $25 per participant), and the plan's allocation method (e.g., pro rata). The following examples are consistent with these principles.

Example 1. The plan divides total recordkeeping costs equally among all individual accounts so that each participant or beneficiary with a plan account will pay $25 per year. One fourth of this amount is subtracted from each individual plan account each quarter.

Example 2. An annual recordkeeping fee of .12 percent of the account balance will be charged to each individual plan account. Each month, an amount equal to .01 percent of the account's ending balance for the month will be deducted from your individual account.

Example 3. An annual recordkeeping fee of .12 percent of the account balance will be charged to each individual plan account. Every month, an amount equal to .01 percent of the account's ending balance for the month will be deducted from your individual account. For example, if your ending account balance for a month is $55,000, then $5.50 will be deducted for that month.

When services, fees, or both are not known at the time of the disclosure, the explanation must reasonably take into account the known facts and circumstances. For example, if a plan administrator reasonably expects the plan to incur legal fees in the upcoming year, such as for legal compliance services, but does not know the precise amount of such fees at the time of the disclosure, an identification of the services that are expected to be performed and the allocation method ordinarily used would be sufficient for purposes of this disclosure. The following example is consistent with these principles.

Example. If the plan incurs any legal expenses, such expenses will be paid from the plan's assets and deducted from individual plan accounts on a pro rata basis.

In these circumstances, the expense amount may be estimated based on the plan's legal expenses in prior years, provided the plan does not have reason to expect that the current year's fees will be substantially different from the prior year's fees, although an estimate is not required under the regulation.

Example. The plan's legal expenses average approximately $1,000 per year. These expenses will be paid from the plan's assets and deducted from individual plan accounts on a pro rata basis. This means that if the plan's assets total $1 million and your account balance is $10,000, you would pay $10 in legal expenses, and a participant with a $20,000 account balance would pay $20.

[DOL Field Assist. Bull. 2012-02R]

Q 19:79 With regard to plan-related information listed in Q 19:60, how should administrative expense disclosures be handled if revenue sharing payments have exceeded the monthly 2-basis point monthly recordkeeping fee in some, but not all, months?

Despite the fact that revenue sharing (or similar) payments, if any, reduce the gross fee amount (2 basis points monthly of the plan's assets, 24 basis points annually), this situation should be treated as if the recordkeeping fees are known at the time of the disclosure. Thus, the explanation must clearly identify the service, the amount or cost of the service, and the plan's allocation method. The following explanation is consistent with these principles.

> **Example.** The plan incurs monthly recordkeeping expenses of up to .02 percent of the plan's assets. These expenses typically will be deducted from [the individual's] account on a pro rata basis. However, these monthly expenses may be paid, in whole or in part, from revenue sharing payments that the plan receives from plan investment options. In the past, these payments have completely paid for these recordkeeping expenses in some months. If revenue sharing payments are received, the plan will pay less than .02 percent of the plan's assets per month, and only those expenses not offset by any revenue sharing payments will be deducted from your account. [DOL Field Assist. Bull. 2012-02R]

Q 19:80 With regard to plan-related information in Q 19:60, must a plan's administrative expenses be disclosed if those expenses are paid either from amounts forfeited under the terms of the plan or from the general assets of the employer sponsoring the plan?

No. The regulation requires an explanation of fees for general plan administrative services (e.g., legal, accounting, recordkeeping) that may be charged against the individual accounts of participants and beneficiaries and are not reflected in the total annual operating expenses of any designated investment alternative. The administrative expenses in this example are not charged against participant and beneficiary individual accounts and also are not reflected in the total annual operating expenses of designated investment alternatives; instead, they are paid either from the plan's assets that have been forfeited or from the general assets of the employer sponsoring the plan. Accordingly, these fees are not required to be disclosed under the regulation. [DOL Field Assist. Bull. 2012-02R]

Q 19:81 With regard to plan-related information in Q 19:60, must a plan's administrative expenses be disclosed if the plan document provides that administrative expenses shall be paid from individual accounts, from forfeitures, or by the employer (at the discretion of the plan administrator), but administrative expenses have always been paid either from the plan's forfeiture account or by the employer, and the plan has a written commitment from the employer that it will pay administrative expenses not covered by forfeitures?

No. Although administrative expenses could be charged against individual accounts if the employer fails to pay them, the fact that the employer has undertaken this obligation relieves the plan of having to disclose the explanation of these expenses. The disclosure is not likely to be a helpful piece of information to participants and beneficiaries if it describes fees and expenses that, in fact, have never been assessed against participants' and beneficiaries' accounts in the past and probably never will be assessed in the future. It may even be confusing to them. The plan administrator would be required to inform participants and beneficiaries if circumstances were to change such that the plan administrator might prospectively charge the plan's administrative expenses against the individual accounts of participants and beneficiaries. [DOL Field Assist. Bull. 2012-02R]

Q 19:82 With regard to plan-related information in Q 19:60, if a plan pays a recordkeeping expense of 10 basis points of its total assets by liquidating shares from participants' and beneficiaries' accounts, does the plan administrator have the discretion to disclose this expense as part of the total annual operating expenses of each of the plan's designated investment alternatives (i.e., as if these recordkeeping expenses actually were being paid from assets of the designated investment alternatives)?

No. A plan administrator does not have this discretion under the regulation. Consequently, a plan administrator may not include the cost of a recordkeeping expense in the total annual operating expenses of a plan's designated investment alternatives, unless the fee is actually paid in such a way (e.g., through revenue sharing) as to reduce the rate of return of the designated investment alternatives. When a fee or expense is charged against the individual accounts of participants and beneficiaries by liquidating shares or deducting dollars, it must be disclosed pursuant to either item 2 or item 3 in Q 19:60. [DOL Field Assist. Bull. 2012-02R]

Q 19:83 With regard to plan-related information listed in Q 19:60, must the revenue sharing explanation itemize or identify the specific plan administrative expenses being paid from the total annual operating expenses of one or more of the plan's designated investment alternatives?

No. The revenue sharing explanation is required when a plan's administrative expenses are paid through revenue sharing arrangements, Rule 12b-1 fees, or sub-transfer agent fees. According to the DOL, some information, even if general, would help participants and beneficiaries to better understand that there are administrative fees and expenses associated with the operation of their plan and that some of those fees and expenses might be indirectly paid by the plan's designated investment alternatives.

The DOL does not require an identification of the specific plan administrative expense or expenses being paid or an identification of the specific designated investment alternative or alternatives making the payment. Rather, a statement that some or all of the plan's administrative expenses are paid indirectly through some or all of the plans' designated investment alternatives will satisfy this specific requirement. It does not preclude, however, a more detailed explanation identifying the specific administrative expense or expenses being underwritten or an identification of the specific designated investment alternative or alternatives from which the payment is being made. [DOL Field Assist. Bull. 2012-02R]

Q 19:84 With regard to plan-related information listed in Q 19:60, if all of a plan's administrative expenses are paid from revenue sharing received by the plan from one or more of the plan's designated investment alternatives, must the plan administrator provide to participants and beneficiaries the revenue sharing explanation?

Yes. Some individuals have interpreted this requirement to apply only if the plan allocates some fees or expenses to individuals' accounts. Under this interpretation, if all administrative expenses are paid from such revenue sharing and there are no actual charges to individual plan accounts, the explanation is not required.

The requirement for a revenue sharing explanation is not contingent on the plan also allocating at least some administrative expenses to participants' accounts. The purpose of the explanation is to inform participants and beneficiaries of plans that pay for some or all administrative services through investment-related charges so that they do not think that there are few or no administrative expenses associated with their participation in the plan. [DOL Field Assist. Bull. 2012-02R]

Q 19:85 With regard to plan-related information listed in Q 19:60, may the plan include the revenue sharing explanation in each quarterly statement, even though revenue sharing payments to the plan are made by the designated investment alternatives only every other quarter?

Yes. The plan may include the revenue sharing explanation in each quarterly statement. [DOL Field Assist. Bull. 2012-02R]

Q 19:86 With regard to plan-related information listed in Q 19:60, what information must be disclosed about brokerage windows, self-directed brokerage accounts, and other similar plan arrangements that enable participants and beneficiaries to select investments beyond those designated by the plan?

First, a plan administrator must provide a general description of any such window, account, or arrangement. The regulation does not state how specific and detailed a description must be to satisfy this requirement. Whether a particular description is satisfactory will depend on the facts and circumstances of the specific plan and the specific window, account, or arrangement. At a minimum, this description must provide sufficient information to enable participants and beneficiaries to understand how the window, account, or arrangement works (e.g., how and to whom to give investment instructions; account balance requirements, if any; restrictions or limitations on trading, if any; how the window, account, or arrangement differs from the plan's designated investment alternatives); and whom to contact with questions.

Second, a plan administrator also must provide an explanation of any fees and expenses that may be charged against the individual account of a participant or beneficiary on an individual, rather than on a plan-wide, basis in connection with any such window, account, or arrangement. This would include: (1) any fee or expense necessary for the participant or beneficiary to start, open, or initially access such a window, account, or arrangement (such as enrollment, initiation, or startup fees), or to stop, close or terminate access; (2) any ongoing fee or expense (annual, monthly, or any other similarly charged fee or expense) necessary for the participant to maintain access to the window, account, or arrangement, including inactivity fees and minimum balance fees; and (3) any commissions or fees (e.g., per trade fee) charged in connection with the purchase or sale of a security, including front- or back-end sales loads if known; but would not include any fees or expenses of the investment selected by the participant or beneficiary (e.g., Rule 12b-1 or similar fees reflected in the investment's total annual operating expenses). In some circumstances the specific amount of certain fees associated with the purchase or sale of a security through a window, account, or arrangement, such as front-end sales loads for open-end management investment companies registered under the Investment Company Act of 1940, may vary across investments available through the window or may not be known by the plan administrator or provider of the window, account, or arrangement in advance of the purchase or sale of the security by a participant or beneficiary. In recognition of that, a general statement that such fees exist and that they may be charged against the individual account of a purchasing or selling participant or beneficiary, and directions as to how the participant can obtain information about such fees in connection with any particular investment, ordinarily will satisfy the requirements. Otherwise, plan administrators might inundate participants and beneficiaries with information about the cost of buying or selling all the various securities available through a window, account, or arrangement, despite the fact that participants and beneficiaries may not have the interest or expertise to purchase or sell each or any such security. Further, the statement should advise participants and beneficiaries to ask the provider of the window, account, or arrangement about any fees, including any undisclosed fees, associated with the purchase or sale of a particular security through a window, account, or arrangement, before purchasing or selling such security.

Third, a plan administrator also must provide participants and beneficiaries with a statement of the dollar amount of fees and expenses that actually were charged during the preceding quarter against their individual accounts in connection with any such window, account, or arrangement. A statement of these fees must include a description of the services to which the charge relates. The description of the services must clearly explain the charges (e.g., $19.99

brokerage trades, $25 brokerage account minimum balance fee, $13 brokerage account wire transfer fee, $44 front-end sales load). [DOL Field Assist. Bull. 2012-02R]

Q 19:87 With regard to plan-related information listed in Q 19:60, if only a small percentage of the participants and beneficiaries currently select such a brokerage window, self-directed brokerage account, or similar arrangement, may the plan administrator provide the required annual fee and expense information only to those participants and beneficiaries who have affirmatively elected to use the window, accounts, or arrangement?

No. The plan administrator must provide the required annual fee and expense information to all participants and beneficiaries so that they have sufficient information to make informed decisions about whether to direct the investment of their assets into such arrangements. The disclosure requirement is not conditioned on a prior investment decision of a specific participant or beneficiary. Similarly, a participant is not required to take a plan loan in order to receive disclosures about the fee and expense information associated with plan loans. [DOL Field Assist. Bull. 2012-02R]

Q 19:88 With regard to investment-related information listed in Q 19:61, must a plan administrator provide the disclosures for a designated investment alternative that is closed to new investments, but that allows participants and beneficiaries to maintain prior investments in the alternative and to transfer their interests to other plan investment alternatives?

Yes. A plan administrator must provide the disclosures to participants and beneficiaries for each designated investment alternative on the plan's investment platform even if the alternative is closed to new money. In the DOL's view, the required disclosures are as important for deciding whether to transfer out of a designated investment alternative as they are for deciding whether to invest in a designated investment alternative. The plan administrator is not required, but may choose, to provide the disclosures about the closed alternative as part of a comparative document furnished only to those participants or beneficiaries who remain invested in that alternative. [DOL Field Assist. Bull. 2012-02R]

Q 19:89 With regard to investment-related information listed in Q 19:61, if a plan administrator furnishes an additional benchmark for a balanced fund by blending more than one appropriate broad-based securities market index, may the plan administrator use the target asset allocation of the fund (e.g., 50 percent stocks, 50 percent bonds) to determine the weightings of the indexes used in creating the additional benchmark?

Yes, if the target is representative of the actual holdings of the designated investment alternative over a reasonable period of time. Disclosing blended benchmark returns, in addition to the required benchmark returns, is permissible provided that the additional benchmark returns are not inaccurate or misleading. Whether a time period is "reasonable" under this standard is dependent on the facts and circumstances. A period that is the same as that covered by the benchmark returns (e.g., 1-, 5-, or 10-year period) would not be unreasonable. Similarly, whether a target asset allocation is representative of the actual holdings of a designated investment alternative is dependent on the facts and circumstances. Target percentages ordinarily would be representative of an alternative's actual holdings if they are nearly equal to the daily average of the alternative's ratios of stocks and bonds (e.g., 50 percent stocks, 50 percent bonds) over a reasonable period of time. The DOL indicated that there are other similarly acceptable methods of determining whether target percentages are representative of actual holdings. [DOL Field Assist. Bull. 2012-02R]

Q 19:90 With regard to investment-related information listed in Q 19:61, what alternatives may be used to comply with the Web site address requirement?

According to the DOL, plan administrators have multiple ways to satisfy their obligation to provide a Web site address. For example, a plan administrator may contract with a third-party administrator or recordkeeper to establish and maintain the Web site for the plan. Alternatively, a plan administrator may use the existing Web site address of the employer who sponsors the plan to make available the required supplemental investment information. The plan administrator also may use Web site addresses provided by the issuers of the designated investment alternative(s) (e.g., the family of mutual funds comprising the plan's investment platform) as long as this address is sufficiently specific to lead the participant to the required information.

Although the plan administrator is responsible for ensuring the availability of a Web site address, a plan administrator will not be responsible for the completeness and accuracy of information used to satisfy the regulation's disclosure requirements, including the Web site address requirement, when the plan administrator reasonably and in good faith relies on information received from or provided by a plan service provider or the issuer of a designated investment alternative. [DOL Field Assist. Bull. 2012-02R]

Q 19:91 With regard to investment-related information listed in Q 19:61, must the Web site address landing page include all the required supplemental investment information regarding a designated investment alternative?

No. The Web site address must be sufficiently specific to lead the participant to supplemental investment-related information regarding designated investment alternatives. The Web site address landing page is not required to include all the supplemental investment-related information required by the regulation. The listed Web site address must, however, be sufficiently specific to provide participants and beneficiaries access to the information without difficulty.

Whether an address is "sufficiently specific" depends on the facts and circumstances. A plan administrator should consider, for example, the user-friendliness of the Web site, the number and complexity of the plan's designated investment alternatives, and the computer literacy of the average plan participant. [DOL Field Assist. Bull. 2012-02R]

Q 19:92 With regard to investment-related information listed in Q 19:61, what return information for a plan's designated investment alternatives must be available at the required Web site address?

Performance data for a plan's designated investment alternatives must be included in the supplemental investment-related information available on the Web site, updated on at least a quarterly basis.

For designated investment alternatives that do not have a fixed return, the Web site address must enable the participants and beneficiaries to obtain the average annual total return for 1-, 5-, and 10-year periods (or for the life of the alternative, if shorter) ending on the date of the most recently completed calendar quarter (or more current information if required by applicable law).

For designated investment alternatives with a fixed or stated return over the term of the investment, a Web site address must be sufficiently specific to provide participants and beneficiaries access to the current fixed or stated rate of return and the term of the investment. In some cases, such as when the issuer reserves the right to adjust the fixed or stated return, the information on the Web site may be different from the information provided on the annual comparative chart.

The regulation does not have a specific requirement for updating the supplemental information. However, the information made available on the Web site should be accurate and reasonably current, since participants and beneficiaries will have continuing access to the required Web site.

A plan administrator may include on the comparative chart or, at the required Web site address, additional information that the plan administrator determines to be appropriate as long as the information is not inaccurate or misleading. The DOL indicated that it would not, for this purpose, consider the inclusion of additional performance data on the Web site, such as year-to-date returns or returns for the most recently completed calendar month or quarter, reported consistently, to be misleading. [DOL Field Assist. Bull. 2012-02R]

Q 19:93 With regard to investment-related information listed in Q 19:61, does the DOL plan to publish a glossary for use in compliance with its regulation?

According to the DOL, it received two submissions from industry groups with sample glossaries. One sample, titled "Sample Glossary of Collective Investment Fund Terms for Disclosures to Retirement Plan Participants," January 2012, was developed by the American Bankers Association and its member banks. This sample, available at *www.aba.com*, defines terms that are commonly used by bank collective investment funds.

The second sample, titled "Sample Glossary of Investment-Related Terms for Disclosures to Retirement Plan Participants," December 2011, was developed by the SPARK Institute and the Investment Company Institute and endorsed by the American Benefits Council, the American Council of Life Insurers, the American Society of Pension Professionals & Actuaries, and the Society for Human Resource Management. This sample is available at *www.sparkinstitute.org*.

The DOL indicated that it does not intend to publish its own sample glossary, and continues to believe that plan administrators, in conjunction with their service providers and issuers of investment alternatives, are in the best position to determine the glossary (or glossaries) appropriate for their participants, taking into consideration their plans' investment alternatives. [DOL Field Assist. Bull. 2012-02R]

Q 19:94 With regard to investment-related information listed in Q 19:61, must a plan administrator provide a single, unified comparative chart, or may multiple charts, supplied by the plan's various service providers or investment issuers, be furnished to participants and beneficiaries?

Plan administrators may provide participants and beneficiaries with multiple comparative charts or documents supplied by the plan's various service providers or investment issuers, as long as the comparative charts or documents are provided to participants and beneficiaries at the same time in a single mailing or transmission, and the comparative charts or documents are designed to facilitate a comparison among designated investment alternatives available under the plan. However, permitting individual investment issuers, or others, to separately distribute comparative documents reflecting their particular investment alternatives would not facilitate a comparison of the core investment information and therefore would not satisfy the requirements. [DOL Field Assist. Bull. 2012-02R]

Q 19:95 With regard to investment-related information listed in Q 19:61, if there is a change to a designated investment alternative's fee and expense information after the plan administrator has provided the annual disclosure (comparative chart) to participants and beneficiaries, does the plan administrator have an obligation to automatically furnish a new comparative chart?

No. The regulation does not require plan administrators to furnish more than one comparative chart annually to participants and beneficiaries. However, fee and expense information must be made available on a Web site, and information made available on the Web site must be accurate and updated as soon as reasonably possible following a change. The Web site also should reflect the date on which it was most recently updated. Further, under extraordinary circumstances, the duties of prudence and loyalty under ERISA Section 404 may require the plan administrator to inform participants and beneficiaries of important changes to investment-related information before the next comparative chart is required under the regulation. [DOL Field Assist. Bull. 2012-02R]

Q 19:96 With regard to investment-related information listed in Q 19:61, for designated investment alternatives with variable rates of return, may a plan administrator furnish on the comparative chart average annual total return information that is more recent than the end of the most recently completed calendar year?

Yes. A plan administrator may provide the average annual total return of each designated investment alternative with variable rates of return for 1-, 5-, and 10-year periods (or for the life of the alternative, if shorter) as of the date of the most recently completed calendar month or quarter. However, to ensure appropriate comparability, the same ending date for a particular period ordinarily would have to be used for all designated investment alternatives under the plan, and the associated benchmark information would have to correspond to the same time period. [DOL Field Assist. Bull. 2012-02R]

Q 19:97 With regard to investment-related information listed in Q 19:61, is a plan administrator required to include "since inception" information for all the plan's designated investment alternatives?

No. A plan administrator is only required to provide "since inception" performance data (including benchmarks) for designated investment alternatives that have been in existence for fewer than 10 years. The regulation provides that performance data and benchmarks must be disclosed for 1-, 5-, and 10-calendar year periods (or for the life of the alternative, if shorter). If a plan administrator discloses performance and benchmark information for each of these 1-, 5-, and 10-year periods, "since inception" information is not required to be disclosed. However, nothing in the regulation precludes a plan administrator from including "since inception" data, provided such information is not inaccurate or misleading. [DOL Field Assist. Bull. 2012-02R]

Q 19:98 What must be provided in terms of a document similar to a prospectus (as described in item 1 of Q 19:64) for designated investment alternatives that are not registered under the Securities Act of 1933 or the Investment Company Act of 1940?

With respect to designated investment alternatives that are registered under either the Securities Act of 1933 or the Investment Company Act of 1940, the plan administrator must provide copies of prospectuses, or the plan administrator may opt to provide short-form or summary prospectuses upon request (or automatically at times specified in Q 19:61). Copies furnished must be based on the latest information available to the plan administrator. Similar documents are required for all other designated investment alternatives under the plan.

Whether a document is "similar" to a prospectus, or a short-form or a summary prospectus, would depend on the particular facts and circumstances, including the type of designated investment alternative for which investment-related information must be disclosed. For example, in connection with a bank collective investment fund, a copy of the fund's "written plan" within the meaning of 12 C.F.R. § 9.18(b)(1) or similar state law ordinarily would satisfy the requirements. Alternatively, similar to short-form or summary prospectuses, bank fund fact sheets ordinarily may be used to satisfy this disclosure requirement, because they typically would contain information corresponding to that contained in short-form or summary prospectuses. When such a document does not already exist, copies of the documents and other materials used by a plan fiduciary to prudently select and monitor the designated investment alternative ordinarily would satisfy the requirements. [DOL Field Assist. Bull. 2012-02R]

Q 19:99 Must the disclosures required under the regulation be furnished as stand-alone documents?

No. While plan administrators have discretion to furnish the required disclosures as stand-alone documents, they also have discretion to furnish the required disclosures along with, or as part of, other documents. Under the regulation, certain disclosures may be provided as part of the plan's summary plan description or a pension benefit statement (see Q 19:65). It does not preclude other means for satisfying disclosure obligations under the final rule. For example, disclosures that must be made before the date on which a participant or beneficiary can first direct his or her investments may be furnished as part of a new employee's enrollment packet. Whatever the means for satisfying the disclosure obligations under the final rule, the disclosures must be furnished in compliance with the applicable timing requirements in the regulation. [DOL Field Assist. Bull. 2012-02R]

Q 19:100 If a plan designates a fiduciary investment manager, within the meaning of ERISA Section 3(38), who may be appointed by participants or beneficiaries to allocate the assets in their individual accounts among the plan's designated investment alternatives, is this investment management service a designated investment alternative under the regulation?

No. Neither the service described above, nor each individual account it manages, is a "designated investment alternative." Thus, the investment-related disclosure requirements in Q 19:61 would not apply to this investment service. However, the disclosure requirements in Q 19:60 would apply. Consequently, the plan administrator must identify the designated investment manager, provide plan-level information regarding fees associated with the service, and provide participants and beneficiaries with a statement, at least quarterly, of the dollar amount of fees and expenses that actually were charged against their individual accounts, along with a description of the services to which the charges relate. According to the DOL, a plan fiduciary will be responsible for the prudent selection and monitoring of the designated investment manager, which is a provider of services to the plan. [DOL Field Assist. Bull. 2012-02R]

Q 19:101 If a plan offers three model portfolios made up of different combinations of the plan's designated investment alternatives, is each model portfolio a designated investment alternative under the regulation?

A model portfolio ordinarily is not required to be treated as a designated investment alternative under the regulation if it is clearly presented to the participants and beneficiaries as merely a means of allocating account assets among specific designated investment alternatives (e.g., "conservative," "moderate," and "growth"). On the other hand, if, in choosing a model portfolio, the plan participant acquires an equity security, unit participation, or similar interest in an entity that itself invests in some combination of the plan's designated investment alternatives, such a model portfolio ordinarily would be a designated investment alternative. In either case, the plan administrator should clearly explain how the model portfolio functions. When a model portfolio is simply a means of allocating account assets among specific, designated investment alternatives, the plan administrator must clearly explain how it differs from the plan's designated investment alternatives. Finally, if a plan offers only model portfolios made up of investments not separately designated under the plan, each model would have to be treated as a designated investment alternative.

Some plans and service providers currently may have the ability to calculate and provide the investment-related information specified in Q 19:61 with respect to model portfolios offered on recordkeeping platforms. While model portfolios ordinarily are not required to be treated as designated investment alternatives, plan administrators may include on the comparative chart additional information that they determine to be appropriate as long as the information is not inaccurate or misleading. [DOL Field Assist. Bull. 2012-02R]

Q 19:102 Does the regulation cover "brokerage windows"?

Yes. The regulation covers "brokerage windows," "self-directed brokerage accounts," and other similar plan arrangements that enable participants and beneficiaries to select investments beyond those designated by the plan. Coverage of brokerage windows under the regulation, however, is limited to the disclosure requirements in Q 19:60 (relating to plan-related information). The disclosure requirements in Q 19:61 (relating to investment-related information) do not apply to brokerage windows, self-directed brokerage accounts, and similar arrangements, because such windows, accounts, and arrangements are not designated investment alternatives, and do not apply to any investment selected by a participant or beneficiary that is not designated by the plan (i.e., any investments made through the window, account, or arrangement). [DOL Field Assist. Bull. 2012-02R]

Q 19:103 If a plan offers an investment platform that includes a brokerage window, self-directed brokerage account, or similar plan arrangement, and the plan fiduciary did not designate any of the funds on the platform as "designated investment alternatives," is the platform or the brokerage window, self-directed brokerage account, or similar plan arrangement a designated investment alternative?

No. Whether an investment alternative is a "designated investment alternative" depends on whether it is specifically identified as available under the plan. The regulation does not require that a plan have a particular number of designated investment alternatives, and nothing in the guidance prohibits the use of a platform or a brokerage window, self-directed brokerage account, or similar plan arrangement in an individual account plan. It also does not change the Section 404(c) regulation or the requirements for relief from fiduciary liability under Section 404(c) of ERISA or address the application of ERISA's general fiduciary requirements to SEPs or SIMPLE IRA plans.

According to the DOL, a plan fiduciary's failure to designate investment alternatives—for example, to avoid investment disclosures under the regulation—raises questions under ERISA Section 404(a)'s general statutory fiduciary duties of prudence and loyalty. Also, fiduciaries of such plans with platforms or brokerage windows, self-directed brokerage accounts, or similar plan arrangements that enable participants and beneficiaries to select investments beyond those designated by the plan are still bound by ERISA Section 404(a)'s statutory duties of prudence and loyalty to participants and beneficiaries who use the platform or the brokerage window, self-directed brokerage account, or similar plan arrangement, including taking into account the nature and quality of services provided in connection with the platform or the brokerage window, self-directed brokerage account, or similar plan arrangement.

The DOL indicated that plan fiduciaries and service providers may have questions regarding the situations in which fiduciaries may have duties under

ERISA's general fiduciary standards apart from those in the regulation. It intends to determine how best to ensure compliance with these duties in a practical and cost-effective manner, including, if appropriate, through amendments of relevant regulatory provisions.

[DOL Field Assist. Bull. 2012-02R]

Q 19:104 If the plan offers a fund-of-funds as a designated investment alternative, and both the acquiring fund and funds in which it invests (acquired funds) are open-end management investment companies registered under the Investment Company Act of 1940, must the acquiring fund's total annual operating expenses reflect the operating expenses of the acquired funds?

Yes. Acquired fund fees and expenses are included in the total annual operating expenses of an acquiring fund, which is disclosed in the prospectus of the acquiring fund filed with the Securities and Exchange Commission (SEC). The annual operating expenses of the acquiring fund must, in addition to its own annual operating expenses, proportionally reflect the annual operating expenses of the acquired funds.

> **Example.** A registered open-end mutual fund that is a designated investment alternative (the acquiring fund) invests evenly in four underlying funds (the acquired funds) each of which also is an open-end mutual fund. The first acquired fund has annual operating expenses of .50 percent, the second and third 1.00 percent, and the fourth 1.50 percent, respectively. The annual operating expenses of the acquired funds would be 1.00 percent ((0.25 × .5) + (0.50 × 1.0) + (0.25 × 1.5)). The acquiring fund, itself, has annual operating expenses of .25 percent of average net assets. Accordingly, the total annual operating expenses of this designated investment alternative would be 1.25 percent of average net assets. This assumes that the acquiring fund's percentage investment in each underlying fund remains the same throughout the year.

Principles similar to those expressed above apply to unregistered designated investment alternatives that invest in acquired funds or trusts. Accordingly, the total annual operating expenses for an unregistered designated investment alternative that is an acquiring fund (e.g., a fund-of-funds or trust-of-trusts) should be calculated in the same manner. [DOL Field Assist. Bull. 2012-02R]

Q 19:105 With regard to Q 19:68, how often must an investment alternative not registered under the Investment Company Act of 1940 calculate their net asset values in order to determine their average net asset value for the year?

The intent of the regulation was to achieve as much symmetry as possible between the calculation of the total annual operating expenses for registered and unregistered designated investment alternatives. Designated investment alternatives that are registered under the Investment Company Act of 1940 must value their net assets at least monthly in order to calculate their average net assets for the year (Instruction 4 to Item 13 of Form N-1A). An unregistered designated investment alternative ordinarily would be in compliance with the regulation if it calculated its net asset value not less frequently than monthly in order to determine the alternative's average net asset value for the year. [DOL Field Assist. Bull. 2012-02R]

Q 19:106 If the payment of plan administrative expenses reduces the value of each unit of the designated investment alternative, but has no impact on the number of units owned by participants and beneficiaries or on the share value of the underlying mutual fund, is this designated investment alternative considered "registered" or "unregistered" for purposes of calculating its total annual operating expenses as described in Q 19:68?

By way of an example, one of a plan's designated investment alternatives is a separately managed trust account that invests solely in shares of a mutual fund that is registered under the Investment Company Act of 1940. When participants and beneficiaries invest in this alternative, they acquire units of the designated investment alternative, not shares in the mutual fund itself. Pursuant to the plan document, the plan administrator pays for some of the plan's general administrative expenses (legal, accounting, recordkeeping) by liquidating assets of the designated investment alternative. This method of paying plan administrative expenses reduces the value of each unit of the designated investment alternative, but has no impact on the number of units owned by participants and beneficiaries or on the share value of the underlying mutual fund.

According to the DOL, the designated investment alternative in this example is an unregistered alternative even though it invests solely in a mutual fund that itself is registered under the Investment Company Act of 1940. Accordingly, in calculating its total annual operating expenses, the plan administrator must follow the methodology for an unregistered alternative. The plan's general administrative expenses mentioned above must be reflected in the designated investment alternative's total annual operating expenses. Because the plan's general administrative expenses are part of the designated investment alternative's total annual operating expenses, they also must be reflected in the designated investment alternative's average annual total return. Because of how this plan pays for its general administrative expenses, the total annual operating expenses and average annual total return of the designated investment alternative will differ from the annual operating expenses and average annual total return of the mutual fund as reported in its prospectus. Plan administrators should keep these discrepancies in mind as they discharge all of their disclosure obligations under the regulation, such as the Web site address disclosures. [DOL Field Assist. Bull. 2012-02R]

Q 19:107 With regard to investment-related information in Q 19:61, if a designated investment alternative purchases insurance to smooth its rate of return, how should the cost of the insurance be disclosed under this regulation?

By way of an example, a plan offers a stable value fund as one of its designated investment alternatives. The manager of the stable value fund purchases an insurance contract that is designed to smooth the rate of return of the alternative's underlying fixed income investments. The annual cost for this insurance is 20 basis points of the alternative's underlying investments. This fund expense is paid from the assets of the fund, which reduces the alternative's rate of return.

According to the DOL, the cost of the insurance must be included in the total annual operating expenses of the designated investment alternative. The regulation defines total annual operating expenses by providing two calculations, one for registered and one for unregistered designated investment alternatives. These calculations are designed to capture the fees and expenses that reduce the alternative's rate of return. In this example, the cost of the insurance component is an expense that is paid by reducing an alternative's rate of return and so must be included in the total annual operating expense of the alternative. [DOL Field Assist. Bull. 2012-02R]

Q 19:108 Did the *first* initial quarterly statement of fees and expenses need to reflect the fees and expenses deducted prior to the third quarter?

No, the initial quarterly statement needed to reflect only the fees and expenses deducted for the calendar-year or plan-year quarter to which the statement relates. The regulation requires that, at least quarterly, participants and beneficiaries are furnished with the dollar amount of any fees and expenses actually deducted from their account along with a description of the services to which the charges relate. The regulation became applicable to individual account plans for plan years beginning on or after November 1, 2011. However, the regulation contains a transitional rule (see Q 19:58) which provides that the initial quarterly disclosure must be furnished no later than 45 days after the end of the quarter in which the first set of initial disclosures are required to be furnished. For example, for calendar-year plans, the rule required that the first quarterly disclosure be furnished no later than 45 days after the end of the third quarter (or Nov. 14, 2012), and that the quarterly disclosure only reflect the fees and expenses actually deducted during the third quarter. [DOL Field Assist. Bull. 2012-02R]

Blackout Notices

In response to the bankruptcy of Enron Corporation, Congress enacted the Sarbanes-Oxley Act of 2002 [Pub. L. No. 107-204, 116 Stat. 745], a far-reaching accounting and corporate governance reform law. Under Sarbanes-Oxley, retirement plan administrators are required to give notice to participants and beneficiaries in advance of a so-called blackout period. The requirements are intended to ensure that plan participants and beneficiaries have advance notice of restrictions on their access to assets credited to their accounts during a period of more than three consecutive business days and can take appropriate steps in anticipation of the restrictions. In 2003, the DOL issued regulations interpreting the blackout notice rules.

Q 19:109 What is a *blackout period* that triggers the advance notice requirements?

A *blackout period* is defined as any period during which the ability of participants or beneficiaries to direct or diversify assets credited to their accounts, to obtain loans from the plan, or to obtain distributions from the plan is temporarily suspended, limited, or restricted *for more than three consecutive business days*.

The most common reasons for a blackout period include changes to recordkeepers, changes to investment offerings, corporate mergers or acquisitions, and spin-offs that impact the company's retirement plan.

A blackout period does not include a suspension, limitation, or restriction that:

1. Occurs by reason of the application of the securities laws as defined in Section 3(a)(47) of the Securities Exchange Act of 1934 (the 1934 Act);
2. Is a regularly scheduled suspension, limitation, or restriction under the plan (or change thereto) that has been disclosed to affected plan participants and beneficiaries through the SPD, SMM, materials describing specific investment alternatives under the plan and limits thereon or any changes thereto, participation or enrollment forms, or any other documents and instruments pursuant to which the plan is established or operated that have been given to such participants and beneficiaries;
3. Occurs by reason of a QDRO or by reason of a pending determination (by the plan administrator, by a court of competent jurisdiction or otherwise) whether a domestic relations order (DRO) is a QDRO; or
4. Occurs by reason of an act or a failure to act on the part of an individual participant or by reason of an action or claim by a party unrelated to the plan involving the account of an individual participant.

[DOL Reg. § 2520.101-3(d)]

Limits on the ability to give investment direction during certain prescribed time frames would be covered under item 2 above to the extent disclosed to affected participants and beneficiaries. Receipt of a tax levy and a dispute over a deceased participant's account are examples that could fall under item 4 above.

Q 19:110 What types of plans are subject to the blackout notice requirements?

Any "individual account" plan or defined contribution plan that provides for an individual account for each participant and provides for benefits based solely on each participant's allocated earnings, losses, and contributions is subject to the blackout notice requirements. The plan need not provide for participant-directed investments to be subject to the requirements. Defined benefit arrangements are not subject to the rules, nor are "one-participant retirement plans." [DOL Reg. § 2520.101-3(d)(2)]

A one-participant retirement plan is a retirement plan that on the first day of the plan year (a) covered only the individual (and his or her spouse), and the individual owned the entire business (whether or not incorporated) or (b) covered only one or more partners (and their spouses) in the plan sponsor. [ERISA § 101(i)(8)(B)]

Q 19:111 Who is required to give and to receive blackout notices?

The plan administrator must provide blackout notices to all participants and beneficiaries whose rights under the plan will be temporarily suspended, limited, or restricted by the blackout period (the "affected participants and beneficiaries"). [DOL Reg. § 2520.101-3(a)]

Q 19:112 What additional requirement applies if employer securities are subject to a blackout period?

When employer securities are subject to a blackout period, the plan administrator must give the issuer of the employer securities advance notice of the blackout period, in addition to giving notice to all affected participants and beneficiaries. Under a separate requirement, the issuer is required to notify its directors and officers and the Securities and Exchange Commission (SEC) of the blackout period (see chapter 6).

The term *issuer* means an issuer as defined in Section 3 of the 1934 Act (15 U.S.C. § 78c), the securities of which are registered under Section 12 of the 1934 Act, or that is required to file reports under Section 15(d) of the 1934 Act, or files or has filed a registration statement that has not yet become effective under the Securities Act of 1933 (15 U.S.C. §§ 77a *et seq.*), and that it has not withdrawn. [DOL Reg. §§ 2520.101-3(a), 2520.101-3(d)(4)]

Q 19:113 What information must a blackout notice contain?

A blackout notice must be written in a manner to be understood by the average plan participant and must include the following:

1. The reasons for the blackout period;
2. A description of the rights otherwise available to participants and beneficiaries under the plan that will be temporarily suspended, limited, or restricted by the blackout period (e.g., right to direct or diversify assets in individual accounts, right to obtain loans from the plan, right to obtain distributions from the plan), including identification of any investments subject to the blackout period;
3. The length of the blackout period by reference to:
   - The expected beginning date and ending date of the blackout period or
   - The calendar week during which the blackout period is expected to begin and end, provided that during such weeks information as to whether the blackout period has begun or ended is readily available, without charge, to affected participants and beneficiaries, such as via a toll-free number or access to a specific Web site, and the notice describes how to access the information;
4. In the case of investments affected, a statement that the participants or beneficiaries should evaluate the appropriateness of their current investment decisions in light of their inability to direct or diversify assets in the accounts during the blackout period;
5. If the notice is not being furnished at least 30 days in advance of the blackout, (a) a statement that federal law generally requires that notice be furnished to affected participants and beneficiaries at least 30 days in advance of the last date on which participants and beneficiaries could exercise the affected rights immediately before the commencement of a blackout period and (b) an explanation of the reasons why at least 30 days advance notice could not be furnished; and
6. The name, address, and telephone number of the plan administrator or other contact responsible for answering questions about the blackout period.

[DOL Reg. § 2520.101-3(b)]

Q 19:114 How must the blackout notice be furnished?

The blackout notice must be in writing and is to be distributed to affected participants and beneficiaries in any manner consistent with the requirements applicable to SPDs and other required disclosures under ERISA (see Q 19:31), including those applicable when electronic media are used (see Qs 19:124, 19:125). [DOL Reg. §§ 2520.101-3(b)(3), 2520.104b-1]

Q 19:115 When must the blackout notice be given?

The blackout notice must be given to all affected participants and beneficiaries at least 30 days, but not more than 60 days, in advance of the last date on which such participants and beneficiaries could exercise the affected rights immediately before the commencement of any blackout period. [DOL Reg. § 2520.101-3(b)(2)]

In the case of a daily-traded plan, the 30-day period can be counted back from the date immediately preceding the commencement of the blackout period. In the case of a plan that permits trading on a monthly basis, notice must be given at least 30 days prior to the month preceding the month in which a blackout period occurs. So, for example, if a plan permits participants to direct investments during the first 15 days of the month and if such plan is suspending participant investment direction from May 1 to May 15, the last date on which participants could take action in anticipation of the blackout is April 15. Accordingly, notice must be given not later than March 16.

In the case of a plan identifying the blackout as beginning "the week of February 9," February 9 will be the beginning of the blackout period for purposes of timing the blackout notice.

Q 19:116 Under what circumstances does the 30-day advance notice requirement not apply?

The requirement to give at least 30 days' advance notice does not apply if any of the following applies:

1. A postponement of the blackout period in order to comply with the notice requirements would result in a violation of the exclusive purpose and prudence requirements of ERISA, and a fiduciary of the plan reasonably so determines in writing;
2. The inability to provide the advance notice of a blackout period is due to events that were unforeseeable or circumstances beyond the reasonable control of the plan administrator, and a fiduciary of the plan reasonably so determines in writing; or
3. The blackout period applies only to one or more participants or beneficiaries solely in connection with their becoming, or ceasing to be, participants or beneficiaries of the plan as a result of a merger, acquisition, divestiture, or similar transaction involving the plan or plan sponsor.

In any of the cases above, the plan administrator must give the notice to all affected participants and beneficiaries as soon as reasonably possible under the circumstances, unless such notice in advance of the termination of the blackout period is impracticable. Determinations under items 1 and 2 above must be dated and signed by the fiduciary. [DOL Reg. § 2520.101-3(b)(2)]

Q 19:117 What happens if there is an unexpected change to the duration of the blackout period?

If there is a change in the duration of the blackout period, the plan administrator shall provide all affected participants and beneficiaries an updated notice explaining the reasons for the change and identifying all material changes in the information contained in the prior notice. Such notice must be provided to all affected participants and beneficiaries as soon as reasonably possible, unless such notice in advance of the termination of the blackout period is impracticable. [DOL Reg. § 2520.101-3(b)(4)]

Q 19:118 What is the effective date of the blackout notice rules?

The blackout notice rules became effective and apply to any blackout period commencing on or after January 26, 2003. [DOL Reg. § 2520.101-3(f)]

Q 19:119 What are the penalties for noncompliance with the blackout notice rules?

Failure to provide a timely blackout notice can result in civil penalties up to $100 per participant per day computed from the date of the administrator's failure or refusal to provide notice of the blackout period up to and including the date that is the final day of the blackout period. The amount assessed is determined by the DOL, taking into consideration the degree and/or willfulness of the failure or refusal to provide notice of a blackout period. [DOL Reg. § 2560.502c-7(b)]

Q 19:120 Has the DOL provided a model blackout notice?

Yes. (See Appendix F for the DOL's model blackout notice.) Use of the DOL's model notice is not mandatory. However, a notice that uses the statements in paragraphs 4 and 5(A) of the model notice will be deemed to satisfy the requirements of items 4 and 5(a), respectively, in Q 19:113. With regard to all other information, compliance with the notice content requirements will depend on the facts and circumstances pertaining to the particular blackout period and plan. [DOL Reg. § 2520.101-3(e)]

Diversification Notices

Q 19:121 What notice is required under the Pension Protection Act of 2006 when plan assets are invested in publicly traded employer securities?

Under the PPA, participants in defined contribution plans (other than certain employee stock ownership plans) must be allowed to diversify investments in publicly traded employer securities. At least 30 days before the first date on which a participant is eligible to exercise his or her diversification rights, the participant must receive a notice that (1) describes his or her diversification rights and (2) provides information on the importance of diversifying retirement plan assets. [ERISA § 101(m)]

The diversification and notice requirements are generally effective for plan years beginning after December 31, 2006. (See chapter 6 for detailed information on the diversification and notice requirements applicable to plans invested in employer securities.)

Use of Electronic Technology

Q 19:122 What is meant by *paperless administration*?

Paperless administration refers to a system in which information is prepared, stored, and communicated in electronic form instead of on paper. In light of various technological advances and the growth of computer use, plan administrators are experiencing the evolution of paperless administration. Paperless administration is currently accomplished through the use of interactive voice response units (VRUs), kiosks, personal computers, and the Internet and intranets.

Various modes of electronic communication allow participants and beneficiaries to access benefit information at times convenient to them. Paperless administration can lead to significant cost savings for plan sponsors by reducing costly paper flow.

Q 19:123 What are some legal issues associated with paperless administration?

Although the use of electronic communication has grown significantly, plan sponsors must consider the legal implications of paperless administration. There are three main legal issues:

1. Written consent and notification requirements;
2. Satisfying disclosure and record retention requirements under ERISA; and
3. Satisfying notice and consent requirements under the Internal Revenue Code.

Plan sponsors must also ensure that the electronic framework properly protects the security of participant transactions and confidentiality of personal information.

Q 19:124 What are some issues that arise from ERISA disclosure requirements?

When a plan administrator is required by ERISA to furnish materials either by direct operation of law or on individual request, the administrator must use measures reasonably calculated to ensure actual receipt by plan participants and beneficiaries. Material required to be furnished must be sent by a method likely to result in full distribution. In-hand delivery to an employee at his or her work site or delivery via first-class mail, for example, is acceptable. It is not acceptable merely to place copies of the material in a location frequented by plan participants. [DOL Reg. § 2520.104b-1(b)(1)]

Presumably, the disclosure requirements were intended to ensure actual receipt of, and continuous access to, plan information by participants and beneficiaries. It should follow that disclosure of such material electronically would be permitted as long as those goals are satisfied.

Q 19:125 What guidance has the DOL issued concerning the use of electronic technologies for complying with ERISA's disclosure requirements?

On April 6, 2011, the DOL issued a request for comments to assist in determining whether and how to expand or modify current rules regarding the electronic distribution of benefit plan information, such as quarterly benefit statements, required to be disclosed under ERISA. The DOL's request for information set forth 30 specific questions on a broad range of topics related to electronic distribution of benefit plan information.

Pending further DOL action, current guidance on the use of electronic technologies for satisfying ERISA's disclosure requirements are based on DOL regulations finalized in April 2002. The rules establish a safe harbor method for furnishing all documents required to be furnished or made available under Title I of ERISA using electronic media. The disclosure requirements are generally deemed satisfied if all of the following conditions are met.

1. The administrator takes appropriate and necessary measures to ensure that the system for furnishing documents results in actual receipt by participants of transmitted information and documents (e.g., uses return receipt electronic mail feature or conducts periodic reviews or surveys to confirm receipt of transmitted information). In addition, with respect to disclosures that contain personal information, the administrator must take reasonable steps to protect confidentiality and avoid unauthorized receipt of or access to the information. Making information available at a kiosk does not satisfy this "actual receipt" requirement.
2. Electronically delivered documents are prepared and furnished in a manner consistent with ERISA's applicable style, format, and content requirements.
3. Each participant is provided notice, through electronic means or in writing, apprising the participant of the document(s) to be furnished electronically, the significance of the document (e.g., the document describes changes in the benefits provided by the plan), and the participant's rights to request and receive a paper copy of each such document.
4. Upon request of any participant, the administrator furnishes a paper copy of any document delivered to the participant through electronic media.

The furnishing of documents through electronic media satisfies the disclosure requirements only with respect to:

1. Participants who have the ability to effectively access documents furnished in electronic form at any location where they are reasonably expected to perform their duties as employees and with respect to whom access to the employer's electronic information system is an integral part of their duties; or
2. Participants, beneficiaries, or anyone entitled to receive documents under Title I of ERISA who consents to electronic receipt under the following conditions:
   - Consent is given or affirmed in a manner that reasonably demonstrates the individual's ability to access the electronic disclosure;
   - The individual provides an address for receipt of electronically furnished documents;
   - Prior to consenting, the individual is given a statement telling him or her the types of documents to which the consent would apply, that consent can be withdrawn at any time at no charge, the procedures for withdrawing consent and for updating the individual's e-mail address, the right to receive a paper version of the document, and any hardware or software requirements for accessing and retaining the documents; and
   - In the event of any changes to hardware or software requirements that create a material risk that the individual will no longer be able to access electronically furnished documents, he or she must be notified of the new requirements, given the right to withdraw consent at no charge and without the imposition of any consequence that was not disclosed at the time of the initial consent, and affirm consent.

[DOL Reg. § 2520.104b-1(c)]

See Qs 19:44 and 19:65 for additional DOL guidance applicable to participant benefit statements and participant investment and fee disclosures and Q 7:56 for additional guidance relating to QDIA notices.

Q 19:126 What standards apply to the use of electronic media for the maintenance and retention of records required by ERISA?

ERISA contains requirements for the maintenance of records for reporting and disclosure purposes and for determining the benefits to which participants and beneficiaries are or may become entitled. For example, certain records related to annual report filings must generally be maintained for at least six years after the filing date under ERISA Section 107. Records relating to the determination of benefits are subject to a more open-ended retention requirement under ERISA Section 209 (see Q 19:136). [ERISA §§ 107, 209]

The record maintenance and retention requirements of ERISA will be satisfied when using electronic media if the following is the case:

1. The electronic recordkeeping system has reasonable controls to ensure the integrity, accuracy, authenticity, and reliability of the records kept in electronic form;
2. The electronic records are maintained in reasonable order and in a safe and accessible place and in such manner as they may be readily inspected or examined (e.g., the recordkeeping system should be capable of indexing, retaining, preserving, retrieving, and reproducing the electronic records);
3. The electronic records are readily convertible into legible and readable paper copy as may be needed to satisfy reporting and disclosure requirements or any other obligation under Title I of ERISA;
4. The electronic recordkeeping system is not subject, in whole or in part, to any agreement or restriction that would, directly or indirectly, compromise or limit a person's ability to comply with any reporting and disclosure requirement or any other obligation under Title I of ERISA; and
5. Adequate records management practices are established and implemented—for example, following procedures for labeling of electronically maintained or retained records; providing a secure storage environment; creating backup electronic copies and selecting an off-site storage location; observing a quality assurance program evidenced by regular evaluations of the electronic recordkeeping system including periodic checks of electronically maintained or retained records; and retaining paper copies of records that cannot be clearly, accurately, or completely transferred to an electronic recordkeeping system.

All electronic records must exhibit a high degree of legibility and readability when displayed on a computer screen and when reproduced in paper form. Original paper records may be disposed of any time after they are transferred to an electronic recordkeeping system that complies with the above requirements, except such original records may not be discarded if an electronic reproduction would not constitute a duplicate record or substitute record under the terms of the plan and applicable state or federal law. [DOL Reg. § 2520.107-1]

Q 19:127 What standards apply to the use of electronic media for notices and consents required under the Internal Revenue Code?

On October 20, 2006, the IRS released final regulations that set forth standards for using an electronic medium (e.g., Web site, e-mail, telephonic system, magnetic disk, and CD-ROM) for Code-based notices and consents. The final regulations are applicable to notices, elections, and consents that must be written or in writing, which include:

- Section 402(f) notices (describing rollover rights) (see chapter 16);
- Section 411(a)(11) notices (describing a participant's benefit commencement rights) (see chapter 16);

- Spousal consents under Section 417(a)(2) (survivor annuity requirements) (see chapter 17); and
- Section 204(h) notices (notification of a significant reduction in the rate of future benefit accrual) (see chapter 9).

The rules, according to the IRS, reflect applicable provisions of the Electronic Signatures in Global and National Commerce Act, or E-SIGN. [Pub. L. No. 106-229, 114 Stat. 464 (2000)]

For any requirement under the Code or regulations that an employee benefit notice or election be in writing or in written form, the standards set forth in the regulations are generally the exclusive rules for providing such communication through the use of an electronic medium. For example, a retirement plan providing a Section 402(f) notice through the use of an electronic medium must satisfy the rules set forth in these regulations. Safe harbor notices (under Sections 401(k)(12)(D) and 401(m)(11)) can be provided electronically, for example, if the rules are met.

For any notice or election that is not required to be in writing or in written form, the standards set forth in these regulations function as a safe harbor. A retirement plan is permitted to satisfy either these regulations or any other applicable guidance issued by the IRS. For example, with respect to creating an electronic system to accept electronic transmissions of beneficiary designations (other than designations requiring spousal consent), a retirement plan is permitted to use the rules under these regulations or continue to follow the standards set forth in IRS Notice 99-1 [1999-2 I.R.B. 8], which is not affected by E-SIGN.

The regulations generally do not apply to any notice, election, consent, disclosure, or obligation required under the provisions of Title I or Title IV of ERISA over which the DOL or the Pension Benefit Guaranty Corporation (PBGC) has interpretative and enforcement authority. For example, the rules described in Q 19:125 apply with respect to ERISA-based disclosure documents, such as summary plan descriptions (SPDs) and summary annual reports (SARs). [71 Fed. Reg. 61,877 (Oct. 20, 2006); Treas. Reg. § 1.401(a)-21]

Q 19:128 To what types of retirement plans do the standards apply?

The final regulations apply to any notice or similar communication provided to or any election made by a participant or beneficiary in the following retirement plans:

- Section 401(a) plans;
- Section 403(a) plans;
- Section 403(b) plans;
- Simplified employee pension (SEP) plans under Section 408(k);
- Savings Incentive Match Plans for Employees (SIMPLEs) under Section 408(p);
- Eligible governmental plans under Section 457(b); and

- Individual retirement arrangements (IRAs), including Roth IRAs under Section 408A and deemed IRAs under Section 408(q).

[Treas. Reg. § 1.401(a)-21(a)(*1*)(i), (a)(2)(i) and (iii)]

Q 19:129 What general requirements must first be met in connection with using electronic media for Code-based notices, consents, and elections?

The following general requirements must first be met in connection with using electronic media for Code-based notices, consents, and elections:

- The specific rules for timing and content applicable to a particular notice and consent must be met (e.g., a safe harbor notice provided using an electronic medium must meet applicable timing and content requirements). It is therefore critical to consider the rules applicable to a particular notice in addition to these regulations.
- The electronic system must take into account the content of a notice. With respect to the content of an applicable notice, the electronic system must be reasonably designed to provide the information in the notice to a recipient in a manner that is no less understandable to the recipient than is a written document delivered on paper. For example, a plan delivering a lengthy Section 402(f) notice would not satisfy this requirement if the plan chose to provide the notice through a pre-recorded message on an automated phone system. However, a plan with few distribution options is permitted to provide a Section 411(a)(11) notice through the use of a pre-recorded message on an automated phone system.
- The regulations require that the electronic system be reasonably designed to alert the recipient, at the time the applicable notice is provided, to the significance of the information in the notice (including the identification of the subject matter of the notice), and to provide instructions needed to access the notice, in a manner that is as readily understandable.

An electronic record of an applicable notice or a participant election must be maintained in a form that is capable of being retained and accurately reproduced for later reference to preserve its legal effect, validity, and enforceability.

Q 19:130 What are the permissible methods of providing notices using electronic media?

The final regulations provide for two methods of notifying participants through the use of electronic media:

1. Notices may be provided to a recipient using an electronic medium after the recipient consents to electronic delivery (the "consumer consent method") (see Q 19:131); and
2. Notices may be provided using a method that does not require consent but does require electronic systems that satisfy certain standards (the "alternative method") (see Q 19:132).

[Treas. Reg. § 1.401(a)-21]

Q 19:131 What are the requirements for using the "consumer consent method"?

Under the "consumer consent method," the participant must consent to receive the communication electronically *before* an applicable notice is provided using an electronic medium. The consent generally must be:

1. Made electronically in a manner that reasonably demonstrates that the participant can access the notice in the electronic form that will be used to provide the notice; or
2. Made using a written paper document, but only if the participant confirms the consent in a manner that reasonably demonstrates that the participant can access the notice in the electronic form to be provided.

Prior to giving consent to receiving the communication electronically, the participant must receive a disclosure statement that outlines the following:

- The right to have the applicable notice in a written paper document or other non-electronic form.
- The scope of the consent (e.g., whether the consent applies to a particular transaction or will apply to all future notices);
- The participant's right to withdraw his or her consent to receive the communication electronically (and how the participant can obtain the communication using paper and any fees imposed for receiving communications on paper);
- The procedure to update information needed to contact the participant electronically;
- The hardware and software requirements needed to access and retain notices. (In the event the hardware or software requirements change, a participant must receive information regarding revised requirements and the right to withdraw consent without fees or consequences, and the participant must reaffirm his or her consent).

Under the consumer consent method, notices may not be provided orally or by means of a recording of an oral communication.

Example. Plan A, a qualified plan, permits participants to request benefit distributions from the plan on Plan A's Web site. Under Plan A's system for such transactions, a participant must enter his or her account number, personal identification number (PIN), and the e-mail address to which the notice is to be sent. The participant's PIN and account number must match the information in Plan A's records in order for the transaction to proceed.

Peter, a participant in Plan A, requests a distribution from the plan on Plan A's Web site. At the time of the request for distribution, a disclosure statement appears on the computer screen explaining that Peter can consent to receive the Section 402(f) notice electronically. The disclosure statement contains information relating to the consent, including how to request a paper copy of the notice, how to withdraw consent, the hardware and software requirements, and the procedures for accessing the Section 402(f) notice, which is in a file format from a specific spreadsheet program. After reviewing the disclosure statement, which satisfies the requirements in the final regulations, Peter consents to receive the Section 402(f) notice via e-mail by selecting the consent button at the end of the disclosure statement. As a part of the consent procedure, an e-mail is sent to Peter's e-mail address to ascertain and confirm that Peter can access the spreadsheet program. The e-mail prompts Peter to answer a question from the spreadsheet program, which is in the attachment to the e-mail. Once Peter has correctly answered the question, the Section 402(f) notice is delivered to Peter by e-mail.

Assuming the general requirements in Q 19:129 are met, Plan A's delivery of the Section 402(f) notice to Peter satisfies the requirements of the consumer consent method.

Q 19:132 What are the requirements of the "alternative method" of providing notices using electronic media?

Under the alternative method, at the time the applicable notice is provided, the participant must be advised that he or she may request that the notice be sent in writing on paper at no charge. In addition, any recipient of the notice must be "effectively able" to access the electronic medium used to provide the notice.

Example 1. Plan B permits participants to request benefit distributions from the plan on the plan's Web site. Under Plan B's system for such transactions, a participant must enter his or her account number and PIN and the e-mail address to which the notice is to be sent. The participant's PIN and account number must match the information in Plan B's records in order for the transaction to proceed. Kelly, an unmarried employee, requests a distribution from the plan on Plan B's Web site. The plan administrator sends Kelly a Section 411(a)(11) notice as an attachment to an e-mail. The e-mail is sent with a request for a computer-generated notification that the message was received and opened. The e-mail instructs Kelly to read the attachment for important information regarding the request for a distribution. In addition, the e-mail states that Kelly may request the Section 411(a)(11) notice be sent on paper, and that if Kelly requests the notice as a written paper document, it will be provided at no charge. Plan B receives notification that the e-mail was received and opened by Kelly.

Plan B requires a participant to enter his or her account number and PIN in order to preclude any person other than the participant from making the election to receive a distribution from the plan. After the authentication process, Kelly completes a distribution request form on the Web site. After the request form is completed, the Web site generates a summary of the information entered on the form and gives Kelly an opportunity to review or modify the distribution request form before the transaction is completed.

Within a reasonable period of time after Kelly consents to the distribution, the plan administrator, by e-mail, sends confirmation of the terms (including the form) of the distribution to Kelly and advises her that, upon request, the confirmation may be provided on a written paper document at no charge.

Plan B retains an electronic copy of the consent to the distribution in a form that is capable of being retained and accurately reproduced for later reference by Kelly.

Plan B's delivery of the Section 411(a)(11) notice and the electronic system used to make Kelly's consent to a distribution satisfy the requirements of the final regulations.

Example 2. Plan D, a qualified profit-sharing plan, permits participants to request distributions through an automated telephone system. Under Plan D's system for such transactions, a participant must enter his or her account number and PIN, and this information must match the information in Plan D's records for the transaction to proceed. Plan D provides only two distribution options—a single-sum payment or annual installments made over 5, 10, or 20 years. Nick, an unmarried participant, requests a distribution from Plan D by following the applicable instructions on the automated telephone system. After Nick has requested the distribution, the automated telephone system recites the Section 411(a)(11) notice over the phone. The automated telephone system also advises Nick that, upon request, the notice may be provided on paper and that, if Nick so requests, the notice will be provided as a written paper document at no charge.

Plan D requires a participant to enter his or her account number and PIN in order to preclude any person other than the participant from making the election. Nick requests a distribution by entering information on the automated telephone system. After completing the request, the automated telephone system provides an oral summary of the information entered and gives Nick the opportunity to review or modify the distribution request before the transaction is completed. Plan D's automated telephone system confirms the distribution request to Nick and advises him that, upon request, he may receive the confirmation on a written paper document at no charge. Plan D retains an electronic copy of the consent to the distribution request in a form that is capable of being retained and accurately reproduced for later reference by Nick.

Because Plan D has relatively few and simple distribution options, the provision of the Section 411(a)(11) notice through the automated telephone system is not less understandable to the participant than is a written paper notice for purposes of paragraph (a)(5)(i) of Treasury Regulations Section 411. In addition, Plan D's automated telephone procedures satisfy the applicable requirements in the final regulations.

Example 3. The facts are the same as those in Example 2, except that pursuant to Plan D's system for processing such transactions, a participant who so requests is transferred to a customer service representative whose conversation with the participant is recorded. The customer service representative reads the Section 411(a)(11) notice from a prepared script and processes the participant's distribution in accordance with the predetermined instructions from the plan administrator.

In Example 3, as in Example 2, because Plan D has relatively few and simple distribution options, the Section 411(a)(11) notice provided through the automated telephone system is not less understandable to the participant than is a written paper notice. Plan D's customer service telephone procedures satisfy the requirements in the final regulations.

Q 19:133 What requirements apply with respect to a participant consent or election made using an electronic system?

The following requirements apply with respect to participant elections made using an electronic system:

1. The participant be "effectively able" to access the electronic medium in order to make the participant election.
2. The electronic system be reasonably designed to preclude any person other than the appropriate individual from making a participant election.
3. The electronic system provides the participant making a participant election with a reasonable opportunity to review, confirm, modify, or rescind the terms of the election before it becomes effective.
4. The individual making a participant election, within a reasonable time period, receives a confirmation of the election either via a written paper document or via an electronic medium under a system that satisfies the applicable notice requirements of either the "consumer consent method" or the "alternative method."

The regulations require that a plan participant be effectively able to access the electronic medium under an electronic system used to make a participant election, but do not require that a plan also permit the election to be made by paper as an alternative to using an electronic system that is available to the participant.

The regulations do not apply with respect to a participant who is not effectively able to access the electronic medium to make a participant election. Accordingly, the plan must offer each such participant the right to make an election using another medium that is accessible to the participant (such as making the election on paper). A plan that fails to offer paper or an electronic medium that a participant is effectively able to access will fail to comply with the participant-election requirements and would likely violate other qualification requirements, such as the requirements that a plan operate in accordance with its terms (by actually making available all distribution options provided by the plan) and the requirements that benefits, rights, and features (including the right to early distribution) must be made available in a nondiscriminatory manner.

Example. Plan E permits participants to request distributions by e-mail on the employer's e-mail system. Under this system, a participant must enter his or her account number, PIN, and e-mail address. The information must match that in Plan E's records for the transaction to proceed. If a participant e-mails the request for a distribution, the plan administrator provides the participant with a Section 411(a)(11) notice by e-mail. The plan administrator also advises the participant by e-mail that he or she may request the Section 411(a)(11) notice as a written paper document, and that, if a written paper document is requested, it will be provided at no charge.

David, a participant in Plan Q, e-mails his request for a distribution and receives the Section 411(a)(11) notice from the plan administrator by reply e-mail. However, David terminates employment with the company before he requests the distribution. Following termination of employment, David no longer has access to his employer's e-mail system.

Plan E does not satisfy the participant election requirements because David is not effectively able to access the electronic medium used to make the participant election. Plan E must provide David with the opportunity to make the participant election through a written paper document or another system that David is effectively able to access, such as an automated telephone system.

See Q 19:132 for other examples.

Q 19:134 Can an electronic medium be used in connection with spousal waivers or other elections and consents required to be witnessed by a plan representative or notary public?

Prior regulations did not permit the use of electronic media for communicating notices or consents that involve signatures that must be witnessed by a plan representative or notary public (e.g., spousal consents in plans that are subject to survivor annuity requirements). (See chapter 17.) The current regulations extend the use of electronic media to the notice and election rules applicable to plans that are subject to the survivor annuity requirements of Code Section 417.

A plan that is subject to the survivor annuity requirements is permitted to use electronic media to provide the notice required by Section 417 to a participant as long as the plan complies with either the "consumer consent method" or the "alternative method" for providing electronic notices described above (see Q 19:130).

With respect to the requirement that participant elections, including spousal consents, be witnessed by a plan representative or a notary public, the regulations provide that:

1. The signature of the individual making the participant election must be witnessed in the physical presence of a plan representative or a notary public.
2. An electronic notarization acknowledging a signature (in accordance with Section 101(g) of E-SIGN and state law applicable to notary publics) will not be denied legal effect if the signature of the individual is witnessed in the physical presence of a notary public.

The regulations did not adopt the suggestion that spousal PINs be permitted in lieu of the physical presence requirement. Because of the potential risk that two spouses could share information regarding PINs, any electronic system that relies solely on separate PINs would not, according to the final regulations, provide the same level of safeguards as provided by the physical presence requirement and would not be reasonably designed to preclude any person other than the appropriate individual from making the election.

It was noted in the final regulations that technology could exist that would provide the same safeguards as the physical presence requirement. In light of that possibility, the IRS may provide that the use of procedures under an electronic system can satisfy the physical presence requirement, but only if those procedures with respect to the electronic system provide the same safeguards for participant elections as those provided through the physical presence requirement.

> **Example.** Plan C, a qualified money purchase pension plan, permits a married participant to request a plan loan through the plan's Web site with the notarized consent of the spouse. Under Plan C's system for requesting a plan loan, a participant must enter his or her account number, PIN, and his or her e-mail address. The information entered by the participant must match the information in Plan C's records for the transaction to proceed. Martha, a married participant, is effectively able to access Plan C's Web site to apply for a plan loan.
>
> Plan C requires a participant to enter his or her account number and PIN in order to preclude any person other than the participant from making the election. Martha completes the loan application on Plan C's Web site. Within a reasonable period of time after submitting the plan loan application, the plan administrator, by e-mail, sends Martha the loan application, including all attachments setting forth the terms of the loan agreement and all other required information. In the e-mail, the plan administrator also notifies Martha that, upon request, the loan application may be sent to her as a paper document at no charge.
>
> Plan C then instructs Martha that, in order for the loan application to be processed, Martha must submit to the plan administrator a notarized spousal consent form. Martha and her spouse, Robert, seek out a notary public, and the notary witnesses Robert's signing of the spousal consent for the loan agreement on an electronic signature capture pad with adequate security. After witnessing Robert's signing the spousal consent, the notary public sends an e-mail to the plan administrator with an electronic acknowledgment that is attached to or logically associated with Robert's signature. The electronic acknowledgment is in accordance with Section 101(g) of E-SIGN and the relevant state law applicable to notary publics.
>
> After the plan administrator receives the e-mail, he or she sends an e-mail to Martha, giving her a reasonable period to review and confirm the completed loan application and to determine whether the loan application should be modified or rescinded. In addition, the e-mail notifies Martha that she may request the completed loan application as a written paper document, and that, if Martha so requests, the written paper document will be provided at no

charge. Plan C retains an electronic copy of the loan agreement, including the spousal consent, in a form that is capable of being retained and accurately reproduced for later reference by all parties.

By requiring that the participant's spouse sign the spousal consent on an electronic signature capture pad in the physical presence of a notary public, the electronic system satisfies the requirement that the system be reasonably designed to preclude any person other than the appropriate individual from making the election and satisfies the requirements under the final regulation.

Q 19:135 What is the effective date of the final regulations applicable to Code-based notices and consents in the electronic context?

The final regulations became effective on October 20, 2006, and generally apply to applicable notices provided, and participant elections made, on or after January 1, 2007.

Record Retention Under ERISA

Q 19:136 How long must records be retained under ERISA?

Reporting and disclosure records are generally subject to the six-year retention requirement of ERISA Section 107. Such records would include forms filed with government agencies (e.g., Form 5500 filings, participant benefits statements, and other documents).

Records relating to the determination of benefits are subject to a more open-ended retention requirement under ERISA Section 209. Those must be maintained with respect to each employee sufficient to determine the benefits due, or which may become due, to him or her. These records could include plan/trust documents, payroll and other employment-related records, distribution forms and notices, and other documents. [ERISA §§ 107, 209]

Chapter 20

Correcting 401(k) Plan Qualification Errors

The size of this publication is an indication of how complicated it is to properly set up and administer a 401(k) plan. Even well-intentioned plan sponsors with good advisers can make inadvertent errors that could result in plan disqualification. The Internal Revenue Service (IRS) has, over the years, introduced a variety of programs designed to promote compliance without resorting to the sanction of disqualification. These programs have been consolidated into the Employee Plans Compliance Resolution System (EPCRS).

Employee Plans Compliance Resolution System 20-2
Table 20-1. Comparison of Programs Under EPCRS 20-4
Self-Correction Program 20-7
Flowchart 20-1. Eligibility for the Self-Correction Program (SCP)—Qualified Plans and 403(b) Plans 20-8
Voluntary Correction Program 20-11
Audit Closing Agreement Program 20-13

Q 20:1 What is the impact of plan disqualification?

The IRS, from its perspective, wants to promote full compliance with all its rules and regulations. The primary tool that it has for accomplishing this is the threat of plan disqualification, which results in loss of the employer's deduction for any contributions to the plan, taxation of trust income, and taxation of individual participants for contributions made on their behalf. The consequences of disqualifying a plan are both serious and far-reaching in that the tax bite is felt not only by the plan sponsor and key personnel, who may have been involved in the error that caused the disqualification, but also by rank-and-file employees who participate in the plan. Perhaps for that reason, the IRS has typically disqualified few plans.

Employee Plans Compliance Resolution System

Q 20:2 What is the *Employee Plans Compliance Resolution System*?

Beginning in 1991, the IRS started introducing various programs designed to promote full compliance while using sanctions that fall short of the full tax impact of plan disqualification. These programs have now been consolidated and are referred to as the Employee Plans Compliance Resolution System (EPCRS). [Rev. Proc. 2013-12, 2013-4 I.R.B. 313]

Section 1101 of the Pension Protection Act of 2006 [Pub. L. No. 109-280, 120 Stat. 780] (PPA) formally authorizes the Treasury Department to establish and implement EPCRS and any other employee plan correction policies, including the authority to waive income, excise, and other taxes and to ensure that taxes, penalties, and sanctions are not excessive and bear a reasonable relationship to a particular failure.

Q 20:3 What programs does the IRS offer under EPCRS to avoid plan disqualification?

Under EPCRS, three IRS programs are available for solving plan qualification defects. They are:

1. Self-Correction Program (SCP);
2. Voluntary Correction Program (VCP); and
3. Audit Closing Agreement Program (Audit CAP).

[Rev. Proc. 2013-12, § 1.03, 2013-4 I.R.B. 313]

Q 20:4 What common features apply to all programs under EPCRS?

Common to all the programs under EPCRS is that a qualification failure is not considered corrected unless full correction is made with respect to all participants and beneficiaries and for all taxable years, including taxable years that are closed. See Table 20-1 for a comparison of the three programs under EPCRS. [Rev. Proc. 2013-12, § 6.02, 2013-4 I.R.B. 313]

Q 20:5 What principles are taken into account in determining whether full correction is accomplished?

In determining whether full correction is accomplished, a plan must use a correction method that is reasonable and appropriate and that restores the plan to the position that it would have been in had the qualification failure not occurred. Restoring the plan to this position also means the restoration of current and former participants and beneficiaries to the benefits and rights they would have had if the qualification failure had not occurred. [Rev. Proc. 2013-12, § 6.02(1) and (2), 2013-4 I.R.B. 313]

Q 20:6 Is there only one reasonable and appropriate correction method for a qualification failure?

No, there may be more than one such method. Whether a particular correction method is reasonable and appropriate should be determined taking into account relevant facts and circumstances and the following principles:

1. The correction method should, to the extent possible, resemble one already provided for in the Internal Revenue Code (Code).
2. The correction method for a qualification failure relating to nondiscrimination should provide benefits to non-highly compensated employees (NHCEs).
3. The correction method should keep assets in the plan except to the extent the law permits corrective distributions to participants or beneficiaries or the return of assets to the employer.
4. The correction method should not violate any other qualification requirement.

[Rev. Proc. 2013-12, § 6.02(2), 2013-4 I.R.B. 313]

Q 20:7 What principles apply in determining corrective allocations and distributions?

The following principles apply in determining corrective allocations and distributions:

1. Corrective allocations should be based on the terms of the plan in effect at the time of failure and should be adjusted for earnings (or losses) and forfeitures that would have been allocated but for the failure. Adjustments for losses are not required, however.
2. A corrective allocation of contributions, forfeitures, or both because of a failure to make a required allocation in a prior limitation year is considered a Code Section 415 annual addition for the limitation year to which the corrective allocation relates.
3. Corrective allocations should come from employer nonelective contributions but may come from forfeitures if the plan permits the use of forfeitures to reduce employer contributions. However, for the purpose of correcting failed ADP and ACP tests, the corrective contribution must satisfy the definition of a qualified nonelective contribution in Treasury Regulations Section 1.401(k)-6.
4. The corrective contribution or distribution should be adjusted for earnings or losses from the date of the failure and not from any later date that would otherwise be permitted under the Code.

Table 20-1. Comparison of Programs Under EPCRS

Feature	*SCP*	*VCP*	*Audit CAP*
Defects subject to correction	Program I: Self-identified significant but nonegregious operational defects within last two years if plan has IRS letter Program II: Insignificant defects found by IRS or employer (meeting most of seven factors)	Self-identified operational, form, demographic, or employer eligibility defects	Operational, form, demographic, or employer eligibility defects found by IRS
Available for operational defects that relate to the diversion or misuse of plan assets?	No	No	No
Available once an IRS audit has commenced?	Yes, but only under Program II	No	Yes
Policies and procedures in effect prior to the defects occurring?	Yes	No	No

Correction	For all years make plan and participants whole; document correction but do not report to IRS	For all years make plan and participants whole (in a way subject to negotiation) within 150 days of compliance letter	For all years make plan and participants whole as required by IRS
Correction by retroactive amendment?	Yes, but only with respect to hardship withdrawals, premature entry into plan, Code Section 401(a)(17) violations, and participant loans	Yes	Yes
Results in	IRS can second-guess correction on examination	Written compliance statement from IRS	Written closing agreement with IRS
Fee or sanction	None	Sanction based on Rev. Proc. 2013-12 table	Negotiated sanction based on deduction for contributions, tax on trust, employee tax on vested contributions, and mitigating factors
Variation	N/A	Special procedures for anonymous and group submissions	N/A

5. Earnings, in the case of a participant who has not made any investment choices, are based on the return of the plan as a whole. For a participant who has made investment choices, earnings are based on the investment return generated by that participant's choices. In either case, if most of the affected participants are NHCEs, the rate of return of the fund with the highest earnings rate may be selected. The plan is not required to adjust corrective contributions for losses. The DOL calculator, which is used to determine interest on employee contributions and loan payments that are not remitted to a 401(k) plan on a timely basis, can be used to determine earnings only if it is not feasible to make a reasonable estimate of what the actual investment results would have been.

[Rev. Proc. 2013-12, § 6.02(4) and (5); Appendix B, § 3.01(3), 2013-4 I.R.B. 313]

Q 20:8 Are there any exceptions to full correction?

In general, no. The inconvenience and burden of full correction are generally insufficient to relieve the employer of its responsibility to fully correct qualification failures. But full correction may not be required in certain situations because it is unreasonable and not feasible. Such situations include the following:

1. Reasonable estimates of benefits are allowed if it is not possible to make a precise calculation or if the probable difference between the approximate and precise amount of benefits is insignificant and the administrative cost of determining the precise amount of benefits would significantly exceed that difference.
2. Corrective distribution of benefits of $75 or less is not required if the cost of processing and delivering the distribution exceeds the amount of the distribution.
3. Corrective distributions are not required if the participant or beneficiary cannot be located after reasonable actions have been taken to locate him or her. If using certified mail to an individual's last known address is not successful, one or more additional search methods, depending on the facts and circumstances, should be used, including a commercial locator service, a credit reporting agency, or Internet search tools. The Social Security Letter Forwarding Service that also could be used for locating missing participants and beneficiaries was discontinued on May 19, 2014.
4. The employer is not required to seek the return of an overpayment to a participant or beneficiary if the overpayment is $100 or less. In addition, the employer is not required to notify the participant or beneficiary that the overpayment is not eligible for rollover.
5. The employer is not required to distribute or forfeit an excess amount (e.g., an excess contribution resulting from a failed ADP test) with respect to a participant if the excess amount is $100 or less. However, if the excess amount exceeds a statutory limit (e.g., the Code Section 402(g) limit on elective deferrals), and the excess amount is distributed, the employer must notify the participant or beneficiary that the distribution is not eligible for rollover.

[Rev. Proc. 2013-12, § 6.02(5), 2013-4 I.R.B. 313]

Q 20:9 Has the IRS prescribed any standard correction methods for common operational errors?

Yes. In Appendices A and B of Revenue Procedure 2013-12 [2013-4 I.R.B. 313], the IRS has prescribed methods for correcting typical operational errors. Although these methods are not intended to be the exclusive methods for correcting these errors, a plan that utilizes any of these methods to correct an operational error will have assurance that the corrections will be acceptable to the IRS.

Q 20:10 Has the IRS provided any other guidance regarding the correction of qualification errors?

Additional information regarding the identification of common qualification errors and their correction can be found on the IRS Web site at *www.irs.gov/Retirement-Plans/Plan-Sponsor/Fixing-Common-Plan-Mistakes*. The IRS also periodically provides in its newsletters informal guidance regarding the correction of errors, recent examples of which dealt with the correction of compensation errors (see Vol. 8, Summer 2011 newsletter) and failures to allocate forfeitures (see Vol. 7, Spring 2010 newsletter). In 2015, the IRS issued two revenue procedures modifying EPCRS. Revenue Procedure 2015-27 [2015-16 I.R.B. 914] made a number of modifications to EPCRS, the most important of which clarified that employers can pursue corrective measures other than recoupment from participants in the event of benefit overpayments. Revenue Procedure 2015-28 [2015-16 I.R.B. 920] provides a new set of corrective contributions if an employer fails to implement participant deferral elections, whether affirmative or pursuant to an automatic contribution arrangement, or it fails to make the 401(k) plan available to an employee who is eligible to participate. See Appendix M for a chart showing methods for correcting missed deferrals. For errors not involving plan qualification, see *http://www.dol.gov/ebsa/compliance_assistance.html* at the DOL Web site and the discussion in chapter 5 of this edition.

Self-Correction Program

Q 20:11 What qualification defects are covered by SCP?

SCP is designed to cover qualification defects that arise from the failure to operate a plan in accordance with its terms. SCP is not available to cure qualification issues arising from defects in the plan document (e.g., a failure to amend for the Economic Growth and Tax Relief Reconciliation Act of 2001, Pub. L. No. 107-16, 115 Stat. 38 (2001)). It is also not available for qualification issues that arise because of a shift in demographics (e.g., a problem with the minimum coverage rules under Code Section 410(b)). Finally, SCP cannot be used to correct operational failures that are egregious or that relate to the diversion of assets. [Rev. Proc. 2013-12, § 4, 2013-4 I.R.B.313] A flowchart showing whether an operational error is eligible for SCP appears on page 20-8.

Flowchart 20-1. Eligibility for the Self-Correction Program (SCP)—Qualified Plans and 403(b) Plans

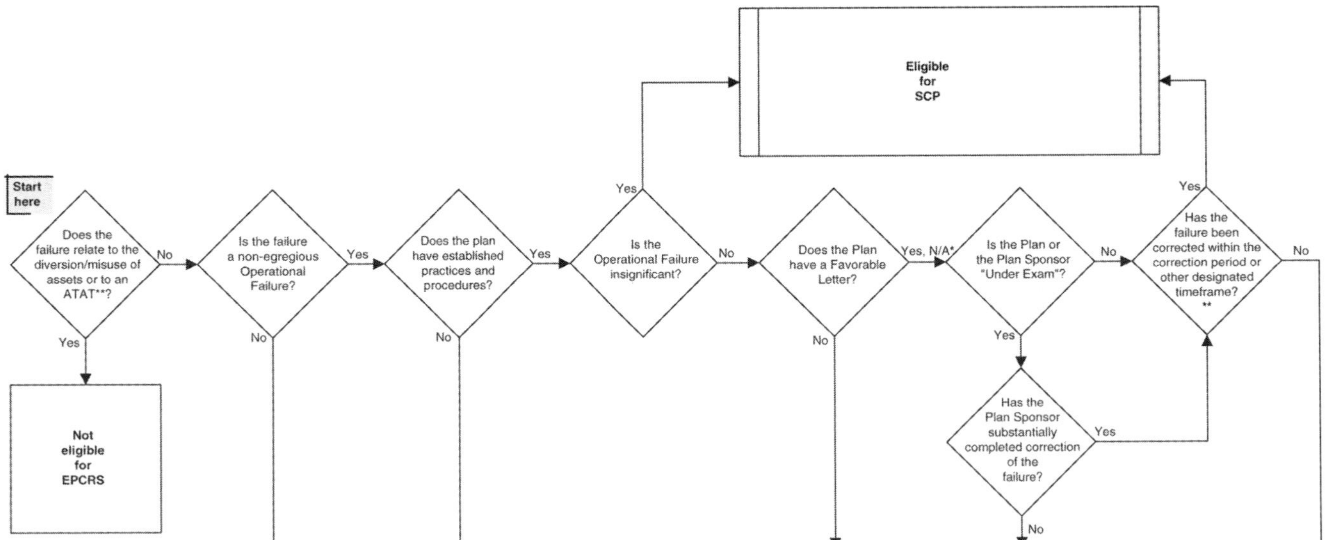

* **N/A** - Plan Document Failures are not applicable to 403(b) Plans.

** In the event that the plan or the plan sponsor has been a party to an Abusive Tax Avoidance Transaction (ATAT), SCP is not available to correct any Operational Failure that is directly or indirectly related to the ATAT.

** Other timeframes apply if failures have been substantially corrected - refer to section 9.02.

Q 20:12 Is there a deadline for correcting operational defects under SCP?

It depends. For failures that are considered significant the operational defect must generally be corrected by the end of the second plan year following the plan year in which the defect arose. Significant operational defects relating to assets transferred to a plan in connection with a merger or acquisition can be corrected up to the last day of the plan year following the plan year in which the merger or acquisition occurs. Failures treated as insignificant can be corrected after these deadlines. [Rev. Proc. 2013-12, §§ 8.01 and 9.02, 2013-4 I.R.B. 313]

Example. ABC Company sponsors a 401(k) plan with a plan year ending December 31. For the plan year ending December 31, 2015, ABC Company does not make the top-heavy minimum contribution it is required to make. In addition, the plan fails to satisfy the actual deferral percentage (ADP) test (see chapter 13). These failures are discovered in March 2017. Assuming ABC Company otherwise satisfies the eligibility requirements for SCP, it has until the end of 2017 to correct the missing top-heavy minimum contribution. Correction of the failed ADP test could wait until December 31, 2018, as the two-year correction period is considered to begin one year after the plan year of failure.

Section 1101 of the Pension Protection Act of 2006 directed the IRS to consider extending the period for self-correcting significant operational defects.

Q 20:13 What factors are considered in determining whether or not an operational failure is insignificant?

The factors to be considered include but are not limited to the following:

1. Whether other failures occurred during the period being examined;
2. The percentage of plan assets and contributions involved in the failure;
3. The number of years the failure occurred;
4. The number of participants affected versus the total number of participants;
5. The number of participants affected versus the total number of participants that could have been affected;
6. Whether correction was made within a reasonable time after the failure's discovery; and
7. The reason for the failure.

If the plan has more than one operational error in a single plan year or operational failures that occur in more than one plan year, the errors will be considered insignificant only if they are insignificant in the aggregate. [Rev. Proc. 2013-12, §§ 8.02, 8.03, 2013-4 I.R.B. 313]

Q 20:14 Must a plan have a favorable IRS letter in order to take advantage of SCP?

Yes. In order to correct significant operational failures (but not insignificant failures) the plan must have a favorable IRS letter. A favorable IRS letter is, in the case of an individually designed plan, a current favorable determination letter. Adopters of master or prototype plans and volume submitter plans will be considered to have favorable letters if the sponsors of these plans have received current favorable opinion or advisory letters. [Rev. Proc. 2013-12, § 4.03, 2013-4 I.R.B. 313]

Q 20:15 Is there any other condition that must be met before SCP can be used to correct an operational failure?

Yes. Prior to the defect, the plan must have had established practices and procedures (whether formal or informal) that were reasonably designed to promote and facilitate overall compliance but, because of an oversight or mistake in applying them or because of their inadequacy, operational violations occurred. [Rev. Proc. 2013-12, § 4.04, 2013-4 I.R.B. 313]

Q 20:16 Is SCP available if the plan is being audited by the IRS?

It is available but, in general, SCP can be used only to correct insignificant operational failures if the plan is being audited by the IRS. [Rev. Proc. 2013-12, § 4.02, 2013-4 I.R.B. 313]

Q 20:17 What procedures are used to take advantage of SCP?

Except for insignificant defects that are detected during an IRS audit, SCP is designed to be initiated by a plan sponsor or plan administrator, without IRS involvement, with respect to any plan eligible for SCP. [Rev. Proc. 2013-12, § 7, 2013-4 I.R.B. 313]

Q 20:18 What is the cost of using SCP?

No sanctions or penalties are payable to the IRS in connection with use of SCP. The only cost to the plan sponsor is the cost of correcting the defect.

Q 20:19 Can an operational error be corrected under SCP by retroactively amending the plan to conform its operation to the plan document as amended?

Under four limited circumstances, a retroactive amendment is permitted. First, a 401(k) plan that made a hardship distribution at a time when such distributions were not available under the terms of the plan can be amended retroactively to add the hardship withdrawal provision. Second, a plan's minimum age and service or entry date requirements can be retroactively amended to reflect the inclusion of an employee who was not eligible to participate under the plan's pre-amendment provisions. Third, a plan can be amended to provide for additional contributions if, in determining contributions, the plan took into account compensation in excess of the Code Section 401(a)(17) limit. Fourth, a plan that made a participant loan at a time when such loans were not available under the plan can be retroactively amended to add a loan provision. As a condition to using a retroactive amendment under these circumstances, the amendment is required to be submitted to the IRS for its approval unless the amendment is achieved through the adoption of an IRS-approved master/prototype or volume submitter plan. [Rev. Proc. 2013-12, §§ 4.05(2), 6.05(1), 2013-4 I.R.B. 313]

Voluntary Correction Program

Q 20:20 What qualification defects are covered by VCP?

VCP is designed to cover all types of qualification defects: operational, plan document, demographic, and employer eligibility (see Q 20:11). It is not available, however, to cure any violations of the exclusive benefit rule (e.g., misuse or diversion of plan assets). [Rev. Proc. 2013-12, § 4.01(2), 2013-4 I.R.B. 313]

Q 20:21 Is there a deadline for correcting defects under VCP?

No, there is no deadline. However, VCP is not available if the plan is being audited by the IRS. [Rev. Proc. 2013-12, § 4.02, 2013-4 I.R.B. 313]

Q 20:22 Must a plan have a favorable IRS letter in order to take advantage of VCP?

No. A favorable IRS letter is not required to take advantage of VCP. [Rev. Proc. 2013-12, § 4.03, 2013-4 I.R.B. 313]

Q 20:23 Must a plan have established practices and procedures in effect in order to utilize VCP?

No. In this respect it differs from SCP. [Rev. Proc. 2013-12, § 4.04, 2013-4 I.R.B. 313]

Q 20:24 Can operational errors be corrected under VCP by retroactively amending the plan to conform its operation to the plan document as amended?

Under VCP a plan sponsor may correct an operational failure by a plan amendment to conform the terms of the plan to the plan's prior operations. As part of the VCP process, the plan sponsor must apply for a determination letter on the retroactive amendment unless the amendment is achieved through the adoption of an IRS-approved master/prototype or volume submitted plan. [Rev. Proc. 2013-12, §§ 4.05(1), 6.05(1), 2013-4 I.R.B. 313] The determination letter requirement, however, does not apply to VCP submissions relating to the failure of a plan to timely adopt good-faith, interim amendments (e.g., an amendment to update the plan for the new final 415 regulations) as provided in Section 5 of Revenue Procedure 2007-44 [2007-28 I.R.B. 54]. (See Q 20:27.) [Rev. Proc. 2013-12, § 6.05(3), 2013-4 I.R.B. 313]

Q 20:25 Are there other specialized procedures under VCP?

Yes. The IRS has established a procedure called the Anonymous Submission Procedure that permits any failure to be addressed without identifying the plan or its sponsor. [Rev. Proc. 2013-12, § 10.10, 2013-4 I.R.B. 313]

The IRS has also established a procedure for group submissions. This procedure enables an eligible organization to address systemic operational and plan document errors that affect at least 20 client plans. An eligible organization includes a sponsor of a prototype plan or an organization that provides administrative services with respect to qualified plans. [Rev. Proc. 2013-12, § 10.11, 2013-4 I.R.B. 313]

Q 20:26 What procedures are used to take advantage of VCP?

The plan sponsor initiates the program by preparing an application to the IRS that contains all the information described in Section 11 of Revenue Procedure 2013-12. [2013-4 I.R.B. 313] Essentially, the plan sponsor must describe the defect and the correction and explain why the problem will not recur.

The IRS will respond to a VCP application with a compliance statement that addresses the failure and the terms of its correction and that contains the IRS's agreement not to disqualify the plan on account of the failure described in the compliance statement. Within 30 days after the statement is issued, a plan sponsor that agrees with the statement must send a signed acknowledgment letter to the IRS. If this acknowledgment is made, the plan sponsor has 150 days after the issuance of the compliance statement to correct the failure. [Rev. Proc. 2013-12, § 10, 2013-4 I.R.B. 313]

Q 20:27 What is the cost of using VCP?

The VCP fee is determined in accordance with the table below. The table contains a graduated range of fees based on the number of participants in the plan. [Rev. Proc. 2013-12, § 12, 2013-4 I.R.B. 313]

Number of Participants	*Amount*
20 or fewer	$ 750
21–50	$1,000
51–100	$2,500

Number of Participants	*Amount*
101–500	$ 5,000
501–1,000	$ 8,000
1,001–5,000	$15,000
5,001–10,000	$20,000
Over 10,000	$25,000

If a VCP submission involves only the failure to satisfy the minimum distribution rules, and the failure involves 50 or fewer participants, then the schedule above does not apply, and the VCP fee is limited to $500. If a VCP submission only involves a limited failure to satisfy loan limitation requirements under Code Section 72(p)(2), the VCP fee is reduced by 50 percent. Plans that are not timely amended for changes in the laws and regulations are generally subject to the schedule above; however, the VCP fee is reduced by 50 percent if the VCP submission occurs no later than one year after the expiration of the remedial amendment period for complying with those changes. Finally, the schedule does not apply to plans that do not timely adopt good-faith, interim amendments as provided in Section 5 of Revenue Procedure 2007-44 [2007-28 I.R.B. 54]. [Rev. Proc. 2013-12, §§ 12.02(2), 12.03, 2013-4 I.R.B. 313] In that case the fee is $375.

In addition to paying these fees, the plan sponsor must fully correct all qualification defects for all years in which the disclosed defects occurred, including years prior to the three-year period the IRS has to disqualify a plan under the statute of limitations.

Under certain circumstances, the IRS will provide relief from excise taxes that result from particular operational errors. The excise taxes that may be abated include those relating to a failure to satisfy the Section 401(a)(9) minimum distribution rules and to make timely distributions of excess contributions and excess aggregate contributions, as well as excise taxes that might arise on account of a corrective contribution that is not deductible by the employer. However, there is no relief from ERISA's Title I fiduciary conduct provisions. These factors must be considered in reviewing the decision to use VCP and in analyzing the costs involved. [Rev. Proc. 2013-12, § 6.09, 2013-4 I.R.B. 313]

Audit Closing Agreement Program

Q 20:28 Under what circumstances will Audit CAP be used?

Audit CAP is available to a plan sponsor if the qualification defect (other than an insignificant operational error that can be handled through SCP) is discovered by the IRS during an audit. All defects that may be corrected under VCP (see Q 20:20) may be corrected under Audit CAP. If the plan sponsor corrects the qualification failures identified by the IRS, pays a sanction, and enters into a closing agreement with the IRS, then the IRS will not disqualify the plan on account of the failures. [Rev. Proc. 2013-12, § 13, 2013-4 I.R.B. 313]

Q 20:29 How is the amount of the Audit CAP sanction determined?

The amount of the sanction is a negotiated percentage of the full amount of the tax liability that would be due the IRS if the plan were disqualified for the years open under the statute of limitations (known as the *maximum payment amount*). In other words, it will include taxes based on the loss of the employer's deduction for plan contributions, taxes on trust earnings, taxes on individual employees for inclusion of plan contributions in their taxable compensation, and any penalties and interest that would accrue on any of these amounts. The negotiated percentage is required to bear a reasonable relationship to the nature, extent, and severity of the failures and must not be excessive. Section 14.02 of Revenue Procedure 2013-12 [2013-4 I.R.B. 313] cites examples of the factors that will be taken into account in arriving at the negotiated percentage.

Chapter 21

Plan Terminations, Mergers, Spinoffs, and Abandoned Plans

An employer may wish to terminate its 401(k) plan for a number of reasons, including the closing or selling of a business, a change in goals for the employer's benefit programs, or the establishment of a new plan. An employer may also wish to consolidate its plans, combine its plan with that of another employer, or divide a single plan into separate plans for subsidiaries or divisions. This chapter discusses how to accomplish those goals. It also discusses when an involuntary or partial termination of a plan will be considered to have occurred. Plan considerations in the context of major business transactions, such as mergers and acquisitions, and issues involving abandoned plans conclude the chapter.

Plan Terminations 21-1
Missing Participants 21-4
Partial Termination 21-8
Mergers and Spinoffs 21-10
Plan Considerations During Major Business Transactions 21-14
Abandoned Plans 21-17

Plan Terminations

Q 21:1 How is an employer's ability to terminate a 401(k) plan restricted?

Employers are generally free to terminate a 401(k) plan at any time, and the authority to terminate a plan is usually incorporated into the plan document. The only restriction on this freedom is the rule requiring a plan to be a permanent, not a temporary, program (see chapter 2). Under this rule, if a plan is terminated for any reason other than business necessity within a few years after it has taken effect, it may not be considered a qualified plan. [Treas. Reg. § 1.401-1(b)(2)] The regulation does not specify what constitutes a few years.

Q 21:2 How does an employer terminate its 401(k) plan?

Termination of a plan is generally done through corporate resolution or other similar authorization adopting an amendment to terminate the plan consistent with plan language addressing plan termination. In a 401(k) plan, there is no general requirement that participants be notified in advance of the termination, although employees may view the change more favorably if they are kept informed. Special notice requirements may be triggered if certain mandatory contributions are being discontinued and/or if the employer files for an IRS determination letter in connection with a plan termination.

There is also no requirement to notify the Internal Revenue Service (IRS) or the Department of Labor (DOL) that the termination of a 401(k) plan is intended.

A single-employer plan may request an IRS determination that the plan is qualified at the time of termination by filing IRS Form 5310. The filing of a Form 5310 will usually result in a delay of the plan termination process since payouts are often held up pending the IRS's determination. It is used most frequently when there are large account balances that will be rolled over to an IRA or another qualified plan. In this circumstance, the delay involved may be worth the assurance that the money distributed will continue to be treated as tax-deferred.

Regardless of whether an IRS determination is requested, the employer must continue filing annual reports for the plan until such time as all assets are distributed to participants. The annual report for the final year of the plan must indicate that it is the last year of filing. The employer also must amend the plan document as necessary for all applicable laws, regardless of whether the plan terminates before or after an amendment deadline (see chapter 3 for information on plan document amendments).

Q 21:3 What is the impact of a plan termination on participants' benefits in the plan?

When a plan is terminated, all benefits must become 100 percent vested as of the date of the termination. [I.R.C. § 411(d)(3); Treas. Reg. § 1.411(d)-2(a)(1)] For example, even if a plan has a vesting schedule applied to its matching contributions so that a participant is not 100 percent vested until he or she has earned six years of service, all funds held in a participant's matching account will become 100 percent vested at plan termination regardless of how many years of service have been earned.

Q 21:4 What is the date of termination for purposes of applying the 100 percent vesting rule?

Generally, an employer can dictate the date a plan is considered terminated. [Treas. Reg. § 1.411(d)-2(c)(3)] This information is usually contained in the resolution or amendment to terminate the plan.

Q 21:5 How do the nondiscrimination rules apply to plan termination?

The effect of any plan termination must be nondiscriminatory. [Treas. Reg. § 1.401(a)(4)-1(b)(4)] For example, a corporation may, in the course of winding down its business affairs, distribute benefits to terminated participants who have left the company in connection with the wind-down. If, after distributing benefits to non-highly compensated employees, the corporation then makes a discretionary profit sharing contribution to the few remaining employees, all of whom are highly compensated, the plan will violate the nondiscrimination rule.

Q 21:6 Under what circumstances can a 401(k) plan not be terminated due to an inability to distribute assets?

A 401(k) plan may not distribute elective contributions to participants, and thus cannot be terminated, if the employer maintains an alternative defined contribution plan. [Treas. Reg. § 1.401(k)-1(d)(4)(i)]

Q 21:7 What is an *alternative defined contribution plan*?

Except as noted below, an *alternative defined contribution plan* is a defined contribution plan that exists at any time during the period beginning with the 401(k) plan's termination date and ending 12 months after the distribution of the 401(k) plan's assets. Employee stock ownership plans (ESOPs), simplified employee pension plans (SEPs), SIMPLE IRAs, and Section 403(b), 457(b), and 457(f) plans are not considered alternative defined contribution plans.

Any other defined contribution plan is not considered an alternative plan if fewer than 2 percent of the employees eligible to participate in the 401(k) plan at the time of its termination are eligible to participate in such other defined contribution plan within 12 months before or after the 401(k) plan's termination. [Treas. Reg. § 1.401(k)-1(d)(4)(i)]

Q 21:8 How must a distribution on plan termination be paid?

A distribution must be in the form of a lump-sum payment. A lump-sum payment is the distribution of the participant's account balance under the 401(k) plan within a single taxable year of the participant. A lump-sum payment includes a distribution of an annuity contract (see chapter 16 for information on payments in the form of an annuity contract). [Treas. Reg. § 1.401(k)-1(d)(4)(ii)] Plan assets must be distributed as soon as administratively feasible following the date of plan termination. Whether a distribution is made as soon as administratively feasible is determined under all the facts and circumstances, but generally, a distribution of assets that is not completed within one year of the date of termination specified by the employer may be viewed by the IRS as not having been made as soon as administratively feasible. A plan under which all assets are not timely distributed will be considered an ongoing plan and remain subject to plan qualification requirements. [Rev. Rul. 89-87, 1989-2 C.B. 81]

Q 21:9 What options does an employer have if benefits cannot be distributed in connection with a plan termination?

If the employer cannot distribute plan assets, it will have either to continue the 401(k) plan or merge it into another plan. If the 401(k) plan is frozen (i.e., amended to eliminate all contributions), the employer must still file annual reports and keep the plan document up to date and in compliance with any changes in the law. These requirements make continuing a frozen plan an unattractive alternative for most employers.

Missing Participants

Q 21:10 What steps should a plan administrator take with respect to a participant who cannot be located when the plan is terminated?

Participants who are either missing or cannot be located when a terminated plan is attempting to distribute all its assets present a significant problem. An ongoing plan can forfeit benefits payable to an unlocatable participant as long as the plan provides for reinstatement of that benefit if a claim is later made. [Treas. Reg. § 1.411(a)-4(b)(6)] However, since a terminating plan cannot provide reinstatement rights, forfeiture does not appear to be an option that would be accepted by the IRS in a qualified plan.

As a result of participants' unresponsiveness, plan administrators are often unable to effectively terminate a plan and are confronted with an array of issues related to their duties under ERISA to search for missing participants and distribute their benefits.

In Field Assistance Bulletin 2014-01, the DOL provides guidance to plan fiduciaries in connection with locating a missing participant in a terminated defined contribution plan and distributing benefits when efforts to communicate with a missing participant fail to secure a distribution election. According to the DOL, the decision to terminate a plan is generally viewed as a "settlor" decision rather than a fiduciary decision relating to the administration of the plan. However, the steps taken to implement this decision, including steps to locate missing participants, are governed by the fiduciary responsibility provisions of ERISA.

A plan fiduciary must therefore take certain steps to locate a missing participant or beneficiary (see Q 21:11) before the plan fiduciary determines that the participant cannot be found and must distribute his or her benefits in accordance with certain steps. In determining any additional steps that may be appropriate with regard to a particular participant (see Q 21:11), a plan fiduciary must consider the size of the participant's account balance and the expenses involved in further search efforts to locate the missing participant. Reasonable expenses associated with locating a missing participant may be charged to a participant's account, provided that the amount of the expenses allocated to this account is reasonable and the method of allocation is consistent with the terms of the plan and the plan fiduciary's duties under ERISA. [DOL Field Assist. Bull. 2014-01]

Q 21:11 What are the search methods prescribed under the DOL's guidance for locating missing participants?

Required Search Steps

A plan fiduciary cannot distribute a missing participant's benefits in accordance with the distribution options discussed in Q 21:12 unless each of the following search methods proves ineffective in locating the missing participant:

1. *Use certified mail.* Certified mail can be used to easily ascertain, at little cost, whether the participant can be located in order to distribute benefits.
2. *Check related plan records.* While the records of the terminated plan may not have current address information, it is possible that the employer or another plan of the employer, such as a group health plan, may have more up-to-date information with respect to a given participant or beneficiary. For this reason, plan fiduciaries of the terminated plan must inquire into the records of related plans to search their records for a more current address for the missing participant. If there are privacy concerns, the plan fiduciary that is engaged in the search can request to contact or forward a letter on behalf of the terminated plan to the participant or beneficiary, requesting the participant or beneficiary to contact the plan fiduciary.
3. *Check with designated plan beneficiary.* In connection with a search of the terminated plan's records or the records of related plans, plan fiduciaries must attempt to identify and contact any individual that the missing participant has designated as a beneficiary (e.g., spouse, children, etc.) for updated information concerning the location of the missing participant. Again, if there are privacy concerns, the plan fiduciary can request the designated beneficiary to contact or forward a letter on behalf of the terminated plan to the participant, requesting the participant or beneficiary to contact the plan fiduciary.
4. *Use free electronic search tools.* Plan fiduciaries must make reasonable use of Internet search tools that do not charge a fee to search for a missing participant or beneficiary. Such online services include Internet search engines, public record databases (such as those for licenses, mortgages, and real estate taxes), obituaries, and social media.

The DOL eliminated the requirement to use IRS or Social Security Administration (SSA) letter-forwarding services that are no longer available. Instead the required search steps were expanded to include the use of free electronic search tools as described above.

Additional Search Steps

If a plan administrator follows the required search steps, but does not find the missing participant or beneficiary, a plan fiduciary must consider whether additional search steps are appropriate. A plan fiduciary should consider the size of a participant's account balance and the cost of further search efforts in deciding if any additional search steps are appropriate. As a result, the specific additional steps that a plan fiduciary takes to locate a missing participant may vary depending on the facts and circumstances. Possible additional search steps include the use of Internet search tools, commercial locator services, credit reporting agencies, information brokers, investigation databases and analogous services that may involve charges. [DOL Field Assist. Bull. 2014-01]

Q 21:12 What distribution methods are acceptable in the missing participant context?

Despite using the DOL prescribed search methods (see Q 21:11), according to the DOL, plan fiduciaries may be unable to locate participants or otherwise obtain directions concerning the distribution of their benefits from terminated defined contribution plans. In these circumstances, plan fiduciaries must consider distribution options in order to effectuate the termination of the plan.

Following are the fiduciary considerations that are relevant to the various options available to plan fiduciaries in the context of missing participants of terminated defined contribution plans:

1. *Individual retirement plan rollovers.* In the DOL's view, plan fiduciaries must always consider distributing missing participant benefits to individual retirement accounts (IRAs). Establishing an IRA is the preferred distribution option because it is more likely than other options to preserve assets for retirement purposes and it results in a deferral of income tax consequences for missing participants.

   The choice of an IRA raises fiduciary issues as to the particular choice of an IRA provider as well as the selection of an initial investment vehicle. The DOL established a safe harbor for plan fiduciaries in connection with the distribution of benefits from a terminated individual account plan (see Q 21:48).

2. *Alternative distribution options.* If a plan fiduciary is unable to locate an IRA that is willing to accept a rollover distribution on behalf of a missing participant or determines not to make a rollover distribution for some other compelling reason based on the particular facts and circumstances, plan fiduciaries may consider either establishing an interest bearing federally insured bank account in the name of a missing participant or transferring missing participants' account balances to state unclaimed

property funds. In this regard, fiduciaries should be aware that transferring a participant's benefits to either a bank account or state unclaimed property fund will subject the deposited amounts to income taxation, mandatory income tax withholding, and a possible additional tax for premature distributions. Moreover, interest accrued would also be subject to income taxation. Plan fiduciaries should not use 100 percent income tax withholding as a means to distribute plan benefits to missing participants.

- *Federally insured bank accounts.* Plan fiduciaries may consider establishing an interest bearing federally insured bank account in the name of a missing participant, provided the participant would have an unconditional right to withdraw funds from the account. In selecting a bank and accepting an initial interest rate, with or without a guarantee period, a plan fiduciary must give appropriate consideration to all available information relevant to such selection and interest rate, including associated bank charges.
- *Escheat to state unclaimed property funds.* As an alternative, plan fiduciaries may also consider transferring missing participants' account balances to state unclaimed property funds in the state of each participant's last known residence or work location in order to complete the plan termination process. Such a transfer would constitute a plan distribution, which ends both the property owner's status as a plan participant and the property's status as plan assets under ERISA. In deciding between distribution into a state unclaimed property fund and distribution into a federally insured bank account, a plan fiduciary should evaluate any interest accrual and fees associated with a bank account against the availability of the state unclaimed property fund's searchable database that may facilitate the potential for recovery. Transfer to state unclaimed property funds must comply with state law requirements.
- *100 percent income tax withholding.* Imposing 100 percent income tax withholding on missing participant benefits, the DOL concluded, would not be in the interest of participants and beneficiaries and therefore would violate ERISA's fiduciary requirements. This option should not be used as a means to distribute benefits to plan participants and beneficiaries.

3. *Miscellaneous issues.* Fiduciaries have expressed concerns about legal impediments that might hinder the establishment of IRAs or bank accounts on behalf of missing participants. These impediments include perceived conflicts with the customer identification and verification provisions of the USA PATRIOT Act. [Pub. L. No. 107-56, 115 Stat. 272] Regulators have issued guidance in a set of questions and answers on the customer identification and verification provision (CIP) of the USA PATRIOT Act, "FAQs: Final CIP Rule," on the various Web sites (*www.occ.gov*; *www.fincen.gov*; *www.fdic.gov*).

In a footnote, the DOL indicated that its guidance assumes that the terminated plan does not provide an annuity option and that no other appropriate defined contribution plans are maintained within the sponsoring employer's corporate group to which account balances from the terminated plan could be transferred.

[DOL Field Assist. Bull. 2014-01]

Q 21:13 What is the additional option created under the Pension Protection Act of 2006 for dealing with missing participants?

Under the Pension Protection Act of 2006 [Pub. L. No. 109-280, 120 Stat. 780] (PPA), a plan administrator of a terminating plan may elect to transfer a missing participant's benefits to the Pension Benefit Guaranty Corporation (PBGC). The PBGC's missing participant program is a program for defined benefit plans. The option to use it for defined contribution plans is new.

It is unclear whether and under what circumstances fiduciary relief will be available in connection with using this program.

The DOL has indicated it will reevaluate its guidance after the PBGC publishes final regulations permitting a distribution to its missing participants program. Other particulars, including the type of information that must be conveyed to the PBGC regarding benefits of missing participants, are also unclear at the time this edition goes to press. This provision of the PPA is effective after the PBGC issues final regulations implementing it. [ERISA § 4050]

In 2013, the PBGC made a public request for information to assist it in making decisions about implementing this program. [78 Fed. Reg. 37,598 (June 21, 2013)]

Partial Termination

Q 21:14 What is a *partial termination*?

A *partial termination* occurs when a group of employees who were covered by a plan are excluded by either plan amendment or severance from service with the employer. [Treas. Reg. § 1.411(d)-2(b)(1)]

Q 21:15 What is the effect of a partial termination?

If a plan is partially terminated, all affected participants become 100 percent vested in their accounts. [I.R.C. § 411(d)(3); Treas. Reg. § 1.411(d)-2(a)(1)] It should be noted that 100 percent vesting in a partial termination is required for affected participants—that is, participants who were actually excluded or who separated from service in connection with the event or during the applicable period (see Q 21:17). [Treas. Reg. § 1.411(d)-2(b)(3)] The IRS has indicated that all participating employees who experienced severance from employment during the applicable period should be made fully vested, including those whose terminations were voluntary. [Rev. Rul. 2007-43, 2007-38 I.R.B. 45]

> **Example.** Company A sells off Division X, and a partial plan termination results. Only employees of Division X will be entitled to 100 percent vesting of their accounts; other employees of Company A who remain in the plan after the sale will be subject to the plan's regular vesting schedule.

Q 21:16 Are there plan events other than termination or partial termination that may require 100 percent vesting?

Yes. If a plan completely discontinues contributions, 100 percent vesting is required. [Treas. Reg. § 1.411(d)-2(a)(1)(ii)] A temporary freezing of benefits, however, will generally not trigger 100 percent vesting. [Treas. Reg. § 1.411(d)-2(d)(1)]

Q 21:17 How does an employer decide when a partial termination has occurred?

It is often very difficult for an employer to determine whether a partial termination has occurred and, if it has, when it occurred. The general rule is that the existence of a partial termination is a facts-and-circumstances determination. [Treas. Reg. § 1.411(d)-2(b)(1)] Some guidance has been developed over the years on this issue, but it still remains an individual determination. As a general guideline, if a significant percentage of employees are excluded from a plan in connection with a major corporate event, a partial termination may occur.

The IRS has indicated that if 20 percent or more of participants turn over in a particular year, there is an assumption that a partial termination has occurred. The turnover rate is determined by dividing the number of participants who had an employer-initiated severance from employment during the applicable period by the sum of all the participants at the start of the applicable period and the employees who became participants during the applicable period. The applicable period is the plan year (or, in the case of a plan year that is shorter than 12 months, the plan year plus the immediately preceding plan year) or a longer period if there is a series of related severances from employment.

All participants—vested as well as nonvested—are taken into account in calculating the turnover rate. Employer-initiated severances from employment do not include purely voluntary terminations and those on account of death, disability, or retirement on or after normal retirement age. A severance will be considered employer-initiated even if caused by events outside the employer's control, such as depressed economic conditions. [Rev. Rul. 2007-43, 2007-28 I.R.B. 45]

The Seventh Circuit reversed an earlier ruling that held that only nonvested participants may be counted for purposes of determining whether a partial plan termination occurred. The reversal was consistent with the IRS's interpretation that both nonvested and vested participants should be counted in making a partial plan determination. The following chart summarizes the parameters set forth by the court in making partial termination determinations. [Matz v. Household Int'l Tax Reduction Inv. Plan, 388 F.3d 570 (7th Cir. 2004)] Although the IRS has not adopted the specific parameters put forth by the court, the parameters in the *Matz* decision are not inconsistent with IRS guidance and reflect the views of a particular court.

If the reduction in participants is:	*Then there is:*
Below 10%	No partial termination
10% more than to less than 20%	A rebuttable presumption of no partial termination
20% to 40%	A rebuttable presumption of partial termination
40% more than to less than 100%	Partial termination
100%	Complete termination

If an employer wants some certainty that it has handled a partial termination or potential partial termination correctly, it should apply for an IRS determination on whether a particular set of facts constitutes a partial termination. For a 401(k) plan, this request is made using IRS Form 5300.

Mergers and Spinoffs

Q 21:18 What is a *merger*?

A *merger* occurs whenever two or more plans are combined into a single plan. [Treas. Reg. § 1.414(*l*)-1(b)(2)] For example, if an employer maintains a profit sharing plan and a 401(k) plan and wishes to combine them into a single plan to save administrative costs, the plans would undergo a merger to achieve that result.

Q 21:19 What rules apply to the allocation of benefits in a merger?

When two or more defined contribution plans are merged, the following conditions must be met:

1. The sum of account balances in each plan as of the date of the merger must equal the fair market value of the entire plan's assets;
2. The assets of each plan must be combined to form the assets of the merged plan; and
3. Immediately after the merger, each participant in the surviving plan must have an account balance equal to the sum of the account balances the participant had in the plans immediately prior to the merger.

[Treas. Reg. § 1.414(*l*)-1(d)]

See Q 21:23 for a discussion of special issues involved with a merger involving a money purchase plan. See chapter 22 regarding mergers involving a 403(b) plan.

Q 21:20 What is a *spinoff*?

A *spinoff* is the splitting of a single plan into two or more plans. For example, if Corporation A sells Division 5 to new Corporation B, that portion of Corporation A's plan covering the employees of Division 5 could be spun off to a new plan established by Corporation B. [Treas. Reg. § 1.414(*l*)-1(b)(4) Reg. § 1.414(*l*)1(b)(4)]

Q 21:21 What rules apply to the allocation of assets in a spinoff?

If defined contribution plans undergo a spinoff, the following rules apply to the allocation of assets:

1. The sum of account balances for each participant in the resulting plans must equal the account balance for that participant in the plan before the spinoff; and
2. The assets in each plan immediately after the spinoff must equal the sum of account balances for all participants in that plan.

[Treas. Reg. § 1.414(*l*)-1(m)]

Q 21:22 What procedures are involved in a merger or spinoff?

A spinoff or merger transaction usually begins with a corporate resolution outlining how the transaction will occur. All plans involved in the transaction will have to be reviewed to determine what amendments are necessary, and a date must be selected for the transaction. The plans must undergo a valuation of assets and the allocation of all funds to participants on that date so that compliance with the rules discussed in Qs 21:19 and 21:21 can be determined.

No special federal filing is typically required when a plan is merged, although Form 5310-A should be consulted to verify that no filing is required. It should be noted, however, that the disappearing plan must file a final return (Form 5500) in the year of the merger. In a 401(k) plan, no notification to participants in advance of a merger or spinoff is required, although as a practical matter an employer may want to keep its employees informed. (See chapter 19 for information on the blackout notice and ERISA Section 404(c) requirements if an administrative blackout and/or fund change will occur in conjunction with a merger or spinoff of assets.)

The plan sponsor need not request an IRS determination letter on a merged or spun-off plan, but if it wishes to do so, it can request the IRS's determination by filing Form 5300 or 5307 (see chapter 3).

Q 21:23 What special considerations are involved if a money purchase plan is merged into a 401(k) plan?

If a money purchase plan is merged into a 401(k) plan, special notice requirements may be triggered under ERISA Section 204(h) and Code Section 4980F. [Rev. Rul. 2002-42, 2002-28 I.R.B. 76] Under those requirements, generally, the plan administrator must provide plan participants, alternate payees, and certain employee organizations written notice of the reduction to future allocations within a specified time before the effective date of the change. The notice must provide sufficient information to allow affected individuals to understand the effect of the change, including the approximate magnitude of the expected reduction. Failure to timely comply with the notice requirements can result in adverse consequences, including the application of excise taxes. [Treas. Reg. § 54.4980F-1] According to the IRS, the merger of a money purchase plan into a 401(k) plan does not result in a partial plan termination necessitating 100 percent vesting if:

- All of the employees who are covered by the merged money purchase plan remain covered under the 401(k) plan;
- The money purchase plan assets and liabilities retain their characteristics under the 401(k) plan; and
- The employees vest in the 401(k) plan under the same vesting schedule that existed under the money purchase plan.

[Rev. Rul. 2002-42, 2002-28 I.R.B. 76]

Because money purchase plan assets retain their character as pension plan-type funds, the balances remain subject to the Code Section 417 joint and survivor rules and more restrictive in-service distribution rules. Separate accounting of these assets is required following the merger.

Q 21:24 What plan provisions should be reviewed when merging or spinning off plans?

A number of problems can arise in the context of a merger or spinoff when the plans involved do not contain identical provisions concerning benefits and other features. For example, if the plans involved have different vesting schedules or eligibility requirements or inconsistent plan years, amendments may have to be made to the merged or spun-off plan to ensure that participants do not lose valuable rights and are credited with appropriate levels of service in the resulting plan.

To the extent that the distribution options or other optional forms of benefits (see chapter 16) in the involved plans are different, measures will have to be taken to ensure that no protected optional forms of benefits are eliminated or reduced as a result of the transaction. [Treas. Reg. § 1.411(d)-4, Q&A 2(a)(3)] Recent rules provide plan sponsors more latitude to eliminate periodic and in-kind distribution options under certain circumstances (see chapter 16).

Example. Plan A, which permits immediate lump-sum distribution of benefits, is merged into Plan B, which requires deferral of any lump-sum payments until normal retirement age. Plan B will have to retain the right for participants in Plan A to take an immediate lump-sum distribution of benefits accrued up to the date of the merger.

Q 21:25 What special distribution concerns are involved in mergers or spinoffs of 401(k) plans?

If a 401(k) plan is merged into a non-401(k) plan and benefits are transferred in connection with that merger, care must be taken to ensure that elective contributions transferred to the merged plan do not become available for immediate distribution to active employees. The 401(k) regulations prevent an employer from avoiding the restriction on in-service withdrawals of elective contributions through the merger or transfer of benefits. [Treas. Reg. § 1.401(k)-1(d)(5)(iv)]

If a 401(k) plan is accepting transferred benefits from a non-401(k) plan, a key issue for review is whether the plan transferring benefits contains a qualified joint and survivor annuity requirement that must be preserved and that is not contained in the 401(k) plan. In those cases, the survivor annuity requirements also must survive any merger or transfer. [Treas. Reg. § 1.401(a)-20, Q&A 5]

Q 21:26 How can the problem of monitoring and harmonizing distribution options be avoided?

The problem of monitoring and harmonizing protected distribution options can be avoided by liberalizing the surviving plan so that it encompasses the most liberal distribution features of all the original plans. If this option is chosen, care must also be taken to preserve survivor annuity requirements to the extent required, as well as restrictions on in-service withdrawals of elective contributions.

Q 21:27 What relief did the IRS provide from distribution option concerns?

In January 2001, rules were finalized that allow a 401(k) plan to eliminate periodic distribution options (e.g., annuities or installments) so long as participants can receive a single-sum distribution that is otherwise identical to the options being eliminated and to eliminate certain in-kind distribution options (see chapter 16).

The rules also liberalize the application of the elective transfer rules for transfers made in connection with certain corporate transactions such as mergers and acquisitions (see chapter 16).

Plan Considerations During Major Business Transactions

Q 21:28 What types of issues might a 401(k) plan sponsor encounter if it is being acquired by or merged into another company?

If Company A is being acquired by or merged into Company B, and both companies sponsor 401(k) plans, the options for handling Company A's 401(k) plan generally fall into four categories:

1. Merge Company A's plan into Company B's plan (see Q 21:29).
2. Continue both Company A's and Company B's plans (see Q 21:30).
3. Freeze Company A's plan (see Q 21:31).
4. Terminate Company A's plan (see Q 21:32).

Dealing with the retirement plans of companies involved in a business transaction is complicated. What can and should be done will vary depending on the particular facts of the situation, including whether the transaction involves a sale of assets or a sale of stock. The buy-sell or merger agreement should specify how retirement plans will be dealt with, including whether the seller's plan will be terminated before the date of a stock purchase, whether the seller's plan will be merged into the buyer's plan on a particular date, or whether the buyer will assume sponsorship of the seller's plan after an asset purchase. It is important that the attorney who drafts the agreement has expertise in the retirement plan area. Whatever the circumstances, advance planning before the acquisition or merger takes place is essential.

Q 21:29 What are some pros and cons of merging the plans?

Advantages of a plan merger are that employees would not have access to their funds as they would if a termination occurred, and there is plan continuity for affected employees. Furthermore, a plan merger may be the only viable option, depending on the nature and timing of the transaction.

Merging plans can pose some risks. If document or operational failures exist in one of the plans and those failures are not corrected, the taint of disqualification can infect the other plan. If a qualification defect is known, that defect should be addressed before the plans are merged. The existence of a qualification defect is not, however, always known in advance. Also, post-merger administration can be more complicated if one of the plans contained more favorable distribution and vesting provisions (see Qs 21:24, 21:25). Rules requiring the crediting of service with the predecessor employer also come into play. [I.R.C. § 414(a)]

Q 21:30 What are some pros and cons of continuing both Company A's and Company B's plans?

Continuing both Company A's and Company B's plans avoids exposing one plan to the potentially disqualifying defects of the other. However, the maintenance of separate plans may raise future minimum coverage and nondiscrimination issues. There is also the added expense of maintaining two plans rather than one.

Q 21:31 What are some pros and cons of freezing Company A's plan?

Under this alternative, no further contributions are made to the frozen plan and, as a result, the minimum coverage and nondiscrimination issues of continuing the plan disappear. The risk of exposing each plan to the other's qualification defects is also avoided. On the downside, all accounts must be 100 percent vested. There is also the added expense of maintaining the plan until all assets are distributed.

Q 21:32 What are some pros and cons of terminating Company A's plan?

If Company A's plan is terminated, plan benefits must be 100 percent vested and distributed to plan participants; however, the complications associated with a plan merger (or the costs associated with maintaining two plans) are avoided.

A plan termination may not always be an option. If the business transaction involves a stock purchase (e.g., Company B purchases the stock of Company A), the termination of Company A's 401(k) plan must occur before the date of the stock purchase. If Company A's plan is not terminated before the purchase and Company B sponsors a 401(k) plan, Company A's plan will be prohibited from terminating the plan and distributing plan assets under the alternative defined contribution plan rules (see Qs 21:6, 21:7).

If the business transaction involves an asset purchase (e.g., Company B purchases the assets of Company A), Company B does not automatically assume sponsorship of Company A's 401(k) plan and may be able to terminate the plan. If Company B does assume sponsorship by formally adopting the plan, it would be unable to terminate it under the alternative defined contribution plan rules.

Q 21:33 Will Company A be able to distribute 401(k) plan assets to employees who go to work for Company B after the transaction?

It depends. Whether Company A can make 401(k) distributions to employees who go to work for Company B (allowing them to roll over those amounts to an IRA or to Company B's plan) will depend on whether a so-called triggering event occurs (see Q 21:34).

Q 21:34 What is a severance of employment in the context of distributing elective contributions?

Prior to January 1, 2002, amounts attributable to elective contributions could be distributed only if the participant attained age 59½, or experienced a separation of service, death, disability, or hardship, or if the plan terminated or disposed of assets or a subsidiary. The IRS applied the *same desk rule* to determine whether a participant experienced a separation of service entitling him or her to receive a distribution.

Generally speaking, under the same desk rule, any participant who, after a merger, acquisition, or other business transaction, continues to perform the same job for the buyer that he or she performed for the seller will not be treated as having separated from service. Therefore, if there is no other triggering event (e.g., plan termination, disposition of assets or of a subsidiary), no distribution may be made.

Distributions of elective contributions made after December 21, 2001, are permitted if there is a "severance from employment," death, disability, attainment of age 59½, hardship, or plan termination. [Treas. Reg. § 1.401(k)-1(d)(1)] A severance of employment occurs when a participant ceases to be employed by the employer that maintains the plan. The employer includes all corporations and other entities treated as the same employer under the controlled group and affiliated service group rules (see chapter 10). An employee would not have a severance from employment if, in connection with a change of employment, the employee's new employer maintains such a plan (e.g., the new employer assumes sponsorship of the plan or accepts a merger of plan assets with respect to the employee). This change effectively eliminates the same desk rule and should simplify the treatment of 401(k) plans in major business transactions.

Q 21:35 What special coverage rule applies in the context of an acquisition or disposition?

Under the minimum coverage requirements, a special rule applies in situations where an employer that sponsors a 401(k) plan is involved in an acquisition or disposition (i.e., an asset or stock acquisition, merger, or other similar transaction). Employers are given some time to adjust to these changes through plan redesign or other methods. Under these rules, the plan will continue to be considered in compliance with minimum coverage requirements during a "transition period." [I.R.C. § 410(b)(6)(C)]

The *transition period* is the period beginning on the date of the transaction and ending on the last day of the first plan year beginning after the date of the transaction. To qualify for special treatment under the transition rule, two conditions must be met:

1. The 401(k) plan of the employer involved in the acquisition, merger, or similar transaction must have satisfied the minimum coverage rules immediately before the acquisition, merger, or similar transaction, and

2. Coverage under the 401(k) plan must not significantly change during the transition period (other than by reason of the change in the members of a group).

[Rev. Rul. 2004-11, 2004-7 I.R.B. 480]

Example. Employer M, a wholly owned subsidiary of Employer Z, sponsors a 401(k) plan maintained on a calendar-year basis. On April 15, 2009, Employer Z sells the stock of Employer M to Employer P. Immediately prior to the sale, Employer M's 401(k) plan satisfies the minimum coverage rules. If no significant change is made to Employer M's 401(k) plan, the plan will automatically satisfy the minimum coverage rules until December 31, 2010.

Two key questions that remain unanswered are:

1. How does Employer M's plan determine whether it satisfied the minimum coverage rules immediately before the transaction? For example, if the transaction occurs mid-year, must a special coverage test be run as of the date of the transaction? Would the coverage testing results from the immediately preceding plan-year-end (PYE) suffice?
2. What would be considered "a significant change" in coverage that would nullify the relief under the transition rule?

The IRS is considering issuing more comprehensive guidance on this matter in the future. (See chapter 11 for information on minimum coverage requirements.)

Q 21:36 What other guidance is expected from the IRS regarding the application of retirement plan qualification requirements in the context of major business transactions such as mergers and acquisitions?

In Notice 2000-3, the IRS indicated that it would develop guidance on the application of various qualification requirements in cases in which a plan sponsor is involved in a major business transaction. Guidance is expected with respect to the nondiscrimination requirements under Code Sections 401(k) and 401(m) and the highly compensated employee definition under Code Section 414(q). It is anticipated that the guidance will take the form of proposed regulations. [IRS Notice 2000-3, 2000-4 I.R.B. 413]

Abandoned Plans

Q 21:37 Has the DOL provided guidance regarding abandoned plans?

Yes. On April 21, 2006, the DOL published final regulations designed to facilitate the termination of abandoned plans and increase the likelihood that participants and beneficiaries would receive retirement benefits. The final regulations establish standards for determining when a plan may be considered abandoned and deemed terminated, procedures for winding up the affairs of the plan and distributing benefits to participants and beneficiaries, and guidance on who may initiate and carry out the winding-up process. [Termination of Abandoned Individual Account Plans, 71 Fed. Reg. 20,820 (Apr. 21, 2006)]

The final regulations:

1. Establish a framework pursuant to which financial institutions and other entities holding the assets of an abandoned plan can terminate the plan and distribute benefits to the plan's participants and beneficiaries, with limited liability. [DOL Reg. § 2578.1]
2. Provide a fiduciary safe harbor for use in connection with making distributions from terminated plans on behalf of participants and beneficiaries who fail to make an election regarding a form of benefit distribution. [DOL Reg. § 2550.404a-3]
3. Establish a simplified method for filing a final report for abandoned plans. [DOL Reg. § 2520.103-13]

Appendices to the final regulations contain model notices for use in connection with compliance with the final regulations. The regulations and the appendices are available on the DOL's Web site (*www.dol.gov/ebsa/compliance_assistance.html#section9*).

In 2008, the final regulations and model notices were amended to reflect that distributions to nonspouse beneficiaries will no longer be required to be made to accounts other than IRAs. [73 Fed. Reg. 58,459 (Oct. 7, 2008)]

In 2012, the DOL proposed amendments to the regulations that would provide a process for a Chapter 7 bankruptcy trustee to terminate a plan, distribute benefits, and pay necessary expenses, including to itself. This process would not be available in the Chapter 11 bankruptcy context. The proposed amendments would:

- Expand the definition of a qualified termination administrator (QTA) to include Chapter 7 bankruptcy trustees and certain eligible designees of such trustees to act as QTAs.
- Revise the model notices to reflect informational requirements specific to Chapter 7 plans and bankruptcy trustees.

Other key changes under the proposed amendments, according to the DOL, would include:

- A Chapter 7 plan would be considered "abandoned" on the date the plan sponsor's bankruptcy proceeding commences (i.e., when a bankruptcy court enters an order for relief pursuant to the U.S. Bankruptcy Code).
- The bankruptcy trustee may terminate and wind up the plan himself or appoint an eligible designee (i.e., a financial institution holding the plan's assets to assume these duties). The bankruptcy trustee retains a duty to monitor the eligible designee, for which the trustee may be compensated.
- A bankruptcy trustee (or eligible designee) would have to determine whether it makes economic sense to collect delinquent contributions (e.g.,

whether the plan would collect more than it costs to collect the delinquencies) and would have a duty to attempt to collect the delinquencies if it makes sense financially to do so.

- A bankruptcy trustee (or eligible designee) would have to report any activity he or she believes may be evidence of other fiduciary breaches that involve plan assets by a prior plan fiduciary (e.g., embezzlement).

The 2012 proposed amendments would also make the following technical changes unrelated to Chapter 7 plans:

- Eliminate the requirement that a QTA, in its statement to the DOL, provides information on any investigation, examination, or enforcement action by the DOL, IRS, or the SEC concerning its (or any affiliate's) conduct as a fiduciary or party in interest within the past 24 months.
- Permit QTAs to transfer the account balances of decedents to an appropriate or a state's unclaimed property fund, regardless of size of account, if the QTA reasonably believes the participant and any named beneficiary are deceased and has included specified information in its notice to the DOL.
- Clarify and update location of instructions for completing the special Form 5500 terminal report (*www.dol.gov/ebsa/publications/APterminalreport.html*).

[77 Fed. Reg. 74,056 (Dec. 12, 2012)]

Q 21:38 Who can determine whether a plan is abandoned and can terminate an abandoned plan under the DOL regulations?

A qualified termination administrator (QTA), whether a person or an entity, can determine whether a plan is abandoned and can terminate an abandoned plan (see Q 21:39). [DOL Reg. § 2578.1(a)]

Q 21:39 Who is eligible to be a qualified termination administrator?

A person or entity can qualify as a termination administrator only if he or she or it holds assets of the plan and is eligible to serve as a trustee or issuer of an individual retirement account (e.g., a bank, trust company, mutual fund company, or insurance company). [DOL Reg. § 2578.1(g)]

See Q 21:37 for proposed amendments that would allow Chapter 7 bankruptcy trustees (and eligible designees) to serve as QTAs.

Q 21:40 When is a plan considered abandoned according to the DOL's regulations?

A plan would be considered abandoned under the regulations if:

1. No contributions to or distributions from the plan have been made for a period of at least 12 consecutive months or where facts and circumstances

known—such as a plan sponsor's liquidation or communications from plan participants and beneficiaries regarding distributions—suggest that the plan is or may become abandoned; and

2. Following a reasonable effort to locate or communicate with the plan sponsor, the QTA determines that the plan sponsor no longer exists, cannot be located, or is unable to maintain the plan. For this purpose, a reasonable effort would include furnishing a notice to the plan sponsor of the intent to terminate the plan and distribute benefits to the plan's participants and beneficiaries (see Q 21:41). [DOL Reg. § 2578.1(b)]

Q 21:41 What information should be contained in the notice to the plan sponsor of an abandoned plan?

The notice to a plan sponsor of an abandoned plan must contain the following information:

- The name and address of the QTA;
- The name of the plan;
- The account number or other identifying information relating to the plan;
- A statement that the plan may be terminated and benefits distributed if the plan sponsor fails to contact the QTA within 30 days;
- The name, address, and telephone number of the person, office, or department that the plan sponsor must contact regarding the plan;
- A statement that if the plan is terminated, notice of such termination will be furnished to the DOL;
- The following statement: "The U.S. Department of Labor requires that you be informed that, as a fiduciary or plan administrator or both, you may be personally liable for costs, civil penalties, excise taxes, etc. as a result of your acts or omissions with respect to this plan. The termination of this plan will not relieve you of your liability for any such costs, penalties, taxes, etc."; and
- A statement that the plan sponsor may contact the DOL for information about the abandoned plan process and the telephone number of the appropriate EBSA contact person.

The regulations contain a model plan sponsor notice (Notice of Intent to Terminate Plan). [DOL Reg. § 2578.1(b)(5)]

Q 21:42 On what date is a plan considered terminated under the rule?

A plan will be deemed terminated on the 90th day following the date of the letter from EBSA acknowledging receipt of the notice of abandonment unless, prior to that, the DOL notifies the QTA that it objects to the termination of the plan or waives the 90-day period. [DOL Reg. § 2578.1(c)]

See Q 21:37 for proposed amendments that would address when a plan would be considered abandoned in the Chapter 7 bankruptcy context.

Q 21:43 What should the QTA include in the notice of plan abandonment to the DOL?

The QTA's notice of abandonment to the DOL must be signed and dated by the QTA and include:

- Information on the QTA including contact information, a statement that the person is qualified to serve as QTA and elects to terminate and wind up the plan, and details on any investigation, examination, or enforcement action by the DOL, IRS, or the Securities and Exchange Commission (SEC) concerning such entity's (or any affiliate's) conduct as a fiduciary or party in interest within the past 24 months;
- The name, address, telephone number, account number, employer identification number (EIN), and plan number of the plan;
- The name and last known address and telephone number of the plan sponsor;
- The estimated number of participants in the plan;
- A statement concerning the findings that the plan is abandoned, the specific steps taken to locate or communicate with the known plan sponsor, and a statement that no objection has been received from the plan sponsor;
- The estimated value of the plan's assets, the length of time plan assets have been held by the QTA if such period of time is less than 12 months, an identification of any assets with respect to which there is no readily ascertainable fair market value, as well as information, if any, concerning the value of such assets, and identification of any known delinquent contributions owed to the plan;
- The name, address, and telephone number of known service providers (e.g., recordkeeper, accountant, lawyer, other asset custodian(s)) and information on services considered necessary to wind up the plan, the name of the service provider(s) that is expected to provide such services, and an itemized estimate of expenses attendant thereto expected to be paid out of plan assets by the QTA; and
- A statement that the information being provided in the notice is true and complete under penalty of perjury.

A model DOL notice (Notification of Plan Abandonment and Intent to Serve as Qualified Termination Administrator) is contained in the regulations. [DOL Reg. § 2578.1(c)(3)]

See Q 21:37 for proposed amendments that would change the notice requirements in the first bulleted item above.

Q 21:44 What procedures under the DOL regulations must a QTA follow when terminating and paying out an abandoned plan?

When terminating and paying out an abandoned plan, a QTA must follow specific procedures under the DOL regulations:

- Undertake reasonable and diligent efforts to locate and update plan records necessary to determine the benefits payable under the terms of the plan to each participant and beneficiary.
- Use reasonable care in calculating the benefits payable to each participant or beneficiary based on plan records.
  - An account that is less than the estimated share of expenses may be forfeited and allocated to defray expenses or to other accounts in accordance with the plan document.
  - Expenses and unallocated assets should be allocated in accordance with the plan document or (if the plan document is not available, is ambiguous, or if compliance is not feasible) on a pro rata (based on account balance) or per capita (equally to all accounts) basis, and unallocated assets (including forfeitures and assets in suspense accounts) should be allocated on a per capita basis.
- Notify the DOL of any contributions (either employer or employee) owed to the plan in conjunction with either the initial or final QTA filing. The DOL does not impose an obligation to collect delinquent contributions that are reported.
- Engage, on behalf of the plan, such service providers as are necessary to wind up the plan and distribute benefits.
- Pay, from plan assets, reasonable expenses to wind up and pay out the plan. Expenses of plan administration shall be considered reasonable if such expenses are for services necessary to wind up the affairs of the plan and distribute benefits and are consistent with industry rates for such or similar services, are not in excess of rates being charged other customers outside the QTA framework, and the payment of such expenses would not constitute a prohibited transaction under ERISA.
- Furnish to each participant or beneficiary of the plan a notice containing the following:
  - The name of the plan;
  - A statement that the plan has been determined to be abandoned by the plan sponsor and therefore has been terminated pursuant to DOL regulations;
  - A statement of the account balance and the date on which it was calculated by the QTA, and the following statement: "The actual amount of your distribution may be more or less than the amount stated in this letter depending on investment gains or losses and the administrative cost of terminating your plan and distributing your benefits";
  - A description of the distribution options available under the plan and a request that the participant or beneficiary elect a form of distribution and inform the QTA (or designee) of that election;
  - A statement explaining that if a participant or beneficiary fails to make an election within 30 days from receipt of the notice, the QTA (or designee) will roll over the account balance of the participant or

beneficiary directly to an IRA or an inherited IRA and the account balance will be invested in an investment product designed to preserve principal and provide a reasonable rate of return and liquidity, or to an interest-bearing federally insured bank account, the unclaimed property fund of the state of last known address, or to an IRA if the distribution amount is $1,000 or less (if permitted under the rules), or to an annuity provider if survivor annuity requirements apply;

— A statement of the fees, if any, that will be paid from the participant or beneficiary's IRA or other account, if such information is known at the time of the furnishing of this notice;

— The name, address, and telephone number of the IRA or other provider, if such information is known at the time of the furnishing of this notice; and

— The name, address, and telephone number of the QTA and, if different, the name, address, and phone number of a contact person (or entity) for additional information concerning the termination and distribution of benefits under this section.

- Furnish above notice to each participant or beneficiary to the last known address of the participant or beneficiary. If a notice is returned to the plan as undeliverable, the QTA shall be consistent with its fiduciary duties to take steps to locate and provide notice to the participant or beneficiary prior to making a distribution. If, after such steps, the QTA is unsuccessful in locating and furnishing notice to a participant or beneficiary, the participant or beneficiary shall be deemed to have been furnished the notice and to have failed to make an election within the 30-day period.
- Distribute benefits in accordance with the form of distribution elected by each participant or beneficiary. If the participant or beneficiary fails to make an election within 30 days of the time the notice is furnished, distribute benefits in accordance with safe harbor rules (see Q 21:48). (Special rules apply if the plan is subject to survivor annuity requirements.) The QTA may designate itself (or an affiliate) as the transferee of such proceeds and invest such proceeds in a product in which it (or an affiliate) has an interest, only if such designation and investment are exempted from the prohibited transaction provisions under Section 408(a) of ERISA (see Q 21:47).
- Furnishes a terminal report (see Q 21:45) and final notice to the DOL no later than two months after the end of the month in which the QTA satisfies the requirements above. The final notice, signed and dated by the QTA, must contain the following information:

— The QTA's name, EIN, and contact information

— The plan's name, account number, EIN, and plan number

— A statement that the plan has been terminated and plan assets distributed

— A statement that plan expenses were appropriately paid out of plan assets

— An explanation if QTA fees exceeded estimated fees by 20 percent
— Information on any known delinquent contributions
— A statement, under penalty of perjury, that the information is true and complete

A QTA is not required to amend a plan to accommodate the termination, and model notices that the QTA may use in connection with notifying participants (Notice of Plan Termination) and the DOL (Final Notice) are contained in the regulations. [DOL Reg. § 2578.1(d)]

In 2008, the model Notice of Plan Termination was revised to reflect that distributions to nonspouse beneficiaries must be made to inherited IRAs. [73 Fed. Reg. 58,459 (Oct. 7, 2008)]

See Q 21:37 for proposed amendment that would allow Chapter 7 bankruptcy trustees (and eligible designees) to serve as QTAs.

Q 21:45 What type of final governmental reporting is required of a QTA under the DOL regulation?

The DOL regulation provides annual reporting relief if the QTA files a special terminal Form 5500, in accordance with the form's instructions pertaining to terminal reports of QTAs, at the same time the final notice is furnished to the DOL under the procedures set forth in Q 21:44. [DOL Reg. § 2520.103-13]

Q 21:46 Is protection from liability provided when guidelines under the DOL regulation are followed?

Yes. The QTA shall be deemed to satisfy its fiduciary responsibilities under ERISA to the extent it complies with the requirements of the regulation. The protection does not extend to the selection and monitoring of any service providers involved in winding up the plan, as well as ensuring the reasonableness of the compensation paid for such services; and the selection of an annuity provider in connection with distributing benefits subject to survivor annuity requirements. A QTA must separately comply with ERISA fiduciary standards with respect to those activities. [DOL Reg. § 2578.1(e)]

The IRS has advised the DOL that it will not challenge the qualified status of any plan terminated under this regulation or take any adverse action against the QTA, the plan, or any participant or beneficiary as a result of such termination, provided the QTA satisfies three conditions:

1. The QTA must reasonably determine whether, and to what extent, the survivor annuity requirements of Sections 401(a)(11) and 417 of the Code apply to any benefit payable under the plan and must take reasonable steps to comply with the requirements (see chapter 17).
2. Each participant or beneficiary has a nonforfeitable right to his or her accrued benefits as of the date of deemed termination, subject to income, expenses, gains, and losses between that date and the date of distribution.

3. Participants and beneficiaries must receive notification of their rights under Section 402(f) of the Code (see chapter 16, in addition to other information in Q 21:44).

Q 21:47 Can a QTA select itself to provide services and be compensated for its services in connection with terminating an abandoned plan?

Yes. A QTA (or its affiliates) may select itself to provide services and be reimbursed for services in connection with terminating an abandoned plan, and for selecting and paying itself in connection with rollovers from abandoned plans, resulting from a participant's failure to provide direction, to IRAs (or other specified accounts) maintained by the QTA. Under a special DOL class exemption, a QTA may also invest rolled-over amounts in its own or an affiliate's proprietary investment product and pay itself investment fees as a result of the investment. The conditions that must be satisfied under the exemption include the following:

1. The QTA must comply with DOL requirements relating to the termination of abandoned plans and timely provide information requested by the DOL regarding the proposed termination.
2. Fees paid to the QTA for termination services must be consistent with industry rates for similar services, based on the expertise of the QTA, and must not exceed rates charged for similar services not involving terminating an abandoned plan.
3. With respect to distributions:
   - The QTA must include a statement in its notice to participants and beneficiaries (see Q 21:44) that if the participant or beneficiary fails to make an election within the 30-day period, the QTA will distribute benefits to an IRA or other account offered by the QTA or affiliate and benefits may be invested in the QTA's or the affiliate's investment product, which is designed to preserve principal and provide a reasonable rate of return and liquidity.
   - The IRA or other account must be established for the exclusive benefit of the account holder, spouse, or beneficiary.
   - The terms of the IRA or other account, including fees and expenses (e.g., establishment and maintenance fees, investment fees, termination and surrender charges), must be no less favorable than those available to other accounts established outside the QTA framework.
   - Distribution proceeds must be invested in "Eligible Investment Products," defined as investments designed to preserve principal and provide a reasonable rate of return, whether or not such return is guaranteed, consistent with liquidity (e.g., money market funds, interest-bearing savings accounts, certificates of deposit, and stable value products that do not substantially restrict access) that are offered by certain entities subject to state or federal regulation (e.g., federally

insured banks, savings associations, or credit unions, insurance companies, or mutual fund companies). (Special rules may apply to distributions of $1,000 or less.)

- The rate of return or investment performance of the IRA or other account must not be less favorable than that of an identical investment that could have been made outside the QTA framework.
- The IRA or other account must not pay a sales commission in connection with an investment in an Eligible Investment Product.
- The IRA or other account holder must be able, within a reasonable period of time without penalty to principal, to transfer his or her account balance to another investment, whether or not affiliated with the QTA.
- Fees, with the exception of establishment charges, may be charged only against income earned and may not exceed reasonable compensation.

4. The QTA maintains records for six years (from the date the QTA provides notice to the DOL of its determination of plan abandonment and its election to serve as QTA), establishing that the conditions of the exemption have been met.

[71 Fed. Reg. 20,856 (Apr. 21, 2006)]

In 2008, the class exemption was amended to require benefits of missing nonspouse beneficiaries be directly rolled over to inherited IRAs. [73 Fed. Reg. 58,629 (Oct. 7, 2008)]

In 2012, the DOL proposed amendments to the class exemption that would:

- Expand the definition of a QTA to include Chapter 7 bankruptcy trustees and eligible designees of such trustees to act as QTAs; and
- Modify the conditions with respect to fees paid to a QTA that would eliminate the "experience of the QTA" component with respect to bankruptcy trustees only because bankruptcy trustees may have limited experience providing services to employee benefit plans, but the amended requirements reinforce that fees must be consistent with industry rates.

[77 Fed. Reg. 74,506 (Dec. 12, 2012)]

Q 21:48 How should distributions to missing participants be handled in a terminated plan (including terminations under the QTA regime)?

A DOL regulation contains a safe harbor under which a fiduciary, including a QTA, can make distributions from a terminated plan to participants who fail to make a distribution election within the 30-day notice period. The safe harbor has three conditions:

1. Each distribution must be rolled over into an IRA or an inherited IRA maintained by an entity that is eligible to serve as an IRA trustee or issuer. The DOL requires IRA rollovers on behalf of nonspouse distributees in

addition to currently required IRA rollovers to spousal distributees. [73 Fed. Reg. 58,459 (Oct. 7, 2008)] This rule reflects the expansion of IRA rollovers to nonspouse beneficiaries under the PPA. (In the case of a distribution by a QTA of $1,000 or less, and the amount is less than the minimum amount required under the QTA's IRA product to the public, the distribution is made to an interest-bearing federally insured bank or savings account, unclaimed property fund of the state in which the participant or beneficiary's last known address is located, or an IRA offered by a financial institution other than the QTA.)

2. Except with respect to distributions to state unclaimed property funds in the QTA context, the fiduciary and transferee entity must enter into a written agreement that provides that:
   - Rolled-over funds must be invested in an investment product designed to preserve principal and provide a reasonable rate of return, whether or not such return is guaranteed, consistent with liquidity (except in the case of distributions by a QTA of $1,000 or less that are invested in interest-bearing federally insured bank or savings accounts);
   - The investment product selected for the rolled-over funds shall seek to maintain a stable dollar value equal to the amount invested in the product by the account and be offered by a state or federally regulated institution (e.g., bank, savings association, credit union, or mutual fund company);
   - Fees and expenses attendant to the account, including investments of such plan, do not exceed fees charged other accounts for comparable services; and
   - The participant or beneficiary shall have the right to enforce the terms of the contractual agreement establishing the account.
3. The distribution must not violate the prohibited transaction rules unless such actions are exempted from ERISA prohibited transaction rules (see Q 21:47).

Distribution notices with specified content must be sent to each participant and beneficiary to the last known address of the participant or beneficiary. If a notice is returned undelivered and the plan fiduciary is unsuccessful in locating the participant or beneficiary after taking additional steps consistent with its duties under ERISA, the participant or beneficiary is deemed to have been furnished the notice and to have failed to make an election within the 30-day period. If the situation involves an abandoned plan, see Q 21:44 for notice content requirements. For other situations, the model notice (Notice of Plan Termination) that is included in the safe harbor regulation, can be used. [DOL Reg. § 2550.404a-3] The model notice was revised to reflect that distributions to nonspouse beneficiaries must be made to inherited IRAs. [73 Fed. Reg. 58,459 (Oct. 7, 2008)]

See Q 21:37 for proposed amendments that would modify requirements in the case of certain deceased participants.

Q 21:49 When do the DOL regulations on terminating abandoned plans become effective?

The DOL's final regulation on terminating abandoned individual account plans became effective May 22, 2006.

Q 21:50 Does the IRS's Employee Plans Compliance Resolution System make provision for abandoned plans?

An abandoned plan that is terminating and that has operational, demographic, or document errors may be corrected under the Voluntary Correction with Service Approval Program (VCP) or Correction on Audit Program (Audit Cap) (see chapter 20) if the party acting on behalf of the plan is an eligible party. [Rev. Proc. 2013-12, § 4.08] In general, an eligible party is a court-appointed representative with authority to terminate the plan and dispose of the plan's assets or, if the abandoned plan is under DOL investigation, a person or an entity who has accepted responsibility for terminating the plan and distributing its assets. [Rev. Proc. 2013-12, § 5.03] Generally, qualification errors must be fully corrected; however, in the case of abandoned plans that are terminating, the IRS retains discretion to require less than full correction. [Rev. Proc. 2013-12, § 6.02(5)(f)] Finally, in the case of VCP, the IRS may, in appropriate cases, waive the fee that is normally charged in a VCP proceeding. [Rev. Proc. 2013-12, § 12.02(4)]

Q 21:51 What legal and regulatory developments in the bankruptcy context could impact the prevalence of abandoned plans?

The Bankruptcy Abuse Prevention and Consumer Protection Act of 2005 [Pub. L. No. 109-8, 119 Stat. 23] clarified that a bankrupt employer that is the plan administrator within the meaning of ERISA is obligated to continue to perform the duties necessary to wind down the plan. This law was designed to curtail the abandonment of plans as a result of bankruptcies. It is effective for bankruptcy filings on or after October 17, 2005.

If a plan becomes abandoned, the DOL has proposed amendments to its abandoned plan guidance that would permit bankruptcy trustees to terminate and wind up the plans of sponsors in liquidation under Chapter 7 of the U.S. Bankruptcy Code. To that end, the definition of a QTA would be expanded to include Chapter 7 bankruptcy trustees and certain eligible designees of such trustees to act as QTAs. The QTA process would not be available in the Chapter 11 bankruptcy context. See Q 21:37 for proposed amendments that would apply to Chapter 7 bankruptcy trustees.

Chapter 22

401(k) Plan Alternatives

A number of qualified and nonqualified arrangements may be used by employers or individuals as an alternative to a 401(k) plan. This chapter explores a number of those alternative plans, discusses the availability of these plans to different types of employers, and describes the features of these alternatives, as well as their relative advantages and disadvantages. Traditional defined benefit and defined contributions plans under Code Section 401(a) are not discussed here. At the end of each section, the alternative plan is compared with a 401(k) plan. Table 22-8 compares the features of 401(k) plans with all of the alternatives discussed in this chapter.

Individual Retirement Arrangements (IRAs) 22-2
Traditional IRAs 22-3
Contributions to Traditional IRAs 22-5
Table 22-1. Limits on Deductible Contributions to Traditional IRAs 22-5
Distributions, Rollovers, and Transfers 22-8
Roth IRAs 22-10
Contributions to Roth IRAs 22-10
Table 22-2. Limits on Contributions to Roth IRAs 22-10
Distributions from Roth IRAs 22-11
Conversions, Rollovers, and Transfers 22-12
Comparison of Traditional IRAs and Roth IRAs 22-13
Table 22-3. 401(k) Plans Compared with IRAs 22-13
Simplified Employee Pensions (SEPs) and Salary Reduction SEPs (SARSEPs) 22-14
Contributions to SEPs and SARSEPs 22-16
Distributions from SEPs and SARSEPs 22-18
Table 22-4. Comparison of SEPs and SARSEPs with 401(k) Plans 22-20
SIMPLE IRAs and SIMPLE 401(k) Plans 22-21
Contributions to SIMPLE IRAs and SIMPLE 401(k) Plans 22-22
Distributions from SIMPLE IRAs and SIMPLE 401(k) Plans 22-24
Table 22-5. Comparison of SIMPLE IRA Plans with SIMPLE 401(k) and Regular 401(k) Plans 22-27
Cash Balance Plans 22-29

Floor-Offset Plans 22-29
Nonqualified Deferred Compensation (NQDC) Plans 22-29
Types of NQDC Plans 22-30
Tax Aspects of NQDC Plans 22-31
Advantages and Disadvantages of NQDC Plans 22-33
Impact of Code Section 409A 22-34
Benefit Security in Unfunded NQDC Plans 22-37
NQDC Plans Versus 401(k) Plans 22-38
Section 403(b) Plans—Tax-Sheltered Annuities 22-38
Eligible Employers and Funding Rules 22-38
Written Plan Document Requirement 22-39
Nondiscrimination Rules 22-41
Contributions to Section 403(b) Plans 22-42
Distributions, Exchanges, and Rollovers 22-43
ERISA Title 1 Issues 22-45
Form 5500 Rules Applicable to ERISA 403(b) Plans 22-48
Using a Section 403(b) Plan with a Qualified Plan 22-50
Section 403(b) Plans Versus 401(k) Plans 22-50
Section 457(b) Eligible Deferred Compensation Plans 22-52
Eligible Employers and Funding Rules 22-52
Section 457(b) Plan Eligibility Requirements 22-53
Eligible 457(b) Plan Contributions 22-54
Distributions, Rollovers, and Transfers 22-55
Table 22-6. Section 457(b) Provisions Applicable to Various Types of Employers 22-59
Violations of Code Section 457(b) 22-60
Section 457(b) Plans Versus Section 401(k) Plans 22-60
Table 22-7. Comparison of Governmental 457(b) and 401(k) Plans 22-60
Table 22-8. Comparison of Retirement Savings Alternatives 22-62

Individual Retirement Arrangements (IRAs)

Traditional individual retirement arrangements (IRAs) were introduced by the Employee Retirement Income Security Act of 1974 (ERISA) to allow eligible individuals to make pre-tax contributions that accrue on a tax-deferred basis to provide retirement benefits. (See Qs 22:1–22:23 for the rules that apply to traditional IRAs.)

The Taxpayer Relief Act of 1997 [Pub. L. No. 105-34, 111 Stat. 738] (TRA '97) created a new form of IRA called the Roth IRA to allow eligible individuals to make after-tax contributions and take qualifying distributions tax free. (See Qs 22:24–22:38 for the rules that apply to Roth IRAs.)

There are also several types of IRAs that employers can make available to employees. These IRAs allow employees to make payroll-deduction contributions into their individual IRAs or allow employers to make tax-deductible contributions to an employee's tax-deferred IRA. Simplified employee pensions (SEPs) were created by the Revenue Act of 1978 [Pub. L. No. 95-600, 92 Stat.

2763] to provide small employers with an incentive to establish retirement plans for their employees. (See Qs 22:39–22:63 for the rules that apply to SEPs.)

Savings Incentive Match Plans for Employees, or SIMPLE IRAs, allow employees to make salary-reduction contributions into an IRA. Employers must either match those salary reduction contributions or make non-elective contributions to the employee's SIMPLE IRA. (See Qs 22:64–22:86 for the rules that apply to SIMPLE IRAs and SIMPLE 401(k)s.)

On January 28, 2014, President Obama announced the creation of the "MyRA," a new retirement account structured as a Roth IRA. Individuals who earn up to $129,000 and couples who earn up to $191,000 per year will be eligible to contribute to a MyRA if the employer offers the MyRA accounts. The initial contribution can be as little as $25 with subsequent payroll deductions as small as $5. As with other IRAs, account owners can contribute a maximum of $5,500 a year (or $6,500 if they are age 50 or older). There are no fees to set up and use the MyRA, and employers have no responsibility for administering them. Assets in the MyRA will be invested in bonds comparable to the "G Fund" (Government Securities Investment Fund) currently offered inside the government's Thrift Savings Plan (TSP). These bonds provide a variable interest rate that trends with government bonds and have a principal guarantee. Once the MyRA account balance reaches $15,000, or after a maximum of 30 years, the account must be transferred to a private Roth IRA. The rules for the MyRA are similar to those for Roth IRAs (Qs 22:24–22:38).

Traditional IRAs

Q 22:1 What is an *individual retirement account*?

An *individual retirement account* is either a trust or a custodial account established in the United States. [I.R.C. § 408(a)] Individual retirement accounts may offer a wide variety of investments, such as stocks, bonds, mutual funds, U.S. gold and silver coins and certain forms of bullion. Life insurance and certain collectibles are not permissible investment options under an individual retirement account. [I.R.C. § 408(m)(3)]

Q 22:2 What is an *individual retirement annuity*?

An *individual retirement annuity* is a flexible premium annuity contract purchased from an insurance company. Depending on the type of contract purchased, fixed rate or variable investment options, or both, will be available. [I.R.C. § 408(b)]

Q 22:3 What is a *Spousal IRA*?

A *Spousal IRA* is a traditional or Roth IRA established by a working spouse on behalf of a spouse earning less than the maximum IRA contribution limit (including age 50 catch-up contributions). [I.R.C. § 219(c)(1)] A contribution may be made up to the maximum total for the employee's own IRA and the Spousal IRA if the spouses file a joint income tax return. [I.R.C. § 219(c)(2)] The contribution may be split between the spouses in any manner as long as no more than the maximum contribution is made to one spouse's account.

Q 22:4 What is an *Inherited IRA*?

An *Inherited IRA* is either a traditional or Roth IRA that passes to a beneficiary at the death of the IRA owner. If the beneficiary is the IRA owner's spouse, the spouse may treat it as his or her own IRA. If anyone other than the IRA owner's spouse is the beneficiary, that beneficiary only inherits the rights to receive income from the IRA, but does not own the IRA itself.

Q 22:5 What rules apply when a spouse inherits an IRA?

A spouse is allowed to treat an Inherited IRA as his or her own IRA. Once the IRA is owned by the spouse, he or she may make contributions to that IRA or may roll the assets over into another IRA. The IRA is no longer considered an Inherited IRA.

Q 22:6 What rules apply to a nonspouse's Inherited IRA?

A nonspouse beneficiary may not assume ownership of an Inherited IRA. The Inherited IRA is merely a distribution vehicle. The beneficiary may not make contributions to it or roll any amounts from the Inherited IRA to another IRA. A nonspouse beneficiary must satisfy the required minimum distribution rules by either beginning to take life expectancy payments by December 31 of the year following the year of the IRA owner's death, or take the entire account balance by December 31 of the fifth year following the death of the IRA owner.

Q 22:7 May nonspousal beneficiaries of employer-sponsored retirement plans roll their account balances to an inherited IRA?

Yes. Beginning in 2007, a nonspousal beneficiary of a deceased participant's qualified retirement plan account (including a 403(a) annuity, a 403(b) annuity, or a governmental 457(b) plan account) can set up an Inherited IRA to receive a tax-free rollover of a plan distribution.

Q 22:8 Are IRA assets subject to bankruptcy?

Traditional IRA and Roth IRA assets up to $1,245,475 as of April 2013 are exempted from the individual debtor's bankruptcy estate pursuant to The Bankruptcy Abuse Prevention and Consumer Protection Act of 2005 [Pub. L. No. 109-8, 119 Stat. 23]. Pursuant to 11 U.S.C. § 104(b)(1), this dollar exemption is adjusted on April 1 at three-year intervals to reflect the change in the Consumer Price Index for All Urban Consumers. The most recent adjustment occurred

April 1, 2013. Rollover contributions and the earnings thereon do not count toward the dollar exemption amount.

Contributions to Traditional IRAs

Q 22:9 What is the maximum IRA contribution by an individual under age 50?

The maximum IRA contribution by an individual who has not attained age 50 by the end of 2015 is the lesser of $5,500 (subject to adjustment in increments of $500 to reflect cost-of-living increases), or the amount of his or her taxable compensation. This maximum contribution amount may be split between a traditional IRA and a Roth IRA. The maximum contribution may be reduced depending upon the individual's modified adjusted gross income (MAGI). [I.R.C. § 219(b)(5)]

Q 22:10 What is the maximum IRA contribution by an individual age 50 or over?

A catch-up contribution of $1,000 is available to individuals who attain age 50 or more by the end of 2015 for a maximum IRA contribution of the lesser of $6,500 or the amount of his or her taxable compensation. The age 50 catch-up amount is subject to adjustment in increments of $500 to reflect cost-of-living increases. The maximum contribution amount may be split between a traditional IRA and a Roth IRA. The maximum contribution may be reduced depending upon the individual's modified adjusted gross income (MAGI). [I.R.C. § 219(b)(5)]

Q 22:11 May individuals age 70½ or older contribute to a traditional IRA?

No. All contributions to a traditional IRA must cease once the individual attains age 70½. [I.R.C. § 219(d)(1)]

Q 22:12 Are contributions to a traditional IRA tax deductible?

Contributions are fully deductible if the individual's adjusted gross income (AGI) does not exceed certain dollar thresholds, and if neither the individual nor his or her spouse is an active participant in an employer's Section 401(a), 403(a), 403(b), 408(k), 408(p), or 501(c)(18) plan. A Section 457(b) plan is not treated as a plan for this purpose. [I.R.C. § 219(g)(5)] If the individual or spouse is an active participant in an employer's plan, the deductible amount may be reduced or eliminated. [I.R.C. § 219(g)(1)-(8)] See Table 22-1 for details.

Table 22-1. Limits on Deductible Contributions to Traditional IRAs

You may claim a full deduction, up to the maximum contribution limit, on your individual federal income tax return for the amount you contributed to your traditional IRA if you (and your spouse) are not covered by a retirement plan at work. Your deduction may be limited if you (or your spouse) are covered by a retirement plan at work and your income exceeds certain levels.

If you are not covered by a retirement plan at work, use this table to determine if your modified AGI affects the amount of your deduction in 2015.

If Your Filing Status Is...	*And Your Modified AGI Is...*	*Then You Can Take...*
single, head of household, or qualifying widow(er)	any amount	a full deduction up to the amount of your contribution limit
married filing separately or jointly with a spouse who is not covered by a plan at work	any amount	a full deduction up to the amount of your contribution limit
married filing jointly with a spouse who is covered by a plan at work	$183,000 or less	a full deduction up to the amount of your contribution limit
	more than $183,000 but less than $193,000	a partial deduction
	$193,000 or more	no deduction
married filing separately with a spouse who is covered by a plan at work	less than $10,000	a partial deduction
	$10,000 or more	no deduction

If you file separately and did not live with your spouse at any time during the year, your IRA deduction is determined under the "single" filing status.

If you are covered by a retirement plan at work, use the following table to determine if your modified AGI affects the amount of your deduction in 2015.

If Your Filing Status Is...	*And Your Modified AGI Is...*	*Then You Can Take...*
single or head of household	$61,000 or less	a full deduction up to the amount of your contribution limit
	more than $61,000 but less than $71,000	a partial deduction
	$71,000 or more	no deduction
married filing jointly or qualifying widow(er)	$98,000 or less	a full deduction up to the amount of your contribution limit
	more than $98,000 but less than $118,000	a partial deduction
	$118,000 or more	no deduction

married filing separately	less than $10,000	a partial deduction
	$10,000 or more	no deduction

If you file separately and did not live with your spouse at any time during the year, your IRA deduction is determined under the "single" filing status.

Q 22:13 How is a prorated IRA deduction calculated?

The prorated IRA deduction is calculated using the following formula:

$$\frac{\text{Maximum IRA deduction} \times (\text{highest number in the range of the bracket} - \text{AGI})}{\$10{,}000}$$

Thus, for a single taxpayer with a 2015 AGI of $63,000, the high range in the bracket is $71,000, and the deductible contribution is calculated as follows:

$$\frac{\$5{,}500 \times (\$71{,}000 - \$63{,}000)}{\$10{,}000} = \$4{,}400$$

Q 22:14 How much may be contributed if both spouses are employed?

If both individuals are employed and each earns in wages more than the maximum IRA contribution amount (including age 50 contributions), each may make a maximum IRA contribution. [I.R.C. § 219(c)]

Q 22:15 When may nondeductible contributions be made to a traditional IRA?

Individuals under age 70½ may make nondeductible contributions to the extent such amounts are not deductible under the limits described in Q 22:12 and Table 22-1. [I.R.C. § 408(o)(2)] Earnings on nondeductible contributions accrue on a tax-deferred basis until withdrawn from the IRA. The individual must report designated nondeductible contributions on his or her tax return. [I.R.C. § 408(o)(4)(A)] In many situations, however, it will be advantageous to contribute to a Roth IRA rather than making nondeductible contributions to a traditional IRA.

Q 22:16 May an employer sponsor an IRA for its employees?

Yes. Contributions made by the employer to the employee's IRA will be deductible by the employer and will be taxable wages to the employee, subject to Federal Insurance Contributions Act (FICA) and Federal Unemployment Tax Act (FUTA) taxes. [I.R.C. § 408(c)] The employee may be able to deduct the IRA contribution under the rules described in Qs 22:12 and 22:13.

Distributions, Rollovers, and Transfers

Q 22:17 When may contributions to a traditional IRA be withdrawn?

The Code does not impose any distribution restrictions on IRA assets. Contributions and accrued earnings may be withdrawn at any time.

Q 22:18 How are distributions from a traditional IRA taxed?

The portion of the distribution that represents tax-deductible contributions, any pre-tax funds that were rolled over into the IRA from an employer-sponsored retirement plan, and investment earnings will be taxed at ordinary income tax rates for the year the distribution was made. [I.R.C. § 408(d)] In addition to regular income tax, distributions taken prior to age 59½ may be subject to a 10 percent federal penalty tax on the taxable portion of the distribution. [I.R.C. § 72(t)]

Q 22:19 What required minimum distribution rules apply to traditional IRAs?

Required minimum distributions (RMDs) from a traditional IRA must begin by April 1 of the year following the year in which the IRA owner reaches age 70½, regardless of whether the owner is still working. [I.R.C. §§ 408(a)(6), 401(a)(9)] RMDs were waived for calendar year 2009 only due to the recession pursuant to the Worker, Retiree, and Employer Recovery Act of 2008 [Pub. L. No. 110-458, 122 Stat. 5092] (WRERA)

Q 22:20 May an IRA owner age 70½ or older take tax-free charitable distributions from an IRA to contribute to charity?

The Pension Protection Act of 2006 [Pub. L. No. 109-280, 120 Stat. 780] created qualified charitable distribution (QCD) transfers. Individuals aged 70½ or older were allowed to make tax-free charitable gifts of up to $100,000 directly from their IRAs to Section 501(c)(3) charities effective August 17, 2006 through the end of 2007. Congress has repeatedly extended QCDs, most recently through 2014, in the Tax Increase Prevention Act of 2014. [Pub. L. No. 113-295, 128 Stat. 4010] At the time this edition goes to press, Congress has not yet extended QCDs for 2015 and beyond.

Q 22:21 May an IRA owner make direct transfers between multiple IRAs in one calendar year?

Yes. An IRA owner is allowed to make unlimited direct trustee-to-trustee transfers (as opposed to 60-day rollovers) between IRAs.

Q 22:22 May an IRA owner make 60-day rollovers between multiple IRAs in one calendar year?

Beginning in 2015, an individual can make only one rollover from an IRA to another (or the same) IRA in any 12-month period, regardless of the number of IRAs owned [I.R.S. Ann. 2014-15, 2014-32] The limit will apply by aggregating all of an individual's IRAs, including SEP and SIMPLE IRAs as well as traditional and Roth IRAs, effectively treating them as one IRA for purposes of the limit. Trustee-to-trustee transfers between IRAs and rollovers from traditional to Roth IRAs ("conversions") are not limited because such transfers are not considered rollovers. [Rev. Rul. 78-406, 1978-2 C.B. 157]

This change is the result of the ruling in *Bobrow v. Commissioner* [T.C. Memo. 2014-21], which rejected the IRS's prior interpretation applying the limitation on an IRA-by-IRA basis. IRS Publication 590-A, *Contributions to Individual Retirement Arrangements (IRAs) 2014*, is being revised accordingly.

If an individual has made an IRA-to-IRA rollover in the preceding 12 months and receives a distribution of pre-tax amounts from an IRA, the distribution is taxable and may be subject to the 10 percent early withdrawal penalty. Such a distribution is not eligible for rollover, and, if a rollover is made, the amount may be treated as an excess contribution and taxed at 6 percent per year as long as the funds remain in the IRA.

Q 22:23 Are rollovers allowed between traditional IRAs and an employer-sponsored plan?

Traditional IRAs may be rolled over into a qualified retirement plan, such as a 401(k) plan, if the retirement plan has language allowing it to accept this type of rollover.

Roth IRAs can only be rolled over to another Roth IRA, not to an employer-sponsored plan.

Almost any type of distribution from an employer-sponsored retirement plan can be rolled into an IRA, except:

- a required minimum distribution
- a deemed distribution from a loan
- a hardship distribution
- a distribution of excess contributions and related earnings
- a distribution that is one of a series of substantially equal payments
- dividends on employer securities
- the cost of life insurance coverage

Distributions from a designated Roth account can only be rolled over to another designated Roth account or to a Roth IRA.

Roth IRAs

Q 22:24 What is a *Roth IRA*?

A *Roth IRA* is similar to a traditional IRA except that contributions are always made with after-tax dollars and qualifying distributions are received tax free. [I.R.C. §§ 408A(a), (b)] (See Q 22:30.)

Q 22:25 May a spousal Roth IRA be established?

Yes. A spousal Roth IRA may be established pursuant to the same eligibility rules and contribution limits that govern a traditional IRA. The married couple must file a joint income tax return, and the compensation of the recipient spouse (for whom the Roth IRA is being established) must be less than the compensation of the contributing spouse. [I.R.C. § 219(c)(2)]

Contributions to Roth IRAs

Q 22:26 How much may be contributed to a Roth IRA?

The limitation on contributions to Roth IRAs are the same as the limitation on contributions to traditional IRAs (see Qs 22:9, 22:10), and are aggregated with any contributions made to a traditional IRA. The Roth IRA contribution amount may be reduced, however, depending on the individual's modified AGI as computed for Roth IRA purposes. See Table 22-2 below for details.

Table 22-2. Limits on Contributions to Roth IRAs

If Your Filing Status Is...	*And Your Modified AGI Is. . .*	*Then You Can Contribute*
married filing jointly or qualifying widow(er)	< $183,000	up to the limit
	≥ $183,000 but < $193,000	a reduced amount
	≥ $193,000	zero
married filing separately and you lived with your spouse at any time during the year	< $10,000	a reduced amount
	≥ $10,000	zero
single, head of household, or married filing separately and you did not live with your spouse at any time during the year	< $116,000	up to the limit
	≥ $116,000 but < $131,000	a reduced amount
	≥ $131,000	zero

If the amount you can contribute must be reduced, calculate your reduced contribution limit as follows.

1. Start with your modified AGI.
2. Subtract from the amount in (1):
   a. $183,000 if filing a joint return or qualifying widow(er),
   b. $0 if married filing a separate return, and you lived with your spouse at any time during the year, or
   c. $116,000 for all other individuals.
3. Divide the result in (2) by $15,000 ($10,000 if you are filing a joint return, a qualifying widow(er), or are married filing a separate return and you lived with your spouse at any time during the year).
4. Multiply the maximum contribution limit (before reduction by this adjustment and before reduction for any contributions to traditional IRAs) by the result in (3).
5. Subtract the result in (4) from the maximum contribution limit before this reduction.
6. The result is your reduced contribution limit.

[I.R.C. § 408A(c)(3)(C)(ii)(III)]

Q 22:27 May individuals age 70½ or older make Roth IRA contributions?

Yes. Individuals age 70½ or older may contribute to a Roth IRA.

Q 22:28 May contributions to a Roth IRA be deducted?

No. Roth IRA contributions are always made with after-tax dollars.

Distributions from Roth IRAs

Q 22:29 When may contributions to a Roth IRA be withdrawn?

After-tax Roth IRA contributions may be withdrawn at any time without federal income tax consequences. [I.R.C. § 408A(d)(4)]

Q 22:30 What is a qualifying distribution from a Roth IRA?

Qualifying distributions are withdrawals of earnings made after a five-year period, beginning with the first year for which a Roth IRA contribution was made, if it satisfies at least one of the following conditions:

- IRA owner is age 59½ or older,
- IRA owner has died or become disabled, or
- Distribution is used to pay for certain first-time homebuyer expenses up to a lifetime limit of $10,000.

[I.R.C. § 408A(d)(2)]

Q 22:31 May nonqualifying distributions be made from a Roth IRA?

Yes. Distributed earnings, however, will be subject to ordinary income tax and, if applicable, a 10 percent early withdrawal penalty tax. Unlike early distributions from traditional IRAs, early distributions from Roth IRAs are considered to be made first from the after-tax basis, which is not subject to tax. [I.R.C. § 408A(d)(4)]

Q 22:32 What required minimum distribution rules apply to Roth IRAs?

Roth IRAs are not subject to required minimum distribution (RMD) rules during the owner's lifetime. After the death of the IRA owner, however, beneficiaries, including surviving spouses, must begin taking distributions in accordance with the rules in Code Section 401(a)(9) applicable to traditional IRAs and qualified employer-sponsored plans. [I.R.C. § 408A(c)(5)]

Conversions, Rollovers, and Transfers

Q 22:33 May a traditional IRA be converted to a Roth IRA?

Yes. Beginning in 2010, owners of traditional IRAs are allowed to convert all or a portion of the pre-tax IRA assets to a Roth IRA regardless of income level pursuant to the Tax Increase Prevention and Reconciliation Act of 2005 [Pub. L. No. 109-222, 120 Stat. 345] (TIPRA). Prior to 2010, only IRA owners with an adjusted gross income (AGI) of no more than $100,000 could convert a traditional IRA to a Roth IRA.

Q 22:34 When are amounts converted to a Roth IRA in 2016 taxed?

Any amount converted from a traditional IRA to a Roth IRA in 2016 is taxed as ordinary income in 2016.

Q 22:35 Should a traditional IRA be converted to a Roth IRA?

Whether a traditional IRA should be converted to a Roth IRA depends upon the number of years the owner expects the money to remain in the Roth IRA and whether the owner believes the tax rate applicable at the time the Roth IRA assets are distributed are likely to be higher than the tax rate that applies in the year the conversion takes place. Income taxes must be paid on the amount converted in the year of the conversion.

Q 22:36 May distributions from an employer-sponsored retirement plan be rolled directly into a Roth IRA?

Yes. All or any portion of an eligible rollover distribution from an employer sponsored retirement plan, such as a 401(k), may be rolled over into a Roth IRA. The amount rolled into the Roth IRA will be taxed as ordinary income in the year the rollover is completed.

Comparison of Traditional IRAs and Roth IRAs

Q 22:37 Does a Roth IRA provide greater tax savings than a traditional IRA?

The answer depends on a number of factors. A Roth IRA can provide higher retirement benefits than a traditional IRA if the tax-free compounding is allowed to work for a number of years. Consider the following examples:

> **Example 1.** Dick makes a $4,000 pre-tax contribution into a traditional deductible IRA. The $4,000 remains invested for 25 years, until Dick turns 60, with a return of 8 percent, for a total account balance of $27,394. If Dick takes a full distribution at a tax rate of 30 percent, he will have $19,180 after taxes.
>
> Jane has $4,000 before taxes to contribute to a Roth IRA. Assuming a tax rate of 30 percent, Jane's after-tax contribution to a Roth IRA is $2,800. Her $2,800 contribution grows at the rate of 8 percent for 25 years, until, at age 60, the account has grown to $19,180. Since any withdrawal will be a qualifying distribution, no taxes will be due.
>
> **Example 2.** Jane is not limited to contributing $2,800 and contributes $4,000 after-tax dollars to a Roth IRA. Assuming a 30 percent tax rate, 25 years later, Jane will have $27,394 in her Roth IRA, which may be distributed tax free.

Example 1 illustrates the mathematical result that there is no difference between the after-tax amounts at distribution when the same pre-tax income is invested in a traditional or Roth IRA when the tax rates are the same. The Roth IRA locks in the tax rate in effect when the contribution is made, so it will produce a higher yield if the tax rates increase, but a lower yield if tax rates fall, between the contribution date and the distribution date.

Example 2 illustrates that a $4,000 after-tax contribution to a Roth IRA will allow for a greater tax savings than a $4,000 pre-tax contribution to a traditional IRA.

Q 22:38 What are the advantages of a Roth IRA over a traditional IRA?

The most significant benefit of a Roth IRA is that qualified distributions are tax free whether made to the original owner or to a beneficiary who inherits the Roth IRA. [I.R.C. § 408A(d)(1)] When nonqualified distributions are taken, contributions are considered to be withdrawn before accumulated earnings, allowing funds to be withdrawn tax free. [I.R.C. § 408A(d)(4)(B)] RMD rules are not imposed on the Roth IRA owner. [I.R.C. § 408A(c)(5)]

Table 22-3. 401(k) Plans Compared with IRAs

Feature	*401(k) Plan*	*IRAs*
Funding	Trust or annuity	Trust/custodial account/ annuity
Deferral limit	$18,000 in 2015	$5,500 in 2015
Age 50 catch-up	$6,000 in 2015	$1,000 in 2015

Table 22-3. 401(k) Plans Compared with IRAs (*cont'd*)

Feature	*401(k) Plan*	*IRAs*
Tax-deferred contributions	Yes	May be deductible
Roth contributions	Yes	Roth IRAs
Employer may contribute	Yes	Yes
Distribute excess	Yes	Yes, 6% excise tax per year
Loans	Yes	No
Distribution restrictions	Yes	No
Rollovers	Yes at distribution	Only one among all IRAs per year
10% penalty tax	Yes	Yes
Minimum distributions	Later of age 70½ or severance	Yes, age 70½, except Roth
Rollovers to Roth IRAs	Yes	Yes, but not to Roth accounts
In-Plan Roth rollovers	Yes	Conversions to Roth IRAs

Simplified Employee Pensions (SEPs) and Salary Reduction SEPs (SARSEPs)

Simplified employee pensions (SEPs) were created by the Revenue Act of 1978 [Pub. L. No. 95-600, 92 Stat. 2763] to provide small employers with an incentive to establish retirement plans for their employees. These plans became much more like qualified plans in 1982 with the passage of the Tax Equity and Fiscal Responsibility Act of 1982 [Pub. L. No. 97-248, 96 Stat. 324] (TEFRA). The employer's administrative responsibilities are minimized with a SEP. The employer simply makes tax-deductible contributions to an employee's tax-deferred traditional IRA account.

Salary Reduction SEPs (SARSEPs), which more closely resemble 401(k) plans, were only available to employers with 25 or fewer employees and only through calendar year 1996. Although no new SARSEPs may be established, existing ones may be continued. [I.R.C. § 408(k)(6)]

Q 22:39 What is a *SEP*?

A *SEP* plan provides employers with a simplified method to make contributions toward their employees' retirement and, if self-employed, their own retirement. Contributions are made directly to an IRA established for each employee. [I.R.C. § 408(k)] Employers must provide simplified reports with respect to the contributions made to a SEP. [I.R.C. § 408(*l*)]

Q 22:40 What is a *SARSEP*?

A *SARSEP* is a simplified employee pension plan established before January 1, 1997 that includes a salary reduction arrangement. Under a SARSEP, employees can establish an IRA and choose to have part of their wages contributed to that IRA. [I.R.C. § 408(k)(6)]. No new SARSEPs have been established after 1996; however, for SARSEPs set up before 1997, eligible employees hired after 1996 must be allowed to participate.

Q 22:41 Could any employer establish a SARSEP?

No. A SARSEP could not be established by a state or local government, any of its political subdivisions, agencies, or instrumentalities or a tax-exempt organization. Only an employer with 25 or fewer eligible participants may continue to operate a SARSEP. [I.R.C. § 408(k)(6)(B)]

Q 22:42 What are the requirements to maintain a SARSEP?

A SARSEP must have been established before 1997 and must meet the following requirements each year: (1) 25 or fewer employees were eligible to participate in the SARSEP in the preceding year [I.R.C. 408(k)(6)(B)]; (2) at least 50 percent of the eligible employees choose to make salary reduction contributions this year [I.R.C. 408(k)(6)(A)]; and (3) the elective deferrals of highly compensated employees (HCEs) meet the SARSEP deferral percentage limitation. [I.R.C. § 408(k)(6)(D)]

Q 22:43 What year is used for the 25 or fewer employee rule?

The 25-employee rule is a look-back rule. [I.R.C. § 408(k)(6)(B)] It is a year-by-year rule. For example, if an employer had 23 eligible employees in 2014, but 27 eligible employees in 2015, salary reduction contributions may be made to the SEPs of the 27 employees for 2014. In 2015, however, no salary reduction contributions may be made for the employees.

Q 22:44 Who is an eligible employee for a SEP or SARSEP?

An eligible employee for a SEP or SARSEP is an individual who meets the following requirements: (1) attained age 21; (2) has worked for the employer in at least three of the last five years; and (3) has received at least $600 in compensation from the employer for 2015, subject to annual cost-of-living adjustments in later years. The employer may impose less restrictive requirements to determine an eligible employee. [I.R.C. § 408(k)(2)]

Q 22:45 Are there employees that may be excluded from a SEP or SARSEP?

Yes, employees who may be excluded from a SEP or SARSEP include (1) employees covered by a union agreement whose retirement benefits were bargained for in good faith by the employees' union and the employer; and (2) nonresident alien employees who have no U.S. source compensation from the employer. [I.R.C. §§ 408(k)(2), 410(b)(3)(C)]

Q 22:46 If an employer has a SEP, can it also have other retirement plans?

Yes. An employer can maintain both a SEP and another retirement plan. Unless the other retirement plan is also a SEP, however, the employer cannot use Form 5305-SEP. The employer must adopt either a prototype SEP or an individually designed SEP. Additionally, the SEP must be aggregated with any qualified plan(s) of the employer for deduction and contribution limits. [I.R.C. § 404(h)]

Contributions to SEPs and SARSEPs

Q 22:47 May an employer enroll employees into SEPs and SIMPLE IRAs automatically?

Yes. The Worker, Retiree, and Employer Recovery Act of 2008 (WRERA) extends the automatic contribution rules enacted as part of the Pension Protection Act of 2006 (PPA) to SEPs.

Q 22:48 How much may the employer contribute to a SEP?

Annual employer contributions to an employee's SEP cannot exceed the lesser of (1) 25 percent of compensation, or (2) $53,000 for 2015 (subject to annual cost-of-living adjustments for later years). [I.R.C. §§ 408(j), 415(c)(1)] The limits in the preceding sentence apply in the aggregate to contributions an employer makes for its employees to all defined contribution plans, which include SEPs. [I.R.C. § 404(h)] Only employee compensation up to $265,000 in 2015 (subject to annual cost-of-living adjustments for later years) may be considered. [I.R.C. §§ 408(k)(3)(C), 401(a)(17)] Contributions must be made in cash. [I.R.C. § 408(a)(1)]

Q 22:49 Must the same percentage of salary be contributed for all SEP participants?

Contributions made to a SEP may not discriminate in favor of HCEs. [I.R.C. § 408(k)(3)] Contributions to each employee's SEP must bear a uniform relationship to the compensation (not in excess of the first $265,000 in 2015). [I.R.C. § 408(k)(3)(C)]

Q 22:50 Are there other limits on SEP contributions?

Yes, if an employer contributes to another defined contribution plan for its employees, such as a 401(k) plan, an annual addition limit applies. The annual addition limit for 2015 is the lesser of $53,000 (subject to annual cost-of-living adjustments for later years) or 100 percent of the employee's compensation. In determining this limit, contributions for employees to all defined contribution plans of the employer, which includes SEPs, must be included. [I.R.C. §§ 404(h), 415(c)(2)]

Q 22:51 May contributions be made to a SEP or SARSEP of a participant over age 70½?

Contributions must be made for each eligible employee in a SEP or SARSEP, even if over age 70½. Such an employee must take minimum distributions, however.

Q 22:52 How much of the contribution made to employees' SEPs or SARSEPs may be deducted on the employer's tax return?

The maximum that may be deducted on the employer's tax return for contributions to its employees' SEPs is the lesser of (1) its contributions or (2) 25 percent of compensation. Compensation considered for each employee is limited to $265,000 for 2015 [I.R.C. § 408(k)(3)(C)] and subject to annual cost-of-living adjustments for later years. [I.R.C. § 408(k)(8)]

Q 22:53 Are employer contributions to a SEP or SARSEP taxable to employees?

No, contributions to employees' SEPs and SARSEPs are not included in the employees' gross income to the extent such contributions do not exceed the maximum contribution limits. [I.R.C. §§ 408(j), 415(c)(2)] These amounts are taxed when distributed. [I.R.C. § 408(d)]

Q 22:54 How much may an employee defer under a SARSEP?

An employee may make an elective deferral up to the lesser of (1) 25 percent of compensation, or (2) $18,000 for 2015 (subject to annual cost-of-living adjustments). The $18,000 limit applies to the total elective deferrals an employee makes for the year to the SARSEP and any 401(k) plan or 403(b) tax-sheltered annuity plan. [I.R.C. §§ 408(k)(6)(A)(iv), 401(a)(30), 402(g)]

Q 22:55 Can catch-up contributions be made to a SARSEP?

Yes, additional "catch-up" elective deferral contributions are allowed for employees who have reached age 50. Catch-up contributions are limited to

$6,000 for 2015 (subject to cost-of-living adjustments thereafter). [I.R.C. §§ 408(k)(6)(A)(iv), 401(a)(30), 402(g)(1)(C); 414(v)]

Q 22:56 May an employer contribute to the SARSEP for its employees?

Yes, the employer may make nonelective contributions to the SEPs of its employees subject to an annual addition limit. [I.R.C. § 404(h)] The annual addition limit is the lesser of (1) 100 percent of the employee's compensation (limited to $265,000 for 2015, subject to annual cost-of-living adjustments or (2) $53,000 for 2015, subject to annual cost-of-living adjustments). In determining this limit, all amounts deferred by the employee and all employer nonelective contributions to the employee's SEP must be included. In addition, contributions made on behalf of an employee to another defined contribution plan sponsored by the employer must be included in determining the annual addition limit. Employer matching contributions are not permitted. [I.R.C. § 408(k)(3)(C)]

Q 22:57 Can designated Roth contributions be made under a SARSEP?

No, designated Roth contributions cannot be made under a SARSEP.

Q 22:58 Can loans be taken from a SEP or SARSEP?

No, since the contributions are made directly to the employee's IRA, loans are not permitted. [I.R.C. §§ 408(e)(3), (4)]

Distributions from SEPs and SARSEPs

Q 22:59 When may funds be withdrawn from a SEP or SARSEP?

Since SEP and SARSEP contributions are made directly into each employee's IRA, the funds may be withdrawn at any time. The employer may not impose any withdrawal restrictions. [I.R.C. § 408(k)(4)]

Q 22:60 What required minimum distribution rules apply to SEPs and SARSEPs?

Required minimum distributions from a SEP or SARSEP must begin by April 1 of the calendar year following the year the individual attains age 70½. [I.R.C. §§ 408(a)(6), (b)(3)]

Q 22:61 How are distributions from SEPs and SARSEPs taxed?

Distributions from SEPs and SARSEPs are taxed at ordinary income tax rates in effect in the year of the distribution. [I.R.C. §§ 72; 408(d)(1)] In addition to regular income tax, distributions taken prior to age 59½ may be subject to a 10 percent federal penalty tax on the taxable portion of the distribution unless one of the exceptions allowed by the IRS applies. [I.R.C. § 72(t)]

Q 22:62 If a SEP or SARSEP fails to meet the applicable requirements, are the tax benefits for the employer and employees lost?

Generally, tax benefits will be lost if the SEP or SARSEP fails to satisfy the Code requirements. The employer may, however, be able to correct failures and thereby continue to provide employees with retirement benefits on a tax-favored basis using the IRS's Employee Plans Compliance Resolution System (EPCRS). Revenue Procedure 2015-27 [2015-16 I.R.B. 914] improves and updates the most recent restatement of EPCRS set forth in Revenue Procedure 2013-12 [2013-4 I.R.B. 313]. The components of EPCRS are the Self-Correction Program (SCP), Voluntary Correction Program (VCP), and Audit Closing Agreement Program (Audit CAP).

Q 22:63 What IRS guidance is available to assist employers in complying with the SEP and SARSEP rules?

The IRS placed on its Web site a SEP Fix-it Guide and a SARSEP Fix-it Guide, each of which provides tips on how to find, fix, and avoid common mistakes in SEP and SARSEP plans. The SEP plan Fix-it Guide is available at *www.irs.gov/Retirement-Plans/SEP-Fix-It-Guide-Common-Problems-Real-Solutions* and the SARSEP plan Fix-it Guide is available at *www.irs.gov/Retirement-Plans/SARSEP-Plan-Fix-It-Guide*.

Table 22-4. Comparison of SEPs and SARSEPs with 401(k) Plans

Feature	*SEP*	*SARSEP*	*401(k)*
Maximum eligibility requirements	Age 21; worked 3 of past 5 years; earned at least $600 (2015 amount)	Same as SEP	Age 21 and 1 year of service
Coverage	All eligible must participate	50% of those eligible must participate; maximum 25 or fewer eligible employees in preceding plan year	Follows Section 410(b) rules regarding minimum coverage
Employer deduction limit	25% of covered payroll (limited to $265,000, not to exceed $53,000 in 2015)	Same	Same
Maximum employee contributions	Not applicable; employer contributions only	Lesser of 25% of compensation or $18,000 (2015); age 50 catch-up contribution of $6,000 (2015 limit)	Lesser of 100% of compensation or $18,000 (2015); age 50 catch-up contribution of $6,000 (2015)
Vesting	100% immediate	100% immediate	Vesting schedule permitted (on employer contributions)
IRS reporting	Form 5305A-SEP establishes model plan	New SARSEPs may not be established after 1996	Annual form 5500 reports required
Access to funds	Available at any time; 10% IRS penalty for premature distribution	Same as SEP	Withdrawals permitted under certain circumstances—retirement, hardship, etc.; loans if employer allows; 10% IRS penalty for premature distribution
Plan documents	IRS model; Master or Prototype	Same as SEP	Master or Prototype; volume submitter; individually designed
Tax treatment of distributions	Ordinary income	Same as SEP	Generally, ordinary income (10-year income averaging for participants who attained age 50 prior to 1986)

SIMPLE IRAs and SIMPLE 401(k) Plans

SIMPLE is an acronym for Savings Incentive Match Plan for Employees. A SIMPLE 401(k) is a type of profit sharing plan under which participants can voluntarily contribute a portion of their salary on a pre-tax basis.

Q 22:64 What is a *SIMPLE IRA plan*?

A SIMPLE IRA plan is an IRA-based plan, maintained on a calendar-year basis that gives small employers a simplified method to make contributions toward their employees' retirement. Employees may choose to make salary reduction contributions to a SIMPLE IRA. Employers must either match those salary reduction contributions or make nonelective contributions to the employee's SIMPLE IRA. All contributions are made directly to an IRA established for each employee. [I.R.C. §§ 408(p)(1), 7701(a)(37)]

Q 22:65 What is a *SIMPLE 401(k) plan*?

A *SIMPLE 401(k) plan* provides a simplified way for small employers with 100 or fewer employees to offer retirement benefits to their employees. A SIMPLE 401(k) plan covers employees who received at least $5,000 in compensation for the preceding year. SIMPLE 401(k) plans are not subject to the annual nondiscrimination tests that apply to traditional 401(k) plans. Similar to a safe harbor 401(k) plan, the employer is required to make employer contributions that are fully vested. Employees covered by a SIMPLE 401(k) plan may not, however, receive any contributions or benefit accruals under any other retirement plans of the employer. [I.R.C. § 401(k)(11)]

Q 22:66 Can any employer establish a SIMPLE IRA or SIMPLE 401(k) plan?

For either a SIMPLE IRA or a SIMPLE 401(k) plan, eligible employers must have no more than 100 employees who have received at least $5,000 in compensation from the employer for the previous year. [I.R.C. §§ 408(p)(2)(C)(i), 401(k)(11)(D)]

Q 22:67 May an employer automatically enroll employees into a SIMPLE IRA?

Yes. The Worker, Retiree, and Employer Recovery Act of 2008 (WRERA) extends the automatic contribution rules enacted as part of the Pension Protection Act of 2006 (PPA) to SEPs and SIMPLE IRAs. In Notice 2009-66 [2009-39 I.R.B. 418], the IRS provided guidance to facilitate automatic enrollment, including a sample plan amendment for use by SIMPLE IRA plans that use a designated financial institution as described in Code Section 408(p)(7).

Q 22:68 Which employees are eligible to participate in a SIMPLE IRA or SIMPLE 401(k) plan?

Employers may not impose an age requirement for the SIMPLE IRA. Any employee who earned at least $5,000 during any two preceding years and is reasonably expected to earn $5,000 in the current year must be allowed to participate in the SIMPLE IRA plan. Under a SIMPLE 401(k) plan, however, employees may be required to perform service for at least one year and attain age 21 before becoming eligible to participate. For both plans, the employer may choose to implement less stringent eligibility requirements. Participants may not "opt out" of a SIMPLE IRA and must receive any employer nonelective contribution for the year provided under the plan. [I.R.C. §§ 408(p)(4)(A), 401(k)(11)(B)(iii)]

Q 22:69 Are there employees who may be excluded from a SIMPLE IRA?

Yes. Employees described in Section 410(b)(3) may be excluded from eligibility under a SIMPLE IRA. These employees are (1) those included in a unit of employees covered by a collective bargaining agreement between employee representatives and one or more employers, and (2) nonresident aliens who received no earned income (within the meaning of Section 911(d)(2)) from the employer that constitutes income from sources within the United States (within the meaning of Section 861(a)(3)). [I.R.C. §§ 408(p)(4)(B), 401(k)(11)(B)(iii)]

Q 22:70 Can an employer maintain a SIMPLE IRA and another qualified plan in the same calendar year?

Generally no. An employer cannot make contributions under a SIMPLE IRA plan for a calendar year if employees receive contributions under a defined contribution plan (other than the SIMPLE IRA) or an accrual in a defined benefit plan maintained by the employer, or a predecessor employer, for any plan year beginning or ending within that calendar year. [I.R.C. § 408(p)(2)(D)]

Q 22:71 Can an employer maintain a SIMPLE 401(k) plan and another qualified plan in the same calendar year?

Although employers cannot maintain any other retirement plan for employees who are eligible to participate in the SIMPLE 401(k), the employer may maintain a different retirement plan to cover those employees who are not eligible to participate in the SIMPLE 401(k) plan. [I.R.C. §§ 401(k)(11)(A)(ii), (C)]

Contributions to SIMPLE IRAs and SIMPLE 401(k) Plans

Q 22:72 What type of contributions may be made to a SIMPLE IRA plan?

Each eligible employee may make salary reduction contributions to a SIMPLE IRA. The employer must either match the salary reduction contributions or make a nonelective contribution. No other contributions may be made under a SIMPLE IRA plan. [I.R.C. § 408(p)(2)(A)]

Q 22:73 How much may an employee defer under a SIMPLE IRA or SIMPLE 401(k) plan?

An employee may defer up to $12,500 for 2015, subject to cost-of-living adjustments for later years. [I.R.C. §§ 408(p)(2)(E); 401(k)(11)(B)] The salary reduction contributions under a SIMPLE IRA plan count toward the overall annual limit on elective deferrals an employee may make to this and any other plans permitting elective deferrals. [I.R.C. § 408(p)(8)]

Q 22:74 Can catch-up contributions be made to a SIMPLE IRA or SIMPLE 401(k) plan?

Yes. Employees age 50 or over can make a catch-up contribution of up to $3,000 for 2015, subject to cost-of-living adjustments for later years. [I.R.C. § 414(v)(2)(C)(ii)]

Q 22:75 Can contributions made under a SIMPLE IRA be made to any type of IRA?

Contributions under a SIMPLE IRA may only be made to a SIMPLE IRA, not to any other type of IRA. A SIMPLE IRA is an individual retirement account described in Section 408(a), or an individual retirement annuity described in Section 408(b), to which the only contributions that can be made are contributions under a SIMPLE IRA plan and rollovers or transfers from another SIMPLE IRA. [I.R.C. § 408(p)(2)(D)]

Q 22:76 May designated Roth contributions be made to a SIMPLE IRA?

No. Designated Roth contributions are not permitted in SIMPLE IRA plans.

Q 22:77 What employer contributions are generally required under a SIMPLE IRA or SIMPLE 401(k) plan?

Under a SIMPLE IRA or SIMPLE 401(k) plan, an employer is generally required to (1) match the participant contributions dollar-for-dollar up to 3 percent of pay or (2) make a 2 percent nonelective contribution for each eligible employee. The employer's nonelective contributions must be made for each eligible employee regardless of whether the employee elects to make salary reduction contributions for the calendar year. The employer may, but is not required to, limit nonelective contributions to eligible employees who have at least $5,000 (or some lower amount selected by the employer) of compensation for the year. The employees are immediately 100 percent vested in any and all contributions. [I.R.C. §§ 408(p)(2), 401(k)(11)(A), (B)]

For the SIMPLE IRA, an employer who elects to make matching contributions may choose to reduce contributions to less than 3 percent but no less than 1 percent for two out of every five years. [I.R.C. § 408(p)(2)(C)(ii)(II)] This option is not available for SIMPLE 401(k)s.

All employer contributions to a SIMPLE 401(k) are subject to the compensation limit in Section 401(a)(17), which is $265,000 for 2015. On the other hand, only nonelective employer contributions to SIMPLE IRAs are subject to the compensation cap. [I.R.C. §§ 408(p)(2)(B)(ii); 401(k)(11)(B)(i)]

Q 22:78 How much of the contributions made to employees' SIMPLE IRAs or SIMPLE 401(k) plans may be deducted on the employer's tax return?

The employer may deduct all contributions made to its employees' SIMPLE IRAs or SIMPLE 401(k) plans. [I.R.C. §§ 404(m), 404(a)(3)]

Distributions from SIMPLE IRAs and SIMPLE 401(k) Plans

Q 22:79 May amounts held in a SIMPLE IRA or SIMPLE 401(k) be withdrawn at any time?

SIMPLE IRAs must permit distributions to be taken at any time. An employer may not require an employee to retain any portion of the contributions in his or her SIMPLE IRA or otherwise impose any withdrawal restrictions. [I.R.C. § 408(p)(3)] With respect to SIMPLE 401(k) plans, in-service hardship withdrawals are allowed. [I.R.C. §§ 401(k)(11)(A)(iii); 408(p)(3)] In either case, premature withdrawals made prior to age 59½ may be subject to a 10 percent penalty tax. [I.R.C. § 72(t)]

Q 22:80 What are the tax consequences when amounts are distributed from a SIMPLE IRA?

Generally, the same tax results apply to distributions from a SIMPLE IRA as to distributions from a traditional IRA. However, a special rule applies to a payment or distribution received from a SIMPLE IRA during the two-year period beginning on the date on which the individual first participated in any SIMPLE IRA plan maintained by the individual's employer (the "two-year period").

Under this special rule, if the additional income tax on early distributions under Section 72(t) applies to a distribution within this two-year period, the rate of additional tax under this special rule is increased from 10 percent to 25 percent. If one of the exceptions to application of the tax under Section 72(t) applies (e.g., for amounts paid after age 59½, after death, or as part of a series of substantially equal payments), the exception also applies to distributions within the two-year period and the 25 percent additional tax does not apply. The two-year period begins on the first day on which contributions made by the individual's employer are deposited in the individual's SIMPLE IRA. [I.R.C. § 72(t)(6)]

Q 22:81 Are loans allowed from a SIMPLE IRA or SIMPLE 401(k)?

Loans are not allowed from a SIMPLE IRA because it is an IRA-based plan. [I.R.C. §§ 408(e)(3), (4)] On the other hand, an employer may include loans as a feature in a SIMPLE 401(k) plan.

Q 22:82 Why might an employer choose a SIMPLE IRA rather than a SIMPLE 401(k)?

Unlike a SIMPLE 401(k) plan, a SIMPLE IRA does not require a complex plan document. Also with a SIMPLE IRA, there is limited ongoing plan sponsor administration and no need to file an annual Form 5500. Additionally, an employer sponsoring a SIMPLE IRA may reduce the amount of elective deferral matching contributions in two of any five years, an option that is not available under a SIMPLE 401(k).

Q 22:83 Why might an employer choose a SIMPLE 401(k) plan rather than a SIMPLE IRA?

Generally, a SIMPLE IRA is less flexible than a SIMPLE 401(k) plan. SIMPLE 401(k) plans may cover a specific group of employees if the employer has a different plan covering other employees. SIMPLE 401(k) plans may offer loans and a SIMPLE 401(k) plan can be converted to a regular 401(k) at any time.

Q 22:84 If a SIMPLE IRA or SIMPLE 401(k) plan fails to meet the plan requirements, are the employer and employee tax benefits lost?

The Pension Protection Act of 2006 [Pub. L. No. 109-280, 120 Stat. 780] created qualified charitable distribution (QCD) transfers. Individuals aged 70½ or older were allowed to make tax-free charitable gifts of up to $100,000 directly from their IRAs to Section 501(c)(3) charities effective August 17, 2006 through the end of 2007. Congress has repeatedly extended QCDs, most recently through 2014, in the Tax Increase Prevention Act of 2014. [Pub. L. No. 113-295, 128 Stat. 4010] At the time this edition goes to press, Congress has not yet extended QCDs for 2015 and beyond.

Q 22:85 What IRS guidance is available to assist employers in complying with the SIMPLE IRA and 401(k) rules?

The IRS has a SIMPLE IRA Plan Fix-it Guide and a 401(k) Fix-it Guide, each of which provides tips on how to find, fix, and avoid common mistakes in SIMPLE IRA plans and 401(k) plans. The SIMPLE IRA Fix-it Guide is available at *www.irs.gov/Retirement-Plans/SIMPLE-IRA-Plan-Fix-It-Guide* and the 401(k) Fix-it Guide is available at *www.irs.gov/Retirement-Plams/401(k)-Plan-Fix-It-Guide.*

Q 22:86 Where can information on retirement plans for small businesses be found?

Comprehensive IRS Small Business Retirement Plan Resources guidance is available on the IRS Web site. Information on choosing a plan, operating and maintaining a plan, correcting plan errors, as well as additional resources can be found at *www.irs.gov/Retirement-Plans/Plan-Sponsor/Small-Business-Retirement-Plan-Resources*.

Table 22-5. Comparison of SIMPLE IRA Plans with SIMPLE 401(k) and Regular 401(k) Plans

Feature	*SIMPLE IRA*	*SIMPLE 401(k)*	*Regular 401(k)*
Eligible employers	100 or fewer employees making $5,000 in prior year (2-year grace period)	Same as SIMPLE IRA, except no governmental employer	Any, except governmental employer
Types of contributions	Employee deferrals	Employee deferrals	Employee deferrals
	Employer match or nonelective	Employer match or nonelective	Employer match; Employer fixed or discretionary
Other qualified plans	No	No (unless for employees not covered by the SIMPLE 401(k))	Yes
401(k)/401(m) discrimination testing	No	No	Yes
Top-heavy testing	No	No	Yes
Elective deferral limit	$12,000 as indexed for cost-of-living increases (2015)	$12,000 as indexed for cost-of-living increases (2015)	$18,000 as indexed for cost-of-living increases (2015)
Age 50 catch-up	$3,000 (2015)	$3,000 as indexed for cost-of- living increases (2015)	$6,000 as indexed for cost-of-living increases (2015)
Level of match	100% of first 3% of compensation	100% of first 3% (subject to Section 401(a)(17) cap)	Any (subject to Section 401(m) test)
Match alternative	Nonelective employer contribution of 2% of compensation	With notice may make 2% nonelective contribution	Any (subject to Section 401(m) test)
Subject to Section 415 limits	No	Yes	Yes
Eligibility requirements	No minimum age or service	Minimum age 21	Same as SIMPLE 401(k)
	Earned $5,000 in any 2 prior years and expected to earn $5,000 this year	1 year service/1,000 hours	

(*Continued*)

Table 22-5. Comparison of SIMPLE IRA Plans with SIMPLE 401(k) and Regular 401(k) Plans (*cont'd*)

Feature	*SIMPLE IRA*	*SIMPLE 401(k)*	*Regular 401(k)*
Vesting	100% immediate	100% immediate	Graded schedules allowed on employer contributions
Withdrawals	No restrictions; 10% pre-$59\frac{1}{2}$ penalty (25% in first 2 years)	Can restrict; 10% pre-$59\frac{1}{2}$ penalty	Same as SIMPLE 401(k)
Form 5500 reporting	No	Yes	Yes
Investment restrictions	No loans No life insurance	None	None

Cash Balance Plans

Q 22:87 What is a *cash balance plan*?

A *cash balance plan* is a type of defined benefit plan that is designed to look like a defined contribution plan. Each participant has a hypothetical account balance with hypothetical contributions and earnings, but the employer assumes the investment risk. Cash balance plans promise a defined benefit through the interest rate credited and contribution guarantees.

In October 2010, the IRS and the Treasury Department issued final and proposed regulations interpreting many of the rules that were enacted in the Pension Protection Act of 2006. [Pub. L. No. 109-280, 120 Stat. 780] Together, the regulations interpret the primary changes made by PPA related to:

- General age discrimination rules,
- Market-rate-of-return limits for interest credits,
- Anti-wear-away protections for plan conversions,
- Three-year vesting, and
- Elimination of whipsaw and other distribution valuation rules.

For the major features, current status, and the advantages and disadvantages of cash balance plans, see Wolters Kluwer's, *Cash Balance Plan Answer Book*, Third Edition.

Floor-Offset Plans

Q 22:88 What is a *floor-offset plan*?

A *floor-offset plan* is a defined benefit pension plan in which the benefit is reduced, or offset, by the benefit provided under a defined contribution plan. This arrangement allows the employer to guarantee floor, or base, benefits regardless of the amount of benefits derived from the defined contribution plan. The employee never receives less than the promised benefit under the defined benefit plan, but will receive more if the defined contribution plan benefit is greater.

For the major features and the advantages and disadvantages of floor-offset plans, see Wolters Kluwer's *Defined Benefit Answer Book*.

Nonqualified Deferred Compensation (NQDC) Plans

A nonqualified deferred compensation (NQDC) plan is any elective or nonelective plan, agreement, method, or arrangement between an employer and an employee (or service recipient and service provider) to pay the employee compensation some time in the future. NQDC plans do not satisfy all of the qualification requirements of Section 401(a) and thus do not provide employers and employees with the tax benefits enjoyed by qualified plans.

NQDC plans are either funded or unfunded, though most are intended to be unfunded because of the tax advantages unfunded plans provide participants. A funded arrangement generally exists if assets are set aside from the claims of the employer's creditors, such as in a trust for the exclusive benefit of participants. For NQDC purposes, what is relevant is whether the employee has a beneficial interest in the assets. If the arrangement is funded, the benefit is likely taxable under Code Sections 83 and 402(b). In a tax audit, the IRS will examine when amounts deferred under the NQDC are includable in the employee's gross income and when those amounts are deductible by the employer.

Types of NQDC Plans

Q 22:89 What types of NQDC plans are available?

NQDC plans have many names and can vary significantly. One broad category of NQDC plans consists of salary reduction or bonus deferral arrangements allowing employees to defer the receipt of otherwise currently includable salary or bonuses. Top-hat plans are NQDC plans maintained for a select group of management or highly compensated employees (HCEs). [ERISA § 201(2)] Some top-hat plans are called supplemental executive retirement plans, or SERPs. Excess benefit plans are NQDC plans providing benefits solely to employees whose benefits under the employer's qualified plan are limited by Section 415. [ERISA § 3(36)]

Q 22:90 What is a *top-hat plan*?

A *top-hat plan* is an unfunded nonqualified plan maintained for the purpose of providing benefits to a select group of management or HCEs. [ERISA § 201(2)] All amounts in the plan are owned by the employer and subject to the employer's general creditors.

Q 22:91 What is an *excess benefit plan*?

An *excess benefit plan* is a nonqualified plan maintained solely for the purpose of providing benefits to employees in excess of the benefits allowed under a qualified plan due to Section 415 limitations (see chapter 9). [ERISA § 3(36)]

Q 22:92 What is an *unfunded plan*?

An *unfunded plan* is an arrangement where the employer owns the assets and the employee has only the employer's promise to pay the deferred compensation benefits at some point in the future. The promise is not secured in any way and employees must be general creditors of the employer without any preferences over other creditors in the event of the employer's bankruptcy or insolvency. Although the employer may transfer amounts to a grantor trust, the assets must remain a part of the employer's general assets, subject to the claims of the employer's creditors. If amounts are set aside from the employer's creditors for the exclusive benefit of the employee, the tax benefits of an unfunded arrangement will be lost.

Q 22:93 What is a *funded plan*?

The plan is a *funded plan* if the amounts deferred under the NQDC have been set aside for the exclusive benefit of the employee, such as in a trust. Amounts must not be available to the employer's general creditors should the employer become bankrupt or insolvent.

Tax Aspects of NQDC Plans

Q 22:94 When are amounts deferred under an unfunded NQDC includable in an employee's gross income?

Amounts deferred under an unfunded NQDC are includable in the employee's gross income in the taxable year in which the amounts are actually or constructively received. Under the constructive receipt doctrine in Section 451(a), income is constructively received by the employee in the taxable year during which it is (1) credited to his account, (2) set apart for him, or (3) otherwise made available so that he may withdraw it at any time. Income is not constructively received, however, if the taxpayer's control of its receipt is subject to substantial limitations or restrictions. [Treas. Reg. § 1.451-2(a)]

Q 22:95 What is an example of how the constructive receipt doctrine works?

Interest in a savings account is an example of the constructive receipt doctrine. Such interest is taxed to the account owner each year even if none of the interest is withdrawn because there is no limitation on the individual's right to withdraw it.

Q 22:96 When are amounts deferred under a funded NQDC includable in an employee's gross income?

Amounts are taxable under a funded NQDC pursuant to the economic benefit doctrine. If an individual receives any economic or financial benefit or property as compensation for services, the value of the benefit or property is includable in the individual's gross income when received. More specifically, the doctrine requires an employee to include in current gross income, the value of assets that have been unconditionally and irrevocably transferred as compensation into a fund for the employee's sole benefit, if the employee has a nonforfeitable interest in the fund. [I.R.C. §§ 83 and 402(b)]

Q 22:97 When are amounts deferred under a NQDC deductible by the employer?

The employer's deduction must match the employee's inclusion of the compensation in income. The amount of deferred compensation the employer deducts must match the amounts reported on the employees' Forms W-2 for the year. The employer's deduction may also be limited by Section 162(m). Interest or earnings credited to amounts deferred under NQDC plans do not qualify as interest deductible under Section 163, but rather represent additional deferred compensation deductible under Section 404(a)(5).

Q 22:98 When are amounts deferred under a NQDC taken into account for FICA tax purposes?

Under either a funded or unfunded NQDC plan, deferred amounts are taken into account for FICA tax purposes at the later of (1) when the services are performed or (2) when there is no substantial risk of forfeiture with respect to the employee's right to receive the deferred amounts in a later calendar year. Thus, amounts are subject to FICA taxes at the time of deferral, unless the employee is required to perform substantial future services in order for the employee to have a legal right to the future payment. If the employee is required to perform future services in order to have a vested right to the future payment, the deferred amount (plus earnings up to the date of vesting) are subject to FICA taxes when all the required services have been performed. FICA taxes apply up to the annual wage base for Social Security taxes and without limitations for Medicare taxes. [I.R.C. § 3121(a)]

Q 22:99 When are amounts deferred under a NQDC taken into account for FUTA tax purposes?

NQDC amounts are taken into account for FUTA purposes at the later of when services are performed or when there is no substantial risk of forfeiture with respect to the employee's right to receive the deferred amounts up to the FUTA wage base. [I.R.C. § 3301]

Q 22:100 What additional restrictions apply to NQDC plans of tax-exempt organizations?

In addition to the basic NQDC plan rules and Code Section 409A, nonqualified plans maintained by tax-exempt entities, including governmental entities, are subject to additional restrictions under Code Section 457(f). In addition to being structured as top-hat plans to avoid violating ERISA's funding requirements, compensation contributed to a Section 457(f) plan must be subject to a substantial risk of forfeiture. The participant receives tax-deferred treatment only so long as receipt of the compensation is conditioned on the future performance of substantial services. [I.R.C. §§ 83, 457(f)(1), 457(f)(3)(B)] The mere fact that an employer's promise to make future payments under the plan is unfunded or unsecured does not constitute a substantial risk of forfeiture.

[Treas. Reg. § 1.83-3] The deferred compensation is taxable in the year in which the substantial risk of forfeiture lapses.

Any earnings credited on amounts deferred under a Section 457(f) plan are includable in the participant's gross income only when paid or made available, so long as the participant's interest in the earnings is not senior to that of the employer's general creditors. [Treas. Reg. § 1.457-11(a)(3)] Distributions are subject to income tax under Code Section 72. [Treas. Reg. § 1.457-11(a)(4)]

Q 22:101 Can a NQDC plan be linked to a defined contribution plan?

Yes, in certain circumstances, a NQDC plan may be designed to wrap around an existing defined contribution plan. For example, if a 401(k) plan has a nonqualified plan wrapped around it, the employer would be permitted to make contributions to the nonqualified plan prior to ADP testing on the 401(k) plan. After ADP testing, the employer may transfer funds contributed for HCEs from the nonqualified plan to the 401(k) plan up to the ADP limit. Employer contributions in excess of the ADP limit would remain in the NQDC arrangement.

A NQDC plan that references the employer's 401(k) plan may contain a provision that could cause disqualification of the 401(k) plan. Code Section 401(k)(4)(A) and Treasury Regulations Section 1.401(k)-1(e)(6) provide that a 401(k) plan may not condition any other benefit (including participation in a NQDC) upon the employee's participation or nonparticipation in the 401(k) plan.

Advantages and Disadvantages of NQDC Plans

Q 22:102 What are the advantages of a NQDC plan to the employer?

NQDC plans provide a number of advantages to the employer. Such plans are very effective in providing retirement benefits to key employees without the need to cover all employees under a qualified plan. The plans can be individually tailored to the needs of the key executives and the employer and are a useful means of recruiting, retaining and rewarding key personnel. Contributions are made at the discretion of the employer and the employer can control the benefits offered under such plans. Since unfunded NQDC plans are exempt from most ERISA rules, administration may be simpler than that of a qualified plan.

Q 22:103 What are the advantages of an unfunded NQDC plan to employees?

No contribution limits apply to unfunded NQDC plans, which is a very attractive feature for key employees. The current deferral of income tax can result in significant tax savings, and death benefits provide protection for the individual's family.

Q 22:104 What are the disadvantages of an unfunded NQDC plan to the employer?

The employer's receipt of a tax deduction on compensation contributed to an unfunded NQDC plan are deferred until benefits become taxable to the employee. Furthermore, the earnings on the funds set aside in the NQDC plan may be immediately taxable to the employer.

Q 22:105 What are the disadvantages of an unfunded NQDC plan to the employee?

A NQDC plan is an unsecured promise to pay benefits in the future. All assets in an unfunded NQDC plan belong to the employer and are subject to the claims of the employer's general creditors. Additionally, employees in a plan subject to Code Section 457(f) are subject to a substantial risk of forfeiture.

Impact of Code Section 409A

Q 22:106 What is Section 409A?

The American Jobs Creation Act of 2004 [Pub. L. No. 108-357, 118 Stat. 1418] (AJCA) added Section 409A to the Code. Section 409A applies to compensation that employees earn in one year but that is not paid until a future year. Section 409A provides that all amounts deferred under a NQDC plan for all taxable years are currently includable in gross income (to the extent not subject to a substantial risk of forfeiture and not previously included in gross income), unless certain requirements are satisfied. Section 409A does not apply to qualified plans (such as a 401(k) plan) or to a 403(b) plan or an eligible 457(b) plan.

Q 22:107 When was Section 409A effective?

Section 409A became effective with respect to amounts deferred in taxable years beginning after December 31, 2004. It also is effective with respect to amounts deferred in taxable years beginning before January 1, 2005, but only if the plan under which the deferral is made is materially modified after October 3, 2004. [Treas. Reg. § 1.409A-6(a)(4)]

Q 22:108 Was the Section 409A compliance deadline extended?

Yes. Treasury and the IRS did not publish the final Treasury regulations explaining Section 409A's detailed requirements until April 10, 2007, with a January 1, 2008, effective date. Subsequently, the effective date for full compliance was postponed to January 1, 2009, by Notice 2007-78 [2007-41 I.R.B. 780] and Notice 2007-86 [2007-41 I.R.B. 990]. Full compliance generally means that a NQDC plan or arrangement must be operated in accordance with a legally binding written document that subjects it to all the rules in the Section 409A final regulations.

Q 22:109 What impact does Code Section 409A have on NQDC plans?

Code Section 409A dictates plan design, plan operation, distribution restrictions, timing on deferral elections, taxation and tax reporting rules for NQDC plans of all types of employers. Generally, Section 409A imposes limitations on: (1) when an employee (or service provider) with the option to defer may make the election to defer compensation; (2) when deferred compensation may be paid; and (3) when a change may be made to the payment date. Section 409A also generally prohibits funding of NQDC plans with offshore trusts or other offshore security devices. [I.R.C. § 409A(b)(3)]

Q 22:110 What are the basic requirements of Code Section 409A?

Code Section 409A is intended to prevent manipulation of the amount of deferred compensation and when it will be paid. The basic rules include the following:

- An employee's election to defer compensation generally must be made before the start of the calendar year in which the compensation is earned.
- The time and form of deferred compensation payments must be elected by the employee, or be contained in plan provisions, before the compensation is earned. Neither the employer nor employee may retain discretion regarding when payment must be made. Further, the time of the payment generally may not be accelerated.
- Deferred compensation may be paid only if:
  - Payment is made at a specified time or pursuant to a fixed schedule,
  - The employee has a separation from service,
  - The employee dies or becomes totally disabled,
  - There is a "change in control" of the employer, or
  - The employee has an unforeseen financial hardship.

Q 22:111 How does coverage under Section 409A affect an employee's taxes?

Section 409A has no effect on the taxation of an employee's deferred compensation as long as the requirements of Section 409A are satisfied. The compensation is taxed in the same manner as it would be taxed if it were not covered by Section 409A.

Q 22:112 What are the consequences of noncompliance with Section 409A?

Section 409A imposes harsh tax penalties for plans and arrangements that do not satisfy its rules. Generally, if a nonqualified deferred compensation plan or arrangement does not comply with Section 409A, the amount deferred will be included in the employee's income immediately, whether or not the amount is currently payable. [I.R.C. § 409A(a)(1)] Additionally, a penalty tax of 20 percent will be imposed on the amount included in income, as well as interest calculated at the IRS interest rate for tax underpayments plus one percent for the period from the date when the amount was first deferred to the date when it is includable in income. [I.R.C. § 409A(b)(2)] Section 409A has no effect on FICA tax.

Q 22:113 Is there an IRS correction program for violations of Section 409A?

Yes. IRS Notice 2010-6 [2010-3 I.R.B. 275 (Jan. 5, 2010)], established a new Section 409A correction program. This program permits a plan sponsor to correct many types of "document" failures relating to Code Section 409A. A document failure generally relates to a provision in a deferred compensation arrangement that does not satisfy the Section 409A requirements.

Notice 2010-6 clarifies that certain noncompliant terms will not be treated as Section 409A "document" failures if the plan is operated in a manner that complies with Section 409A.

Q 22:114 What requirements must be satisfied to use the correction program in Notice 2010-06?

Under Notice 2010-06, the requirements that must be satisfied to use the correction program include:

- The "document" failures must be inadvertent and unintentional.
- The employer must correct all deferred compensation arrangements having the same type of error.
- The employer is not currently being audited by the IRS. However, there was a transition rule that applied to employers through 2011. The employer was treated as not being under audit unless the specific plan provision being amended was identified as a problem in an IRS audit.
- The affected employee's income tax return is not currently being audited by the IRS.
- Both the employer and the employee must attach information regarding the correction to their respective income tax returns for the taxable year in which the correction was made.

Q 22:115 Are penalties reduced or eliminated if an employer corrects a Section 409A violation using the procedures provided in Notice 2010-06?

Yes. If an employer corrects a Section 409A "document" error using the procedures in Notice 2010-6, the Section 409A penalties are reduced or totally eliminated. As a general rule, no Section 409A penalties apply if: (1) the "document" failure was corrected by December 31, 2010, or (2) the "document" failure was corrected after December 31, 2010, but the corrected plan provision did not affect the operation of the plan within one year after the correction.

In other situations, reduced Section 409A penalties may apply. For example, a 50 percent penalty may apply if the improper payment event that was corrected occurs within one year after the correction.

On November 30, 2010, the IRS issued Notice 2010-80 [2010-51 I.R.B. 853], modifying its existing procedures for voluntarily correcting failures to comply with Section 409A of the Internal Revenue Code (Code). Some of the changes included in Notice 2010-80 will make the correction procedure significantly less burdensome.

The Section 409A final regulations are exceedingly detailed. For additional information on Code Section 409A, see Downey, Smith & Connors, *Nonqualified Deferred Compensation Answer Book* (Wolters Kluwer Law & Business).

Benefit Security in Unfunded NQDC Plans

Q 22:116 What is a *rabbi trust*?

A *rabbi trust* is an irrevocable grantor-type trust used to secure the payment of deferred compensation benefits under an unfunded NQDC plan. The trust is referred to as a rabbi trust because the first IRS letter ruling with respect to this type of trust involved a rabbi whose congregation had made contributions to such a trust for his benefit. [Priv. Ltr. Rul. 8113107 (Dec. 31, 1980)] The employer gives up all rights to the assets and may not terminate the trust. As a grantor trust, however, all income is taxed to the employer at the corporate rate.

Q 22:117 What is the purpose of a rabbi trust?

The purpose of establishing a rabbi trust is to offer some level of security to the employees with respect to their nonqualified benefits. Employee deferrals are placed in the trust and such funds may not revert to the employer until all benefit obligations are fully discharged. Trust assets must be used to pay benefits under the plan unless the employer becomes insolvent. In the case of bankruptcy or insolvency, the trustee must hold the assets for the benefit of the employer's general creditors.

Q 22:118 Has the IRS issued a model rabbi trust document?

The IRS has issued guidance setting forth model rabbi trust provisions that provide a safe harbor for taxpayers who adopt and maintain grantor trusts in connection with unfunded deferred compensation arrangements. [Rev. Proc. 92-64, 1992-2 C.B. 422, *modified in part by* Notice 2000-56, 2000-2 C.B. 393, 10/06/2000]

NQDC Plans Versus 401(k) Plans

Q 22:119 When might a NQDC plan be used as an alternative to a 401(k) plan?

An employer that is mainly concerned with providing the maximum benefits possible to key employees would choose a NQDC plan over a 401(k) plan. Highly compensated employees are allowed to defer up to 100 percent of compensation.

Q 22:120 When might a NQDC plan be used to supplement a 401(k) plan?

NQDC plans are often used to supplement an employer's 401(k) plan. The NQDC allows highly compensated employees to defer amounts in excess of the 401(k) contribution limits.

Section 403(b) Plans—Tax-Sheltered Annuities

A 403(b) plan is a tax deferred arrangement under which employees of eligible employers may exclude salary reduction contributions and earnings from gross income until distributed from the plan. [I.R.C. § 403(b)] The following Q&As incorporate changes made to Code Section 403(b) by the final IRS regulations issued in 2007.

Eligible Employers and Funding Rules

Q 22:121 What types of organizations may establish and maintain Section 403(b) plans?

Organizations whose primary purpose is religious, charitable, scientific, literary, educational, or safety testing, as described in Section 501(c)(3), and public school systems are eligible to establish and maintain a 403(b) plan for their employees. [I.R.C. §§ 403(b)(1)(A)(i), (ii)] Certain state and local hospitals with Section 501(c)(3) standing are also eligible employers. [Rev. Rul. 67-290, 1967-2 C.B. 183]

Q 22:122 What funding vehicles may be used in a Section 403(b) plan?

Eligible employers, other than those maintaining church plans, must fund their plan with annuity contracts purchased from an insurance company [I.R.C. § 403(b)(1); Treas. Reg. § 1.403(b)-3(a)] and/or custodial accounts offering only mutual fund investments [I.R.C. § 403(b)(7)]. Church plans have the option of using a third type of funding vehicle called a retirement income account. [I.R.C. § 403(b)(9)] No other funding options are available. Final Section 403(b) regulations issued in 2007 prohibited the use of separate life insurance policies to fund 403(b) plans.

Written Plan Document Requirement

Q 22:123 Must a Section 403(b) plan be maintained and operated pursuant to a written plan document?

Yes. The final § 403(b) regulations require all § 403(b) arrangements to be maintained pursuant to a written defined contribution plan document. Pursuant to IRS Notice 2009-3, the written plan must have been in place no later than December 31, 2009. [2009-52 I.R.B. 250] The written plan must satisfy the regulatory requirements of § 403(b) in both form and operation. [Treas. Reg. § 1.403(b)-3(b)(3); I.R.C. § 401(a)(1)(D); ERISA § 404(a)(1)] There is no requirement to seek IRS approval of the written plan.

Q 22:124 What provisions must be incorporated into Section 403(b) plans?

The written plan must contain all the material terms and conditions for eligibility, benefits, contribution limitations, the annuity contracts or custodial accounts available for funding, and the timing and form of benefit payments. Any optional plan features that the employer wishes to make available to employees must also be contained in the written plan. Section 403(b) plans should include:

- The specific annuity contracts and/or custodial accounts available to receive elective deferrals and contributions. [I.R.C. §§ 403(b)(1)(A); 403b)(7)] Revenue Procedure 2007-71 provides transition relief for grandfathered contracts. [2007-52 I.R.B. 1184 (Nov. 27,2008)]
- All § 403(b) contracts are aggregated and treated as one contract. [I.R.C. § 403(b)(5); Treas. Reg. § 1.403(b)-3(b)(1)]
- Employee's rights under the contract must be nonforfeitable. [I.R.C. § 403(b)(1)(C); Treas. Reg. § 1.403(b)-3)(a)(2)]
- Contract must be nontransferable. [Treas. Reg. § 1.403(b)-3(a)(5)]
- Elective deferral limits. [I.R.C. § 402(g); Treas. Reg. § 1.403(b)-5(b)]
- Elective deferrals must be universally available to all eligible employees. [Treas. Reg. § 1.403(b)-5(b)]
- Roth contributions and the earnings must be separately accounted for and cannot receive forfeitures. [I.R.C. § 402A(b); Treas. Reg. § 1.403(b)-3(c)]
- Roth in-plan rollovers of distributable pre-tax amounts and transfers of nondistributable pre-tax amounts allowed.
- Employer contribution limits. [I.R.C. §§ 415(c); 403(b)(1); Treas. Reg. § 1.403(b)-5(a)(1)]
- Includable compensation as defined in § 403(b)(3).
- Discrimination tests required on employer contributions. [I.R.C. §§ 403(b)(12); 403(b)(1)(D)]
  - Church plans exempt from discrimination testing. [I.R.C. § 403(b)(12)(B); Treas. Reg. § 1.403(b)-3(a)(3)]

  - Governmental plans exempt from discrimination testing. [I.R.C. § 403(b)(12)(C); Treas. Reg. § 1.403(b)-5(a)(5)]
- Rollovers pursuant to § 401(a)(30) requirements. [I.R.C. § 403(b)(1)(E)]
- Years of service as defined in § 403(b)(4). [Treas. Reg. § 1.403(b)-4(e)]
- Elective deferral distribution restrictions. [I.R.C. § 403(b)(11)]
- Employer contribution distribution restrictions. [Treas. Reg. § 1.403(b)-6(b).
- Required minimum distributions rules pursuant to § 401(a)(9). [I.R.C. § 403(b)(10); Treas. Reg. § 1.403(b)-3(a)(6)]
  - RMDs waived for 2009. [I.R.C. § 401(a)(9)(H); WRERA]
  - Governmental plans may use a reasonable, good-faith interpretation of the rule. [PPA; Prop. Treas. Reg. § 1.401(a)(9)-6, Q&A-16]
- Trustee transfers from governmental § 403(b) to purchase service credits in a governmental defined benefit plan. [I.R.C. § 403(b)(13); Treas. Reg. § 1.403(b)-10(b)(4)]
- Death benefits under USERRA for qualified military. [I.R.C. § 403(b)(14)]

Q 22:125 May an employer include a provision in the plan document to terminate the 403(b) plan?

Yes. The final Section 403(b) regulations permit an employer to include a provision in the plan document allowing the plan to be terminated, but only if all benefits are distributed to participants and beneficiaries as soon as administratively feasible. [Treas. Reg. § 1.403(b)-10(a)]

Q 22:126 Is there a prototype plan program for 403(b) plans?

Yes. On March 29, 2013, the IRS issued Revenue Procedure 2013-22 [2013-18 I.R.B. 1], which establishes a program for the pre-approval of Section 403(b) plan documents. The IRS will issue an opinion or advisory letter as to whether the form of a 403(b) prototype or volume submitter plan meets the requirements of Section 403(b). The program was effective April 29, 2013, and the IRS began accepting applications on June 28, 2013.

In Revenue Procedure 2014-28, issued on March 25, 2014, the IRS postponed the 403(b) document submission deadline from April 30, 2014 to April 30, 2015. Also, in response to comments from plan sponsors and practitioners, the eligibility requirements for the program were modified to allow more plan sponsors and employers to participate in the 403(b) pre-approved program by lowering the required number of employers expected to adopt their pre-approved plan from 30 to 15.

Q 22:127 How does the 403(b) Pre-approved Plan Program affect a plan's remedial amendment period?

By adopting a 403(b) pre-approved plan by the deadline, which will be established and announced by the IRS, the Pre-approved Plan Program allows an eligible employer to retroactively correct defects in the form of its written 403(b) plan back to the first day of the plan's remedial amendment period, which is the later of January 1, 2010, or the plan's effective date.

The employer's adoption of a pre-approved 403(b) plan that has a favorable opinion of advisory letter automatically corrects any defects in its prior written 403(b) plan but not defects in any documents incorporated by reference in to the prior plan. Interim amendments are not required for a plan to be eligible for this remedial amendment period.

403(b) plan sponsors who did not adopt a written plan before December 31, 2009 may use the 403(b) Voluntary Program Submission Kit to correct this error.

Nondiscrimination Rules

Q 22:128 How do the minimum participation and coverage rules apply to Section 403(b) plans?

Employer nonelective and matching contributions into a § 403(b) plan made by a non-governmental, non-church employer must meet the same minimum participation and coverage rules applicable to 401(k) plans. [I.R.C. § 403(b)(12)(A)(i)] The final 403(b) regulations issued in 2007 repealed the nondiscrimination safe harbors of IRS Notice 89-23.

Q 22:129 What nondiscrimination rule applies to 403(b) elective deferrals?

The only nondiscrimination rule that applies to elective deferrals is the universal availability rule under which all eligible employees choosing to defer a minimum of $200 per year must be allowed to make elective deferrals immediately upon hire. [I.R.C. § 403(b)(12)(A)(ii)] No age or service conditions may be imposed on elective deferrals. Employers must notify their employers of their right to make elective deferrals, when to make an election, and when and how often during the year they can change that election. [Treas. Reg. § 1.403(b)-5(b)(2)] Church 403(b) plans are exempt from the universal availability requirement, but government 403(b) plans must comply.

Q 22:130 What categories of employees may be excluded from making elective deferrals?

Employees that may be excluded from making 403(b) plan elective deferrals are: (1) those who are eligible to defer under another employer plan, such as a 457(b) plan or a 401(k) plan; (2) nonresident aliens; (3) students performing services as described in Section 3121(b)(10); and (4) employees who normally work fewer than 20 hours per week.

Q 22:131 Are there nondiscrimination rules that apply to employer contributions?

Yes, non-governmental and non-church plans must meet the nondiscrimination requirements for both employer nonelective and matching contributions. [I.R.C. § 403(b)(12)] (See chapter 13.)

An employer's nonelective contributions must satisfy Code Sections 401(a)(4), 410(b), 407(a)(17), and 401(m) in the same manner as a qualified plan under Code Section 401(a).

Contributions to Section 403(b) Plans

Q 22:132 Who may make contributions to a Section 403(b) plan?

All eligible employees must be allowed to make salary reduction contributions immediately upon hire under the universal availability rule. [I.R.C. § 403(b)(12)] An eligible employer may also make nonelective contributions or matching contributions.

Q 22:133 Is there a dollar cap on employee elective deferrals?

Yes. The dollar cap under Section 402(g) applies to elective deferrals made to 403(b) plans. After 2006, the dollar cap has been adjusted periodically in increments of $500 to reflect cost-of-living increases; in 2015, the cap is $18,000. [I.R.C. §§ 402(g)(1)(B); 403(b)(1)(E); 401(a)(30); Treas. Reg. § 1.403(b)-4(c)]

Q 22:134 Are there special catch-up provisions that apply only to 403(b) plans?

Yes. An increased "special catch-up" provision is available to employees who (1) have completed 15 years of service with the current educational organization, hospital, home health service agency, church, convention or association of churches, or health and welfare service agency and (2) have underutilized elective deferral amounts from prior years. The special catch-up amount is determined by a formula and for any calendar year cannot exceed the lesser of (1) $3,000; (2) $15,000 less amounts previously used for special catch-up; or (3) $5,000 multiplied by the number of years of service, less elective deferrals made in prior years under the current employer's plan. [I.R.C. § 402(g)(7)]

Q 22:135 May employees make age 50 catch-up contributions?

Yes. A participant who has attained age 50 or over by the end of the calendar year may make additional elective deferrals of $6,000 in 2015. The age 50 catch-up amount is adjusted periodically in increments of $500 to reflect cost-of-living increases. [I.R.C. § 414(v)(2)(B)(i); Treas. Reg. § 1.403(b)-4(c)]

Q 22:136 May an employee make both the special 403(b) catch-up contribution and the age 50 catch-up contribution in the same year?

Yes. However, under the final Section 403(b) regulations, any amounts contributed in excess of the basic elective deferral limit are treated first as special 403(b) catch-up contributions and any additional amounts are treated as age 50 catch-up contributions. [Treas. Reg. § 1.403(b)-4(c)(3)(iv)]

Q 22:137 May employees make Roth contributions to a 403(b) plan?

Since January 2006 employers have been allowed to amend their 403(b) plans to include Roth 401(k) accounts. [I.R.C. § 402A] The amounts participants contribute to a designated Roth account are includable in gross income in the year of the contribution, but eligible distributions from the account (including earnings) generally are tax free. The employer must separately account for all contributions, gains, and losses to this designated Roth account until the account balance is completely distributed. There is only a single contribution limit for the 403(b) plan aggregated between pre-tax and Roth deferrals.

Q 22:138 Must Section 403(b) elective deferrals be treated as annual additions?

Yes. Annual additions include employee elective deferrals and after-tax contributions, employer nonelective and matching contributions, and allocated forfeitures. The aggregate of annual additions may not exceed the Section 415(c) limit for the calendar year, which in 2015 is $53,000. [Treas. Reg. § 1.403(b)-4(b)] Age 50 catch-up contributions are disregarded in applying the Section 415(c) limit.

Q 22:139 What types of employer contributions are allowed into a 403(b) plan?

Employers are allowed to make matching and nonelective contributions into a 403(b) plan. Additionally, nonelective employer contributions can be made to a participant's account for up to five years after the participant's severance from employment. Allowable contributions for each of the five years is the lesser of the dollar limit in effect under Section 415 during the year the contribution is made and the participant's includable compensation for his or her final year of employment. [Treas. Reg. § 1.403(b)-4(d)]

Distributions, Exchanges, and Rollovers

Q 22:140 What distribution restrictions apply to elective deferrals in a 403(b) plan?

Generally, elective deferrals in a 403(b) plan cannot be distributed until the participant attains age 59½ or severs from employment, except for hardship or disability. Withdrawals taken prior to age 59½ may be subject to a 10 percent penalty tax unless certain exceptions apply. [I.R.C. § 72(t)]

Q 22:141 Are employer contributions subject to distributions restrictions?

Yes. Pursuant to the final Section 403(b) regulations, employer contributions may not be distributed before the earlier of the participant's severance from employment or upon the occurrence of some event specified in the plan document, such as the passage of a fixed number of years, the attainment of a stated age, or disability. [Treas. Reg. § 1.403(b)-6]

Q 22:142 May Section 403(b) assets be exchanged among annuity contracts issued by different insurers?

Beginning January 1, 2009, pursuant to the final Section 403(b) regulations, a new kind of "transfer" called a *contract exchange* allows participants and beneficiaries to exchange one 403(b) contract for another with a provider approved by the employer to receive contract exchanges under the plan, provided all the following conditions are met:

1. The plan provides for contract exchanges;
2. The participant or beneficiary has an accumulated benefit immediately after the exchange that is at least equal to the accumulated benefit immediately before the exchange, not including fees or expenses of transfer;
3. The receiving contract is subject to distribution restrictions that are at least as stringent as those in the prior contract; and
4. The employer sponsoring the plan has entered into an information-sharing agreement with the provider accepting the exchange.

Q 22:143 May distributable amounts in a participant's pre-tax 403(b) account be rolled into a designated Roth account in the same plan?

Yes. Section 2112 of the Small Business Jobs Act of 2010 [Pub. L. No. 111-203, 124 Stat. 2504 (Sept. 27, 2010)] added a new design option for 401(k) and 403(b) plans effective September 29, 2010, and for governmental 457(b) plans effective January 1, 2011. This new in-plan rollover option permits a participant to roll an eligible rollover distribution from a pre-tax account to a designated Roth account within the same plan. The amount transferred into the Roth account is taxable in the year the transfer is made. IRS Notice 2010-84 [2010-51 I.R.B. 872] provides guidance to facilitate implementation of this provision. This provision is optional, and plan sponsors wishing to make it available must amend their plan documents to add it.

Q 22:144 May nondistributable amounts in a participant's pre-tax 403(b) account be transferred into a designated Roth account in the same plan?

Yes. The American Taxpayer Relief Act of 2012 [Pub. L. No. 112-240, 126 Stat. 2313 (Jan. 2, 2013)] permits pre-tax amounts in a 403(b) plan to be transferred to Roth amounts within the plan, regardless of whether the amounts are otherwise distributable. The amount transferred into the Roth account is taxable in the year the transfer is made. This provision is effective for transfers made after December 31, 2012, and is optional for plan sponsors. The IRS issued Notice 2013-74 [2013-52 I.R.B. 819 (Dec. 11, 2013)] to provide guidance for in-plan Roth transfers of amounts that are otherwise nondistributable as well as in-plan Roth rollovers of amounts that are eligible distribution amounts.

Q 22:145 May pre-tax assets in a 403(b) plan be rolled into a Roth IRA?

Yes. A participant who is entitled to take an eligible rollover distribution may roll all or a portion of his or her pre-tax assets directly to a Roth IRA. The pre-tax amount rolled into the Roth IRA is taxable in the year of the rollover. Roth IRAs cannot be rolled into Roth 403(b) plan accounts. [I.R.C. § 402A(c)(3)]

ERISA Title 1 Issues

Q 22:146 Is a Section 403(b) plan subject to Title 1 of ERISA?

Whether a 403(b) plan is subject to Title 1 of ERISA depends upon the type of entity sponsoring the 403(b) plan and, in some cases, the level of involvement of the employer in maintaining the plan. Governmental and nonelecting church plans have a blanket exemption from ERISA Title 1. [ERISA §§ 4(b)(1) and 4(b)(2)]

Tax-exempt sponsors of 403(b) plans are subject to Title 1 of ERISA unless they satisfy the safe harbor voluntary plan requirements. [ERISA Reg. § 2510. 3-2(f); DOL Field Assist. Bull. 2007-2 and DOL Field Assist. Bull. 2010-01]

Q 22:147 What rules must be met for a safe harbor exemption from ERISA?

A 403(b) plan offered by a non-governmental, non-church Section 501(c)(3) organization is subject to ERISA unless the arrangement satisfies all the requirements of a safe harbor plan described in ERISA Regulations Section 2510.3-2(f), DOL Field Assistance Bulletin 2007-2 (FAB 2007-2), and DOL Field Assistance Bulletin 2010-01 (FAB 2010-01).

ERISA Regulation Section 2510.3-2(f) provides that a program for the purchase of an annuity contract described in Section 403(b) shall not be deemed to be "established or maintained by an employer," and thus will not be an ERISA plan, if

- the plan exists only pursuant to salary reduction agreements or agreements to forego an increase in salary;

- employee participation is completely voluntary;
- all rights under the annuity contract are enforceable solely by the employee, by the beneficiary of such employee, or by any authorized representative of such employee or beneficiary;
- the sole involvement of the employer is limited; and
- the employer receives no direct or indirect consideration or compensation in cash or otherwise other than reasonable reimbursement to cover expenses properly and actually incurred in performing the employer's duties pursuant to salary reduction agreements.

Q 22:148 What DOL guidance on safe harbor 403(b) plans was issued in conjunction with the IRS final regulations?

In conjunction with the issuance of the final IRS and Treasury regulations, the DOL's Employee Benefits Security Administration (EBSA) issued FAB 2007-2 on July 24, 2007. FAB 2007-2 explains how the final 403(b) regulations affect the status of 403(b) plans under the DOL safe harbor regulation at 29 C.F.R. Section 2510.3-2(f). FAB 2007-2 guides an employer through activities it may and may not conduct in order to keep its ERISA safe harbor exemption. An employer may conduct administrative reviews of the plan structure and operation for tax compliance defects; fashion and propose corrections; develop improvements to the plan's administrative processes; obtain the cooperation of independent entities involved in the plan needed to correct tax defects; and keep records of its activities.

Q 22:149 What activities may employers engage in pursuant to FAB 2007-02 without violating the safe harbor?

Under FAB 2007-2, an employer seeking to retain its ERISA safe harbor exemption may:

- Certify to an annuity provider a state of facts within the employer's knowledge, such as employee addresses, attendance records or compensation levels;
- Transmit to the annuity provider another party's certification as to other facts, such as a doctor's certification of the employee's physical condition;
- Adopt a single plan document to coordinate administration among different issuers, and to address tax matters that apply, such as the universal availability requirement;
- Periodically review the documents making up the plan (plan document, annuity contracts, etc.) for conflicting provisions and for compliance with the Code and the Treasury regulations.

Q 22:150 What types of employer activity may violate the safe harbor?

According to FAB 2007-2, the following forms of employer involvement would be outside the safe harbor:

- Taking responsibility for, or making, discretionary determinations in administering the plan, such as authorizing plan-to-plan transfers, processing distributions, satisfying applicable qualified joint and survivor annuity requirements, making determinations regarding hardship distributions, QDROs, and eligibility for or enforcement of loans; and
- Negotiating with annuity providers or account custodians to change the terms of their products for purposes other than compliance with the Code and regulations, such as setting conditions for hardship withdrawals.

Q 22:151 What actions may employers take under the additional guidance provided in Field Assistance Bulletin 2010-01 without violating the safe harbor?

Under DOL Field Assistance Bulletin (FAB) 2010-01, employers intending to satisfy the safe harbor may:

- Elect to offer loans and other optional features so long as the 403(b) provider, not the employer is responsible for any discretionary decisions;
- Elect not to offer loans or other optional features and prohibit contracts or accounts with such features to reduce employer's costs and involvement;
- Select or require the provider of each contract or account to take responsibility for discretionary decisions; and
- Draft the plan document to de-select 403(b) providers that do not meet tax requirements.

Q 22:152 What employer actions are outside the safe harbor under FAB 2010-01?

Under FAB 2010-01, employers intending to satisfy the safe harbor must not:

- Make any discretionary determinations or exercise discretionary control over the plan, such as approving distributions, loans, hardship withdrawals, etc.;
- Appoint or otherwise retain a third-party administrator to make such discretionary decisions;
- Use discretionary authority to exchange or move funds from existing 403(b) providers; or
- Select a single 403(b) provider unless:
  - Employees are permitted to transfer or exchange their accounts to another 403(b) provider in accordance with IRS regulations (which would require an Information Sharing Agreement with each of those providers); or
  - The sole provider offers a wide array of investment products, and the employer can demonstrate that the increased administrative burdens and costs of offering more than one provider would cause the employer to freeze or terminate the plan.

Q 22:153 Will the safe harbor exemption from ERISA be violated if 403(b) matching contributions are placed in a 401(a) plan?

Yes. In Advisory Opinion 2012-02A, the DOL ruled that if employer contributions to a separate qualified 401(a) plan are conditioned upon the employee making salary reduction contributions to a 403(b) plan, the safe harbor exemption would be violated causing the 403(b) plan to be subject to ERISA. Placing the matching contributions into an ERISA Section 401(a) plan violates the rule that employee participation in the 403(b) plan be completely voluntary and exceeds the level of allowable employer involvement allowed in a safe harbor plan.

Form 5500 Rules Applicable to ERISA 403(b) Plans

Q 22:154 What Form 5500 rules apply to Section 403(b) plans?

Prior to the 2009 plan year, a 403(b) plan was required only to file a brief, informational Form 5500. Beginning in 2009, 403(b) plans are required to file a full Form 5500, with all information and schedules, and to conduct a plan audit, just like 401(k) and other qualified plans. The forms must be filed electronically. Many small plans (generally, those with fewer than 100 participants) that meet certain investment conditions can file the 5500-SF short form and are exempt from the audit requirement. [29 C.F.R. §§ 2520.103-1(c), 2520.104-46]

Q 22:155 Which 403(b) contracts or accounts can be excluded for Form 5500 purposes?

DOL Field Assistance Bulletin 2009-02 provides that the administrator of a 403(b) plan need not treat annuity contracts and custodial accounts as part of the employer's Title I plan or as plan assets for purposes of ERISA's annual reporting requirements, provided that:

- The contract or account was issued to a current or former employee before January 1, 2009;
- The employer ceased to have any obligations to make contributions (including employee salary reduction contributions), and in fact ceased making contributions to the contact or account before January 1, 2009;
- All the rights and benefits under the contract or account are legally enforceable against the insurer or custodian by the individual owner of the contract or account without any involvement by the employer; and
- The individual owner of the contract is fully vested in the contract or account.

Q 22:156 Which employees can be excluded for Form 5500 purposes?

For Form 5500 annual reporting purposes, plans do not need to count current or former employees with assets only in contracts or accounts that are excludable from the plan's Form 5500 or Form 5500 SF, under the above-mentioned transition relief as participants covered under the plan. The DOL also said that it will not reject a Form 5500 with an adverse or qualified auditor's opinion if the accountant expressly states that the sole reason for such an opinion was because such pre-2009 contracts were not covered by the audit or included in the plan's financial statements.

Q 22:157 What employer actions could require a pre-2009 contract to be included for Form 5500 purposes?

DOL Field Assistance Bulletin 2010-01 reiterates the rule that qualifying pre-2009 contracts are not considered plan assets for Form 5500 purposes and clarifies several additional points. Under FAB 2010-01, contracts that otherwise could be excluded under FAB 2009-02 must instead be included on the Form 5500 if

- The employer must consent or exercise discretion over employee's exercise of rights under the contract or account;
- The employer must certify employee's eligibility for a distribution or approve hardships or loans;
- The employer forwards employee's loan repayments to the 403(b) provider; or
- The contract or account is received in an exchange after 2008.

Q 22:158 What clarifications did FAB 2010-01 provide with respect to excludable contracts?

Under FAB 2010-01, contracts meeting the requirements of FAB 2009-02 may in fact be excluded from Form 5500 reporting in the following circumstances:

- The employer provides information to 403(b) provider on active or former employee's employment status;
- Employees remit loan payments directly to the 403(b) provider; or
- The only contribution remitted to the 403(b) provider in 2009 was the final 2008 contribution.

FAB 2010-01 indicates that the transitional relief of FAB 2009-02 applies to employers making a "good faith" effort to transition for the 2009 plan year and extends the relief beyond the 2009 reporting year so long as the contracts excluded from reporting continue to meet the requirements.

Q 22:159 What guidance has the IRS provided to assist employers in complying with the 403(b) rules?

In Revenue Procedure 2013-12 [2013-12 I.R. B. 313], the IRS updated its Employee Plans Compliance Resolution System (EPCRS) to include 403(b) plans effective April 1, 2013. Sponsors of 403(b) plans may generally correct the same operational errors and plan documentation problems as sponsors of qualified retirement plans through EPCRS. For more information on the updated EPCRS program for 403(b) plans, see the *403(b) Answer Book* published by Wolters Kluwer Law & Business.

In addition, the IRS's 403(b) Fix It Guide assists plan sponsors to find, fix, and avoid ten common errors. The guide is available at *http://www.irs.gov/Retirement-Plans/403(b)-Plan-Fix-It-Guide.*

Using a Section 403(b) Plan with a Qualified Plan

Q 22:160 How may a Section 403(b) plan be used in conjunction with a qualified plan?

If the employer is eligible to maintain a 403(b) plan, it may offer both a 403(b) plan and a 401(a) qualified plan. Some employers use a 403(b) plan for employee salary reduction contributions and a 401(a) plan for employer non-elective contributions. The advantages of this approach are (1) the qualified plan could use permitted disparity in allocating employer contributions, and (2) employees participating in both plans receive the benefit of two annual addition limits. [I.R.C. § 415(k)(4)]

The DOL has indicated, however, that employer 403(b) matching contributions that are contributed to the 401(a) plan will cause the 403(b) plan to be subject to ERISA. If an employer offers both a 403(b) plan and a 401(k) plan to the same set of employees, the elective deferral limits must be aggregated. [I.R.C. § 402(g)]

Section 403(b) Plans Versus 401(k) Plans

Q 22:161 What features of a 403(b) plan might be seen as advantages over 401(k) plans?

Features of 403(b) plans that may be seen as advantages over 401(k) plans include:

- No average deferral percentage (ADP) test applies to Section 403(b) deferrals. Compare the 401(k) plan rules in Section 401(k)(3).
- Higher special 403(b) catch-up deferral limits are allowed for some employees who have 15 or more years of service with their current qualified employer and have prior underutilized contribution amounts. [I.R.C. § 402(g)(7)]
- The two separate Section 415 limits that generally apply to an employer's 401(a) and 403(b) plans may allow employees to receive higher employer contributions. The nondiscrimination rules will apply. [Treas. Reg. §§ 1.415-7(h); 1.415-8(d)]
- Employers are allowed to make contributions into a Section 403(b) annuity for up to five years after the participant has severed from employment. [Treas. Reg. § 1.403(b)-4(d)]
- Pre-1988 elective deferrals in a Section 403(b) annuity contract (but not a custodial account) are exempt from the elective deferral distribution restrictions.

- Pre-1987 Section 403(b) monies are exempt from the required minimum distribution rules at age 70½ if proper accounting is maintained. [I.R.C. § 403(b)(10); Treas. Reg. § 1.403(b)-2]
- Participants are allowed to make in-service contract exchanges between 403(b) investment providers if the employer has multiple vendors eligible to receive contributions or has entered into an Information Sharing Agreement with one or more vendors for the receipt of contract exchanges.
- Tax-exempt 403(b) plans may receive an exemption from ERISA if the plan meets certain voluntary plan safe harbor requirements of ERISA Regulations Section 2510.3-2(f), DOL Field Assistance Bulletin 2007-2, and DOL Field Assistance Bulletin 2010-01.
- Church plans described in Section 3121(w) are not required to comply with the Code's nondiscrimination requirements. [I.R.C. §§ 403(b)(1)(D), 403(b)(12)(B)]
- Statutory treatment of one-time irrevocable elections to defer amounts under § 403(b). [I.R.C. §§ 402(g)(3), 403(b)(12)(A); Treas. Reg. § 1.401(k)-1(a)(3)(iv)]
- Certain compliance defects affect only some 403(b) participants, or some 403(b) accounts, but generally do not disqualify the entire plan.

Q 22:162 What features of 401(k) plans might be seen as advantages over 403(b) plans?

The features of 401(k) plans that might be seen as advantages over 403(b) plans include:

- Section 401(k) plans are not subject to the elective deferral universal availability rule. [I.R.C. § 410(a) and (b)]
- Deferral of state income tax in Massachusetts, New Jersey and possibly other states that currently tax 403(b) deferrals when contributed.
- Broader availability of investment options since 401(k) plans are not limited to annuity contracts and custodial accounts offering only mutual funds.
- Potentially broader availability of vendors and products, since 403(b) plans may be a more limited market than 401(k) plans.
- Greater employer ability to control administration and compliance due to centralized recordkeeping.
- No individual excise tax on contributions in excess of the Section 415 limit.

Q 22:163 When might an employer use a 403(b) plan as an alternative to a 401(k) plan?

Between July 2, 1985 and December 31, 1996, tax-exempt employers were precluded from establishing 401(k) plans pursuant to the Tax Reform Act of 1986 [Pub. L. No. 99-514, 100 Stat. 2085] [I.R.C. § 401(k)(4)(B)(i)] Thus, many employers that established 403(b) plans may want to continue to maintain them instead of switching to a 401(k) plan because:

- The 403(b) plan cannot be merged into the 401(k) plan. Plan sponsors cannot convert a 403(b) plan into a 401(k) plan or vice versa.
- Employees cannot transfer or roll over their accounts from the 403(b) plan to the 401(k) plan until the participant is entitled to a take distribution, and the 401(k) plan would have to permit such rollovers.
- Employers may only terminate a 403(b) plan if all 403(b) monies are distributed to participants and beneficiaries as soon as practicable. Since most 403(b) vendors do not allow assets to be distributed due to plan termination, the 403(b) plan is treated as "frozen," not terminated.
- Implementing a 401(k) plan as a successor plan to an on-going or frozen 403(b) plan requires ongoing maintenance of two plans, including two sets of Form 5500s each year for plans subject to ERISA.

Section 457(b) Eligible Deferred Compensation Plans

A Section 457(b) plan is a deferred compensation arrangement available only to employees of states, political subdivisions, agencies and instrumentalities of a state, and tax-exempt employers. The arrangement allows employees to exclude elective deferrals contributed into the plan from gross income. Significant differences exist between the rules that apply to governmental versus non-governmental plans. Such differences are described in the questions that follow and summarized in Table 22-7.

Eligible Employers and Funding Rules

Q 22:164 What types of organizations are eligible to sponsor a 457(b) plan?

Eligible employers include (1) a state, political subdivision of a state, and any agency or instrumentality of a state or political subdivision of a state, and (2) any other organization (other than a governmental unit) exempt from tax. [I.R.C. § 457(e)(1)]

Q 22:165 Who owns and holds the assets of a Section 457(b) plan?

Since the enactment of the Small Business Jobs Protection Act [Pub. L. No. 111-240, 124 Stat. 2504] (SBJPA), governmental 457(b) plan assets must be held in a trust, custodial account, or annuity contract for the exclusive benefit of employees. [I.R.C. § 457(g); Treas. Reg. § 1.457-8(a)]

The assets of 457(b) plans maintained by non-governmental tax-exempt employers must not be held in trust for the benefit of participants. All plan assets must remain solely the property of the employer, subject to the claims of the employer's general creditors. [I.R.C. § 457(b)(6); Treas. Reg. § 1.457-8(b)]

Q 22:166 May Section 457(b) plan assets be invested in life insurance policies?

Yes. The trust of a governmental 457(b) plan must retain all incidents of ownership of the life insurance policy and be the sole beneficiary of the policies. Unlike privately held life insurance, any amount paid or made available under an eligible plan as death benefits or life insurance proceeds included in gross income just like other pre-tax distributions from the participant's account. [Treas. Reg. § 1.457-10(d)] A death benefit plan under Section 457(e)(11) is not an eligible plan.

A tax-exempt employer who includes life insurance in its 457(b) plan must be the owner and sole beneficiary of the policy. The cost of life insurance protection purchased by a tax exempt employer with amounts deferred under an eligible 457 plan is not taxed to the participant prior to distribution, as long as the employer:

- Retains all the incidents of ownership in the policy;
- Is the sole beneficiary under the policy; and
- Is under no obligation to transfer the policy or pass through the proceeds of the policy under Treas. Reg. § 1.457-8(b)(1).

Section 457(b) Plan Eligibility Requirements

Q 22:167 What are the general eligibility requirements under Section 457(b)?

The following requirements must be met in order for the plan to be treated as an eligible plan under Code Section 457(b):

- The plan must be established and maintained by an eligible employer;
- The plan must be administered pursuant to a written plan document;
- Only individuals who perform services for an eligible employer may participate (employees and independent contractors, if the plan so provides);
- Contribution limits must not be exceeded;
- Compensation may be deferred for any payroll period only if an agreement providing for such deferral is in existence before the first day of the month in which such wages are paid unless the participant is a new employee and a deferral agreement is entered into on or before the first day of employment;
- Distributions must be restricted until the participant severs employment, attains age $70^1/_2$, suffers an unforeseeable emergency, or meets the requirements for an in-service de minimis distribution;
- Transfers from a governmental Section 457(b) plan for the purchase of defined benefit service credits are only allowed if certain restrictions are met;
- The required minimum distribution requirements of Section 401(a)(9) must be met; and

- All governmental Section 457(b) plans must satisfy the trust requirement in Code Section 457(g).

Unlike Section 457(b) plans maintained by governmental and church employers, a 457(b) plan maintained by a non-governmental, non-church employer must be a top-hat plan open only to a select group of management or highly compensated employees and may not be funded.

Eligible 457(b) Plan Contributions

Q 22:168 Who is eligible to make elective deferrals into a Section 457(b) plan?

Employees and independent contractors performing services for a governmental employer may make elective deferrals into a 457(b) plan. [I.R.C. §§ 457(e)(2), 457(e)(5)]

Only a select group of management or highly compensated employees may be allowed to participate in a 457(b) plan offered by a non-governmental, non-church tax-exempt employer. [ERISA § 201(2)]

Q 22:169 What are the deferral limits in an eligible Section 457(b) plan?

Elective deferrals are limited to the lesser of 100 percent of compensation or the dollar limits under Section 457(e)(15) for eligible 457(b) plans maintained by both governmental and tax-exempt employers. Since 2002, the dollar limits have been equal to the limits that apply to 401(k) plans under Section 402(g), $18,000 in 2015. Deferrals under Section 457(b) are not, however, combined with other types of elective deferrals for purposes of the Section 402(g) or 415(c)(1)(A) limits. [I.R.C. §§ 402(g)(3), 415(c)(2)]

Q 22:170 Are special 457(b) catch-up contributions allowed?

Yes. Eligible 457(b) plans of both governmental and tax-exempt employers may contain a provision allowing participants with underutilized amounts under the employer's plan to make special catch-up contributions for one or more of the last three taxable years ending prior to the year the participant attains normal retirement age. [I.R.C. § 457(b)(3)] The annual special catch-up limit is the lesser of two times the annual dollar limit ($36,000 in 2015) or the sum of the limit that normally applies for the year ($18,000 in 2015) plus unused amounts from prior years under the employer's plan. [I.R.C. § 457(b)(3)]

Q 22:171 Are age 50 catch-up contributions allowed?

Beginning in 2002, eligible 457(b) plans of governmental employers only may contain a provision allowing participants who turn age 50 or over during the calendar year to make catch-up contributions of $6,000 in 2015. [I.R.C. § 414(v)] The special 457(b) catch-up and the age 50 catch-up may not be used in the same calendar year, but the participant may use whichever produces the greater contribution.

Age 50 catch-up contributions are not allowed in a non-governmental 457(b) plan. [I.R.C. § 457(e)(18)]

Q 22:172 When may the deferrals begin or the deferral amount be changed?

Unlike other cash or deferred arrangements, deferral agreements under the 457(b) plan of both governmental and tax-exempt employers must be executed prior to the beginning of the month in which the deferral will be deducted from the employee's paycheck. [I.R.C. § 457(b)(4)] The plan may allow new employees to defer during their first month at work if the salary reduction agreement is executed on or before the first day of employment. [Treas. Reg. § 1.457-4(b)]

Q 22:173 May employees make Roth contributions to a 457(b) plan?

Since January 1, 2011, governmental employers have been allowed to amend their 457(b) plans to include Roth accounts as described in Code Section 402A pursuant to the Small Business Jobs Act of 2010 [Pub. L. No. 111-240, 124 Stat. 2504] (SBJPA). [I.R.C. §§ 402(g)(3), 415(c)(2)]

There is only one elective deferral limit aggregated between the pre-tax and Roth deferrals into a 457(b) plan. Roth contributions to a designated Roth account are includable in gross income in the year of the contribution. Qualified distributions from the Roth account (including earnings) are generally tax-free. The employer must separately account for all contributions, gains and losses to this designated Roth account until this account balance is completely distributed.

Non-governmental tax-exempt employers may not allow Roth contributions into their 457(b) plans.

Distributions, Rollovers, and Transfers

Q 22:174 What restrictions apply to Section 457(b) plan distributions?

Amounts deferred into either a governmental or tax-exempt employer's 457(b) plan, and the earnings thereon, may not be made available until the earlier of:

- The participant's severance from employment [I.R.C. § 457(d)(1)(A)(ii)]
- The occurrence of an unforeseeable emergency [I.R.C. § 457(d)(1)(A)(iii)]
- The calendar year in which the participant attains age 70½ [I.R.C. § 457(d)(1)(A)(i)]
- A de minimis distribution from an account balance not exceeding $5,000 [I.R.C. §§ 457(d)(3), 457(e)(9)(A), 411(a)(11)(A)]

Q 22:175 When must distributions from 457(b) plans commence?

Distributions from 457(b) plans of both governmental and tax-exempt employers must commence on the participant's required beginning date (RBD), which is April 1 of the year following the year the participant severs employment with the plan sponsor, or attains age 70½, whichever is later. [I.R.C. §§ 401(a)(9)(C), 457(d)(2)]

Q 22:176 May distributable amounts in a participant's pre-tax 457(b) account be rolled into a designated Roth account in the same plan?

Yes. Section 2112 of the Small Business Jobs and Credit Act of 2010 added a new design option for governmental 457(b) plans effective January 1, 2011. This in-plan rollover option permits a participant to roll an eligible rollover distribution from his or her pre-tax account into a designated Roth account within the same plan. The amount transferred into the Roth account is taxable in the year the transfer is made. The IRS issued guidance in Notice 2010-84 to facilitate implementing this provision. This provision is optional and plan sponsors wishing to make it available must amend their plan documents to add it.

Non-governmental tax-exempt employers may not allow designated Roth accounts in their eligible 457(b) plans.

Q 22:177 May amounts in a participant's pre-tax 457(b) account that are *not* eligible for rollover be transferred into a designated Roth account in the same plan?

Yes. The American Taxpayer Relief Act of 2012 [Pub. L. No. 112-240, 126 Stat. 2313 (Jan. 2, 2013)] permits pre-tax amounts in an eligible governmental 457(b) plan to be transferred to Roth amounts within the plan, regardless of whether the amounts are otherwise distributable. The amount transferred into the Roth account is taxable in the year the transfer is made. This provision is effective for transfers made after December 31, 2012, and is optional for plan sponsors. On December 11, 2013, the IRS issued Notice 2013-74 [2013-52 I.R.B. 819] providing guidance on in-plan Roth transfers of amounts otherwise non-distributable as well as in-plan Roth rollovers of amounts that are eligible distribution amounts.

Non-governmental, tax-exempt employers may not allow designated Roth accounts in their 457(b) plans.

Q 22:178 May pre-tax assets in a governmental 457(b) plan be rolled into a Roth IRA?

Yes. Participants in an eligible governmental 457(b) plan may roll an eligible rollover distribution from a pre-tax plan account directly to a Roth IRA. The amount rolled into the Roth IRA is taxable in the year of the rollover. Roth IRAs cannot be rolled into Roth plan accounts.

No rollovers are allowed into or out of eligible 457(b) plans maintained by non-governmental, tax-exempt employers. [I.R.C. §§ 402(c)(8)(B), 457(e)(16)]

Q 22:179 May amounts be rolled from a 457(b) plan to another employer's plan?

Yes. Distributions from a governmental 457(b) plan may be rolled over to any other "eligible retirement plan" that will accept such amounts or to an IRA. [I.R.C. §§ 402(c)(8)(B), 457(e)(16)]

No rollovers are allowed into or out of a 457(b) plan maintained by a non-governmental, tax-exempt employer. [I.R.C. §§ 402(c)(8)(B), 457(e)(16)]

Q 22:180 Are hardship withdrawals from a Section 457(b) plan permitted?

Yes. Eligible 457(b) plans may allow unforeseeable emergency withdrawals in the event of severe financial hardship. The unforeseeable emergency standard is more restrictive than hardship withdrawals under 401(k) plans. The distribution must be limited to an amount reasonably required to satisfy the emergency need and cannot be made to the extent the hardship is or may be relieved through reimbursement compensation, or insurance, by liquidation of assets or by stopping deferrals under the plan. [Treas. Reg. § 1.457-6(c)(1)(ii),(iii)]

Q 22:181 How must unforeseeable emergency be defined in the plan document?

The plan document must define unforeseeable emergency as severe financial hardship to a participant resulting from

- Illness or accident of the participant, spouse, dependent, or primary beneficiary;
- Loss of participant's property due to casualty;
- Medical expenses, including nonrefundable deductibles;
- Cost of prescription drugs;
- Funeral expenses of a spouse, dependent, or primary beneficiary;
- Other similar extraordinary and unforeseeable circumstances beyond the participant's control.

[Treas. Reg. § 1.457-6(c)(2)(i)]

Q 22:182 What distribution requirements apply to amounts rolled into a governmental Section 457(b) plan?

The plan document governs when amounts rolled into the 457(b) plan may be distributed. Unless restricted in the document, rollover amounts may be distributed at any time. If the amount was rolled over from a qualified plan (such as a 401(k) plan or an IRA subject to the 10 percent penalty tax on premature withdrawals), the penalty will continue to apply when the rollover amount is distributed from the 457(b) plan unless another exemption under Code Section 72(t) applies.

No rollovers are allowed into a plan maintained by a non-governmental tax-exempt employer.

Q 22:183 When do assets in a 457(b) plan become taxable to the participant?

Pre-tax amounts deferred into a 457(b) plan of a governmental employer are not taxed until actually distributed from the plan.

Income taxes become due for participants in a top-hat 457(b) plan of a tax-exempt employer when the amounts are either paid or "made available" to them. Since all 457(b) plans state that benefits are available at severance from employment, a participant will be taxed immediately upon leaving employment even if no distribution is taken unless he or she makes an irrevocable election to delay distribution to a fixed future date. Only one additional election of a later future distribution date may be made.

Q 22:184 How are distributions from a Section 457(b) plan taxed?

Distributions of pre-tax 457(b) plan assets are taxed as ordinary income. The 10 percent premature withdrawal penalty does not apply to 457(b) assets. There is no special income tax treatment available. These rules apply to 457(b) plans of both governmental and tax-exempt employers. If the participant fails to take the required minimum amount due as of the required beginning date, a 50 percent excise tax will apply. [I.R.C. § 4974]

Q 22:185 May a Section 457(b) plan be frozen or terminated?

Yes, under the final regulations, a 457(b) plan may be frozen or terminated. An eligible governmental or tax-exempt employer may include a provision in its plan to eliminate future deferrals for existing participants or to limit participation to existing participants and employees, and the assets remain in the plan until a distributable event occurs under the Code and the plan document. An eligible plan may also contain a provision permitting the employer to terminate the plan so long as deferred amounts are distributed to participants and beneficiaries or transferred to another eligible plan. [Treas. Reg. § 1.457-10(a) and (b)]

Table 22-6. Section 457(b) Provisions Applicable to Various Types of Employers

	Issue	*Governments*	*Church Plans**	*Non-Profits*
1.	Eligible employees	All	All	Top-hat group
2.	Asset ownership	Trust	Employer	Employer
3.	Employer's creditors	No	Yes	Yes
4.	Constructive receipt rule	No	Yes	Yes
5.	Taxed when "made available"	No	Yes**	Yes**
6.	Elective deferral limits	Yes	Yes	Yes
7.	Special 457(b) catch-ups	Yes	Yes	Yes
8.	Age 50 catch-up	Yes	No	No
9.	Deferral coordinated with 401(k)	No	No	No
10.	Roth contributions	Yes	No	No
11.	Rollovers/§ 402(f) notice	Yes	No	No
12.	In-Plan Roth rollovers/ transfers			
13.	De minimis payouts	Yes	Yes	Yes
14.	Loans	Yes	No	No
15.	QDRO rules	Yes	Yes	Yes
16.	Transfer to DB plan/ Purchase service credits	Yes	No	No
17.	Distribution restrictions	Yes	Yes	Yes
18.	RMD rules	Yes	Yes	Yes
19.	Tax reporting form	1099-R	W-2	W-2
20.	Low-income saver tax credit	Yes	No	No

* Must not be a church or qualified church-controlled organization as defined in Section 3121(w)(3)(A) and (B) respectively.

** Must make irrevocable elections at severance of employment and can make only one additional election of a set future distribution date.

Violations of Code Section 457(b)

Q 22:186 What happens if a Section 457(b) plan does not meet the requirements?

Section 457(f) contains the rules that apply if an eligible deferred compensation plan violates any of the requirements of Sections 457(a) through (e). If the employer allows participants to contribute an amount that exceeds the deferral limit or allows participants to violate the distribution restrictions, the IRS may declare the plan ineligible and Section 457(f) will apply. [I.R.C. § 457(f)(1)] If the employer ceases to be an eligible employer, the plan must be terminated so as to avoid adverse tax consequences with respect to future contributions. [Treas. Reg. § 1.457-10(a)(3)]

Section 457(b) Plans Versus Section 401(k) Plans

Q 22:187 When might an employer use a Section 457(b) plan as an alternative to a 401(k) plan?

The type of entity will determine whether the employer is eligible for a 457(b) or a 401(k) plan (see Q 22:164 and chapter 1). Table 22-7 compares the features of 457(b) and 401(k) plans and Table 22-8 compares the features of the various types of retirement savings alternatives analyzed in this chapter.

Table 22-7. Comparison of Governmental 457(b) and 401(k) Plans

	Governmental 457(b)Plan	*401(k) plan*
Eligible Employers	State and local governments	For-profit/Tax-Exempts
Eligible Participants	Employees and independent contractors	Employees only
Funds Held in Trust	Yes	Yes
Automatic Enrollment	Yes, subject to state law	Yes for ERISA plans
First day of month rule	Yes	No
Deferral Limits	Lesser of 100% of compensation or $18,000 (for 2015)	Same
Catch-up contributions	Special § 457 catch-up and Age 50 catch-up	Age 50 catch-up only
Roth Accounts	Yes	Yes
In-Plan Roth Rollovers/Transfers	Yes	Yes
Rollovers	Yes	Yes
Discrimination testing	No	Yes for ERISA plans

Table 22-7. Comparison of Governmental 457(b) and 401(k) Plans (*cont'd*)

Withdrawals	Unforeseeable emergency, in-service de minimis, age 70½, sever employment, and rollover account	Hardship, age 59½, sever employment, or rollover account
Tax treatment	Ordinary Income	Ordinary Income (grandfathered 10-year forward averaging and capital gains)
10% penalty tax on early withdrawal	No	Yes
Low income saver's credit	Yes	Yes

Table 22-8. Comparison of Retirement Savings Alternatives

	Non-SIMPLE 401(k) Plan	*Roth and Traditional IRA*	*SEP*	*SIMPLE IRA*	*Cash Balance Plan*	*Floor Plan*	*Age-Weighted and Cross-Tested PS Plans*	*403(b) Plan*	*Govern-mental 457(b) Plan*	*NQDC Plan*	*After-tax Savings*
Eligibility											
Minimum age	21	None	21	None	21	21	21	None	None	None	None
Waiting period	1 year	None	Worked 3 of last 5 years. Earned more than $550	Earned $5,000 in 2 pre-ceding years	1 year, 2 years if 100% vested	1 year, 2 years if 100% vested	1 year, 2 years if 100% vested	None	None	None	None
Employee deferral limit	$18,000*	$6,000†	N/A	$12,000*	0	0	0	$18,000*	$18,000*	No limit	0
Age 50 catch-up contributions	$6,000	$1,000	N/A	$3,000	N/A	N/A	N/A	$6,000	$6,000	N/A	N/A
Vesting schedule	Permitted on employer contribution	100%	100%	100%	Permitted	Permitted	Permitted	Permitted on employer contribution	100%	Permitted	N/A
Employer deduction	25% of payroll	N/A	25% of payroll	Amount contri-buted	Actuarially deter-mined	Actuarially deter-mined	25% of payroll	N/A	N/A	When benefits are paid	N/A
Eligible employers	All, except government	N/A	All	Up to 100 employees earning at least $5,000	All	All	All	Public schools; nonprofit hospitals; 501(c)(3) corpora-tions	Government units	All, except govern-ment units	N/A

(*Continued*)

Table 22-8. Comparison of Retirement Savings Alternatives (*cont'd*)

	Non-SIMPLE 401(k) Plan	*Roth and Traditional IRA*	*SEP*	*SIMPLE IRA*	*Cash Balance Plan*	*Floor Plan*	*Age-Weighted and Cross-Tested PS Plans*	*403(b) Plan*	*Governmental 457(b) Plan*	*NQDC Plan*	*After-tax Savings*
Taxation of lump-sum distributions	Ordinary income (grand-fathered 10-year forward averaging)	Ordinary income (except Roth IRA)	Ordinary income	Ordinary income	Ordinary income (grand-fathered 10-year forward averaging)	Ordinary income (grand-fathered 10-year forward averaging)	Ordinary income	Ordinary income	Ordinary income	Ordinary income	N/A
Required minimum distribution (50% penalty)	Uniform life table	Uniform life table (except Roth IRA during the owner's lifetime)	Uniform life table	Uniform life table	Uniform life table	Uniform life table	Uniform life table	Uniform life table	Uniform life table	N/A	N/A
Premature withdrawals	10% penalty	10% penalty	10% penalty	10% penalty (25% first 2 years)	10% penalty	10% penalty	10% penalty	10% penalty	N/A**	N/A	N/A
Investment options	ERISA fiduciary standards	No insurance No collectibles; no loans	No insurance No collectibles no loans	No insurance No collectibles; no loans	ERISA fiduciary standards	ERISA fiduciary standards	ERISA fiduciary standards	Annuity contracts, mutual	No restrictions	No restrictions	No restrictions
Annual IRS reporting	Form 5500	Form 5498	Form 5498	Form 5498	Form 5500	Form 5500	Form 5500	Form 5500 if ERISA plan	None	None	
FICA tax applies	Yes	Yes	No	Yes	No	No	No	Yes	No	Yes	Yes
Subject to PBGC & actuarial valuation	No	No	No	No	Yes	Yes	No	No	No	No	No

*Indexed for cost-of-living increases in $500 increments after 2006.
**Unless attributable to an amount rolled in from a plan or IRA subject to the 10 percent premature distribution penalty.
†Indexed for cost-of-living increases in $500 increments after 2009.

Appendix A

Sample Safe Harbor 401(k) Plan Notice

This sample safe harbor 401(k) plan notice is a tool to assist plan sponsors in meeting the safe harbor notice requirements. A plan sponsor would need to customize the sample notice consistent with the terms and operations of its plan. Plan sponsors must provide notices to participants according to the following rules:

- Notices must be provided between 30 and 90 days before the beginning of each plan year.
- For a new employee, an initial notice must be provided during the 90-day period ending on the date the employee becomes a plan participant (entry date). If that is not practicable, the notice must be provided as soon as practicable after that date and the employee is permitted to elect to defer from all types of compensation that may be deferred under the plan earned beginning on the date the employee becomes eligible.

NOTICE TO PARTICIPANTS IN THE
[*Plan Name*]

The [*Plan Name*] includes features that allow both participants and the Company to make contributions to the Plan. In order to allow you to make an informed decision on the level of your own contributions, if any, and to meet certain "safe harbor" nondiscrimination requirements, the Company must declare the type of contribution it will make within a reasonable period of time before the beginning of the Plan year [*insert Plan year* (__________-__________)]. This notice is intended to meet that requirement.

Safe Harbor Contributions [*customize information consistent with the terms of the Plan*]

The Company will contribute __________________________ (include information on formula).

[*Also insert information about plan to which contribution will be made if other than this Plan.*]

[*Also insert the following for additional flexibility to reduce or suspend safe harbor contributions mid-year:*

The Company retains the right to reduce or suspend the safe harbor [*insert matching or non-elective*] contributions under the Plan. If the Company chooses to do so, you will receive a supplemental notice explaining the reduction or suspension of the safe harbor [*insert matching or non-elective*] contribution at least 30 days before the change is effective. The Company will contribute any safe harbor [*input matching or non-elective*] contributions you have earned up to that point. At this time, the Company has no such intention to suspend or reduce the safe harbor [*insert matching or non-elective*] contribution.]

Other Company Contributions [*customize information consistent with terms of the Plan*)]

The Company may make profit sharing contributions. This contribution is totally optional, is allocated to all participants eligible to share under the terms of the Plan, and is subject to the vesting schedule described in the Plan.

Salary Deferral Contributions [*customize information consistent with the terms of the Plan*]

You may contribute up to _____% of your pay but in no event more than the annual calendar limit on the amount of salary deferral contributions ($_______ for 20_____). However, your salary deferral contributions, when combined with Company contributions, cannot exceed 100% of your pay (or $_______, if less). Your salary deferral contributions will be withheld from your pay and deposited to the Plan. If you would like to make salary deferral contributions, please ask the Company for an enrollment form. [*insert other appropriate procedures for making deferral changes*]. You may change your salary deferral percentage at [*insert periods deferral changes are permitted*].

To learn more about your Plan's definition of eligible pay, please review the discussion of pay or compensation in the Plan's Summary Plan Description (SPD).

Withdrawal Provisions [*customize information consistent with the terms of the Plan*]

In general, amounts accumulated in the Plan are available after you terminate employment with the Company. However, your _______________ [*specify*] may be withdrawn after _______________ [*specify period*].

Vesting Provisions [*customize information consistent with the terms of the plan*]

Salary deferral and safe harbor match contributions are 100% vested at all times. You will also be 100% vested in the Company's profit sharing contributions if ________________________ [*state conditions*]. If you terminate employment for any other reason, you will be entitled to receive only the vested portion of the Company's profit sharing contributions as provided in the following schedule:

Years of Service Vested Percentage

This notice is intended to provide an overview of certain key aspects of the Plan. Should there be discrepancies between the contents of this notice and the Plan document, the terms of the Plan shall govern. Please refer to your Summary Plan Description (SPD) for more information about the Plan, or contact the Plan Administrator at ________________________ to obtain information about the Plan (including an additional copy of the SPD).

Sample Safe Harbor 401(k) Supplemental Notice

Below is sample language for a Safe Harbor 401(k) Supplemental Notice if a safe harbor contribution is reduced or suspended mid-year according to applicable regulations.

The purpose of this notice is to notify participants in the ________________ Plan that effective ____________, 20__, the Plan has been amended to [*insert reduce or suspend*] safe harbor [*insert match or non-elective*] contributions. [*Insert consequences of the amendment that reduces or suspends future safe harbor contributions.*] Because safe harbor [*insert match or non-elective*] contributions will be [*insert reduced or suspended*], participants will have the opportunity at any time before ____________, 20__, to change the amount they have elected to contribute to the Plan. Any participant who wishes to make a change, can do so by submitting a new salary deferral election _____________________ (describe procedure/s for making salary deferral election changes).

Contact your Plan Administrator if you have questions regarding this Notice.

Appendix B

Automatic Contribution Arrangement Comparison Chart and Sample Notices

Automatic Contribution Arrangement Comparison Chart B-2

Sample Notice for Plans with an Automatic Contribution Arrangement (ACA) B-3

Sample Notice for Plans with an Eligible Automatic Contribution Arrangement (EACA) B-4

Sample Notice for Plans with a Qualified Automatic Contribution Arrangement (QACA) B-9

Sample Notice for Safe Harbor QACA Plans with an Eligible Automatic Contribution Arrangement (EACA) B-13

Automatic Contribution Arrangement Comparison Chart

This chart and the sample notices that follow do not constitute legal, tax, or financial advice, and are intended only as informal reference.

Feature	ACA	EACA	QACA
Automatic salary deferral percentage	Yes	Yes	Yes
Automatic annual deferral escalation	Optional	Optional	Required under the Internal Revenue Code
Participant notice requirement	Yes	Yes	Yes
Salary deferrals fully vested	Yes	Yes	Yes
90-day withdrawal option	No	Yes	Only if Plan satisfies EACA requirements
Required employer contributions	No	No	Yes
Required vesting schedule for employer contributions	No	No	Yes, must fully vest after no more than 2 years of service.
Qualified default investment alternative (QDIA) required	Optional	Optional	Optional
ERISA preemption of state anti-garnishment laws for Plans subject to ERISA	Yes[1]	Yes[1]	Yes[1]
Nondiscrimination testing safe harbor	No	No	Yes
Automatic extension on excise tax for corrective distributions to 6 months	No	Only if all eligible employees are covered under the EACA	N/A

[1] Prior to the enactment of the Pension protection Act of 2006 (PPA), there was no clear guidance on whether ERISA preempted contrary state garnishment and other state laws when a Plan has an automatic contribution arrangement. The PPA provided that ERISA preempts any contrary state garnishment and other state laws if a Plan with an automatic contribution arrangement elects a qualified default investment alternative (QDIA) as the plan's default investment option. In final regulations issued on October 24, 2007, the DOL took the position that any plan using an automatic contribution arrangement and providing the specified notice to participants receives ERISA preemption of contrary state garnishment and other state laws, even if the Plan does not use a QDIA as its default investment option.

Sample Notice for Plans with an Automatic Contribution Arrangement (ACA)

The following sample notice is a tool to assist plan sponsors in notifying participants of the plan's automatic enrollment feature, both initially and on an annual basis. A plan sponsor will need to customize the sample notice consistent with the terms and operations of its plan. Participants should have a reasonable period of time, after receipt of the initial notice and before the first elective contribution is made, to make a deferral election. Notices with information about the automatic enrollment feature should also be provided to participants on an annual basis.

Note: If the plan intends to invest defaulted contributions in a qualified default investment arrangement under ERISA Section 404(c)(5), additional notice requirements will apply.

[*Insert Plan Name*] Plan
Automatic Enrollment Notice

Beginning ____________, _____, _____ [*insert effective date of automatic contribution arrangement*], ________________ [*insert name of Employer*] (Company) is making saving for retirement under our 401(k) Plan even easier. We are offering an automatic enrollment feature.

If you have not made a contribution election, you will be enrolled automatically in the Plan starting with your first paycheck after the effective date of the automatic enrollment feature. This means that amounts will be taken from your pay and contributed to the Plan. These automatic contributions will be a certain percentage of your eligible pay each pay period as described in this notice. However, you may choose a different percentage. You can choose to contribute more, less, or even nothing. [*Modify paragraph, as appropriate, to reflect whether auto enrollment feature will apply only to new hires after the effective date of the feature.*]

This notice gives you important information regarding the Plan's automatic enrollment feature. You can find out more about the Plan in another document, the Plan's Summary Plan Description (SPD).

1. Does the Plan's automatic enrollment feature apply to me?

The Plan's automatic enrollment feature will not apply to you if you already made an election pursuant to Plan procedures to make contributions to the Plan or to not contribute. If you made an election, your contribution level will not automatically change. If you want to change your contribution level or do not want to make contributions to the Plan by ______________________. [*Insert procedures for making a contribution election.*] [*Note to plan sponsors: This paragraph should be modified for any particulars related to the plan's auto enrollment feature—for example, if deferral percentages that are less than the default percentage are being raised to the default percentage.*]

2. If I do nothing, how much will be taken from my pay and contributed to the Plan?

If you do not make a contribution election pursuant to Plan procedures, _________% [*insert percentage*] of your eligible pay for each pay period will be taken from your pay and contributed to the Plan. Your contributions to the Plan are taken out of your pay and are contributed to your Plan account.

Contributions will be taken out of your pay if you do nothing. But you are in charge of the amount that you contribute. You may decide to do nothing and become automatically enrolled, or you may choose to contribute an amount that better meets your needs.

3. How will my Plan account be invested?

The Plan allows you invest your account in a number of different investment funds. Unless you choose a different investment fund or funds, your Plan account will be invested in _____________ [*insert name of default investment option*]. You may change how your Plan account is invested among the Plan's offered investment funds. To learn more about the Plan's investment funds and procedures for changing how your Plan account is invested, please contact the Plan Administrator using the information at the end of this notice.

If you have any questions about how the Plan works or your rights and obligations under the Plan, or if you would like a copy of the SPD or other Plan documents, please contact the Plan Administrator at:______________________.

Sample Notice for Plans with an Eligible Automatic Contribution Arrangement (EACA)

Section 414(w) of the Internal Revenue Code provides for certain benefits for a 401(k) Plan that includes an EACA. A 401(k) plan containing an EACA may enable a participant whose deferrals are made under the automatic contribution arrangement to withdraw those deferrals during the 90-day period following the date the first automatic contribution is taken out of his or her paycheck. It also affords the plan additional time to distribute to highly compensated employees (HCEs) excess contributions resulting from a failed nondiscrimination test. The Plan has the option to comply with Section 404(c)(5) of ERISA. That section provides a fiduciary safe-harbor for defaulted investments in a qualified default investment alternative (QDIA). In order to obtain fiduciary protection for defaulted investments, a Plan sponsor must satisfy a number of conditions under the QDIA final regulations, including, but not limited to:

- Assets must be invested in a qualified default investment alternative (QDIA) as defined under the regulations;
- Participants must be given the opportunity to direct investments, but failed to do so;

- Participants must be given initial and annual notices that meet specified requirements;
- Certain materials must be provided to participants upon request;
- Participants must be allowed to transfer investments in the QDIA to other plan investments with the same frequency as participants who elected to invest in the QDIA, but not less frequently than once within any three-month period, and any transfer or withdrawal requested during the first 90 days of a default investment into a QDIA cannot be subject to any fees or expenses (including surrender charges, liquidation or exchange fees, redemption fees, and similar expenses charged in connection with the liquidation or transfer from the investment); and
- The plan must offer a "broad range of investment alternatives," as defined under the regulations.

The following sample notice is a tool to assist plan sponsors in meeting the notice requirements that apply to an EACA. A plan sponsor will need to customize the sample notice consistent with the terms and operations of its plan. The notice must be provided to participants covered under the EACA according to the following rules:

- **Current Participants**: No earlier than 90 days and no later than 30 days before the beginning of each plan year.
- **Future Participants**: During the 90-day period ending on the date an employee becomes a Plan participant (entry date). If that is not practicable, the notice must be provided as soon as practicable after that date and the employee is permitted to elect to defer from all types of compensation that may be deferred under the plan earned beginning on the date the employee becomes eligible.

Note: If the EACA does not contain a 90-day permissive withdrawal provision and includes a QDIA Feature, then the notice elements satisfying QDIA requirements must be provided at least 30 days in advance of the participant's entry date. If notices are not provided in that timeframe, QDIA protection would start 30 days after delivery of notice instead of immediately.

Disclaimer: If protection under ERISA Section 404(c)(5) is desired, the plan sponsor is responsible for satisfying the QDIA requirements. Because the rules are complex, the plan sponsor is encouraged to consult its investment and/or legal advisors for specific guidance. Nothing contained herein constitutes legal or investment advice upon which any party may rely.

[*Insert Plan Name*] Plan (Plan)
Automatic Enrollment Notice

Beginning ____________, _____, _____ [*insert effective date of automatic contribution arrangement*], ______________ [*insert name of Employer*] (Company) is making saving for retirement under our 401(k) Plan even easier. We are offering an automatic enrollment feature.

The new automatic enrollment feature will not change your contribution level if you already elected the level of your contributions to the Plan or elected not to contribute. Your earlier election will continue to be followed.

[*Note to plan sponsors: The paragraph above must be modified if previously elected deferral percentages on the effective date that are less than the default percentage are being raised to the default percentage.*]

If you have not made a contribution election, you will be enrolled automatically in the Plan starting with your first paycheck after the effective date of the automatic enrollment feature. This means that amounts will be taken from your pay and contributed to the Plan. These automatic contributions will be a certain percentage of your eligible pay each pay period as described in this notice. However, you may choose a different percentage. You may choose to contribute more, less, or even nothing.

This notice gives you important information about certain Plan rules, including the Plan's automatic enrollment feature and the Company safe harbor contributions. The notice covers these points:

- Whether the Plan's automatic enrollment feature applies to you;
- What amounts will be automatically taken from your pay and contributed to the Plan;
- What amounts, if any, the Company will contribute to your Plan account;
- How your Plan account will be invested;
- When your Plan account will be vested (i.e., not lost when you leave your job), and when you can access your Plan account; and
- How you can change your contributions.

You can find out more about the Plan in another document, the Plan's Summary Plan Description (SPD).

1. Does the Plan's automatic enrollment feature apply to me?

The Plan's automatic enrollment feature will not apply to you if you already made an election pursuant to Plan procedures to make contributions to the Plan or to not contribute. If you made an election, your contribution level will not automatically change. However, you may always change your contribution level ______________ [*insert periods available for making deferral elections*] by [*insert procedures for making a contribution election*].

If you have not elected a contribution level, you will be enrolled in the Plan. This means money will be automatically taken from your pay and contributed to your Plan account. If you do not want to be enrolled, you must___________ [*insert procedures for making a contribution election*] by ______________ [*insert date/specified timeframe for new employees*].

[*Note to plan sponsors: The paragraphs above must be modified if previously elected deferral percentages on the effective date that are less than the default percentage are being raised to the default percentage, and/or if only certain employees will be covered under the EACA.*]

2. If I do nothing, how much will be taken from my pay and contributed to the Plan?

If you do not make a contribution election pursuant to Plan procedures, ____% [*insert percentage*] of your eligible pay for each pay period will be taken from your pay and contributed to the Plan. To learn more about the Plan's definition of eligible pay, you can review the discussion of compensation or pay in the SPD.

Your contributions to the Plan are taken out of your pay and they are contributed to your Plan account and can grow over time with earnings.

Contributions will be taken out of your pay if you do nothing. However, you are in charge of the amount that you contribute. You may decide to do nothing and become automatically enrolled, or you may choose to contribute an amount that better meets your needs. You can change your contributions by________ [*insert procedure for making a contribution election*].

If you want to contribute more to your account than would be provided automatically, there are limits on the maximum amount. These limits are described in the Plan's SPD.

3. In addition to the contributions taken out of my pay, what amounts will the Company contribute to my Plan account?

Besides contributing the amounts taken from your pay, the Company will make other contributions to your Plan account.

[*Note to plan sponsors: The preceding question and answer should be included only if employer contributions are made to the Plan.*]

4. How will my Plan account be invested?

The Plan allows you to invest your account in a number of different investment funds. Unless you choose a different investment fund or funds, your Plan account will be invested in ________________ [*insert name of default investment option*].

[*Below* or *Attached*] is a general description of the ____________ [*insert name of default investment option*]'s investment objectives, risk and return characteristics, and fees and expenses.

[*Note to plan sponsors: In order for the Plan's default investment to satisfy Section 404(c)(5) of ERISA, the default investment option must be a QDIA under DOL Reg. Section 2550.404c-5. You must describe the Plan's QDIA, including its investment objectives, risk and return characteristics, and fees and expenses, and must describe other circumstances, if any, under which assets may be invested in the QDIA. If more than one QDIA is being used for the Plan and/or for different timeframes, you must identify and provide information on the QDIA being used in each particular circumstance. If the default investment is being changed with respect to existing assets, you must provide an explanation of the transition of current assets to the new QDIA.*]

You may change how your Plan account is invested, among the Plan's offered investment funds, by ______________________ [*insert procedures for making an investment election*].

[*Note to Plan sponsors: In order for the Plan's default investment to satisfy Section 404(c)(5) of ERISA, you must describe any restrictions, fees, or expenses that apply when participants or beneficiaries transfer assets from the QDIA to other investment fund.*]

To learn more about the Plan's investment funds and procedures for changing how your Plan account is invested, please contact the Plan Administrator using the information at the end of this notice.

5. When will my Plan account be vested?

Your contributions are 100% vested at all times. You will also be 100% vested in our contributions if you terminate employment after attaining the Plan's normal retirement age, _____ [*upon becoming disabled, or as a result of death; insert these only if your plan provides for 100% vesting under these circumstances*]. If you terminate employment for any other reason, you will be entitled to receive only the vested portion of our contributions under the following schedule or schedules:

[*Input vesting schedule for each type of employer contribution.*]

[*Note to plan sponsors: The preceding question and answer must be modified if employer contributions are not made to the Plan.*]

6. When will my Plan account be available to me?

In general, amounts accumulated in your account are available after you terminate employment with the Company. [*Describe here the types of contributions that can be withdrawn during employment and the circumstances under which the withdrawals may occur.*]

7. Can I change the amount of my contributions?

You can always change the amount you contribute to the Plan. If you know now that you do not want to contribute to the Plan (and you haven't already elected not to contribute), you will want to elect zero contributions. That way, you avoid any automatic contributions.

[*Note to plan sponsors: Include the paragraph below if Plan will allow 90-day permissive withdrawals. Modify, as appropriate, if withdrawals will be allowed in a timeframe shorter than 90 days (but not shorter than 30 days).*]

But, if you do not make an election in time to prevent automatic contributions, you can withdraw the automatic contributions for a short time, despite the general limits on Plan withdrawals. During the 90 days after automatic contributions are first taken from your pay, you can withdraw the prior automatic contributions by contacting the Plan Administrator. The amount you withdraw will be adjusted for any gain or loss and may be reduced by the amount of any fee charged to process your distribution. If you take out your automatic contributions, you lose Company contributions, if any, that matched the automatic contributions. Also, your withdrawal will be subject to federal income tax (but not the extra 10% tax that normally applies to early distributions). If you take out automatic contributions, the Company may treat you as having chosen to make no further contributions. If so, you can always choose to continue or restart your contributions by making a contribution election pursuant to Plan procedures.]

If you have any questions about how the Plan works or your rights and obligations under the Plan, or if you would like a copy of the SPD or other Plan documents, please contact the Plan Administrator at:

[*Plan administrator name*]

[*Address*]

[*Telephone number*]

[*Email address*]

Sample Notice for Plans with a Qualified Automatic Contribution Arrangement (QACA)

Section 401(k)(13) and Section 401(m)(12) of the Internal Revenue Code enable a 401(k) plan (referred to as a QACA) to avoid discrimination testing of employee elective deferrals and, if applicable, employer matching contributions made to the plan. The following notice is a tool to assist plan sponsors in meeting the notice requirements applicable to "safe harbor" plans. A plan sponsor will need to customize the sample notice consistent with the terms and operations of its plan. The notice must be provided to participants according to the following rules:

- **Current Participants**: No earlier than 90 days and no later than 30 days before the beginning of each plan year.
- **Future Participants**: During the 90-day period ending on the date an employee becomes a Plan participant (entry date). If that is not practicable, the notice must be provided as soon as practicable after that date

and the employee is permitted to elect to defer from all types of compensation that may be deferred under the plan earned beginning on the date the employee becomes eligible.

[*Note to plan sponsors: This notice assumes the default investment option is not intended to be a qualified investment alternative (QDIA) under ERISA Section 404(c)(5). Additional notice requirements will apply if QDIA protection is being sought.*]

[*Insert Plan Name*] Plan (Plan)
Automatic Enrollment Notice

Beginning ____________, _____, _____ [*insert effective date of automatic contribution arrangement*], ______________ [*insert name of Employer*] (Company) is making saving for retirement under our 401(k) Plan even easier. We are offering an automatic enrollment feature.

The new automatic enrollment feature won't change your contribution level if you already elected the level of your contributions to the Plan or elected not to contribute. Your earlier election will continue to be followed.

[*Note to plan sponsors: The preceding paragraph must be modified if previously elected deferral percentages on the effective date that are less than the default percentage are being raised to the default percentage.*]

If you have not made a contribution election, you will be automatically enrolled in the Plan starting with your first paycheck after the effective date of the automatic enrollment feature. This means that amounts will be taken from your pay and contributed to the Plan. These automatic contributions will be a certain percentage of your eligible pay each pay period as described in this notice. However, you may choose a different percentage. You may choose to contribute more, less, or even nothing.

This notice gives you important information about some Plan rules, including the Plan's automatic enrollment feature and Company safe harbor contributions. The notice covers these points:

- Whether the Plan's automatic enrollment feature applies to you;
- What amounts will be automatically taken from your pay and contributed to the Plan;
- What amounts the Company will contribute to your Plan account;
- How your Plan account will be invested;
- When your Plan account will be vested (i.e., not lost when you leave your job), and when you can access your Plan account; and
- How you can change your contributions.

You can find out more about the Plan in another document, the Plan's Summary Plan Description (SPD).

1. Does the Plan's automatic enrollment feature apply to me?

The Plan's automatic enrollment feature will not apply to you if you already made an election pursuant to Plan procedures to make contributions to the Plan or to not contribute. If you made an election, your contribution level will not automatically change. But, you can always change your contribution level [*insert periods available for making deferral elections*] by [*insert procedures for making a contribution election*].

[*Note to plan sponsors: The preceding paragraph must be modified if previously elected deferral percentages on the effective date that are less than the default percentage are being raised to the default percentage. It should also be modified if an election expires under the plan (e.g., at some future date and/or after a 6-month hardship withdrawal suspension) and, thus, require an employee to make a new affirmative election if he or she wants the prior rate of elective contributions to continue.*]

If you have not elected a contribution level, you will be enrolled in the Plan. This means money will be automatically taken from your pay and contributed to your Plan account. If you do not want to be enrolled, you need to __________ [*insert procedures for making a contribution election*] by [*insert date/specified timeframe for new employees*].

2. If I do nothing, how much will be taken from my pay and contributed to the Plan?

If you do not make a contribution election pursuant to Plan procedures, ________% [*insert percentage not less than 3%*] of your eligible pay for each pay period will be taken from your pay and contributed to the Plan. This will continue through the end of the Plan year following the Plan year in which the automatic contribution is first taken. After that Plan year, your contribution level will increase by ____% [*insert percentage*] each year (unless you choose a different level), until it reaches ____% [*insert percentage not to exceed 10%*] of your eligible pay. To learn more about the Plan's definition of eligible pay, you can review the discussion of compensation or pay in the SPD.

[*Note to plan sponsors: As appropriate and allowable under the final regulations, modify the timing for deferral increases in the paragraph above.*]

Your contributions to the Plan are taken out of your pay and they are contributed to your Plan account and can grow over time with earnings.

Contributions will be taken out of your pay if you do nothing. But you are in charge of the amount that you contribute. You may decide to do nothing and become automatically enrolled, or you may choose to contribute an amount that better meets your needs. You can change your contributions by_________ [*insert procedure for making a contribution election*].

If you want to contribute more to your account than would be provided automatically, there are limits on the maximum amount. These limits are described in the Plan's SPD.

3. In addition to the contributions taken out of my pay, what amounts will the Company contribute to my Plan account?

Besides contributing the amounts taken from your pay, the Company will make other contributions to your Plan account. The Company will make a safe harbor ______________________ [*insert* matching *or* non-elective] contribution equal to ______________________ [*insert contribution formula*]. [*If applicable, insert other contribution types and conditions for other types of employer contributions.*]

[*Also insert the following for additional flexibility to reduce or suspend safe contributions mid-year; see also Appendix A for sample language for the supplemental notice required under applicable regulations:*

The Company retains the right to reduce or suspend the safe harbor [*insert matching or non-elective*] contributions under the Plan. If the Company chooses to do so, you will receive a supplemental notice explaining the reduction or suspension of the safe harbor [*insert matching or non-elective*] contribution at least 30 days before the change is effective. The Company will contribute any safe harbor [*insert matching or non-elective*] contributions you have earned up to that point. At this time, the Company has no such intention to suspend or reduce the safe harbor [*insert matching or non-elective*] contribution.]

4. How will my Plan account be invested?

The Plan lets you invest your account in a number of different investment funds. Unless you choose a different investment fund or funds, your Plan account will be invested in ______________________ [*insert name of default investment option*].

You can change how your Plan account is invested, among the Plan's offered investment funds, by ______________________ [*insert procedures for making an investment election*].

To learn more about the Plan's investment funds and procedures for changing how your Plan account is invested you can contact the Plan Administrator using the information at the end of this notice.

5. When will my Plan account be vested?

Your contributions are 100% vested at all times. You will also be 100% vested in our contributions if you terminate employment after attaining the Plan's normal retirement age, _____ [*upon becoming disabled, or as a result of death; insert these only if your Plan provides for 100% vesting under these circumstances*]. If you terminate employment for any other reason, you will be entitled to receive only the vested portion of our contributions under the following schedule or schedules:

[*Input vesting schedule for each type of employer contribution, including the employer safe harbor contribution*]

6. When will my Plan account be available to me?

In general, amounts accumulated in your account are available after you terminate employment with the Company. [*Describe here the types of contributions that can be withdrawn during employment and the circumstances under which the withdrawals may occur.*]

7. Can I change the amount of my contributions?

You can always change the amount you contribute to the Plan. If you know now that you do not want to contribute to the Plan (and you haven't already elected not to contribute), you will want to elect zero contributions. That way, you avoid any automatic contributions.

If you have any questions about how the Plan works or your rights and obligations under the Plan, or if you would like a copy of the Plan's SPD or other Plan documents, please contact the Plan Administrator at:

[*Plan administrator name*]

[*Address*]

[*Telephone number*]

[*Email address*]

Sample Notice for Safe Harbor QACA Plans with an Eligible Automatic Contribution Arrangement (EACA)

A 401(k) plan that is a safe harbor plan enables the 401(k) plan (referred to as a QACA) to avoid discrimination testing of employee elective deferrals and, if applicable, employer matching contributions. A safe harbor plan that is an EACA can provide that a participant whose deferrals are made under the automatic contribution arrangement may withdraw those deferrals during the 90-day period following the date the first automatic contribution is taken out of his or her paycheck. If the plan sponsor desires fiduciary protection for defaulted investments, the plan must comply with Section 404(c)(5) of ERISA. That section provides a fiduciary safe harbor for defaulted investments in a qualified default investment alternative (QDIA). In order to obtain fiduciary protection for defaulted investments, a plan sponsor must satisfy a number of conditions under the QDIA final regulations including, but not limited to:

- Assets must be invested in a QDIA as defined under the regulations;
- Participants must be given the opportunity to direct investments, but failed to do so;
- Participants must be given initial and annual notices that meet specified requirements;
- Certain materials must be provided to participants upon request;

- Participants must be allowed to transfer investments in the QDIA to other plan investments with the same frequency as participants who elected to invest in the QDIA, but not less frequently than once within any three-month period, and any transfer or withdrawal requested during the first 90 days of an investment defaulted into a QDIA cannot be subject to any fees or expenses (including surrender charges, liquidation or exchange fees, redemption fees and similar expenses charged in connection with the liquidation or transfer from the investment); and
- The plan must offer of a "broad range of investment alternatives" as defined under the regulations.

The following sample notice is a tool to assist plan sponsors in meeting the notice requirements that apply to a safe harbor QACA with an EACA. A plan sponsor will need to customize the sample notice consistent with the terms and operations of its plan. The notice must be provided to participants according to the following rules:

- **Current Participants**: No earlier than 90 days and no later than 30 days before the beginning of each plan year.
- **Future Participants**: During the 90-day period ending on the date an employee becomes a plan participant (entry date). If that is not practicable, the notice must be provided as soon as practicable after that date and the employee is permitted to elect to defer from all types of compensation that may be deferred under the plan earned beginning on the date the employee becomes eligible.

Note: If the EACA does not contain a 90-day permissive withdrawal provision and QDIA protection is being sought, then the notice elements satisfying QDIA requirements must be provided at least 30 days in advance of the participant's entry date. If notices are not provided in that timeframe, QDIA protection would start 30 days after delivery of notice instead of immediately.

Disclaimer: If protection under ERISA Section 404(c)(5) is desired, a plan sponsor is responsible for satisfying the QDIA requirements. Because the rules are complex, a plan sponsor is encouraged to consult its investment and/or legal advisors for specific guidance. Nothing contained herein constitutes legal or investment advice upon which any party may rely.

[*Insert Plan Name*] Plan (Plan)
Automatic Enrollment Notice

Beginning ___________, _____, _____ [*insert effective date of automatic contribution arrangement*], ______________ [*insert name of Employer*] (Company) is making saving for retirement under our 401(k) Plan even easier. We are offering an automatic enrollment feature.

The new automatic enrollment feature won't change your contribution level if you already elected the level of your contributions to the Plan or elected not to contribute. Your earlier election will continue to be followed.

[*Note to plan sponsors: The preceding paragraph must be modified if previously elected deferral percentages on the effective date that are less than the default percentage are being raised to the default percentage.*]

If you have not made a contribution election, you will be enrolled automatically in the Plan starting with your first paycheck after the effective date of the automatic enrollment feature. This means that amounts will be taken from your pay and contributed to the Plan. These automatic contributions will be a certain percentage of your eligible pay each pay period as described in this notice. But, you can choose a different percentage. You can choose to contribute more, less, or even nothing.

This notice gives you important information about some Plan rules, including the Plan's automatic enrollment feature and Company safe harbor contributions. The notice covers these points:

- Whether the Plan's automatic enrollment feature applies to you;
- What amounts will be automatically taken from your pay and contributed to the Plan;
- What amounts the Company will contribute to your Plan account;
- How your Plan account will be invested;
- When your Plan account will be vested (i.e., not lost when you leave your job), and when you can access our Plan account; and
- How you can change your contributions.

You can find out more about the Plan in another document, the Plan's Summary Plan Description (SPD).

1. Does the Plan's automatic enrollment feature apply to me?

The Plan's automatic enrollment feature will not apply to you if you already made an election pursuant to Plan procedures to make contributions to the Plan or to not contribute. If you made an election, your contribution level will not automatically change. However, you can always change your contribution level ____________________ [*insert periods available for making deferral elections*] by ____________________ [*insert procedures for making a contribution election*].

[*Note to plan sponsors: The paragraph above must be modified if previously elected deferral percentages on the effective date that are less than the default percentage are being raised to the default percentage. It should also be modified if an election expires under the plan (e.g., at some future date and/or after a 6-month hardship withdrawal suspension) and, thus, require an employee to make a new affirmative election if he or she wants the prior rate of elective contributions to continue.*]

If you have not elected a contribution level, you will be enrolled in the Plan. This means money will be automatically taken from your pay and contributed to your Plan account. If you do not want to be enrolled, you need to__________ [*insert procedures for making a contribution election*] by ____________ [*insert date/specified timeframe for new employees*].

2. If I do nothing, how much will be taken from my pay and contributed to the Plan?

If you do not make a contribution election pursuant to Plan procedures, _____% [*insert percentage not less than 3%*] of your eligible pay for each pay period will be taken from your pay and contributed to the Plan. This will continue through the end of the plan year following the plan year in which the automatic contribution is first taken. After that plan year, your contribution level will increase by _____% [*insert percentage*] each year (unless you choose a different level), until it reaches _____% [*insert percentage not to exceed 10%*] of your eligible pay. To learn more about the Plan's definition of eligible pay, you can review the discussion of compensation or pay in the SPD.

[*Note to plan sponsors: As appropriate and allowable under the final regulations, modify the timing for deferral increases in the paragraph above.*]

Your contributions to the Plan are taken out of your pay and they are contributed to your Plan account and can grow over time with earnings.

Contributions will be taken out of your pay if you do nothing. But you are in charge of the amount that you contribute. You may decide to do nothing and become automatically enrolled, or you may choose to contribute an amount that better meets your needs. You can change your contributions by _______________ [*insert procedure for making a contribution election*].

If you want to contribute more to your account than would be provided automatically, there are limits on the maximum amount. These limits are described in the Plan's SPD.

3. In addition to the contributions taken out of my pay, what amounts will the Company contribute to my Plan account?

Besides contributing the amounts taken from your pay, the Company will make other contributions to your Plan account. The Company will make a safe harbor _______________ [*insert* matching *or* non-elective] contribution equal to _______________ [*insert contribution formula*]. [*If applicable, insert other contribution types and conditions for other types of employer contributions*].

[*Also insert following for additional flexibility to reduce or suspend safe harbor contributions mid-year (see also Appendix A for sample language for the supplemental notice required under applicable regulations):*

The Company retains the right to reduce or suspend the safe harbor [*insert matching or non-Elective*] contributions under the Plan. If the Company chooses to do so, you will receive a supplemental notice explaining the reduction or suspension of the safe harbor [*insert matching or non-elective*] contribution at least 30 days before the change is effective. The Company will contribute any safe harbor [*insert matching or non-elective*] contributions you have earned up to that point. At this time, the Company has no such intention to suspend or reduce the safe harbor [*insert matching or non-elective*] contribution.]

4. How will my Plan account be invested?

The Plan allows you to invest your account in a number of different investment funds. Unless you choose a different investment fund or funds, your Plan account will be invested in ______________________ [*insert name of default investment option*].

[*Below* or *Attached*] is a general description of the ____________ [*insert name of default investment option*]'s investment objectives, risk and return characteristics, and fees and expenses.

[*Note to plan sponsors: In order for the Plan's default investment to satisfy Section 404(c)(5) of ERISA, the default investment option must be a QDIA under DOL Reg. Section 2550.404c-5. You must describe the Plan's QDIA, including its investment objectives, risk and return characteristics, and fees and expenses, and must describe other circumstances, if any, under which assets may be invested in the QDIA. If more than one QDIA is being used for the Plan and/or for different timeframes, you must identify and provide information on the QDIA being used in each particular circumstance. If the default investment is being changed with respect to existing assets, you must provide an explanation of the transition of current assets to the new QDIA.*]

You can change how your Plan account is invested, among the Plan's offered investment funds, by ______________________ [*insert procedures for making an investment election*].

[*Note to plan sponsors: In order for the Plan's default investment to satisfy Section 404(c)(5) of ERISA, you must describe any restrictions, fees, or expenses that apply when participants or beneficiaries transfer assets from the QDIA to other investment fund.*]

To learn more about the Plan's investment funds and procedures for changing how your Plan account is invested, please contact the Plan Administrator using the information at the end of this notice.

5. When will my Plan account be vested?

Your contributions are 100% vested at all times. You will also be 100% vested in our contributions if you terminate employment after attaining the Plan's normal retirement age, ____________ [*upon becoming disabled, or as a result of death; insert these only if your plan provides for 100% vesting under these circumstances*]. If you terminate employment for any other reason, you will be entitled to receive only the vested portion of our contributions under the following schedule or schedules:

[*Input vesting schedule for each type of employer contribution, including the employer safe harbor contribution.*]

6. When will my Plan account be available to me?

In general, amounts accumulated in your account are available after you terminate employment with the Company. [*Describe here the types of contributions that can be withdrawn during employment and the circumstances under which the withdrawals may occur.*]

7. Can I change the amount of my contributions?

You can always change the amount you contribute to the Plan. If you know now that you do not want to contribute to the Plan (and you haven't already elected not to contribute), you will want to elect zero contributions. That way, you avoid any automatic contributions.

[*Note to plan sponsors: Include the paragraph below if Plan will allow 90-day permissive withdrawals. Modify, as appropriate, if withdrawals will be allowed in a timeframe shorter than 90 days (but not shorter than 30 days).*]

However, if you do not make an election in time to prevent automatic contributions, you can withdraw the automatic contributions for a short time, despite the general limits on Plan withdrawals. During the 90 days after automatic contributions are first taken from your pay, you can withdraw the prior automatic contributions by contacting the Plan Administrator. The amount you withdraw will be adjusted for any gain or loss and may be reduced by the amount of any fee charged to process your distribution. If you take out your automatic contributions, you lose Company contributions, if any, that matched the automatic contributions. Also, your withdrawal will be subject to federal income tax (but not the extra 10% tax that normally applies to early distributions). If you take out automatic contributions, the Company may treat you as having chosen to make no further contributions. If so, you can always choose to continue or restart your contributions by making a contribution election pursuant to Plan procedures.

If you have any questions about how the Plan works or your rights and obligations under the Plan, or if you would like a copy of the SPD or other Plan documents, please contact the Plan Administrator at:

[*Plan administrator name*]

[*Address*]

[*Telephone number*]

[*Email address*]

Appendix C

Sample Plan Sponsor Fiduciary Manual, Fiduciary Checklist, ERISA Section 404(c) Compliance Checklist, and QDIA Notice

Sample Plan Sponsor Fiduciary Manual C-1
Sample Plan Sponsor Fiduciary Checklist C-8
Sample ERISA Section 404(c) Compliance Checklist C-10
Sample Qualified Default Investment Alternative (QDIA) Notice C-12
Sample ERISA Section 404(a) Participant Disclosure Checklist C-14

Sample Plan Sponsor Fiduciary Manual

This manual provides the plan sponsor, a fiduciary of a participant directed retirement plan, with general information on complying with its fiduciary responsibilities under the Employee Retirement Income Security Act of 1974 (ERISA).[1]

The Plan Fiduciary

As the sponsor of your qualified retirement plan, you are offering your employees a great savings opportunity, and you have assumed some responsibility as well. As plan sponsor, you have a number of fiduciary duties and a standard

[1] This guide is intended to provide general educational information regarding the fiduciary responsibilities and liabilities of retirement plan fiduciaries. It does not constitute legal advice upon which plan sponsors may rely upon, and plan sponsors are encouraged to consult their own counsel for specific guidance on their plan's fiduciary issues.

of conduct imposed upon you by ERISA. By understanding your fiduciary role and responsibilities, you can handle your fiduciary duties appropriately.

A plan fiduciary is ultimately responsible for maintaining the plan, and your employees place their trust in you to keep the plan in full compliance with applicable law. This obligation is an important one but may not be as daunting as you think. With careful attention to your responsibilities, the plan fiduciary role, although challenging, can be rewarding as well.

Who Is a Plan Fiduciary?

Under ERISA, fiduciary status is attributed to anyone specifically named as a fiduciary in the plan document and to persons performing certain functions on behalf of the plan. A plan sponsor is always considered a plan fiduciary by virtue of maintaining and administering the plan. Although a person may be a fiduciary only with respect to the areas of plan operation over which he or she exercises discretionary authority, the plan sponsor typically fulfills a variety of roles with respect to plan operation and exercises authority by selecting and monitoring the providers retained to provide services to the plan.

Other plan fiduciaries include:

- Any person specifically named as a fiduciary in the plan document (this may include the plan administrator, an administrative committee, or the plan trustee);
- Any person with discretionary control over the administration of the plan;
- Any person with discretionary control over the investment of plan assets;
- Any person rendering investment advice with respect to the plan's investment options for a fee or other compensation; and
- An Investment Manager under ERISA who has the power to manage, acquire, or dispose of plan assets and who acknowledges in writing that he or she is a fiduciary with respect to plan assets.

Who Is NOT a Plan Fiduciary?

If the person performing services for the plan has no discretionary authority or control over the plan or plan assets, that person will not be a plan fiduciary in most cases. The services provided by the following persons generally do not cause the person to be a plan fiduciary:

- Attorneys, accountants, actuaries, and consultants;
- Persons performing ministerial or administrative functions for the plan as directed by the plan fiduciary; and
- Service providers, such as recordkeepers.

Co-fiduciary Liability

Some plan sponsors are under the mistaken impression that selecting one or more persons to serve as a plan fiduciary eliminates any further fiduciary responsibility or liability. As the plan sponsor, however, you remain a fiduciary regardless of the number of other plan fiduciaries you may select. Also, ERISA imposes co-fiduciary liability in certain situations. You may be held responsible for the acts or omissions of other co-fiduciaries. For example, if you know that another plan fiduciary has committed a fiduciary breach and you knowingly participate in that act or omission, you may also be liable for that breach. Likewise, if you have knowledge of a breach by another plan fiduciary and you fail to make reasonable efforts to remedy the breach, you could be held responsible for that breach.

A Plan Fiduciary's Roles and Responsibilities

A plan fiduciary has a variety of roles and duties with respect to the plan and must perform those duties prudently and in the best interest of plan participants and beneficiaries. ERISA can be used by plan fiduciaries to guide them toward a sound, well-maintained plan. The ERISA principles plan fiduciaries are expected to follow include:

- **Prudent Man Rule**—You are not required or expected to be an expert in every aspect of plan administration, but ERISA does require you to act with the care, prudence, skill, and diligence that a knowledgeable person would use in a similar situation. This means that you must carry out your duties in accordance with good judgment and sound processes when handling the affairs of the plan. This may require the hiring of experts to aid in making decisions with or for the plan. Such experts may include trustees, attorneys, accountants, and investment managers, to name a few. The plan sponsor's fiduciary liability, however, cannot be waived merely because an expert was hired. Careful selection of the expert is necessary to comply with ERISA's prudent man rule and the performance of all persons retained must be continually monitored.
- **Prudent Selection of Service Providers**—Choosing the service providers for your plan, and ensuring that those providers continue to provide valuable service for a reasonable fee over time, is a fiduciary decision that must be made in accordance with the plan document and the prudent man standard of care. You are not charged with selecting the lowest cost plan, and cheaper is not always better. A prudent fiduciary will know what service are being provided to the plan for the dollar amount incurred and will compare the cost of those services to the market.
- **Loyalty**—One of the most important of your fiduciary duties is that of loyalty to the plan participants and beneficiaries. As an employee you may be inclined to put the interests of the company ahead of the interests of the plan. ERISA specifically requires you to put your duty as a plan fiduciary

ahead of your corporate responsibilities when you are making a decision as a plan fiduciary. Called the "exclusive benefit rule," you must act solely in the best interests of the plan and its participants and beneficiaries.

- **Follow the Plan Document**—The plan document is the contract between the plan sponsor and the plan participants and beneficiaries. The plan document is your manual for operating and administering the plan and you must keep it updated to comply with ERISA and the Internal Revenue Code.
- **Avoid Prohibited Transactions**—As a plan fiduciary you must avoid causing the plan to engage in any transaction that you know may constitute a direct or indirect:
  - — sale, exchange, or lease between the plan and a party in interest;*
  - — lending money or other extension of credit between the plan and a party in interest;
  - — furnishing goods, services, or facilities between the plan and a party in interest;
  - — transferring or using plan assets for your benefit or that of any other plan fiduciary or party in interest; or
  - — dealing with employer securities or property in violation of ERISA.
- **Diversify the Menu of Investment Options Offered Under the Plan**—The prudent man standard requires plan fiduciaries to evaluate the investment options to be made available under the plan and to offer a diverse range of investment options to plan participants. Diversification may be accomplished by offering investment options with materially different risk and return characteristics and investment objectives.
- **Monitor Investments and Service Providers**—The menu of investment options offered to plan participants, as well as the experts retained to assist you, must be evaluated periodically. With respect to the investment options, a written investment policy statement defines the criteria to be used in selecting, retaining, and terminating a fund. If a fund does not meet the criteria set out in the investment policy statement, appropriate action must be taken. Likewise, with respect to trustees, administrators, attorneys, and others you have chosen to perform services to the plan, periodic evaluation is necessary to ensure that they are performing prudently.
- **Compliance with Participant Disclosure Requirements**—Special rules apply to plans with participant-directed investments. Under the DOL rules, plan fiduciaries must provide participants with certain plan- and investment-related information, including fee and expense information. The rules are designed to provide participants with information to make informed investment decisions.

---

* Parties in interest include plan fiduciaries and service providers, certain company owners, officers and directors, certain relatives of individuals who are parties in interest, and certain other related organizations or entities.

- **Develop Prudent Fiduciary Processes and Procedures**—Developing a prudent process for managing and administering the plan and documenting compliance with that process increase your chances of limiting your fiduciary liability. In addition to the bullet points listed above, these fiduciary procedures could include:
  - — Compliance with a written investment policy statement;
  - — Compliance with ERISA Section 404(c);
  - — Compliance with ERISA's reporting and disclosure rules; and
  - — Development and delivery of effective, easy-to-understand employee communications.

Breaches of Fiduciary Duty

As a fiduciary, you may be personally liable if you are considered to be in breach of your fiduciary duties under ERISA. Breach of fiduciary duty may result in participant lawsuits, monetary penalties, or the intervention of the Department of Labor (DOL) in your plan. You may be considered in breach of your fiduciary duties, for example, if you:

- Fail to comply with the exclusive benefit rule by entering into self-dealing transactions, such as using plan assets for your own or your company's benefit;
- Fail to exercise your responsibilities to the plan in a responsible manner;
- Fail to diversify the menu of investment options offered under the plan;
- Fail to monitor the plan's investment options and replace funds as necessary pursuant to your investment policy; or
- Engage in a prohibited transaction.

Penalties for Breach of Fiduciary Responsibility

A number of civil and criminal penalties may be applied to fiduciaries that breach their responsibilities to the plan participants and beneficiaries. For example:

- Plan fiduciaries can be held personally liable for any losses or may be required to restore profits to the plan resulting from a breach of fiduciary duty.
- Plan fiduciaries may be subject to removal as a fiduciary by the DOL.
- Plan fiduciaries may be assessed monetary penalties or may have personal criminal penalties or imprisonment imposed upon them for willful violations of fiduciary responsibility.

Written Investment Policy Statement

The DOL encourages plan fiduciaries to implement prudent policies for the selection and monitoring of investment options. Consolidating the criteria to be used in the selection and monitoring process into a written set of guidelines will assist you in following a prudent course. Documenting your compliance with those guidelines will also go a long way toward protecting you from liability.

A central theme is that fiduciaries must discharge their duties prudently and that the exercise of prudence in this context requires a deliberative process resulting in the best informed decisions possible under the circumstances.

The purpose of an Investment Policy Statement is to set forth the goals and objectives of the investment options to be made available to the plan participants. It should provide a framework of guidelines for monitoring and evaluating the plan's investment options, including a procedure for terminating and replacing any nonperforming fund.

An effective Investment Policy Statement might include, among other things:

- A statement regarding the investment objectives applicable to long-term retirement plan savings;
- A methodology for selecting a broad, diversified array of investment options providing different levels of risk and historical returns;
- The criteria to be used for selecting investment options that will enable participants to select investment options that are appropriate for their personal savings goals;
- The performance standards that the selected funds will be expected to meet in order to be retained in the investment menu;
- The criteria to be used to evaluate the fees and expenses of each fund;
- The plan's processes for monitoring and evaluating plan investments, including the frequency, content, and person(s) responsible for the review;
- The names and responsibilities of those plan fiduciaries charged with selecting and monitoring the plan's investments; and
- Compliance with ERISA Section 404(c), if applicable.

Compliance with ERISA Section 404(c)

As previously discussed, the plan fiduciary of a participant directed plan is responsible for selecting the menu of investment options to be made available to plan participants.

ERISA Section 404(c) does, however, offer relief from liability for losses resulting from the individual investment choices made by plan participants. This relief is available only if certain rules are met. As the plan sponsor, it is your responsibility to monitor and maintain your plan's compliance with Section 404(c). First, you must give notice to plan participants that the plan is designed to comply with Section 404(c) and that plan fiduciaries may be relieved of liability for any participant investment losses. This notice is often considered the "trigger" that establishes the date when Section 404(c) protection becomes available.

In addition to the notice to participants, there are three general conditions that a participant directed plan must satisfy in order to take advantage of the fiduciary relief available under Section 404(c):

- The plan must offer at least three diversified investment alternatives ("core funds"), each of which has materially different risk and return characteristics and enables participants to minimize risk through diversification;
- The plan must permit transfers among these three core funds at least quarterly; and
- The plan must give participants enough information to permit informed decision making. (The regulation is very specific about what information must be given to participants automatically and upon request. Effective for plan years beginning on or after November 1, 2011, information that must be provided under the ERISA Section 404(a) Participant Disclosure Requirements (applicable to participant-directed plans regardless of 404(c) status) is integrated into the Section 404(c) disclosure requirements.)

Special requirements apply if Section 404(c) is intended to extend to investments in default funds and employer securities.

Section 404(c) relief is available during blackout periods and in connection with a change in investment options if special requirements are met.

With respect to blackouts, protection is available if:

1. The plan complied with Section 404(c) requirements prior to the blackout, and
2. Plan fiduciaries complied with ERISA requirements in connection with authorizing and implementing the blackout period.

In connection with a change in investment offerings (a "qualified change in investment options"), protection is available if the following conditions are met:

1. The plan complied with Section 404(c) requirement prior to the effective date of the change;
2. Participants are given 30 to 60 days' notice prior to the effective date of the change informing them about the new investment options and explaining what will happen if they do not make an affirmative election;
3. The account is mapped to funds with similar risk and return characteristics; and
4. The participants or beneficiaries do not make affirmative elections contrary to the change before the effective date of the change.

Monitoring Plan Success

Plan fiduciaries are not responsible for ensuring that participants make the right decisions about saving, investing, and spending to end up with adequate income for retirement. As a practical matter, the more satisfied participants are with their plan experience, the less likely they will be to blame others for a negative outcome. Monitoring participant behavior (for example, participation/

deferral rates, investment choices, loans/withdrawals) might be helpful in monitoring plan success.

Sample Plan Sponsor Fiduciary Checklist

The following checklist is designed to assist you in fulfilling your fiduciary responsibilities. As always, however, you should consult with your ERISA counsel or other experts in determining whether this list is appropriate or sufficient for your plan. Use the checkboxes below to assist with your compliance monitoring.

- ❑ An up-to-date, IRS-approved plan document is being used.
- ❑ A copy of the IRS Favorable Determination Letter, and/or Prototype Opinion or Advisory Letter is available.
- ❑ The plan document is amended for all legislatively required changes.
- ❑ The plan is being operated in accordance with new legal requirements that may not yet be reflected in plan documents.
- ❑ The plan trustees have been properly appointed and the plan's trust agreement has been properly executed.
- ❑ All plan fiduciaries have been identified and their fiduciary responsibilities have been defined and documented.
- ❑ Service contracts exist with all plan fiduciaries and service providers clearly outlining their services and fees, consistent with regulations under ERISA Section 408(b)(2).
- ❑ Periodic meetings are held with all plan fiduciaries to review their fiduciary responsibilities and provide fiduciary training as appropriate.
- ❑ A fidelity bond is maintained covering fiduciaries and all persons handling plan assets.
- ❑ If deemed appropriate, fiduciary liability insurance coverage has been purchased as a protection against personal liability.
- ❑ You are operating every aspect of the plan in compliance with plan document provisions, paying special attention to compensation and eligibility.
- ❑ All salary reduction deferrals and loan repayments are being collected and invested into the plan as soon as administratively practicable.
- ❑ The fees being paid by the plan are reasonable based upon the investment options and services being provided.
- ❑ The plan maintains and abides by a written investment policy statement.
- ❑ The plan fiduciaries have selected a broad range of investment options for your plan.
- ❑ The plan fiduciaries monitor the investment options periodically to ensure that the funds continue to meet the requirements set out in your investment policy statement.

- ❑ All experts and providers retained to provide services to the plan are monitored periodically to ensure they are meeting the performance standards set for them.
- ❑ You document each of your meetings, the results of your review and monitoring of investments and service providers, and the decisions made with respect to the plan.
- ❑ You document your review and the decisions made with respect to the investment options to be deleted or retained by the plan.
- ❑ You have provided an up-to-date Summary Plan Description to all employees. Redistribute the Summary Plan Description or distribute a Summary of Material Modifications whenever plan design changes dictate. Provide Summary Annual Reports and any required notices based on plan design.
- ❑ You are providing benefit statements to participants that meet applicable content and timeliness requirements (at least quarterly if participants direct investments) as well as any other required notices and disclosures under ERISA and the Code.
- ❑ If your participants direct investments, you are providing participant disclosures (related to fees and investments) that meet applicable DOL requirements under ERISA Section 404(a).
- ❑ You have effective, easy-to-understand participant communications on all important aspects of the plan that educate participants about the plan, the importance of saving for retirement, and the basics of investing.
- ❑ Any required compliance testing has been completed and you have timely filed an accurately completed Form 5500.
- ❑ If you are utilizing multiple service providers for your plan, you have a defined communication process to ensure that services are integrated in a timely, accurate, and cost efficient manner.
- ❑ You have a process in place to respond to participant claims against the plan that is in compliance with ERISA.
- ❑ If the plan intends to rely on ERISA Section 404(c), you comply with the 404(c) requirements.
- ❑ You have considered a review of plan metrics on a periodic basis (participation or deferral rates, investment diversification, loans or withdrawals) and possible changes to plan design, services, and products to improve metrics.
- ❑ If you are a large plan filer (generally a plan with 100 or more participants), you have included an accountant's opinion with your 5500 report.
- ❑ You have ensured payments made from plan assets or from a Plan Expense Account (PEA, also referred to as an ERISA Spending Account) were for allowable expenses and have determined the appropriate treatment of assets remaining in a PEA or other plan-level account.

- ❑ The plan has not engaged in a transaction with a party in interest (i.e., prohibited transaction) that is not exempt.

Sample ERISA Section 404(c) Compliance Checklist

ERISA Section 404(c) applies to individual account plans. To the extent that you permit your plan participants (or beneficiaries) to exercise control over the assets in their individual accounts, you will not be liable for losses resulting from investment choices made by a participant (or beneficiary). As mentioned above, the plan fiduciary is responsible for the selection of the investment lineup and for transactions involving voting, tender, and similar rights to the extent those rights are not passed through to plan participants. Special requirements apply if Section 404(c) protection is intended to extend to investments in a default fund or employer stock. Protection under Section 404(c) is available if you comply with the requirements contained in ERISA Section 404(c).

Special additional requirements apply if Section 404(c) protection is intended to extend to investments during a blackout, or to changes in investment options. Those requirements are not reflected in this checklist.

Plan Design Requirements

- ❑ The plan offers three or more funds that are diversified, have materially different risk and return characteristics, enable the participants to achieve aggregate risk and return characteristics within the range normally appropriate for each participant, and enable participants to minimize risk through diversification.
- ❑ Plan participants are given the opportunity to give investment instructions (in writing or otherwise with an opportunity to receive written confirmation of instructions) to an identified plan fiduciary who is obligated to comply with such instructions.
- ❑ Plan participants are given the opportunity to make investment changes at least quarterly and with a frequency that is appropriate in light of market volatility.
- ❑ If 404(c) protection is intended to extend to assets invested in a default fund, plan participants must have been given an opportunity to, and failed to, direct the investment of the assets; assets are invested in a qualified default investment arrangement (QDIA) that satisfies applicable regulations; and transfers are allowed as frequently as other plan investments (but not less frequently than once within any three-month period); and any transfer or withdrawal is not subject to certain restrictions, fees, or expenses during the first 90 days.

Disclosure Requirements

The following information is provided to participants:

- ❑ An explanation that the plan is intended to be a Section 404(c) plan and that plan fiduciaries may be relieved of liability for any loss that is the direct and necessary result of investment instructions given by the participant.
- ❑ Information required under the participant disclosure requirements (i.e., requiring certain investment- and fee-related disclosures) applicable to participant-directed plans is provided to participants pursuant to DOL Regulations Section 2550.404a-5 (see chapter 19 of *401(k) Answer Book, 2016 Edition* and Sample ERISA Section 404(a) Participant Disclosure Checklist in this appendix).
- ❑ If the plan offers employer securities, a description of the procedures for maintaining the confidentiality of transactions and the exercise of voting, tender, and similar rights, and the name, address, and phone number of the plan fiduciary responsible for ensuring compliance with the procedures.
- ❑ If 404(c) protection is intended to extend to a QDIA, participants must receive:
  - — Information related to voting, tender, and similar rights to the extent those rights are passed through to participants, and information relating to the QDIA that must be provided upon request under the participant disclosure requirements applicable to participant-directed plans (see chapter 19 of the *401(k) Answer Book, 2016 Edition*).
  - — Timely initial and annual QDIA notices containing:
    - A description of the circumstances under which assets will be invested in a QDIA (and, if applicable, an explanation of any automatic enrollment feature and the right to elect not to make contributions or to contribute at a different percentage);
    - An explanation of the right to direct the investment of assets in their accounts;
    - A description of the QDIA's investment objectives, risk and return characteristics (if applicable), and fees and expenses;
    - A description of the right to direct the investment of assets to any other investment alternative under the plan, including a description of any applicable restrictions, fees, or expenses in connection with such transfer; and
    - An explanation of where information on other investment alternatives under the plan can be obtained.

Note. In November 2010, the DOL proposed amendments to the QDIA requirements that would require more specificity concerning investments in QDIAs, including target date or similar investments, as well as clarify other informational requirements. At the time this edition went to press, the amendments were still in the proposed stage and had not been finalized.

Sample Qualified Default Investment Alternative (QDIA) Notice

Section 404(c)(5) of ERISA provides a fiduciary safe harbor for defaulted investments in a qualified default investment alternative (QDIA). To obtain fiduciary protection for defaulted investments, a plan sponsor must satisfy a number of conditions under the QDIA final regulations, including, but not limited to:

- Investment of assets in a "qualified default investment alternative" (QDIA) as defined under the regulations;
- Participants must be given the opportunity to direct investments, but failed to do so;
- Participants must be given initial and annual notices that meet specified requirements;
- Certain materials provided to the plan, such as prospectuses, must be provided to participants upon request;
- Participants must be allowed to transfer investments in the QDIA to other plan investments with the same frequency as participants who elected to invest in the QDIA, but not less frequently than once within any three-month period, and any transfer or withdrawal requested during the first 90 days of an investment defaulted into a QDIA cannot be subject to any fees or expenses (including surrender charges, liquidation or exchange fees, redemption fees and similar expenses charged in connection with the liquidation or transfer from the investment); and
- The plan must offer a "broad range of investment alternatives" as defined under the regulations.

The following sample QDIA notice is provided to assist plan sponsors in meeting the notice condition described above. A plan sponsor will need to customize the sample notice consistent with the terms and operations of its plan. For example, the plan sponsor will need to provide details about the plan's QDIA, as directed in italicized notes, and fill in any blanks as appropriate. Plan sponsors must provide initial and annual QDIA notices to participants according to the following rules:

- Initial notices must be provided at least 30 days prior to the date of plan eligibility, or 30 days prior to the date of any first defaulted investment in the QDIA. If the plan is an eligible automatic contribution arrangement (EACA) with a 90-day permissive withdrawal option, the initial notice can be provided on or before the date of plan eligibility.
- Annual notices must be provided at least 30 days prior to each subsequent plan year.

Fiduciary relief may be available with respect to existing defaulted investments that meet the QDIA rules, are moved to a QDIA, and/or are eligible for grandfathered QDIA treatment under the QDIA rules, after notice is provided and assuming other conditions of the regulation are met.

Disclaimer: If protection under ERISA Section 404(c)(5) is desired, the plan sponsor is responsible for satisfying the QDIA requirements. Because the rules are complex, the plan sponsor is encouraged to consult its investment and/or legal advisors for specific guidance. Nothing contained herein constitutes legal or investment advice upon which any party may rely.

[*Plan Name*] Plan (Plan)
Qualified Default Investment Arrangement (QDIA) Notice

[*Date*]

This notice gives you important investment information related to your account under the [*insert plan name*] (the "Plan"). You should read the notice very carefully to understand how your Plan account assets will be invested if you do not make an investment election. You can find out more about the Plan in other documents, the Plan's Summary Plan Description (SPD), and any Summary of Material Modifications (SMM).

The Plan lets you invest your account in a number of different investment funds. Unless you choose a different investment fund or funds, your Plan account will be invested in the ______________________ [*insert Name of QDIA(*s*)*].

[*Note to plan sponsors: The investment selected as the default investment option for participants who failed to provide investment elections must satisfy the Department of Labor regulations for QDIAs. If more than one QDIA is being used for the Plan and/or for different timeframes, you must identify and provide information on the QDIA being used in each particular circumstance. If you are seeking protection for pre-12/24/07 defaulted investments in a grandfathered QDIA fund, for example, you must identify both the grandfathered and new QDIA funds and describe the circumstances under which monies will be invested in each fund. If the default investment is being changed with respect to existing assets, you must provide an explanation of the transition of current assets to the new QDIA.*]

[*If applicable, add/customize as appropriate:* If you are an existing Plan participant, your balance in the __________ [*name of fund*] prior to__________ [*date*] will be moved to _____________ [*name of QDIA(s)*] unless you provide investment instructions by _____________ [*date*]. Balances in ______________________[*name of grandfathered QDIA fund*] as of December 23, 2007, will remain invested in the _____________ [*name of grandfathered QDIA fund*] until you provide instructions to invest those monies in another Plan investment option.]

[Below *or* Attached] is a general description of the _____________ [*name of QDIA(s)*]'s investment objectives, risk and return characteristics, fees, and expenses. [*Note to plan sponsors: You must provide a description of the Plan's QDIA(s), including its investment objectives, risk and return characteristics (if applicable), and fees and expenses, and must describe other circumstances, if any, under which assets may be invested in the QDIA.*] More detailed information may be available in the prospectus for the _____________ [*insert name of QDIA(s)*], if applicable, which you can get by contacting the Plan Administrator.

[*Note to plan sponsors: Additional notice requirements must be met if the plan includes an automatic contribution arrangement.*]

You can change how your Plan account is invested, among the Plan's offered investment funds, by ______________________ [*insert description of how a participant may change his/her investment elections*]. [*Note to plan sponsors: You must insert information on how a participant can direct assets invested in QDIA(s) to other investments in the Plan. You must also describe any allowable restrictions, fees, or expenses that apply when participants or beneficiaries transfer assets from the QDIA(s) to other investment funds.*]

To learn more about the Plan's investment funds and procedures for changing how your Plan account is invested you can refer to ______________ [*identify source*]. Also, you can contact the Plan Administrator at:

[*Plan administrator name*]

[*Address*]

[*Telephone number*]

[*Email address*]

Note. In November 2010, the DOL proposed amendments to the QDIA requirements that would require more specificity concerning investments in QDIAs, including target date or similar investments. At the time this edition went to press, the amendments were still in the proposed stage and had not been finalized.

Sample ERISA Section 404(a) Participant Disclosure Checklist

When plan participants (and beneficiaries) have control over their investments in their retirement plan accounts, they must receive certain information to allow for informed decision-making under ERISA Section 404(a). The Plan Administrator identified in the plan document is responsible for the providing the required information under the rules.

The following checklist sets forth the general requirements. Because the rules are complex, Plan Administrators are encouraged to consult their legal advisors for specific guidance regarding the requirements.

1. Initial and Annual Disclosures

On or before the date a participant (or beneficiary) is first eligible to direct investment of his or her account and at least annually thereafter, the following information must be provided:

A. General Plan Information

- ❑ An explanation of the circumstances under which participants may give investment instructions.
- ❑ An explanation of any specific limitations imposed by the plan on providing instructions, including any restrictions on transfers to or from a designated investment alternative. (A designated investment alternative (DIA) is any plan-designated investment option made available to participants to invest in. It does not include brokerage windows, self-directed brokerage accounts, or similar arrangements that enable participants to select investments beyond those designated in the plan.)
- ❑ Description or reference to plan provisions relating to the exercise of voting or other rights pertaining to a DIA, as well as any restrictions on such rights.
- ❑ Identification of any DIA offered by the plan.
- ❑ Identification of any designated investment managers.
- ❑ A description of any brokerage window, self-directed brokerage accounts, or similar arrangement that enable participants to select investments beyond those designated by the plan.

B. Plan Expense Information

- ❑ An explanation of any fees and expenses for general plan administrative services (e.g., recordkeeping) that, to the extent not otherwise reflected in the total annual operating expenses of any DIA, may be charged against the individual participant accounts and the basis on which such charges will be allocated (e.g., pro rata, per capita) to, or affect the balance of, each individual account.
- ❑ An explanation of any fees that may be charged against a participant's account for services provided on an individual, versus a plan-wide basis (e.g., plan loan fee, fee for investment advice, fees for brokerage window, transfer fees) and which are not reflected in the annual operating expenses of any DIA.

C. Investment-Related Information

Participants (and beneficiaries) must receive investment-related information with respect to the designated investment alternatives made available in the plan. This information must be presented in a comparative format so that participants can readily compare the available options, and prominently displays the date, as well as:

- ❑ A statement indicating name, address, telephone number of the plan administrator (or designee) to contact for information available upon request.

- ❑ A statement that additional investment-related information including more current performance information) is available at the listed Internet website.
- ❑ A statement explaining how to request and obtain, free of charge, paper copies of information required to be available on a website.

A model disclosure form is available on the Department of Labor's Web site at *www.dol.gov/ebsa/participantfeerulemodelchart.doc.*

Important: Different disclosure rules apply depending on whether the investment has a variable rate of return or fixed rate of return, or is an annuity with a guaranteed stream of income. There are also special rules for qualifying employer securities. Not all types of investments are covered in this checklist.

- ❑ **Identifying information**—The name of the investment option, as well as its investment category (e.g., money market fund, balanced fund, large cap stock fund)
- ❑ **Performance data/Benchmarks**

  Variable Return Investments:

  - ❑ The average annual total return for 1, 5, and 10 calendar-year periods (or for the life of the investment alternative, if shorter) and as compared to the performance of an appropriate broad-based securities market index for the same time periods.
  - ❑ A statement indicating that an investment's past performance is not necessarily an indication of future performance.

  Fixed Return Investments:

  - ❑ The fixed or stated annual rate of return and the term of the investment.
  - ❑ If the issuer has the right to adjust the return prospectively during the term, the current rate of return, the minimum rate guaranteed under the contract, if any, and a statement that the issuer may adjust the rate prospectively and how to obtain (e.g., telephone, Web site) the most recent rate of return required under the rules.
- ❑ **Fee and expense information**

  Variable Return Investments:

  - ❑ The total annual operating expense expressed both as a percentage (expense ratio) and as a dollar amount for a 1-year period per $1,000 invested (e.g., 0.25% or $2.50 per $1,000).
  - ❑ The amount and description of shareholder-type fees (fee charged directly against a plan's investment, such as commissions and sales charges, which are not included in the total annual operating expenses of any DIA) and a description of any restriction or limitation that may be applicable to a purchase, transfer, or withdrawal of the investment in whole or in part.
  - ❑ A statement indicating that fees and expenses are only one of several factors to be considered when making an investment decisions.

- ❑ A statement that the cumulative effect of fees and expenses can substantially reduce the growth of a participant's retirement account and that participants can visit EBSA's Web site for an example demonstrating the long-term effect of fees and expenses.

Fixed Return Investments:

- ❑ The amount and description of any shareholder-type fees.
- ❑ A description of any restriction or limitation that may be applicable to a purchase, transfer or withdrawal of the investment in whole or in part.

❑ **Glossary**— A general glossary of terms to assist participants in understanding the DIAs, or a website address that is sufficiently specific to provide access to such a glossary with a general explanation of the purpose of the address.

❑ **Website**—A website address that is sufficiently specific to provide participants access to the following information regarding the DIA:

- ❑ Name of investment issuer
- ❑ Objectives and goals
- ❑ Principal strategies and risks (does not apply to fixed return investments)
- ❑ Portfolio turnover rate (does not apply to fixed return investments)
- ❑ Performance data updated at least quarterly
- ❑ Fee and expense information
- ❑ Additional information if the DIA has an annuity-type feature.

2. Quarterly Disclosures

- ❑ The dollar amount of fees and expenses actually charged the preceding quarter to the participant's account for administrative services and for individual services.
- ❑ A general description of services provided for the fee/s.
- ❑ If applicable, an explanation that some of the plan's administrative fees for the preceding quarter were paid from the total annual operating expenses of one or more the plan's DIAs (e.g., through revenue-sharing arrangements, Rule 12-b1 fees, sub-transfer agent fees).

3. Disclosure in the Event of Change or Upon Request

- ❑ Provide a description of any changes to the general plan information and plan expense information described above 30 to 90 days in advance of the effective date of the change.
- ❑ Upon request of a participant, provide the following investment-related information relating to DIAs: Copies of prospectuses, financial statements or reports provided to the plan, statement of the value of a share or unit, and list of assets comprising the portfolio and the value (or proportion) of each such asset.

Appendix D

Key Indexed Limits (2014–2015)

Limit	*2015*	*2014*	*Application*
Salary Deferrals	$18,000	$17,500	Maximum salary deferral amount in calendar year
Age 50 Catch-Ups	$6,000	$5,500	Maximum age 50 catch-up contribution amount in calendar year
Section 415 Annual Additions	Lesser of $53,000 or 100% of compensation	Lesser of $52,000 or 100% of compensation	Maximum individual annual additions in a defined contribution plan
Compensation Cap	$265,000	$260,000	Maximum compensation that may be taken into account when determining contributions and for deduction purposes
SIMPLEs	$12,500	$12,000	Maximum annual contribution amount to SIMPLE plans
SIMPLE Age 50 Catch-Ups	$3,000	$2,500	Maximum age 50 catch-up contribution in calendar year
Highly Compensated Employee (HCE)	$120,000	$115,000	Pay threshold for "highly compensated employee" determinations
Threshold Officers	$170,000	$170,000	Officers earning more than this dollar amount treated as key employees for top-heavy testing
Maximum Taxable Wage Base	$118,500	$117,000	Maximum amount of earnings taxable for Social Security purposes

Limit	*2015*	*2014*	*Application*
IRA Contributions	$5,500	$5,500	Maximum annual contribution amount to IRA
IRA Age 50 Catch-Ups	$1,000	$1,000	Maximum age 50 catch-up contribution in calendar year

Appendix E

Key Indexed Limits Affected by the Economic Growth and Tax Relief Reconciliation Act of 2001 (EGTRRA)

Limit	*2001 (Pre-EGTRRA)*	*After 2001 (Post-EGTRRA)*	*Application*
Salary Deferrals	**$10,500**	$11,000 – 2002 $12,000 – 2003 $13,000 – 2004 $14,000 – 2005 $15,000 – 2006 (limit will be adjusted for inflation after 2006 in $500 increments)	Maximum salary deferral amount in calendar year
Age 50 Catch-Up Contributions	**N/A**	$1,000 – 2002 $2,000 – 2003 $3,000 – 2004 $4,000 – 2005 $5,000 – 2006 (limit will be adjusted for inflation after 2006 in $500 increments)	Maximum age 50 catch-up contribution amount in calendar year
415 Annual Additions	**Lesser of $35,500 or 25% of compensation**	Lesser of $40,000 or 100% of compensation (dollar limit will be adjusted for inflation in $1,000 increments)	Maximum individual annual additions in a defined contribution plan
Compensation Cap	**$170,000**	$200,000 (limit will be adjusted for inflation in $5,000 increments)	Maximum compensation that may be taken into account when determining contributions and for deduction purposes
Officers	**$70,000**	$130,000 (limit adjusted for inflation in $5,000 increments)	Officers earning more than this dollar amount treated as key employees for top-heavy testing
IRA Contributions	**$2,000**	$3,000 – 2002 through 2004 $4,000 – 2005 through 2007 $5,000 – 2008 (limit adjusted for inflation after 2008 in $500 increments)	Maximum annual contribution amount to IRA

Limit	*2001 (Pre-EGTRRA)*	*After 2001 (Post-EGTRRA)*	*Application*
Age 50 Catch-Up Contributions (IRA)	**N/A**	$ 500 – 2002 through 2005 $1,000 – 2006 and thereafter	Maximum age 50 catch-up contribution amount in calendar year (IRA)
SIMPLEs	**$6,500**	$ 7,000 – 2002 $ 8,000 – 2003 $ 9,000 – 2004 $10,000 – 2005 (limit adjusted for inflation after 2005 in $500 increments)	Maximum annual contribution amount to SIMPLE plans
Age 50 Catch-Up Contributions (SIMPLE)	**N/A**	$ 500 – 2002 $1,000 – 2003 $1,500 – 2004 $2,000 – 2005 $2,500 – 2006 (limit adjusted for inflation after 2006 in $500 increments)	Maximum age 50 catch-up contribution amount in calendar year (SIMPLE)

Appendix F

DOL Model Blackout Notice

Important Notice Concerning Your Rights Under the ***[Plan Name]***

[*Date of notice*]

1. This notice is to inform you that the [*name of plan*] will be [*enter reasons for blackout period, as appropriate*: changing investment options, changing recordkeepers, etc.].
2. As a result of these changes, you will be unable temporarily to [*enter as appropriate*: direct or diversify investments in your individual accounts (if only specific investments are subject to the blackout, those investments should be specifically identified), obtain a loan from the plan, or obtain a distribution from the plan]. This period, during which you will be unable to exercise these rights otherwise available under the plan, is called a "blackout period." Whether or not you are planning retirement in the near future, we encourage you to carefully consider how this blackout period may affect your retirement planning, as well as your overall financial plan.
3. The blackout period for the plan [*enter as appropriate*: is expected to begin on [*enter date*] and end [*enter date*]/is expected to begin during the week of [*enter date*] and end during the week of [*enter date*]. During these weeks, you can determine whether the blackout period has started or ended by [*enter instructions for using toll-free number or accessing Web site*].
4. [*In the case of investments affected by the blackout period, add the following:* During the blackout period you will be unable to direct or diversify the assets held in your plan account. For this reason, it is very important that you review and consider the appropriateness of your current investments in light of your inability to direct or diversify those investments during the blackout period. For your long-term retirement security, you should give careful consideration to the importance of a well-balanced and diversified investment portfolio, taking into account all your assets, income and investments. [*If the plan permits investments in individual securities, add the following:* You should be aware that there is a risk to holding substantial portions of your assets in the securities of any one

company, as individual securities tend to have wider price swings, up and down, in short periods of time, than investments in diversified funds. Stocks that have wide price swings might have a large loss during the blackout period, and you would not be able to direct the sale of such stocks from your account during the blackout period.]

5. [*If timely notice cannot be provided add:* (A) Federal law generally requires that you be furnished notice of a blackout period at least 30 days in advance of the last date on which you could exercise your affected rights immediately before the commencement of any blackout period in order to provide you with sufficient time to consider the effect of the blackout period on your retirement and financial plans. (B) [*Enter explanation of reasons for inability to furnish 30 days' advance notice.*]

6. If you have any questions concerning this notice, you should contact [*enter name, address, and telephone number of the plan administrator or other contact responsible for answering questions about the blackout period*].

Appendix G

IRS Model Diversification Notice for Plans Holding Publicly Traded Employer Securities

Notice of Your Rights Concerning Employer Securities

This notice informs you of an important change in federal law that provides specific rights concerning investments in employer securities (company stock). Because you may now or in the future have investments in company stock under the [*insert name of plan*], you should take the time to read this notice carefully.

Your Rights Concerning Employer Securities

For plan years beginning after December 31, 2006, the Plan must allow you to elect to move any portion of your account that is invested in company stock from that investment into other investment alternatives under the Plan. This right extends to all of the company stock held under the Plan, except that it does not apply to your account balance attributable to [*identify any accounts to which the rights apply only after three years of service*] until you have three years of service. [*Insert description of any advance notice requirement before a diversification election becomes effective.*] You may contact the person identified below for specific information regarding this new right, including how to make this election. In deciding whether to exercise this right, you will want to give careful consideration to the information below that describes the importance of diversification. All of the investment options under the Plan are available to you if you decide to diversify out of company stock.

The Importance of Diversifying Your Retirement Savings

To help achieve long-term retirement security, you should give careful consideration to the benefits of a well-balanced and diversified investment portfolio. Spreading your assets among different types of investments can help you achieve a favorable rate of return, while minimizing your overall risk of losing money. This is because market or other economic conditions that cause one category of assets, or one particular security, to perform very well often cause another asset category, or another particular security, to perform poorly. If you invest more than 20% of your retirement savings in any one company or industry, your savings may not be properly diversified. Although diversification is not a guarantee against loss, it is an effective strategy to help you manage investment risk.

In deciding how to invest your retirement savings, you should take into account all of your assets, including any retirement savings outside of the Plan. No single approach is right for everyone because, among other factors, individuals have different financial goals, different time horizons for meeting their goals, and different tolerances for risk. Therefore, you should carefully consider the rights described in this notice and how these rights affect the amount of money that you invest in company stock through the Plan.

It is also important to periodically review your investment portfolio, your investment objectives, and the investment options under the Plan to help ensure that your retirement savings will meet your retirement goals.

For More Information

If you have any questions about your rights under this new law, including how to make this election, contact [*enter name and contact information*].

Appendix H

Model Participant Disclosure Regarding Eligible Investment Advice Arrangements (EIAAs)

Fiduciary Adviser Disclosure

This document contains important information about [*name of Fiduciary Adviser*] and how it is compensated for the investment advice provided to you. You should carefully consider this information in your evaluation of that advice. [*name of Fiduciary Adviser*] has been selected to provide investment advisory services for the [*name of Plan*]. [*Name of Fiduciary Adviser*] will be providing these services as a fiduciary under the Employee Retirement Income Security Act (ERISA). [*Name of Fiduciary Adviser*], therefore, must act prudently and with only your interest in mind when providing you recommendations on how to invest your retirement assets.

Compensation of the Fiduciary Adviser and Related Parties

[*Name of Fiduciary Adviser*] (is/is not) compensated by the plan for the advice it provides. (If compensated by the plan, explain what and how compensation is charged (e.g., asset-based fee, flat fee, per advice)). (If applicable, [*name of Fiduciary Adviser*] is not compensated on the basis of the investment(s) selected by you.) Affiliates of [*name of Fiduciary Adviser*] (*if applicable, enter,* and other parties with whom [*name of Fiduciary Adviser*] is related or has a material financial relationship) also will be providing services for which they will be compensated. These services include: [*enter description of services, e.g., investment management, transfer agent, custodial, and shareholder services for some/all the investment funds available under the plan.*]

When [*name of Fiduciary Adviser*] recommends that you invest your assets in an investment fund of its own or one of its affiliates and you follow that advice, [*name of Fiduciary Adviser*] or that affiliate will receive compensation from the investment fund based on the amount you invest. The amounts that will be paid by you will vary depending on the particular fund in which you invest your assets and may range from ________% to ____%. Specific information concerning the fees and other charges of each investment fund is available from [*enter source, such as: your plan administrator, investment fund provider (possibly with Internet Web site address)*]. This information should be reviewed carefully before you make an investment decision. (if applicable enter, [*name of Fiduciary Adviser*] or affiliates of [*name of Fiduciary Adviser*] also receive compensation from non-affiliated investment funds as a result of investments you make as a result of recommendations of [*name of Fiduciary Adviser*]. The amount of this compensation also may vary depending on the particular fund in which you invest. This compensation may range from ________% to ____%.

Specific information concerning the fees and other charges of each investment fund is available from [*enter source, such as: your plan administrator, investment fund provider (possibly with Internet Web site address)*]. This information should be reviewed carefully before you make an investment decision. [*If applicable, enter,* In addition to the above, [*name of Fiduciary Adviser*] or affiliates of [*name of Fiduciary Adviser*] also receive other fees or compensation, such as commissions, in connection with the sale, acquisition or holding of investments selected by you as a result of recommendations of [*name of Fiduciary Adviser*]. These amounts are: [*enter description of all other fees or compensation to be received in connection with sale, acquisition or holding of investments*]. This information should be reviewed carefully before you make an investment decision.

[*If applicable enter,* When [*name of Fiduciary Adviser*] recommends that you take a rollover or other distribution of assets from the plan, or recommends how those assets should subsequently be invested, [*name of Fiduciary Adviser*] or affiliates of [*name of Fiduciary Adviser*] will receive additional fees or compensation. These amounts are: [*enter description of all other fees or compensation to be received in connection with any rollover or other distribution of plan assets or the investment of distributed assets*]. This information should be reviewed carefully before you make a decision to take a distribution.

Consider Impact of Compensation on Advice

The fees and other compensation that [*name of Fiduciary Adviser*] and its affiliates receive on account of assets in [*name of Fiduciary Adviser*] (*enter if applicable*, and non-[*name of Fiduciary Adviser*]) investment funds are a significant source of revenue for the [*name of Fiduciary Adviser*] and its affiliates. You should carefully consider the impact of any such fees and compensation in your evaluation of the investment advice that [*name of Fiduciary Adviser*] provides to you. In this regard, you may arrange for the provision of advice by another adviser that may have no material affiliation with or receive no compensation in connection with the investment funds or products offered under the plan. This type of advice is/is not available through your plan.

Investment Returns

While understanding investment-related fees and expenses is important in making informed investment decisions, it is also important to consider additional information about your investment options, such as performance, investment strategies, and risks. Specific information related to the past performance and historical rates of return of the investment options available under the plan (has/has not) been provided to you by [*enter source, such as: your plan administrator, investment fund provider*]. (*If applicable enter,* If not provided to you, the information is attached to this document.) For options with returns that vary over time, past performance does not guarantee how your investment in the option will perform in the future; your investment in these options could lose money.

Parties Participating in Development of Advice Program or Selection of Investment Options

[*Name and describe role of affiliates or other parties with whom the fiduciary adviser has a material affiliation or contractual relationship that participated in the development of the investment advice program (if this is an arrangement that uses computer models) or the selection of investment options available under the plan.*]

Use of Personal Information

[*Include a brief explanation of the following—*

- *What personal information will be collected;*
- *How the information will be used;*
- *Parties with whom information will be shared;*
- *How the information will be protected; and*
- *When and how notice of the Fiduciary Adviser's privacy statement will be available to participants and beneficiaries.*]

Should you have any questions about [*name of Fiduciary Adviser*] or the information contained in this document, you may contact [*name of contact person for fiduciary adviser, telephone number, address*].

Appendix I

IRS Rollover Chart

IRS ROLLOVER CHART

Roll From \ Roll To	Roth IRA	IRA (traditional)	SIMPLE IRA	SEP-IRA	457(b) (government)	Qualified Plan[1] (pre-tax)	403(b) (pre-tax)	Designated Roth Account (401(k), 403(b), or 457(b))
Roth IRA	Yes[2]	No	No	No	No	No	No	No
IRA (traditional)	Yes[3]	Yes[2]	No	Yes[2]	Yes[4]	Yes	Yes	No
SIMPLE IRA	Yes[3], after two years	Yes[2], after two years	Yes[2]	Yes[2], after two years	Yes[4] after two years	Yes, after two years	Yes, after two years	No
SEP-IRA	Yes[3]	Yes[2]	No	Yes[2]	Yes[4]	Yes	Yes	No
457(b) (government)	Yes[3]	Yes	No	Yes	Yes	Yes	Yes	Yes[3,5]
Qualified Plan[1] (pre-tax)	Yes[3]	Yes	No	Yes	Yes[4]	Yes	Yes	Yes[3,5]
403(b) (pre-tax)	Yes[3]	Yes	No	Yes	Yes[4]	Yes	Yes	Yes[3,5]
Designated Roth Account (401(k), 403(b), or 457(b))	Yes	No	No	No	No	No	No	Yes[6]

[1] Qualified plans include, for example, Profit Sharing, 401(k), Money Purchase, and Defined Benefit plans.
[2] Only one rollover in any 12-month period.
[3] Must include in income.
[4] Must have separate accounts.
[5] Must be an in-plan rollover.
[6] Any amounts distributed must be rolled over via direct (trustee-to-trustee) transfer to be excludable from income.
For more information regarding retirement plans and rollovers, visit Tax Information for Retirement Plans Community on IRS Web site (*www.irs.gov*).

Appendix J

401(k) Plan Compliance Calendar

The following calendar includes dates for key recurring events in a 401(k) plan using a December 31 plan year end. In many cases where the deadline falls on a weekend or holiday, the deadline will be extended to the next business day. Refer to relevant sections of this book for definitions and additional detail.

January 31

Deadline for sending Form 1099-R to participants who received distributions during the prior calendar year.

Deadline for filing Form 945 with the IRS to report income tax withheld during the prior calendar year (or by February 10 if all withheld taxes were paid timely).

February 14

Deadline for providing fourth-quarter individual benefit statements to participants in participant-directed plans. The quarterly fee disclosure due under the new participant fee disclosure rule is also due on this date and can be included in the statement. Deadline for non-calendar-year plans is 45 days following the end of the quarter to which the statement relates.

February 28 (or 29 in a leap year)

Deadline for filing Form 1099-R in paper format with the IRS to report distributions made in the previous calendar year (or by March 31 if filing electronically).

March 15

Deadline for processing corrective distributions for failed actual deferral percentage/actual contribution percentage (ADP/ACP) tests without incurring 10 percent excise tax. Note: for non-calendar-plan years, the deadline is 2½ months following the plan year-end.

For corporations operating on a calendar year tax year, deadline for filing corporate tax return, and contribution deadline for deductibility (without extension). For non-calendar-year corporations, the deadline is 2½ months following the end of the tax year.

For corporate tax returns, deadline for requesting an automatic filing extension until September 15. For non–calendar-year corporations, the deadline is 2½ months following the end of the tax year for an automatic extension of six months

March 31

Deadline to file Form 1099-R in electronic format with the IRS to report distributions made in the previous calendar year.

April 1

Deadline for making initial required minimum distributions.

April 15

Deadline for processing corrective distributions of excess deferrals under Code Section 402(g).

Deadline for filing sole proprietor and/or partnership tax returns. For non–calendar-year plans, the deadline is 3½ months following the end of the tax year.

Deadline for requesting an automatic filing extension to September 15 for partnerships and to October 15 for sole proprietors. For non–calendar-year plans, the deadline is 3½ months following the end of the tax year to obtain a five-month extension for partnerships or a six-month extension for sole proprietors.

May 14

Deadline for providing first-quarter individual benefit statements to participants in participant-directed plans. The quarterly fee disclosure due under the new participant fee disclosure rule is also due on this date and can be included in the statement. Deadline for non–calendar-year plans is 45 days following the end of the quarter to which the statement relates.

June 30

Deadline for processing corrective distributions for failed ADP/ACP test from a plan with an eligible automatic contribution arrangement (EACA) without incurring the 10 percent excise tax. For non–calendar-year plans, the deadline is six months following the end of the plan year.

July 29

Deadline for sending any Summary of Material Modifications (SMMs) to participants. For non–calendar-year plans, the deadline is 210 days after the plan year to which the amendment relates.

July 31

Due date for filing Form 5500 (without extension). For non–calendar-year plans, the deadline is the last day of the seventh month following the end of the plan year.

Deadline to request an automatic 2½-month extension to file Form 5500 using Form 5558. For non-calendar-year plans, the deadline is the normal Form 5500 filing due date without extensions.

Last day to file Form 5330, Return of Excise Taxes Related to Employee Benefit Plans, which is used to report and pay excise taxes on prohibited transactions that occurred in the prior year. For non-calendar-year plans the deadline is the last day of the seventh month following the end of the tax year of the filing taxpayer. If Form 5330 is used to report excise tax on excess contributions or excess aggregate contributions, the filing deadline is 15 months after the plan year to which the contributions relate.

Deadline for providing individual benefit statements to participants in plans that do not have an extension for filing Form 5500 and do not allow for participant direction of investments. For non-calendar-year plans, the deadline is the due date of the Form 5500 return with extensions.

August 14

Deadline for providing second-quarter individual benefit statements to participants in participant-directed plans. The quarterly fee disclosure due under the new participant fee disclosure rule is also due on this date and can be included in the statement. For non-calendar-year plans the deadline is 45 days following the end of the quarter to which the statement relates.

September 15

Extended deadline for filing corporate or partnership tax returns, and for making tax deductible plan contributions. For non-calendar-year corporations or partnerships the deadline is 8½ months following the end of the tax year.

Deadline for filing Form 5500 where corporate or partnership tax year and plan year are the same and a corporate or partnership tax year extension has been granted. For non-calendar-year plans and partnerships, the deadline is 8½ months following the end of the tax year.

Deadline for providing individual benefit statements to participants in non-participant-directed plans where the corporate or partnership tax years are the same, and an extension for filing Form 5500 has been granted. For non-calendar-year plans, the deadline is the due date of the Form 5500 return, with extensions.

September 30

Deadline for distributing the Summary Annual Report (SAR) to participants if no extension for filing Form 5500 applies. For non-calendar-year plans, the deadline is 2 months after the Form 5500 filing due date.

October 2

Earliest date for providing the annual 401(k) safe-harbor, QACA safe-harbor, QDIA, EACA, or ACA notice. For non-calendar-year plans, the earliest date is 90 days before the beginning of the plan year. See Appendices A, B, and C for sample notices.

October 15

Deadline for filing Form 5500 when a Form 5558 filing extension has been granted. For non-calendar- plan years, the deadline is 9½ months following the end of the plan year.

Deadline for providing individual benefit statements to participants in non–participant-directed plans where a Form 5500 filing extension has been granted through a Form 5558 filing. For non–calendar-year plans, the deadline is the due date of the Form 5500 return, with extensions.

Deadline for adopting a retroactive amendment to correct a Code Section 410(b) coverage or Section 401(a)(4) nondiscrimination failure occurring in the previous plan year. For non–calendar-year plans, the deadline is 9½ months after the end of the plan year.

Deadline for sole proprietors to file tax return and to make tax-deductible contributions.

November 14

Deadline for providing third-quarter individual benefit statements to participants in participant-directed plans. The quarterly fee disclosure due under the new participant fee disclosure rule is also due on this date and can be included in the statement. For non–calendar-year plans, the deadline is 45 days following the end of the quarter to which the statement relates.

SAR due to participants in plans where Form 5500 deadline was extended due to corporate or partnership tax-filing extension. For non–calendar-year corporations or partnerships, the deadline is 10½ months following the end of the tax year.

December 2

Latest date for providing a 401(k) safe-harbor, QACA safe-harbor, QDIA, EACA or ACA notice. For non–calendar-year plans, the latest date is 30 days before the beginning of the plan year.

December 15

Extended deadline for distributing SAR to participants if Form 5500 extension was granted as the result of a Form 5558 filing. For non–calendar-plan years, the deadline is 11½ months following the plan year.

December 31

Deadline for making corrective distributions for failed ADP/ACP test in previous plan year without jeopardizing qualified status of the plan. A 10 percent excise tax will apply.

Deadline for making QNECs or QMACs to correct failed ADP or ACP tests in previous plan year in plans using current year testing.

Deadline for an amendment to convert an existing 401(k) plan to a safe harbor design (regular or QACA) in the next plan year. See the following notice requirements.

Deadline for amending a plan to remove safe harbor status for the next plan year. See the following notice requirements.

Deadline for amending plan for changes implemented during the plan year (certain exceptions apply, e.g., adding salary deferrals, cutback of an accrued benefit).

Deadline for making required minimum distributions to participants whose required beginning date has already occurred.

For non–calendar-plan years, the deadline is the last day of the plan year.

At Least Once in Every 14-Month Period

Deadline for providing the fee and investment information required to be disclosed to participants in participant-directed plans.

Other Deadlines Triggered by Plan Events or Design Features

Newly Eligible Participants

**EACA Notice*: No earlier than 90 days before the employee becomes eligible to participate and not later than a date affording the employee a reasonable period of time after receipt of the notice to make an election. In an immediate entry plan, notice will be considered timely if given as soon as possible after the employee's eligibility date and the employee can elect to defer on compensation earned from the date of eligibility. See Appendix B for sample notice.

**Safe-Harbor or QACA Notice*: No earlier than 90 days before the employee is eligible to participate and no later than a reasonable period of time before the employee is eligible. In an immediate entry plan, notice will be considered timely if given as soon as possible after the employee's eligibility date and the employee can elect to defer on compensation earned from the date of eligibility. See Appendices A and B for sample notices.

**QDIA Notice*: At least 30 days before the employee is eligible to participate or make an initial investment in a QDIA or, if the plan contains an EACA and allows for 90-day permissible withdrawals, on or before the date of plan eligibility. See Appendix C for sample notice.

*Notice is only required in plans offering these features.

Summary Plan Description (SPD): Within 90 days after becoming a participant in the plan.

Participant Disclosure Initial Notice: Under the participant disclosure rules, employees who are eligible to enter the plan, or beneficiaries with the right to make investment decisions for their beneficiary account, must receive an initial disclosure notice on or before the date they can first direct investment of their account.

Terminating Participants

Special Tax Notice: Must be provided to all participants receiving an eligible rollover distribution 30 to 180 days before the distribution is made. The 30-day requirement can be waived by the participant in many circumstances (see chapter 16).

Right to Defer Notice: Generally must be provided 30 to 180 days before the date benefits are to be paid, although the 30-day rule can be waived by the participant in some circumstances. The participant's consent to receive a distribution must be given after the participant receives the notice and no more than 180 days before the distribution occurs.

Tax Withholding Notice: Participants receiving distributions that are not eligible rollover distributions must be notified of their right to elect out of the withholding requirement. For periodic distributions, notice must be provided not earlier than six months before the first payment and not later than the date of the first payment. The notice must be repeated at least once each calendar year. For non-periodic distributions, notice must be provided no earlier than six months before the distribution and no later than a date giving the participant a reasonable period of time to elect out of withholding.

Qualified Joint and Survivor Annuity (QJSA) Notice: For plans subject to the survivor annuity rules, a written explanation of the QJSA must be provided to participants within 30 to 180 days before their annuity starting date.

Qualified Pre-retirement Survivor Annuity (QPSA) Notice: For plans subject to the survivor annuity rules, a written explanation of the QPSA must generally be provided during a period beginning on the first day of the plan year in which the participant attains age 32 and ending on the last day of the plan year in which the participant attains age 34. If the individual becomes a participant after this period, notice must be provided no later than one year after participation commences. If a participant separates from service prior to attaining age 35, notice must be provided within one year of the participant's separation from service.

Claims for Additional Benefits: If a participant makes a claim for additional benefits in accordance with the plan's claims review procedures, the Plan Administrator has 90 days to make a determination on the claim, which can be extended an additional 90 days upon written notification to the claimant. If a claim is denied, the claimant must have at least 60 days following the denial to file an appeal.

Remitting Salary Deferral Contributions

Salary deferral contributions must be turned over to the plan trustee on the earliest date they can reasonably be segregated from corporate assets, but no later than the 15th business day of the month following the payroll month. For plans with fewer than 100 participants, contributions are deemed to be remitted timely if paid within 7 business days after the payroll date (or, for amounts such as loan repayments, which may be paid directly to the employer, within 7 days of receipt by the employer).

Annual and Quarterly Participant Disclosures

At least once in every 14-month period, participants, eligible employees, and beneficiaries with the right to direct investment of their account must receive the annual investment and fee disclosures required under the participant disclosure rules. (See chapter 19 for discussion of a transition rule regarding these disclosures).

Under the participant disclosure rules, which went into effect for plan years starting on or after November 1, 2011, participants must receive a statement at least quarterly describing certain fees and services associated with their plan accounts.

Blackout Notices

Blackout periods, defined as a period of more than three consecutive business days during which participants' ability to transact in their accounts is suspended, typically occur due to a change in recordkeepers, a merger or spin off, or a change in investment offerings. Notice must be provided within 30 to 60 days in advance of when blackout occurs. See Appendix F for model notice.

Qualified Domestic Relations Orders (QDRO)

The Plan Administrator must promptly notify the participant and alternate payee when an order is received and inform them of the plan's procedures for reviewing orders. The Plan Administrator must make a determination regarding the qualified status of an order within a reasonable period of time.

Employer Stock Diversification Notice

In certain plans offering publicly traded employer securities as an investment option, a notice describing the participant's right to diversify must be provided at least 30 days in advance of the date the participant is eligible to exercise his or her diversification rights. See Appendix G for model notice.

Eligible Investment Advice Arrangements (EIAA)

Financial advisors providing fiduciary investment advice pursuant to an EIAA must provide required disclosures before providing any investment advice to a participant. See Appendix H for a model EIAA notice.

Mid-Year Suspension or Reduction of Safe Harbor Contributions

In the event that safe harbor matching or non-elective contributions will be suspended or reduced mid-year in accordance with IRS rules, participants must receive notice of the change at least 30 days in advance of its effective date.

Appendix K

DOL Model Comparative Chart

ABC Corporation 401(k) Retirement Plan Investment Options—January 1, 20XX

This document includes important information to help you compare the investment options under your retirement plan. If you want additional information about your investment options, you can go to the specific Internet Web site address shown below or you can contact [*insert name of plan administrator or designee*] at [*insert telephone number and address*]. A free paper copy of the information available on the Web site[s] can be obtained by contacting [*insert name of plan administrator or designee*] at [*insert telephone number*].

Document Summary

This document has three parts. Part I consists of performance information for plan investment options. This part shows you how well the investments have performed in the past. Part II shows you the fees and expenses you will pay if you invest in an option. Part III contains information about the annuity options under your retirement plan.

Part I. Performance Information

Table 1 focuses on the performance of investment options that do not have a fixed or stated rate of return. Table 1 shows how these options have performed over time and allows you to compare them with an appropriate benchmark for the same time periods. Past performance does not guarantee how the investment option will perform in the future. Your investment in these options could lose money. Information about an option's principal risks is available on the Web site[s].

Table 1 —Variable Return Investments

Name/ Type of Option	Average Annual Total Return as of 12/31/XX				Benchmark			
	1yr.	5yr.	10yr.	Since Inception	1yr.	5yr.	10yr.	Since Inception
Equity Funds								
A Index Fund/ S&P 500 www.website address	26.5%	.34%	−1.03%	9.25%	26.46%	.42%	−.95%	9.30%
					S&P 500			
B Fund/Large Cap www.website address	27.6%	.99%	N/A	2.26%	27.80%	1.02%	N/A	2.77%
					US Prime Market 750 Index			
C Fund/Int'l Stock www.website address	36.73%	5.26%	2.29%	9.37%	40.40%	5.40%	2.40%	12.09%
					MSCI EAFE			
D Fund/Mid Cap www.website address	40.22%	2.28%	6.13%	3.29%	46.29%	2.40%	−.52%	4.16%
					Russell Midcap			
Bond Funds								
E Fund/Bond Index www.website address	6.45%	4.43%	6.08%	7.08%	5.93%	4.97%	6.33%	7.01%
					Barclays Cap. Aggr. Bd.			
Other								
F Fund/GICs www.website address	.72%	3.36%	3.11%	5.56%	1.8%	3.1%	3.3%	5.75%
					3-month US T-Bill Index			
G Fund/Stable Value www.website address	4.36%	4.64%	5.07%	3.75%	1.8%	3.1%	3.3%	4.99%
					3-month US T-Bill Index			
Generations 2020/Lifecycle Fund www.website address	27.94%	N/A	N/A	2.45%	26.46%	N/A	N/A	3.09%
					S&P 500			
					23.95%	N/A	N/A	3.74%
					Generations 2020 Composite Index*			

* Generations 2020 composite index is a combination of a total market index and a US aggregate bond index proportional to the equity/bond allocation in the Generations 2020 Fund.

Table 2 focuses on the performance of investment options that have a fixed or stated rate of return. Table 2 shows the annual rate of return of each such option, the term or length of time that you will earn this rate of return, and other information relevant to performance.

Table 2—Fixed Return Investments			
Name/ Type of Option	**Return**	**Term**	**Other**
H 200X/GIC www.website address	4%	2 Yr.	The rate of return does not change during the stated term.
I LIBOR Plus/Fixed-Type Investment Account www.website address	LIBOR +2%	Quarterly	The rate of return on 12/31/xx was 2.45%. This rate is fixed quarterly, but will never fall below a guaranteed minimum rate of 2%. Current rate of return information is available on the option's Web site or at 1-800-yyy-zzzz.
J Financial Services Co./Fixed Account Investment www.website address	3.75%	6 Mos.	The rate of return on 12/31/xx was 3.75%. This rate of return is fixed for six months. Current rate of return information is available on the option's Web site or at 1-800-yyy-zzzz.

Part II. Fee and Expense Information

Table 3 shows fee and expense information for the investment options listed in Table1 and Table 2. Table 3 shows the Total Annual Operating Expenses of the options in Table 1. Total Annual Operating Expenses are expenses that reduce the rate of return of the investment option. Table 3 also shows Shareholder-type Fees. These fees are in addition to Total Annual Operating Expenses.

Table 3—Fees and Expenses			
Name/ Type of Option	**Total Annual Operating Expenses**		**Shareholder-Type Fees**
	As a %	Per $1000	
Equity Funds			
A Index Fund/ S&P 500	0.18%	$1.80	$20 annual service charge subtracted from investments held in this option if valued at less than $10,000.
B Fund/ Large Cap	2.45%	$24.50	2.25% deferred sales charge subtracted from amounts withdrawn within 12 months of purchase.
C Fund/ International Stock	0.79%	$7.90	5.75% sales charge subtracted from amounts invested.
D Fund/ Mid Cap ETF	0.20%	$2.00	4.25% sales charge subtracted from amounts withdrawn.
Bond Funds			
E Fund/Bond Index	0.50%	$5.00	N/A
Other			
F Fund/GICs	0.46%	$4.60	10% charge subtracted from amounts withdrawn within 18 months of initial investment.
G Fund/ Stable Value	0.65%	$6.50	Amounts withdrawn may not be transferred to a competing option for 90 days after withdrawal.
Generations 2020/Lifecycle Fund	1.50%	$15.00	Excessive trading restricts additional purchases (other than contributions and loan repayments) for 85 days.

Table 3—Fees and Expenses		
Name/ Type of Option	**Total Annual Operating Expenses**	**Shareholder-Type Fees**
Fixed Return Investments		
H 200X/GIC	N/A	12% charge subtracted from amounts withdrawn before maturity.
I LIBOR Plus/ Fixed-Type Invest Account	N/A	5% contingent deferred sales charge subtracted from amounts withdrawn; charge reduced by 1% on 12-month anniversary of each investment.
J Financial Services Co./ Fixed Account Investment	N/A	90 days of interest subtracted from amounts withdrawn before maturity.

The cumulative effect of fees and expenses can substantially reduce the growth of your retirement savings. Visit the Department of Labor's Web site for an example showing the long-term effect of fees and expenses at *http://www.dol.gov/ebsa/publications/401k employee.html.* Fees and expenses are only one of many factors to consider when you decide to invest in an option. You may also want to think about whether an investment in a particular option, along with your other investments, will help you achieve your financial goals.

Part III. Annuity Information

Table 4 focuses on the annuity options under the plan. Annuities are insurance contracts that allow you to receive a guaranteed stream of payments at regular intervals, usually beginning when you retire and lasting for your entire life. Annuities are issued by insurance companies. Guarantees of an insurance company are subject to its long-term financial strength and claims-paying ability.

Table 4—Annuity Options			
Name	**Objectives/ Goals**	**Pricing Factors**	**Restrictions/ Fees**
Lifetime Income Option www.website address	To provide a guaranteed stream of income for your life, based on shares you acquire while you work. At age 65, you will receive monthly payments of $10 for each share you own, for your life. For example, if you own 30 shares at age 65, you will receive $300 per month over your life.	The cost of each share depends on your age and interest rates when you buy it. Ordinarily the closer you are to retirement, the more it will cost you to buy a share. The cost includes a guaranteed death benefit payable to a spouse or beneficiary if you die before payments begin. The death benefit is the total amount of your contributions, less any withdrawals.	Payment amounts are based on your life expectancy only and would be reduced if you choose a spousal joint and survivor benefit. You will pay a 25% surrender charge for any amount you withdraw before annuity payments begin. If your income payments are less than $50 per month, the option's issuer may combine payments and pay you less frequently, or return to you the larger of your net contributions or the cash-out value of your income shares.
Generations 2020 Variable Annuity Option www.website address	To provide a guaranteed stream of income for your life, or some other period of time, based on your account balance in the Generations 2020 Lifecycle Fund.	You have the right to elect fixed annuity payments in the form of a life annuity, a joint and survivor annuity, or a life annuity with a term certain, but the payment	Maximum surrender charge of 8% of account balance. Maximum transfer fee of $30 for each transfer over 12 in a year. Annual service charge of $50 for account balances below $100,000.

Table 4—Annuity Options			
Name	**Objectives/ Goals**	**Pricing Factors**	**Restrictions/ Fees**
	This option is available through a variable annuity contract that your plan has with ABC Insurance Company.	Amounts will vary based on the benefit you choose. The cost of this right is included in the Total Annual Operating Expenses of the Generations 2020 Lifecycle Fund, listed in Table 3 above. The cost also includes a guaranteed death benefit payable to a spouse or beneficiary if you die before payments begin. The death benefit is the greater of your account balance or contributions, less any withdrawals.	
Please visit www.ABCPlanglossary.com for a glossary of investment terms relevant to the investment options under this plan. This glossary is intended to help you better understand your options.			

Appendix L

Sample DOL Guide to 408(b)(2) Initial Disclosures

See chapter 5 for proposed DOL regulation that would require a fee disclosure guide.

ABC Service Provider, Inc. (ABC) Guide to Services and Compensation Prepared for the XYZ 401(k) Plan

The following is a guide to important information that you should consider in connection with the services to be provided by ABC to the XYZ 401(k) Plan.

Should you have any questions concerning this guide or the information provided to you concerning our services or compensation, please do not hesitate to contact [*enter name of person and/or office*] at [*enter phone number and/or email address*].

Required Information	Location(s)
Description of the services that ABC will provide to your Plan.	Master Service Agreement § 2.4, p. 1
A statement concerning the services that ABC will provide as [*an ERISA fiduciary*][*a registered investment adviser*].	Master Service Agreement § 2.6, p. 2
Compensation ABC will receive from your Plan ("direct" compensation).	Master Service Agreement § 3.2, p. 4
Compensation ABC will receive from other parties that are not related to ABC ("indirect" compensation).	Master Service Agreement § 3.3, p. 4 Stable Value Offering Agmt § 3.1, p. 4

Required Information	Location(s)
Compensation that will be paid among ABC and related parties.	Master Service Agreement § 3.5, p. 6
Compensation ABC will receive if you terminate this service agreement.	Master Service Agreement § 9.2, p. 11
The cost to your Plan of recordkeeping services.	Master Service Agreement § 3.4, p. 5
Fees and Expenses relating to your Plan's investment options. *Total Annual Operating Expenses	(1) Capital and Income Fund Trans. Fees: InvestCo Prospectus, Fund Summary, p. 2 TAOE: *InvestCo Prospectus, Fund Summary, p. 2 (2) International Stock Fund Trans. Fees: www.weblink/ABCProspInv2/trans.com TAOE: www.weblink/ABCProspInv2/taoe.com (3) Small Cap Fund Trans. Fees: www.ABCweblink/ProspInv3/trans.com TAOE: www.weblink/ABCProspInv3/taoe.com (4) Bond Market Index Fund Trans. Fees: www.weblink/ABCProspInv4/trans.com TAOE: www.weblink/ABCProspInv4/taoe.com (5) Stable Value Fund Trans. Fees: Stable Value Offering Agmt, § 2.4, p. 3 TAOE: Stable Value Offering Agmt, § 2.3, p. 3 (6) Money Market Fund Trans. Fees: www.weblink/ABCProspInv6/trans.com TAOE: www.weblink/ABCProspInv6/taoe.com

Appendix M

Fixing Common Plan Mistakes—Correcting Missed Deferrals

FAQ: Fixing Common Plan Mistakes—Correcting Missed Deferrals

Q&As for informational purposes only. Plan Sponsors should consult their tax and/or legal advisor for specific guidance.

Q. Has the IRS provided guidance regarding how to correct a failure to permit an employee to make a deferral election, to implement an employee's deferral election, or to correctly administer a plan's automatic enrollment provision?

A. IRS guidance on the methods for correcting a failure to permit an employee to make a deferral election, to implement a participant's deferral election and/or a plan's automatic enrollment provision includes:

- Revenue Procedure 2013-12 containing the detailed guidance on the IRs's Employee Plans Compliance Resolution System (EPCRS) and can be accessed at http://www.irs.gov/irb/2013-04_IRB/ar06.html
- Revenue Procedure 2015-28 setting forth additional guidance under EPCRS and can be accessed at: http://www.irs.gov/pub/irs-drop/rp-15-28.pdf
- Information on correcting a failure to permit an employee to make a deferral election can be accessed at: http://www.irs.gov/Retirement-Plans/Plan-Sponsor/Fixing-Common-Plan-Mistakes—Correction-for-Exclusion-of-Employees-for-Elective-Contributions-or-After-Tax-Employee-Contributions
- Information on correcting a failure to implement an employee's deferral election can be accessed at: http://www.irs.gov/Retirement-Plans/Fixing-Common-Plan-Mistakes—Correcting-a-Failure-to-Effect-Employee-Deferral-Elections

- Information on correcting a plan's automatic enrollment provision can be accessed at: http://www.irs.gov/Retirement-Plans/Fixing-Common-Plan-Mistakes—Correcting-a-Failure-to-Implement-the-Plan's-Automatic-Enrollment-Provisions

Each particular fact pattern must be assessed to determine the appropriate correction method(s) under available IRS guidance. Depending on the nature of the failure, more than one option may be available to correct the failure. The chart that follows is a road map for making those assessments and identifying available options under IRS guidance.

Remember that failures occurring more than 3 years ago (including the current plan year) may need to be corrected under the IRS's VCP program if the failures in the aggregate are considered significant as provided in Section 8 of Revenue Procedure 2013-12. The significance of failures is a determination to be made by the plan sponsor and its advisers.

IRS Guidance	*Failure to permit an employee to make a deferral election*	*Failure to implement an employee's deferral election*	*Failure to implement a plan's automatic enrollment provision*	*Notice Requirement & Earnings Calculation*	*Matching Requirement (if plan has matching provision)*
	Example of error: John's entry date is April 1 but the employer does not allow him to make a deferral election.	**Example of error:** Amy makes a deferral election of 5% of compensation, but the employer fails to implement the election.	**Example of error:** Jim's entry date is July 1 and he does not make a deferral election. The employer fails to implement the plan's automatic enrollment provision that provides for deferral of 3% of pay in absence of an affirmative election.		
Options under Revenue Procedure 2013-12 (EPCRS)	No QNEC required if the participant still has the remaining 9 months in the plan year to defer, and error is limited to only the first 3 months of plan year.	No QNEC required if the participant still has the remaining 9 months in the plan year to defer, and error limited to only the first 3 months of plan year.	It is not clear under this guidance whether QNEC is not required if the participant still has the remaining 9 months in the plan year to defer, and error is limited to only the first 3 months of plan year.	**All Options:** No Notice Required **All Options:** For Earnings Calculation, if investment election is known—use Actual Investment Return or Best Performing Fund (if mostly NHCEs); if investment election is unknown—may	**All Options:** If the plan has a match, provide a corrective matching contribution based on the amount that would have been deferred but for the failure (even if no QNEC is needed for missed deferrals) according to the matching formula in the plan.

IRS Guidance	*Failure to permit an employee to make a deferral election*	*Failure to implement an employee's deferral election*	*Failure to implement a plan's automatic enrollment provision*	*Notice Requirement & Earnings Calculation*	*Matching Requirement (if plan has matching provision)*
	If participant is not permitted to make a deferral election and plan is not a safe harbor plan: Corrective QNEC based on 50% of missed deferral (calculated: ADP of the group of participants (NHCE or HCE) to which the participant belongs times compensation). If participant is not permitted to make an election and plan is a safe harbor (SH) plan, corrective QNEC depends on the type of safe harbor contribution provided: If SH nonelective, then a corrective QNEC equal to 1.5% of compensation. If SH matching contribution, then corrective QNEC equal to 1.5% of the compensation or, if greater, 50% of	If participant made a deferral election that is not implemented (whether or not plan is a safe harbor plan): Corrective QNEC based on 50% of the participant's missed deferral (participant's deferral election times compensation).	If automatic enrollment notice is not provided and plan is not a safe harbor plan: Corrective QNEC based on 50% of missed deferral (ADP of the group of participants (NHCE or HCE) to which the participant belongs times compensation). If automatic enrollment notice is not provided and plan is a safe harbor (SH) plan, corrective QNEC depends on the type of safe harbor contribution provided: If SH nonelective, then corrective QNEC equal to 1.5% of compensation. If SH matching contribution, then corrective QNEC equal to 1.5% of compensation or, if	use plan's overall rate of return. May reflect losses but may choose not to.	

IRS Guidance	*Failure to permit an employee to make a deferral election*	*Failure to implement an employee's deferral election*	*Failure to implement a plan's automatic enrollment provision*	*Notice Requirement & Earnings Calculation*	*Matching Requirement (if plan has matching provision)*
	the maximum deferral percentage for which the employer provides a matching contribution of 100% multiplied by compensation.		greater, 50% of the maximum deferral percentage for which the employer provides a matching contribution of 100% multiplied by compensation. If automatic enrollment notice is provided (whether or not plan is a SH plan): Corrective QNEC based on 50% of the participant's missed deferral (automatic deferral percentage times compensation).		
Options under Revenue Procedure 2015-28 (additional methods added to EPCRS)	Correction applies to plans that do not have automatic enrollment provisions. Also available to plans with automatic enrollment provisions where deferrals are not started in time.	Correction applies to plans that do not have automatic enrollment provisions. Also available to plans with automatic enrollment provisions where deferrals are not started in time.	Correction applies to all failures (including failure to implement an employee's affirmative deferral election or to permit an employee to make a deferral election) involving a plan with an automatic enrollment provision.	**All Options:** Notice required to the affected participant within 45 days after the date on which correct deferrals	**All Options:** If the plan has a match, provide a corrective matching contribution according to the

IRS Guidance	*Failure to permit an employee to make a deferral election*	*Failure to implement an employee's deferral election*	*Failure to implement a plan's automatic enrollment provision*	*Notice Requirement & Earnings Calculation*	*Matching Requirement (if plan has matching provision)*
	No QNEC required if the correct deferrals begin no later than the earlier of (i) the first payment of compensation made on or after the three-month period that begins when the failure first occurred for the affected eligible employee or (ii) if the employer was notified of the failure by the affected eligible employee, the first payment of compensation made on or after the last day of the month after the month of notification.	No QNEC required if the correct deferrals begin no later than the earlier of (i) the first payment of compensation made on or after the three-month period that begins when the failure first occurred for the affected eligible employee or (ii) if the employer was notified of the failure by the affected eligible employee, the first payment of compensation made on or after the last day of the month after the month of notification.	No QNEC if the correct deferrals begin no later than the earlier of (i) the first payment of compensation made on or after the last day of the 9 ½ month period after the end of the plan year in which the failure first occurred for the affected eligible employee or (ii) if the employer was notified of the failure by the affected eligible employee, the first payment of compensation made on or after the last day of the month after the month of notification.	begin and address the following: (1) general information regarding the failure, such as percentage that should have been deferred and date deferrals should have begun, (2) statement that deferrals have started or will start shortly, (3) a statement that corrective matching contributions, if any, have been made or will be made, (4) an explanation that the participant may choose to	matching formula in the plan. Must be made and based on the match contribution that would have been made had no failure occurred (even if no QNEC is needed for missed deferrals) within the timing requirements for significant operational failures (the last day of the second plan year following the plan year for which the failure occurred).

IRS Guidance	*Failure to permit an employee to make a deferral election*	*Failure to implement an employee's deferral election*	*Failure to implement a plan's automatic enrollment provision*	*Notice Requirement & Earnings Calculation*	*Matching Requirement (if plan has matching provision)*
	A QNEC equal to one-half of the amount calculated per Option under Revenue Procedure 2013-12 (see above) if: Correct deferrals begin no later than the earlier of (1) the first payment of compensation made on or after the last day of the second plan year following the plan year in which the failure occurred or (2) if the employer was notified of the failure by the affected eligible employee, the first payment of compensation made on or after the last day of the month after the month of notification.	A QNEC equal to one-half of the amount calculated per Option under Revenue Procedure 2013-12 (see above) if: Correct deferrals begin no later than the earlier of (1) the first payment of compensation made on or after the last day of the second plan year following the plan year in which the failure occurred or (2) if the employer was notified of the failure by the affected eligible employee, the first payment of compensation made on or after the last day of the month after the month of notification.		increase his or her deferrals to make up for the missed deferrals, (5) name of the plan and contact information. **All Options:** For Earnings Calculation, if an affected participant has not made an investment election, the plan's default investment can be used to calculate earnings owed to the participant, provided any losses are not used to offset contributions	

IRS Guidance	*Failure to permit an employee to make a deferral election*	*Failure to implement an employee's deferral election*	*Failure to implement a plan's automatic enrollment provision*	*Notice Requirement & Earnings Calculation*	*Matching Requirement (if plan has matching provision)*
				that are owed as part of the correction. Alternatively, an employer may use the earnings calculation method provided under Revenue Procedure 2013-12 (see above).	
	Examples of Fixes on IRS Web site: http://www.irs.gov/Retirement-Plans/Plan-Sponsor/Fixing-Common-Plan-Mistakes---Correction-for-Exclusion-of-Employees-for-Elective-Contributions-or-After-Tax-Employee-Contributions	Examples of Fixes on IRS Web site: http://www.irs.gov/Retirement-Plans/Fixing-Common-Plan-Mistakes---Correcting-a-Failure-to-Effect-Employee-Deferral-Elections	Examples of Fixes on IRS Web site: http://www.irs.gov/Retirement-Plans/Fixing-Common-Plan-Mistakes---Correcting-a-Failure-to-Implement-the-Plan's-Automatic-Enrollment-Provisions		

Glossary

ABP Test: See **Average Benefit Percentage Test.**

ACA: See **Automatic Contribution Arrangement.**

Accrued Benefit: The portion of the retirement benefit that has been earned since an employee began to participate in a plan. In a defined contribution plan (including a 401(k) plan), the accrued benefit for a participant is the value of all accounts maintained on behalf of the participant, including the value of insurance contracts on the life of the participant. In a defined benefit plan, the accrued benefit is the portion of the benefit payable at normal retirement age that the participant has currently earned.

ACP Test: See **Actual Contribution Percentage Test**.

Active Management: A portfolio management strategy that seeks to exceed the returns of a selected market index. Active managers rely on research, market forecasts, and their own judgment and experience in making investment decisions. (Compare with **Index Investing**.)

Actual Contribution Percentage Test (ACP Test): A test that measures whether employer matching contributions and employee after-tax contributions discriminate in favor of highly compensated employees.

Actual Deferral Percentage Test (ADP Test): A test that measures whether elective contributions (salary deferrals) in a 401(k) plan discriminate in favor of highly compensated employees.

Actuarial Equivalence: A form of benefit that differs in time, period, or manner of payment from the normal form of benefit provided by the plan, but is equivalent in value to the normal form of benefit. For example, a 401(k) plan provides a lump sum as the normal form of benefit and the participant has an account balance of $100,000. Depending on the factors in the plan, the actuarially equivalent life annuity benefit may provide the participant with an annual annuity for life equal to $12,200 commencing at age 65.

ADP Test: See **Actual Deferral Percentage Test**.

Advisory Letter: A letter issued by the IRS indicating its approval of a volume submitter plan.

Affiliated Service Group: A group of organizations that, by virtue of business relationships, are treated for various employee benefit requirements as a single employer but do not share sufficient common ownership to be a controlled group.

Age 50 Catch-Up Contributions: Additional elective contributions that are permitted to individuals who have attained age 50 and who, in the case of a 401(k) plan, 403(b) plan, or 457 plan, are prevented from making contributions because of legal or plan restrictions.

Age-Weighted Profit-Sharing Plan: A type of profit sharing plan in which contributions are allocated to participants on a basis that considers both age and compensation.

Aggressive Growth Fund: A fund that seeks to provide maximum long-term capital growth primarily from stocks of smaller companies or narrow market segments.

Alternate Payee: Any spouse, former spouse, child, or other dependent of a participant who is recognized by a domestic relations order as having a right to receive all, or a portion of, the participant's accrued benefit.

American Taxpayer Relief Act of 2012: Enacted on January 2, 2013, ATRA added In-Plan Roth Transfers/Conversions.

Annual Additions: Amounts that are credited to a participant's account during the limitation year under Code Section 415, exclusive of interest, earnings, rollovers, and loan payments.

Annuity: A series of periodic payments (e.g., for the life of the participant). Annuity payments may be level or may be subject to an annual cost-of-living adjustment. (See **Joint and Survivor Annuity**.)

Anti-Assignment Rule: The portion of the Internal Revenue Code that restricts the accrued benefits of participants from being pledged or assigned, either voluntarily or involuntarily.

Anti-Cutback Rule: A provision in the Internal Revenue Code that prohibits an employer from reducing accrued or protected benefits.

Anti-Kickback Rule: A provision in ERISA prohibiting a fiduciary from receiving consideration in connection with a plan transaction.

Asset Allocation: The process of deciding how investment dollars will be apportioned among available asset classes.

Asset Allocation Fund: A fund that invests its assets in a wide variety of investments which may include domestic and foreign stocks and bonds, and government securities. Some asset allocation funds keep the proportions allocated among different investments relatively constant; others alter the mix.

Asset Class: A grouping of investment types that share similar risk and return characteristics. The three primary asset classes are stocks, bonds, and cash investments.

Audit CAP: A program under which a qualified plan negotiates a penalty with the IRS as an alternative to plan disqualification on account of plan document or operational defects identified by the IRS during a plan audit. It also covers demographic failures (e.g., failure to satisfy minimum coverage requirements), but is not available for violations relating to the diversion or misuse of plan assets. (See also **EPCRS**.)

Automatic Contribution Arrangement (ACA): A plan design whereby participants are automatically enrolled in a 401(k) plan at a deferral rate specified in the plan document unless they affirmatively opt out of the arrangement. A notice requirement must be met, and the plan may use a default fund that is a Qualified Default Investment Alternative (QDIA).

Automatic Enrollment: See **Negative Election**.

Average Benefit Percentage Test (ABP Test): One of two tests necessary to determine whether a plan meets the Average Benefit Test. (See **Nondiscriminatory Classification Test**.)

Average Benefit Test: One of two alternative tests used for purposes of determining whether a plan meets the minimum coverage requirements under Code Section 410(b). (See **Ratio-Percentage Test**.)

Balanced Fund: A fund that seeks to provide current income and long-term growth from a combination of stocks and bonds.

Balance Forward Accounting: See **Pooled Accounting**.

Beneficiary: The person to whom all or a portion of a deceased participant's account balance is payable.

Bond: A type of debt instrument issued by corporations, governments, and government agencies. The issuer makes regular interest payments and promises to pay back, or redeem, the face value of the bond at a specified time called the maturity date.

Bond Fund: A fund that invests primarily in bonds; generally, corporate, municipal, or U.S. government debt obligations. Bond funds usually emphasize income rather than growth.

Bundled Services: A package of complete administrative and investment services provided to 401(k) plan sponsors by a single entity.

C Corporation: A regular corporation that elects to be taxed at the corporate, rather than individual, level. (See **S Corporation**.)

Cafeteria Plan: A plan that allows employees to choose between taxable and nontaxable benefits; also known as a Section 125 or flexible benefits plan. Typical nontaxable benefits would include health insurance, group term life, and dental benefits. Taxable benefits would always include the option to choose cash, although a taxable benefit such as auto or homeowner's insurance could be offered. A 401(k) plan may be offered as an option under a cafeteria plan.

Cash Balance Plan: A defined benefit plan in which the accrued benefit is defined in terms of a hypothetical account balance that is increased yearly by hypothetical contributions and earnings.

Cash-or-Deferred Arrangement (CODA): Generally known as a 401(k) plan, a qualified profit sharing or stock bonus plan that allows participants to elect to receive cash or to have the employer contribute amounts on their behalf to a plan.

Cash Investments: Short-term loans to a borrower with a very high credit rating, including short-term bank certificates of deposit (CDs), money market instruments, and U.S. Treasury bills. Cash investments are usually considered to have negligible (though not zero) market and credit risk.

Claims Procedure: The steps a participant must follow when making a claim for benefits or appealing for review of a denial of a benefit claim.

Closely Held Corporation: A corporation that has a relatively small number of shareholders and whose stock is not traded on a public stock exchange.

CODA: See **Cash-or-Deferred Arrangement**.

Code: The Internal Revenue Code of 1986, as amended.

Collective Trust Fund: A vehicle in which assets of qualified plans, generally sponsored by unrelated employers, are pooled for investment purposes. The funds are typically managed by trust departments of financial institutions.

Collectively Bargained Plans: Retirement plans that are established and maintained pursuant to a collective bargaining agreement. If more than one employer is required to contribute to the plan, the plan may become a multiemployer plan under Code Section 414(f).

Common-Law Employee: An individual who performs services for the employer in an employment relationship.

Compensation: The amount of a participant's remuneration that is considered for purposes of certain employee benefit requirements.

Contributory Plan: A qualified plan that mandates employee contributions as a condition of participation; may be in the form of a defined benefit or defined contribution plan.

Controlled Group of Corporations: Two or more corporations, that, by virtue of common ownership, are treated as a single entity for purposes of certain employee benefit requirements under Code Section 414(b).

Corrective Distribution: A mechanism for distributing excess deferrals, excess contributions, and excess aggregate contributions in order to satisfy statutory limits or ADP and ACP tests. Corrective distributions provide a fail-safe mechanism for a plan to avoid disqualification.

Cost Recovery: A method for a participant to recoup previously taxed amounts from a qualified plan.

Credit Risk: The possibility that a bond issuer will default; that is, fail to repay principal or interest to a bond holder in a timely manner or at all. Also known as default risk. (Compare to **Market Risk**.)

Daily Valuation: A system of accounting that provides for the allocation of earnings and losses to a participant's account on a daily basis.

Death Benefit: The portion of a participant's accrued benefit that is payable to a named beneficiary upon the participant's death.

Deferral Contribution: See **Elective Deferral (Contributions)**.

Deficit Reduction Act of 1984 (DEFRA): An act of Congress passed to reduce the budget deficit. A portion of this bill contained the Tax Reform Act of 1984.

Defined Benefit Plan: A retirement plan that promises a specific benefit at retirement usually defined in terms of such factors as salary and years of service. Since the benefit is not determined by allocated contributions and investment earnings as in a defined contribution plan, the sponsor—not the employee—bears the investment risk.

Defined Contribution Plan: A type of qualified plan in which a participant's benefits are based solely on the participant's account balance; the account balance depends on the level of employer and employee contributions and the earnings on those contributions.

Delinquent Filer Voluntary Compliance (DFVC) Program: Relief program for late filers or nonfilers of Form 5500 returns.

DEFRA: See **Deficit Reduction Act of 1984**.

Department of Labor (DOL): One of the government entities responsible for the administration of ERISA.

Determination Letter: A letter issued by the IRS that states whether a submitted plan meets the qualification requirements of the Internal Revenue Code.

DFVC: See **Delinquent Filer Voluntary Compliance (DFVC) Program**.

Direct Rollover: Payment of an eligible rollover distribution directly to the trustee of an eligible retirement plan or individual retirement account (IRA).

Discretionary Contributions: Any employer contributions to a 401(k) or profit sharing plan that are not mandated by the terms of the plan.

Discretionary Nonelective Contribution: Employer contributions to a 401(k) plan that are not tied to elective contributions; also known as profit sharing contributions or simply employer contributions.

Discrimination: The undue favoring of highly compensated employees in plan provisions or operations.

Disqualification: The IRS sanction for failure to satisfy the qualification requirements of the Internal Revenue Code. Penalties for disqualification may include loss of tax-exempt status of the trust, loss of tax deductions, and taxable income to employees.

Disqualified Person: The Internal Revenue Code term for an individual who is prohibited from engaging in certain transactions with the plan. (See **Party-in-Interest**.)

Diversification: A strategy for investing in different asset classes to reduce the risks inherent in investing in a single class.

DOL: Department of Labor.

EACA: See **Eligible Automatic Contribution Arrangement.**

Early Withdrawal Penalty: A 10 percent penalty (in addition to ordinary income taxes owed) on money withdrawn from a tax-advantaged retirement plan usually before age 59½. The penalty does not apply in special circumstances such as death, disability, or withdrawals in the form of an annuity or payment over the recipient's (and spouse's) life expectancy.

Economic Growth and Tax Relief Reconciliation Act of 2001 (EGTRRA): A tax package signed into law in 2001 containing numerous retirement plan provisions.

EGTRRA: See **Economic Growth and Tax Relief Reconciliation Act of 2001.**

EIAA: See **Eligible Investment Advice Arrangement.**

Elective Deferrals (Contributions): The amount of a participant's voluntary reduction in pay; otherwise known as salary deferrals. An election to defer pay must be made in advance. The employer then contributes the deferral to the 401(k) plan.

Elective Transfer: Process under which an employee, under certain circumstances, can direct the transfer of his or her account balance from one plan to another. Unlike direct rollovers, elective transfers are not considered distributions.

Eligible Automatic Contribution Arrangement (EACA): An automatic contribution arrangement under which a participant may withdraw, during a limited period of time, deferrals made pursuant to the arrangement. An EACA may also provide a 401(k) plan additional time to refund excess contributions and excess aggregate contributions.

Eligible Employee: Any employee who is eligible to become a participant in the plan pursuant to the terms of the plan document.

Eligible Investment Advice Arrangement (EIAA): An arrangement created by the Pension Protection Act of 2006 whereby participants can receive fiduciary-level investment advice, financial advisors can receive fees from the funds they are providing advice on without violating ERISA's prohibited transaction rules, and plan sponsors or other hiring fiduciaries can be relieved of fiduciary liability for the individual advice given to participants. Numerous requirements apply.

Eligible Retirement Plan: An individual retirement account (IRA) or a retirement plan to which a rollover of an eligible rollover distribution may be made.

Eligible Rollover Distribution: A distribution of all or part of a participant's interest in a plan except for certain periodic distributions, minimum distributions, and corrective distributions.

Employee: Any individual employed by the employer maintaining the plan or any affiliated employer required to be aggregated with the employer under Code Sections 414(b), 414(c), 414(m), and 414(o). A leased employee may also be deemed an employee for purposes of these rules. (See **Affiliated Service Group** and **Leased Employee**.)

Employee Contributions: Contributions made by an employee to a qualified plan from funds that have previously been taxed. (See **Mandatory Contribution** and **Voluntary Contributions**.)

Employee-Directed Plan: A plan that permits employees to direct the investment of their account balances.

Employee Plans Compliance Resolution System (EPCRS): An IRS created system of correction programs that allow sponsors of qualified retirement plans to correct document, operational, and demographic defects that would otherwise result in disqualification. EPCRS consists of the following programs: SCP, VCP, and Audit Cap.

Employee Retirement Income Security Act of 1974 (ERISA): An act of Congress encompassing both Internal Revenue Code provisions, which determine when a plan is tax qualified, and Department of Labor provisions, which govern the rights of participants and beneficiaries and the obligations of plan fiduciaries.

Employee Stock Ownership Plan (ESOP): A plan designed to invest primarily in employer securities. Unlike other types of qualified plans, an ESOP may borrow funds to acquire employer securities.

Employer Contribution: See **Nonelective Contributions** and **Matching Contributions**.

Employer-Sponsored IRA: An IRA program for employees that is set up and maintained by the employer. (See **Individual Retirement Account (IRA)**.)

Employer Securities: Shares of stock, bonds, or debentures issued by a corporation sponsoring the plan, including securities of a parent or subsidiary.

EPCRS: See **Employee Plans Compliance Resolution System**.

ERISA: See **Employee Retirement Income Security Act of 1974**.

ERISA Bond: Bond required under ERISA to cover plan fiduciaries and other plan officials who handle plan assets.

ERISA Spending Account: A mechanism for using payments received from plan investments to cover a broad array of plan expenses. In some situations, a bookkeeping account is set up independent of the plan trust to collect fund revenues to pay plan expenses at the direction of a plan fiduciary. In others, fund revenue is held in an account within the plan trust from which plan expenses are paid.

ESOP: See **Employee Stock Ownership Plan.**

Excess Aggregate Contributions: The amount by which matching contributions and voluntary employee contributions made on behalf of highly compensated employees exceeds the amount permitted by the ACP nondiscrimination test contained in Code Section 401(m).

Excess Benefit Plan: An unfunded or funded nonqualified plan maintained solely for the purpose of providing benefits in excess of the limits imposed under Code Section 415.

Excess Contributions: The amount by which elective contributions made on behalf of highly compensated employees exceeds the amount permitted by the ADP nondiscrimination test contained in Code Section 401(k).

Excess Deferrals: The amount by which elective deferrals made on behalf of an employee by all employers exceeds the annual cap in effect for that taxable year.

Excise Tax: A nondeductible tax imposed on the occurrence of an event.

Excludable Employee: An employee who does not need to be counted when performing minimum coverage testing under Code Section 410(b).

Family Attribution: Rules attributing ownership of a company from an owner to a member of the owner's family for purposes of determining controlled groups, highly compensated employees, and key employees.

Federal Insurance Contributions Act (FICA): An act of Congress requiring employers and employees to pay into a federal fund that provides for retirement and welfare benefits.

Federal Unemployment Tax Act (FUTA): An act of Congress that imposes a tax on employers to fund cash benefits to former employees undergoing temporary periods of unemployment.

Fee-Sharing Arrangement: A practice in which plan investment funds offer fees to service providers that provide services to defined contribution plans.

FICA: See **Federal Insurance Contributions Act.**

Fiduciary: Under ERISA, any person who (1) exercises any discretionary authority or control over the management of a plan or the management or disposition of its assets, (2) renders investment advice for a fee or other compensation with respect to the funds or property of a plan or has the authority to do so, or (3) has any discretionary authority or responsibility in the administration of a plan. The DOL proposed rules that would modify this definition.

5 Percent Owner: An employee who owns, directly or indirectly, more than 5 percent of the value or voting power of the stock of the employer or, if the employer is not a corporation, more than 5 percent of the capital or profits interest. A 5 percent owner is both a highly compensated employee and a key employee.

Fixed-Income Fund: A fund with the objective of providing current income, primarily from fixed-income securities or bonds.

Floor Plan: A defined benefit plan that provides a minimum level of benefits for all participants in conjunction with a defined contribution plan.

Forfeitures: The portion of a participant's benefit that may be lost if the participant separates from service before becoming 100 percent vested.

404(c) Plan: See **Section 404(c) Plan**.

Frozen Plan: A qualified plan that holds benefits for future distribution but does not permit current contributions or accruals.

Funding Policy: See **Investment Policy**, though the latter usually refers to a specific policy for investing assets and the former to the funding of the plan.

FUTA: See **Federal Unemployment Tax Act**.

GATT: The General Agreement on Tariffs and Trade, part of the Uruguay Round Agreements Act.

GIC: See **Guaranteed Investment Contract**.

Global Fund: A fund that invests in both U.S. and non-U.S. securities.

Growth and Income Fund: A fund whose aim is to provide a balance of long-term growth and current dividend income.

Growth Fund: A fund whose main objective is long-term growth in capital from investing primarily in growth stocks. (See **Growth Stocks**.)

Growth Stocks: The stocks of companies that have experienced or are expected to experience rapid growth in revenue or earnings and are expected to continue such growth for an extended period. Such stocks typically have relatively low dividend yields and sell at relatively high prices in relation to their earnings and book value. A fund that emphasizes growth stocks is called a growth fund.

Guaranteed Investment Contract (GIC): A contract sold by an insurance company that guarantees payment of interest on the amount invested for a particular duration.

GUST: An acronym applied to the four laws GATT, USERRA, SBJPA, and TRA '97.

Hardship Withdrawal: An in-service withdrawal from a 401(k) plan because of the immediate and heavy financial need of a participant that cannot be satisfied from other resources. The conditions for a hardship withdrawal of elective contributions can be determined through either a safe harbor or a facts-and-circumstances method.

HEART Act: See **Heroes Earnings and Assistance Relief Tax (HEART) Act**.

Heroes Earnings and Assistance Relief Tax (HEART) Act: Legislation passed in 2008 that made changes impacting welfare and retirement benefits available to military personnel.

HCE: See **Highly Compensated Employee**.

Highly Compensated Employee (HCE): An employee who, during either the determination year or lookback year, was a 5 percent owner of the employer or, during the lookback year, earned more than $80,000 (indexed) and (optionally) was in the top-paid group.

Income Fund: A fund that seeks current income rather than growth of capital. Income funds typically invest in bonds or high-yielding stocks or both.

Index: An indicator that reflects the value of a representative grouping of securities. For example, Dow Jones Industrial Average or Standard & Poor's 500 Index.

Index Fund: A fund that seeks to parallel the performance of a particular stock or bond market index.

Index Investing: An investment strategy that structures a portfolio so that its holdings replicate a specific stock or bond market index and are thus expected to provide a return that tracks with that specific benchmark. Index funds offer investors a passive approach to investing; advantages associated with passive management are low investment costs and minimal portfolio turnover. (Compare to **Active Management**.)

Individual Account Plan: A plan in which individual accounts are established for each participant. A participant's benefit is determined solely on the basis of contributions to his or her account and the investment experience of those contributions. Participants are not guaranteed any particular benefit amount. (See **Defined Contribution Plan**.)

Individual Retirement Account (IRA): An individual retirement account or an individual retirement annuity that holds assets on a tax-deferred basis.

Individually Designed Plan: A plan tailored specifically to an individual employer that is not a master or prototype plan or a volume submitter plan.

Inflation Risk: The possibility that increases in the cost of living will reduce or eliminate the real returns on a particular investment.

Inherited IRA: An IRA created through a direct rollover of the account balance of a deceased participant whose beneficiary is a trust or an individual other than the participant's spouse.

In-House Administration: The performance of plan administration services by employees of the entity sponsoring the plan.

In-Plan Roth Rollover or Transfer/Conversion: A plan feature that allows participants to convert pre-tax accounts into Roth accounts inside their 401(k) plans.

In-Service Withdrawal: A withdrawal of plan benefits prior to separation from service with the employer.

Integrated Plan: A plan that makes adjustments in contributions or benefits for amounts available through Social Security. (See **Permitted Disparity**.)

Interested Parties: Individuals who must be notified when application is made for a determination letter on a plan.

Interest Rate Risk: The risk that a security will decline in price because of changes in market interest rates.

Internal Revenue Service (IRS): The agency of the Treasury Department with the responsibility for administering, interpreting, and enforcing the Internal Revenue Code.

International Fund: A fund that invests in securities traded in markets primarily outside the United States. (Contrast with **Global Fund**.)

Internet: A collection of intercommunicating computer networks accessible to the general public.

Investment Policy: A statement that sets forth investment objectives and constraints as well as the methods by which those objectives will be attained and measured. (See also **Funding Policy**.)

Investment Style: A broad indicator of a fund's investment emphasis. For U.S. stock funds investment style usually indicates whether a fund emphasizes stocks of large-, medium-, or small-capitalization companies and whether it emphasizes stocks with growth or value characteristics or a blend of those characteristics.

IRA: See **Individual Retirement Account**.

IRC: Internal Revenue Code of 1986, as amended.

IRRA: See **IRS Restructuring and Reform Act of 1998**.

IRS: See **Internal Revenue Service**.

IRS Restructuring and Reform Act of 1998 (IRRA): Act containing technical corrections to TRA '97 and SBJPA, many of which deal with Roth IRAs.

Joint and Survivor Annuity: An annuity that is paid for the life of a participant, with a survivor annuity available for the life of his or her spouse. A qualified joint and survivor annuity must offer a survivor benefit that is not less than 50 percent nor more than 100 percent of the annuity received by the participant.

Keogh Plan: A qualified retirement plan covering a self-employed person.

Key Employee: A participant who at any time during the preceding year (1) owned more than 5 percent of the employer, (2) earned more than $150,000 and owned more than 1 percent of the employer, or (3) earned more than $130,000 and was an includable officer. The dollar threshold in (3) is adjusted annually for cost-of-living increases.

KSOP: A stock bonus plan in which elective contributions and/or employer contributions may be invested in employer stock.

Leased Employee: An individual (not an employee) who provides services under the primary direction and control of the recipient of the services pursuant to an agreement with a leasing organization, on a substantially full-time basis for a period of at least one year. Leased employees are counted as employees for purposes of the minimum coverage rules, as well as determining key employees and highly compensated employees.

Leveraged ESOP: An employee stock ownership plan that takes out a loan to purchase employer stock.

Limited Liability Company (LLC): An entity designed to be taxed as a partnership. For 401(k) plan purposes, the members of the LLC are treated like partners and the non-members are treated like partnership employees.

Lookback Rules: Rules used in determining who is a highly compensated or key employee. Employees who meet the definition of a highly compensated or key employee for a lookback year will be counted as highly compensated or key employees in the current year.

Look-Through Fund: A fund in which the underlying assets of a pooled fund are taken into account in determining whether ERISA's diversification requirements have been satisfied.

Lump-Sum Distribution: A distribution that qualifies for forward averaging (where available). The basic requirements are that the distribution be made within one taxable year of the recipient, that it include the entire balance to the credit of the employee, and that it be made on account of the employee's death, attainment of age 59½, separation from service (except for the self-employed), or disability (self-employed persons only).

Managed Account Service: A service that automatically allocates assets in a participant's individual account among the available investment alternatives based on certain factors (e.g., participant's age, target retirement date, life expectancy, risk tolerance). A managed account service may take into account other financial data relevant to the participant (e.g., assets held outside the plan), if input by the participant.

Manager Risk: The possibility that a fund's portfolio manager may fail to execute a fund's investment strategy or style effectively and consistently so that the fund fails to achieve its statement objective.

Mandatory Aggregation: Plans, or portions of plans, that must be tested together when applying the average benefit percentage test.

Mandatory Contribution: An after-tax employee contribution required as a condition of participation in qualified plans.

Mandatory Disaggregation: Parts of plans that must be tested separately for minimum coverage and nondiscriminatory testing purposes. Mandatory disaggregation applies to plans covering both collective bargaining and non-collective bargaining employees, plans with different contribution types, multiple-employer plans, and ESOPs.

Market Risk: The possibility that stock or bond prices over broad segments of the market will fluctuate. (Compare to **Credit Risk**.)

Master Plan: An IRS-approved plan that the sponsor of the plan makes available for adoption by employers and for which a single funding medium (e.g., a trust or custodial account) is established, as part of the plan, for joint use of all adopting employers. A master plan is adopted by an employer by completing an adoption agreement that tailors the plan to the needs of the individual employer. (See **Prototype Plan**.)

Matching Contribution: An employer contribution in a 401(k) plan that is linked to an elective deferral contribution or, less typically, an after-tax employee contribution. For example, an employer might match elective contributions up to 4 percent of pay on a dollar-for-dollar basis.

Minimum Distribution Requirements: Rules governing when distributions from a qualified plan must commence and the maximum time period over which benefit payments can be made. Generally, distributions must commence by April 1 of the year following the later of the calendar year in which the employee attains age 70½ or retires (the delay until retirement is only for non-5 percent owners) and generally must be paid over a period based in part on the life expectancy of the employee.

Money Market Fund: A fund that invests in highly liquid short-term securities, including bank certificates of deposit (CDs), commercial paper, and Treasury Bills (T-Bills). (See **Cash Investments**.)

Money Purchase Plan: An individual account plan in which the employer has a fixed obligation to make annual contributions to the plan, usually based on a percentage of pay.

Multiemployer Plan: A plan maintained under a collective bargaining agreement that covers employees of different employers within the same industry.

Multiple-Employer Plan: A plan sponsored by a group of employers that do not have sufficient common ownership to be considered a controlled group or affiliated service group. This type of plan is not established pursuant to a collective bargaining agreement as is the case with a multiemployer plan.

Mutual Fund: An investment company that combines the money of its numerous shareholders to invest in a variety of securities in an effort to achieve a specific objective over time.

Negative Election: A 401(k) plan design feature in which a certain percentage or dollar amount of an eligible employee's compensation is automatically deferred unless the employee designates a different amount or affirmatively elects not to contribute (also known as **Automatic Enrollment**).

New Comparability: Any method of allocating nonelective contributions in a defined contribution plan that demonstrates compliance with the general test under the Code Section 401(a)(4) regulations on the basis of actuarially equivalent benefits.

NHCE: See **Non-Highly Compensated Employee**.

No-Load Fund: A fund that sells its shares without charging a sales commission or load, though 12b-1 marketing costs may be assessed.

Noncontributory Plan: A plan to which employees do not make contributions.

Nondiscrimination: A requirement that a qualified plan not unduly favor highly compensated employees. The nondiscrimination requirements of the Code are found in Code Sections 401(a)(4), 401(k), 401(m), and 410(b).

Nondiscriminatory Classification Test: A component test of the average benefits test under Code Section 410(b). The nondiscriminatory classification test requires a plan to benefit a class of employees that is both reasonable and nondiscriminatory. (See **Average Benefit Percentage Test (ABP Test)**.)

Nonelective Contributions: Employer contributions (other than matching contributions) made without regard to elective contributions.

Nonforfeitable Benefits: Benefits under a plan to which a participant has an unconditional right.

Non-Highly Compensated Employee (NHCE): An employee who is not a highly compensated employee.

Non-Key Employee: An employee who is not a key employee.

Nonqualified Deferred Compensation Plan: A retirement plan to which the qualification requirements under the Internal Revenue Code do not apply. Depending on how they are designed and operated, these plans have varying tax advantages and may be subject to minimal requirements under ERISA.

OASDI: See **Old Age, Survivors, and Disability Insurance**.

OBRA '87: The Omnibus Budget Reconciliation Act of 1987.

Officer: An employee who is an administrative executive in regular and continued service. An officer may be a key employee.

Old Age, Survivors, and Disability Insurance (OASDI): A program under Social Security. Also refers to that portion of the employment taxes paid under Chapter 21 of the Code used to fund this program. (See **FICA**.)

1 Percent Owner: An employee who owns, directly or indirectly, more than 1 percent of the value or voting power of the stock of a corporation, or, if the employer is not a corporation, more than 1 percent of the capital or profits interest. A 1 percent owner who has compensation in excess of $150,000 is considered a key employee.

Opinion Letter: A letter issued by the IRS indicating its approval of a prototype or master plan.

Optional Forms of Benefit: Distribution alternatives available for the payment of an employee's accrued benefit.

Other Right or Feature: A feature of a plan that is more than an administrative detail and that might reasonably be expected to be of meaningful value to participants (e.g., right to direct investments).

Owner-Employee: A self-employed person who owns more than 10 percent of a noncorporate employer. (See **Self-Employed Person**.)

Paperless Administration: A system in which information is prepared, stored, and communicated in electronic form instead of in paper form.

Partial Termination: The exclusion, either by plan amendment or severance from service with the employer, of a substantial (usually 20 percent or more) group of employees who are covered by a plan.

Participant: An employee or former employee who has an accrued benefit under the plan.

Participant-Directed Plan: A plan under which participants determine the investment of their account balance.

Participant Loan: A loan from the plan to a participant.

Party in Interest: An ERISA term referring to certain parties who have a close relationship to the plan and, as a consequence, are prohibited from engaging in certain transactions with the plan in the absence of a statutory or an administrative exemption. (See **Disqualified Person**.)

Pension Protection Act of 2006 (PPA): A law enacted in 2006 that made wide-ranging changes to the retirement plan laws.

Pension Simplification Act of 1996: Contained in the Small Business Job Protection Act of 1996.

Permissible Withdrawal: A deferral that is made pursuant to an eligible automatic contribution arrangement (EACA) and that is withdrawn by the participant by a plan-established deadline that is not greater than 90 days of the first deferral.

Permitted Disparity: Rules under Code Section 401(*l*) that permit a plan to recognize the Social Security contributions made by the employer on behalf of employees in determining the allocation of nonelective contributions. Permitted disparity allows a greater share of such contributions to be allocated to highly paid participants. (See **Integrated Plan**.)

Plan Administrator: The party named in the plan document with responsibility to ensure the plan is being operated in accordance with its terms.

Plan Year: The period for which the records of the plan are kept.

Political Risk: The potential for price fluctuations in securities sold in foreign countries due to political or financial events in those countries.

Pooled Accounting: A system of accounting that provides for the allocation of plan earnings and losses to a participant's accounts on an annual or more frequent basis.

Pooled Fund: A fund that is managed by a registered investment company, registered investment advisor, bank, or insurance company and that is offered as an investment choice in a participant-directed plan.

PPA: See **Pension Protection Act of 2006**.

Profit Sharing Plan: A plan under which contributions made by the employer are allocated to participants pursuant to a definite predetermined formula. Contributions are generally discretionary and may be made without regard to profits.

Prohibited Transaction: A transaction between the plan and a party-in-interest (disqualified person).

Prohibited Transaction Exemptions: Statutory or administrative exemptions that permit transactions between plans and parties-in-interest to occur that would otherwise be prohibited.

Protected Benefit Rights and Features: Optional forms of benefits and other features of a plan that cannot be eliminated with respect to benefits already accrued under the plan.

Prototype Plan: An IRS-approved plan generally sponsored by a bank, insurance company, mutual fund, plan administration firm, or law firm that is made available for adoption by the clients of the sponsor.

PS-58 Cost: The taxable value of the pure life insurance protection in a plan that provides for insured death benefits.

QACA: See **Qualified Automatic Contribution Arrangement**.

QDIA: See **Qualified Default Investment Alternative**.

QDRO: See **Qualified Domestic Relations Order**.

QJSA: See **Qualified Joint and Survivor Annuity**.

QMACs: See **Qualified Matching Contributions**.

QNECs: See **Qualified Nonelective Contributions**.

QOSA: See **Qualified Optional Survivor Annuity**.

QPSA: See **Qualified Pre-retirement Survivor Annuity**.

QSLOB: See **Qualified Separate Line of Business**.

Qualified Automatic Contribution Arrangement (QACA): A plan design whereby participants are automatically enrolled in the plan at a deferral rate specified in the plan document unless they affirmatively opt out of the arrangement and that also is designed to qualify for relief from certain nondiscrimination testing. A QACA is exempt from nondiscrimination testing of elective and/or matching contributions if it meets minimum contribution levels for both employee (elective) contributions, as well as employer (matching or nonelective) contributions.

Qualified Default Investment Alternative (QDIA): A default fund satisfying the conditions of a Department of Labor regulation under ERISA Section 404(c)(5), which entitles plan fiduciaries to fiduciary relief for the investment results of participant accounts defaulted into the QDIA.

Qualified Distribution: A distribution from a Roth account that is made on account of death, disability, or attainment of age 59½, and is made after the five-year period beginning on January 1 of the year that a contribution was first made to the Roth account.

Qualified Domestic Relations Order (QDRO): A domestic relations order that entitles an alternate payee to receive some or all of a participant's benefits under a plan.

Qualified Joint and Survivor Annuity (QJSA): The QJSA is an annuity for the life of the participant with a survivor annuity for the life of the spouse. The survivor annuity is a plan-specified percentage not less than 50 percent and not more than 100 percent of the amount of the annuity that is payable during the joint lives of the participant and spouse. In the case of an unmarried participant, the QJSA is an annuity for the life of the participant.

Qualified Matching Contributions (QMACs): Matching contributions that are 100 percent vested at all times and that are subject to restrictions on distributability.

Qualified Nonelective Contributions (QNECs): Nonelective contributions that are 100 percent vested at all times and that are subject to restrictions on distributability.

Qualified Optional Survivor Annuity (QOSA): For plan years beginning on or after January 1, 2008, plans are required to offer a QOSA in the event a participant waives the Qualified Joint and Survivor Annuity (QJSA). If the survivor annuity under the QJSA is less than 75 percent of the amount of the annuity that is payable during the joint lives of the participant and spouse, the QOSA is 75 percent of the amount that is payable during their joint lives. If the survivor annuity under the QJSA is equal to or greater than 75 percent, the QOSA is 50 percent.

Qualified Plan: A plan the provisions of which satisfy Code Section 401(a). Sometimes used more broadly to include plans that qualify under other Code sections.

Qualified Pre-retirement Survivor Annuity (QPSA): If a married participant dies before his or her annuity starting date, his or her benefits are paid to the surviving spouse unless waived. A QPSA is an immediate annuity for the life of the surviving spouse purchased with not less than 50 percent and not more than 100 percent of the value of the participant's account balance as of the date of death, as specified in the plan document.

Qualified Separate Line of Business (QSLOB): A line of business that meets certain IRS requirements and thus may be treated as a distinct unit for purposes of applying certain nondiscrimination requirements.

Qualified Start-Up Costs: A limited tax credit that can be taken by small employers for the expenses incurred to establish and administer a plan for the first three years of its existence.

Qualifying Employer Securities: Stock, marketable obligations, and certain interests in a publicly traded partnership of the employer. In an employee stock ownership plan (ESOP), qualifying employer securities are classes of common stock that are readily tradable or stock whose voting and dividend rights are equivalent to the most favorable voting and dividend rights of any class of the employer's common stock.

Qualifying Plan Assets: Categories of plan assets under the Form 5500 audit rules for small plans.

Rabbi Trust: A vehicle to secure payment of nonqualified plan benefits.

Ratio-Percentage Test: One of two alternative tests used for purposes of determining whether a plan meets the minimum coverage requirements under Code Section 410(b). (See **Average Benefits Test**.)

Recharacterization: A mechanism that treats excess contributions as employee contributions in order to correct an ADP test that does not meet the requirements of the law.

Registered Investment Adviser (RIA): A person who is an investment advisor and is registered either with the Securities and Exchange Commission under the Investment Advisers Act of 1940 or with the state where the advisor maintains its principal office and business.

Remedial Amendment Period: The period of time during which a qualified retirement plan must be amended to conform to new legislation or other rules in order to retain its qualified status. This period is usually stated in the legislation, though it is often extended by subsequent legislation or revenue procedures. However, if a plan terminates prior to the date amendments otherwise must be adopted, the plan must be amended to conform to the applicable new rules in effect on the date the plan is terminated.

Required Minimum Distribution: The amount that must be withdrawn each year from all retirement plans once a participant reaches age 70½ or, if later, terminates employment. (The delay until termination of employment is for non-5 percent owners).

Reversion of Employer Contributions: The return of plan assets to the employer. A reversion can occur only under limited circumstances.

RIA: See **Registered Investment Adviser**.

Risk: The possibility of deviation from a particular target; from an investor's perspective, the chance of financial loss or not attaining investment goals. Risk is often measured as the amount of unpredictable variability in the return on an investment.

Risk Tolerance: An investor's personal ability or willingness to endure declines in the prices of investments. Sometimes measured by risk tolerance questionnaires.

RMD: See **Required Minimum Distribution**.

Rollover: A plan contribution made by an employee, attributable to a distribution from a qualified plan, a governmental 457 plan, a 403(b) plan, and the taxable portion of a traditional IRA.

Rollover IRA Account: An individual retirement account that is funded with an eligible rollover distribution from a qualified plan.

Roth 401(k): A type of 401(k) plan account in which salary deferral contributions are made using after-tax dollars. Distributions from a Roth 401(k) account that are *qualified distributions* are not subject to income tax.

Roth IRA: A type of IRA funded with after-tax dollars, qualifying distributions from which are excludable from income tax.

Salary Deferral: See **Elective Deferrals (Contributions)**.

Savings Incentive Match Plan for Employees (SIMPLE): A special plan involving simplified legal requirements for businesses with 100 or fewer employees. (See also **SIMPLE 401(k) Plan** and **SIMPLE IRA Plan**.)

S Corporation: A small business corporation in which the shareholders elect to be taxed like a partnership with profits and losses passing directly through to the shareholders. Income is not taxed at the corporate level. (See **C Corporation**.)

Safe Harbor 401(k) Plan: A 401(k) plan exempt from nondiscrimination testing of elective and/or matching contributions in exchange for providing certain minimum levels of 100 percent vested matching or nonelective contributions.

Safe Harbor Rules: Regulations that specify plan provisions or plan operational characteristics by virtue of which more complex rules or tests need not be considered.

Salary Reduction Arrangement: A cash-or-deferred arrangement under which an employee elects to reduce a portion of his or her regular salary or wages and to have that portion contributed by the employer to a 401(k) plan.

Salary Reduction Simplified Employee Pension Plan (SARSEP): A simplified employee pension under Code Section 408(k) that permits employees to make elective contributions to their IRAs. New SARSEPs may not be established after December 31, 1996.

SAR: See **Summary Annual Report**.

SARSEP: See **Salary Reduction Simplified Employee Pension Plan**.

Saver's Credit: Tax credit available to individuals at certain income levels for retirement plan contributions up to a specific limit.

Savings or Thrift Plan: A contributory defined contribution plan where the employer's obligation to make contributions depends on whether the employee makes a contribution out of after-tax compensation. Thrift plans are subject to the Section 401(m) nondiscrimination requirements.

SBJPA: See **Small Business Job Protection Act of 1996**.

SCP: See **Self-Correction Program**.

SEC: Securities and Exchange Commission.

Section 401(k) Plan: A plan in which employees may elect to make pre-tax or Roth contributions to an employer-sponsored plan in lieu of receiving cash. (See **Cash-or-Deferred Arrangement**.)

Section 403(b) Plan: An elective contribution arrangement available to employees of public schools and to employees of certain entities that are tax exempt under Code Section 501(c)(3). A 403(b) plan may also provide for employer contributions. (See **Tax-Sheltered Annuities (TSA)**.)

Section 404(c) Plan: Any defined contribution plan meeting regulatory requirements in which a participant exercises control over the assets in his or her account such that a participant will not be considered a fiduciary by reason of that control, and no other fiduciary shall be held liable for losses resulting from that control. After Section 404(c) of ERISA.

Section 457 Plan: An elective contribution arrangement available to states, political subdivisions of a state, or any agency or instrumentality of a state and certain non governmental organizations exempt from taxation.

Self-Correction Program (SCP): A program for correcting operational (but generally not document) defects by the end of the second plan year following the year in which the defect arose (or later, if, given all the facts and circumstances, the defects are considered insignificant). No fees or filings with the IRS are required. (See also **EPCRS**.)

Self-Directed Option: An investment option permitting participants to invest their plan assets in an unlimited number of investment options through either a full brokerage account or a mutual fund window (also known as an open-ended option or plan).

Self-Employed Person: An individual who has net earnings from self-employment with respect to a trade or business in which the personal services of the individual are a material income-producing factor.

SEP: See **Simplified Employee Pension Plan**.

Separate Line of Business (SLOB): A line of business that is organized and operated separately from the remaining businesses of the employer and that meets certain requirements.

Shareholder-Employee: An employee who owns more than 5 percent of the capital stock of a corporation that is taxed as a Subchapter S small business corporation.

SIMPLE: See **Savings Incentive Match Plan for Employees**.

SIMPLE 401(k) Plan: A 401(k) plan that can be sponsored by employers with 100 or fewer employees and that is exempt from ADP and ACP testing and the top-heavy rules in exchange for prescribed 100 percent vested employer contributions and a lower limit on salary deferrals. Cannot be used in conjunction with any other active qualified plan covering the same employees.

SIMPLE IRA Plan: Also called SIMPLE retirement account plan. A salary deferral plan that can be sponsored by employers with 100 or fewer employees and that is exempt from discrimination testing and top-heavy rules but subject to prescribed employer contributions and a $6,000 (indexed) cap on deferrals. All contributions are made to IRAs. Cannot be used in conjunction with any other active qualified plan of the same sponsor(s).

Simplified Employee Pension Plan (SEP): A retirement plan where employer contributions are made to the individual retirement accounts (IRAs) of the participants.

SLOB: See **Separate Line of Business.**

Small Business Job Protection Act of 1996 (SBJPA): Contains the Pension Simplification Act of 1996.

Small Business Jobs Act of 2010: Added In-Plan Roth Rollovers.

Sole Proprietor: The owner of 100 percent of an unincorporated business.

SPD: See **Summary Plan Description.**

Spousal IRA: An additional IRA contribution made by a working spouse on behalf of a nonworking spouse.

Standardized Plan: A prototype plan that is designed to satisfy automatically the Internal Revenue Code's minimum coverage and nondiscrimination requirements.

Stock: A security that represents part ownership, or equity, in a corporation.

Stock Bonus Plan: A defined contribution plan similar to a profit sharing plan except that distributions must generally be made in company stock. A stock bonus plan may contain a cash-or-deferred arrangement.

Stock Fund: A fund whose holdings consist mainly of stocks.

Strategic Alliance: A group of two or more service providers that have entered into an agreement that enables them to offer a unified package of plan services.

Summary Annual Report (SAR): A report of overall plan financial information provided to each participant in a format published by the DOL. The information is derived from the Form 5500 series annual report.

Summary Plan Description (SPD): A written description of the plan designed to provide a participant or beneficiary with a comprehensive but understandable overview of how the plan operates.

TAMRA: Technical and Miscellaneous Revenue Act of 1988.

Target Date Fund: A type of asset allocation fund where the participant's age over time is taken into account in determining investment positions.

Tax Equity and Fiscal Responsibility Act of 1982 (TEFRA): Created minimum distribution requirements, reduced the limits on contributions and benefits in plans, established parity between corporate and noncorporate or Keogh plans, treated certain plan loans as taxable distributions, and added the top-heavy rules.

Taxable Year: The 12-month period selected by an employer to report income for tax purposes.

Tax Reform Act of 1984 (TRA '84): See **Deficit Reduction Act of 1984 (DEFRA)**.

Tax Reform Act of 1986 (TRA '86): The first wholesale revision of the tax code since 1954. As a result, the Code is now named the "Internal Revenue Code of 1986."

Taxpayer Relief Act of 1997 (TRA '97): Act containing a number of retirement plan provisions simplifying plan administration and creating new retirement planning options—notably the Roth IRA.

Tax-Sheltered Annuities (TSA): Also known as 403(b) annuities. This is a mechanism for employees of certain not-for-profit organizations to elect to defer compensation in a qualified retirement plan on a pre-tax basis.

TEFRA: See **Tax Equity and Fiscal Responsibility Act of 1982**.

Third-Party Administrator: A plan administrator who is unrelated to the sponsoring employer.

Top-Hat Plan: An unfunded nonqualified plan for a select group of management or highly compensated employees.

Top-Heavy Plan: A qualified retirement plan in which more than 60 percent of the benefits are for key employees. Top-heavy plans must provide minimum benefits or contributions for non-key employees.

TRA '84: See **Deficit Reduction Act of 1984 (DEFRA)**.

TRA '86: See **Tax Reform Act of 1986**.

TRA '97: See **Taxpayer Relief Act of 1997**.

Trades or Businesses under Common Control: Two or more corporations, partnerships, or sole proprietorships that, by virtue of common ownership, are treated as a single entity for purposes of certain employee benefit requirements under Code Section 414(c).

Treasury Regulations: Regulations written by the IRS interpreting the Internal Revenue Code are technically Treasury Regulations. The IRS is part of the Department of the Treasury, and the Internal Revenue Code authorizes the Secretary of the Treasury to promulgate regulations.

Trustees: The parties named in a trust document who have responsibility to hold assets for the participants. Some trust documents also give investment responsibility to the trustees.

Truth-in-Lending: Federal law governing consumer credit transactions that provides for uniform disclosure of annual credit cost, finance charges, amount financed, and total payments to be made.

TSA: See **Tax-Sheltered Annuities**.

12b-1 Fee: A fee for advertising, marketing, and distribution services of a mutual fund.

Unbundled Administration: The process by which different individuals or companies perform various aspects of plan administration. (Compare with Bundled Services.)

Unincorporated Business: A business organization that is not a corporation, such as a partnership or sole proprietorship.

User Fees: The fees charged by the IRS to review determination letter applications as to the qualified status of the form of retirement plans or to consider a VCP application.

USERRA: The Uniformed Services Employment and Reemployment Rights Act of 1994.

Value Stocks: Those stocks that have relatively high dividend yields and that sell at relatively low prices in relation to their earnings or book value. Funds that emphasize value stocks are sometimes called "value" funds.

VCP: See **Voluntary Correction with Service Approval**. (See also **Employee Plans Compliance Resolution System (EPCRS)**.)

Vested Benefits: Benefits that become nonforfeitable with respect to a participant as the result of the passage of time or the occurrence of an event such as retirement or plan termination.

Volume Submitter: A type of retirement plan document for which a specimen plan is submitted to the IRS for approval. The submitter must certify that at least 30 employers will adopt the plan. The user fees for filing IRS determination letter applications are less than those for an individually designed document.

Voluntary Contributions: Participant contributions made to a plan on an after-tax basis. These contributions are treated as Section 415 annual additions and are subject to Section 401(m) nondiscrimination requirements.

Voluntary Correction with Service Approval (VCP): A program that allows an employer to correct operational, plan document, and demographic errors that do not involve diversion or misuse of plan assets. Participation in the program is initiated by the employer and, in addition to correction of the error, requires payment of a fee to the IRS.

Voluntary Fiduciary Correction Program (VFCP): A program to encourage applicants to voluntarily self-correct certain violations of ERISA.

Worker, Retiree, and Employer Recovery Act of 2008 (WRERA): Act signed on December 23, 2008, which made technical corrections and clarifications to the Pension Protection Act of 2006 (PPA), provided minimum distribution relief for 2009, and other various changes.

WRERA: See **Worker, Retiree, and Employer Recovery Act of 2008**.

Year of Service: A 12-month period in which an employee completes a specified number of hours of service, commonly 1,000 hours; however, the plan document can require fewer hours. A year of service can also be determined on an elapsed time basis.

Internal Revenue Code Sections

[*References are to question numbers.*]

Key Code Sections 401(a): The basic requirements for a retirement plan to be qualified for special treatment under the Internal Revenue Code. (See chapter 2.)

401(a)(4): The general nondiscrimination rule. A qualified plan may not discriminate in favor of highly compensated employees with respect to contributions or benefits. (See chapter 12.)

401(a)(17): Cap on compensation that may be considered in determining benefits under a qualified retirement plan. (See chapter 10.)

401(a)(26): The minimum participation requirement. Each plan must benefit the lesser of 50 employees or 40 percent of all employees of the employer. It no longer applies to 401(k) and other defined contribution plans. (See chapter 11.)

401(a)(31): The requirement that distributees must be offered a direct rollover election on all eligible rollover distributions. (See chapter 16.)

401(k): The requirements for a qualified cash or deferred arrangement that must be followed in order to give participants a choice between receiving currently taxable cash compensation or deferring tax by electing to contribute amounts to a profit sharing or stock bonus plan. (See especially chapters 1 and 2.)

401(m): The nondiscrimination test for employer matching contributions and after-tax employee contributions. (See chapter 13.)

402(g): The limit on the amount of elective deferrals a participant may exclude from current taxation. The limit is adjusted annually for cost of living increases. This section also describes the mechanism for returning elective deferrals that exceed the limit. (See chapter 9.)

403(b): Describes how employees of certain tax-exempt nonprofit organizations can defer receipt of currently taxable compensation by means of salary deferrals (also known as tax-sheltered annuities). (See chapter 22.)

410(b): The specific minimum coverage requirements for a qualified retirement plan. Consists of two alternate tests, the ratio percentage test and the average benefit test. (See chapter 11.)

411(d): The anti-cutback rules that protect a participant from having rights or benefits accrued under a plan taken away. (See chapter 16.)

415: The overall maximum limits on contributions and benefits with respect to participants under qualified plans. (See chapter 9.)

416: The top-heavy rules requiring accelerated vesting and minimum benefit or contribution standards in the event that more than 60 percent of a plan's benefits are for key employees. (See chapter 14.)

417: The minimum survivor annuity requirements, which affect the form and timing of distributions and provide for spousal consent to distributions from the plan. (See chapter 17.)

457: Deferred compensation arrangements for employees and independent contractors of state and local governments. (See chapter 22.)

3405: Income tax withholding on 401(k) plan distributions, including the 20 percent withholding requirements. (See chapter 16.)

I.R.C. §

25B . . . 1:63
25B(b) . . . 8:61
25B(b)(3) . . . 2:20
25B(c) . . . 2:22
25B(d)(1) . . . 2:23
25B(d)(2) . . . 2:23
72 . . . 22:61, 22:100
72(b) . . . 18:37
72(d)(1)(B) . . . 18:37
72(d)(1)(E) . . . 18:37
72(d)(2) . . . 18:42
72(e)(8) . . . 18:41
72(e)(8)(D) . . . 16:106, 18:43
72(m)(7) . . . 18:86
72(p) . . . 15:15, 15:21, 15:23, 15:24, 15:26, 16:112, 18:23, 18:50, 18:53, 18:61
72(p)(1) . . . 15:15
72(p)(2) . . . 20:27
72(p)(2)(A) . . . 15:15
72(p)(2)(B) . . . 15:15
72(p)(2)(C) . . . 15:15
72(p)(3) . . . 15:39
72(t) . . . 1:60, 2:49, 9:19, 9:53, 13:80, 15:18, 15:56, 16:27, 18:39, 18:86, 22:18, 22:61, 22:79, 22:80, 22:140, 22:182
72(t)(2)(A)(ii) . . . 18:86
72(t)(2)(A)(iii) . . . 18:86
72(t)(2)(A)(iv) . . . 18:86, 18:106
72(t)(2)(A)(v) . . . 18:86
72(t)(2)(A)(vi) . . . 18:86
72(t)(2)(A)(vii) . . . 18:86
72(t)(2)(B) . . . 18:86
72(t)(2)(C) . . . 17:59, 18:86
72(t)(2)(G) . . . 16:27, 18:86
72(t)(2)(G)(ii) . . . 16:29
72(t)(2)(G)(iii) . . . 16:28
72(t)(3)(B) . . . 18:86, 18:106
72(t)(4) . . . 18:106
72(t)(4)(A)(ii) . . . 18:108
72(t)(6) . . . 22:80
72(t)(10) . . . 18:86
83 . . . 22:96, 22:100
119 . . . 10:106
125 . . . 9:49, 10:93, 15:49
132(f) . . . 10:93
151(f)(2) . . . 2:22
162(m) . . . 22:97
163 . . . 22:97
165 . . . 15:46
204(h) . . . 19:127
213 . . . 18:86
213(d) . . . 15:46
219(b)(5) . . . 1:62, 22:9, 22:10
219(c) . . . 22:14
219(c)(1) . . . 22:3
219(c)(2) . . . 22:3, 22:25
219(d)(1) . . . 22:11
219(g)(1)–(8) . . . 22:12
219(g)(5) . . . 22:12
318 . . . 10:82
318(a) . . . 10:36

I.R.C. §

401 . . . . 10:23
401(a) 1:53, 2:148, 2:141, 2:144, 2:150, 2:153, 19:128, 22:12, 22:62, 22:84, 22:131, 22:153, 22:160, 22:161
401(a)(1)(D) 22:123
401(a)(2) 2:153, 2:167, 9:66
401(a)(4) 2:94, 2:108, 2:110, 2:112, 2:113, 2:116, 2:126, 2:140, 2:148, 3:28, 3:36, 6:81, 7:6, 10:39, 10:103, 11:6, 11:32, 14:6, 22:131
401(a)(9) 2:125, 3:17, 9:20, 13:33, 13:76, 13:80, 16:15, 16:16, 16:38, 16:45, 16:47, 16:57, 16:60, 18:107, 20:27, 22:19, 22:124, 22:167
401(a)(9)(A) 16:44
401(a)(9)(C) 16:30, 22:175
401(a)(9)(C)(ii)(I) 16:31
401(a)(9)(H) 22:124
401(a)(11) 2:236, 16:7, 16:19, 16:41, 16:90, 21:46
401(a)(12) 2:159
401(a)(13) 2:155, 2:238, 17:64
401(a)(13)(C) 2:156, 5:57
401(a)(14) 16:16
401(a)(17) 2:43, 2:225, 10:39, 10:99, 10:104–10:106, 20:7, 20:19, 22:48
401(a)(17)(A) 10:104, 22:48
401(a)(17)(B) 10:105
401(a)(27) 2:166
401(a)(28)(C) 6:74
401(a)(30) 2:165, 9:6, 9:22, 22:54, 22:55, 22:124, 22:133
401(a)(31) 2:168, 3:17, 16:67
401(a)(31)(A) 16:64
401(a)(31)(B) 16:69
401(a)(35) 1:62, 3:21, 6:55, 6:56, 6:58, 6:59, 6:62
401(a)(37) 1:73, 2:187
401(b) 9:8
401(c) 2:71, 10:63
401(c)(1) 10:81
401(f) 2:150, 4:4
401(h) 9:42
401(k) 2:148, 6:55
401(k)(1) 1:28, 6:73
401(k)(2)(B) 2:266, 2:267
401(k)(3) 13:80, 22:161
401(k)(4)(A) 2:94, 22:101
401(k)(4)(B) 1:26
401(k)(4)(B)(i) 22:163
401(k)(4)(B)(ii) 2:145–2:147
401(k)(4)(B)(iii) 2:147
401(k)(8) 1:63
401(k)(11) 2:96, 2:220, 13:1, 13:80, 22:65
401(k)(11)(A) 22:77
401(k)(11)(A)(ii) 22:71
401(k)(11)(A)(iii) 22:79
401(k)(11)(B) 22:73, 22:77
401(k)(11)(B)(i) 22:77
401(k)(11)(B)(iii) 22:68, 22:69
401(k)(11)(C) 22:71
401(k)(11)(D) 22:66
401(k)(12) 2:89, 2:96, 2:239, 2:245, 13:1, 13:80
401(k)(12)(D) 19:127
401(k)(12)(E) 2:266
401(k)(12)(E)(i) 2:255
401(k)(13) 1:58, 2:56, 13:1
401(k)(13)(B) 2:52
401(k)(13)(D) 2:97
401(k)(13)(D)(ii) 2:61, 2:62
401(k)(13)(D)(iii)(II) 2:64
401(*l*) 2:159, 12:2, 12:15
401(m) 2:8, 2:137, 2:274, 3:17, 6:55, 11:5, 11:25, 15:25, 22:84, 22:131
401(m)(2) 13:80
401(m)(2)(A) 13:53
401(m)(4)(A) 2:86
401(m)(6)(A) 1:63
401(m)(6)(C) 13:65
401(m)(10) 2:96, 2:220, 13:1
401(m)(11) 2:239, 2:245, 13:1, 19:127
401(m)(12) 2:56, 13:1
402(b) 22:96
402(b)(4) 11:31
402(c)(1) 16:52
402(c)(2) 16:53, 16:57, 16:82
402(c)(3) 16:81
402(c)(4) 16:56, 16:57, 18:68
402(c)(4)(C) 15:52, 16:111
402(c)(6) 16:61
402(c)(8) 16:53, 16:67, 16:117
402(c)(8)(B) 22:178, 22:179
402(c)(9) 16:62, 18:34
402(c)(11) 1:60, 16:62, 16:82, 18:35
402(e)(1) 16:62
402(e)(1)(A) 17:59
402(e)(1)(B) 17:59
402(e)(4)(A) 18:28
402(e)(4)(B) 18:28
402(e)(4)(D) 18:15
402(e)(4)(D)(ii) 18:17, 18:18
402(e)(4)(D)(v) 18:18
402(e)(4)(D)(vii) 18:21
402(e)(4)(D)(vii) 18:21
402(e)(4)(E) 18:29
402(f) 1:73, 16:92, 18:68, 19:127, 19:129, 19:131, 21:46, 22:185

I.R.C. §

402(g) 1:74, 2:33, 2:43, 2:74, 2:261, 2:267, 9:31, 9:34, 18:54, 18:61, 20:8, 22:54, 22:124, 22:133, 22:160, 22:169
402(g)(1) 9:1, 9:2
402(g)(1)(B) 22:133
402(g)(1)(C) 22:55
402(g)(2)(A)(ii) 18:55
402(g)(3) 9:3, 22:161, 22:169, 22:173
402(g)(3)(C) 1:27
402(g)(7) 22:134, 22:161
402A 22:137, 22:173
402A(b) 22:124
402A(c)(2) 9:4
402A(c)(3) 18:67, 22:145
402A(c)(4) 2:84, 18:67
402A(d)(1) 18:59
402A(d)(2) 9:23, 18:60
403(a) 16:67, 19:128, 22:7, 22:12, 22:62, 22:84
403(b) 1:51, 1:53, 1:60, 1:78, 2:23, 2:25, 9:3, 9:6, 9:8, 9:38, 10:93, 11:25, 16:52, 16:54, 16:82, 18:77, 18:103, 19:75, 19:128, 21:7, 21:19, 22:7, 22:12, 22:54, 22:62, 22:84, 22:106, 22:121–22:134, 22:136–22:148, 22:151–22:163
403(b)(1) 22:122, 22:124
403(b)(1)(A) 22:124
403(b)(1)(A)(i) 22:121
403(b)(1)(A)(ii) 22:121
403(b)(1)(C) 22:124
403(b)(1)(D) 22:124, 22:161
403(b)(1)(E) 22:124, 22:133
403(b)(3) 22:124
403(b)(4) 22:124
403(b)(5) 22:124
403(b)(7) 22:122, 22:124
403(b)(8) 16:53
403(b)(9) 22:122
403(b)(10) 22:124, 22:161
403(b)(11) 22:124
403(b)(12) 22:124, 22:131, 22:132
403(b)(12)(A) 22:161
403(b)(12)(A)(i) 22:128
403(b)(12)(A)(ii) 22:129
403(b)(12)(B) 22:124, 22:161
403(b)(12)(C) 22:124
403(b)(13) 22:124
403(b)(14) 22:124
403(d)(3) 16:53
404 . . . . . 1:31, 2:24, 6:74, 9:55, 13:72
404(a)(3) 9:55, 22:78
404(a)(3)(A) 9:56
404(a)(3)(A)(ii) 9:65
404(a)(3)(A)(iv) 9:57
404(a)(3)(A)(v) 9:75
404(a)(5) 22:97

I.R.C. §

404(a)(6) 9:67, 15:59
404(a)(7) 9:73
404(a)(7)(C) 1:63
404(a)(9) 9:60
404(a)(12) 9:61
404(h) 22:46, 22:48, 22:50, 22:56
404(k) 9:60, 16:57, 18:31, 18:93
404(k)(2)(A)(iii) 2:29
404(*l*) 9:62, 10:106
404(m) 22:78
404(n) 9:59
406(a)(3) 10:9
407(a)(17)22:131
408 . . . . . 19:5
408(a) 22:1, 22:75
408(a)(1) 22:48
408(a)(3) 6:38
408(a)(6) 22:19, 22:60
408(b) 22:2, 22:75
408(b)(2) 4:105
408(b)(3) 22:60
408(c) 16:74, 22:16
408(d) 22:18, 22:53
408(d)(1) 22:61
408(d)(3)(C) 16:99
408(e)(3) 22:58, 22:81
408(e)(4) 22:58, 22:81
408(j) 22:48, 22:53
408(k) 19:128, 22:12, 22:39, 22:62, 22:84
408(k)(2) 22:44, 22:45
408(k)(3) 22:49
408(k)(3)(C) 22:48, 22:49, 22:52, 22:56
408(k)(4) 22:59
408(k)(6) 9:3, 9:49, 22:40
408(k)(6)(A) 22:42
408(k)(6)(A)(iv) 22:54, 22:55
408(k)(6)(B) 22:41, 22:42, 22:43
408(k)(6)(D) 22:42
408(k)(8) 22:52
408(*l*) 22:39
408(m)(3) 22:1
408(o)(2) 22:15
408(o)(4)(A) 22:15
408(p) 9:3, 9:49, 19:128, 22:12, 22:62, 22:84
408(p)(1) 22:64
408(p)(2) 22:77
408(p)(2)(A) 22:72
408(p)(2)(A)(iii) 2:226
408(p)(2)(B)(ii) 22:77
408(p)(2)(C)(i) 22:66
408(p)(2)(C)(ii) 2:226
408(p)(2)(C)(ii)(II) 22:77
408(p)(2)(D) 2:229, 22:70, 22:75
408(p)(2)(E) 9:36, 22:73
408(p)(3) 22:79

I.R.C. §

408(p)(4)(A) 22:68
408(p)(4)(B) 22:69
408(p)(7) 22:67
408(p)(8) 22:73
408(q) 2:120, 2:189, 16:74, 16:77, 19:128
408(q)(1)(A) 2:127
408A 19:128
408A(a) 22:24
408A(b) 22:24
408A(c)(3)(C)(ii)(III) 22:26
408A(c)(5) 22:32, 22:38
408A(d)(1) 22:38
408A(d)(2) 22:30
408A(d)(3)(A)(iii) 18:102
408A(d)(4) 22:29, 22:31
408A(d)(4)(B) 22:38
408A(e) 1:60
409(e) 6:74
409(e)(2) 6:65
409(e)(3) 6:65
409(h) 6:74
409(*l*) 6:52
409(o) 6:74
409A 22:100, 22:106–22:113, 22:115
409A(a)(1) 22:112
409A(b)(2) 22:112
409A(b)(3) 22:109
410 . . . . . 10:23, 10:39
410(a) 2:148, 13:36, 22:162
410(a)(1) 2:180
410(a)(1)(A) 2:170
410(a)(1)(B)(i) 2:172
410(a)(2) 2:171
410(a)(3)(A) 2:173
410(a)(4) 2:33
410(a)(5)(B) 2:185
410(a)(5)(D) 2:184
410(a)(5)(E) 2:188
410(b) 2:33, 2:98, 2:148, 2:165, 2:222, 2:229, 2:230, 3:36, 6:81, 9:31, 10:62, 12:8, 13:38, 14:5, 14:6, 14:35, 20:11, 22:131, 22:162
410(b)(3) 22:69
410(b)(3)(B) 11:25
410(b)(3)(C) 22:45
410(b)(6)(C) 21:35
411 . . . . . 2:148, 10:23, 10:39
411(a)(2) 1:63
411(a)(2)(B) 2:194, 14:29
411(a)(4)(A) 2:197
411(a)(5)(A) 2:195
411(a)(6)(C) 2:204
411(a)(6)(D) 2:203
411(a)(6)(E) 2:206
411(a)(8) 2:193

I.R.C. §

411(a)(11) 2:148, 16:16, 16:22, 16:23, 19:127, 19:129, 19:132, 19:133
411(a)(11)(A) 22:174
411(a)(11)(D) 16:24
411(d)(3) 21:3, 21:15
411(d)(6) 3:16, 3:17, 12:35, 15:42, 16:79, 18:72
411(d)(6)(D) 2:135, 16:12
412 . . . . . 14:20
412(c) 2:254
412(c)(2)(A) 2:253
414 . . . . . 2:221
414(a) 21:29
414(b) 10:1, 10:23, 14:3, 15:15
414(c) 10:1, 10:23, 14:3, 15:15
414(*l*) 2:159, 6:55
414(m) 14:3, 15:15
414(m)(2)(A) 10:24
414(m)(2)(B) 10:24, 10:30
414(m)(4) 10:39
414(m)(5) 10:24, 10:37
414(m)(6)(B) 10:36
414(n)(2) 10:65
414(n)(3) 10:72
414(n)(3)(B) 14:4
414(n)(5) 10:73, 10:74
414(n)(5)(C)(ii) 10:75
414(p)(1)(A) 17:51
414(p)(1)(B) 17:52
414(p)(2) 17:54
414(p)(3) 17:55
414(p)(4) 17:63
414(p)(5) 17:61
414(p)(6) 4:4, 17:56
414(p)(7) 17:57
414(p)(8) 17:53
414(q) 10:88, 21:36
414(q)(1) 10:76, 10:78
414(q)(4) 10:90
414(q)(8) 14:15
414(s) 2:67, 2:259, 2:267, 3:36, 3:37, 10:92–10:96, 10:102, 10:103, 10:106, 12:3, 13:12, 13:60
414(s)(2) 10:93
414(u)(1) 1:70, 2:99, 9:5, 9:45
414(u)(2) 1:66, 2:77
414(u)(2)(A)(ii) 2:92
414(u)(3) 1:69
414(u)(7) 1:67, 2:77, 9:50
414(u)(8) 2:99
414(u)(8)(A) 2:100, 2:189
414(u)(8)(B) 2:200
414(u)(9) 1:73
414(u)(12)(A) 1:71
414(u)(12)(B) 1:72
414(v) 22:55, 22:171

I.R.C. §

414(v)(2) . . . 2:223
414(v)(2)(B)(i) . . . 22:135
414(v)(2)(B)(ii) . . . 9:37
414(v)(2)(C)(ii) . . . 22:74
414(v)(3) . . . 9:31
414(v)(4) . . . 9:31
414(w) . . . 1:58
414(w)(2) . . . 7:43
414(w)(2)(B) . . . 7:49
414(w)(4) . . . 1:58
414(x) . . . 2:270
414(x)(2)(A) . . . 2:271
414(x)(2)(B) . . . 2:272
414(x)(2)(C) . . . 2:272
414(x)(2)(D) . . . 2:273
414(x)(3) . . . 2:274
414(x)(4) . . . 2:274
415 . . . 1:46, 2:43, 2:74, 2:116, 2:137, 2:163, 2:258, 2:267, 3:17, 3:36, 6:74, 9:14, 9:28, 9:30, 9:31, 9:39, 9:41, 9:46, 9:48, 9:49, 9:51–9:53, 9:74, 9:76, 10:23, 10:39, 10:74, 10:90, 10:106, 11:5, 13:27, 13:40, 13:72, 13:80, 14:17, 15:25, 16:57, 18:61, 20:7, 22:84, 22:139, 22:160–22:162
415(c) . . . 2:164, 9:51, 9:54, 10:106, 22:124, 22:138
415(c)(1) . . . 9:39, 22:48
415(c)(1)(A) . . . 22:169
415(c)(2) . . . 22:50, 22:53, 22:169, 22:173
415(c)(3) . . . 1:71, 2:267, 9:49, 10:92, 10:99, 10:102, 14:17
415(c)(6) . . . 9:44
415(d) . . . 9:40, 10:78, 10:105
415(h) . . . 10:23
415(k)(4) . . . 22:160
416 . . . 2:148, 3:36, 9:31, 10:23, 10:39
416(c)(2)(A) . . . 2:263, 14:38
416(g)(3)(A) . . . 14:25
416(g)(3)(B) . . . 14:25
416(g)(4)(B) . . . 14:28
416(g)(4)(E) . . . 14:1, 14:28
416(g)(4)(H) . . . 2:65, 14:38
416(i)(1)(A) . . . 14:9, 14:13–14:15
416(i)(1)(B)(iii)(I) . . . 14:10
416(i)(1)(C) . . . 14:10
416(i)(1)(D) . . . 14:17
417 . . . 1:60, 2:236, 9:76, 16:90, 19:134, 21:23, 21:46
417(a)(2) . . . 19:127
417(a)(2)(A) . . . 17:29
417(a)(3) . . . 17:24
417(a)(6) . . . 1:61, 17:22
417(a)(6)(A) . . . 16:19, 17:23, 17:27
417(b) . . . 17:11

I.R.C. §

417(e)(1) . . . 16:24
417(g) . . . 17:12
419(u)(9)(A) . . . 2:93
451(a) . . . 22:94
457 . . . 1:27, 1:51, 1:53, 1:60, 1:78, 2:23, 9:3, 9:49, 16:52, 16:53, 16:67
457(a)–(e) . . . 22:186
457(b) . . . 19:93, 21:7, 22:7, 22:12, 22:106, 22:130, 22:143, 22:164–22:187
457(b)(3) . . . 22:170
457(b)(4) . . . 22:172
457(b)(6) . . . 22:165
457(d)(1)(A)(i) . . . 22:174
457(d)(1)(A)(ii) . . . 22:174
457(d)(1)(A)(iii) . . . 22:174
457(d)(2) . . . 22:175
457(d)(3) . . . 22:174
457(e)(1) . . . 22:164
457(e)(2) . . . 22:168
457(e)(5) . . . 22:168
457(e)(9)(A) . . . 22:174
457(e)(11) . . . 22:166
457(e)(15) . . . 22:169
457(e)(16) . . . 16:53, 22:178, 22:179
457(e)(18) . . . 22:171
457(f) . . . 21:7, 22:100, 22:105, 22:186
457(f)(1) . . . 22:100, 22:186
457(f)(3)(B) . . . 22:100
457(g) . . . 22:165, 22:167
501(a) . . . 6:15
501(c)(3) . . . 1:27, 11:25, 22:20, 22:121, 22:147
501(c)(18) . . . 22:12
512 . . . 6:82
851(a) . . . 6:59
861(a)(3) . . . 22:69
911(d)(2) . . . 22:69
1401 . . . 18:3
1563 . . . 6:59
1563(a) . . . 6:59
2001 . . . 18:92
2010 . . . 18:92
3101(a) . . . 18:4
3101(b) . . . 18:4
3101(b)(2)18:4
3102(a) . . . 18:5
3102(b) . . . 18:5
3111(a) . . . 12:17, 18:4
3111(b) . . . 18:4
3121(a) . . . 22:98
3121(a)(5)(A) . . . 18:2
3121(b)(10) . . . 22:130
3121(d) . . . 18:3
3121(v)(1)(A) . . . 16:107, 18:2
3121(w) . . . 22:161

I.R.C. §

3121(w)(3)(A) 22:185
3121(w)(3)(B) 22:185
3301 . . . . 22:99
3301(1) 18:11
3301(2) 18:11
3302(a)(1) 18:8, 18:11
3302(b) 18:11
3306(b)(5)(A) 18:9
3306(c) 18:10
3306(r)(1)(A) 16:107, 18:9
3401(a) 9:4, 10:106
3401(h)(2) 16:49
3405 . . . . 9:53
3405(a) 16:108
3405(a)(4) 16:127
3405(b) 16:108, 16:129
3405(c) 2:168, 16:108
3405(c)(3) 16:117
3405(e) 16:122
3405(e)(3) 16:128
3405(e)(8) 16:123
3405(e)(9) 16:124
3405(e)(10)(B) 16:131
3405(e)(10)(B)(i) 16:133
3405(e)(12) 16:135
3405(e)(13) 16:136
4972 . . . . 9:65
4974 . . . . 22:184
4974(a) 18:88
4974(d) 18:88
4975 . . . . 5:57, 5:146
4975(a) 5:73
4975(b) 5:73
4975(c)(1)(E) 5:61
4975(c)(1)(F) 5:61
4975(e)(7) 6:74

I.R.C. §

4975(e)(8) 6:52
4975(f)(5) 5:74
4975(f)(6)(B)(iii) 15:1
4979 . . . . 2:50, 13:35
4979(f) 1:58, 1:63
4979(f)(1) 18:58
4979(f)(2) 13:19, 18:57
4980F 9:76, 21:23
6001 . . . . 15:44
6051(a) 18:7
6057(b) 19:23
6058 . . . . 19:21
6058(b) 19:21
6302(g) 16:138
6331 . . . . 18:86
6621(a)(2) 5:145
6651(a) 16:140
6651(d) 16:140
6652(d)(2) 19:23
6652(e) 19:14, 19:21
6652(h) 16:133, 16:134
6654 . . . . 16:132
6656 . . . . 16:140
6663 . . . . 16:140
6672 . . . . 16:140
6721 . . . . 18:95
7201 . . . . 16:140
7202 . . . . 16:140
7203 . . . . 16:140
7204 . . . . 16:140
7205 . . . . 16:140
7206 . . . . 16:140
7207 . . . . 16:140
7528(b)(2) 3:34
7701(a)(37) 22:64
7701(a)(46) 11:25

United States Code

[References are to question numbers.]

1 U.S.C. §

7 . . . 17:34

11 U.S.C. §

104(b)(1) . . . 22:8

15 U.S.C. §

77a *et seq.* . . . 19:112
77b(1) . . . 6:66
77c . . . 6:66
77d . . . 6:66
77e . . . 6:66
78c . . . 19:112
78p . . . 6:67, 6:68, 6:69

21 U.S.C. §

3101–3128 . . . 18:1

23 U.S.C. §

3301–3311 . . . 18:8

29 U.S.C. §

1002(14) . . . 5:72
1002(21) . . . 5:2, 8:21
1002(38) . . . 4:5, 5:133
1008(b)(1) . . . 15:2
1021(a) . . . 4:4
1022 . . . 19:28
1023(a)(3)(A) . . . 4:4, 19:5
1024(b)(4) . . . 19:52
1025(a) . . . 4:4
1027 . . . 4:4
1056(d) . . . 4:4
1059 . . . 4:4
1101(a) . . . 6:59
1101(b) . . . 5:121
1101(c)(3) . . . 5:70
1102 . . . 4:2, 5:37
1102(a) . . . 5:26
1102(b)(1) . . . 5:39
1103 . . . 4:3, 4:52
1103–1104 . . . 2:146
1103–1105 . . . 2:130
1103(a) . . . 5:28, 5:29
1104 . . . 2:150, 4:52
1104(a) . . . 5:45
1104(a)(1)(B) . . . 5:45
1104(a)(1)(C) . . . 5:45
1104(a)(1)(D) . . . 5:37, 5:45
1104(b) . . . 5:44
1104(c) . . . 5:70
1105 . . . 5:45
1105(a) . . . 5:65
1105(a)(3) . . . 5:66
1105(b) . . . 5:132
1105(c)(1) . . . 4:6
1105(d) . . . 5:70
1106 . . . 5:45, 5:71
1106(a)(1) . . . 5:61
1106(a)(1)(B) . . . 15:2
1106(b) . . . 8:37
1107(a)(2) . . . 6:45
1108(a) . . . 5:117
1108(b) . . . 5:117
1108(b)(2) . . . 4:52
1108(d)(2)(C) . . . 15:1

29 U.S.C. §

1109 . . . . 5:57
1109(a) 5:73, 15:14
1110 . . . . 5:70, 5:128
1110(b) 5:122
1112 . . . . 5:45
1112(a) 5:47
1112(b) 5:47
1131 . . . . 19:20
1132 . . . . 5:57
1132(c) 19:55
1132(c)(1) 19:54
1132(c)(2) 19:14
1132(g) 5:68
1132(*l*) 5:57, 5:73, 5:146

29 U.S.C. §

1133 . . . . 4:4
1144(a) 5:64

38 U.S.C. §

43 . . . . 15:34
4301–4333 . . . . 1:65–1:70

50 U.S.C. §

527 . . . . 15:34

ERISA

[References are to question numbers.]

Key ERISA Section:

404(c): This provision relieves plan fiduciaries from some fiduciary responsibility for plan investments if participants have a certain amount of control over the assets in their accounts. (See chapter 7.)

ERISA §

3(2) 1:42
3(4) 1:42
3(5) 1:42
3(14) 5:72
3(16) 5:4
3(16)(A) 19:1
3(18)(A) 6:63
3(21) 5:2, 5:3, 8:21
3(36) 22:89, 22:91
3(38) 4:5, 5:3, 5:133, 6:59, 7:41, 19:77, 19:100
3(38)(A) 7:41
3(38)(B) 7:41
3(38)(C) 5:28, 7:41
4(b)(1) 22:146
4(b)(2) 22:146
25B 2:19
45E 2:10
101(a) 4:4
101(i)(8)(B) 1:61, 19:110
101(m) 6:60, 19:121
102 . . . . 19:28
103 . . . . 6:82
103(a)(3)(A) 4:4, 19:5
104(b)(5) 1:61
105(a) 1:61, 4:4, 19:40, 19:41
105(a)(2)(C) 19:42
107 . . . . 4:4, 19:126, 19:136
191(m) 6:62
201(2) 22:89, 22:90, 22:168
204(h) 9:76, 19:24, 21:23

ERISA §

204(j) 6:55, 6:56, 6:58, 6:59, 6:62
205(c)(7)(A) 1:61
206(d) 4:4
206(d)(3)(J) 17:61
209 . . . . 4:4, 19:126, 19:136
401(b) 5:121
401(c)(3) 5:70
401(m) 6:55
402 . . . . 5:37
402(a) 4:2, 5:25
402(a)(2) 7:41
402(b)(1) 5:39
402(f) 19:24
403 . . . . 4:52
403(a) 2:150, 4:3, 5:28, 5:29
403(a)(1) 6:72
403(b) 1:78, 4:70
403(c) 2:130
403(c)(2)(A) 2:154
403(c)(2)(B) 2:154
403(c)(2)(C) 2:154
404 . . . . 2:130, 4:52, 4:66, 19:95, 19:103
404(a) 4:115, 5:45, 6:51, 6:65, 16:76, 19:56, 19:65
404(a)(1) 22:123
404(a)(1)(A) 5:86
404(a)(1)(B) 5:45
404(a)(1)(C) 5:45
404(a)(1)(D) 5:37, 5:45, 6:82

ERISA §

404(b) 2:150, 5:45, 6:82
404(c) 1:58, 1:59, 1:61, 4:26, 4:115, 5:41, 5:70, 5:134, 5:135, 5:138, 5:161, 6:43, 6:45, 6:50, 6:65, 6:71, 6:78, 6:83, 6:89, 7:1, 7:2, 7:4, 7:8, 7:15–7:24, 7:28, 7:29, 7:31, 7:34–7:42, 7:60, 7:61, 7:63, 7:71–7:73, 7:75–7:76, 8:3, 8:20, 8:34, 8:35, 19:12, 19:24, 19:26, 19:56, 19:73, 19:103, 21:22
404(c)(1) 1:59, 7:71, 7:72
404(c)(5) 1:58, 1:59, 2:37, 2:41, 5:133, 6:43, 7:40
404(c)(5)(B)(i) 6:45
404a-5 . . . . 4:4
405 . . . . 2:130, 5:45
405(a) 5:65, 5:132
405(a)(3) 5:66
405(b) 5:131
405(c)(1) 4:6
405(d) 5:3, 5:70, 5:133
405(g)(1) 5:96
405(g)(10) 5:96
406 . . . . 5:45, 5:71, 5:86, 6:82, 7:63
406(a)(1) 5:61
406(a)(1)(B) 15:2
406(a)(1)(E) 6:51
406(a)(2) 6:51
406(b) 8:37
406(b)(1) 8:37
406(b)(3) 8:37
407(a)(1)(A) 6:51
407(a)(2) 6:51
407(b) 6:54
407(b)(1) 6:51
407(b)(2) 6:51
407(d)(1) 6:52
407(d)(3)(A) 6:53
407(d)(3)(B) 6:51, 6:53
407(d)(5) 6:52, 7:16
407(e) 6:52

ERISA §

407(f)(1) 6:52
408(a) 5:117, 21:44
408(b) 5:117
408(b)(1) 15:2, 19:5
408(b)(2) 4:52, 4:66, 4:70, 4:105, 5:86, 5:87, 19:58
408(b)(14) 5:95, 8:37
408(b)(15)–(20) 1:59
408(d)(2)(C) 15:1
408(e) 6:51, 6:63
408(g) 1:59, 5:95, 8:37
408(g)(3) 5:99
408(g)(5) 5:101
408(g)(6) 5:100
408(g)(7) 5:102
408(g)(11) 5:97, 5:98, 5:102
409 . . . . 5:57
409(a) 5:73, 15:14
409(b) 5:62
410 . . . . 5:70, 5:128
410(b) 5:122
412 . . . . 5:45, 5:52, 19:5
412(a) 1:62, 5:47
412(b) 5:47
414(*l*) 6:55
501 . . . . 19:20
501(a) 16:146
502 . . . . 5:57
502(a) 16:144
502(c) 19:35, 19:55
502(c)(1) 19:54
502(c)(2) 19:14
502(c)(4) 2:39
502(g) 5:68
502(*l*) 5:57, 5:73, 5:121, 5:126, 5:146
503 . . . . 4:4
514(a) 2:155, 5:64
514(e) 1:58
514(e)(1) 2:40
514(e)(2) 2:37
514(e)(3) 2:38
4050 . . . . 21:13

Pension Protection Act of 2006

[*References are to question numbers.*]

PPA §

generally 5:47, 7:76
812 . . . . 8:61
822 . . . . 16:54
824 . . . . 1:60, 16:54
826 . . . . 1:60, 15:46
829 . . . . 16:54
833 . . . . 8:61

PPA §

902 . . . . 2:36
902(g) 2:51, 2:68
904 . . . . 14:29
1001 . . . . 1:63
1101 . . . . 20:2, 20:12
1103 . . . . 1:61
1107 . . . . 3:21

Cases

[References are to question numbers.]

Abbot v. Lockheed Martin Corp. 4:115
Bobrow v. Commissioner 22:22
Braden v. WalMart Stores, Inc. 4:115
Bussian v. RJR Nabisco 5:63
Calderon v. Amvescap PLC 5:159
Charters v. John Hancock Life Ins. Co. . . . 4:115
Columbia Air Servs., Inc. v. Fidelity Mgmt. Trust Co. 4:115
Commissioner v. *See name of opposing party*
Corbett v. Marsh & McLennan Cos. 5:159
DiFelice v. U.S. Airways, Inc. 4:115
Donovan v. Cunningham 5:61
Eddy v. Colonial Life Ins. Co. of Am. 5:68
Guidry v. Sheet Metal Workers Nat'l Pension Fund 2:158
Haddock v. Nationwide Fin. Servs., Inc. 4:115
Hecker v. Deere & Co. 4:114, 4:115
Howell v. Motorola, Inc. 4:115
Jenkins v. Yager 7:36
Jones v. Harris Assocs., LP 4:115
Kanawi v. Bechtel Corp. 4:114
Keystone Consol. Indus. Inc.; Commissioner v. 5:82
Langbecker v. Electronic Data Sys. 4:115
LaRue v. DeWolff, Boberg & Assocs., Inc. 5:69
Massachusetts Mut. Life Ins. Co. v. Russell 5:67, 5:69
Matz v. Household Int'l Tax Reduction Inv. Plan 21:17
Mazur v. Gaudet 5:122
Mertens v. Hewitt Assocs. 5:60
Morrisey v. Curran 5:62
Obergefell v. Hodges 17:34, 17:40, 17:44, 17:68
Packer Eng'g, Inc. v. Kratville 5:130
Patterson v. Shumate 2:157
Pratt v. Maurice L. Brown Co. Employee Sav. Plan 4:29
Schoonmaker v. Employee Sav. Plan of Amoco Corp. 17:60
Tibble v. Edison Int'l 4:115
Tittle v. Enron Corp. 5:138
Tussey v. ABB, Inc. 4:115, 5:85
Walker v. Mass. Fin. Servs. Co. 5:159
Walsh v. Marsh & McLennan Cos. 5:159
Windsor, United States v. 3:25, 17:34–17:39, 17:42, 17:43
WorldCom Inc. ERISA Litig., In re 5:31, 5:138
Zarate v. Bank One Corp. 5:159

Code of Federal Regulations

[*References are to question numbers.*]

C.F.R. §

12 C.F.R. § 9.18(b)(1) 19:98
12 C.F.R. § 226.3(g) 15:38
17 C.F.R. § 240.15d-21 . . . . 6:66
20 C.F.R. § 1002.259 . . . . 1:65
20 C.F.R. § 1002.262 . . . . 1:68
29 C.F.R. § 2509.75-5 . . . . 4:55
29 C.F.R. § 2510.3-2(f) 22:146, 22:147, 22:148, 22:161
29 C.F.R. § 2520.103-1(c) 22:154
29 C.F.R. § 2520.104-46 . . . . 22:154
29 C.F.R. § 2550.404a-2(c) 6:34, 16:77
29 C.F.R. § 2550.404a-2(d) 16:78
29 C.F.R. § 2550.404a-4 . . . . 16:42
29 C.F.R. § 2550.404a-5 . . . . 4:4
29 C.F.R. § 2550.408b-2 . . . . 4:55
29 C.F.R. § 2550.408b-2(c) 4:69, 5:94
29 C.F.R. § 2550.408b-2(c)(1)(ii) 4:70
29 C.F.R. § 2550.408b-2(c)(1)(iii) 4:72, 4:77
29 C.F.R. § 2550.408b-2(c)(1)(iii)(A) 4:79
29 C.F.R. § 2550.408b-2(c)(1)(iii)(A)(2) 4:80
29 C.F.R. § 2550.408b-2(c)(1)(iii)(B) 4:81
29 C.F.R. § 2550.408b-2(c)(1)(iii)(C) 4:83
29 C.F.R. § 2550.408b-2(c)(1)(iii)(D)(1) . . . 4:73
29 C.F.R. § 2550.408b-2(c)(1)(iii)(D)(2) . . . 4:76, 4:80
29 C.F.R. § 2550.408b-2(c)(1)(iv)(C)(1) . . . 4:90
29 C.F.R. § 2550.408b-2(c)(1)(iv)(C)(2) . . . 4:91
29 C.F.R. § 2550.408b-2(c)(1)(iv)(C)(3) . . . 4:92, 4:94
29 C.F.R. § 2550.408b-2(c)(1)(iv)(C)(4) . . . 4:94
29 C.F.R. § 2550.408b-2(c)(1)(iv)(D) 4:81, 4:85
29 C.F.R. § 2550.408b-2(c)(1)(iv)(E) 4:88
29 C.F.R. § 2550.408b-2(c)(1)(iv)(F) 4:79, 4:80
29 C.F.R. § 2550.408b-2(c)(1)(iv)(F)(2) . . . 4:86
29 C.F.R. § 2550.408b-2(c)(1)(v) 4:97
29 C.F.R. § 2550.408b-2(c)(1)(v)(A) 4:69, 4:98
29 C.F.R. § 2550.408b-2(c)(1)(vi) 4:98
29 C.F.R. § 2550.408b-2(c)(1)(vi)(B)(2) 4:98
29 C.F.R. § 2550.408b-2(c)(1)(vi)(G) 4:96
29 C.F.R. § 2550.408b-2(c)(1)(vii) 4:99
29 C.F.R. § 2550.408b-2(c)(1)(viii)(A) 4:74
29 C.F.R. § 2550.408b-2(c)(1)(viii)(B) 4:77
29 C.F.R. § 2550.408b-2(c)(1)(viii)(B)(3) . . . 4:95
29 C.F.R. § 2550.408b-2(c)(1)(viii)(C) 4:87, 4:88
29 C.F.R. § 2550.408b-2(c)(1)(viii)(D) 4:82
29 C.F.R. § 2550.408b-2(c)(1)(viii)(E) 4:71
29 C.F.R. § 2550.408b-2(c)(1)(viii)(F) 4:75
29 C.F.R. § 2550.408b-2(c)(1)(ix) 4:99
29 C.F.R. § 2550.408b-2(c)(1)(xii) 4:67
29 C.F.R. § 2560.503-1(b) 16:142
29 C.F.R. § 2560.503-1(e) 16:141
29 C.F.R. § 2560.503-1(f)(1) 16:143
29 C.F.R. § 2560.503-1(f)(3) 16:143
29 C.F.R. § 2560.503-1(g) 16:144
29 C.F.R. § 2560.503-1(h)(1) 16:145
29 C.F.R. § 2560.503-1(h)(2) 16:145
29 C.F.R. § 2560.503-1(h)(4) 16:145
29 C.F.R. § 2560.503-1(i) 16:147
29 C.F.R. § 2560.503-1(j) 16:146
29 C.F.R. § 2580.412 . . . . 5:52

Treasury Regulations

[References are to question numbers.]

Treas. Reg. §

1.72-16(b)(1) 18:46
1.72-16(b)(2) 18:46
1.72-16(c) 18:33
1.72(p)-1 . . . . 15:28
1.72(p)-1, Q&A 3 . . . . 15:15, 15:16
1.72(p)-1, Q&A 4(a) 15:19
1.72(p)-1, Q&A 5 . . . . 15:32
1.72(p)-1, Q&A 6 . . . . 15:32
1.72(p)-1, Q&A 7 . . . . 15:32
1.72(p)-1, Q&A 8 . . . . 15:32
1.72(p)-1, Q&A 9 . . . . 15:33
1.72(p)-1, Q&A 9(b) 15:34
1.72(p)-1, Q&A 10 . . . . 15:19
1.72(p)-1, Q&A 11 . . . . 15:18
1.72(p)-1, Q&A 13 . . . . 15:21
1.72(p)-1, Q&A 14 . . . . 15:20
1.72(p)-1, Q&A 19 . . . . 15:22, 15:23
1.72(p)-1, Q&A 19(b)(2) 15:24
1.72(p)-1, Q&A 19(b)(3) 15:24
1.72(p)-1, Q&A 20 . . . . 15:36
1.72(p)-1, Q&A 21 . . . . 15:25
1.72(p)-1, Q&A 22 . . . . 15:15, 15:23
1.72(p)-1, Q&A 22(c) 15:26
1.83-3 . . . . 22:100
1.401-1(a)(2) 2:143, 2:149
1.401-1(a)(3)(i) 2:150
1.401-1(b)(1)(ii) 2:151, 15:58
1.401-1(b)(2) 2:152, 21:1
1.401(a)-1(b)(4) 21:5
1.401(a)(4)-2 . . . . 2:101
1.401(a)(4)-2(b)(1) 12:1
1.401(a)(4)-2(b)(2) 12:2
1.401(a)(4)-2(b)(3) 12:4
1.401(a)(4)-2(b)(3)(i)(A) 2:103, 12:5
1.401(a)(4)-2(b)(3)(i)(B) 2:103, 12:6
1.401(a)(4)-2(b)(4)(iii) 12:7
1.401(a)(4)-2(b)(4)(vi)(D)(3) 12:8
1.401(a)(4)-2(c)(1) 12:9, 12:10
1.401(a)(4)-2(c)(2)(i) 12:11
1.401(a)(4)-2(c)(2)(ii) 12:12
1.401(a)(4)-2(c)(3) 12:13
1.401(a)(4)-4 . . . . 16:3
1.401(a)(4)-4(a) 6:81, 12:26, 12:30
1.401(a)(4)-4(b) 6:81
1.401(a)(4)-4(b)(1) 12:31
1.401(a)(4)-4(b)(2) 12:32
1.401(a)(4)-4(b)(2)(ii)(A) 12:33
1.401(a)(4)-4(b)(2)(ii)(B) 12:34
1.401(a)(4)-4(b)(2)(ii)(C) 12:34
1.401(a)(4)-4(b)(2)(ii)(D) 12:34
1.401(a)(4)-4(b)(2)(ii)(E) 12:34, 15:3
1.401(a)(4)-4(b)(3) 12:35
1.401(a)(4)-4(c) 6:81, 12:36
1.401(a)(4)-4(c)(2), Ex. 2 . . . . 6:81
1.401(a)(4)-4(e)(1)(i) 12:27
1.401(a)(4)-4(e)(2) 12:28
1.401(a)(4)-4(e)(3) 7:6, 7:7, 12:29
1.401(a)(4)-4(e)(3)(iii)(G) 13:49
1.401(a)(4)-8 . . . . 2:107, 2:119
1.401(a)(4)-8(b) 12:14
1.401(a)(4)-8(b)(1)(vi) 2:114, 14:36
1.401(a)(4)-8(b)(2) 2:108
1.401(a)(4)-10(c) 15:3
1.401(a)(4)-11(b)(1) 2:140
1.401(a)(4)-11(g)(3)(iv) 11:34
1.401(a)(4)-11(g)(3)(vii) 11:32, 11:33
1.401(a)(4)-12 . . . . 12:3
1.401(a)(9)-2, Q&A 2(e) 16:30
1.401(a)(9)-2, Q&A 4 . . . . 16:43
1.401(a)(9)-3, Q&A 1 . . . . 16:35
1.401(a)(9)-3, Q&A 1(a) 16:34
1.401(a)(9)-3, Q&A 2 . . . . 16:35
1.401(a)(9)-3, Q&A 3(b) 16:39
1.401(a)(9)-3, Q&A 4 . . . . 16:35
1.401(a)(9)-4, Q&A 1 . . . . 16:36
1.401(a)(9)-4, Q&A 3 . . . . 16:37
1.401(a)(9)-4, Q&A 5 . . . . 16:37
1.401(a)(9)-5, Q&A 1 . . . . 16:45

Treas. Reg. §

1.401(a)(9)-5, Q&A 3 . . . . 16:46
1.401(a)(9)-5, Q&A 4 . . . . 16:45
1.401(a)(9)-5, Q&A 4(b) 16:45
1.401(a)(9)-5, Q&A 5 . . . . 16:47
1.401(a)(9)-5, Q&A 5(b) 16:38
1.401(a)(9)-5, Q&A 6 . . . . 16:38, 16:47
1.401(a)(9)-6, Q&A 17 . . . . 16:46
1.401(a)(9)-8, Q&A 13 . . . . 16:32
1.401(a)(9)-8, Q&A 16 . . . . 16:33
1.401(a)-12 . . . . 2:159
1.401(a)-13(b) 2:155
1.401(a)-13(b)(2) 2:156
1.401(a)-13(d)(1) 2:156
1.401(a)-13(d)(2) 2:156, 15:14
1.401(a)-13(e) 2:156
1.401(a)-13(g)(2) 17:58
1.401(a)-13(g)(3) 17:63
1.401(a)-14(a) 16:13
1.401(a)-14(b) 16:15
1.401(a)-14(c) 16:14
1.401(a)(17)-1(a)(3)(i) 10:105
1.401(a)(17)-1(b)(1) 10:106
1.401(a)(17)-1(c)(1) 10:106
1.401(a)-20, Q&A 3(a) 17:1
1.401(a)-20, Q&A 3(b)(1) 17:49
1.401(a)-20, Q&A 5 . . . . 21:25
1.401(a)-20, Q&A 5(a) 17:2, 17:3
1.401(a)-20, Q&A 5(b) 17:4
1.401(a)-20, Q&A 8(a) 17:9
1.401(a)-20, Q&A 8(b) 17:18
1.401(a)-20, Q&A 10(b) 17:14
1.401(a)-20, Q&A 17(a) 17:16
1.401(a)-20, Q&A 17(b) 17:17
1.401(a)-20, Q&A 20 . . . . 17:10
1.401(a)-20, Q&A 22(b) 17:15
1.401(a)-20, Q&A 24(a) 17:45
1.401(a)-20, Q&A 24(a)(1) 15:41
1.401(a)-20, Q&A 24(b) 17:46
1.401(a)-20, Q&A 24(d) 17:47
1.401(a)-20, Q&A 25(a) 17:11
1.401(a)-20, Q&A 27 . . . . 17:48
1.401(a)-20, Q&A 29 . . . . 17:32
1.401(a)-20, Q&A 30 . . . . 17:31
1.401(a)-20, Q&A 31(a) 17:19, 17:20, 17:29, 17:30
1.401(a)-20, Q&A 31(b) 17:20, 17:29, 17:30
1.401(a)-20, Q&A 31(c) 17:30
1.401(a)-20, Q&A 32 . . . . 17:50
1.401(a)-20, Q&A 33 . . . . 17:50
1.401(a)-20, Q&A 33(b) 17:21
1.401(a)-20, Q&A 35 . . . . 17:26
1.401(a)-20, Q&A 36 . . . . 17:24
1.401(a)-21 . . . . 2:242, 3:35, 15:16, 19:127, 19:130
1.401(a)-21(a) 16:22
1.401(a)-21(a)(1)(i) 19:128

Treas. Reg. §

1.401(a)-21(a)(2)(i) 19:128
1.401(a)-21(a)(2)(iii) 19:128
1.401(a)-21(b) 16:22, 16:90
1.401(a)-21(c) 16:22, 16:90, 17:28
1.401(a)-21(d) 16:23, 17:18
1.401(a)-21(d)(6) 15:41, 17:29, 17:45
1.401(a)(26)-2(a) 11:1
1.401(a)(31)-1, Q&A 1 . . . . 16:64
1.401(a)(31)-1, Q&A 3 . . . . 16:65, 16:87
1.401(a)(31)-1, Q&A 4 . . . . 16:87
1.401(a)(31)-1, Q&A 6 . . . . 16:88
1.401(a)(31)-1, Q&A 8 . . . . 16:93
1.401(a)(31)-1, Q&A 9 . . . . 16:64, 16:66
1.401(a)(31)-1, Q&A 10 . . . . 16:85
1.401(a)(31)-1, Q&A 11 . . . . 16:66
1.401(a)(31)-1, Q&A 12 . . . . 16:91, 16:94
1.401(a)(31)-1, Q&A 13 . . . . 16:68
1.401(a)(31)-1, Q&A 14 . . . . 2:137
1.401(a)(31)-1, Q&A 14(a) 16:68
1.401(a)(31)-1, Q&A 15 . . . . 16:96
1.401(a)(31)-1, Q&A 16 . . . . 15:31, 16:86
1.401(a)(35)-1 . . . . 6:56, 6:58, 6:59
1.401(a)(35)-1(f)(2) 6:55
1.401(b)-5(d)(5) 11:23
1.401(k)-1(a)(1) 1:28
1.401(k)-1(a)(2)(iii) 2:46
1.401(k)-1(a)(3) 2:27
1.401(k)-1(a)(3)(ii) 2:34
1.401(k)-1(a)(3)(iii)(C)(1) 2:30
1.401(k)-1(a)(3)(iii)(C)(2) 2:31
1.401(k)-1(a)(3)(iv) 2:70, 22:161
1.401(k)-1(a)(3)(v) 2:32
1.401(k)-1(a)(4)(ii) 2:75
1.401(k)-1(a)(6)(ii) 2:91
1.401(k)-1(a)(6)(iii) 2:71, 2:72
1.401(k)-1(a)(6)(iv) 2:73
1.401(k)-1(b)(4)(iii)(A) 10:60
1.401(k)-1(b)(4)(iv)(A) 10:62
1.401(k)-1(b)(4)(v)(A) 10:62
1.401(k)-1(b)(4)(v)(B) 10:62
1.401(k)-1(b)(4)(v)(C) 10:62
1.401(k)-1(c) 2:189
1.401(k)-1(d) 15:57
1.401(k)-1(d)(1) 15:60, 21:34
1.401(k)-1(d)(2) 15:60
1.401(k)-1(d)(3) 15:44
1.401(k)-1(d)(3)(ii)(B) 15:54
1.401(k)-1(d)(3)(iii)(A) 15:45
1.401(k)-1(d)(3)(iii)(B) 15:46
1.401(k)-1(d)(3)(iv) 15:53
1.401(k)-1(d)(3)(iv)(B) 15:47
1.401(k)-1(d)(3)(iv)(C) 15:47
1.401(k)-1(d)(3)(iv)(D) 15:47
1.401(k)-1(d)(3)(iv)(E) 15:48
1.401(k)-1(d)(3)(iv)(F) 15:49
1.401(k)-1(d)(4)(i) 21:6, 21:7

Treas. Reg. §

1.401(k)-1(d)(4)(ii) 21:8
1.401(k)-1(d)(5)(iv) 21:25
1.401(k)-1(e)(2)(ii) 2:69
1.401(k)-1(e)(2)(ii) 2:69
1.401(k)-1(e)(4)(iii) 2:147
1.401(k)-1(e)(5) 2:172
1.401(k)-1(e)(6) 22:101
1.401(k)-1(e)(6)(i) 2:94
1.401(k)-1(f)(1)(i) 2:79, 2:80
1.401(k)-1(f)(1)(ii) 2:78
1.401(k)-1(f)(3) 2:82
1.401(k)-1(f)(4) 2:83
1.401(k)-1(f)(4)(ii) 16:66
1.401(k)-1(f)(5)(ii) 2:81
1.401(k)-2(1)(6)(ii) 13:14
1.401(k)-2(a) 13:2
1.401(k)-2(a)(1)(iii) 13:36
1.401(k)-2(a)(1)(iii)(A) 13:38
1.401(k)-2(a)(2) 13:3
1.401(k)-2(a)(2)(ii) 13:4, 13:5, 13:8
1.401(k)-2(a)(3) 13:3
1.401(k)-2(a)(3)(i) 13:7
1.401(k)-2(a)(3)(ii) 13:10
1.401(k)-2(a)(4) 2:76
1.401(k)-2(a)(5)(iv) 13:7
1.401(k)-2(a)(5)(v) 13:4
1.401(k)-2(a)(5)(vi) 2:49, 13:4
1.401(k)-2(a)(6)(i) 13:13
1.401(k)-2(a)(6)(iv)(A) 13:43
1.401(k)-2(a)(6)(iv)(B) 13:44
1.401(k)-2(a)(6)(iv)(C) 13:45
1.401(k)-2(b)(1) 13:15
1.401(k)-2(b)(1)(iii) 13:16
1.401(k)-2(b)(2)(ii) 13:17
1.401(k)-2(b)(2)(iii) 13:18
1.401(k)-2(b)(2)(iv)(B) 13:25
1.401(k)-2(b)(2)(iv)(C) 13:25
1.401(k)-2(b)(2)(iv)(D) 13:26
1.401(k)-2(b)(2)(v) 13:23, 18:57
1.401(k)-2(b)(2)(vi) 18:86
1.401(k)-2(b)(2)(vi)(A) 13:29, 13:31, 13:32
1.401(k)-2(b)(2)(vi)(B) 13:29
1.401(k)-2(b)(2)(vi)(C) 13:30
1.401(k)-2(b)(2)(vii)(A) 13:28
1.401(k)-2(b)(2)(vii)(B) 13:27
1.401(k)-2(b)(2)(vii)(C) 13:33
1.401(k)-2(b)(3)(ii) 13:19
1.401(k)-2(b)(3)(iii)(A) 13:22
1.401(k)-2(b)(3)(iii)(B) 13:21
1.401(k)-2(b)(3)(iv)(D) 13:24
1.401(k)-2(b)(5)(i) 13:35
1.401(k)-2(b)(5)(ii) 13:34, 18:58
1.401(k)-2(b)(5)(iii) 13:35
1.401(k)-2(c)(1) 13:5
1.401(k)-2(c)(2)(i) 13:9
1.401(k)-2(c)(2)(iii) 2:240

Treas. Reg. §

1.401(k)-3 . . . . 2:254
1.401(k)-3(b) 2:246, 2:247
1.401(k)-3(b)(2) 2:259
1.401(k)-3(c) 2:246, 2:247
1.401(k)-3(c)(3) 2:248
1.401(k)-3(c)(4) 2:248
1.401(k)-3(c)(5)(ii) 2:260
1.401(k)-3(c)(6) 2:258
1.401(k)-3(d)(2)(ii) 2:243
1.401(k)-3(d)(2)(iii) 2:244
1.401(k)-3(d)(3) 2:241
1.401(k)-3(e)(1) 2:240, 2:269
1.401(k)-3(e)(2) 2:240
1.401(k)-3(f) 2:249
1.401(k)-3(g) 2:253
1.401(k)-3(h)(2) 2:265
1.401(k)-3(h)(4) 2:268
1.401(k)-3(j)(1) 2:67
1.401(k)-3(j)(1)(i) 2:52
1.401(k)-3(j)(1)(ii) 2:52
1.401(k)-3(j)(1)(iii) 2:66
1.401(k)-3(j)(2) 2:57
1.401(k)-3(j)(2)(i) 2:59
1.401(k)-3(j)(2)(ii) 2:58
1.401(k)-3(k)(2) 2:60
1.401(k)-3(k)(3) 2:63
1.401(k)-3(k)(4) 2:53, 2:55
1.401(k)-3(k)(4)(iii) 2:54
1.401(k)-4(b) 2:221
1.401(k)-4(c) 2:228
1.401(k)-4(d) 2:225
1.401(k)-4(e)(1) 2:227
1.401(k)-4(e)(2) 2:223, 2:225
1.401(k)-4(e)(3) 2:225, 2:230
1.401(k)-4(e)(4) 2:231
1.401(k)-4(f) 2:233
1.401(k)-4(g) 2:237
1.401(k)-6 . . . . 2:27, 2:193,
13:11–13:13, 20:7
1.401(*l*)- 1(c)(4) 12:15
1.401(*l*)- 1(c)(15) 12:15
1.401(*l*)- 2(a)(1) 12:15
1.401(*l*)- 2(b) 12:17
1.401(*l*)- 2(d) 12:16
1.401(*l*)- 2(d)(4) 12:18
1.401(*l*)- 5(b) 12:23
1.401(*l*)- 5(c)(1) 12:24
1.401(m)-1(a)(2) 2:86
1.401(m)-1(a)(3) 13:58
1.401(m)-1(a)(3)(i)(C) 13:66
1.401(m)-1(b)(4)(v) 10:62
1.401(m)-2(a)(1) 13:47
1.401(m)-2(a)(1)(iii) 13:62
1.401(m)-2(a)(2) 13:48
1.401(m)-2(a)(2)(ii) 13:55
1.401(m)-2(a)(3) 13:48

Treas. Reg. §

1.401(m)-2(a)(3)(ii) 13:57
1.401(m)-2(a)(4)(ii) 13:49
1.401(m)-2(a)(5)(ii) 13:50
1.401(m)-2(a)(5)(ii)(B) 13:51
1.401(m)-2(a)(5)(ii)(C) 13:52
1.401(m)-2(a)(5)(iii) 13:14, 13:49
1.401(m)-2(a)(5)(v) 13:49
1.401(m)-2(a)(5)(vi) 13:49
1.401(m)-2(a)(6) 13:62, 13:78
1.401(m)-2(a)(6)(ii) 13:61
1.401(m)-2(a)(6)(iii) 13:61
1.401(m)-2(b)(1) 13:62
1.401(m)-2(b)(1)(iii) 13:63
1.401(m)-2(b)(2)(ii) 13:64
1.401(m)-2(b)(2)(iii) 13:65
1.401(m)-2(b)(2)(iv)(B) 13:69
1.401(m)-2(b)(2)(iv)(C) 13:69
1.401(m)-2(b)(2)(iv)(D) 13:68, 13:70
1.401(m)-2(b)(2)(v) 13:67
1.401(m)-2(b)(2)(vi) 18:57, 18:86
1.401(m)-2(b)(2)(vi)(A) 13:74, 13:75
1.401(m)-2(b)(2)(vi)(B) 13:73
1.401(m)-2(b)(3)(i) 13:77
1.401(m)-2(b)(3)(ii) 13:72
1.401(m)-2(b)(3)(iii) 13:76
1.401(m)-2(b)(3)(v)(B) 13:63, 13:71
1.401(m)-2(b)(4) 13:78
1.401(m)-2(b)(4)(ii) 18:58
1.401(m)-2(b)(4)(iii) 13:78
1.401(m)-2(c)(1) 13:53
1.401(m)-2(c)(2) 13:56
1.401(m)-3(d) 2:250
1.401(m)-3(d)(3) 2:250
1.401(m)-3(d)(6) 2:258
1.401(m)-3(f)(1) 2:269
1.401(m)-3(h) 2:253, 2:254
1.401(m)-3(j)(2) 2:265
1.401(m)-3(j)(4) 2:268
1.401(m)-3(j)(6) 2:262
1.401(m)-5 . . . . 13:59, 13:60
1.402(c)-2, Q&A 2 . . . . 16:67
1.402(c)-2, Q&A 3 . . . . 16:56, 18:101
1.402(c)-2, Q&A 4 . . . . 16:57
1.402(c)-2, Q&A 4(a) 9:21
1.402(c)-2, Q&A 4(d) 15:18, 16:112
1.402(c)-2, Q&A 5(a) 16:58
1.402(c)-2, Q&A 5(c) 16:59
1.402(c)-2, Q&A 6 . . . . 16:59
1.402(c)-2, Q&A 7 . . . . 16:60
1.402(c)-2, Q&A 9 . . . . 15:31, 16:112
1.402(c)-2, Q&A 11 . . . . 16:80
1.402(f)-1, Q&A 1 . . . . 16:89, 16:91
1.402(f)-1, Q&A 1(b) 16:92
1.402(f)-1, Q&A 2(a) 16:90
1.402(f)-1, Q&A 3 . . . . 16:91, 16:94
1.402(g)-1(a) 9:7

Treas. Reg. §

1.402(g)-1(b) 9:3
1.402(g)-1(b)(5) 9:4
1.402(g)-1(d)(1) 9:2
1.402(g)-1(e)(1) 9:6
1.402(g)-1(e)(1)(ii) 9:14
1.402(g)-1(e)(2) 9:6
1.402(g)-1(e)(2)(i) 9:7
1.402(g)-1(e)(2)(ii) 9:11
1.402(g)-1(e)(3) 9:10
1.402(g)-1(e)(4) 9:8, 9:9
1.402(g)-1(e)(5)(i) 9:12
1.402(g)-1(e)(5)(ii) 9:13
1.402(g)-1(e)(5)(iii) 9:13
1.402(g)-1(e)(6) 9:15
1.402(g)-1(e)(7) 9:16
1.402(g)-1(e)(8) 18:86
1.402(g)-1(e)(8)(i) 9:17, 9:18, 9:19, 18:55
1.402(g)-1(e)(8)(iii) 9:22
1.402(g)-1(e)(8)(iv) 9:21, 9:22, 9:23, 18:65
1.402(g)-1(e)(9) 9:20
1.402(g)-2(b) 9:34
1.402A-1, Q&A 2 . . . . 18:61
1.402A-1, Q&A 3 . . . . 18:62
1.402A-1, Q&A 4 . . . . 18:60
1.402A-1, Q&A 4(a) 18:60
1.402A-1, Q&A 4(b) 18:77
1.402A-1, Q&A 5 . . . . 18:67
1.402A-1, Q&A 5(c) 18:77
1.402A-1, Q&A 7 . . . . 15:56
1.402A-1, Q&A 8 . . . . 15:56, 18:64
1.402A-1, Q&A 9(b) 18:81
1.402A-1, Q&A 10 . . . . 18:66
1.402A-1, Q&A 11 . . . . 15:30, 18:61, 18:63, 18:66
1.402A-1, Q&A 12 . . . . 15:30
1.402A-2, Q&A 1 . . . . 18:80
1.402A-2, Q&A 2 . . . . 18:80
1.403(b)-2 . . . . 22:161
1.403(b)-3(a) 22:122
1.403(b)-3(a)(2) 22:124
1.403(b)-3(a)(3) 22:124
1.403(b)-3(a)(5) 22:124
1.403(b)-3(a)(6) 22:124
1.403(b)-3(b)(1) 22:124
1.403(b)-3(b)(3) 22:123
1.403(b)-3(c) 22:124
1.403(b)-4(b) 22:138
1.403(b)-4(c) 22:133, 22:135
1.403(b)-4(c)(3)(iv) 22:136
1.403(b)-4(d) 22:139, 22:161
1.403(b)-4(e) 22:124
1.403(b)-5(a)(1) 22:124
1.403(b)-5(a)(5) 22:124

Treas. Reg. §

1.403(b)-5(b) 22:124
1.403(b)-5(b)(2) 22:129
1.403(b)-6 . . . . 22:141
1.403(b)-6(b) 22:124
1.403(b)-10(a) 22:125
1.403(b)-10(b)(4) 22:124
1.404(a)-3(d) 4:43
1.404(a)-9(c) 9:58
1.408(q)-1(b) 2:121
1.408(q)-1(c) 14:23
1.408(q)-1(d)(1) 2:122
1.408(q)-1(d)(2) 2:123
1.408(q)-1(e) 2:125
1.408(q)-1(f)(1) 2:124
1.408(q)-1(f)(2)(i) 2:123
1.408(q)-1(f)(4) 2:128
1.408(q)-1(f)(6) 2:126
1.408(q)-1(g) 2:129
1.408A-10, Q&A 4 . . . . 18:77
1.409A-6(a)(4) 22:107
1.410(a)-4(b)(1) 2:178
1.410(a)-5(c)(1) 2:181
1.410(a)-5(c)(3) 2:183
1.410(a)-7 . . . . 2:176
1.410(b)-2(b)(2) 11:4
1.410(b)-2(b)(3) 11:9
1.410(b)-2(b)(5) 11:2
1.410(b)-2(b)(6) 11:2
1.410(b)-2(b)(7) 11:2
1.410(b)-2(f) 11:2
1.410(b)-3(a)(1) 11:5
1.410(b)-3(a)(2)(i) 11:5
1.410(b)-3(a)(2)(ii) 11:5
1.410(b)-4(a) 11:10
1.410(b)-4(b) 11:11
1.410(b)-4(c)(2) 11:12
1.410(b)-4(c)(3) 11:12
1.410(b)-4(c)(3)(ii) 11:16
1.410(b)-4(c)(4)(i) 11:13
1.410(b)-4(c)(4)(ii) 11:14
1.410(b)-4(c)(4)(iii) 11:15
1.410(b)-5(a) 11:18
1.410(b)-5(b) 11:19
1.410(b)-5(c) 11:20
1.410(b)-5(d)(3)(i) 11:21
1.410(b)-5(d)(3)(ii) 11:22
1.410(b)-5(e)(3) 11:23
1.410(b)-6(a)(2) 11:24
1.410(b)-6(b)(1) 11:25
1.410(b)-6(b)(2) 11:25
1.410(b)-6(c) 11:25
1.410(b)-6(d) 11:25
1.410(b)-6(d)(2)(i) 11:25
1.410(b)-6(d)(2)(iii)(B)(1) 11:25
1.410(b)-6(e) 11:25
1.410(b)-6(f) 11:25

Treas. Reg. §

1.410(b)-6(g) 11:25
1.410(b)-7(b) 10:60
1.410(b)-7(c)(1) 10:62
1.410(b)-7(c)(2) 10:62
1.410(b)-7(c)(3) 13:15
1.410(b)-7(c)(4)(ii)(A) 10:62
1.410(b)-7(c)(4)(ii)(B) 10:62
1.410(b)-7(c)(4)(ii)(C) 10:62
1.410(b)-7(d) 11:6, 11:17
1.410(b)-7(d)(4) 11:8
1.410(b)-7(e)(1) 11:21
1.410(b)-7(e)(2) 11:21
1.410(b)-8(a) 11:26
1.410(b)-8(a)(2) 11:27
1.410(b)-8(a)(3) 11:28
1.410(b)-8(a)(4) 11:29
1.410(b)-9 . . . . 11:25
1.411(a)-1(a)(1) 2:191
1.411(a)-1(a)(2) 2:193
1.411(a)-4(b)(6) 21:10
1.411(a)-5(a) 2:199
1.411(a)-5(b)(3) 2:197
1.411(a)-5(b)(3)(v) 2:198
1.411(a)-5(i) 19:132
1.411(a)-6(c)(1)(i) 2:202
1.411(a)-7(d)(4) 2:213
1.411(a)-7(d)(4)(iii) 2:214
1.411(a)-7(d)(4)(iv) 2:216
1.411(a)-7(d)(4)(iv)(C) 2:218
1.411(a)-7(d)(4)(v) 2:217
1.411(a)-7(d)(5) 13:62
1.411(a)-7(d)(6)(iii)(C) 2:219
1.411(a)-8(a) 2:207
1.411(a)-11(c) 16:16
1.411(a)-11(c)(2) 4:60
1.411(a)-11(c)(2)(i) 16:17
1.411(a)-11(c)(2)(iii)(A) 16:19
1.411(a)-11(c)(2)(iii)(B) 16:20
1.411(a)-11(c)(2)(iii)(B)(3) 16:21
1.411(a)-11(c)(4) 16:24
1.411(a)-11(c)(5) 16:25
1.411(a)-11(c)(6) 16:26
1.411(d)-2(a)(1) 2:191, 21:3, 21:15
1.411(d)-2(a)(1)(ii) 21:16
1.411(d)-2(b)(1) 21:14, 21:17
1.411(d)-2(b)(3) 21:15
1.411(d)-2(c)(3) 21:4
1.411(d)-2(d)(1) 21:16
1.411(d)-3(a)(3) 2:210
1.411(d)-3(b)(1)(i) 16:3, 16:6
1.411(d)-3(b)(3)(i) 16:2
1.411(d)-3(g)(6)(ii) 16:1
1.411(d)-4, Q&A 1(b)(1) 16:1
1.411(d)-4, Q&A 1(d) 16:2
1.411(d)-4, Q&A 1(d)(4) 15:42

Treas. Reg. §

1.411(d)-4, Q&A 2(a) 16:6
1.411(d)-4, Q&A 2(a)(1) 16:3, 16:6
1.411(d)-4, Q&A 2(a)(3) 21:24
1.411(d)-4, Q&A 2(b)(2)(iii) 16:8
1.411(d)-4, Q&A 2(b)(2)(v) 16:7
1.411(d)-4, Q&A 2(b)(2)(vii) 15:42
1.411(d)-4, Q&A 2(b)(2)(x) 16:7
1.411(d)-4, Q&A 2(e) 16:7
1.411(d)-4, Q&A 3(a)(3) 16:9
1.411(d)-4, Q&A 3(b) 2:135, 16:12, 17:2
1.411(d)-4, Q&A 3(b)(2) 2:139
1.411(d)-4, Q&A 4 . . . . 16:4
1.411(d)-4, Q&A 4(a) 16:3
1.411(d)-4, Q&A 4(b) 16:5
1.411(d)-4, Q&A 6(a) 16:5
1.414(c)-2(a) 10:2
1.414(c)-2(b)(1) 10:3
1.414(c)-2(b)(2) 10:4
1.414(c)-2(c)(1) 10:5
1.414(c)-2(c)(2) 10:6
1.414(c)-2(d) 10:7
1.414(c)-3(a) 10:8
1.414(c)-3(b)(1) 10:9
1.414(c)-3(b)(3) 10:9
1.414(c)-3(b)(4) 10:9
1.414(c)-3(b)(5) 10:9
1.414(c)-3(b)(6) 10:9
1.414(c)-3(c)(1) 10:9
1.414(c)-3(c)(2) 10:9
1.414(c)-3(c)(3) 10:9
1.414(c)-3(c)(4) 10:9
1.414(c)-3(d)(2) 10:10
1.414(c)-3(d)(3) 10:11
1.414(c)-3(d)(6) 10:12
1.414(c)-4(b)(1) 10:13
1.414(c)-4(b)(2) 10:15
1.414(c)-4(b)(3) 10:17
1.414(c)-4(b)(4) 10:16
1.414(c)-4(b)(5)(i) 10:18
1.414(c)-4(b)(5)(ii) 10:19
1.414(c)-4(b)(6)(i) 10:20
1.414(c)-4(b)(6)(ii) 10:20
1.414(c)-4(c)(1) 10:21
1.414(c)-4(c)(2) 10:21
1.414(c)-4(c)(3) 10:13
1.414(c)-5(b) 10:22
1.414(g)-1(b)(1) 19:1
1.414(*l*)-1 . . . . 19:21
1.414(*l*)-1(b)(1) 10:59
1.414(*l*)-1(b)(2) 21:18
1.414(*l*)-1(b)(4) 21:20
1.414(*l*)-1(d) 21:19
1.414(*l*)-1(m) 21:21
1.414(r)-1(b)(2)(iv)(B) 10:41
1.414(r)-1(b)(2)(iv)(C) 10:41

Treas. Reg. §

1.414(r)-1(b)(2)(iv)(D) 10:41
1.414(r)-1(c)(2)(ii) 11:7
1.414(r)-2(a) 10:42
1.414(r)-2(b)(1) 10:43
1.414(r)-2(b)(2) 10:42
1.414(r)-2(b)(3)(i) 10:43
1.414(r)-2(b)(3)(ii) 10:44
1.414(r)-2(b)(3)(iii) 10:45
1.414(r)-3(a) 10:46
1.414(r)-3(b)(2) 10:46
1.414(r)-3(b)(3) 10:46
1.414(r)-3(b)(4) 10:46, 10:47
1.414(r)-3(b)(5) 10:46, 10:51
1.414(r)-3(c)(5)(i) 10:49
1.414(r)-5(a) 10:53
1.414(r)-5(b)(1) 10:54
1.414(r)-5(b)(2) 10:55
1.414(r)-5(b)(4) 10:54
1.414(r)-5(c) 10:56
1.414(r)-5(d) 10:56
1.414(r)-5(e) 10:56
1.414(r)-5(f) 10:56
1.414(r)-5(g) 10:56
1.414(r)-6 . . . . 10:53
1.414(r)-7(b)(2)(i) 10:57
1.414(r)-7(c)(2) 10:57
1.414(r)-7(c)(3) 10:57
1.414(r)-7(c)(4) 10:57
1.414(r)-8(b)(2) 11:21
1.414(r)-11(b)(2) 10:48
1.414(r)-11(b)(3) 10:52
1.414(r)-11(b)(4) 10:58
1.414(s)-1(a)(2) 10:103
1.414(s)-1(c)(2) 10:92
1.414(s)-1(c)(3) 10:92
1.414(s)-1(c)(5) 10:94
1.414(s)-1(d)(1) 10:95
1.414(s)-1(d)(2) 2:67, 2:258, 2:267
1.414(s)-1(d)(2)(iii) 10:97
1.414(s)-1(d)(3)(i) 10:98
1.414(s)-1(d)(3)(ii) 10:99
1.414(s)-1(d)(3)(iv)(A) 10:99
1.414(s)-1(d)(3)(iv)(B) 10:100
1.414(s)-1(d)(3)(v) 10:101
1.414(s)-1(g)(1) 10:102
1.414(v)-1(b)(1)(i) 9:28
1.414(v)-1(b)(1)(ii) 9:25
1.414(v)-1(b)(1)(iii) 9:29
1.414(v)-1(b)(2)(i)(B)(1) 9:27
1.414(v)-1(c)(2)(i) 9:24
1.414(v)-1(c)(2)(iii) 9:24
1.414(v)-1(d) 9:31
1.414(v)-1(d)(2) 13:4
1.414(v)-1(d)(3) 14:24
1.414(v)-1(e)(1)(i) 9:33

Treas. Reg. §

1.414(v)-1(e)(2) 9:32
1.414(v)-1(e)(4) 9:32
1.414(w)-1(b)(2) 2:43
1.414(w)-1(b)(2)(i)(A) 9:26
1.414(w)-1(d) 2:49, 18:93
1.414(w)-1(d)(1)(ii) 18:86
1.414(w)-1(d)(1)(iv) 9:3
1.414(w)-1(e)(3) 2:45
1.415-7(h) 22:161
1.415-8(d) 22:161
1.415(c)-1(b) 9:42
1.415(c)-1(b)(1)(ii) 13:27
1.415(c)-1(b)(1)(iii) 9:43
1.415(c)-1(b)(1)(iv) 9:43
1.415(c)-1(b)(2)(ii) 9:43
1.415(c)-1(b)(2)(ii)(C) 9:69, 9:70, 9:71
1.415(c)-1(b)(2)(ii)(D) 9:14
1.415(c)-1(b)(3) 9:43
1.415(c)-1(e) 9:42
1.415(c)-1(f) 9:44
1.415(c)-2(b) 9:46
1.415(c)-2(b)(1) 9:49
1.415(c)-2(c) 9:46
1.415(c)-2(d)(2) 9:48
1.415(c)-2(d)(3) 9:48, 9:49
1.415(c)-2(d)(4) 9:48, 9:49
1.415(c)-2(e)(3) 9:47
1.415(c)-2(e)(4) 9:47
1.415(c)-2(f) 10:106
1.415(d)-1(b)(2)(iii) 9:41
1.415(f)-1(a)(2) 9:42
1.416-1, Q&A M-7 . . . . 14:32–14:34, 14:38
1.416-1, Q&A M-8 . . . . 14:40
1.416-1, Q&A M-10 . . . . 14:39
1.416-1, Q&A M-12 . . . . 14:41
1.416-1, Q&A M-18 . . . . 14:38
1.416-1, Q&A M-20 . . . . 14:38
1.416-1, Q&A T-1(a) 14:1
1.416-1, Q&A T-1(b) 14:3
1.416-1, Q&A T-1(c) 14:2
1.416-1, Q&A T-1(d) 14:4
1.416-1, Q&A T-6 . . . . 14:5
1.416-1, Q&A T-7 . . . . 14:6
1.416-1, Q&A T-9 . . . . 14:2
1.416-1, Q&A T-11 . . . . 14:7, 14:8
1.416-1, Q&A T-13 . . . . 14:12
1.416-1, Q&A T-14 . . . . 14:15, 14:16
1.416-1, Q&A T-16 . . . . 14:11
1.416-1, Q&A T-17 . . . . 14:10
1.416-1, Q&A T-20 . . . . 14:10, 14:11
1.416-1, Q&A T-22 . . . . 14:18, 14:19
1.416-1, Q&A T-23 . . . . 14:18
1.416-1, Q&A T-24 . . . . 14:20
1.416-1, Q&A T-25 . . . . 14:21
1.416-1, Q&A T-26 . . . . 14:22

Treas. Reg. §

1.416-1, Q&A T-30 . . . . 14:25
1.416-1, Q&A T-31 . . . . 14:26
1.416-1, Q&A T-32 . . . . 14:27
1.416-1, Q&A V-2 . . . . 14:30
1.416-1, Q&A V-3 . . . . 14:31
1.417(a)(3)-1 . . . . 17:24
1.417(a)(3)-1(c)(3) 17:25
1.417(a)(3)-1(c)(4) 17:25
1.417(e)-1(b)(1) 17:16
1.417(e)-1(b)(2)(i) 16:24
1.417(e)-1(b)(3) 17:27
1.417(e)-1(b)(3)(ii) 16:19, 16:90
1.451-2(a) 22:94
1.457-4(b) 22:172
1.457-6(c)(1)(ii) 22:180
1.457-6(c)(1)(iii) 22:180
1.457-6(c)(2)(i) 22:181
1.457-8(a) 22:165
1.457-8(b) 22:165
1.457-8(b)(1) 22:166
1.457-10(a) 22:185
1.457-10(a)(3) 22:186
1.457-10(b) 22:185
1.457-10(d) 22:166
1.457-11(a)(3) 22:100
1.457-11(a)(4) 22:100
1.1563-1(a) 10:2
1.1563-1(a)(2)(i) 10:3, 10:4
1.1563-1(a)(3)(i) 10:5, 10:6
1.1563-1(a)(4) 10:7
1.1563-2(a) 10:8
1.1563-2(b)(1) 10:9
1.1563-2(b)(2)(i) 10:9
1.1563-2(b)(2)(ii) 10:9, 10:10, 10:11
1.1563-2(b)(2)(iii) 10:9
1.1563-2(b)(2)(iv) 10:9
1.1563-2(b)(3) 10:9
1.1563-2(b)(4)(i) 10:9
1.1563-2(b)(4)(ii) 10:9, 10:12
1.1563-2(b)(4)(iii) 10:9
1.1563-3(b)(1) 10:13
1.1563-3(b)(2) 10:15
1.1563-3(b)(3) 10:17
1.1563-3(b)(4) 10:16
1.1563-3(b)(5)(i) 10:18
1.1563-3(b)(5)(ii) 10:19
1.1563-3(b)(6)(i) 10:20
1.1563-3(b)(6)(ii) 10:20
1.1563-3(c)(1) 10:21
1.1563-3(c)(2) 10:21
1.1563-3(c)(3) 10:13
1.7476-1(b) 3:35
1.7476-2(c) 3:35
31.3102-1(d) 18:5
31.3405(c)-1, Q&A 1 . . . . 16:109, 16:121
31.3405(c)-1, Q&A 2 . . . . 16:110

Treas. Reg. §

31.3405(c)-1, Q&A 4 . . . 16:118
31.3405(c)-1, Q&A 5 . . . 16:118
31.3405(c)-1, Q&A 7 . . . 16:120
31.3405(c)-1, Q&A 7(a) . . . 16:119
31.3405(c)-1, Q&A 9 . . . 16:115
31.3405(c)-1, Q&A 11 . . . 16:113, 16:114, 16:116
31.3405(c)-1, Q&A 12 . . . 16:116
31.3405(c)-1, Q&A 14 . . . 16:66
31.3405(c)-1, Q&A 16 . . . 16:95
31.6051-1(a)(1)(i) . . . 18:7
31.6071(a)-1(a)(1) . . . 16:137
31.6302-1(h) . . . 18:13
31.6302-1(h)(2)(iii) . . . 16:109, 16:138, 18:6
31.6302(c)-3(a)(2) . . . 18:13
31.6302(c)-3(b) . . . 18:13
35.3405-1, Q&A D-35 . . . 16:131
35.3405-1T, Q&A B-3 . . . 16:135
35.3405-1T, Q&A B-7 . . . 16:126
35.3405-1T, Q&A D-1 . . . 16:131
35.3405-1T, Q&A D-5 . . . 16:133
35.3405-1T, Q&A D-9 . . . 16:134
35.3405-1T, Q&A D-10 . . . 16:134
35.3405-1T, Q&A D-12 . . . 16:135
35.3405-1T, Q&A D-18 . . . 16:132
35.3405-1T, Q&A D-22 . . . 16:135
35.3405-1T, Q&A D-26 . . . 16:135
35.3405-1T, Q&A F-1 . . . 16:122
35.3405-1T, Q&A F-2 . . . 16:122
54.4974-1 . . . 2:67
54.4974-2, Q&A 1 . . . 18:88
54.4979-1(c)(1) . . . 2:44
54-4980F-1 . . . 21:23
301.6058-1(a)(4) . . . 19:13
301.6652-3(a)(3) . . . 19:19

Prop. Treas. Reg. §

1.401(a)(9)-6, Q&A-16 . . . 22:124
1.401(a)(35)-1 . . . 6:62
1.401(k)-1(f)(1)(ii) . . . 2:72
1.401(k)-3(g)(1)(ii) . . . 2:254
1.401(k)-3(j)(2) . . . 2:57
1.401(k)-3(j)(2)(i) . . . 2:59
1.401(k)-3(k)(3) . . . 2:63
1.401(k)-4(e)(3) . . . 2:88
1.401(m)-3(h)(1)(ii) . . . 2:254
1.402(e)-2(d)(1)(ii)(B) . . . 18:19
1.402(e)-2(d)(1)(ii)(C) . . . 18:18
1.402(f)-1 . . . 16:90
1.411(a)-1(b)(3)(ii) . . . 16:19

Prop. Treas. Reg. §

1.411(a)-11(c)(2)(i) . . . 16:17
1.411(a)-11(c)(2)(iii)(B) . . . 16:21
1.411(a)-11(c)(2)(vi) . . . 16:18
1.414(m)-1(c) . . . 10:25
1.414(m)-2(a) . . . 10:25
1.414(m)-2(b) . . . 10:28
1.414(m)-2(b)(2) . . . 10:29
1.414(m)-2(c)(1) . . . 10:30
1.414(m)-2(c)(2)(i) . . . 10:31
1.414(m)-2(c)(2)(ii) . . . 10:31
1.414(m)-2(c)(2)(iii) . . . 10:31
1.414(m)-2(c)(2)(iv) . . . 10:32
1.414(m)-2(c)(2)(v) . . . 10:33
1.414(m)-2(c)(3) . . . 10:34
1.414(m)-2(e) . . . 10:26
1.414(m)-2(f)(1) . . . 10:27
1.414(m)-2(f)(2) . . . 10:27
1.414(m)-2(g) . . . 10:35
1.414(m)-5(b) . . . 10:37
1.414(m)-5(c)(1) . . . 10:38
1.414(n)-1(b)(1) . . . 10:71
1.414(n)-1(b)(5) . . . 10:66
1.414(n)-1(b)(10)(i) . . . 10:67
1.414(n)-1(b)(10)(ii) . . . 10:68
1.414(n)-1(b)(13) . . . 10:69
1.414(n)-2(f)(1) . . . 10:74
1.414(w)-1(b)(3) . . . 2:42
1.414(w)-1(c) . . . 2:47, 2:48
1.417(e)-1(b)(3)(ii) . . . 16:90

Temp. Treas. Reg. §

1.411(a)-8T(b)(1) . . . 2:208
1.411(a)-8T(b)(2) . . . 2:209
1.411(a)-8T(b)(3) . . . 2:208
1.414(q)-1T, Q&A 3(c)(2) . . . 10:79
1.414(q)-1T, Q&A 6(a) . . . 10:80
1.414(q)-1T, Q&A 6(c) . . . 10:80
1.414(q)-1T, Q&A 7(a) . . . 10:81
1.414(q)-1T, Q&A 7(b) . . . 10:81
1.414(q)-1T, Q&A 8 . . . 10:82
1.414(q)-1T, Q&A 9(a) . . . 10:83
1.414(q)-1T, Q&A 9(b) . . . 10:84, 14:15
1.414(q)-1T, Q&A 9(c) . . . 10:87
1.414(q)-1T, Q&A 9(e) . . . 10:85
1.414(q)-1T, Q&A 9(f) . . . 10:86
35.3405-1T, Q&A A-9 . . . 16:126
35.3405-1T, Q&A B-8 . . . 16:126
35.3405-1T, Q&A D-11 . . . 16:135
35.3405-1T, Q&A F-2 . . . 16:115
35.3405-1T, Q&A F-7 . . . 16:122

Department of Labor Regulations, Opinions, and Field Bulletins

[*References are to question numbers.*]

DOL Reg. §

825.215(d)(4) 2:188, 2:206
2509.08-2 . . . . 6:85, 6:86
2509.75-4 . . . . 5:131
2509.75-5, FR-10 . . . . 5:66
2509.75-8, D-2 . . . . 5:5
2509.75-8, D-3 . . . . 5:30
2509.94-2(1) 6:65
2509.96-1 . . . . 7:25, 8:21
2509.96-1(d) 8:23, 8:31
2509.96-1(d)(1) 8:24
2509.96-1(d)(1)(ii) 8:25
2509.96-1(d)(2) 8:26
2509.96-1(d)(3) 8:27
2509.96-1(d)(3)(i) 8:28
2509.96-1(d)(3)(ii) 8:28
2509.96-1(d)(3)(iii) 8:28
2509.96-1(d)(3)(iv) 8:28
2509.96-1(d)(4) 8:29
2509.96-1(d)(4)(i) 8:30
2509.96-1(d)(4)(ii) 8:30
2509.96-1(d)(4)(iii) 8:30
2509.96-1(d)(4)(iv) 8:30
2509.96-1(d)(4)(v) 8:30
2509.96-1(e) 8:33, 8:34
2510.3-2(f) 22:146, 22:147, 22:161
2510.3-21(c) 5:6, 8:21, 8:22
2510.3-21(c)(1) 8:31
2510.3-102 . . . . 5:33, 5:81
2510.3-102(a) 5:75
2510.3-102(a)(1) 15:43
2510.3-102(a)(2) 5:81
2520.101-3(a) 19:111, 19:112
2520.101-3(b) 19:113
2520.101-3(b)(2) 19:115, 19:116
2520.101-3(b)(3) 19:114
2520.101-3(b)(4) 19:117

DOL Reg. §

2520.101-3(d) 19:109
2520.101-3(d)(2) 19:110
2520.101-3(d)(4) 19:112
2520.101-3(e) 19:120
2520.101-3(f) 19:118
2520.102-2 . . . . 19:25
2520.102-2(c) 19:27
2520.102-3 . . . . 19:26
2520.102-3(d) 7:24
2520.103-1 . . . . 4:64
2520.103-1(b)(5) 19:5
2520.103-1(d) 19:5
2520.103-8 . . . . 19:5
2520.103-13 . . . . 21:37, 21:45
2520.104-41(c) 19:5
2520.104-46(b)(1) 19:5
2520.104-46(d) 19:5
2520.104b-1 . . . . 19:114
2520.104b-1(b)(1) 19:31, 19:124
2520.104b-1(c) 19:125
2520.104b-2(a) 19:29
2520.104b-2(b)(1) 19:32
2520.104b-2(b)(2) 19:32
2520.104b-3(a) 19:33, 19:34
2520.104b-3(b) 19:33
2520.104b-10(d)(3) 19:37
2520.104b-10(e) 19:39
2520.104b-30 . . . . 19:53
2520.107-1 . . . . 19:126
2530.200b-2(a) 2:175
2530.200b-2(b) 2:175
2530.200b-2(c) 2:175
2530.200b-3(c) 2:176
2530.200b-3(d) 2:176
2530.200b-3(e) 2:176
2530.200b-3(f) 2:176
2530.200b-4(a)(1) 2:186, 2:205

DOL Reg. §

2530.200b-4(a)(2) 2:187
2530.200b-4(a)(3) 2:205
2530.202-2 . . . . 2:174
2530.203-2(a) 2:196
2530.206 . . . . 17:67
2550.401-1 . . . . 6:82
2550.404a-2(c) 6:42
2550.404a-3 . . . . 21:37, 21:48
2550.404a-4 . . . . 5:165
2550.404a-5 . . . . 4:4, 5:45, 7:22, 7:23
2550.404a-5(a) 19:56
2550.404a-5(b)(1) 19:59
2550.404a-5(b)(2) 19:57
2550.404a-5(c) 19:60
2550.404a-5(d) 19:61
2550.404a-5(d)(2) 19:62
2550.404a-5(d)(3) 19:63
2550.404a-5(d)(4)(i) 7:23
2550.404a-5(e) 19:65
2550.404a-5(e)(3) 19:62
2550.404a-5(f) 19:59
2550.404a-5(h)(1) 19:67
2550.404a-5(h)(2) 19:67
2550.404a-5(h)(3) 19:68
2550.404a-5(h)(4) 19:66
2550.404a-5(h)(5) 19:68
2550.404a-5(i)(1) 19:69
2550.404a-5(i)(2) 19:70
2550.404a-5(i)(3) 19:71
2550.404a-5(j) 19:58
2550.404b-1 . . . . 5:46
2550.404c-1 . . . . 7:1, 7:2, 7:28
2550.404c-1 Preamble 6:40, 7:7, 7:15, 7:31, 7:32
2550.404c-1(a)(2) 7:3, 7:4
2550.404c-1(b) 7:5
2550.404c-1(b)(2)(i)(A) 7:30
2550.404c-1(b)(2)(i)(B) 7:21, 7:22
2550.404c-1(b)(2)(ii)(A) 7:33
2550.404c-1(b)(2)(ii)(B) 7:32
2550.404c-1(b)(2)(ii)(C)(1) 7:26
2550.404c-1(b)(2)(ii)(C)(2) 7:27
2550.404c-1(b)(2)(ii)(C)(3) 7:27
2550.404c-1(b)(3)(i) 7:9
2550.404c-1(b)(3)(i)(C) 7:14
2550.404c-1(b)(3)(ii) 7:14
2550.404c-1(c)(1)(ii) 7:20
2550.404c-1(c)(2) 7:18
2550.404c-1(c)(4) 7:25
2550.404c-1(d)(2) 7:34
2550.404c-1(d)(2)(ii) 7:32
2550.404c-1(d)(2)(ii)(E)(4) 7:16, 7:17
2550.404c-1(d)(2)(ii)(E)(4)(vi) 6:65
2550.404c-1(d)(2)(iii) 7:19

DOL Reg. §

2550.404c-1(d)(2)(iv) 7:35
2550.404c-1(d)(3) 7:35
2550.404c-1(e)(1) 7:12
2550.404c-1(f)(4) 7:17
2550.404c-1(g) 7:39
2550.404c-5 . . . . 5:135, 6:44, 6:45, 7:54
2550.404c-5(a) 7:61
2550.404c-5(a)(2) 7:62
2550.404c-5(b) 7:63
2550.404c-5(c) 7:42
2550.404c-5(c)(5) 7:43
2550.404c-5(d) 7:54
2550.404c-5(e) 7:41
2550.404c-5(e)(4)(i)(C) 7:48
2550.404c-5(e)(4)(iv) 7:49
2550.404c-5(e)(4)(v) 7:50
2550.404c-5(e)(4)(vi) 7:53
2550.404c-5(f)(2) 2:40
2550.408b-1 . . . . 15:2
2550.408b-1(a)(3)(i) 15:13
2550.408b-1(a)(3)(ii) 15:7
2550.408b-1(a)(4), Ex. 2 . . . . 15:3
2550.408b-1(a)(4), Ex. 6 . . . . 15:11
2550.408b-1(b)(1) 15:3
2550.408b-1(b)(2) 15:3
2550.408b-1(c)(1) 15:4
2550.408b-1(c)(2) 15:4
2550.408b-1(d) 15:5
2550.408b-1(e) 15:6
2550.408b-1(f)(1) 15:8
2550.408b-1(f)(2) 15:9
2550.408b-2 . . . . 4:52, 4:55
2550.408g 5:103
2550.408g-1 . . . . 5:104
2550.408g-1(a)(3) 5:116
2550.408g-1(b)(3) 5:106
2550.408g-1(b)(3)(i)(D) 5:105
2550.408g-1(b)(4) 5:106
2550.408g-1(b)(4)(i)(F) 5:107
2550.408g-1(b)(4)(i)(G) 5:107
2550.408g-1(b)(4)(ii) 5:108
2550.408g-1(b)(4)(iii) 5:108
2550.408g-1(b)(4)(iv) 5:109
2550.408g-1(b)(4)(v) 5:108
2550.408g-1(b)(5) 5:110
2550.408g-1(b)(6) 5:111
2550.408g-1(b)(7) 5:112
2550.408g-1(b)(8) 5:113
2550.408g-1(b)(9) 5:113
2550.408g-1(d) 5:113
2550.408g-1(f) 5:115
2560.502c-2 . . . . 19:14
2560.502c-2(a) 19:19
2560.502c-2(b)(3) 19:16

DOL Reg. §

2560.502c-2(b)(3) 19:16
2560.502c-2(e) 19:17
2560.502c-7 . . . . 6:61
2560.502c-7(b) 19:119
2578.1 . . . . 21:37
2578.1(a) 21:38
2578.1(b) 21:40
2578.1(b)(5) 21:41
2578.1(c) 21:42, 21:43
2578.1(c)(3) 21:43
2578.1(d) 21:44
2578.1(e) 21:46
2578.1(g) 21:39

DOL Prop. Reg. §

2510.3-18 . . . . 6:63
2510.3-21(a)(1) 5:8
2510.3-21(a)(2) 5:11
2510.3-21(b)(1)(i) 5:15
2510.3-21(b)(1)(ii) 5:17
2510.3-21(b)(2) 5:18
2510.3-21(b)(3) 5:19
2510.3-21(b)(4) 5:20
2510.3-21(b)(5) 5:21
2510.3-21(b)(6) 5:22, 8:21, 8:23
2510.3-21(b)(6)(i) 8:24
2510.3-21(b)(6)(ii) 8:26
2510.3-21(b)(6)(iii) 8:28
2510.3-21(b)(6)(iv) 8:30
2510.3-21(d) 5:23
2510.3-21(f)(1) 5:9
2510.3-21(f)(6) 5:10
2510.3-21(f)(7) 5:10
2510.3-21(f)(8) 5:10
2520.105-2(b) 19:51
2550.404a-5 . . . . 19:56
2550.408b-2(c)(1)(iv)(H) 4:106

DOL Adv. Op.

81-12A 15:13
81-69A 5:82
89-30A 15:3
90-05A 5:82
93-24A 5:84
94-32A 4:59, 17:66
97-03A 4:53–4:55, 5:38
97-15A 5:91, 8:37
97-16A 5:90, 5:91
2001-01A 4:53–4:55, 4:62, 5:38
2001-09A 5:91, 8:37
2002-02A 15:43
2002-08A 5:131
2003-09A 5:91
2005-10A 8:37
2005-23A 5:8, 5:25
2012-02A 22:153
2012-03A 1:42, 4:126
2012-04A 1:42

DOL Field Assist. Bull.

2002-3 . . . . 5:84
2003-2 . . . . 5:76
2003-3 . . . . 4:55, 4:56–4:60, 17:66
2004-3 . . . . 5:30, 5:31
2004-03 . . . . 6:72
2006-01 . . . . 5:160
2006-03 . . . . 6:60, 19:43–19:48, 19:65
2006-107 . . . . 6:54
2007-01 . . . . 4:25, 5:116, 5:137, 8:37
2007-02 . . . . 22:146–22:150, 22:161
2007-03 . . . . 19:45
2008-01 . . . . 5:33–5:35, 5:80
2008-03 . . . . 7:44, 7:45, 7:47, 7:49, 7:51, 7:52, 7:55–7:59, 7:64–7:69
2008-04, Q 1 . . . . 5:48
2008-04, Q 2 . . . . 5:48
2008-04, Q 3 . . . . 5:55
2008-04, Q 4 . . . . 5:54
2008-04, Q 5 . . . . 5:49
2008-04, Q 6 . . . . 5:53
2008-04, Q 7 . . . . 5:49
2008-04, Q 8 . . . . 5:56
2008-04, Q 11 . . . . 5:56
2008-04, Q 15 . . . . 5:52
2008-04, Q 17 . . . . 5:50
2008-04, Q 18 . . . . 5:51
2008-04, Q 19 . . . . 5:51
2008-04, Q 20 . . . . 5:51
2008-04, Q 21 . . . . 5:51
2008-04, Q 22 . . . . 5:55
2008-04, Q 23 . . . . 5:55
2008-04, Q 30 . . . . 5:55
2008-04, Q 31 . . . . 5:55
2008-04, Q 33 . . . . 5:55
2009-02 . . . . 22:155, 22:157, 22:158
2009-03 . . . . 7:23
2010-01 . . . . 22:146, 22:147, 22:151–22:152, 22:157–22:158, 22:161
2012-02R 4:70, 4:87, 7:22, 19:58, 19:74–19:108
2014-01 . . . . 21:10–21:12

Miscellaneous IRS Announcements, Notices, Memoranda, Rulings, and Procedures

[*References are to question numbers.*]

IRS Announcements

2001-106, 2001-44 I.R.B. 416 . . . . 2:19, 8:61
2001-120, 2001-50 I.R.B. 583 . . . . 8:61
2007-59, 2007-25 I.R.B. 1448 . . . . 2:269
2008-23, 2008-14 I.R.B. 731 . . . . 3:18
2008-56, 2008-26 I.R.B. 1192 . . . . . 18:31, 18:93
2011-82, 2011-52 I.R.B. 1052 . . . . 3:28
2012-3, 2012-4 I.R.B. 335 . . . . 3:23
2012-44, 2012-49 I.R.B. 663 . . . . 15:62
2014-16, 2014-17 I.R.B. 983 . . . . 3:23
2015-19, 2015-32 I.R.B. 157 . . . . 3:28

IRS Notices

83-23, 1983-2 C.B. 418 . . . . 16:32
84-11, 1984-2 C.B. 469 . . . . 10:64, 10:69
84-11, 1984-2 C.B. 469, Q&A 6 . . . . 10:66
84-11, 1984-2 C.B. 469, Q&A 7 . . . . 10:67
87-7, 1987-1 C.B. 420 . . . . 16:136
87-13, 1987-1 C.B. 432 . . . . 18:44
89-23, 1989-1 C.B. 654 . . . . 22:128
89-25, 1989-1 C.B. 662 . . . . 18:86, 18:107
97-45, 1997-2 C.B. 296 . . . . 10:88, 10:91
97-75, 1997-2 C.B. 337 . . . . 16:48
98-1, 1998-1 C.B. 327 . . . . 13:6, 13:54
99-1, 1999-2 I.R.B. 8 . . . . 19:127
2000-3, 2000-4 I.R.B. 413 . . . . 21:36
2000-56, 2000-2 C.B. 393 . . . . 22:118
2001-42, 2001-30 I.R.B. 70 . . . . 3:16
2001-57, 2001-2 C.B. 279 . . . . 3:16
2002-1, 2002-1 C.B. 283 . . . . 3:34
2002-2, 2002-2 I.R.B. 285 . . . . 9:60
2002-8, 2002-4 I.R.B. 398 . . . . 18:47

IRS Notices

2003-49, 2003-32 I.R.B. 294 . . . . 3:34
2004-10, 2004-6 I.R.B. 433 . . . . 18:94
2005-5 Q&A 2, 2005-3 I.R.B. 337 . . . . 16:70
2005-5 Q&A 3, 2005-3 I.R.B. 337 . . . . 16:69
2005-5 Q&A 4, 2005-3 I.R.B. 337 . . . . 16:69
2005-5 Q&A 10, 2005-3 I.R.B. 337 . . . . 16:75
2005-5 Q&A 11, 2005-3 I.R.B. 337 . . . . 16:74
2005-5 Q&A 12, 2005-3 I.R.B. 337 . . . . 16:79
2005-5 Q&A 13, 2005-3 I.R.B. 337 . . . . 16:73
2005-5 Q&A 14, 2005-3 I.R.B. 337 . . . . 16:72
2005-5 Q&A 15, 2005-3 I.R.B. 337 . . . . 16:71
2006-107, 2006-51 I.R.B. 1114 . . . . . . 6:60, 6:62
2007-7, 2007-5 I.R.B. 395 . . . . 15:46, 16:62, 18:35
2007-7, Q&A 11, 2007-5 I.R.B. 395 . . . . . . 16:97
2007-7, Q&A 13, 2007-5 I.R.B. 395 . . . . . 16:100
2007-7, Q&A 15, 2007-5 I.R.B. 395 . . . . . . 16:70
2007-7, Q&A 16, 2007-5 I.R.B. 395 . . . . . . 16:98
2007-7, Q&A 17, 2007-5 I.R.B. 395 . . . . . 16:101
2007-7, Q&A 17(c)(2), 2007-5 I.R.B. 395 . . . . 16:103
2007-7, Q&A 18, 2007-5 I.R.B. 395 . . . . . 16:102
2007-7, Q&A 19, 2007-5 I.R.B. 395 . . . . . 16:101, 16:103
2007-78, 2007-41 I.R.B. 780 . . . . 22:108
2007-86, 2007-41 I.R.B. 990 . . . . 22:108
2008-30, 2008-12 I.R.B. 638 . . . . 18:102
2008-30, Q&A 6, 2008-12 I.R.B. 638 . . . . . 16:110
2008-30, Q&A 7, 2008-12 I.R.B. 638 . . . . . 16:99
2008-30, Q&A 8, 2008-12 I.R.B. 638 . . . . . 17:12
2008-30, Q&A 11, 2008-12 I.R.B. 638 . . . . . 17:33
2008-30, Q&A 12, 2008-12 I.R.B. 638 . . . . . 17:24
2008-30, Q&A 13, 2008-12 I.R.B. 638 . . . . . 17:13
2008-108, 2008-50 I.R.B. 1275 . . . . 3:24
2009-3, 2009-52 I.R.B. 250 . . . . 22:123

IRS Notices

2009-66, 2009-39 I.R.B. 418 . . . . 22:67
2009-71, 2009-35 I.R.B. 262 . . . . 2:270
2009-75, 2009-39 I.R.B. 436 . . . . 18:102
2009-82, 2009-41 I.R.B. 491 . . . . 3:22, 16:40, 16:57, 18:35
2009-82, Q&A 7, 2009-41 I.R.B. 491 . . . . 16:108
2009-97, 2009-52 I.R.B. 972 . . . . 3:21
2010-06, 2010-3 I.R.B. 275 . . . . . 22:113–22:115
2010-15, 2010-6 I.R.B. 3903:22 2010-15 Q&As 1–4, 2010-6 I.R.B. 390 . . . . 1:73
2010-15 Q&As 5–8, 2010-6 I.R.B. 390 . . . . . 1:73
2010-15, Q&A 9, 2010-6 I.R.B. 390 . . . . 1:71
2010-15 Q&A 10, 2010-6 I.R.B. 390 . . . . . . 1:71, 9:46
2010-15 Q&As 11–16, 2010-6 I.R.B. 390 . . . . 1:72
2010-15 Q&As 11–14, 2010-6 I.R.B. 390 . . . . 16:49, 16:50
2010-15 Q&A 15, 2010-6 I.R.B. 390 . . . . 16:51
2010-15 Q&A 16, 2010-6 I.R.B. 390 . . . . . . 16:63
2010-80, 2010-51 I.R.B. 853 . . . . 22:115
2010-84, 2010-51 I.R.B. 872 . . . . . . 18:67–18:76, 22:143, 22:176
2010-84, Q&A 1, 2010-51 I.R.B. 872 . . . . 2:84, 18:67, 18:70
2010-84, Q&A 3, 2010-51 I.R.B. 872 . . . . . 18:72
2010-84, Q&A 6, 2010-51 I.R.B. 872 . . . . . 18:71
2010-84, Q&As 7–10, 2010-51 I.R.B. 872 . . . . 18:73
2010-84, Q&A 11, 2010-51 I.R.B. 872 . . . . . 18:74
2010-84, Q&A 12, 2010-51 I.R.B. 872 . . . . . 18:75
2010-84, Q&A 13, 2010-51 I.R.B. 872 . . . . . 18:76
2010-84, Q&A 15, 2010-51 I.R.B. 872 . . . . . 18:69
2010-84, Q&A 17, 2010-51 I.R.B. 872 . . . . . 18:69
2010-84, Q&A 18, 2010-51 I.R.B. 872 . . . . . 18:69
2010-84, Q&A 19, 2010-51 I.R.B. 872 . . . . . 18:69
2011-6, 2011-3 I.R.B. 315 . . . . 19:12
2011-86, 2011-45 I.R.B. 698 . . . . 3:34
2013-74, 2013-52 I.R.B. 819 . . . . . . 2:269, 18:67, 18:68, 22:144, 22:177
2013-74, Q&A 1, 2013-52 I.R.B. 819 . . . . 2:84, 18:70
2013-74, Q&A 3, 2013-52 I.R.B. 819 . . . . . . 18:72
2013-74, Q&A 4, 2013-52 I.R.B. 819 . . . . . . 18:73
2013-74, Q&A 5, 2013-52 I.R.B. 819 . . . . . . 18:69
2013-74, Q&A 8, 2013-52 I.R.B. 819 . . . . . . 18:78
2013-74, Q&A 11, 2013 I.R.B. 819 . . . . 18:65
2014-19, 2014-10 I.R.B. 619 . . . . 3:25
2014-19, 2014-17 I.R.B. 979 . . . . . . 17:34, 17:42, 17:43
2014-24 I.R.B. 110C 2:269

IRS Notices

2014-35, 2014-23 I.R.B. 1072 . . . . 19:15
2014-54, 2014-41 I.R.B. 670 . . . . 16:106
2014-66, 2014-__ I.R.B. ___ 6:28, 7:53
2014-74, 2014-5 I.R.B. 937 . . . . 16:92

Private Letter Rulings

8113107 . . . . 22:116
9124034 . . . . 4:61
9124035 . . . . 4:61
9124036 . . . . 4:61
9124037 . . . . 4:61
9144041 . . . . 2:154
200404050 . . . . 9:70
201229012 . . . . 9:63

Revenue Rulings

56-497, 1956-2 C.B. 284 . . . . 1:1
61-164, 1961-2 C.B. 99 . . . . 2:151
63-180, 1963-2 C.B. 189 . . . . 1:1
65-295, 1965-2 C.B. 148 . . . . 9:63
66-110, 1966-1 C.B. 12 . . . . 18:47
67-290, 1967-2 C.B. 183 . . . . 22:121
68-24, 1968-1 C.B. 150 . . . . 15:59
68-89, 1968-1 C.B. 402 . . . . 1:1
69-494, 1969-2 C.B. 88 . . . . 6:64
71-90, 1971-1 C.B. 115 . . . . 2:149
71-224, 1971-1 C.B. 124 . . . . 15:55
71-295, 1971-2 C.B. 184 . . . . 15:59
74-466, 1974-2 C.B. 131 . . . . 2:143
76-259, 1976-2 C.B. 111 . . . . 14:41
80-145, 1980-1 C.B. 89 . . . . 9:61
80-155, 1980-1 C.B. 84 . . . . 6:64, 6:82
81-100, 1981-1 C.B. 326 . . . . 6:15
89-14, 1989-1 C.B. 111 . . . . 15:14
89-87, 1989-2 I.R.B. 81 . . . . 21:8
90-105, 1990-2 C.B. 69 . . . . 9:68
91-4, 1991-1 C.B. 57 . . . . 2:154, 9:66
2000-8, 2000-7 I.R.B. 617 . . . . 2:35
2002-42, 2002-28 I.R.B. 76 . . . . 9:77, 21:23
2002-45, 2002-29 I.R.B. 116 . . . . 9:69, 9:70, 9:71
2002-46, 2002-29 I.R.B. 117 . . . . 9:68
2002-62, 2002-42 I.R.B. 710 . . . . 18:107, 18:108
2003-105, 2003-40 I.R.B. 696 . . . . 18:47
2004-10, 2004-8 I.R.B. 484 . . . . 4:60
2004-11, 2004-7 I.R.B. 480 . . . . 11:3, 21:35
2004-13, 2004-7 I.R.B. 485 . . . . 2:264, 14:38
2006-38, 2006-29 I.R.B. 80 . . . . 5:75
2007-43, 2007-28 I.R.B. 45 . . . . 21:15, 21:17
2009-31, 2009-39 I.R.B. 395 . . . . 2:33
2009-32, 2009-39 I.R.B. 398 . . . . 2:33
2009-65, 2009-39 I.R.B. 413 . . . . 2:34

Revenue Rulings

2010-15, 2010-6 I.R.B. 390 . . . . 2:93
2012-3, 2012-8 I.R.B. 383 . . . . 17:6, 17:7
2013-17, 2013-38 I.R.B. 1 . . . . 17:34, 17:43, 17:68
2014-9, 2014-17 I.R.B. 975 . . . . 2:137

Revenue Procedures

92-64, 1992-2 C.B. 422 . . . . 22:118
92-93, 1992-2 C.B. 505 . . . . 9:53
93-42, 1993-2 C.B. 260 . . . . 11:30
2001-55, 2001-2 C.B. 552 . . . . 3:15
2002-21, 2002-2 C.B. 911 . . . . 2:144
2002-73, 2002-49 I.R.B. 932 . . . . 3:15
2003-13, 2003-4 I.R.B. 317 . . . . 2:122
2003-16, 2003-4 I.R.B. 359 . . . . 16:81
2003-72, 2003-38 I.R.B. 578 . . . . 3:15
2006-27, § 6.02(1), 2006-22 I.R.B. 945 . . . . 20:5
2006-27, § 6.02(2), 2006-22 I.R.B. 945 . . . . 20:5, 20:6
2007-44, § 2.05, 2007-28 I.R.B. 54 . . . . 3:17
2007-44, § 2.13, 2007-28 I.R.B. 54 . . . . 3:18
2007-44, § 5, 2007-28 I.R.B. 54 . . . . 20:24, 20:27
2007-44, § 5.03, 2007-28 I.R.B. 54 . . . . 3:17
2007-44, § 5.05(2), 2007-28 I.R.B. 54 . . . . . 3:17
2007-44, § 6.05, 2007-28 I.R.B. 54 . . . . 3:17
2007-44, § 9, 2007-28 I.R.B. 54 . . . . 3:20
2007-44, § 17, 2007-28 I.R.B. 54 . . . . 3:19
2007-71, 2007-51 I.R.B. 1184 . . . . 22:124
2008-50, 2008-35 I.R.B. 464 . . . . 22:84
2011-49, § 3.02(5), 2011-44 I.R.B. 608 . . . . 3:13
2011-49, § 4.01, 2011-44 I.R.B. 608 . . . . 3:2, 3:5
2011-49, § 4.02, 2011-44 I.R.B. 608 . . . . 3:2, 3:5
2011-49, § 4.07, 2011-44 I.R.B. 608 . . . . 3:3
2011-49, § 4.08, 2011-44 I.R.B. 608 . . . . 3:4
2011-49, § 4.09, 2011-44 I.R.B. 608 . . . . 3:6
2011-49, § 4.10, 2011-44 I.R.B. 608 . . . . 3:6
2011-49, § 13.01, 2011-44 I.R.B. 608 . . . . 3:9
2011-49, § 13.02, 2011-44 I.R.B. 608 . . . . 3:9
2011-49, § 13.05, 2011-44 I.R.B. 608 . . . . 3:9
2011-49, § 13.06, 2011-44 I.R.B. 608 . . . . . . 3:10
2011-49, § 19, 2011-44 I.R.B. 608 . . . . 3:36
2011-49, § 19.03, 2011-44 I.R.B. 608 . . . . . . 3:11
2011-49, § 19.03(3), 2011-44 I.R.B. 608 . . . . 3:8
2013-12, 2013-4 I.R.B. 313 . . . . 20:2, 20:7, 22:62, 22:84, 22:159
2013-12, § 1.03, 2013-4 I.R.B. 313 . . . . 20:3
2013-12, § 4, 2013-4 I.R.B. 313 . . . . 20:11

Revenue Procedures

2013-12, § 4.01(2), 2013-4 I.R.B. 313 . . . . 11:36, 20:20
2013-12, § 4.02, 2013-4 I.R.B. 313 . . . . 20:16, 20:21
2013-12, § 4.03, 2013-4 I.R.B. 313 . . . . 20:14, 20:22
2013-12, § 4.04, 2013-4 I.R.B. 313 . . . . 20:15, 20:23
2013-12, § 4.05(1), 2013-4 I.R.B. 313 . . . . 20:24
2013-12, § 4.05(2), 2013-4 I.R.B. 313 . . . . . 20:19
2013-12, § 4.08, 2013-4 I.R.B. 313 . . . . 21:50
2013-12, § 5.03, 2013-4 I.R.B. 313 . . . . 21:50
2013-12, § 6.02, 2013-4 I.R.B. 313 . . . . 20:4
2013-12, § 6.02(1), 2013-4 I.R.B. 313 . . . . . . 20:5
2013-12, § 6.02(2), 2013-4 I.R.B. 313 . . . . 20:5, 20:6
2013-12, § 6.02(4), 2013-4 I.R.B. 313 . . . . . . 20:7
2013-12, § 6.02(5), 2013-4 I.R.B. 313 . . . . 20:7, 20:8
2013-12, § 6.02(5)(f), 2013-4 I.R.B. 313 . . . . 21:50
2013-12, § 6.05(1), 2013-4 I.R.B. 313 . . . . 20:19, 20:24
2013-12, § 6.05(3), 2013-4 I.R.B. 313 . . . . . 20:24
2013-12, § 6.06(2), 2013-4 I.R.B. 313 . . . . . . 9:52
2013-12, § 6.09, 2013-4 I.R.B. 313 . . . . 20:27
2013-12, § 7, 2013-4 I.R.B. 313 . . . . 20:17
2013-12, § 8.01, 2013-4 I.R.B. 313 . . . . 20:12
2013-12, § 8.02, 2013-4 I.R.B. 313 . . . . 20:13
2013-12, § 8.03, 2013-4 I.R.B. 313 . . . . 20:13
2013-12, § 9.02, 2013-4 I.R.B. 313 . . . . 20:12
2013-12, § 10, 2013-4 I.R.B. 313 . . . . 20:26
2013-12, § 10.10, 2013-4 I.R.B. 313 . . . . . . 20:25
2013-12, § 10.11, 2013-4 I.R.B. 313 . . . . . . 20:25
2013-12, § 11, 2013-4 I.R.B. 313 . . . . 20:26
2013-12, § 12, 2013-4 I.R.B. 313 . . . . 20:27
2013-12, § 12.02(2), 2013-4 I.R.B. 313 . . . . 20:27
2013-12, § 12.02(4), 2013-4 I.R.B. 313 . . . . 21:50
2013-12, § 12.03, 2013-4 I.R.B. 313 . . . . . . 20:27
2013-12, § 13, 2013-4 I.R.B. 313 . . . . 20:28
2013-12, § 14.02, 2013-4 I.R.B. 313 . . . . . . 20:29
2013-12, app. A, 2013-4 I.R.B. 313 . . . . 20:9
2013-12, app. B, 2013-4 I.R.B. 313 . . . . 20:9
2013-12, app. B, § 3.01(3), 2013-4 I.R.B. 313 . . . . 20:7
2013-22, 2013-18 I.R.B. 1 . . . . 22:126, 22:127
2014-27, 2014-27 I.R.B. 41 . . . . 22:126, 18:94
2014-32, 2014-23 I.R.B. 1073 . . . . 19:15
2015-6, 2015-1 I.R.B. 194 . . . . 3:32
2015-6, §6.15, 2015-1 I.R.B. 194 . . . . 3:33
2015-6, §17, 2015-1 I.R.B. 194 . . . . 3:35
2015-6, §18, 2015-1 I.R.B. 194 . . . . 3:35
2015-6, §21, 2015-1 I.R.B. 194 . . . . 3:30
2015-8, 2015-1 I.R.B. 235 . . . . 3:34
2015-27, 2015-16 I.R.B. 914 . . . . 20:10
2015-28, 2015-16 I.R.B. 920 . . . . 20:10

INDEX

[*References are to question numbers and Appendixes.*]

A

Abandoned plans
  Bankruptcy Abuse Prevention and Consumer Protection Act of 2005, 21:51
  bankruptcy context, legal and regulatory developments in, 21:37, 21:51
  Employee Plans Compliance Resolution System (EPCRS), 21:50
  final regulations, 21:37–21:51
  termination of plan, 21:37–21:51
    bankruptcy trustee as QTA, 21:37, 21:51
    compensating QTA, 21:47
    date plan is considered terminated, 21:42
    determination that plan is abandoned, 21:38
    DOL guidance, 21:37
    effective date for regulations, 21:49
    liability, protection, 21:46
    missing participants, distributions to, 21:48
    notice to plan sponsor, 21:41, 21:43
    paying out, procedures to follow, 21:44
    qualified termination administrators (QTAs), 21:37, 21:38–21:39, 21:43–21:47
    reporting requirements, 21:45
    when plan is considered abandoned, 21:40

Above par, defined, 6:5

ACAs. *See* Automatic contribution arrangements (ACAs)

Access, effect on participation, 2:18

Account balance
  participant loans, used to secure, 15:9
  survivor annuity requirements
    transferee plan, 17:4
  top-heavy plans, minimum vesting, 14:31

Accrued benefits, present value, 14:20–14:28
  catch-up contributions, taken into account, 14:24
  distributions to participants, effect on determination of, 14:25

Acquisitions. *See* Mergers and acquisitions, corporate

Actively managed fund, defined, 6:21

Actual contribution percentage (ACP) test, 13:47–13:80
  actual contribution ratio (ACR), determination of, 13:49
    calculating actual contribution ratios, 13:60–13:61
    generally, 13:53
    matching contributions, disregarding, 13:50
    NHCE matching rate, 13:52
    representative matching rate, defined, 13:51
  avoiding, 13:1
  calculating actual contribution ratios, 13:60–13:61
  comparison of ADP and ACP tests, 13:80
  compensation, definition of, 13:60
  correcting failures, 13:62–13:63, 13:80
  current-year testing method, 13:53–13:54
  elective contributions, 13:61
  eligible employees, defined, 13:59
  employee contributions, 13:58–13:59
    after-tax contributions, 13:47
  excess aggregate contributions
    corrective distributions, 13:67, 13:72–13:78
    determining, 13:64–13:66
    discriminatory distribution, 13:71
    distributing, 13:67–13:78
    forfeited matching contributions, 13:72

Actual contribution percentage (ACP) test *(cont'd)*
excess aggregate contributions *(cont'd)*
gap period, 13:68–13:70
income allocable to, 13:68–13:70
recharacterization, 13:66
failures, corrections, 13:62–13:63, 13:80
governmental 401(k) plans, 2:148
group of eligible employees, calculation of ACP, 13:48
highly compensated employee, 13:55, 13:57
IRS approval, 13:54
matching contributions, 13:47, 13:61
ACR, disregarding in determining, 13:50
NHCE matching rate, 13:52
representative matching rate, defined, 13:51
non-highly compensated employee, 13:55, 13:56
matching contributions, 13:50
not satisfied, 13:62
prior year *vs.* current-year testing method, 13:53–13:54
qualified nonelective contributions (QNECs), 13:61, 13:78, 13:80
representative matching rate, defined, 13:51
restructuring of 401(k) plan, 13:79
safe harbor 401(k) plan and, 2:241, 2:245, 2:263
ACP test avoidance, 2:250
advantages and disadvantages, 2:245
after-tax contributions, 2:262
SIMPLE 401(k) plans, 13:1
special adjustments, 13:55–13:57
top-heavy rules, 2:263

Actual deferral percentage (ADP) test, 13:2–13:46
actual deferral ratio, determination of, 13:4, 13:7
avoiding, 13:1
calculating actual deferral ratios, 13:12–13:14
catch-up contributions, ADP limit, 9:29
communications with employees and, 8:1
comparison of ADP and ACP tests, 13:80
compensation, definition of, 13:12
correction of failures, 13:15–13:16
current-year testing method
IRS approval, 13:6
NHCE actual deferral ratios, 13:5
prior-year *versus,* 13:4–13:6
early participation rule, restructuring and, 13:38
elective contributions
satisfying ADP test, 13:2
treated as matching contributions, 13:7
eligible employees, 13:11
excess aggregate contributions, recharacterizing, 13:19
excess contributions
age 59½, distributions made before, 13:32
corrective distributions, 13:23–13:35
determining, 13:17–13:18
distributing, 13:23–13:35
gap period, 13:24, 13:26
income allocable, 13:23–13:26
recharacterizing, 13:19–13:22
required minimum distributions and, 13:33
Roth deferrals, excess contributions consisting all or in part of, 13:30
tax treatment, 13:29–13:31
failures, 1:8
correction, 13:15–13:16
governmental 401(k) plans, 2:148
group of eligible employees, calculated for, 13:3
HCE actual deferral ratio calculated differently, 13:10
non-highly compensated employee
initial plan year, calculation for, 13:9
not satisfied, 13:15
prior year *vs.* current-year testing method, 13:4–13:6
QMACs, 13:13–13:14
applicable contribution rate of NHCE, 13:45
elective contributions treated as matching contributions, 13:7
QNECs, 13:13–13:14
allocation of QNEC, 13:39–13:46
applicable contribution rate of NHCE, 13:45
bottom-up approach, 13:40–13:42, 13:45
correcting ADP test by, 13:39–13:46
elective contributions, treated as matching contributions, 13:7
per capita basis of allocation, 13:46
proportionate basis of allocation, 13:46
representative contribution rate of NHCE, 13:44
specific groups of NHCEs, allocations targeted to, 13:43
restructuring for, 13:36–13:38
safe harbor 401(k) plan and, 2:245, 2:246, 2:267
SIMPLE 401(k) plans, 13:1
special adjustments, 13:7–13:10
tax treatment of corrective distributions, 12:28
types of contributions to determine ratio, 13:7

Actuarial assumptions
accrued benefits, present value, 14:22

Adequate consideration, defined, 6:63

Adequate diversification, defined, 5:46

Adjusted balance method. *See* Balance forward accounting

Administration of plan
abandoned plans, determination of, 21:38
bundled administration
advantages, 4:16
disadvantages, 4:17
costs, 2:8
allocation of, 4:51
calculating total costs, 4:47–4:50
factors adding to, 4:11
payment of, 4:51
disadvantages to employer, 1:8
expenses
allocating, 4:51, 4:56, 4:57
benchmarking plan costs, 4:129
DOL final rule on service provider fee disclosure, 4:66–4:104
DOL's position on use of plan assets, 4:53
ERISA treatment of use of plan assets, 4:52
former employees, fees charged to accounts of, 4:60
generally, 4:41
legal and regulatory initiatives concerning fees, 4:63–4:126
plan assets used to pay, 4:53, 4:55
reasonable amount, 4:128
reimbursing plan for expenses paid by plan, 4:61
revenue-sharing amounts outside plan trust, 4:126
settlor fees, breaking out from other fees when combined in single charge, 4:62
settlor functions, 4:54
types of expenses to charge directly to participant, 4:59
fees, generally, 4:42. *See also* Expenses *above, this group*
disclosure, 4:114–4:127
generally, 4:42
identifiable costs
defined, 4:42
participant directed plan, 4:42
who pays, 4:43
in-house administration
advantages, 4:12
disadvantages, 4:13
multiemployer plans, 1:38
performance costs
defined, 4:44
participant directed plan, 4:45
services. *See* Service requirements
third party administrator
advantages, 4:14
disadvantages, 4:15

Administrative scrutiny requirement, QSLOBs, 10:53

ADP test. *See* Actual deferral percentage (ADP) test

Advisers
uniform standard of care, 1:81

Affiliate
defined, 4:74
disclosure of compensation disclosure, 4:92
fee disclosure requirements, 4:73
indirect compensation, 4:83

Affiliated service groups
nondiscrimination rules, 10:24–10:40
A-org, 10:28, 10:34, 10:36
B-org, 10:30, 10:36
constructive ownership rules, 10:36
employee benefit requirements, 10:39
first service organization, 10:25, 10:29, 10:34, 10:36
formal determination as to whether group of organizations constitutes affiliated service group, 10:40
historically performed services, 10:34
management functions, 10:38
management organization, 10:37
multiple affiliated service groups, aggregation of, 10:35
organization defined, 10:26
service organization defined, 10:27
service receipts percentage, 10:32
significant portion of business, 10:31
total receipts percentage, 10:33
types of groups, 10:24

After-tax savings
401(k), over, 1:17

Age 50
IRAs, maximum contributions, 22:9–22:10

Age 55
premature distribution tax, exception, 18:86

Age 59½
distributions made before, excess contributions, 13:32

Age 70½
individual retirement arrangements (IRAs), contributions, 22:11
rollovers, 18:100
Roth IRA contributions, 22:27
salary reduction SEPs (SARSEPs), contributions, 22:51

Age 70½ *(cont'd)*
simplified employee pensions (SEPs), contributions, 22:51

Age discrimination
PPA changes, 1:64

Age requirements
minimum coverage rules, 11:25
safe harbor 401(k) plan, 2:256
SIMPLE 401(k) plans, 2:232

Age-weighted formula, 2:104–2:105. *See also* Contributions
defined benefit plans, in lieu of, 2:115
design-based safe harbor, in lieu of, 2:115
drawbacks of, 2:116
situations for use of, 2:117

Aggregation groups, top-heavy testing
permissive aggregation group, 14:6–14:8
required aggregation group, 14:5

Aggressive stock fund, defined, 6:23

Airline pilots
minimum coverage rules, disregarding for, 11:25

AJCA. *See* American Jobs Creation Act of 2004 (AJCA)

Allocation, 2:101–2:119
contributions
age-weighted formula, 2:104–2:105
conversion to benefits, 2:107
design-based safe harbor, 2:101–2:102, 2:105
discretionary contributions, 2:16
equivalent benefit accrual rates, 2:107
integrated method, 2:104
matching contributions, 2:16
new comparability method, 2:104, 2:106, 2:111–2:116, 2:118, 2:119
nonelective contributions, 2:101, 2:104
points system, 2:101–2:103
proportional method, 2:104
earnings and expenses, 4:28–4:31
accounts of participants, allocating to, 4:28
balance forward accounting, 4:28–4:31
daily valuation, 4:28, 4:32–4:40
methods. *See* Contributions

Alternate payees
QDROs
administrative expenses associated with reviewing, charge to, 17:66
benefits distributed to, 17:63
defined, 17:47
lump-sum distributions, 18:21
rights of, 17:55
tax consequences of distributions to, 17:59
Roth account set up for, 18:81

Alternative defined contribution plans, 21:6, 21:7

Alternatives to 401(k) plans, 22:1–22:187. *See also* Cash balance plans; Code Section 403(b) plans; Code Section 457(b) plans; Nonqualified deferred compensation plans; SIMPLE IRA plans; Simplified employee pensions (SEPs); Individual retirement arrangements (IRAs)

Amendment to plan. *See* Plan amendment

American Jobs Creation Act of 2004 (AJCA), 22:106

American Savings Education Council (ASEC), 8:17

American Taxpayer Relief Act of 2012, 18:67, 18:90

Amortization
participant loans during leaves of absence, level amortization requirement and, 15:33

Ancillary benefit, nondiscrimination rules, 12:28

Annual additions, 9:39–9:45
defined, 2:164, 9:42
indexing for inflation, 9:40
limitation years ending on date other than December 31, 9:40
limits
Code Section 415 limits, 9:39–9:45
compensation under Code Section 415, 9:46–9:48
correcting violations, 9:52–9:53
definition, 9:42
design considerations, 9:51
maximum deferral percentage, 9:54
veterans' reemployment rights under USERRA, 9:45
what are not considered, 9:43

Annual reporting requirement. *See* Form 5500 series

Annuities
deferred, in target date funds, 6:28, 7:53
investment-related information, participant investment and fee disclosures, 19:70

Annuity contracts
Code Section 403(b) plans, 9:8
unallocated deferred annuity contract, investment in, 7:53
variable. *See* Variable annuity contracts

Annuity starting date, defined, 17:10

Anonymous Submission Procedure
VCP, 20:25

Anti-alienation rules
participant loans, violations, 15:14

Anti-assignment rule
exceptions
amounts owed to employer, 2:158
bankruptcy of participant, 2:157
recognized by IRS, 2:156
generally, 2:155

Anti-cutback rules
design considerations, 16:10
exceptions, 16:7
in-kind distributions, elimination of right to receive, 16:8
mergers, 16:11
optional form of benefit, 16:6–16:12
participant not entitled to receive benefits, 16:12
reduction or elimination of, 16:6
spinoffs, 16:11
transfers not subject to, 16:12
vesting, interaction of rules relating to changes in vesting schedules, 2:210
waiver by employee, 16:9

A-org
constructive ownership rules, 10:36
defined, 10:28
historically performed services, 10:34

Appeals
claims for benefits, denial of, 16:146
determination of appeal, timing, 16:147

Application fees, determination letters, 3:34

Appraisal services and fiduciary status, 5:21

Appropriateness of 401(k) plans, 1:29–1:34

ASC 820, 19:12

Asset allocation. *See also* Asset allocation funds
accomplishment of, 6:48
defined, 6:46
importance of, 6:47
models, 8:27–8:28
strategy, 6:46–6:48

Asset allocation funds
defined, 6:25
and qualified default investment alternatives (QDIAs), 6:25
utilization of, increased, 1:48

Assets. *See* Asset allocation; Plan assets

At a discount, defined, 6:5

At a premium, defined, 6:5

Attorneys' fees, recovery of, 5:68

Audit
applicability of requirement, 19:5
eligible investment advice arrangements (EIAAs), 5:101
fiduciary audit, defined, 5:138
IRS and DOL Form 5500 reporting, 19:5
requirement, 19:5
SCP, 20:16

Audit Closing Agreement Program (Audit CAP), 22:62
abandoned plans, 21:50
circumstances for use of, 20:28
determination of sanction, 20:29
maximum payment amount, 20:29

Automated phone system, 16:22

Automatic contribution arrangements (ACAs)
comparison chart, Appendix B
corrective distributions, 18:58
creation of, 2:36
defined, 2:37
eligible automatic contribution arrangements (EACAs), 2:41–2:51
advantages to adoption of, 2:50
availability to participants, 2:44
covered employee, defined, 2:45
defined, 2:41
effective date of PPA provisions, 2:51
notice, 2:42
permissible withdrawal provisions, 2:48–2:49
reason to add to plan, 2:47
tax consequences of permissible withdrawal, 2:49
time to add to plan, restrictions, 2:46
uniformity requirement, 2:43
notice to employee, 2:38
failing to provide, penalty, 2:39
sample notices, Appendix B
penalties
notice, failure to provide, 2:39
QACA. *See* Qualified automatic contribution arrangements (QACAs)
reason to add to plan, 2:40
Worker, Retiree, and Employer Recovery Act of 2008 (WRERA), 1:74

Automatic enrollment plans, 2:34–2:35
PPA changes, 1:10, 1:58, 2:34–2:40. *See also* Automatic contribution arrangements (ACAs)
requirements, 2:35
Roth contributions, 2:81

Automatic payroll deduction IRAs
proposed legislation, 1:78

Average benefit percentage test
calculation, 11:19
each group, actual benefit percentage of calculated, 11:20
defined, 11:18
employee's benefit percentage, calculation of, 11:23
testing group defined, 11:21
testing period defined, 11:22

Average benefits safe harbor, QSLOBs, 10:56

Average benefits test, 11:9

B

Baby boomers
housing market and, 8:56
Social Security and, 8:57

Back-end loads, defined, 6:97

Balanced fund, defined, 6:19

Balance forward accounting
adjusted balance method, 4:30
described, 4:28
earnings and expenses, 4:30
equitable allocation, 4:31
methods used, 4:30
ending balance method, 4:30
frequency of valuation, 4:29
regular defined contribution method, 4:30
time weighted method, 4:30

Balance to the credit of participant, lump-sum distributions, 18:18

Bankruptcy
abandoned plans
prevalence of, 21:51
termination of, 21:37
anti-assignment rule and, 2:157
participant loans, 15:37
trustees as QTAs, 21:37, 21:51

Bankruptcy Abuse Prevention and Consumer Protection Act of 2005, 2:153, 15:37, 21:51
account balance protections, 2:238
anti-assignment rule exception, 2:157
individual retirement arrangements (IRAs), 22:8
participant loans, 15:37

Below par, defined, 6:5

Beneficiary
breach of fiduciary duty, 5:67
death proceeds, rolling over
non-spouse beneficiary, 18:35
spousal beneficiary, 18:34
designated beneficiaries
designated beneficiary rule, defined, 16:38
estate or trust as beneficiary, 16:37
inherited IRAs, rollovers to, 16:98
minimum distribution requirements, 16:35–16:39
surviving spouse as sole beneficiary, 16:39
distributions
lump-sum distributions, election as beneficiary, 18:26
minimum distribution requirements. *See* Required minimum distributions *below, this group*
present value of accrued benefits, 14:26
non-spouse
death proceeds, 18:35
inherited IRA, 16:97–16:98, 22:6
required minimum distributions
designated beneficiary, 16:35–16:39
estate or trust as beneficiary, 16:37

Benefits
accrued, present value, 14:20–14:28
alternate payees, QDRO, 17:63
compensation used for calculating, 2:162
optional form of benefit. *See* Optional form of benefit
postponement of, 16:14–16:22
consent of participant, 16:17–16:22
early retirement provision, 16:14
electing delay, 16:15
failure to defer receipt of distribution, 16:18
length of delay, 16:13
notice, 16:17–16:22
right-to-defer notice, 16:19–16:22
summary notice, 16:21
superseding plan provisions, 16:16
termination of plan, impact of, 21:3

Benefits, rights, and features. *See also* Nondiscrimination testing
self-directed options and, 6:81

Best interest contract exemption (BICE), 5:24, 5:118–5:120, 8:37

general requirements, 5:120
relief available, 5:119

BICE. *See* Best interest contract exemption (BICE)

Blackout notices, 19:109–19:120
change in duration of period, 19:117
daily-traded plans, 19:115
defined contribution plans, 19:110
definition, 19:109
effective date of rules, 19:118
employer securities subject to, 19:112
furnishing of notice, 19:114

individual account plans, 19:110
information contained in notice, 19:113
issuer, defined, 19:112
model blackout notice, DOL, 19:120, Appendix F
noncompliance penalties, 19:119
one-participant retirement plan, 19:119
30-day advance notice requirement not applicable, 19:116
types of plans subject to, 19:110
when notice must be given, 19:109
who is required to give and receive, 19:111

Blackout periods
participant direction of investments, fiduciary protection from liability during, 7:35, 7:71
risks involved in incurring, 4:19
Sarbanes-Oxley Act of 2002, 6:68, 6:69

Bonds, 6:5–6:7
above par, defined, 6:5
below par, defined, 6:5
coupon rate, defined, 6:5
debentures, defined, 6:5
defined, 6:5
at a discount, defined, 6:5
federal government bonds, 6:7
at a premium, defined, 6:5
risks and returns associated with investing in bonds, 6:6
Treasury bills, 6:7
Treasury bonds, 6:7
Treasury inflation-protected securities (TIPs), 6:7
Treasury notes, 6:7

Bonuses, elective contributions, 2:76

B-org
constructive ownership rules, 10:36
defined, 10:30

Bottom-up approach, allocation of QNEC
ADP test, 13:40–13:42, 13:45

Breach of fiduciary duty
co-fiduciary, breaches committed by, 5:65, 5:66
consequences, 5:57–5:70
controversy, 5:59
indemnification, 5:130
LaRue decision, 5:69
liability, 5:57, 5:60–5:65, 5:70
minimizing risk of, 5:70
nonfiduciaries, liability of, 5:60
occurrence before fiduciary's appointment, 5:62
payment directly to plan to settle claim for, 5:58
punitive damages to beneficiary, 5:67
recovery of attorneys' fees and costs, 5:68
unwitting violation, 5:61

Break-in-service rules, 2:181–2:189
defined, 2:182
five-year rule, vesting, 2:204
generally, 2:181
100 percent vested break-in-service rule, 2:185
one-year break in service
computation period, 2:187
defined, 2:186
maternity or paternity leaves of absence, 2:188
operation, 2:183
vesting, 2:202, 2:205
rule of parity, 2:184
two-year break in service, 2:185
vesting, 2:201–2:206
veterans' reemployment rights under USERRA, 2:189

Broad range standard. *See* Participant-directed plans

Brokers
designated, 6:84
disclosure requirements, 4:81
participant-directed plans, special rules, 4:86
investment services, 4:21
SEC study of uniform fiduciary standard of care, 4:21
"suitability standard," 4:21
uniform standard of care, 1:81, 1:82

Brother-sister controlled group
nondiscrimination testing, 10:5, 10:9

Bundled administration
advantages, 4:16
disadvantages, 4:17

Business profits, contributions based on, 2:166

Business transactions, major, 21:28–21:36
continuing plans of both company, 21:30
distribution of assets, 21:33
distribution of elective contributions, 21:34
acquisition, special coverage rule, 21:35
disposition, special coverage rule, 21:35
freezing plans, 21:31
IRS guidance, 21:36
same desk rule, 21:34
severance of employment, 21:34
termination of plan, 21:32
triggering events, 21:33, 21:34

C

Cash balance plans
defined, 22:87

Cash investments
defined, 6:8
risks and returns, 6:9

Cash or deferred arrangement
election
affirmative nature of, 2:34
defined, 2:28
ESOP, arrangement under included, 2:29
exceptions, 2:31
frequency, allowable, 2:69
negative elections, 2:34
one-time election, 2:32
performance of services, contributions made prior to, 2:30
unused paid time off, dollar equivalent of, 2:33
growth of, 1:2
unused paid time off, dollar equivalent of, 2:33

Cashout/buyback rule, defined, 2:213

Catch-up contributions
accrued benefits, taken into account for determination of, 14:24
availability of, 9:2, 9:33
Code Section 403(b) plans, 22:134–22:136
same year, contribution of both special catch-up and age 50 catch-up, 22:136
special catch-up, 22:134
designated Roth contributions, 9:35
EGTRRA changes
SIMPLE 401(k) plans, 1:51
excess deferrals, 9:24
ADP limit, 9:29
availability of, 9:2, 9:33
determination of limit, 9:30
different employers, plans of, 9:34
legal limit, defined, 9:28
plan limit, 9:25–9:27
separate portion of plan year, calculation of plan limit, 9:27
SIMPLE 401(k) plan, 9:37
tax treatment, 9:31
universal availability requirement, 9:33
plan limit, excess deferrals, 9:25–9:27
defined, 9:25
determination of, 9:26
separate portion of plan year, 9:27
revocation of election made under TEFRA Section 242(b)(2), 16:33
Roth contributions, 9:35
salary reduction SEPs (SARSEPs), 22:55
SIMPLE 401(k) plans, 22:74
EGTRRA changes, 1:51
elective deferrals, 9:37
SIMPLE IRA plans, 22:74
tax treatment, 9:31
universal availability requirement, 9:33

Certificates of deposits (CDs), 6:8

Certified mail
missing participants, 21:11

Charitable contributions
IRA, distributions from, 22:20

Checking account, setting up, 5:84

Civil unions, 17:42

Claims for benefits, 16:141–16:147
defined, 16:141
denial of
appeals stage, 16:146, 16:147
notification, 16:144
90-day period, 16:143
reasonable procedures, 16:142
requirements, 16:142
review procedure, 16:145
timing, 16:143

Code Section 403(b) plans, 22:121–22:163
advantages of, 22:161
as alternative to 401(k) plan, 22:163
annual additions, deferrals treated as, 22:138
annuity contracts, excess deferrals, 9:8
catch-up contributions, 22:134–22:136
same year, contribution of both special catch-up and age 50 catch-up, 22:136
special catch-up, 22:134
contributions
catch-up contributions, 22:134–22:136
dollar cap elective deferrals, 22:133
overall Section 415 limit on contributions, 22:138
who may make, 22:132
dollar cap elective deferrals, 22:133
elective deferrals, 22:133
eligible employers, 22:121
ERISA, subject to, 22:146–22:153
reporting requirements, 22:154
safe harbor exemption, 22:147–22:153
Title 1, 22:146
excess deferrals, 9:8
excludable contracts
safe harbor exemption from ERISA, 22:152
401(k) plans, either maintained, 2:25
401(k) plans *vs.*, 22:161–22:163
features of 401(k) plans as advantageous, 22:162
features of 403(b) plans as advantageous, 22:161
funding vehicles used, 22:122
good faith effort
safe harbor exemption from ERISA, 22:158
guidance, 1:79, 22:159
issues, Treasury guidance, 1:79

matching contributions, 22:131
minimum coverage rules, 22:128
minimum participation rules, 22:128
nondiscrimination rules, 22:128–22:131, 22:132
online guide for compliance with rules, 22:159
overall Section 415 limit on contributions, 22:138
plan document requirement, 1:79
pre-approval program, 22:126
prototype plan program, 1:79, 22:126
provisions incorporated into plans, 22:124
and qualified default investment alternatives (QDIAs), 7:68
qualified plan, use with, 22:160
remedial amendment period, 22:127
reporting requirements
ERISA, plans subject to, 22:155
Revenue Procedure 2007-71, 22:124
safe harbor exemption from ERISA, 22:147–22:153
DOL guidance issued in conjunction with IRS final regulations, 22:148
employer activity violating safe harbor, 22:150
excludable contracts, 22:155
excluded employees, 22:156
Field Assistance Bulletin 2007-02, 22:146–22:150, 22:161
Field Assistance Bulletin 2009-02, 22:155, 22:157, 22:158
Field Assistance Bulletin 2010-01, 22:146, 22:147, 22:151–22:152, 22:157–22:158, 22:161
Form 5500 relief, 22:154–22:157
good faith effort, 22:158
pre-2009 contracts, 22:156
salary reduction contributions, nondiscrimination rules, 22:132
termination of plan, 21:7, 22:125
types of organizations establishing and maintaining, 22:121
universal availability, 22:132
written plan document requirement, 22:123

Code Section 404 deduction limits
applicable to 401(k) plan, 9:55
compensation defined, 9:61
defined benefit plans, 9:73
design considerations, 9:72–9:77
elective contributions, 9:59
existing profit sharing plans, 9:74
KSOPs (401(k) stock ownership plans), 9:60
maximum deductible amount
compensation limit, 9:61
determination of, 9:58, 9:62, 9:63
EGTRRA, changes by, 9:56
limitation, 9:61
more contributed, 9:65
plan year, 9:64
taxable year, 9:64
two or more profit sharing plans sponsored by employer, 9:57
money purchase plan, 9:75
existing plan in addition to 401(k) plan, 9:76
merger into 401(k) plan, 9:77
nondeductible contributions, 9:66
target plan, 9:75
timing of deductions, 9:67–9:68
two or more profit sharing plans sponsored by employer, 9:57

Code Section 409A
nonqualified deferred compensation plans, 22:106–22:115
basic requirements of Code Section 409A, 22:110
benefit security, unfunded plans, 22:116–22:118
compliance deadline, extension of, 22:108
correction program, IRS, 22:113–22:115
effective date, 22:107
generally, 22:106
impact on plans, 22:109
noncompliance, consequences, 22:112
Notice 2010-06, 22:113–22:115
tax considerations, 22:111–22:115
unfunded plans, benefit security, 22:116–22:118

Code Section 414(s), compensation defined, 10:92–10:103

Code Section 415 limits
annual additions, 9:39–9:45
defined, 9:42
EGTRRA changes, 1:51
compensation for purpose of 25 percent of compensation limit, 9:46
correcting a violation, 9:52–9:53
returning elective deferrals, 9:52
definitions of compensation, 9:48
design of 401(k) plan, 9:51
elective deferrals, 9:49
maximum deferral percentage, defined, 9:54
returning elective deferrals, 9:52
severance, amounts paid after treated as compensation, 9:47

Code Section 457 plans
Roth IRAs, availability, 1:79

Code Section 457(b) plans, 22:164–22:187
assets, who owns and holds, 22:165
catch-up contributions, 22:170–22:171

Code Section 457(b) plans *(cont'd)*
deferrals
amount, change of, 22:172
eligibility to make, 22:168
limits, 22:169
distributions, 22:174–22:185
commencement of benefits, 22:175
hardship, 22:180–22:181
restrictions, 22:174
rollovers, 22:176, 22:182
tax considerations, 22:184
eligible employers and funding rules, 22:164–22:166
eligible plans, 22:167
401(k) plans *vs.*, 22:187
frozen plans, 22:185
hardship withdrawals, 22:180–22:181
life insurance policies, plan assets invested in, 22:166
plan assets
life insurance policies, invested in, 22:166
who owns and holds, 22:165
rollovers, 22:176
governmental Code Section 457(b) plan, 22:182
SBJPA, 22:165
tax considerations
distributions, 22:184
termination of plan, 21:7, 22:185
types of organizations eligible to sponsor, 22:164
violations, 22:186

Code Section 457(f) plans
termination of plan, 21:7

Collectibles
self-directed options, investments, 6:82

Collective funds
investment fees, 6:103

Collective investment trust funds
fees, 4:121

Collectively bargained plans
mandatory disaggregation rules, 10:62
minimum coverage rules, disregarding for, 11:25
multiemployer 401(k) plans, 1:38

Collective trust funds, defined, 6:15

Combined benefit/401(k) plan design
creation of, 1:63

Commercial paper, 6:8

Communication program
advantages of saving in 401(k) plans, 8:2
approaches to, 8:15
assessing information needs of participants, 8:7
availability of funds, 8:2
choosing own investments, information needed for, 8:3
computer-based planning tools, 8:16
advantages of, 8:16
available tools, 8:17
online resources, 8:17
consumption-oriented employee, 8:10
contents of, 8:2–8:5
disadvantages to employer, 1:8
eligibility, 8:2
examples emphasizing investment return, 8:12
factual information, 8:5
follow-up, 8:19
goals, measurable, 8:8
implementing, 8:6–8:20
information, most important, 8:2
information needs, differing, 8:9
initial communication, importance of, 8:1
investment orientation, moving to, 8:11
investment return, emphasizing, 8:12
limits on contributions, 8:2
multiple contacts, approaches, and messages, 8:13, 8:15
structuring of, 8:18
quarterly reports, 8:14
Retirement Readiness report, 8:20
savings orientation, moving to investing orientation, 8:11
yearly contacts, number of, 8:14
younger employee, 8:10

Compensation
actual contribution percentage (ACP) test, definition, 13:60
actual deferral ratios, calculating, 13:12
allocation among affiliates and subcontractors, 4:92
average percentages
determination of, 10:99–10:101
HCE *vs.* NHCE group, 10:101
calculating plan contributions or benefits, for, 2:162
Code Section 401(a)(17) limits, 10:106
Code Section 414(s), satisfying
calculating contributions under the plan, 10:103
definitions of, 10:92–10:103
excluding specified percentage of employee's compensation, 10:97
nondiscrimination requirement, generally, 10:98
reasonable definition, 10:96–10:97
Code Section 415, under, 9:46–9:49
severance, amounts paid after treated as compensation, 9:47

deferred
advantages, 1:14
tax environment, 1:15
ten years, for, 1:16
definitions
Code Section 415, under, 9:48
HEART Act, compensation defined under, 1:71
qualified automatic contribution arrangements (QACAs), 2:67
top-heavy plans, minimum contribution, 14:33
Uniformed Services Employment and Re-Employment Rights Act of 1994 (USERRA), 9:50
W-2 definition, 9:48
design-based safe harbors
points, determination of employee's, 12:5
uniform allocation formula, 12:3
direct compensation, 4:90
Form 5500 series
direct compensation, information, 19:9
eligible indirect compensation (EIC), information, 19:9
indirect compensation, information, 19:9
indirect compensation, 4:83, 4:91
key employees, 14:17
limits, 2:163, 10:104–10:105
nondiscrimination testing, 10:92–10:106
salary deferral for ten years, 1:16
self-employed individuals, 10:102
service providers, fees paid to
allocation among affiliates and subcontractors, 4:92
compensation, defined, 4:88
direct compensation, defined, 4:69
form or manner compensation on disclosed, 4:95, 4:96
indirect compensation, defined, 4:83, 4:91
terminations, 4:94

Competition
global, 1:12
motivation and, 1:4

Compliance
costs, 2:8
401(k) compliance calendar, Appendix J
individual participant benefit statements, 19:49–19:50
qualified plan status. *See* Employee Plans Compliance Resolution System (EPCRS)

Computer-based planning tools
communication program, 8:16, 8:17

Computer model approach, EIAAs. *See* Eligible investment advice arrangements (EIAAs)

Conflicts of interest
investment service providers, 4:23
service providers
disclosure, 4:93, 5:94
investment service providers, 4:23

Congress
fees, actions with regard to, 4:63

Consent. *See also* Spousal consent
electronic media
Code-based, 19:127–19:129, 19:135
"consumer consent method," 19:131
plan distributions, 16:23
spousal waivers, 19:134
excess contributions and allocable income, distributions, 13:28

Consolidation
protection of participants, 2:159
reporting and disclosure, 19:21

Constructive ownership rules
affiliated service groups, nondiscrimination testing, 10:36
controlled groups, nondiscrimination testing, 10:13–10:21
corporate interest, attribution of, 10:16
entity attribution rule, defined, 10:14
estate or trust organization interest, attribution of, 10:17
exemptions from tax under Code Section 501(a), 10:22
family attribution rule, 10:18
lineal ascendant or descendant, attribution to, 10:20
option attribution rule, defined, 10:13
partnership interest, attribution of, 10:15
spouse owning organization, attribution of interest in, 10:19

Constructive receipt doctrine, 22:95

Consumer Protection Act of 2005, 2:238

Consumption-oriented employee, communication program, 8:10

Contributions
after-tax employee contributions, vesting, 2:193
age-weighted formula, 2:104–2:105
allocation to participants, 2:109
defined benefit plans, in lieu of, 2:115
design-based formula, differences, 2:105
design-based safe harbor formula, in lieu of, 2:115
determination of, 2:108
disadvantages, 2:116
nondiscrimination tests, satisfaction of, 2:108, 2:110
situations for use of, 2:117

Contributions (*cont'd*)
allocation methods
age-weighted formula, 2:104–2:105
conversion to benefits, 2:107
design-based safe harbor, 2:101–2:102, 2:105
equivalent benefit accrual rates, 2:107
integrated method, 2:104
new comparability method, 2:104, 2:106, 2:111–2:116, 2:118, 2:119
nonelective contributions, 2:101, 2:104
points method, 2:104
points system, 2:101–2:103
proportional method, 2:104
allocation of responsibilities, 5:80
business profits, based on, 2:166
catch-up. *See* Catch-up contributions
Code Section 404 deduction limits. *See* Code Section 404 deduction limits
Code Section 415 limits. *See* Code Section 415 limits
compensation used for calculating, 2:162
continuing contributions, 2:152–2:154
conversion to benefits, 2:107
deemed IRA contributions, 2:120–2:130
acceptance of, 2:127
availability of feature, 2:126
deductibility, 2:128
defined, 2:120
distribution rules, 2:125
document requirements, 2:122
ERISA requirements, 2:130
exclusive benefit requirement, 2:130
failure to satisfy qualification requirements, 2:129
requirement to accept, 2:127
separation from other assets, 2:123
trustee, restrictions on who can serve as, 2:124
types of IRAs to which contributions may be made, 2:121
deferral contributions. *See* Elective contributions *below, this group*
deposit of in trust, 5:75
elective contributions
actual deferral ratios, determining, 13:7
ADP test, 13:2
affirmative nature of, 2:34
age 50 reached by end of year, 9:24
annual cap period, 9:2
bonuses, 2:76
business transactions, major, 21:34
Code Section 404 deduction limits, 9:59
currently available to employee, when amount is considered, 2:70
currently available to partner, when amount is considered, 2:71
currently available to sole proprietor, when amount is considered, 2:72
deductions, 9:68
defined, 2:27
employee contributions, considered as, 2:75
ESOP, arrangement under included, 2:29
exceptions, 2:31
excess deferrals. *See* Excess deferrals
frequency of election, allowable, 2:69
hardship withdrawals. *See* Hardship withdrawals
limitations, 2:165
negative elections, 2:34
one-time election, 2:32
performance of services, contributions made prior to, 2:30
Roth contributions treated as, 2:79
safe harbor 401(k) plans, 2:245
same desk rule, 21:34
segregated from employer assets, 5:75
self-employed individual, deferral of cash advance payments made during plan year, 2:73
severance of employment, 21:34
special limitations, 2:74
unused paid time off, dollar equivalent of, 2:33
USERRA, veterans' reemployment rights under, 2:77
vesting, 2:193
elective deferrals
limitations, 9:1–9:35
elective salary deferrals. *See also* Elective contributions *above, this group*
returning, 9:52
employee contributions
accrued benefits, 14:23
actual contribution percentage (ACP) test, 13:58–13:59
elective contributions considered as, 2:75
excess aggregate contributions recharacterized as, 13:66
employer contributions
qualified automatic contribution arrangements (QACAs), requirement, 2:60
employer securities, diversification rights, 6:56
encumbered property, contributions of, 5:82
equivalent benefit accrual rates (EBARs), 2:107, 2:113
excess aggregate contributions. *See* Excess aggregate contributions
excess contributions. *See* Excess contributions

excess deferrals. *See* Excess deferrals
fiduciary or trustee ensuring deposit in timely manner, 5:33
fiduciary, property contributions to, 5:82
individual retirement (IRA) plans. *See* Deemed IRA contributions *above, this group*
integrated method of allocation, 2:104
last-day requirements, 2:98
limits, 9:1–9:77
  amount allocated to participant, 2:164
  annual addition limits, 9:39–9:45
  changes by EGTRRA, 1:51
  Code Section 404 deduction limits, 9:55–9:59
  Code Section 415 annual addition limits, 9:39–9:45
  deduction limits, 9:55–9:59
  elective contributions, 9:1–9:35
  restorative payments, 9:69–9:71
matching contributions, 2:86–2:93
  choosing, 2:16
  Code Section 403(b) plans, 22:131
  computing cost of, 2:7
  cost of, 2:6
  deductions, 9:68
  defined, 2:86
  defined benefit plans, 9:73
  discretionary basis in safe harbor 401(k) plan, made on, 2:89, 2:90
  discretionary basis in SIMPLE 401(k) plans, made on, 2:88
  discretionary basis, made on, 2:87–2:90
  fixed or discretionary, 2:12
  forfeited, tax treatment, 13:72
  highly compensated employees, 2:251
  market downturn of 2008, effect of, 1:46
  match cap, 2:6
  military service, death or disability while performing, 2:93
  non-highly compensated employee, 2:251
  ongoing or made at year's end, 2:13
  participation, impact on, 2:11
  participation rates and, 1:46
  partners, made on behalf of, 2:91
  qualified automatic contribution arrangement (QACA), plan containing, 2:90
  rate of match, 2:251
  safe harbor 401(k) plan, 2:237, 2:247, 2:251, 2:253, 2:257
  self-employed individual, 2:91
  SIMPLE 401(k) plans, 2:230
  top-heavy minimum contribution obligation, 14:45
  true-up match contributions after end of plan year, 2:14
  USERRA, veterans' reemployment rights under, 2:92
  vesting rules, 1:56
minimum contributions, top-heavy plans. *See* Top-heavy plans
minimum hours requirements, 2:98
monitoring, responsibility of fiduciary, 5:80
new comparability formula, 2:104
  allocation to participants, 2:111
  defined benefit plans, use in lieu of, 2:115
  design-based formula, differences, 2:106
  design-based safe harbor formula, use in lieu of, 2:115
  disadvantages of, 2:116
  nondiscrimination rules, 2:112
  nondiscrimination testing, 2:113
  nondiscriminatory, plans containing treated as, 2:119
  restrictions on use of, 2:114
  situations for use of, 2:118
nondeductible contributions, 9:66
nonelective contributions
  allocation methods, 2:101–2:119
  choosing, 2:16
  considerations, 2:15
  defined, 2:94
  eligibility requirements, 2:95–2:98
  in-service contributions, 15:55, 15:58
  last-day requirements, 2:98
  "maybe" safe harbor, 2:249
  military service, death or disability while performing, 2:100
  minimum hour requirements, 2:98
  safe harbor, 2:249
  veterans' reemployment rights under USERRA, 2:99
partnerships. *See* Partnerships
points method of allocation, 2:104
pre-tax
  tax considerations, 18:14–18:45
profits, based on, 2:166
proportional method of allocation, 2:104
qualified automatic contribution arrangement (QACA), plan containing, 2:90
  eligibility requirements, 2:97
qualified matching contributions (QMACs). *See* Qualified matching contributions
qualified nonelective contributions (QNECs). *See* Qualified non-elective contributions
remitting, safe harbor standard, 5:81
restorative contributions, 9:69–9:71
  defined, 9:70
  requirements, 9:71
return of contributions to employer, 2:154
rollover contributions. *See* Rollovers
Roth contributions, 2:78–2:85
  automatic enrollment, part of plan providing for, 2:81
  circumstances, 2:79

Contributions (*cont'd*)
Roth contributions (*cont'd*)
conversion of pre-tax elective contributions into Roth contributions, 2:84
defined, 2:78
elective contributions treated as, 2:79
elective deferrals, treatment as, 9:4
how long participants have been able to make contributions, 2:85
only Roth option offered, 2:80
pre-tax elective contributions converted to Roth contributions, 2:84
requirements, 2:83
separate account, allocation to, 2:82
Roth 401(k) plans. *See* Roth 401(k) plans
salary deferrals
automatic contribution rules, 22:47
fiduciary or trustee ensuring deposit in timely manner, 5:33
salary reduction SEPs (SARSEPs)
age 70½, employee, 22:51
catch-up contributions, 22:55
deductibility of contributions, 22:52
designated Roth contributions, 22:57
elective deferrals, 22:54
employer contributions, 22:48, 22:56
nonelective contributions by employer, 22:56
tax consequences, 22:53
SIMPLE 401(k) plans
suspension of during plan year, 2:237
simplified employee pensions (SEPs)
age 70½, employee, 22:51
annual addition limit, 22:50
deductibility of contributions, 22:52
percentage of salary contributed, 22:49
taking back contributions by employer, 2:153
taxable year, 9:67
top-heavy plans. *See* Top-heavy plans
true-up match contributions after end of plan year, 2:14
types of, 2:26–2:140
voluntary and mandatory contributions, separate accounting for, 18:42

Controlled group
affiliated service groups. *See* Affiliated service groups
nondiscrimination rules, definition, 10:1
nondiscrimination testing
brother-sister controlled group, 10:5, 10:9
combined groups, 10:7
constructive ownership rules, 10:13–10:21
controlling interest defined, 10:4
corporation interest, attribution of, 10:16
disregarding interests, 10:8
effective control, 10:6
employee benefit requirements, 10:23
employee's interest in organization, 10:12
entity attribution rule, 10:14
estate or trust organization interest, attribution of, 10:17
exemptions from tax under Code Section 501(a), 10:22
family attribution rule, 10:18
generally, 10:1
kinds of groups, 10:2
limit on attribution, 10:21
lineal ascendant or descendant, attribution to, 10:20
officer, 10:9, 10:11
option attribution rule, 10:13
parent-subsidiary controlled group, 10:3, 10:9
partnership interest, attribution of, 10:15
principal owner, 10:9, 10:10
significance of controlled groups, 10:23
spouse owning organization, attribution of interest in, 10:19

Corporate/government bond fund, 6:18

Corporations
constructive ownership rules, 10:16
controlled groups. *See* Controlled group

Correction Upon Audit. *See* Audit Based Closing Agreement Program (Audit CAP)

Corrective distributions
automatic contribution arrangements (ACAs), 18:58
excess contributions, ACP test, 13:67, 13:72–13:78
Pension Protection Act of 2006 (PPA), 13:74
excess deferrals, 9:8–9:16
conditions participant required to meet before permitting distribution of, 9:9
eligible rollover distribution, 9:21
gap period, 9:12
premature distribution tax and, 9:19
Roth contributions, 9:18
Roth deferrals, 13:30
tax treatment, 9:17–9:21
time for, 9:10
Pension Protection Act of 2006 (PPA)
tax treatment, effect on, 13:31, 13:74
required minimum distributions and, 13:33
Roth contributions, 9:18
Roth distributions, 18:65

Cost-of-living adjustments, 1:6

Coupon rate, defined, 6:5

Coverage requirements
minimum coverage rules
age conditions, disregarding employees, 11:25
air pilots, disregarding, 11:25
automatically satisfying, 11:2
automatic avoidance of minimum coverage failure, 11:37
average benefits test, 11:9
benefiting, definition of, 11:5
change of employer, transition period, 11:3
Code Section 403(b) plans, 22:128
collective bargaining employees, disregarding, 11:25
combination of plans to satisfy nondiscriminatory classification test, 11:17
combining plans, 11:6–11:7
disregarding certain employees, 11:24–11:25
employee's benefit percentage, calculation of, 11:23
facts and circumstances, nondiscriminatory classification, 11:16
failure to satisfy, 11:31–11:37
governmental 401(k) plans, 2:148
NHCE concentration percentage, 11:15
nondiscriminatory classification test, 11:10–11:17
nonresident aliens, disregarding, 11:25
QSLOBs, 11:8, 11:21, 11:25
rate group, 12:13
ratio percentage test, 11:4–11:8
reasonable classification, 11:11
retroactive correction when rules not satisfied, 11:32, 11:34–11:36
safe harbor percentage, 11:13
satisfaction of, testing for, 11:25
service conditions, disregarding employees, 11:25
terminating employees, disregarding, 11:25
testing for, 11:26–11:30
trade or business, change of employer, 11:3
unsafe harbor percentage, 11:14
minimum coverage testing, 11:2–11:37
alternatives to testing methodologies, 11:30
annual testing method, 11:29
average benefits test, 11:9
daily testing method, 11:27
IRS alternatives to testing methodologies, 11:30
nondiscriminatory classification test, 11:10–11:17
quarterly testing method, 11:28
ratio percentage test, 11:4–11:8

Covered employee
defined, eligible automatic contribution arrangements (EACAs), 2:45

Covered service providers
affiliates of, 4:73, 4:74, 4:83
compensation disclosures, 4:96
defined, 4:72
identification of, 5:94
indirect compensation, 4:83, 4:91
information to disclose, 4:84, 5:94
initial disclosure statement, 4:97
noncompliance with rules, 4:100
recordkeeper disclosures, 4:85
service provider is not a covered service provider, 4:104
subcontractors of, 4:73, 4:75, 4:83
termination of contracts or arrangements, 4:94

Criminal penalties
IRS and DOL Form 5500 reporting, 19:20

Criminal violations
voluntary Fiduciary Correction Program (VFCP), 5:148

Cross-testing rules
safe harbor 401(k) plan, 2:265
volume submitter plan, 3:13

Cumulative disparity limit, 12:24

Current availability
nondiscrimination testing, 12:31–12:35
self-directed options, 6:81

Current-year testing method
actual contribution percentage (ACP) test, 13:53–13:54
actual deferral percentage (ADP) test, 13:5
IRS approval, 13:6

D

Daily-traded plans
blackout notices, 19:115

Daily valuation
advantages
participant, to, 4:35
sponsor, to, 4:33
defined, 4:32
disadvantages
participant, to, 4:36, 4:37
sponsor, to, 4:34
generally, 4:28
service provider features, 4:39, 4:40
voice response unit, 4:38

Damages
breach of fiduciary duty, punitive damages to beneficiary, 5:67

Death benefits
incidental, 2:151
lump-sum distributions, 18:32. *See also* Lump-sum distributions
required minimum distributions, post-death benefits, 16:34
spousal death benefit, 17:50

Death of participant
federal estate tax, 18:90–18:92
involuntary distributions, 16:25
lump-sum distributions, 18:32
military service, during performance of
matching contributions, 2:93
nonelective contributions, 2:100
vesting, 2:193
premature distribution tax, exception, 18:52, 18:86
required minimum distributions (RMDs), 16:34, 16:47

Debentures, defined, 6:5

Deemed distribution, loans treated as. *See* Participant loans

Deemed IRA contributions. *See* Contributions

Default investment funds, 6:39–6:45
DOL guidance, 6:42, 6:44
fiduciary liability for assets invested, 6:40
participant direction of investments
compliance with Section 404(c) and, 7:61
conditions that must be met, 7:42
failure to make investment election, 7:40
notices regarding, information contained, 7:54
qualified default investment alternatives (QDIAs), 7:41–7:70
relief not available, 7:63
Pension Protection Act of 2006 (PPA), 6:42–6:43
qualified default investment alternatives (QDIAs), 6:43–6:45
requirement to offer, 6:39
types of funds used as, 6:41, 6:42, 6:44

Defense of Marriage Act, 1:81, 17:42
constitutionality of, 17:34, 17:41, 17:68
marital status, 17:34, 17:42
status of, 17:34, 17:41

Deferrals. *See* Contributions

Deficit Reduction Act of 1984 (DEFRA)
estate tax exclusion, 18:90

Defined benefit plans
age-weighted formula, contributions, 2:115
both 401(k) plan and defined benefit plans offered, type of employer, 1:7
cash balance plans, converting to. *See* Cash balance plans
Code Section 404 deduction limits, 9:73
combined benefit/401(k) plan design. *See* Combined benefit/401(k) plan design
contributions, deductions, 1:52
defined contribution plans *also* maintained
amended deduction limits, PPA, 1:63
matching contributions, 9:73
multiemployer plans replacing, 1:36
new comparability formula, contributions, 2:115
participation in both 401(k) plan and, 14:41
present value of accrued benefits
actuarial assumptions, 14:22
determination, 14:21
replacement of, 1:6
supplement of, 1:6
top-heavy plans
minimum contributions, 14:41
present value of accrued benefits, 14:21, 14:22

Defined contribution method, balance forward accounting, 4:30

Defined contribution plans
alternative defined contribution plans
defined, 21:7
termination of plan, 21:6, 21:7
annual benefit payable from, limits
EGTRRA changes, 1:51
blackout notices, 19:110
defined benefit plans *also* maintained
amended deduction limits, PPA, 1:63
nonqualified deferred compensation plans, link to, 22:101
Pension Protection Act of 2006 (PPA)
defined benefit plans *also* maintained, amended deduction limits, 1:63
present value of accrued benefits, determination, 14:20
termination of plan
alternative defined contribution plans, 21:6, 21:7

DEFRA. *See* Deficit Reduction Act of 1984 (DEFRA)

Delinquent Filer Voluntary Compliance (DFVC) Program, 19:15

Demographics
employee, 1:8
design considerations, 2:1
future of 401(k) plans, 1:47

Department of Labor (DOL)
abandoned plans, 21:37–21:51
advanced notice of proposed rulemaking (ANPRM), 19:41
Advisory Opinions, 8:37

automatic rollovers, DOL regulations, 16:77–16:78
default investment funds
  types of funds used, guidance, 6:42, 6:44
definition of fiduciary, proposed guidance for, 5:7–5:24
eligible investment advice arrangements (EIAAs), 4:25
  guidance, 5:102–5:103
fees, action regarding, 4:64, 4:117
guidance, 1:80, 5:7–5:24
investment advice. *See* Investment advice
investment services, guidelines for selection and monitoring of providers, 4:25
model blackout notice, 19:120, Appendix F
model comparative chart, Appendix K
mutual funds
  fiduciaries, payments to, 5:91
  nonfiduciaries, payments to, 5:90
participant investment and fee disclosures, 19:56–19:73, 19:74–19:108
  acquired-fund fees and expenses, 19:104
  acquiring-fund fees and expenses, 19:104
  administrative expenses, 19:80–19:81, 19:83–19:84, 19:106
  annuity contract or custodial account, 19:75
  average annual total return, defined, 19:68
  benchmarks, 19:61, 19:89
  blended benchmark returns, disclosure of, 19:89
  brokerage windows, information about, 19:86–19:87, 19:102, 19:103
  checklist, Appendix C
  closed investment alternatives, information about, 19:88
  comparative charts or documents, 19:94–19:96
  compliance, 19:58, 19:59
  delivery of disclosures, DOL guidance, 19:65
  designated investment alternative, 19:63, 19:66, 19:69–19:72, 19:75–19:77, 19:88, 19:96, 19:98, 19:103–19:105
  designated investment manager, 19:77, 19:100
  detail required of explanations, 19:78
  electronic media, use of, to satisfy disclosure requirements, 19:65
  ERISA Section 404(c), impact of regulations, 19:73
  fees and expenses, explanation of, 19:78
  form of disclosure, DOL guidance, 19:65
  fund-of-funds, 19:104
  glossary of investment-related terms, samples, 19:93
  impracticability of obtaining necessary information, 19:75
  initial quarterly statement of fees and expenses, 19:108
  insurance cost, 19:107
  investment-related information provided, 19:61–19:64, 19:69, 19:88–19:97
  at least annually thereafter, defined, 19:67
  at least quarterly, defined, 19:67
  model portfolios, 19:101
  multiple investment alternatives, platform with, 19:103
  net asset value, calculation of, 19:105
  participant-directed and trustee-directed investments, plan with both, 19:74
  plan-related information provided, 19:60, 19:77–19:87
  plans subject to, 19:57
  prospectuses or similar documents, 19:98
  quarterly statement of fees and expenses, 19:108
  recordkeeping expenses, 19:79, 19:82
  responsibility for compliance, 19:59
  revenue-sharing explanation, 19:83–19:85
  revenue-sharing payments in excess of recordkeeping fee, 19:79
  Section 403(b) plans that are ERISA-covered plans, 19:75
  self-directed brokerage accounts, information about, 19:86–19:87, 19:102
  "since inception" data, 19:97
  single document disclosing plan-related and investment-related information, 19:76
  stand-alone documents not required, 19:99
  supplemental investment-related information on Web site, 19:92
  target asset allocations, 19:89
  total annual operating expenses, calculation of, 19:106
  total annual operating expenses, defined, 19:68
  trustee-directed investments, plan with, 19:74
  unregistered designated investment alternatives, 19:98, 19:104–19:106
  variable rates of return, 19:96
  Web site requirements, 19:90–19:92, 19:95
  windows, information about, 19:86–19:87, 19:102, 19:103
participant loans, regulation of, 15:2, 15:13, 15:14
plan fee arrangements, DOL addressing potential prohibited transactions, 5:93
qualified default investment alternatives (QDIAs), 6:44
regulatory agenda, 1:80

Department of Labor (DOL) *(cont'd)*
rollovers, automatic, 16:77–16:78
service provider fee disclosure, 4:63–4:104
settlor functions, 4:54
termination of plan
abandoned plans, 21:37–21:51
use of plan assets to pay administrative expenses, 4:53

Deposits
salary deferrals
fiduciary or trustee ensuring deposit in timely manner, 5:33
in trust, 5:75

Designated beneficiary. *See* Beneficiary

Designated investment alternative
defined, 4:87
participant investment and fee disclosures, 19:63, 19:66, 19:69–19:72, 19:75–19:77, 19:88, 19:96, 19:98, 19:103–19:105

Designated investment manager, 19:77, 19:100

Designated Roth contributions. *See* Roth contributions

Design-based safe harbors
defined, 12:1
loss of status, 12:7
nonelective contributions, allocation of, 12:7
points, determination of employee's, 12:5
top-heavy minimum contribution, 12:8
uniform allocation formula, 12:2
compensation, what is considered, 12:3
uniform point system plan, 12:4–12:6

Design considerations, 2:1–2:272
allocation methods, 2:101–2:119. *See also* Allocation
anti-cutback rules and, 16:10
Code Section 403(b) plans, 22:121
annual additions, deferrals treated as, 22:138
catch-up contributions, 22:134–22:136
Code Section 401(k) plans, either maintained, 2:25
contributions, who may make, 22:132
dollar cap elective deferrals, 22:133
eligible employers, 22:121
funding vehicles used, 22:122
matching contributions, 22:131
minimum coverage rules, 22:128
minimum participation rules, 22:128
nondiscrimination rules, 22:128–22:131, 22:132
overall Section 415 limit on contributions, 22:138
provisions incorporated into plans, 22:124
salary reduction contributions, nondiscrimination rules, 22:132
types of organization establishing and maintaining, 22:121
Code Section 404 deduction limits, 9:72–9:77
Code Section 415 limits, 9:51
Code 457(b) plans, 22:164–22:166
assets, who owns and holds, 22:165
catch-up contributions, 22:170–22:171
deferral amount, change of, 22:172
deferral limits, 22:169
deferrals, eligibility to make, 22:168
eligible employers, 22:164
life insurance policies, plan assets invested in, 22:166
SBJPA, 22:165
contributions. *See* Contributions
demographics, employee, 2:1
distribution features, 16:10
dual-income households, members of, 2:3
eligible combined plans, 2:270–2:272
expenses
administration expense, 2:8, 4:53
compliance costs, 2:8
credit against taxes owed, use as, 2:10
enrollment costs, 2:8
financial considerations, 2:5
installation of plan, 2:8
matching contributions, costs of, 2:6, 2:7
ongoing administration costs, 2:8
options affecting, 2:5–2:10
plan assets, paid from, 2:9
recordkeeping costs, 2:8
limited liability companies (LLCs), 1:33
lower-paid participants, credit against taxes to encourage participation
amount of credit, 2:20
eligible individual, defined, 2:22
generally, 2:19
permanence of credit, 2:21
qualified retirement savings contribution, defined, 2:23
matching contributions affecting participation, 2:11
choice of allocating funds to matching or discretionary, 2:16
fixed or discretionary, 2:12
ongoing or made at year's end, 2:13
true-up match contributions after end of plan year, 2:14
multiemployer plans, 1:38
nonelective contributions, 2:15, 2:94–2:100
one participant covered in plan, 2:24
options and objectives, 2:1–2:25
participation
access to plan funds, 2:18
options impacting, 2:11–2:25

partnership, for, 1:32
pay levels of employees, 2:3
professional businesses, 1:34
prohibited transactions occurring in design process, 5:83
qualification requirements, 2:141–2:168
qualified automatic contribution arrangements (QACAs), 2:52–2:68
application of, 2:66
and compensation definition, 2:67
defined, 2:52
effective date of PPA provisions, 2:68
employer contributions, requirement, 2:60
failure of employee to make affirmative election, 2:54
non-highly compensated employee, employment on last day of plan, 2:62
notice to employees, 2:53, 2:55
and qualified percentage, 2:52, 2:57–2:59
reason to add QACA to plan, 2:56
safe harbor match formula, 2:61–2:64
safe harbor plans, differences in compensation definition, 2:67
top-heavy rules, 2:65
repayment rights, 2:216–2:219
Roth contributions. *See* Roth contributions
safe harbor 401(k) plans, 2:239–2:269. *See also* Safe harbor 401(k) plans
saver's credit
amount of, 2:20
eligible individuals, 2:22
generally, 2:19
permanence of, 2:21
qualified retirement savings contribution, defined, 2:23
SIMPLE 401(k) plans, 2:220–2:238. *See also* SIMPLE 401(k) plans
size of workforce, 2:2
small businesses, 1:34
transfers, 2:131, 2:134–2:135, 2:138–2:140
turnover, employee, 2:4
25 percent deductible limit, 9:72

Determination letters
applications, 3:32–3:35
employee, notification, 3:35
fees, 3:34
generally, 3:32
not necessary, 3:36
where to send, 3:33

Determination years, 10:91

Deterred Compensation Plan, 2:145

DFVC. *See* Delinquent Filer Voluntary Compliance (DFVC) Program

Different industries safe harbor, QSLOBs, 10:56

Direct compensation, 4:90

Directed trustee, 6:72
defined, 5:29
responsibilities regarding investing plan assets, 5:31
status as fiduciary, 5:30

Direct rollovers. *See* Rollovers

Disability
HEART Act, 1:71, 1:73
military service, during performance of
matching contributions, 2:93
nonelective contributions, 2:100
premature distribution tax, exception, 18:86

Disaster recovery
and premature distribution tax, 18:86

Disclosure requirements. *See* Reporting and disclosure

Discrimination, self-directed options, 6:81

Disqualification. *See* Plan disqualification

Disqualified persons, 5:71–5:73

Distributions
accelerating payment of retirement benefits, disadvantages of, 18:110
accumulating funds, advantages of, 18:111
cash distribution, rollover of, 16:80
Code Section 457(b) plans. *See* Code Section 457(b) plans
consent, electronic media, 16:23
deemed IRA contributions, 2:125
electronic media, consent, 16:23
eligible rollover. *See* Rollovers
employer securities, 18:28–18:31
equal periodic payments, computation of, 18:107
filing requirements
correction of Form 1099-R, 18:98
failure to file, penalty, 18:95
generally, 18:93
magnetic media, filing, 18:96
paper returns, 18:97
Form 1099-R, magnetic media, 18:96
in-service. *See* In-service distributions
installment
gross income exclusion, determination, 18:37
investment in contract, gross income exclusion, 18:37
taxation, 18:36–18:38
involuntary
alternate payee's consent in QDRO case, 16:26
circumstances, 16:25
death of participant, 16:25
life insurance proceeds in death payout, 18:33

Distributions *(cont'd)*
lump-sum. *See* Lump-sum distributions
mergers, 21:25
monitoring and harmonizing options, 21:26
option concerns, IRS relief, 21:27
minimum distribution requirements. *See* Required minimum distributions (RMDs)
participant loan converted to, 18:52
planning, 18:99–18:113
PPA changes to rules, 1:60
premature. *See* Premature distribution
qualification requirements, 2:167–2:168
qualified reservist distributions. *See* Qualified reservist distributions
required beginning date, 16:30–16:40
required minimum distributions. *See* Required minimum distributions (RMDs)
Roth 401(k) plans. *See* Roth distributions
Roth IRAs, required minimum distributions (RMDs), 22:32
SIMPLE 401(k) plans, 2:234–2:235
joint and survivor annuity requirements, 2:236
required minimum distributions (RMDs), 2:235
restrictions, 2:234
SIMPLE IRA plan, differences, 2:238
SIMPLE IRA plans
required minimum distributions (RMDs), 2:235
SIMPLE 401(k) plans, differences, 2:238
spinoffs, 21:25
monitoring and harmonizing options, 21:26
option concerns, IRS relief, 21:27

Diversification
adequate, 5:46
employer securities, diversification rights, 6:55–6:62
conditions placed on investments, 6:58
contributions applicable, 6:56
effective dates, 6:62
employee stock ownership plans (ESOPs) and, 6:55
notice requirements, 6:60, 6:61, Appendix G
options offered to participants, 6:57
penalties for noncompliance with notice requirements, 6:61
pooled investment vehicles, 6:59
PPA, impact of, 6:55
publicly-traded employer securities, defined, 6:59
restrictions placed on investments, 6:58
individual participant benefit statements, 19:48
mutual funds, 6:12
notice, publicly traded employer securities, 19:121
Pension Protection Act of 2006 (PPA)
notice, plan assets invested in publicly traded employer securities, 19:121
publicly traded employer stock, diversification notice, 19:121

Dividends, ESOPs. *See* Employee stock ownership plans (ESOPs)

Doctrine of constructive receipt, 22:95

Document. *See* Plan document

Documentation to be retained
under ERISA, 19:136
for hardship withdrawals, 15:51
for loan programs, 15:17, 15:32
for principal residence loans, 15:17, 15:32

Dodd-Frank Wall Street Reform and Consumer Protection Act of 2010
generally, 1:81
impact of, 1:76
SEC study requirements, 4:21

DOL. *See* Department of Labor (DOL)

DOMA. *See* Defense of Marriage Act

Domestic partners
spousal consent, 17:41

Domestic relations orders (DROs). *See also* Qualified domestic relations orders (QDROs)
consequences of making payment to participant while order is under review, 17:57
defined, 17:52
failure to qualify as QDRO, 17:67
plan administrator's responsibility, 17:56
review and qualification of, 17:56–17:57

Dominant line of business method of allocation, QSLOBs, 10:57

DROs. *See* Domestic relations orders (DROs)

Dual-income households, members of, 2:3

Due diligence. *See* Procedural due diligence

E

Early participation rule
restructuring, ADP test, 13:38

Early retirement
earliest retirement age, defined, 17:13
provision, postponement of benefits, 16:14

EBARs. *See* Equivalent benefit accrual rates (EBARs)

Economic Growth and Tax Relief Reconciliation Act of 2001 (EGTRRA 2001), 1:50–1:57
benefit limits, 1:51
catch-up contributions, non-SIMPLE 401(k) plans, 1:51
Code Section 404 deduction limits
maximum deductible amount, 9:56
Code Section 415 annual additions dollar limit, 1:51
contribution limits, 1:51
defined benefit plans
annual benefit payable from, limits, 1:51
contributions to, 1:52
effective dates, 1:57
elective deferral limits, 1:51, 9:1
design of plan and, 9:51
employee stock ownership plans (ESOPs)
dividends, 1:52
employers' deduction limits, 1:52
estate tax, 18:90
failure to amend for, 20:11
401(k) plan changes, 1:50
future of 401(k) plans, 1:49
indexed limits affected by, Appendix E
individual retirement arrangements (IRAs), 1:54
matching contributions, vesting rules, 1:56
maximum deferral percentage, 9:54
multiple use test, 1:56
participant loans, who may borrow, 15:1
plan administrator, simplification of rules for, 1:56
plan documents
remedial amendment period, 3:17
updating of, 3:16
remedial amendment period, updating plans, 3:17–3:20
rollovers, 1:53, 16:53
Roth 401(k) plans, 1:24
distributions, 18:84
same desk rule, 1:56
SIMPLE 401(k) plan, annual cap on deferrals, 9:36
SIMPLE plan limits, 1:51
small employers, use of qualified plans by, 1:55
top-heavy plans
five-year look-back rule, elimination of, 1:56

Economic trends, future of 401(k) plans, 1:48

Education
target date funds, fiduciary concerns, 5:163

Educational expenses
hardship withdrawals to pay, 15:46

EESA. *See* Emergency Economic Stabilization Act of 2008

EFAST 2, 19:6
generally, 19:10
information, where to obtain, 19:11

Effective availability test
self-directed options, 6:81

EFTPS. *See* Electronic Federal Tax Payment System (EFTPS)

EGTRRA. *See* Economic Growth and Tax Relief Reconciliation Act of 2001 (EGTRRA 2001)

EIAAs. *See* Eligible investment advice arrangements (EIAAs)

EIC. *See* Eligible indirect compensation (EIC)

$80,000, compensation in excess of, 10:77, 10:78

Elapsed time method used for calculating service, 2:176, 2:177

Election
avoiding income tax withholding on eligible rollover distribution, 16:110
cash or deferred arrangement, 2:28–2:34, 2:69
delay of benefit payments, 16:15
direct rollover, 16:84
eligible rollover distributions, on, 16:64
restrictions, 16:88
electronic media
Code-based, 19:127–19:129
requirements, 19:133
spousal waivers, 19:134
eligible rollover distributions, 16:64, 16:94
given effect, withholding rules, 16:135
lump-sum distribution, future election rights, 18:26
TEFRA
Code Section 242(b)(2), revocation, 16:33
required beginning date, 16:32
top-paid group, 10:89
vesting, 2:209

Elective contributions. *See* Contributions

Elective deferrals
defined, 9:3
excess deferrals. *See* Excess deferrals
limits
changes by EGTRRA, 1:51
cost-of-living increases and, 9:1
design of plan and, 9:51
safe harbor 401(k) plans, 2:245, 2:261
veterans' reemployment rights under USERRA, 9:5
returning salary deferral contributions, 9:52
Roth IRA contributions treated as, 9:4

Elective deferrals *(cont'd)*
segregated from employer assets, 5:75
veterans' reemployment rights under USERRA, 2:77
limits, 9:5

Elective transfer, defined, 2:135

Electronic delivery
consents, plan distributions, 16:23
right-to-defer notice, postponement of benefits, 16:22

Electronic disclosure request for information, 1:80

Electronic Federal Tax Payment System (EFTPS)
FICA tax payments, 18:6
FUTA tax payments, 18:13

Electronic filing. *See also* Electronic media
Form 1099-R, 18:94
paperless administration, defined, 19:122

Electronic media
consents
Code-based, 19:127–19:129, 19:135
"consumer consent method," 19:131
spousal waivers, 19:134
disclosure requirements, satisfaction of, 19:65
elections
Code-based, 19:127–19:129
requirements, 19:133
ERISA and
disclosure requirements, 19:124–19:125
recordkeeping, 19:126
individual participant benefit statements, 19:44
notary public, elections and consents, 19:134
notices
"alternative method," 19:132
Code-based, 19:127–19:129, 19:135
effective date, 19:135
eligibility, safe harbor 401(k) plan, 2:242
methods, 19:130
requirements, 19:133
plan representatives, election and consents, 19:134
recordkeeping
ERISA and, 19:126
spousal consent, participant loans, 15:41
spousal waivers, 19:134
survivor annuity requirements, 17:24

Electronic Signatures in Global and National Commerce Act (E-SIGN), 19:134

Eligibility computation period, defined, 2:174

Eligibility rights, 2:169–2:180
age eligibility, 2:170, 2:171
commencement of participation, 2:178
part-time employees, 2:180
service requirements, 2:172–2:178
waiver of participation, 2:179

Eligible automatic contribution arrangements (EACAs), 2:41–2:51
advantages to adoption of, 2:50
automatic enrollment, 22:47
availability to participants, 2:44
covered employee, defined, 2:45
creation of, 2:36
defined, 2:41
effective date of PPA provisions, 2:51
notice, 2:42
permissible withdrawal provisions, 2:48–2:49
premature distribution tax, exception, 18:86
QDIAs, combination of notice with, 7:55–7:59
reason to add to plan, 2:47
requirements, 2:43
tax consequences of permissible withdrawal, 2:49
time to add to plan, restrictions, 2:46

Eligible combined plans, 2:270–2:272
defined, 2:272
establishment of, eligibility, 2:271
exemptions, 2:272
vesting requirements, 2:273

Eligible indirect compensation (EIC)
reporting, 19:9

Eligible individual account plans, defined, 6:53

Eligible investment advice arrangements (EIAAs), 4:25
advice pursuant to EIAA, information taken into account, 5:106–5:109
annual audit requirement, 5:111
audit requirement, 5:101
computer model approach, 5:99, 5:107–5:109, 5:114
certification, 5:108–5:109
post-model advice, 5:114
conditions applicable, 5:113
conditions to obtain relief, 5:98
creation of, 1:59
defined, 5:95
disclosure standards, 5:112
DOL guidance, 4:25, 5:102–5:104, 5:112–5:116
effective date for final EIAA rule, 5:115
exemption, 5:116, 5:117
financial adviser, who can serve as, 5:97
generally, 8:37

independent fiduciary, standards for obtaining authorization from, 5:110
model participant disclosure, Appendix H
notice requirements, 5:100
post-model advice, 5:114
prohibited transactions, 5:95–5:120
audit requirement, 5:101
computer model approach, 5:99
conditions to obtain relief, 5:98
definition, 5:95
DOL guidance, 5:102–5:103
exemptions, 5:117–5:120
financial adviser, who can serve as, 5:97
notice requirements, 5:100
reasonable compensation, 5:102
relief available, 5:96
securities law disclosure rules, compliance with, 5:102
reasonable compensation, 5:102
regulations (DOL), 5:104–5:116
relief available, 5:96
reporting and disclosure
model participant disclosure, Appendix H
scope of the level fee requirement, 5:105
securities law disclosure rules, compliance with, 5:102

Eligible rollover distributions. *See* Rollovers

E-mail consent
right-to-defer notice, postponement of benefits, 16:22

Emergency Economic Stabilization Act of 2008
premature distribution tax, 18:86

Emerging market funds, 6:24

Employee
age eligibility, 2:170, 2:171
allocation rate
amounts considered, 12:12
determining, 12:11
benefit to, 1:10
competitive environment, 1:12
defined, top-heavy plans, 14:4
demographics, 1:8
disadvantages to, 1:13
full-time services for at least one year, 10:67, 10:68
highly compensated employee. *See* Highly compensated employee
leased employee. *See* Leased employees
non-highly compensated employee. *See* Non-highly compensated employee
part-time employees, eligibility rights, 2:180
personal savings program, supplementing, 1:11
primary direction or control of recipient, 10:70
restrictions on eligibility to participate. *See* Eligibility rights
self-employed individuals, nondiscrimination rules, 10:63

Employee Plans Compliance Resolution System (EPCRS), 5:147, 17:37, 20:2–20:8, 22:62, 22:159
abandoned plans, 21:50
allocations, corrective, 20:7
Audit CAP, 20:28–20:29, 22:62
common operational errors, standard correction methods, 20:9
correction methods, numbers of, 20:6
defined, 20:2
distributions, corrective, 20:7
exceptions to full correction, 20:8
programs under, 20:3
common features of, 20:4
principles taken into account, 20:5
reciprocity under, 5:147
SCP, 20:11–20:19, 22:62
search methods to locate participant or beneficiary, 20:8
standard correction methods, 20:9
VCP and, 20:20–20:27, 22:62

Employee Retirement Income Security Act (ERISA). *See* ERISA

Employee stock ownership plans (ESOPs)
diversification rights and, 6:55
dividends
cash or deferred arrangements, dividends distributed to or invested pursuant to election, 2:29
EGTRRA changes, 1:52
premature distribution tax and, 18:86
mandatory disaggregation rules, 10:62
minimum coverage rules, average benefit percentage test, 11:21
nondiscrimination rules, 10:62
termination of plan, 21:7

Employer
competitive pressures, 1:4
defined, top-heavy plans, 14:3
disadvantages of sponsoring plan, 1:8
401(k) plan benefit to employer, 1:3
governmental employer
defined, 2:146
401(k) plans, 2:147, 2:148
Section 457(b) deferred compensation plan, 2:145
indemnification of fiduciary, 5:131
multiemployer plans. *See* Multiemployer plans
tax-related objectives, 1:5

Employer securities, 6:50–6:71
adequate consideration, 6:63
blackout periods, 19:112
considerations for investment option, 6:71
danger of being heavily invested, 6:70
defined, 18:29
distributions, 18 28–18:31
diversification requirements, 6:55–6:62
conditions placed on investments, 6:58
contributions applicable, 6:56
effective dates, 6:62
employee stock ownership plans (ESOPs) and, 6:55
notice requirements, 6:60, 6:61, Appendix G
options offered to participants, 6:57
penalties for noncompliance with notice requirements, 6:61
pooled investment vehicles, 6:59
PPA, impact of, 6:55
publicly-traded employer securities, defined, 6:59
restrictions placed on investments, 6:58
dividends paid, reporting, 18:31
eligible individual account plan defined, 6:53
ERISA fiduciary rules, 6:51
fair market value, 6:72
as investment option
PPA changes to rules, 1:62
investment-related information, participant investment and fee disclosures, 19:69
KSOPs (401(k) stock ownership plans), funds borrowed to purchase from C corporation, 9:44
net unrealized appreciation, 18:28
offering in plan, 6:50–6:71
options after receiving, 18:30
participant direction of investments, 7:15–7:17
qualifying employer securities
defined, 6:52
restrictions, 6:54
reporting and disclosure
dividends paid, 18:31
restrictions, 6:54
Roth distributions, 18:66
Sarbanes-Oxley Act of 2002
blackout periods, 6:68, 6:69
generally, 6:68
short-swing profit rules
publicly traded employer stock, 6:67
voting rights, 6:65
withholding, 16:116

Encumbered property, contributions of, 5:82

Ending balance method, balance forward accounting, 4:30

Enrollment costs, 2:8

Enron
ERISA Section 404(c), 7:76
fiduciary audit and, 5:138
issues involved, 7:75
legislation ensuing from, 7:75

Entities that may adopt 401(k) plans, 1:26–1:28

Entity attribution rule, defined, 10:14

EPCRS. *See* Employee Plans Compliance Resolution System (EPCRS)

Equal periodic payments
change of election after receiving, 18:108
computation of, 18:107
substantially equal periodic payments
eligible rollover distributions, 16:57–16:59
premature distribution tax, exception, 18:86

Equivalency method used for calculating service, 2:176

Equivalent benefit accrual rates (EBARs)
conversion to, 2:107
general nondiscrimination test and, 2:113

ERISA (Employee Retirement Income Security Act)
anti-assignment rule, 2:155
bond requirements, 5:47–5:56
exemptions from, 5:52
form of bond, applicable rules, 5:55
funds or other property of a plan, defined, 5:50
handling of funds or other property, when bond is required, 5:51, 5:53
losses covered by, 5:48
plan assets, paid from, 5:56
responsibility for ensuring persons are bonded, 5:53
restrictions on who can issue, 5:54
term of bond, applicable rules, 5:55
who must be covered, 5:47, 5:48
breach of fiduciary duty
punitive damages to beneficiary, 5:67
recovery of attorneys' fees and costs, 5:68
budget accounts. *See* ERISA spending accounts
cash or deferred arrangements, 1:1
deemed IRAs, 2:130
delegation of responsibilities by plan administrator, 4:6
disclosure rules
covered plans, 4:70
fiduciaries, 4:79
registered investment advisors, 4:79

electronic media
disclosure requirements, 19:124–19:125
recordkeeping, 19:126
employer securities, 6:51
Federal Insurance Contributions Act (FICA) and, 18:3
funds or other property of a plan, defined, 5:50
handling of funds or other property, when bond is required, 5:51, 5:53
individual retirement arrangements, 22:1–22:23
investment advice under, 8:22–8:23
issues arising, 8:37
investment manager, delegating fiduciary responsibility to, 5:130
record retention under, 19:136
Section 404(c) defense, 4:115, 7:73. *See also* Participant direction of investments
use of plan assets to pay administrative expenses, 4:52

ERISA spending accounts, 4:123
defined, 4:124
legal issues, 4:125
revenue-sharing amounts outside plan trust, 4:126

Errors
disclosures, 4:99, 5:94

E-SIGN (Electronic Signatures in Global and National Commerce Act), 19:134

ESOPs. *See* Employee stock ownership plans (ESOPs)

Estate or trust as beneficiary
required minimum distributions (RMDs), 16:37

Estate or trust organization interest, attribution of
constructive ownership rules, controlled groups, 10:17

Estate tax
death distributions, 18:90
amount of tax, 18:92

ETFs. *See* Exchange traded funds (ETFs)

Excess aggregate contributions
actual deferral percentage (ADP) test
recharacterization, 13:19
corrective distribution, 13:72–13:78
defined, 18:56
determining, 13:64–13:66
discriminatory distribution, 13:71
distributing, 13:67–13:78
forfeited matching contributions, 13:72
gap period, 13:68–13:70
income allocable to, 13:68–13:70
pre-tax excess aggregate contributions, taxation to participant, 18:57
recharacterization, 13:66
taxation to employer, 18:58

Excess benefit plans, defined, 22:91

Excess contributions
actual deferral percentage (ADP) test
age 59½, distributions made before, 13:32
corrective distributions, 13:24–13:35
determining, 13:17–13:18
distributing, 13:24–13:35
employer contributions, treatment as, 13:27
gap period, 13:24, 13:26
income allocable, 13:23–13:26
recharacterization, 13:19–13:22
required minimum distributions and, 13:33
Roth deferrals, excess contributions consisting all or in part of, 13:30
tax treatment, 13:29–13:31
defined, 18:56
excess aggregate contributions. *See* Excess aggregate contributions
gap period, 13:24, 13:26
Pension Protection Act of 2006 (PPA)
corrective distributions, 13:31, 13:74
premature distribution tax, exception, 18:86
pre-tax excess contributions, taxation to participant, 18:57
recharacterization
actual deferral percentage (ADP) test, 13:19–13:22
PPA, effect of, 13:22
taxation to employer, 18:58

Excess deferrals
allocable income, 9:11–9:13
annual cap
exceeding, 9:6
period applicable to, 9:2
circumstances when allowed, 9:24
Code Section 403(b) annuity contracts, contributions to, 9:8
consent, employee or spousal, 9:16
corrective distributions
conditions participant required to meet before permitting distribution of, 9:9
eligible rollover distribution, 9:21
gap period, 9:12
Roth contributions, 9:18
tax treatment of, 9:17–9:21
time for, 9:10
defined, 18:53
distribution of, 9:15
employer contributions, as, 9:14

Excess deferrals *(cont'd)*
failure to correct, 9:22
Roth contributions, 9:23
401(k) plans, corrective distributions, 9:8, 9:10
gap period, 9:12
pre-tax excess deferrals, taxation to participant, 13:54
Worker, Retiree, and Employer Recovery Act of 2008 (WRERA), 1:74
income allocable to, 9:11–9:13
premature distribution tax
corrective distribution and, 9:19
exception, 18:86
pre-tax excess deferrals, taxation to participant, 18:55
recharacterization of, 9:15
required minimum distributions (RMDs), 9:20
Roth contributions
consisting of excess deferrals, 9:7
failure to correct, 9:23
SARSEPs, contributions to, 9:8
SIMPLE retirement accounts, contributions to, 9:8
Worker, Retiree, and Employer Recovery Act of 2008 (WRERA)
gap-period income, 9:12

Exchange traded funds (ETFs)
defined, 6:31

Excise taxes
Code Section 404 deduction limits, avoidance of tax on nondeductible contributions, 9:66
reporting and disclosure, 19:24
Roth distributions 18:82

Exclusive benefit requirement
deemed IRA contributions, 2:130

"Expense ratio," 4:48

Expenses of plan
administration expense, 2:8, 4:53
compliance costs, 2:8
credit against taxes owed, use as, 2:10
enrollment costs, 2:8
financial considerations, 2:5
installation of plan, 2:8
matching contributions, costs of, 2:6, 2:7
ongoing administration costs, 2:8
options affecting, 2:5–2:10
plan assets used to pay, 2:9
recordkeeping costs, 2:8
tax credits, use as, 2:10

F

Family and Medical Leave Act of 1993 (FMLA)
break-in-service rules and, 2:188, 2:206

Family attribution rules, 10:18

FASB Statement of Financial Accounting Standards
FAS No. 157, 19:12

Federal estate tax, death distributions, 18:90–18:92

Federal government bonds, 6:7

Federal Insurance Contributions Act (FICA)
amounts subject to, 18:2
collection of tax, 18:5
computation of tax, 18:4
definition, 18:1
IRAs, 22:16
nonqualified deferred compensation plans, 22:98
payment of tax, 18:6
reporting, 18:7
withholding
amounts subject to, 18:2
employees subject to, 18:3

Federal Thrift Savings Fund, 1:27

Federal Unemployment Tax Act (FUTA)
amounts subject to tax, 18:9
computation of tax, 18:11
employees subject to tax, 18:10
IRAs, 22:16
nonqualified deferred compensation plans, 22:99
payment of tax, 18:13
reporting, 18:12

Fees. *See also* Expenses of plan
administration of plan
allocating expenses, 4:51, 4:56, 4:57
asset-based fees, impact on performance costs, 4:48
benchmarking costs, 4:128
determination letter application, 3:34
DOL's position on use of plan assets, 4:53
ERISA treatment of use of plan assets, 4:52
"expense ratio," 4:48
former employees, fees charged to accounts of, 4:60
generally, 4:41
identifiable costs, 4:42
other administrative costs, 6:100
reasonable amount, 4:128

reimbursing plan for expenses paid by plan, 4:61
settlor functions, 4:54
total costs, calculation of, 4:50
types of expenses to charge directly to participant, 4:58
asset-based fees, impact on performance costs, 4:48
collective investment trust funds, 4:121
complicated nature of, reason for, 4:49
former employees, fees charged to accounts of, 4:60
Congress, actions by regarding, 4:53
DOL action, 4:64, 4:117
ERISA spending accounts, 4:123
defined, 4:124
legal issues, 4:125
revenue-sharing amounts outside plan trust, 4:126
evaluation of, tools available, 4:118
fee leveling, 4:58
fiduciaries
mutual funds, payment of fees from, 5:91
Government Accountability Office (GAO), 5:94
improper fees, 5:161
information, disclosure to plan participants, 1:80
insurance company proceeds, 4:122
investment fees
back-end loads, defined, 6:97
collective funds, 6:103
front-end loads, defined, 6:97
generally, 6:95
management fees, defined, 6:99
mutual funds, 6:96, 6:101, 6:102
12b-1 fees, 1:81, 6:98, 6:101. *See also* 12b-1 fees
variable annuity contract, 6:104
legal and regulatory initiatives, 4:63–4:126
leveling, 4:58
litigation involving, 4:114
significant rulings, 4:115
market downturn, effect on plan fees, 4:63
methods for paying plan fees, 4:57
basis point fee assessed at plan level, 4:57
flat dollar fee assessed at plan level, 4:57
participant, payment by, 4:57
per head fee, 4:57
plan assets, allocation across, 4:57
plan sponsor, payment by, 4:57
revenue sharing, 4:57
transaction-based, 4:57
mutual funds, 6:13, 6:96
determination of amount, 6:102
expense ratio, 6:101
"fund of funds," multiple mutual funds combined into, 4:120
improper fees, 5:161
multiple mutual funds, 4:120
plan fees paid from, 4:119–4:120, 5:91
nonfiduciaries
mutual funds, payment of fees from, 5:90
participant direction of investments
charging directly to participants' accounts, 7:33
transfer fees, 7:28
payment of, 4:41–4:128
plan fee arrangements, DOL addressing potential prohibited transactions, 5:93
plan loans, 15:40
plan participant, charged directly to, 4:59
plan revenue and costs, mismatch between, 4:49
qualified default investment alternatives (QDIAs), 7:55
reasonable, 4:115, 4:125
redemption fees
allocation of proceeds, 5:160
fiduciary responsibilities in relation to market timing, 5:159
financial intermediary, defined, 5:158
market timing, imposition of to limit, 7:29
SEC's rule regarding, current status, 5:158
reporting and disclosure
service providers, 4:65, 4:66–4:105. *See also* Reporting and disclosure *for detailed treatment*
revenue sharing arrangements, paid through, 4:58, 4:119
review of fees and services, 4:103
Securities and Exchange Commission (SEC) initiatives, 4:116
service providers
additional disclosures after initial statement, 4:98
affiliates, 4:73, 4:74, 4:92
compensation, 4:88, 4:90, 4:96
conflicts of interest, 4:93, 5:94
covered plans, 4:70
covered service providers. *See* Covered service providers
direct compensation, 4:90
DOL guidance, 1:80
DOL interim final rule, 4:66–4:104, 5:94
effective date, 4:67
ERISA fiduciaries, 4:79
error correction, 4:99, 5:94
failure to disclose, 4:99
fiduciaries planning investment products, 4:80
Form 5500, Schedule C disclosures, 4:105
form or manner of disclosure, 4:95
fund investment managers, 5:89
guide or index as part of initial disclosure, 1:80, 4:106–4:113

Fees *(cont'd)*
service providers *(cont'd)*
indirect compensation, 4:83, 4:91
information to be disclosed, 4:84, 4:87
initial disclosures, 4:69, 4:97
investment products, 4:76
noncompliance consequences, 4:100
$1,000 limit, 4:77, 4:78
purpose and scope of fee disclosure rule, 4:66
recordkeeping services, 4:82, 4:85, 4:86
registered investment advisors, 4:79
responsible plan fiduciaries, 4:71
rules for describing plan services, 4:88
service providers who are not covered service providers, 4:104
subcontractors, 4:73, 4:75, 4:92
terminations, 4:94
written requirement, 4:68
statements upon request, provision of, 19:53
"sub-transfer agency" (sub-ta) fees, 4:120, 4:123, 6:106
tools available for evaluating, 4:118
transfer fees, participant direction of investments, 7:28
12b-1 fees, 4:120, 4:123
defined, 6:98
limitations, 1:81
mutual funds, 6:106
mutual fund's expense ratio, 6:101
regulation and disclosure, 6:98
U.S. Government Accountability Office (GAO), 4:63
variable annuity contracts, 4:122, 6:104

FICA. *See* Federal Insurance Contributions Act (FICA)

Fiduciary, 5:1–5:60
adequate diversification, 5:46
allocation of responsibilities, 5:37, 5:80
audit, defined, 5:138
avoiding fiduciary status, 5:12
breach of duty
co-fiduciaries, breaches committed by, 5:65, 5:66
failing to act, 5:63
indemnification, 5:130
LaRue decision, 5:69
liability, 5:57, 5:60–5:65, 5:70
nonfiduciaries, liability of, 5:60
occurrence before fiduciary's appointment, 5:62
payment directly to plan to settle claim for, 5:58
punitive damages to beneficiary, 5:67
recovery of attorneys' fees and costs, 5:68
unwitting violation, 5:61
checklist, Appendix C
compensation to, 5:84
concerns related to specific investment products, 5:153–5:165
consent of person to be fiduciary or to be treated as fiduciary, 5:27
decisions on investments, 5:39
decisions that are fiduciary in nature, 5:38
default fund, assets deposited in to reduce liability, 5:135
defined, 5:1–5.6. See also DOL new proposed rules on fiduciary status below, this group
3(16) fiduciary, 5:4
3(21) fiduciary, 5:2
3(38) fiduciary, 5:3
delegation of responsibility, 5:132
directed trustee
contributions, ensuring deposit in timely manner, 5:33
defined, 5:29
FAB 2008-01, 5:33–5:35, 5:80
liability, protection from, 5:32
responsibilities regarding investing plan assets, 5:31
salary deferrals, ensuring deposit in timely manner, 5:33
status as fiduciary, 5:40
disclosure requirements
DOL interim final rule, 4:79
plan investment products, 4:80
DOL new proposed rules on fiduciary status, 5:7–5:24
activities considered fiduciary activity, 5:8
"affiliate," defined, 5:10
carve-outs, 5:14–5:23
compensation incident to the transaction, 5:10
current standard *vs.*, 5:12
employees of plan sponsor, 5:14, 5:18
exceptions, 5:14–5:23
fee or other compensation, advice provided for, 5:10
financial reports and valuations, 5:14, 5:21
functional test, 5:11
indirect compensation, 5.10
investment education, 5:14, 5:22, 8:35, 8:37
mutuality component, removal of, 5:12
other exceptions, 5:23
platform providers, 5:14, 5:19
"recommendation," defined, 5:9
selection and monitoring assistance, 5:14, 5:20
seller's carve-out, 5:14, 5:15, 5:16
service provider distinctions and, 5:13
small plans or individuals, 5:16
swap transactions, 5:14, 5:17

duties and obligations, 5:45–5:60
employer securities, 6:51
ERISA bond requirements, 5:47–5:56
  exemptions from, 5:52
  form of bond, applicable rules, 5:55
  funds or other property of a plan, defined, 5:50
  handling of funds or other property, when bond is required, 5:51
  losses covered by, 5:48
  plan assets, paid from, 5:56
  responsibility for ensuring persons are bonded, 5:53
  restrictions on who can issue, 5:54
  term of bond, applicable rules, 5:55
  who must be covered, 5:47, 5:49
ERISA Section 404(c) compliance checklist, Appendix C
fees, payment from mutual funds, 5:91, 5:92
float income, use of, to pay for plan expenses, 5:85
funding policy and method, 5:39–5:42
  development of, 5:40
guaranteed lifetime income investments, fiduciary concerns, 5:165
indemnification, 5:129–5:131
independent fiduciary, 5:110
investment advice for a fee. *See also* DOL new proposed rules on fiduciary status *above, this group*
  current definition, 5:6
  proposed new definition, 5:10
investment manager fiduciary, defined, 5:3
investment of plan assets, 5:39
investment policy coverage, 5:41
liability
  assets deposited in plan's default fund, reduction of liability, 5:135
  default investment funds, assets invested in, 6:40
  directed trustee, steps to protect from, 5:32
  investment education, 8:33–8:34
  managing fiduciary liability, 4:93–4:115
  managing personal liability, 5:136–5:137
  participant-directed plans, 7:2
  participant direction of investments, 5:134, 5:135, 7:34–7:39
liability insurance, 5:121–5:128
manual, sample, Appendix C
multiple functions, 5:36
mutual funds
  investigations, response to, 6:94
  payments from, 5:91, 5:92
  revenue sharing, responsibilities of plan fiduciaries in understanding, 5:162
named fiduciary
  defined, 5:26
  role of, 4:2
noncompliance to plan sponsor or other fiduciary, 4:100
participant-directed plans, protection, 7:2, 7:6, 7:7
participant direction of investments, 5:134, 5:135
  restrictions on participant rights, 7:32
participant loans, involvement in, 15:12
Pension Protection Act of 2006 (PPA)
  bond limit, 5:47
  changes to rules, 1:59
  default fund, assets deposited in to reduce liability, 5:135
plan administrator, 5:4
platform provider exception, fiduciary status, 5:19
procedural due diligence, 5:136
property, contributions of, 5:82
protection, participant-directed plans, 7:2, 7:6, 7:7
PTE 2003-39, 5:58, 5:59
qualified professional asset managers (QPAMs), 5:27
readiness of participants for retirement, fiduciary audit and, 5:138
responsibilities
  allocation of, 5:37
  trustee, 5:28
responsible plan fiduciary disclosure rules, 4:71, 5:94
revenue sharing, responsibilities of plan fiduciaries in understanding, 5:162
risk management services, 4:7
selection
  factors in selection, 5:43
  procedures to follow, 5:44
self-directed options, 6:84
specific investment products, concerns related to, 5:153–5:165
status as fiduciary
  directed trustee, 5:30
  DOL new proposed rules,
5:7–5:24. *See also* DOL new proposed rules on fiduciary status *above, this group*
  investment advice for a fee, current definition, 5:6
  investment manager fiduciary, defined, 5:3
  and risk, 5:25
and target date funds, 5:163, 5:164
uniform standard of care, 1:81, 1:82
unwitting violation of ERISA's fiduciary duties, 5:61
Voluntary Fiduciary Correction Program (VFCP). *See* Voluntary Fiduciary Correction Program (VFCP)

Fiduciary Rule, proposed changes to definition, 1:80

Financial Industry Regulatory Authority (FINRA), 1:82
participant communications, 8:3
"Smart 401(k) Investing?," 8:3

Financial intermediary, defined, 5:158

FINRA. *See* Financial Industry Regulatory Authority (FINRA)

First service organization
constructive ownership rules, 10:36
defined, 10:25
historically performed services, 10:34
regularly performing services, determination, 10:29

Five percent owner, 10:77, 10:82
required minimum distributions (RMDs), 16:31
top-heavy plans, 14:10

Fixed number of years, in-service distributions, 15:59

Fixed-rate investments
participant direction of investments, 7:12

Fixed-return investments
investment-related information, participant investment and fee disclosures, 19:71

Float earnings, 5:84, 5:85
plan expenses, payment of, 5:85

Floor-offset plans, defined, 22:88

FMLA. *See* Family and Medical Leave Act of 1993 (FMLA)

Foreign addresses, participants with
withholding, 16:136

Foreign affiliate, nondiscrimination testing, 10:9

Forfeiture. *See* Vesting

Form 945, 16:137

Form 1040
premature distribution tax, 18:89

Form 1099-DIV, 18:31

Form 1099-R, 16:95, 16:139
correction of, 18:98
distributions, 18:93–18:96
electronic format, 18:94
employer securities, 18:31
in-service withdrawals, 18:45
installment distributions, 18:38
life insurance, 18:49
magnetic media, 18:96
participant loans, 18:53
penalty for failure to file, 18:95
premature distribution tax, 18:87

Form 5300, 3:32, 10:40

Form 5307, 3:32

Form 5310, 21:2

Form 5310-A, 19:21, 21:22

Form 5329, 18:87, 18:89

Form 5330, 5:57, 19:24

Form 5500-EZ, 19:4

Form 5500 series. *See also* Reporting and disclosure
audit requirement, 19:5
challenges involved in filing, 19:12
Code Section 403(b) plans
safe harbor exemption from ERISA, 22:154–22:156
Delinquent Filer Voluntary Compliance (DFVC) Program, 19:15
direct compensation, information, 19:9
due date for filing, 19:13
electronic filing, 19:10–19:11
eligible indirect compensation (EIC), information, 19:9
employer securities, 6:64
enforcement program for assessment of penalties, 19:14
fee disclosure, 4:65
generally, 19:2
indirect compensation, information, 19:9
late deposits, 5:67, 19:12
multiple-employer plans, 1:40, 1:43
open MEPs, 1:43
participant direction of investments, 7:38
penalties for late filing, 19:14
plan characteristics codes, 19:12
PPA changes to rules, 1:61
schedules,
explained, 19:6
Schedule C, information required, 4:105, 5:94, 19:9
small plans, 19:3
summary annual reports (SARs), 19:38
terminating plan, 19:22

Form 5500-SF, 5:67, 19:3
Code Section 403(b) plans
safe harbor exemption from ERISA, 22:154
electronic filing, 19:10–19:11

Form 5558, 19:13, 19:24

Form 8955-SSA
Delinquent Filer Voluntary Compliance (DFVC) Program, 19:15
late filing, penalty for, 19:8
purpose of, 19:7

Form W-4, 16:127

Former employees
fees, administration of plan, 4:60

Freezing plan, 21:31

Front-end loads, defined, 6:97

Frozen plans
business transactions, major, 21:31
Code Section 457(b) plans, 22:185

FSO. *See* First service organization

Full brokerage account, self-directed option, 6:76

Funded plan, defined, 22:93

Funding policy and method, 5:39–5:42
application of, 5:42
coverage by, 5:41
development, 5:40, 5:42
plan assets investment, 5:39
updating, 5:42

"Fund of funds," multiple mutual funds combined into, 4:120

FUTA. *See* Federal Unemployment Tax Act (FUTA)

Future of 401(k) plans
demographic trends, 1:47
economic trends, 1:48
guaranteed lifetime income, access to investment options providing, 1:48
prospects for 401(k) plans, 1:49

G

GAO. *See* U.S. Government Accountability Office (GAO)

Gap period
elimination of need to calculate earnings, 1:63
excess aggregate contributions, 13:68–13:70
excess contributions, 13:24, 13:26
excess deferrals, 9:12
pre-tax excess deferrals, taxation to participant, 18:54
Worker, Retiree, and Employer Recovery Act of 2008 (WRERA), 1:74

GATT (General Agreement on Tariffs and Trade), 3:15

GICs. *See* Guaranteed investment contracts (GICs)

Glide path of target date funds, 6:28

Global funds, 6:24

Government Accountability Office (GAO)
fees, actions with regard to, 4:63, 5:94

Governmental plans
cash or deferred arrangements, generally, 1:27
401(k) plan sponsorship, 2:147, 2:148
Section 457(b) deferred compensation plan, 2:145

Growth and income stock fund, defined, 6:22

Growth fund, defined, 6:23

Growth stocks, defined, 6:2

Guaranteed investment contract fund
costs, 6:105

Guaranteed investment contracts (GICs)
defined, 6:34

Guaranteed lifetime income investments
access to investment options providing, 1:48
fiduciary concerns, 5:165

Guaranteed withdrawal benefits, 6:35

GUST remedial amendment period, 3:15, 3:16

H

Hardship withdrawals
all other plans maintained by employer, defined, 15:49
Code Section 457(b) plans, 22:180–22:181
combining standards, 15:50
considered made, 15:44
distribution from employer contributions, 15:55
documentation to be retained, 15:51
educational expenses, payment of, 15:46
events test, 15:45–15:46
general standard, 15:45
primary beneficiary under the plan, defined, 15:46
safe harbor standard, 15:46
general standard
combining standards, 15:50
events test, 15:45
needs test, 15:47
safe harbor standard *vs.*, 15:50
Hurricane Sandy relief, 15:62
limit on amount, 15:54
medical care expenses, payment of, 15:46
needs test, 15:47–15:49
all other plans maintained by employer, defined, 15:49
general standard, 15:47
safe harbor standard, 15:48
Pension Protection Act of 2006 (PPA), 1:60

Hardship withdrawals (*cont'd*)
primary beneficiary under the plan, defined, 15:46
retention of records, 15:51
rollovers, 1:53
Roth elective deferral accounts, 15:56
Roth 401(k) accounts, 18:64
safe harbor standard, 15:54
combining standards, 15:50
events test, 15:46
general standard *vs.*, 15:50
needs test, 15:48
self-certification, 15:51
substantiation of, 15:51
tax consequences, 15:52–15:53
withholding rules, 16:111

HCE percentage ratio, 10:55
qualified separate lines of business (QSLOBs), 10:57

HCEs. *See* Highly compensated employees

Heroes Earnings Assistance and Tax Relief Act of 2008 (HEART Act), 1:71–1:73
compliance, plan amendment, 3:22
death and disability benefits, 1:73
differential wage payments, 1:71
disabled participant, 1:71
master and prototype plans
plan document, updating of, 3:23
plan amendment to comply with, 3:22
qualified reservist distributions, 1:72, 16:27
volume submitter plans
plan document, updating of, 3:23

Highly compensated employees
ACP test, 13:55, 13:57
actual deferral ratio calculated differently, 13:10
compensation, defined, 10:90
defined, 10:76
determination of, 10:81
determination years, 10:91
dollar thresholds, adjustment of, 10:78–10:79
$80,000, compensation in excess of, 10:77, 10:78
five percent owner, 10:77, 10:82
flowchart determining, 10:91
limited to employees of entity sponsoring plan, 10:80
look-back year, 10:91
application of dollar thresholds to, 10:79
matching contributions, 2:251
nondiscrimination testing, 10:76–10:91
participant loans, 15:4
plan years beginning after 1996, 10:77
rate group, 12:10
seven months, working less than, 10:86
top-paid group
defined, 10:83
determining membership in, worksheet, 10:84
membership in, 10:87–10:89
number of employees in, 10:84
selection of, 10:87
seven months, working less than, 10:86
17½ hours per week, working less than, 10:85

Historical performance test
affiliated service groups, 10:34
leased employees, 10:65

History of 401(k) plans, 1:1–1:2

Home ownership
individual retirement planning, 8:56
principal residence, loan to purchase, 15:32

Hours of service
defined, 2:175
elapsed time methods, 2:176, 2:177
equivalency method, 2:176
methods for determining, 2:176

Hurricane Sandy relief
hardship distributions, 15:62
plan loans, 15:62

I

Identifiable costs
defined, 4:42
participant directed plan, 4:42
who pays, 4:43

I Got Caught CAP. *See* Audit Based Closing Agreement Program (Audit CAP)

Incidental death benefits, 2:151

Includable officer, top-heavy testing
defined, 14:13
limit on number of, 14:14, 14:16

Income acceleration rule
in-plan Roth rollovers, 18:76

Indemnification
defined, 5:129
employer, indemnification of fiduciary by, 5:131
fiduciaries, 5:70, 5:129–5:131
breach of duty, 5:130
definition, 5:129
employer, indemnification by, 5:131

Independent fiduciary
eligible investment advice arrangements (EIAAs), 5:113

Independent ratings services, investment funds, 6:93

Indexed limits
EGTRRA, affected by, Appendix E
2013-2014, Appendix D

Index fund, defined, 6:20

Indexing for inflation, 9:40

Indian tribal governments
age discrimination, PPA changes, 1:64
401(k) sponsorship, 2:147

Indirect compensation, 4:83, 4:91

Individually designed plans
advantages and disadvantages, 3:14
plan amendment
HEART Act, updating of plan document for, 3:24
PPA, updating of plan document for, 3:24
"spouse" definition after *Windsor* decision, 3:25
WRERA, updating of plan document for, 3:24
plan document
HEART Act, updating for, 3:24
PPA, updating for, 3:24
spouse, definition of, 3:25
updating plans, 3:20
WRERA, updating for, 3:24

Individual participant benefit statements, 19:40–19:51
compliance, 19:49–19:50
diversification, 19:48
electronic media, use of, 19:44
information required
diversification, 19:48
flexibility, 19:42
generally, 19:41
investing, 19:48
participant directed plan, multiple documents used, 19:43
investing, information, 19:48
language, DOL-approved, 19:48
limitations, 19:47
participant direction of investments
limitations and restrictions, 19:47
multiple documents used for required information, 19:43
Pension Protection Act of 2006 (PPA), 19:40
restrictions, 19:47
when statements given to participants, 19:45

Individual retirement annuity, defined, 22:2

Individual retirement arrangements (IRAs), 22:1–22:23
advantages of saving in 401(k) plans rather than, 8:2, 8:3
age 70½, contributions, 22:11
annual installment exception, 18:109
assets, charitable contributions of, 22:20
Bankruptcy Abuse Prevention and Consumer Protection Act of 2005, 22:8
bankruptcy estate, exemption from, 22:8
both spouses employed, contribution allowed, 22:14
charitable distributions from, 22:20
contributions
age 50, limit on contributions for those over, 22:10
age 50, limit on contributions for those under, 22:9
age 70½, persons reaching, 22:11
charitable distributions from IRA, 22:20
deductions, 22:12–22:13
defined, 22:1
maximum contribution amount, 22:9–22:10
prorated deduction, calculation, 22:13
coverage for deductible traditional IRA contributions, 22:12
death proceeds
non-spouse beneficiary rolling over, 18:35
spousal beneficiary rolling over, 18:34
deductions
contributions, 22:12–22:13
deemed IRA contributions. *See* Contributions
direct transfers between multiple IRAs, 22:21
distributions
bankruptcy, as subject to, 22:19
commencement, 22:17
required minimum distribution rules, 22:19
taxation, 22:18
EGTRRA, changes in rules, 1:54
employer-sponsored IRA program, 22:16
Roth IRAs, rollovers to, 22:36
FICA, 22:16
FUTA, 22:16
individual retirement annuity defined, 22:2
inherited IRAs
defined, 22:4
non-spouse inheriting, applicable rules, 22:6
rollovers by beneficiaries, 22:7
spouse inheriting, applicable rules, 22:5
inherited IRAs, rollovers to, 16:62, 16:82, 16:97–16:103
defined, 16:99
direct rollovers, 16:97–16:98
establishment of, 16:100

Individual retirement arrangements (IRAs) *(cont'd)*
inherited IRAs, rollovers to *(cont'd)*
non-spouse beneficiaries, direct rollovers, 16:97–16:98
required beginning date, death after, 16:102
required beginning date, death before, 16:101
required minimum distributions (RMDs), 16:101, 16:103
title, 16:100
missing participants, rollovers, 21:12
multiple IRAs
direct transfers in one year, 22:21
rollover, one per year, 1:79, 22:22
nondeductible contributions, 22:15
non-spouse beneficiaries, direct rollovers, 16:97–16:98
required minimum distributions (RMDs), 22:19
rollovers
abandoned plans, 21:48
automatic rollover rules, 16:74–16:76
employer-sponsored plan, rollovers to and from, 22:23
inherited IRAs. *See* Inherited IRAs *above, this group*
missing participants, 21:12
multiple IRAs, one rollover per year, 22:22
Roth IRAs, conversions to. *See* Roth IRAs
SEP IRAs. *See* Simplified employee pensions (SEPs)
SIMPLE IRA plans. *See* SIMPLE IRA plans
spousal IRA, defined, 22:3
tax considerations
distributions, 22:18
Tax Increase Prevention Act of 2014, 22:20
traditional IRAs
contributions to, 22:9–22:16
distributions, 22:17–22:19
generally, 22:1–22:2
Roth IRAs compared, 22:37–22:38
transfers, trustee-to-trustee, 22:21
withholding rules, 16:117

Individual retirement planning, 8:38–8:61
future salary and inflation, 8:38–8:41
home ownership, 8:56
inflation, 8:38–8:41
asset classes keeping pace with, 8:55
importance of taking into account, 8:54
investment risk management, 8:59–8:60
longevity risk, 8:58
long-term investment return, 8:47–8:53
disadvantage to investing solely in asset classes with higher average return, 8:48
higher expected average return, 8:48
higher-yielding asset classes, variable risk return, 8:50
increasing expected return, 8:47
managing risk while achieving objectives, 8:51
riskiness of asset class, determining, 8:49
risk tolerance, 8:52–8:53
standard deviation of annual return, 8:49
outliving retirement savings, risk management, 8:46
replacement ratios, 8:44–8:46
retirement ages, choosing, 8:42
Retirement Readiness report, 8:20
risk management, 8:59–8:60
risk tolerance, 8:52–8:53
saver's credit, 8:61
PPA changes, 1:63
Social Security, 8:56, 8:57
tools, retirement planning, 8:43
types of, 8:38–8:43

Industry segments safe harbor, QSLOBs, 10:56

Inflation
falling behind, 8:39, 8:40
historic levels as guide to future, 8:41
housing, investments, 8:56
keeping pace with, 8:40
outpacing, 8:39, 8:40
retirement planning, 8:38–8:41
asset classes keeping pace with inflation, 8:55
future salary and inflation, 8:38–8:41
taking into account, importance of, 8:54
salary outpacing, 8:39, 8:40
Treasury inflation-protected securities (TIPs), 6:7

Information upon request, 19:51–19:55

Inherited IRAs
defined, 22:4
non-spouse inheriting, applicable rules, 22:6
rollovers by beneficiaries, 22:7
rollovers to, individual retirement arrangements (IRAs), 16:62, 16:82, 16:97–16:103
defined, 16:99
direct rollovers, 16:97–16:98
establishment of, 16:100
non-spouse beneficiaries, direct rollovers, 16:97–16:98
required beginning date, death after, 16:102
required beginning date, death before, 16:101

required minimum distributions (RMDs), 16:101, 16:103
title, 16:100
spouse inheriting, applicable rules, 22:5

In-house administration
advantages, 4:12
disadvantages, 4:13

In-kind contributions
prohibited transactions, 5:82

In-kind distributions
anti-cutback rules, 16:8
right to receive, elimination of, 16:8

In-service distributions, 15:57–15:61
elective contributions, 15:60
employer contribution accounts, 15:55, 15:58
fixed number of years, 15:59
hardship, 15:55
nonelective contributions, 15:58, 15:60
restrictions of accessibility, 15:61
when may 401(k) accounts be distributed, 15:57

In-service withdrawals, 18:39–18:45
basis recovery rules, 18:40, 18:43
described, 18:44
cost basis, 18:40
mandatory contributions, accounting for, 18:42
reporting, 18:45
safe harbor 401(k) plan, 2:266
taxation while employed, 18:39
TRA '86, 18:41, 18:43
voluntary contributions, accounting for, 18:42

Installation of plan, costs, 2:8

Installment distributions. *See* Distributions

Insurance. *See also* Life insurance
benefits to plan participants, 2:151
fiduciary liability insurance, 5:121–5:128
determination of which insurance company to use, 5:127
eligibility for coverage under, 5:125
linked insurance policy, 5:123
prohibited transactions, losses resulting from, 5:128
purpose of, 5:124
20 percent civil penalty, 5:126

Insurance companies
proceeds, fees, 4:122

Integrated method of allocation, contributions, 2:104

Internal Revenue Service (IRS)
current-year testing method, approval, 13:54
determination letters, 3:32–3:37
Electronic Federal Tax Payment System (EFTPS). *See* Electronic Federal Tax Payment System (EFTPS)
employee notification, 3:35
fee for, 3:34
not necessary, 3:36
where to send, 3:33
Notice 2010-80, 22:115
plan document, advance approval, 3:26–3:37
publicly traded employer securities, model diversification notice, Appendix G
regulatory agenda, 1:79
withheld income taxes reported, 16:137

International funds, types of, 6:24

Interpretive Bulletin 96-1 (DOL), 7:25, 8:21, 8:32–8:35, 8:37

Investment advice
asset allocation models, 8:27–8:28
defined, 5:6, 5:10, 8:23
Department of Labor, 8:21–8:38
Advisory Opinions, 8:37
asset allocation models, 8:27–8:28
education constituting advice, 8:21, 8:37
education *vs.* investment advice, 8:21, 8:23, 8:31–8:32
general financial and investment information, 8:26
interactive investment materials, 8:29–8:30
Interpretive Bulletin 96-1, 8:21, 8:32–8:35, 8:37
investment-related information and material not considered advice, 8:23
plan information, 8:24–8:25
plan sponsor, 8:33, 8:35–8:37
safe harbors, 8:32
education *vs.* investment advice, 8:21, 8:23, 8:31–8:32
ERISA
characterized under, 8:22
investment-related information and material not considered advice, 8:23
issues arising, 8:37
for a fee. *See also* Fiduciary
current definition, 5:6
proposed new definition, 5:10
general financial and investment information, 8:26
interactive investment materials, 8:29–8:30
offering, 8:36–8:37
outside professional, offering advice from, 8:36
Pension Protection Act of 2006 (PPA), 8:37
plan information, 8:24–8:25

Investment Advisers Act of 1940, 5:133

Investment change frequency
participant direction of investments, 7:26–7:29
market timing, actions to limit, 7:29
transfer fees, funds with, 7:28
transfer restrictions, funds with, 7:28
volatility levels, differing, 7:27

Investment Company Act of 1940, 5:154, 7:41
money market funds, 6:17
participant investment and fee disclosures, 19:58

Investment education
advice *vs.* education, 8:31–8:32
fiduciaries, 8:33–8:34

Investment in the contract
lump-sum distributions, 18:23

Investment manager fiduciary, defined, 5:3

Investment managers. *See also* Fiduciary
defined, 5:133
delegating fiduciary responsibility to, 5:133
role of, 4:5

Investments, 6:1–6:107. *See also* Investment advice; Investment vehicles; Participant direction of investments
asset allocation strategy, 6:46–6:48
audit, fiduciary, 5:138
decision, 5:39
directed trustees, 6:72
disclosure requirements, 4:87
employer securities, 6:50–6:71
fees
back-end loads, defined, 6:97
collective funds, 6:103
front-end loads, defined, 6:97
generally, 6:95
management fees, defined, 6:99
mutual funds, 6:96, 6:101, 6:102
12b-1 fees, 6:98, 6:101
variable annuity contract, 6:104
KSOPs, 6:73–6:74
"other" administrative or operating costs, 6:100
primary asset classes, 6:1–6:9
regulations, 6:107
reporting requirements, 6:66–6:69
revenue sharing, 6:106
SEC registration, 6:66–6:69
selection and monitoring, 6:88–6:93
comparison with similar investments, 6:91
considerations, 6:88
independent ratings services, 6:93
investment monitoring program, 6:90
monitoring, 6:92
type offered, 6:89
self-directed options, 6:75–6:84
service provider disclosures, 4:76

Investment services, 4:20–4:27
brokers, 4:21
conflicts of interest, potential, 4:23
distinctions between brokers and registered investment advisors, 4:21
DOL guidelines for selection and monitoring of providers, 4:25
questions to ask when selecting investment service provider, 4:24, 4:26–4:27
registered investment advisers, 4:21
selecting, 4:20–4:27
services offered by investment service providers, 4:22
suitability of investment provider, determining, 4:24–4:27
types of providers offering, 4:20

Investment vehicles, 6:10–6:45
asset allocation funds, 6:25
utilization of, increased, 1:48
collective trust funds, 6:15
default investment funds, 6:39–6:45
DOL guidance, 6:42, 6:44
fiduciary liability for assets invested, 6:40
Pension Protection Act of 2006 (PPA), 6:42–6:43
qualified default investment alternatives (QDIAs), 6:43–6:45
requirement to offer, 6:39
types of funds used as, 6:41, 6:42, 6:44
exchange traded funds, 6:31
guaranteed investment contracts (GICs), 6:34
guaranteed withdrawal benefits, 6:35
investment funds offered, common types, 6:16
life insurance contracts, 6:38
lifetime income products, 6:35–6:37
mutual funds, 6:11–6:13. *See also* Mutual funds
options offered, 6:10
real estate funds, 6:30
separately managed account, 6:14
target date funds, 6:26, 6:27
variable annuities, 6:32

Involuntary distributions. *See* Distributions

IRA. *See* Individual retirement arrangement (IRAs)

IRRA. *See* IRS Restructuring and Reform Act of 1998 (IRRA)

IRS. *See* Internal Revenue Service (IRS)

IRS Restructuring and Reform Act of 1998 (IRRA) plan documents, amendment, 3:15

J

Joint and survivor annuities. *See also* Qualified joint and survivor annuity (QJSA)
PPA changes to rules, 1:60
SIMPLE 401(k) plan, 2:232

Joint and survivor rules
governmental 401(k) plans, 2:148
rollovers, consent if vested balance not exceeding $5,000, 16:73

K

Key employees. *See also* Top-heavy plans
compensation, 14:17
defined, 14:9
five percent owner, 14:10
includable officer
defined, 14:13
limit on number of, 14:14, 14:16
minimum contributions on behalf of, 14:37
number of employees, determination of, 14:15
officer, 14:12
one percent owner, 14:11

KSOPs (401(k) stock ownership plans)
C corporations
employer securities, funds borrowed to purchase, 9:44
special deduction rules, 9:60
defined, 6:73
employer securities, funds borrowed to purchase from C corporation, 9:44
special deduction rules, 9:60
stock bonus rules, 6:74

L

Language requirements
summary plan description (SPD), 19:27

***LaRue* decision,** 5:69

Last-day requirements
contributions, 2:98

Late-day trading
concerns, reasons for, 5:154
defined, 5:154

Leased employees
defined, 10:65
money purchase plan, 10:74
nondiscrimination rules, 10:64–10:75
agreement between recipient and leasing organization, 10:66
consideration as employee, 10:64
covering individual under recipient's 401(k) plan, 10:72
defined, 10:65
disregarding of plan by recipient, 10:73
employee, consideration as, 10:69
full-time services for at least one year, 10:67, 10:68
historical performance test, 10:65
leasing organization, employee of, 10:71
non-highly compensated employee, 10:75
primary direction or control of recipient, 10:70
safe harbor plan, 10:74

Leaves of absence
participant loans and, 15:33
military service, leave for, 15:34

Legislation
abandoned plans, 21:37–21:51
proposed, 1:78

Letter-forwarding services, elimination of
missing participants, 21:11

Levy, IRS
anti-assignment rules and, 2:156
premature distribution tax, exception, 18:86

Life expectancy
longevity risk, 8:58
required minimum distributions (RMDs), 16:45

Life insurance
amount at risk, 18:47
limited, 2:151
policies
Code Section 457(b) plans, 22:166
proceeds, payment of, 18:33
PS-58 costs, 18:23, 18:33, 18:47
premature distribution tax, exception, 18:86
taxable cost of protection reporting, 18:49
taxation
generally, 18:46
second to die, 18:47
survivor whole life taxation, 18:48
taxable cost computed, 18:47

Life insurance contract, defined, 6:38

Lifetime income products, 6:35–6:37
defined, 6:35
factors to consider, 6:36, 6:37
plan sponsors, considerations for, 6:36
regulatory considerations, 6:37

Limited liability companies (LLCs)
sponsorship of 401(k) plan, 1:33

Lineal ascendant or descendant, attribution to, 10:20

Lines of business. *See* Qualified separate lines of business (QSLOBs)

Linked insurance policy, 5:123

Liquidity, mutual funds, 6:12

LLCs. *See* Limited liability companies (LLCs)

Loans. *See* Participant loans

Lockdown periods, risks involved in incurring, 4:19

Longevity risk, 8:58

Long-term investment return. *See* Individual retirement planning

Look-back rules
- salary reduction SEPs (SARSEPs), 22:43
- top-heavy plans, 1:56

Look-back year, 10:79
- defined, 10:91

Look-through funds
- participant direction of investments, 7:14

Lump-sum distributions
- balance to the credit of participant, 18:18
- computation of tax, 18:25
- death benefits, 18:32
- defined, 15
- election as beneficiary, 18:26
- excluded items from taxation, 18:23
- future election rights, 18:26
- investment in the contract, 18:23
- minimum distribution allowance (MDA), 18:24
- older participants, 18:22
- payment, generally, 18:14
- plans considered, 18:17
- prior distribution, 18:19
- QDROs, alternate payees, 18:21
- reporting, 18:27
- small distributions qualifying for additional favorable treatment, 18:24
- subsequent payments, 18:19
- tax considerations, 18:14–18:27, 18:104
- tax options for qualified participants, 18:20
- ten-year forward income averaging option, 18:20
- termination of plan, 18:16
- TRA '86, 18:22

M

Magnetic media, filing on, 18:96

Management fees, defined, 6:99

Management functions, affiliated service groups, 10:38

Mandatory disaggregation testing
- application of, 10:62
- separate asset pool, 10:61

Marketable obligation, defined, 6:52

Market downturn of 2008
- matching contributions, effect on, 1:46
- plan fees, effect on, 4:63

Market timing, 5:155–5:160
- concern, reasons for, 5:155
- defined, 5:155
- limitation of, actions, 7:29
- redemption fees
  - allocation of proceeds, 5:160
  - fiduciary responsibilities, 5:159
  - imposition of, 7:29
- Securities and Exchange Commission (SEC), 5:156–5:158

Mass submitter plans, 3:4. *See also* Regional prototype plans

Master and prototype plans, 3:2–3:8
- advantages, 3:7, 3:8
- comparisons with other plans, 3:12
- defined, 3:2
- differences, 3:5
- disadvantages, 3:7, 3:8
- installation costs, 2:8
- mass submitter master or prototype plan, 3:4
- options, 3:6
- plan amendment
  - HEART Act, updating of plan document for, 3:23
  - PPA, updating of plan document for, 3:23
  - WRERA, updating of plan document for, 3:23
- plan document
  - HEART Act, updating for, 3:23
  - PPA, updating for, 3:23
  - WRERA, updating for, 3:23
- prototype plan program
  - Code Section 403(b) plans, 1:79, 22:126
  - pre-approval program, 22:126
- regional prototype plans, consolidation with, 3:2
- requirements for sponsors, 3:3
- Self-Correction Program (SCP), 20:14
- standardized and nonstandardized, 3:6, 3:7
- updating plans, 3:18

Match cap, 2:6

Matching contributions. *See* Contributions

Material information, defined, 19:16

Maternity leave
- eligibility, 2:188
- vesting, 2:206

Maximum deferral percentage
defined, 9:54

"Maybe" safe harbor nonelective contribution, 2:249

Medical expenses
hardship withdrawals to pay, 15:46
premature distribution tax and, 18:86

Merger of plan
allocation of benefits, 21:19
defined, 21:18
distribution concerns, 21:25
monitoring and harmonizing options, 21:26
relief from, 21:27
IRS guidance, 21:36
issues encountered, 21:28
procedures involved, 21:22
pros and cons, 21:29
protection of participants, 2:159
reporting and disclosure, 19:21
review of plan provisions, 21:24

Mergers and acquisitions, corporate
anti-cutback rules, 16:11
IRS guidance, 21:36
issues encountered, 21:28

Mergers and acquisitions (M&A) safe harbor
QSLOBs, 10:56

Merrill Lynch Trust Co., 5:31

Military service
differential wage payments
eligible rollover distributions to participants on active duty for more than 30 days, 16:63
participants called to active military service, 16:50–16:51
eligible rollover distributions to participants on active duty for more than 30 days
differential wage payments *also* received, 16:63
participant loans during, 15:34
participants called to active military service, 16:49–16:51
differential wage payments, 16:50–16:51
qualified reservist distributions. *See* Qualified reservist distributions
rollovers to participants on active military duty for more than 30 days, 16:63

Minimum coverage rules. *See* Coverage requirements

Minimum coverage testing. *See* Coverage requirements

Minimum distribution requirements. *See* Required minimum distributions (RMDs)

Minimum hours requirements
contributions, 2:98

Minimum or maximum benefits safe harbor
qualified separate lines of business (QSLOBs), 10:56

Minimum participation rules. *See* Participation

Ministerial functions, 5:5

Missing participants
certified mail, 21:11
distribution methods, 21:12
escheat to state unclaimed property, 21:12
federally insured bank accounts, 21:12
free electronic search tools, 21:11
letter-forwarding services, elimination of, 21:11
location of participant, steps to take, 21:10, 21:11
rollovers, 21:12
search methods, 20:8, 21:11
search steps, 21:11
termination of plan, 21:10–21:13
abandoned plans, 21:48
distribution methods, 21:12
location of participant, steps to take, 21:10
Pension Protection Act of 2006 (PPA), 21:13
search methods, 21:11
withholding, 21:12

Missing spouse
survivor annuity requirements, spousal consent, 17:48

Money market fund
amended rules, 6:17
defined, 6:17
"floating" net asset value, 1:81, 6:17
liquidity fee, 6:17
reform proposals, 6:17

Money purchase plans
Code Section 404 deduction limits, 9:75
existing plan in addition to 401(k) plan, 9:76
merger into 401(k) plan, 9:77
leased employees, 10:74
merger into 401(k) plans, 9:77, 21:23
survivor annuity requirements, 17:1
vesting, merger into 401(k) plan, 9:77

Multiemployer Pension Plan Amendments Act (MPPAA), 1:35

Multiemployer plans, 1:35–1:38
administration of plan, 1:38
defined benefit plans, replacing, 1:36
generally, 1:35
mandatory disaggregation rules, 10:62

Multiemployer plans *(cont'd)*
nondiscrimination rules, 10:62
nondiscrimination testing, 1:38
plan design, 1:33
prohibited transactions, late deposits of salary deferral contributions, 5:76
start-up costs, 1:38
structure of 401(k) plan, 1:36
supplemental 401(k) plan, structure of, 1:37
"union only" funds, 1:38
unique features, 1:38

Multiple affiliated service groups, aggregation of, 10:35

Multiple destinations, rollovers to, 16:106

Multiple-employer plans, 1:39–1:43
benefits of joining MEP, 1:40
how MEPs work, 1:39
mandatory disaggregation rules, 10:62
nondiscrimination rules, 10:62
open MEPs, 1:41–1:43
defined, 1:41
DOL ruling, significance of, 1:43
filing requirements, 1:43
legal concerns, 1:42

Multiple use test, 1:56

Mutual funds, 5:153–5:162, 6:11–6:13
actively managed fund, defined, 6:21
advantages of offering in plans, 6:12
aggressive stock fund, defined, 6:23
balanced fund defined, 6:19
concerns, reasons for, 5:153–5:162
considerations of offering in plans, 6:13
convenience, 6:12
corporate/government bond fund defined, 6:18
defined, 6:11
diversification, 6:12
emerging market funds, 6:24
expense ratio, 6:101
fees, 6:13, 6:96
determination of amount, 6:102
expense ratio, 6:101
"fund of funds," multiple mutual funds combined into, 4:120
multiple mutual funds, 4:120
paid from, 4 119–4:120, 5:91
fiduciaries, payments to, 5:91, 5:92
flexibility, 6:12
global funds, 6:24
government entities regulating, 6:107
growth and income stock fund defined, 6:22
growth fund defined, 6:23
guarantees, lack of, 6:13
improper fees, 5:161
independent ratings services, 6:93
index fund defined, 6:20
information, 6:12
international funds, types of, 6:24
issues. *See also* Enron; WorldCom
fiduciaries, response to, 6:94
late-day trading
concerns, reasons for, 5:154
defined, 5:154
liquidity, 6:12
manager risk, 6:13
market timing, 5:155–5:160
concern, reasons for, 5:155
defined, 5:155
multiple mutual funds, fees, 4:120
nonfiduciaries, payments to, 5:90
professional management, 6:12
regional funds, 6:24
regulation, government entities, 6:107
revenue sharing
responsibilities of plan fiduciaries in understanding, 5:162
types, 6:106
statutory prospectus, disclosure requirements, 7:23
summary prospectus, disclosure requirements, 7:23

Mutual fund window, self-directed option, 6:76

***My*RA accounts,** chapter 1, 22:24–22:38

N

National Association of Securities Dealers (NASD), 4:21

Native American tribes. *See* Indian tribal governments

NAV. *See* Net asset value (NAV)

Negative elections, cash or deferred election, 2:34

Net asset value (NAV)
calculation of, 19:105
"floating," for money market funds, 1:81, 6:17

New comparability method, allocation of contributions, 2:104
defined benefit plan, use in lieu of, 2:115
design-based formula, differences, 2:106
design-based safe harbor formula, use in lieu of, 2:115
nondiscrimination rules, 2:112
nondiscrimination testing, 2:113
nondiscriminatory, plans containing treated as, 2:119

participants, allocation to, 2:111
restrictions on use of, 2:114
situations for use of, 2:118

NHCE. *See* Non-highly compensated employee

90-day period, claims for benefits, 16:143

No action letters
Voluntary Fiduciary Correction Program (VFCP), 5:146

Nondiscrimination rules. *See also* Highly compensated employee
age-restricted target date funds, 6:28
basic requirements, 2:157
Code Section 403(b) plans, 22:132
collectively bargained plans, mandatory disaggregation rules, 10:62
deferred annuities, target date funds with, 6:28
different contribution types, plans of, mandatory disaggregation rules, 10:62
employer contributions, 22:131
ESOPs, mandatory disaggregation rules, 10:62
history of, 1:2
mandatory disaggregation rules, 10:61
matching contributions by employer, 22:131
multiemployer plans, 1:38
mandatory disaggregation rules, 10:62
multiple-employer plans, mandatory disaggregation rules, 10:62
new comparability formula, 2:112
non-church plans, 22:131
nonelective contributions by employer, 22:131
non-governmental plans, 22:131
permitted disparity. *See* Permitted disparity
purpose of, 2:160
QSLOBs. *See* Qualified separate lines of business (QSLOBs)
separate asset pool, mandatory disaggregation rules, 10:61
target date funds that include deferred annuities, 6:28
termination of plan, 21:5
testing. *See* Nondiscrimination testing

Nondiscrimination testing, 10:1–10:106, 12:1–12:36
ACP test. *See* Actual contribution percentage (ACP) test
ADP test. *See* Actual deferral percentage (ADP) test
affiliated service groups, 10:24–10:40
A-org, 10:28, 10:34, 10:36
B-org, 10:30, 10:36
constructive ownership rules, 10:36
employee benefit requirements, 10:39
first service organization, 10:25, 10:29, 10:34, 10:36
formal determination as to whether group of organizations constitutes, 10:40
historically performed services, 10:34
management functions, 10:38
management organization, 10:37
multiple affiliated service groups, aggregation of, 10:35
organization defined, 10:26
service organization defined, 10:27
service receipts percentage, 10:32
significant portion of business, 10:31
total receipts percentage, 10:33
types of, 10:24
age-weighted formula, 2:108, 2:110
allocation rate, determination of, 12:11
amounts taken into account, 12:12
ancillary benefit, 12:28
average benefits test, 11:9
benefits, rights, and features, 12:26–12:36
ancillary benefit, 12:28
current availability, 12:31–12:35
defined, 12:26
disregarding conditions, 12:33–12:34
effective availability requirement, 12:36
elimination of, 12:35
optional form of benefit, 12:27
other rights or features, 12:2, 12:29
prospectively eliminated, 12:35
provided on nondiscriminatory basis, 12:30
brother-sister controlled groups, 10:5, 10:9
Code Section 414(s), compensation defined, 10:92–10:103
compensation, described, 10:92–10:106
constructive ownership rules, 10:36
controlled groups
brother-sister, 10:5, 10:9
combined groups, 10:7
constructive ownership rules, 10:13–10:21
controlling interest defined, 10:4
corporation interest, attribution of, 10:16
defined, 10:1
disregarding interests, 10:8, 10:9
effective control, 10:6
employee benefit requirements, 10:23
employee's interest in organization, 10:12
entity attribution rule, 10:14
estate or trust organization interest, attribution of, 10:17
exemptions from tax under Code Section 501(a), 10:22
family attribution rule, 10:18
limit on attribution, 10:21
lineal ascendant or descendant, attribution to, 10:20

Nondiscrimination testing *(cont'd)*
controlled groups *(cont'd)*
officer, 10:9, 10:11
option attribution rule, 10:13
parent-subsidiary, 10:3, 10:9
partnership interest, attribution of, 10:15
principal owner, 10:9, 10:10
significance of controlled groups, 10:23
spouse owning organization, attribution of interest in, 10:19
current availability, 6:81, 12:31–12:35
design-based safe harbor, 12:1–12:8
uniform point system plan, 12:4–12:6
effective availability, 6:81
benefits, rights, and features, 12:36
employees, described, 10:63–10:75
highly compensated employees, 10:76–10:91
employers, described, 10:1–10:58
affiliated service groups, 10:24–10:40
controlled groups, 10:1–10:22
qualified separate lines of business (QSLOBs), 10:41–10:58
foreign affiliate, employees of, 10:9
general nondiscrimination test, 12:9–12:14
allocation rate, determination of, 12:11–12:12
defined, 12:9
minimum coverage rules, 12:13
rate group, 12:10, 12:13
satisfaction on basis of allocation rates, 12:14
governmental 401(k) plans, 2:148
highly compensated employees, 10:76–10:91
historically performed services, leased employees, 10:65
history of, 1:2
leased employees, 10:64–10:75
agreement between recipient and leasing organization, 10:66
consideration as employee, 10:64
covering individual under recipient's 401(k) plan, 10:72
defined, 10:65
employee, consideration as, 10:69
full-time services for at least one year, 10:67, 10:68
historical performance test, 10:65
leasing organization, employee of, 10:71
non-highly compensated employee, 10:75
plan disregarded by recipient, 10:73
primary direction or control of recipient, 10:70
safe harbor plan, 10:74
minimum coverage testing, ratio percentage test, 11:4–11:8
multiemployer plans, 1:38
new comparability formula, 2:113
nondiscriminatory classification test, 11:10–11:17
rate group, minimum coverage rules, 12:13
optional form of benefit, 12:27
parent-subsidiary controlled groups, 10:3, 10:9
permitted disparity. *See* Permitted disparity
plans, described, 10:59–10:62
qualified separate lines of business (QSLOBs), 10:41–10:58
mandatory disaggregation rules, 10:62
rolled-over benefits, 2:140
safe harbor 401(k) plan after-tax contributions, 2:262
satisfaction on basis of allocation rates, 12:14
self-employed individuals, 10:63, 10:102
separate asset pool
defined, 10:59
more than one, 10:60
SIMPLE 401(k) plans, 2:224
single employer, 10:1
transferred benefits, 2:140
uniform point system plan, 12:4–12:6

Nondiscriminatory classification test, 11:10–11:17
combination of plans to satisfy, 11:17
defined, 11:10
facts and circumstances, 11:16
NHCE concentration percentage, 11:15
nondiscriminatory classification, defined, 11:12
rate group, minimum coverage rules, 12:13
reasonable classification, defined, 11:11
safe harbor percentage, 11:13
unsafe harbor percentage, 11:14

Nonelective contributions. *See* Contributions

Nonfiduciary
breach, 5:60
decisions that are not fiduciary in nature, 4:25
mutual funds, payment of fees from, 5:90
non-ERISA grounds, liable on, 5:64
settlor functions, 4:25

Non-highly compensated employee (NHCE)
ACP test, 13:55, 13:56
matching contributions, 13:50–13:52
ADP test
actual deferral ratios and, 13:5
adjustment of non-highly compensated employee to HCE, 13:8
applicable contribution rate of NHCE, 13:45
calculation for initial plan year, 13:9
current plan year data, 13:5

QNECs, 13:43–13:45
representative contribution rate of NHCE, 13:44
specific groups of NHCEs, allocations targeted to, 13:43
concentration percentage, 11:15
contributions, matching contributions, 2:251
defined, 10:75
qualified nonelective contributions, 11:33

Non-highly compensated employees
qualified automatic contribution arrangements (QACAs), 2:62

Nonperiodic distributions
defined, 16:128
notice, 16:134
rate of withholding, 16:129

Nonqualified deferred compensation plans, 22:89–22:120
advantages to employee, 22:103
advantages to employer, 22:102
benefit security
rabbi trust, 22:116–22:118
unfunded plans, 22:116–22:118
Code Section 409A, 22:106–22:115
basic requirements, 22:110
compliance deadline, extension of, 22:108
correction program, IRS, 22:113–22:115
defined, 22:106
effective date, 22:107
impact on plans, 22:109
noncompliance, consequences, 22:112
Notice 2010-06, 22:113–22:115
tax considerations, 22:111–22:115
constructive receipt doctrine, 22:95
defined contribution plan, link to, 22:101
disadvantages to employee, 22:105
disadvantages to employer, 22:104
doctrine of constructive receipt, 22:95
excess benefit plans, defined, 22:91
FICA, taken into account for, 22:98
401(k) plans *vs.*, 22:119–22:120
supplementing 401(k) plans, 22:120
funded plan, defined, 22:93
FUTA, taken into account for, 22:99
gross income inclusion
amounts deferred under funded NQDC, 22:96
amounts deferred under unfunded NQDC, 22:94
rabbi trust, 22:116–22:118
supplementing 401(k) plans, 22:120
tax considerations, 22:94–22:101
Code Section 409A, 22:111–22:115
employer, amounts deferred under deductible by, 22:97
FICA, taken into account for, 22:98
FUTA, taken into account for, 22:99
gross income inclusion, amounts deferred under funded NQDC, 22:96
gross income inclusion, amounts deferred under unfunded NQDC, 22:94
tax-exempt organizations, 22:100
top-hat plans, 22:90
types of, 22:89
unfunded plans
benefit security, 22:116–22:118
defined, 22:92

Nonresident aliens
minimum coverage rules, disregarding for, 11:25

Nonstandardized plan, 3:6, 3:7, 3:37

Normal retirement age, defined, 2:192

Notary public
spousal waivers, electronic media, 19:134

Notice
abandoned plans, 21:41, 21:43
automatic contribution arrangements (ACAs), 2:38, Appendix B, Appendix C
failing to provide notice, penalty, 2:39
blackout notices. *See* Blackout notices
default investments
participant direction of investments, 7:54
direct rollovers, 16:89–16:92
information contained in notice, 16:91
model notice, 16:92
periodic installments, eligible rollover distributions paid in, 16:94
reasonable period of time to provide notice, 16:90
diversification
publicly traded employer securities, 19:121
electronic media, 2:242
"alternative method," 19:132
Code-based, 19:127–19:129, 19:135
effective date, 19:135
methods, 19:130
requirements, 19:133
eligible automatic contribution arrangements (EACAs), 2:42
eligible investment advice arrangements (EIAAs), 5:100
employer securities, diversification rights, 6:60, Appendix G
participant direction of investments
default investments, 7:54
postponement of benefits. *See* Notice and consent; Postponement of benefits
qualified automatic contribution arrangements (QACAs)
matters addressed in notice, 2:55
requirements, 2:53

Notice *(cont'd)*
qualified default investment alternatives (QDIAs), 6:45, 7:55–7:59
EACA, combination of notice with, 7:57–7:58
electronic distribution rules, 7:56
fees and expenses, information regarding, 7:55
grandfathered QDIA, 7:64
information conveyed in notices, 7:54
pass-through of investment materials, 7:56
QACA, combination of notice with, 7:57–7:58
safe harbor 401(k) notice, combining with, 7:59
sample notice, Appendix C
30 days before effective date, distribution of notice, 7:64
timing requirements, 7:58
rollovers
automatic rollover rules, 16:71
Roth IRAs, 16:92
safe harbor 401(k) plan, combination of notice with QDIA, 7:59
safe harbor 401(k) plan, eligibility, 2:262
electronic media, 2:242
information required, 2:243
sample notice, Appendix A
summary plan description (SPD) provided in lieu of, 2:244
Voluntary Fiduciary Correction (VFC) Program
steps to using notice, 5:143
withholding, electing out of, 16:132
nonperiodic distributions, 16:134
periodic distributions, 16:133

Notice and consent, postponement of benefits, 16:17–16:22
failure to defer receipt of distribution, 16:18
information included in summary notice, 16:132
right-to-defer notice, 16:19–16:22
form taken, 16:22
summary notice, 16:21

Notice of Plan Termination
model notice, 21:44

O

Officers
controlled groups, nondiscrimination testing, 10:9, 10:11
includable officer, top-heavy plans, 14:13, 14:14, 14:16
nondiscrimination testing, 10:11
top-heavy testing, 14:12

Offset, participant loans
deemed distributions, differences, 15:21
difference between deemed distribution, 15:21
eligible rollover distributions, 16:86
rollover rules, 15:31

On demand valuation, 4:28

One-participant retirement plan
blackout notices, 19:110
defined, 19:4
synchronization of, 1:74

One percent owner, top-heavy plans, 14:11

One-stop shopping administration. *See* Bundled administration

Open MEPs (multiple-employer plans), 1:41–1:43. *See also* Multiple-employer plans
defined, 1:41
DOL ruling, significance of, 1:43
filing requirements, 1:43
legal concerns, 1:42

Optional form of benefit, 16:1–16:29
anti-cutback rules, 16:6–16:12
defined, 16:1
employer discretion, 16:4–16:5
failure to defer receipt of distribution, 16:18
features not optional forms of benefit, 16:2
nondiscrimination testing, 12:27
postponement of, 16:14–16:22
consent of participant, 16:17–16:22
early retirement provision, 16:14
electing delay, 16:15
failure to defer receipt of distribution, 16:18
length of delay, 16:13
notice, 16:17–16:22
right-to-defer notice, 16:19–16:22
summary notice, 16:21
superseding plan provisions, 16:16
reduced or eliminated by plan amendment, 16:6
rules applicable, 16:3

Option attribution rule, defined, 10:13

Oral trusts, 2:143

Organization, defined, 10:26

Orphaned plans. *See* Abandoned plans

Ownership. *See* Affiliated service groups; Controlled group; Employer

P

Paid time off (PTO)
dollar equivalent as elective deferral contribution, 2:33

Paperless administration, defined, 19:122

Parent-subsidiary controlled group
nondiscrimination testing, 10:3
disregarding interests, 10:9

Participant-directed plans, 7:1–7:8. *See also* Participant direction of investments
all accounts, selection of investments for, 7:6
defined, 7:1
disclosure rules, 4:86
DOL regulation and, 7:3–7:5
employees and beneficiaries, rights of, 7:7
fiduciary, 5:134, 5:135
protection, 7:2, 7:6, 7:7
how plans become 404(c) plans, 7:8
identifiable costs, 4:42
individual participant benefit statements
multiple documents used for required information, 19:43
performance costs, 4:45
self-directed options. *See* Self-directed options
"triggers," 7:8

Participant direction of investments, 7:1–7:76
blackout period, protection, 7:35, 7:71
broad range of investment alternatives, 7:9–7:14
fixed-rate investments, 7:12
group of funds satisfying requirements, example, 7:10
individual stocks or assets, 7:13
look-through funds, 7:14
satisfaction of requirement, 7:9–7:11
change in investment options, extension of protection to, 7:72
compliance checklist, Appendix C
default elections, 7:31
default investments
compliance with Section 404(c) and, 7:61
conditions that must be met, 7:42
failure to make investment election, 7:40
notices regarding, information contained, 7:54
qualified default investment alternatives (QDIAs), 7:41–7:70
relief not available, 7:63
disclosure requirements, 7:21–7:25
generally, 7:21
mutual fund summary prospectus, 7:23
obligation of employers to provide investment advice or education, 7:25
special requirements, 7:24
specific information, 7:22
elections. *See* Investment elections *below, this group*
employer securities under, 7:15–7:17
Enron
issues involved, 7:75
legislation ensuing from, 7:76
ERISA Section 404(c) tested as defense in lawsuit, 7:73
fiduciary liability, 7:34–7:39
blackout period, protection, 7:35, 7:71
compliance with DOL's regulation, 7:37
effective date of DOL regulation, 7:39
Form 5500, 7:38
litigation, 7:74
noncompliance with ERISA Section 404(c), 7:36
relief from, 7:34
reporting, 7:38
fixed-rate investments, 7:12
Form 5500, 7:38
independent exercise of control, 7:18–7:19
individual participant benefit statements
limitations and restrictions, 19:47
individual stocks or assets, 7:13
investment change frequency, 7:26–7:29
market timing, actions to limit, 7:29
transfer fees, funds with, 7:28
transfer restrictions, funds with, 7:28
volatility levels, differing, 7:27
investment elections, 7:30–7:33
default elections, 7:31
fees charging directly to participants' accounts, 7:33
procedures used to obtain, 7:30
restrictions by fiduciaries, 7:32
investment managers independent exercise of control requirement and, 7:19
litigation involving, 7:50–7:76
look-through funds, 7:14
mutual fund summary prospectus, 7:23
noncompliance with ERISA Section 404(c), 7:36
notice, default investments, 7:54
participant-directed plans, 7:1–7:8
all accounts, selection of investments for, 7:6
defined, 7:1
DOL regulation and, 7:3–7:5
employees and beneficiaries, rights of, 7:7
fiduciary, 5:134, 5:135, 7:2, 7:6, 7:7
how plans become 404(c) plans, 7:8
identifiable costs, 4:42

Participant direction of investments, *(cont'd)*
participant-directed plans *(cont'd)*
individual participant benefit statements, multiple documents used for required information, 19:43
performance costs, 4:45
self-directed options. *See* Self-directed options
"triggers," 7:8
Pension Protection Act of 2006 (PPA)
blackout period, protection, 7:71
change in investment options, extension of protection to, 7:72
default investment funds, 7:40
legislation resulting from, 7:76
qualified default investment alternatives (QDIAs). *See* Qualified default investment alternatives (QDIAs)
reporting, 7:38
tender rights, 7:20
voting rights, 7:20
WorldCom
issues involved, 7:75
legislation ensuing from, 7:76

Participant disclosure. *See* Reporting and disclosure

Participant loans, 15:1–15:43
account balance used to secure loan, 15:9
adequately secured, 15:8
anti-alienation rules, violations of, 15:14
availability
highly compensated employee, greater amounts to, 15:4
reasonably equivalent basis, 15:3
bankruptcy, 15:37
changing loan program, 15:42
consistency rule, 15:26
converted to distribution, 18:52
creditworthiness of borrower, 15:10
deductibility of interest paid, 15:39
deemed distribution, loans treated as, 15:18–15:29
amount taxed, 15:19
applicable taxes, 15:18
avoiding complications, 15:29
consistency rule, 15:26
initial default amount, 15:26
interest, 15:22–15:23
offset, difference, 15:21
pooled in fund, 15:28
problems, 15:28
refinancing of outstanding loans, 15:36
repayments, 15:25
reporting requirements, 15:20
Roth accounts, 15:30
segregated loans, 15:28
some or all of loan treated as, 15:27
subsequent loan, impact of deemed loan on ability to obtain, 15:24
documentation to be retained, 15:17, 15:32
DOL regulation, 15:2, 15:13, 15:14
electronic medium, 15:16
elimination or changing loan program, 15:42
enforceable agreement, what constitutes, 15:16
failing to satisfy DOL loan rules, 15:14
fees, 15:40
plan participant, charged directly to, 4:59
fiduciary involved in administering the loan program, 15:12
hardship withdrawals. *See* Hardship withdrawals
Hurricane Sandy relief, 15:62
initial default amount, 15:26
leave of absence, participant on, 15:33
level amortization requirement, 15:33
limits on numbers of, 15:35
military leave, 15:34
number of, limits, 15:35
offset
difference between deemed distribution and, 15:21
eligible rollover distributions, 16:86
rollovers, 15:31
withholding, 16:112–16:114
paperless loans, 15:16
principal residence, to buy, 15:17, 15:32
provisions in plan document, 15:5
QMACs and, 15:61
QNECs and, 15:61
rate of interest
reasonable, 15:6
review, 15:7
reasonably equivalent basis, 15:3
records to be retained, 15:17, 15:32
refinancing of outstanding loans, 15:36
repayments
deemed distributions, treated as, 15:25
when must be remitted to plan, 15:43
reporting, 18:53
restrictions, 15:11
retention of records, 15:17, 15:32
review of plan interest rate, 15:7
Roth accounts, 15:30
salary reduction SEPs (SARSEPs), 22:58
SIMPLE 401(k) plans, 22:81
SIMPLE IRA plans, 22:81
simplified employee pensions (SEPs), 22:58
spousal consent, 15:16, 15:41
subsequent loan, impact of deemed loan on ability to obtain, 15:24
survivor annuity requirements, 17:45–17:47

taxation, 15:15–15:29
avoidance of, 15:15
conversion to distribution, 18:52
deemed distribution, loans treated as, 15:18–15:29
electronic medium, 15:16
enforceable agreement, what constitutes, 15:16
failure to meet requirements, 15:18–15:29
loans subject to rules, 15:16
obligation to 401(k) plan, 18:51
paperless loans, 15:16
reporting, 18:53
when taxable, 18:50
terminated participant, 15:31
terms of, 15:5–15:14
truth-in-lending disclosure rules, 15:38
who may borrow, 15:1
withholding rules, 16:112–16:114
eligible rollover distribution, loan offset amount, 16:114

Participation
access to plan funds affecting, 2:18
age eligibility, 2:170, 2:171
commencement, 2:178
disadvantages to employee, 1:13
eligibility computation period defined, 2:174
fixed or discretionary matching employer contributions, 2:12
403(b) plans or 401(k) plans, either maintained, 2:25
hours of service, 2:175–2:177
length of service requirement, 2:172
lower-paid participants, credit against taxes to encourage participation
amount of credit, 2:20
eligible individual, defined, 2:22
generally, 2:19
permanence of credit, 2:21
qualified retirement savings contribution, defined, 2:23
matching employer contribution affecting, 1:46, 2:11
minimum participation rules, 11:1
Code Section 403(b) plans, 22:128
governmental 401(k) plans, 2:148
prior to January 1, 11:1
one participant covered in plan, 2:24
rates, survey of average, 1:45
restrictions on employee eligibility, 2:169
saver's credit
amount of, 2:20
eligible individuals, 2:22
generally, 2:19
permanence of, 2:21
qualified retirement savings contribution, defined, 2:23
waiver by employee, 2:179
year of service defined, 2:173

Partnerships
compensation currently available to partner, 2:71
constructive ownership rules, controlled groups, 10:15
designing a 401(k) plan, considerations in, 1:32
matching contributions made on behalf of partners, 2:91

Part-time employees, participation, 2:180

Party in interest, 5:71–5:73

Pass-through voting, 6:65

Paternity leave
eligibility, 2:188
vesting, 2:206

Payroll taxes, 18:1–18:13
FICA taxes, 18:1–18:7
FUTA taxes, 18:8–18:13

Penalties. *See specific topic*

Pension and Welfare Benefits Administration (PWBA)
VFCP Program. *See* Voluntary Fiduciary Correction Program (VFCP)

Pension benefit plans, 1:42

Pension Protection Act of 2006 (PPA)
automatic enrollment plans
changes to, 1:10, 1:58, 2:34–2:40. *See also* Automatic contribution arrangements (ACAs)
generally, 2:34
cash balance plans, 22:87
changes made, 1:64
combined benefit/401(k) plan design, creation of, 1:63
corrective distributions, tax treatment, 13:31, 13:74
default investment funds, 6:42–6:43
changes in law, 6:43
participant direction of investments, 7:40
defined benefit plans
defined contribution plans *also* maintained, 1:63
defined contribution plans
defined benefit plans *also* maintained, amended deduction limits, 1:63
disclosure requirements, changes to rules, 1:61
distributions, changes to rules, 1:60
diversification
notice, plan assets invested in publicly traded employer securities, 19:121

Pension Protection Act of 2006 (PPA) *(cont'd)*
eligible automatic contribution arrangements (EACAs), 1:74, 2:41–2:51, 5:95
eligible investment advice arrangements (EIAAs), 1:59, 4:25, 8:37
employer securities
diversification rights, 6:55
as investment options, 1:62
ERISA requirements, changes to rules, 1:61
estate tax exclusion, 18:90
excess aggregate contributions
pre-tax excess aggregate contributions, taxation to participant, 18:57
excess contributions
corrective distributions, tax treatment, 13:31, 13:74
pre-tax excess contributions, taxation to participant, 18:57
recharacterization, 13:22
excess deferrals
gap period earnings, 1:74
fiduciaries
bond limit, 5:47
changes to rules, 1:59
default fund, assets deposited in to reduce liability, 5:135
Form 5500 series
changes to, 1:61
gap period earnings
need to calculate, elimination of, 1:63
hardship distributions, changes to rules, 1:60
individual participant benefit statements, 19:40
information upon request, 19:51
interim good faith amendments to comply, 3:21, 3:22
investment advice, 8:37
joint and survivor annuities, changes to rules, 1:60
master and prototype plans
plan document, updating of, 3:23
missing participants, 21:13
notice requirements, changes to rules, 1:61
one-participant retirement plan, synchronization of, 1:74
participant direction of investments
blackout period, protection, 7:71
change in investment options, extension of protection to, 7:72
default investments, 7:40
legislation resulting from, 7:76
participation
lower-paid participants, credit against taxes to encourage participation, 2:19
plan amendment to comply, 3:21
plan document, compliance, 3:21
prohibited transactions, changes to rules, 1:59
qualified automatic contribution arrangements (QACAs)
effective date of provisions, 2:68
qualified domestic relations orders (QDROs), expansion of rules, 1:63
qualified joint and survivor annuity (QJSA), 17:12
qualified pre-retirement survivor annuity (QPSA), 17:13
qualified reservist distributions, 16:27
reporting and disclosure
changes to rules, 1:61
simplified reporting, 19:3
small plans, 19:3
small plans, simplified reporting, 19:3
reservists, distributions to, 1:60
rollovers
changes to rules, 1:60
death proceeds, non-spouse beneficiary, 18:35
termination of employment, 16:54
Roth 401(k) plans, 1:24
distributions, 18:84
Roth IRAs
changes to rules, 1:60
saver's credit, 1:63, 2:21
signing of, 1:2
SIMPLE IRA plans
automatic enrollment, 22:47, 22:67
simplified employee pensions (SEPs)
automatic enrollment, 22:47
statements upon request, 19:51
termination of employment, rollovers, 16:54
top-heavy plans, minimum vesting, 14:29
vesting
contributions not subject to 100 percent vesting requirement, 2:194
maximum vesting periods, 1:63
top-heavy plans, minimum vesting, 14:29
volume submitter plans
plan document, updating of, 3:23
withdrawals, changes to rules, 1:60
Worker, Retiree, and Employer Recovery Act of 2008 (WRERA), technical corrections, 1:74

Performance costs
asset-based fees, impact of, 4:48
defined, 4:44
participant directed plan, 4:45

Periodic distributions
defined, 16:126
notice, 16:133
rate of withholding, 16:127

Permissive aggregation group, top-heavy plans, 14:6–14:8

Permitted disparity, 12:15–12:25
- annual overall limit, computation of, 12:23
- basic rules, 12:15–12:18
- cumulative disparity limit, 12:24
- defined, 12:15
- excess contribution percentage and base contribution percentage, between, 12:17
- implications of limits, 12:25
- integration level, 12:16
- more than one plan, 12:22–12:25
- nondiscrimination rules. *See lines throughout this topic*
- operation of, 12:21
- reduction required, 12:18
- safe harbor 401(k) plan, 2:265
- use of
  - appropriateness of, 12:19
  - operation of, 12:21
  - reason for, 12:20

Pilots
- minimum coverage rules, disregarding for, 11:25

Plan administrator
- delegation of responsibilities, 4:6
- Economic Growth and Tax Relief Reconciliation Act of 2001 (EGTRRA 2001), 1:56
- fiduciary duties, 5:4
- role of, 4:4

Plan amendment
- Heroes Earnings Assistance and Tax Relief (HEART) Act of 2008
  - compliance, 3:22
- individually designed plans
  - HEART Act, updating of plan document for, 3:24
  - PPA, updating of plan document for, 3:24
  - WRERA, updating of plan document for, 3:24
- master and prototype plans
  - HEART Act, updating of plan document for, 3:23
  - PPA, updating of plan document for, 3:23
  - WRERA, updating of plan document for, 3:23
- operational defect, correction of, 20:19
- optional form of benefit, reduction or eliminated, 16:6
- Pension Protection Act of 2006 (PPA)
  - compliance, 3:21
  - interim good faith amendments to comply, 3:21, 3:22
- remedial amendment period, 3:15–3:17
  - Code Section 403(b) plans, 22:127
  - extended remedial amendment period, 3:19
- Roth 401(k) plans
  - in-plan Roth rollovers. adoption of, 18:69
- SCP, retroactive amendment, 20:19
- VCO, retroactive amendment, 20:24
- VCP, retroactive amendment, 20:24
- volume submitter plans
  - HEART Act, updating of plan document for, 3:23
  - PPA, updating of plan document for, 3:23
  - WRERA, updating of plan document for, 3:23
- Worker, Retiree, and Employer Recovery Act of 2008 (WRERA)
  - compliance, 3:22

Plan assets
- access encouraging plan participation, 2:18
- administrative expenses, use of to pay, 4:53, 4:55
- allocation models, 8:27–8:28. *See also* Asset allocation
- bonds paid from, 5:56
- Code Section 457(b) plans
  - life insurance policies, invested in, 22:166
  - who owns and holds, 22:165
- deposit of salary deferrals in trust
  - late deposits, 5:75–5:81
- expenses, use to pay, 4:52
- investments. *See* Investments
- qualification requirements, holding for, 2:150
- segregated from employer assets, 5:75
- separate asset pools, 10:59, 10:60
- transfers of, reporting and disclosure, 19:21
- use to pay plan expenses, 2:9, 4:53, 4:55

Plan disqualification
- Audit CAP. *See* Audit Based Closing Agreement Program (Audit CAP)
- EPCRS and
  - common features of programs, 20:4
  - correction methods, numbers of, 20:6
  - definition, 20:2
  - exceptions to full correction, 20:8
  - principles taken into account, 20:5
  - programs under, 20:3
- impact of, 20:1

Plan document, 3:1–3:37
- advance IRS approval, 3:26–3:37
  - advantages of, 3:29–3:31
  - determination letter application, 3:28, 3:33–3:37

Plan document *(cont'd)*
alternatives, generally, 3:1
amendments
EGTRRA requirements, 3:16
GUST, for, 3:15, 3:16
Code Section 403(b) plans, 1:79
determination letter application, 3:28, 3:33–3:37
employee notification, 3:35
fee for, 3:34
not necessary, 3:36
where to send, 3:33
GUST, amendment for, 3:15, 3:16
individually designed plans, 3:14
HEART Act, updating for, 3:24
PPA, updating for, 3:24
updating plans, 3:20
WRERA, updating for, 3:24
IRS approval
advance, 3:26–3:37
determination letter application, 3:28, 3:33–3:37
obtaining, 3:32
master and prototype plans
advantages and disadvantages, 3:7, 3:8
comparisons with other plans, 3:12
defined, 3:2
differences, 3:5
HEART Act, updating for, 3:23
options, 3:6
PPA, updating for, 3:23
WRERA, updating for, 3:23
Pension Protection Act of 2006 (PPA)
amendments to comply, 3:21
pre-approved plans, extended remedial amendment period, 3:19
remedial amendment period, 3:17
extended remedial amendment period, 3:19
standardized and nonstandardized plans, 3:6, 3:7
tax qualification, 3:29
updating plans, 3:17–3:20
individually designed 401(k) plans, 3:20
master and prototype plans, 3:18
volume submitter plan, 3:18
volume submitter plans
comparisons with other plans, 3:12
defined, 3:9
determination letter not necessary, 3:36
failure to have operational reliance, 3:37
format, 3:11
HEART Act, updating for, 3:23
vs. mass submitter, defined, 3:10
PPA, updating for, 3:23
WRERA, updating for, 3:23

Plan loans. *See* Participant loans

Plan operations
audit, fiduciary, 5:138

Plan repayment provision, defined, 2:216

Plan services. *See* Services of plan

Plan sponsor
costs
allocation of, 4:51
calculating total costs, 4:47–4:50
payment of, 4:51
fiduciary duties, 5:4
reporting and disclosure, compliance with key requirements, 1:9
service provider fee disclosure rule, responsibilities under, 4:101

Plan-to-plan transfers, 14:27, 16:12

Points system, allocation of contributions, 2:101–2:103

Pooled investment vehicles, diversification rights, 6:59

PPA. *See* Pension Protection Act of 2006 (PPA)

Predecessor plan, defined, 2:198

Premature distribution tax, 18:85
avoiding 10 percent tax, 18:105–18:109
exceptions to, 18:86
in-plan Roth rollovers, 18:75
reporting, 18:87

Preparer Tax Identification Numbers (PTINs), 19:12

Principal owner, controlled groups, 10:9, 10:10

Principal residence, participant loan used to purchase, 15:32

Prior year *vs.* current-year testing method
actual contribution percentage (ACP) test, 13:53–13:54
actual deferral percentage (ADP) test, 13:4–13:6

Procedural due diligence, 5:136

Professional businesses
design considerations, 1:34

Professional employee organization (PEO), 1:39

Profits, contributions based on, 2:166

Profit sharing plans
Code Section 404 deduction limits
existing plan, 9:74
maximum deductible amount, 9:57
two or more profit sharing plans sponsored by employer, 9:57

money purchase plan, 9:75
existing plan in addition to 401(k) plan, 9:76
merger into 401(k) plan, 9:77
target plan, 9:75

Prohibited transaction exemption (PTE)
best interest contract exemption, 5:25, 5:118–5:120, 8:37
DOL guidance, proposed, 5:118
fiduciaries (PTE 2003-39), 5:58, 5:59

Prohibited transactions. *See also* Prohibited transaction exemption (PTE)
audit, fiduciary, 5:138
checking account of plan, setting up, 5:84
class exemption, 5:117
compensation received without engaging in, 5:88
correction, 5:74
late deposits of salary deferral contributions, 5:78
defined, 5:71
design process, 5:83
disqualified persons, 5:71–5:73
eligible investment advice arrangements (EIAAs), 5:95–5:117
advice pursuant to EIAA, information taken into account, 5:106–5:109
annual audit requirement, 5:111
audit requirement, 5:101
computer model approach, 5:99, 5:107–5:109, 5:114
conditions to obtain relief, 5:98
defined, 5:95
disclosure standards, 5:112
DOL guidance, 4:25, 5:104, 5:112–5:116
financial adviser, who can serve as, 5:97
independent fiduciary, standards for obtaining authorization from, 5:110
notice requirements, 5:100
post-model advice, 5:114
proposed regulations (DOL), 5:95–5:117
reasonable compensation, 5:102
relief available, 5:96
scope of the level fee requirement, 5:105
securities law disclosure rules, compliance with, 5:102
encumbered property, contributions of, 5:82
exemption, 5:117
failure to remit salary deferral contributions, 5:75–5:81
fees
fiduciaries, from mutual funds, 5:92
float income used to pay plan expenses, 5:85
individual exemption, 5:117
in-kind contributions, 5:82
insurance purchased to cover losses resulting from, 5:128
late deposits of salary deferral contributions, 5:75–5:81
concerns of DOL with timeliness, reasons for, 5:79
correction, 5:78
multiemployer plans, 5:76
reporting to DOL, 5:77
multiemployer plans
late deposits of salary deferral contributions, 5:76
mutual funds, payments from, 5:91
fiduciaries, to, 5:91, 5:92
nonfiduciaries, to, 5:90
parties in interest, 5:71–5:73
penalties, 5:73
plan fee arrangements, DOL addressing potential prohibited transactions, 5:93
PPA changes to, 1:59
revenue sharing and other fee arrangements, 5:86–5:89
salary deferral contributions, failure to remit. *See* Late deposits of salary deferral contributions *above, this group*
service providers
affiliated with fund investment managers, payment of fees to, 5:89
fees paid to, 5:86–5:89
statutory exemption, 5:117
types of, 5:71–5:73
Voluntary Fiduciary Correction (VFC) Program, 5:147

Proportional method of allocation, contributions, 2:104

Pro rata method of allocation, QSLOBs, 10:57

Prospects for 401(k) plans, 1:49

Prototype plans. *See* Master and prototype plans

PS-58 costs, 18:23, 18:33
definition, 18:47
premature distribution tax, exception, 18:86

PTO. *See* Paid time off (PTO)

Publicly traded employer stock
defined, 6:59
diversification notice, 19:121
short-swing profit rules, 6:67

Q

QACA. *See* Qualified automatic contribution arrangements (QACAs)

QCDs. *See* Qualified charitable distribution (QCD)

QDIAs. *See* Qualified default investment alternatives (QDIAs)

QDROs. *See* Qualified domestic relations orders (QDROs)

QJSA. *See* Qualified joint and survivor annuity (QJSA)

QMACs. *See* Qualified matching contributions (QMACs)

QNECs. *See* Qualified nonelective contributions (QNECs)

QOSA. *See* Qualified optional survivor annuity (QOSA)

QPAMs. *See* Qualified professional asset manager (QPAM)

QPSA. *See* Qualified pre-retirement survivor annuity (QPSA)

QRDs. *See* Qualified reservist distributions

QSLOBs. *See* Qualified separate lines of business (QSLOBs)

QTAs. *See* Qualified termination administrators (QTAs)

Qualification errors, correction of, 20:1–20:29. *See also specific program*
- identification of common qualification errors, 20:10

Qualification requirements, 2:141–2:219
- advantages, 2:142
- annual limits, 2:164
- anti-assignment rule, 2:155
  - amounts owed to employer, exceptions for, 2:158
  - bankruptcy of participant, exceptions for, 2:157
  - exceptions, 2:156
  - IRS, exceptions recognized by, 2:156
- asset holding, 2:150
- assignment of benefits, 2:155–2:158
- benefit limits, 2:163–2:166
- break-in-service rules, 2:181–2:189
- communication to employees, 2:149
- compensation limits, 2:164
- continuing contributions, 2:152–2:154
- design, affecting, 2:141
- distributions, 2:167–2:168
- eligibility rights, 2:169–2:180
- employer, establishment and maintenance of plan by person other than, 2:144
- formal requirements, 2:143–2:151
- governmental employers, 2:145–2:148
- insurance benefits to participants, 2:151
- merger or consolidation, protection in, 2:159
- nondiscrimination requirements
  - basic requirements, 2:161
  - purpose of, 2:160
- oral trusts, 2:143
- permanent and continuing arrangement, 2:148
- repayment rights, 2:216–2:219
- returned contribution, 2:152
- rollovers, 2:168
- taking back contributions made to plan, 2:153
- vesting, 2:190–2:215
- written plan requirement, 2:143

Qualified automatic contribution arrangements (QACAs)
- application of, 2:66
- and compensation definition, 2:67
- creation of, 2:36
- defined, 2:52
- design considerations, 2:52–2:68
  - application of, 2:66
  - and compensation definition, 2:67
  - defined, 2:52
  - effective date of PPA provisions, 2:68
  - employer contributions, requirement, 2:60
  - failure of employee to make affirmative election, 2:54
  - non-highly compensated employee, employment on last day of plan, 2:62
  - reason to add QACA to plan, 2:56
  - safe harbor match formula, 2:61–2:64
  - safe harbor plans, differences in compensation definition, 2:67
  - top-heavy rules, 2:65
- effective date of PPA provisions, 2:68
- eligibility requirements, 2:97
- employer contributions, requirement, 2:60
- failure of employee to make affirmative election, 2:54
- hardship withdrawal, 15:54
- matching contributions made on discretionary basis, 2:90
- non-highly compensated employee, employment on last day of plan, 2:62
- notice
  - matters addressed in notice, 2:55
  - requirement, 2:53
  - sample notice, Appendix C
- plans containing. *See lines throughout this topic*

QDIAs, combination of notice with, 7:57–7:58
qualified percentage
defined, 2:57
generally, 2:52
increase, date for initial, 2:58
maximum qualified percentage, 2:58
reason to add QACA to plan, 2:56
safe harbor match formula, 2:61–2:64
safe harbor plans, differences in compensation definition, 2:67
top-heavy plans, 2:65, 14:48

Qualified charitable distribution (QCD), 22:20, 22:84

Qualified default investment alternatives (QDIAs), 5:19, 6:43–6:45, 7:41–7:70
annuity as cash component of, 7:53
asset allocation funds and, 6:24
assets invested prior to effective date, 7:65, 7:66
automatic furnishing of information, 7:60
automatic prospectus delivery requirement, elimination of, 7:42
capital preservation fund as QDIA, 7:49, 7:51–7:52
collective trust fund qualifying as QDIA, 7:53
DOL guidance, 6:44
EACAs, combination of notice with, 7:55–7:59
effective date, 7:70
eligible arrangements, 6:44
fiduciary liability, relief of, 5:135
grandfathered QDIA, 7:50, 7:64
litigation, proceeds from invested in QDIA, 7:67
named fiduciary of plan treated as managing QDIA, 7:48
and 90-day permissible withdrawals, 1:74
nonelective contributions invested in QDIA, 7:67
notice requirement, 6:45, 7:55–7:59
EACA, combination of notice with, 7:57–7:58
electronic distribution rules, 7:56
fees and expenses, information regarding, 7:55
grandfathered QDIA, 7:64
pass-through of investment materials, 7:56
QACA, combination of notice with, 7:57–7:58
safe harbor 401(k) notice, combining with, 7:59
30 days before effective date, distribution of notice, 7:64
timing requirements, 7:58
120-day capital preservation QDIA, 7:51
plan sponsor as manager, 7:52
participant direction of investments
assets invested prior to effective date, 7:65, 7:66
automatic furnishing of information, 7:60
automatic prospectus delivery requirement, elimination of, 7:42
capital preservation fund as QDIA, 7:49, 7:51–7:52
collective trust fund qualifying as QDIA, 7:53
definition, 7:41
effective date, 7:70
generally, 7:42
grandfathered QDIA, 7:50, 7:64
information conveyed in notices, 7:54
investment funds, 7:47
litigation, proceeds from invested in QDIA, 7:67
long-term QDIAs, 7:41, 7:47
named fiduciary of plan treated as managing QDIA, 7:48
newly "defaulted" participants, 7:45
90-day period, transfers and withdrawals, 7:43–7:46
nonelective contributions invested in QDIA, 7:67
notice requirement, 7:55–7:59
120-day capital preservation QDIA, 7:51
plan sponsor, committee established by, 7:48
qualified nonelective contributions (QNECs) invested in QDIA, 7:67
relief not available, 7:63
request, information provided upon, 7:60
requirements, satisfaction of, 7:61
"round-trip" restrictions, 7:46
settlement, proceeds from invested in QDIA, 7:67
stable value fund as QDIA, 7:50
tax-sheltered annuities, protection available to, 7:68
transfer out of QDIA by participant, 7:43
two different QDIAs sponsored, 7:69
variable annuity qualifying as QDIA, 7:53
zero fixed income, products with, 7:41, 7:47
PPA law changes, 6:43
QACAs, combination of notice with, 7:55–7:59
qualified nonelective contributions (QNECs) invested in QDIA, 7:67
relief not available, 7:63
request, information provided upon, 7:60
requirements, satisfaction of, 7:61
settlement, proceeds from invested in QDIA, 7:67

Qualified default investment alternatives (QDIAs) *(cont'd)*
stable value fund as QDIA, 7:50
and target date funds, 5:163, 6:26
tax-sheltered annuities, protection available to, 7:68
two different QDIAs sponsored, 7:69
unallocated deferred annuity contract qualifying as QDIA, 7:53
variable annuity qualifying as QDIA, 7:53

Qualified domestic relations orders (QDROs), 17:51–17:68
administrative expenses associated with reviewing, 17:66
alternate payees
administrative expenses associated with reviewing, charge to, 17:66
benefits distributed to, 17:63
defined, 17:53
lump-sum distributions, 18:21
rights of, 17:61
tax consequences of distributions to, 17:59
anti-assignment rule, exceptions to, 2:156
change in administrator, 17:62
defined, 17:51
drafting process, distributions during, 17:60
failure of DRO to qualify, 17:67
form of benefit no longer available, 17:65
information contained in, 17:54
involuntary distributions, alternate payee's consent, 16:26
issue, time of, 17:67
lump-sum distributions, 18:21
payment pursuant to order that is not qualified, 17:64
Pension Protection Act of 2006 (PPA)
expansion of rules, 1:63
plan documentation, 17:58
premature distribution tax, exception, 18:86
provisions of plan, 17:3
rollover options, 16:62
same-sex partners, 17:42, 17:68
"spouse" defined, 17:42, 17:68
tax consequences of distributions to alternate payees, 17:59
terms of, 17:54–17:55

Qualified joint and survivor annuity (QJSA)
alternative to, 17:12
annuity starting date, 17:14
commencement of payments, 17:16
defined, 17:11
earliest retirement age, 17:17
loan outstanding at time QJSA payable, 17:47
Pension Protection Act of 2006 (PPA), 17:12
QOSA elected to receive instead of, spousal consent, 17:33
requirements, 17:9
waivers, 17:18
requirements, 17:20
timing, 17:23
written explanation, 17:27

Qualified matching contributions (QMACs)
ADP test, 13:13–13:14, 13:45
elective contributions, treated as matching contributions, 13:7
defined, 13:13
participant loans and, 15:61
vesting, 2:193
minimum vesting, 14:29

Qualified nonelective contributions (QNECs)
ACP test, 13:61, 13:78, 13:80
ADP test, 13:13–13:14
allocation of QNEC, 13:39–13:46
applicable contribution rate of NHCE, 13:45
bottom-up approach, 13:40–13:42, 13:45
correcting by making QNECs, 13:39–13:46
defined, 13:13
elective contributions, treated as matching contributions, 13:7
per capita basis of allocation, 13:46
proportionate basis of allocation, 13:46
representative contribution rate of NHCE, 13:44
specific groups of NHCEs, allocations targeted to, 13:43
non-highly compensated employees, 11:33
participant loans and, 15:61
qualified default investment alternatives (QDIAs), investments in, 7:67
quantity allowed, 2:17
top-heavy plans, 14:46
vesting, 14:29
vesting, 2:193
minimum vesting, 14:29

Qualified optional survivor annuity (QOSA)
election to receive instead of QJSA, spousal consent, 17:33
provision of, 17:12, 17:13

Qualified plan status. *See* Employee Plans Compliance Resolution System (EPCRS)

Qualified pre-retirement survivor annuity (QPSA)
annuity starting date, 17:14
commencement of payments, 17:15
defined, 17:10
earliest retirement age, 17:17
generally, 17:9
loan outstanding at time QPSA payable, 17:47

Pension Protection Act of 2006 (PPA), 17:13
requirements, 17:9
waivers, 17:18
requirements, 17:19
terminated participants, 17:22
when participant may waive, 17:21
written explanation, 17:26

Qualified professional asset manager (QPAM), 5:27

Qualified reservist distributions, 16:27–16:29
defined, 16:28
generally, 1:72
Heroes Earnings Assistance and Tax Relief Tax (HEART) Act of 2008, 1:72, 16:27
participants called to active military service
differential wage payments, 16:51
Pension Protection Act of 2006 (PPA), 16:27
premature distribution tax, exception, 18:86
return of payments to plan, 16:29

Qualified retirement plans
proposed legislation, 1:78

Qualified Roth distributions. *See* Roth distributions

Qualified separate lines of business (QSLOBs)
allocation of employees, 10:57
average benefit percentage test, 11:21
average benefits safe harbor, 10:56
defined, 10:41
different industries safe harbor, 10:56
dominant line of business method of allocation, 10:57
HCE percentage ratio method of allocation, 10:57
industry segments safe harbor, 10:56
line of business
defined, 10:42
designation of, 10:43
percentage of services provided, 10:50
property or services, types of, 10:44–10:45
providing services to, when considered as, 10:49
residual shared employee, 10:58
separate management, 10:51
separate workforce, 10:47
top-paid employees, 10:52
mandatory disaggregation rules, 10:62
mergers and acquisitions (M&A) safe harbor, 10:56
minimum coverage requirements, 11:8, 11:25
minimum or maximum benefits safe harbor, 10:56
nondiscrimination testing, 10:41–10:58
mandatory disaggregation rules, 10:62
pro rata method of allocation, 10:57
ratio percentage test, 11:8
regulatory safe harbors, 10:56
residual shared employee, 10:58
separate line of business
administrative scrutiny requirement, 10:53
defined, 10:46
HCE percentage ratio, 10:55
statutory safe harbor, 10:54
substantial-service employee, 10:48

Qualified termination administrators (QTAs), 21:37, 21:38–21:39, 21:43–21:48
bankruptcy trustee as, 21:37

Qualifying employer securities
restrictions, 6:54

Quarterly reports
communication program, 8:14

R

Rabbi trust
defined, 22:116
model rabbi trust document, 22:118
purpose of, 22:117

Rate group, highly compensated employee, 12:10

Ratio percentage test, 11:4–11:8
benefiting under 401(k) plan, defined, 11:5
combining plans to satisfy, 11:6–11:7
defined, 11:4
QSLOBs, 11:8

Real estate funds, defined, 6:30

Real estate investment trusts (REITs), 6:30

Recharacterization
excess aggregate contributions
ACP test, 13:66
ADP test, 13:19
excess contributions, ADP test, 13:19–13:22
excess deferrals, 9:15

Reciprocity under VFCP and EPCRS, 5:147

Recordkeeping
costs, 2:8
disclosure requirements, 4:81, 4:85, 4:86
electronic media
ERISA and, 19:126
recordkeeping services defined, 4:82
retention of records under ERISA, 19:136

Recordkeeping (*cont'd*)
services of plan
industry, effect of consolidation, 4:10

Redemption fees. *See* Fees

Regional funds, 6:24

Regional prototype plans
master and prototype plans, consolidation with, 3:2

Registered investment advisers
disclosure requirements, 4:79
investment services, 4:21
standard of care, 4:21

Registration requirements, employer securities, 6:54

Regulatory developments, 1:79–1:80

Rehired employees
break-in-service rules. *See* Break-in-service rules
vesting, 2:199

REITs. *See* Real estate investment trusts (REITs)

Repayment rights
funds used to restore account balances, 2:219
interest on previously forfeited amounts, 2:217
limits on, 2:218
plan repayment provision, 2:216

Replacement ratios at retirement
adequacy of retirement, measurement of, 8:44
definition, 8:45
outliving retirement savings, risk management, 8:46
risk management, 8:46

Reporting and disclosure, 19:1–19:135
abandoned plans, 21:45
blackout notices. *See* Blackout notices
change in plan status, notification to IRS, 19:23
Code Section 403(b) plans
ERISA, subject to, 22:154
communication program, 8:4
consolidation, 19:21
deemed distribution, loans treated as, 15:20
direct rollovers, 16:95
distributions, generally, 18:93
electronic disclosure request for information, 1:80
electronic media
disclosure under ERISA, 19:124–19:125
legal issues, 19:123
paperless administration, defined, 19:122
eligible investment advice arrangements (EIAAs), 5:112
model participant disclosure, Appendix H
employer securities
dividends paid, 18:31
ERISA Section 404(c), impact of regulations, 19:73
excise taxes, 19:24
fee information, disclosure to plan participants, 1:80
fees, service providers, 4:65, 4:66–4:105
additional disclosures after initial statement, 4:98
affiliates, 4:73, 4:74, 4:92
and allocation of fiduciary responsibilities, 5:37
compensation, 4:90, 4:91, 4:96
conflicts of interest, 4:93, 5:94
covered plans, 4:70
covered service providers. *See* Covered service providers
direct compensation, 4:90
DOL guidance, 1:80
DOL interim final rule, 4:66–4:105, 5:94
effective date, 4:67
ERISA fiduciaries, 4:79
error correction, 4:99, 5:94
failure to disclose, 4:99
fiduciaries planning investment products, 4:80
Form 5500, Schedule C disclosures, 4:105
form or manner of disclosure, 4:95
fund investment managers, 5:89
indirect compensation, 4:83, 4:91
information to be disclosed, 4:84, 4:88
initial disclosures, 4:69, 4:97
investment products, 4:76
noncompliance consequences, 4:100
$1,000 limit, 4:77, 4:78
plan fee arrangements, DOL addressing potential prohibited transactions, 5:93
purpose and scope of fee disclosure rule, 4:66
recordkeeping services, 4:82, 4:85, 4:86
registered investment advisors, 4:79
responsible plan fiduciaries, 4:71
rules for describing plan services, 4:89
service providers who are not covered service providers, 4:104
subcontractors, 4:73, 4:75, 4:92
terminations, 4:94
written requirement, 4:68
FICA tax, 18:7
FUTA tax, 18:12
individual participant benefit statements. *See* Individual participant benefit statements
in-service withdrawals, 18:45

installment distributions, 18:38
investment-related information, participant investment and fee disclosures, 19:61–19:64
annuity options, 19:70
designated investment alternative, 19:63, 19:66, 19:69–19:72
employer securities, designated investment alternative, 19:69
fixed-return investments, 19:71
information upon request, 19:64
target date funds, 19:72
investments, 6:66–6:67
IRS and DOL Form 5500 reporting
audit requirement, 19:5
basic annual reporting requirement, 19:2
changes, effect of, 19:12
criminal penalties, 19:20
due date, 19:13
enforcement policy, DOL, 19:15
incomplete filings, 19:16
late deposits, 19:12
late filing, 19:14, 19:17, 19:18
material information, defined, 19:16
plan characteristics codes, 19:12
responsibility for payment of penalties, 19:19
schedules, 19:6
who is responsible, 19:1
key requirements, 1:9
late deposits, 19:12
of salary deferral contributions, 5:77
life insurance protection, 18:49
lump-sum distributions, 18:27
merging of plan, 19:21
noncompliance
to service provider, 4:100
one-participant retirement plan, defined, 19:4
paperless administration, defined, 19:122
participant direction of investments, 7:21–7:25, 7:38
generally, 7:21
mutual fund summary prospectus, 7:23
obligation of employers to provide investment advice or education, 7:25
special requirements, 7:24
specific information, 7:22
participant disclosure, 19:25–19:121
blackout notices, 19:109–19:110
checklist, Appendix C
diversification notices, 19:121
ERISA Section 404(c), impact of regulations, 19:73
individual participant benefit statements, 19:40–19:51
information upon request, 19:52–19:55, 19:64
investment-related information, 19:61–19:64, 19:69, 19:88–19:97
participant investment and fee disclosures, 19:56–19:73, 19:74–19:108
plan-related information, 19:60, 19:77–19:87
summary annual report (SAR), 19:37–19:39
summary of material modifications (SMM), 19:33–19:36
summary plan description (SPD), 19:25–19:32. *See also specific headings for detailed treatment*
participant investment and fee disclosures, 19:56–19:73, 19:74–19:108
acquired-fund fees and expenses, 19:104
acquiring-fund fees and expenses, 19:104
administrative expenses, 19:80–19:81, 19:83–19:84, 19:106
annuity contract or custodial account, 19:75
average annual total return, defined, 19:68
benchmarks, 19:61, 19:89
blended benchmark returns, disclosure of, 19:89
brokerage windows, information about, 19:86–19:87, 19:102, 19:103
checklist, Appendix C
closed investment alternatives, information about, 19:88
comparative charts or documents, 19:94–19:96
compliance, 19:58, 19:59
delivery of disclosures, DOL guidance, 19:65
designated investment alternative, 19:63, 19:66, 19:69–19:72, 19:75–19:77, 19:88, 19:96, 19:98, 19:103–19:105
designated investment manager, 19:77, 19:100
detail required of explanations, 19:78
electronic media, use of, to satisfy disclosure requirements, 19:65
ERISA Section 404(c), impact of regulations, 19:73
fees and expenses, explanation of, 19:78
form of disclosure, DOL guidance, 19:65
fund-of-funds, 19:104
glossary of investment-related terms, samples, 19:93
impracticability of obtaining necessary information, 19:75
initial quarterly statement of fees and expenses, 19:108
insurance cost, 19:107
investment-related information provided, 19:61–19:64, 19:69, 19:88–19:97

Reporting and disclosure *(cont'd)*
participant investment and fee disclosures *(cont'd)*
at least annually thereafter, defined, 19:67
at least quarterly, defined, 19:67
model portfolios, 19:101
multiple investment alternatives, platform with, 19:103
net asset value, calculation of, 19:105
participant-directed and trustee-directed investments, plan with both, 19:74
plan-related information provided, 19:60, 19:77–19:87
plans subject to, 19:57
prospectuses or similar documents, 19:98
quarterly statement of fees and expenses, 19:108
recordkeeping expenses, 19:79, 19:82
responsibility for compliance, 19:59
revenue-sharing explanation, 19:83–19:85
revenue-sharing payments in excess of recordkeeping fee, 19:79
Section 403(b) plans that are ERISA-covered plans, 19:75
self-directed brokerage accounts, information about, 19:86–19:87, 19:102
"since inception" data, 19:97
single document disclosing plan-related and investment-related information, 19:76
stand-alone documents not required, 19:99
supplemental investment-related information on Web site, 19:92
target asset allocations, 19:89
total annual operating expenses, calculation of, 19:106
total annual operating expenses, defined, 19:68
trustee-directed investments, plan with, 19:74
unregistered designated investment alternatives, 19:98, 19:104–19:106
variable rates of return, 19:96
Web site requirements, 19:90–19:92, 19:95
windows, information about, 19:86–19:87, 19:102, 19:103
participant loans, 18:53
Pension Protection Act of 2006 (PPA)
changes to rules, 1:61
simplified reporting, 19:3
plan assets, transfers of, 19:21
plan fee arrangements, DOL addressing potential prohibited transactions, 5:93
premature distributions, 18:87
required minimum distributions (RMDs), 16:48
penalty, 18:89
retention of records under ERISA, 19:136
Roth distributions, 18:83
SARs. *See* Summary annual report (SAR)
services and compensation, disclosure of, Appendix L
simplified reporting, 19:3
small plans, 19:3
simplified reporting, 19:3
SMM. *See* Summary of material modifications (SMM)
SPDs. *See* Summary plan description (SPD)
target date funds, 1:80, 1:81
termination of plan, 19:22
abandoned plans, 21:45

Representative contribution rate of NHCE
ADP test, 13:44

Request for Information (RFI)
guaranteed benefit and lifetime income products, 6:35

Required aggregation group, top-heavy plans, 14:5

Required minimum distributions (RMDs), 16:30–16:48
annuity contract provided as payment option, 16:42
calendar year, amount paid, 16:45
corrective distributions and, 13:33
death of employee, 16:47
deferral of benefits, allowable time for, 16:30
designated beneficiary, 16:35–16:39
election revoked under TEFRA Section 242(b)(2), 16:33
employee's required beginning date
before, 16:43
exception to rule, 16:32
estate or trust as beneficiary, 16:37
excess deferrals, 9:20
five percent owner, 16:31
five-year rule, 16:35
how long benefits may be deferred, 16:30
individual retirement arrangements (IRAs), 22:19
inherited IRAs, rollovers to, 16:102, 16:104
length of deferment, 16:30
length of time, 16:44
life expectancy, 16:45
payment options, 16:41–16:48
penalty for failure to distribute, 18:88, 18:89
post-death benefits, 16:34
reporting requirements, 16:48
required beginning date, 16:30–16:40
Roth IRAs, 22:32
salary reduction SEPs (SARSEPs), 22:60
simplified employee pensions (SEPs), 22:60

tax considerations, 18:88–18:89
value of employee's interest, 16:46
waivers, 16:40
Worker, Retiree, and Employer Recovery Act of 2008 (WRERA), 16:40
technical corrections, 18:88, 18:100

Reservists
distributions to, PPA changes, 1:60
qualified reservist distributions. *See* Qualified reservist distributions

Residence
participant loan used to purchase, 15:32

Residual shared employees, QSLOBs, 10:58

Responsible plan fiduciary, 4:71, 5:94

Restorative contributions, 9:69–9:71
defined, 9:70
requirements, 9:71

Restructured 401(k) plans
ACP test, 13:79
ADP test, 13:36–13:38

Retention of records
under ERISA, 19:136
for hardship withdrawals, 15:51
for loan programs, 15:17
for principal residence loans, 15:17, 15:32

Retirement age
choosing, individual retirement planning, 8:42
earliest retirement age, defined, 17:17
normal retirement age, defined, 2:192

Retirement planning. *See* Individual retirement planning

Retirement Readiness reports and review, 4:22, 5:138, 8:7, 8:20

Retirement savings rates, lowness of, 1:48

Revenue Act of 1978, 1:2
simplified employee pensions, 22:39–22:63

Revenue Procedure 2007-71, 22:124

Revenue sharing
investment funds, 6:106
mutual funds, responsibilities of plan fiduciaries, 5:162

RFI. *See* Request for Information (RFI)

RIAs. *See* Registered investment advisers

Right-to-defer notice, postponement of benefits, 16:19–16:22

Risk management
investment risk, retirement planning, 8:59–8:60

Risk tolerance
determining, 8:53
long-term investment return, 8:52–8:53
measurement of, 8:53

"Robo advice," 5:119

Rollovers
acceptance of, 2:136
advantages, 16:104
after-tax and pre-tax amounts, accounts with, 16:106
age 70½, 18:100
automatic rollover rules, 16:69–16:79
amounts attributable to rollover contributions, 16:72
avoidance, 16:79
DOL guidance, 16:77–16:78
IRAs, 16:74–16:76
joint and survivor rules, consent if vested balance not exceeding $5,000, 16:73
notice to participants, 16:71
$1,000 or less, 16:78–16:79
safe harbor, 16:78
cash distribution, 16:80
chart, Appendix I
Code Section 457(b) plans, 22:179. *See also* Code Section 457(b) plans
governmental Code Section 457(b) plan, 22:182
contribution eligibility for rollover, 2:137
defined, 16:52
direct rollovers, 16:64–16:68
acceptance of, whether required, 16:68
cutoff date, 16:93
defined, 2:132, 16:65
elections, 16:83–16:87
eligible retirement plan, 16:67
eligible rollover distributions, 16:64–16:68, 16:82
how accomplished, 16:87
income tax reporting, 16:95
loan offset amount that is eligible rollover distribution, 16:86
mandatory, 16:69–16:70
model notice, 16:92
non-spouse beneficiaries, inherited IRAs, 16:97–16:98
notice, 16:89–16:92, 16:94
option, 16:64–16:68
procedures, 16:88–16:96
reasonable period of time to provide notice, 16:90
restrictions, 16:66
revocation, 16:93
Roth IRAs, 22:36
spousal consent for election, 16:84
transfer of benefits, 16:96

Rollovers *(cont'd)*
disadvantages, 16:105
EGTRRA, changes in rules, 1:53
eligibility, ensuring, 2:137
eligible retirement plan, more than one, 16:85
eligible rollover distributions, 16:55–16:63
availability of option, 16:62
corrective distributions of excess deferrals as, 9:21
death proceeds, 18:34, 18:35
defined, 16:55
direct rollover, 16:64–16:68, 16:82
election out of withholding, 16:110
exceptions to rule defining, 16:57
generally, 16:55
loan offset amounts, 16:86, 16:114
military duty, distribution to participant on duty for more than 30 days, 16:63
minimum distribution not eligible rollover distribution, 16:60
payment changes, 16:59
periodic installments, 16:94
property other than cash, 16:61
requirement, 2:168
substantially equal periodic payments, 16:57–16:59
withholding, 16:109
individual retirement arrangements (IRAs)
abandoned plans, 21:48
automatic rollover rules, 16:74–16:76
inherited IRAs, rollovers to, 16:62, 16:82
missing participants, 21:12
ineligible distributions, 16:121–16:123
inherited IRAs
beneficiaries, rollovers by, 22:7
in-plan Roth rollovers, 18:68–18:76. *See also* Roth 401(k) plans *for detailed treatment*
loan offset amount that is eligible rollover distribution, 16:86
mandatory distributions
circumstances, 16:69
defined, 16:70
DOL guidance, 16:77–16:78
limiting to avoid automatic rollover rules, 16:79
notice to participants, 16:71
$1,000 or less, 16:78–16:79
safe harbor, 16:78
military duty, distribution to participant on duty for more than 30 days, 16:63
missing participants, 21:12
multiple destinations, to, 16:106
nondiscrimination testing, 2:140
notice
Roth IRAs, 16:92
partial distribution, 18:101
participant loans, offset, 15:31
Pension Protection Act of 2006 (PPA)
changes to rules, 1:60
death proceeds, non-spouse beneficiary, 18:35
premature distribution, tax, 18:85
present value of accrued benefits, 14:27
pre-tax accounts, advantages, 18:99
pre-tax and after-tax amounts, account with both, 16:106
QDRO, 16:62
qualification requirements, 2:168
Roth 401(k) plans, 1:22
considerations in making rollover decision, 18:103
eligibility, 18:67
five-year holding period, 18:77, 18:78, 18:80
in-plan Roth rollovers, 18:68–18:76. *See also* Roth 401(k) plans *for detailed treatment*
tax planning, 18:79
Roth IRAs
in-plan Roth IRAs, 1:79
tax considerations, 18:20

Roth contributions, 2:78–2:85
automatic enrollment, part of plan providing for, 2:81
catch-up contributions consisting of designated Roth contributions, 9:35
circumstances, 2:79
conversion of pre-tax elective contributions into Roth contributions, 2:84
corrective distributions, 9:18
defined, 2:78
designated Roth contributions. *See also lines throughout this topic*
required minimum distributions, 16:48
salary reduction SEPs (SARSEPs), 22:57
SIMPLE IRA plan, 22:76
elective contributions treated as, 2:79
excess deferrals
consisting of Roth contributions, 9:7
failure to correct, 9:23
how long participants have been able to make contributions, 2:85
only Roth option offered, 2:80
pre-tax elective contributions converted to Roth contributions, 2:84
requirements, 2:83
separate account, allocation to, 2:82

Roth deferrals
excess contributions, corrective distributions
actual deferral percentage (ADP) test, 13:30

Roth distributions
alternate payee, Roth account set up for, 18:81
corrective distributions, 18:65
deemed distributions, taxation, 18:63
employer securities, 18:66
excise taxes, 18:82
five-year holding period, 18:77, 18:78, 18:80
generally, 18:59
hardship distributions, 18:64
partial distributions, 18:62
qualified Roth distribution defined, 18:60
reporting of distributions, 18:83
rollovers, 18:67–18:80
in-plan Roth rollovers, 18:68–18:76
taxation of, 18:59–18:84
alternate payee, Roth account set up for, 18:81
corrective distributions, 18:65
deemed distributions, taxation, 18:63
employer securities, 18:66
excise taxes, 18:82
five-year holding period, 18:77, 18:78, 18:80
generally, 18:59
hardship distributions, 18:64
partial distributions, 18:62
qualified Roth distribution defined, 18:60
reporting of distributions, 18:83
rollovers, 18:67–18:80
types of distributions not considered qualified distributions, 18:61

Roth 401(k) plans
alternate payee, Roth account set up for, 18:81
choice between pre-tax 401(k) account or Roth 401(k) account, considerations, 18:113
considerations
plan participant, deciding whether to participate, 18:113
plan sponsor, decision to offer, 18:112
contribution option, 1:10. *See also* Roth contributions
analysis of, 1:18–1:25
earnings, anticipated, 1:21
EGTRRA extension, 1:24
factors to consider, 1:18
income tax payment, 1:19
maximizing deferrals, 1:19
number of years until benefits needed, 1:22
qualified, when account becomes, 1:25
rollovers, 1:22
tax diversification, 1:23
tax rates, anticipated for postretirement, 1:20
contributions. *See* Roth contributions
distributions. *See* Roth distributions
hardship withdrawals, 15:56
in-plan Roth rollovers, 18:68–18:76, 18:78
amount allocable to taxable portion, determination of, 18:76
calculation of holding period, 18:78
conditions applicable, 18:68
direct rollovers, 18:70
distribution, treatment as, 18:72
holding period, 18:78
income acceleration rule, 18:74
income tax rules, 18:74
plan amendment to adopt, 18:69
retroactive amendment to adopt, 18:69
60-day rollovers, 18:70
tax consequences, 18:73–18:76
10 percent premature distribution tax, 18:75
undoing of, 18:71
participant loans, 15:30
plan amendment
in-plan Roth rollovers. adoption of, 18:69
qualified Roth distributions. *See* Roth distributions
rollovers, 1:22
considerations in making rollover decision, 18:103
eligibility, 18:67
five-year holding period, 18:77, 18:78, 18:80
in-plan Roth rollovers, 18:68, 18:76, 18:78. *See also* In-plan Roth rollovers *above, this group*
tax considerations, 18:103
tax planning, 18:79

Roth IRAs, 22:24–22:38. *See also* Roth contributions; Roth distributions; Individual retirement arrangements
advantages of saving in 401(k) plan rather than, 8:2
advantages over traditional IRAs, 22:38
age 70½, contributions by persons reaching, 22:27
amount contributed, 22:26
Code Section 457 plans, availability in, 1:79
considerations in making rollover decision, 18:102
contributions
age of individuals making, 22:27
amount contributed, 22:26
limits on, 22:26
nondeductibility of, 22:28
treatment as elective deferrals, 9:4
withdrawal of, 22:29

Roth IRAs *(cont'd)*
conversions to, 22:33–22:36
rollovers from employer-sponsored retirement plans, 22:36
tax treatment, 22:34
traditional IRA conversion to Roth IRA, 22:33–22:35
defined, 22:24
distributions, 22:29–22:32
elective deferrals, designated contributions treated as, 9:4
employer-sponsored retirement plans, distributions from, 22:36
in-plan rollovers, 1:79
model notice, 16:92
nonqualifying distribution, 22:31
Pension Protection Act of 2006 (PPA) changes to rules, 1:60
qualifying distribution, 22:30
required minimum distributions (RMDs), 22:32
rollovers
considerations in making rollover decision, 18:102
employer-sponsored retirement plans, distributions from, 22:36
in-plan, 1:79
model notice, 16:92
options, 16:62
tax considerations, 18:20
savings compared to traditional IRAs, 22:37
60-day rollover, 2:133
exceptions to, 16:81
option not available, 16:82
splitting of contributions between IRA and, 22:9–22:10
spousal Roth IRAs, 22:25
termination of employment, 16:52–16:106
Pension Protection Act of 2006 (PPA), changes, 16:54
traditional IRAs compared, 22:37–22:38
types of, 2:131
vesting, 2:193
withholding, employer securities, 16:116
Worker, Retiree, and Employer Recovery Act of 2008 (WRERA)
death proceeds, non-spouse beneficiary, 18:35

Rule of parity
defined, 2:184
vesting, 2:203

Rural cooperatives
401(k) sponsorship, 2:147

S

Safe harbor 401(k) plans, 2:239–2:269
ACP test
after-tax contributions, 2:262
avoidance of, 2:245, 2:250
adoption of, 2:240
ADP test, avoidance of, 2:245, 2:246
advantages, 2:245
after-tax contributions, nondiscrimination testing and, 2:262
age requirements, 2:256
amendments, mid-year, 2:269
avoiding top-heavy status by converting to, 14:47
compensation used for purposes of contributions, 2:259
contributions
after-tax, nondiscrimination testing and, 2:262
compensation used for purposes of, 2:259
elective deferral contributions, limit on, 2:245
employer contributions, generally, 2:237, 2:247
matching contributions. *See* Matching contributions *below, this group*
restrictions, 2:258
timing of, 2:260
cross-tested profit sharing formula, counting in, 2:265
defined, 2:239
disadvantages, 2:245
discretionary basis, made on
eligibility requirements, 2:95–2:98
matching contributions, 2:89, 2:90
dollar limit on elective deferrals, 2:261
eligible employees, 2:241
examples illustrating, 2:267
in-service withdrawals, 2:266
leased employees, 10:74
matching contributions
additional contributions, 2:252, 2:264
conditions, 2:257
enhanced matching formula, 2:248
made on discretionary basis, 2:89, 2:90
rate of match, 2:251
requirements, 2:237, 2:248
stopping contributions during plan year, 2:253, 2:254
vesting, 2:255
"maybe" safe harbor nonelective contribution, 2:249
mid-year amendments, 2:269
notice, combination with QDIAs, 7:59

notice of eligibility, 2:241
electronic media, 2:242
information required, 2:243
sample notice, Appendix A
summary plan description provided to employee in lieu of, 2:244
participation in other retirement plans, 2:268
permitted disparity, 2:265
QDIAs, combination of notice with, 7:59
qualified automatic contribution arrangements (QACAs), 14:48
differences in compensation definition, 2:67
service requirements, 2:256
top-heavy rules, 2:263–2:264
vesting, 2:193, 2:255

Safe harbor match formula
qualified automatic contribution arrangements (QACAs), 2:61–2:64

Safe harbors
age-weighted formula in lieu of design-based safe harbor formula, 2:115
allocation methods, design-based safe harbor, 2:101–2:102, 2:105
Code Section 403(b) plans
ERISA, exemption from, 22:147–22:152
contributions, standard for remitting, 5:81
design-based safe harbor
age-weighted formula in lieu of, 2:115
allocation methods, 2:101–2:102, 2:105
defined, 12:1
loss of status, 12:7
new comparability formula in lieu of, 2:115
top-heavy minimum contribution, 12:8
uniform allocation formula, 12:2, 12:3
uniform point system plan, 12:4–12:6
hardship withdrawals
events test, 15:46
needs test, 15:48
QACA, 15:54
investment advice, 8:32
"maybe" safe harbor nonelective contribution, 2:249
minimum coverage rules
safe harbor percentage, 11:13
unsafe harbor percentage, 11:14
new comparability formula in lieu of design-based safe harbor formula, 2:115
QSLOBs
regulatory safe harbors, 10:56
statutory safe harbor, 10:54
rollovers, mandatory distributions, 16:78
uniform allocation formula
compensation, 12:3
defined, 12:2
uniform point system plan, 12:4–12:6

Salary. *See* Compensation

Salary deferral. *See* Contributions

Salary reduction SEPs (SARSEPs)
catch-up contributions, 22:55
compliance with rules, IRS guidance, 22:63
contributions
age 70½, employee, 22:51
catch-up contributions, 22:55
deductibility of contributions, 22:52
designated Roth contributions, 22:57
elective deferrals, 9:3, 22:54
employer contributions, 22:48, 22:56
excess deferrals, 9:8
nonelective contributions by employer, 22:56
tax consequences, 22:53
defined, 22:40
designated Roth contributions, 22:57
distributions
failure to meet applicable requirements, 22:62
required minimum distributions (RMDs), 22:60
tax considerations, 22:61
when funds may be withdrawn, 22:59
elective deferrals, 22:54
eligible employees, 22:44
excluded employees, 22:45
Fix-it Guide (IRS), 22:63, 22:85
look-back rule, 22:43
participant loans from, 22:58
qualified default investment alternatives (QDIAs)
Worker, Retiree, and Employer Recovery Act of 2008 (WRERA), 1:74
required minimum distributions (RMDs), 22:60
requirements to maintain, 22:42
25 or fewer employee rule, 22:43
who can establish, 22:41

Same desk rule, 21:34
elimination of, 1:56

Same-sex marriages
QDROs, 17:41, 17:68
spousal consent, 17:41
spousal status. *See* Spousal status
state law treatment of, 17:40, 17:42, 17:44
survivor annuity rules, 17:41

SAR. *See* Summary annual report

Sarbanes-Oxley Act of 2002
blackout periods, 6:68, 6:69. *See also* Blackout periods
generally, 6:68

SARSEPs. *See* Salary reduction SEPs (SARSEPs)

Saver's credit, 8:61
amount of, 2:20, 3:61
communication to participants, 8:61
credit used against taxes owned, 2:10
defined, 8:61
eligible individuals, 2:23
generally, 2:19
permanence of, 2:21
PPA changes, 1:63
qualified retirement savings contribution, defined, 2:23
rates, 8:61

SBJA. *See* Small Business Jobs Act of 2010 (SBJA)

SBJPA. *See* Small Business Job Protection Act of 1996 (SBJPA)

Scope of the level fee requirement
eligible investment advice arrangements (EIAAs), 5:105

SCP. *See* Self-Correction Program (SCP)

SCRA. *See* Servicemembers Civil Relief Act of 2003 (SCRA)

Search methods for locating participant or beneficiary, 20:8, 21:11

SEC. *See* Securities and Exchange Commission (SEC)

SECA. *See* Self-Employment Contributions Act (SECA)

Section 403(b) plans. *See* Code Section 403(b) plans

Section 404(c) plans. *See* Participant direction of investments

Section 415 limits. *See* Code Section 415 limits

Section 457(b) plans. *See* Code Section 457(b) plans

Section 457(f) plans. *See* Code Section 457(f) plans

Securities and Exchange Commission (SEC)
fees, initiatives regarding, 4:116
market timing, 5:156–5:158
study of uniform fiduciary standard of care, 4:21

Securities Exchange Act of 1934, 4:21, 6:67

Self-certification
hardship withdrawals, 15:51
home purchase, loan for, 15:17, 15:32

Self-Correction Program (SCP), 20:11–20:19, 22:62
audit by IRS and, 20:16
condition that must be met, 20:15
cost of using, 20:18
deadline for correcting operational defects, 20:12
factors considered in determining significance of operational failure, 20:13
favorable IRS letters, 20:14
master and prototype plans, 20:14
procedures used, 20:17
qualification defects covered by, 20:11
retroactive amendment to plan, 20:19
volume submitter plans, 20:14

Self-directed options
administrative complications, 6:79
collectibles, investment in, 6:82
considerations, 6:78–6:82
costs, increased, 6:79
current availability test, 6:81
defined, 6:75
discrimination issues, 6:81
effective availability test, 6:81
fiduciaries, 6:86
full brokerage account, 6:76
investment policies, 6:75–6:84
motivation for, 6:77
mutual fund window, 6:76
policy, 6:85–6:87
provisions, 6:87
Section 404(c), ERISA, 6:83
setting up, 6:76
strategies, 6:84
structure, 6:84
troublesome investments, 6:82
unlimited investment options, 6:80
written investment policies, 6:85

Self-employed individuals
compensation, 10:102
deferral of cash advance payments made during plan year, 2:73
elective contributions, 2:73
employee, consideration, 10:63
matching contributions, 2:91
nondiscrimination testing, 10:63, 10:102
withholding, 18:3

Self-Employment Contributions Act (SECA), 18:3

SEP. *See* Simplified employee pensions (SEPs)

Separate asset pools
defined, 10:59
mandatory disaggregation rules, 10:61
more than one, 10:60

Separated accounts, 6:32

Separate lines of business. *See* Qualified separate lines of business (QSLOBs)

Separately managed accounts, defined, 6:14

SEP IRAs. *See* Simplified employee pensions (SEPs)

Servicemembers Civil Relief Act of 2003 (SCRA), 15:34

Service organization, defined, 10:27

Service providers
audit, fiduciary, 5:138
Covered Service Providers
affiliates, 4:73, 4:74, 4:83
compensation disclosures, 4:96
defined, 4:72
identification of, 5:94
indirect compensation, 4:83, 4:91
information to disclose, 4:84, 5:94
initial disclosure statement, 4:97
noncompliance with rules, 4:100
recordkeeper disclosures, 4:85
service provider is not a covered service provider, 4:104
subcontractors of, 4:73, 4:75, 4:83
termination of contracts or arrangements, 4:94
disclosure requirements
compensation, disclosure of, Appendix L
guide or index as part of, 1:80, 4:106–4:113
participant-directed plans, special rules, 4:86
sample guide to initial disclosures, Appendix L
services, disclosure of, Appendix L
fees, 4:66–4:128
additional disclosures after initial statement, 4:98
affiliates, 4:73, 4:74, 4:92
calculation of, 4:102
checklist for responding to service provider disclosures, 4:101
compensation, 4:90, 4:91, 4:96
conflicts of interest, 4:93, 5:94
covered plans, 4:70
covered service providers. *See* Covered service providers
direct compensation, 4:90
DOL guidance, 1:80
DOL final rule, 4:66–4:105, 5:94
effective date, 4:67
ERISA fiduciaries, 4:79
ERISA spending accounts, payments from, 4:130
error correction, 4:99, 5:94
failure to disclose, 4:99
fiduciaries planning investment products, 4:80
Form 5500, Schedule C disclosures, 4:105
form or manner of disclosure, 4:95
fund investment managers, 5:89
indirect compensation, 4:83, 4:91
information to be disclosed, 4:84, 4:88
initial disclosures, 4:69, 4:97
investment products, 4:76
methods for payment of, 4:57
noncompliance consequences, 4:100
$1,000 limit, 4:77, 4:78
plan fee arrangements, DOL addressing potential prohibited transactions, 5:93
plan sponsor responsibilities under fee disclosure rule, 4:101
purpose and scope of fee disclosure rule, 4:66
reasonableness of fee, determination of, 4:102
recordkeeping services, 4:82, 4:85, 4:86
registered investment advisors, 4:79
responsible plan fiduciaries, 4:71
review of fees and services, 4:103
rules for describing plan services, 4:89
service providers who are not covered service providers, 4:104
subcontractors, 4:73, 4:75, 4:92
terminations, 4:94
written requirement, 4:68
fiduciary services, 5:4
fund investment managers, affiliated with, payment of fees to, 5:89
guide or index as part of fee and service disclosure
changes to information in guide, disclosure of, 4:111
effective date, 4:113
information included in guide, 4:108
proposed rule, 1:80, 4:106–4:113
reason for guide requirement, 4:112
as separate document, 4:110
service providers subject to requirement, 4:107
when guide would need to be provided, 4:109
monitoring of, 5:137
noncompliance to plan sponsor or other fiduciary, disclosure, 4:100
questions to ask, 4:18
review of fees and services, frequency of, 4:103
selection of, 5:137
switching service providers, considerations, 4:19
third-party providers, 4:14–4:15
Web site, features plan sponsor might look for, 4:39, 4:40

Service receipts percentage, defined, 10:32

Service requirements
break-in-service rules. *See* Break-in-service rules
generally, 2:172
length of service, 2:172–2:173
minimum coverage rules, 11:25
safe harbor 401(k) plan, 2:256
SIMPLE 401(k) plans, 2:232

Services of plan, 4:1–4:128. *See also* Service providers
bundled administration, 4:16–4:17
choices, 4:8
cost, factors adding to, 4:11
factors considered by employer, 4:9, 4:11
fees and expenses, 4:41–4:128. *See also* Fees
fiduciary risk management services, 4:7
in-house administration, 4:12–4:13
investment manager, role of, 4:5
investment services, 4:20–4:27
brokers, 4:21
conflicts of interest, potential, 4:23
distinctions between brokers and registered investment advisors, 4:21
DOL guidelines for selection and monitoring of providers, 4:25
questions to ask when selecting investment service provider, 4:24, 4:26–4:27
registered investment advisers, 4:21
selecting, 4:20–4:27
services offered by investment service providers, 4:22
suitability of investment provider, determining, 4:24–4:27
types of providers offering, 4:20
named fiduciary, role of, 4:2
objectives of employer, 4:9
operating plan, 4:1
plan administrator, role of, 4:4, 4:6
plan trustee, role of, 4:3, 4:6
recordkeeping industry, effect of consolidation in, 4:10
selection of services, 4:8–4:19
third-party administrator, 4:14–4:15

Settlor decisions, 5:38

Settlor fees, 4:62

Settlor functions, 4:54, 5:38

Severance of employment
elective contributions, distribution of, 21:34

Severance pay
compensation, treatment as, 9:47

Short-swing profit rules
publicly traded employer stock, 6:67

SIMPLE 401(k) plans, 2:220–2:238
ACP testing, avoiding, 13:1
ADP testing, avoiding, 13:1
age requirements, 2:228
annual cap on elective deferrals, 9:36
exceeded, 9:38
another qualified plan maintained *also* in same calendar year, 22:71
automatic enrollment, 22:67
contributions, 22:72–22:78
catch-up contributions, 22:74
deductibility, amount, 22:78
deferrals, amount allowed, 22:73
employer contributions required, 22:77
suspension of during plan year, 2:237
types of contributions, 22:72
defined, 2:220, 22:65
distributions, 2:234–2:235, 22:79–22:86
compliance with rules, IRS guidance, 22:85
joint and survivor annuity requirements, 2:236
participant loans, 22:81
required minimum distributions (RMDs), 2:235
restrictions, 2:234
SIMPLE IRA plan, differences, 2:238
withdrawals, time for, 22:79
dollar limit applied to elective contributions, 2:223
elective deferrals
annual cap exceeded, 9:38
limitation on amount of, 9:37
eligible employees, 22:68
eligible employers, 2:221
employees covered, 2:222
employer contributions
generally, 2:225
more than required, 2:227
SIMPLE IRA, compared, 2:226
failure to meet plan requirements, 22:84
ineligibility to participate, 2:229
joint and survivor annuity requirements, 2:236
limits, EGTRRA changes, 1:51
matching contributions
conditions on receipt of, 2:230
discretionary basis, made on, 2:88
nondiscrimination test, 2:224
nonelective contributions
eligibility requirements, 2:96
other retirement plans, participation of employees in, 2:228
ineligibility to participate in SIMPLE 401(k) plan, 2:229
participant loans, 22:81
participation in other plans, 2:228
reason for choosing, 22:82, 22:83

reduced elective deferral limit, 2:224
requirements to establish, 22:66
service requirements, 2:232
size of workforce and, 2:2
top-heavy rules, avoiding, 14:43
two percent nonelective contributions, conditions on receipt of, 2:231
vesting, 2:193, 2:233

SIMPLE IRA plans
another qualified plan maintained *also* in same calendar year, 22:70
automatic enrollment, 22:47, 22:67
contributions, 22:72–22:78
allowed, 22:75
catch-up contributions, 22:74
deductibility, amount, 22:78
deferrals, amount allowed, 22:73
designated Roth contributions, 22:76
employer contributions required, 22:77
types of contributions, 22:72
defined, 22:64
designated Roth contributions, 22:76
distributions, 22:79–22:86
compliance with rules, IRS guidance, 22:85
participant loans, 22:81
required minimum distributions (RMDs), 2:235
SIMPLE 401(k) plans, differences, 2:238
tax consequences, 22:80
withdrawals, time for, 22:79
eligible employees, 22:68
employer contributions
SIMPLE 401(k) plan, compared, 2:226
excluded employees, 22:69
failure to meet plan requirements, 22:84
participant loans, 22:81
Pension Protection Act of 2006 (PPA)
automatic enrollment, 22:47
qualified default investment alternatives (QDIAs)
and Worker, Retiree, and Employer Recovery Act of 2008 (WRERA), 1:74
reason for choosing over SIMPLE 401(k) plan, 22:82
reason for choosing SIMPLE 401(k) plans over, 22:83
requirements to establish, 22:66
size of workforce and, 2:2
termination of plan, 21:7

SIMPLE retirement accounts
elective deferrals, 9:3
excess deferrals, 9:8

Simplified employee pensions (SEPs)
automatic enrollment, 22:47
compliance with rules, IRS guidance, 22:63
contributions
age 70½, employee, 22:51
annual addition limit, 22:50
deductibility of contributions, 22:52
percentage of salary contributed, 22:49
Worker, Retiree, and Employer Recovery Act of 2008 (WRERA), technical corrections, 22:47
defined, 22:39
distributions
failure to meet applicable requirements, 22:62
required minimum distributions (RMDs), 22:60
tax considerations, 22:61
when funds may be withdrawn, 22:59
eligible employees, 22:44
excluded employees, 22:45
Fix-it Guide (IRS), 22:63, 22:85
other retirement plans *also* maintained by employee, 22:46
participant loans from, 22:58
Pension Protection Act of 2006 (PPA)
automatic enrollment, 22:47
required minimum distributions (RMDs), 22:60
60-day rollover
exceptions to, 16:81
termination of plan, 21:7
Worker, Retiree, and Employer Recovery Act of 2008 (WRERA), technical corrections
contributions, 22:47

SLOB rules. *See* Qualified separate lines of business (QSLOBs)

Small businesses
design considerations, 1:34
information on retirement plans, 22:86
qualified plans
economic sense of, 1:29
EGTRRA, 1:55

Small Business Job Protection Act of 1996 (SBJPA)
Code Section 457(b) plans, 22:165
future of 401(k) plans, 1:49
leased employees, primary direction or control of recipient, 10:70
lump-sum distributions, 18:14
plan documents, amendment, 3:15
Roth contributions, pre-tax elective contributions converted to, 2:84

Small Business Jobs Act of 2010 (SBJA)
Roth 401(k) plans, rollovers, 18:67

Small plans
reporting and disclosure
one-participant retirement plan, defined, 19:4
simplified reporting, 19:3

"Smart 401(k) Investing?," 8:3

SMM. *See* Summary of material modifications

Social Security
- benefits expected from, 8:57
- online account access, 8:57
- planning for retirement, 8:56, 8:57

Sole proprietor
- compensation currently available to, 2:72
- 401(k) plan, appropriateness of, 1:31

SPD. *See* Summary plan description

Spinoffs
- allocation of assets, 21:21
- anti-cutback rules, 16:11
- defined, 21:20
- distribution concerns, 21:25
  - monitoring and harmonizing options, 21:26
  - relief from, 21:27
- procedures involved, 21:22
- review of plan provisions, 21:24

Spousal consent
- civil unions, 17:42
- direct rollovers, election, 16:84
- domestic partners, 17:42
- electronic media, participant loans, 15:41
- excess contributions and allocable income, distributions, 13:28
- legally separated or abandoned spouse, 17:48
- missing spouse, 17:48
- participant loans, 15:16, 15:41
  - electronic media, 15:41
  - survivor annuity requirements, 17:49
- plan sponsors' response to Supreme Court's decision, 17:43, 17:44
- prior waiver, revocation, 17:30
- QOSA elected to receive instead of QJSA, 17:33
- revocable, 17:31
- rollovers
  - direct rollovers, election, 16:84
  - joint and survivor rules, consent if vested balance not exceeding $5,000, 16:73
- spousal death benefit, 17:50
- subsequent spouse, 17:32
- survivor annuity requirements, 17:29–17:47
- who is considered spouse, 17:41

Spousal IRAs
- contributions by both spouses, 22:14
- defined, 22:3

Spousal rights. *See* Qualified domestic relations orders (QDROs); Spousal status; Survivor annuity requirements

Spousal Roth IRAs, 22:25

Spousal status
- definition of "spouse," 3:25, 17:34–17:38, 17:43, 17:68
- determination of status, 17:34
- plan benefits affected by definition of "spouse," 17:41
- same-sex marriages, 1:79, 17:34–17:38
  - amendment of 401(k) plans, 3:25, 17:38, 17:39, 17:43
  - effective date of *Windsor* decision, 17:35
  - noncompliance operationally by effective date of *Windsor* decision, 17:37
  - recognition of, 17:34, 17:40
  - spousal benefits offered prior to effective date of *Windsor* decision, 17:36
  - state law treatment of, 17:40, 17:42, 17:44
  - "state of celebration" rule, 17:34, 17:44
  - "state of domicile," reliance on, to deny benefits, 17:39
- steps required of plan sponsors, 17:43, 17:44

Stable value funds, 6:33
- defined, 6:33
- structure of, 6:33

Standardized plan, 3:6, 3:7

Start-up costs, 2:2
- multiemployer plans, 1:38

Statements upon request, 19:51–19:55
- documents to be requested, 19:52
- fees for providing reports or documents, 19:53
- terminated participant, 19:51

Stocks
- defined, 6:1
- growth stocks defined, 6:2
- risks and returns associated with stock ownership, 6:4
- value stocks defined, 6:3

Subaccounts, 6:32

Subcontractors
- defined, 4:75
- disclosure of compensation allocation, 4:92
- fee disclosure, 4:73
- indirect compensation, 4:83

Substantially equal periodic payments
- eligible rollover distributions, 16:57–16:59
- premature distribution tax, exception, 18:86

Substantial-service employee, defined, 10:48

"Sub-transfer agency" (sub-ta) fees, 4:120, 4:123, 6:106

Summary annual report (SAR)
- information included, 19:37
- language requirements, 19:39
- non-English speaking participants, 19:39
- when to provide, 19:38

Summary of material modifications (SMM)
failure to provide in timely basis, 19:35
information provided, 19:34
notification of changes in plan, 19:33

Summary plan description (SPD), 19:25–19:32
defined, 19:25
disclaimer, benefits of including, 19:36
distribution, 19:31
entitlement to receive, 19:28
failure to provide on timely basis, 19:35
filing with DOL, 19:30
information included, 19:26
language requirements, 19:27
non-English speaking participants, 19:27
safe harbor 401(k) plans, SPD supplied in lieu of notice, 2:244
timing for receipt, 19:29
updating, 19:32

Supplemental 401(k) plan, structure of, 1:37

Survivor annuity requirements, 17:1–17:50
account balance is payable in full upon death, 17:49
annuity starting date, 17:14
commencement of payments, 17:15, 17:16
earliest retirement age, 17:17
electronic media, 17:28
financial effects of various forms of benefits, written explanation, 17:25
legally separated or abandoned spouse, 17:48
loans, 17:45–17:47
secured loan, outstanding, 17:47
missing spouse, 17:48
plan sponsors' response to Supreme Court's decision, 17:43, 17:44
plans subject to, 17:1
QJSA. *See* Qualified joint and survivor annuity (QJSA)
QPSA. *See* Qualified pre-retirement survivor annuity (QPSA)
same-gender partners, 17:42
spousal consent, 17:29–17:41
spousal death benefit, waiver of, 17:50
"spouse" defined for 401(k) plan, 17:34–17:44
subsequent spouse, 17:32
transferee plans
all plan participants, 17:3
defined, 17:2
participant's entire account balance, 17:4
waivers, 17:18–17:23, 17:50
spousal consent, 17:30, 17:32
written explanation, 17:24–17:28

T

Target date funds
age-restricted, 6:28
collective fund option, 6:25
customized funds, 6:26
deferred annuities in, 6:28, 7:53
defined, 6:26
disclosures, 1:80, 1:81
fiduciary concerns, 5:163
glide path, 6:28, 6:29
guidance on selection and monitoring of, 5:164, 6:28, 6:29
investment-related information, participant investment and fee disclosures, 19:72
monitoring of, 5:164, 6:28
mutual fund option, 6:26
name including date, 6:27
nondiscrimination requirements, 6:28
and qualified default investment alternatives (QDIAs), 6:26, 6:28, 7:53
regulatory considerations, 6:27
selection of, 5:164, 6:28
tips for ERISA plan fiduciaries, 5:163, 5:164
unallocated deferred annuity contracts, investment in, 7:53

Target pension plan
Code Section 404 deduction limits, 9:75

TARP. *See* Treasury Department's Troubled Asset Relief Program (TARP)

Tax considerations, 18:1–18:113
actual deferral percentage (ADP) test
corrective distributions, 12:28
after-tax savings, 1:17
alternate payees, QDRO, 17:59
catch-up contributions, 9:31
Code Section 415 limits, correcting a violation, 9:53
Code Section 457(b) plans
distributions, 22:184
contributions, pre-tax, 18:14–18:45
corrective distributions, tax treatment of, 9:17–9:21
deferred compensation, 1:15
distributions, 18:14–18:45
Code Section 457(b) plans, 22:184
death, on, 18:32–18:35
employer securities, 18:28–18:31
in-service withdrawals, 18:39–18:45
installment, 18:36–18:38
lump-sum distributions, 18:14–18:27
planning, 18:99–18:113
premature distributions, 18:85–18:87
required minimum distributions (RMDs), 18:88–18:89

Tax considerations *(cont'd)*
eligible automatic contribution arrangements (EACAs)
permissible withdrawal, 2:49
employer, tax-related objectives, 1:5
excess contributions, 18:56–18:57
excess deferrals, 18:54–18:55
federal estate tax, death distributions, 18:90–18:92
FICA. *See* Federal Insurance Contributions Act (FICA)
FUTA. *See* Federal Unemployment Tax Act (FUTA)
hardship withdrawals, 15:52–15:53
individual retirement arrangements (IRAs)
distributions, 22:18
in-plan Roth rollovers, 18:73–18:76, 18:78
in-service withdrawals, 18:39–18:45
installment distributions, 18:36–18:38
life insurance, 18:46–18:49
lump-sum distributions, 18:14–18:27, 18:104
nonqualified deferred compensation plans, 22:94–22:101
Code Section 409A, 22:111
doctrine of constructive receipt, 22:95
employer, amounts deferred under deductible by, 22:97
FICA, taken into account for, 22:98
FUTA, taken into account for, 22:99
gross income inclusion, amounts deferred under funded NQDC, 22:96
gross income inclusion, amounts deferred under unfunded NQDC, 22:94
tax-exempt organizations, 22:100
participant loans, 18:50–18:53. *See also* Participant loans *for detailed treatment*
payroll taxes, 18:1–18:13
FICA taxes, 18:1–18:7
FUTA taxes, 18:8–18:13
premature distributions, 18:85–18:87
annual installment exception, 18:106
10 percent tax, avoiding, 18:105–18:109
qualified domestic relations order (QDRO), 17:59
Roth distributions, 18:59–18:84
alternate payee, Roth account set up for, 18:81
corrective distributions, 18:65
deemed distributions, taxation, 18:63
employer securities, 18:66
excise taxes, 18:82
five-year holding period, 18:77, 18:78, 18:80
generally, 18:59
hardship distributions, 18:64
partial distributions, 18:62
qualified Roth distribution defined, 18:60
reporting of distributions, 18:83
rollovers, 18:67–18:80
types of distributions not considered qualified distributions, 18:61
Roth 401(k) plans, rollovers, 18:103
Roth IRAs, rollovers, 18:102
salary deferral for ten years, 1:16
salary reduction SEPs (SARSEPs)
distributions, 22:61
employer contributions, 22:53
SIMPLE IRA plans, distributions, 22:80
simplified employee pensions (SEPs), distributions, 22:61
taxable year for contributions, 9:67

Tax credits
expenses of plan used as, 2:10
saver's credit. *See* Saver's credit

Tax-exempt employees
cash or deferred arrangements, generally, 1:27

Tax-exempt organizations
nonqualified deferred compensation plans, 22:100

Tax Increase Prevention and Reconciliation Act of 2005 (TIPRA), 22:33

Taxpayer Relief Act of 1997 (TRA '97)
breach of fiduciary duty, 5:57
plan documents, amendment, 3:15
Roth IRA, 22:24–22:38
summary plan descriptions (SPDs), 19:30

Tax Reform Act of 1984 (TRA '84)
cash or deferred arrangements, 1:2

Tax Reform Act of 1986 (TRA '86)
basis recovery rules, 18:43
change, 18:41
described, 18:44
grandfathered rules, 18:44
cash or deferred arrangements, 1:2
in-service withdrawals, 18:41, 18:43, 18:44
lump-sum distributions, older participants, 18:22
qualified domestic relations orders (QDROs), 17:65

Tax Relief, Unemployment Insurance Reauthorization and Job Creation Act of 2010
estate tax, 18:90
IRAs, charitable distributions from, 22:20
OASDI, 18:4

Tax-sheltered annuities (TSAs). *See* Code Section 403(b) plans

T-bills. *See* Treasury bills

TEAMTRA. *See* Tax Extenders and Alternative Minimum Tax Relief Act of 2008 (TEAMTRA)

Technology, costs and, 4:11

TEFRA (Technical and Miscellaneous Revenue Act of 1988)
estate tax, 18:90
required minimum distributions (RMDs), 16:32
Code Section 242(b)(2), revocation, 16:33

Tender rights
participant direction of investments, 7:20

Termination of employment
claims for benefits, 16:141–16:147. *See also* Claims for benefits
distributions subsequent to, 16:1–16:147
optional forms of benefits, 16:1–16:29
required minimum distributions (RMDs), 16:30–16:48
rollover rules, 16:52–16:106
withholding, 16:107–16:140
minimum coverage rules and, 11:25
participant loans, 15:31
Pension Protection Act of 2006 (PPA), changes
rollover rules, 16:54
QPSA, waiver, 17:22
rehired employees, vesting, 2:199
rollover rules, 16:52–16:106
Pension Protection Act of 2006 (PPA), changes, 16:54
statements upon request, 19:51

Termination of plan, 21:1–21:9
abandoned plans, 21:37–21:51
compensating QTA, 21:47
date plan is considered terminated, 21:42
determination that plan is abandoned, 21:38
DOL guidance, 21:37
effective date for regulations, 21:49
final regulations, 21:37–21:51
liability, protection, 21:46
missing participants, distributions to, 21:48
notice to plan sponsor, 21:41, 21:43
paying out, procedures to follow, 21:44
qualified termination administrators (QTAs), 21:38–21:39, 21:43–21:48
reporting requirements, 21:45
when plan is considered abandoned, 21:40
acquisition, special coverage rule, 21:35
alternative defined contribution plan, 21:6, 21:7
benefits
distributed, 21:6
impact on, 21:3
not distributed, 21:9
business transactions, major, 21:32
Code Section 403(b) plans, 1:79, 22:125
Code Section 457(b) plans, 21:7, 22:185
Code Section 457(f) plans, 21:7
compensation of disclosures, 4:94
date of termination
100 percent vesting rule and, 21:4
defined contribution plans
alternative defined contribution plans, 21:6, 21:7
disposition, special coverage rule, 21:35
distributions
alternative defined contribution plans, 21:6, 21:7
elective contributions, 21:34
payment of, 21:8
elective contributions, 21:6
employee stock ownership plans (ESOPs), 21:7
how plan is terminated, 21:2
lump-sum distributions, 18:16
missing participants, 21:10–21:13
abandoned plans, 21:48
distribution methods, 21:12
location of participant, steps to take, 21:10
Pension Protection Act of 2006 (PPA), 21:13
nondiscrimination rules, 21:5
100 percent vesting rule, date of termination and, 21:4
partial termination, 21:14–21:17
defined, 21:14
effect of, 21:15
facts-and-circumstances of determination, 21:17
occurrence, determination of, 21:17
100 percent vesting, 21:16
Pension Protection Act of 2006 (PPA)
missing participants, 21:13
procedure, 21:2
qualified termination administrators (QTAs), 21:38–21:39, 21:43–21:47
reporting and disclosure, 19:22
abandoned plans, 21:45
restriction of employer's ability to terminate plan, 21:1
SEPs, 21:7
SIMPLE plans, 21:7
tax-sheltered annuities (TSAs), 21:7
vesting
100 percent vesting rule, date of termination and, 21:4

Third-party administrators
advantages, 4:14
disadvantages, 4:15
questions to ask, 4:18

Time-weighted method, balance forward accounting, 4:30

TIPRA. *See* Tax Increase Prevention and Reconciliation Act of 2005 (TIPRA)

Top-hat plans
defined, 22:90

Top-heavy minimum contributions, 12:8

Top-heavy plans, 14:1–14:48
determination date, 14:18, 14:19
governmental 401(k) plans, 2:148
includable officer
defined, 14:13
limit on number of, 14:14, 14:16
key employees
compensation, 14:17
defined, 14:9
five percent owner, 14:10
includable officer, 14:13, 14:14, 14:16
minimum contributions on behalf of, 14:37
number of employees, determination of, 14:15
officer, 14:12
one percent owner, 14:11
minimum contributions, 14:32–14:41
allocated forfeitures, 14:34
amounts taken into account, 14:38
compensation defined, 14:33
discretionary profit sharing contribution, 14:44
elective contributions on behalf of key employees, 14:37
elective contributions only, 14:42
employer matching contribution, 14:45
excess of three percent of compensation, 14:36
key employees, on behalf of, 14:37
non-key employees, 14:39–14:41
requirements, 14:32
three percent of compensation, 14:35–14:37
minimum vesting, 14:29–14:32
account balance, 14:31
disregarded service, 14:30
Pension Protection Act of 2006 (PPA), 14:29
requirements, 14:29
officer, 14:12
includable officer, 14:13, 14:14, 14:16
permissive aggregation group, 14:6–14:8
present value of accrued benefits, 14:20–14:28
disregarding accrued benefits for certain participants, 14:28
qualified automatic contribution arrangements (QACAs), 14:48
qualified nonelective contributions (QNECs), 14:46
vesting, 14:29
required aggregation group
60 percent of sum of accrued benefits, less than, 14:8
60 percent of sum of accrued benefits, more than, 14:7
safe harbor 401(k) plan, 2:263–2:264
avoiding top-heavy status by converting to, 14:47
qualified automatic contribution arrangements (QACAs) added to, 14:48
SIMPLE plan, converting to, 14:43
strategies, 14:42–14:48
testing, 14:1–14:28
aggregation groups, 14:5–14:8
compensation, 14:17
determination, 14:1
determination date, 14:18, 14:19
employee defined, 14:4
employer defined, 14:3
how plan becomes top heavy, 14:2
includable officer, 14:13, 14:14, 14:16
key employees, 14:9–14:17
number of employees, determination of, 14:15
officer, 14:12
permissive aggregation group, 14:6–14:8
present value of accrued benefits, 14:20–14:28
required aggregation group, 14:5
vesting. *See* Minimum vesting *above, this group*

Top-paid employees
qualified separate lines of business (QSLOBs), 10:52

Top-paid group, highly compensated employee, 10:83–10:89
defined, 10:83
determining membership in, worksheet, 10:84
election, 10:89
membership in, 10:87–10:89
number of employees in, 10:84
selection of, 10:87
seven months, working less than, 10:86
17½ hours per week, working less than, 10:85

Total receipts percentage, defined, 10:33

TRA '84. *See* Tax Reform Act of 1984 (TRA '84)

TRA '86. *See* Tax Reform Act of 1986 (TRA '86)

TRA '97. *See* Taxpayer Relief Act of 1997 (TRA '97)

Transferee plans
defined, 17:2
survivor annuity requirements
all plan participants, 17:3
participant's entire account balance, 17:4

Transfers
considerations, 2:138–2:140
defined, 2:134
elective transfer defined, 2:135
nondiscrimination testing, 2:140

Treasury bills, 6:8
described, 6:7

Treasury bonds, described, 6:7

Treasury Department
guidance, new, 1:79

Treasury inflation-protected securities (TIPs), 6:7

Treasury notes, described, 6:7

True-up match contributions, 2:14

Trustees
directed trustee, 6:72
contributions, ensuring deposit in timely manner, 5:33
defined, 5:29
FAB 2008-01, 5:33–5:35
liability, protection from, 5:32
responsibilities regarding investing plan assets, 5:31
status as fiduciary, 5:30
plan trustee, role of, 4:3
responsibility, 5:28

Trust, salary deferral contributions deposited to, 5:75

Truth-in-lending disclosure rules, 15:38

Turnover, employee, 2:4

12b-1 fees, 4:123, 6:98
limitations, 1:81

20 percent withholding requirement, 16:113, 16:118

Two percent nonelective contributions, conditions on receipt of
SIMPLE 401(k) plans, 2:231

U

Unforeseeable emergencies, hardship withdrawals
Code Section 457(b) plans, 22:180–22:181

Unfunded plan, defined, 22:92

Uniform allocation formula
compensation, 12:3
defined, 12:2

Uniformed Services Employment and Re-Employment Rights Act of 1994 (USERRA)
actions employee must take to secure rights under, 1:65
adjustment of contributions for earnings, 1:69
affecting 401(k) plans, 1:65–1:70
annual additions, limits on, 9:45
break-in-service rules, 2:189
compensation upon rehire, 1:67
compensation, what is considered, 9:50
and current-year testing, 13:4
death or disability while performing military service
matching contributions, 2:93
elective contributions, 2:77
elective deferral contributions, 1:66
elective deferral limits, 2:77, 9:5
employer contributions, 1:68–1:70
matching contributions, 2:92
death or disability while performing military service, 2:93
nonelective contributions
death or disability while performing military service, 2:100
veterans' reemployment rights under USERRA, 2:99
plan documents, amendment, 3:15
testing, ADP and ACP, 1:70
vesting rights, 2:200
veterans' reemployment rights under USERRA
nonelective contributions, 2:99

Uniform point system plan, 12:4–12:6

Uniform standard of care, brokers and advisers, 1:81, 1:82

Unincorporated business, appropriateness of 401(k) plan, 1:30

"Union only" funds
Multiemployer plans, 1:38

Unit investment trusts, 6:32

Universal availability requirement
catch-up contributions, 9:33

USERRA. *See* Uniformed Services Employment and Re-Employment Rights Act of 1994 (USERRA)

U.S. Government Accountability Office (GAO)
fees, actions with regard to, 4:63

Utilization of 401(k) plans
number of companies in United States offering, 1:44
participation rates, 1:45

V

Value stocks, defined, 6:3

Variable annuity contracts
- defined, 6:32
- fees, 4:122, 6:104
- group variable annuities, 6:32–6:33
- guaranteed benefit and lifetime income products, 6:35
- questions to ask, 6:32

VCO. *See* Voluntary Correction of Operational Failures (VCO)

VCP. *See* Voluntary Correction with Service Approval Program (VCP)

VCS. *See* Voluntary Correction of Operational Failures Standardized (VCS)

Vesting, 2:190–2:215
- after-tax employee contributions, 2:193
- anti-cutback rules, interaction of rules relating to changes in vesting schedules, 2:210
- break-in-service rules, 2:201–2:206
- cashout/buyback rule, 2:213
- contributions 100 percent vested, 2:193–2:194
- defined, 2:190
- disregarding any years of service, 2:197, 2:198
- elective contributions, 2:193
- eligible combined plans, 2:273
- five-year rule, 2:204
- forfeiture, 2:211–2:215
  - amount allowed, 2:214
  - cashout/buyback rule, 2:213
  - disposition, 2:215
  - funds used to restore account balances, 2:219
  - interest on previously forfeited amounts, 2:217
  - nonvested portion, 2:211
  - safe harbor contributions, no offsetting of, 2:215
  - timing, 2:212
- matching contributions, 1:56
- maternity or paternity leaves of absence, 2:206
- military service, death of participant during performance of, 2:191
- minimum vesting, governmental 401(k) plans, 2:148
- money purchase plan, merger into 401(k) plan, 9:77
- nonvested portion, forfeiture of, 2:211
- normal retirement age, defined, 2:192
- 100 percent vesting, 2:193–2:194
  - date of termination and, 21:4
  - partial termination, 21:16
- one-year break-in-service rule
  - defined, 2:205
  - described, 2:202
  - maternity or paternity leaves of absence, 2:206
- participant's entire interest in plan, 2:191
- Pension Protection Act of 2006 (PPA)
  - contributions not subject to 100 percent vesting requirement, 2:194
  - maximum vesting period, changes, 1:63
- percentage
  - previous vesting schedule, 2:208
  - vesting schedule amended to reduce vesting percentage, 2:207
- predecessor plan defined, 2:198
- previous vesting schedule
  - account balances determined under, 2:208
  - election period, 2:209
  - vested percentages determined under, 2:208
- qualified matching contributions (QMACs), 2:193
  - minimum vesting, 14:29
- qualified nonelective contributions (QNECs), 2:193
- rehired employees, 2:199
- rollovers, 2:193
  - consent if vested balance not exceeding $5,000, 16:73
- rule of parity, 2:203
- safe harbor 401(k) plans, 2:193, 2:255
- SIMPLE 401(k) plans, 2:193, 2:233
- termination and rehire, 2:199
- top-heavy plans. *See* Top-heavy plans
- USERRA, under, 2:200
- vesting computation period, 2:196
- veterans' reemployment rights under USERRA, 2:200

Veterans' reemployment rights under USERRA
- annual additions, limits on, 9:45
- break-in-service rules, 2:185
- compensation, what is considered, 9:50
- death or disability while performing military service
  - matching contributions, 2:93
  - nonelective contributions, 2:100
- elective contributions, 2:77
- elective deferrals, 2:77, 9:5
- matching contributions, 2:92
  - death or disability while performing military service, 2:93
- nonelective contributions, 2:99
  - death or disability while performing military service, 2:100
- vesting rights, 2:200

VFCP. *See* Voluntary Fiduciary Correction Program (VFCP)

Voice response unit (VRU), 4:38, 19:122

Volatility levels
participant direction of investments, 7:27

Volume submitter plans
changes to, 3:13
comparisons with other plans, 3:12
cross-tested allocation formulas, 3:13
defined, 3:9
determination letter applications for, 3:28
failure to have operational reliance, 3:37
format, 3:11
installation costs, 2:8
vs. mass submitter, defined, 3:10
master/prototype plans and, 3:13
plan amendment
HEART Act, updating of plan document for, 3:23
PPA, updating of plan document for, 3:23
WRERA, updating of plan document for, 3:23
plan document
HEART Act, updating for, 3:23
PPA, updating for, 3:23
WRERA, updating for, 3:23
Self-Correction Program (SCP), 20:14
updating plans, 3:18

Voluntary Correction of Operational Failures (VCO)
retroactive amendment, correction by, 20:24

Voluntary Correction with Service Approval Program (VCP), 20:20–20:27, 22:62
abandoned plans, 21:50
Anonymous Submission Procedure, 20:25
application to IRS, 20:26
cost of using, 20:27
deadline for correcting defects, 20:21
favorable IRS letter, 20:22
group submissions, 20:25
practices and procedures, 20:23
procedures, 20:25, 20:26
qualification defects covered by, 20:20
retroactive amendment, correction by, 20:24
specialized procedures under, 20:25

Voluntary Fiduciary Correction Program (VFCP), 5:139–5:152
additional information, where to find, 5:152
circumstances for use of, 5:149
criminal violations, 5:148
described, 5:139
effective date, 5:140
generally, 5:74
general principles, 5:144
late deposits of salary deferral contributions, 5:78
late remittance problem, example of correction of, 5:145
no action letters, 5:146
notice, steps to using, 5:143
prohibited transaction, violation being corrected as, 5:147
reciprocity under, 5:147
relief offered for using, 5:146
risks involved in using, 5:148
understanding, value of, 5:148
violations corrected through, 5:142
when not to use, 5:150
who can use, 5:141

Voting rights
employer securities, 6:65
participant direction of investments, 7:20

VRU. *See* Voice response unit (VRU)

VS mass submitter, defined, 3:10

W

Waivers
required minimum distributions (RMDs), 16:40
spousal waivers, electronic media, 19:134
survivor annuity requirements, 17:18–17:23

Web site of service provider, features plan sponsor might look for
participant Web site, 4:39
plan sponsor Web site, 4:40

Withdrawals
hardship. *See* Hardship withdrawals
Hurricane Sandy relief, 15:62
in-service. *See* In-service withdrawals
PPA changes to rules, 1:60
restrictions, 15:61

Withholding
amounts reported to payee, 16:139
contributions, required on, 16:107
deposits of federal income tax withholding, 16:138
distributions, required on, 16:108
electing out of
notice on nonperiodic distributions, 16:134
notification of right, 16:131
payor, by, 16:135
periodic distributions, notice, 16:133
who may, 16:130
withholding notice, 16:132
eligible rollover distributions
election out of withholding, 16:110
income tax, 16:109

Withholding *(cont'd)*
employer securities, 16:109, 18:2
FICA taxes, 18:2, 18:3
foreign addresses, participants with, 16:136
hardship withdrawals, 16:111
IRA, 16:117
IRS, reported to, 16:137
missing participants, 21:12
nonperiodic distribution
notice, 16:134
rate of withholding, 16:129
old rules, 16:122, 16:125
participant loans, 16:112–16:114
eligible rollover distribution, loan offset amount, 16:114
periodic distribution
defined, 16:126
notice, 16:133
required
on contributions, 16:107
on distributions, 16:108
responsibility
adequate information, 16:120
enforcing the mandatory 20 percent withholding, 16:118
taxes, interest, or penalties, 16:119
rollover, distributions not eligible for, 16:121–16:123
self-employed individuals, 18:3
termination of employment, 16:107–16:140
distributions ineligible for rollover, 16:121–16:123
electing out of withholding, 16:130–16:135
loan offset amount, 16:112–16:114
penalties, 16:140
periodic distributions, 16:126–16:127
procedures, 16:136–16:140
responsibility for withholding, 16:118–16:120
special distributions, 16:115–16:117
20 percent withholding requirement, 16:113, 16:118
Worker, Retiree, and Employer Recovery Act of 2008 (WRERA), 16:108

Worker, Retiree, and Employer Recovery Act of 2008 (WRERA)
and automatic contribution arrangements (ACAs), 1:74
automatic enrollment feature, 2:34
compliance, plan amendment, 3:22
contributions
salary reduction SEPs (SARSEPs), 22:47
simplified employee pensions (SEPs), 22:47
economic relief provided by, 1:75
excess deferrals
gap-period income, 9:12
gap-period earnings, excess deferrals, 1:74
master and prototype plans
plan document, updating of, 3:23
one-participant retirement plan, synchronization of, 1:74
plan amendment to comply with, 3:22
PPA technical corrections included in, 1:74
required minimum distributions (RMDs), 16:40, 18:100
penalty for failure to distribute, 18:88
rollovers
death proceeds, non-spouse beneficiary, 18:35
salary reduction SEPs (SARSEPs)
automatic enrollment, 22:47
contributions, 22:47
simplified employee pensions (SEPs)
automatic enrollment, 22:47
contributions, 22:47
volume submitter plans
plan document, updating of, 3:23
withholding, 16:108

WorldCom
fiduciary audit and, 5:138
issues involved, 7:75
legislation ensuing from, 7:76
litigation, 5:31, 6:72

WRERA. *See* Worker, Retiree, and Employer Recovery Act of 2008 (WRERA)

Written explanation, survivor annuity requirements, 17:24–17:28

Written plan requirement, 2:143, 6:85
Code Section 403(b) plans, 22:123
service providers, fees, 4:68
survivor annuity requirements, 17:28

Y

Yearly contacts, number of communication program, 8:14

Year of service
defined for eligibility, 2:173
defined for vesting, 2:195